Making Sense of Nonsense: Navigating Through the West's Current Quagmire

For those who feel vaguely uneasy about the current direction of our culture and our politics, but can't put their finger on the problem, the fifty-five chapters of this book are a wake-up call, and they bring into focus reasons for our current malaise. The editor and principal author, Scott D. G. Ventureyra, is joined by more than twenty others who explore perennial themes of philosophy and theology enlivened by accounts of personal experience in the quest for the true and the good amidst the drama of the decay of the West. Topics range from faith and science to gender ideology to the attack on freedom and dignity of persons, to COVID-19 and the New World Order. Pick this volume up for a lively discussion of the distemper of our times, and for reflections on the prospects for redemption.

—David J. Klassen, LL.B., Ph.D.

The Western world is intent on defeating reality to vaunt utopian narratives. The authors of this impressive work offer a necessary assessment of this "culture war," while also forging a path for a return to the essential and eternal truths of human existence. A copy of this notable book should be on every shelf.

—Nirmal Dass, publisher, *The Postil Magazine*

I knew something was deeply wrong with the world prior to 2020, but 2020 confirmed it. With the changes in views about sex, marriage, and the economy, we are seeing a direct confrontation with traditional Western Christian values. This continues to be confirmed for those who have eyes to see what politics, medicine, science, and technology are doing to cultural consciousness led by globalist elite groups (just read the Davos report for yourself!). This really hit home for me when politicians told us in Spring 2020 that all the hospitals were full to capacity with COVID-19 patients and I was not permitted to visit my father in the intensive care unit. Well I gained entrance, and what I saw was shocking! It was largely empty! The politicians were lying. And, many were buying it! What was really happening was a wholesale neglect with no process in place to treat COVID-19 patients. This coupled with the ongoing race riots and the constant in your face challenge to traditional ethics of both sex and Western values. All of it is a part of a reset. A reset of values with the intent to replace Christian foundations through coercive tactics. We are experiencing this now in the society as well as in our evangelical churches. *Making Sense of Nonsense* confronts many of the issues, motivations, and challenges that continue to upset not only our economy and social interactions but our values. With an honest look at the issues from a variety of perspectives, *Making Sense of Nonsense* will furnish the reader with a host of issues backed by research that aid us in thinking better about the problems in medicine, technology, economics, society and how they are interwoven, so that we might be better equipped to engage the new world staring us square in the face. The motivations are no longer disguised attempts to deceive. At best the motivations are hidden in plain sight for all to see. For those who have ears to hear, let him hear and see the nonsense before us.

—Joshua R. Farris, Rev. Dcn., Ph.D, Professor of Theology of Science, Missional University

MAKING SENSE OF NONSENSE

MAKING SENSE OF NONSENSE

NAVIGATING THROUGH THE WEST'S CURRENT QUAGMIRE

Edited by Scott D. G. Ventureyra

TFP
True Freedom Press

MAKING SENSE OF NONSENSE:
Navigating Through the West's Current Quagmire

First published in Ottawa, Ontario, Canada
in 2022 by True Freedom Press.
https://www.scottventureyra.com/true-freedom-press
truefreedompress@gmail.com

PAPERBACK ISBN: 978-1-7773435-0-7
HARDCOVER ISBN: 978-1-7773435-5-2
EBOOK ISBN: 978-1-7773435-6-9

Disclaimer Notice

To all those noble souls who throughout history stood up for love, truth, and freedom, including the martyrs of today.

"Long is the way and hard, that out of Hell leads up to light."
—John Milton, Paradise Lost

Contents

Preface xxiii
Scott D. G. Ventureyra

Overview xxxi
Scott D. G. Ventureyra

Section I: Setting the Stage: Humanity at the Crossroads?

Chapter 1: The Decay of the West 3
Scott D. G. Ventureyra
Disregarded Warnings to the West 4
Soviet Dissident: Aleksandr Solzhenitsyn 5
Former KGB Propagandist: Juri Bezmenov 7
North Korean Defector and Human Rights Activist: Yeonmi Park (Park Yeon-mi) 12
Descent into Hell 13
Scientific Materialism 14
The Death of God 15
The Denigration of the Human Person 16
Further Symptoms of the West's Affliction 16
Economic Socialism 16
Cultural Marxism 20
Postmodernism 20
Identity Politics 20
The Persecution of Christians and Christianity 22
Orwell Meets Derrida 25
Bibliography 28

Chapter 2: Progression or Regression: Political Correctness, Censorship, and the Information War 33
Scott D. G. Ventureyra
The Left: Progressive or Regressive? 33
The Perils of Political Correctness 35
The Varieties of Cancel Culture 36
In Defense of Free Speech 38

The Information War 39
Technology and the Spread of Information 39
The Influence of Big Tech Oligarchs and the Mainstream Media 39
The Cases of Kyle Rittenhouse and Nick Sandman 42
The Times Are They a-Changin'? 43
Destination Unknown? 44
Bibliography 44

Chapter 3: The Campus Culture Wars: Symptom of a Holy War 49
Rick Mehta
Bibliography 52

Chapter 4: Thinking about Tolerance 53
Scott D. G. Ventureyra
Bibliography 60

Section II: On Truth

Part I: Faith, Reason, Science, and Experience

Chapter 5: Dawkins's Unholy Trinity—Incoherency, Hypocrisy, and Bigotry 67
Scott D. G. Ventureyra
"Man of Science" Promotes Bigotry 69
Questions Dawkins Does Not Answer 71
Bibliography 72

Chapter 6: An Approach to the Santa Legend 74
Scott D. G. Ventureyra
Bibliography 77

Chapter 7: The Peterson-Craig Encounter: A Missed Opportunity? 78
Scott D. G. Ventureyra
Natural Law Theory 78
Methodological Naturalism vs Metaphysical Naturalism 79
The Existence of God 80
On the Historicity of Jesus Christ and His Resurrection 81
Peterson's Epistemology of Truth 81
A More In-depth Dialogue with Craig 82
Bibliography 83

Chapter 8: **Lightning Crashes +LĪVE+** 85
Scott D. G. Ventureyra
Bibliography 90

Chapter 9: **The Atheist Truth-Seeker: A Reflection on Mario Augusto Bunge's Life and Work** 92
Scott D. G. Ventureyra
Postmodernism 93
Scientific Materialism 94
A Kind of Kinship 95
Love of Wisdom 95
Bibliography 96

Chapter 10: **My Godfather's Road to Damascus** 97
Scott D. G. Ventureyra
A Road Less Travelled 97
Bibliography 102

Part II: God, Philosophy, Theology, and Science

Chapter 11: **Warranted Skepticism? Putting the Center for Inquiry's Rationale to the Test** 105
Scott D. G. Ventureyra
Introduction 105
Emotions a Motivation for Non-Belief? 107
The Epistemology of Sagan's Dictum 108
Philosophy, Science, and the Question of God 110
The Presumption of Atheism and Sagan's Dictum 114
Proper Basicality and Sagan's Dictum 116
Test Case: Jesus' Resurrection 118
Conclusion 119
Bibliography 120

Chapter 12: **The Governor General's Hubris and Anti-Intellectualism** 122
Scott D. G. Ventureyra
Faith and Science 122
The Difficulty with the "Origin of Life" 124
Randomness vs. chance 125
God's Hand 126
Trudeau's Oversight 127
God and the Astronauts 128
Bibliography 129

Chapter 13: **Science and Christian Theology** 131
Scott D. G. Ventureyra
A Historical Consideration 132
The Interaction Between Science and Theology 134
Intelligibility, Science, and God 135
Bibliography 136

Part III: Science versus Scientism

Chapter 14: **The Lawyer Who Put the Logic of Darwinism on Trial: Phillip E. Johnson's Gift to Posterity** 141
Scott D. G. Ventureyra
Evolving Our Thinking about Evolution 141
Mere Dilettante or Skillful Logician? 143
The Legacy 143
Bibliography 144

Chapter 15: **On Scientism** 145
Hugh Hunter
Bibliography 151

Chapter 16: **Is Science the Only Path to Truth?** 152
Phil Fernandes and Matthew J. Coombe
The Assumptions and Limitations of Science 152
Dawkins' Mistaken View of Faith and Reason 154
Bibliography 156

Section III: On the Human Person

Part I: Abortion and Euthanasia

Chapter 17: **The Sanctity of Life in Light of the Incarnation** 161
Scott D. G. Ventureyra
Remembering the Unborn 162
The Incarnation: A Christological Argument against Abortion 163
Raising Awareness Among Christians 164
Bibliography 165

Chapter 18: **Demolishing Secular Pretensions: Assisted Suicide, the Media, and Relativism** 167
Scott D. G. Ventureyra
Bibliography 169

Chapter 19: Euthanasia and Assisted Suicide: Eugenics in Disguise 170
Brenna Bloodworth
Bibliography 176

Part II: Crimes against Our Children

Chapter 20: Sexualization of Children: Lifting the Last Taboo 183
David Bellusci, O.P.
Introduction 183
Alfred Kinsey 183
John Money 185
Sexualizing Children: Opponents 186
Sexualization of Children: Political Maneuvers 188
Education and Ideology 189
Hollywood: Re-educating Children 191
Where Do We Go from Here? 193
Moral Credibility 195
Bibliography 195

Chapter 21: Child Trafficking: Feeding Sexual Addicts 198
David Bellusci, O.P.
Introduction 198
Child Sexual Trafficking 198
Pornography 199
From Soft-Core to Hard-Core 200
Slipping into Extreme Pornography 201
Desensitization and Pseudo-Child Pornography (PCP) 203
Child Pornography 204
Child Sex Trafficking 205
Child Trafficking: Deception, Manipulation, and Coercion 207
Combating Child Sexual Trafficking 210
Bibliography 211

Part III: On Healthy Living: Lessons from Others and Personal Experience

Chapter 22: The Corruption of the Pharmaceutical Companies 215
James Harris
The Landing: My Personal Journey down the Healthcare Industry's Rabbit Hole 215
Pharmaceutical Industry Sales in—Humanity out 217
Money over Medicine 219
Pharmaceutical production using misguided models 220

Enter the Blue Zone 222
Final Thoughts: Sticking to the Landing 225
Bibliography 225

Chapter 23: **Phil Lynott in Retrospect: From Tragedy to Christian Hope** 227
Scott D. G. Ventureyra

Chapter 24: **Fell on a Black Day: A Reflection on Chris Cornell's Suicide** 230
Scott D. G. Ventureyra
Bibliography 232

Part IV: On Gender Ideology

Chapter 25: **Abortion Inequalities: Does Abortion-Choice Treat Women and Men as Equals?** 235
John D. Ferrer
Abortion-choice Favours a Sexual Ethic That Disadvantages Women 237
It Permits Sex-selective Abortion 238
It Reduces the Pool of Marriageable Males 239
It Undercuts Other Attempts to Strengthen Marriage and Family 240
It Fosters "Love 'em and leave 'em" Relationships 241
Pro-choice Ideology Implies Women Are Naturally Unequal to Men 241
Abortion Choice Policy Treats Maternity as a Detriment 241
It Interprets Sexual Differences in Favour of Men 242
A Pro-life Ethic Can Correct against Those Problems 243
Women's Equality Deserves Better than Abortion 244
Bibliography 245

Chapter 26: **Perpetuating the Gender Myth in Sports** 247
Scott D. G. Ventureyra
Good Ol' Identity Politics 247
Biological and Psychological Sex Differences 248
Sex Differences in Tennis—the "Battle of the Sexes" 249
Bibliography 252

Chapter 27:	**Unpacking Toxic Masculinity**	254
	Stella Shihman	
	Bibliography	258
Chapter 28:	**Gender Ideology and the Deconstructing of Deconstructionism: Peterson versus Derrida**	260
	Scott D. G. Ventureyra	
	Bill C-16—What Is It?	261
	Jordan Peterson: "Defender of Truth"	262
	Derrida: "Wishful Mortician of the Absolute"	264
	A Discussion on Free Speech, Political Correctness, and Bill C-16	271
	Conclusion	279
	Bibliography	281
Chapter 29:	**The Gender Revolution and Its Global Imposition**	286
	Pablo Muñoz Iturrieta	
	The Gender Revolution	287
	The Social Imposition of Gender Ideology	288
	The Destruction of the Political Foundations of the West	294
	Conclusion	295
	Bibliography	297

Part V: The Unrelenting Assault on Human Freedom

Chapter 30:	**The Tragic Story of Imre Szép: Disproportionate Justice and What Cannot Be Unseen**	301
	Paul Satori	
Chapter 31:	**Living and Surviving Socialism**	307
	Stella Shihman	
	Bibliography	313
Chapter 32:	**Turning a Blind Eye: Denial of Left-Wing Pathologies**	315
	Trevor Blackwell	
	Bibliography	323
Chapter 33:	**Learning to Think Critically about Culture and Combating Wokeism**	324
	Oren Amitay and Scott D. G. Ventureyra	
	Editor's Note	324
	Mao's China Hitting Closer and Closer to Home	325

Journalism and Journalists' Ever Crumbling Integrity 327
Alexandria Ocasio Cortez's Massive Lie About January 6 329
Democrats Demand Unthinking Compliance 330
The Left's Intolerance 331
Free Pass to Leftist Posts on Twitter 332
On Pedophilia 333
On Free Speech 333
Capital Rioters Charged 334
Democrats' Hunger for Power and Authoritarian Rule 334
Unwarranted Attacks on Julian Assange and Edward Snowden 335
Questioning Narratives and Thinking Critically 336
Bibliography 336

Chapter 34: Canada's Free Speech Wars 338
Scott D. G. Ventureyra
Compelled Speech Demanded by Ontario's Bar Association 339
Wilfrid Laurier University's Suffocation of Free Speech 339
Fallout from the WLU Controversy 341
The Associated Ills of Postmodernism 342
Free Speech and the Human Person 344
Bibliography 345

Chapter 35: On Peterson's Revoked Fellowship to Cambridge Divinity School 348
Scott D. G. Ventureyra
Why the Revocation? 348
Cambridge's Legacy Disgraced 352
Bibliography 353

Chapter 36: On Anti-Religious Indoctrination 355
Scott D. G. Ventureyra
Anti-Religious Indoctrination 355
Examples of Anti-Religious Indoctrination 356
How to know Recognize Anti-Religious Indoctrination 359
How to Counteract Such Indoctrination 360
Bibliography 362

Chapter 37: Not Like Our Elders' Movement 363
C. C. Harvey
Meet the New Boss: The Racial Justice Juggernaut 363

A Foundation for Political Activism 365
Grassroots Unity & Collective Action 366
Antiracism is Neoracism? 366
Whiteness in Different Colours 368
Individualism as a White Trait 368
Not Like Our Elders 370
Kneeling for Black Lives 372
Bibliography 373

Chapter 38: How Educational Institutions Imprison the Minds of Our Youth 375
Scott D. G. Ventureyra
Introduction 375
The Hijacking of Truth 377
Truth & Justice Supplanted by Social Justice 382
Justice vs Social Justice 382
OISE (Ontario Institute for Studies in Education)—Social Justice Think Tank 384
Health and Physical Education 387
Background on Curriculum 388
The Follies of Gender Ideology 391
Maritain's Emphasis on Truth Centered Education 393
Conclusion 394
Bibliography 395

Chapter 39: The Death of Man: The Coming Death of Western Civilization 400
Phil Fernandes
Nietzsche: Prophet for the Twentieth Century 400
C. S. Lewis: The Abolition of Man 402
Schaeffer: The Post-Christian Era and the Death of Man 404
Concluding Remarks 407
Bibliography 408

Part VI: The New World Order & COVID-19

Chapter 40: Lessons Lost to History 413
Travis Louisseize
Bibliography 420

Chapter 41: The Great Reset and the New World Order 422
Phil Fernandes
See No Evil 423
The Biblical View of Government 424
The Twentieth-Century Move Towards Global Government 425
Key Globalist Organizations 429
Key Globalist Leaders 430
The Bill Clinton Administration 431
The George W. Bush Administration 432
The Barak Obama Administration 432
Cultural Marxism—The New Civil Religion 433
The Great Reset 436
Leading Opponents of the New World Order 438
Conclusion: The Current Situation 439
Bibliography 440

Chapter 42: Reflections on the COVID-19 Pandemonium 443
Scott D. G Ventureyra
Some Preliminaries 445
Early Negligence in Canada 448
A Period of Mass Confusion 450
Human Corruption and Evil 451
Unthinking Compliance 452
Social Engineering? 453
Cognitive Dissonance and Self-Deception 453
COVID-19 "Vaccination" and Appalling Absurdities Related to Child Custody (Decision-Making) 454
COVID Stockholm Syndrome 461
COVID-19 as Religion 463
The Nature and History of Science 465
The Fallibility of Medicine and Doctors 467
Mainstream Media's Duplicity and Lack of Integrity 468
On COVID Censorship 471
Big Tech Censorship and Manipulation 471
Censorship of Dissenting Scientific and Medical Experts 474
Medical Experts Threatened Over COVID 479
Ensuring Compliance of Health Practitioners 479
The Imposition of Bill C-10 482
Exposing COVID-19 Vaccine Companies 484
Project Veritas 484
Luciferase and Graphene Oxide in the Pfizer Vaccine? 487
Goodbye to Reason and Morality 488

A Divided World 488
"Oh! What Ethics! What Heroes!" 491
Betraying Your Moral Conscience 492
More Lies 496
Unceasing Absurdities 498
Awareness as a Way Forward? 499
Bibliography 501

Chapter 43: Mind-Control Tactics and Fear Mechanisms Deployed during the COVID-19 Pandemic 516
Valérie A. G. Ventureyra
Bibliography 523

Chapter 44: The Psychosocial Cost of Extreme Measures regarding Mental Health 524
Martina J. Speck
Bibliography 530

Chapter 45: COVID-19: A Pandemic of Malfeasance and Incompetence: Unpopular Truths and Propagated Lies 537
Scott D. G. Ventureyra and Enrique C. G. Ventureyra
The Origin of SARS-CoV-2 539
The Publicly Released Fauci Emails 539
On PCR Testing 554
Symptomatic, Asymptomatic, and Pre-symptomatic Spread 562
The Myth of Asymptomatic Transfer 563
Continued Absurdity or the Crumbling of the Narrative? 564
With Vs. From COVID 565
Has SARS-CoV-2 Been Isolated/Purified? 566
The Environmental Theory 569
On Lockdowns 571
On the Inutility of Masks 573
Size Matters 575
Side-Effects of Masks 576
The Politicization of Masks 578
The Demonization of Early COVID-19 Treatments 579
Hydroxychloroquine 580
Ivermectin 582
No Transparency with Big Pharma 584
Incompetence and Medical Malfeasance 585
Natural Immunity Matters 587
On the COVID-19 "Vaccines" 589

Incessant Psychological Attacks 590
On a Personal Front 590
The Fideistic Anesthesiologist 591
Further Absurdities 593
But is it a Vaccine? 594
Is it Gene Therapy? 595
Three Vital Questions 600
Is it Necessary? 600
Is it Dangerous? 600
Is it Effective? 605
Unjustly Stigmatizing the Unvaccinated 609
Where's the Baloney Detector? 613
Bibliography 616

Chapter 46: The Aftermath of a False Pandemic: Thoughts on Experimental Vaccines 639
Enrique C. G. Ventureyra
Final Thoughts 648
Bibliography 650

Part VII: Human Hope: The *Imago Dei* and Human Resilience

Chapter 47: Shattering Martin Luther King Jr.'s Dream 659
Scott D. G. Ventureyra
Bibliography 662

Chapter 48: Friends and Politics 664
Benjamin Blake Speed Watkins
What Do You Mean? 664
Resolving Disagreement as Our Aim 665
Mirroring as Technique 667
Patience Is a Virtue 667
Bibliography 668

Chapter 49: A Message to All Humanity, All Governments, All Royal and Financial Elites (One-Percent Group) 669
Ton Laurijssen

Chapter 50: Embracing Intuition 676
Andrew H. Gill
Intuition and Law Enforcement 676
Our Relationship to Animals and Intuition 677

Intuition and Relationships 679
Intuition and Corporations: The Missing Soul 680
Intuition and Big Pharma 680
Bibliography 681

Chapter 51: Reflections on the *Rocky* Saga and the Intrinsic Value of the Human Person 683
Scott D. G. Ventureyra
Relevant Background to the *Rocky* Saga 684
Adonis's Struggles 685
Rocky's Reconciliation 686
Ivan Drago's Re-Emergence and Awakening 686
Bibliography 687

Chapter 52: Cobra Kai: Self-Defense and the Defense of Others 688
Scott D. G. Ventureyra
Synopsis 688
The Search for a Father Figure 690
Bullying, Self-Defense, Moral Responsibility, Adaptation, and Transformation 692
Bibliography 697

Chapter 53: A Korean Pastor Inspires Us to Love without Limits 698
Scott D. G. Ventureyra
Bibliography 701

Chapter 54: The Indomitable Spirit of Man: Seeking Unity through the Enduring Message of Terry Fox 702
Scott D. G. Ventureyra
Bibliography 708

Chapter 55: The Gift of Self and the Renewal of Humanism and Culture 709
Nikolaj Zunic
Introduction: Do We Live in An Age of Crisis? 709
Love as the Path to Knowing God 711
The Need for a New Humanism 716
The Gift of Self as the Fulfillment of Self 721
Conclusion 725
Bibliography 726

Epilogue: Where Do We Go from Here? 729
Scott D. G. Ventureyra

Appendices 763
Contributors 777
Index 785

Preface

Scott D. G. Ventureyra

Originally, I had signed a contract and planned on publishing this volume with a large publishing house in the United States. I had reached out to the publisher out of concern that they may not want to publish some of the material in this volume that contradicts the accepted narrative regarding COVID-19. It turns out that I was correct. This publishing house, whatever their reasons, is blindly defending and upholding all mandates and recommendations imposed by America's Center for Disease Control (CDC) and the governments that follow the accepted narrative. I then decided to remove anything related to COVID, but then realized they may disapprove of any controversial position that contradicts "woke" culture, so I decided to cancel my contract altogether. I then decided to go with my own "press." Phil Fernandes, a Christian philosopher and contributor to this volume, explains how such publishing houses are unwilling to entertain controversial perspectives:

> I've been speaking out against the New World Order since the early 1990s. In Christian academic circles I was always considered a nut. Though many Christian laypeople are now seeing the light, most Christian publishers still have their heads buried in the sand. The church has almost completely forfeited its prophetic voice. It was okay for C.S. Lewis to talk about this stuff in the 1940s, and for Schaeffer to address these issues in the 1970s; but now, as we draw closer to global government, we are censored even by Christian publishers. If we quote the pro-globalist/NWO statements of George H.W. Bush or Obama or the Clintons, we're censored. If we quote the anti-globalist statements of Ron Paul or Pat Buchanan or Donald Trump, we are once again censored. Christian publishers desire to be accepted by the world even while the world is crushing the church. That's why your own publishing company will probably be your best bet.[1]

The book is extensively researched with close to 1,800 references. Since I have adopted the footnoting and bibliographic style of the above-mentioned publishing house, it would have been much too time consuming to convert

1 Phil Fernandes, Email message to Scott Ventureyra, August 21, 2021.

everything to my preferred style. If you want to do further research and verify some of the references, it is important that you match the footnote, which is in a short form, with the corresponding chapter's bibliographic entry with the full citation. For the Preface and Epilogue, I have included the full citation in the footnotes: a method which is much more commonsensical and practical than the one adopted by the aforementioned publishing house. But alas, commonsense and practicality do not seem to be their forte.

This is the third book published by True Freedom Press. Its first publication was a satirical book about the 2020 American presidential candidate Joseph Robinette Biden: *The Safe Bet: The 2020 Presidential Case for Joe Biden: A Brilliant Campaign and Forty-Seven Years of Unparalleled Dedication.*[2] It can be purchased on Amazon. True Freedom Press promotes free speech and freedom of expression. With the pervasiveness of censorship throughout the legacy media, Big Tech platforms such as Facebook, Twitter, Instagram, Google and others, university campuses, work settings, and even places of worship—true free-thinkers are increasingly seeking alternative platforms and methods of communication. True Freedom Press offers an alternative to this Orwellian nightmare that has become so commonplace throughout western consciousness.

It is an avenue for conservatives, theists, libertarians, free-thinkers, and others to express their positions in an open and honest fashion without fear of being stifled by political correctness. Little do many realize that political correctness is an oppressive tool to prevent dissenting views. The term itself originated with Leon Trotsky and was used by genocidal tyrants like Mao Zedong.

True Freedom Press upholds a traditional understanding of tolerance, one which defends an individual's right to hold a particular position and express it freely even if it offends others. To write freely is to have the ability to offend. The truth may offend at first, but it should be embraced for the sake of authentic living and expression.

Enrique Discépolo's famous song "Cambalache," written in 1934 and later popularized by tango singer Julio Sosa, captures the essence of the times we are living in. Even though it is a reaction to the "Infamous Decade" (a reference to the corruption in Argentina from 1930 to 1940, involving electoral fraud, persecution of political opposition, and other issues related the Great Depression—*all of which sounds eerily familiar*), it indeed perfectly captures the political and cultural climate of today. He brilliantly describes how relativism and immorality are two sides of the same coin. A translation of the second verse reads:

> Today it is the same to be decent or a traitor! To be an ignoramus, a genius, a pickpocket, a generous person, or a swindler! All are the same!

2 https://www.amazon.com/2020-Presidential-Case-Joe-Biden/dp/1777343518/ref=sr_1_2?dchild=1&keywords=ventureyra&qid=1608824719&sr=8-2.

> None is better! It is the same being a moron or a great professor! There are no failing grades or recognitions of merit; the immoral have caught up with us.[3]

Although he is describing the ridiculousness, corruption, immorality, and evil of the twentieth century, I believe we have even descended into greater depths of absurdity and malice in our current century. But any astute student of history should not be surprised. The fallenness of human nature does not suddenly change because of certain "advancements," whether scientific or technological or in general societal practices.

In recent years, there has been a concerted attack on many precepts of Western civilization relating to the concept of God, truth, Christianity, morality, sex, the family, and even modern science, especially biology. The concern of this volume is to explore these and other attacks through the tools of philosophy, theology, science, and intuition. It seeks to bring clarity to the ongoing struggle of Western civilization to preserve its values and traditions. Although the vision for this project emerged in the spring of 2020, it bears the fruit of years of labor. Some of the material in this volume has been presented at conferences throughout North America, while some of the chapters are modified articles that were published in various journals and magazines.

Some of the chapters in this volume emanate from a place of frustration with our educational system, and Christian churches, whether Catholic, Orthodox, or Reformed, for a lack of rigorous engagement with intellectual and cultural issues. Even though exceptional Christian and non-Christian thinkers have been effective in defending Western values through arguments and evidence, much of Christendom has acquiesced to the changing trends of our culture. Amidst it all, those who control the levers of power—the mainstream media, the entertainment industry, and the Big Tech oligarchs, alongside governmental bodies who determine what information is worth knowing—are pushing a bankrupt narrative that embodies a strange mélange of scientific materialism, social justice, and relativism, which functions as a series of axes chopping away at the foundation of Western civilization. To be sure, this is not a book solely devoted to Christian thought, but the latter is a significant aspect of the cultural war that has been ongoing for decades.

The authors of this volume largely agree that the world is heading in the wrong direction. Too many people across the globe are unthinkingly accepting a narrative that runs contrary to truth, reason, evidence, justice, and goodness. This work seeks to bring clarity and order to much of the madness that is currently shaping countless people's minds. Although many of these subjects have been addressed numerous times and in numerous ways, I believe the

3 My translation.

authors of this volume bring something unique. The chapters contained in this volume vary greatly in their breadth, tackling topics related to culture, politics, science, society, philosophy, theology, and spirituality. Within these chapters, many contentious issues are addressed, including but not limited to abortion, assisted suicide, truth, tolerance, relativism, postmodernism, Marxism, communism, socialism, gender ideology, theology, science, scientism, civil liberties, free speech, COVID-19, and academic freedom. Each author brings a unique perspective, drawn from academic training, life experience, reason, belief, and intuition, to confront a deep malaise that is threatening human civilization. This malaise has greatly affected our ability as a collective consciousness to reason and deliberate correctly on moral issues. Since the beginning of the COVID crisis in March of 2020, our freedoms have been trampled on by authoritarian governmental rule through medical tyranny under the pretext of compassion for the vulnerable. As C.S. Lewis aptly stated:

> Of all tyrannies, a tyranny sincerely exercised for the good of its victims may be the most oppressive. It would be better to live under robber barons than under omnipotent moral busybodies. The robber baron's cruelty may sometimes sleep, his cupidity may at some point be satiated; but those who torment us for our own good will torment us without end for they do so with the approval of their own conscience.
>
> Even the most well-meaning people can do great damage if they lose perspective. The road to hell is paved with good intentions, as they say.[4]

The situation is only worsening day by day with the imposition of vaccine mandates and vaccine passports. Even the Vatican requires a Green Pass. Such mandates have no basis in Scripture, as exemplified by James 5:14–16, where the sick are to be prayed for and saved, not segregated and punished (in this case those deemed to be sick).

Since March of 2020, individuals and their families have been brought to their knees because of government tyranny. Businesses have shut down permanently. Suicide rates have increased. If an individual imposed the same tactics on his family members as governments have on their citizens, they would question his sanity. Governments have used fear tactics, bribes, guilt, shame, blame, and now the threat of unemployment, all for refusing to accept an injected gene therapy with unknown long-term effects. Do people really believe that governments are taking this course of action because they sincerely care about the well-being of their citizens? Frighteningly, some people believe without question that they do. Yet the intent is to divide and control. By and

4 C.S. Lewis, "The Humanitarian Theory of Punishment," in *God in the Dock: Essays on Theology and Ethics*, ed. Walter Hooper (London: HarperOne, 1994), 121.

large, the medical establishment has ignored the significance of the adverse effects of the COVID-19 "vaccine."

Many have complied because they want this tyrannical rule to end, but it is precisely because of people's compliance that it will never end. Little do they realize that unless they receive the endless boosters necessitated by the waning protection of these vaccines, they will end up with the same legal vaccination status as the unvaccinated. Now a new alleged COVID variant, Omicron, has medical bureaucrats question whether the "vaccine" will be effective against it. Nevertheless, growing evidence indicates that natural immunity is more robust than that conferred by double-vaccination. There is also a threat to some parents' access to and even custody over their children because of their views on COVID-19 and vaccine mandates. This is more reminiscent of the Soviet Union, Nazi Germany, or Mao's China than of any democratic nation in the twenty-first century, but here we are. It is an affront to reason to take these extreme measures for a virus that has a recovery rate well over 99 percent. President John F. Kennedy famously stated in his inaugural address of January 20, 1961: "In the long history of the world, only a few generations have been granted the role of defending freedom in its hour of maximum danger. I do not shrink from this responsibility—I welcome it. I do not believe that any of us would exchange places with any other people or any other generation."[5]

As I write this, we are rapidly approaching that maximum hour of danger which JFK so eloquently spoke about. The draconian measures imposed on sovereign citizens of the world are in direct violation of our human rights and the Nuremberg Code. Historians will look upon this period with disbelief. Despite all our scientific achievements and technological advancements, we are still incapable of shaking off our tribal proclivities towards unthinking compliance with brutal authoritarian rule and its associated fear tactics. As Spanish philosopher George Santayana put it: "Those who cannot remember the past are condemned to repeat it."[6] The deadliest virus we face is one of the mind which spreads at unprecedented rates, mutating into unimaginable absurd variations. All one has to do is check the comments under a CBC article or CNN video.

Even though the contributors to this volume hold to different worldviews, conceptions of God, economic policies, COVID-19 outlooks, and political views, they share a strong belief in an individual's right to free expression without fear of reprisal and in the important role that reason, science, logic, intuition, and lived experience play in navigating through such difficult

5 Inaugural address of President John F. Kennedy (Washington, D.C., January 20, 1961). https://www.jfklibrary.org/archives/other-resources/john-f-kennedy-speeches/inaugural-address-19610120.

6 George Santayana, *The Life of Reason: Reason in Common Sense (New York:* Scribner's, 1905), 284.

subjects. It is worth noting that the organization, structure, and selection of chapters fall solely on the shoulders of the editor; individual authors are not aware of the contents of other chapters and as such may not be in agreement, nor should they be held accountable for any views other than the ones expressed in their respective chapters. Although I myself may not agree with every part of every chapter, I believe that each idea presented is at least worth examining. We arrive at a great understanding when we engage with those we disagree with. The purpose of this volume is to provide a wide-ranging resource in thinking critically through a host of issues affecting the future of our shared humanity. Each chapter can stand on its own or be read in unison with others to form a global picture of the crises we face. By no means is it meant to offer the definitive text on any of the examined subjects. Nevertheless, it is our hope that this body of work will help our readers confront major existential questions regarding the world we live in and the future world people of good will yearn for. It is also our sincere hope that this book will inspire further questions, research, and a call to change. Indeed, the authors share a common desire for authentic human flourishing and progress.

Gone are the days when students were captivated by the Holy Scriptures, the works of Plato, Aristotle, Augustine, and Aquinas, or timeless literary classics such as the *Iliad, Don Quixote*, the *Divine Comedy*, or *The Brothers Karamazov.* Instead, our youth look to sources which lack virtue, substance, mystery, and depth. In spite of this, in recent years, the phenomenon of the world-renowned psychologist and opponent of politically correct culture Jordan Peterson has had a profound effect on our youth and others. Age-old wisdom and common-sense truths, although repackaged, are resonating with men and women both young and old, since this yearning for meaning and responsibility has not fully vanished. Yet these are not currently offered in many of our churches and educational institutions. Regrettably, activism and tribal foolishness have taken their place.

In the absence of God, truth, and reason, we are left in a relativistic quagmire, where falsehoods reign tyrannically. This book endeavors to make sense out of nonsense—to reason through the ever-crumbling structures of the West. It is of no coincidence that many secular yet astute commentators and public figures like Jordan Peterson, Gad Saad, David Rubin, Stefan Molyneux, and Douglas Murray are moving from the left to the center (or right-of-center). They are also demonstrating a greater openness to Christian values and even truths. This is a direct effect of the immoral, corrupt, and bankrupt practices and ideologies emanating from the left. Given this context, it should come as no surprise that a secular, quasi-scientific-materialist thinker like Jordan Peterson who is attempting to affirm objective morality nonetheless seriously struggles with the truth of Christ's divinity and resurrection (something which I predicted in an essay which I delivered to him personally several years ago and is now a chapter of this volume, titled "The Peterson-Craig Encounter: A Missed Opportunity?"). Truth exists, and it does matter. Peterson's evolving position is a sure indication of this. Truth matters in every domain of existence, despite popular culture's persistent claim that everything is relative or subjective. But what is the solution? This author believes it is found in a return to our Christian roots, since Christianity is one of the few forces capable of confronting and defeating much of the world's evil. (This is a personal view and does not speak to the views of several of the contributors of this volume.) In order to make sense of nonsense we must have a light to navigate out of the current quagmire the West finds itself in. Make no mistake, once you cut away all superficial analyses of politics and culture, you will discover that, *au fond*, this is a spiritual battle: "Finally, be strong in the Lord and in the strength of his power. Put on the whole armor of God, so that you may be able to stand against the wiles of the devil. For our struggle is not against enemies of blood and flesh, but against the rulers, against the authorities, against the cosmic spiritual forces of evil in the heavenly places" (Eph 6:10–20).

Scott D. G. Ventureyra
Ottawa, Ontario
March 2022

Overview

Scott D. G. Ventureyra

I will now provide an overview of the sections and parts of this volume. The first section, titled "Setting the Stage," provides a diagnosis of the current predicament of the West. Destructive ideologies are gnawing away at the edifices of the West. It is undeniable that the West is in decay. Over the past few decades, communist dissenters have warned the West about the perils of totalitarianism. Tragically, citizens of the free world are blindly following in the footsteps of these tyrannical states. The very oppression that people fled from for freedom is being imported into sovereign Western nations. The attacks upon the foundations of Western civilization are predominantly coming from within, from elites, politicians, educators, entertainers, and most recently so-called medical experts. Tolerance has been subverted into something that is unrecognizable. It is now commonplace to blatantly state that someone who holds a differing viewpoint is intolerant, but isn't that the point of a Western democracy—to debate ideas we disagree about?

The section on "Truth" deals with issues related to philosophy, theology, and science. The authors discuss the overreach of certain scientific claims and methodologies, the nature of reality, what is reasonable to believe in, and how experience can guide us. Confusion on these points taints our understanding of philosophy, theology, and science.

In the final section, devoted to the human person, various authors examine the many threats that affect the future of humanity, both individually and collectively. Subjects treated include abortion, euthanasia, crimes against children, a variety of issues pertaining to physical and mental health, gender ideologies, the COVID-19 crisis, vaccination mandates and passports, and the struggle for freedom in its various manifestations. It is also worth noting the connection between chapter 10 and chapter 30 in regard to my godfather's life. Chapter 30 is about his self-realizations and the suffering he experienced as a young medical student, while Chapter 10 sheds light on his long path towards truth and redemption. Both stories are worth recounting given the "Jekyll and Hyde" switch in our governments' treatment of patients and health workers before and after vaccination mandates. In 1943, early in my godfather's medical career, he was coerced into assisting in cruel and morally reprehensible medical experiments. When he emigrated to Canada, he then had the freedom to follow his moral conscience for the rest of his medical career. Unfortunately, many are not following their conscience or the Hippocratic oath these days.

After the rather dire picture of human existence painted throughout Section III, Part VII: "Human Hope: The *Imago Dei* and Human Resilience" gives a glimpse of hope through examining the various gifts and graces bestowed upon humanity. It is a look toward the endurance of the human spirit. On the one hand, some of this hope relies on concrete things such as self-reliance, love for oneself and others, reason, compassion, understanding, and action. On the other hand, this hope relies on belief in the reality of the invisible and spiritual realm that aids us on our quest to understand reality and fulfill our ultimate purpose in this life. It is this conjoining of the mundane and the spiritual which embodies the human response to suffering and evil. It is a trust and assurance beyond physical reality, as Hebrew 1:11 emphasizes: "Now faith is the assurance of things hoped for, the conviction of things not seen."

Section I:

Setting the Stage: Humanity at the Crossroads?

Chapter 1

The Decay of the West

Scott D. G. Ventureyra

Sixteen years before becoming the 40th president of the United States, Ronald Reagan gained national attention as a new and important conservative voice in America with his famous 1964 speech, "A Time for Choosing" (also known as "The Speech"). In this speech, he made the following reflection:

> You and I are told increasingly we have to choose between a left or right. Well, I'd like to suggest there is no such thing as a left or right. There's only an up or down: [up] man's old-aged dream, the ultimate in individual freedom consistent with law and order, or down to the ant heap of totalitarianism. And regardless of their sincerity, their humanitarian motives, those who would trade our freedom for security have embarked on this downward course.[1]

Reagan's incisive observation is still as relevant today as it was back then, perhaps even more so now. This is seen forcefully amidst the destruction wrought by progressive woke culture and the COVID situation. Woke culture has propagated countless falsehoods aimed at destroying our freedom of speech and conscience. Common sense, logic, science, hard work, prosperity, and property rights have been demonized as harmful, oppressive tools enslaving people. Truth is being upturned at every opportunity. We are told that war is peace, oppression is freedom, male is female (female is male), racial equality is racism, the healthy are ill, and so on. We are increasingly told, essentially, that 2+2=5, and if we disagree with this and other untruths, we are to be ostracized and punished. It is not unlike George Orwell's description of the Party's philosophy of government for Oceania in his dystopian novel *Nineteen Eighty-Four*:

> In the end, the Party would announce that two and two made five, and you would have to believe it. It was inevitable that they should

1 Reagan, "A Time for Choosing (The Speech)." You could substitute the word "health" for "security" now.

> make that claim sooner or later: the logic of their position demanded it. Not merely the validity of experience, but the very existence of external reality, was tacitly denied by their philosophy. The heresy of heresies was common sense. And what was terrifying was not that they would kill you for thinking otherwise, but that they might be right. For, after all, how do we know that two and two make four? Or that the force of gravity works? Or that the past is unchangeable? If both the past and the external world exist only in the mind, and if the mind itself is controllable—what then?[2]

This attitude runs rampant through our educational and political institutions, where truth is deemed to be irrelevant and might decides what is right. Historically, those on the side of truth, goodness, and justice never had to resort to such tactics of obfuscation, propaganda, disinformation, misinformation, and manipulation. People escape countries run by oppressive regimes and flee to Western democracies, in the hope of living a free, prosperous, and happy life. Tragically, these Western democracies are turning into the very oppressive states that people have sought freedom from. To the reasonable person, it should be obvious why you only see boats fleeing from Cuba, for instance, to the US and not vice versa. We are truly heading downwards, as Reagan warned us over half a century ago.

Disregarded Warnings to the West

Throughout the 1970s and 1980s, two Soviet dissenters, Aleksandr Solzhenitsyn and Yuri Bezmenov, offered different insights into how and why the Western world would succumb to communism if it did not awake from its slumber. The philosophy or a-theology of communism has many elements, but the following definition is best suited for the purposes of this book:

> Communism is neither a trend of thought, nor a doctrine, nor a failed attempt at a new way of ordering human affairs. Instead, it should be understood as a devil—an evil specter forged by hate, degeneracy, and other elemental forces in the universe… The communist evil specter, with its countless mutations, is full of guile. Sometimes it uses slaughter and violence to destroy those who refuse to follow it. Other times, it takes recourse in the language of "science" and "progress," offering a wonderful blueprint of the future in order to deceive people. Sometimes it presents itself as a profound field of learning and makes people believe that it is the future direction of mankind. Other times, it uses the slogans of "democracy," "equality," and "social justice" to infiltrate the fields

2 Orwell, *Nineteen Eighty-Four*, 72–73.

> of education, media, art, and law, bringing people under its banner without their awareness. At yet other times, it calls itself "socialism," "progressivism," "liberalism," "neo-Marxism," and other leftist terms.[3]

Unfortunately, these warnings have been largely ignored throughout our recent cultural descent. Today, in the United States, we have a young woman who fled North Korea, Yeonmi Park, who carries forward this dissenting flag, warning the West of the perils of such pernicious ideologies.

Soviet Dissident: Aleksandr Solzhenitsyn

Aleksandr Solzhenitsyn (1918–2008) won the Nobel Prize in Literature in 1970. He served the world as a beacon of light, truth, and hope. He suffered at the hands of both Adolph Hitler and Joseph Stalin. He had been imprisoned in 1945 for distributing anti-Soviet propaganda. During his time in the gulags, he had the opportunity to reflect deeply upon his life. Solzhenitsyn endured tremendous amounts of psychological, physical, and spiritual torment. But, instead of allowing his resentfulness, despair, and bitterness to consume him, he underwent a radical transformation. He took inventory of the things he had done wrong and found ways to repair the failures of his past life. Inspired by this experience, he wrote the three-volume *Gulag Archipelago* from 1958 to 1968, publishing it in 1973. This masterful work served as an intellectual death knell to the pernicious ideology of communism.

This intense introspection, delving into the deep and terrifying recesses of our own moral consciousness, is where true freedom lies. The deep significance of Solzhenitsyn's life and message is that at every turn we are capable of both good and evil. It is the willful turn towards good which helps not only us, but others and the world in general. Despite the collapse of the Soviet Union, Solzhenitsyn feared that free societies would devolve into ones of oppression. During the summer of 1975, Solzhenitsyn gave three speeches in the United States: two to labor organizations and one to Congress. A year later he was interviewed by the BBC and delivered a speech over British radio. The transcripts of these speeches were collected in a volume fittingly titled *Warning to the West*, which was published in 1976. He warned us about the direction that Western civilization was heading when he stated:

> Human nature is full of riddles and contradictions; its very complexity engenders art—and by art I mean the search for something more than simple linear formulations, flat solutions, oversimplified explanations.

3 Editorial Board of "Nine Commentaries on the Communist Party," *How the Specter of Communism Is Ruling Our World*, *xv*–xvi.

> One of these riddles is: how is it that people who have been crushed by the sheer weight of slavery and cast to the bottom of the pit can nevertheless find strength to rise up and free themselves, first in spirit and then in body; while those who soar unhampered over the peaks of freedom suddenly appear to lose the taste for freedom, lose the will to defend it, and, hopelessly confused and lost, almost begin to crave slavery. Or again: why is it that societies which have been benumbed for half a century by lies they have been forced to swallow find within themselves a certain lucidity of heart and soul which enables them to see things in their true perspective and to perceive the real meaning of events; whereas societies with access to every kind of information suddenly plunge into lethargy, into a kind of mass blindness, a kind of voluntary self-deception.[4]

The last portion of the final sentence is timely, given how people in the West have become not only deluded but also distracted from reality with the help of the media and the entertainment industry and through the direct access to vast amounts of information, so much so that they are unable to discern a modicum of truth when it appears before their eyes.

Although I had never endured life under a brutal oppressive totalitarian regime, over the past two years I have come to taste the foulness of autocratic rule as exercised by Canadian politicians throughout the ongoing health crisis:[5] something that can only set a bad precedent for the rulers of free citizens. I can nonetheless relate to the words of Solzhenitsyn through the experience of others. Over the years, I have spoken to many individuals who fled countries like Cuba, Hungary, Romania, and Russia, seeking asylum in Western democracies. These people were always flabbergasted when I would explain to them how much support there was for Marxism in the Western academy and popular culture. In my childhood, when my parents would travel, a kind, loving, and intelligent woman from Cuba named Georgina would look after me for weeks at a time. She always reminded me to be grateful for the free and peaceful life I had in Canada. She spoke to me of the horrors she endured at the hands of the communist regime in Cuba before she fled for a better life. She was always thankful for this new life, although the communist propaganda still ran deep in her son's veins. My godfather, a neurosurgeon who fled from communism in Hungary, also spoke of the brutality and oppression he endured under a fascist regime. I have included an excerpt depicting one of his experiences in this volume. Political propagandists like Michael Moore, self-congratulating professors like Michael Eric Dyson, and media personalities such as CNN anchor Don Lemon do not speak from the real experience of real people who

4 Solzhenitsyn, *Warning to the West,* 125–126.

5 There is also a volume on COVID-19 that corresponds with this one.

suffered under oppressive totalitarian regimes. Rather they follow an ideological script that is far removed from reality. Fascist and communist regimes are often enough different sides of the same coin.

Solzhenitsyn also warned about the descent into moral relativism that is one of the key characteristics of any communist system:

> Communism has never concealed the fact that it rejects all absolute concepts of morality. It scoffs at any consideration of "good" and "evil" as indisputable categories. Communism considers morality to be relative, to be a class matter. Depending on circumstances and the political situation, any act, including murder, even the killing of hundreds of thousands, could be good or could be bad. It all depends on class ideology. And who defines this ideology? The whole class cannot get together to pass judgment. A handful of people determine what is good and what is bad. But I must say that in this respect Communism has been most successful. It has infected the whole world with the belief in the relativity of good and evil. Today, many people apart from the Communists are carried away by this idea. Among progressive people, it is considered rather awkward to use seriously such words as "good" and "evil." Communism has managed to persuade all of us that these concepts are old-fashioned and laughable. But if we are to be deprived of the concepts of good and evil, what will be left? Nothing but manipulation of one another. We will sink to the status of animals.[6]

All we need to do is look at the entertainment industry and the arbitrariness of many governmental policies. Indeed, the West has been swept away, although not consistently, by both metaphysical and moral relativism, often in issues surrounding truth, life, gender, or sexuality.

Former KGB Propagandist: Juri Bezmenov

Juri Bezmenov (1939–1993) was a journalist and a former KGB informant and propagandist who defected to Canada in the 1970s. Bezmenov had become somewhat forgotten, although there has been a resurgence and growing presence of his thought online, as some of his claims have been vindicated in recent years, especially with our current health and cultural crises. In an interview hosted by G. Edward Griffin[7] in 1984 titled "Soviet Subversion of the Free-World Press: A

6 Solzhenitsyn, *Warning to the West*, 57–58.

7 G. Edward Griffin is an American author, filmmaker, and lecturer. His *The Creature from Jekyll Island* (1994) is an expose of the corruption associated with the US Federal Reserve system. Unsurprisingly, Wikipedia and other mainstream sources have dubbed him a conspiracy theorist.

Conversation with Yuri Bezmenov," Bezmenov explains how he was discredited through a joint effort between Prime Minister Pierre Elliot Trudeau and Soviet ambassador Aleksandr Yakovlev:

> In about five years, [the] KGB eventually discovered that I [was] working for Canadian broadcasting. I made a very big mistake. I started working for [the] overseas service of [the] CBC, which is similar to Voice of America, in [the] Russian language, and of course [the] monitoring service in [the] USSR picked up every new voice—[with] every new announcer they would make it a point to discover who he is—and in five years, sure enough, slowly but surely, they discovered that I am not Tomas [David] Schuman, that I am Yuri Alexandrovich Bezmenov, and that I am working for Canadian broadcasting, and undermining [the] beautiful detente between Canada and [the] USSR. And the Soviet ambassador Aleksandr Yakovlev made it his personal effort to discredit me; he complained to Pierre Trudeau, who is known to be a little bit soft on socialism [actually he was a great sympathizer with communist states like China and Cuba (with very friendly relations with Fidel Castro)—ed.], and the management of CBC behaved in a very strange, cowardly way, unbecoming of representatives of an independent country like Canada. They listened to every suggestion that [the] Soviet ambassador gave, and they started shameful investigation, analyzing [the] content of my broadcasts to [the] USSR. Sure enough, they discovered that some of my statements were probably too... would be offending to the Soviet politburo. So I had to leave my job.[8]

Bezmenov spoke frequently on the concept of ideological subversion, which he defined as "the process of changing the perception of reality in the minds of millions of peoples all over the world."[9] The General Secretary of the Communist Party of the Soviet Union and onetime head of the KGB Yuri Andropov (1914–1984) referred to the process of ideological subversion as "the final struggle for the minds and hearts of the people."[10] There are four stages of ideological subversion:

- Demoralization: educate an entire generation in Marxist ideology.
- Destabilization: of the economy, foreign relations, and defense systems.
- Crisis: violent change of power structure and the economy.
- Normalization: period of stability (until the next cycle reaches crisis point).[11]

8 Knight, "Useless Dissident: Interview with Yuri Bezmenov."

9 Schuman, *Love Letter to America*, 5. Tomas Schuman was the pseudonym used by Juri Bezmenov.

10 Schuman, *Love Letter to America*, 5.

11 Schuman, *Love Letter to America*, 21.

It is not difficult to see how the West, including the United States, went through the first stage decades ago, often by its own hands under the influence of communist subverters. I wonder to myself whether recent developments in the ongoing cultural war in parts of the West have transitioned, partly or wholly, from destabilization to crisis. One need only contemplate all the rioting carried out by groups like Black Lives Matter (BLM) and antifa.[12] On the whole, this was never condemned by mainstream media, or by prominent Democrats like Joe Biden and Kamala Harris. Even worse, it was justified and spun. They gaslit their own people into believing falsehoods ("it was just peaceful protesting") and accepting double standards. In Canada, dozens of churches have been burned down since the discovery of hundreds of unmarked graves on sites that were once church-run residential schools for indigenous children. Indigenous leaders have condemned such actions by "activists." All the while, rapidly, silently, and surely, Communist China increases its economic power and influence on the global stage while strengthening its defense systems. The seeds of division in the West are growing day by day.

When Bezmenov was lecturing and writing about ideological subversion, the communist subverters were the Soviets. Today, it is the Chinese Communist Party who are the subverters. In general, their principles are the same, but unlike the Soviets, Communist China left socialism behind and has embraced capitalism. The spread of private ownership and free markets has lifted millions of Chinese out of poverty. China has been able to sustain economic development because government intervention has decreased, and privately-owned enterprises have increased dramatically since the 1990s. This has accelerated China's presence as a superpower on the world stage. Moreover, throughout recent decades they have acquired properties all over the world and infiltrated mainstream media, social media platforms, and the entertainment industry.[13]

Unfortunately, Bezmenov's assessment of the indoctrination that has occurred throughout America is quite accurate; I can attest to it in my home country (Canada) through countless experiences in the workplace, academia, and everyday life. A particularly noticeable aspect of this is the brainwashing that occurs as part of ideological subversion:

> It's a great brainwashing process, which goes very slow[ly] and is divided [into] four basic stages. The first one [is] demoralization; it takes from 15 [to] 20 years to demoralize a nation. Why that many years? Because this is the minimum number of years which [is required] to educate one generation of students in the country of your enemy, exposed to the ideology of the enemy. In other words, Marxist-Leninist ideology is being pumped into the soft heads of at least three generations of

12 Matthews, "Flashback 2020: Six Months of Antifa/BLM Looting, Rioting, and Chaos."

13 Rogers, "China Has Already Infiltrated America's Institutions."

> American students, without being challenged, or counter-balanced by the basic values of Americanism (American patriotism).
>
> The result? The result you can see. Most of the people who graduated in the sixties (drop-outs or half-baked intellectuals) are now occupying the positions of power in the government, civil service, business, mass media, [and the] educational system. You are stuck with them. You cannot get rid of them. They are contaminated; they are programmed to think and react to certain stimuli in a certain pattern. You cannot change their mind, even if you expose them to authentic information, even if you prove that white is white and black is black, you still cannot change the basic perception and the logic of behavior. In other words… the process of demoralization is complete and irreversible. To [rid] society of these people, you need another twenty or fifteen years to educate a new generation of patriotically-minded and commonsense people, who would be acting in favor and in the interests of United States society.[14]

Individuals who have been so deeply demoralized are practically incapable of seeing truth, and a new, patriotically minded generation is the only way to overcome the devastation wrought by this process. We see this beginning with strong counter-cultural conservative movements in the US such as Turning Point USA:

> For the last 25 years…actually, it's over-fulfilled because demoralization now reaches such areas where previously not even Comrade Andropov and all his experts would even dream of such a tremendous success. Most of it is done by Americans to Americans, thanks to a lack of moral standards.
>
> As I mentioned before, exposure to true information does not matter anymore. A person who was demoralized is unable to assess true information. The facts tell nothing to him. Even if I shower him with information, with authentic proof, with documents, with pictures; even if I take him by force to the Soviet Union and show him [a] concentration camp, he will refuse to believe it, until he [receives] a kick in his fan-bottom. When a military boot crashes his… then he will understand. But not before that. That's the [tragedy] of the situation of demoralization.
>
> So basically America is stuck with demoralization and unless… even if you start right now, here, this minute, you start educating [a] new generation of American[s], it will still take you fifteen to twenty years to turn the tide of ideological perception of reality back to normalcy and patriotism.[15]

14 Knight, "Useless Dissident."
15 Knight, "Useless Dissident."

The COVID-19 health crisis has also played a major role in inflicting unprecedented chaos, division, and sheer harm on people around the world. What has precipitated all of this is not so much the SARS-CoV-2 virus but the "cure," namely, the side-effects brought on by politicians and health experts: draconian lockdowns, mask mandates, physical ("social") distancing, limits on social gatherings and even religious ceremonies, and now vaccine passports and mandates. This is most glaring among those around us who are willing to trade their civil liberties for false promises of security and health by politicians and putative health experts who have become drunk on power and money. Indeed, a dystopian delusion has penetrated the hearts and minds of countless individuals. The combination of fear, uncritical thinking, and unthinking compliance has become ubiquitous throughout a significant portion of the population. A deadly virus of the mind has invaded the fabric of Western civilization. This delusion is in the process of destroying the freest and most prosperous societies that humanity has ever known. The rampant censorship of certain medical doctors and scientists, the growing segregation (vaccinated versus unvaccinated), propaganda, indoctrination, and going door to door demanding compliance are reminiscent of the Soviet Union or Nazi Germany, not a 21st-century democracy.

The communist subverters and influencers run rampant, but ultimately the death of the West will come by its own hands, through self-strangulation. It is the "useful idiots" such as the anti-patriotic leftists who will bring this about, with the help of "leaders" such as Canadian Prime Minister Justin Trudeau, American President Joseph Biden, French President Emmanuel Macron, German Chancellor Angela Merkel. It is precisely as Bezmenov explains:

> In the context of the USA, most of these nasty things are done to America by Americans... with the IDEOLOGICAL help of the Communist subverters. Most of the actions are overt, legitimate, and easily identifiable. The only trouble is they are "stretched in time." In other words, the process of subversion is such a long-term process that an average individual, due to the short time-span of his historical memory, is unable to perceive the process of subversion as a CONSISTENT and willful effort. That is exactly how it is intended to be: like the small hand of your watch. You know it moves, but you CANNOT SEE it moving.
>
> The main principle of ideological subversion is URNING A STRONGER FORCE AGAINST ITSELF. Just like in the Japanese martial arts: you do not stop the blow of a heavier, more powerful enemy with an equally forceful blow. You may simply hurt your hand. Instead you catch the striking fist with your hand and PULL the enemy in the direction of his blow until he crashes into a wall or any other heavy object in his way.
>
> America is obviously a "stronger force" that Communism is unable to defeat. But it is possible to conquer this nation using the

> preconditions I have described, created by Americans themselves, and diverting America's attention away from these mortally dangerous preconditions. The situation is similar to a house, the owners of which have stored explosives and inflammable materials INSIDE. To destroy this house the enemy docs not have to intrude physically into it. It is enough to start a fire next door and wait till the wind blows in the right direction.
>
> Meanwhile the enemy may "throw in some great ideas" for the owners to argue about in order to take their attention off the actual fire: environmental protection, gay liberation, or emancipation of house pets are the types of noncritical arguments that divert America's attention from the real danger. Smart people would notice the fire and remove the inflammable objects and materials BEFORE the house catches the fire. Useful idiots will keep arguing about whether it is constitutional or not to pay firefighters, or the equality of husband and wife in domestic chores (who should remove the combustibles), until the actual explosion blows their enfeebled brains all over the neighbourhood.[16]

Unfortunately, not enough people are realizing that their attention is being diverted through critical race theory (CRT), gender ideology, the current world health crisis, and the like. To be sure, all are important issues that need to be appropriately addressed, but at the same time distractions from the inner divisions and turmoil within the fabric of the West. I fear that those in the West who have not already awakened to these realities will remain in their slumber as their beloved countries self-implode.

North Korean Defector and Human Rights Activist: Yeonmi Park (Park Yeon-mi)

The experience of Yeonmi Park (Park Yeon-mi), a young woman who fled the brutal dictatorship of North Korea in 2007, should add further credence to Solzhenitsyn's and Bezmenov's assessments and warnings. Yeonmi claims that the future of America is as bleak as that of North Korea.[17] Having been subjected to the slave trade in China after fleeing North Korea,[18] she knows firsthand what real oppression and suffering entail. She was reprimanded by professors at Columbia University for expressing enjoyment of classic literature such as the writing of Jane Austen, who was labeled as having a "colonial mindset" and belonging to a group of white authors who were bigoted racists looking to brainwash their readers. The hypocrisy of these ivory-tower

16 Schuman, *Love Letter to America*, 40.
17 Sahakian, "North Korean defector says 'even North Korea was not this nuts.'"
18 Sahakian, "North Korean defector."

intellectuals is nothing short of astounding, considering they are in the business of indoctrinating their students in how and what to think. They are the epitome of privilege and entitlement. They look nothing short of ridiculous when reprimanding someone like Yeonmi for their reading preferences. Yeonmi's experience at Columbia University led her to think that Western universities have become bastions of indoctrination. She was left with the following realization: "Wow, this is insane. I thought America was different, but I saw so many similarities to what I saw in North Korea that I started worrying."[19] In this interview on Fox News, she also stated that Americans are *choosing* to be brainwashed: "North Koreans, we don't have Internet, we don't have access to any of these great thinkers, we don't know anything. But here, while having everything, people choose to be brainwashed. And they deny it."[20] It is a tragic state of affairs to say the least. It takes someone who can appreciate freedom to acknowledge the madness that the West is undergoing. Yeonmi, although generations younger than Solzhenitsyn and Bezmenov, is providing the same warnings to a later generation, hopefully a more receptive one.

Intertwined ideologies such as Marxism, socialism, and communism are inherently anti-human, especially once all the falsehoods are exposed and their "alluring" promises are stripped away. There is no greater threat to these ideologies than truth, lived experience, and history. To anyone who is grateful for their freedom, the words of Ronald Reagan (then the governor of California) on the fragility of freedom are as true today as when he first uttered them:

> Perhaps you and I have lived too long with this miracle to properly be appreciative. Freedom is a fragile thing and it's never more than one generation away from extinction. It is not ours by way of inheritance; it must be fought for and defended constantly by each generation, for it comes only once to a people. And those in world history who have known freedom and then lost it have never known it again.[21]

Descent into Hell

Three pillars of Western civilization—Greco-Roman philosophy and government, Christianity, and modern science—are withering away. The core ideas that helped build the West, such as the Judeo-Christian conception of God, truth, goodness, justice, human rights, democracy, reason, logic, science, tolerance, and capitalism, are all under attack. In recent years, the attacks have intensified, leading many to accept a confused and distorted understanding of

19 Sahakian, "North Korean defector."
20 Sahakian, "North Korean defector."
21 Reagan, Inaugural Address.

the world. The history and complexities of this attack, past and present, have been the subject of much discussion and controversy.

Western civilization's decline has a complex history that cannot be given a comprehensive treatment here. However, a brief sketch to set the stage for the subsequent parts and chapters of this volume will be provided. Even though secularism and non-traditional religiosity (new-age and neo-pagan belief systems) have been on the rise for centuries, from the so-called Age of Enlightenment forward, with various deist and atheist philosophies that challenged Christian truths and values, it is the developments of the nineteenth and twentieth century that came to profoundly alter the socio-economic and cultural milieu of the West. Some of these challenges and developments will be discussed below.

Scientific Materialism

The guise of atheism most commonly propagated in contemporary times is scientific materialism. It is the view that physical reality, as investigated through the scientific method in the natural sciences, is all that *really* exists. It leaves no room for theology and suppresses many metaphysical questions. It has had a tremendous impact on the Western psyche. It is also widely held in popular culture. Consequently, it has been unthinkingly accepted by many people, highly educated or not. However, despite its push in popular culture through scientific popularizers such as Neil deGrasse Tyson, Lawrence Krauss, Richard Dawkins, and Stephen Hawking, it has also been met with significant challenges in recent years. The truth is that philosophy and theology are indispensable to science;[22] and that science itself is not based on materialism, even though the study of matter is fundamental to understanding the universe. The philosophical and scientific challenges to materialism are significant.[23] Indeed, a major presupposition behind the scientific revolution was that the universe was created by a rational God in an intelligible and comprehensible way for humans to understand. This correspondence between human rationality and the intelligibility of the universe is indispensable to scientific inquiry. In spite of this, scientific materialism has inhibited many from considering the possibility of the existence of the supernatural and has led us toward a culture of relativism

22 Ventureyra, *On the Origin of Consciousness*, chapter 2. The rest of the book also builds a cumulative case against scientific materialism and metaphysical naturalism, known as the Cumulative Evolutionary Natural Theological Argument from Consciousness (CENTAC).

23 For a contemporary treatment of the problems with scientific materialism see Nagel, *Mind & Cosmos*. For a treatise outlining scientific evidence with theological implications, see Meyer, *The Return of the God Hypothesis*.

and death, which denigrates and devalues human life and the inherent dignity of the human person.[24]

The Death of God

In the late 19th century, Friedrich Nietzsche brought to the fore the concept of the death of God. It famously appears in the "Parable of the Madman" (whom commentators have identified as Nietzsche himself) in his book *The Gay Science* (1882):

> God is dead. God remains dead. And we have killed him. How shall we comfort ourselves, the murderers of all murderers? What was holiest and mightiest of all that the world has yet owned has bled to death under our knives: who will wipe this blood off us? What water is there for us to clean ourselves? What festivals of atonement, what sacred games shall we have to invent? Is not the greatness of this deed too great for us? Must we ourselves not become gods simply to appear worthy of it?[25]

The cultural milieu of his time celebrated what it saw as the triumph of science over superstition. Nietzsche identified the "death of God" with the Enlightenment, which was thought to be the historical high point of human reason with its associated scientific discoveries. Moreover, the advent of Darwinism in his time further cemented the erosion of a belief in a personal Creator God. In essence, Nietzsche foresaw that in the twentieth century, this victory of instrumental rationality over religious "superstition" (more precisely Christianity) would inevitably result in humanity's most murderous massacre. In addition, he also realized that humanity had essentially lost its capacity or will to sustain objective moral values and duties; this was what he likened to the death of God. Thus, Nietzsche in a prophetic way ushered in an age of nihilism, rather like Fyodor Dostoyevsky's character Ivan Karamazov in *The Brothers Karamazov* (1880—two years before Nietzsche's *The Gay Science*):

> And Rakitin doesn't like God, oof, how he doesn't! That's the sore spot in all of them! But they conceal it. They lie. They pretend. "What, are you going to push for that in the department of criticism?" I asked. "Well, they won't let me do it openly," he said, and laughed. "But," I asked, "how will man be after that? Without God and the future life? It means everything is permitted now, one can do anything?" "Didn't you know?" he said. And he laughed. "Everything is permitted to the intelligent

24 Moreland and Rae, *Body & Soul.*

25 Nietzsche, *The Gay Science*, 181.

> man," he said. "The intelligent man knows how to catch crayfish, but you killed and fouled it up," he said, "and now you're rotting in prison!" He said that to me. A natural-born swine! I once used to throw the likes of him out—well, and now I listen to them.[26]

The death of God, whether in philosophical musings or in practice, did indeed make all things permissible, especially in the eyes of twentieth-century despots. One only needs to look toward the abhorrent actions of Nazi Germany, the Soviet Union, Mao Zedong's China, Pol Pod's Cambodia, and the United States' Japanese internment camps to find that this is as an undeniable truth.

The Denigration of the Human Person

In the fourth century B.C., Protagoras claimed that "man is the measure of all things." What he meant was that when he denies God or any absolute moral law, man becomes his own arbiter of truth. We are left in a Nietzschean universe, where everything is a will to power—might makes right, as our leftist friends have asserted repeatedly throughout history. This is a logical consequence of materialism and its offshoot, relativism. If there is no transcendent lawgiver, then there is no objective morality, no matter how sophisticated the moral theory. This reasoning has played out consistently in debates revolving around human dignity and the sanctity of life. This denigration of the human person is evident in debates over abortion, euthanasia, child abuse, and eugenics, and in the indoctrination of students with radical and harmful ideologies, the immoral profiteering of the pharmaceutical companies at humanity's expense, and the transgender confusion.

Further Symptoms of the West's Affliction

Economic Socialism

Economic socialism finds its basis in Marxism, the political-economic theory developed by Karl Marx (1818–1883) with the collaboration of Friedrich Engels (1820–1895) in the mid-19th century. Although there are many debates among Marxists on how to understand and interpret Marxism, the following description will suffice for our purposes—Marxism is a philosophy which combines a dialectical materialism with a political-economic theory. In essence, dialectical materialism is the view that metaphysical materialism

26 Dostoevsky, *The Brothers Karamazov*, 589.

is true, i.e., that all things in the universe, including human beings, are reducible to *matter in motion*, coupled with the notion that progress emerges through struggle. This is directly related to the aforementioned metaphysical materialism. In Marxism, class struggle is determined by economics and social class. It calls for an abrupt change in the hierarchical economic structure overturning private ownership: from capitalism to socialism and eventually communism. The core of the struggle would be between social classes: bourgeoisie versus proletariat, and capitalist versus worker. Marx and Engels envisioned the change from private ownership to socialism and communism as being possible solely through violent revolution: "The Communists disdain to conceal their views and aims. They openly declare that their ends can be attained only by the forcible overthrow of all existing social conditions. Let the ruling classes tremble at the Communistic revolution. The proletarians have nothing to lose but their chains. They have the world to win. WORKING MEN OF ALL COUNTRIES UNITE!"[27]

Unlike capitalism, where more people reap benefits from their toil and innovation, socialism leaves everyone equally destitute, except those governing, who live lives of luxury. Under capitalism, people are incentivized to work hard, and innovation is rewarded. The individual exercises power over the market by purchasing goods and services, rather than the state regulating which products and services will be available to the public.

Unfortunately, we are living in a time when university professors, politicians, and Hollywood celebrities are forcefully pushing the ideology of socialism;[28] these people, followers of Karl Marx, want to push the agenda of Joseph Stalin while they themselves live like Warren Buffet.[29] Leftists at university campuses, LGTBQ+ activists, and BLM supporters will ignorantly wear t-shirts of Ernesto de Guevara (Che Guevara), who was a lying, murderous psychopath, a racist, and homophobe.[30] The hypocrisy and ignorance of these people is astounding. If they would only take the time to study economics and history, or listen to the experiences of those who have fled from communist states, they would see the many pitfalls of socialism. This is a perfect example of the hypocrisy and incoherence of the modern "bourgeoisie." The late conservative political philosopher Roger Scruton (1944–2020) gave perhaps the most accurate assessment about these power-hungry people (particularly in the case of intellectuals): "It is not the truth of Marxism that explains the willingness of intellectuals to believe it, but the power that it confers on intellectuals, in their attempts to control the world. And since it is futile to reason someone out of

27 Marx and Engels, *The Communist Manifesto*, 39.
28 D'Souza, *United States of Socialism.*
29 Lott, "Lifestyles of the rich and socialist."
30 Alvarez, "Who Celebrates Che Guevara?"

a thing that he was not reasoned into, we can conclude that Marxism owes its remarkable power to survive every criticism to the fact that it is not a truth-directed but a power-directed system of thought."[31]

Such a motivation is especially reprehensible given the known failures and perils of socialism, most recently witnessed in the destruction of Venezuela,[32] which offers but a glimpse of full-blown socialism at work, where in 2018 the inflation rate hit 830,000 percent[33] and the minimum wage rose over 3,000 percent. This meant you required exorbitant amounts of money to buy extraordinarily little; in other words, you were better off replacing cash with toilet paper. Of course, the Marxist apologists will argue that this does not represent authentic socialism, nor do many of the other failed socialist experiments. How many times do we have to run this failed experiment? How many millions more must die? The truth is that economic systems require incentive-based structures to promote efficient economies, something socialism simply cannot produce, for in this system there is no incentive. And in case you are wondering, no, Scandinavian countries are not socialist.[34]

But how much of a failure has economic socialism been? We can count at least 25 countries—in the former Soviet bloc, Asia, South America, Latin America, and Africa—that have implemented socialism. Historically, socialism has been coupled with not only with totalitarianism but with murderous regimes the likes of which humanity had never seen before, as was the case in the Soviet Union, Mao's China, and Nazi Germany, which had its own brand of socialism: National Socialism. With or without such egregious crimes against humanity, all 25 of these experiments were utter failures. In science, what happens when experiments contradict the hypothesis? The hypothesis must be abandoned or altered. Researchers would not do well in accepting funding after so many failed attempts. And yet generations of students in tax-funded universities, in the departments of the humanities and social sciences, are taught to believe in socialism. If taxpayers fully realized this, I do not think they would be incredibly pleased. What are we to think of the stark differences between North and South Korea and between East and West Germany? You cannot get better test cases than these, since each presents almost identical variables—similar geography and climate, the same people, culture, and background—with two different economic systems; North Korea and East Germany were socialist, and South Korea and West Germany went toward capitalism. The capitalist countries fared

31 Scruton, *A Political Philosophy*, 149.

32 Di Martino, "How Socialism Destroyed Venezuela."

33 Martin, "Venezuela's inflation rate just hit 830,000%—and is likely to keep rising."

34 Dorfman, "Sorry Bernie Bros But Nordic Countries Are Not Socialist."

much better than the socialist.[35] The same goes for China, India, and Russia, all socialist countries that have now turned to capitalism; although not perfect, they are markedly better off now, with much more prosperity and opportunity.

Now recently, in July of 2021, there have been large uprisings in Cuba. The people of Cuba have had enough of decades of oppression. Ever since the 1959 revolution in Cuba led by Fidel Castro and Che Guevara, Cuba has been declined economically. However, the silence by Western leftists, including Justin Trudeau and Joseph Biden has generally been deafening. In fact, when Castro died in 2016, Canadian leaders like Trudeau and Jagmeet Singh praised his dictatorial rule. Castro was responsible for anywhere between 35,000 and 141,000 people dead and imprisoned countless others.[36] These figures are comparable to those of the Soviet Union per capita. What's the reason for the Cuban protests, the likes of which have not been witnessed in decades? It is not what some Western leftists think: Trudeau's diplomats recently praised Cuba's Communist Party for embracing social rights and freer speech, and laid the blame for human rights abuses on the pandemic.[37] Government crackdown on protesters has left many families unable to locate loved ones:

> Relatives are not being informed of the whereabouts of those detained within a reasonable period of time: Since 16 July, Amnesty International has spoken to multiple relatives of families detained in the context of the protests on 11 July. They told the organization that the authorities had not informed them of the whereabouts of their relatives. In one case, the family had not been informed of the relative's whereabouts for 96 hours. In another case, a family member indicated they had not been able to locate their relative for 6 days. In none of the cases had relatives received a phone call from detainees. We issued an Urgent Action calling for their immediate and unconditional release.[38]

Despite the horrific treatment of Cuban citizens by this ruthless communist regime, leftist organizations such as BLM (an avowed Marxist movement) and Democrat politicians such as Alexandria Ocasio-Cortez blame the Cuban's people strife on a "cruel embargo" by the US, instead of the real culprits.[39]

35 Gramlich, "East Germany has narrowed economic gap with West Germany since fall of communism"; Bajpai, "North Korean vs. South Korean Economies."

36 See a table of deaths throughout the twentieth century at the hands of communist dictatorships: Communist Democide 1900–1987, https://www.hawaii.edu/powerkills/COM.TAB1.GIF.

37 *Blacklock's Reporter*, "Hail Cuba Rights, Speech."

38 Amnesty International, "Cuba protests: latest information."

39 Cathell, "AOC blames Cuban suffering on US 'contributions,' calls for end to 'cruel' embargo."

Cultural Marxism

In 1930, the school of thought known as the Frankfurt School of Critical Theory emerged. Its leading thinkers included Max Horkheimer, Theodor Adorno, Herbert Marcuse, and Erich Fromm. Their thought can be classified as a prototypic cultural Marxism[40] or neo-Marxism.[41] The Bolshevik revolution and the rise of Nazism and fascism deeply shaped these thinkers' attempt to integrate Marxism with other social theories.[42] What is important to realize about the Frankfurt School is that it rejects basic tenets of what are broadly understood as important aspects of *traditional theories*, namely the application of universal laws of logic, coherence, and empirical confirmation—and thus any objective understanding of the world.

Postmodernism

Subsequently, a different but related school of thought began to emerge: postmodernism. With this new movement or way of "thinking," not only were the concepts of God and truth and the major doctrines of Christianity challenged, but also science, reason, and authentic progress. This would also include our traditional understanding of human rights, tolerance, capitalism, individualism, and truth—as will be examined throughout this volume. Under this "epistemology," if one can call it that without denigrating the term, reality is not objective but rather constructed by its observers. These social-constructionist ideas combine with cultural Marxism to produce notions such as critical race theory (CRT), feminism, and gender ideology.

Identity Politics

Postmodernists and cultural Marxists are also pushing a so-called social justice agenda, one that has penetrated institutions such as government, the entertainment industry, academia (both secular and Christian), and both elementary and secondary education. The game of identity politics as being played out throughout the West is creating an unprecedented divisiveness among its citizens. Leftists believe they can change reality by yelling the loudest. Roger Scruton observes that "Leftists believe, with the Jacobins of the French Revolution, that the goods of this world are unjustly distributed, and that the

40 McManus, "The Frankfurt School and Postmodern Philosophy."
41 Mendenhall, "Cultural Marxism Is Real."
42 *Encyclopedia Britannica*, "The Frankfurt School: German Research Group."

fault lies not in human nature but in usurpations practiced by a dominant class. They define themselves in opposition to established power, the champions of a new order that will rectify the ancient grievance of the oppressed."[43] They seek to blame institutions such as family, nation-state, Church, the scientific enterprise, and law.

One of the inanest examples of identity politics is manifested within the totalitarianism of the transgender activism movement. In December of 2019, for instance, J.K. Rowling was lambasted for stating the obvious: that one's sex is real and immutable.[44] This is an example of radical leftists eating the more moderate leftists. Rowling is someone who writes gender-inclusive books and is quite left-leaning in most of her views, but this does not satisfy the trans-activists. In July of 2021, a trans-activist on Twitter threatened Rowling with a pipe bomb in her mailbox, to which she responded: "To be fair, when you can't get a woman sacked, arrested, or dropped by her publisher, and cancelling her only made her book sales go up, there's really only one place to go."[45] The most recent victim has been comedian Dave Chappelle, who refuses to acquiesce to trans-activists' irrational demands.

The medical profession is kowtowing to transgender ideology and compromising the health of young children by promoting the idea that sex is mutable and that pumping them with hormones is a moral thing to do;[46] this is tantamount to child abuse of the worst kind;[47] and whistle-blowers have warned that gender dysphoria is being over-diagnosed.[48] President Biden's administration has been pushing a radical transgender agenda through allowing males who identify as females to compete alongside females.[49]

As consistent with cancel culture, those who speak against this insanity are consistently silenced and others are terrified to speak against it.[50] Good psychologists—those who maintain some level of sanity, like Oren Amitay in Toronto—have been "cancelled" for speaking the truth on transgenderism,[51] an insane ideology that is totalitarian in how it is enforced, but lacking any credible scientific, medical, philosophical, or theological backing. Just how totalitarian? An Iowa man was sentenced to prison for fifteen years for burning an LGBTQ+ flag. It is an unkind thing to attack a group in such a way, but is

43 Scruton, *Fools, Frauds and Firebrands: Thinkers of the New Left*, 3.

44 Coleman, "JK Rowling sparks controversy for tweet on gender: 'Sex is real.'"

45 Rowling, Twitter post, July 19, 2021.

46 Cantor, "American Academy of Pediatrics policy and trans- kids: Fact-checking."

47 Cretella, "I'm a Pediatrician. How Transgender Ideology Has Infiltrated my Field and Produced Large-Scale Child Abuse."

48 Donnelly, "Children's transgender clinic hit by 35 resignations in three years as psychologists warn of gender dysphoria 'over-diagnoses.'"

49 Mushnick, "Political correctness could threaten women's sports."

50 Dreher, "The Trojan Horse of Gender Ideology."

51 Amitay, "Telling the truth on trans issues got me cancelled."

the sentence proportionate to the crime? Nevertheless, the greatest pushback is coming from those who have suffered from transgender ideology; the first gender "detransition" conference has taken place.[52]

The Persecution of Christians and Christianity

The persecution of Christians throughout Asia, the Middle East, and Africa has been met with a deafening silence in the West.[53] This has been especially true throughout the COVID-19 world health crisis.[54] The mainstream news in the West has paid little to no attention to this horrible situation, which nearly counts as a genocide; it was only two years ago, after many years of silence, that a mainstream media outlet like the BBC gave this the attention it deserves, even if it failed to sustain it.[55] To be clear, I am not arguing that Christianity is the only religion that is being persecuted. However, I would argue Christians are currently the most persecuted religious group in the world, and at a level close to genocide. For example, in Nigeria, 3,000 Christians have been reported to be killed throughout 2021.[56] The media typically never covers any news about the strife that Arab Christians face in the Holy Land. These Christians are often caught in the crossfire between Jews and Muslims. The media will emphasize some facet of the Arab-Israeli conflict while ignoring the plight of Palestinian Christians, who have decreased from 15% of the population to 2% in the area. An organization based out of Canada is helping over 50 Christian families in the Holy Land through redistributing handicrafts they design.[57]

Throughout the summer of 2021, we have witnessed in Canada the burning of dozens of churches by far-left activists after the announcement made by the Canadian government and mainstream media regarding the discoveries of burial sites located near former residential schools.[58] Mainstream media has pushed a false narrative regarding these burial sites, which are in fact graveyards still in active use. Sophie Pierre, a former chief of the St. Mary's Indian Band and former student of the Kootenay Residential School at St. Eugene Mission just outside Cranbrook, British Columbia, where the 182 unmarked graves were allegedly recently discovered, stated: "To just assume that every unmarked grave inside a graveyard is already tied to a residential school, we've got to be a little bit more respectful of our people who are buried in our graveyards...

52 McLean, "At world's first gender 'detransition' conference."
53 Ibrahim, "The genocide of Christians in Burkina Faso."
54 Sawdy, "The Signs of Our Times: Christian persecution."
55 Gardner, "Iraq's Christians 'close to extinction.'"
56 Zeisloft, "Over 3,000 Christians reportedly killed in Nigeria so far this year."
57 See Handicrafts Holy Land Christians website: www.holylandchristians.ca.
58 Dzsurdzsa, "A map of the 57 churches that have been vandalized or burned."

We just buried one of our people there last month… Anyone who died in my community would be buried there."[59]

Hatred for traditional Christianity and what it embodies is prevalent throughout the West, within governments and social groups and throughout the academy. However, there has recently been an increase in attacks on churchgoers with the draconian COVID-19 restrictions and lockdowns. Sanitary policies have indeed become fascistic. By May of 2021, three Canadian pastors had been arrested for violating COVID-19 policies.[60] On May 8, 2021, the Calgary Police (sanitary fascists) made an example of Pastor Artur Pawlowski and his brother, Dawid Pawlowski, by arresting them in a dramatic fashion; they spent 30 hours in solitary confinement for allegedly not following church capacity limits set by the Albertan government.[61] Videos of Pawlowski casting police and health inspectors out of his church on Easter weekend went viral. He called these police officers and health inspectors "Nazis," "Gestapo," "Communists," "Psychopaths," and "Fascists."[62] Throughout North America a number of pastors have been either fined or incarcerated for exercising their freedom to practice their religions publicly, under the guise of violating unlawful sanitary COVID-19 fascistic policies. As of September 14, 2021, the government of Alberta (Alberta Health Services) has found Artur and David guilty of violating Alberta health policies: "the health provider asked that the pastor be jailed for 21 days and that his brother be sentenced to 10 days. The court is also being asked to fine Artur Pawlowski $2,000 and impose $15,000 in costs."[63] All of this for engaging in "wrongthink," even though at the time there were no restrictions on churches and the lockdown had ended.[64] This is the type of behaviour one would expect from Communist China. Governments are meant to serve and protect their citizens, not to dictate how they live. Instead, they are preventing us from living physically, mentally, and spiritually healthy lives. Artur told Bench Justice Adam Germain: "I am here before this court as a political prisoner of conscience… I have heard from my grandparents about similar tactics from the time of the Nazis, persecuting churches and the clergy. Canada has fallen. Sure you can lock us up and throw the key away, but our political imprisonment will

59 Merkowsky, "Official reveals 'unmarked graves' in Canada are part of an overgrown cemetery."

60 Showalter, "3rd Canadian pastor arrested for holding worship services violating COVID-19 orders."

61 Westen, "Pastor Artur Pawlowski, arrested for refusing to shut church, tells all"; Pawlowski, "Pastor arrested for opening church speaks out," interviewed by Laura Ingraham.

62 Pawlowski, "Pastor who stood up to police in viral video speaks out," interviewed by Mark Steyn.

63 Graveland, "Unrepentant Calgary pastor convicted of COVID restriction violations says he is political prisoner."

64 Levant, "BIZARRE: Judge orders Pastor Artur Pawlowski to condemn himself."

shout even louder about the hypocrisy."[65] Subsequently, because of a bizarre ruling made by Justice Germain, Pawlowski was required to utter the following words when referring to the pandemic:

> I am aware that the views I am expressing to you on this occasion may not be views held by the majority of medical experts in Alberta... While I may disagree with them, I am obliged to inform you that the majority of medical experts favor social distancing, mask-wearing, and avoiding large crowds to reduce the spread of COVID-19... Most medical experts also support participation in a vaccination program unless for a valid religious or medical reason you cannot be vaccinated. Vaccinations have been shown statistically to save lives and to reduce the severity of COVID-19 symptoms.[66]

On November 25, 2021, Alberta's Court of Appeal overturned Justice Germain's unconstitutional order to gag Artur Pawlowski's, Dawid Pawlowski's, and Alberta businessman Christ Scott's right to freedom of speech. Horrifyingly, in 2022, for 51 days, Artur Pawlowski was incarcerated and was put into solitary confinement for weeks and feared for his life because higherups incentivized other inmates to attack him (luckily their moral compass prevented them from doing so). Luckily, for now, justice has been restored for these men.[67]

Nonetheless, to suggest these examples are even remotely comparable to the levels of persecution we hear of in China, or the Middle East would be an insult to our brothers and sisters there, who are enduring unspeakable acts. Nevertheless, those hostile to religion do not realize that the Church and her truth are the historical bedrock for the view that the human person has intrinsic value, as well as the progress and development of the scientific revolution. The powers that be in the West would rather replace the Judeo-Christian belief system with Marxism, climate alarmism, or some neo-paganistic earth-worshipping religion. Leftists even welcome radical Islam without understanding what it truly entails. To aggravate things even more, politicians such as Barack Obama and Hillary Clinton state that "Easter worshippers" rather than Christians are being persecuted at the hands of Islamic terrorists. See, for instance, Clinton's tweet regarding the attack upon Christians in Sri Lanka during Easter 2019: "On this holy weekend for many faiths, we must stand united against hatred and violence. I'm praying for everyone affected by today's horrific attacks on Easter worshippers and travelers in Sri Lanka."[68]

It is worth mentioning that several days after the overturn of the Pawlowskis' gagging order, Artur Pawlowski launched the Solidarity Movement of Canada

65 Graveland, "Unrepentant Calgary pastor convicted of COVID restriction violations says he is political prisoner."

66 Foley, "Canadian appeals court lifts enforcement of compelled speech order on Pastor Artur Pawlowski."

67 Foley, "Canadian appeals court lifts enforcement of compelled speech order on Pastor Artur Pawlowski."

68 Clinton, Twitter post, April 21, 2019, 1:17 PM.

as a way to unite people against COVID medial tyranny.[69] The movement was inspired by Poland's solidarity movement which emerged in August of 1980, led by anti-communist activist Lech Walesa. A key factor in the movement's success was the prior election of Karol Wojtyla (John Paul II) as pope in 1978. Together with the US presidency of Ronald Reagan, John Paul II's pontificate was instrumental in the defeat of communism. Christians often function more powerfully under persecution. As Walesa states in reference to Communist demoralization strategy in Poland: "In fact our souls contain exactly the opposite of what they wanted. They wanted us not to believe in God, and our churches are full. They wanted us to be materialistic and incapable of sacrifice. They wanted us to be afraid of the tanks, of the guns, and instead we don't fear them at all."[70] Similarly, we can all find strength in times of persecution, as Pawlowski has shown us.

Orwell Meets Derrida

While it is true that the Soviet Union dissolved internally from 1988 to 1991, there remains a pernicious philosophy that is infecting human minds across the globe, now more widespread and powerful than it ever was under Soviet rule, and still officially enshrined in totalitarian regimes like the Chinese Communist Party. This evil specter of communism embodies an a-theology that eats away like an acid at the edifice of Western civilization, along with every great and noble idea that it has generated or even fathomed. It is seductive since it gnaws away at the human will, intellect, and sense of morality, building concession through chaos and confusion. If we allow it, it will write out humanity's epitaph.

What happens when George Orwell's notion of "big brother" and Jacques Derrida's "method" of deconstructionism as applied to social issues collide? Something that is very sinister; a collective madness that penetrates Western civilization. But what are these ideas about? And what does their collision entail? The postmodern philosopher Jacques Derrida espoused an approach to textual analysis known as deconstructionism. However, its application has been extended far beyond textual analysis. Derrida made a thought-provoking confession in his work *Moscou aller-retour* on deconstructionism as it relates to political activism, where he pinpoints, of all things, Marxism: "Deconstruction never had meaning or interest, at least in my eyes, than as a radicalization, that is to say, also within the tradition of Marxism in a certain spirit of Marxism."[71] Similarly, Derrida's fellow postmodern philosopher Michel Foucault uses

69 Soos, "'I am a Canadian, free to speak without fear.'"

70 Crozier, *The Rise and Fall of the Soviet Empire*, 358.

71 Derrida, *Mouscou aller-retour*. See also Hicks, Explaining Postmodernism, 5.

Marxism as a tool for political activism: "I label political everything that has to do with class struggle, and social everything that derives from and is a consequence of the class struggle, expressed in human relationships and institutions."[72]

This reveals the true agenda behind postmodernism and deconstructionism. Furthermore, postmodernism is utterly relativist in its morality and epistemology. As philosopher John Searle has observed, it is a world that is turned upside down. It is the ones who were "suppressed" who now act as the suppressors; however, they do not achieve dominance through rational argumentation but rather through decrying oppression and marginalization. Those who claim to be powerless have ironically gained power through their "powerlessness." These are overt attacks on the very fabric of the West's Judeo-Christian roots, the basis for the scientific revolution, the foundations of law, and the intrinsic value and dignity of all human persons.

In George Orwell's novel *Nineteen Eighty-Four*, the character Big Brother, who heads the totalitarian state of Oceania, subjects his citizens to perpetual surveillance through the scrutiny of the authorities via telescreens. In the West we are experiencing mass surveillance through the state (local and federal governments) and social media outlets such as Twitter, Facebook, YouTube, and Instagram. It is not enough that mainstream media with its propaganda, or as others would call it "fake news," is in the business of misinforming and indoctrinating the public. Moreover, Canadian Prime Minister Trudeau's Liberal government has made a commitment to regulate "hate speech" on social media, but of course, a precise definition of 'hate speech' is never given. Bill C-36, "An Act to Amend the Criminal Code," is the most recent legislation to regulate speech online.[73] This is just another excuse to censor people who hold unpopular views. The Liberals have also sought to update the language of section 13 of Bill C-36 with the following statement: "It is a discriminatory practice to communicate or cause to be communicated hate speech by the means of the Internet or other means of telecommunication in a context in which the hate speech is likely to foment detestation or vilification of an individual or group of individuals on the basis of a prohibited ground of discrimination."[74]

The question remains: what is hate speech and who defines it? Government? No thanks. We are never provided a precise definition, but at most something ambiguous and susceptible to manipulation in countless ways. This poses a tremendous threat to our freedom of expression, freedom of speech, and freedom of conscience. It is worth noting that the term "hate" is nowhere to

72 Foucault, *Foucault Live (Interviews 1961–1994)*, 104.

73 Wakerell-Cruz, "Trudeau Liberals unveil NEW internet censorship bill to remove 'hate' from the internet."

74 House of Commons Canada, Bill C-36.

be found in Canadian jurisprudence. However, "hatred" is defined in case law. What the Criminal Code does prohibit is "hate propaganda,"[75] defined as "any writing, sign or visible representation that advocates or promotes genocide..." Undoubtedly, free speech is under assault, and Trudeau, sometimes known as postmodernism's poster-boy,[76] is a leading figure in this assault. An arbitrary definition of "hate speech" can lead to such absurd situations as a "transgender woman" being accused of hate speech claiming via a t-shirt to be still male.[77] Thus, on the one hand, you have a denial of metaphysical and moral truths alternating with attempts to affirm such truths—something which is logically incoherent—and on the other hand, you have massive surveillance and censorship to ensure you do not deny these untruths. It is worse than an Orwellian nightmare; it is a relativistic morass founded on nonsense which is forcefully submerging its citizens in a sea of absurdities. In the aforementioned examples, we can see the ramifications of these two abhorrent ideas, especially when combined.

Politics, culture, science, and philosophy undergird something much deeper than appears on the surface. It will require readers to dig deeply within themselves, since the struggle is ultimately internal although appearing externally; it is a struggle for moral responsibility and human dignity. *Au fond*, this is a spiritual war, where human civilization is the battleground for a struggle that involves good and evil predating human existence.

We are at a critical juncture in human history; the following questions lie before us: will we be able to overcome the lesser angels of our nature? Will we be able to override the savage and tribalist vestiges of our evolutionary past that stifle genuine and authentic human progress? Will truth, science, reason, logic, love, and justice prevail? To answer those questions in the affirmative it will take individuals who have become aware of this decadence, so that we can properly navigate through this current quagmire. If we remain deep in slumber and "woke" rather than awakened, we will be forced to face the impending death of our great civilization; we risk descending into the bottomless nether regions inhabited by the likes of Karl Marx, Margaret Sanger, Andrea Dworkin, Judith Butler, Theodor Adorno, Jacques Derrida, Michel Foucault, and other sinister characters who commiserate with each other for eternity.

75 Government of Canada, Justice Laws Website.

76 Craig, "Canada and Postmodernism's Poster Boy." A term that was coined by James Porter Craig (a pseudonym for a Canadian scholar).

77 Lyons, "Transgender woman accused of 'hate speech' after wearing t-shirt stating she is still biologically male."

Bibliography

Alvarez, Gloria. "Who Celebrates Che Guevara?" *Prager University*, August 2, 2021. https://www.prageru.com/video/who-celebrates-che-guevara/.

Amitay, Oren. "Telling the truth on trans issues got me cancelled: one psychologist's story." *The Post Millennial*, September 17, 2019. https://www.thepostmillennial.com/telling-the-truth-on-trans-issues-got-me-cancelled-one-psychologists-story/.

Amnesty International. "Cuba protests: latest information." https://www.amnesty.org/en/latest/news/2021/07/cuba-protests-updates/.

Bajpai, Prableen. "North Korean vs. South Korean Economies: What's the Difference?" *Investopedia*, October 19, 2020. https://www.investopedia.com/articles/forex/040515/north-korean-vs-south-korean-economies.asp.

Bezmenov, Yuri. "Subversion of the Free World Press—Yuri Bezmenov." YouTube video, April 29, 2021. https://www.youtube.com/watch?v=sQN4c3uN_tA.

Blacklock's Reporter staff. "Hail Cuba Rights, Speech." *Blacklock's Reporter*, July 21, 2021. https://www.blacklocks.ca/hail-cuba-on-rights-speech/.

Cantor, James. "American Academy of Pediatrics policy and trans- kids: Fact-checking." *Sexology Today!* October 17, 2018. http://www.sexologytoday.org/2018/10/americanacademy-of-pediatrics-policy.html?fbclid=IwAR0hsgeCfBpu0qT5F_cFrZLy698q6haeMZgXgtJbqQjMHj40eIICFzB68cQ.

Cathell, Mia. "AOC blames Cuban suffering on US 'contributions,' calls for end to 'cruel' embargo." *The Post Millennial*, July 16, 2021. https://thepostmillennial.com/aoc-blames-cuban-suffering-on-us-contributions-calls-for-end-to-cruel-embargo.

Clinton, Hillary. Twitter post, April 21, 2019, 1:17 PM. https://twitter.com/HillaryClinton/status/1120013694073810944.

Coleman, Justine. "JK Rowling sparks controversy for tweet on gender: 'Sex is real.'" *The Hill*, December 19, 2019. https://thehill.com/blogs/in-the-know/in-the-know/475312-jk-rowling-sparks-controversy-for-defending-stating-that-sex-is.

Craig, James Porter. "Canada and Postmodernism's Poster Boy." *Catholic Insight*, July 1, 2017. https://catholicinsight.com/canada-postmodernisms-poster-boy/.

Cretella, Michelle. "I'm a Pediatrician. How Transgender Ideology Has Infiltrated My Field and Produced Large-Scale Child Abuse." *The Daily Signal*, July 3, 2017. https://www.dailysignal.com/2017/07/03/im-pediatrician-transgender-ideology-infiltrated-field-produced-large-scale-child-abuse/.

Crozier, Brian. *The Rise and Fall of the Soviet Empire*. New York: Prima Lifestyles, 1999.

D'Souza, Dinesh. *United States of Socialism: Who's Behind It, Why It's Evil, How to Stop It.* New York: All Points Books, 2020.

Derrida, Jacques. *Mouscou aller-retour.* Saint Etienne: De l'Aube, 1995.

Di Martino, Daniel. "How Socialism Destroyed Venezuela." *E21*, March 21, 2019. https://economics21.org/how-socialism-destroyed-venezuela.

Donnelly, Laura. "Children's transgender clinic hit by 35 resignations in three years as psychologists warn of gender dysphoria 'over-diagnoses.'" *The Telegraph*, December 12, 2019. https://www.telegraph.co.uk/news/2019/12/12/childrens-transgender-clinic-hit-35-resignations-three-years/?fbclid=IwAR2FKIK6E6_apn0Kn5YX4Mmoh3RjBccU6cjx6eKOmXrGWIa_6cy8fSuVW3k.

Dorfman, Jeffrey. "Sorry Bernie Bros But Nordic Countries Are Not Socialist." *Forbes*, June 8, 2018. https://www.forbes.com/sites/jeffreydorfman/2018/07/08/sorry-bernie-bros-but-nordic-countries-are-not-socialist/?sh=4b6d3ccd74ad.

Dostoevsky, Fyodor. *The Brothers Karamazov.* Translated by Richard Pevear and Larissa Volokhonsky. San Francisco: North Point Press, 1990.

Dreher, Rod. "The Trojan Horse Of Gender Ideology." *The American Conservative*, December 18, 2019. https://www.theamericanconservative.com/dreher/trojan-horse-gender-ideology/.

Dzsurdzsa, Cosmin. "A map of the 57 churches that have been vandalized or burned since the residential schools announcement." *True North*, July 15, 2021. https://tnc.news/2021/07/15/a-map-of-every-church-burnt-or-vandalized-since-the-residential-school-announcements/.

Editorial Board of "Nine Commentaries on The Communist Party." *How the Specter of Communism Is Ruling Our World*, volume 1. New York: The Epoch Times, 2020.

Editors of the *Encyclopedia Britannica.* "The Frankfurt School: German Research Group." *Encyclopedia Britannica*, August 22, 2019. https://www.britannica.com/topic/Frankfurt-School.

Foley, Ryan. "Canadian appeals court lifts enforcement of compelled speech order on Pastor Artur Pawlowski." *The Christina Post,* November 30, 2021. https://www.christianpost.com/news/appeals-court-lifts-compelled-speech-order-on-artur-pawlowski.html.

Foucault, Michel. *Foucault Live (Interviews 1961–1994)*, edited by Sylvère Lotringer and translated by Lysa Hochroth and John Johnston. New York: Semiotexte, 1989.

Gardner, Frank. "Iraq's Christians 'close to extinction.'" *BBC News*, May 23, 2019. https://www.bbc.com/news/world-middle-east-48333923?fbclid=IwAR2trYqzr0mLhxNjdROXa8LiNIZHEZWThzWJJlb7U91oWgrrgprmE26ks54.

Government of Canada. Justice Laws Website. Criminal Code. (R.S.C., 1985, c. C-46). http://laws-lois.justice.gc.ca/eng/acts/C-46/section-319.html.

Gramlich, John. "East Germany has narrowed economic gap with West Germany since fall of communism, but still lags." *Pew Research Center*,

November 16, 2019. https://www.pewresearch.org/fact-tank/2019/11/06/east-germany-has-narrowed-economic-gap-with-west-germany-since-fall-of-communism-but-still-lags/.

Graveland, Bill. "Unrepentant Calgary pastor convicted of COVID restriction violations says he is political prisoner." *National Post*, September 14, 2021, https://nationalpost.com/news/canada/canada-has-fallen-calgary-pastor-unrepentant-at-his-sentencing-for-covid-19-breach?utm_term=Autofeed&utm_medium=Social&utm_source=Facebook&fbclid=IwAR2J_DJYM43VvMWGfI3DQ0HYbuWi-CPl-QnsAELbPyrLKA47FZHIf04dpXI#Echobox=1631670466.

House of Commons Canada. "BILL C-36: An Act to amend the Criminal Code and the Canadian Human Rights Act and to make related amendments to another Act (hate propaganda, hate crimes and hate speech)." First Reading, June 23, 2021. https://parl.ca/Content/Bills/432/Government/C-36/C-36_1/C-36_1.PDF.

Ibrahim, Raymond. "The Genocide of Christians in Burkina Faso." *Front Page Magazine*, December 19, 2019. https://www.frontpagemag.com/fpm/2019/12/genocide-christians-burkina-faso-raymond-ibrahim/.

Knight, Keith. "Useless Dissident: Interview with Yuri Bezmenov: Part One." Transcript of interview. November 24, 2008. https://archive.org/stream/YuriBezmenovExKGBPsychologicalWarfareTechniquesSubversionAndControlOfTheWestUSSRCommunism_201810/InterviewWithYuriBezmenovByG.EdwardGriffin-parts1-3-43_djvu.txt.

Levant, Ezra. "BIZARRE: Judge orders Pastor Artur Pawlowski to condemn himself." *Rebel News*, October 13, 2021. https://www.rebelnews.com/bizarre_judge_orders_pastor_artur_pawlowski_to_condemn_himself.

Lott, Maxim. "Lifestyles of the rich and socialist: American celebs who blast capitalism while making millions." *Fox News*, April 30, 2019. https://www.foxnews.com/entertainment/lifestyles-of-the-rich-and-socialist-american-celebs-capitalism-millionaires.

Lyons, Izzy. "Transgender woman accused of 'hate speech' after wearing t-shirt stating she is still biologically male." *The Telegraph*, December 22, 2019. https://www.telegraph.co.uk/news/2019/12/22/transgender-woman-accused-hate-speech-wearing-t-shirt-stating/.

Martin, Will. "Venezuela's inflation rate just hit 830,000% — and is likely to keep rising." *Business Insider*, November 8, 2018. https://www.businessinsider.com/venezuela-inflation-rate-hyperinflation-2018-11.

Marx, Karl and Friedrich Engels. *The Communist Manifesto.* Translated by Samuel Moore. New York: Oxford University Press, 1992.

Matthews, Stacey. "Flashback 2020: Six Months of Antifa/BLM Looting, Rioting, and Chaos." *Legal Insurrection*, January 9, 2021. https://legalinsurrection.com/2021/01/flashback-2020-six-months-of-antifa-blm-looting-rioting-and-chaos/.

McLean, Dorothy Cummings. "At world's first gender 'detransition' conference, women express regret over drugs, mutilation." *LifeSite News*, December 2, 2019. https://www.lifesitenews.com/news/at-worlds-first-gender-detransition-conference-women-express-regret-over-drugs-mutilation.

McManus, Matt. "The Frankfurt School and Postmodern Philosophy." *Quillette*, January 3, 2019. https://quillette.com/2019/01/03/the-frankfurt-school-and-postmodern-philosophy/#:~:text=He%20argues%20that%20there%20is,skeptical%20epistemologies%20of%20the%20postmodernists.

Mendenhall, Allen. "Cultural Marxism Is Real." *The James G. Martin Center for Academic Renewal*, January 4, 2019. https://www.jamesgmartin.center/2019/01/cultural-marxism-is-real/.

Merkowsky, Clare Marie. "Official reveals 'unmarked graves' in Canada are part of an overgrown cemetery." *LifeSite News*, July 9, 2021. https://www.lifesitenews.com/news/official-reveals-unmarked-graves-in-canada-are-part-of-an-overgrown-cemetery.

Meyer, Stephen C. *The Return of the God Hypothesis: Three Scientific Discoveries That Reveal the Mind behind the Universe.* New York: HarperOne, 2021.

Moreland, J.P. and Scott B. Rae. *Body & Soul: Human Nature & the Crisis in Ethics.* Downers Grove: InterVarsity Press, 2000.

Mushnick, Phil. "Political correctness could threaten women's sports." *New York Post*, January 30, 2021. https://nypost.com/2021/01/30/bidens-transgender-policy-could-threaten-womens-soccer/.

Nagel, Thomas. *Mind & Cosmos: Why the Materialist Neo-Darwinian Conception of Nature Is Almost Certainly False.* New York: Oxford University Press, 2012.

Nietzsche, Friedrich. *The Gay Science*. Translated by Walter Kaufmann. New York: Vintage Press, 1974.

Orwell, George. *Nineteen Eighty-Four*. New York: Penguin Books, 1954.

Pawlowski, Artur. "Pastor arrested for opening church speaks out." Interviewed by Laura Ingraham. *Fox News*, May 15, 2021. https://www.youtube.com/watch?v=Zz5zGm3gJKg.

———. "Pastor who stood up to police in viral video speaks out." Interviewed by Mark Steyn. Fox News, April 6, 2021. https://www.youtube.com/watch?v=uXefE-Z3H6M.

Reagan, Ronald. "A Time for Choosing (The Speech)." October 27, 1964. YouTube video. https://www.youtube.com/watch?v=qXBswFfh6AY.

———. Inaugural Address (Public Ceremony). January 5, 1967. https://www.reaganlibrary.gov/archives/speech/january-5-1967-inaugural-address-public-ceremony.

Rogers, Mike. "China has already infiltrated America's institutions." *The Hill*, March 2, 2021. https://thehill.com/opinion/international/541196-china-has-already-infiltrated-americas-institutions.

Rowling, J. K. Twitter post, July 19, 2021, 3:59 AM. https://twitter.com/jk_rowling/status/1417031300498829315.

Sahakian, Teny. "North Korean defector says 'even North Korea was not this nuts' after attending Ivy League school." *Fox News,* June 14, 2021. https://www.foxnews.com/us/north-korean-defector-ivy-league-nuts.

Sawdy, MichaEL. "The Signs of Our Times: Christian Persecution." *Biblical Signs in the Headlines,* May 20, 2021. https://biblicalsigns.com/2021/05/20/the-signs-of-our-times-christian-persecution/.

Schuman, Tomas D. *Love Letter to America.* Los Angeles: Almanac Panorama, 1984.

Scruton, Roger. *A Political Philosophy: Arguments for Conservatism.* London: Continuum Books, 2006.

Scruton, Roger. *Fools, Frauds and Firebrands: Thinkers of the New Left.* New York: Bloomsbury, 2015.

Soos, Adam."'I am a Canadian, free to speak without fear.'" *Rebel News,* November 29, 2021. https://www.rebelnews.com/i_am_a_canadian_free_to_speak_without_fear.

Showalter, Brandon. "3rd Canadian pastor arrested for holding worship services violating COVID-19 orders." *The Christian Post,* May 18, 2021. https://www.christianpost.com/news/3rd-canadian-pastor-arrested-after-violating-covid-19-orders.html.

Solzhenitsyn, Alexander. *Warning to the West.* New York: Farrar, Straus and Giroux, 1976.

Ventureyra, Scott D. G. *On the Origin of Consciousness: An Exploration through the Lens of the Christian Conception of God and Creation.* Eugene, OR: Wipf and Stock, 2018.

Wakerell-Cruz, Roberto. "Trudeau Liberals unveil NEW internet censorship bill to remove 'hate' from the internet." *The Post Millennial,* June 24, 2021. https://thepostmillennial.com/trudeau-liberals-unveil-new-internet-censorship-bill-to-remove-hate-from-the-internet.

Westen, John-Henry. "Pastor Artur Pawlowski, arrested for refusing to shut church, tells all." *LifeSite News,* May 21, 2021. https://www.lifesitenews.com/blogs/pastor-artur-pawlowski-arrested-for-refusing-to-shut-church-tells-all.

Zeisloft, Ben. "Over 3,000 Christians Reportedly Killed In Nigeria So Far This Year." *The Daily Wire,* July 27, 2021. https://www.dailywire.com/news/over-3000-christians-reportedly-killed-in-nigeria-so-far-this-year?utm_source=facebook&utm_medium=social&utm_campaign=benshapiro&fbclid=IwAR32WvujvkE3EG8i7ZrCdPmSnrL6xshZqn0butuM2i_3x4X0MQ1nCy8ewlE.

Chapter 2

Progression or Regression? Political Correctness, Censorship, and the Information War

Scott D. G. Ventureyra

The Left: Progressive or Regressive?

The economist and cultural critic Thomas Sowell astutely observed that "ours may become the first civilization destroyed, not by the power of our enemies, but by the ignorance of our teachers and the dangerous nonsense they are teaching our children."[1] This is the direction we have been heading in for decades now. And it is only getting worse.

A word on human progress; progress in this context is not to be confused with the left's idea of social progressivism which seeks to erode much of western civilization's traditional institutions. By the left I mean those who hold to some of the defining characteristics of leftism, such as anti-capitalist, anti-nationalist, and anti-patriotic sentiments, anti-free speech inclinations, adherence to climate alarmism,[2] radical views on race, class, gender, ableness, and sex, and a general contempt for religion. Although these characteristics are not exhaustive of leftism/leftists, and it is important to acknowledge that there are variances from person to person, these several beliefs, desires and attitudes are often displayed by those who espouse an adherence to leftist ideologies—often manifest in the phenomenon of *wokeness* and the rise of the *social justice warrior (SJW)*. The term SJW can be used to describe anyone who believes they exhibit some sort of moral superiority over anyone who opposes their crusade to resolve perceived social injustices of contemporary society. Although there is nothing wrong with defending what one believes in, in an impassioned way, there is something troubling about the method that is commonly utilized whereby emotions are elevated above reason and feelings over facts—shouting and calls to violence are often defended. It is this sort of tribalistic mentality combined

1 Sowell, "Random Thoughts."

2 For a good exposé of problems and inanities associated with climate alarmism see Schellenberger, *Apocalypse Never*.

with ideological possession[3] which is leading to an unprecedented divisiveness within western culture. Much of the social justice movement is structured online to distribute propaganda, censor speech, and reprimand anyone who dares challenge any politically correct position, for example, that gender is on a spectrum; this is something that evolutionary psychologist Gad Saad refers to as biophobia—a fear of explaining human traits in terms of biology; anyone who challenges the status quo is likely to be punished by losing their employment. With regards to *wokeness*, mathematician James Lindsay astutely observed in a roundtable last year that "Wokeness is a fusion of the critical theory school of neo-Marxism, which is a form of identity politics, and radical activism that has a very particular worldview that separates the world into liberationists versus oppressors or oppressed versus oppressors."[4]

These realities are not just endemic to university campuses, but also prevalent throughout social media and increasingly at workplaces, whether private or public. It is worth noting that such illiberal positions are at odds with classical liberalism. As Dennis Prager has put it: "liberalism has far more in common with conservatism than it does with leftism. The left has appropriated the word 'liberal' so effectively that almost everyone—liberals, leftists, and conservatives—thinks they are synonymous."[5]

The writings in this volume uphold western traditions and values. Not often acknowledged is the fact that progressivism is a misnomer adopted by the left. Regressivism, on the other hand, is an accurate descriptor for retrograde ideas promulgated by the radical left, such as legalization of third-trimester abortions (up until the moment of birth), the idolization of communism and socialism, censorship and free-speech infringements for dissidents, the advocacy of puberty blockers and "medical transitioning" of minors, climate-alarmist hysteria, and rejoicing in the demise of their opponents.[6] Anyone who stops to think critically about these malevolent and ignorant ideologies realizes that they are a return to a form of moral barbarism, and a devolution of the human mind to the primordial soup. While it is true that egregiously wicked ideas

3 When someone is ideologically possessed it is completely depersonalized. There is no relation with the ideology and the personal thought of the individual, but rather a regurgitation of a set of principles and/or beliefs related to a particular ideology.

4 Taken from James Lindsay's commentary in the discussion titled "Wokeism at Work." See also Pluckrose and Lindsay, *Cynical Theories*.

5 Prager, "Leftism Is Not Liberalism. Here Are the Differences."

6 Keep in mind that these are the same people who are likely to call a dissenting viewpoint *hate speech*. Here are just two examples out of many. First, the left's celebration of Jordan Peterson's health struggles over the past two years: Emmons, "Social justice lunatics celebrate Jordan Peterson's struggles." Second, Sarah Parcak's angry Tweet against Rush Limbaugh, who passed away on February 17, 2021: "When a terrible piece of scum who caused immeasurable harm to millions dies, there is no sympathy. Only a desire that they suffered until their last breath." See Clark, "Here Are the Professors Disparaging Rush Limbaugh's Passing."

and people have plagued humanity for millennia, and periods of both great decadence and brilliance have come, gone, and returned, as the author of the book of Ecclesiastes recognized: "What has been will be again, what has been done will be done again; there is nothing new under the sun" (Eccl 1:9); still, there is, nonetheless, something undeniably different about the times we live in.

The Perils of Political Correctness

Those who kowtow to political correctness typically identify as champions of pluralism and diversity, except when it pertains to diversity of thought. Political correctness has unleashed a ubiquitous malady throughout western civilization at the expense of our freedoms, liberties, and now history itself. Universities have become places of complacency, where at every turn students demand trigger warnings and safe spaces in order to cope with what are perceived as microaggressions. It is as evolutionary psychologist Gad Saad has recognized in his most recent book, *The Parasitic Mind: How Infectious Ideas Are Killing Common Sense*: "The West is currently suffering from such a devastating pandemic, a collective malady that destroys people's capacity to think rationally. Unlike other pandemics where biological pathogens are to blame, the current culprit is composed of a collection of bad ideas, spawned on university campuses, that chip away at our edifices of reason, freedom, and individual dignity."[7]

There is an undeniable narcissism and intellectual vacuity backed by an endless myriad of unsubstantiated claims found in the upper echelons of our society's "intelligentsia." Anti-reason, anti-scientific attitudes, and a pervasive lack of openness and intellectual curiosity have permeated the humanities and social sciences throughout universities. As the economist Thomas Sowell observed in his work *Ever Wonder Why? and Other Controversial Essays*: "Of all ignorance, the ignorance of the educated is the most dangerous. Not only are educated people likely to have more influence, they are the last people to suspect that they don't know what they are talking about when they go outside their narrow fields."[8] At every turn, in western culture, we have famous personalities lecturing us on race, gender, sexuality, religion, and the environment. It is an affront to reason, since many of these people have not taken the time to educate themselves on these topics. The university is *the* place where these cultural trends typically originate. Regrettably, the university, which was once a place of debate and ingenuity, is gradually transforming into a bedrock for political correctness and social activism.

7 Saad, *The Parasitic Mind*, xi.
8 Sowell, *Ever Wonder Why? and Other Controversial Essays*, 455.

The Varieties of Cancel Culture

Political correctness is an assault on not only human persons but also on history. Ironically, in the godless culture we live in today, there are unreflective puritans who wish to execute moral authority over all others while not applying the same level of scrutiny to their own actions. It is a classic case of hypocrisy. They seek to disparage the legacies and contributions to society of such eminent figures as Martin Luther King Jr., Francisco Ayala (one of the most eminent evolutionary biologists of our time), philosopher of mind John Searle, and Christian evangelist and apologist Ravi Zacharias, among many others—all of whom have been accused of sexual improprieties. These individuals may very well be guilty of some wrongful acts, as the evidence indicates, but is that reason to disparage their contributions to humanity?

Others have been censored for having Christian, conservative and/or commonsense views. Their transgressions are not in the camp of uninvited sexual advances, but from countering the *accepted narrative* propagated by most individuals and media outlets. For example, psychologist Oren Amitay was banned from Twitter and *cancelled* by colleagues and the LGBTQ+ community a couple of years ago for taking a prudent expert opinion about gender identity.[9] Gina Carano, the star of Disney's *The Mandalorian*, was dismissed by Lucasfilm for expressing her conservative views on social media.[10] There are many other examples like these. After all, if Twitter and other big tech platforms could permanently ban President Donald Trump,[11] then who can they not cancel? The big tech oligarchs exercise more power than many governments. Actor Rowan Atkinson of Mr. Bean fame rightfully likened the woke mob to a medieval one looking for someone to burn.[12]

In March of 2010, I recall the social justice mob protesting and making it physically unsafe for Ann Coulter to speak at the University of Ottawa—this troubled me, since I had always understood the university to be a place to debate ideas, not to protect one from them.[13] Professors throughout the Western world have not been exempted from cancel culture for exercising their academic freedom. But long before Jordan Peterson was a household name, scientists who questioned the tenets of Neo-Darwinism and defended intelligent design, even privately, were losing their positions at universities for upholding such

9 Amitay, "Telling the truth on trans issues got me cancelled: one psychologist's story"; Cross Country Checkup, "When it comes to boycotting opinions."

10 See Carano, *The Ben Shapiro Show: Sunday Special*, Ep. 111.

11 Guardian Staff, "Twitter says Trump ban is permanent."

12 Fleet, "Rowan Atkinson compares woke cancel culture to 'medieval mob looking for someone to burn.'"

13 Ventureyra, "Invocation of Fear."

views.[14] The Coulter incident was the first time I had experienced such a thing firsthand. It is imprudent to cheer on the cancellation of those we disagree with, since we never know when we will be silenced next. In 2009, Richard Dawkins helped de-platform Ben Stein as a commencement speaker at the University of Vermont. In a twist of irony, in 2017, Dawkins was disinvited from an interview by a Berkeley radio station for his past comments on Islam.[15] Here are a number of recent examples: Rick Mehta, professor of psychology at Acadia University, lost his tenured position for exercising free speech;[16] Kathleen Lowrey, professor of anthropology at the University of Alberta, was fired for stating that biological sex is real;[17] Ricardo Duchesne, a professor of sociology at the University of New Brunswick, was accused by 100 colleagues of being a white supremacist for his views on immigration and consequently took an early retirement;[18] and finally, Bret Weinstein of Evergreen State University was chased off campus after he dared to object to a social justice warrior's demand that all white people leave the campus for one day.[19]

As of late, the PC police have also managed to cancel the Aunt Jemima syrup brand, despite the real Aunt Jemima's grandson's justified enragement over the destruction of her legacy.[20] Six Dr. Seuss books will cease to be printed because of allegedly racist content.[21] Ironically, Dr. Seuss books were praised by the Obamas throughout Barack's presidency.[22] Woke activists will stop at nothing to demonstrate their deluded and narcissistic sense of moral superiority. It is important to consider that human persons are products of their times. People make mistakes and misjudgments, but cancelling their work or their names from history, especially with respect to their contributions, will not be of service to anyone. I believe good contributions stand on their own, apart from an individual person's failings: truth is truth. Awareness of a person's shortcomings while appreciating their gifts and achievements is a more balanced way forward. On a Christian understanding of human nature, we are fallen and finite creatures, but also bear the *imago Dei*; thus, we have the capacities to do both good and evil. Nevertheless, these champions of social "justice" and this cancel culture should take heed of Jesus's words:

14 See *Expelled: No Intelligence Allowed.*

15 Klinghoffer, "Dawkins (Not) at Berkeley—The Best Irony."

16 Mehta, *The Saad Truth*, interview by Gad Saad.

17 Perse, "University of Alberta fires anthropology professor for saying biological sex is real."

18 CFT Team, "Canadian Professor Fired for Defending 'Uniqueness' of White European Civilization."

19 Dreher, "The Hunting of Bret Weinstein."

20 Konkol, "Aunt Jemima's Great-Grandson Enraged Her Legacy Will Be Erased."

21 See an excellent poem demonstrating the lunacy of wokeism: Robson, "There is nothing in Dr. Seuss that a leftist can't love."

22 Jacobs, "Barack and Michelle Obama praised, quoted Dr. Seuss during presidency."

23 This is just one example of many. See Rambaran, "Ulysses S. Grant statue toppled in San Francisco."

> Do not judge, or you too will be judged. For in the same way you judge others, you will be judged, and with the measure you use, it will be measured to you. Why do you look at the speck of sawdust in your brother's eye and pay no attention to the plank in your own eye? How can you say to your brother, "Let me take the speck out of your eye," when all the time there is a plank in your own eye? You hypocrite, first take the plank out of your own eye, and then you will see clearly to remove the speck from your brother's eye. (Mt 7:1–5)

Even worse, we now see the erasing of history by Black Lives Matter—not the sentiment but the Global Network Foundation—through the toppling of statues, like that of Ulysses Grant,[23] a Republican president who fought against the party of Jim Crow and the KKK, the Democrats.[24] It is a very odd phenomenon among Democrats and other progressives (more properly, regressives) who wish to cancel any person or organization of the past or present based on any perceived hint of racism, sexism, or classism, since they do not hold their own party responsible for its undeniable atrocities. One wonders: why aren't the social justice warriors crying foul against the Democrat Party and chanting for its dissolution? It is not difficult to see the double standard that is at play, which is so typical of a regressive mentality that has become all too common for leftists. One wonders if this is attributable to sheer ignorance or something more sinister looming in the background, as George Orwell eerily predicted in *Nineteen Eighty-Four*: "Every record has been destroyed or falsified, every book rewritten, every picture has been repainted, every statue and street building has been renamed, every date has been altered. And the process is continuing day by day and minute by minute. History has stopped."[25]

In Defense of Free Speech

As a matter of principle, if it were liberals or leftists who were being silenced, I would still criticize such silencing. For instance, I decry the censorship that occurred against musicians throughout the 1980s. To this day, I applaud the brilliant defense of freedom of expression and speech that the lead singer of Twisted Sister, Dee Snider, presented against Tipper Gore and the Parents Music Resource Center in 1985.[26] Censorship is antithetical to Western principles and values. Constructive dialogue should always be encouraged, instead of the all-too-common celebration of our enemies' demise, something which occurs time and time again with posts on social media. The exchange of truth for tribalism

24 Admin, "The Democratic Party's History of Slavery, Jim Crow, and the KKK."

25 Orwell, *Nineteen Eighty-Four*, 137.

26 Taysom, "When Dee Snider fought against censorship in the 1980s."

will be the death of our shared humanity. People should remain cognizant that any one of us could be on the chopping block of censorship, especially if the standards are so low and inconsistent.

The Information War

Technology and the Spread of Information

Harmful ideas are spreading at unprecedented rates. We live in a period where not only falsehoods are heralded as truths everywhere, but those who speak the truth are punished and censored. This is all facilitated by the capability to transfer exorbitant amounts of information, disinformation, and misinformation at truly exceptional rates. The drastic developments in technology and big tech platforms have allowed for us to communicate with one another with great ease across space and time. We transfer monetary funds through online banking systems and blockchain with not only incredible speed but also convenience. The internet and the latest technologies are to the Gutenberg Press what modern space shuttles are to the first vehicles powered by gas engines in the late 19th century. Technology itself is morally neutral, but it can be used for both good and evil purposes. These unprecedented developments in technology also make it easier and more efficient for governments to monitor their citizens. Indeed, as technology increases, governments can execute more power over their citizens, while people's privacy decreases.

The Influence of Big Tech Oligarchs and the Mainstream Media

Few would doubt that we are in an information war.[27] This has been true for many years. Technological developments in the past 30 years have only equipped us with heavier artillery to engage in combat. We are living throughout a peculiar period, where big-tech billionaire oligarch CEOs in Silicon Valley such as Twitter's Jack Dorsey, Facebook's Mark Zuckerberg, Google's Sundar Pichai, Amazon's Jeff Bezos, and Apple's Tim Cook exercise an unprecedented control over our access to information and consequently our minds.[28] Couple this with the mainstream media's constant spin, distortions, blatant lies, and

27 Stupples, "The next war will be an information war, and we're not ready for it." Regardless of what one thinks of Alex Jones, in 1999, he founded www.infowars.com, which, despite being banned from every social media platform, has been able to maintain a large following. He is just one of many in the alternative media who has made a career combatting the mainstream media (MSM).

28 Miele, "Big Tech Oligarchs vs. the Free."

hypocrisy, and you have a recipe for utter disaster.[29] It is like what linguist and political commentator Noam Chomsky has dubbed "manufacturing consent," but much worse.[30] This far surpasses anything that Chomsky could have envisioned. The situation has exponentially worsened in recent years, putting Western democracy in grave danger. Although there is a heightened awareness of the spread of falsehoods by the mainstream news in collusion with social media platforms, many people continue to be oblivious to it. Nevertheless, distrust of the media is growing day by day.[31]

Whether or not one believes there was systemic election fraud in the 2020 American presidential election,[32] there are forms of "legal fraudulence" utilized for the purpose of swaying (here used as a euphemism for stealing) votes. For instance, in October of 2020, Twitter completely censored a bombshell story by the New York Post[33] which exposed the corruption of Joseph R. Biden and his son Hunter Biden. It prevented American users from re-Tweeting the story. This was a blatant example of election interference.[34] Moreover, in the following month, tech expert and researcher for the American Institute for Behavioral Research and Technology Dr. Robert Epstein, who is not a conservative or a fan of Donald Trump, told Tucker Carlson on *Fox News* that at least six million votes were stolen through Google's algorithmic manipulations:

> Google's search results were strongly biased in favor of liberals and democrats. This was not true on Bing or Yahoo. The bias was being shown to pretty much every demographic group we looked at, including conservatives. In fact, conservatives got slightly more liberal bias in their search results than liberals did. How do you account for that?... These manipulations that we've so far quantified could easily have shifted at least six million votes in one direction. That's the bare minimum at this point that I'm confident of. The maximum we haven't even begun to estimate because we have so much data to look at.[35]

Epstein revealed: "We also found what seems to be a smoking gun. That is, we found a period of days when the vote reminder on Google's homepage was

29 There are notable anchors who are exceptions to the overall corruption of MSM, such as Tucker Carlson, who present a more balanced picture than activist anchors such as Don Lemon and Chris Cuomo.

30 See Herman and Chomsky, *Manufacturing Consent.*

31 Knight Foundation, "Gallup/Knight Poll: Americans' Concerns About Media Bias Deepen"; Luther, "America's Trust in the Mainstream Media Hits an ALL-TIME LOW"; Vondracek, "Republicans and Democrats agree: America has lost confidence in mainstream."

32 For a recent exploration of collusion to take the election from the American people, see Hemingway, *Rigged: How the Media, Big Tech, and the Democrats Seized Our Elections.*

33 Nelson, "Senate committee investigating alleged Hunter Biden drive."

34 Bokhar, "Twitter Censors Links to *New York Post*'s Hunter Biden Bombshell."

35 Epstein, "What effect did Big Tech have on the 2020 presidential election?"

being sent only to liberals—not one of our conservative field agents received a vote reminder during those days."[36] The reason Epstein has spoken out is that he sees big tech as the greatest threat to Western democracy, as he emphatically states in an article for *The American Spectator*:

> So go for it, Big Tech (says my liberal voice). Marginalize Trump to keep America safe and to help us get back on track to honoring our country's founding motto, E Pluribus Unum. But there's a problem with this logic. The attack on our Capitol building on January 6 was disturbing, but it was not a serious threat to our democracy. Twelve hours after the attack began, the joint session of Congress was back in business, and many of the key players in the attack have now been arrested. But when unelected executives at private tech companies—companies that are in no way accountable to the citizens of the United States—are making consequential decisions about what content tens of millions of people can see online and what content they cannot see and about which public figures are allowed to use their platforms and which public figures are not (even the duly elected president of the United States!), democracy no longer exists.[37]

Recent evidence suggests that Mark Zuckerberg was heavily involved in "influencing" the 2020 merging of public election offices with privately funded resources and personnel. Although the election was considered "free," it was not fair, because of manipulation of legal loopholes. The Chan-Zuckerberg Initiative through the Center for Technology and Civic Life (CTCL) and the Center for Election Innovation and Research (CEIR) funneled $419.5 million into a number of local-government election offices. This sort of "private" funding was previously unknown in American electoral history. This will have serious ramifications for future elections; it marks an assault on the republic. As William Doyle of the Caesar Rodney Election Research Institute (CRERI) explains:

> Big CTCL and CEIR money had nothing to do with traditional campaign finance, lobbying, or other expenses that are related to increasingly expensive modern elections. It had to do with financing the infiltration of election offices at the city and county level by left-wing activists, and using those offices as a platform to implement preferred administrative practices, voting methods, and data-sharing agreements, as well as to launch intensive outreach campaigns in areas heavy with Democratic voters.[38]

36 Epstein, "What effect did Big Tech have on the 2020 presidential election?"

37 Epstein, "When Big Tech Flexes, Everyone's Freedom Is Threatened." His lecture on this topic is worth a watch: "Unethical Algorithms of Massive Scale."

38 Doyle, "The 2020 Election Wasn't Stolen, It Was Bought by Mark Zuckerberg."

One continuously sees the double standards at play. In 2014, conservative author and commentator Dinesh D'Souza was indicted for using a "straw donor" to donate $20,000 to a Republican politician, Wendy Long, for her Senate race in 2012. He was subsequently sentenced to five years of probation and eight months in a community confinement center with weekly "counselling" sessions alongside a $30,000 fine. He was targeted by a vindictive Barack Obama, who was incapable of rebutting D'Souza's pointed criticisms of his many shortcomings. Interestingly, well-known leftist comedian Rosie O'Donnell committed the same crime as D'Souza on five separate occasions but did not face any repercussions.[39] The double standards for the left seem to never end. Nevertheless, a modicum of justice was restored when President Trump pardoned D'Souza in 2018.

The Cases of Kyle Rittenhouse and Nick Sandman

Much of the MSM has painted a false picture of Kyle Rittenhouse, who killed two men and wounded a third with a rifle during a chaotic night of violent protesting in August of 2020 in Kenosha, Wisconsin. Rittenhouse has been defamed by many leftists and the legacy media as a white supremacist and agitator of violence. Even President Biden made negative comments about Rittenhouse suggesting he was a white supremacist. However, there is no evidence that Rittenhouse is a racist. Senator Tom Cotton has demanded a public apology from Biden.[40] Moreover, the video that surfaced of the killings clearly demonstrates that Rittenhouse acted in self-defense. Rittenhouse was acquitted of all charges.[41] Unsurprisingly, the media never highlighted the criminality of the men Rittenhouse defended himself from. For instance, Joseph Rosenbaum was a known sex offender with eleven counts of child molestation and other charges.[42]

Nick Sandmann endured similar treatment from the media. In January of 2019, based on a short video showing him and Native American activist Nathan Phillips, the media painted Sandman, a student at Covington Catholic High School, as a racist agitator. Videos that surfaced days later showed a very distinct picture of the event. There are many parallels between Kyle Rittenhouse's ordeal and that of Nick Sandmann. Both were depicted as something they were not and attacked for it. They both have had their lives threatened because of the media's recklessness. Rightfully, Sandman successfully sued several media

39 Savitsky, "Dinesh D'Souza got a felony conviction for illegal campaign donations; will Rosie O'Donnell get same treatment?"

40 Keene, "Tom Cotton demands Biden 'publicly apologize' to Kyle Rittenhouse."

41 Salo, "Kyle Rittenhouse acquitted of all charges in Kenosha shooting."

42 Piwowarczyk, "Joseph Rosenbaum: Sex Offender 2002 Arizona Criminal Complaint."

outlets for defamation. In a recent op-ed, Sandmann urged Rittenhouse to do the same.[43] Sandmann had the following words to say about the media's carelessness and malice:

> From my own experience, the death threats, feeling of no future ahead, and that millions of people hate you, is enough to alter you in many concrete ways and permanently.
>
> Make no mistake: even the strongest of people cannot resist the mental impact when the media war machine targets you.
>
> With Kyle's name dragged through the mud, and the clear effect it is having on him, many have started to ask the question whether Kyle should sue for defamation.
>
> While I am by no means an attorney, I have gained some experience on the ins and outs of defamation and can offer an educated guess on what the outcome would be if Kyle were to sue.[44]

The Times Are They a-Changin'?

In March 2021, Texas governor Greg Abbott decided to fight back against the attacks on the civil liberties affected by COVID-19 policies by ending mask mandates and reopening businesses[45] and against the censorship of conservative voices by social media.[46] Likewise, the governor of Florida, Ron DeSantis, signed legislation to ban mask mandates, lockdowns, and vaccine passports.[47] He is also fighting to keep divisive racial ideologies like critical race theory (CRT) out of the education system.[48] The world needs more leaders like Abbott and DeSantis who are willing to stand up to the enemies of civil liberties. In Canada, we have very few politicians who are willing to defend civil liberties, among them the leader of the People's Party of Canada, Maxime Bernier,[49] conservative politician Derek Sloan,[50] Members of Provincial Parliament Randy Hillier[51] and Roman Baber[52]. Unfortunately, it is now difficult to distinguish between

43 Sandmann, "The corrupt liberal media came for me, just like they came for Kyle Rittenhouse, and if he decides to sue I say go for it and hold the media accountable."

44 Sandmann, "The corrupt liberal media came for me, just like they came for Kyle Rittenhouse, and if he decides to sue I say go for it and hold the media accountable."

45 Stieber, "Texas Governor Ends Statewide Mask Mandate."

46 GQ Pan, "Texas Governor Backs Bill Prohibiting Social Media Censorship of Conservative Speech."

47 Durkee, "Florida Gov. DeSantis Latest to Block All Local Covid-19 Orders—Including Mask Mandates."

48 Jones, "DeSantis Reveals What Critical Race Theory Hysteria Is All About."

49 People's Party of Canada website: https://www.peoplespartyofcanada.ca/.

50 Derek Sloan's website: https://www.dereksloan.ca/.

51 Randy Hillier's website: https://www.randyhilliermpp.com/.

52 Roman Baber's website: https://romanbabermpp.ca/

three major parties of Canada: the Liberal Party, the Conservative Party, and the National Democrat Party. Political commentator Spencer Fernando has rightly pointed out that the independent media has become the official opposition.[53] It is only a handful of politicians, and the independent media, standing against political tyranny.

Destination Unknown?

Where do we go from here? Not down our current path. Without freedom of inquiry, freedom of the press, freedom of speech, and freedom of conscience, we will become soulless, subservient automatons. Progress is impossible without any advancement toward a desired destination. Censorship and its offspring, political correctness, do nothing to facilitate progress or regulate hate; rather, they stifle love and freedom. Freedom should never be taken for granted. With freedom comes responsibility, but also disagreement.

Bibliography

Amitay, Oren. "Telling the truth on trans issues got me cancelled: one psychologist's story." *The Post Millennial,* September 19, 2019. https://thepostmillennial.com/telling-the-truth-on-trans-issues-got-me-cancelled-one-psychologists-story/.

Bokhar, Allum. "Twitter Censors Links to New York Post's Hunter Biden Bombshell." *Breitbart,* October 14, 2020. https://www.breitbart.com/tech/2020/10/14/twitter-censors-links-to-new-york-post-biden-bombshell/.

Carano, Gina, interviewed by Ben Shapiro. *The Ben Shapiro Show: Sunday Special,* Ep. 111, February 21, 2021. https://www.youtube.com/watch?v=mxObG659Sc0.

CFT Team. "Canadian Professor Fired for Defending 'Uniqueness' of White European Civilization." *Christians for Truth,* June 6, 2019. https://christiansfortruth.com/canadian-professor-fired-for-defending-uniqueness-of-white-european-civilization/.

Clark, Chrissy. "Here Are the Professors Disparaging Rush Limbaugh's Passing." *The Daily Wire,* February 17, 2021. https://www.dailywire.com/news/here-are-the-professors-disparaging-rush-limbaughs-passing.

Cross Country Checkup. "When it comes to boycotting opinions, 'cancel culture' is preventing dialogue from occurring: psychologist." *CBC Radio,* November 3, 2019. https://www.cbc.ca/radio/checkup/has-cancel-culture-

53 Fernando, "Independent Media Has Become the Real Opposition to the Government."

gone-too-far-1.5344590/when-it-comes-to-boycotting-opinions-cancel-culture-is-preventing-dialogue-from-occurring-psychologist-1.5345798.

"The Democratic Party's History of Slavery, Jim Crow, and the KKK." *Social Justice Survival Guide*, January 8, 2018. https://www.socialjusticesurvivalguide.com/2018/01/08/the-democratic-partys-history-slavery-jim-crow-kkk/.

Doyle, William. "The 2020 Election Wasn't Stolen, It Was Bought by Mark Zuckerberg." *The Federalist*, October 12, 2021. https://thefederalist.com/2021/10/12/the-2020-election-wasnt-stolen-it-was-bought-by-mark-zuckerberg/.

Dreher, Rob. "The Hunting of Bret Weinstein." *The American Conservative*, May 25, 2017. https://www.theamericanconservative.com/dreher/hunting-of-bret-weinstein-evergreen-state/.

Durkee, Alison. "Florida Gov. DeSantis Latest to Block All Local Covid-19 Orders—Including Mask Mandates." *Forbes*, May 3, 2021. https://www.forbes.com/sites/alisondurkee/2021/05/03/florida-gov-desantis-latest-to-block-all-local-covid-19-orders-including-mask-mandates/?sh=9560a3fa3a7f.

Emmons, Libby. "Social justice lunatics celebrate Jordan Peterson's struggles." *The Post Millennial*, February 9, 2020. https://thepostmillennial.com/social-justice-lunatics-celebrate-jordan-petersons-struggles/.

Epstein, Robert. "Unethical Algorithms of Massive Scale." Lecture, Stanford Center for Professional Development, June 8, 2017. https://www.youtube.com/watch?v=-7qT_38iRSc.

———. interviewed by Tucker Carlson. "What effect did Big Tech have on the 2020 presidential election?" *Tucker Carlson Tonight, Fox News*, November 24, 2020. https://video.foxnews.com/v/6211866665001#sp=show-clips.

———. "When Big Tech Flexes, Everyone's Freedom Is Threatened." *The American Spectator*, January 28, 2021. https://spectator.org/trump-twitter-google-big-tech/.

Fernando, Spencer. "Independent Media Has Become the Real Opposition to the Government." October 18, 2021. https://spencerfernando.com/2021/10/18/independent-media-has-become-the-real-opposition-to-the-government/?fbclid=IwAR1SufiPZTaCcOvwszrWuCI85U41mJh7rhvFbDlVViWMe8IW36mge0bsNHI.

Fleet, Holly. "Rowan Atkinson compares woke cancel culture to 'medieval mob looking for someone to burn.'" *Express*, January 5, 2021. https://www.express.co.uk/celebrity-news/1379930/rowan-Atkinson-cancel-culture-woke-snowflakes-twitter-news-latest-update.

Frankowski, Nathan, dir. *Expelled: No Intelligence Allowed.* Los Angeles: Premise Media Corporation/Rampant Films, 2008.

"Gallup/Knight Poll: Americans' Concerns About Media Bias Deepen, Even as They See It as Vital for Democracy." Knight Foundation. https://

knightfoundation.org/press/releases/gallup-knight-poll-americans-concerns-about-media-bias-deepen-even-as-they-see-it-as-vital-for-democracy/.

Griffin, G. Edward. *The Creature from Jekyll Island: A Second Look at the Federal Reserve*. Fifth ed. New York: American Media, 2010.

Guardian Staff. "Twitter says Trump ban is permanent—even if he runs for office again." *The Guardian*, February 10, 2021. https://www.theguardian.com/us-news/2021/feb/10/trump-twitter-ban-permament-social-media.

Hemingway, Mollie. *Rigged: How the Media, Big Tech, and the Democrats Seized Our Elections*. Washington, D.C.: Regnery, 2021.

The Heritage Foundation. "Wokeism at Work: How 'Critical Theory' and Anti-Racism Training Divide America." YouTube video, July 17, 2020. https://www.youtube.com/watch?v=D6mwDvEqpI0&feature=emb_logo.

Herman, Edward S. and Noam Chomsky. *Manufacturing Consent: The Political Economy of the Mass Media*. New York: Pantheon Books, 1988.

Jacobs, Emily. "Barack and Michelle Obama praised, quoted Dr. Seuss during presidency." *New York Post*, March 3, 2021. https://nypost.com/2021/03/03/barack-and-michelle-obama-praised-dr-seuss-during-presidency/.

Jones, Sarah. "DeSantis Reveals What Critical Race Theory Hysteria Is All About." *Intelligencer*, June 23, 2021. https://nymag.com/intelligencer/2021/06/desantis-reveals-truth-about-critical-race-theory-hysteria.html.

Keene, Houston. "Tom Cotton demands Biden 'publicly apologize' to Kyle Rittenhouse." *Fox News*, November 19, 2021. https://www.foxnews.com/politics/cotton-biden-apologize-rittenhouse.

Klinghoffer, David. "Dawkins (Not) at Berkeley—The Best Irony." *Evolution News*, June 24, 2017. https://evolutionnews.org/2017/07/dawkins-not-at-berkeley-the-best-irony/.

Konkol, Mark. "Aunt Jemima's Great-Grandson Enraged Her Legacy Will Be Erased." *MSN*, June 18, 2020. https://www.msn.com/en-us/news/crime/aunt-jemimas-great-grandson-enraged-her-legacy-will-be-erased/ar-BB15FQwX.

Luther, Daisy. "America's Trust in the Mainstream Media Hits an ALL-TIME LOW and 'Journalists' Are Shocked." *SGT Report*, January 30, 2021. https://www.sgtreport.com/2021/01/americas-trust-in-the-mainstream-media-hits-an-all-time-low-and-journalists-are-shocked/.

Mehta, Rick, interviewed by Gad Saad. "My Chat with Rick Mehta - Academic Freedom Under Threat." *The Saad Truth*, September 14, 2018. https://www.youtube.com/watch?v=m5_MXChEG6s.

Miele, Frank. "Big Tech Oligarchs vs. the Free." *RealClear Politics*, October 19, 2020. https://www.realclearpolitics.com/articles/2020/10/19/big_tech_oligarchs_vs_the_free_world_144474.html.

Nelson, Steve. "Senate committee investigating alleged Hunter Biden drive, smoking-gun email." *New York Post*, October 14, 2020. https://nypost.com/2020/10/14/senate-committee-investigating-hunter-biden-hard-drive-email/.

Orwell, George. *Nineteen Eighty-Four*. New York: Penguin Books, 1954.

Pan, GQ. "Texas Governor Backs Bill Prohibiting Social Media Censorship of Conservative Speech." *The Epoch Times*, March 5, 2021. https://www.theepochtimes.com/texas-governor-backs-bill-prohibiting-social-media-censorship-of-conservative-speech_3722584.html?fbclid=IwAR0uMK-dMw1d_b2xfPlYLGesn05a6QGcsHC4Clq_FAg27hV-vz2Fsq-3AmI.

Perse, Erin. "University of Alberta fires anthropology professor for saying biological sex is real." *Post Millennial*, June 4, 2020. https://thepostmillennial.com/university-of-alberta-fires-anthropology-professor-for-saying-biological-sex-is-real.

Piwowarczyk, Jim. "Joseph Rosenbaum: Sex Offender 2002 Arizona Criminal Complaint." *Wisconsin Right Now*, March 11, 2021. https://www.wisconsinrightnow.com/2021/03/11/joseph-rosenbaum-sex-offender/.

Pluckrose, Helen and James Lindsay. *Cynical Theories: How Activist Scholarship Made Everything about Race Gender, and Identity-and Why This Harms Everybody*. Durham, NC: Pitchstone, 2020.

Prager, Dennis. "Leftism Is Not Liberalism. Here Are the Differences." *The Daily Signal*, September 12, 2017. https://www.dailysignal.com/2017/09/12/leftism-not-liberalism-differences/.

Rambaran, Vandana. "Ulysses S. Grant statue toppled in San Francisco." *Fox News*, June 20, 2020. https://www.foxnews.com/us/ulysses-grant-statue-toppled-san-francisco.

Robson, John. "There is nothing in Dr. Seuss that a leftist can't love but the woke hate him anyway." *National Post*, March 2, 2021. https://nationalpost.com/opinion/john-robson-there-is-nothing-in-dr-seuss-that-a-leftist-cant-love-but-the-woke-hate-him-anyway.

Saad, Gad. *The Parasitic Mind: How Infectious Ideas Are Killing Common Sense*. Washington, D.C.: Regnery, 2020.

Salo, Jackie. "Kyle Rittenhouse acquitted of all charges in Kenosha shooting." *New York Post*, November 19, 2021. https://nypost.com/2021/11/19/kyle-rittenhouse-acquitted-of-all-charges-in-kenosha-shooting/.

Sandmann, Nick. "The corrupt liberal media came for me, just like they came for Kyle Rittenhouse, and if he decides to sue I say go for it and hold the media accountable." *Daily Mail*, November 16, 2021. https://www.dailymail.co.uk/news/article-10208119/kyle-rittenhouse-trial-NICHOLAS-SANDMANN-media-defamation.html.

Savitsky, "Dinesh D'Souza got a felony conviction for illegal campaign donations; will Rosie O'Donnell get same treatment?" *Fox News*, May 7, 2018. https://www.foxnews.com/entertainment/dinesh-dsouza-got-a-felony-conviction-for-illegal-campaign-donations-will-rosie-odonnell-get-same-treatment.

Schellenberger, Michael. *Apocalypse Never: Why Environmental Alarmism Hurts Us All.* New York: HarperCollins, 2020.

Sowell, Thomas. *Ever Wonder Why? and Other Controversial Essays*. Stanford: Hoover Institute Press, 2006.

———. "Random Thoughts." *The Jewish World Review*, May 24, 2000. https://www.jewishworldreview.com/cols/sowell052400.asp.

Stieber, Zachary. "Texas Governor Ends Statewide Mask Mandate, Allows All Businesses to Fully Reopen." *The Epoch Times*, March 2, 2021. https://www.theepochtimes.com/texas-governor-ends-statewide-mask-mandate-allows-all-businesses-to-fully-reopen_3717796.html.

Stupples, David. "The next war will be an information war, and we're not ready for it." *The Conversation*, November 26, 2015. https://theconversation.com/the-next-war-will-be-an-information-war-and-were-not-ready-for-it-51218.

Taysom, Joe. "When Dee Snider fought against censorship in the 1980s." *Far Out Magazine*, October 25, 2020. https://faroutmagazine.co.uk/twisted-sister-dee-snider-censorship-battle/.

Ventureyra, Scott. "Invocation of Fear." *The Ottawa Citizen*, March 26, 2010. https://www.scottventureyra.com/_files/ugd/f90fdb_a14d5d483c8f45d4b6f594d2cd3b16c4.pdf

Vondracek, Christopher. "Americans' distrust in media at alarming levels, poll reveals." *The Washington Times*, August 4, 2020. https://www.washingtontimes.com/news/2020/aug/4/americans-distrust-in-media-at-alarming-levels-pol/.

Chapter 3

The Campus Culture Wars: Symptom of a Holy War

Rick Mehta

In 1971, John Lennon released one of his most famous songs: "Imagine." In it, Lennon sings about his dream of our world becoming a utopia in which there are no countries, no religion, and no possessions. Fast forward to 2020: *Time Magazine* has published an article about a Great Reset. The often-heard mantra of the World Economic Forum is repeated on the *Time Magazine* website: "The COVID-19 pandemic has provided a unique opportunity to think about the kind of future we want. *Time* partnered with the World Economic Forum to ask leading thinkers to share ideas for how to transform the way we live and work."[1] Many of these ideas overlap with John Lennon's vision. Because I could find little evidence of these "leading thinkers" consulting with the people who would be affected by their ideas, I have little choice but to conclude that these dreamers and thinkers wish to impose their ideas on the masses without their knowledge or consent.

Is this the first time that people with grandiose ideas have gone out of their way to impose their vision on their societies? Hardly. But I believe that the scale on which they are attempting to achieve their goals is unprecedented.

As citizens in the free world, we can easily feel helpless and become despondent. However, readers should ask themselves whether the widespread corruption that they are observing in the world now is something that has already been foreseen. Is it possible that the behavioural scientists who understand human nature in political and historic contexts have pieced together the core components of the intricate web of deceit that threatens to enslave humanity? Is it possible that the weapon that humanity needs to fight back is also staring us in the face, but much of humanity has an ideological blind spot that prevents them from seeing it? This article will attempt to answer these questions.

On October 6, 2016, the moral psychologist Jonathan Haidt delivered a lecture titled "Two Incompatible Values at American Universities." In this lecture, Haidt talks about the problem of a lack of viewpoint diversity in universities and how this lack of diversity is relevant to the culture war that

1 *Time Magazine* in Partnership with Sompo Holdings, "The Great Reset."

is transpiring on university campuses throughout the United States. A core theme that emerges from his talk is that one group of ideologues has become dominant at university campuses in the free world and that our campuses are now in the midst of an ideological takeover.

Similar to takeovers in other contexts, the good people are staying silent or are complicit, apparently with the false belief that their silence will save them or their complicity reward them. The culture war transpiring on university campuses seems reminiscent of a line from the Remembrance Day Program held at Acadia University in 2019: "Unhappily, there are people who wish to enslave the world to their own power or doctrines, and we [the free thinkers] are forced to defend the principles and freedoms that we know and cherish."

Haidt also argues that universities have to choose between two mutually exclusive options: the pursuit of truth and the pursuit of social justice. While Haidt raises an important issue, I believe that his argument would have been clearer and more precise if he had presented it in terms of universities having to choose between the pursuit of truth and the pursuit of falsehoods, with the term "social justice" being an all-encompassing window dressing for the falsehoods. This wording might have helped viewers bring to mind the old adage that a pig wearing lipstick is still just a pig. This criticism aside, Haidt correctly argues that justice becomes corrupted when the word "justice" is qualified by the word "social." This raises the questions "what is truth?" and "what is social justice?"

According to the Bible, Jesus Christ is the Truth and the Life. Some readers may question the relevance of the Bible in the context of a culture war. Out of all the religions in the world of which I am aware, Christianity is the only one in which God's representative on Earth claims to *be* the Truth. This may explain why the Bible has traditionally been one of the two objects on which people in the West may swear before they testify in court—the other option being a book of laws, which, for the purposes of this article, can be thought of as a secular equivalent of the Bible; Christians try not to impose their faith on others. If Jesus Christ encompasses truth and life, Satan—by virtue of being the opposite of Jesus Christ—encompasses lies and deception, with lies and deception ultimately leading to death.

The components of social justice are equity, diversity, and inclusion. Given that Satan embodies death, it should not come as a surprise to anyone when I point out that if the components are rearranged as diversity, inclusion, and equity, the acronym that arises is DIE. This is because, according to the Bible, Satan always hides in plain sight and, as I will demonstrate, social justice is the work of Satan. The argument that I plan to make is that the culture war the Western world is witnessing is actually a symptom of a much greater Holy War.

In late 2016, the Canadian psychology professor Jordan B. Peterson made a famous stand against Bill C16. His concerns were that the bill was allowing imprecisely defined terms such as "gender identity" and "gender expression" to be enshrined in federal law and that the wording of the bill was a threat to Canadians' rights under the Charter of Rights and Freedoms to freedom of expression.

In January 2020, I received the course materials for the Catechumenate section of a course that I was required to take if I wanted to be received into the Roman Catholic faith. When I was reviewing the course materials, I came across Catechumenate 16; interestingly, its short form is C16. When I read Catechumenate, I noticed that it called on Christians to the cause of social justice. However, I noticed that the sections of the Bible that were quoted to substantiate this claim made reference only to justice. Because Satan, much like Jesus Christ, hides in plain sight, all one has to do is find the lie to uncover him.

A natural question to ask is, aside from certain Roman Catholic catechetical programs and university campuses in the free world, where else can Satan be found? I would argue: the legal profession in Canada. At the provincial level of Canada, for example, the components of social justice are being promoted by the Nova Scotia Barristers' Society. At the national level, it is well-known that the Supreme Court of Canada is stacked with judges who are activists with an agenda, as opposed to judges who are fair and neutral when they enforce the law. I will highlight one ruling: Weber v. Ontario Hydro, 1995. In it, the Supreme Court of Canada ruled that unionized employees cannot take their employers to court because these employees already have legal representation by their unions. A major problem with this ruling is that it has given unions full carriage rights over their members' cases but ensures that unions are not accountable to their members. Because it is highly unlikely that Jesus Christ would condone a ruling such as this one, the only reasonable conclusion that readers can make is that the Supreme Court of Canada did Satan's bidding in their ruling and that millions of unionized employees are unwittingly paying the price for the Supreme Court's actions.

Satan, like communist regimes, sometimes works through so-called useful idiots. Another method is to contaminate that which has been clean. While I was at the Kentville Court House in 2019, I noticed that people now "have the option" of swearing on the Koran. This should be of concern to all people who value freedom because Islam has long been the political enemy of not only Christians, but also societies that value freedom. Based on the evidence, it is reasonable to conclude that Satan is having an influence not only at universities in the Western world, but also at all levels of Canada's legal system.

In fields such as optometry and vision research, 20/20 refers to "perfect vision." Interestingly, the year 2020 was one in which people had begun to reveal their true character so that others could see them clearly (the COVID-19 situation brought this to the fore). The notion of people's true faces coming to light seems reminiscent of the Biblical Book of Revelation, whose theme is that God wins the war against Satan.

This article started by asking whether the widespread corruption that we are observing today has already been foreseen. I would argue that the answer is "yes." The Bible does make reference to a plague. However, it is possible that the plague in question is not a virus, but instead is the corruption that has taken over the institutions that people trust, such as science and medicine.

The next question this article addressed was whether it is possible that behavioural scientists who understand human nature in political and historic contexts have pieced together the core components of the intricate web of deceit that threatens to enslave humanity. I would argue that the answer to this question is also "yes." In Jonathan Haidt's talk, he focuses on the change of the political composition of the professoriate since 1989, the year the Berlin Wall fell. However, I believe that the changes to the professoriate started in the 1960s with the civil rights movement being used as a pretext to set the stage for academia being ruled by people on the left end of the political spectrum.

The last question is whether it is possible that the weapon that humanity needs to fight back is staring us in the face but we are blind to it. I would argue that the answer is that the answer again is "yes." With the rise of secularism that started to become pronounced in the 1960s, politics became the new religion. The Bible, however, explicitly forbids the worship of false idols. While the Bible spells out in detail what happens to societies that turn away from God, it also states explicitly that God is forgiving. It is perhaps for this reason that one of the lines from the Canadian national anthem is, "God keep our land glorious and free," and that the American currency makes reference to trusting God.

My search for truth led me to become a Christian, and I would argue that the Bible is a paradox in that it is at once remarkably simple and intricately complex. The Old Testament contains numerous stories of societies on the verge of collapse and dissenters patiently waiting for their societies to listen to them. The New Testament, in contrast, provides a lens through which to interpret the Old. There is also much wisdom to be gained from the Proverbs and Psalms; these sections of the Bible stand alone and are relatively easy to process.

In closing, there is another Great Reset that is possible for those who seek it: Crying out to a God who will welcome us with open arms and forgive us for all that we have done wrong. This Great Reset will not promise us a utopia on Earth, but it will give people the keys to joy, life-satisfaction, and meaningful relationships with our fellow human beings.

Bibliography

Time Magazine in Partnership with Sompo Holdings. "The Great Reset." 2020-2021. https://time.com/collection/great-reset/.

Chapter 4

Thinking about Tolerance

Scott D. G. Ventureyra

Several years ago, a good friend (unfortunately an ex-friend now) and I had a disagreement over several things written by a Christian scholar regarding Islam. As a Christian with a Muslim mother, he was upset by the content of the article, which challenged the nature of political Islam and its growing presence in Western consciousness. In the end, my friend seemed to reduce religion to a mere personal taste instead of truth. He also said that one ought to focus on bolstering their own faith rather than engage in polemics regarding other faiths. This is a politically correct stance to take in a multi-cultural country. But doesn't that betray freedom of inquiry, thought, and debate? This was not the first time I had such a conversation. Indeed, many friends and acquaintances get upset at the notion that one religion or viewpoint could be singled out as correct. Essentially, my friend was playing into the hands of what has become known as the "new tolerance." This and many other engagements I have had with people over the years regarding religion and truth inspired me to participate in a Roundtable on Tolerance at the Dominican University College in Ottawa, Ontario, that was held on April 24, 2015. This chapter takes some of the main points from that presentation into consideration.

With respect to Western political philosophy, present-day ideas of tolerance or toleration were initiated during what is known as the War of Religions between Catholics and Protestants.[1] The failure to impose a single religion throughout Europe led to the principal of tolerance. This was the purpose of the 1598 Edict of Nantes, by which the French king promised "*liberté de conscience*" that would allow the Protestant minority to stay in France, although this was revoked in 1685.[2] Tolerance in the context of the Edict of Nantes referred to respecting and allowing the existence of heterodox confessions and differing religious behaviour.

The idea of tolerance was later defended by John Locke in 1689 in *A Letter Concerning Toleration*.[3] Locke maintained that church and state held separate

1 Kimlycka, "Toleration," 877.

2 Wangegffelen, *L'edit de Nantes. Une histoire europeene de la toleranace.*

3 Horton, "Toleration," 895.

functions: the government upheld external interests related to life, liberty, and welfare whereas the church was concerned with internal interests such as salvation. This notion that was exclusive to religious polemic has since the 19th and 20th centuries been extended to all facets of society: racial, sexual, political, and social.[4] A few arguments in favour of tolerance include "the fallibility of one's beliefs, the impossibility of coercion into religious belief, respect for human freedom, the danger of civil strife and the value of diversity."[5] In contemporary North American society we now find ourselves in a much more complex and diverse interconnection of conflicting faith traditions and ideological viewpoints—over the past two years, we have witnessed heightened divisions in politics as well as issues revolving around the COVID-19 crisis. Ironically, any dissenting view from the accepted COVID narrative is met with censorship, derision, tarnishing of reputation, or loss of employment. This is anything but tolerant.[6]

It is thought, at least among certain thinkers and segments of the population in North America, that our belief in tolerance requires qualification or modification. Years ago, over the period of three days, *CBC Radio* hosted a debate and discussion titled *The Trouble with Tolerance*[7] where the following questions were considered: "What does tolerance look like?"; "Why is it that in Canada, in order to honour somebody else's tradition, I have to dishonour my own?"; "Is Canada too tolerant for its own good?"; "Do you have to be tolerant of intolerant people?"; and "How far can we tolerate tolerance?" Yet such discussions and debates exemplify how far the concept of tolerance has penetrated into North American consciousness. Still, as I seek to demonstrate, we have diverged significantly from the understanding of tolerance as proposed by both the Edict of Nantes and Locke.

The notion of tolerance is so deeply entrenched in Western consciousness that to question it may seem for many unthinkable or even intolerable. The idea of tolerance is held in very high esteem by the majority of westerners. Even though it is held uncritically, tolerance has over the years evolved into a "fundamental norm" and consequently has been elevated to "a central political category."[8] Most of us in North America want to be tolerant, and the concept of tolerance seems to have been raised to the status of a "highest good"[9] trumping

4 Horton, "Toleration," 895.

5 Kimlycka, "Toleration," 877.

6 Here are two examples—the first, Dr. Robert Malone, who helped invent the technology behind the mRNA vaccine: Barkoukis, "'The Single Most Qualified' mRNA Expert Censored after Discussing Concerns over Vaccines"; and the second, Francis Christian, a professor of medicine at the University of Saskatchewan who expressed concern over the issue of informed consent for 12-to-17-year-olds: Giles, "USask suspends doctor calling for 'informed consent' for mRNA vaccines."

7 CBC, *The Trouble with Tolerance.*

8 De Wit, "Why Tolerance Cannot Be Our Principal Value."

9 In philosophy, the principle of goodness in which all moral values are included or from which they are derived; the highest or supreme good.

other beliefs and ideas. This is because tolerance is often viewed as a virtue, *if* applied to what we deem *ought* to be tolerated.[10] But the trouble lies not only in suggesting what *ought* to be tolerated but—more fundamentally, for our purposes—in clearly defining tolerance itself.

In recent years, we have seen a dramatic shift in our conception of tolerance. It has gone from meaning the acceptance of the *existence* of differing views to meaning now the acceptance of different views. We jump from the ability to articulate beliefs and claims that we do not agree with to the claim that all beliefs are equally valid. My friend unknowingly fell victim to this latter view, the "new" tolerance. This is precisely the point that many thinkers have made in recent years, including D.A. Carson in his book *The Intolerance of Tolerance*[11]:

> The new tolerance suggests that actually accepting another's position means believing that position to be true or at least as true as your own. We move from allowing the free expression of contrary opinions to the acceptance of all opinions; we leap from permitting the articulation of beliefs and claims with which we do not agree to asserting that all beliefs and claims are equally valid. Thus we slide from the old tolerance to the new.[12]

The problem is compounded in contemporary popular culture, where the old and the new meanings are sometimes interchangeably used. The difficulty lies in discerning which one is being used.[13] For instance, if one says that "Christians tolerate other religions"—what does one mean by this statement? Does it mean that Christians accept the existence of other religions or that they accept other religions as being equally true? What if someone declares that "Christians are so intolerant?" Does this mean that Christians want all dissenting positions to be eradicated or does it mean that Christians insist that through the atoning sacrifice of Christ we are saved? The answer to these questions depends on our understanding of tolerance and intolerance.[14] In today's climate it is deemed intolerant to question or not accept leftist propaganda on sex, gender, sexuality, immigration, religion, critical race theory, economics, the main narrative on COVID, or any other holy tenet of the left. If any of the "accepted" narratives surrounding these contentious domains is doubted then one is deemed to be sexist, transphobic, homophobic, xenophobic, Islamophobic, racist, a greedy capitalist, conspiracy theorist, or just a bigot.

10 Newman, *The Foundations of Religious Tolerance*, 6.

11 Carson, *The Intolerance of Tolerance*, 3. Carson goes through several dictionary definitions to trace this shift in the definition of tolerance.

12 Carson, *The Intolerance of Tolerance*, 3–4.

13 Carson, *The Intolerance of Tolerance*, 4.

14 For an excellent explanation of how the meaning of tolerance has dramatically shifted, see Koukl, "The Intolerance of Tolerance."

On the older view of tolerance, one may allow a dissenting view in spite of disapproving of it.[15] There are three assumptions associated with this older notion of tolerance: objective truth exists, there is disagreement about truth, and the best way to persuade people of truth is through reason, not coercion or force—where the best ideas win the day based on their merit.

On the other hand, the "new tolerance" argues that no one has a claim to exclusivity since all views are equally valid. What's more, anyone who disagrees with such a view is deemed intolerant. Now, we enter another level of complexity, because under the new version of tolerance there is also a new view of intolerance. Carson observes that "intolerance is no longer a refusal to allow contrary opinions to say their piece in public, but must be understood to be any questioning of contradicting the view that all opinions are equally valid. To question such postmodern axioms is by definition intolerant. For such questioning there is no tolerance whatsoever for it is classed as intolerance and must therefore be condemned. It has become the supreme vice."[16]

Interestingly, along this line of thought, the Dominican University College's late research professor Leslie Armour is alleged to have stated: "Our idea is that to be a virtuous citizen is to be one who tolerates everything except intolerance."[17] What is implied by this new tolerance is that any adherence to absolutism is prohibited except for the absolutism of its prohibition. Tolerance reigns supreme, but not when anyone disagrees with this strange definition of tolerance.[18] Hence, the inconsistency is revealed—all absolutes are discarded while one is inconspicuously smuggled in.

It is worth pointing out that implicit in the very notion of tolerance is truth. We can tolerate other viewpoints because we disagree with them. In affirming some position as correct, we must at most tolerate others which we think of as incorrect. Hence, an assumption of truth and falsity is associated with tolerance. You cannot tolerate something you already agree with. The new version of tolerance argues for an incoherent view that promotes relativism. The "new tolerance" is logically incoherent, since tolerance itself assumes believing someone else's position is false, or else you would not tolerate it. Again, my friend and countless others seem to have fallen victim to this fallacious form of reasoning.

Given the incoherence of a relativistic view that attempts to affirm the equal validity of a number of contradictory positions, the possibility of truth is revealed when applied to religious claims because of the ability to discern this fallacy. There are simply no good grounds to affirm all religions or all viewpoints as equally valid. It is logically possible that all religions or viewpoints may be

15 Carson, *The Intolerance of Tolerance*, 6.

16 Carson, *The Intolerance of Tolerance*, 12.

17 Quoted in Harvey, "Wanted: Old Fashioned Virtue."

18 Carson, *The Intolerance of Tolerance*, 13.

false, but by the same token one indeed may be correct, which as an objective truth would rule out the possibility of relativism. Yet it is not intolerant to assert the truth of a single religion or viewpoint, since this does not preclude the existence of other religions or viewpoints or forbid others from accepting them. If anything, the view expounded by the "new tolerance" reveals itself to be intolerant, since it does not take an honest account of the significant differences between religious traditions. Similarly, the late philosopher Jay Neuman suggests in his book *Foundations of Religious Tolerance* that the claims made by a religious relativist are untenable:

> The religious relativist, while claiming to take most religions seriously [by giving them equal status], does not take any seriously. He does not appreciate how much is at stake in religious disagreements. But religious faith involves the most powerful commitments, and if it does not appear to in our own society, perhaps that is only because most of our fellow citizens who profess to be religious are not really religious. I happen to believe that the particular religious opinions I hold are more reasonable than any others that I have been exposed to. If I did not believe this, I would give them up in favour of different ones. I shall continue to enjoy the company of [people] of other faiths, and I shall continue to appreciate the importance with them to achieve common goals. But I will not accept the relativist's view that their religious commitments are as profound as my own, if only because I cannot. And if my understanding of human nature is reasonably correct, then I can speculate with some confidence that if the religious relativist tries to make people tolerant by converting them to relativism, he will fail again and again.[19]

I will make three proposals to help move the conversation regarding tolerance a step forward. The first is to distinguish between persons and ideas. As moral truth seekers, we should rid ourselves of the *ad hominem* fallacy. We should most certainly challenge others' views that we disagree with, but in a respectful manner. You can explain why someone is wrong without attacking the person. As already mentioned, it is a confusion to suggest that one is intolerant by virtue of disagreeing with someone's position. Moreover, we have seen that labeling someone intolerant for this reason is incoherent, since tolerance presupposes that one disagrees with the other. Instead, we must love someone even through disagreement. However, under the "new tolerance" people have demanded not only that they be loved but their ideas as well.[20] We should discriminate

19 Newman, *The Foundations of Religious Tolerance*, 72–73.

20 See Dallas Willard, quoted in Stetson and Conti, *The Truth about Tolerance*, 139. Willard has recognized such notions as having disastrous consequences with respect to moral matters.

against ideas but not against people. The Judeo-Christian theological belief that humans are created in the image and likeness of God provides one with good grounds for affirming dignity and value in all people, even if their beliefs are false or their behavior abhorrent. This particular theological belief could be applied in a practical way to people of good will who do not necessarily believe in such a theological doctrine but are still convinced that the "new tolerance" is terribly flawed. The intrinsic value of every human person calls for us to love them in spite of any profound disagreements we may have.

In addition to pointing out the several flaws of the "new tolerance" already discussed, another way to help challenge people who adhere to such views is to appeal to the notion of progress. Most people value and appreciate progress; we are not static beings. One could demonstrate that progress is not possible under the "new tolerance." The mere fact that this relativistic position views all positions as equally valid implies this. One may change positions under the rubric of the relativism associated with the "new tolerance," but not thereby become more tolerant or a better person. Moral relativists deny that we ought to act a certain way or strive for a particular goal in order to progress. In essence, morals can never improve or worsen. A particular position can shift, but there is no improvement or worsening.[21] In reality, progress is predicated upon the ability to discuss competing ideas and decide which is most promising. The "new tolerance" cannot facilitate such progress.

A final way to clarify the nature of tolerance is to consider the concept of non-tolerance.[22] Tolerance should be pragmatic, in the sense that it ought not imply moral silence or agnosticism, since responsible ethical beings should point out if someone's ideas are false or rest on shaky grounds.[23] As Brian Stetson and Joseph Conti recognize, silence is cowardly in such situations: "such a person is acting out of a defect in personal character or a capitulation to the cultural force of political correctness, not a sense of friendship or broadminded humanity."[24] It is important to realize that tolerance cannot be viewed as an absolute but has serious limits. The concept of intolerance is somewhat ambiguous: it can be taken to mean being insufficiently tolerant of something that should be tolerated. Stetson and Conti suggest that *non-tolerance*, on the other hand, indicates "refusing to make or keep legal a morally objectionable practice."[25] We should take a non-tolerant (rather than intolerant) position towards criminal

21 Beckwith and Koukl, *Relativism: Feet Firmly Planted in Mid-Air*, 66–67. The authors consider what they call seven fatal flaws of relativism. My comments about the inability to progress were inspired by their exposition of flaw 5: "relativists can't improve their morality."

22 Stetson and Conti, *The Truth about Tolerance*, 147–156.

23 Stetson and Conti, *The Truth About Tolerance*, 145.

24 Stetson and Conti, *The Truth About Tolerance*, 145.

25 Stetson and Conti, *The Truth About Tolerance*, 155.

acts "that are justly and properly unlawful,"[26] such as rape, murder, racial discrimination, fraud, partial-birth abortions, and many other moral evils.

However, an often unobserved application of non-tolerance threatens our civil liberties: government, the medical establishment, and educational institutions muzzle dissenters by assaulting their constitutional rights and freedoms, like freedom of the press, freedom of speech, and freedom of conscience. Throughout this book we will see various examples of such assaults. Such blatant attacks on our humanity and our civil rights are frequently and widely enabled by cowardice. All too often, unfortunately, people who are knowledgeable and articulate lack the courage to face any backlash, whereas people who may have the courage to confront cultural bullies lack the knowledge and the ability to do so effectively. Both situations make it difficult to disseminate important ideas to a wide audience. What is needed is the intersection of knowledge with courage, which is indeed a rare occurrence. Today, we can take the COVID-19 situation as an example, with some medical doctors and scientists afraid to speak against the accepted narrative. Still, a number of Canadian medical doctors, like Francis Christian and Chris Milburn, have lost their jobs, and scientists like Byram Bridle have been harassed for following their own moral conscience in dissenting.[27] The same goes for Canadian politicians such as Derek Sloan, Randy Hillier, and Maxime Bernier who have taken a vocal stance against some of the draconian restrictions imposed by federal and provincial governments, much of which has been shown to be unscientific. Tolerance in this sense takes opposed ethical viewpoints very seriously. In a truly progressive and self-critical society it would be done through open debate in a respectful manner, in opposition to the climate of the "new tolerance." Contrary to popularly and uncritically held belief, serious debate does not reflect bigotry or intolerance but rather genuine concern and love for those who may be affected in their health, life and livelihoods if scientists and doctors continue to remain silent in the face of what they know to be evil. We must not tolerate such assaults on our freedoms, but rather resist and defend these values and mechanisms that hold liberal democracies in place.

In the end, the promotion of relativism does not take any religion or viewpoint seriously, since it reduces religion to mere preferences. The new tolerance stifles dialogue and suppresses truth. Those who appreciate true progress must fight against these pernicious ideas. Under relativism, progress is impossible. As Christians, we cannot compromise on truth for the sake of political correctness or to appease other's beliefs we know to be incorrect. This would betray the Gospel message. It is outright cowardly and works against

26 Stetson and Conti, *The Truth About Tolerance*, 155.

27 Attkison, "CENSORED: Pro-vaccine doctor Francis Christian, over Covid-19 vaccine safety concerns."

the cultivation of true Christian virtues. The Christian road is a difficult one. Speaking the truth and living consistently under a Christian worldview will sever friendships, obliterate careers, and perhaps even cost you your life. However, I believe that defending truth and making our friends and relatives understand the many flaws in contemporary thinking, although an uphill battle, is worthwhile. We are called to be lights to the world. Correct thinking is a necessary light that can shine brightly in a period of vast confusion and darkness. Ultimately, what lies beyond mere tolerance is love.

Bibliography

Armour, Leslie. "Wanted: Old Fashioned Virtue." *Montreal Gazette*, February 19, 1995.

Attkison, Sharyl, "CENSORED: Pro-vaccine doctor Francis Christian, over Covid-19 vaccine safety concerns." *Sharyl Attkisson*, June 24, 2021. https://sharylattkisson.com/2021/06/censored-pro-vaccine-doctor-francis-christian-over-covid-19-vaccine-safety-concerns/.

Barkoukis, Lea. "'The Single Most Qualified' mRNA Expert Censored after Discussing Concerns over Vaccines." *Townhall*, June 24, 2021. https://townhall.com/tipsheet/leahbarkoukis/2021/06/24/the-single-most-qualified-mrna-expert-censored-after-discussing-concerns-over-vaccines-n2591500.

Beckwith, Francis J. and Gregory Koukl. *Relativism: Feet Firmly Planted in Mid-Air*. Grand Rapids, MI: Baker Books, 1998.

Carson, D.A. *The Intolerance of Tolerance*. Grand Rapids: William B. Eerdmans, 2012.

CBC, *The Trouble with Tolerance*. February, 2007. http://www.cbc.ca/player/Radio/Ideas/ID/2650568328/.

De Wit, Theo W.A. "Why Tolerance Cannot Be Our Principal Value." *Bijdragen, International Journal in Philosophy and Theology* 71 (2013): 377–390.

Giles, David. "USask suspends doctor calling for 'informed consent' for mRNA vaccines." *Global News*, June 23, 2021. https://globalnews.ca/news/7975431/usask-doctor-francis-christian-mrna-vaccines/.

Horton, John. "Toleration." *Concise Routledge Encyclopedia of Philosophy*, edited by Edward Craig. New York: Routledge, 2000.

Kimlycka., Will. "Toleration." In *The Oxford Companion to Philosophy*, edited by Ted Honderich. Oxford: Oxford University Press, 1995.

Koukl, Greg. "The Intolerance of Tolerance." *PragerU*, March 16, 2020. https://www.youtube.com/watch?v=ENKJBDMOjt4.

Newman, Jay. *The Foundations of Religious Tolerance*. Toronto: University of Toronto Press, 1982.

Stetson, Brad and Joseph G. Conti, *The Truth about Tolerance*. Downers Grove, IL: InterVarsity, 2005.

Wangegffelen, Thierry. *L'edit de Nantes. Une histoire europeene de la toleranace. XVIe -XXe siècle.* Paris: Le Livre de Poche, 1998.

Section II:

On Truth

Part I:

Faith, Reason, Science, and Experience

Chapter 5

Dawkins's Unholy Trinity—Incoherency, Hypocrisy, and Bigotry[1]

Scott D. G. Ventureyra

In November of 2014, the BBC interviewed E. O. Wilson (a highly reputable professor emeritus of entomology at Harvard) asking him about his disagreements on natural selection with Richard Dawkins. He responded: "There is no dispute between me and Richard Dawkins and there never has been, because he's a journalist, and journalists are people that report what the scientists have found and the arguments I've had have actually been with scientists doing research."[2] Although Dawkins possesses a PhD in zoology, his scientific research largely ended in the 1970s, according to his publication list. Since then, he has been, as Wilson states, nothing more than a science journalist. Yet Dawkins has consistently declared that "there is no serious scientist who doubts that evolution is a fact." My motivation here is not to dispute the findings of evolutionary biology but to point out Dawkins's hypocrisy. The truth is that there are many scientists, even biologists, who deny that evolution is a fact but are light years ahead of Dawkins in terms of research and peer-reviewed publications. Here are just a few verifiable examples: Dean H. Kenyon, John C. Sanford, and Henry F. Schaefer III. Clearly Dawkins is not in a position to make declarations as to what constitutes a "serious scientist."

In his book *River out of Eden: A Darwinian View of Life*, he succinctly explains the implications of a physicalist universe: "In a universe of electrons and selfish genes, blind physical forces and genetic replication, some people are going to get hurt, other people are going to get lucky, and you won't find any rhyme or reason in it, nor any justice. The universe that we observe has precisely the properties we should expect if there is, at bottom, no design, no purpose, no evil, no good, nothing but pitiless indifference."[3] Nothing Dawkins has written

1 This is a modification of the following article: Scott Ventureyra, "Dawkins' Unholy Trinity: Incoherency, Hypocrisy and Bigotry," *Crisis*, November 26, 2014, https://www.crisismagazine.com/2014/dawkins-unholy-trinity-incoherency-hypocrisy-bigotry.

2 BBC, "EO Wilson talks evolution and Richard Dawkins spat."

3 Dawkins, *River out of Eden*, 133.

since then indicates that he has changed his mind. If he hasn't, then he still believes that in our universe there is no good or evil. And yet Dawkins made headlines nine years later with a proclamation that it's immoral for a mother not to abort a foetus that has Down's syndrome: "Abort it and try again. It would be immoral to bring it into the world if you have the choice."[4] Has Dawkins changed his mind? Has he decided we can say certain actions (like abortion) are not "indifferent" but either "good" or "bad"—for the troubled mother, or for others in her family, or, on any of a number of grounds, for society? Seven years later, in 2021, his position remains the same.[5]

Several questions arise from Dawkins's recent declaration in light of his atheistic materialism. First, how can something be declared immoral when the universe is ultimately comprised of "pitiless indifference"? Something is either amoral or immoral: it cannot be both at the same time. Secondly, do objective moral standards exist without God? And third, how do we make sense of the content, significance, and knowledge of morality in the absence of God? These are questions Dawkins must address in order to avoid incoherence. Perhaps he could consult Friedrich Nietzsche, who declared that the death of God meant the annihilation of all meaning and value in life. Nietzsche, unlike Dawkins, was a critical and consistent atheist. The most amusing element of Dawkins's incoherency is that he unwittingly affirms that God exists through agreement with the first two premises of the moral argument for God's existence as defended by Christian philosopher William Lane Craig:

1. If God does not exist, objective moral values and duties do not exist.
2. Objective moral values and duties do exist.
3. Therefore, God exists.[6]

A detailed explanation of this can be found in Craig's chapter in *God Is Good, God Is Great* dealing with the new atheism and arguments for God.

It had been quite some time since I had given the new atheists and their rhetoric much thought. This was changed recently by an acquaintance who had an unusual admiration for Dawkins and his "argumentation" against religious belief and God. He reasoned that anyone who did not agree with Dawkins's logic was either ignorant or completely brainwashed by religious superstition and fear tactics. Although many atheists hold this view uncritically, I still found it remarkable that anyone could hold such a view at all—especially years after the publication of *The God Delusion*. Following the publication of Dawkins's "magnum opus," many refutations were published in book form or appeared on

4 Hawkins, "Richard Dawkins: 'Immoral' not to abort if foetus has Down's syndrome."
5 Dawkins, Interview with Brandon O'Connor.
6 Craig, "Richard Dawkins on Arguments for God," 18.

YouTube. I thought that no thinking non-believer could hold to most of these new popularizations of atheism. Moreover, one can easily find debates dismantling popular atheistic arguments one by one, including Dawkins's encounter with John Lennox (a professor of mathematics and philosophy) in 2008.[7] If people want to think clearly about these issues, many resources are at their fingertips.

"Man of Science" Promotes Bigotry

Despite all this, Dawkins has continued to promote his ideas. On March 24, 2012, at the "Reason Rally" in Washington, D.C., he urged atheists and agnostics to mock religious believers. He encouraged them to question Roman Catholics' belief in transubstantiation: "For example, if they say they're Catholic: Do you really believe, that when a priest blesses a wafer, it turns into the body of Christ? Are you seriously telling me you believe that? Are you seriously saying that wine turns into blood?" He then incited non-believers to "mock them" and "ridicule them! In public!" if they responded in the affirmative. He also encouraged them to ridicule belief in the virgin birth and the resurrection. Christians have good historical grounds for believing in the resurrection.[8] However, Dawkins rarely shows interest in rational discourse about religious claims. Instead, he would rather encourage bigotry among his followers.

Dawkins takes pride in thinking he is a man of science. He believes that science is a self-correcting discipline. He also perpetuates the myth that a scientist would rather die at the stake than knowingly maintain a false idea. Does he know that scientists sometimes fudge their data in hope of being published and recognized for their work? I wonder if he is ignorant of the fact that sometimes peer-review journals ensure orthodoxy over quality. In 2008, an article in the *Financial Times* argued that peer-review journals are becoming increasingly sloppy, by rejecting scientifically valid papers while accepting invalid ones: "The process is under assault from critics who say it is ineffective at filtering out poor research, while it perpetuates predictable work at the expense of more imaginative thinking. In the long run we all suffer, argues Don Braben of University College London, because economic growth depends on unpredictable scientific advances."[9]

Much worse than this is what we have even seen in the past two years, more vividly than ever, in how pharmaceutical companies have compromised the integrity of scientific and medical journals—this is something that will be explored in more detail in our section on COVID-19.

7 Fixed Point Foundation, "Richard Dawkins vs John Lennox | The God Delusion Debate."
8 Ladydifadden, "Transcript of Richard Dawkins's speech from Reason Rally 2012."
9 Cookson and Jack, "Science stifled? Why peer review is under pressure."

In *The God Delusion*, Dawkins gives the example of a scientist admitting that the Golgi Apparatus is in fact real after denying its existence, demonstrating that scientists let go of their pride for the sake of scientific progress. He admits that if evidence were forthcoming against evolution, he would admit that he was wrong. This is an interesting admission considering the slew of invalid arguments found throughout his book. These have been pointed out by philosophers and theologians such as Alvin Plantinga, William Lane Craig, Paul Copan, Alister McGrath, Scott Hahn, and Benjamin Wiker.[10] For example, on pages 157–58 of *The God Delusion*, Dawkins lays out the main argument of the book. It contains six premises that do not logically follow to the conclusion. It goes like this:

1. One of the greatest challenges to the human intellect has been to explain how the complex, improbable appearance of design in the universe arises.
2. The natural temptation is to attribute the appearance of design to actual design itself.
3. The temptation is a false one because the designer hypothesis immediately raises the larger problem of who designed the designer.
4. The most ingenious and powerful explanation is Darwinian evolution by natural selection.
5. We don't have an equivalent explanation for physics.
6. We should not give up the hope of a better explanation arising in physics, something as powerful as Darwinism is for biology.

Therefore, God almost certainly does not exist.[11]

Craig has thoroughly shown why the argument is invalid in *Contending with Christianity's Critics*. One wonders why Dawkins, who claims to be a man of reason and science, hasn't rebutted Craig's refutation. And if he can't respond to the criticisms, why hasn't he admitted this publicly? If not solely for the sake of truth and scientific integrity? One wonders whether book sales are more important than truth. It should come as no surprise that Dawkins has avoided a one-on-one discussion or debate with Craig.

In 2011, he was invited to defend *The God Delusion* in a public debate against Craig at Birmingham University. Dawkins never attended, and preferred to obfuscate the real issues with ad hominem attacks on Craig, accusing him of being an "apologist for genocide" for Craig's defence of God's commandment in Deuteronomy 20:15–17 in a piece in *The Guardian* the day

10 Cf. Plantinga, "The Dawkins Confusion"; McGrath and McGrath, *The Dawkins Delusion*; Hahn and Wiker, *Answering the New Atheism*; Copan and Craig, *Contending with Christianity's Critics*; Copan, *Is God a Moral Monster?*

11 Dawkins, *The God Delusion*, 157–158.

before. Atheist philosopher Daniel Came has stated in response to Dawkins's piece, also published in *The Guardian*: "It is quite obvious that Dawkins is opportunistically using these remarks as a smokescreen to hide the real reasons for his refusal to debate with Craig—which has a history that long predates Craig's comments on the Canaanites."[12]

Questions Dawkins Does Not Answer

How does one assess Dawkins's thought in light of his many intellectual shortcomings? It is well known that Dawkins has claimed that "Darwin made it possible to be an intellectually fulfilled atheist." He has stated that Darwin's theory of evolution by natural selection has fuelled his atheism. It seems to me that he must have an extraordinarily low standard for being intellectually fulfilled. If evolutionary biology is to be treated as a scientific discipline, then it remains neutral regarding religious and metaphysical questions. Many secular evolutionary biologists have speculated that the whole process of evolution is purposeless, wasteful, and directionless. They have notoriously utilized metaphorical language that is not necessitated by scientific observation to describe natural selection as "a blind watchmaker." Yet such reflections are philosophical and not scientific. This creates a conflation between methodological naturalism and metaphysical naturalism. So, Dawkins's atheism is based on a naïve interpretation of evolutionary biology.

Even if, for argument's sake, Dawkins were to have the correct interpretation of evolutionary biology, there remain many important questions to be answered regarding the nature of reality, such as: Why is there something rather than nothing? What is the best explanation of the finitude of the past? What is the best explanation for the finely tuned laws and initial conditions of physics and chemistry that permit life? What is the correlation between existence and scientific observability? What is the best explanation for the specified information necessary for the origin of a self-replicating system? What explains the high level of consciousness that humans possess? How can we account for the correspondence of our minds with reality that permits us the use of logic and language? What is the source of objective morality? These are questions that reasonably transcend the purview of Darwinian biology. Without a coherent system to address these questions it is difficult to see how someone can be intellectually fulfilled. Furthermore, the distinguished naturalist philosopher Thomas Nagel has identified numerous flaws in Dawkins's reductive materialism.[13]

12 Came, "Richard Dawkins's refusal to debate is cynical and anti-intellectualist."

13 Nagel, *Mind and Cosmos*.

Given all this, how is it even possible that Dawkins is consistently recognized as one of the top public intellectuals of our time? We know it is not based on rational argumentation or scientific reasoning. His views should be met with scorn, not with unmerited popular adulation. Ultimately, I believe that it is because we live in an age of theological and philosophical illiteracy. Critical reasoning has been swept aside by emotive responses to religious claims and practices, so much so that during graduate school I remember some theologians (albeit third-rate ones) embracing Dawkins's shallow reasoning against religion. Some may think it is better to ignore Dawkins. But all that does is permit the perpetuation of ignorance.

One thing Dawkins is extremely good at is self-promotion and selling copies of his books by the millions. The best way to counter this is to educate people in critical thinking and to encourage erudite philosophical and theological thought. As we have seen, Dawkins has ridiculed his critics for not being serious scientists, but many of them tower over him in terms of publications and research. He has, unknowingly, implicitly admitted God's existence through his sloppy reasoning. He has urged the mockery of Christians and their beliefs without ever providing one shred of evidence against those beliefs. He has never been able to even engage in a serious intellectual discussion about the historicity of Jesus' resurrection. And he continues to shy away from defending his views publicly against serious critics like Bill Craig. I suppose John Lennox's spanking was enough for one lifetime. Dawkins surely does not merit the self-given title "bright."

Dawkins's level of hypocrisy should severely undermine his credibility. Unfortunately, self-styled skeptics and "free thinkers" like the acquaintance I mentioned above will continue to uncritically accept Dawkins's superficial argumentation. But hopefully those with an open mind will gain a new perspective. The only way to defeat this ignorance is through education. It is our responsibility to humanity. It is regrettable that Dawkins will most likely continue to mock the Holy Trinity while worshipping at the altar of his own unholy trinity: incoherency, hypocrisy, and bigotry.

Bibliography

BBC. "EO Wilson talks evolution and Richard Dawkins spat." *BBC News*, November 7, 2014. https://www.bbc.com/news/av/science-environment-29959821.

Came, Daniel. "Richard Dawkins's refusal to debate is cynical and anti-intellectualist." *The Guardian*, October 22, 2011. https://www.theguardian.com/commentisfree/belief/2011/oct/22/richard-dawkins-refusal-debate-william-lane-craig.

Cookson, Clive and Andrew Jack. "Science stifled? Why peer review is under pressure." *Financial Times*, June 11, 2008. https://www.ft.com/content/4409911c-37df-11dd-aabb-0000779fd2ac.

Craig, William Lane and Chat Meister. "Richard Dawkins on Arguments for God." In *God Is Great, God Is Good: Why Believing in God Is Reasonable and Responsible*, 13-31. Downers Grove: IVP, 2009.

Copan, Paul and William Lane Craig, eds. *Contending with Christianity's Critics: Answering the New Atheists & Other Objectors*. Nashville: B&H Academic, 2009.

Copan, Paul. *Is God a Moral Monster? Making Sense of the Old Testament God*. Grand Rapids: Baker Books, 2011.

Dawkins, Richard. *The God Delusion*. New York: Houghton Mifflin Harcourt, 2006.

Dawkins, Richard. Interview with Brandon O'Connor. *RTE Radio 1*, May 9, 2021. https://www.rte.ie/radio/radioplayer/html5/#/radio1/21951189.

Dawkins, Richard. *River out of Eden: A Darwinian View of Life*. New York: Basic Books, 1995.

Fixed Point Foundation. "Richard Dawkins vs John Lennox | The God Delusion Debate." YouTube video, February 8, 2017. https://www.youtube.com/watch?v=zF5bPI92-5o.

Hahn, Scott and Benjamin Wiker. *Answering the New Atheism: Dismantling Dawkins's Case against God*. Steubenville, OH: Emmaus Road, 2008.

Hawkins, Kathleen. "Richard Dawkins: 'Immoral' not to abort Down's foetuses." *BBC News*, August 21, 2014. https://www.bbc.com/news/blogs-ouch-28879659.

Ladydifadden. "Transcript of Richard Dawkins's speech from Reason Rally 2012." Ladydifadden, March 28, 2012. https://ladydifadden.wordpress.com/2012/03/28/transcript-of-richard-dawkins-speech-from-reason-rally-2012/.

McGrath, Alister and Joanna Collicutt McGrath. *The Dawkins Delusion? Atheist Fundamentalism and the Denial of the Divine*. Downers Grove: IVP, 2007.

Nagel, Thomas. *Mind and Cosmos: Why the Materialist Neo-Darwinian Conception of Nature Is Almost Certainly False*. Oxford: Oxford, 2012.

Plantinga, Alvin. "The Dawkins Confusion." *Books & Culture: A Christian Review*, March/April 2007. https://www.booksandculture.com/articles/2007/marapr/1.21.htm.

Chapter 6

An Approach to the Santa Legend[1]

Scott D. G. Ventureyra

Many people who "celebrate" Christmas come from all sorts of religious and non-religious backgrounds, but do not recognize or accept the real significance of Christmas. As Christians, we really should try our best not to be swept up by the artificiality and emptiness of consumerism that is so common around Christmastime. And most importantly, we mustn't lose sight of the centrality of Christ's birth.

I want to raise an issue which is often neglected by many Christians, concerning the character of Santa Claus. Who is he, really? I believe that the figure of Santa Claus has taken on a significance with troubling theological implications, if not dealt with carefully.

The story of Santa originates with St. Nicholas, a bishop from Myra in what was known as Asia Minor (present-day Turkey). St. Nicholas was a generous and kind man who helped the poor and distributed gifts. Throughout the Western world, from the 16th century onward, St. Nicholas evolved into Santa Claus. This character of Santa that we have come to identify as having a long white beard and hair, wearing a red and white robe and hat, black boots, and glasses, who lives in the North Pole and flies around the world on Christmas Eve, on a sleigh led by Rudolf the red-nosed reindeer and eight other reindeer, has evolved into a quasi-divine fantastical legend involving miraculous powers, such as quasi-omniscience, quasi-omnipresence, and quasi-omnibenevolence. The question is: should such a belief be encouraged for our children?

To be sure, on the one hand, the metaphor of Santa Claus in principle can inspire awe, mystery, and anticipation in children, which are certainly valuable things. Nathan Stone wrote a wonderful piece for *Crisis* which takes this line of thought.[2] We need only examine the works of C. S. Lewis and J. R. R. Tolkien to know that myth and imagination certainly have many uses, including the illustration of deep Christian truths. Probably one of the most masterful minds

1 This is a modified version of Scott Ventureyra, "An Approach to the Santa Legend," *Catholic Insight*, December 24, 2017, https://catholicinsight.com/approach-santa-legend/.

2 Stone, "In Defense of Santa Claus."

to demonstrate this was the Swiss psychiatrist Carl Jung, with his study of archetypes as they are developed in the collective unconscious—something that contemporary professor and clinical psychologist Jordan Peterson has spent much time lecturing and writing about. One can explore these themes in great depth through Peterson's YouTube videos. Peterson is leading many young men back to their Christian roots through his evocative presentations which explore biblical metaphors and archetypes.

I do not deny that these approaches can be useful, but we must also be on guard against, for instance, the Neo-Atheists who like to equate belief in Santa Claus with belief in God. We live in a culture deeply imbued with both scientific and metaphysical materialism. Just as much as we must restore belief in myth and a proper awe of reality, I think we must confront these other challenges as well. If we do not do this with good measure, it can have somewhat dangerous theological consequences. One need only take a poll of how Christians' beliefs are deeply shaken upon entering university.

For our purposes, let us examine how disbelief in Santa Claus can lead to disbelief in theological truths. Take for instance, the lyrics to the song "Santa Claus Is Coming to Town," which attributes to its subject special foreknowledge and even a capacity for higher moral judgment.

I have told my daughter Julianna that Santa only gets these miraculous powers from God. It was the best compromise I could come up with, since the story of Santa had been inculcated in her from an early age. Years ago, when I made a comment about the packaging of presents, she said, "Well, it doesn't matter, since Santa's elves are making them from scratch in the North Pole, unless everybody has been lying to me." Her skeptical mind had started to analyze elements of the story. My fear was and has always been the loss of her innocence and wonderment at the world.

Recently, I was made aware that my daughter had lost her belief in a literal Santa figure who delivers gifts to children all over the world. Readers may wonder why I had not explained the nonexistence of a literal Santa to her earlier on. The reason is twofold: one minor and one major reason. The minor reason is out of respect for her mother, who has been significantly invested in our daughter's belief in Santa. The major reason was to preserve her innocence for as long as I possibly could. Upon becoming aware that she has ceased to believe in Santa, I still worried what effect this would have on her faith.

Perhaps, since her moment of disbelief, she may have started doubting the existence of God. We must be honest with ourselves, given our cultural climate: this is certainly a strong possibility for most Christian children. I know, from personal experience, that once I began to lose my enchantment with the world, so too began my skepticism of theological truths. Even though my objections were not tempered by good argumentation, as is the case with many disbelievers, they were rooted in some healthy skepticism. In order to help cope with this, I want to outline some brief arguments/strategies to help other Christian parents cope with such a situation, if it were to arise.

The first thing to point out to your child, who may begin to question God's existence because of disbelief in a *literal* Santa, is that most adults who do not believe in a *literal* Santa still believe in God. Second, the reason we do not believe in a *literal* Santa is that we have no evidence of his existence (which furthermore would violate some basic rules of physics and metaphysics). Has anyone ever witnessed him on Christmas Eve travelling the world on his sleigh and distributing presents? Have we seen any evidence of his toy factory at the North Pole? What about elves? Indeed, we do not believe in Santa Claus because we lack any evidence of such a person truly existing. Now, a skeptic may object and argue, "well, it could be that Santa is invisible and so are the reindeer and elves." A somewhat clever strategy, even though it still does little to demonstrate why no presents are ever delivered by this invisible being, since parents are the ones placing the presents under the tree on Christmas Eve. Moreover, this perpetually invisible being would not resemble Santa anymore, but rather some transcendent quasi-angelic spiritual being.

In contrast, we have plenty of good arguments and evidence to demonstrate the existence of God. We have many signs pointing to a transcendent reality. Take for instance, that the past is finite with a definite beginning, which calls for its explanation in an a-temporal and transcendent cause, as argued in the Kalam Cosmological Argument. There are plenty of others, such as the principle of sufficient reason (Leibniz's contingency argument), the teleological argument, the axiological (moral) argument, the argument from consciousness, the ontological argument, the usefulness of mathematics in the natural sciences which outlines the intelligibility of the universe, the historical evidence of Jesus' resurrection and His own divine self-understanding, and many others.[3] Interestingly, once the deep implications of these arguments are pondered and realized, they can help renew and even deepen our enchantment with the world and our faith. Reason is not opposed to faith; they are inextricably linked in profound ways. The deeper my understanding of these arguments, the deeper my faith has grown. Thus, I do believe we must help reverse our culture's disenchantment with the universe, and besides the use of legends and imaginative apologetics with fantasy narratives, à la Lewis and Tolkien, we must also foster a faith grounded in reason.

Furthermore, I believe there are plenty of places for adults to find "awe" in the world, not least in nature itself. We need only look at the scientific discoveries of the past 100 years. Ponder Big Bang cosmology, quantum mechanics, the intricacy of a cell and its components, the miracle of human life

3 See Sennett and Groothuis, *In Defense of Natural Theology*; Wilkins and Moreland, *Jesus under Fire*.

and consciousness, and so on. This is where we can find not just the evidence of God's handiwork but also His beauty and majesty that allow for one of the greatest miracles of all: the Incarnation.

So, my advice to parents is to try to delicately balance their children's propensity for belief in the "magical" and the wonderful which Santa and other myths truly embody—which, no doubt, provide hope and anticipation—with true knowledge of God, especially when they raise important questions of the faith. In other words, there is certainly goodness that comes from belief in the myth of Santa for children, and from the archetypal genre of such myths for adults. This in my view can restore a forgotten childlike innocence and visceral amazement at existence. Yet as parents we must be prepared to give proper reasons to our children for theological truths for the time when they fall into disbelief in the literal Santa, which is also of great importance. The balance between upholding truth and preserving innocence, in our shattered world, is the difficult challenge we face, but one we must not shy away from. Both in synergy will help draw us ever closer to God.

Both parents and children must always be prepared to give a reason for the hope that lies within them, (1 Pt 3:15). I encourage parents to investigate some of the arguments I listed, through the provided resources. What could be a greater way to honor God than imparting truth and love to our children?

Bibliography

Sennett, James F. and Douglas Groothuis, eds. *In Defense of Natural Theology: A Post-Humean Assessment.* Downers Grove: InterVarsity, 2005.

Stone, Nathan. "In Defense of Santa Claus." *Crisis*, December 21, 2017. https://www.crisismagazine.com/2017/defense-santa-clause.

Wilkins, Michael J. and J. P. Moreland. *Jesus under Fire: Modern Scholarship Reinvents the Historical Jesus.* Grand Rapids: Zondervan, 1995.

Chapter 7

The Peterson-Craig Encounter: A Missed Opportunity?[1]

Scott D. G. Ventureyra

On January 26, 2018, Wycliffe College, a graduate school federated with the University of Toronto, hosted a discussion on the question "Is there meaning to life?" The three participants included philosopher and theologian William Lane Craig, atheist philosopher Rebecca Goldstein, and clinical psychologist and professor of psychology Jordan Peterson. This encounter—especially the highly anticipated interaction between Craig and Peterson—made me reflect more deeply on the areas where I have taken issue with Peterson's understanding of philosophical and theological issues.

None of what I am about to say is meant to denigrate Peterson or the tremendous cultural impact he is having. I do believe that almost single-handedly, Peterson is rescuing a decadent Western culture and a tragically lost generation of men. Without affirming belief in God, ironically, on this front he is accomplishing more than many Christian preachers and Catholic Church hierarchs, including the Bishop of Rome. It should be noted, I am not saying there are no other thinkers who are involved in this battle; there are, but not with the unprecedented appeal and influence of Peterson. I also know that his research in his field is top-notch. I can also see how effective he would be as a clinical psychologist. But we are called to speak the truth; here is my analysis of his understanding of philosophical and theological issues as they pertain to Christian truth.

Natural Law Theory

I had hoped that Craig would press Peterson on the grounds of natural law theory. However, Craig, as a Protestant, most likely does not agree with the tenets of natural law theory, although he is one of the most influential

1 This is a modified version of Scott Ventureyra, "The Peterson-Craig Encounter: A Missed Opportunity?" *Crisis Magazine*, February 23, 2018, https://www.crisismagazine.com/2018/peterson-craig-encounter-missed-opportunity.

Christian philosophers defending natural theology. He has brilliantly defended the axiological argument, which would be of tremendous aid to Peterson, if only as a thought experiment.

Natural law theory entails a set of normative guidelines for human behavior and action that are not man-made but endowed by a transcendent source such as God. Human reason can ascertain these laws of nature. They exist independently of the laws of any given state or socio-cultural milieu. Craig did express an appreciation of Peterson's affirmation of objective moral standards and duties against moral relativism. The issue is whether Peterson has any foundation to make these affirmations, since they cannot be grounded in naturalism. Naturalism alone has nothing to offer as an explanation of objective moral values and duties. As Craig pointed out, if morality is the by-product of undirected naturalistic socio-biological evolution, it is merely contingent on how we have evolved; there is no necessary and objective morality. As the late Harvard paleontologist Stephen Jay Gould observed, if we re-ran the evolutionary "tape" of history, we would get different sorts of creatures emerging, since evolution is not a deterministic but a contingent process. The same would be true of moral values.

Peterson spoke of a Cartesian moment, namely his realization of something he could not doubt. The existence of human evil is the most indubitable fact of reality for Peterson. By coming to this realization, he then comes to understand there must be good as well. Therefore, Peterson understands that there is a mode of discernment between good and evil. Peterson comes to a moral understanding through reasoning. Yet this presupposes the existence of a moral lawgiver, even though the problem of evil seeks to undermine the very existence of an all-powerful, all-knowing, and all-loving God. I believe it is atheists rather than believers who are faced with the biggest difficulty here. On the one hand, they must confront the nihilist who denies any objective meaning and value in the absence of God; and on the other, the theist who has coherent grounds for affirming objective meaning and value. To do so, one would have to reason through morality, evil, and suffering in a framework of natural law—devoid of supernatural revelation. Indeed, in the dialogue portion, Peterson affirms a Platonic sort of moral realm, thus acknowledging the insufficiency of naturalism to account for morality. There is, indeed, a deep tension for Peterson between a naturalistic outlook and an intuited transcendent reality.

Methodological Naturalism vs Metaphysical Naturalism

Methodological naturalism is the exclusion of supernatural explanations of the natural world, whereas metaphysical naturalism asserts that the supernatural realm does not exist. In his dialogue with Craig and Goldstein, and elsewhere,

Peterson refers to the power of the naturalistic method in science—which I take to mean methodological naturalism. Its power is real, but methodological naturalism has its limitations and cannot answer the deep questions of theology or metaphysics, which are two disciplines he seems to conflate.

Metaphysical naturalism seems patently false in light of the many good arguments in favor of God's existence. Methodological naturalism has its power but also severe limitations, and it remains logically neutral on questions such as the existence of God, objective moral values and duties, and the nature and origin of consciousness itself. Catholic philosopher Edward Feser has given a brilliant analogy for the limitations of methodological naturalism. He likens methodological naturalism to a metal detector.[2] A metal detector is extremely useful for detecting metal, but nothing else. Thus, it does not follow that, if the metal detector detects A, B, and C, then only A, B, and C exist. It could be that D, E, or F also exists, but the metal detector is not meant to detect non-metallic entities. Similarly, methodological naturalism has a limited scope and is not a reliable method for studying non-material phenomena.

The Existence of God

Another troubling aspect of Peterson's naturalistic outlook is that, as he stated in the discussion period (and in his book *Maps of Meaning: The Architecture of Belief*),[3] he views the transcendent as "irrational." But why? The relationship between faith and reason, science and theology is highly complex. It would be more appropriate to discuss belief in the transcendent as supra-rational. The transcendent is not to be understood by reason alone, but this doesn't make it irrational. It merely transcends the rational. Peterson has been frustratingly ambiguous on his belief in God and Christianity.

It is true, as Peterson suggests, that people have many different ideas about God, but there are clear and cogent philosophical discussions of His nature and existence. Has Peterson not read the works of such great Christian philosophers as St. Augustine, St. Anselm of Canterbury, St. Thomas Aquinas, Richard Swinburne, and Alvin Plantinga? Is he not aware that such works exist? There has been much ink spilled defending the coherence of the concept of God and defining precisely what God means. In one of his lectures, when asked about the existence of God, Peterson refers to the singularity and Big Bang cosmology. The latter in connection with God's existence is one of Craig's areas of expertise.[4]

2 Feser, "Reading Rosenberg, Part II."
3 Peterson, *Maps of Meaning.*
4 See Faith HKU, "God and the Big Bang—Prof William Lane Craig @HKU."

On the Historicity of Jesus Christ and His Resurrection

Peterson suggests that he is afraid of being "boxed in" when it comes to his belief or nonbelief in Christianity. He has also made the dubious claim that the historicity of Jesus is questionable. The truth is that the historicity of Jesus is on more solid ground even than the existence of Socrates. We have more firsthand accounts of Jesus than any other figure of antiquity. The New Testament books are more than 99.5-percent textually pure. In other words, throughout the 20,000 lines of the New Testament, only 40 lines are of questionable authenticity; this amounts to 400 words. And, significantly, these 400 words do not affect any Christian doctrine. This is much more accuracy than any Socratic text possesses. This does not mean we can demonstrate the existence of Jesus beyond a shadow of a doubt, but it rests on strong evidentiary grounds. The New Testament critic and self-professed agnostic Bart Ehrman has gone out of his way to argue for the historicity of Jesus's existence against certain culturally illiterate figures in his book *Did Jesus Exist? The Historical Argument for Jesus of Nazareth*.

There are also plenty of cogent arguments defending the dual nature of Christ[5] and Jesus' divine self-awareness. Furthermore, there are stronger arguments for a supernatural resurrection of Jesus than for a natural one. Peterson seems to affirm a naturalistic one in this video. The majority of scholars engaging in New Testament studies (including a vast number of nonbelievers), particularly those concentrating on the events of the resurrection, agree upon three well-established facts that constitute historical evidence for the resurrection of Jesus: the empty tomb of Jesus, the appearances of Jesus to his disciples, and the origin of the Christian faith. For a rigorous study of a novel historiographical approach to the resurrection, I recommend Michael Licona's *The Resurrection of Jesus: A New Historiographical Approach*.[6]

Peterson's Epistemology of Truth

I think much of Peterson's difficulty with God's existence comes from his epistemology. Peterson's epistemological approach to truth is two-pronged. The first prong is what he refers to as objective truth–truth as conventionally understood, whatever is in accordance with reality. The second prong, which the general thrust of his thought and discourse revolves around, is the notion of pragmatic truth. This is determined by a question of value, how one should act in the world.[7] Closely tied to this is Darwinian survivability, since Peterson

5 See Morris, *The Logic of God Incarnate*.

6 Licona, *The Resurrection of Jesus*.

7 Ping? Pong!, "Jordan Peterson on pragmatic truth 1."

connects this pragmatic truth to the ability to exist and reproduce; it confers a selective advantage and functional utility.

Nevertheless, Darwinian survivability does not provide any veritable linkage between knowledge of truth and the brute fact of mere existence and reproduction. Physicist Paul Davies eloquently illustrates this tension in his book *The Mind of God: The Scientific Basis for a Rational World.* Davies wonders how we can even comprehend the rationality and structure of reality—why it should be comprehensible to us, especially from an evolutionary survival standpoint:

> The mystery in all this is that human intellectual powers are presumably determined by biological evolution and have absolutely no connection with doing science. Our brains have evolved in response to environmental pressures, such as the ability to hunt, avoid predators, dodge falling objects, etc. How fortuitous that our minds (or at least the minds of some) should be poised to fathom the depths of Nature's secrets.[8]

Thus, Peterson's conception of pragmatic truth is wholly insufficient to explain our capacity for knowledge of objective truth. Unfortunately, Peterson's understanding of truth is mostly usurped by his fixation on its connection to pragmatism and Darwinism. This fixation resulting in confusion was demonstrated in a debate with neo-atheist Sam Harris titled "What is true?" The problem for Peterson is that his notion of pragmatic truth is nested not only in Darwinism but also in a framework of good and evil. Although sometimes, as in his course lectures based on his book *Maps of Meaning*, he makes reference to objective meaning, he seems to completely neglect it in other instances. The discussion that ensued between Harris and Peterson involved some sophomoric fumbling in ascertaining what truth *really* is. The safest place to start is with the laws of logic; for instance, without the validity of the law of non-contradiction, correct thinking would be impossible. Without it, how would we make assessments and conclusions about anything?

A More In-depth Dialogue with Craig

There is no Christian philosopher who has more rigorously engaged academically with the big questions of metaphysics and theology—while also being involved heavily in university debates and the wider culture—than Craig. Sam Harris has said that Craig is the "one Christian apologist who seems to have put the fear

8 Davies, *The Mind of God*, 149.

of God into many of my fellow atheists." *The Best Schools* named Craig one of the 50 most influential living philosophers.[9] His first doctorate, supervised by John Hicks, a leading philosopher at the University of Birmingham, dealt (like many of his subsequent publications) with what I consider the most convincing argument for God's existence, the Kalam Cosmological Argument (KCA).[10] His second doctorate—on the most fundamental question in Christian theology, the historicity of the resurrection of Jesus—was supervised by arguably the most influential Protestant theologian of the twentieth century, Wolfhart Pannenberg, at the University of Munich. Pannenberg set the theological world on fire in the 1960s with his now classic book *Jesus—God and Man*.

Craig is also a leading philosopher of time who has explored God's relationship to time—defending the notion that God is timeless without the existence of the universe and temporal with the existence of the universe. He also worked on divine foreknowledge and human freedom, the challenge of Platonism to divine aseity, and most recently the doctrine of Christ's atonement. An in-depth dialogue between Peterson and Craig could help Peterson realize that the existence of God, the divinity of Christ, and Christ's resurrection are reasonable to believe in. Although not absolutely compelling, they best explain the data available to us.

As a psychologist and observer of the history of totalitarian regimes, Peterson recognizes all too well that Christianity best explains the data of the universe and the plight that humanity finds itself in. How much better would it be for Peterson to live his life acknowledging that Christianity really is true rather than merely acting as if it were true? As St. Paul wrote: "And if Christ has not been raised, your faith is futile, and you are still in your sins" (1 Cor 15:17). It seems as though Peterson is stuck in the merely archetypal understanding of biblical truths—which indeed has its place—and is not giving other profound questions the proper care they deserve. Will he become the most reluctant convert in Canada, as C. S. Lewis was many years ago in England?

Bibliography

Craig, William Lane. *The Kalam Cosmological Argument*. Eugene, OR: Wipf and Stock, 2000.

Davies, Paul. *The Mind of God: The Scientific Basis for a Rational World*. New York: Simon & Schuster, 1992.

Ehrman, Bart. *Did Jesus Exist? The Historical Argument for Jesus of Nazareth*. New York: HarperOne, 2013.

9 TBS Staff, "The 50 Most Influential Living Philosophers."

10 Craig, *The Kalam Cosmological Argument*.

Faith HKU. "God and the Big Bang—Prof William Lane Craig @ HKU." YouTube video, March 22, 2016. https://www.youtube.com/watch?v=oFyoiyAlLoM.

Feser, Edward. "Reading Rosenberg, Part II." *Edward Feser*, November 3, 2011. https://edwardfeser.blogspot.com/2011/11/reading-rosenberg-part-ii.html.

Licona, Michael. *The Resurrection of Jesus: A New Historiographical Approach.* Westmont: InterVarsity, 2010.

Morris, Thomas V. *The Logic of God Incarnate*. Eugene, OR: Wipf and Stock, 2001.

Pannenberg, Wolfhart. *Jesus—God and Man.* 2nd ed. Translated by Lewis L. Wilkins and Duane A. Priebe. Philadelphia: Westminster Press, 1977.

Peterson, Jordan B. *Maps of Meaning: The Architecture of Belief.* London: Routledge, 1999. https://archive.org/details/peterson_mapsofmeaning-ru/peterson_mapsofmeaning-en/page/n175/mode/2up.

Ping? Pong! "Jordan Peterson on pragmatic truth 1." YouTube video, February 8, 2017. https://www.youtube.com/watch?v=SyopcVoK0EA.

TBS Staff. "The 50 Most Influential Living Philosophers." *The Best Schools*, updated March 31, 2021. https://thebestschools.org/features/most-influential-living-philosophers/.

Wycliffe College at the University of Toronto. "Is There Meaning to Life? Jordan Peterson, Rebecca Goldstein, William Lane Craig." YouTube video, January 26, 2018. https://www.youtube.com/watch?v=pDDQOCXBrAw&t=10s.

Chapter 8

Lightning Crashes +LĪVE+ [1]

Scott D. G. Ventureyra

Increasingly, in Western society, a narrative is being defended that runs contrary to anything biblical or supernatural, to the point that it should not only be doubted but also scoffed at. One example follows from the discovery that people of Lebanese ancestry share 90% or more of their genetics with the Canaanites,[2] the biblical arch-enemies of the Israelites. The Israelites were commanded by God to exterminate the Canaanites (Deut 7:1–2; 20:16–18). The opportunity commonly seized by journalists is to show that thereby "science" yet again disproves one of the claims of the Bible, in this case, that the Israelites wiped out the Canaanites.[3] More than ever, journalists today have been attacking straw men while demonstrating a serious lack of rigour (all this is aside from the endless fake news propagated by mainstream media). Although the findings of the genetic lineage shared by modern Lebanese people and the Canaanites are indeed fascinating, there is a small problem. The Biblical account does not claim that all the Canaanites were exterminated, since they survived Joshua's invasion. The first chapter in Judges lists areas in which the Canaanites persevered: "Neither did Zebulun drive out the Canaanites living in Kitron or Nahalol, so these Canaanites lived among them, but Zebulun did subject them to forced labor. Nor did Asher drive out those living in Akko or Sidon or Ahlab or Akzib or Helbah or Aphek or Rehob. The Asherites lived among the Canaanite inhabitants of the land because they did not drive them out" (Jgs 1:30–32). Thus, all the recent journalistic pieces about the Canaanites being exterminated are patently false according to the Hebrew Scriptures themselves.

This is just one example of the pervasive narrative against biblical claims, infesting newspapers, documentaries, TV shows, lecture halls, and even the

1 This is a modified version of Scott Ventureyra, "Lightning Crashes LiVE," *Catholic Insight*, August 22, 2017, https://catholicinsight.com/lightning-crashes-live/.

2 Romey, "Living Descendants of Biblical Canaanites Identified via DNA."

3 Johnston, "Bible says Canaanites were wiped out by Israelites"; Best, "Bronze Age DNA disproves the Bible's claim that the Canaanites were wiped out"; Newitz, "Genetic evidence suggests the Canaanites weren't destroyed after all."

song lyrics of popular bands such as +LĪVE+. Attacks on Christianity are so widespread that they find themselves in verses of songs. Let me first explain who +LĪVE+ is and their connection to the spiritual in general and Christianity in particular.

For anyone familiar with the band +LĪVE+, the title of this piece is a play on words. "Lightning Crashes" was a 1994 hit single by +LĪVE+, which, together with other songs from the album *Throwing Copper*, brought significant attention to the band, which remained in the limelight for a number of years and has enjoyed a successful career since then. +LĪVE+ has been active continuously since its founding in 1989, with only a three-year hiatus from 2009 to 2012; the lead singer, Ed Kowalczyk, had left the band for seven years to pursue a solo career, during which time the other members of +LĪVE+ (Chad Gracey, Patrick Dahlheimer, and Chad Taylor) joined members of Candlebox (lead singer Kevin Martin and guitarist Sean Hennesy) to form The Gracious Few.

On July 14, 2017, +LĪVE+ was set to perform at Ottawa's annual *Bluesfest*, which has been cancelled for both 2020 and 2021 because of the COVID situation. After a long day at work and a session of tennis, I had made a last-minute decision to attend the show. I parked right in front of my *alma mater*, the Dominican University College, and made the ten-minute trek, through an increasingly heavy rain, to the *Bluesfest* venue. I had seen +LĪVE+ three previous times, twice at *Bluesfest* and once in Hull, Quebec, at the Robert Guertin Centre. Their performances were always instrumentally and vocally tight. They've also always exuded high energy. They started off the 2017 concert with their hard-driving hit song "All Over You," from *Throwing Copper*. They continued with two songs from their 1991 album *Mental Jewelry*: "Operation Spirit (The Tyranny of Tradition)" and "Pain Lies on the Riverside." At the conclusion of the latter, the rain had significantly intensified, to the point where water was flowing several inches high from where I was standing. Despite my umbrella, my shoes and the rest of my clothing were completely soaked at this point. The show was cut short in the middle of the third song since lightning "crashed" through the amplification.[4] Subsequently, the main stage was closed, and a red emergency message appeared on screens throughout the *Bluesfest* grounds, urging people to leave calmly. Only two and a half songs were played, and the show was over.

The inspiration and real motivation for writing this chapter is to offer a reflection upon the second song that +LĪVE+ performed that night, but first it will be worthwhile to examine their progression since its original release in 1991. Take, for instance, the lyrics to the song "They Stood up for Love," a track from their 2000 album *The Distance to Here*, which at all glances seems to refer to God's immanence and transcendence. One could make the case

4 See Maxwell, "Lightning Crashes Bluesfest."

that the lyrics contain hints of panentheism which has often attracted certain Christian philosophers and theologians. The song, in my estimation, contains many valuable elements for reflection. It has the existential cry for God. It is reminiscent of when Augustine states in his *Confessions*: "Our hearts are restless until they find their rest in you." In other words, we can never fully be at peace until we not only accept the truth of Christ but align ourselves with His will, which is to bring forth goodness, love, truth, justice, and righteousness. Kowalczyk's words in the song show that humans do not focus on the real essence of life but instead on trivialities. It reminds me of the great mathematician and Christian philosopher Blaise Pascal's grand work *Pensées*, where he considers the absurdity of how modern people live their lives avoiding the true consequences of life:

> I know not who put me into the world, nor what the world is, nor what I myself am. I am in terrible ignorance of everything. I know not what my body is, nor my senses, nor my soul, not even that part of me which thinks what I say, which reflects on all and on itself, and knows itself no more than the rest. I see those frightful spaces of the universe which surround me, and I find myself tied to one corner of this vast expanse, without knowing why I am put in this place rather than in another, nor why the short time which is given me to live is assigned to me at this point rather than at another of the whole eternity which was before me or which shall come after me. I see nothing but infinities on all sides, which surround me as an atom, and as a shadow which endures only for an instant and returns no more. All I know is that I must soon die, but what I know least is this very death which I cannot escape.[5]

Thus, given the various deep existential realizations contained within the song of God's immanence in the world and its importance to our lives, it seems that Kowalczyk and members of +LĪVE+ acknowledge the true significance of not only a personal God's existence, but also His action in our lives.

Moving forward toward their 2003 album *Birds of Pray*, there are some interesting lyrics by Kowalczyk in the song "Heaven." In the song he focuses on the importance of faith over many of life's distractions.[6] Kowalczyk also elevates faith over reason, but the two need not be separated; God, evidence, and truth cannot be opposed to one another, as Kowalczyk seems to deny; faith and evidence need not be opposed to one another. So although, regrettably, he seems to be expounding some sort of fideism, he nonetheless emphasizes the importance of belief in God, heaven, and truth. The last two phrases are redolent of C. S. Lewis's famous saying: "I believe in Christianity as I

5 Pascal, *Pensées*.
6 Kowalcyk, "Heaven."

believe that the sun has risen not only because I see it, but because by it I see everything else."[7]

Now, to one of the songs performed at the concert: "Operation Spirit (The Tyranny of Tradition)," found on *Mental Jewelry*, an album that reflected the influence of various schools of thought. The alternate title of the song itself gives an inkling of its anti-Christian sentiment. Kowalcyk reduces Jesus to wishful thinking and irrelevant to the struggles of his life.

This song, like much of contemporary Western culture, which is inundated with multicultural and secular pretensions, fits into an ever-growing narrative that denies core Christian doctrines such as the hypostatic union, i.e., the union of Christ's divine and human natures. I had never heard them perform this song live and I wondered to myself why they had decided to do so here—especially considering that they have, I presume (from the lyrics of subsequent songs), experienced a spiritual progression in their lives, seemingly in the direction of Christianity since the release of *Mental Jewelry*. If they had not embraced Christianity, I thought, they may have been on track to do so, as "They Stood up for Love" and "Heaven" arguably indicate.

Mental Jewelry suggests the influence of the Indian philosopher Jiddu Krishnamurti.[8] Krishnamurti at one point had been associated with the occultist Theosophical Society, founded by the esoteric and controversial theosophist Helena Blavatsky.[9] Blavatsky and her associates had deep pantheistic inclinations. They also denied the historicity of the Gospels. Blavatsky viewed them as containing some truths about spiritual initiation, with Christhood occupying the seventh of ten levels of spiritual development. The following quotation presents Blavatsky's take on the Gospels and Jesus Christ:

> For me Jesus Christ, i.e., the Man-God of the Christians, copied from the Avatâras of every country, from the Hindu Krishna as well as the Egyptian Horus, was never a historical person. He is a deified personification of the glorified type of the great Hierophants of the Temples, and his story, as told in the New Testament, is an allegory, assuredly containing profound esoteric truths, but still an allegory... The legend of which I speak is founded, as I have demonstrated over and over again in my writings and my notes, on the existence of a personage called Jehoshua (from which Jesus has been made) born at Lüd or Lydda about 120 years before the modern era.[10]

7 Lewis, "Is Theology Poetry?," 164–165.

8 Boldman, Review of *Mental Jewelry*.

9 The relationship between Krishnamurti and his philosophies to theosophy and Blavastky are rather complex, see Matiana, "Krishnamurti and Theosophy: Where Do They Differ, Where Do They Agree?"

10 Blavatsky, *H. P. Blavatsky: Collected Writings*, Vol. IX, 224–225.

Much modern denial of the historical existence of Jesus goes back to Blavatsky. The works of Richard Carrier and Robert M. Price followed in her footsteps on this point, as did Tom Harpur (a lapsed Anglican minister) in *The Pagan Christ: Rediscovering the Lost Light*, published in 2004. Nonetheless, denial of the historicity of Jesus has also been sharply criticized by even non-believing New Testament scholars such as Bart Ehrman (an agnostic) in his work *Did Jesus Exist?: The Historical Argument for Jesus of Nazareth*.[11] There are many resources that build a solid historiographical case for not only the existence of Jesus but also the events and facts surrounding His resurrection.[12]

Krishnamurti eventually distanced himself from the Theosophical Society, but his views may have very well been influenced by his early involvement with it.[13]

"Operation Spirit," like many of +LĪVE+'s songs, describes what appears to be a man's existential crisis. Kowalczyk and his bandmates were roughly twenty years old when the song was released. The lyrics reflect a self-destructive attitude praising anxiety and pain. There is an emphasis on suffering; the beauty of life is being consumed by bitterness. But this is mere angst and discontent with the Christian faith, rather than an actual argument against Jesus' divinity. One can only speculate that a young man here feels anger toward Christ because of unfilled prayers. And yet sometimes it is what we ask for that needs to be re-examined. Or perhaps it is a rebellion against God fuelled by immoral proclivities? I know that I, as a teenager who was straying from his faith, once showed the lyrics to this song to a very devout Catholic friend, who was extremely appalled that I would ever show him such lyrics. At the time, I was facing my own spiritual crisis. I was trying to justify or find comfort in my doubt of the Catholic faith, spawned by years of secular indoctrination at the hands of an educational system where unbelieving teachers foisted their beliefs upon unsuspecting students. Once this is combined with a pop culture that denigrates human sexuality to the level of mere insatiable and selfish pleasures of the flesh, one need not wonder too hard why so many young people stray from the Christian faith in high school and university. In the end, I was trying to wish God away in order to follow ignoble pursuits. I was grasping at any means necessary to deny Christian truths; sometimes science infused by metaphysical naturalism was a weapon for such a cause, as were lyrics to songs such as these. Little did I know what devastating effects secular indoctrination and metaphysical untruths would have upon my life. It was not until much later that I was forced to face the truth of God's existence, Jesus' authentic claims to divinity, and the evidence for the resurrection (all of which have been well supported in writing by many Christian philosophers and

11 Ehrman, *Did Jesus Exist? The Historical Argument for Jesus of Nazareth.*

12 Licona, *The Resurrection of Jesus.*

13 Matiana, "Krishnamurti and Theosophy: Where Do They Differ, Where Do They Agree?"

theologians).[14] These considerations and my personal experiences lead me back to the way, the truth, and the life. I had suffered from what secular philosopher Thomas Nagel had dubbed "the cosmic authority problem" in his book 1997 book *The Last Word*:

> My guess is that this cosmic authority problem is not a rare condition and that it is responsible for much of the scientism and reductionism of our time. One of the tendencies it supports is the ludicrous overuse of evolutionary biology to explain everything about life, including everything about the human mind. Darwin enabled modern secular culture to heave a great collective sigh of relief, by apparently providing a way to eliminate purpose, meaning, and desiring as fundamental features of the world. Instead, they become epiphenomena, generated incidentally by a process that can be entirely explained by the operation of the non-teleological laws of physics on the material of which we and our environments are all composed. There might still be thought to be a religious threat in the existence of the laws of physics themselves, and indeed the existence of anything at all, but it seems to be less alarming to most atheists.[15]

One wonders whether Kowalczyk and the other members of +LĪVE+ had suffered or still suffer from the cosmic authority problem. For me, it was the interplay of faith and reason that led me away from the position expounded in "Operation Spirit." I invite those who, like Kowalczyk, have doubts about God or the truth of Christianity to examine the philosophical, theological, and historical arguments associated with Jesus' divine self-understanding and the resurrection. That night's incident cannot but make me wonder whether the lightning that crashed +LĪVE+'s concert was a flagrant example of God's providential plan.

Bibliography

Best, Shivali. "Bronze Age DNA disproves the Bible's claim that the Canaanites were wiped out." *Daily Mail*, July 8, 2017. https://www.dailymail.co.uk/sciencetech/article-4733046/Canaanites-ancestors-modern-day-people-Lebanon.html.

Blavatsky, Helena P. *H. P. Blavatsky: Collected Writings*, Vol. IX. Wheaton: Theosophical Publishing House, 1962.

14 Anyone interested in examining some of the evidence for these claims can look to William Lane Craig's ministry as a starting point: http://www.reasonablefaith.org/.

15 Thomas Nagel, *The Last Word*, 130–31.

Boldman. Gina. Review of *Mental Jewelry. AllMusic.* https://www.allmusic.com/album/mental-jewelry-mw0000272911.

Ehrman, Bart. *Did Jesus Exist? The Historical Argument for Jesus of Nazareth.* New York: HarperOne, 2013.

Harpur, Tom. *The Pagan Christ: Rediscovering the Lost Light.* Toronto: Thomas Allen Publishers, 2004.

Johnston, Ian. "Bible says Canaanites were wiped out by Israelites but scientists just found their descendants living in Lebanon." *The Independent*, September 7, 2017. http://www.independent.co.uk/news/science/bible-canaanites-wiped-out-old-testament-israelites-lebanon-descendants-discovered-science-dna-a7862936.html.

Lewis, C. S. "Is Theology Poetry?" In *They Asked for a Paper*. London: Geoffrey Bless, 1962.

Licona, Michael R. *The Resurrection of Jesus: A New Historiographical Approach.* Downers Grove: InterVarsity, 2010.

Matiana. "Krishnamurti and Theosophy: Where Do They Differ, Where Do They Agree?" *Theosophy.* https://blavatskytheosophy.com/krishnamurti-and-theosophy/.

Maxwell, Owen. "Lightning Crashes Bluesfest." *Ottawa Life Magazine*, July 15, 2017. https://www.ottawalife.com/article/lightning-crashes-bluesfest?c=2.

Newitz, Annalee. "Genetic evidence suggests the Canaanites weren't destroyed after all." *Ars Technica*, July 27, 2017. https://arstechnica.com/science/2017/07/genetic-evidence-suggests-the-canaanites-werent-destroyed-after-all/.

Pascal, Blaise. *Pensées*. Translated by W. F. Trotter. Mineola: Dover Publications, 1958.

Romey, Kristin. "Living Descendants of Biblical Canaanites Identified Via DNA." *National Geographic*, July 27, 2017. http://news.nationalgeographic.com/2017/07/canaanite-bible-ancient-dna-lebanon-genetics-archaeology/.

Chapter 9

The Atheist Truth Seeker: A Reflection on Mario Augusto Bunge's Life and Work[1]

Scott D. G. Ventureyra

On February 24, 2020, at 100 years of age, physicist and philosopher Mario Augusto Bunge passed on to the next life. Bunge received a PhD in physico-mathematical sciences from Universidad Nacional de La Plata (Argentina) in 1952 (the same university where my father completed his medical degree in 1970). He held sixteen honorary doctorates and four honorary professorships. He was also a prolific author, having written over four hundred papers and eighty books. He is one of the most cited Spanish-speaking scientists and philosophers in history, as well as one of the most famous physicists of the past two hundred years. His groundbreaking *Causality: The Place of the Causal Principle in Modern Science* (1959) was translated into seven languages. In it, he argued for an expanded principle of determinism to be applied to modern science. He spoke and wrote vociferously against what he considered pseudoscience. He was critical of Marxism, postmodernism, psychoanalysis, alternative medicine, logical positivism, and existentialism.

Remarkably, Bunge was a self-trained philosopher. He was a rare thinker. As an atheist and scientific materialist, he took philosophy and the natural and social sciences seriously. Many scientific materialists throughout the past hundred years or so have had an irrational aversion to philosophy because of their ignorance of it. But, of course, for any *bona fide* intellectual this would be contradictory to reason, since philosophy is fundamental and indispensable to the scientific method. (I have argued this in chapter 2 of my book *On the Origin of Consciousness*.) He worked diligently to remove cultural ignorance of philosophy, in part through his lectures and writings geared toward medical doctors in understanding the importance of philosophy. He saw a synergy between metaphysics and science. Volumes 3 and 4 of his *Treatise on Basic Philosophy* emphasized the importance of metaphysics.

1 This is a modified version of Scott Ventureyra, "A Reflection on Mario Augusto Bunge's Life and Work," *Catholic Insight*, March 20, 2020, https://catholicinsight.com/a-reflection-mario-augsto-bunges-life-and-work/.

Postmodernism

We do not have the space to explore all of the ideologies, pseudo-sciences, and modes of thought Bunge critiqued, so I'll focus on just one: postmodernism. Postmodernism can be viewed as a disastrous thought experiment or what physicists Alan Sokal and Jean Bricmont accurately dubbed "fashionable nonsense." It is important to note that postmodern "philosophers" such as Jacques Derrida, Michel Foucault, Francois Lyotard, and their faithful disciples have vehemently denied objective truth, metaphysics, and consequently any meta-narrative. Meta-narratives are fundamental to any coherent worldview. They have sought to reduce the philosophy of history, the history of philosophy, and history in general to a power struggle as opposed to a pursuit of truth. Incoherently, by denying ultimate truth, they affirm it; there's no escaping this logical misstep. Philosophical pursuits, if we can call them that, under a postmodern epistemological guise, are to be localized and subjective. In other words, they are relativistic. Nevertheless, one of the fruits of postmodernism lies in its ability to force one to more precise analyses and deductions, based on questions of specificity. The view I have just expounded here aligns well with Bunge's as expressed in his *Between Two Worlds: Memoirs of a Philosopher-Scientist*: "A philosophy without ontology is invertebrate; it is acephalous without epistemology, confused without semantics, and limbless without axiology, praxeology, and ethics. Because it is systemic, my philosophy can help cultivate all the fields of knowledge and action, as well as propose constructive and plausible alternatives in all scientific controversies."[2] Bunge scathingly writes the following about postmodernism:

> Over the past three decades or so very many universities have been infiltrated, though not yet seized, by the enemies of learning, rigor, and empirical evidence: those who proclaim that there is no objective truth, whence "anything goes," those who pass off political opinion as science and engage in bogus scholarship. These are not unorthodox original thinkers; they ignore or even scorn rigorous thinking and experimenting altogether. Nor are they misunderstood Galileos punished by the powers that be for proposing daring new truths or methods. On the contrary, nowadays many intellectual slobs and frauds have been given tenured jobs, are allowed to teach garbage in the name of academic freedom, and see their obnoxious writings published by scholarly journals and university presses. Moreover, many of them have acquired enough power to censor genuine scholarship. They have mounted a Trojan horse inside the academic citadel with the intention of destroying higher culture from within.[3]

2 Bunge, *Between Two Worlds: Memoirs of a Philosopher-Scientist*, 406.
3 Bunge, "In Praise of Intolerance to Charlatanism in Academia," 96.

This point could not have been more brilliantly made. The situation has only drastically worsened since 1995. Our unthinking culture gravitates more and more towards relativism; we see this with the cancel culture and the attempt to annihilate free speech and reason. (Over the past two years, we saw this with politicization of medicine and science by pseudo-doctors like Anthony Fauci and Theresa Tam who urge us to "follow the science," even though it is forbidden to question or appropriately assess the science.) What makes things significantly more sinister is that the general population is unaware of their tax dollars being used to fund this rubbish. Wishful morticians of the absolute (as I sometimes refer to postmodernists) toy with the very fabric of Western civilization, and yet take advantage of its fruits—a hypocrisy of the highest order. It is like the social activist who decries capitalism and yet does so by using state-of-the-art technology. It is an irreverent form of narcissism and pathological to its core. It lies somewhere between ignorance, malevolence, and insanity. Such lunacy can only teach one how not to think or act. In 1996, Sokal brilliantly exposed postmodernism's abuse of science and reason with a submission of a hoax article, with the absurd title "Transgressing the Boundaries: Towards a Transformative Hermeneutics of Quantum Gravity," to *Social Text*, a prominent postmodern cultural studies journal.

In more recent years, such abuse has been exposed even more forcefully by magazine editor Helen Pluckrose, mathematician James Lindsay, and philosopher Peter Boghossian through a series of purposely nonsensical articles that were published in prominent postmodernism and grievance studies journals. Lindsay and Pluckrose chronicle and analyze their infiltration of postmodernism journals.[4]

Scientific Materialism

Although I reject scientific materialism (a position that Bunge defends) and have argued against this philosophy in many of my writings, I must admit Bunge argues for this position more persuasively than any of the neo-atheists or contemporary scientists could ever hope to. Despite profound disagreements in this area, I had asked Bunge to endorse my book on consciousness in 2018. I was surprised not only that he replied, but also that he did so with such promptness, a testament to his lucidity and technological savvy. Here is his reply:

> Hello Dr Ventureyra,
> Thank you for thinking that I might endorse your book, but that won't be possible, because I have argued repeatedly for a scientific materialist

4 Pluckrose & Lindsay, *Cynical Theories*.

view of the mental.
Sincerely,
mb

A Kind of Kinship

In spite of our disagreements, I have felt some affinity to Bunge's work on account of its rigour, profundity, and innovation. I had also have felt some kinship with the man without ever having met him. Like me, Bunge was both Argentinian and Canadian. Nonetheless, in one of his last interviews he said he did not think much about Argentina, since within the last hundred years it ceased to be an important country because of multiple dictatorships and economic, political, and social crises. I cannot say I disagree with this assessment.

Bunge also seemed to be a quirky man with a good sense of humour. For example, in a 2009 interview for *elPeriódico.com*, the reporter asked Bunge about his secret to looking so youthful at ninety years old and he responded: "That's because I avoid alcohol, tobacco, and postmodernism." It seems inescapable that good thinkers will unceasingly poke at and beat postmodernism. In light of this sense of humour, I can't help but think of a joke from a scene in the Netflix movie *The Two Popes,* involving a (fictitious) conversation between Argentine Cardinal Bergoglio (now Pope Francis; played by Jonathan Pryce) and Pope Benedict XVI (played by Anthony Hopkins): "Do you know how an Argentinian commits suicide? He climbs to the top of his ego and jumps off!" Inflated egos seem to be a feature of academics throughout the world, but perhaps especially in Argentina.

My friend William Sweet, a prominent Canadian philosopher and a fellow member of the Canadian Jacques Maritain Association, recently recounted an amusing story about Bunge. Before the 1995 Quebec referendum, at the yearly meeting of the Canadian Philosophical Association, Bunge in the presence of some philosophers who were Quebec separatists made a toast: "to the unity of Canada!" A colleague quickly made another toast: "to the unity of Professor Bunge!" One can only imagine the separatists' faces after Bunge's toast. Bunge was a man who spoke his mind without much reservation.

Lover of Wisdom

Whether we agree or disagree with Bunge on any number of philosophical or scientific issues, one thing is clear: he thought deeply and passionately about some of the most difficult problems in metaphysics, epistemology, and philosophy of science. He sought to integrate philosophy and science with what he identified as a "scientific philosophy." This would be not too dissimilar to Teilhard de Chardin's "scientific theology." I myself have sought to integrate science, philosophy, and theology. To understand the world and ourselves, we need a holistic approach. He and I shared the view that knowledge should be unified.

He also emphasized the importance of passion for philosophers in their pursuit of philosophical wisdom—he attributed his clear mental faculties toward the end of his life to such a passion. He was a true philosopher, that is, a true a lover of wisdom; a person who Plato in the *Symposium* would describe as being between the wise and the ignorant. Even though most people do not make good philosophers, all human beings philosophize; and we cannot be found to be anywhere else than between wisdom and ignorance. This is a sign of our limitations and a reminder that we should always remain humble and hungry for knowledge. Bunge pursued truth through his passion for writing and teaching. He has left us with many important intellectual contributions. In these trying times of extreme ignorance and irrationality, rational theists can find allies in rational secular thinkers like Bunge since they affirm the existence of truth, goodness, and justice. The theist can in a strange way find closer proximity to the rational atheist than theists who adhere to postmodernism or the "accepted" COVID narrative, for instance. Nevertheless, perhaps now his journey has led him to discover eternal truth: that there is a reality that transcends the physical.

Bibliography

Bunge, Mario. *Between Two Worlds: Memoirs of a Philosopher-Scientist.* Switzerland: Springer, 2016.

———. Email message to Scott Ventureyra. October 6, 2018.

———. "In Praise of Intolerance to Charlatanism in Academia." *Annals of the New York Academy of Sciences* 775, no.1 (June 1995): 96. https://doi.org/10.1111/j.1749-6632.1996.tb23131.x.

Pluckrose, Helen and James Lindsay. *Cynical Theories: How Activist Scholarship Made Everything about Race, Gender, and Identity—and Why This Harms Everybody*. Durham, NC: Pitchstone, 2020.

Chapter 10

My Godfather's Road to Damascus[1]

Scott D. G. Ventureyra

"I am a once-again Christian. I wanted to thank you for your love and kindness. You were instrumental to my return to Christianity. God bless you." These were the words spoken to me in January of 2015 by my then 94-year-old godfather, who had spent most of his adult life as an agnostic. (He passed away on July 24, 2015.)[2] Although I had prayed for this moment for a long time, these beautiful words took me by surprise. I think he may have meant to say "born-again" Christian, but nonetheless the message was loud and clear. He had accepted Christ back into his life. The winding and often treacherous roads that led him back to the way, the truth, and the life made for a remarkable journey.

A Road Less Travelled

My godfather, who for his own reasons preferred his name not be used, led quite an eventful life suffused with many poignant moments. He was born in Eastern Europe and became involved in the Hungarian Revolution of 1956, where he fought valiantly against the Soviet invasion. In 2006, on the 50th anniversary of the revolution, he was awarded the order of the Hungarian Republic's Officer's Cross. After the revolution, he immigrated to Canada as a refugee and, in the ensuing years, worked as a neurosurgeon across Canada. He rose to positions of authority and respect in both the clinical and academic worlds, publishing numerous articles, book chapters, and books. He was recognized as an innovator and lived a productive life of tremendous self-sacrifice and noble enterprises.

As with all events, connections, friendships, and relationships, I came to know him through a series of complex, contingent events. When I think about the events that led to the development of our relationship, I think

1 For the original see: Scott Ventureyra, "Once Again a Christian," *Convivium*, August 1, 2015, https://www.convivium.ca/articles/once-again-a-christian/.

2 Dr. Leslie P. Ivan. Obituary.

of the fact that my father was inspired to pursue neurosurgery by Frigyes Karinthy's *A Journey around My Skull.* Karinthy was of the same Hungarian nationality as my godfather. This calling eventually led my father to Ottawa to practise neurosurgery at the Children's Hospital of Eastern Ontario (CHEO). The man who would become my godfather acted as a valuable mentor in helping to harness my father's abilities as a clinician, surgeon, and academic researcher, which in turn steered him toward a gratifying career in neurosurgery. Additionally, it is interesting to note that Karinthy was the first to expound the concept of six degrees of separation, whereby all people and things are connected through six steps or less. All the more intriguing when I ponder the interconnections and synchronicities of our lives through the influence of Karinthy's work on my father.

There could have been one different turn and perhaps everything would have ended much differently. I feel this way when I look back on situations and events that have shaped my academic endeavours in philosophy and theology. My refined philosophical and theological knowledge helped me open my godfather's heart and mind to the Holy Spirit. Yet despite a series of contingent events, it is God who undergirds the history of being. It is also God who ceaselessly helps shape us through the circumstances of our lives.

Despite a life in large part dedicated to saving innocent children's lives, my godfather's was marred with loss, suffering, and tragedy. He fathered six children, including two daughters from his first marriage. He lost his first wife after immigrating to Canada. Fortunately, he met his second wife not long after. She was a blessing to him over many difficult years and remained a dedicated wife to his death. They coauthored books together and raised six loving children. Unfortunately, two children died from pancreatic cancer: a daughter from his first marriage and a son, just before Christmas 2014. There must be a feeling of abandonment by God for any father who loses a child, but even more so for a surgeon who spends his days saving other children's lives.

He had his own share of health issues, and underwent bypass surgery. He was diagnosed with cancer in the late 1970s, but luckily it was caught early, without the need for chemotherapy. He suffered hindrances to his vision, affecting two of his greatest passions: reading and writing. Toward the end, he endured a multitude of other health issues. In December 2014, he was placed in intensive care for a month.

My godfather was quite familiar with suffering and the evils of this broken world. The emotional problem of evil is very vivid and can become overwhelming in the life of the sufferer. Nevertheless, in order to be able to provide a rational explanation to the nonbeliever of why God permits evil, one must separate the emotional and the logical aspects of the problem of evil. Interestingly, once evil is acknowledged, so must be the good and, consequently, the moral law that provides the ability to discern between the two. Ultimately, it presupposes the existence of a moral lawgiver even though the problem seems to tell against the very existence of an all-powerful, all-knowing and all-loving God. I believe it is atheists rather than believers who are faced with the biggest difficulty here. On the one hand, they must confront the nihilist who denies any objective meaning and value in the absence of God; and on the other, the theist who has coherent grounds for affirming objective meaning and value.

Human evil is ultimately explicable by human free will, since all the evil caused by human beings can be traced back to either individuals or collections of them. There have been many theodicies offered by Christian philosophers and theologians over the centuries. It is important to note that Christianity involves doctrines that strongly suggest the concurrence of God and suffering. Contrary to the beliefs of popular culture, in Christianity the main purpose of this life is to know God, not to experience unbridled happiness. God wills to bring us into eternal salvation so that the sufferings of this world infinitely pale in comparison to the glory and eternal bliss that await us.

I shared many discussions with my godfather for almost a decade. I provided him with a wealth of resources challenging his agnosticism, including some of my own writings. In 2007, in an email correspondence, he explained his religious upbringing. He told me about his grandfather being a Calvinist minister in a small town in Hungary and how this faith was carried forward from his father to him. He remained a Calvinist until an encounter with a professor. This is how he describes his "de-conversion":

> I was brought up in the Calvinist faith and had been religious until I met my teacher of neurology and neurosurgery, an outstanding scientist and a man who followed Christian ethics but was agnostic, whose motto was "theories should be built only on evidence." The influence of this man weakened my faith, but I remained a Christian agnostic, believing that neither atheism nor the existence of God can be proved on the available evidence. All my life I have been searching for God, but certain influences—my ancestry, my teacher, and seeing too much mindless slaughter of innocent people—shook my faith. Reaching the end of my life today, I cannot state with confidence that being an agnostic is wrong. But I can say that, to me, neither the existence nor the denial of God was proved to me from the available evidence.

I was curious about the conclusions made by a highly intelligent man about the existence of God. Having arrived at an opposite conclusion after examining the available evidence, I thought that I should share my knowledge with him and see where it could lead.

Fast-forward a couple of years to a correspondence in 2009 regarding arguments for God's existence. My godfather wrote: "Unfortunately, the same arguments [classical theistic arguments such as the cosmological, ontological, and teleological] made me an agnostic, which is the only way to remain neutral when the truth is supported only by opposing theories rather than facts; nevertheless, I agree with you to be humble since ultimately to claim anything with absolute certainty is to be arrogant."

The problem, I pointed out, with this reasoning is that theories, although subject to change, are an accumulation of facts. Theories are typically discarded or augmented if they don't fit the evidence. However, in philosophy, you never want to rely on theories alone in arguments for or against God's existence since it leads to a God-of-the-gaps. What is most viable is to incorporate the findings of a scientific theory in a premise of philosophical argument in order to avoid such traps.

In September 2012, my godfather made the following statement concerning a series of debates between Christian and non-believing scholars: "The CDs you gave me a long time ago to listen to were interesting but did not change my agnostic leaning, although I realize that [Richard] Dawkins is very rigid and unfair with agnostics. I am 92 years old, stopped searching, but am upset seeing how much violence is generated by religious bigotry."

His main objections were the insufficiency of evidence for God's existence or non-existence and the amount of seemingly pointless human suffering. So, over the years, I felt his position would remain fixed despite all the material and sound argumentation I provided him alongside my many prayers.

Anyone who says apologetics is obsolete or irrelevant in our day couldn't be more mistaken. Countless thinking people want logical responses to difficult questions about the Christian faith. The apostles engaged in such polemics with other Jews, and Saint Paul provided a defence of the faith contra the gentiles. Apologetics is a Biblical mandate, as 1 Peter 3:15–16 instructs us: "But in your hearts revere Christ as Lord. Always be prepared to give an answer to everyone who asks you to give the reason for the hope that you have. But do this with gentleness and respect, keeping a clear conscience, so that those who speak maliciously against your good behavior in Christ may be ashamed of their slander." This is in direct reference to defending the truth of Jesus' resurrection and the hope of our future resurrection.

While it is true that one of the greatest apologetic tools is a life of sincere Christian discipleship, this does not take away the need for arguments and reason. An apologist should avoid being argumentative but rather should provide good reasons for the sake of persuasion and conversion. For a large part of the 19th and the early part of the 20th century, there was a severe anti-intellectualism that pervaded Christianity. Christians tended to rely mostly on feelings and emotions instead of rational grounds for the beliefs they held. Vestiges of this persist to this day.

Luckily, the use of logic was not a point of contention in our discussions. This facilitated his openness to Christian truths. Ultimately, I challenged his long-held assumption that Christianity did not rest on good rational grounds.

I challenged his position of agnosticism, which makes a claim about reality just as any other belief does. Standard agnosticism indicates that one comes to a particular metaphysical conclusion, namely that one cannot infer the existence or nonexistence of God based on the current state of knowledge. Yet the agnostic bears the burden of proof just as the theist or atheist does. This point is neglected in these sorts of discussions; the position that there is currently an insufficiency of knowledge pointing in either direction must itself be supported by evidence.

I then questioned his assumptions revolving around the problem of evil, suffering and wars, the relationship between science and theology, arguments for God's existence, the evidence for the historicity of Jesus' resurrection and claims to His divine self-understanding, and a host of other issues.

Over the years, I bought my godfather some important books, including *There Is a God* by the philosopher Antony Flew,[3] who, on the evidence of modern science, renounced atheism not long before his death; and *Reasonable Faith* by William Lane Craig,[4] which is one of the most convincing contemporary works of Christian apologetics.

Shortly before his death, I visited my godfather a number of times with my daughter. You could see his love and admiration of children because of their purity and innocence. I witnessed his passion for helping others, particularly children, in his interactions with my daughter.

He spoke about the loss of his only son. I could see in his eyes the hope of resurrection and reunification with his son as he stared at the picture of him on his dresser. A couple of weeks before his announcement of returning to Christ, he remarked that the suffering associated with that loss was almost unbearable for the first two days, but on the third day he felt an extreme tranquility. It seemed as though he was making an allusion to Jesus' resurrection. Perhaps it was an inner certainty about a future meeting with his son.

I bought him a crucifix to provide him comfort. I said it was a symbol of God's unconditional love for him. He would always pray next to it. The cross is a strong reminder that God humbled Himself to become man and enter into human history. The death and suffering of Jesus on the cross and His resurrection was the ultimate triumph over evil. The greatest injustice of history was the crucifixion of Christ, a completely blameless and sinless man who died for us. It is this very God who suffers with His creation.

3 Flew with Abraham Varghese, *There Is a God: How the World's Most Notorious Atheist Change His Mind.*

4 Craig, *Reasonable Faith: Christian Truth and Apologetics.*

I suspect that much of my godfather's time alone permitted him to reflect upon his life and God. It was an honour to learn that I was "instrumental" in his return to Christ. The Lord blessed me with such a privilege. Courageous resilience in the face of tremendous suffering while still keeping an open heart and mind to humbly return to truth reminds us that God is always with us. We should never forget that God draws near to those who draw near to Him.

Bibliography

Craig, William Lane. *Reasonable Faith: Christian Truth and Apologetics.* 3rd ed. Wheaton: Crossway, 2008.

Flew, Antony with Roy Abraham Varghese. *There Is a God: How the World's Most Notorious Atheist Change His Mind.* New York: HarperOne, 2007.

Karinthy, Frigyes. *A Journey around My Skull.* New York: NYRB Classics, 2008.

Part II:

God, Philosophy, Theology, and Science

Chapter 11

Warranted Skepticism? Putting the Center for Inquiry's Rationale to the Test[1]

Scott D. G. Ventureyra

Introduction

Several years ago, the Center for Inquiry (CFI), an international secular humanist organization,[2] placed a series of advertisements on public buses throughout North America and England. These included a quote from the late astronomer and host of the 1980s TV series *Cosmos: A Personal Voyage*, [3] Carl Sagan: "Extraordinary claims require extraordinary evidence." Although Sagan popularized the principle, the notion itself seems to have originated with David Hume, who stated in *An Enquiry Concerning Human Understanding* that "a wise man...proportions his belief to the evidence. In such conclusions as are founded on an infallible experience, he expects the event with the last degree of assurance and regards his past experience as a full *proof* of the future existence of that event."[4] Much has been written on Hume's principle, which is essentially an assault on the concept of miracles.[5] In recent years, philosophers have debated the legitimacy of Hume's claim. John Earman has heavily criticized it and deemed it without merit in his book *Hume's Abject Failure*,[6] whereas Robert

1 For the original see: Scott Ventureyra, "Warranted Skepticism? Putting the Center for Inquiry's Rationale to the Test,"*American Journal of Biblical Theology* 16 (36), September 6, 2015, https://biblicaltheology.com/Research/VentureyraS04.pdf.

2 The organization holds conferences and events with many prominent atheist philosophers and scientists such as Stephen Law, Daniel Dennett, Keith Parsons, John Shook, Richard Dawkins, and Lawrence Krauss. In 2009, the reflective atheist philosopher Austin Dacey left the organization and published a thoughtful critique of some of its motives. See Dacey, "Decomposing Humanism: Why Replace Religion?"

3 This show has been recently remade; it is now titled *Cosmos: A Spacetime Odyssey* and is hosted by astrophysicist Neil Tyson deGrasse.

4 Hume, *An Enquiry Concerning Human Understanding,* 10.4.

5 Particularly, Hume attacked Jesus' resurrection, observing that dead people stay dead.

6 See Earman, *Hume's Abject Failure: The Argument against Miracles.*

Fogelin[7] has vigorously defended Hume's view.[8] My intention is not to immerse myself in such debates but to criticize the CFI's applicabilion of Sagan's dictum. However, in the final section I will briefly examine why such line of reasoning in general is unreasonable and ultimately fallacious when directed towards, for example, the miracle of Jesus' resurrection.

The CFI is an influential secular organization throughout the western world, so I believe it is important to seriously engage with their assertions and arguments, which can easily persuade young unequipped minds, both within and outside the Church, in particular. The purpose of this chapter is to take the CFI's mission statement to task in its critique of supposed extraordinary claims, specifically those that are defensible through rational argumentation (God's existence); i.e., to question whether they are actually promoting rigorous critical thought through the utilization of science and reason. We will also consider whether they are actually fostering freedom of inquiry or merely insulating themselves from criticism. The purpose is to provide not a rigorous defense of belief in God but a critique of the CFI's methodology, and to argue that one must be critical of one's own position as well, as I believe the CFI is not.[9] Although I will briefly outline reasons theism is reasonable to believe in, I will not examine the reasons with any great depth, as such an endeavour is beyond the scope of this article.

I propose to present my case against the CFI's position by examining the following: (i) emotions and non-belief; (ii) the epistemology of Carl Sagan's dictum; (iii) philosophy, science, and the question of God; (iv) the presumption of atheism and its relation to Sagan's dictum; (v) properly basicality with respect to Sagan's dictum; and (vi) a test case of Jesus' resurrection in light of argumentation against the CFI's position.

For the sake of clarity, I take materialism[10] to mean the philosophical view that all that exists is matter and that everything, including consciousness and information, is created by interactions of matter. I will also take naturalism

7 Fogelin, *A Defense of Hume on Miracles.*

8 Wielenberg, *God and the Reach of Reason,* 126; see also Sennett and Groothuis, *In Defense of Natural Theology,* for a thorough treatment and critique of Hume's views on miracles and natural theology in general.

9 I take this as a presupposition within the article since I am not providing a rigorous defense of every argument I mention. Many Christian apologists have taken into account conceivable objections to their arguments and have demonstrated why their position is still reasonable to accept, arguing that it is ultimately more probable than its denial. The CFI and many atheists do not do this, nor do they seem to think it is necessary to do so, since they presume atheism. Alvin Plantinga has mentioned atheists' lack of consistency, i.e., that the burden of proof they place on Christian philosophers is never consistent with the burden they place on their own arguments.

10 It is worth noting that there are theists, particularly Christians, who are materialists/physicalists; they believe in God but not in things like souls. This is a minority position but a position nonetheless. Christian materialists/physicalists include Nancy Murphy and Peter van Inwagen. So, the category of materialism isn't as tidy as one would hope.

to mean the philosophical view that nature is all that exists, i.e., that nothing beyond nature exists. Although materialism and naturalism are distinction, I will for the purposes of this article use the terms interchangeably, since in their essence both deny the supernatural and spiritual realms.

Emotions a Motivation for Non-Belief?

The above-mentioned advertisement also mentioned a slew of claims that are deemed extraordinary by the CFI, such as God, Christ, Allah, UFOs, and Bigfoot. The CFI-related website for extraordinary claims (https://extraordinarybus.wordpress.com) includes many more. I would agree that many of the extraordinary claims involving elves, gnomes, fairies, mermaids, dragons, witches, and wizards listed on the site have very little evidence if any to support them. In fact, a large number of people have no vested interest in many of these claims. The CFI deliberately intertwines many religious claims together with fairy tales. It is quite clear that their goal is to undermine and even ridicule religious belief, so that, as their mission statement declares, they may "foster a secular society based on science, reason, freedom of inquiry, and humanist values."[11] The problem arises when uninformed readers of the bus ads and website get the wrongful impression that claims about the existence of God are on par with fairy tale characters. For many atheists, such an organization provides comfort for their disdainful and often unwarranted rejection of religious beliefs, both based more on emotion than on reasoned argumentation. One could argue that the emotional response occurs before the justification for naturalism is articulated. A case in point could be made of a respected philosopher like Thomas Nagel, who candidly admits that he has an aversion to and even fears the concept of a theistic God (something also known as the cosmic authority problem). He hopes that such a God does not exist.

> I want atheism to be true and am made uneasy by the fact that some of the most intelligent and well-informed people I know are religious believers. It isn't just that I don't believe in God, and naturally, hope that I'm right in my belief. It's that I hope there is no God! I don't want there to be a God; I don't want the universe to be like that.
>
> My guess is that this cosmic authority problem is not a rare condition and that it is responsible for much of the scientism and reductionism of our time. One of the tendencies it supports is the ludicrous overuse of evolutionary biology to explain everything about life, including everything about the human mind. Darwin enabled modern secular culture to heave a great collective sigh of relief, by apparently providing

11 Center for Inquiry, "About the Center for Inquiry."

> a way to eliminate purpose, meaning, and design as fundamental features of the world.[12]

It seems as though at least the first paragraph's sentiment is shared by a significant number of atheists, whether they admit it or not. Nevertheless, it should be noted that some of the greatest thinkers throughout history have spent a significant amount of time demonstrating the existence of God and the coherence of His nature.[13] This fact alone does not make their claims true, but it places them on a higher epistemic level than fairy tales. A significant proportion of the world believes in a transcendent reality that may or may not include a personal God. Atheists must therefore maintain that the majority of people either are delusional or have something wrong with their cognitive faculties. But is such the case?

The Epistemology of Sagan's Dictum

Before we delve into a critique of the CFI's position, let us begin by examining Sagan's dictum a bit more closely, since it plays a central role in the CFI's polemical rhetoric. On the surface, the quote seems to reflect a healthy and reasonable type of skepticism, one that I have no problem advocating. In everyday living, most adults employ a basic level of skepticism, as when purchasing a new house, for instance: one would want to be sure that the house lacks serious electrical, plumbing, or structural problems. These days most people would demand an inspection to ensure that the house is in good condition. No one would expect a buyer to rely on the word of the seller on the condition of the house—even if the seller is honest, perhaps they are unaware of certain problems or damages. On the

12 Nagel, *The Last Word*, 130–131.

13 Arguments for God's existence have had a revival since the 1960s with thinkers such as Alvin Plantinga, William Alston, Stuart Hackett, Richard Swinburne, Dallas Willard, William Lane Craig, and J.P. Moreland. This is in part due to the collapse of verificationism, which suggested that for a sentence to have meaning it should be empirically verifiable, i.e., by the senses, and therefore that knowledge of God was impossible and statements about God meaningless. The interesting thing about the verification principle is that it was revealed to be incoherent itself, by its own very criteria, since it could not be verified by the senses. It seems to me that European Continental philosophy has been out of touch with this resurgence of theistic arguments or has met it with resistance. This was glaringly obvious to me in the response I received from French philosopher and theologian Philippe Capelle-Dumont at his lecture titled "*Le Retour de Dieu en Philosophie*?" in April of 2014 at the Dominican University College in Ottawa, when I asked him about the renaissance of Christian philosophy and the reaction from continental-European philosophy. I believe there is much groundwork to be done in helping create solidified bridges between the Anglo-American analytic tradition and the Continental European philosophy with respect to epistemological and metaphysical approaches to the question of God. I believe the current impasse boils down to talking past one another. As Canadians we may be at an advantage to bridge such chasms, since we are more balanced in our exposure to both schools of thought.

other hand, we take many things for granted in certain contexts. For instance, someone in Israel may be skeptical about going on public transportation for fear of a bomb threat, whereas in Canada, where such occurrences are not a common experience, such a skepticism would not be warranted. That is not to say that such a thing could not transpire in Canada, but the occurrence of a bomb exploding on a public bus here is fairly improbable. These examples show that the evaluation of certain claims as either ordinary or extraordinary can be to a degree subjective. Everyone incorporates particular presuppositions in their everyday living, whether consciously or not. Some of these presuppositions might be well articulated. For instance, to return to the bomb threat example, in Canada an implicit presupposition would be that public transport buses will neither have bombs planted in them set to detonate nor have suicide bombers on them ready to explode themselves. However, in certain parts of Israel, the opposite may be presupposed as something not out of the ordinary. So, this raises some epistemological issues with Sagan's dictum—how do we know what can be deemed extraordinary as opposed to ordinary? What counts as evidence? Can Sagan's dictum be applied objectively?

In order to address these questions, it will be worth examining the meaning of the words "extraordinary" and "evidence." The former is defined by the Merriam-Webster's dictionary as something that goes "beyond what is usual, regular or customary." What is meant by evidence? According to Merriam-Webster, it is "something that furnishes proof." We could take that to be synonymous with corroboration, attestation, validation, and confirmation. If we accept these definitions, Sagan's point is that any claim of what is outside of the norm would require evidence that is also outside of the norm. This seems quite broad and dependent on one's subjective interpretation of what is outside the norm and what counts as extraordinary evidence. In this case it seems as though our subjective experience will play a significant role in how we interpret claims and evidences as extraordinary or not. Every individual has (besides genetic makeup) all sorts of experiential influences, including a host of environmental factors, such as places lived, culture, socio-economic situation, education, beliefs, and food and chemical intake. Such factors can impact how we perceive and understand reality; they play a pivotal role in one's criteria extraordinary claims and extraordinary evidence. It is difficult to completely remove one's self from one's experience. The application of Sagan's dictum to claims about God and religion is especially ambiguous. For instance, a person who claims to have had a spiritual experience of God will most likely, unless they are a fideist, be convinced of particular arguments for the truth of God's existence—or at the very least, see a coherence among them which could provide warrant for such beliefs.[14] On the other hand,

14 Below, I will discuss some such arguments, including something known as a properly basic belief.

perhaps a non-religious person in the absence of such an experience would deny that any of those arguments have any validity. Both are undoubtedly influenced by their subjective experiences, but when it comes to rational discussion we must attempt to look at the evidence before us, as impartially as possible. Although at times it may be a difficult task, it is what is required in any intellectual endeavour.

Philosophy, Science, and the Question of God

Skepticism is a useful tool, especially when it is not biased towards a specific claim. The more evidence for a claim, the more compelling it becomes. However, when dealing with abstract philosophical notions, one may not have direct access to evidence as with a house inspection or wondering whether a bus has a bomb planted on it. One cannot always use a strictly empirical approach to find truth in the validity of a particular claim.

I would argue that both philosophical and scientific inquiry, particularly in the historical sciences, are better served through the utilization of rational empiricism. Rational empiricism is the idea that the possibility of knowledge depends on both *a priorio* and *a posteriori* elements, therefore combing both rational and empirical methods of knowing. Philosopher Stuart Hackett explains this notion:

> Rational empiricism, as I profess it, is the doctrine that knowledge is possible only because it involves the combination of two elements: a mind that comes to experience with a structure of thought in terms of which it is necessarily disposed to understand that experience—this is the a priori or "before-experience" element; data upon which this structure of thought terminates to gain specific knowledge of particulars—this is the a posteriori or "after-experience" element.[15]

Thus, neither pure empiricism nor pure rationalism is tenable in either philosophical and scientific inquiry; i.e., it is insufficient to rely solely on either one's sense experience (or independence from it) to gain accurate knowledge of the world.[16] A conjoint of the two is of most value (especially in gaining knowledge of God, whether through natural reason or supernatural revelation). Moreover, as I will argue below, this type of epistemological approach is useful in both scientific and philosophical inquiry and in the intersection of the two (i.e., the proper use of science in philosophical arguments, not merely asserting scientific conclusions without further explanation).

15 Hackett, *The Resurrection of Theism*, 37.
16 Hackett, *The Resurrection of Theism*, 37.

It is important to note that historical scientists utilize what is known as abductive reasoning—the use of presently acting causes to make reasonable inferences about the past. Both Charles Darwin and Charles Lyell made use of such reasoning. It is particularly useful in making inferences to the best explanation to rule out competing hypotheses.[17] Inference to the best explanation has its uses in determining the cause of singular occurrences in the past: the origin of the universe, the origin of life, the Cambrian explosion, the origin of consciousness, and even the resurrection of Jesus. Abductive reasoning, unlike deductive reasoning, does not guarantee the conclusion with certainty, nor does it, like inductive reasoning, suggest a conclusion as highly likely. However, despite this, abductive reasoning is very useful in ascertaining past events. This is a perfectly acceptable method of providing evidence for the existence of God in an overall philosophical argument (more will be said on this below). Moreover, the aforementioned singular events are the sort of thing you would expect if a personal God were to exist and wanted to reveal Himself to conscious beings.

It would be naive, as some natural scientists (such as the biologist Richard Dawkins and the physicist Stephen Hawking) seem to think, that the question of God's existence could be determined solely by the scientific method.[18] God as understood in classical theism is an immaterial being who by definition cannot be examined by empirical tools. Only the effects of God's action, from primary and secondary causes, can be examined in such a fashion.

Scientists such as Hawking seem to expound what is known as a *strong scientisim.*[19] However, it is worth mentioning that some conceptions of God or gods throughout history have been demonstrated to be false or at least highly implausible through primarily empirical methods. For instance, ancient Greek pagans could over time notice that their gods did not inhabit Mount Olympus as was claimed and could at least rule out their inhabitation of such an area. Primitive anthropomorphic conceptions of gods or demi-gods are more vulnerable than a transcendent conception of God to empirical critique. To verify claims of the existence of a transcendent God that may or may not be immanent as well is a more challenging task than to verify ones that seem to be part of the material world or at least inhabit it (such as Zeus). In this sense, the scientific method has its limitations by definition and cannot fully adjudicate such questions. However, that is not to say that reason cannot help adduce and bring precision to such questions. That would require a mediating philosophy.

17 Lipton, *Inference to the Best Explanation*, 1.

18 Dawkins, *The God Delusion*, 55, 59; Hawking and Mlodinow, *The Grand Design*, 5.

19 This is the view that we should only believe things deemed scientific, i.e., only scientific truths exist, and what can't be tested by the scientific method isn't true. This should be contrasted with weak scientism, which allows for other truths but still regards science as the highest and most important method of knowing.

Science, as defined by methodological naturalism, must operate with the material world; anything outside of that is necessarily beyond the purview of natural science.[20] This raises the demarcation problem[21] in the philosophy of science, but for our purposes we will not delve into this. It should be noted that when scientists such as Richard Dawkins or Stephen Hawking are attempting to use science to answer questions such as the existence of God, they are actually expounding their own brand of philosophy[22], albeit a naive one.

When one attempts to rule out the existence of God solely through the tools of the natural sciences, there inevitably occurs an obvious conflation of methodological naturalism with metaphysical naturalism. A well-thought-out, sophisticated type of philosophy, when coupled with science, provides a better tool for weighing the competing claims of religious (Christianity, Judaism, Islam, Hinduism) and non-religious (materialism, naturalism, agnosticism, secular humanism, atheism) outlooks. Thus, the rational-empirical approach is useful. Robert J. Spitzer in his book *New Proofs for the Existence of God* explains why science alone cannot decide questions pertaining to God's existence:

> First, unlike philosophy and metaphysics, science cannot deductively prove [or disprove] a creation or God. This is because natural science deals with the physical universe and with the regularities which we call "laws of nature" that are obeyed by the phenomena within that universe. But God is not an object or phenomenon or regularity within the physical universe; so science cannot say anything about God. Moreover, science is an empirical and inductive discipline. As such, science cannot be certain that it has considered all possible data that would be relevant to a complete explanation of particular physical phenomena or the universe itself.[23]

20 That is beyond the dictates of methodological naturalism. Scientists often conflate methodological naturalism with metaphysical naturalism—the view that all that exists is nature.

21 This is the problem of distinguishing and defining science. Typically, historians and philosophers of science are better equipped than opposed to scientists to answer such questions, as Stephen Meyer explains on pages 400–401 of *Signature of the Cell*:

> As they say of the catcher in baseball, the philosopher and the historian of science has a view of the whole field of play, meaning he or she is less likely to fall into the error of defining all of science by practices used in one corner of the scientific world. I already had some inkling of this from my work as a geophysicist. I was aware that historical and structural geology use distinct (if partially overlapping) methods. But as I delved into the demarcation question, I discovered that different sciences use a wide variety of methods.

For a thorough treatment, see Meyer, *Signature in the Cell*, 400–401, 419, 430–431. Meyer provides a series of useful resources from a variety of thinkers concerning this issue.

22 van Inwagen, "Can Science Disprove the Existence of God?," 41; see also van Inwagen, «La Science Peut-Elle Prouver L'inexistence de Dieu?» 285–302.

23 Spitzer, *New Proofs for the Existence of God*, 22.

So, in order to avoid the overused God-of-the-gaps criticism, it should be realized that science alone does not get you to a sound argument about God; it is the use of scientific evidence in a philosophical premise of an overall argument that builds the case for God's existence. For example, an argument such as the Kalam Cosmological Argument (KCA)[24] states that:

1. Whatever begins to exist has a cause
2. The universe began to exist.

Therefore, the universe has a cause.

This argument is hotly debated in peer-reviewed philosophical journals among philosophers of religion.

To properly tackle metaphysical questions such as God's existence, one must recognize that a scientific model or theory on its own cannot justify a certain belief system. It is once you couple science with philosophy that you have a serious argument. As philosopher Peter van Inwagen rightly recognizes:

> When it comes to classifying arguments, philosophy trumps science: if an argument has a single 'philosophical' premise (a single premise that requires a philosophical defense), it is a philosophical argument. But an argument is a scientific argument only if *all* its premises are either propositions that have been established by science or else propositions so trivial that they require no defense.[25]

So, the evidence for big bang cosmology would be used to justify the second premise of the KCA, but nowhere is this seen as a God-of-the-gaps argument; it is a sound deductive argument where the conclusion follows logically from the premises. The onus is on the one who disagrees with the argument to demonstrate which of the premises is false and why. So, it should be evident that science in itself remains neutral on the question of God, as stated above; science can only be used to fortify premises as evidence in philosophical argumentation for God, which is not itself a matter of science.

Consequently, one would have to ask—what sorts of things would I expect to follow from a particular claim? If God exists, as the cause of the universe (both determinant and sustaining), immaterial, spaceless, eternal, omniscient, omnipotent and omnibenevolent—what sorts of things would I expect also to be true in reality? Each posited attribute of God must be examined for its possibility. It is important to note that, for instance, one argument may establish one attribute of God, as perhaps being the cause of the universe, without

24 It is the most examined argument in contemporary times for the existence of God, popularly defended by William Lane Craig.

25 van Inwagen, "Can Science Disprove the Existence of God?," 41.

establishing God's all-loving nature. Typically, what is needed to establish multiple attributes is a cumulative method of argumentation. Some atheists will have the unreasonable assumption that an argument such as the KCA is meant to establish the existence of the Christian God, but of course that is not the purpose of such an argument.[26] Another important question that arises is what sorts of things could be deemed consistent or inconsistent with how we come to observe and know reality given the existence of such a God. It seems that at first glance, some things may be more consistent with the existence of God than His non-existence.

The Presumption of Atheism and Sagan's Dictum

A significant proportion of atheists (or adherents to natural religious views) from all avenues of life, whether academicians or not, past and present, have been surreptitious in insulating themselves from criticism. There exists an inherent presupposition, namely that nature is all that exists, and consequently metaphysical materialism is the only rational proposition, with the burden of proof resting on their opponents to show otherwise. Unfortunately, what seems to be revealed by the statement "extraordinary claims require extraordinary evidence" is what is known as the presumption of atheism. Thus, to pose the question again, can Sagan's dictum be applied objectively? It seems that perhaps it can, but not as the CFI is using it. The statement itself, especially when applied to a one-directional skepticism (against religious beliefs or the existence of God), contains the assumption that anything dealing with God or the supernatural does not have any evidence or at least any good evidence in its favour. This view is commonly known as the *presumption of atheism*.[27] On this view, because of the lack of evidence in favour of God's existence, it is logical to presume that God does not exist. It seems as though this is the assumption at the core of the statement as applied towards solely supernatural claims. Yet, burden of proof for the presumption of atheism seems far too high to sustain. It is much too audacious to suggest there is no evidence at all for claims about God's existence or that the evidence is insufficient. How can the atheist come to know such a thing? The atheist must either show that if God existed, God would have provided more evidence than is provided, since the

26 Stephen Law, philosopher and editor of the Cambridge University Press journal *Think*, has claimed that something like the KCA does not establish the existence of a benevolent God but could establish the existence of a malevolent God. I would agree with Law here at one level, but the KCA is not meant to establish the moral nature of the cause of the universe.

27 Craig, "Theistic Critiques of Atheism," 70.

theist's purportedly evidential claims are considered to be insufficient or even non-existent. William Lane Craig elucidates this notion further:

> This is an enormously heavy burden of proof for the atheist to bear, for two reasons: (1) On at least Christian theism the primary way in which we come to know God is not through evidence but through the inner work of his Holy Spirit, which is effectual in bringing persons into relation with God wholly apart from evidence. (2) On Christian theism God has provided the stupendous miracles of the creation of the universe from nothing and the resurrection of Jesus from the dead, for which events there is good scientific and historical evidence—not to mention all the other arguments from natural theology. In this light, the presumption of atheism is presumptuous indeed![28]

For the sake of argument, it seems that even as an atheist or agnostic, one could see the coherence of the view that God created the universe out of nothing in its relation to modern big bang cosmology. This seems to be fortified by the Borde, Guth, and Vilenkin paper "Inflationary space-times are not past-complete," in which all three physicists draw the strong conclusion that all eternally inflating models point to having a necessary beginning, that is, a definite finite past.[29] Moreover, there are other contemporary arguments from natural theology, such as a modern formulation of the teleological argument involving the fine-tuning of the physical laws, constants and initial conditions present with the universe. Furthermore, given certain propositions and notions such as the existence of the universe and its creation out of nothingness, it does not seem so extraordinary that there could exist a transcendent cause. Perhaps the postulation of the universe's past eternality or uncaused nature, given the indications of the finitude of the past as evidenced by modern cosmology, is the more extraordinary claim. At the very heart of the application of Sagan's dictum, although not made explicit, is a belief in materialism held *a priori* before even examining the evidence contrary to it. To give a brief illustration of the presumption of atheism and its ability to cloud one's judgment in metaphysical issues, we can consider an atheist philosopher's reply to a profound question in a debate over God's existence. In 2008 debate between William Lane Craig and John Shook, Craig probed Shook over what could possibly exist beyond nature, if anything, and Shook responded, "more nature."[30] This response cannot be taken seriously: if nature is all there is, there is not more nature, since it would already embody the totality of reality—it demonstrates his unwillingness to even

28 Craig, "Theistic Critiques of Atheism," 70–71.

29 Borde, et al., "Inflationary spacetimes are not past-complete," 3.

30 See a video on the debate between Dr. William Lane Craig and Dr. John Shook over the question "Does God Exist?"

allow for the possibility of a supernatural reality. This is just a typical example of how atheists, even perfectly good working philosophers such as Shook, attempt to insulate themselves from criticism. Moreover, as a further point, naturalists suggest not only that methodological naturalism has an impeccable track record in the natural sciences but also that metaphysical naturalism is the best way to make sense of reality.

The truth of the matter is that Christian theology, not materialism, is what played a vital role in the rise of modern science. The presupposition of Christian theology that the universe comes from a benevolent and omniscient creator gives one justification to rely on one's own cognitive faculties to correspond with how reality actually is; it is foundational to scientific understanding. In fact, the very comprehensibility of the universe and its laws, which is necessary for scientific discovery, makes better sense under a universe that was created by a mind as opposed to from just matter or nothingness. This is especially clear from the works of great scientists such as Isaac Newton, Johannes Kepler, Rene Descartes, Galileo Galilei, and Nicolas Copernicus, who posited that the structure of physical reality could be knowable.[31]

The CFI seems to be practicing one-sided skepticism. True skepticism in its purest form would question everything. However, many nonbelievers who stylize themselves as skeptics typically do so only from one direction, seeking to discredit and undermine anything that pertains to the supernatural. Ironically, when the CFI practices such an arbitrary form of skepticism, it betrays reason. Not only does it betray forms of knowing it claims comprise the basis of knowledge; it also stifles freedom of inquiry. That is not to say that there are no non-religious thinkers who do not attempt to practice bi-directional or multi-directional skepticism. To be sure, there are reputable atheistic philosophers who have put forth some sophisticated a-theological arguments from the problem of evil, the alleged incoherency of theism, and non-culpability for non-belief (known as the argument from divine hiddenness). However, the CFI does not seem interested in building a positive case for its a-theological views, particularly with the application of Sagan's dictum, but instead wants to solely attack anything presupposed to be being irrational, particularly whatever is supernatural.

Proper Basicality and Sagan's Dictum

To be sure, there are many arguments that point away from the position of materialism and metaphysical naturalism. These include the ontological argument, the cosmological argument in variant forms (including the KCA),

31 Grant, "Science and Theology in the Middle Ages," 59.

the argument from reason, the teleological argument, the moral argument, the anthropic argument, the transcendental argument, and the argument from consciousness, the best explanation for the origin of information for a self-replicating system and the origin of consciousness. There are many writings that explore these arguments in great detail. Many of them are highly defensible and have modern formulations.[32] It is worth noting that outside positive arguments for and against the existence or coherence of a theistic God, there is also the concept of properly basic beliefs, which seeks to ground belief in God and provide a warrant for religious experience. It is inescapable that human experience is permeated with many beliefs that cannot be proven or disproven,[33] including belief in the external physical world, our own minds, other minds[34], the intelligibility of the world, and that the past was not suddenly created with the appearance of age. Such beliefs have been deemed self-evident axioms (or properly basic beliefs) by some Christian philosophers, such as Alvin Plantinga and William Alston. The belief in God is such a belief.[35] So, given this conception, belief itself (particularly in the aforementioned examples) is intrinsic to humans. If belief in God counts as a properly basic belief in the sense used by Plantinga and Alston, then belief in God counts as an ordinary rather than extraordinary claim. Moreover, perhaps it could also be argued that claims for materialism and naturalism, on this view, could be deemed extraordinary since they lie outside of human experience. Such naturalistic outlooks require extraordinary evidence and should not just be presumed from the outset, as is typically done. Naturalists, at least many involved with the CFI, seem to conflate nature with the totality of reality, while ignoring all the signposts to transcendence (e.g., the origin of the universe, the laws of physics, information, and consciousness).

As William Lane Craig noted, the inner witness of the Holy Spirit is what is foundational for bringing human beings into relationship with God. Furthermore, if belief in God is properly basic, then such a belief is perfectly rational and the converse could be potentially deemed otherwise. The arguments I have just sketched to point towards a transcendent reality, i.e., the God of theism, against the claims of materialism. Although not strict proofs,

32 See Craig and Moreland, *Blackwell Companion to Natural Theology* for a contemporary treatment of arguments for God's existence.

33 I understand proof and disproof in this context to be applicable strictly to mathematics and formal logic. In my estimation, the terms have been hijacked by popular culture without justification.

34 Alvin Plantinga cleverly argues that belief in other minds is on the same epistemic grounds as belief in God, who entails among many other attributes a disembodied mind, ultimately demonstrating that atheists cannot consistently deny God's existence as such while adhering to belief in other minds, let alone their own. For a thorough reflection see Plantinga, *God and Other Minds.*

35 Plantinga, *Warranted Christian Belief*, 180.

these arguments, especially when taken together cumulatively, provide an evidential basis for a transcendent and immaterial reality more powerful than the grounds for the postulation that material nature is all that exists. It makes one wonder why it never occurs to the CFI that their secular views may indeed be extraordinary, resting outside our everyday experience of spiritual realities.

Test Case: Jesus' Resurrection

Science cannot adjudicate whether the supernatural exists. As long as the possibility of God is plausible, then so are miracles. One must be careful not to artificially rule miracles out through the presumption of atheism. We have already seen, in the section on the presumption of atheism, that such a burden cannot be adequately sustained. Science by definition, under methodological naturalism, examines naturalistic causes. Miracles such as Jesus' resurrection are supernatural events that are beyond the purview of such methodologies. It must be made clear, however, that this does not mean they do not occur.

As mentioned in the introduction, I do not intend to extensively enter into the debates between philosophers such as John Earman and Robert Fogelin. But Sagan's dictum has been undoubtedly heavily influenced by Hume's own philosophical analyses of miracles in the 17th century, which attempts to demonstrate their impossibility. Academia, as Earman has put it, has too often been "genuflecting at Hume's altar."[36] Indeed, there has been an uncritical acceptance of Hume's argumentation for well over two centuries, which has infected biblical exegesis as well as scientific and historical analyses based on a rationale that is highly questionable. It is no surprise that scholars such as Rudolf Bultmann have affirmed the position that miracles are outside of historical and biblical studies. Likewise, the famous New Testament critic Bart Ehrman rejects the possibility of miracles offhand, regardless of any background knowledge: since he rejects God's existence and the evidence for it, he therefore also rejects miracles. The problem with this, as we have seen, is that God's existence is more probable than not, especially when we consider the KCA (including all the other unexamined arguments for God's existence) and proper basicality (i.e., the inner witness of the Holy Spirit). In essence, Ehrman's reasoning is circular since he presumes the impossibility of miracles as a *fait accompli*.

The fact is that probability calculus and Bayes' theorem have shown the fallaciousness of Hume's arguments, which wasn't as readily apparent beforehand. Although such argumentation would be in itself the subject of a paper, in a nutshell, the argument suggests that given the background knowledge

36 Earman, *Hume's Abject Failure: The Argument against Miracles* (Oxford: Oxford University Press, 2000), vi.

of a particular claim—in this case, the historical evidence of the resurrection of Jesus: the empty tomb, the disciples having experiences of Jesus appearing to them, and the origin of the disciples' belief that Jesus was raised from the dead[37]—it is more probable that such an event in fact occurred than that it did not. In other words, for a particular event to be improbable, the background knowledge should provide compelling disconfirming evidence, but this is clearly not the case with respect to Jesus' resurrection. This demonstrates that Ehrman's reasoning is wholly biased against miracles in spite of the evidence—his presuppositions influence and guide his conclusions. Philosopher Stephen Law, who takes an agnostic position on the remarkable claim of Jesus' nonexistence, applying Sagan's dictum to the resurrection; Craigs shows why Law's conclusion does not hold weight and is actually improbable:

> This sounds so commonsensical, doesn't it? But in fact it is demonstrably false. Probability theorists studying what sort of evidence it would take to establish a highly improbable event came to realize that if you just weigh the improbability of the event against the reliability of the testimony, we'd have to be skeptical of many commonly accepted claims. Rather what's crucial is the probability that we should have the evidence we do if the extraordinary event had not occurred. This can easily offset any improbability of the event itself. In the case of the resurrection of Jesus, for example, this means that we must also ask, "What is the probability of the facts of the empty tomb, the post-mortem appearances, and the origin of the disciples' belief in Jesus' resurrection, if the resurrection had not occurred?" It is highly, highly, highly improbable that we should have that evidence if the resurrection had not occurred.[38]

So, even with the example of a particular historical miracle such as Jesus' resurrection, the extraordinary claim is its negation as opposed to its confirmation, given the background knowledge. In other words, the view that Jesus was not raised from the dead constitutes an extraordinary claim without the evidence to back it up.

Conclusion

It has become a typical tactic for a number of naturalists to attempt to avoid criticisms by suggesting they do not need any arguments in favour of naturalism

37 For such evidence and argumentation, see *Jesus' Resurrection: A Debate between William Lane Craig and Gerd Ludemann*, ed. Copan and Tacelli (Downers Grove, IL: InterVarsity, 2000).

38 Craig deals extensively with Sagan's dictum in this response to Stephen Law: http://www.reasonablefaith.org/stephen-law-on-the-non-existence-of-jesus-of-nazareth#_edn3; see Craig, *Reasonable Faith*.

or materialism since they believe it to be self-evident. However, they do so in the absence of any proper warrant. Once carefully examined, the CFI's tactics ironically work to discredit part of its own mission statement, which gives the false impression that it is bolstered on reason, science, and free inquiry. Instead, a closed-mindedness is revealed, with a failure to acknowledge the weaknesses in their own position. The skepticism they drive against supernatural beliefs seems wholly unwarranted and motivated more by emotions than by calm and objective reason. This is evident from a thorough look at the epistemology of Sagan's dictum and the use of philosophy and science to assess the question of God. When applying Sagan's dictum to the existence of God it becomes apparent that naturalistic conclusions are the extraordinary claims lacking extraordinary evidence. Moreover, such is the case also for claims against the miracle of Jesus' resurrection, as Craig has so aptly demonstrated. What is ultimately revealed is the unjustifiedly presumptuous nature of atheism, which seems to be motivated by an aversion to the concept of God (the cosmic authority problem), especially given the absence of compelling reasons to accept non-belief as a rational proposition.

Any intellectual debate will require each side to present arguments in favour of its position. If it is a debate regarding the existence of God, it is inadequate just to present evidence against a particular proposition; rather, one must also present arguments and evidences in favour of the position they maintain to be true. Indeed the secular humanist position against God's existence lacks extraordinary evidence for such an extraordinary claim! So the atheist, as much as the theist, must present a positive case for their belief system. Progress will be reached by both sides through the acknowledgement of their own shortcomings and through the admission of weaknesses, as opposed to attempting to constantly insulate themselves from legitimate criticisms as if they do not exist.

Bibliography

Borde, Arvind, et al. "Inflationary spacetimes are not past-complete." *Physical Review Letters*, vol. 90, no. 15 (2003).

Center for Inquiry. "About the Center for Inquiry." http://www.centerforinquiry.net/about.

Copan, Paul and Ronald K. Tacelli, eds. *Jesus' Resurrection: A Debate between William Lane Craig and Gerd Ludemann.* Downers Grove, IL: InterVarsity, 2000.

Craig, William Lane. *Reasonable Faith.* 3rd ed. Wheaton: Crossway Books, 2008.

———. "Theistic Critiques of Atheism." In *The Cambridge Companion to Atheism*, edited by Michael Martin. Cambridge: Cambridge University

Press, 2007.

Dacey, Austin. "Decomposing Humanism: Why Replace Religion?" October 29, 2009. http://www.religiondispatches.org/archive/atheologies/1963/decomposing_humanism%3A_why_replace_religion.

Dawkins, Richard. *The God Delusion.* New York: Houghton Mifflin Company, 2006.

Earman, John. *Hume's Abject Failure: The Argument against Miracles.* New York: Oxford University Press, 2000.

Fogelin, Robert J. *A Defense of Hume on Miracles.* Princeton, New Jersey: Princeton University Press, 2005.

Grant, Edward. "Science and Theology in the Middle Ages." In *God and Nature: Historical Essays on the Encounter between Christianity and Science,* edited by David C. Lindberg and Ronald L. Numbers. Los Angeles: University of California Press, 1986.

Hackett, Stuart C. *The Resurrection of Theism: Prolegomena to Christian Apology.* Eugene, OR: Wipf and Stock, 2009.

Hawking, Stephen and Leonard Mlodinow. *The Grand Design.* New York: Random House, 2010.

Hume, David. *An Enquiry Concerning Human Understanding.* Oxford: J.B. Bebbington, 1861.

Inwagen, Peter van. "Can Science Disprove the Existence of God?" *Philosophic Exchange* 34 (2004): art. 3.

Lipton, Peter. *Inference to the Best Explanation.* New York: Routledge, 1991.

Meyer, Stephen C. *Signature in the Cell: DNA and the Evidence for Intelligent Design.* New York: Harper One, 2009.

Nagel, Thomas. *The Last Word.* New York: Oxford University Press, 2001.

Plantinga, Alvin. *God and Other Minds: A Study of the Rational Justification of Belief in God* (Ithaca: Cornell University Press, 1967).

———. *Warranted Christian Belief.* Oxford: Oxford University Press, 2000.

Sennett, James F. and Douglas Groothuis, eds. *In Defense of Natural Theology: A Post-Humean Assessment.* Downers Grover, IL: InterVarsity, 2005.

Spitzer, Robert J. *New Proofs for the Existence of God: Contributions of Contemporary Physics and Philosophy.* Grand Rapids, Michigan: William B. Eerdmans Publishing Company, 2010.

Wielenberg, Erik J. *God and the Reach of Reason: C.S. Lewis, David Hume and Bertrand Russell.* Cambridge: Cambridge University Press, 2007.

Chapter 12

The Governor General's Hubris and Anti-Intellectualism[1]

Scott D. G. Ventureyra

On November 1, 2017, Governor General (GG) Julie Payette was a keynote speaker at the Canadian Science Policy Conference in Ottawa. She touched upon a variety of issues, including climate change, horoscopes, the origin of life, alternative medicine, and "divine intervention." In this chapter, I would like to focus on her comments regarding religion and science, on which she stated: "We are still debating and still questioning whether life was a divine intervention or whether it was coming out of a natural process, let alone, oh my goodness, a random process." She also suggests that religious beliefs about the origin of life, among others, should be unfathomable in a "learned society."[2]

This statement is so deliciously bad that it is hard to know where to begin in response, since I feel as though I am a mosquito at a nudist colony. In this sloppily thought-out sentence, the GG not only assaulted and disparaged complex religious issues in a highly irresponsible manner, but she also trivialized the beliefs of millions of Canadians. One wonders what the supreme governor of the Church of England, Queen Elizabeth II, whom she supposedly represents, would think. The GG's mandate is to represent the Queen and not to give partisan views on what people should believe or not believe in a free society. Furthermore, I think she is highly misinformed on the relationship between science and faith.

Faith and Science

The GG raised a number of issues pertaining not only to science, but to theology, the science-theology dialogue, and philosophy of science. These

1 For the original see: Scott Ventureyra, "The Governor General's Hubris and Anti-Intellectualism," *Catholic Insight*, November 8, 2017, https://catholicinsight.com/the-governor-generals-hubris-and-anti-intellectualism/.

2 Urback, "Governor General to deride people for their beliefs?"

comments deeply disturbed me, since I have thought long and hard about the relationship between science and theology. Unfortunately, she caricatured the two great disciplines. She espoused the typical view of scientism, which sets up religion against science. However, most likely unbeknownst to the GG, there are nuanced positions on the relationship between science and religion, including what the physicist-theologian Robert John Russell dubbed "Creative Mutual Interaction," whereby science and theology inform one another.[3] There is also what the late nuclear physicist, theologian and pioneer of the science-theology interaction Ian Barbour labelled *dialogue* and *integration*, outlining many of the complexities concerning the relations between the two.[4]

Treatment of deep questions such as the origin of life and God's interaction with physical reality require careful thought. One is not entirely clear what the GG meant by "life": did she mean the origin of information necessary for building the first replicating system? Or is it a generic expression for discussing evolution in general, i.e., common descent—the view that all organisms are descended from one (the standard view) or several (the unorthodox view) common ancestors, regardless of the mechanisms involved (natural selection, random mutation, horizontal gene transfer, endosymbiosis, self-organization, etc.)? Common descent is what most people think of when they think of evolution, and this is quite compatible with God's guidance or "intervention," but we'll come back to this term later. If she meant the origin of life, as a scientist and especially as an engineer she should appreciate the high level of sophistication of even "low life." Living in the twenty-first century, we find ourselves in an era of utter awe and discovery with the rapid advancement of natural sciences and the exponential development of technology, all of which serve as indispensable aids to scientific, philosophical, and theological inquiry. Through this ever-evolving correspondence between our understanding of the natural sciences and technological development, it is astonishing, for instance, to observe the features of "low life" (micro-organisms) endowed with specified complexity, something that has only become possible because of our advancement in technology. Most remarkable is the fact that we can unravel a world far more complicated than any computer or device we have been able to design. This is especially true with the informational content embedded on the spine of the double-helical DNA molecule. Indeed, our technology has allowed us to discover an exquisite world of biological "nano-technology" that is far more sophisticated than our own, yet vastly more primitive (e.g., even primordial single-celled organisms such as eukaryotes or prokaryotes bacteria), exhibiting much lower orders of specified complexity and obvious cognitive

3 Ventureyra, *On the Origin of Consciousness*, chapter 1.

4 Barbour, *When Science Meets Religion: Enemies, Strangers or Partners?*

capacities than humans possess. Such advancements provoke us to reflect deeply on our philosophical and theological outlooks.

The Difficulty with the "Origin of Life"

The GG should have at least some acquaintance with the tremendous obstacles that origin-of-life studies face. For instance, philosopher of science Stephen C. Meyer, in his seminal book on the origin of life, *Signature in the Cell*, builds a case for agent causation using standard scientific modes of reasoning. He uses abductive reasoning, which is standard in the historical sciences. This is precisely the same method used by Charles Darwin in his *On the Origin of Species* and geologist-lawyer Charles Lyell, who in his *Principles of Geology* expounded his doctrine of uniformitarianism, which deeply influenced Darwin's theory of evolution by natural selection. Abduction also involves making an inference to the best explanation among competing hypotheses. Meyer employs precisely this method, using the origin of life to explain the origin of the first replicating system. He states:

> The inability of genetic algorithms, ribozyme engineering, and prebiotic simulations to generate information without intelligence reinforced what I had discovered in my study of other origin-of-life theories. Undirected materialistic causes have not demonstrated the capacity to generate significant amounts of specified information. At the same time, conscious intelligence has repeatedly shown itself capable of producing such information. It follows that mind—conscious, rational intelligent agency—what philosophers call "agent causation," now stands as the only cause known to be capable of generating large amounts of specified information starting from a nonliving state… If there are no other known causes—if there is only one known cause—of a given effect, then the presence of the effect points unambiguously back to the (uniquely adequate) cause.[5]

We can summarize Meyer's findings with the following argument:

1. The origin of information needed to build the first replicating system is due to either natural law, chance, a combination of chance and natural law, or design.
2. It is neither due to natural law or chance nor to a combination of the two.
3. Therefore, it is due to design.

5 Meyer, *Signature in the Cell*, 341.

I wonder if the GG knows of this line of argumentation and considers it fitting for a "learned society."

Randomness vs. chance

What about the issue of randomness? Did the GG mean by this "chance"? It is not clear. No one thinks that life originated by chance or "randomly." Most origin-of-life specialists agree that some "law" imposing order must be necessary, but as we saw above, the combination of chance and natural law is insufficient according to Meyer's systematic argument. But even if life originated by chance or randomness, for argument's sake, why isn't it possible that God pre-ordained the laws of physics and front-loaded information into the universe, in order to allow for this singular event to take place through cosmic evolution? This is the position of thrice-doctored scientist-theologian-dentist Denis Lamoureux, who was the first tenured professor of science and religion in Canada. Perhaps the GG believes she is more learned than a philosopher like Meyer and an actual working scientist, such as Lamoureux, who publishes his findings in peer-reviewed journals and makes his arguments in carefully thought-out books? It is difficult to say.

Philosopher Brendan Sweetman, in his book *Evolution, Chance and God: Understanding the Relationship between Evolution and Religion*, focuses on the concepts of chance, randomness, and determinism in relation to evolution, as he states:

> Central to my thinking will be the claim that, contrary to one influential, even prevailing, view in the general discussion, evolution does not operate by or involve a significant element of chance. This means that there is no chance operating in either physics or biology: I will defend, with certain qualifications concerning human free will and any action by God in creation, the position of determinism with regard to the operations of the physical universe… I have become convinced in my reading and thinking about evolution that, with certain qualifications, there is no chance or random occurrences involved in the process, and that leading thinkers in biology, philosophy and theology who claim there is, or who assume there is, or who have made chance a key part of the way they understand or explain the theory, are seriously mistaken. Moreover, this mistake has far-reaching implications and consequences for the evolution/religion discussion.[6]

6 Sweetman, *Evolution, Chance and God*, 15.

So, far from being a matter of mere chance or randomness, evolution may be basically deterministic. All this is to say that there is debate among scientists, philosophers, and theologians over the role of chance and randomness. Even the famous atheist Richard Dawkins emphasizes the non-random aspect of evolution: natural selection as the key to evolutionary change. Moreover, it is worth pointing out that randomness does not mean that something is without a cause.

God's Hand

Finally, what about intervention? This term has spawned countless articles and discussions in the science-theology dialogue. But what does it mean? It turns out thinkers have not come to a consensus. The question of intervention directly concerns the notion of divine action. Traditionally, since the 17th century, an intervention is an act of God understood as an instance of special creation or action after the initial creation of the universe. Intervention, it seems, could mean any action that God takes upon the created order. It is sometimes described as a suspension of the laws of physics. One could ask why God would suspend the laws He created at one point, in order to intervene at another. The concept of divine intervention may seem unpalatable to many, particular theologians, because of the accompanying stigma of being labelled scientifically ignorant. But perhaps an intervention of God, or to put it in more acceptable terms, God's "action," is where a resolution may lie. In order to be intellectually honest with oneself, one must be able to at least entertain the possibility. What about God operating through the informational structure of the universe? Life as we know it depends on information-rich systems (specified information). We also know through information theory that information transcends the material component, so in essence this is a way God could interact with life and even complex brains without suspending or breaking the laws of nature. This could also be seen as an intervention, even if operating at the quantum level, but not one where God contravenes the laws of nature that He initially created.

Interestingly, it turns out that anyone who believes in God is a creationist regardless of how God chose to create. This is true whether His action is detectable or not. Nevertheless, I hope that I have been able to show that these questions raised by the GG are highly contentious and complex. I doubt she really has any clue how complex the matter really is and how many nuanced positions there are. But she should know better than to disparage people's beliefs. She should also be mindful of her mandate.

Either God was involved in creation or He wasn't. The ways by which He was involved can be explored, but what the GG is suggesting, namely that God had no involvement, is a claim that is not only unsubstantiated but extremely presumptuous indeed. She has no arguments for this, since science has zero to say about God *per se* because God by definition is transcendent to space, time, matter, and energy and therefore unobservable through the scientific method. Only the *effects* of God's action can be examined by science.

Trudeau's Oversight

Prime Minister Justin Trudeau, in his usual fashion, gave reflexive support for the GG, saying: "And I am extraordinarily proud of the strength and the story of our Governor General, Julie Payette, who has never hidden away her passion for science and her deep faith that knowledge, research and the truth is a foundation for any free, stable, successful society. And I applaud the firmness with which she stands in support of science and the truth."[7] I wonder what the PM considers truth, since he so often contradicts himself. For instance, he identifies as a Catholic but is a ruthless totalitarian against those who are pro-life, as seen with his treatment of pro-life Liberals and the 2017 fiasco with the Liberal MPs walking out on conservative pro-lifer Rachel Harder.

It is worth pointing out that from the time of her controversial speech to early 2021, a lot changed for Payette. It seems that her arrogance has caught up to her: she was forced to resign as GG for her public humiliations, toxic attitude, and aggressive conduct towards her staff.[8] Sadly, Canadian taxpayers must foot the bill for her lifetime pension of nearly $150,000 and an additional $206,000 for expenses each year.

Aside from his oversight in appointing Payette as the GG of Canada, Trudeau has at least been consistent: his cabinet and outside appointments are comprised of individuals who embody corruption, incompetence, mediocrity, or all or several of these less-than-desirable traits. Personifications of these traits include environment minister Catherine McKenna, who openly mocked Canadians for their credulousness;[9] health minister Patt Hajdu, ignorant of basic medicine and science (calling the use of Vitamin D to combat the flu and Covid-19 "fake news");[10] finance minister Chrystia Freeland, with zero knowledge of economics and finance; former finance minister Bill Morneau, guilty of unprecedented financial corruption; public health officer[11] Dr. Theresa Tam with her ludicrous endorsement of extreme COVID restrictions; and minister of science Kirsty Duncan, who panders to gender ideology, just to mention a

7 Wherry, "Scheer blasts Trudeau for supporting Governor General."

8 Cousins, "Gov. Gen. Julie Payette resigns, says 'I am sorry' after 'tensions have arisen at Rideau Hall.'"

9 Goldstein, "Screeched-in McKenna commits a classic political gaffe."

10 Malcolm, "No, Minister Hajdu, the Vitamin D conversation isn't 'fake news.'"

11 BBC News, "Bill Morneau: Canada finance minister quits amid charity probe."

few. Thus, Trudeau being extraordinarily proud of appointing someone who does not have any merit—if anything it should warrant concern—but I digress. I would suggest that in the future the GG, and the PM for that matter, should better inform themselves on complex and sensitive issues. It would save them much embarrassment.

I fully support science, but it should be emphasized that experimental science emanated from a Judeo-Christian worldview, and not any other. It did not stem from atheism or ancient materialism, nor from Islam, Buddhism, or Hinduism. I wonder if the GG or the PM is aware of this fact of history. There is good reason why science stemmed from the Western Judeo-Christian world, since it entails the view that the world was created by an all-knowing and all-loving God, and structured so as to be intelligible. This intelligibility is what allows rational inquiry and scientific study—so that humans who possess intelligence can understand the workings of God, so to speak, whether through evolution or through "divine intervention." This is the view that was held by the modern architects of science such as Galileo, Newton, Kepler, and Copernicus.

God and the Astronauts

Interestingly, Payette's keenness on pitting science versus religion and ridiculing the latter is not a shared disposition among many astronauts of higher qualifications and repute. Take for instance the moon landing of July 20, 1969: before astronauts Neil Armstrong and Buzz Aldrin were to take man's first steps on the moon, Aldrin took Holy Communion.[12] Aldrin was not able to make this a public memorial since NASA feared another atheist lawsuit from the "most hated woman in America," the atheist activist Madalyn Murray O'Hair. Aldrin was going to read Psalm 8: "When I consider Thy heavens, the work of Thy fingers, the moon and the stars which Thou hast ordained, what is man that Thou are mindful of him?" Instead, Aldrin kept his comments more generalized to cater to different beliefs. Out of the astronauts who went to the moon, Aldrin was the most educated, with a PhD from MIT. 52 years after this historic event, Aldrin is still alive (aged 91). It worth noting that since then, other astronauts have also engaged in religious rituals in space. In 1994, three Catholics astronauts who were onboard the Space Shuttle Endeavor took Holy Communion. Ilan Ramon, an Israeli astronaut, recited the Jewish Shabbat Kiddush prayer in space, then tragically died in the Space Shuttle Columbia. In 2017, Russian cosmonaut Sergei Ryzhikovtook brought a relic of St. Serafim (an Orthodox saint) to space.

12 Blakemore, "Buzz Aldrin Took Holy Communion on the Moon. NASA Kept it Quiet."

Thus, contrary to Payette's hubris, science and religion complement one another. Credentialed and educated astronauts not only have sincere faith in a personal God but are humbled in the presence of God's majesty through the vastness of His wondrous creation. I would extend an invitation to both Julie Payette and the PM for a debate on the nature of science, the science-theology interaction, issues in the philosophy of science, or even the reasonableness of faith and the existence of God. This, however, would require them to finally substantiate many of their audacious claims. I wonder if they are prepared to have a discussion in the spirit of truth, instead of resolving important issues by fiat. This is how real progress and understanding are possible, in a true "learned society." Pitting science against faith is so typical of our highly secularized society. Exposing such intellectual laziness and canned statements would help the general population realize that neither science nor reason is really opposed to faith and theology. The only thing that supersedes Justin Trudeau and Julie Payette's ignorance is their arrogance.

I will end with a famous quote that Payette should take heed of, from an agnostic, astronomer, and planetary physicist who worked for NASA, Robert Jastrow (1925–2008), in his book *God and the Astronomers*:

> It is not a matter of another year, another decade of work, another measurement, or another theory; at this moment it seems as though science will never be able to raise the curtain on the mystery of creation. For the scientist who has lived by his faith in the power of reason, the story ends like a bad dream. He has scaled the mountain of ignorance; he is about to conquer the highest peak; as he pulls himself over the final rock, he is greeted by a band of theologians who have been sitting there for centuries.[13]

Bibliography

Barbour, Ian G. *When Science Meets Religion: Enemies, Strangers or Partners?* New York: HarperCollins, 2000.

BBC News. "Bill Morneau: Canada finance minister quits amid charity probe." *BBC News*, August 18, 2020. https://www.bbc.com/news/world-us-canada-53815645.

Blakemore, Erin. "Buzz Aldrin Took Holy Communion on the Moon. NASA Kept it Quiet." *History.com*, July 20, 2019. https://www.history.com/news/buzz-aldrin-communion-apollo-11-nasa.

13 Jastrow, *God and the Astronomers*, 107

Cousins, Ben. "Gov. Gen. Julie Payette resigns, says 'I am sorry' after 'tensions have arisen at Rideau Hall.'" *CTV News*, January 21, 2021. https://www.ctvnews.ca/politics/gov-gen-julie-payette-resigns-says-i-am-sorry-after-tensions-have-arisen-at-rideau-hall-1.5276646.

Goldstein, Lorrie. "Screeched-in McKenna commits a classic political gaffe." *Toronto Sun*, May 27, 2019. https://torontosun.com/opinion/columnists/goldstein-screeched-in-mckenna-commits-a-classic-political-gaffe.

Jastrow, Robert. *God and the Astronomers.* 2nd ed. New York: W.W. Norton & Company, 1992.

Malcolm, Candice. "No, Minister Hajdu, the Vitamin D conversation isn't 'fake news.'" *Toronto Sun*, April 24, 2021. https://torontosun.com/opinion/columnists/malcolm-no-minister-hajdu-the-vitamin-d-conversation-isnt-fake-news.

Meyer, Stephen C. *Signature in the Cell: DNA and the Evidence for Intelligent Design*. New York: HarperOne, 2009.

Sweetman, Brendan. *Evolution, Chance and God: Understanding the Relationship between Evolution and Religion*. New York: Bloomsbury, 2015.

Urback, Robyn. "In what universe is it appropriate for a Governor General to deride people for their beliefs?" *CBC News*, November 2, 2017. https://www.cbc.ca/news/opinion/governor-general-speech-julie-payette-climate-change-1.4384481.

Ventureyra, Scott D. G. *On the Origin of Consciousness: An Exploration through the Lens of the Christian Conception of God and Creation*. Eugene, OR: Wipf and Stock, 2018.

Wherry, Aaron. "Scheer blasts Trudeau for supporting Governor General after 'divine intervention' comment." *CBC News*, November 3, 2017. https://www.cbc.ca/news/politics/scheer-trudeau-payette-divine-intervention-1.4385895.

Chapter 13

Science and Christian Theology[1]

Scott D. G. Ventureyra

Popular consciousness in the West has affirmed over and over again, like the beating of a drum, that natural science and theology are in bitter conflict. At the end of 2018, evolutionary biologist Jerry Coyne made this claim in a predictable piece,[2] claiming that the two are incompatible and are at war with one another. In recent years, scientific materialists—at full throttle—have pushed forward the notion that natural science is a beacon of light and that religion is at best an archaic fairy tale that offers nothing more than false hope, and is at worst a collective madness which stagnates human progress and reason, causing the majority of wars and irreparable psychological damage to human beings. The truth is that explicitly atheistic regimes have been the cause of much more bloodshed than all religious wars combined; only seven percent of all wars have been explicitly religious (i.e., 123 of the 1,763 violent conflicts over 3,500 years).[3]

This sort of superficial analysis reminds me of the book *Contact*, written by the late astronomer Carl Sagan, which was adapted into a motion picture in 1997. Sagan perpetuated this myth that theology and natural science are engaged in an ongoing struggle. The movie follows Ellie Arroway (played by Jodie Foster, who I presume was to some degree the female embodiment of Sagan himself), an astronomer who is obsessed with bringing the SETI (search for extra-terrestrial intelligence) program to its fruition, and her love interest Palmer Joss (played by Matthew McConaughey), a theologian who argues that science and technology have failed to provide any remedy to humanity's existential angst.

In a scene relevant to our discussion, Arroway conjectures that science has demonstrated God's nonexistence, since science operates by proving things and

1 For the original, see Scott Ventureyra, "Science and Christian Theology Mutually Inform One Another," *Crisis Magazine*, January 29, 2019, https://www.crisismagazine.com/2019/science-and-christian-theology-mutually-inform-one-another.

2 Coyne, "Yes, there is a war between science and religion."

3 Day, "Atheists abandon 'religion causes war' argument."

no proof exists for God. Joss retorts by asking Arroway to prove her love for her deceased father. Joss's point is sound: science cannot account for the subjective experience of love. Empirical observation of the causal connections between emotional states and the neurochemical and physiological events within the brain and other parts of the human body just provide one level of analysis (i.e., a physical explanation) and not the substance or object of one's love; love involves an act of the will and intellect, which is irreducible to the material.

Having recently watched *Contact* again after a number of years, I've pondered how I would tackle Arroway's assertion. To my dismay, many individuals across different Christian denominations have received impoverished and misguided responses to legitimate questions. The relationship between the sciences and theology is a fundamental obstacle for many inquisitive minds (at least on the surface). On the other hand, it has also distressed me to witness the lackadaisical approach of many believers when it comes to the articulation and understanding of arguments and reasons that support the Christian faith. Indeed, Christianity is undergoing an intellectual crisis; philosophical and theological illiteracy is pervasive in our culture. The average believer would be surprised to learn that there are a number of compelling reasons to accept the existence of God (including the Christian conception of God). It would also astonish many lay Christians to learn that science and theology are not in conflict but inform one another. I have sought to demonstrate the plausibility of these two propositions in my book *On the Origin of Consciousness*.[4]

A Historical Consideration

An early historical example of how theology and science can be integrated is found in the work of the sixth-century Christian philosopher John Philoponus.[5] A thinker who remains obscure outside of academic circles and who specialized in ancient Greek philosophy, Philoponus was known for his both polemical and non-polemical commentaries on the works of Aristotle. Following this unique approach, he wrote a substantial amount of material combating Aristotle's notion of the eternality of the world. Philoponus's belief that God created the universe out of nothing played a significant role in challenging the reigning philosophy of his time. Many Christians and Jews were embarrassed by the doctrine of *creation ex nihilo* and were divided over whether God created from pre-existing matter through reorganizing it or created matter itself from nothing. The reason for this embarrassment was precisely the natural philosophical consensus that pointed toward an eternal past. As philosopher and renowned

4 Ventureyra, *On the Origin of Consciousness.*

5 Wildberg, "John Philoponus."

Philoponus commentator Richard Sorabji notes: "Up to AD 529, Christians were on the defensive. They argued that a beginning of the universe was not impossible. In 529, Philoponus swung round into the attack. He argued that a beginning of the universe was actually mandatory, and mandatory on the pagans' own principles."

Instrumental to Philoponus's approach was a separation between Creator and creation. This belief allowed him to argue not only that the past was finite, but also that the sun was made of fire, which he acknowledged as a terrestrial substance as opposed to a celestial substance. Thus, Philoponus established that heavenly bodies are not divine and are subject to decomposition, thereby collapsing a central Aristotelian doctrine in the face of a Christian doctrine. Philoponus's Christian worldview permitted him to also create a coherent system of thought where he could provide argumentation and evidence to support his belief system—one that proved fruitful to scientific discovery. Historians of science have noted that Philoponus's rigor positively influenced the future direction of cosmology.

Philoponus proposed a syllogistic argument for the existence of God:

1. Whatever comes to be has a cause of its coming to be.
2. The universe came to be.
3. Therefore, the universe has a cause of its coming to be.

Thus, Philoponus's understanding of reality, which was heavily influenced and guided by his Christian faith, bore several fruits that are relevant to this very day. His theological and philosophical reasoning has been confirmed by modern empirical science, which affirms that the universe is not eternal. This affirmation is made through two lines of reasoning: the standard Big Bang model which argues for the expansion of the universe and the second law of thermodynamics. Remarkably, there are hints of both of these in Philoponus's thought. Even though the evidence provided by the empirical sciences is typically provisional and can indeed change in the future, we have good reasons to believe in the beginning of the universe as established by modern science. Philoponus, in the sixth century, exemplifies the strong consonance between science and theology in the early Middle Ages. His argument for the finitude of the past has come to be known as the Kalam Cosmological Argument.[6] Today, its foremost defender is philosopher and theologian William Lane Craig.

6 "The Kalam Cosmological Argument—Part 1: Scientific."

The Interaction between Science and Theology

Belief in the intelligibility and rationality of reality came to shape much scientific empiricism, as well as the use of mathematics to describe natural processes. Indeed, theological insights and understanding inspired many developments in modern scientific thought. This is especially true of great scientific minds such as Isaac Newton, Johannes Kepler, René Descartes, Galileo Galilei, and Nicolas Copernicus, who all held that the structure of physical reality was knowable. The explicitly theological conviction that there is intelligibility and comprehensibility in reality because of God's role as Creator inspired scientists to adopt a type of reverse-engineering mode of thinking (whereby humans could possibly even modify and perfect creation) in order to understand how things were created (this was precisely the mode of thinking practiced by Isaac Newton). This would help us to perceive how the universe functioned. The point here is that, from the early modern period until the early twentieth century, scientists were directly aided by theological thoughts and notions in discerning the operations of nature. The inescapable conclusion here is that modern science was born out of a Christian worldview: these theological notions set a framework for scientific research and discovery. Throughout history theological thought and science have gone hand in hand more often than not.

Due to the collapse of the verification principle, the intersection of natural science and theology enjoys a burgeoning discourse, with the potential for valuable new discoveries and insights. Despite popular caricatures setting the two great fields at odds with one another, they have had much to say to one another in mutual cooperation throughout history (as demonstrated with Philoponus's insights and arguments). Such cooperation continues to this very day. Ever since the 1960s, a number of peer-reviewed journals devoted to this dialogue have sprung into existence. They include *CTNS: Theology and Science Journal*, *The European Journal of Science and Theology*, *Zygon: Journal of Science and Religion*, and the latest addition: *Philosophy, Theology and the Sciences*. Indeed, the field is growing and gaining interest from scholars of a variety of disciplines.

There have also been a series of typologies outlining the relationship between science and theology offered by scientists and theologians such as Ian Barbour, Ted Peters, Willem Drees, John Haught, and Robert John Russell. Of these, the most promising method is Russell's Creative Mutual Interaction (CMI). What is novel and promising about this method is that not only do scientific research programs influence theological research programs, but theological research programs, in turn, influence scientific research programs. Russell uses a *theology of nature* for his CMI. In my book *On the Origin of Consciousness*, I have transposed this and utilized instead a *natural theology* for my CMI method. Natural theology functions as a rational endeavour to adduce God's existence and purpose in nature by understanding the natural world (through using philosophical tools and the best scientific evidence available, sans the aid of biblical revelation). By contrast, a theology of nature like Russell's begins with the Christian tradition via religious experience, and historical and biblical revelation. Furthermore, a theology of nature suggests that certain Christian doctrines may require revision in light of modern scientific findings. Both approaches have their fruits and purposes.

Intelligibility, Science, and God

One intriguing argument emanating from the 1970s is found in the work of philosopher and theologian Bernard Lonergan: *Insight: A Study of Human Understanding*. It lends support to the claim that Christian thought was a vital component of the emergence of modern scientific thought (as was argued above). He demonstrates God's existence from intelligibility. I will relate it also to a scientific argument. Lonergan's own argument is stated thus:

> If the real is completely intelligible, then complete intelligibility exists. If complete intelligibility exists, the idea of being exists. If the idea of being exists, then God exists. Therefore, the real is completely intelligible, and so God exists.[7]

It is worth pointing out that finite intelligibility is grounded upon complete intelligibility. The fact that we are able to formulate general laws of science, use mathematics and logic, communicate, and discern truth in its different manifestations is a reflection of an unbounded intelligibility—the sort of thing we should expect if there is any correspondence between reality and our minds.

Philosopher and theologian Jay Richards and astrophysicist Guillermo Gonzalez have developed an argument that provides the scientific basis for Lonergan's onto-epistemic argument. In their book *The Privileged Planet*, Gonzalez and Richards lay out a scientific argument with deep metaphysical implications. They provide a host of different lines of evidence to suggest that the earth occupies a special place in the cosmos. Their argument goes against the popular notion, held by many scientists and popularized by Carl Sagan, that the Earth has no special or privileged place in the cosmos and is merely an insignificant cosmic accident, which Sagan dubbed a "pale blue dot." His book[8] and the saying were inspired by a famous photograph taken of Earth on February 14, 1990, by the Voyager 1 space probe, which depicts

7 Lonergan, *Insight*, 696.
8 Sagan, *Pale Blue Dot*.

Earth as a tiny speck in the vastness of space and bands of sunlight. This is strongly connected to the misnamed Copernican Principle, which Gonzalez and Richards refute as well. Gonzalez and Richards argue that there is a deep correlation between habitability and scientific observability. The fact that we exist on a particularly special type of planet (i.e., Earth) is also related to the fact that we are in such a place, with a purpose, to observe the universe and discover, measure, and understand much of the cosmos. They provide examples of the correlation between habitability and measurability. They illustrate, in a scientific manner, the very intelligibility which Lonergan describes as being intrinsic to a reality grounded upon the ultimate source of all intelligibility.

Thus, we have examined various lines of reasoning which demonstrate that neither science nor reason is in conflict with theology. God's existence is supported by logic and scientific argumentation. In fact, the real culprit for the dissonance between science and religion is the atheological worldview of metaphysical naturalism, the belief that nature is all there is and that no supernatural beings exist. It is a philosophical prejudice that has little grounding in actual science and is increasingly challenged on both philosophical and scientific grounds. A believer in a Creator God should not find this surprising, but it is comforting to know that contemporary scientists are increasingly recognizing the debt modern science owes to theology.

Bibliography

Coyne, Jerry. "Yes, there is a war between science and religion." *The Conversation*, December 18, 2019. https://theconversation.com/yes-there-is-a-war-between-science-and-religion-108002?utm_source=twitter&utm_medium=twitterbutton&fbclid=IwAR0KGEIWBnYFHMu0Bp7IyEk-h5n7fkMVhWIi-Fb0CBiWpC0TrT4CTcR1P5g.

Day, Vox. "Atheists abandon 'religion causes war' argument." *Vox Popoli*, August 13, 2012. https://voxday.blogspot.com/2012/08/atheists-abandon-religion-causes-war.html.

Drcraigvideos. "The Kalam Cosmological Argument—Part 1: Scientific." YouTube video, September 1, 2013. https://www.youtube.com/watch?v=6CulBuMCLg0.

Gonzalez, Guillermo and Jay Richards. *The Privileged Planet: How Our Place in the Cosmos is Designed for Discovery*. Washington: Regnery, 2004.

Lonergan, Bernard. *Insight: A Study of Human Understanding*. Collected Works of Bernard Lonergan, vol.3, edited by Frederick E. Crowe and Robert M. Doran. Toronto: University of Toronto Press, 1992.

Sagan, Carl. *Pale Blue Dot: A Vision of the Human Future in Space*. New York: Random House, 1994.

Ventureyra, Scott D. G. *On the Origin of Consciousness: An Exploration through the Lens of the Christian Conception of God and Creation*. Wipf and Stock, 2018.

Wildberg, Christian. "John Philoponus." *Stanford Encyclopedia of Philosophy*, last revised October 26, 2018. https://plato.stanford.edu/entries/philoponus/.

Part III:

Science versus Scientism

Chapter 14

The Lawyer Who Put the Logic of Darwinism on Trial: Phillip E. Johnson's Gift to Posterity[1]

Scott D. G. Ventureyra

On the second of November 2019, at the age of 79, Phillip E. Johnson died at his home in California. Johnson was a gifted and productive author. By his late twenties he was a professor of law at the University of California, Berkeley. He studied at both Harvard and the University of Chicago. In his 30s he underwent a divorce and became rather disillusioned with his life. Although well-published in his field, he began to see the meaninglessness of life in the absence of any ultimate purpose. At the age of 38 he converted to Christianity; this profoundly changed the way he viewed life, the universe, and humanity's place within it.

Evolving Our Thinking about Evolution

In 1987, during his sabbatical in London, Johnson stumbled upon two diametrically opposed books on evolution written by scientists. The first was *The Blind Watchmaker*, by the vociferous atheist-zoologist Richard Dawkins, which is still one of the best popular books making the case for Darwinism. The other, *Evolution: A Theory in Crisis,* was written by a little-known Australian geneticist and medical doctor, Michael Denton, who was an agnostic. Johnson was more persuaded by the argumentation put forward by Denton. Denton's book was at the time the most thorough scientific critique of Neo-Darwinism. Johnson saw Dawkins's rhetoric as a mask for covering deep-seated scientific problems in a failing theory.

Several years after this period of deep reflection on Darwinism of various stripes, Johnson published his seminal book *Darwin on Trial*, which was

1 For the original see Scott Ventureyra, "The Lawyer Who Put the Logic of Darwinism on Trial: Phillip E. Johnson's Gift to Posterity," *Catholic Insight*, November 23, 2019, https://catholicinsight.com/the-lawyer-who-put-the-logic-of-darwinism-on-trial-phillip-e-johnsons-gift-to-posterity/.

reviewed widely, albeit critically, by both scientists and philosophers, including the late paleontologist Stephen J. Gould. Soon after, he was dubbed the godfather of intelligent design (ID). For those unfamiliar with ID, it is the study of the universe and what it contains as the products of intelligence. It holds that intelligence (mind) better explains the existence of complex-information-rich structures and processes than an undirected natural processes.

Please note that this essay is not an endorsement of all of what Johnson had argued for, nor a denial of evolutionary processes or of evolution in the sense of universal common descent; rather, it is an acknowledgement of his profound impact since the 1990s on the debate regarding origins. I am confident in stating that even his strongest detractors cannot deny that he framed questions pertaining to the origin of life, organisms, organelles, etc., in a fresh new light which brought a critique of naturalism's unnecessary stronghold on science—in the sense of metaphysical naturalism, the view that nature is all that exists. Methodological naturalism, on the other hand, is a method employed in the sciences which only makes use of natural causes to explain all phenomena. The two are distinct, but Johnson argued that the former, for all intents and purposes, was equivalent to the latter. Although I do not full embrace that position, Johnson rightfully rejected the famous biologist Richard Lewontin's candid statement in a review of Carl Sagan's book *The Demon-Haunted World: Science as a Candle in the Dark*, about scientific materialism and its allegedly necessary stranglehold on science:

> It is not that the methods and institutions of science somehow compel us to accept a material explanation of the phenomenal world, but, on the contrary, that we are forced by our a priori adherence to material causes to create an apparatus of investigation and a set of concepts that produce material explanations, no matter how counter-intuitive, no matter how mystifying to the uninitiated.
>
> Moreover, that materialism is absolute, for we cannot allow a Divine Foot in the door. The eminent Kant scholar Lewis Beck used to say that anyone who could believe in God could believe in anything. To appeal to an omnipotent deity is to allow that at any moment the regularities of nature may be ruptured, that miracles may happen.[2]

Additionally, Johnson centralized the importance of the question of how biological and chemical evolution happened for a popular audience—something that scientists to date have failed to provide plausible and detailed accounts of. It is noteworthy that a growing number of scientists, including evolutionary biologists, have questioned the efficacy of the modern synthetic version of Charles Darwin's theory, Neo-Darwinism, which holds the combination of

2 Lewontin, "Billions and Billions of Demons."

random mutation and natural selection as a means to explain the existence of every living organism and its biological features.

Mere Dilettante or Skilful Logician?

Phillip Johnson was often dismissed by his critics for not being a scientist. This is a facile way of dismissing inconvenient arguments, i.e., to demonize one's opponent as a mere dilettante. For instance, the late physicist Mark Perakh who authored the book *Unintelligent Design*, devoted a whole chapter, titled "A Militant Dilettante in Judgment of Science," to critiquing Johnson's work. It is interesting to note that Charles Darwin's formal postsecondary educational background was in medicine and theology, not biology. Likewise, his mentor, Charles Lyell, the founder of modern geology and a famous advocate of uniformitarianism—the notion that the earth was shaped by slow processes still acting today—was originally a lawyer by trade. So, it is possible for an outsider or a non-trained scientist to have a long-lasting impact within a scientific domain. Johnson's contribution to the origins debate was not a scientific one but one of applying logic to sweeping claims. This is where his training as a legal expert helped cut through much of the presuppositions which bolster the thinking of countless evolutionary biologists and their scientistic and naturalistic inclinations.

The Legacy

In *Darwin on Trial,* Johnson was able to demolish the popular misconception which seeks to set theological claims against scientific knowledge. There are many approaches and typologies to examine the relationship between science and theology, as exemplified in Ian Barbour's seminal text *Religion and Science.* Johnson himself sought to critique aspects of Darwinism while leaving the door open to the question of design, which had been predominantly closed to scientists with respect to their research. For most of the twentieth century there had been a bifurcation between a scientist's beliefs, if they were a theist, and their research—an arrangement popularized by Stephen J. Gould with his NOMA approach,[3] which placed science and theology in separate non-overlapping domains. Yet scientists had always brought presuppositions regarding the world into their research, whether knowingly or unknowingly.

3 "Non-overlapping magisteria."

In recent years, scientists and philosophers have been emboldened by Johnson's legacy. Consequently, they have sought to bring to the fore the notion of design into the origins debate and their scientific research; the Biologic Institute in Seattle would be an example.

Since Johnson published *Darwin on Trial* there have been scores of seminal documentaries produced, such as *Unlocking the Mystery of Life* and *The Privileged Planet*, and books and articles supporting ID and critiquing Neo-Darwinism and naturalism more broadly. He was able to organize and unite thinkers with the same dissatisfaction with naturalism (both methodologically and metaphysically), such as Michael J. Behe, Stephen C. Meyer, William A. Dembski, Jonathan Wells, Michael Denton, and many others.

Johnson was able to rally a number of good speculative scientists and philosophers who had similar objections to scientific materialism and Neo-Darwinism in particular. The discontents, although in some cases inspired by theological presuppositions, were always scientific in their approach. Johnson ignited a quiet revolution within the halls of academia throughout the world, with a growing number of scientists chipping away at the edifice of both methodological and metaphysical naturalism. Johnson's gift to posterity was the revival of the design question, not only among a group of renegade scientists and free thinkers, but also within popular consciousness for the past 25 years. As Johnson had always insisted, good science follows the evidence wherever it leads, and good pedagogy asks the right questions. As he stated in his book *The Right Questions: Truth, Meaning & Public Debate*: "the questions I am asking are the ones they should be asking, and…their education to this point has prepared them to ask the wrong questions [instead of] the right ones."[4] In the face of the COVID-19 crisis throughout the world, Johnson's approach would be useful to scientists, medical doctors, and everyday citizens; applied early on, it could have altered the whole trajectory of the crisis. Nevertheless, we bid farewell to Johnson, the man who has been rightfully dubbed "Darwin's nemesis."

Bibliography

Lewontin, Richard C. "Billions and Billions of Demons." *The New York Review*, January 9, 1997. https://www.nybooks.com/articles/1997/01/09/billions-and-billions-of-demons/.

Johnson, Phillip E. *The Right Questions: Truth, Meaning & Public Debate.* Downers Grove: InterVarsity Press, 2002.

Chapter 15

On Scientism

Hugh Hunter

Whatever you think about Darwinism, you can't deny its simple appeal. Everyone knows that there is variation within groups, and that some variations confer an advantage upon the creatures that receive them. That's the first of Darwinism's two ingredients. The second was Thomas Malthus' observation that animal populations increase until there is no more food. The simplicity of Darwinism lies in connecting these two thoughts. The perpetual competition for limited food means that those with advantageous variations will eat while others starve, which will overall select for advantageous variations, thereby leading over time to the emergence of entirely new species. It seemed so intuitive that as soon as T. H. Huxley read *The Origin of the Species* he was annoyed with himself for not having been the one to make the connection.[1] To put the point in philosophical terms, Darwinism is a way of getting from less to more, from chaos to order. There is obviously an order of nature. How is it that the carnivorous fox is so well adapted to hunt all those local rabbits? How is it that the rabbits themselves live among plentiful grass which they are adapted to eat? As David Hume put it in *Dialogues Concerning Natural Religion*: "the curious adapting of means to ends, throughout all nature, resembles exactly, though it much exceeds, the productions of human contrivance; of human designs, thought, wisdom, and intelligence."[2] It is hard to overstate how important the argument leading from nature's order to a divine Orderer was to Christian apologists right up until Charles Darwin published his book. Hume, himself not a Christian, found the argument from natural order impossible to dismiss. But Darwin set nature's apparent order in a new perspective: the fox and the rabbit are as they are because millions of proto-foxes and proto-rabbits failed and starved and suffered and died. If you could survey these millions of failures, you would be cured of the sense that nature has much in common with a human artisan.

1 Stove, *Darwinian Fairytales*, 31.

2 Hume, *Dialogues and Natural History of Religion*, Part 2, 45.

This Darwinian blow sent Christian common sense reeling. It was the beginning of a century and a half of scientific ascendancy in which Christianity and common sense were ever on the back foot. Of course, many scientists were themselves believers as well as men of common sense. But self-appointed spokesmen for natural science launched a flurry of attacks on the notion of human freedom, the existence of a soul, the value of family, the importance of meaning at work, of a spiritual element in our national struggle, and of hierarchy in our lives. The idea that the nation should be like an extended family was mocked as obsolete. Sexual morality was first said to be old-fashioned, and then replaced with an inverted new moral framework. As scientists pushed into new areas, some began to accuse them of overreach. Our name for this is "scientism." Scientism is the overapplication of science to areas where it does not belong, whether by overzealous scientists or (more often) by their ill-informed fans.

One way of defending against scientism has been to try to draw a boundary: science can come this far but no farther. This talk of boundaries brings to mind the idea of non-overlapping magisteria, as articulated by the Jewish paleontologist Stephen Jay Gould upon reading a papal encyclical. Science and religion, Gould thought, are in separate but adjacent domains of authority. "The net of science covers the empirical universe: what is it made of (fact) and why does it work this way (theory). The net of religion extends over questions of moral meaning and value. These two magisteria do not overlap."[3] Gould cheerfully admits that there will be a border, perhaps a somewhat troubled border between science and faith. For example, religious people will insist that as a matter of *fact*, there is some moment at which a body becomes associated with a soul. But this raises the question of why "moral meaning and value," along with all the other things that religious people believe, can't be facts and theories in their own right. Isn't it just a fact that murder is wrong? Can't we have a theory about the nature of the afterlife?

Gould envisions a border separating his non-overlapping magisteria, so that the domain of human knowledge will resemble countries on a map. A better model might be the ocean, which is composed of many layers of water, each layer containing its own currents and creatures, all collectively making up the whole. An insight from Gilbert Ryle can help us to see things this way. The insight is that not every form of science threatens us with scientism, but only some forms. Nowadays they are, I would say, physics (which promotes a materialist reductionism) and psychology (which suggest that our beliefs and attitudes are shaped by forces outside ourselves). It was not ever thus. Darwinist biology used to seem threatening for a while, but then the recognition spread that biology has little to say about the soul or mind, the thing that makes us

3 Gould, "Non-overlapping Magisteria," 12.

human. Later, economists had everyone worried that perhaps economic class determined all. In Ryle's telling,

> There seemed to be a deadly rivalry between what economists said about the motives and policies of human beings and what ordinary people said about the motives and policies of the people with whom they lived—and it was the latter story that seemed doomed to be condemned. The brother, whom I ordinarily describe as hospitable, devoted to his branch of learning, and unexcited about his bank-balance, must be a dummy-brother if I am to take science seriously. My real brother, my Economic Brother, is concerned only to maximize his gains and minimize his losses. Those of his efforts and outlays which do not pay are done in ignorance of the state of the market or else from stupidity in making his calculations about it.[4]

Nowadays, not even self-described Marxists worry that the brother described by economics is the *real brother*. Somehow, the science of economics has returned to its proper layer; scientism has been avoided. So let us try to spell out our understanding of economics and see whether we can apply it to other sciences too.

We understand, it seems to me, that the brother described by economics is the real person but described *at an economic level*. The economist isn't *wrong* about my brother. It's just that my brother exists at many levels. My brother's martial arts teacher or his PhD supervisor might give descriptions of him as well, and though these need not intersect or overlap with the economic description, they might all be true at once. When we say that my brother bought his house because of "economic constraints," nobody worries about whether these economic constraints affected his free will or his moral responsibility. The world admits of description at many levels, and we have come to be content to let economics be just another level.

The way to reconcile common sense with physics and psychology, then, is to once again place these on the levels where they belong. We must learn to think of the constraints of physics and psychology as we think of the constraints of economics or martial arts, which are entirely compatible with common sense.

Take as an example the question of free will. It is a tenet of common sense, I think, that human beings exercise free will. This belief is sometimes challenged by physicists, who insist that the universe must be explained in terms of physical cause and effect. The world and we as parts of it are like a great machine, and machines allow for determinism and perhaps quantum indeterminacy, but not free choice. Free will is also sometimes challenged by psychologists, who suppose that many of our choices have hidden, evolutionary

4 Ryle, *Dilemmas*, 69.

sources. You didn't propose because you fell in love with her beauty, it was because her facial symmetry and long full hair spoke to your instinctual sense of her low mutational load. Physicists and psychologists would be right if they pointed out that neither particles nor evolutionary motivations are the terms in which to express a theory of free will. They are guilty of scientism, I think, if they conclude that for this reason no such theory of free will can be expressed *at all*. When we ask about free will we are asking about the nature of the causal order, and answers will be found on the seabed of metaphysics. The best (I would add, in the old Empiricist tradition, the only) experience we have of causal force is of ourselves as agents, and it is in terms of this experience that we conceive of the causal structure that physics and psychology and all the other sciences take for granted. On the metaphysical seabed, there is every reason to suppose that our wills are free.

Thinking of science and other disciplines as like ocean levels is, I find, a sufficient bulwark against scientism. When the spokesmen of natural science overreach, I try to take their claims in the levels where they belong. I know that creatures from one level of the ocean often cannot sustain the pressure at another level, and so will necessarily seem monstrous and bloated if they are examined anywhere but where they belong. Like these sea creatures, theories need to stay in their proper levels, where their normal implications and proportions can be maintained. That is the solution to keeping science from becoming scientism.

Up until now I have been trying to sketch a defence against scientism. But we can say more. Ever since Christian common sense first had its nose bloodied by Darwinism, scientism has rested on two intellectual pillars. First, we are told, science has greatly increased our understanding of the nature of the world. And second, science has helped us to live better lives overall. These two pillars are pretty much what people mean by "scientific progress." If you think scientific progress is so wonderful that we should have more of it, as much of it as possible, in as many areas as possible, then you have found your way to scientism. That is why putting the notion of progress in question is a way to mount an offensive against scientism.

First then, is it true that science helps us to better understand the world? Certainly, science helps us to better predict and control the world. Self-described scientific "realists" think that the best explanation for scientists' ability to predict and control the world is that they are coming to understand it ever better. But consider whether this is true in your own experience. The folk remedy may be surrounded by superstition; the martial artist may go on and on about your "chi." Yet folk medicine and martial arts *work*. They work not because of but despite their theories. In just the same way, the fact that science works and grants us prediction and control is no evidence at all that scientific theories are true. Think of how well you can predict and control your body and how little you understand exactly what goes on in it. Now extend that from just your body to the entire universe and you have arrived at the grotesque fallacy of scientific "realism." As Bas van Fraassen, a philosopher of science who opposes realism, put it, "it is not an epistemological principle that one might as well hang for a sheep as for a lamb."[5] It is the second pillar where we might expect the defender of scientism to make his stand. Hasn't science indisputably made our lives *better*? To this question I am inclined to answer no, that is not indisputable. In some ways, our lives are clearly better than those of our ancestors: anaesthetics and optometry, for example, have removed two terrible scourges. But whether these changes amount to a net improvement seems to me to be very much open to debate. The curmudgeonly philosopher John Gray points out that this was true right from the start: "We think of the Stone Age as an era of poverty and the Neolithic as a great leap forward. In fact the move from hunter-gathering to farming brought no overall gain in human well-being or freedom. It enabled larger numbers to live poorer lives. Almost certainly, Paleolithic humanity was better off."[6] For the last century and a half, that is, roughly since Darwin, science has received much of the credit that we used to reserve for faith. There is, perhaps, no more authoritative way to begin a sentence today than "scientists say…" Of late we have found ourselves confined to our homes and our livelihoods devastated on the say-so of scientists. Our time has experimented with following where science leads, and we, of all people, ought to be able to say whether we are like those early men whose easy lives broke on the invention of the wheel.

One is tempted to say that we are better off. Food shortages no longer haunt us, and even our poorest are clothed and can get shelter and medical care. Personal parasites are mostly a thing of the past. Infant mortality has been greatly reduced. Even many among the poor live lives of comfort beyond what was possible in the Middle Ages, even for kings. Considered from the point of view of our material existence, things have certainly improved.

Widen your perspective to include also what we might call our spiritual health, and it is not so clear that things have improved. We are lonely. Our families and fraternal organizations have been atomized. Western millennials don't have many children, and that trend doesn't seem likely to change. The reflexive patriotism that many of us grew up with is now a punchline. Mobs are eager to tear down the statues of great white men, and the descendants of these men feel mostly apathy. In Canada and the United States, more than 40 percent of the population are at any one time medicated: whatever ailments modernity has cured, we seem sicker than ever.

I know that in this scientistic age, many people's eyes glaze over at this talk of spiritual health. I imagine them responding brusquely, *if you're lonely, buy a dog*. So, at the risk of veering into scientism myself, let me illustrate my point with an experiment.

In the late 1950s John Calhoun began to experiment with rodents to build what he called a "utopia" or "paradise." He supplied rats or mice in a large cage with all the food they wanted. If Malthus had been right, the rodents should have reproduced until they filled the cage. To Calhoun's surprise, the rats and mice in these experiments did not breed until they filled the space. They bred until their space was, for them, unbearably crowded. And then something completely unexpected began to happen.

Males became aggressive, some moving in groups, attacking females and the young. Mating behaviours were disrupted. Some males became exclusively homosexual. Others became pansexual and hypersexual, attempting to mount any rat they encountered. Mothers neglected their infants, first failing to construct proper nests, and then carelessly abandoning and even attacking their pups. In certain sections of the pens, infant mortality rose as high as 96 percent, the dead cannibalized by adults. Subordinate animals withdrew psychologically, surviving in a physical sense but at an immense psychological cost. They were the majority in the late phases of growth, existing as a vacant, huddled mass in the centre. The crowded rodents had lost the ability to co-exist harmoniously, even after the population numbers once again fell to low levels.[7] Eliminating the material needs of Calhoun's rodents didn't empower or advance them. It broke them. The parallel between comfortable man in overcrowded Western cities and comfortable rodents in an overcrowded cage was not lost on Calhoun. With the exception of cannibalism (for now?) we see our civilizations, what is left of them, in the rodents. Perhaps drawing a line from rodent to man is scientism, but I fear it may be an example of something older, a point at which nature mirrors the big in the small and the complex in the simple. What Renaissance scholars called a microcosm.

In this microcosm we can see what our technocrat rulers have done to the West, at least in part due to their scientism. Natural science is exclusively concerned with material things, and in consequence it cannot express even the modest spiritual dimensions of a rodent. Technocrats draw on natural science and consequently view their subjects as existing only in the material dimension. Many people have come to view themselves that way as well. Their thinking is constrained, forced onto the spectrum of materialist philosophies, at one end of which is liberalism, at the other communism. The one upholds directionless equality of opportunity, and the other directionless equality of outcome. Western man staggers between these extremes, correcting an excess of one with more of the other and finding happiness in neither. Left unaddressed is the yearning for hierarchy, for beauty, for purpose, for meaning, for community, and for virtue. That is why our hope, if we have any, lies in a rejection of the materialism that leads to scientism.

Bibliography

Fraassen, Bas van. *The Scientific Image*. Oxford: Oxford University Press, 1980.

Gould, Stephen Jay. "Nonoverlapping Magisteria." *Filozoficzne Aspekty Genezy* (2014) 11: 7–21.

Gray, John. *Straw Dogs*. New York: Farrar, Strauss and Giroux, 2003.

Hume, David. *Dialogues and Natural History of Religion*, edited by J. C. A. Gaskin. Oxford: Oxford University Press, 1993.

Ramsden, Edmund and Jon Adams. "Escaping the Laboratory: The Rodent Experiments of John B. Calhoun & Their Cultural Influence." *Journal of Social History* (Spring 2009): 761–792.

Ryle, Gilbert. *Dilemmas*. Cambridge: Cambridge University Press, 1960.

Stove, David. *Darwinian Fairytales*. New York: Encounter Books, 1995.

Chapter 16

Is Science the Only Path to Truth?

Phil Fernandes and Matthew J. Coombe

The Assumptions and Limitations of Science

Atheists like Richard Dawkins often imply that science is the only valid way for man to find truth.[1] However, these atheists are simply mistaken. In order for scientific investigation to begin, scientists must make several assumptions—assumptions that cannot be proven through science (i.e., through the five senses). These assumptions are philosophical in nature; they deal with abstract reasoning rather than sense perception.

For the scientist to begin his work he must assume a real world exists outside his mind, his senses are reliable and not deceiving him, and truth and honesty are real.[2] A scientist cannot prove through experimentation that the real world exists outside his mind; for in his attempt to prove this, he must assume its existence before he uses his five senses to study this world.

To do science, a scientist must trust the data discovered through his five senses. Science does not prove the basic reliability of the five senses—it presupposes it. Likewise, the scientist assumes real truths exist that can be found through science, and that the results of his experimentation should be honestly reported. Yet truth cannot be placed in a test tube; it cannot be weighed or visually examined. Science presupposes truth is real but has no way of proving it is real. And honesty is a moral virtue that also cannot be examined through the five senses. In short, the existence of a real world outside the human mind, the basic reliability of sense perception, the existence of truth, and the reality of moral virtues like honesty cannot be proven through science. These are not scientific issues at all—they are philosophical assumptions that the scientist must make to justify the scientific endeavor.[3]

1 Dawkins, *The God Delusion*, 14, 58–66. See also Haught's description of scientific naturalism, a view held by Dawkins and rejected by Haught, in *God and the New Atheism*, 41.

2 Lennox, *God's Undertaker*, 31–45. See also Moreland, *Christianity and the Nature of Science*, 103–138.

3 Lennox, *God's Undertaker*, 31–45; Moreland, *Christianity and the Nature of Science*, 103–138.

Another reason science is not the only avenue through which truth can be found is the self-refuting nature of such a claim. The statement "Truth can only be found through the five senses" is a self-refuting statement. It cannot be true, for the statement itself cannot be proven to be true by the five senses. Therefore, there are other ways of finding truth than through the five senses (i.e., science).[4] This shows us that science is limited in its scope—there are truths that exist that cannot be discovered through the five senses alone. These would include moral laws, the concept of truth, virtues like love, and the concept of meaning in life.[5] Despite the fact that radical atheists like Dawkins want to proclaim science the sole arbiter of truth and knowledge, there are some truths and issues that are simply outside the field of science. These truths are in the domains of philosophy and religion. To argue that science alone can find truth is an extremely dogmatic stance that cannot be justified by the evidence.

The pragmatic limits of scientism are also troublesome. Scientism is not concerned with truth, but rather an unwavering commitment to "science-like-truth." The desire for science-like-truth is good, but within scientism such a desire results in a presupposition against other kinds of truths. J. P. Moreland argues that even the weak form of scientism "still implies that science is by far the most authoritative sector of human knowing."[6] Pragmatically, this presupposition results in scientific models and paradigms wherein the scientist's bias blinds him to his own contradictions: "We have seen that in science there is no direct route by logical reasoning from data to theory. Theories arise in acts of creative imagination in which models often play a role."[7] If one employs a creative imagination to posit a model for science (scientism), but the formulation of the model is replete with bad philosophies and contradictions, not even an absolute desire for science-like-truth can save the scientist.

Dawkins is a naturalist—he believes that all explanations must be physical explanations. This makes him a proponent of what has been labeled "scientism."[8] Scientism goes beyond the limited scope of science and demands that only natural or physical explanations be accepted—no non-physical or supernatural explanations are allowed—they are ruled out a priori (i.e., before any investigation of the evidence). While true science examines physical effects and goes wherever the evidence leads (whether it be a natural or supernatural cause), scientism dismisses any possibility of a supernatural or non-physical cause at the outset. Hence, scientism is not good science; it is a dogmatic bias against possible supernatural or non-natural causes. Scientism is a prejudiced

4 Geisler and Feinberg, *Introduction to Philosophy: A Christian Perspective*, 50–51.

5 Lennox, *God's Undertaker*, 38–43.

6 Moreland, *Scientism and Secularism*, 30.

7 Barbour, *Religion and Science*, 116.

8 Haught, *God and the New Atheism*, 17. See also D'Souza, *What's So Great about Christianity*, 160–164.

look at the evidence—it is not an objective, unbiased attempt to find truth.[9] Therefore, the failure of naturalism (i.e., scientism) to justify itself must be noted. Ronald Nash shows the futility of naturalism's attempt to justify itself by referring to the work of C. S. Lewis and Richard Taylor.[10] Nash argues that all our knowledge depends upon the validity of human reason; for if our reasoning ability is not valid, then we have no reason to trust the conclusions drawn by our reason. No scientific discoveries or claims to knowledge can be trusted if our reason does not work. If naturalism is true, then there is no basis for our faith in human reason.[11] Nash discusses an illustration given by Richard Taylor. Suppose a lady is on a train entering Wales and she sees white stones on a hillside spelling out "Welcome to Wales." This lady is free to believe, however unlikely it may be, that the white stones randomly spelled out those letters and that no intelligence placed the stones in that specific order to communicate the message that travelers are now entering Wales. But if she believes that the order of the white stones was a product of random causes, then she has no basis for trusting what the white stones tell her. She has no basis for believing the message is true and she is now entering Wales. The same dilemma occurs for the naturalist. The naturalist, like Richard Dawkins, is free to believe that human reasoning ability got here by chance and is not a product of rational causes. But then the naturalist has no reason to trust what his reason tells him. Naturalists believe our reason got here by chance; therefore, they have no reason to believe that their reason works. Hence, naturalists have no reason to believe that naturalism is true. In short, if naturalism is true then there is no way to know that it is true.[12] Dawkins' naturalism is accepted on blind faith. Apparently, he is not the unbiased, rational "Bright" that he claims to be.[13] While he ridicules religious people for their faith, even Dawkins has his own faith. But his faith is blind and not supported by the evidence.

Dawkins' Mistaken View of Faith and Reason

Dawkins' naturalism stems from his mistaken view of faith and reason. He wrongly assumes that, by definition, faith and reason are mutually exclusive. He believes that, by definition, religious faith is blind, and science alone is rational.[14] This is clearly a straw-man argument. Many religious people, like

9 Haught, *God and the New Atheism*, 17; D'Souza, *What's So Great about Christianity*, 160–164.

10 Nash, "Miracles and Conceptual Systems," 115–131.

11 Nash, "Miracles and Conceptual Systems," 127–130.

12 Nash, "Miracles and Conceptual Systems," 130–131.

13 Dawkins, *The God Delusion*, 338.

14 Lennox, 15–16.

the authors of this chapter, consider their faith to be based firmly on strong evidence. That Dawkins assumes all religious faith is non-rational or irrational does not mean that this is the case.

Even scientists must exercise faith. Scientists, as mentioned above, place faith in the reliability of the five senses and the existence of a real physical world independent of their minds. These cannot be proven through the five senses alone. In a debate with Oxford scholar John Lennox, Dawkins admitted that he has good reasons for the faith he has in his wife, thus contradicting his own view.[15] Hence, faith and reason are not mutually exclusive. When someone drives his car over a cement bridge suspended hundreds of feet above the ground, he is displaying great faith in man's technology to build adequate bridges. This is not blind faith, but a faith built upon evidence. Many Christians believe that their faith is not blind and that it is based upon evidence.

In fact, contrary to what Dawkins believes, a case can made that all people are religious. If when the Christian says, "God exists," he is uttering a religious statement, then when the atheist declares, "God does not exist," he is also uttering a religious statement. The subject does not change simply by the negating of an affirmation. If the belief that there is a God is a religious belief, then the belief there is no God is also a religious belief. As noted earlier, this point can be confirmed in several ways.

First, Webster's Dictionary provides as one of the definitions of religion: "a specific fundamental set of beliefs and practices generally agreed upon by a number of persons or sects."[16] On this wide definition of religion, since atheists and agnostics share common fundamental beliefs and practices, they are clearly in the "religious" camp.

Second, the 1961 Torcaso versus Watkins United States Supreme Court decision declared secular humanism to be as much a religion as theistic religions.[17] The court noted that traditional Buddhism is agnostic concerning the existence of God, yet no one denies that traditional Buddhism is a religion. Hence, one does not have to believe in God to be religious.

Third, the first *Humanist Manifesto*, written in 1933 and signed by some of the world's leading atheists and agnostics, declared secular humanism to be a religion.[18] Secular humanism is a belief system based on the belief that there is no God and that the universe got here through naturalistic causes alone.

Hence, all people are religious; all people hold deeply cherished beliefs and build their lives upon the foundation of those beliefs. Even the apathetic person builds his life upon his apathy. Even the skeptic is dogmatic about his skepticism. "Nothing human is alien to the religious." This is as true for the

15 This occurred in a 2007 debate between John Lennox and Richard Dawkins.

16 *Random House Webster's College Dictionary*, 1113.

17 Geisler, *Is Man the Measure?*, 164.

18 Kurtz, *Humanist Manifestos I and II*, 3, 7–10.

atheist as it is for the Christian or another theist. Therefore, Dawkins' dogmatic belief that religious people have irrational faith whereas atheists accept only what can be rationally proven is simply not true. Dawkins is as religious as Christians or theists. The question is not, "Should I be religious?" Everyone, including Dawkins, already is. Instead, the question should be, "Is my religion based on the evidence or refuted by the evidence?" If Dawkins is not religious, then why does he write with so much passion and religious fervor?

In conclusion, scientism itself is a religion—it leaves the domain of true science which goes wherever the evidence leads. Scientism naively accepts the philosophical worldview called naturalism, a worldview that fails to account for the validity of human reason. And the validity of human reason is essential to the development of a worldview that is built upon the evidence. Scientism fails—science is clearly not the only way to find truth.

Bibliography

Barbour, Ian G. *Religion and Science: Historical and Contemporary Issues*. San Francisco: HarperSanFrancisco, 1997.

Dawkins, Richard. *The God Delusion*. London: Black Swan, 2016.

D'Souza, Dinesh. *What's So Great about Christianity*. Washington, DC: Regnery Publishing, 2007.

Geisler, Norman L. *Is Man the Measure?* Grand Rapids, MI: Baker Book House, 1983.

Geisler, Norman L. and Paul D. Feinberg. *Introduction to Philosophy: A Christian Perspective*. Grand Rapids: Baker Book House, 1980.

Haught, John F. *God and the New Atheism*. Louisville, KY: Westminster John Knox Press, 2008.

Kurtz, Paul, ed. *Humanist Manifestos I and II*. Amherst, NY: Prometheus Books, 1973.

Lennox, John C. *God's Undertaker: Has Science Buried God?* Oxford: Lion Books, 2007.

Moreland, J. P. *Christianity and the Nature of Science*. Grand Rapids, MI: Baker Book House, 1989.

———. *Scientism and Secularism*. Wheaton, IL: Crossway, 2018.

Nash, Ronald. "Miracles and Conceptual Systems." In *In Defense of Miracles*, edited by Douglas R. Geivett and Gary R. Habermas, 115–131. Downers Grove: InterVarsity, 1997.

Random House Webster's College Dictionary. New York: Random House, 1999.

Section III:

On the Human Person

Part I:

Abortion and Euthanasia

Chapter 17

The Sanctity of Life in Light of the Incarnation[1]

Scott D. G. Ventureyra

> "I've noticed that everybody that is for abortion has already been born."
> —Ronald Reagan, 40th President of the USA

Although President Reagan's famous statement at first blush comes across as a truism, it is a rather profound reflection about those who advocate for abortion. It exposes simultaneously an abortionist's hypocrisy and inconsistency. They who were granted life not by their choice ironically inveigh against the most fundamental right—the right to live—for those without a say in the matter.

Every year, Catholics, Anglicans, and Lutherans celebrate the Feast of the Holy Innocents on December 28,[2] remembering the extermination of young boys (two years and younger) in Bethlehem, which was ordained by King Herod the Great in a bid to kill the King of Kings: Jesus (Mt 2:16–18). In modern times, we face a much more ominous and widespread massacre. In a similar fashion, we should keep in memory all those created in His image and likeness who never had the opportunity to be born. In 2019, there were 83,576 abortions reported in Canada.[3] Recently, it was discovered that thousands have gone unreported. Be that as it may, from 1990 to 2014, the abortion rate worldwide ranged from 49.7 million to 56.3 million.[4] The Guttmacher Institute has estimated that between 2010 and 2014, the yearly world abortion rate increased to an average of 55.9 million.[5] If we take the lowest average of 49.7 million abortions per year, over

1 For the original see, Scott Ventureyra, "The Sanctity of Life in Light of the Incarnation," *Catholic Insight*, November 28, 2018, https://catholicinsight.com/the-sanctity-of-life-in-light-of-the-incarnation/.

2 Eastern Orthodox Christians celebrate it on December 29 and Eastern Syrian Christians on January 10.

3 Abortion Rights Coalition of Canada, "Abortion Statistics in Canada." Interestingly, there has been a steady decrease of abortions from 2011 to 2019. The reasons for this could be many, such as younger men reportedly not having sex. The accuracy of these figures would be the subject of entirely separate study. Nevertheless, to see rates decrease, whatever the reason, is encouraging even if it is not due to an increase in a collective moral awareness.

4 Sedgh, et al., "Abortion incidence between 1990 and 2014: global, regional, and subregional levels and trends," 263.

5 Singh, et al., "Abortion Worldwide 2017: Uneven Progress and Unequal Access."

a five-year span, then we would have a total of 248.5 million aborted infants worldwide. Given this bleak figure, it is worth considering that estimated death rates from World War I range between 8 million and 21 million, and for World War II between 56 million and 85 million. If we tally up the highest estimates, the total would be 106 million. Moreover, the worldwide abortion rate from 1990 to 2014 is also significantly higher than the slaughter committed by Adolf Hitler (17 million), Hideki Tojo (5 million), Josef Stalin (23 million), Mao Zedong (78 million), and Pol Pot (1.7 million) all who amassed a total of 124.7 million deaths.[6] Appallingly, the abortion rate for the aforementioned five-year period was close to double those perpetrated by these genocidal maniacs. Now, one may argue that this is an unfair comparison, since the massacre that millions upon millions faced from these despots were of fully grown humans. I don't intend to enter into a discussion on the science of fetal pain, even though there is a growing scientific literature indicating that unborn humans can feel pain as early as twelve weeks.[7] These figures pertain to the most fundamental and basic human right, the right to life. This precept is consistent with a deontological approach to the sanctity of life, whereby abortion is considered to be morally prohibited (exception when the mother's life is in clear danger). On such grounds, regardless of the circumstances surrounding a pregnancy, whatever reasoning may be made in favour of abortion, it is trumped by one's right to live. Once this fundamental right is stripped then any number of other rights become expendable. Tragically, what is supposed to be the safest place on Earth (the mother's womb) has actually become the most inhospitable and hostile place for the most vulnerable.

Remembering the Unborn

Several years ago, on Remembrance Day, at Immaculate Heart of Mary Church in Ottawa, which I have attended since I was child, Father Joe LeClair delivered a powerful sermon. Father LeClair is a controversial figure who, in the past, has made some poor decisions with grave legal consequences, but he has a talent for engaging people on emotionally difficult subjects. His sermon linked the deaths of World War I and II with all the forgotten unborn children. LeClair's message was simple but poignant. He asked the congregants to remember these forgotten children who never received the opportunity to live outside their mother's womb. He also spoke of his niece who has Down syndrome and how her life has been a blessing to his whole family.[8] Unfortunately, in our culture,

6 Carlos, "Top Ten Most Evil Dictators of All Time (in order of kill count)."

7 For a series of references and a discussion on this topic of fetal pain, see Charlotte Lozier Institute, "Fact Sheet: Science of Fetal Pain."

8 See chapter in this volume titled "Dawkins' Unholy Trinity: Incoherency, Hypocrisy and Bigotry" for Dawkins' abhorrent statement regarding morality and abortion.

we seem to think we can dispense with people who may be "inconvenient." Some may think it is more convenient to abort a child, for any possible reason, than to take full responsibility for their actions. It was interesting that at this Mass, a friend of mine who many years ago had an abortion had asked to attend with me, something that she had never done before. Divine providence utilized Father LeClair as a vehicle to communicate to her and others who may have had a similar experience: while God willingly takes the unborn back to Himself, those who are unrepentant will be accountable for their choice.

The Incarnation: A Christological Argument against Abortion

The miracle of the Incarnation exemplifies the extraordinary biological process of human birth. God could have chosen many different conceivable ways of entering the world, but He chose to come in the most vulnerable form, as a dependent infant who required his mother's love and care. Just as we experience pain and suffering, God made Himself susceptible to both human and natural evil through His Incarnation. Christ submitted Himself to God's providence, subjecting Himself to many of life's cruel and contingent occurrences. Indeed, God the Son took the human form of Jesus, with a fully human nature. Christ embodies both fully divine and human natures through the hypostatic union.

The conception of Christ provides a Christological argument against abortion. The New Testament shows that Christ's assumption of human nature commenced at his conception. This is illustrated in Luke 1:26-37 with Gabriel's annunciation to Mary of the miracle of Christ's conception: "The Holy Spirit will come on you, and the power of the Most High will overshadow you. So the holy one to be born will be called the Son of God." If we deny that at conception Christ took a fully human nature in Mary's womb, where does this lead us? What if His human nature was assumed after conception, perhaps gradually, throughout the pregnancy, or at the moment of birth? Was Christ's human nature separate from His divine nature? If there are two persons in Christ, this would bring about an ancient heresy known as Nestorianism (a notion developed by the patriarch-theologian Nestorius); this heresy denies the hypostatic union and argues that there are two distinct persons within Christ: God, the divine Son, and the man Jesus, who at some point was adopted by the Son later on.[9] This was condemned at the Council of Ephesus in 431 and at the Council of Chalcedon in 451.

Human persons are both matter and form, i.e., composites of body and soul. The most convincing position regarding Christ's dual nature is that His human

9 Kelly, "Nestorius."

body and soul come into being simultaneously. This is true whether one adopts a traducian position (where a human person's soul is naturally transmitted through the souls of the parents) or a creationist one (where all souls are created directly by God). If personhood (the coming-into-being of the soul) occurs after conception but not simultaneously with the body, then this would reveal an offshoot of the heretical position of Apollinarianism—in this particular case, that Christ had no human soul until some time after conception. Thus, the body existed without a soul. These Christological issues can be circumvented if we follow the Church teaching: "The unique and altogether singular event of the Incarnation of the Son of God does not mean that Jesus Christ is part God and part man, nor does it imply that he is the result of a confused mixture of the divine and the human. He became truly man while remaining truly God. Jesus Christ is true God and true man."[10]

Raising Awareness among Christians

In Canada, the position adopted on abortion by the Liberal Party and other "progressives" is utterly wrongheaded. For instance, Prime Minister Justin Trudeau is highly intolerant of any dissent on abortion. In 2014, he didn't allow any pro-life candidates to run for the Liberal Party. Even though Trudeau claims to be a Catholic, he is a staunch supporter of abortion and assisted suicide. Instead of concerning himself with issues within Canada, he and the Liberal Party have been using Canadian tax dollars to promote leftist ideology, through the allocation of $650 million (in 2017 alone) to promote "reproductive rights" and fight anti-abortion laws globally.[11] He also plans on spending 1.4 billion dollars on this from 2023 forward.[12] By such behavior, Trudeau combines ignorance and immorality. Aside from the fact that the Liberal Government is amassing a tremendous amount of unsustainable debt, they could reallocate such funds for more pressing and legitimate issues, such as helping businesses and individuals struggling from the draconian restrictions imposed by both provincial and federal governments because of COVID-19. It is not the responsibility of the Canadian government to promote the annihilation of the unborn abroad, or at home, for that matter.

In late September of 2017, Liberal Members of Parliament (MPs) walked out on Rachel Harder, a pro-life MP who was picked as woman committee chair for the Conservative Party of Canada. This disregard for not only truth but also common decency, dialogue, and understanding has become pervasive

10 *Catechism of the Catholic Church*, 117.

11 Carbert, "Canada spending $650-million on reproductive rights."

12 Carbert and Woo, "Trudeau announces hundreds of millions in foreign aid for women's health."

across Canada. In a similar vein, there has been legislations passed in Ontario by the Liberal provincial government, led at the time by the radical Kathleen Wynne, to establish ridiculous "safe access zones" of 50 to 150 meters around abortion clinics for the purpose of preventing "harassment." In 2018, Father Tony Van Lee was arrested for praying near a "safe zone."[13] In fact, harassment laws already prevent attempts to block access to clinics. The new law is just another way for abortion proponents to silence pro-life demonstrators and protect the current abortion laws. Finally, a few years ago, the Liberals required applicants for the Canada Summer Jobs program to state they were pro-abortion. However, as a political ploy to retain Judeo-Christian and pro-life voters, they recently dropped this anti-abortion test, which sought to punish pro-life organizations.

It is important to note that as neonatal science advances, the prolife case grows stronger.[14] It is with good reason that organizations such as Planned Parenthood do not offer ultrasounds for prenatal care.[15] The best currently available treatise on this is Francis Beckwith's excellent *Defending Life: A Moral and Legal Case against the Abortion Choice.*[16] Those in favour of abortion cannot consistently support human rights, nor can they be consistent Christians who respect all life. So-called progressives (I prefer the term "regressive") should note that terminating an unborn life is a form of discrimination based on age and geographic location.

Whenever we respect life and let the unborn live, we truly honour and follow God's command to love Him with all our heart, soul, strength, and mind (Luke 10:27). When reflecting upon the miracle of the Incarnation, we must be mindful that just as Christ's conception was indeed a miracle, so is the conception of every human person (whether they have been afforded the chance to be born or not).

Bibliography

Abortion Rights Coalition of Canada. "Abortion Statistics in Canada." Updated March 28, 2021. http://www.arcc-cdac.ca/backrounders/statistics-abortion-in-canada.pdf.

Beckwith, Francis J. *Defending Life: A Moral and Legal Case against Abortion Choice.* Oxford: Oxford University Press, 2007.

Carbert, Michelle. "Canada spending $650-million on reproductive rights, including fighting global anti-abortion laws." *Globe and Mail,* March 8,

13 Risdon, "Police charge 83-year-old pro-life priest."
14 Lewis, "Pro-abortion, anti-science."
15 Chretien, "Planned Parenthood caught on video."
16 Beckwith, *Defending Life.*

2017. https://www.theglobeandmail.com/news/politics/ottawa-announces-650-million-for-sexual-and-reproductive-health/article34237503/.

Carbert, Michelle and Andrea Woo. "Trudeau announces hundreds of millions in foreign aid for women's health, amid 'attacks' on abortion rights." *Globe and Mail,* June 4, 2019. https://www.theglobeandmail.com/politics/article-trudeau-announces-billions-in-foreign-aid-for-maternal-and-child/.

Carlos, Juan. "Top Ten Most Evil Dictators of All Time (in order of kill count)." *Juan Carlos.* https://www.jcpe.tv/top-ten-most-evil-dictators-of-all-time-in-order-of-kill-count/.

Catechism of the Catholic Church. 2nd ed. Vatican City: Libreria Editrice Vaticana, 1997.

Charlotte Lozier Institute. "Fact Sheet: Science of Fetal Pain." February 9, 2021. https://lozierinstitute.org/fact-sheet-science-of-fetal-pain/.

Chretien, Claire. "Planned Parenthood caught on video: 'We only do ultrasounds' for abortion." *LifeSite News,* January 31, 2017. https://www.lifesitenews.com/news/breaking-undercover-video-shows-planned-parenthoods-nationwide-will-only-do.

Kelly, John N. D. "Nestorius." *Encyclopedia Britannica,* May 9, 2021. https://www.britannica.com/biography/Nestorius.

Lewis, Brenna. "Pro-abortion, anti-science." *Students for Life,* August 1, 2018. https://studentsforlife.org/2018/08/01/pro-abortion-anti-science/.

Risdon, James. "Police charge 83-year-old pro-life priest who was praying too close to Canadian abortion mill." *LifeSite News,* October 25, 2018. https://www.lifesitenews.com/news/police-charge-83-year-old-pro-life-priest-who-was-praying-too-close-to-cana.

Sedgh, Gilda, et al. "Abortion incidence between 1990 and 2014: global, regional, and subregional levels and trends." *Lancet* 388 (May 2016): 258–267. https://www.thelancet.com/action/showPdf?pii=S0140-6736%2816%2930380-4.

Singh, Susheela, et al. "Abortion Worldwide 2017: Uneven Progress and Unequal Access." *Guttmacher Institute.* https://www.guttmacher.org/report/abortion-worldwide-2017.

Chapter 18

Demolishing Secular Pretensions: Assisted Suicide, the Media, and Relativism[1]

Scott D. G. Ventureyra

Several discussions with a friend on the subject of human dignity and the sanctity of life led to a reflection on the legalization of assisted suicide in Canada. My friend, although a lapsed Christian, means well. He longs for self-transcendence, but as many people do, he searches for it through false avenues. It consistently seems to elude him, but I pray that he will receive God's grace (as I do for many others). Sometimes this friend seems so close but still so far from recognizing truth. He is an unfortunate casualty of the complete morass of Western culture. This quagmire we find ourselves in is due in large part to the unmitigated control of the media over society, through newspaper articles, TV shows, movies, and the like. For instance, many journalists writing for major newspapers are expected to follow a script which often ridicules religious beliefs while bolstering liberal secular viewpoints.

It is a time where unreflective thought is frequently celebrated. Slogans and caricatures of real issues posted on Facebook and Twitter feeds are considered to be enlightened wisdom. Indeed, individuals in general, even though thinking they are free to decide and vote, have been the victims of systematic brainwashing through the internet and various other media outlets. The question is, can democracy truly cope with such monsters? With this type of manipulation and control, the answer seems quite grim. Despite the ease of access to all sorts of information, including credible and valuable sources, through the internet, society as a whole has lost its ability to think critically and sift the good from the bad. This is also a sad reflection on many who consider themselves to be university-educated. The corrective to this problem is education emphasizing critical thinking, through which we can be liberated from the shackles of liberal secular ideology that has dominated so many of our academic institutions for the past 50 years or so.

1 For the original, see Scott Ventureyra, "Demolishing Secular Pretensions: Assisted Suicide, the Media, and Relativism," *Catholic Insight*, March 26, 2016, https://catholicinsight.com/demolishing-secular-pretensions-assisted-suicide-the-media-and-relativism/.

Often, when we find ourselves in moments when we think that we cannot help someone like my above-mentioned friend, there is an opening, no matter how slight. My friend responded to an article I sent him by John Paul Meenan: "The Totalitarian Imposition of Euthanasia in Canada," with some questions that opened the possibility for dialogue. He asked why one should not be allowed to kill themselves if they want to, particularly if they are not physically capable. Then he proceeded to ask what the "big picture" was surrounding such issues. What follows is part of my response to him.

Doctors are not "compelled" to provide assisted suicide. However, part of the big picture includes doctors being implicated in it through "effective" and "timely" referrals despite their personal or religious beliefs. This does not set a good precedent; things could easily get worse in the foreseeable future. It makes doctors who have a moral conscience against such practices into accomplices. It is a form of totalitarianism.[2] Those interested in informing themselves should read the "Interim Guidance on Physician-Assisted Death" published by the College of Physicians and Surgeons of Ontario.[3]

In the end, it all comes down to what is ethically right. If we are just accidental, unplanned assemblages of matter where consciousness and the "self" are merely a delusion, then ultimately questions about life and death are of no consequence. This is the presumption underlying the Canadian legislation of pernicious unreflective secular dogmas. North America is turning into a greater mess every day. It reflects an ongoing celebration of the culture of death, at both extremes of human life. It is an abolition of the human person and our supposed dignity. One will only begin to understand how society will slowly descend into the depths of nihilism as things move more and more in this direction. It is also a culture of relativism (which is impossible to live out consistently), where slogans such as "that's his/her choice" and "it has nothing to do with me" are mindlessly repeated. Once it begins to affect you personally, you start to see that moral relativism does not work. It is ironic to see those who deem themselves "progressive" typically uphold moral and religious relativism. Thus, as self-described progressives, they cannot improve their morality. There is no moral reform since this presupposes an objective standard of acting, but that is what is denied by relativists. If there is no better method of behaving, then there can be no improvement. After all, it is ultimately "his/her choice." There are no real moral standards, just preferences. Nevertheless, evil has to be denounced for what it is. That is why questions about God and the afterlife are fundamental

2 See Meenan, "The Totalitarian Imposition of Euthanasia in Canada." See College of Physicians and Surgeons of Ontario, "Interim Guidance on Physician-Assisted Death Online Survey Report and Analysis."

3 College of Physicians and Surgeons of Ontario, "Interim Guidance on Physician-Assisted Death."

to ethical issues. Otherwise, as Protagoras declared, "man is the measure of all things." In the apocalyptic lyrics of King Crimson's song "Epitaph," a similar pronouncement is made regarding the deadliness of knowledge when it isn't grounded in objective morality. The poignant words of "Epitaph" beautifully capture the state in which contemporary Western culture finds itself in.

Years ago, another friend, who is a Muslim and contributor to this volume, made a comment that stuck with my friend mentioned above: "everything in this life is a test." Indeed, I pointed out to the latter friend that this was absolutely right; that is, there are eternal consequences to our actions in this life.

God provides us with opportunities to make an impact on the lives of others. Sometimes we do not see the direct or potential impact of our action, but we must always be prepared to be a witness to the Gospel through our varied talents in whatever way we can. It is my hope that my friend will give more thought to issues of life, death (suicide), and God. This will help us to do God's will and help others to draw closer to Him. Let us be reminded of St. Paul's much-needed words: "We demolish arguments and every pretension that sets itself up against the knowledge of God, and we take captive every thought to make it obedient to Christ" (2 Cor 10:5).

Bibliography

College of Physicians and Surgeons of Ontario. "Interim Guidance on Physician-Assisted Death Online Survey Report and Analysis." February 8, 2016. http://policyconsult.cpso.on.ca/wp-content/uploads/2016/02/CPSO-Interim-Guidance-on-Physician-Assisted-Death-Survey-Report.pdf.

Meenan, John Paul. "The Totalitarian Imposition of Euthanasia in Canada." *Crisis*, March 7, 2016. https://www.crisismagazine.com/2016/the-totalitarian-imposition-of-assisted-suicide-in-canada.

Chapter 19

Euthanasia and Assisted Suicide: Eugenics in Disguise

Brenna Bloodworth

Euthanasia and assisted suicide (collectively referred to as EAS) policies are gaining traction throughout the world as the practice becomes increasingly normalized and accepted at the behest of policy makers and "right to die" advocates. The implications posed by rapidly progressing EAS policies are often left out of public discussion, providing little opportunity to examine the risks of such policies and whether or not they are truly being proposed in the best interests of the people.

There is one major difference between euthanasia and assisted suicide: assisted suicide only has doctors provide the patient with a lethal drug, which the patient administers themselves, whereas euthanasia sees the physician administer the lethal dose of the drug to the patient. Both methods have one very significant thing in common—they are in clear violation of the centuries-old Hippocratic Oath, which states: "I will not give a lethal drug to anyone if I am asked, nor will I advise such a plan." Of course, the Hippocratic Oath has been altered and modernized many times over the years, but a physician's duty to do no harm largely remains a core principle to which all physicians swear.[1] Despite this, assisted suicide and euthanasia have occurred for many centuries, even when and where they have been clearly outlawed. During the 19th and 20th centuries, euthanasia was widely discussed in terms of the principles of Darwinism and eugenics. The term "euthanasia" was embraced and used in Nazi Germany to describe the "mercy" killings of over 300,000 mentally and physically disabled people, who were seen to not fit the image of the ideal human.[2] This tragedy made euthanasia an incredibly sensitive subject in Germany and throughout the world, leaving the practice of euthanasia and any other type of mercy killing prohibited in most parts of the world until the early 1990s.

1 Ahlzen, "Suffering, Authenticity, and Physician Assisted Suicide."

2 Berenbaum, "T4 Program."

The extreme push for equality in the treatment of people facing various forms of illness and respect of an individual's bodily autonomy has led to euthanasia and assisted-suicide becoming a topic of heavy debate among healthcare providers, governments, policy makers, and religious groups, and has led a small number of countries to decriminalize and implement some form of the practice.[3] These laws were largely passed as means to allow terminally ill patients to end their life as a means to cease their inevitable suffering, or to void doctors of liability should a patient choose to refuse treatment, resulting in death. However, as EAS policies have evolved over the past few decades, the lines between euthanasia or assisted suicide and murder have become increasingly blurry, raising the question whether what were once intended to be supportive policies to help alleviate unbearable and untreatable suffering have evolved into the killing of people suffering from treatable mental health conditions,[4] masking a hidden agenda—eugenics.[5]At least eight countries throughout the world have legalized and actively implemented some method of EAS, including Canada, Belgium, Switzerland, Germany, Finland, the Netherlands, and some parts of the United States.[6] Only five of these countries have legalized euthanasia in the strict sense. Except in Switzerland and the Netherlands, these policies have only been introduced within the past thirty years. A few other countries have opted to allow "passive" euthanasia, in respect of a person's "right to die," which voids doctors of liability for taking no action should a patient decide to refuse treatment for their terminal condition[7] but does not allow any lethal drug to be provided or administered. Most countries have criminalized all forms of EAS due to the significant moral and ethical dilemmas involved.[8]A major factor in determining eligibility to make a request for assisted death in any country which it is allowed is typically that the patient is of sound mind, with the mental capacity to make the decision independently and rationally, and fully understands the implications of their choice.[9] Though a person may be facing death as a result of their illness, choosing assisted dying often means foregoing treatment that could increase quality of life or longevity. Choosing death ultimately means ending a life earlier than it needs to end. Opening the door to euthanasia and assisted dying for people with mental illness immediately raises the concern that such a decision will be made by someone who may not have the capacity to make such a decision. Although it is often defended on the grounds of equality and bodily autonomy, and many safeguards are in place that are intended to ensure that a mentally ill person is making the decision

3 ProCon.org, "Euthanasia & Physician-Assisted Suicide (PAS) around the World."

4 Tuffrey-Wijne, et al., "Euthanasia and assisted suicide for people with an intellectual disability"; Mehlum, et al., "Euthanasia and assisted suicide in patients with personality disorders."

5 Kim, "Lives Not Worth Living in Modern Euthanasia Regimes."

6 ProCon.org, "Euthanasia & Physician-Assisted Suicide (PAS) around the World."

7 ProCon.org, "What Is Passive Euthanasia?"

rationally, these safeguards have been repeatedly shown to be insufficient or ineffective, resulting in the deaths of many people who, to put it simply, had the full potential to live healthy, happy, and meaningful lives.[10]

For a mentally ill person to access EAS, two physicians typically must agree that the patient seeking EAS will not otherwise improve in their condition, even with treatment.[11] Alarmingly, documents have shown that in many cases where EAS has been approved for people suffering from mental illness, no other treatment options had been attempted, rendering the determination that the patients were incapable of improvement unjust and without due rationale.[12] In fact, one study reported that in 2013, nearly two percent of documented cases of euthanasia were done without any explicit request having been made. The same study also found that less than half the people euthanized in Belgium have it documented and reported to the appropriate registry.[13] Unfortunately, these failed safeguards lead to very few criminal convictions of the involved physicians,[14] though their determination of the patient's prognosis and resulting actions are essentially a Nazi-Germany-style "mercy" killing.

In the Netherlands, one of the first two countries to allow access to EAS for people with mental illness, children as young as twelve years old, referred to as "mature minors," are able to request EAS with parental consent. Children who are sixteen and seventeen years old can make the request themselves, as long as their parents are aware and involved in the process, and eighteen-year-olds can request EAS without parental knowledge or consent.[15] Similarly, Belgium also has no minimum age for mature minors to make EAS requests, but requires that children under the age of twelve wishing to access EAS must be suffering from a terminal illness. In both of these countries, EAS policies now allow euthanasia of people living with intellectual disability, cognitive disabilities, autism, behavioural disorders,[16] and even loneliness,[17] for both adults and mature minors. The circumstances causing unbearable suffering that lead patients who live with these conditions to request EAS are not always a direct result of their condition. Unfortunately, financial and socioeconomic

8 Banović and Turanjanin, "Euthanasia: Murder or Not: A Comparative Approach."

9 Annabel, et al., "Concepts of mental capacity for patients requesting assisted suicide."

10 Mehlum, et al., "Euthanasia and assisted suicide in patients with personality disorders"; Pereira, "Legalizing euthanasia or assisted suicide: the illusion of safeguards and controls."

11 Verhofstadt, et al., "Psychiatric patients requesting euthanasia: Guidelines for sound clinical and ethical decision making."

12 Kasper, et al., "Euthanasia in Belgium: Shortcomings of the Law."

13 Chambaere, et al., "Recent trends in euthanasia and other end-of-life practices in Belgium."

14 Lewis, et al., "Accusations of Murder and Euthanasia in End-of-Life Care."

15 Vrakking, et al., "Regulating physician-assisted dying for minors in the Netherlands."

16 Waddell, "Autism and Assisted Suicide"; Stainton, "Disability, vulnerability and assisted death."

17 Jones and Simpson, "Medical Assistance in Dying: Challenges for Psychiatry."

difficulties and inequalities have also been documented as causes of the feelings of hopelessness behind some EAS requests.[18] It is astounding to think that because the proper support cannot feasibly be offered by the treating physician, they are left to agree that there is no reasonable alternative that could improve their patient's life.

For what purpose would any rational person see it as acceptable to aid in the death of a person suffering from mental illness, especially a child, when this is not in their best interest or the only alternative to a life without suffering? For the purpose of eugenics, the alleged improvement of the human race through selective breeding and the elimination of disease, disability, or other undesirable human traits.[19] It is no secret that mental illness is most likely to be passed down from generation to generation, or that it requires a tremendous amount of money and resources for any healthcare system to support it. By offering assisted death to people dealing with mental illness, a great financial burden on the healthcare system is alleviated,[20] while the potential for mental illness to continue in further generations through breeding is reduced and, eventually, eliminated.

While the world is grappling with COVID and mental health issues have dramatically risen among all populations since the crisis first began for much of the world at the beginning of 2020,[21] the concept of offering access to assisted death to people dealing with mental illness is an issue that should not be ignored. Within the span of only a few months, while most countries have imposed tyrannical lockdown measures aimed at saving lives—coincidently, the lives of the many of the same vulnerable populations whose killing EAS policies are increasingly legalizing—various governments are currently gathering to introduce or expand their own EAS policies. In December 2020, Spain and Chile approved legalization of both euthanasia and assisted suicide; in early 2021 Canada moved to expand eligibility for EAS to people living with mental illness beginning in 2023, and has been considering expanding EAS eligibility to "mature minors" for several years;[22] and in April 2021 France began to explore the possibility of legalizing EAS. To the surprise of many, due to the country's grim history with mercy killing, Germany's top court also legalized assisted suicide in 2020.[23] During the supposed "fourth wave" of COVID nearly two years later, what patient-centered support EAS is intended to provide is further

18 Stoll, et al., "Perceived Burdensomeness and the Wish for Hastened Death."

19 Cheyfitz, "Who Decides? The Connecting Thread of Euthanasia"; Bingham, "Involuntary Sterilisation, Eugenics, and Physician."

20 Emanuel and Battin, "What are the potential cost savings from legalizing physician-assisted suicide?"

21 Abbott, "COVID's mental-health toll: how scientists are tracking a surge in depression."

22 Council of Canadian Academies, "The State of Knowledge on Medical Assistance in Dying for Mature Minors," 117–119.

23 Horn, "The right to a self-determined death as expression of the right to freedom of personal development."

confused as such support becomes secondary in importance to supporting those fearing death from COVID. The increasingly illogical fight against the disease has resulted in Germany's Euthanasia Association announcing in December 2021 the requirement of vaccination, or becoming ill with and recovering from COVID, in order to be eligible to access EAS.[24] Though the prospect of misused or abused EAS policies resulting in unnecessary death for a person dealing with mental illness, autism, intellectual disability, or loneliness is terrifying it itself, one might wonder what could come next. Can it get any worse? Unfortunately, it does. Aside from such policies progressing to include even physical disabilities, as seen in Belgium,[25] such policies raise the question who gets to decide when the person with an eligible condition has a surrogate decision-maker. As is the case when it comes to any other health care decision,[26] surrogate decision makers will eventually be granted the right to request EAS for their dependent in the push for equal access to "treatment" options. In the case of people facing terminal illness, for which EAS policies originated, it is already ingrained in most countries' EAS policies that such a person who is without the mental capacity and with a substitute decision maker, the surrogate is indeed granted the ability to request EAS.[27]

Should countries continue to follow each other's lead in the development of such policies, we are heading down a slippery slope indeed. Deaths by EAS have increased dramatically over the past ten years,[28] with EAS deaths accounting for nearly five percent of all deaths in the Netherlands in 2015.[29] We are currently heading at a rapid pace towards the normalization and acceptance of mercy killing, and it is all being done under the guise of support and respect of bodily autonomy. Despite governments and policy makers showing significantly increased willingness to implement EAS policies over the years, the greater number of health care providers and disability advocates have spoken out and remained against it.

A 2017 study found that twenty-four out of twenty-nine declarations made by healthcare organizations around the world, most recently in 2016 by the World Medical Association, have strongly condemned the practice of EAS.[30] Catalina Devandas-Aguilar, the United Nations Special Rapporteur on the rights of persons with disabilities, released a report to the UN in December 2019 in which she warned, "If assisted dying is made available for persons

24 Chaya, "Covid vaccine now mandatory to get euthanized in Germany."

25 Nicol, "Medical Assistance in Dying: The Law in Selected Jurisdictions outside Canada."

26 DeMartino, et al., "Who Decides When a Patient Can't?"; Harrison, "Treatment decisions regarding infants, children and adolescents," 9

27 Reddy and Hahn-Chaet, "AMA Code of Medical Ethics' Opinions Related to End-of-Life Care"; Government of Canada, "Options and decision-making at end of life."

28 Nicol, "Medical Assistance in Dying: The Law in Selected Jurisdictions outside Canada."

29 Kouwenhoven, et al., "Developments in euthanasia practice in the Netherlands."

30 Inbadas, et al., "Declarations on euthanasia and assisted dying."

with health conditions or impairments, but who are not terminally ill, a social assumption could be made that it is better to be dead than to live with a disability," and further goes on to state, "People have the right to live and to die with dignity, but we cannot accept that people choose to end their lives because of social stigma, isolation or lack of access to personal assistance or disability-related services"[31]—a point which governments and policy-makers throughout the world have begun to ignore as EAS policies continue to expand to include such populations.

Throughout history, people have fought to protect our most vulnerable populations. We have fought against the stigmatization of mental illness; we have fought to eliminate segregation and promote inclusion of people with disabilities; we have worked tirelessly to make advancements in health care to extend and better the lives of people with chronic illness. Despite the progress made, many of these populations have remained marginalized due to inadequate funding and policies that leave support difficult to access, and now we have begun advocating to end the very same lives we have fought so hard to save. If nothing is done to alter the current trajectory of EAS policies, we are heading into very dangerous territory and putting many lives at further risk.

Health care providers and disability advocates are continuously fighting to bring attention to the lack of appropriate support available to people who may be seeking EAS. Some studies even noted that no alternative treatment options were offered to some patients seeking EAS not because such options do not exist, but because they are often not accessible by the patient, whether for financial or geographical reasons, or due to lengthy wait times.[32] In Oregon, a patient only needs to be informed of other treatment options, but no attempts to offer or pursue them are required.[33] These challenges take their toll not only on patients themselves, but also on their family and friends, and the physicians involved.[34]

More must be done to respect the dignity of individuals and their potential to live, by providing timely and equitable access to any mental, physical social, or financial supports necessary to improve and maintain quality of life. Euthanasia or assisted suicide is without a doubt an unconscionable "treatment" option for persons living with mental illness and other disabilities. Death is not a solution to the challenges they face, but a solution to the now widely perceived burden of their lives. This perspective is both cruel and irresponsible

31 Devandas-Aguilar, "Report from the Special Rapporteur on the rights of persons with disabilities."

32 Verhofstadt, et al., "When unbearable suffering incites psychiatric patients to request euthanasia."

33 Disability Rights Education & Defense Fund, "Why Assisted Suicide Must Not Be Legalized."

34 Evenblij, et al., "Physicians' experiences with euthanasia"; Brody, "Physician-Assisted Suicide: Family Issues."

and has the power to fuel an incredibly dangerous way of thinking. The past and present state of euthanasia and EAS policies throughout the world offer many stark reminders of the dangers that will be faced by people living with mental illness or disability should we continue on this trajectory, and it will occur on a scale greater than we've ever seen before. If history has taught us anything, this is not a direction in which we should allow our governments to continue to lead us. The normalization and acceptance of mercy killing will equate to the normalization and acceptance of eugenics. This cannot be viewed or defined as support while people's basic needs for having a life worth living continue to be neglected.

Bibliography

Abbott, Alison. "COVID's mental-health toll: how scientists are tracking a surge in depression." *Nature* 590 (2021): 194–5. https://doi.org/10.1038/d41586-021-00175-z.

Ahlzen, R. "Suffering, Authenticity, and Physician Assisted Suicide." *Medicine, Health Care and Philosophy* 23, 3 (2020): 353–359. https://doi.org/10.1007/s11019-019-09929-z.

Banović, Božidar, et al. "Euthanasia: Murder or Not: A Comparative Approach." *Iranian Journal of Public Health* 43, 10 (2014): 1316–1323.

Berenbaum, Michael. "T4 Program." *Encyclopedia Britannica*, February 16, 2001. https://www.britannica.com/event/T4-Program.

Bingham, Gail. "Involuntary Sterilisation, Eugenics, and Physician-assisted Dying: Lessons for New Zealand." *Journal of Law and Medicine* 27, 3 (2020): 707–717.

Brody, Howard. "Physician-Assisted Suicide: Family Issues." *Michigan Family Review* 1, 1 (1995): 19–28. https://quod.lib.umich.edu/m/mfr/4919087.0001.103.

Chambaere, K., et al. "Recent trends in euthanasia and other end-of-life practices in Belgium." *The New England Journal of Medicine* 372, 12 (2015): 1179–1181. https://doi.org/10.1056/NEJMc1414527.

Chaya, Lynn. "Covid vaccine now mandatory to get euthanized in Germany." *National Post*, December 2, 2021. https://nationalpost.com/news/covid-19-vaccine-now-mandatory-to-get-euthanized-in-germany.

Cheyfitz, Kirk. "Who Decides? The Connecting Thread of Euthanasia, Eugenics, and Doctor-Assisted Suicide." *OMEGA—Journal of Death and Dying* 40, 1 (2000): 5–16. https://doi.org/10.2190/DJFU-AAWP-M3L4-4ALP.

DeMartino, Erin S., et al. "Who Decides When a Patient Can't? Statutes on Alternate Decision Makers." *The New England Journal of Medicine* 376, 15

(2017): 1478–1482. https://doi.org/10.1056/NEJMms1611497.

Devandas-Aguilar, Catalina. "Report from the Special Rapporteur on the rights of persons with disabilities." UN General Assembly, December 17, 2019. https://www.un.org/ga/search/view_doc.asp?symbol=A/HRC/43/41.

Disability Rights Education & Defense Fund. "Why Assisted Suicide Must Not Be Legalized." https://dredf.org/public-policy/assisted-suicide/why-assisted-suicide-must-not-be-legalized/#alternatives.

Emanuel, Ezekiel J. and Margaret P. Battin. "What are the potential cost savings from legalizing physician-assisted suicide?" *The New England Journal of Medicine* 339, 3 (1998): 167–172. https://www.nejm.org/doi/full/10.1056/NEJM199807163390306.

Evenblij, Pasman, et al. "Physicians' experiences with euthanasia: a cross-sectional survey amongst a random sample of Dutch physicians to explore their concerns, feelings and pressure." *BMC Family Practice* 20, 177 (2019). https://doi.org/10.1186/s12875-019-1067-8.

The Expert Panel Working Group on MAID for Mature Minors, Council of Canadian Academies. "The State of Knowledge on Medical Assistance in Dying for Mature Minors," 2018. https://cca-reports.ca/wp-content/uploads/2018/12/The-State-of-Knowledge-on-Medical-Assistance-in-Dying-for-Mature-Minors.pdf.

Government of Canada. "Options and decision-making at end of life." https://www.canada.ca/en/health-canada/services/options-decision-making-end-life.html.

Harrison, C. "Treatment decisions regarding infants, children and adolescents." *Paediatrics & Child Health* 9, 2 (2004): 99–103. https://academic.oup.com/pch/article/9/2/99/2648514.

Horn, Ruth. "The right to a self-determined death as expression of the right to freedom of personal development: The German Constitutional Court takes a clear stand on assisted suicide." *Journal of Medical Ethics* 46, 6 (2020): 416–417. https://doi.org/10.1136/medethics-2020-106197.

Inbadas, Zaman, et al. "Declarations on euthanasia and assisted dying." *Death Studies* 41,9 (2017): 574–584. https://www.tandfonline.com/doi/full/10.1080/07481187.2017.1317300.

Jones, Roland M., and Alexander I. F. Simpson. "Medical Assistance in Dying: Challenges for Psychiatry." *Frontiers in Psychiatry* 9 (2018): 678. https://www.frontiersin.org/articles/10.3389/fpsyt.2018.00678/full.

Kim, Scott. "Lives Not Worth Living in Modern Euthanasia Regimes." *Journal of Policy and Practic in Intellectual Disabilities* 16, 2 (2019): 134–136. https://doi.org/10.1111/jppi.12300.

Kouwenhoven, Thiel, et al. "Developments in euthanasia practice in the Netherlands: Balancing professional responsibility and the patient's autonomy." *The European Journal of General Practice* 25, 1 (2019): 44–48.

https://doi.org/10.1080/13814788.2018.1517154.

Mehlum, Schmahl, et al. "Euthanasia and assisted suicide in patients with personality disorders: a review of current practice and challenges." *Borderline Personality Disorder and Emotion Dysregulation* 7, 15 (2020). https://doi.org/10.1186/s40479-020-00131-9.

Merino, Aruanno, et al. "'The prohibition of euthanasia' and medical oaths of Hippocratic Stemma." *Acta Bioethica* 23 (2017): 171–178. https://doi.org/10.4067/S1726-569X2017000100171.

Nicol, Julia. "Medical Assistance in Dying: The Law in Selected Jurisdictions outside Canada." *Library of Parliament*, Publication No. 2015-116-E (2015). https://lop.parl.ca/sites/PublicWebsite/default/en_CA/ResearchPublications/201511 6E.

Pereira, José. "Legalizing euthanasia or assisted suicide: the illusion of safeguards and controls." *Current Oncology* 18, 2 (2011): 38–45. https://www.mdpi.com/1718-7729/18/2/883.

Price, McCormack, et al. "Concepts of mental capacity for patients requesting assisted suicide: a qualitative analysis of expert evidence presented to the Commission on Assisted Dying." *BMC Medical Ethics* 15, 32 (2014). https://doi.org/10.1186/1472-6939-15-32.

ProCon.org. "Euthanasia & Physician-Assisted Suicide (PAS) around the World." https://euthanasia.procon.org/euthanasia-physician-assisted-suicide-pas-around-the-world/.

———. "What Is Passive Euthanasia?" https://euthanasia.procon.org/questions/what-is-passive-euthanasia/.

Raus, Vanderhaegen, et al. "Euthanasia in Belgium: Shortcomings of the Law and Its Application and of the Monitoring of Practice." *The Journal of Medicine and Philosophy: A Forum for Bioethics and Philosophy of Medicine* 46, 1 (2021): 80–107. https://academic.oup.com/jmp/article-abstract/46/1/80/6118631?redirectedFrom=fulltext.

Reddy, Rajadhar, and Danielle H. Chaet. "AMA Code of Medical Ethics' Opinions Related to End-of-Life Care." *AMA Journal of Ethics* 20, 8 (2018): 738–742. https://journalofethics.ama-assn.org/article/ama-code-medical-ethics-opinions-related-end-life-care/2018-08.

Stainton, Tim. "Disability, vulnerability and assisted death: commentary on Tuffrey-Wijne, Curfs, Finlay and Hollins." *BMC Medical Ethics* 20, 89 (2019). https://bmcmedethics.biomedcentral.com/articles/10.1186/s12910-019-0426-2.

Stoll, Ryan, et al. "Perceived Burdensomeness and the Wish for Hastened Death in Persons with Severe and Persistent Mental Illness." *Frontiers in Psychiatry* 11 (2021). https://www.frontiersin.org/articles/10.3389/fpsyt.2020.532817/full.

Tuffrey-Wijne, Curfs, et al. "Euthanasia and assisted suicide for people with an intellectual disability and/or autism spectrum disorder: an examination of nine relevant euthanasia cases in the Netherlands (2012–2016)." *BMC Medical Ethics* 19, 17 (2018). https://bmcmedethics.biomedcentral.com/articles/10.1186/s12910-018-0257-6.

Verhofstadt, Assche, et al. "Psychiatric patients requesting euthanasia: Guidelines for sound clinical and ethical decision making." *International Journal of Law and Psychiatry* 64 (2019): 150–161. https://www.sciencedirect.com/science/article/pii/S0160252719300068?via%3Dihub.

———. "When unbearable suffering incites psychiatric patients to request euthanasia: qualitative study." *The British Journal of Psychiatry: The Journal of Mental Science* 211, 4 (2017): 238–245. https://doi.org/10.1192/bjp.bp.117.199331.

Vrakking, Heidi, et al. "Regulating physician-assisted dying for minors in the Netherlands: views of paediatricians and other physicians." *Acta Paediatrica* 9 (2007): 117–121. https://onlinelibrary.wiley.com/doi/10.1111/j.1651-2227.2006.00004.x.

Waddell, Michael M. "Autism and Assisted Suicide." *Journal of Disability & Religion* 24, 1 (2020): 1–28. https://www.tandfonline.com/doi/abs/10.1080/23312521.2019.1694463.

Part II:

Crimes against Our Children

Chapter 20

Sexualization of Children: Lifting the Last Taboo

David Bellusci, O.P.

Introduction

In this chapter I will show that the sexualization of children can be traced to John Money, Alfred Kinsey, and Sigmund Freud. Normalising sexual behaviour associated with children continues in the context of entertainment with the portrayal and exploitation of girls and boys in music and film where children are innocently sexual objects.[1] In the last decades, where sexuality has been politicised by LGBTQ+Q advocates demanding gay-straight alliances in schools, same-sex parenting in classroom syllabi, and transgender "rights" for the child, the responsibility of moral education is increasingly detached from the parent(s) and left to states endorsing sexualizing ideologies.[2] Anthropological and psychological support for pedophilic orientation leads to further doubting the criminality of pedophilia, a "disorder" to be re-examined—removing the last taboo.

Alfred Kinsey

In the 1940s the zoologist-turned-sexologist Alfred Kinsey produced the "Kinsey Report," publishing two books, *Sexual Behaviour in the Human Male* (1948) and *Sexual Behaviour in the Human Female* (1953), with support from the Rockefeller Foundation.[3] Drawing from his research and that of his colleagues—with the "consent" of children—Kinsey claimed

1 This paper does not deal with the criminal issue of child pornography or child trafficking but with social elements that contribute to these crimes.

2 Anderson, *When Harry Became Sally*, 131–132, 142–143.

3 "The Rockefeller Foundation has contributed a major portion of the cost of the program during the past six years" (Kinsey, et al., *Human Male*, ix). "The Rockefeller Foundation has contributed through grants made to the National Research Council's Committee" (Kinsey, et al., *Human Female*, ix).

that sexual relations with children do not cause psychological damage.[4] Kinsey regards the child's education as the conditioning factor for not having sexual contact with adults when there is no physical harm.[5] With the research carried out on both male and female children and observing/recording their sexual behaviour, Kinsey sought to desensitise and re-educate the public with a renewed understanding of child sexuality based on his "empirical" studies. Kinsey's claims relating to child consent in adult sexual encounters is problematic: How is the consent of a child possible without some kind of manipulation by the adult?[6]

Kinsey's exploration of child sexuality was pioneered by Freud in the latter's study of the psychosexual development of the child. Freud identifies the early stages of human development in terms of psycho-sexual stages: oral, anal, phallic, and genital.[7] The emphasis on sexual energy stemming from libido impulses places human affective and emotional development within the structure of human sexuality. Although Kinsey appears to continue to the Freudian project, Kinsey's objectives differ from Freud's.[8] Kinsey and Freud were contemporaries; Freud's case studies served his psychoanalytic treatment of patients. Kinsey as a zoologist and anthropologist acknowledged Freud's contribution in the field of child sexuality, but as that of a psychoanalyst.[9] Kinsey's research opened the path to sex as pleasure and sex as recreation. Kinsey asserts that the person, rather than being driven by unconscious sexual impulses, consciously seeks to satisfy their sexual drives. For his research, besides the Rockefeller Foundation, Kinsey also counted on the support of Hugh Heffner, who at the time was introducing soft pornography into the mainstream—*Playboy*. The sex logic of the period was that "men were playboys and women were playthings."[10]

4 Kinsey, *Human Female,* 120–121.

5 Kinsey's claims are based on his 1948 work involving the observation/recordings of pre-adolescent males and his 1953 study on females, including memory, observation, and recordings.

6 Controversial Table 34 raises questions of the criminal nature of Kinsey's research where children are used (1948), 180. Kinsey refers to 182 pre-adolescent boys (1948), 179. See below, Reisman and her response to Kinsey's criminal/fraudulent studies on children.

7 Freud, "Development of the Libido and Sexual Organizations," 271–287; Gay, *Freud,* 145–148.

8 Kinsey, *Human Male*, 180; Kinsey, *Human Female*, viii.

9 Freud is acknowledged in the Introduction to *Human Female*, 8.

10 Nerozzi, *L'uomo nuovo*, 26.

John Money

As Kinsey sought to liberalise human sexuality, freeing the person from socio-religious sexual codes, John Money actively worked toward the same objectives, although with political motives.[11] Influenced by Kinsey where the term "sexual paraphilias" replaced "sexual abnormalities," Money conceived sexual acts not as deviations from "normal" behaviour or perversions but as individual preferences.[12] John Money, not unlike Alfred Kinsey, claimed that the pedophile experience did not "necessarily have a negative influence on the child" so long as no harm takes place and consent is given. Money also maintained that gender was not biological but a construct.[13] In Money's world, any sexual relation would be legal, including pedophilia, because the eroticisation of humanity would melt away aggressive tendencies. The need to educate children in sexuality was part of Money's vision of a "brave new world."[14] Neither pedophilia nor ephebophilia is voluntary; "no more a matter of voluntary choice than are left-handedness or colour blindness." The best one can do is accept this reality, with enlightened minds to pass appropriate laws.[15] Sexuality extends from the construction of gender-to-gender roles where women find themselves disadvantaged seeking equality. Money worked from a socio-political angle with preconceived scientific data based especially on Freud and Kinsey. His research confirmed the pre-established gender perceptions which he attempted to demonstrate in the infamous case of Bruce/Brenda. Money envisioned a world free from the archaic and intolerant imposition of religious codes; a brave new world with

11 Kinsey, *Human Female*, viii; Nerozzi, *L'uomo nuovo*, 36; Perucchietti and Marletta, *Unisex*, 46–47.

12 Money, introduction to Sandfort, *Boys on Their Contacts with Men.*

13 At Johns Hopkins, where he was professor of pediatrics and medical psychology, Money created the Clinic for Gender Identity in 1965. Money's first experiment turned out tragically: a twin boy, Bruce Reimer, who had been accidentally mutilated during a circumcision procedure was to be brought up not with the original name, but as "Brenda." Money claimed that gender identity was a matter of how the child is reared, not biology. Money believed his theory would be proved with the twins Brian and Brenda, now a girl. But by nine years old, Brenda became "masculine" and "rebellious," and in her adolescence she found out the truth of her biological birth. Brenda then returned to her original gender and took the name David. The power and control Dr. Money had over the entire Reimer family had psychological consequences when David came to understand he was the subject of scientific experiments in gender re-assignment. The tragic story of David ultimately ended in suicide but was first turned into an ideological fiction by Colapinto in *As Nature Made Him,* giving the impression of a happy transformation from male to female, as falsely suggested by the scientific community—until David went public. Interviews with David and his mother show a "successful" sexual reassignment was hardly the case. See Chudeau Productions, "David Reimer interviews."

14 Peruchietti and Marletta, *Unisex,* 46–47.

15 Money, introduction to *Boys on Their Contacts with Men.*

people free to pursue recreational sex, including precocious preparation for the sexual life of children.[16] Money's Introduction to Theo Sandfort's *Boys on Their Contacts with Men* attempts to legitimise pedophilia. In Money's view, sexual education for children assures a healthy sexuality in adult years, after the example of chimpanzees: when isolated in youth, they do not engage in erotic games and become sexually incompetent.[17] For this reason, he claimed, at school children need to be educated not only in theory, but also in practise.[18]

Sexualizing Children: Opponents

Judith Reisman's paper "Kinsey and the Homosexual Revolution" attacks Kinsey's criminal studies.[19] Reisman rhetorically asks whether children can be molested in the name of science. In response to E. Pomeroy's letter, Reisman quotes Pomeroy in a footnote referring to Kinsey's experiments: "sources have added to their written or verbal reports photographs, and in a few instances, cinema."[20] Reisman adds that "the Kinsey Institute is on record as possessing a selection of child pornography films and photographs."[21] Writing over twenty years ago, Reisman asserts, "It should come as no surprise then to those on our campuses, and in the halls of legislative, judicial and educational power, that as our nation has followed Kinsey and his disciples, we too have been increasingly coarsened to conscience and honor."[22] Reisman identified the downward spiral of legitimising sexual perversion with the Kinsey revolution: "Kinsey, for his part, refashioned the way humankind looked upon sexuality and separated this most powerful of human acts from its labor-intensive *procreational* function, pronouncing true human sexuality in the new human nature to be free, self-fulfilling, and *recreational*."[23] In the same article, Reisman considers the extent to which scientists serve their funders, and patrons who are a small but powerful elite. But human behavioural sciences are not hard science; they can be manipulated and are frequently misused to undermine traditional values.[24]

16 Nerozzi, *L'uomo nuovo*, 36.

17 Money, introduction to *Boys on Their Contacts with Men.*

18 Money, introduction to *Boys on Their Contacts with Men.*

19 Reisman, "Homosexual Revolution," 23.

20 Pomeroy was one of Kinsey's research assistants. Reisman, "Homosexual Revolution," 28n21.

21 Reisman, "Homosexual Revolution," 28n21.

22 Reisman, "Homosexual Revolution," 28.

23 Reisman, "Homosexual Revolution," 28.

24 Reisman, "Homosexual Revolution," 22.

In the name of "science," Reisman observes, scientists could "teach pederasts and pedophiles techniques for sexually abusing children for science."[25] Could "scientists" not use their power, influence, and support to change sex crime laws?[26] "While no one noted that 317 infants and children were 'tested' for Kinsey's child sex data, educators repeated his conclusions—that children were sexual from birth, hence, school sex education, Kinsey style, should be mandated."[27] Kinsey's experiments involved molesting children given his sexual premises but also gave the psychosexual basis and later political justification to decriminalise sodomy. This is Reisman's point: with the questionable nature of the data coming from Table 34 that is either criminal or fraudulent, Kinsey's assertions leading to *Sexual Behaviour in the Human Male* immediately made headlines used for publicity purposes "to institutionalize Kinsey's claims."[28] Reisman takes a clear position on the criminality of Kinsey's experiments: "To trust anything these men or their disciples produce is to put one's faith in those who use the language of science to accomplish personal, criminal, and/or sexual interests."

Alfred Kinsey and John Money continued where Freud left off in developing a vision of the person as shaped by libido. Alice Miller, a Polish-Swiss child psychologist and outspoken critic of Freud, asserts her views in *Thou Shalt Not Be Aware: Society's Betrayal of the Child.* In the chapter "Is There Such a Thing as 'Infantile Sexuality'?" Miller observes, "In order to survive, a little child needs love, care, attention, and tenderness from the adult."[29] Miller also adds, "He will do anything in order to get them and keep them." The child will also satisfy the adult's desires—or at least not frustrate them—because offending the adults signifies the possibility of rejection.[30] Miller goes on to state, "Yet, we should be surprised that whereas it is now so easy for many people to take for granted the absurd idea that a child wants to have sexual relations with a grownup, in all of psychoanalytic theory there is very rarely any mention of the effect a child has on sexually unfulfilled parents."[31] Miller extends her critique of Freudian psychoanalysis to the Oedipal complex: "The Oedipus theory made it possible to continue

25 Reisman, "Homosexual Revolution," 22.

26 Reisman, "Homosexual Revolution," 22.

27 Reisman, "Homosexual Revolution," 23.

28 Reisman, "Homosexual Revolution," 25.

29 Miller, *Thou Shalt Not Be Aware,* 119.

30 Miller, *Thou Shalt Not Be Aware,* 119.

31 This psychoanalytic sexualization of the child is evident in the work of the Neo-Freudian Melanie Klein: "Moreover, the main object of all sexual desires—in the girl, the father; in the boy, the mother—also rouse hate and revenge, because these desires are disappointed." See Klein and Riviere, *Love, Hate and Reparation,* 64.

to treat the child, now seen as having sexual desire, as the object of adults' didactic (or therapeutic) efforts."[32]

Sexualization of Children: Political Manoeuvres

In the 2013 American Psychiatric Association (APA) manual, pedophilia is listed as an orientation and not a pathology. This means that pedophilia is not considered a mental disturbance or an illness that needs to be treated.[33] With worldwide outrage over the approval of pedophilia, the APA added distinctions to the terminology, but the confusing language concerning pedophilia appears to be taking the same route as homosexuality, from criminality to in-born orientation, to social permissibility.

It would be naive to believe gender equality, gay/lesbian rights, gender reassignment, and pedophilia are unrelated. They are aspects of the same anthropological-political project that was spearheaded by Kinsey. Peruchietti and Marletta maintain that in the last decades there appears to have been a move towards normalising if not legalising pedophilia, gradually lifting the last taboo of western society.[34] The Kinsey/Money revolution received support and funding from the sex industry itself (as Hugh Heffner demonstrated with *Playboy*) as well as the Rockefeller Foundation and schools like Indiana University, where Kinsey taught Sex Education, and Johns Hopkins, where John Money worked. The circulation of a new view of human sexuality also needed the support of the APA to influence lawmakers.

Although Kinsey thought of himself as continuing where Freud left off in terms of the psychosexual understanding of the person from infancy onwards, Freud's psychoanalytical approach was based on case studies and treating patients. Kinsey, instead, essentially redefined human sexual anthropology.

32 Miller, *Thou Shalt Not Be Aware,* 146.

33 This change resembles that whereby in 1973 the APA removed homosexuality as a pathology. The distinction between an orientation and an act is significant because of the criminal implications: sexual desires are not criminal (even though they may be sinful) but acting on desires may be criminal (and sinful). In the case of homosexual acts and pedophilic acts, the former have been decriminalised while the latter remain criminal. Therefore, juridical recognition is now given to same-sex unions/marriages in most western societies, and LGBTQ+ lobbyists in the EU and the UN continue to pressure governments to make changes in favour of LGBTQ+ rights. Pedophilia is no longer considered a pathology but an orientation "like any other." As already noted, the claim made by Kinsey and Money is that the person is born a pedophile (although Money maintains that sexual identity—"gender"—is constructed). The new Diagnostic and Statistical Manual of Mental Disorders—DSM-5 or DSM-V—distinguishes between pedophilia and pedophilic disorder. Another distinction has been made; pedophilic disorder is regarded as a paraphilia and not a sexual orientation. *Psychology Today* staff, "Pedophilia."

34 Peruchietti and Marletta, *Unisex,* 148.

Freud's unconscious sexual impulses that drove human behaviour became Kinsey's conscious sexual needs that needed to be fulfilled and required socio-political recognition. Kinsey's intention to normalise sexual behaviour regarded as pathological and/or criminal could only be achieved with the help of the APA. What is abnormal, a pathology requiring treatment, becomes progressively normalised—or a paraphilia. In the 1970s, militant homosexuals accused the APA of discrimination; APA meetings were boycotted; and eyewitnesses Ronald Bayer and William Dannemeyer relate the use of intimidation, belligerence, and accusation of false credentials to impose changes at the APA convention of 1971. At the APA's 1973 convention, the decision was made to remove "homosexuality" as a "sickness" from the DSM. Reasons given were not scientific but political. These changes brought about by the APA show how perceived sexual norms can be changed: not by scientific research but by a mob.[35] If this can be achieved with homosexual activity, why not with other sexual pathologies? Just as gay/lesbian activists have successfully changed social perception of sexuality, marriage, and sex education. The right to gender re-assignment and the rights of children to have their sex changed without parental intervention moves into the arena of child sexuality and the law, where rights of the child trump the moral responsibility and concerns of the parents.

Education and Ideology

Education is the primary means to sexually indoctrinate children, even before they reach college. In Ontario, Kathleen Wynne's Liberal Government introduced a contentious sex education programme that reflects Wynne's own LGBTQ+ agenda as a lesbian. Sixth-grade pupils are already expected to be taught about masturbation and gender diversity. But they will have been prepared for gender identity in Grade 3.[36] Some alleviation came under the Conservative government of Doug Ford; from 2019, parents could have their children opt out of the controversial sex education programme. One cannot ignore the political force of the LGBTQ+ activists whose demands for rights has now extended to classroom curricula. In Berlin, Germany, a dispute erupted over a 140-page sex education guide for kindergarten teachers, entitled "Murat Plays Princess, Alex Has Two Mothers, and Sophie is Now Called Ben: Sexual

35 Peruchietti and Marletta, *Unisex,* 66.

36 Government of Ontario, "Health and Physical Education." In Grade 3, children are taught to "identify the characteristics of healthy relationships," and this includes "accepting differences, being inclusive": "gender identity, sexual orientation…make each person unique." The Grade 3 child is also expected to understand that "some have two mothers or two fathers." See Pete Balinski, "A Grade-by-Grade Breakdown of Kathleen Wynne's Graphic New Sex-Ed Program."

and Gender Diversity as Topics of Inclusive Early Education Pedagogy."[37] While defended by Berlin's Queer Format,[38] the Conservative and Alternative for Germany parties officially protested in Berlin's Senate. The issue for the latter party was "hypersexualising" children. Similarly, British Minister of Education Nicky Morgan defended an explicit sex education program for 11-year-olds giving details on pornography and rape.[39] Morgan claimed to be motivated not by the LGBTQ+ movement but with women fighting against violence, especially in light of the Rotherham sex scandal that began with a Pakistani-Muslim ring in the 1980s. Rotherham police authorities failed to investigate the sexual crimes.[40] The explicit sex education programme that included rape, domestic violence, pornography, female genital mutilation, and online sex abuse was criticized; sex education should be left to parents, not to the Ministry of Education.

The media joins health authorities and LGBTQ+ activists in the push to alter perceptions of morality. As social taboos increasingly break down across continents on issues from abortion to same-sex marriage, from the adoption of children by same-sex couples to "transgender rights" for children, an increasing sexualization of children spreads throughout the world. In its totalitarian style the EU attempts to impose its ideologies on non-compliant states such as Poland and Hungary.[41] These former Soviet satellite states claim that the EU resembles the repressive dictatorships under which they once suffered. Between repackaged Marxism and Hollywood's pedophile Mecca, the sexualization of children continues to be driven by LGBTQ+ rights activists and the film and music industries.[42]

37 Chase, "Berlin row over sex education guide for kindergarten teachers," *Deutsche Welle*, February 27, 2018.

38 Queer Format, a Berlin-based LGBTQ+ institute, has been promoting LGBTQ+ indoctrination in Berlin's schools since the 1980s.

39 Doyle, "Schools Minister Backs Explicit Sex Education for Children Aged 11."

40 The sexual offenses were against girls aged 12-16 and included rape, gang rape, and sexual trafficking. Beyond the horror of the sexual abuse, the police shockingly failed to respond to these crimes, which had been known for over ten years. An estimated 1,400 children, mainly white British girls, had been abused.

41 A global sex education programme, Comprehensive Sexuality Education, began under Barak Obama's administration, with support from the Planned Parenthood Federation and the global organisation International Planned Parenthood. Besides sexualising children and undermining parent/child relations, the programme promotes gender ideology. See Slater, "Parents, Beware: The Global Assault on the Health and Innocence of Children." President Trump in August 2020 put a "pause" to funding the World Health Organisation, which also promotes abortion and radical sex education.

42 In August 2020, Disney confirmed that *The Owl House* series will have a bisexual lead character. Morales, "Disney Confirms Its First Bisexual Lead Character Who Is Also Multicultural."

Hollywood: Re-educating Children

Hollywood directors, producers, and managers have a surprising number of sexual predators of children in their ranks. Amy Berg's documentary *An Open Secret* treated the issue of pedophilia in Hollywood circles. Dawn Chimielewski of the *Los Angeles Times* found that young children who are aspiring actors are often targets.[43] these children leave home for Hollywood when their parents cannot afford to move but wish to support their child's acting career aspirations; these parents relinquish their authority to adult figures in the movie industry. The greatest problem in Hollywood "was, is, and will be pedophilia" among older men with power or connections to power.[44] With the promise of roles, children are hooked into parties and wealth. Many of these children have never drunk, have never taken drugs, and have never had sex before arriving in the Hollywood pedophilia scene.[45] The children who are abused in swimming pools, showers, and beds are too afraid to say anything, as they may lose their career; and studios try to make sure this does not go public. Children who speak out will have to give up their career. While Amy Berg's documentary is the "tip of the iceberg," other factors are "pushing the iceberg into the water." Hollywood is where you do whatever you want: parents are trusting when they shouldn't be; there is no adult supervision, and no retribution for crimes committed. Amy Berg's documentary demonstrates that the Hollywood film/sex industry "normalises pedophilia."

The industry that strives to distort and shape people's perception of reality is the same industry that has given social approval to the homosexual and transgender lifestyle. Increasingly, the sexualization of children serves to legitimise pedophilia. In the 2015 music video for "Elastic Heart," 28-year-old Australian singer-songwriter Shia LaBoeuf and 12-year-old Maddie Ziegler perform an erotic dance. Both are dressed in skin-tone clothes highlighting nude-like bodies, with the cage setting, the suggested naked bodies, and the sensuous physical contact conveying to the viewer a sexualised child. The female voice of Shia is identified with the female figure of Ziegler as she and LaBoeuf engage in a musical erotic caged dance. LaBeouf's hairy, sweaty chest and Ziegler's petite little girl's body connect, "confined" under a cage dramatizing an erotic pedophilic encounter. Such performances give legitimacy to sexualised scenes with a child under the cover of artistic creativity.

43 Chmielewski and Ryan, "Molester Helped Cast Child Actors."

44 Berg, *An Open Secret.*

45 Berg, *An Open Secret.* The American director/producer Bryan Singer (*X-Men, Superman Returns, Dr. House*) had sexual abuse allegations made against him involving minors in 1997, 2014, 2017, and 2019. The allegations involved filming nude adolescents, sex with adolescents, and rape of adolescents, and were denied withdrawn, or settled out of court.

In 2020, the Superbowl half-time show included caged girls in a performance that was claimed to be an expression of the "empowerment of women."[46] The alleged celebration of Latino culture in Miami was to be found offensive by Latinos and non-Latinos alike: Jennifer Lopez appears on the scene with the pink lights reflecting the Empire State Building, where New York's new abortion law was applauded.[47]. The entertainment aired on family time makes a political statement endorsing the killing of preborn babies. Jennifer Lopez moves into a scene where the camera zooms onto her buttocks as she performs in the name of women's empowerment. Lopez then climbs up a pole and stretches out her arms, mocking the symbol of the Cross. The performance served to convey the underlying sexual ideologies advanced by the orgiastic dances of men and women, with masturbating hand gestures from Lopez, who had her vagina covered with a strip of black leather.[48] While this may satisfy the "adult entertainment" industry, one is left to wonder what motivates airing this during a "family" program. After celebrating the death of innocent babies and mocking Christianity's central symbol, the empowerment performance simulated masturbation and orgies, with little girls released from cages and brought onto the stage. The message is that the little girls will become empowered women by sexualising themselves and their bodies. The future of "women's empowerment" is the sex industry.[49] As sex becomes increasingly recreational for an increasingly younger population under the influence of the sexualising media and LGBTQ+ activists, only laws need to change to make sex with minors fully acceptable.

The blurring of children's play and adult sexual manipulation is evident in the 2018 French film *Un frère*.[50] The movie presents Tom, a 15-year-old boy, and Felix, 17, who spends time at Tom's family's summer home. Felix apparently was struggling with his girlfriend, who "lost" their baby. Bertille, Tom's little sister, is a playful and innocent presence in the film, while the sexually assertive Felix craftily initiates the adolescent virgin Tom into sex. One can sense the blurring between childlike play and sex-play. Felix believes Tom is finally ready to have anal sex with him. While the scenes never show nudity, they are suggestive of it. Tom does not resist Felix in any way; after all, Tom has been psychologically and emotionally prepared by Felix for this final

46 February 2, 2020. The official Superbowl video removed sexually provocative scenes.

47 New York State passed a law permitting abortion after 24 weeks of pregnancy until the end of term in 2019.

48 In the Biblical scene at Sinai the Golden Calf was worshiped in the orgiastic dance of the Israelites (Gen 32:6).

49 Widburg, "The Superbowl LIV Halftime Show was polished, highly produced—and vulgar": "With all of this sexually explicit dancing, it was bizarre to have the show end with a chorus of sweet-faced girls (including J-Lo's own daughter) doing the usual women's empowerment shtick."

50 The video is free and intended to be made widely accessible to children and adolescents to teach them about adolescent sexual (homosexual) experiences.

sexual encounter. Is the film endorsing rape? Tom does not show consent to what is happening to him, and one can only wonder whether a 15-year-old can even consent to manipulation. Had Felix been two years older, he could have been charged with sexual abuse, as could an older adult in Felix's place. Felix is both sexually assertive and provocative. What is the message of the film: Sex is play? Rape is OK? If you are under 18 or 19 you can play sex games even if "consent" is ambiguous? We are not left to know what happens to Tom—whether he is scarred by such an event. Discovering one's sexuality at an early age is what matters for the producers, who believe that fifteen-year-olds are interested in sexual experiences—this is part of play.[51] The 2020 French film *Mignonnes,* or *Cuties,* has been released on Netflix. The hyper-sexualization of 11-year-old girls is paradoxically depicted in this film that supposedly aims at combatting the treatment of girls as sexualised objects.[52] *Cuties* sexualises children and employs stereotypes, especially of black children, and "the pornographic industry is built on these stereotypes."[53] Numerous studies show that such sexualised media leads children and adolescents to engage in sex earlier, to have more sexual partners, and to engage in anal or oral sex.[54]

Where Do We Go from Here?

One finds the ongoing sexualization of the child drawing from psychoanalytic interpretations of child behaviour (Freud), the anthropological dimension of human sexuality (Kinsey), and the socio-political implications of sexuality and gender theory (Money) that have now been pushed by Hollywood, music and film stars, and the LGBTQ+ movement, with further legitimacy offered by the APA, creating a society where the sexualization of children is increasingly seen as acceptable—only laws need to change, as John Money asserted.

California has recently introduced a law whereby a 14-year-old can have anal sex with a male ten years older.[55] Since vaginal sex was already permitted in such a case, it appeared that the previously existing law was discriminatory

51 The National Center on Sexual Exploitation, "Press Conference: Addressing the Sexual Exploitation of Men and Boys." Boys that are sexually abused have an eight times higher likelihood of being sexually trafficked than girls that have not. But the sexual trafficking of boys tends to be given less attention than that of girls.

52 National Center on Sexual Exploitation, "Netflix Promotes Sexualization of Children, Racist Stereotypes with New Film *Cuties*."

53 Canadian Women's Health Network, "Hypersexualisation of Young Girls: Why Should We Care?"

54 Brown and L'Engle, "X-Rated," 129–151; Wingood, et al., "Exposure to X-rated movies," 1116–1119; Braun-Courville and Rojas, "Exposure to sexually explicit web sites," 156–162.

55 California Legislative Bill Text SB-145: Sex Offenders Registration.

against the LGBTQ+ activists. Now a 24-year-old male may have homosexual sex with a 14-year-old, with the charge of abuse left to a judge's discretion.[56] The law is clearly meant to draw attention to the alleged discrimination against those over 24 years old, who are not currently covered by the law. Once the "discriminatory" nature of a 10-year limit is recognised—analogous to discrimination against homosexuality—any adult over 24 years old may have sex with a 14-year-old boy. From Hollywood, California's pedophile Mecca, the movie industry will continue to promote, defend, and finance the sexualization of children, continuing the Alfred Kinsey experiment in zoology and human anthropology that started in the late 1930s, trying to establish that sex is recreational.

One is left with the danger of removing this last taboo: sexualising children. In March 2018, Madeleine van der Bruggen gave a talk on pedophilia through the TEDx platform.[57] A psychologist and criminologist, Van der Bruggen approached her topic in a spirit of "let's be mature about this, even though emotional reactions are understandable." For Van der Bruggen, pedophiles need to talk, but out of fear keep everything hidden. They do not act upon their impulses because of fear of the law. Van der Bruggen acknowledges pedophiles need to seek help, yet she asserts pedophilia is not what these people chose but their "orientation."[58] Homosexuality was accepted by the APA as something that the person did not choose, with the right to act on these unchosen impulses a psychological consequence. Kinsey had a similar claim for pedophiles; they cannot change their orientation and they do no harm to children. Based on how the APA approached orientation, asserting pedophilia as an "orientation" seems likely to open the path to the sexualization of children. The liberalising of sexual activity leaves pedophilia as the last taboo to become normalised. The pattern should sound familiar: compassion is needed to understand and help the person who suffers; question whether the laws that cause such suffering are unjust; demonstrate the laws existing laws are discriminatory; introduce a new law creating a just society based on cherished democratic principles. As with abortion, same-sex marriage, and gender reassignment of children, normalised pedophilia follows this trajectory.

56 Under SB-145, if a young adult has gay sex with a minor 14 or older who is less than 10 years younger, a judge will have the discretion whether to place the individual on the sex offender registry. Senator Scott Wiener (D-San Francisco) stated, "This eliminates discrimination against LGBTQ youth in our criminal justice system." See Margolis, "CA Legislature Passes Bill."

57 Van der Bruggen, "Let's Be Mature about Pedophilia."

58 As already argued in the body of this paper, Freud, Kinsey, and Money.

Moral Credibility

Academic research at universities such as Indiana University and Johns Hopkins, backed up by funding from foundations and research grants, with LGBTQ+ activists wielding political power and Hollywood further sexualizing children through the film industry, started us on a path toward social approval of pedophilia—lifting the last taboo. What realistic solution can be offered that recognises the sacredness of the child and human sexuality?

The Roman Catholic Church is the only institution with the moral resources to challenge the sexualization of children. Catholicism bases its morality on natural law and Sacred Scripture. Yet Catholicism has been silenced by the media: sins of clerics involving child sexual abuse have dominated news broadcasts relating to the Catholic Church, stifling the voice of the Catholic hierarchy on moral issues. The institution that has the moral duty to confront the sexualization of children in the media, in academia, in film and music, and in the LGBTQ+ agenda is buried under accusations against clerics. Secular societies of the West can show their moral high ground while hypocritically dragging the Church in the mud. The child is sacred. And so is human sexuality. But who will teach this?

Bibliography

Anderson, Ryan T. *When Harry Became Sally: Responding to the Transgender Moment.* Encounter Books: New York and London, 2018.

Balinski, Pete. "A Grade-by-Grade Breakdown of Kathleen Wynne's Graphic New Sex-Ed Program." *LifeSiteNews,* February 24, 2015. https://www.lifesitenews.com/news/a-grade-by-grade-breakdown-of-kathleen-wynnes-graphic-new-sex-ed-program.

Berg, Amy, dir. *An Open Secret.* 2014.

Braun-Courville, D., and M. Rojas. "Exposure to sexually explicit web sites and adolescent sexual attitudes and behaviors." *Journal of Adolescent Health* 45 (2009): 156–162.

Brown, J., and K. L'Engle. "X-Rated: Sexual attitudes and behaviors associated with U.S. early adolescents' exposure to sexually explicit media." *Communication Research* 36 (2009): 129–151.

California Legislative Bill Text SB-145: Sex Offenders Registration. https://leginfo.legislature.ca.gov/faces/billTextClient.xhtml?bill_id=201920200SB145.

Canadian Women's Health Network. "Hypersexualization of Young Girls: Why Should we Care?" http://www.cwhn.ca/en/hypersexualizationprimer.

Chase, Jefferson. "Berlin row over sex education guide for kindergarten teachers."

Deutsche Welle, February 27, 2018. https://www.dw.com/en/berlin-row-over-sex-education-guide-for-kindergarten-teachers/a-42759631.

Chmielewski, Dawn, and Harriet Ryan. "Molester Helped Cast Child Actors." *Los Angeles Times,* November 17, 2011. https://www.latimes.com/archives/la-xpm-2011-nov-17-la-fi-ct-casting-director-20111118-story.html.

Chudeau Productions. "David Reimer interviews." December 30, 2018. https://vimeo.com/308805171?embedded=true&source=video_title&owner=89408345.

Colapinto, John. *As Nature Made Him.* Harper: New York, 2001.

Doyle, Jack. "Schools Minister Backs Explicit Sex Education for Children Aged 11: Education Secretary Nicky Morgan Gives Green Light to Controversial Resource Providing Schoolchildren with Information about Pornography and Rape." *Daily Mail,* September 27, 2014. http://www.ivanfoster.net/pdf/DailyMail_Sex%20education.pdf.

Freud, Sigmund. "Development of the Libido and Sexual Organizations." In Sigmund Freud, *A General Introduction to Psychoanalysis.* Translated by G. Stanley Hall. Wordsworth: Hertfordshire, 2012.

Gay, Peter. *Freud.* Norton: New York and London, 2006.

Government of Ontario. "Health and Physical Education." 2015. http://www.edu.gov.on.ca/eng/curriculum/elementary/health.html.

Kinsey, Alfred C., et al. *Sexual Behavior in the Human Male.* Philadelphia and London: Saunders, 1948.

———. *Sexual Behavior in the Human Female.* Philadelphia and London: Saunders, 1953.

Klein, Melanie, and Joan Riviere. *Love, Hate, and Reparation.* Norton: New York, 1964.

Margolis, Matt. "CA Legislature Passes Bill Easing Punishment for Pedophiles because of 'LGBTQ+Q Equality,' or Something." *PJ Media,* September 3, 2020. https://pjmedia.com/news-and-politics/matt-margolis/2020/09/03/ca-legislature-passes-bill-easing-punishment-for-pedophiles-because-of-LGBTQ+q-equality-or-something-n885940.

Miller, Alice. *Thou Shalt Not Be Aware.* New York: Farrar, Straus and Giroux, 1981.

Money, John. Introduction to Theo Sandfort, *Boys on Their Contacts with Men.* Elmhurst, NY: Global Academic Publishers, 1987.

Morales, Adrianne. "Disney Confirms Its First Bisexual Lead Character Who Is Also Multicultural." *CNN,* August 15, 2020. https://edition.cnn.com/2020/08/15/us/disney-bisexual-trnd/index.html.

National Center on Sexual Exploitation. "Netflix Promotes Sexualization of Children, Racist Stereotypes with New Film *Cuties.*" April 21, 2020. https://endsexualexploitation.org/articles/netflix-promotes-sexualization-of-children-racist-stereotypes-with-new-film-cuties/.

National Center on Sexual Exploitation. "Press Conference: Addressing the Sexual Exploitation of Men and Boys." September 8, 2017, Washington, DC. https://endsexualexploitation.org/boysandmen/.

Nerozzi, Dina. *L'uomo nuovo.* Soveria Mannelli: Rubbettino, 2008.

Perucchietti, Enrica, and Gianluca Marletta. *Unisex: cancellare l'identità sessuale.* Arianna: Bologna, 2020.

Psychology Today staff. "Pedophilia," *Psychology Today,* February 22, 2019. https://www.psychologytoday.com/us/conditions/pedophilia.

Reisman, Judith. "Kinsey and the Homosexual Revolution."*Journal of Human Sexuality* (1996): 21–28.

Slater, Sharon. "Parents, Beware: The Global Assault on the Health and Innocence of Children." *Daily Signal,* August 10, 2020. https://www.dailysignal.com/2020/08/10/parents-beware-the-global-assault-on-the-health-and-innocence-of-children/.

Widburg, Andrea. "The Superbowl LIV Halftime Show was polished, highly produced—and vulgar." *American Thinker,* February 3, 2020. https://www.americanthinker.com/blog/2020/02/.

Wingood, J. G., et al. "Exposure to X-rated movies and adolescents' sexual and contraceptive related attitudes and behaviors." *Pediatrics* 107 (2001): 1116–1119.

Van der Bruggen, Madeleine. "Let's Be Mature about Pedophilia." TEDx Talks, April 13, 2018. https://www.youtube.com/watch?v=egiBgmvv8wA.

Chapter 21

Child Trafficking: Feeding Sexual Addicts

David Bellusci, OP

Introduction

In this paper I claim that an unmistakable connection exists between pornography, prostitution, and child sexual trafficking.[1] This connection is evident in that pornography sex addicts have moved rapidly in a downward spiral that reflects out-of-control behaviour.[2] This loss of control is manifested in an addictive pattern of sexual desensitization seeking extreme outlets in the form of child pornography. Child prostitution and child sexual trafficking are driven by child pornography. This means child sexual trafficking is fundamentally geared towards feeding adult consumers of pornography.

Child Sexual Trafficking

Trafficking in Persons (TIP) involves "the recruitment, transportation, harbouring and/or control of movement of persons for the purpose of exploitation, typically for sexual exploitation or forced labour."[3] The issue with minors differs from that of adults because adults need to prove they are victims while children are protected by the law punishing those who violate laws trafficking minors. The Palermo Protocol prohibits the "trafficking of children (which is defined as a person being under 18 years of age) for purposes of sexual exploitation of children."[4] TIP can take many forms, including sexual exploitation and forced labour.[5] Statistics

1 I would like to thank the staff at the Marion Alloway Library, Trinity Western University, for locating and retrieving numerous articles for this paper.

2 For a discussion on "out of control behaviour" as a sign of sexual addiction see Carnes, *Don't Call It Love*, 1–14.

3 Government of Canada, Department of Justice, *A Handbook for Criminal Justice Practitioners on Trafficking in Persons*.

4 "Palermo Protocol," *Protocol to Prevent, Suppress.*

5 United Nations Office on Drugs and Crime, *Global Report.* The report was unveiled by the US Embassy to the Holy See by Secretary of State Michael Pompeo, Ivanka Trump, and US Ambassador John Richmond, describing the US government's efforts to end human trafficking around the world. US Embassy to the Holy See, *Trafficking in Persons Report.*

Canada provides details concerning the exploitation of children. Most exploited victims are female, and one quarter are less than 18 years old—which means that 25% of sexual trafficking involves minors.[6] The disturbing statistics reveal the sharp increase of TIP involving minors, children, and adolescents. In her research on pornography, Pamela Paul notes that "between 1996 and 2004, the total number of child porn cases handled by the FBI cyber-crime investigators increased twenty-three-fold. By 2003 there were more than 80,000 reports of internet-related pornography made to Cyber-Tipline, a service provided by the National Center for Missing and Exploited Children (NCMEC), up 750% in five years."[7] Both the American and Canadian statistics show that radical increase associated with the sexual exploitation and trafficking of children. The exponential increase in sexual trafficking of minors corresponds to the escalation in pornography consumption.

Pornography

The moral issue concerning pornography is straightforward: pornography is unethical because it instrumentalizes and dehumanizes the person, whether an adult or a child, for one purpose: sexual gratification. This slippery slope had already been anticipated in the prophetic statement of Pope Paul VI in 1968: "Man, growing used to contraceptive practises, may finally lose respect for the woman and, no longer caring for her physical and psychological equilibrium, may come to the point of considering her as a mere instrument of selfish enjoyment."[8] Pope John Paul II would echo the condemnation of the instrumentalization of the body for sexual gratification. He distinguishes the true "communion of persons" (*communio personarum*), from the concupiscence that drives an attraction "toward utilitarian dimensions, in whose sphere of influence one human being 'makes use' of another human being, 'using her' only to satisfy his own 'urges.'"[9] Rachael Denhollander, an attorney and survival advocate, also employs a language of "communion" and "intimacy" between persons as the alternative to treating a person as "object" or "instrument."[10]

A human anthropology grounded in metaphysics differs from the materialist anthropology taught and advanced by Alfred Kinsey.[11] Kinsey's work

6 Ibrahim, *Trafficking in Persons.*

7 Paul, *Pornified*, 190.

8 Pope Paul VI, *Humanae Vitae*, §17.

9 Pope John Paul II, *Man and Woman He Created Them*, 292.

10 For Rachel Denhollander the question is not how much pornography is all right but rather how to put an end to pornography altogether. National Center on Sexual Exploitation, "Taking on Big Porn."

11 The former is, namely, an anthropology grounded in Aristotelian-Thomistic metaphysics recognizing the human being as both bodily and spiritual.

promoted a materialist vision of the person, a body without a spiritual soul.[12] The Kinseyan doctrine of recreational sex spread and was transmitted to and through his associates, colleagues, and students. Judith Reisman, an outspoken critic of Alfred Kinsey, identified the ethical, social, and political implications of the Kinseyan school.[13]

From Soft-Core to Hard-Core

Looking at the development of *Playboy*, *Penthouse*, and *Hustler*, we can see a clear continuum as the magazines become increasingly explicit.[14] *Playboy* was already risqué when it first appeared in 1953, with "teasing" photos set against respectable academic content, relying on advertising for revenues.[15] *Penthouse* appeared in 1969 with the objective to compete with *Playboy* using the same format but with more sexually explicit content. Moving towards hard-core pornography as promised, *Hustler* appeared in 1974. The soft-porn mainstream market now had a hard-core alternative.[16] The appearance of a hard-core magazine reflected the continuum moving towards more explicit images; the legal battles defending pornography had already been fought by *Playboy* and *Penthouse*.[17] Why does a person turn to pornography to begin with?[18] It can be adolescent curiosity, a college student wanting sexual release, the frustrated spouse seeking escape, adult loneliness—or, using Kinseyan terminology,

12 See my paper *Sexualization of Children* in this same volume, where I give the implications and controversies surrounding Alfred Kinsey's research.

13 See Reisman, "Kinsey and the Homosexual Revolution," 21–28.

14 For details on the development of the pornographic industry, see Dines, *Pornland*, chapter 1.

15 Paul, *Pornified*, 11.

16 Paul, *Pornified*, 12.

17 Paul, *Pornified*, 15.

18 Paul, *Pornified*, chapter 1. The feminist/sociological/Marxist critique turns the question of pornography from a human problem into a man vs. woman dichotomy, "us/them," "oppressor/oppressed." As a result, female pornography or sex addicts find themselves isolated since pornography is presented as a "male problem" (from my own experience working with female sexual addicts). Where women are addicted to pornography, findings show that they view "violent," "rough," or "aggressive" pornography at a higher rate than men. See Stringer, *Unwanted*, 120-21. Dines, *Pornland*, 81, criticized Catholic high school students whom she had visited because the boys were not willing to engage with the subject of pornography after viewing an explicit film and labeling Dines as a "man-hater." Dines believed these high school boys lost an opportunity for growth. Dines herself lost the opportunity to engage with, and help educate, adolescent boys. Guinn observes that in a conference developed by Captive Daughters and the International Human Rights Law Institute the scholars in this field are "political 'progressives' often operating from a 'radical feminist' perspective... [most] participants tended to identify progressivism as a leftist political orientation that often verged on Marxist...favoring strong social welfare programs to address social ills resulting from patriarchy and oppression." See Guinn, *Driving the Demand*, 15.

"recreational sex."[19] The *Playboy-Penthouse-Hustler* downward spiral should have taught consumers—our society—something about pornography: it's addictive. Pornography is about sexual pleasure and pleasure seeks repetition. But the euphoric "high" depends on the visual stimuli; so, from soft-core to hard-core to extreme-core, "particularly on the internet, men find themselves veering off into forms of pornography they *never* thought they could find appealing. Those who start off with soft-core develop a taste for harder-core pornography."[20] Sexual addicts acknowledge the same sexual pattern: what was sexually gratifying at an earlier stage has lost that intensity of gratification. And so, one moves from hetero-sex to same-sex to violent sex and finally to child sex. In the words of a child porn addict, "there's a rush you get form doing something that is forbidden. That's part of the attraction."[21]

Slipping into Extreme Pornography

During the *Playboy*, *Penthouse*, and *Hustler* years, having to go out to purchase a magazine in public may have kept the number of porn users limited. Of course, the magazines could be delivered, but the consumer was subjected to public knowledge. A "respectable" person would think twice before going into a shop to stand in queue purchasing a *Playboy* magazine, or having it delivered, and for minors it was illegal. Availability on video created an ever-growing market for pornography between 1975 and 1995.[22] With the internet in the 1990s, pornography skyrocketed; the global worth approximately was $96 billion in 2006.[23] The dramatic increase can be attributed in part to the triple-A engine: Access, Anonymity, Affordability.[24] But is the "triple-A engine" the only reason for the dramatic increase? In fact, access, anonymity, and affordability exacerbate the underlying issues of compulsive behaviour associated with sexual addiction.[25]

The rapid spread of pornography reflects the sexualised cultures that western societies have become.[26] The dramatic increase in pornographic

19 Paul devotes chapters 1 and 3 to what leads men to pornography and how pornography effects men, respectively. Paul provides stories of pornographic consumption accompanied by statistics, but she does not probe into the underlying or motivating psychological factors.

20 Dines, *Pornland*, 22, 160–161.

21 Herbeck, "'I had become a monster.'"

22 Dines, *Pornland*, 47.

23 Dines, *Pornland*, 47.

24 Cooper, *Sex and the Internet*, 5.

25 The problem of sexual addiction needs to be addressed at both psychological and spiritual levels. For a pastoral psycho-therapeutic approach see Bellusci, *Love Deformed, Love Transformed*, chapters 3, 5.

26 Paul, *Pornified*, 49.

consumption means that sex is "pushed": our attention is captured by media entertainment only if it's "sexy, hot, exciting, dangerous, illicit, fun, titillating, new, more, more…" Distribution of pornography has been facilitated by online consumption—"in homes, on TVs, beamed into cell phones, watched in cars, forwarded via email."[27] From sexting to cyber-sex and increasing consumer demand for pornography, desensitization occurs. Studies show sexual addiction now starts as early as fourteen years old.[28]

The phenomenon of reduced sexual intensity with repeated viewing of pornography is referred to as "desensitization." The images no longer create the neuro-chemical effect they once had. With the weakened dopamine effect, arousal is decreased or altogether lost. Reduced adrenaline and increased time spent viewing leads to the viewer "extreme" pornography that will provide the dopamine and testosterone levels needed for the heightened "ecstasy."[29] Neuroscience gives an account of two types of pleasure: one involves excitement—appetite—that is dopamine-related; and the other, satisfaction—consummation—release of endorphins that creates "euphoria."[30] The thought of "extreme" pornography may have been disgusting or disturbing at first: violence, same-sex porn, attraction to adolescents, and where the porn consumers were not expecting to go: child porn. "Men who view a lot of pornography talk about their disgust the first time they chanced upon an unpleasant image or unsolicited child porn."[31] Pornography consumers do not start viewing pornography with the intent of watching men reenacting rape, or women wanting violent sex, or feeling drawn to bestiality, or turning to child porn. Paul maintains that desensitisation is a major stage in becoming addicted to porn.[32] Moving to extreme pornography is rationalised by "everyone does it"; with such justification, activities contrary to one's previous morals and standards become acceptable.[33] Masturbating to images that the viewer had previously found "disgusting" is an "out of control" behaviour; viewing "extreme" pornography of "violence," "bondage," and child porn to derive pleasure indicates that desensitization has taken place. The Internet effectively triggers more extreme forms of pornography, and for those who had not ever been interested in child porn, it facilitates the virtual sexual experience with the risk that it goes further and becomes "real."[34] Child pornography already abuses

27 Paul, *Pornified*, 49.

28 Eberstadt and Layden, *The Social Costs of Pornography*, 29.

29 Struthers, *Wired for Intimacy*, 104. See chapter 4, "Your Brain on Porn," for the technical neuro-chemical and neuro-biological details of how pornography affects the (male) brain.

30 Doidge, *The Brain That Changes Itself*, 108.

31 Paul, *Pornified*, 88.

32 Paul, *Pornified*, 227.

33 Cline, *Pornography's Effects*.

34 Dines, *Pornland*, 94–95.

children in its very production; but it also puts children at risk from men who consume child porn as a bridge to child sexual abuse.[35]

Desensitization and Pseudo-Child Pornography (PCP)

Before viewing child pornography, the addict may be viewing young women who are presented as adolescent girls. These may be legally adults, but they appear in pornography as minors, so the transition from adult woman to adolescent girl reflects the gradual slippery slope without breaking any laws. Technically neither the woman being filmed or photographed nor the viewer is breaking any laws when age of consent is "respected." This is referred to as Pseudo-Child Pornography (PCP) and becomes a pathway to child pornography.[36] The eroticising of young adolescents becomes first a social phenomenon to make rationalising it permissible and create the "appetite" for more, since "craving" is an integral component of the pornography market.

Between 2004 and 2006 teen sex and teen porn have increased 61% and 45%, respectively.[37] Hypersexualised youth first made its appearance in the fashion industry with the 15-year-old Brook Shields advertising for Calvin Klein. In the 1990s, Calvin Klein advertising used teenagers in poses suggestive of child pornography, which brought the US Justice Department to investigate whether any laws had been broken. Klein escaped prosecution and continued his provocative selling strategy with prepubescent boys and girls wearing only underwear.[38] Advertising, magazine covers, and pop culture looked increasingly pornographic, supplying a desensitized consumer market that gradually went "hard core."[39]

PCP sites become the link to child pornography. Those who have been coerced to work for the PCP sites are of legal age. But the viewers believe they are looking at child pornography. The sole objective of PCP is to deceive the user so into thinking that "he is masturbating to sexual images involving a

35 Dines, *Pornland*, 161.

36 Dines, *Pornland*, 143.

37 Dines, *Pornland*, 143.

38 Dines, *Pornland*, 142.

39 Pubescent boys and girls were used in 1999 for Klein's advertising, pulled after a public outcry. Porn culture is evident in MTV, which began in 1981 targeting youth and young adults. Themes and music content led to censorship controversies. "MTV has edited a number of music videos to remove references to drugs, sex, violence, weapons, racism, homophobia, and/or advertising. Many music videos aired on the channel were either censored, moved to late-night rotation, or banned entirely from the channel." See "MTV—Censorship." Larry Flynt's *Hustler/Barely Legal* first started as magazine porn in 1979, then developed as a web site with video porn in 2008, reflecting the title, "barely legal." To avoid prosecution, Flynt used PCP. See Dines, *Pornland*, 143.

minor."[40] As Dines asserts, "These sites may satisfy the user for a time, [but] desensitization eventually leads to boredom and the need for harder core and more extreme porn."[41] The next step is to turn to real child porn. In this case a younger child is really used—illegally. The desensitized user experiences the "thrill" of the secrecy that accompanies child porn.[42] The rate of child porn users who themselves victimise children varies significantly from 40% to 85% and remains dangerously high.[43]

Child Pornography

In Canada, child pornography is defined as the following: i) any representation of a person who is, or is depicted as being, under the age of 18 years, engaged in explicit sexual activity; (ii) any representation whose dominant characteristic is the depiction of the sexual organs or anal region of a person under the age of 18 years for a sexual purpose; (iii) written, visual, and audio material that advocates or counsels unlawful sexual activity with a person under the age of 18; (iv) written, visual, and audio material whose dominant characteristic is the description of unlawful sexual activity with a person under the age of 18 for a sexual purpose.[44]

With internet accessibility, from 1996 to 2004 child pornography cases according to an FBI cyber-crime investigation had increased from 80,000 reported cases in 2003 up 750% in five years.[45] Large quantities of pornography are made available through "file sharing," primarily through peer-to-peer file-sharing networks. The National Center for Missing and Exploited Children reported an increase from 1,393 child pornography sites in 1998 to 25,759 in 2002.[46] In the United Kingdom the Internet Watch Foundation found that "3,000 to 3,500 child pornography sites are added to the World Wide Web each year."[47]

40 Dines, *Pornland*, 146.

41 Dines, *Pornland*, 159.

42 One sexual addict I had worked with experienced pornography as the "excitement of being defiant."

43 Dines, *Pornland*, 159.

44 Government of Canada, Department of Justice, "Age of Consent to Sexual Activity."

45 Caruso, "Internet Fuels"; Paul, *Pornified*, 190.

46 Paul, *Pornified*, 191.

47 Paul, *Pornified*, 196.

Child Sex Trafficking[48]

The National Center for Missing and Exploited Children identifies several groups at risk for child trafficking: children who are chronically missing or frequently run away (three times); children who have experienced sexual abuse, especially if unaddressed or unreported, or leading to a child being removed from home; children who experienced prior sexual assault or rape; children with substance abuse issues or living with someone with substance abuse.[49]

Child trafficking and prostitution feed pornography consumers.[50] The fact that governments do not recognise the pornography-trafficking connection is reflected in laws permitting pornography, or obscenity laws that are ignored or difficult to prove violations of, creating a thriving sex market. Based on 1993–2001 findings on rape and pornography and the adequacy of existing laws, the UK acknowledged existing laws on pornography were inadequate; France maintained pornography was punished; the Netherlands claimed pornography had a restraining influence on adults; Norwegian studies noted more hard-core pornography was being consumed and prostitution with increasing child pornography; Belgium adopted a "landmark law" against trafficking in persons, prostitution, and pornography; in Singapore pornography is banned, as is advertising that enacts the portrayal of women as sex objects.[51]

In the 1980s and '90s, anti-pornography advocates such as Catharine MacKinnon and Andrea Dworkin recognised "pornography as a form of violence against women that violated their civil rights such that it could and should be legislated against."[52] Feminist opposition emerged arguing that "efforts to control pornography represented a dangerous step onto the slippery slope of censorship that could ultimately threaten the political freedoms of women."[53] The Dworkin-MacKinnon arguments were rejected in the courts, which accepted the "free speech" claims made by the counter-movement.[54] Another risky feminist claim grounded in Kinseyan sexuality is that pornography was "liberating."[55] "Sex work" was also defended legitimate

48 The National Center for Child Sexual Exploitation, "About the National Center on Sexual Exploitation."

49 Another risk factor argued by LGBTQ+ advocates is homes where the child's sexuality is stigmatized. This claim identifies a particular group of children when many children are vulnerable due to poverty. When California passed Bill SB-145 legalizing gay sex between 14-year-olds and adults up to ten years older, this undermined the protection of children, since manipulation of a minor is difficult to establish due to grooming techniques. See "Child Sex Trafficking."

50 Peters, et al., "Slave and Porn Star," 14.

51 MacKinnon, "Pornography as Trafficking," 1008.

52 Guinn, *Driving the Demand*, 16.

53 Guinn, *Driving the Demand*, 16.

54 Guinn, *Driving the Demand*, 16. Guinn does not identify this "counter-movement."

55 Once again Guinn does not state whether these are "Kinseyan" (my expression) feminists or some other branch.

work deserving of legal protection.[56] With these counter-arguments working to crush the anti-pornography movement, it should not come as a surprise that pornography and prostitution are mediated by illegal sexual trafficking to satisfy both the demand for pornography and its extreme outcome. The short-sightedness of these counter-claims reflects a purely material understanding of the human body, one might say of "zoological" inspiration, that has drastic consequences not only for women but also for children. The lack of understanding of the body as both corporeal and spiritual is reflected in materialist claims that can be traced to Kinsey's work. As MacKinnon says, "Most denials of the role of pornography in these dynamics come down to some version of a mind-body distinction…as though sexuality is neither body or mind when it is both."[57] Sadly enough, societies allowing child pornography, prostitution, or trafficking have morally degenerated, leaving especially children vulnerable, even if apparent cosmetic attempts to protect children are in place in what is a moral paradox.

The criminal aspect intensifies the excitement for the consumer: the virtual is real. For the manipulated, deceived, or coerced victims, the filmed sex acts are the hellish experience of being raped. In her statement on trafficking in persons, founder and president of Global Centurion Laura J. Lederer asserts that TIP is essentially modern-day slavery where men, women, and children are "subjected to inhumane treatment, exploited as commercial sex objects, and forced to work as slaves."[58] MacKinnon, who examined the legal aspect of pornography, identifies pornography as a form of trafficking.[59] MacKinnon convincingly shows that,

> As with all prostitution, the women and children in pornography are, in the main, not there by choice but because of a lack of choices. They usually "consent" to the act only in the degraded and demented sense of the word (common also to the law of rape in which a person who despairs at stopping what is happening, sees no escape, has no real alternative, was often sexually abused before as a child, may be addicted to drugs, is homeless, hopeless, is often trying to avoid being beaten or killed, is almost always economically desperate, acquiesces in being sexually abused for payment, even if, in most instances, it is payment to someone else).[60]

56 Guinn, *Driving the Demand*, 17. Guinn does not state whether these were feminists regarding prostitution as "legitimate sex work."

57 MacKinnon, "Pornography as Trafficking," 1000.

58 Lederer, "Trafficking in Persons Report."

59 MacKinnon, "Pornography as Trafficking," 993–1012.

Where a vulnerable child is trafficked and reduced to slavery while feeding pornography, it is prostitution. Adults in the sex industry, in fact, started as sex "slaves."[61] The triangular model of sexual trafficking is based on a business model: supply, demand, and distribution.[62] The purpose of sexual trafficking is to transport women and children into prostitution.[63] To make pornography of a woman or child is to turn them into prostitutes. The sex acts are real; these slaves are consumed "as and for sex."[64] The viewer may seem more distanced in sexual gratification because of the digital reproduction, but the acts remain real for the exploited children involved.[65] Pornography creates the demand for prostitution and thus involves trafficking a boy or girl.[66]

Research has shown that where prostitution is legal—Australia, Ireland, the Netherlands, and Sweden—sexual trafficking increases.[67] In fact the legalisation has reinforced the links between prostitution and sexual trafficking; this is because legalisation promotes the growth of the sex industry. With prostitution being legal in the Netherlands, child prostitution has also increased between 1997 and 2007, and of 15,000 adolescents prostituting themselves, primarily young girls, one-third of them originate from other countries, particularly Nigeria.[68] Germany, where prostitution is also legal, has shown consistent hypocrisy in handling sexual trafficking.[69]

Child Trafficking: Deception, Manipulation, and Coercion

In the 1980s, North Hollywood "madams" were asked to provide 12- and 13-year-old girls for prostitution services.[70] Because of the amount offered for these girls, some madams complied. Girls were brought in from Mexico deceived into believing they would be working as housekeepers. Men on the LA streets asked to meet with girls from 5 to 10 years old. In LA, teenage

60 MacKinnon, "Pornography as Trafficking," 995.

61 MacKinnon, "Pornography as Trafficking," 998.

62 Lederer, "Trafficking in Persons Report."

63 MacKinnon, "Pornography as Trafficking," 998.

64 MacKinnon, "Pornography as Trafficking," 997.

65 MacKinnon, "Pornography as Trafficking," 997.

66 MacKinnon, "Pornography as Trafficking," 999.

67 Bindel, "The Dangers of False Distinctions," 69.

68 Bindel, "The Dangers of False Distinctions," 70.

69 When the World Soccer Cup was held in Germany in 2006, venues serving as brothels in Berlin and other cities, besides finding sponsors for condoms, facilitated sexual trafficking and rape, especially of women arriving from Russia, Ukraine, and other Eastern European countries. Chris Smith, the Republican Chair of the US House of Representatives, had asked the Bush administration to categorise Germany as a "tier-three" country," which would place sanctions on Germany under anti-trafficking legislation. See Dinmore, "Germany 'aiding prostitution.'"

70 Corwin, "Life on the Street."

prostitution escalated in the 1970s due to new laws; the police could no longer pick up suspected runaways and call their homes. The legal age of consent was also lowered. About half the male prostitutes on Santa Monica Boulevard are minors.[71] Deception? Manipulation? Coercion? How is consent determined with adolescents and changing legislation on age of consent? It appears that the laws themselves exacerbate the problem of child trafficking.

One of the earliest cases of sexual trafficking of adolescent girls was the Rotherham Sex Scandal, which took place in England from the late 1980s to 2010s—over twenty years of sexual trafficking.[72] The tragedy of Rotherham, besides the victimised girls, was that the local authorities had been informed or tipped off but refused to take action. Bringing to light the Pakistani-Muslim ring of sex traffickers was seen as creating ethnic tension and destabilising the communities involved. Rotherham's "secrecy" was caused by political correctness and a social conditioning of peaceful co-existence. Jayne Seymour identified a local grooming network employing identifiable trafficking strategies: befriending, supplying with drugs and alcohol, and finally rape.[73] Girls aged 10 to 16 were picked up by taxi drivers from care homes and schools. They were gang-raped, forced to watch rape, and threatened with being burned and the rape of their mothers and sisters. The Rotherham scandal shows how silence and secrecy only exacerbate the problem of sexual trafficking.[74]

In October 1999, an American living in Phenom Penh, Cambodia, advertised his website as a "Rape Camp," featuring Asian sex slaves used for bondage, discipline, and humiliation. The women used on the website were blindfolded, gagged, or bound with ropes while being used in sex acts.[75] Child prostitution is common in Cambodia, with roughly one-third of all women or girls under age 17 in prostitution.[76] One study counted 2,291 underage girls in prostitution, some younger than 12 years old.[77] Poverty is often cited as a cause of prostitution where females are "sold" to seven to ten men per day.[78] Increasing numbers of Vietnamese children are trafficked to Cambodia;

71 According to Corwin's article, they were "kicked out of the house" when their parents discovered they were homosexual, and they then left for Hollywood.

72 I have treated the Rotherham Scandal in my paper in this volume entitled "Sexualization of Children."

73 Seymour, *Broken and Betrayed*.

74 A sexual abuse case in Vienna in 2016 involved an Iraqi who violently sodomized a 10-year-old Serbian boy in the swimming-pool changing room. The Iraqi claimed to have experienced a "sexual emergency." The rape of the Serbian boy was ignored by the press. The silence on the matter shows the failure to educate both migrants and citizens on cultural differences and misconceptions. See *RT*, "Iraqi refugee raped 10yo boy."

75 Hughes, "Welcome to the Rape Camp," 30.

76 Hughes, "Welcome to the Rape Camp," 34.

77 Hughes, "Welcome to the Rape Camp," 34.

78 Hughes, "Welcome to the Rape Camp," 34.

sex abusers demand younger girls because they believe they are less likely to be infected with HIV.[79] The intense competition among internet subscriber sites represents the single part of e-commerce with approximately 40,000 individually run operations. In an attempt to attract buyers, operators supply new material and more extreme images, such as bondage, torture, bestiality, and child pornography.[80] These extreme pornographic needs supply the demand—fulfilling the objectives of "Rape Camp."

A child trafficking ring behind a global internet pornography service reported in the *New York Times* was traced to Eastern Europe; fifteen individuals in New Jersey who subscribed to the service were arrested.[81] Regpay Limited, based company in Minsk, Belarus, operated fifty child pornography websites with subscription profits of $3 million. It was considered a major player of the child pornography industry.[82] In a related article, *The Buffalo News* revealed disturbing details: "Pictures on the internet showing toddlers being raped. They show a girl hanging upside down and gagged while being sexually abused. Children are forced to perform sex acts in "real time."[83] While most of the victims are girls, many boys are also targeted for child pornography: "a majority of the children are under 13 years old."[84] Even at rehabilitation centers children are approached, as in the Ukrainian capital, Kiev, by pornographers.[85] A child pornography ring responds to escalating internet demands, reflecting a global human crisis generating a multi-billion-dollar industry. Russia appears to be the center of illegal activity in terms of child pornography production; the United States that of consumption.[86] The underlying message in Russia, as in other parts of the world where poverty is widespread, is that "economic desperation leads to child exploitation." In Russia, apart from the age of consent (14), to own or share child pornography in one's home is legal. But the consumers of the pornography in Russia, as in Eastern European, are few compared to in the US, where most of it is distributed and consumed. If the demand did not exist, neither would the production.

In Karachi, Pakistan, six members of an internet pornography ring blackmailed, raped, and filmed dozens of young and underage victims and were arrested by the Pakistani Federal Investigation Agency.[87] The charges were

79 Hughes, "Welcome to the Rape Camp," 35.

80 Hughes, "Welcome to the Rape Camp," 37.

81 Smothers, "15 Arrested."

82 Michel and Schulman, "Russia aMichel and Schulman point out that half the company's customers were from the US.

83 Michel and Schulman, "Russia and US-bound," A6.

84 Michel, "Day Three."

85 Michel, "Day Three."

86 Michel and Schulman, "Russia and US-bound," A6.

87 Hasmi, "FIA arrests members of porn ring."

connected to "same-sex abuse." The charges involved "raping, sodomising, and filming" young boys—creating and circulating pornographic videos. Since videos had been produced, the victims were subsequently threatened with blackmail, a common strategy used by pornographers to silence their victims. The Pakistani authorities were made aware of the ring when one of the victims reached out. The ring used mobile applications and websites to track LGBTQ+ youth seeking employment opportunities. The unsuspecting victims clicked on ads offering employment interviews. At the interview site, the victims were subjected to sexual abuse at gunpoint, with the filmed abuse made available on child pornography sites.

Combating Child Sexual Trafficking

With the immediate accessibility of pornography on the internet, the transition from soft porn to hard porn to extreme porn—the downward spiral due to desensitisation—continues to create a demand for sexual trafficking of minors. *Demand*, a 2007 video produced by Shared Hope International, shows how the pornography industry creates a "demand" for extreme pornography and prostitution of minors. Pornography, prostitution, and child sex trafficking are inseparable. The demands of freedom-of-expression activists on the grounds that sex is "liberating" and claims of the legitimacy of sex work exacerbate the vulnerability of minors and the problem of child sex trafficking. As long as pornography and prostitution are not tackled, especially in a sexual "rights" climate, a demand for extreme pornography will continue, to be fulfilled by the manipulation, deception, and coercion of minors.

Advertising, the music and film industries, and internet pornography create a sexualised culture. Pornography, which has now become a billion-dollar global industry, raises the question whether child sexual trafficking here to stay. Radical changes in thinking are needed if any social reforms are to come about. At the political level, we must consider whether "sexual rights" are not exacerbating the problem of the ongoing sexualization of men and women, boys and girls; at a social level, the need to understand that pornography, prostitution, and trafficking are not a woman's issue or man's problem, but a humanitarian crisis where men and women need to be engaged in combating pornography and protecting children; finally, education is needed in human anthropology that is grounded in metaphysics—an understanding of the person as a spiritual being and not only a material one. Perhaps the reality that lies ahead is one that Saint Augustine identified in the *City of God*: the citizens will choose to belong either to the City of the World or to the City of God.

Bibliography

Bellusci, David C. *Love Deformed, Love Transformed.* Eugene, OR: Wipf and Stock, 2019.

Bindel, Julie. "The Dangers of False Distinctions between Pornography, Prostitution, and Trafficking." In *Driving the Demand,* edited by David E. Guinn. Culver City, CA: Captive Daughters Media, 2007.

Carnes, Patrick. *Don't Call It Love.* New York: Bantam, 1991.

Caruso, David B. "Internet Fuels Child Porn Trafficking." *Computer Crime Research Center.* http://www.crime-research.org/news/16.01.2005/902/.

Cline, Victor B. *Pornography's Effects on Adults and Children.* New York: Morality and Media, n.d.

Cooper, Al. *Sex and the Internet.* New York: Routledge, 2002.

Corwin, Miles. "Life on the Street: New Wave of Prostitution with More Violence Is Overwhelming L.A. Authorities." *Los Angeles Times,* December 8, 1985.

Dines, Gail. *Pornland: How Pornography Has Hijacked Our Sexuality.* Boston: Beacon, 2010.

Dinmore, Guy. "Germany 'aiding prostitution during World Cup.'" *Financial Times,* May 1, 2006. https://www.ft.com/content/bfae11a6-d95b-11da-8b06-0000779e2340.

Doidge, N. *The Brain That Changes Itself: Stories of Personal Triumph from the Frontiers of Brain Science.* New York: Viking, 2007.

Eberstadt, Mary, and Mary Anne Layden. *The Social Costs of Pornography.* Princeton, NJ: Witherspoon Institute, 2010.

Government of Canada, Department of Justice. "Age of Consent to Sexual Activity." https://www.justice.gc.ca/eng/rp-pr/other-autre/clp/faq.html.

Government of Canada, Department of Justice. "What Is Trafficking in Persons?" https://www.justice.gc.ca/eng/rp-pr/cj-jp/tp/hcjpotp-gtpupjp/p1.html.

Guinn, David E., ed. *Pornography: Driving the Demand in International Sex Trafficking.* Culver City, CA: Captive Daughters Media, 2007.

Hasmi, Talha. "FIA arrests members of porn ring for alleged involvement in raping, filming boys." *Geo News,* September 22, 2020. https://www.geo.tv/latest/309268-fia-arrests-members-of-porn-ring-for-alleged-involvement-in-raping-filming-boys.

Herbeck, Dan. "'I had become a monster'; Former teacher in prison for child pornography discusses his obsession and the nightmare it caused." Part 2. *Buffalo News,* October 18, 2005.

Hughes, Donna M. "'Welcome to the Rape Camp': Sexual Exploitation and the Internet in Cambodia." *Journal of Sexual Aggression* 6 (2008): 29–51.

Ibrahim, Dyna. "Trafficking in Persons in Canada, 2016." *Statistics Canada.* https://www150.statcan.gc.ca/n1/pub/85-005-x/2018001/article/54979-eng.htm.

Lederer, Laura J. "Trafficking in Persons Report." *Global Centurion*, July 14, 2014. https://www.globalcenturion.org/2014-trafficking-in-persons-report-statement-by-laura-j-lederer/.

MacKinnon, Catharine A. "Pornography as Trafficking." *Michigan Journal of International Law* 26/4 (2005): 993–1012.

Michel, Lou. "Day Three: A child victim's story of betrayal and despair." *Buffalo News*, October 17, 2007.

Michel, Lou, and Susan Schulman. "Russia and US-bound in illegal cyber-trafficking." *Buffalo News*, October 14, 2007.

National Center on Child Sexual Exploitation "About the National Center on Sexual Exploitation." https://endsexualexploitation.org/about/.

National Center on Child Sexual Exploitation. "Taking on Big Porn: Exposing the Abuse, Sex Trafficking and Harms to Children." https://vimeo.com/442185169/f2e8fd2f37?utm_source=newsletter&utm_medium=email&utm_campaign=NCOSE_Vimeo_Summit_TakingonBigPorn.

National Center for Missing and Exploited Children. "The Issues: Child Sex Trafficking." https://www.missingkids.org/theissues/trafficking.

Paul, Pamela. *Pornified*. Holt: New York, 2005.

Peters, Robert W. et al. "Slave and Porn Star." *Journal of Human Rights and Civil Society* 5 (2012): 1–20.

Pope John Paul II. *Man and Woman He Created Them: A Theology of the Body.* Translated by Michael Waldstein. Boston: Pauline Books and Media, 2006.

Pope Paul VI. *Humanae Vitae.* Boston: Pauline Books and Media, 1968.

Reisman, Judith. "Kinsey and the Homosexual Revolution. "*Journal of Human Sexuality* (1996): 21–28.

RT. "Iraqi refugee raped 10yo boy in Austria, says it was 'sexual emergency.'" February 6, 2016. https://www.rt.com/news/331594-iraqi-refugee-raped-boy/.

Seymour, Jayne. *Broken and Betrayed.* London: Pan, 2016.

Smothers, Ronald. "15 Arrested in New Jersey in Child Pornography Inquiry." *New York Times*, January 16, 2004.

Stringer, Jay. *Unwanted.* Carol Stream, IL: Tyndale, 2018.

Struthers, William. *Wired for Intimacy: How Pornography Hijacks the Male Brain.* Downers Grove, IL: Intervarsity, 2009.

United Nations General Assembly. "Protocol to Prevent, Suppress, and Punish, Trafficking in Persons, Especially Women and Children." November 15, 2000. https://www.ohchr.org/Documents/ProfessionalInterest/ProtocolonTrafficking.pdf.

United Nations Office on Drugs and Crime. "Global Report on Trafficking in Persons." June 25, 2020. https://va.usembassy.gov/trafficking-in-persons-report-2020/.

Wikipedia. "MTV—Censorship." https://en.wikipedia.org/wiki/MTV#Censorship.

Part III:

On Healthy Living: Lessons from Others and Personal Experience

Chapter 22

The Corruption of the Pharmaceutical Companies

James A. Harris

"True health care reform cannot happen in Washington. It has to happen in our kitchens, in our homes, in our communities. All health care is personal."

—Mehmet Oz

The Landing: My Personal Journey down the Healthcare Industry's Rabbit Hole

My curiosity about the world of the healthcare industry stemmed from one of many incidents in my life, where I suffered from a debilitating knee injury while practicing martial arts. I was performing a simple jumping spinning hook kick that I had performed routinely before, but somehow my body had failed to remember one of the most important techniques when performing this kick—the landing.

My foot wasn't positioned well to land properly from the air, so on impact I twisted my knee joint and stretched many ligaments in the process. The pain was so excruciating that my family doctor immediately recommended I see an orthopaedic surgeon for knee surgery. The doctor took x-rays of my knee and then explained that surgery was the standard protocol for such an injury. This seemed like welcoming news, until he informed me that it would take approximately six to eight months to heal after the surgery was completed. "Six to eight months!" I remember thinking; "that's way too long for me to put my very active lifestyle on hold!" The news was absolutely devastating and exhausting to even think about. Just the thought of using crutches for so long gave me a headache. This mental exhaustion would turn out to be a significant factor in my rapid recovery less than two weeks after the scheduled knee surgery.

My appointment for surgery was at 2:00 PM in mid-January of 2005. Due to the mental stressors of undergoing surgery and being essentially handicapped for six months *if* the surgery was successful, I decided to take a quick power nap to relax. Maybe I was more exhausted than I felt at the time, because

I remember waking up at 2:43 PM. It was too late—I had missed my 2:00 appointment! Interestingly enough, I wasn't upset at all about missing the surgery appointment. Perhaps because I believed deep down that there had to be a better way to fix this knee injury. My mind then shifted from the surgery to other possible solutions. I settled on going to the local Fitness Depot to buy a treadmill machine and slowly walk my knee back into shape. After all, this is what we always see on television when people are recovering from such injuries and learning to walk properly again, right?

When I arrived at the Fitness Depot, a store manager asked me what I was looking for. I explained my ideal non-surgical solution of getting a treadmill to walk my knee back into shape, to which he smiled and said; "Why don't you first try glucosamine supplements before spending so much money on this machine? It's what's recommended for people who have hip replacement surgery to speed up the healing process." At the time, I had never heard of glucosamine, so I asked him to write it down on a piece of paper; I would pick up a bottle from the drug store to see if it helped.

The glucosamine supplements turned out to be just the miracle drug I needed. In less than two weeks of taking the supplements, my knee was back to normal. I remember feeling elated, shocked, and somewhat infuriated. Why, I thought, would doctors recommend such an expensive and invasive surgery, which would essentially handicap someone for well over six months, when possibly all they needed was some glucosamine supplements? There must be more to this medical mishap story. Thus began my journey down the industry's bottomless rabbit hole of corruption. Not all healthcare professionals have our best interest in mind when it comes to healing. This was also the seed catalyst I needed planted in my mind for me to fully understand and accept that the body can and will "heal itself," as long as the proper nutrients and mindset are there to help it do so.

This chapter will explore some of the research on this issue. We will begin by investigating the condition of today's pharmaceutical industry and the role it plays in the healthcare system. It will show that the two industries are deeply intertwined, with often systemic conflicts of interest, sometimes at the expense of the public's health. We will start to see a clearer picture of why so many people are suffering with chronic illnesses like diabetes, high blood pressure, heart disease, and dementia despite our profound medical and technological advancements. We will examine how this crisis developed and how it may be solved. There are many unanswered essential questions, like whether some medications and surgeries are regularly recommended solely for monetary purposes (just like the surgery I was advised was essential for my knee to heal)—just so this industry can continue to thrive financially.

It's certainly important to acknowledge the amazing medical professionals who have not lost their moral compass in the dark haze of our healthcare industry. There's some absolutely fantastic research continuously being done to save lives. According to the National Institute of Health (NIH), approximately 500,000 children's lives are saved every single year by Oral Rehydration Therapy (ORT) alone—a relatively inexpensive means of treating diarrheal dehydration, which is the leading cause of childhood death in societies where ORT is not available. However, it is equally essential to highlight the enormous number of medical mistakes and abuses within these industries, in order to help remedy this crisis—in May of 2016 the *British Medical Journal* (BMJ) published an article with the headline "Medical error—the third leading cause of death in the U.S." The article estimated that as many as 250,000 deaths per year in the United States were caused by *medical mistakes*.

We will also explore some potential solutions to this healthcare crises by looking at the some of the healthiest cities on the planet, called "Blue Zones." What are these cities doing so differently from the rest of the world? Is it possible that their methodology of healthy living can somehow be implemented in other communities to increase longevity? If the healthcare industry's leaders are interested in having healthy populations, then this sort of healthy lifestyle should be embraced wholeheartedly. It is sometimes said that "a customer cured is a customer lost." If this is the medical mantra, then we are certainly in trouble. In any case, we certainly can and must do better for the simple sake of future generations. Let us now look at some of the sinister sales of drugs and vaccines being plastered and promoted all over the mainstream media by the pharmaceutical industry—"Big Pharma." These experimental chemicals are rarely tested properly and are often rushed to the market under the guise of safety. What originally starts off as only one minor medical issue then becomes several major side-effect concerns, which often require more medications to be prescribed in turn—so the cycle keeps on going. At what point do we start to say, "enough is enough!"

Pharmaceutical Industry Sales in—Humanity out

According to the Federal Trade Commission, the pharmaceutical industry uses more widespread advertising than any other industry in the United States.[1] Recently, both the American College of Physicians and the American Medical Association called for a limitation of pharmaceutical industry's marketing procedures. Despite this, the industry did not alter its ways, maintaining that its ad campaigns were "educational," and that people were able to make their own decisions about what they purchased.[2] However, it is evident that

1 Greenan, *Report of the Presiding Officer on Proposed Trade Regulation Rule.*
2 Payer, *Disease-Mongers*, 66.

the advertisements produced by the pharmaceutical industry are designed for the very purpose of making it difficult for people to make these decisions independently.

One of the most ubiquitous tactics employed by the pharmaceutical industry is selling drugs which produce side effects, hoping that consumers will purchase more drugs to treat the side effects. For example, some drugs that were prescribed for arthritis caused gastrointestinal bleeding. The pharmaceutical companies' response to this was to create more drugs to treat these stomach problems.[3] Many other drugs which claim to treat symptoms also cause other health problems. These adverse reactions to drugs are not seen as a risk by the pharmaceutical companies; they are viewed as an opportunity to sell more drugs. This strategy is obviously harmful to the consumer but is only a small part of the problem we're facing.

The number of "experts" (including physicians, medical writers, researchers, and other medical professionals) who accept money from pharmaceutical companies is unbelievably large. When a study was done at UCLA in 1992, the authors wanted to select a group of these experts as reviewers. Initially, they had intended to exclude all experts who had received more than $300 in the past two years from the pharmaceutical industry. However, this criterion was soon waived because they could not find a sufficient number who fit this criterion.[4] It was found that 71 percent of the reviewers who had initially been selected to take part in the study had received a substantial amount of money from the pharmaceutical industry in the past two years.[5]

Even more alarming is the fact that more than half of these experts had received over $5,000.[6] In the face of this, it would be foolish to assume that the pharmaceutical industry does not, to some degree, control the medical professionals in whom the American public places its trust. Another widely used marketing tactic is the promotion of unnecessary products. For example, a slew of ads were published a few years ago which suggested that people get their cholesterol level tested because it could be dangerously high. Cholesterol-lowering drugs such as lovastatin were prescribed for people with cholesterol levels that were considered to be too high. However, a number of these drugs produced health hazards which were, in many cases, worse than the cholesterol-related diseases they were supposedly intended to prevent.[7] According to Dr. Ralph Lach, "the cholesterol hysteria currently sweeping our country and its physicians is clearly the machination of the pharmaceutical industry."[8]

3 Payer, *Disease-Mongers*, 65.
4 Payer, *Disease-Mongers*, 68.
5 Payer, *Disease-Mongers*, 68.
6 Payer, *Disease-Mongers*, 68.
7 Payer, *Disease-Mongers*, 66.
8 Payer, *Disease-Mongers*, 6.

Many studies have shown that "cholesterol-lowering" drugs increase the risk of other diseases by the same amount that they claim to decrease heart disease, and therefore are not beneficial in the long run.[9] Cholesterol-lowering drugs, however, are not the only often non-beneficial drugs endorsed by the pharmaceutical industry. Many other examples exist. For example, according to a research study by the University of Kentucky and the University of Wisconsin, 60 percent of cold sufferers use antibiotics, while only 20 percent are helped by them.[10] These drugs, therefore, are fundamentally unnecessary. Their advertisements deceive the consumer into spending an exorbitant amount of money needlessly. In addition, they deceive consumers into thinking that they are helpful in "curing" them, when they actually are not.

Furthermore, there are the financial incentives for medical doctors, who may feel they are underpaid compared to their specialized colleagues (such as surgeons). To compensate, many doctors truncate visits to ten or fifteen minutes and increase the number of patients they see on any given day. Working in such haste certainly increases cognitive mistakes; it also limits a doctor's ability to impart the most basic information about treatment. A study of 45 doctors caring for 909 patients found that two-thirds of the physicians did not tell the patient how long to take the new medication or what side effects it may cause. Nearly half of the doctors failed to specify the dose and frequency of a medication.[11]

Money over Medicine

In 2010, antidepressants were the second most commonly prescribed medications (just behind cholesterol-lowering agents), costing patients about $10 billion altogether. The rate of antidepressant use across all ages exploded from 1988 to 2008, increasing nearly 400 percent. One study showed that medical professionals other than psychiatrists wrote 80 percent of these prescriptions, often without any specific psychiatric diagnoses.[12] Dr. Andrew Weil, M.D., explains in his book *Mind over Meds* how too many people are being prescribed medications today unnecessarily:

> Moreover, when used long term, many of the most widely prescribed medications can actually prolong or worsen the conditions they are meant to relieve. The reason has to do with *homeostasis*, a basic principle of physiology that designates a living organism's tendency to maintain

9 Payer, *Disease-Mongers*, 66.
10 Greenan, "Flash! Colds and Antibiotics: A Weak Link," 94.
11 Groopman, "How Doctors Think," 86.
12 Weil, *Mind over Meds*, 124.

> equilibrium (The word *homeostasis* derives from Greek roots, meaning "standing still."). If an external force disturbs the body's balance, the body reacts against it to regain balance. Reduce caloric intake and your body compensates by slowing metabolism—to the great frustration of dieters. Most of our medications counteract or suppress aspects of physiology. You can quickly get a sense of this by considering the names of drug categories. We use anti-spasmodics, anti-hypertensive, anti-depressants, anti-inflammatories, anti-this and anti-that. Strong counteractive medications are indeed useful for short-term management of health conditions resulting from severe imbalances of body function. When they are continued long term, however, especially without attention to the root causes of illness, they are likely to ensnare patients in the homeostatic trap. The body reacts against the pharmacological actions, making it difficult to lower dosage or discontinue medication because of rebound symptoms.[13]

It is becoming abundantly clear that many of these prescription medications are disturbing the body's physiology, throwing it totally out of balance. In some cases, they trigger the immune system to overreact in order to restore homeostasis. Even "synthetic" vitamins are considered to be antigens—foreign invaders against the body's natural defence mechanisms. We can no longer afford the convenience of inexpensive processed foods. We must get our nutrients from all-natural sources (organic whole food, etc.) irrespective of cost if we want to be healthy long-term. Exposing our bodies to one chemical after another in order to treat an adverse reaction to a medication defies common sense! We have to start treating the root cause (which can certainly be psychological in many cases) instead of just masking the symptoms with so many toxic pharmaceuticals.

Another major concern with the pharmaceutical industry is the methods used to create these chemicals in the first place. We are often trying to test new drugs by making a correlation between human beings and genetically modified rodents—who have similar genes to ours but significantly shorter life spans, which are not being taken into consideration.

Pharmaceutical Production Using Misguided Models

Many drugs are tested on animals—mostly rats or genetically altered mice. In some cases, these animals are appropriate models for human disease because we have some genes in common with them. To date, roughly four thousand genes in humans and mice have been studied, and just a few of them were

13 Weil, *Mind over Meds*, 124.

found to be existing in only one species. But these unique genes result in all kinds of biological differences, ranging from how genes get turned on and off to important qualities like lifespan. Lifespan in mice is only two to three years; any self-respecting mouse would be insulted by the suggested correlation. Yet we humans are embracing the research unequivocally!

The significance of their shorter life span is that it isn't sufficient enough to allow them to endure the kind of stress a human does over the course of seventy or eighty years. They are not subjected to inflammation, oxidation, insulin resistance, or vascular assaults in the same way we are. Thus, this testing model simply can't replicate the complicated biology of neurological diseases like Alzheimer's in the human brain.[14] In fact, none of the current models used today are accurate representatives of these complex neurological diseases. In mouse models, false amyloid lesions lead to false results. In neuro-lattice models, an incomplete picture leads to an incomplete treatment. As any scientist will tell you, an inaccurate model will only yield inaccurate results.[15]

If our testing models for pharmaceuticals are flawed, then we are only producing drugs that potentially have devastating long-term effects on the human body. Researchers are well aware that there is no commonality of pathways in genetically altered mice and humans, but they continue to work with a flawed model. This is why so many clinical trials fail—our animal models don't even come close to representing the diseases like Alzheimer's we're trying to cure.[16]

For example, there are only five medications approved by the FDA for the treatment of Alzheimer's symptoms today. Cholinesterase inhibitors (Aricept, Exelon, and Razadyne) are used in early-to-moderate cases, designed to target short-term memory loss, confusion, and impaired thinking and reasoning. These drugs do not stop Alzheimer's from progressing but may lessen the symptoms, for about six to twelve months on average.[17] In more advanced Alzheimer's patients Memantine (Namenda) can help block a specific type of neuron receptor called NMDA, which binds to glutamate—the most common neurotransmitter in our brains.[18] Finally, there's a newly concocted drug called Namzaric—a mixture of the previous two mentioned (Aricept and Namenda), sometimes prescribed to those with moderate-to-severe Alzheimer's. All these drugs can have debilitating side effects like nausea, vomiting, dizziness, nightmares, and headaches. Yet they have no effect whatsoever on the progression of Alzheimer's.[19]

14 Sherzai and Sherzai, *The Alzheimer's Solution*, 32–33
15 Sherzai and Sherzai, *The Alzheimer's Solution*, 33.
16 Sherzai and Sherzai, *The Alzheimer's Solution*, 33.
17 Sherzai and Sherzai, *The Alzheimer's Solution*, 30.
18 Sherzai and Sherzai, *The Alzheimer's Solution*, 30.
19 Sherzai and Sherzai, *The Alzheimer's Solution*, 30.

The pharmaceutical industry is one of the most powerful industries on the planet today. It has complete control over the mainstream media (MSM), with the exception of a few independent outlets. Social media platforms like Facebook and Google are censoring any medical professionals who dare to go against the narrative put forth by them.

This misguided mindset forces one to seek health advice from other, more reliable sources. What is important is that we understand that the human body is equipped with a powerful immune system that is innately designed to protect the body at all cost from invading pathogens. The same immune system is so determined to annihilate invaders that it can often go awry and begin to damage the body itself, as happens in autoimmune diseases, such as lupus and rheumatoid arthritis.[20] Our primary job is to keep the immune system healthy with proper nutrition, diet, and exercise. Processed foods are for the most part depleted of nutrition—which allopathic doctors are being taught isn't much of a factor in our health. Yet the lack of proper nutrition has been proven to be the leading cause of immune deficiency worldwide.[21]

The good news is that the tide is turning in favour of a more natural holistic approach to medicine and people are taking their health into their own hands. *Time* magazine recently released a special edition entitled "Alternative Medicine: The New Mainstream." This indicates that society itself is the real health authority. In this edition, an article by Alice Park is titled "Just What the Doctor Ordered: The medical community is starting to consider the possibility that food is the best medicine." In the next section we will look at Blue Zone communities that have taken healthy diet, stress management, and exercise to a whole new level of understanding, health, and longevity.

Enter the Blue Zone

Loma Linda, California, a small city located sixty miles east of Los Angeles, is widely considered one of the healthiest places on the planet. A third of its roughly twenty-five thousand residents are Seventh Day Adventists whose faith deeply promotes health and wellness. The religion encourages vegetarianism, regular exercise, stress management, and community service. Smoking, drinking, and even caffeine consumption are discouraged. This unusually healthy lifestyle results in the faith's followers living longer (ten years, on average) and healthier lives than the rest of the population.[22]

20 Vanderhaeghe and Bouic, *The Immune System Cure,* 9.
21 Groopman, *How Doctors Think,* 124.
22 Walsh, "Nothing to Sneeze About," 40.

Loma Linda is also America's only "Blue Zone," a term popularized by Dan Buettner in *The Blue Zone*, his bestselling book about lifestyle and longevity. Blue Zones are communities in which people live much longer and healthier lives due to optimal nutrition, exercise, stress management, and social support. Buettner says there are nine tenets of healthy living in Blue Zones:

1. A lifestyle that involves natural movement throughout the day.
2. A deep sense of purpose or meaning.
3. Skilful stress management.
4. Avoiding overeating and eating late at night.
5. A primarily plant-based diet.
6. Enjoying a drink or two with friends (Adventists prefer non-alcoholic drinks).
7. Connection to a faith community.
8. Living near family and finding a lifelong partner.
9. Access to social networks that support living.[23]

Communities with such a comprehensive healthy lifestyle are extremely rare. There are only five of them on the planet: Sardinia, Italy; Okinawa, Japan; Ikaria, Greece; Nicoya, Costa Rica; and Loma Linda, California. Buettner's revolutionary research on the healthy lifestyle behaviours of these diverse communities has since inspired researchers to investigate the underlying science. Many cities across the world have subsequently adopted features of the Blue Zone lifestyle, hoping that their residents will experience the same incredible health and longevity.[24]

There's a very inspiring story worth mentioning here, of a native of one of these Blue Zone cities, Stamatis Moraitus. He was diagnosed with terminal lung cancer while living in the United States. He decided to go back home to his native island of Ikaria, Greece. The plan was to have an inexpensive funeral (around 200 dollars) and be buried alongside his ancestors. Despite the nine months which "nine oncologists" confirmed he had left to live, he ended up surviving for forty more years without any standardized medical treatment. Moraitus died cancer-free in 2013, outliving all nine oncologists who gave him only a few months to live after his initial diagnosis. His story was reported in the *New York Times*:

> In 1943, a Greek war veteran named Stamatis Moraitis came to the United States for treatment of a combat-mangled arm. He'd survived a gunshot wound, escaped to Turkey and eventually talked his way onto the Queen Elizabeth, then serving as a troopship, to cross the Atlantic.

23 Walsh, "Nothing to Sneeze About," 42.
24 Bjerklie, "The New Roads to Wellness," 4.

Moraitis settled in Port Jefferson, N.Y., an enclave of countrymen from his native island, Ikaria. He quickly landed a job doing manual labor. Later, he moved to Boynton Beach, Fla. Along the way, Moraitis married a Greek-American woman, had three children and bought a three-bedroom house and a 1951 Chevrolet.

One day in 1976, Moraitis felt short of breath. Climbing stairs was a chore; he had to quit working midday. After X-rays, his doctor concluded that Moraitis had lung cancer. As he recalls, nine other doctors confirmed the diagnosis. They gave him nine months to live. He was in his mid-60s.

Moraitis considered staying in America and seeking aggressive cancer treatment at a local hospital. That way, he could also be close to his adult children. But he decided instead to return to Ikaria, Greece (one of the five Blue Zone cities), where he could be buried with his ancestors in a cemetery shaded by oak trees that overlooked the Aegean Sea. He figured a funeral in the United States would cost thousands, a traditional Ikarian one only $200, leaving more of his retirement savings for his wife, Elpiniki. Moraitis and Elpiniki moved in with his elderly parents, into a tiny, whitewashed house on two acres of stepped vineyards near Evdilos, on the north side of Ikaria. At first, he spent his days in bed, as his mother and wife tended to him. He reconnected with his faith. On Sunday mornings, he hobbled up the hill to a tiny Greek Orthodox chapel where his grandfather once served as a priest. When his childhood friends discovered that he had moved back, they started showing up every afternoon. They'd talk for hours, an activity that invariably involved a bottle or two of locally produced wine. I might as well die happy, he thought.

In the ensuing months, something strange happened. He says he started to feel stronger. One day, feeling ambitious, he planted some vegetables in the garden. He didn't expect to live to harvest them, but he enjoyed being in the sunshine, breathing the ocean air. Elpiniki could enjoy the fresh vegetables after he was gone.

Six months came and went. Moraitis didn't die. Instead, he reaped his garden and, feeling emboldened, cleaned up the family vineyard as well. Easing himself into the island routine, he woke up when he felt like it, worked in the vineyards until mid-afternoon, made himself lunch, and then took a long nap. In the evenings, he often walked to the local tavern, where he played dominoes past midnight. The years passed. His health continued to improve. He added a couple of rooms to his parents' home so his children could visit. He built up the vineyard until it produced 400 gallons of wine a year. Today, three and a half decades later, he's 97 years old—according to an official document he disputes; he says he's 102—and cancer-free. He never went through chemotherapy, took drugs or sought therapy of any sort. All he did was move home to Ikaria.[25]

25 Buettner, "The Island Where People Forget to Die."

Final Thoughts: Sticking to the Landing

On January 15, 2015, almost 10 years to the day after my knee injury and subsequent missed surgery appointment, I was running late for a morning meeting and decided to take a shortcut through the lawn of the building—which unbeknownst to me had patches of slippery snow-covered ice. I eventually slipped and fell sideways on the ice and heard a cracking sound. My ankle was clearly twisted out of place, but I managed to adjust it back. After about two weeks, I was still feeling intense pain and decided to have x-rays taken just in case it was worse than I thought. The orthopaedic surgeon looked at me and said: "It's a clear fracture right down the middle!" He also showed me the cracked bone leading down to the ankle. Then he said, "I have no idea how you've been walking on this injury for two weeks." He prescribed a removable cast for my left leg and said I should use it for a month and then come back to see him. I removed the annoying cast the next day but did go back to see him a month later for the follow-up. He noticed I wasn't wearing the cast and said, "You're very brave, but you have to realise that if your bones don't heal properly, we may have to bring you in for surgery." I responded to him while looking at my x-rays on the monitor, which were showing no sign of the crack that was there before. "Yes sir, I was told by another orthopaedic surgeon 10 years ago that surgery was essential for these types of injuries." I went home, took my 'glucosamine' supplements, and fell asleep. It seemed that even after a decade, the narrative hadn't changed, perhaps because medical schools have not changed. This is why health education is so vital to any project. It is the foundation upon which everything else is built, because if we are not mentally and physically healthy there is not much we can do to help others—whether by activism, protest, or politics. It is my hope that this drop in the ocean of understanding, about the corruption within the pharmaceutical and healthcare industries as a whole, sheds a bit more light on this topic so our medical professionals can, without fear of losing their careers, start to honour their sworn Hippocratic oath to "First do no harm!"

Bibliography

Bjerklie, David. "The New Roads to Wellness," in Alternative Medicine: The New Mainstream, Special edition, *Time* (January 1, 2020): 4–7.

Buettner, Dan. "The Island Where People Forget to Die." *New York Times*, October 12, 2012. https://www.nytimes.com/2012/10/28/magazine/the-island-where-people-forget-to-die.html?_r=2&.

Greenan, James P. "Flash! Colds and Antibiotics: A Weak Link." *FTC*, October 1996.

———. *Report of the Presiding Officer on Proposed Trade Regulation Rule: Concerning the Advertising of Over-the Counter Antacids*. Washington, D.C.: Federal Trade Commission, 1979.

Groopman, Jerome. *How Doctors Think*. Boston and New York: Houghton Mifflin Harcourt, 2008.

Payer, Lynn. *Disease-Mongers: How Doctors, Drug Companies, and Medical Insurers are Making You Feel Sick*. New York: John Wiley and Sons, 1992.

Sherzai, Dean and Ayesha Sherzai. *The Alzheimer's Solution: A Breakthrough Program to Prevent and Reverse the Symptoms of Cognitive Decline at Every Age*. New York: HarperCollins, 2019.

Vanderhaeghe, Lorna R. and Patrick J. D. Bouic. *The Immune System Cure: Nature's Way to Super-Powered Health*. New York: Kensington Publishing, 2000.

Walsh, "Nothing to Sneeze About," "The New Roads to Wellness," in *Alternative Medicine: The New Mainstream*, Special edition, *Time* (January 1, 2020): 40–44.

Weil, Andrew. *Mind over Meds*. New York: Little, Brown and Company, 2017.

Chapter 23

Phil Lynott in Retrospect: From Tragedy to Christian Hope

Scott D. G. Ventureyra

The thirty-sixth anniversary of Phil Lynott's death gives us the opportunity to reflect on a tragic life that could have been transformed. On January 4, 1986, at the age of 36, Lynott died of heart failure and pneumonia caused by a heroin overdose and many bouts of heavy drinking. He was the frontman, founding member, bassist, and main songwriter of Thin Lizzy, a prolific rock band from Ireland that gained prominence during the 1970s and 1980s. Although they released many songs and memorable albums, they were best known for their 1976 mega-hit "The Boys Are Back in Town."

All too often the lives of rock 'n' roll icons like Lynott end with tremendous sorrow. Other notable examples include the death of Scott Weiland (former frontman of Stone Temple Pilots) in December of 2015 and the heart-breaking death of Tony Sly, the talented frontman of the punk rock band No Use for a Name, in the summer of 2012. And on and on, as if, sadistically, programmed into the genetics of these individuals and the fabric of the universe they inhabit. These ostensibly tortured souls succumb to inescapable proclivities combined with a seemingly endless supply of deadly substances. So, the scientific-materialist narrative goes, right? Christian truth, however, points in a different direction, where grace and true freedom can break such individuals free from lives bent on destruction.

Although self-inflicted because of an indulgence in dangerous excesses, such a pathway to tragedy, unless escaped, nonetheless leaves family, friends, and fans in a bleak enveloping void. Not surprisingly, even somewhat poignantly prophetic, Lynott modelled himself after dead rock stars such as Elvis Presley, Jimi Hendrix, Janis Joplin, and Jim Morrison, who had succumbed to similar self-fulfilled finalities. The eerie cry for help in his song "Got to Give It Up" attests to the realization of the severity of his addictions. Unfortunately, he did not fully commit himself to finding a way out. Lynott knew the consequences of his actions and the inevitability of his impending death, at a relatively young age, caused by a successive chain of poor decisions. Oddly, it was as though he embraced it through his morbid fascination with the tragic endings of others. It reminds me of the great singer Jeff Buckley (who did not have severe addictions himself), who had an untimely death akin to his own father, Tim Buckley. There is a proleptic feel to the words of these men when considered after their deaths.

Without a doubt, Lynott was a talented musician and a brilliant songwriter. His brokenness inspired him to write many great musical compositions. He possessed a tremendous knack for articulating one's very own sentiments and sorrows in wonderful verse. Three songs stand out the most. "Running Back" speaks of a dissolved relationship with playfully sarcastic humour that expresses the pain subsisting past the end of the relationship. Some of Lynott's songs were positive and optimistic. "Do Anything You Want To" is a good example.

Finally, *Southbound* is a song about new beginnings that possesses an infectiously melodic guitar riff coupled with a nostalgic evocative quality. It brings back many memories. Some old and some more recent, including images of driving my car while playing it with the windows down on a tranquil summer evening as my daughter sings along.

Despite these magnificent songwriting talents, the deaths of rock icons such as Lynott serve as one of the many stark reminders of the perils of our fallen world. The universe and everything in it are not as they were originally intended by God. The deeply imbued remnants of our original selfishness inherited by the fallen created order and all living things in it leave us in a devastating despair, if left solely to our own devices. Even in his pitiful state, Lynott realized there was no escape outside of Christ. In his song "The Holy War," he recognizes the wages of sin through a cosmic battle between God and the devil where we are all active participants.

Shortly before his death he repented of his selfish life. His mother saw at his deathbed, for the first time, the hidden scars of addiction on the soles of his feet. It is my hope that this repentance was a true one and that Lynott was saved by the only One who can save us from ourselves. Indeed, God's mercy is always within our grasp if we truly repent.

Ultimately, there is a positive message that can be taken from Lynott's death over thirty-six years ago. Let us not ignore the signs of despair we see in others around us. It is Christ-like to extend a hand to help one who is struggling with addiction. Of course, people must have the desire to help themselves in order for us to make any meaningful impact on them. Nevertheless, we can reach out in subtle ways, showing love and compassion, as Jesus did with sinners of all stripes. Jesus boldly declares in Luke 5:32, "I have not come to call the righteous, but sinners to repentance." Jesus came for *all*, since as Romans 3:23 declares, "for all have sinned and fall short of the glory of God." The point not to be missed is that Christ came for the very sinners who recognized their need of His salvific gift. Lynott may have only truly recognized this in the face of death. Sometimes it is in this confrontation with despair that we can attain *kenosis*: the act of self-emptying and becoming one with Christ. Let us pray that every single one of us become aligned to God's will.

Chapter 24

Fell on a Black Day: A Reflection on Chris Cornell's Suicide

Scott D. G. Ventureyra

Chris Cornell, the frontman of the Seattle grunge rock bands Soundgarden and Audioslave, was declared dead on May 18, 2017. It soon emerged that the cause of death was suicide by hanging. His suicide was shocking not only to his fans but even to his wife, Vicky, who allegedly stated that Chris had not demonstrated any signs of depression prior to his final concert in Detroit on May 17 with Soundgarden.[1]

Chris was one of my favourite singers when I was growing up. Over the years, I found myself appreciating his work more and more, including his collaboration with some members of Rage Against the Machine, which resulted in the formation of Audioslave. His work as a solo artist further showed his creativity as a gifted songwriter. He had an impressive four-octave vocal range combined with a unique talent for authoring poignant lyrics and thoughtfully composed music. His versatility is reflected in an array of songs such "Can't Change Me," "Like a Stone," and the beautiful acoustic ballad "Sunshower" for the *Great Expectations* soundtrack, not to mention the many songs he wrote for Soundgarden. He recorded an exceptional interpretation of Michael Jackson's "Billie Jean." He also performed a beautiful rendition of "Ave Maria" which displays his extraordinary vocal range. One could go on and on about his musical achievements, but this is not the purpose of this chapter.

Initially, when I thought of writing a piece on Chris, I considered focusing on the notion that we never know when we will die and that we must cherish

1 Since then, there have been many claims spreading online that Cornell and Chester Bennington (lead singer of Linkin Park), who committed suicide on July 20, 2017, did not commit suicide but instead were murdered. See Lerintiu, "Interview with music rock journalist Randy 'Rocket.'" The claim is that they were both involved, alongside Anthony Bourdain and Avicii, in a documentary about child trafficking titled *The Silent Children*, as per this Facebook page: https://www.facebook.com/ktspredhuntersllc/posts/166141601795776. I do not offhand dismiss these claims, but at the present time I have no corroborating evidence. This also would not take away from the message of this article, namely that people should turn to God in moments of despair and suffering.

every moment by giving God thanks for the gift of life. However, further developments could not permit me to continue with this line of thought. Suicide is a difficult subject to broach, but I cannot conclude that he was merely determined by his genetics and environment to execute such an act, although it now seems the usage of Ativan for relieving anxiety may have impaired his judgment. But is that a sufficient explanation? Some are speculating that Soundgarden's cover of Led Zeppelin's song "In My Time of Dying," which was their last song of the set the day before he died, was Chris' goodbye to the world.[2] Something tells me he was very cognizant of what was to transpire next.

Depression and mental illness are very difficult subjects to tackle, but I am persuaded that there are always ways out of certain predicaments, that is, if one wants a way out. I am neither a hard nor a soft determinist (compatibilist);[3] I really do believe we are morally responsible for our actions, which, in my estimation, make us both praiseworthy and blameworthy; neither neuroscience nor physics precludes this. I think we have good philosophical and theological reasons to affirm genuine free will. After all, why would we praise Cornell's musical abilities if it were not him who freely and creatively composed and performed such wonderful music? Are we to praise matter in motion, i.e., the unintended firing of neurons to produce something that utterly transcends physics? Neither the informational content of music nor the subjective experience of it can be reduced to the mere sounds produced by the instruments or vocal cords. We can also ask why we would condemn serial murderers and child rapists if we are wholly determined by genetic makeup and environmental factors. It is quite simple: if no one has any moral responsibility, then we do not have the right to praise or blame anyone. Throughout our lives we cultivate virtues and vices. We do not become the persons we are overnight. In a world without God, the afterlife, and free will, things *just are*, whether we like them or not; as Richard Dawkins has observed, such an understanding of the universe is filled with "nothing but blind pitiless indifference."

I am sorry for Chris's children, wife, family, friends, and fans. As a huge fan, I am also saddened, in a selfish way, since I would have loved to hear more recordings and live performances. However, more importantly, as a follower of Christ it saddens me to think of his despair, depression, or confusion, or whatever it was that led him to this path of irreparable damage. Apparently, Chris became part of the body of Christ through his conversion to Greek Orthodoxy, but one never truly knows the heart or mind of another person. Let us hope that there was a genuine moment of repentance before it was too late, for we cannot know the hidden thoughts of any individual. Let us also hope that in those final moments, Chris reached out to the Redeemer of all, instead

2 Vincent, "'I guess that was his goodbye.'"
3 Timpe, "Free Will."

of as in his famous line from "Like a Stone" where he reaches out like a pagan to any angel or god.

There is this indubitable and inescapable hidden pathos in every one of us, whether we acknowledge it or not. Some of us attempt to suffocate it with alcohol, drugs, sex, or countless other distractions that become false idols. False idols are worshipped whenever we put any created thing above God. However, this struggle that is manifested through various ills can only ever be overcome by the Source of all, the ultimate uncreated reality, which is God. This is why St. Augustine observed that "our hearts are restless until they rest in [God]." Perhaps Chris had a similar realization when he wrote his cryptic lyrics in "Like a Stone" where he alludes to waiting for death, and perhaps for God.

Unfortunately, most people in such a plight will continue on their path of self-destruction and can only stop through acknowledgement of our predicament and its only true remedy. Personal autonomy and reliance on created things has never been, nor can ever be, the answer. True hope is found in everlasting life, through Christ's ultimate redemptive act. We must put our trust in Him and nothing else. Instead of his final decision, I wish that Chris would have "tried to live" that day.

Bibliography

Lerintiu, Monica K. "Interview with music rock journalist Randy "Rocket" Cody of THE METAL DEN." *Romania Journal*, January 20, 2020. https://www.romaniajournal.ro/spare-time/exclusive-yes-100-i-believe-both-chris-cornell-and-chester-bennington-were-murdered/.

Timpe, Kevin. "Free Will." *Internet Encyclopedia of Philosophy*. http://www.iep.utm.edu/freewill/.

Vincent, Alice. "'I guess that was his goodbye': Chris Cornell's [*sic*] covered Led Zeppelin's In My Time of Dying for his final song." *The Telegraph*, May 19, 2017. http://www.telegraph.co.uk/music/news/guess-goodbye-chris-cornells-covered-led-zeppelins-time-dying/.

Part IV:

On Gender Ideology

Chapter 25

Abortion Inequalities: Does Abortion Choice Treat Women and Men as Equals?

John D. Ferrer

The short answer to the question in the title is no. Abortion treats men and women as fundamentally unequal. It does this in a few different ways. A more immediate problem, however, is that this fundamental inequality is really hard to spot. The abortion debate is typically a foggy slog through a swamp of euphemisms, insults, distractions, and other obscuring rhetoric. As a pro-life male I typically hear that rhetoric in the form of at least one of these five abortion-choice rebuttals. They come almost every time abortion enters the conversation. Yet each of these talking points is liable to consume the entire conversation, leaving no room to consider how abortion creates inequalities that disadvantage women.

- "No womb, no say."—I am a man, so allegedly, I don't have a right to devote my life to protecting innocent children-in-utero or try to halt what is likely the deadliest crime against humanity in world history. Never mind that around half of all abortion victims are male, and the effects of abortion reverberate across the whole family and society, not just women.[1] "Masturbation is murder."—Haploid sperm cells, allegedly, are biologically equivalent to diploid embryos. Never mind that no self-respecting biologist agrees.
- "No one knows when human life begins."—According to many abortion-choice advocates either the scientific consensus is a vast conspiracy, or we just don't need to consult any of the experts from the last 50 years or so, especially not the embryologists, fetologists, and biologists who have settled on the conception definition for the origin of human life.

1 See Lee and Lucky, "No Utero, No Opinion"; Ferrer, "59 Reasons Why Men Need to Speak Out about Abortion."

- "What about rape and threats to the mother's life?"—These are legitimate "tough cases," which would cover maybe 2-4% of abortions. Abortion-choicers tend to think those cases should justify the other 96-98% of abortions too. But almost all pro-life bills allow exceptions for these cases. And those issues were grounds for legal abortion *before* Roe v. Wade, so they don't really justify the Roe v. Wade era policy.
- "My body, my right."—Bodily autonomy is the flagship of the pro-choice movement, yet it has never been clearly or sufficiently demonstrated that autonomy entails a license to kill one's own children-in-utero. Barring an overwhelming justification for this manner of fiat death-sentence, we cannot ethically support it. We shouldn't pass death sentences when there's reasonable doubt, especially when it's a ton of reasonable doubt about whether abortion is even remotely humanitarian.

I'm not claiming to have "solved" all these pro-choice rebuttals. But they are not anything new either. And when they are compared to the plain and apparent wrongness of deliberately killing innocent, non-threatening humans, the pro-choice position needs a much better defense for abortion than is currently available. The violinist argument,[2] blood donation,[3] and the burning lab experiment,[4] for example, do not cut it. As it stands, socially conscious humanitarians are not rationally justified in accepting a liberal abortion-choice policy.

Why not? Well, we cannot morally support a policy that's immoral. And it's immoral to allow the killing of innocent, non-threatening, non-combatant children-in-utero. It's not self-defense. It's selfish. It's not excising a tumor. It's cutting up a human. It's not expelling a parasite. It's destroying one's offspring. Humanitarian ethics demands we abstain from killing innocent humans unless and until all reasonable doubts over pro-choice policy have been resolved. We should not be issuing death sentences on the basis of a "maybe." And when those

2 The violinist argument refers to an article by Judith Jarvis Thomson postulating a feeble violinist who conscripts a woman, against her will, to share her kidney for nine months so he can live on. Thomson, "A Defense of Abortion." One among many compelling critiques against this argument is the de facto guardian argument from Wagner, "De Facto Guardian and Abortion: A Response to the Strongest Violinist."

3 Blood donation is a variant on the organ-donation argument (i.e., the violinist argument). It too is deeply problematic; see Brahm, "Blood Donation and Bodily Rights Arguments."

4 The "burning lab" thought experiment originally illustrated a point about human cloning. See Annas, "A French Homunculus in a Tennessee Court." But it gained notoriety in recent years as an illustration of abortion-choice dilemma. Rebutting the cloning argument is Damschen and Schönecker, "Saving Seven Embryos or Saving One Child?" Rebutting the abortion argument are George and Tolleffson, "Embryos and Five-Year-Olds: Whom to Rescue?"; and Ferrer, "A Simple Answer to a Burning Question."

death sentences are issued to the order of hundreds of thousands of innocent fetal humans every year, the moral case for abortion-choice crumbles under the weight of it all. Standing upright in the rubble of failed pro-choice attacks, the pro-life case like is tall statue, untarnished, in brilliant clarity.

When pro-choicers face up to the scope and scale of abortion,[5] or when they dare to dwell on the abortion procedures themselves, it's not hard to see why they might revert to the talking points above. The glare is blinding. A thick rhetorical fog can dim that glare.

But that same fog also hides a deeper divide between the pro-choice and pro-life camps. Rarely do abortion debates dispel that cloud of rhetoric enough to finally show how our camps disagree fundamentally. We are deeply divided on the issue of gender equality.

Abortion-choice Favors a Sexual Ethic That Disadvantages Women

To understand how abortion-choice ethics disadvantage women, it's important to get a sense of the distinguishing values between pro-lifers and pro-choicers.

Broadly speaking, anti-abortionists or "pro-lifers" are social conservatives, who affirm a family-focused ethic of responsible sexuality: modesty, chastity, and the sanctity of marriage. We know that people violate these norms all the time, but we can show grace and lend a helping hand while a teen mom tries to regain her footing. And we still uphold these traditional family values because we see them as good for their own sake and as giving strong, well-proven goals to aim for in guarding our hearts, strengthening families, stabilizing communities, and building the nation.[6] Plus, we can hold to an ethic of sexual responsibility as we walk people through the healing process in the wake of a marital affair, a porn addiction, an unplanned pregnancy, or even just a bad breakup. No sexual ethic, in this life, is going to be perfectly adhered to. But we don't need to detonate the entire bridge of responsible sexual ethics just because people swerve sometimes.

On the other side are abortion-choice advocates, also known as "pro-choicers." Typically identifying as social liberals, pro-choicers support libertine sexual ethics as a form of bodily autonomy. In other words, only the individual woman should have any say about what she does with her body. So long as she's using her body in ways that are harmless to the public, or private to herself or

5 Ferrer, "The Big Kill."

6 On the importance of sexual restraint/responsibility for society see Unwin, *Sex and Culture*. For briefer comments in that vein see Durston, "Why Sexual Morality May Be Far More Important Than You Ever Thought."

to consenting adults, then the going rule is "her body, her choice." This does not mean abortion-choice advocates are intentionally "anti-family" or "anti-community," but just that bodily autonomy tends to get more emphasis from this side than family or community responsibilities. Abortion-choice ideology is a predictable result when bodily autonomy is prized higher than social duties.

For pro-choicers, liberal abortion-choice policy is seen as a victory because women are claiming another "right," privilege, or power over their own body. They translate abortion choice policy into personal empowerment and greater freedom. Even if different levels of society were better off because of abortion (which is questionable), that's not the driving force behind abortion-choice policy. Individual self-interest is the fulcrum on which abortion policy turns. It might seem, then, that abortion-choice policy empowers women by granting wider access to liberty, choice, and opportunity.

But note that in abortion-choice ideology, the emphasis is on choice, not on responsibility. While this "choice" is supposed to liberate women, unless it is balanced by responsibility it's not really "liberty" at all but license, or even anarchy. License and anarchy are not healthy prescriptions.

It Permits Sex-selective Abortion

Abortion-choice ideology is reluctant to tell women to be responsible with their bodies, as that can sound like a loss of freedom, explicit oppression, or even "patriarchy."[7] As social liberals, pro-choicers typically value equality, human rights, and humanitarian ethics, yet liberal abortion-choice policy blatantly contradicts these values. Consider how abortion permits discrimination.

In my own experience, pro-choicers typically have never thought about how the current policy permits race-based, sex-selective, and ability-based abortion. Discriminating against members of the human race on the basis of race, sex, and ability is literally racism, sexism, and ableism. This can be a jolting realization for social liberals who tend to see conservatives as the racists, sexists, and bigots.

Focusing on sexism, sex-selective abortion is perhaps the clearest example of discrimination against women in modern times. In China and India, sex-selective abortion has reached epidemic proportions.[8] And with immigration patterns, it would not be surprising to see sex-selective abortion rising in Western Europe and North America. Yet libertine sexuality is too important to abortion-choice ideology. Its supporters cannot surrender this ideological hill even for

7 Neither side typically objects to telling men to be responsible with their bodies. We can grant this moral precept as a point of agreement between pro-life and pro-choice camps.

8 Li Lu and Xing, "The Consequences of Son Preference and Sex-selective Abortion in China."

the sake of uprooting this kind of explicit sexism. Abortion-choice ideology is married, pun intended, to sexual license—without responsibility—even to the point of permitting sexist killing.

It Reduces the Pool of Marriageable Males

Libertine sexuality also works against women's interests by undercutting marriage and family. Many women, conservative and liberal alike, still long to settle down and raise a family with the loving support of a loyal husband. Historically, traditional marriage and family models have a mixed but largely effective record of domesticating males, protecting and supporting females, and rearing children. Again, we are talking in broad terms here, but it's not hard to see that it's far easier for people to flourish in life when they had a stable home life with a mom and dad, in a traditional marriage, with evening meals, quality time, and so forth. The social and psychological studies supporting this point are easy enough to find, so I won't belabor you with them here.

Libertine sexuality, however, is not about harnessing and directing typical male aggression to make it useful for raising a family. If anything, libertine sexuality plays to the strengths of that particular sub-species of males who are trying to sleep around with as many women as they can, for as long they can get away with it, and as long as it's sanctioned by society. They are not necessarily criminal degenerates, but they have no serious interest in marriage, procreation, or fatherhood as long as they can keep up their adolescent sexscapade. Some of these misdirected aggressors could even make decent fathers and husbands—hence the feminine penchant for liking the "bad boys," sensing something sexy in their untamed strength. But so long as those overgrown boys can keep settling for sex addiction, meaningless hook-ups, and exploiting gullible women—and the wider culture excuses that behavior—they won't ever get around to the hard work of building their masculine identity into something redemptive for the sake of family and community. They will be useless, even harmful, to the institution of family.

Neither is libertine sexuality about protecting and supporting family-focused women who want their kids to have a father. Of course, the guys themselves are individually worse off for spiraling into sex addiction or hedonistic distraction. But the harm extends to women and children who suffer in the absence of upstanding men. Women are justified in wanting a committed, responsible, fully adult man for a husband and for a father to their kids. Of course, some women never want to marry or settle down and some opt for alternative lifestyles. But even among progressive liberal women, the maternal instinct is still quite strong. The desire to settle down and raise a family, with a dashing warrior-poet Prince Charming at her side—that's a dreamy ideal for countless women on every side of the political aisle. Those women, however, will have an even harder time finding a Prince Charming, or even a Mr. Okay, as long as a libertine sexual ethic reigns across western culture. Libertine sexuality isn't about disciplining the stereotypical male libido, or training people to be better husband or wife material, or imparting parenting and family skills. Libertine sexual ethics are more about shedding inhibitions, ideologies, and religious traditions that kept you from having as little or as much consensual sex as you want.

It Undercuts Other Attempts to Strengthen Marriage and Family

You may be thinking: "Responsible sexuality is just one facet of culture; we can't expect it to do all the heavy lifting in raising people up to marriage and family." True enough. Healthy marriages and families mostly consist of friendship, conflict resolution, communication skills, and things like that. Sexual ethics could be just a small part of all that. But libertine sexuality also tends to poke holes in every other effort to reinforce marriage and family.

For example, committing to libertine sexuality precludes any serious (non-hypocritical) commitment to religious traditions like Christianity, Islam, Judaism, and most streams of Buddhism and Hinduism, as these religions historically prohibit sex outside of marriage, prostitution, adultery, etc. Yet religious upbringing is one of the most tried-and-true ways to enculturate men and women into the social standards needed for healthy marriages and families. It's difficult to overstate the importance of the spirit of sacrifice it inculcates.

Libertine sexuality can also make parents look like hypocrites when they instruct their children to be more conservative and careful about sex than the parents were at that age. And the marriage itself can be undercut when the couple finds their marriage bed haunted, so to speak, by the ghosts of lovers past. Knowing that one's partner may have had much better sex with an ex-lover can create conflict, unseemly competition, and discontentment.

And of course, children are already able to access pornography and almost every kind of sexual vice imaginable online. When young people imbibe a libertine sexual ethic, they lack the maturity of adulthood to safeguard them from dangerous excess, misuse, and abuse. As long as the parents and children believe in libertine sexual ethics, they have one less guardrail to keep them from falling down that mountain.

It Fosters "Love 'em and leave 'em" Relationships

Libertine sexual ethics also mean women can be exploited by men who talk about romance and commitment, to "rope them in" and then dump them as soon as they've had their way. It's "love 'em and leave 'em." As long as sex is recast primarily as a recreational activity, unrelated to pregnancy, with no responsibility or commitment, there's little incentive in sight for immature males to strive for more than just hook-ups, or serial monogamy, or "sleeping around." It takes a lot of work to settle down, get married, and raise a family. And libertine sexual ethics have a deflating effect on that work capacity.

It doesn't take a rocket surgeon to see why this happens. When men don't have to get married to have sex with an attractive female acquaintance, they are less likely to get married. For adult males, few things are more motivating than sex.[9] Scores of women, however, aren't terribly interested in hook-up culture, preferring instead to prepare for marriage and family. But, as the old saying goes, "Why buy the cow if you can get the milk for free?" Libertine sexual ethics mean an endless supply of free milk.

But sexual ethics aren't the only tectonic divide between the two camps. There might be an even deeper fissure separating pro-choice and pro-life camps.

Pro-choice Ideology Implies Women Are Naturally Unequal to Men

Consider the most basic universal difference between women and men. Women make babies. Biological females, in their anatomy, psychology, and bio-chemistry, are specially equipped to gestate and deliver babies. While some women choose not to, and other women are prevented from it, absolutely no biological male has ever been able to birth a baby. This is the most glaring distinction of womanhood in all of biology. Abortion-choice advocates have to account for this fact, without degrading womanhood, if they hope to promote gender equality.

Abortion Choice Policy Treats Maternity as a Detriment

Yet time and again pro-choicers interpret this uniquely feminine ability as more a detriment than a distinction, more burden than blessing. Carrying children-

9 A monumental book that makes this point better than I could is Gilder, *Men and Marriage*. The distinctive views on sex typical of men and women also appear in evolutionary psychology. See Wright, *The Moral Animal*, 33–179.

in-utero to birth is seen largely as a disadvantage, making women naturally unequal. From that perspective, abortion-choice policy is the solution to that natural inequality. Women need a surgical option (abortion) to be able to have practical equality with men.

Pro-lifers, on the other hand, see this maternal capacity not as a detriment but as a dignity. Pregnancy and childbirth are uniquely beautiful abilities of women, for which they deserve care and protection so that dignity doesn't turn into a detriment. Of course, we can all agree that sad and regrettable circumstances can turn pregnancy into a burdensome trial; still, maternity isn't primarily a problem to be solved but an empowerment to be protected.

Remember, all our freedoms entail responsibilities. If the uniquely feminine ability to carry and birth babies is a "problem to solve," then abortion-choice policy might seem like a viable solution. But if child-bearing is uniquely empowering to women, then abortion-choice policy instead pressures people to reinterpret that power as a weakness. Womanhood, then, is construed as a fundamentally unequal state, an unfortunate outcome of biology that can only be cured by superimposing medical access and procedures on a woman.

It Interprets Sexual Differences in Favour of Men

All sides should be able to agree that men and women, biologically speaking, are fundamentally different. Pro-lifers can view differences between the sexes as distinct but equally valuable endowments from nature. Equal human rights allow for natural differences between men and women. Pro-choicers, however, implicitly interpret these basic differences as favoring men. If maternity is more liability than asset, and libertine ethics are the reigning paradigm for sex, then men do have the advantage.

Stated another way, if abortion-choice policies treat maternity mostly as a liability, then women can be led to believe that they need abortion access to have the same reproductive rights as men. Technically, that's false. Men aren't allowed to abort their children in the womb since men don't carry children in their womb. But setting that technicality aside, men can walk away from an unwanted pregnancy, and that's a privilege (allegedly) that abortion-choice extends to women.

Even in the modern era of feminism, birth control pills, and the sexual revolution, women are still disproportionately affected by pregnancy. Abortion policy, therefore, is an attempt to even the odds so that women and men can approach sex in roughly the same way. Before abortion-choice policy, men had the natural advantage, since they could walk away from any unwanted pregnancies. Women didn't have as much freedom to be casual about sex. Even "the pill," condoms, and other contraception aren't foolproof. Plus, women—more than men—are liable to bring different and competing goals to the relationship, for example, wanting intimacy, romance, and long-term commitment. Popular wisdom tells us that men use romance to leverage for sex and women use sex to leverage for romance.

Libertine sexuality, however, exalts sex as the primary commodity, without regard for marriage, children, family, or social responsibility. Women are at a disadvantage when they long for those things more than sex. Men can long for those things too, but history testifies that men are typically more driven by sex than women are. And medical science testifies that men can reach orgasm more easily and tend to orgasm more often. Men, having more testosterone, tend to have the stronger hormonal drive for sex, too. Men can even pretend to be a virgin, or a veteran—whichever serves their persuasive purposes. But for an obviously pregnant woman, the virginity question is answered already. And, of course, men will never be saddled with pregnancy or experience the pressing existential calculus of weighing a "one night stand" against the prospect of getting "knocked up." Even with the threat of child-support payments, which might help level the playing field, that's not a strong threat as long as abortion-choice is the social norm. The guy can just pressure her till she gets an abortion. He could even pay for an abortion, and walk away, thinking that the cost of an abortion is his only material responsibility to her, even if she chooses to have the baby.

In that way, libertine sexual ethics exalts casual attitudes about sex. And men tend to be more adept at that then women. Women are wired and built for maternity in a way that men are not. Despite all the cultural changes over the years, women and men still tend to approach sex with different and often competing interests. And as long as a libertine sexual ethic is accepted, uncritically, as the going paradigm, then men will tend to have the advantage since they have less maternal baggage slowing them down.

A Pro-life Ethic Can Correct against Those Problems

There are two glaring problems with that libertine inequality. First, we don't have to accept a libertine sexual ethic in the first place. We can opt for a (pro-life) ethic of sexual responsibility instead. We can balance sexual choice within a mature framework of chastity, modesty, and the sanctity of marriage. That way individual interests and family interests are weighed together, and we don't have to pit one against the other.

Second, we don't have to grant that a typically "masculine" approach to sex is the standard. Masculine *and* feminine approaches to sex can complement each other in service to higher goals instead of just short-sighted selfish pleasure. Yes, guys can walk away from an unwanted pregnancy in a way that women cannot.

Abortion-choice policy, however, doesn't correct that wrong; it multiplies it. It treats child abandonment as the reference point and helps women to be just as irresponsible as deadbeat dads. But abandoning a mother-with-child is a failing, a moral evil, and a hole in our social and legal system. We shouldn't be multiplying wrongs for the sake of balance; we should be eliminating those wrongs. If we multiply anything it should be goods, privileges, and benefits instead.

Contrary to abortion-choice policy, we should be finding ways to hold fathers accountable for their children from the moment of conception. Leaving pregnant mothers high and dry is not a manly privilege. It's boyish cowardice. It's a moral vice. It's what males do when they have failed to grow and mature into real men (i.e., gentlemen).

Neglecting one's young should be unthinkable, not encouraged. But with abortion-choice policy, it's as if the option for child abandonment were a social standard that should be doled out equally between men and women. It's not. Child neglect and abandonment are no better than abortion. And pro-life ideology isn't just anti-abortion, it's pro-life for mothers, children, and fathers alike. Children need more than just their mothers, they need their fathers too.

Women's Equality Deserves Better than Abortion

Clearly, I don't think abortion serves the family very well. Abortion is to family as divorce is to marriage. Families and marriages can recover, but a break means aching hearts, broken trust, and weaker homes.

I know I've been shifting lanes pretty freely between "pro-family" and "pro-life." Just to be clear, "pro-life" isn't identical to "pro-family," but they are typically found together, since pro-lifers recognize how important family is in providing a safe and secure place for raising those un-aborted children. Pro-choicers aren't necessarily anti-family either. Their abortion-choice policy, however, tends to be planned *non*-parenthood. And abortion doesn't offer any great incentive to settle down, get married, plan for a newborn, take on a second job, or ask for raise, or to embrace the full responsibility of protecting and caring for the lives you create.

As for sexual ethics, sex is too powerful and too consequential to be unleashed as in libertine sexual ethics. Sex is a great good, but so is fire. We do better to exercise responsibility, like lighting a fire in a fireplace, instead of setting fields ablaze in a wildfire of libertine sexual expression.

Women are also equal to men. They don't need a particular surgery or medical procedure to have equality. They are innately equal to men in dignity and worth. Pregnancy isn't a disease. Children aren't punishment. And womanhood is a great good in itself, with no need to adapt, adjust, or conform to stereotypically "masculine" approaches to love, sex, and relationships (e.g., casual sex, aloofness, aggression, child abandonment, and spreading seed).

Because women are naturally equal to men, and abortion access isn't necessary to achieve that equality, abortion is a fabricated privilege and not a natural right. It doesn't give women any more equality than they already had. Plus, abortion undercuts the dignity of motherhood. It does untold harm to family and parenthood. And in America, it has already claimed the lives of ten times more human beings than the Holocaust. Abortion is easily the deadliest act of violence against humanity of all time. That's hardly a "victory" for women, or anybody for that matter.

The dignity of womanhood rests not in killing but in caring; in celebrating distinctions, not in denigrating differences. We can do better than abortion.

Bibliography

Annas, George. "A French Homunculus in a Tennessee Court." *Hastings Center Report* 19, 6 (1989): 20–22.

Brahm, Timothy. "Blood Donation and Bodily Rights Arguments." YouTube video, April 18, 2019. https://www.youtube.com/watch?v=YmBrUcpOxDw&feature=youtu.be.

Damschen, Gregor and Deiter Schönecker. "Saving Seven Embryos or Saving One Child? Michael Sandel on the Moral Status of Human Embryos." *Journal of Philosophical Research* 32 (2007): 239–245.

Durston, Kirk. "Why Sexual Morality May Be Far More Important Than You Ever Thought." *Quest,* December 1, 2019. https://www.kirkdurston.com/blog/unwin?fbclid=IwAR0qKHT18JB8oUrdBGl9EFdiZyb8v4F-UsTnOrhZJXIvUdyCQ9oCg3Sc4MU.

Ferrer, John D. "59 Reasons Why Men Need to Speak Out about Abortion." *Abortion History Museum,* October 15, 2018. https://abortionhistorymuseum.com/2018/10/15/59-reasons-why-men-need-to-speak-out-about-abortion/.

———. "The Big Kill." *Salvo* 34 (Fall 2015).

———. "A Simple Answer to a Burning Question." *Abortion History Museum,* November 8, 2017. https://abortionhistorymuseum.com/2017/11/08/a-simple-answer-to-a-burning-question/.

George, Robert P. and Christopher O. Tolleffson. "Embryos and Five-Year-Olds: Whom to Rescue?" *The Public Discourse,* Oct 19, 2017. https://www.thepublicdiscourse.com/2017/10/20332/.

Gilder, George. *Men and Marriage.* Rev. ed. Gretna, LA: Pelican, 1992.

Hesketh, Therese, Li Lu, and Zhu Wei Xing. "The Consequences of Son Preference and Sex-selective Abortion in China and Other Asian Countries." *Canadian*

Medical Association Journal 183, 12 (September 6, 2011): 1374-7.

Lee, Skyler and Ethan Lucky, "No Utero, No Opinion: Why Men Must Speak Out about Abortion." *Human Defense Initiative*, May 29, 2018. https://humandefense.com/no-uterus-no-opinion/.

Sandel, Michael. "The Ethical Implications of Human Cloning." *Jahrbuch fur Wissenschaft und Ethik* 8 (2003): 5–10.

Thomson, Judith J. "A Defense of Abortion." *Philosophy and Public Affairs* 4 (Autumn 1971): 47–66.

Unwin, J. D. *Sex and Culture*. London: Oxford, 1934. Wagner, Stephen. "De Facto Guardian and Abortion: A Response to the Strongest Violinist." *Life Report Blog*, April 13, 2013. http://doc.jfaweb.org/Training/DeFactoGuardian-v03.pdf.

Wright, Robert. *The Moral Animal: Why We Are the Way We Are: The New Science of Evolutionary Psychology*. Illus. ed. New York: Vintage, 1995.

Chapter 26

Perpetuating the Gender Myth in Sports[1]

Scott D. G. Ventureyra

On September 8, 2018, Serena Williams had a mental breakdown at the US Open women's finals. Her behaviour was inexcusable and demonstrated a great disrespect for the game, the officials, and her opponent, Naomi Osaka. The umpire, Carlos Ramos, issued her three code violations: first, a warning for receiving coaching (which her coach, Patrick Mouratoglou, admitted to); second, a point penalty for breaking her racket; and finally, a game for verbally abusing Ramos by calling him a liar and a thief. Ramos was doing his job and strictly followed the Grand Slam Rulebook Code of Conduct.[2] This is not the first time Williams has been out of line at the US Open. In 2009, she threatened to shove a ball down the throat of a lines woman who called a foot-fault on her. This does not sound like very lady-like conduct.

Good Ol' Identity Politics

After the match, in an attempt to justify her narcissistic behaviour, she accused Ramos of sexism. Many articles have appeared backing up Williams.[3] The Women's Tennis Association and the United States Tennis Association also backed up Williams, while the International Tennis Federation and Roger Federer (the greatest tennis player of all time) backed up Ramos. What is worth noting is that Williams's claim is at odds with the evidence, as tennis correspondent Simon Briggs affirms: "there were 86 code violations handed out to male players at the US Open, and only 22 to women. Now, a more detailed analysis of the past 20 years of grand-slam events has revealed a long-term split of 1,534 to 526."[4] Bob Christianson, a 67-year-old umpire who has

1 For the original, see Scott Ventureyra, "Perpetuating the Gender Myth in Sports," *Crisis Magazine,* September 21, 2018, https://www.crisismagazine.com/2018/perpetuating-the-gender-myth-in-sports.

2 ESPN, "2018 US Open Highlights: Serena Williams' dispute."

3 Quinn, "Alexis Ohanian Responds to 'Blatantly Racist & Misogynistic.'"

4 Briggs, "Carlos Ramos returns to umpire's chair."

worked 38 consecutive majors, had the following to say about the allegation of sexism: "That's the worst brouhaha I've witnessed in my 40-plus years of tennis officiating… I did a lot of McEnroe matches. He wouldn't go on and on, minute after minute. He would have, at some point, calmed down because he feared a game penalty. But [Williams] didn't."[5] It is also worth noting that Fabio Fognini,[6] a top Italian tennis player, was rightfully kicked out of last year's US Open for spewing profanities at a female umpire after a bad loss to a fellow countryman. This took him out of the third round of doubles at the US Open. Again, contrary to Williams's allegations, this clearly shows that there are strict consequences for both male and female tennis players.

It seems the ideologues call treating women equally to men (or perhaps more leniently) sexism. It is the tiresome tactic that the politically correct and ideologically possessed left always utilize when things don't go their way. It goes something like this: "disagree with our ideology and we will call you a sexist, bigot, racist, fascist, Nazi, xenophobe, transphobe, homophobe…" It is merely a tactic to create fear of expressing opposing viewpoints and to stifle any constructive dialogue. It is the toxicity of groupthink. Ironically, what is often revealed is that the ones laying the charges are typically guilty of them, an example of psychological projection.

We know the sexist charge against Ramos is a dishonest attempt to cover for abhorrent behavior, since a 30-plus year veteran of the sport cannot possibly claim to be ignorant of the rules. If we really want to talk about double standards, why is it that the payout for men and women is exactly the same at the Grand Slams? Men have to play best of five sets, whereas women only have to play best of three. How is that fair? This is a clear example of equality of outcome (or equity) being denied: the playing field between men and women is unequal in favor of female players. This injustice in pay ignores the fact that men's tennis attracts much larger crowds and generates much more money for the sport. Nevertheless, 14 out of the 30 top-paid tennis players of all time are women.[7]

Biological and Psychological Sex Differences

The social constructionist position promoted by the postmodernist left denies biological differences. The breathtaking inanity of university instructors such as Nicholas Matte (seen in a panel discussion in 2016 with Jordan Peterson on Steve Paikin's Canadian public television show *The Agenda*), who claimed there

5 Miller, "Officials are scared."

6 Mitchell, "Fabio Fognini thrown out of US Open over obscene remarks at umpire."

7 Gaines and Loudenback, "Maria Sharapova retires as the 8th highest-paid tennis player of all time."

is no such thing as biological sex, is quite widespread. Regrettably, this is the sort of falsehood that has been enshrined in Canadian law with the passage of Bill C-16, which deals with gender identity and expression. According to it, anyone can be male, female, both, neither, or whatever they wish at the time they wish it.

What is worth noting is that in more gender-equal countries, the sex differences with respect to personality become wider. Authors of a recent scientific paper in the *International Journal of Psychology* "speculate that as gender equality increases both men and women gravitate towards their traditional gender roles."[8] This is not at all what one would expect.

So, what are we to say about biological differences between men and women? In our climate of political correctness, it is a huge faux pas to state what is scientific and commonsensical. It is as one philosopher, John Searle, has described Jacques Derrida's postmodern philosophy of deconstructionism: "the world turned upside down."[9] Several years ago, Germund Hesslow, a professor of neurophysiology at Lund University, was accused of making "transphobic" and "anti-feminist" statements[10] for merely stating that men and women are biologically different. Scientific fact is consistently being questioned to advance political agendas. There are undeniable scientific differences between male and female. These facts need to be established and accepted before there can be any legitimate philosophical analysis of, or political debate over, those sex differences. The differences are real, as Melvin Porter, a scientist, explains: "The physiological differences in the sexes are biological as well as chemical-driven. It is the quantity of the testosterone and estrogen in the blood of both sexes and the ratio of the two hormones present that affect the physiological activities in both sexes as well as the physical attributes of the male and female human body."[11] This flies in the face of the social constructionist agenda.

Sex Differences in Tennis—the "Battle of the Sexes"

Charges of sexism have not been confined to code violations but have also been made about the differences between men and women in sports. This is largely due to the second- and third-wave feminist movements. Early feminism, which fought against inequalities in the law (e.g., the suffragette movement), is quite distinct from the second- and third-wave feminist movements of the 1960s to the 1990s, which sought to upend cultural inequalities, gender

8 Giolla and Kajonius, "Sex differences in personality are larger in gender equal countries."
9 Searle, "The Word Turned Upside Down."
10 RT Staff, "Swedish professor accused of bigotry."
11 Porter, "Biological Differences between Men and Women."

norms, and the role of women in society. Depending on how far second-wave feminism and later modes are taken, they can have both positive and negative effects for society.[12] Modern women are increasingly avoiding the feminist label because of the term's extremist connotations and prefer instead terms like "equal opportunist" or "egalitarian" that reflect the movement's earlier mainstream agenda.

As a consequence of modern feminist agitation, there has been a lot of attention paid to differences between male and female athletes, especially in tennis. This has been particularly true since the 1970s. The first battle of the sexes was between former world number-one and Wimbledon champion Bobby Riggs, who was 55 at the time, and the number-one female player, Margaret Court, who was 30 years old. Riggs won that match easily, 6-2, 6-1. The second battle of the sexes involved Riggs again, now against Billie Jean King, who was 29. This match had a lot of hype around it. King won the best of five sets in three relatively easy ones. At the time, King was considered an advocate for women's equality. Nevertheless, it has been argued that Riggs threw the match because of gambling debts owed to the mafia.[13] King wisely refused a rematch. A huge deal was made of her "victory," despite the 26-year difference and the fact that Riggs was not competing professionally nor training like King. (In 2017, a motion picture was made about the King-Riggs match titled *Battle of the Sexes*, featuring Steve Carell.)

Other examples are lesser known: for example, in 1992, a battle of the sexes occurred between Jimmy Connors, who was 40, and Martina Navratilova, 35, where Connors only had one serve and had to cover the doubles alley. Connors won 7-5 and 6-2. More recently, in 1998 the Williams sisters claimed they could beat any man outside the top 200 in the world. This did not end well for them. Karsten Braasch, who was ranked 203rd at the time, took on their challenge.[14] He beat Serena 6-1 and Venus 6-2, after having a couple of drinks and smoking on changeovers. Braasch stated after the match, "They wouldn't have had a chance against anyone inside the top 500 because today I played like someone ranked 600th to keep it fun." In 2017, the politically correct (PC) police were upset over the legendary seven-time Grand Slam champion John McEnroe's comment that Serena would be about 700th on the men's circuit.[15] The PC lynch mob expected McEnroe to say that Serena was the best of all time, instead of just the best female. McEnroe rightly pointed out that such an expectation is outright ridiculous.[16] An apology was demanded from McEnroe

12 Saad, "The Pros and Cons of Feminism."

13 Natta Jr., "The Match Maker Bobby Riggs, the Mafia and the Battle of the Sexes."

14 The Observer Staff, "How to... beat both Williams sisters in one afternoon."

15 Garcia-Navarro, "Tennis Great John McEnroe Says He's Seeking 'Inner Peace.'"

16 A1Cvenom, "Tennis Legend Triggers Panel over Gender Differences."

and to his credit he refused. I also believe that McEnroe was generous with the 700 number. Some Ottawa players I know could very well beat her. Despite displaying indignation at McEnroe's comment,[17] she herself has admitted that she has no chance to win a single game against top male players[18] such as Andy Murray.

The radical feminists believe, as a consequence of their shoddy logic, that men and women are the same in every way, which is not only unscientific but unjust to females. For example, consider cases in which transgender females and males are allowed to compete in categories outside the sex they were "assigned" at birth. Either way, biological women end up on the losing end. Perhaps the PC mob should take heed from the words of Concordia University marketing psychology professor Gad Saad:

> From the onset of the movement, many radical feminists rapidly converged on the erroneous idea that if women are to be treated equally in all walks of life, it is important to demonstrate that men and women are indistinguishable beings. Hence, all sex differences short of one's genitalia were attributed to socialization. An average three-year-old knows this position to be laughable yet this is a central mantra in Women's Studies programs and related feminist literature. See *Professing Feminism: Cautionary Tales from the Strange World of Women's Studies* by Daphne Patai and Noretta Koertge for endless examples of irrational and blatantly falsifiable feminist positions.[19]

Men and women should be equal under the law, yet they are distinguishable biological beings. It is idiotic to wish away sex differences and create imaginary narratives about the power of socialization in shaping all sex differences. It does not take a sophisticated Darwinist to recognize that we are a sexually dimorphic and sexually reproducing species. By definition, this means that men and women possess some innate biologically based differences.

Fundamental differences between the male and female species, allowing for the proliferation of organisms and their distinctive features which are crucial to adaptability and survivability, are intrinsic to evolutionary development. This was all planned by the sovereign Creator, ever since the incipient moment of creation. To ignore these differences will be perilous to the survival of humanity.

17 Williams, Twitter.

18 Hart, "Wimbledon 2013: Serena Williams believes playing Andy Murray in a battle of the sexes 'would be fun.'"

19 Saad, "The Pros and Cons of Feminism."

Bibliography

Battle of the Sexes (tennis), *Wikipedia*, updated, March 30, 2021. https://en.wikipedia.org/wiki/Battle_of_the_Sexes_(tennis).

Briggs, Simon. "Carlos Ramos returns to umpire's chair after Serena Williams row as statistics back him up." *The Telegraph*, September 14, 2018. https://www.telegraph.co.uk/tennis/2018/09/13/carlos-ramos-returns-chair-serena-williams-row-statistics-back/.

Cvenom, Al. "Tennis Legend Triggers Panel Over Gender Differences." YouTube video, June 28, 2017. https://www.youtube.com/watch?v=hDPK8ds1D-o.

ESPN. "2018 US Open Highlights: Serena Williams' dispute overshadows Naomi Osaka's final win." YouTube video, September 8, 2018. https://www.youtube.com/watch?v=uiBrForlj-k&t=727s.

Gaines, Cork and Tanza Loudenback. "Maria Sharapova retires as the 8th highest-paid tennis player of all time." *Business Insider*, updated February 26, 2020. https://www.businessinsider.com/tennis-players-highest-paid-all-time-men-women-2017-1.

Garcia-Navarro, Lulu. "'But Seriously,' Tennis Great John McEnroe Says He's Seeking 'Inner Peace.'" *NPR*, June 25, 2017. https://www.npr.org/2017/06/25/534149646/but-seriously-tennis-great-john-mcenroe-says-hes-seeking-inner-peace.

Giolla, Erik Mac and Petri J. Kajonius. "Sex differences in personality are larger in gender equal countries: Replicating and extending a surprising finding." *International Journal of Psychology* 54, no. 6 (December 2019): 705-711. https://doi.org/10.1002/ijop.12529.

Hart, Simon."Wimbledon 2013: Serena Williams believes playing Andy Murray in a battle of the sexes 'would be fun.'" *The Telegraph*, June 27, 2013. https://www.telegraph.co.uk/sport/tennis/wimbledon/10146362/Wimbledon-2013-Serena-Williams-believes-playing-Andy-Murray-in-a-battle-of-the-sexes-would-be-fun.html.

Miller, Bryce. "'Officials are scared': Veteran tennis official seething over Serena Williams spat." *Stuff*, September 15, 2018. https://www.stuff.co.nz/sport/tennis/107109630/officials-are-scared-veteran-tennis-official-seething-over-serena-williams-spat.

Mitchell, Kevin. "Fabio Fognini thrown out of US Open over obscene remarks at umpire." *The Guardian*, September 2, 2017. https://www.theguardian.com/sport/2017/sep/02/fabio-fognini-thrown-out-us-open-obscenities-umpire.

Natta Jr., Don Von. "The Match Maker Bobby Riggs, the Mafia and the Battle of the Sexes." *ESPN*, updated March 26, 2020. http://www.espn.com/espn/feature/story/_/id/9589625/the-match-maker.

Porter, Melvin. "Biological Differences between Men and Women." *Owlcation*, November 25, 2018. https://owlcation.com/stem/The-Biological-Explanation-of-Human-Sex-Differences.

Quinn, Dave. "Alexis Ohanian Responds to 'Blatantly Racist & Misogynistic' Cartoon of Wife Serena Williams." *People*, September 14, 2018. https://people.com/sports/alexis-ohanian-responds-serena-williams-cartoon/.

RT Staff. "Swedish professor accused of bigotry for saying men and women 'biologically different.'" *RT*, September 17, 2018. https://www.rt.com/news/438638-swedish-professor-biologically-different/.

Saad, Gad. "The Pros and Cons of Feminism: The difference between benevolent feminism and hostile feminism." *Psychology Today*, August 10, 2009. https://www.psychologytoday.com/us/blog/homo-consumericus/200908/the-pros-and-cons-feminism.

Searle, John. "The Word Turned Upside Down." *The New York Review of Books*, October 23, 1983. https://www.nybooks.com/articles/1983/10/27/the-word-turned-upside-down/.

The Observer Staff. "How to… beat both Williams sisters in one afternoon." *The Observer*, September 2, 2001. https://www.theguardian.com/observer/osm/story/0,,543962,00.html.

Williams, Serena. Twitter, June 26, 2017. https://twitter.com/serenawilliams/status/879466071404810241?lang=en.

Chapter 27

Unpacking "Toxic Masculinity"

Stella Shihman

By today's standards, a decorated war veteran like my late maternal grandfather would have been considered to manifest toxic masculinity. At least some of the traits he cultivated and exhibited would likely qualify. When he fought the Nazis—actual ones—during World War II, he surely resorted to extreme physical force or violence. When he came back from the war after his parents and sisters had been murdered, wounded in the many battles he heroically took part in, he cultivated and exhibited traditional masculine traits like stoicism, self-reliance, emotional restrain, and dominance. He was an unshakable pillar that held the family together, and took care of my late grandmother and their three children during the post-war era in the Soviet Union.

Listing the aforementioned character traits leads to asking what constitutes "toxic masculinity." Is there a consensus? Well, not entirely so, it appears. The term has come to signify traditional male attributes that are perceived as harmful to women, men themselves, and society as a whole; such qualities include self-reliance, dominance, and competitiveness.[1] Some posit that it entails destructive tendencies like bullying and aggression and sexual and domestic violence, as well as expressions of misogyny and homophobia. It may also encompass the desire to win, risk-taking behaviour, the need for emotional control, high importance placed on one's career as a defining characteristic, and pursuit of social status.[2] There are significant qualitative differences between these traits, and while some are evidently negative and destructive, othersare not.

The concept of masculinity varies across time and place, and it may be more fitting to speak of "masculinities." *Essentialist* definitions delineate accounts of men's lives based on a core feature that defines the *masculine.* Freud adopted such an approach when he equated *masculinity* with activity and *femininity* with passivity. Masculinity has also been articulated as "Zeus energy," ideals embedded in myths of gods and heroes, and maleness that is defined by "hard

1 Hess, "Sexism May Be Bad for Men's Mental Health."
2 Hess, "Sexism May Be Bad for Men's Mental Health."

and heavy phenomena."[3] In medieval Europe, for example, masculinity was Christian and chivalric.[4] The *positivist* approach emphasizes finding facts, and defines masculinity as what men are. This definition forms the basis of femininity-masculinity scales in psychology, wherein statistical discrimination between groups of women and men validates the scales' items. This approach also serves as the foundation for ethnographic accounts of masculinity that rely on describing patterns in men's lives in a given cultural context, and then equating that to patterns of masculinity.[5] *Normative* definitions of masculinity propose a standard: they ascribe what men ought to be. Examples include characters like John Wayne and Clint Eastwood, and men typically portrayed in action movies—Bruce Willis comes to mind. The normative approach recognizes that different men meet the standard to varying degrees. Another well-known example of a normative definition is the prescription that men ought to be breadwinners; that's contrary to women who, notably in past decades, were largely thought of as homemakers. Lastly, *semiotic* definitions outline masculinity through a system of symbolic difference in which masculine and feminine are contrasted. As such, masculinity is defined as "not-femininity."[6]

The phrase "toxic masculinity" was coined by Professor Stephen Bliss; it originated as part of the Mythopoetic Men's Movement in the 1980s and 1990s. The movement offered an alternative vision of masculinity in response to feminist challenges to traditional male authority.[7] By organizing male-only workshops, drumming circles, and wilderness retreats, the movement promoted masculine spirituality in order to rescue a protective "warrior" masculinity from toxic masculinity.[8] Through spiritual searching, communing with nature, and exploring emotions, Bliss emphasized discovery of the authentic self in a man. The goal was to cultivate male-positive behaviours, leading men to become happier and better versions of themselves.[9] The intent in speaking of "toxic masculinity" was to highlight male behaviours that are detrimental primarily to men.[10]

The modern-day interpretation of "toxic masculinity" has shifted from bad behaviours affecting the psychological state of men to the effects those behaviours have on other people and society at large.[11] While some boys and men of varying ages are pathologically masculine, so to speak, and they manifest

3 Connell, *Masculinities*, 68.

4 Richards, "From Christianity to Paganism: The New Middle Ages and the Values of 'Medieval' Masculinity," 213–234.

5 Connell, *Masculinities*.

6 Connell, *Masculinities*.

7 See sources in Wikipedia, "Toxic Masculinity."

8 Salter, "The Problem with a Fight against Toxic Masculinity."

9 Mullen, "Toxic Masculinity Was First Coined."

10 Smith, "The Truth about Toxic Masculinity."

11 Smith, "The Truth about Toxic Masculinity."

it via bullying, destroying, and preying on vulnerable people, many others or even most are displaying healthy masculinity by giving an outlet to their innate energy and aggression via games and sports, via building rather than destroying, and via protecting rather than exploiting weak and vulnerable individuals.[12]

Any human trait or tendency appears to have at least two possible outlets, taking specific energy and channelling it towards either a positive outcome—typically one that is socially acceptable—or a negative one. A duality of expression. Relating this idea to the life of my late grandfather who fought as part of the Red Army, it's evident that one can use physical strength (or what can be considered violence) to thwart existential threats rather than pose them. Presumably very few, if any, would disagree about the necessity of using force to stop those who engage in perpetual destruction (Nazi Germany). Moreover, one can employ traditional traits like stoicism and fortitude to "pick oneself up" following a tragedy like war, to start a new life, to build a home and create a family, and to provide for them and for future generations. A man can use his strength and power to assume responsibility, to become a provider and a protector, rather than use that strength for exploitative and destructive ends. That is why "traditional masculinity" need not to be conflated with "toxic masculinity," or, more fittingly, detrimental personality traits that may have more in common with personality disorders—such as an antisocial personality disorder or psychopathy—than with masculinity per se.

It's worth noting that certain aspects or levels of *hegemonic masculinity*—a term used by R. W. Connell to refer to the culturally dominant form of masculinity—can in fact be socially detrimental if men adhere to them rigidly and uncompromisingly. This version of masculinity is known in many parts of the world as "manbox" and can be said to consist of four key principles: (1) No sissy stuff, (2) Be a big wheel, (3) Be a sturdy oak, and (4) Damn the torpedoes, full speed ahead.[13] "No sissy stuff" is a directive for boys and men to avoid demonstrating any traits or behaviours closely associated with women and femininity, such as being emotionally expressive. "Be a big wheel" is a directive for boys and men to strive for success and high status, wherein competitiveness and ambition play key roles. "Be a sturdy oak" is a directive for boys and men to be able to function independently, to strive for inexpressiveness of feelings, and to let their actions speak instead of words. Lastly, "Damn the torpedoes, full speed ahead" is a directive to be aggressive and take risks, placing focus on short-term goals and effects.[14]

On an individual level, a man who adheres devoutly to "manbox" masculinity may exhibit "toxicity" due to an inability to adapt to individual

12 Sommers, "Masculinity Is More Than a Mask."
13 Smiler, *Is Masculinity Toxic?*, 26.
14 Smiler, *Is Masculinity Toxic?*, 26.

variations and cultural changes, which may negatively affect social interactions. Moreover, research points to a positive correlation between men's rigidity in adhering to certain prescriptions of traditional masculinity and negative health outcomes, such as higher rates of suicide, substance abuse, violence, and early death.[15] Specifically, pushing away emotions and ignoring them may lead to reduced mental health; it may explain—at least in part—why more men than women die from opioid overdoses, are more likely to underutilize mental health services, and are more likely to die from suicide.[16] Extreme, uncompromising takes on masculinity can be detrimental to men. Having said that, it should be noted that the same prescriptions which can be harmful or limiting in their extremes can also be of utility, beneficence, and honour in their non-extreme expressions. For example, in risking their bodies and lives, men who serve in the military or work as first respondents may be acting on the directive "Be a sturdy oak" and possibly "Be a big wheel" in defending and caring for others. Across the world, by and large, men are not particularly interested in being promiscuous and irresponsible; rather, they want to be seen as honourable, to be in control of their lives, and to have a good job.[17] Once more, using the example of my late grandfather in relation to "Be a sturdy oak," the prescription doesn't need to be inherently negative; a man can be guided by it in order to better the lives of the people he loves and cares for (e.g., via providing for them), rather than employing it for dominance and control.

Beyond the suspect exercise of conjoining the words "toxic" and "masculinity" into one cohesive definition, it's worth noting that masculine ideals or "masculinities" have not been the same over the course of Western history. The three Ps—providing, protecting, and procreating—that define modern American manhood haven't always been the standard across times and places. However, according to some anthropologists, one concern pertaining to masculinity that has been somewhat consistent is the fear of having it taken away. Certain researchers in the field are concerned about the concept of "toxic masculinity" for it implies that manhood itself is to some extent faulty. Instead, they assert that toxic behaviour pertains to a subset of men—typically those with low self-esteem—who lash out as a reaction to perceived threats to their masculinity. Otherwise put, there's nothing inherently wrong with masculine traits and behaviour; rather, the lashing out of some men may be due to fear that their masculinity can be taken away.[18]

To summarize, while the term "toxic masculinity" has limited utility in delineating or calling out traits like intolerance, violence, misogyny, and even

15 Dastagir, "Psychologists Call 'Traditional Masculinity' Harmful."
16 Sheppard, "The Dangerous Effects of 'Toxic Masculinity.'"
17 Smiler, *Is Masculinity Toxic?*, 26,
18 Vinopal, "Toxic Masculinity Is a Myth."

political discord and war, the absence of a clear definition and haphazard conflation of "traditional masculinity" with "toxic masculinity"—evident in activists blending the two and calling for the eradication of traditional masculinity similarly to sexism and racism—is problematic.[19] It is also unclear to what extent expressions of "toxic masculinity" are akin to displays of personality disorders or, perhaps, are reflective of a specific subset of men who may be lashing out at what they perceive as attacks on their masculinity. Also, to the degree that rigid traditional or hegemonic masculinity can lead to extreme behaviours, it can also entail leadership, strength, and courage in service of others. In commingling traditional masculine traits with deviant ones and disparaging masculinity as a whole, there's harm to be inflicted on boys and men who find themselves unable to live up to new, progressive gender expectations. Those boys and men may be biologically-inclined or "wired" to be more daring, competitive, innately aggressive, confident, and self-reliant. To the extent that socialization plays into gender differences, it doesn't have complete explanatory power for said differences; some differences between men and women are rooted in biology and hormonal influences.[20] Having interacted with my grandfather growing up, and having heard others speak of him posthumously, I have experienced firsthand how traditional masculine traits can be anything but toxic. Seeing those values and corresponding behaviours in service of other people, it is quite plausible that what has been depicted as "toxic masculinity" are unusual, extreme manifestations or violent deviations from how traditional masculine traits are generally expressed. It is a deviation from the concept of masculinity as a whole. Those who shape the language and culture nowadays should be wary of using "toxic masculinity" irresponsibly to include a wide range of men who exhibit traditional values and norms, thereby damning them to the detriment of society.

Bibliography

Connell, R. W. *Masculinities*. 2nd ed. Berkeley & Los Angeles: University of California Press, 2005.

Dastagir, Alia E. "Psychologists Call 'Traditional Masculinity' Harmful, Face Uproar from Conservatives." *USA Today*, January 10, 2019. https://www.usatoday.com/story/news/investigations/2019/01/10/american-psychological-association-traditional-masculinity-harmful/2538520002/.

Ferguson, Chris. "How 'Toxic Masculinity' Is Hurting Boys." *Houston Chronicle*, March 26, 2018. https://www.houstonchronicle.com/local/gray-matters/

19 Ferguson, "How 'Toxic Masculinity' Is Hurting Boys."
20 Ferguson, "How 'Toxic Masculinity' Is Hurting Boys."

article/toxic-masculinity-gender-norms-harmful-boys-12782202.php.

Hess, Peter. "Sexism May Be Bad for Men's Mental Health." *Popular Science.* November 21, 2016. https://www.popsci.com/research-shows-that-toxic-masculinity-is-harmful-to-mens-mental-health/.

Mullen, Gretchen. "Toxic Masculinity Was First Coined in the Context of Male-Positivity in 1980s: Shepherd Bliss." *Skeptic Review*, January 16, 2019. https://skepticreview.com/2019/01/16/toxic-masculinity-was-first-used-as-a-male-positive-term-in-the-80s-shepherd-bliss.

Richards, Jeffrey. "From Christianity to Paganism: The New Middle Ages and the Values of 'Medieval' Masculinity." *Cultural Values* 3, 2 (March 2009): 213–234. https://www.tandfonline.com/doi/abs/10.1080/14797589909367162.

Salter, Michael. "The Problem with a Fight against Toxic Masculinity." *The Atlantic*, February 27, 2019. https://www.theatlantic.com/health/archive/2019/02/toxic-masculinity-history/583411/.

Sheppard, Sarah. "The Dangerous Effects of Toxic Masculinity." *VeryWellMind*, November 12, 2020. https://www.verywellmind.com/the-dangerous-mental-health-effects-of-toxic-masculinity-5073957.

Smiler, Andrew. *Is Masculinity Toxic? A Primer for the 21st Century*. Thames & Hudson, 2019.

Smith, Kurt. "The Truth about Toxic Masculinity." *Medium*, March 5, 2020. https://medium.com/equality-includes-you/the-truth-about-toxic-masculinity-5057352eb668.

Sommers, Christina Hoff. "Masculinity Is More Than a Mask." *Time*, January 13, 2014. https://time.com/2974/masculinity-is-more-than-a-mask/.

Vinopal, Lauren. "Toxic Masculinity Is a Myth. But Insecure Men Lash Out at Women." *Fatherly*, July 22, 2021. https://www.fatherly.com/health-science/toxic-masculinity-fake-male-insecurity/.

Wikipedia. "Toxic Masculinity." Last modified May 28, 2021. https://en.wikipedia.org/wiki/Toxic_masculinity.

Chapter 28

Gender Ideology and the Deconstructing of Deconstructionism: Peterson versus Derrida[1]

Scott D. G. Ventureyra

In this chapter, I will reflect upon political correctness and its implications for freedom of speech in Canada, as it pertains to gender ideology. There has been much controversy over Bill C-16 and the surrounding legislation (this will be explained in detail below). Throughout 2016, Jordan B. Peterson, professor of psychology at the University of Toronto, expressed his opposition to Bill C-16 and its implications for free speech. Peterson argues that free speech is the *mechanism* by which democracies have survived over the centuries.[2] He has further argued that the imposition of language on sovereign people can have devastating effects.[3] For example, there is a clear distinction between legislation against what one *ought* not to say, such as screaming "fire!" in a crowded cinema, and mandating what one *must* say, as in the case of Bill C-16, with the use of compelled gender-neutral pronouns.

To understand the background of Bill C-16, I propose to examine two distinct philosophical approaches to gather insights as to what is at stake in and motivating these cultural trends. First, I will examine the thought of Jordan Peterson, who can be dubbed the "defender of truth." The second involves the thought of postmodern epistemologist Jacques Derrida. Derrida can be dubbed the "wishful mortician of the absolute" for his methodology of deconstructionism. These distinct approaches will help us understand complex issues surrounding Bill C-16 and free speech.

1 This chapter is based on a presentation I delivered at Ryerson University on May 27, 2017, for the Canadian Jacques Maritain Association on "Philosophy, Religion, and the Meaning of Nationhood in the 21st century."

2 More will be said on this understanding of free speech below in the section on Peterson.

3 Peterson often cites the disastrous consequences of totalitarian regimes and their impositions on speech and many other freedoms. He sees the passing of Bill C-16 as one step in such a direction. For a brilliant firsthand eyewitness account of Soviet Communist totalitarianism, often discussed by Peterson, see Solzhenitsyn, *The Gulag Archipelago.*

Bill C-16—What Is It?

Bill C-16 is a law that was passed by the Canadian Parliament. It passed the legislative process of the House of Commons and the Senate. It received Royal Assent on June 19, 2017.[4] It was introduced in May of 2016 by the Liberal government of Prime Minister Justin Trudeau, but it has had a lengthier history under preceding bills C-276[5] and C-279[6]—both introduced by the Liberals and the New Democratic Party (NDP). Bill C-16 amends the Canadian Human Rights Act and the Criminal Code. The bill adds gender expression and identity as a protected ground to the Canadian Human Rights Act, and also to Criminal Code provisions. As the legislative summary of Bill C-16 states: "The bill is intended to protect individuals from discrimination within the sphere of federal jurisdiction and from being the targets of hate propaganda, as a consequence of their gender identity or their gender expression."[7] Bill C-16 has been summarized in the following way:

> The bill is intended to protect individuals from discrimination within the sphere of federal jurisdiction and from being the targets of hate propaganda,[8] as a consequence of their gender identity or their gender expression. The bill adds "gender identity or expression" to the list of prohibited grounds of discrimination in the Canadian Human Rights Act and the list of characteristics of identifiable groups protected from hate propaganda in the Criminal Code. It also adds that evidence that an offence was motivated by bias, prejudice or hate based on a person's gender identity or expression constitutes an aggravating circumstance for a court to consider when imposing a criminal sentence.[9]

The terms "gender identity" and "gender expression" refer to how an individual understands their own gender and how they *choose* to express it. Furthermore, the legislative summary of Bill C-16 asserts:

> People may identify with a concept of gender that is aligned with the sex they were assigned at birth, or they may identify with a gender

4 Parliament of Canada, Bill C -16: An Act to amend the Canadian Human Rights Act and the Criminal Code.

5 Parliament of Canada, Bill C-276: An Act to amend the Canadian Human Rights Act and the Criminal Code (gender identity and gender expression).

6 Parliament of Canada, Bill C-279: An Act to amend the Canadian Human Rights Act and the Criminal Code (gender identity).

7 Bill C-279.

8 Parliament of Canada, Hate Speech and Freedom of Expression: Legal Boundaries in Canada, 3.1.

9 Bill C-16.

that is different from their sex assigned at birth or simply self-identify with a non-traditional or non-stereotypical concept of gender.[10] The most commonly used term to describe people who self-identify with a non-traditional concept of gender is "transgender," though some individuals prefer to be described as intersex, cross-gender, gender-diverse, or gender queer, among other terms. The term "transsexual" is often used to describe people who do not identify with the sex they were assigned at birth and seek to have their gender and their sex align through medical intervention, such as by taking hormones or undergoing surgery.[11]

Jordan Peterson: "Defender of Truth"

Peterson's epistemological approach to truth is two-pronged, but for the purposes of this paper we will focus solely on what I have labelled the first prong.[12] The first prong adheres to what he refers to as objective truth—this you can think of as a conventional definition of truth as whatever is in accordance with reality. On my own view, Bill C-16, political correctness, and free speech must be understood in light of this sense of truth, which is best understood as philosophical realism, or a correspondence theory of truth[13]—a traditional model which dates back to Plato and Aristotle. Philosophers who hold to a correspondence theory of truth maintain that truth is demonstrated by a correspondence between cognitive representations and reality, as Thomas Aquinas understood, where truth is the equation of thing and intellect.[14] One of the most well-known definitions of truth is found in Aristotle's *Metaphysics*: "To say of what is that it is not, or of what is not that it is, is false, while to say of what is that it is, and of what is not that it is not, is true."[15] Peterson seems to equate generic truth with "scientific

10 Ontario Human Rights Commission, Policy on preventing discrimination because of gender identity and gender expression, section 3.

11 Legislative Summary of Bill C-16.

12 This two-prong approach is not something stated by Peterson himself, but rather an understanding I have developed from listening to many of his lectures and interviews, and reading articles written about him. The second prong is where a large portion of Peterson's attention is explicitly fixed (whereas the first prong is implicit/presupposed), i.e., the notion of pragmatic truth. Essentially his understanding of a pragmatist approach to truth is one of action, which follows a question of value, namely, of how one should act in the world. For his own explanation of a "realist" understanding of truth and a pragmatic one, see https://www.youtube.com/watch?v=SyopcVoK0EA and https://www.youtube.com/watch?v=RnPuqvg1mv8.

13 For a thorough explanation of the correspondence theory of truth see David, "The Correspondence Theory of Truth."

14 Aquinas, *ST* I, Q 16, A 2; *De Veritate*, Q 1, A 1-3.

15 Aristotle, *Metaphysics*, 1011b25.

truth" or what is known as "scientific realism," but I would maintain this is largely a philosophical question which can be aided by scientific knowledge in terms of knowing what the universe is composed of and how laws and organisms' function within it. Furthermore, this implies intelligibility which as far as I can discern would be impossible without an ultimate grounding for intelligibility which would be a Source of ultimate rationality as found in a being such as God.[16]A useful place to start in ascertaining truths is with the laws of logic, which are implicit in Aristotle's definition of truth: for instance, without the validity of the law of non-contradiction, correct thinking would be impossible. Without it, how would we make assessments or conclusions about anything? It is when Peterson applies this understanding of truth, as we shall see below, that his assessment of Bill C-16 has been clearest. Peterson makes great use of the concept of Logos; he understands the significance of what such a concept represents to Western civilization, including Greek philosophy and Christian theology. Undoubtedly, Logos is a vital concept to both western philosophy and theology. Its roots can be traced to Heraclitus, who used the term to signify both order and knowledge.[17] In Christian theology, Logos is the "word," as in the prologue of the Gospel of John (1:1–5)—the second person of the Trinity. Logos is also identified as Jesus in the Gospel of John (1:14–15).

Peterson rightfully acknowledges the place of the concept of Logos in the West as the principle of reason and of creating order out of chaos.[18] He understands that Logos, truth, and speech are all bound up together, as he states in his Manning Centre talk in February 2017:

> The Logos is the sacred element of Western culture, what does that mean? It means that your capacity for speech is divine. It is the thing that generates order from chaos... Don't underestimate the power of truth, there is nothing more powerful. Now in order to speak what you might regard as the truth, you have to let go of the outcome... I'm going to state what I think, as clearly as I can, and I'm going to live with the consequences, no matter what they are... Nothing brings a better world into being than the stated truth. Now you might have to pay a price for that but that's fine, you're going to pay a price for every bloody thing you do and everything you don't do, you don't get to choose to not pay a price, you get to choose which poison you're going to take, that's it. So, if you're going to stand up for something, stand up for your truth, it'll shape you... It's not safe to speak, but also not safe not to speak. It's a balance of risks, you want to pay the price for being who

16 Lonergan, *Insight: A Study of Human Understanding*, 696–698.

17 Hussey, "Epistemology and Meaning in Heraclitus," 33–59.

18 Peterson, *Maps of Meaning*, 100–111.

> you are and stating your mode of being or do you want to pay the price for being a bloody serf. One that's enslaved him or herself, well that's a major price, man, that thing unfolds for decades; you'll be a miserable worm at the end of about twenty years of that. No self-respect, no power, no ability to voice your opinions, nothing left but resentment because everyone is against because of course you've never stood up for yourself, it's like say what you think carefully, pay attention to your words, it's a price you want to pay, if you're going to believe the truth, it's the cornerstone of society.[19]

Peterson can be dubbed defender of truth against the confusion wrought by postmodernists, particularly Derrida and his method of deconstructionism, which as we will see has played a role into the chaotic confusion and the incoherence littered throughout Bill C-16 and the surrounding legislation.

Derrida: "Wishful Mortician of the Absolute"

Derrida's philosophy is anti-metaphysical:[20] he believes metaphysics is not possible. He views humans as being confined to linguistic bubbles. He has been dubbed the "Father of Deconstructionism."[21] Derrida is a very difficult philosopher to understand; his writings are frequently self-contradictory and ambiguous, which in part could be because of the inadequacy of the translations combined with the peculiarity of his views. Deconstructionism is a method of hermeneutics;[22] it seeks to abandon conventional rules of textual analysis. It is a search through reading and rereading a text to find a novel, more profound, and perhaps overlooked meaning. It is important to understand, as Norman Geisler observes, that deconstruction "is not a negation from dismantling the text but rather it is a critique that remodels the text, rather than a grammatical-literal-historical foundation associated with the text under consideration."[23] Geisler has provided a useful summary of several key features that characterize Derrida's deconstructionism:

- *Conventionalism*—meaning is relative (not absolute or complete) to a culture or situation. There is no meaning prior to language.

19 See the Manning Centre Conference talk—"Censorship on Campus."

20 See Derrida, *Margins of Philosophy*, 195. Jacques Derrida's main texts include *Speech and Phenomena and Other Essays in Husserl's Theory of Signs*; *Of Grammatology*; *Writing and Difference*; *Dissemination*; *Glas*.

21 See Stein, "Life with the Father of Deconstructionism."

22 I affirm this since for all intents and purposes it is a method of analysis, despite the fact that Derrida denied that deconstructionism was a method, critique, or analysis. See Wood and Bernasconi, eds., *Derrida and Différance*; Beardsworth, *Derrida & The Political*, 4.

23 Geisler, *A History of Western Philosophy*, vol. 2, 404.

- *Perspectivalism*—truth is conditioned by one's perspective.
- *Referentialism*—there is no perfect reference or one-to-one correspondence between words and the meanings they confer. Therefore, meaning is ultimately *untransferable* between the writer and reader, suggesting that context radically limits all meaning.
- *Differentialism*—rational structures leave something out where the reader approaches the text with suspicion looking for some "differences" and in search for "something" that is "not there."
- *Linguistic solipsism*—inability to escape the limits of language. Linguistic concepts can be broadened but limits of language keep the reader corralled.
- *Semantic progressivism*—all possible meanings are never exhausted. A text can always be further deconstructed.[24]

All these positions make it impossible to ascertain any objective meaning of a text. While it is certainly one thing to grant the obvious, namely, that a text can be interpreted in many different ways, this does not entail that a text should be rendered unintelligible through the use of these unwarranted claims, which are asserted by Derrida without persuasive argumentation. Philosopher Brendan Sweetman, similarly, has observed the difficulty in analyzing Derrida's deconstructionism:

> I am especially concerned to attempt to state Derrida's main thesis *clearly*, for it seems to me that this is one of the main difficulties with the philosophy of deconstructionism. Derrida and his disciples seldom provide a clear account of the main points of their philosophy. There are varying reasons for this, of course, not least their claim that they are not asserting a philosophical theory, or even a position, at all. This reluctance to state clearly what is they wish us to take away from their thought has the effect of at once isolating deconstructionism from philosophical debate, while at the same time protecting it from critical examination.[25]
>
> To add to this ambiguity and even incoherence, it should be noted that in all of Derrida's texts (roughly around 60 that have been translated to English), he purposely uses his terms differently in each, which can be seen as part of the "deconstructive strategy."[26]

24 Geisler, *History of Philosophy Western Philosophy,* vol. 2, 405–406.

25 Sweetman, "The Deconstruction of Western Metaphysics: Derrida and Maritain on Identity," 236.

26 Reynolds, "Jacques Derrida (1930–2004)."

Deconstructionism and its influence have become increasingly widespread since its inception in the 1960s. Unfortunately, thorough critiques have been much harder to come by,[27] as John M. Ellis notes in *Against Deconstruction*:

> But at the moment a debate scarcely exists: books and articles that use and advocate deconstruction are abundant, but apart from a handful of reviews and review articles there is very little in print that might represent the anti-deconstructionist side of the debate. Any sense of a continuing dialogue and interchange between the two sides is completely lacking. This is surely strange, given deconstruction's prominence. And it is regrettable—or ought to be—whatever position one might wish to take on the issues…
>
> Why then does the usual exchange between proponents and opponents barely exist in this case? Much of the answer must surely be found in the fact that deconstructionists have generally reacted with hostility and even outrage to any serious criticism of deconstruction and thus to any possibility of an exchange with their intellectual opponents. Give this initial response, it is almost inevitable that any riposte will be aimed, not at the argument that has been made, but at the credentials and motives of opponents; and, not uncommonly, this has resulted in deconstructionists seeming to want to set standards for participation in the debate that would effectively exclude skeptics from it… The tendency to avoid argument by attacking the bona fides of the adversary has, it must be admitted, had its effect on the opposition, which must also be held responsible for the inhibited condition of the debate; there is far more grumbling about deconstruction in the corridors of academic institutions than ever finds its way into print.[28]

Ellis's assessment, which took place in 1989, sounds uncannily similar to the current assaults on free speech that are commonplace at university campuses throughout North American and Europe, and to any dissenting voice from the accepted COVID narrative. To any astute observer, it should be abundantly clear that when proponents of a particular school of thought refuse to engage in debate through substantive argumentation and instead rely on ad hominem attacks, it is most likely due to the lack of substance of

27 Here are some of the very few critiques of deconstruction: Ellis, *Against Deconstruction*; Dutton, "Debunking Deconstruction"; Searle, "The World Upside Down"; Sweetman, "The Deconstruction of Western Metaphysics: Derrida and Maritain on Identity"; Sweetman, "Postmodernism, Derrida and Différance." These are others which are broader criticisms of postmodernism: Lundin, *The Culture of Interpretation*; Morningstar, "How to Deconstruct Almost Anything—My Postmodern Adventure"; Sokal and Bricmont, *Fashionable Nonsense*; Hicks, *Explaining Postmodernism*; Habermas, *The Philosophical Discourse of Modernity.*

28 Ellis, *Against Deconstruction*, viii.

their claims. Young students[29] at university campuses have learned well from their college professors, who in turn have been mimicking the antics of the postmodern "intellectuals" who laid the groundwork for their intersectional political and social movements. It should also be apparent that postmodernism in general and deconstruction in particular are not at all interested in logic, coherence, dialogue, and truth (either explicitly or implicitly), since their focus is on power.

Fittingly, Derrida's postmodern interlocutors interpret Derrida's writings from a deconstructionist perspective. Julian Wolfreys, a commentator on Derrida, suggests that to thematize, organize, or attempt to understand Derrida in a logical fashion "is what Derrida describes as *logocentric*. It is a dominant form of thinking in the history of Western thought, or metaphysics from Plato at least, to the present day. And such thinking is precisely what, in tireless and endlessly inventive fashion, Derrida exposes for its limitations."[30] We are told further that:

> One cannot gather up Derrida's text and give some simplistic order or context to it. Derrida has shown, patiently and repeatedly, that no context is ever finite. No context excludes other contexts. One can never exhaust the resources of a context. Whatever idea or notion is found to have particular contexts will never remain in place in that context. It will instead transport itself into other contexts, transforming its meaning and identity.[31]

Wolfrey's evaluation, of course reveals the common features of deconstructionism, namely, perspectivalism and semantic progressivism. There are serious implications to the idea that one can interpret and reinterpret texts in an endless number of ways. Even if this is possible, does it follow that each of the interpretations and shifting contexts are equally valid? This seems to be patently false, since any number of interpretations can lead to absurdities; this was well illustrated through the physicist Alan Sokal's experiment with a postmodern journal, which came to be known as the "Sokal Affair,"[32] or as Derrida called it, the "Sokal Hoax." It is important to note that this was not an isolated case. In May 2017, a paper with the preposterous title "The Conceptual

29 I use the term "young students" as a euphemism for "social justice warriors."

30 Wolfreys, *Derrida: A Guide for the Perplexed*, ix–x.

31 Wolfreys, *Derrida: A Guide for the Perplexed*, x.

32 In 1996, Sokal submitted an article to a postmodern journal to test the rigour and the integrity of the journal. In it article he argued that quantum gravity is a social and linguistic construct. See Sokal, "Transgressing the Boundaries: Toward a Transformative Hermeneutics of Quantum Gravity." Sokal then published an essay explaining that his article in *Social Text* was a hoax. See Sokal, "A Physicist Experiments with Cultural Studies."

Penis as a Social Construct" was published in a gender studies journal.[33] Its claims are breathtakingly nonsensical, which goes to show how ideologically possessed the editorial board of this journal must have been:

> The conceptual penis presents significant problems for gender identity and reproductive identity within social and family dynamics, is exclusionary to disenfranchised communities based upon gender or reproductive identity, is an enduring source of abuse for women and other gender-marginalized groups and individuals, is the universal performative source of rape, and is the conceptual driver behind much of climate change.[34]

I quote this simply to illustrate that further absurdities and problems arise when such thinking is applied to social activism. This is especially clear in the case of identities of individuals and oppressed people. This we will return to in our assessment of Bill C-16.

Inherent to deconstructionism is an obvious disdain for logic and the fabric of the West. This is precisely why Derrida coined the neologism "phallogocentrism," which is a reference to the privileging of the masculine, that is, the phallus, in the construction of meaning.[35] It is a combination of the terms "phallocentrism," which refers to the masculine or patriarchal point of view, and "logocentrism," the use of language to ascribe meaning to the world.[36] Furthermore, Derrida suggests that phonocentrism, the prioritization of the spoken word over the written word, is an essential component of phallogocentrism.[37] Gender and women's studies have widely used the term "phallogocentrism" in no small measure because of the influence of Derrida.[38] The criticism is that logocentrism is a patriarchal tool used by men to oppose other groups, including women and children. It is an absurd claim, since logic itself can be used by children and women and furthermore is fundamental to any sort of communication, academic discipline, and everyday reasoning and practically all other human endeavours. The claim is utterly vacuous but ironically uses logic and turns out to be self-refuting.

33 For the original article, written under pseudonyms, see the following link (it was taken down from the journal's website for obvious reasons): Lindsay & Boyle, "The Conceptual Penis as a Social Construct": https://www.skeptic.com/downloads/conceptual-penis/23311886.2017.1330439.pdf. For a discussion of the article see Peter Boghossian, Ed.D. (aka Peter Boyle, Ed.D.) and James Lindsay, PhD (aka Jamie Lindsay, PhD), "The Conceptual Penis as a Social Construct: A Sokal-Style Hoax on Gender Studies."

34 Lindsay & Boyle, "The Conceptual Penis as a Social Construct," 5–6.

35 See Reynolds, "Jacques Derrida (1930–2004)."

36 See Niall Lucy, *A Derrida Dictionary*, 70–72.

37 See Derrida, "Plato's Pharmacy," in Derrida, *Dissemination*, 61–171.

38 Reynolds, "Jacques Derrida (1930–2004)."

It is interesting to note that philosopher Richard Rorty observes that pragmatism, which we have already mentioned in our analysis of Peterson, leads to political conservatism and deconstruction to political radicalism. Jonathan Culler observes that the "pragmatist view of truth…treats conventionally accepted norms as foundations, deconstruction goes on to point out that 'norms are produced by acts of exclusion.'"[39] Rorty raises questions about the nature of Derrida's writing:

> The quarrel about whether Derrida has arguments thus gets linked to a quarrel about whether he is a private writer—writing for the delight of us insiders who share his background, who find the same rather esoteric things as funny or beautiful or moving as he does—or rather a writer with a public mission, someone who gives us weapons with which to subvert "institutionalized knowledge," and thus social institutions… Those who read Derrida to get ammunition, and a strategy, for the struggle to bring about social change.[40]

This assessment seems to be in line with what we are experiencing with Bill C-16, political correctness, and free speech. So, what are the implications of Derrida's method of deconstruction? It would be the end of Western philosophy and metaphysics if implemented. Derrida thought one could continue endlessly deconstructing and reinterpreting. But Derrida's implicit presuppositional claims contain self-contradictory claims, such as "the history of philosophy is closed" or "metaphysics has to come to an end"—in order to make such claims one cannot avoid using philosophy and metaphysics. Moreover, how can the positions implicit to deconstructionism (perspectivalism, referentialism, differentialism, and semantic progressivism) hold unless Derrida knows something about reality or that he knows one thing about reality with certainty? Logic dictates that if these positions could be logically affirmed, they would be demonstrated to be false. Well, then, what is Derrida doing? Is it merely poetry and as Rorty says: that he merely finds his claims to be "funny" or "beautiful"? If that's the case, then objective meaning is still intact, together with metaphysics and philosophy, in spite of all the postmodern doublethink employed. His use of metaphysics is just unavoidable. The same can be said about logic: he assumes logical statements so that can he reject them. Again, Rorty comes to Derrida's defence:

> The only thing that can displace an intellectual world is another intellectual world—a new alternative, rather than an argument against an old alternative. The idea that there is some neutral

39 Rorty, "Is Derrida a Transcendental Philosopher?," 236.
40 Rorty, "Is Derrida a Transcendental Philosopher?," 236.

> ground on which to mount an argument against something as big as "logocentrism" strikes me as one more logocentric hallucination. I do not think that demonstrations of "internal incoherence" or of "presuppositional relationships" ever do much to disabuse use of bad old ideas or institutions. Disabusing gets done, instead, by offering us sparkling new ideas, or utopian visions of glorious new institutions. The result of genuinely original thought, on my view, is not so much to refute or subvert our previous beliefs as to help us forget them by giving us substitutes for them. I take refutation to be a mark of unoriginality, and I value Derrida's originality too much to praise him in those terms.[41]

According to this, it seems to me, one is welcome to interpret Derrida as they please whether there is a deeper meaning or not. To understand Derrida is to get a glimpse at him casting aside Western philosophical tradition, that is logocentrism—solely through declaration (through allegedly ignoring it) albeit inconsistently; this is what seems to be essential to Derrida and his deconstructionist approach. Indeed, if Derrida were somehow correct in his method of deconstruction, he would not even be able to articulate a position if he were somehow right. It is as if Derrida is attempting to firmly plant his feet in mid-air. Nevertheless, for every commentator on Derrida who attempts to be consistent in applying deconstructionism, there is a new interpretation with endless supposed depths and contexts of meaning. How are we then to explain the various commonalities in interpreting Derrida if objectivity is not possible? Can anything truly be affirmed? If so, how come? If not, why not? How can one implicitly claim that one cannot reason (through rejecting logocentrism), then proceed to write texts allegedly making affirmations, conclusions, interpretations, and reinterpretations? The game continues but Derrida, his deconstructionist followers, and the postmodernists to this very day have all refused to play by the rules. Derrida's method of deconstruction would be like playing tennis without the net, or without rackets and tennis balls; perhaps the tennis court could be understood as a bunch of arbitrary lines symbolizing some esoteric message no one can decipher. But one may ask: what is understanding? What are lines? Even further, perhaps, one does not even show up to the court at all, because what is tennis anyway? But do we not know what tennis is? It is a game created by white privileged French Europeans in the 12th century to oppress the poor. Says who? Maybe tennis needs new rules, but are rules not categories of outdated oppressive structures? Should we not dispense with categories, or should there be endless categories for the marginalized and the oppressed? What if you are overweight, too short, too slow, lack talent—how is this at all fair? Tennis is a severely exclusionary and

41 Rorty "Is Derrida a Transcendental Philosopher?," 237

oppressive way of getting exercise; it is reserved only for the athletically gifted. Therefore, it should be eradicated.

As nonsensical and self-contradictory as the postmodern method of deconstructionism really is, it is nonetheless, as Rorty admits, within American circles a fuel for political radical activism. A thought-provoking confession was made by Derrida on deconstructionism in his work *Moscou aller-retour* as it relates to connecting the abstractions and methodological issues in his epistemology to political activism, where he pinpoints, of all things, Marxism: "Deconstruction never had meaning or interest, at least in my eyes, than as a radicalization, that is to say, also within the tradition of a certain Marxism in a certain spirit of Marxism."[42] Perhaps we are seeing the true agenda behind deconstructionism. Despite protestations that deconstructionism has been falsely applied to social and political activism, we have the real agenda uttered by the architect of postmodern deconstructionism himself. Sweetman has also observed that "Derrida's thesis, however, is not restricted to books or art works, for texts may consist of any set of ever-changing meanings. Hence, the world, and almost any object or combination of objects in it, could be regarded as a 'text.'"[43] Philosopher Stephen Hicks' assessment of why postmodernism even emerged as a possibility is especially helpful here: "The failure of epistemology made postmodernism possible, and the failure of socialism made postmodernism necessary."[44]

Thus, appropriately, although not without troubling implications, Derrida and his deconstructionist efforts are merely wishful attempts at instantiating the death of the absolute. Derrida's fumbling and incoherence demonstrate the contrary. We now may consider the following question: how does this all relate to Bill C-16 and the current discussions surrounding it?

A Discussion on Free Speech, Political Correctness, and Bill C-16

As mentioned above, Bill C-16 achieved Royal Assent on June 19, 2017—making it legally enforceable. The question now arises, what happens when you apply deconstructionism to gender? Philosopher John Searle has denoted one key strategy of deconstructionism:

> First, and most important, the deconstructionist is on the lookout for any of the traditional binary oppositions in Western intellectual history,

42 Derrida, *Moscou aller-retour*. See also Hicks, *Explaining Postmodernism*, 5.

43 Sweetman, "The Deconstruction of Western Metaphysics: Derrida and Maritain on Identity," 236.

44 Hicks, *Explaining Postmodernism*, i.

> e.g., speech/writing, male/female, truth/fiction, literal/metaphorical, signified/signifier, reality/appearance. In such oppositions, the deconstructionist claims that the first or the left-hand term is given a superior status over the right-hand term, which is regarded "as a complication, a negation, a manifestation, or a disruption of the first." These hierarchical oppositions allegedly lie at the very heart of logocentrism with its obsessive interest in rationality, logic, and the search for truth.
>
> The deconstructionist wants to undermine these oppositions, and so undermine logocentrism, by first reversing hierarchy, by trying to show that the right-hand term is really the prior term and that the left-hand term is just a special case of the right-hand term; the right-hand term is the condition of possibility of the left-hand term. This move gives some very curious results. It turns out that speech is really a form of writing, understanding a form of misunderstanding, and that what we think of as meaningful language is just a free play of signifiers or an endless process of grafting texts onto texts.[45]

As we can see, deconstruction elicits a rejection of binary categorization such as male/female—as associated with traditional sex designations.

The first thing to note is that Bill C-16 was not passed by conventional democratic means, since sponsors of the bill did not allow public hearings.[46] The second point is that the bill has nothing to do with discrimination and everything to do with the suppression of free speech. At this point, it will be worthwhile to return to Peterson's notion that free speech is not merely a value such as justice or mercy but rather a *mechanism*.[47] What Peterson means is that freedom of speech is the method by which humans can interact with one another through discussion, dialogue, and debate in order to resolve disagreements. It is the way we can reach a consensus on contentious issues rather than resorting to primordial and barbaric acts of violence, as has been witnessed, time and time again, throughout human history. It is an appeal to our rational capacities. This is why Logos is such a vital concept: it embodies speech, reason and logic. It is our connection with the divine, this connection from which the Judeo–Christian tradition can be seen as bearing the image-likeness stamp of God. This capacity for higher-level reasoning is what separates us from the rest of the animal kingdom. What we have seen with the suppression of free speech on college campuses reflects a regression in our humanity. In place of discussing issues and tolerating dissent, one's ability to express dissent has been stifled.

45 Searle, "The World Upside Down," 171.

46 Warmington, "No public hearings on gender identity protection bill."

47 For Peterson's explanation of free speech being a mechanism see his University of Toronto debate on "Free Speech, Political Correctness and Bill C-16" on November 19, 2016, https://www.youtube.com/watch?v=68NHUV5me7Q&feature=youtu.be.

Postmodernism, as Searle has observed, is a world that is upside-down. It is the ones who were "suppressed" who now act as the suppressors; however, they do not achieve dominance through rational argumentation but rather through decrying oppression and marginalization. Those who claim to be powerless have ironically gained power through their "powerlessness." The attack on free speech, aux fond, is an attack on the human person since it undermines our capacity for peaceful resolution through rational discussion and deliberation. As Hicks suggests in an article on free speech, which further corroborates the idea that it is more than merely a value, it is crucial to the survival of a democratic society because it fosters individual responsibility:

> Beliefs and thoughts are each individual's responsibility, just as making a living and putting together a happy life are the individual's responsibility. The purpose of government is to protect individuals' rights to pursue these activities. Thoughts and speech do not, no matter how false and offensive they are, violate anyone's rights. Therefore, there is no basis for government intervention… Free speech is a check on the abuses of government power. History teaches us to worry about the abuse of government power, and one indispensable way of checking such abuse is to allow people to criticize the government and to prohibit the government from preventing such criticism.[48]

One may also wonder why the stifling of free speech has come from what may be dubbed the "hard" or "far" left and why those who are more centrist, on the right, or conservative have been defending free speech. Hick explains this ironic move on the part of the "left" (which is seen politically in Canada through the Liberal Party and the NDP and is rampant throughout the social sciences and humanities[49]):

> I want to point out, first, that all of the speech codes around the country [applicable to the US and Canada, and even Europe and Australia] are proposed by members of the far Left, even though the same far Left for many years complained about the heavy-handedness of university administrations and championed freedom from university restrictions. So there is an irony in the shift of tactics in the Left's campaign for authoritarian, politically correct speech-restrictions.

All of the speech codes around the country are proposed by members of the far Left.

48 Hicks, "Free Speech and Postmodernism."

49 For an article exposing the postmodernist and relativistic inclinations of PM Justin Trudeau and the Liberal Party, see Porter Craig, "Canada and Postmodernism's Poster Boy."

> The question accordingly is: Why, in recent years, have academic Leftists switched their critique and their tactics so dramatically? I have spoken about aspects of this topic before—for example, in my two lectures on postmodernism—and I have written a book on the topic [*Explaining Postmodernism*]. In my judgment, a key part of explaining why the Left now advocates speech codes is that in recent decades the Left has suffered a series of major disappointments. In the West, the Left has failed to generate significant far-Left socialist parties, and many socialist parties have become moderate. Major experiments in socialism in nations such as the Soviet Union, Vietnam, and Cuba have been failures. Even the academic world has shifted sharply towards liberalism and free markets. When an intellectual movement suffers major disappointments, you can expect it to resort to more desperate tactics.[50]

Thus, we see postmodern thinkers shifting their attention from economic equality to identity politics as a way of creating an equalizer.

In response to Bill C-16 in 2016, Peterson posted three lectures[51] explaining the various problems with this legislation. In the first video, he explains that he fears being brought in front of the Human Rights Commission for the things he is saying and teaching, which could be deemed as "hate speech" because of a sloppily worded bill. Hate is a notoriously difficult word to define. It is hopelessly vague and could lead to the prosecution of innocent people. Peterson has argued that the Canadian government has essentially enshrined social constructionism in law. This, he suspects, will lead to a persecution of biologists for making politically incorrect claims regarding sex designation and sexual orientation. Moreover, Peterson has also pointed out that "gender expression" sounds an awful lot like fashion; thus criticism of fashion (dress, hair, makeup, body language, voice, etc.) is now considered a crime,[52] which is absurd. Peterson noted that both provincial[53] and federal legislation[54] already cover gender identity and gender expression. Lawyer Jared Brown corroborated much of what Peterson has stated[55] and has explained how you can be imprisoned for refusing to use invented gender pronouns, now that Bill

50 Hicks, "Free Speech and Postmodernism."

51 These videos can be found the following links (all of which are private now): Video 1: https://www.youtube.com/watch?v=fvPgjg201w0, Video 2: https://www.youtube.com/watch?v=f-7YGGCE9es,Video 3: https://www.youtube.com/watch?v=W2u62u4entc.

52 See Ontario Human Rights Commission, Policy on preventing discrimination because of gender identity and gender expression, section 3.

53 Ontario Human Rights Commission, Policy on preventing discrimination because of gender identity and gender expression, section 3.

54 Quite disturbingly, the link to the Canadian Department of Justice was removed back in 2017: http://www.justice.gc.ca/eng/404.html.

55 See Brown's legal analysis of Bill C-16, https://litigationguy.wordpress.com/2016/12/24/bill-c-16-whats-the-big-deal/.

C-16 has been passed by the Canadian Senate. Bill C-16 will also allow men to use women's washrooms and change rooms. Both Brown and Peterson were expert witnesses against the passing of Bill C-16, which unfortunately sailed through without any amendments.[56] The video of their expert testimonies to date has almost received two million views, which is exceedingly high for a senate hearing. (Unfortunately, this infringement on freedom of speech and freedom of conscience is no more evident than in the treatment of anyone who dissents from the COVID lies.)

Despite claims to the contrary, Bill C-16 pushes compelled speech on Canadians and is an example of how one group's freedoms compromise another's, as Queen's University law professor Bruce Pardy observes:

> Human rights are now a zero-sum game. Giving rights to some means taking them from others… Freedom of expression is a traditional, negative human right. When the state manages expression, it threatens to control what we think. Forced speech is the most extreme infringement of free speech. It puts words in the mouths of citizens and threatens to punish them if they do not comply. When speech is merely restricted, you can at least keep your thoughts to yourself. Compelled speech makes people say things with which they disagree.
>
> Bill C-16, like provincial human rights codes, does not make specific reference to speech. In the Senate, supporters of C-16 fell over each other denying that the legislation would compel language. When Justice Minister Jody Wilson-Raybould testified before the Senate's Legal and Constitutional Affairs Committee, she specifically denied that the bill would force the use of gender-neutral pronouns. There are reasons to doubt her sincerity. First, human rights commissions say otherwise. Along with human rights tribunals, they have primary control over the meaning and application of code provisions, something the justice minister must know. Human rights commissions are not neutral investigative bodies but advocacy agencies with expansive agendas. In comparison, courts and governments play only a minor role in interpreting these statutes.[57]

If we just take a look at, for example, how gender identity is defined, we can discern a host of problems: "Gender identity is each person's internal and individual experience of gender. It is their sense of being a woman, a man, both, neither, or anywhere along the gender spectrum."[58] Peterson states in

56 For Peterson's expert testimony at the Senate hearing on Bill C-16 which took place May 17, 2017, see https://www.youtube.com/watch?v=KnIAAkSNtqo.

57 Pardy, "Meet the new 'human rights.'"

58 Ontario Human Rights Commission, Policy on preventing discrimination because of gender identity and gender expression, section 3.

his video that such an elastic definition of gender has not only been poorly written into legislation but also been poorly thought out, which should be a major cause for worry. What is meant by "neither"? How can a human person be neither a man nor a woman? This may be a reference to gender fluidity and the idea of "gender blender," namely that persons can identify as whatever they please at any given moment. It could also be a reference to "otherkins" (trans-speceism)[59]—persons who identify as animals or a hybridization of animal and human. In any event, the denial of male or female is invalid in light of binary biological sex. Where is the evidence for this denial? Is this in reference to intersex individuals? It is not clear at all. What is meant by "both"? It seems to be demonstrably incoherent as currently expressed in legislation, and vague language makes for very poor law. Peterson states that the separation of gender from one's biological sex is a proposition and not a fact, with next to zero scientific support. The main fear is that bad legislation like this may hinder further scientific discussions on such issues, if not outright prohibit them as "hate speech." It is also important to note that the postmodern view of human nature is one of social constructionism.[60] A few questions can be raised about non-binary genders. Are they a social construct? And if they are, how can one claim them to be a right? In gender studies, the notion that gender is a social construct is widely accepted. It involves gender identity, that is, one's personal experience of one's own gender. We are also told that gender identity is not a stable, static trait—rather, being socially constructed, it may vary over time for an individual.[61] Now, if it is a social construct then it is dependent on the recognition of others whether one is a transman, transwoman, or any other "transgender" category—but recall it is a subjective experience of a "person's internal and individual experience of gender." Thus, if it is left to the individual's "sense" then it arguably aligns with a radical subjectivity of how one feels from

59 Roberts, "Otherkin Are People Too; They Just Identify as Nonhuman."

60 Lindsey, *Gender Roles*, chapter 1.

61 On Steve Paikin's show *The Agenda* on TVO, in an episode titled "Gender, Rights and Freedom of Speech," which aired October 27, 2016 (http://tvo.org/video/programs/the-agenda-with-steve-paikin/genders-rights-and-freedom-of-speech), Peterson was criticized for his refusal to use gender-neutral pronouns by a transgender man (what I mean by that is someone who was "sexually assigned female genitalia at birth who prefers to be referred to as 'they'"), a professor of gender studies at the University of Toronto and a transgender activist law professor at the University of Ontario. Interestingly, the only one sympathetic to Peterson's position was Theryn Meyer, a transgender woman who opposes Bill C-16 and the imposition of compelled speech. Interestingly, most transgendered/transsexual individuals want to be called the opposite sex (the one they identify as) and therefore do not ascribe to all these gender-neutral pronouns—a point often overlooked. It is also worth noting that the gender studies professor made the following outlandish statement: "there is actually no such thing as a biological sex." No one knows what this really means; aside from speculating that it might have something to do with deconstructionism and attempting to apply it to genetics and evolutionary biology, one is left uncertain.

moment to moment, rather than being contingent upon others' acceptance (as is the case with social construction).

The upshot is that Peterson refuses to utter the neologisms of gender-neutral pronouns such as 'thon,' 'hiz' and 'hizer', 'ne' and 'nir', 'ze' and 'zir', and 'xe' and 'xyr' as substitutions for standard pronouns such as 'his' and 'hers', 'him' and 'her', 'he' and 'she', or even 'they' to refer to individual students: "I won't mouth the words of ideologues, because when you do that you become a puppet for their ideology." He compared the bill to the work of "totalitarian and authoritarian political states."[62] What is also troubling about legislating people to refer to transgender individuals with gender-neutral pronouns is that there are by some estimations at least 63 genders:[63] this would be an impossible feat.[64] Perhaps one designation such as 'they' could be a concession, but 63? One potential way of simplifying this whole ordeal is to only refer to someone by name; until you know someone's name, perhaps it is best not to assign them a pronoun. But again, this goes against standard societal conventions of how we interact daily with one another; we have evolved certain mechanisms that allow us to recognize when we are interacting with a male or female. At times, this distinction may be vague, but for the most part it is quite accurate. Peterson explains, in an article for the *Toronto Sun*, the unreasonableness behind the law demanding we use such pronouns:

> It is simply not reasonable for a stranger—say, a student in one of my classes—to request that I learn, speak and remember a whole set of personal descriptors as a precondition for our interactions. It is certainly not reasonable to demand that I do so—and it is absolutely unreasonable for that demand to have been given the force of law. You don't get to exercise control over my speech.
>
> The demand for use of preferred pronouns is not an issue of equality, inclusion or respect for others. It's a wolf in sheep's clothing. It's a purposeful assault on the structure of language. It's a dangerous incursion into the domain of free speech. It's narcissistic self-centeredness. It's part and parcel of the Political Correctness madness that threatens to engulf our culture.[65]

It should be further pointed out that those who kowtow to political correctness typically identify as champions of pluralism and diversity, except when it pertains to diversity of thought. Political correctness has unleashed

62 McParland, "Are zee ready for the dictatorship of the gender warriors?"

63 aPath.org, "63 Genders."

64 For a thorough article dealing with Dr. Peterson and the gender pronoun battle, see Ventureyra, "Canada's Boldest Professor Defies the Gender Police."

65 Peterson, "Why I won't use 'preferred' pronouns—and why you shouldn't either."

a ubiquitous malaise throughout Western civilization at the expense of our freedoms and liberties. Universities have become a place of complacency, where at every turn students require trigger warnings and safe spaces in order to cope with perceived microaggressions.[66]

Ironically, the transgender community as a whole does not seem too pleased about this unwanted exposure. They are not a homogenous community and have wide variances in political, social, and religious outlooks—just like any other segment of the population. If anything, this has the potential to have negative ramifications in their lives instead of improving them. This also goes to demonstrate the wrongfulness of identity politics and intersectional ideology, which in my estimation are highly discriminatory, since they do not take the individual person into full account but rather lump together or collectivize a series of "marginalized" individuals in order to support a political agenda.

Recall my point regarding the implications of Derrida's deconstructionism and endless possibilities of categories as it applies to "texts" being transposed into the social and political realm.[67] This can have an endless chaotic affect when applied to social activism with respect to alleged oppressed and marginalized groups. Consider that apart from transgender people, there are other "trans" categories. As we mentioned above, there are trans-speciesist (otherkins). There are also people who are "transracial": for example, Rachel Dolezal has identified as white at certain points of her life and black at others.[68] There are "transager/ transgender" individuals like StefonKnee Wolscht, who is the father of 4 children but now lives as a 6-year-old girl.[69] There is the case of transableism where able-bodied individuals desire to become disabled.[70] Keep also in mind that with transgenderism there is the notion of fluidity, by which one can fluctuate between male, female, both, and neither at a moment's decision, from

66 See Ventureyra, "A brief reflection on M-103 and Islamophobia," 6. I saw this as a problem at the University of Ottawa a number of years ago with the cancellation of Ann Coulter's talk; see Ventureyra, "Invocation of Fear." Similarly, Professor Graeme Hunter wrote a piece for the *National Post* arguing that shutting down speakers is anti-intellectual; see Hunter, "Coulter exposes Ottawa's Shame-On U." For a recent but controversial analysis of the phenomenon of political correctness, see Adams, *Retaking America*. For the devastating implications of political correctness and thought/ speech policing, see Charlton, *Thought Prison*. For an incisive historical outlook concerning political correctness, see Hughes, *Political Correctness*. For understanding the widespread reach of political correctness and its associated culprits in the university setting, I recommend watching a lecture by Gad Saad (professor of marketing at Concordia University), titled "How Political Correctness Limits the Free Exchange of Ideas on Campus," which was given at the University of Ottawa in February 2016: https://www.youtube.com/watch?v=G5-oG0L6ZnU. In this lecture Professor Saad covers the language police, the rejection of intellectual diversity, identity politics, micro-aggressions, trigger warnings, safe spaces, cultural appropriation, etc.

67 For works applying deconstruction to the realm of politics, see McQuillan, *The Politics of Deconstruction*; McQuillan, *Deconstruction Reading*.

68 See Dolezal, *In Full Color*.

69 Goldenberg, "Transgender AND Transager."

70 See Boesveld, "Becoming disabled by choice, not chance."

day to day, hour to hour, minute to minute. What's next? What if we combine various "trans" categories with their various manifestations? We would get all kinds of combinations. Who is to say this is wrong? The question arises, does deconstructionism when applied to the issue of gender and radical subjectivity (i.e., of how one feels or identifies) inevitably lead to a *reductio ad absurdum*? Once we accept transgenderism are we committed to accepting all other "trans" categories? Consider the following syllogistic argument:

1. If transgenderism is true, then so are other "trans" categories (trans-speciesism, transageism, transableism, etc.).
2. Other "trans" categories (trans-speciesism, transageism, transableism etc.) are false.
3. Therefore, transgenderism is false.

It seems that once we accept transgenderism, then we must accept the plethora of other "trans" categories; but in the absence of any good argument that one should accept transgenderism, we are well within our rights to reject all these "trans" categories. This is not to say that we do not acknowledge the legitimacy of people's feelings. We must be empathetic and sympathetic toward those who struggle or are different than us, but in rational discourse these concepts are mere constructions without any biological correspondence.[71]

Conclusion

Derrida's confused deconstructionism has some deep ramifications when applied to the human person. Deconstructionism has infiltrated our faculties of humanities throughout the Western world. It has emboldened radical social activists, also known as "social justice warriors," that are indoctrinated by university professors. This radical leftist ideology has spread like a virus. Many professors, professionals, and others are afraid to speak out against political correctness. But it is not a time for people to be silent and complacent. Everyone should refuse compelled speech; the law should not be able to dictate what one ought to say. The postmodernist ideology as it applies to social issues, as exemplified by cultural Marxism, has not only penetrated our secular institutions and government but also Catholic universities, as many professors have also applied postmodernist thought to

71 Intersexuality is often raised in defense of transgenderism, but first, this is a real physical and biological reality; and second, these individuals typically desire to be either male or female, not a nonbinary category.

Catholic philosophy and theology. This must be stopped before it grows even more out of hand.

Without acknowledging the existence of truth, there can be no debate that leads to genuine human flourishing. Our self-worth does not come from a confused psychological identity crisis but is based on our common dignity, an inalienable value that transcends all socio-cultural impositions. Thus, we all need to act as champions of truth. We must stand against such tyranny at all levels of society regardless of our religious commitments. All who value freedom of speech as a means of resolving disagreement and discovering truth must stand against tyranny by supporting Peterson and his defence of free speech. When Peterson applies objective notions of truth is when these wrongheaded ideas like the application of Derrida's deconstructionism can be dispelled. We have every reason to reject postmodernism and its offspring of deconstructionism since there are no good reasons to affirm it. Moreover, it is not only incoherent but chaotic in its effects on politics and social ideas. I believe that, in addition to logical refutations (no matter how much the postmodernists resist engaging in logic), they should be taken to task on all their fallacious claims. The reasoning student will immediately see the vacuity of their claims and philosophy. Moreover, I encourage thinkers to ridicule the absurdities that come along with postmodernism. They should also attempt to publish papers in postmodern journals, following Sokal's example years ago. Helen Pluckrose and James Lindsay in their recent book *Cynical Theories* expose the corruption and lack of scholarship found in grievance studies. They published a series of satirical papers in peer-reviewed journals to demonstrate this. They even published a feminist rendition of portions of Adolf Hitler's *Mein Kampf* for *Affilia: Journal of Women and Social Work*.[72] This is one case where I believe ridicule and mockery can be effective. As Thomas Jefferson famously stated: "Ridicule is the only weapon which can be used against unintelligible propositions. Ideas must be distinct before reason can act upon them."[73]

Free speech, which is a mechanism for opening up dialogue to help peacefully correct the wrongs of our society, is under attack. It is the West's last stand before something more ominous is to come. Recently, comedian Dave Chapelle has come to recognize that the transgender issue is not about discriminating against transgender individuals, but about corporations and certain activists with financial interests, who would like to monitor what is acceptable speech. Chappelle has rightly taken a stand against such an imposition.[74] If we are silenced, then what hope is there for correcting the wrongs of our society?

72 Melchior, "Fake News Comes to Academia: How three scholars gulled academic journals to publish hoax papers on 'grievance studies.'"

73 Jefferson, "Thomas Jefferson to Francis Adrian van der Kemp."

74 Jones, "Dave Chappelle says he's willing to speak to transgender community but will not bend 'to anyone's demands.'"

But why should a postmodernist care about free speech and rational discourse? In the end, as Nietzsche observed, in *The Will to Power*, human inclinations have more to do with power than with truth. The postmodernists following such thinking would rather not discuss or debate; they prefer to impose their views by fiat: do not let them do it.[75] It is time for people to wake up from their slumber and defend truth, logic, and the human person while exposing illogical and pernicious ideologies that have infiltrated our government and educational institutions under the mask of "compassion" and "equal rights."

Bibliography

Adams, Nick. *Retaking America: Crushing Political Correctness.* New York: Post Hill Press, 2016.

aPath.org. "63 Genders." https://apath.org/63-genders/.

Aristotle. *The Complete Works of Aristotle*, 2 vols. Revised Oxford Translation. Edited by J. Barnes. Princeton University Press, 1984.

Beardsworth, Richard. *Derrida & The Political.* London: Routledge.

Bernasconi, Robert. *Derrida and Différance.* Evanston, IL: Northwestern University Press, 1988.

Boesveld, Sarah. "Becoming disabled by choice, not chance: 'Transabled' people feel like impostors in their fully working bodies." *National Post,* June 3, 2015. https://nationalpost.com/news/canada/becoming-disabled-by-choice-not-chance-transabled-people-feel-like-impostors-in-their-fully-working-bodies.

Boghossian, Peter, and James Lindsay. "The Conceptual Penis as a Social Construct: A Sokal-Style Hoax on Gender Studies." *Skeptic Magazine.* https://www.skeptic.com/reading_room/conceptual-penis-social-contruct-sokal-style-hoax-on-gender-studies/.

Charlton, Bruce G. *Thought Prison: The Fundamental Nature of Political Correctness.* Buckingham, UK: University of Buckingham Press, 2015.

Craig, James Porter. "Canada and Postmodernism's Poster Boy." *Catholic Insight,* July 1, 2017. https://catholicinsight.com/canada-postmodernisms-poster-boy/.

75 This chapter is dedicated to Professors Jordan B. Peterson and Gad Saad for their vigorous defense of free speech and for being a voice of sanity in a time when insanity rules our academic/educational institutions, government, and overall culture. It is also dedicated to Professor Stephen Hicks for his brilliant exposure of the postmodernist agenda. I am thankful to these three professors for awakening me from my slumber, years ago. I always felt something was amiss but did not realize how deeply entrenched in postmodernism professors in the social sciences and humanities even at Catholic institutions truly were. If only their wisdom and courage would be carried forward by other professors and people of good will, then we would find a way out of the totalitarian imposition of this cultural Marxist agenda foisted upon us by radical leftists.

David, Marian. "The Correspondence Theory of Truth." *The Stanford Encyclopedia of Philosophy*, May 28, 2015. https://plato.stanford.edu/entries/truth-correspondence/.

Derrida, Jacques. *Dissemination*. Translated by B. Johnson. Chicago: University of Chicago Press, 1981.

———. *Glas*. Translated by J. P. Leavey, Jr. and R. Rand. Lincoln, NE: University of Nebraska Press, 1986.

———. *Margins of Philosophy*. Translated by Alan Bass. Chicago: University of Chicago Press, 1982.

———. *Moscou aller-retour*. Saint Etienne: De l'Aube, 1995.

———. *Of Grammatology*. Translated by G. Spivak. Baltimore: Johns Hopkins, 1976.

———. *Writing and Difference*. Translated by Alan. Bass. Chicago: University of Chicago Press, 1978.

———. *Speech and Phenomena and Other Essays in Husserl's Theory of Signs*. Translated by D. B. Allison. Evanston, IL: Northwestern University Press, 1973.

Dolezal, Rachel. *In Full Color: Finding My Place in a Black and White World*. Dallas: BenBella Books, 2017.

Dutton, Dennis. "Debunking Deconstruction." *Philosophy and Literature* 13 (1989): 430–434.

Ellis, John M. *Against Deconstruction*. Princeton, NJ: Princeton University Press, 1988.

Geisler, Norman. *A History of Western Philosophy, Volume II: Modern and Postmodern from Descartes to Derrida*. Matthews, NC: Bastion Books, 2016.

Goldenberg, Ashlee Rae. "Transgender AND Transager: 52-Year-Old Father Lives as a 6-Year-Old Girl." *mrcTV*, December 7, 2015. http://www.mrctv.org/blog/52-year-old-father-lives-6-year-old-girl.

Habermas, Jürgen. *The Philosophical Discourse of Modernity: Twelve Lectures*, edited by Frederick Laurence. Cambridge, UK: Polity Press, 2005.

Hicks, Stephen R. C. *Explaining Postmodernism: Skepticism and Socialism from Rousseau to Foucault*. Milwaukee, WI: Scholargy, 2004.

———. "Free Speech and Postmodernism." *The Atlas Society*, June 21, 2010. https://atlassociety.org/students/students-blog/3703-free-speech-and-postmodernism.

Hughes, Geoffrey. *Political Correctness: A History of Semantics and Culture*. Oxford: Wiley-Blackwell, 2010.

Hunter, Graeme. "Coulter exposes Ottawa's Shame-On U." *National Post*, March 26, 2010. http://nationalpost.com/full-comment/graeme-hunter-coulter-exposes-ottawas-shame-on-u/.

Hussey, Edward. "Epistemology and Meaning in Heraclitus." In *Language and Logos*, edited by M. Schofield and M. C. Nussbaum, 33–59. Cambridge:

Cambridge University Press, 1982.
Jefferson, Thomas. "Thomas Jefferson to Francis Adrian Van der Kemp." *Founders Online*, National Archives, July 30, 1816. https://founders.archives.gov/documents/Jefferson/03-10-02-0167.
Jones, Zoe Christen. "Dave Chappelle says he's willing to speak to transgender community but will not bend 'to anyone's demands.'" *CBS News*, October 26, 2021. https://www.cbsnews.com/news/dave-chappelle-transgender-closer-controversy/.
Kay Melchior, Jillian. "Fake News Comes to Academia: How three scholars gulled academic journals to publish hoax papers on 'grievance studies.'" *Wall Street Journal*, October 2, 2018. https://www.wsj.com/articles/fake-news-comes-to-academia-1538520950.
Lindsay, Jamie and Peter Boyle. "The Conceptual Penis as a Social Construct." *Cogent Social Sciences* (2017), 3. https://www.skeptic.com/downloads/conceptual-penis/23311886.2017.1330439.pdf.
Lindsey, Linda. *Gender Roles: A Sociological Perspective*. New York: Routledge, 2015.
Lonergan, Bernard. *Insight: A Study of Human Understanding. Collected Works of Bernard Lonergan*, vol. 3, edited by Frederick E. Crowe and Robert M. Doran. Toronto: University of Toronto Press, 1992.
Lucy, Niall. *A Derrida Dictionary*. Oxford, UK: Blackwell, 2004.
Lundin, Roger. *The Culture of Interpretation: Christian Faith and the Postmodern World*. Grand Rapids, MI: William B. Eerdmans, 1993.
McParland, Kelly. "Are zee ready for the dictatorship of the gender warriors?" *National Post,* October 27, 2016. http://nationalpost.com/opinion/kelly-mcparland-are-zee-ready-for-the-dictatorship-of-the-gender-warriors.
McQuillan, Martin. *Deconstruction Reading Politics*. New York: Palgrave Macmillan, 2008.
———, ed. *The Politics of Deconstruction: Jacques Derrida and the Other Philosophy*. London: Pluto Press, 2007.
Morningstar, Chip. "How to Deconstruct Almost Anything—My Postmodern Adventure." June 1993. http://www.fudco.com/chip/deconstr.html.
Ontario Human Rights Commission. Policy on preventing discrimination because of gender identity and gender expression. https://www3.ohrc.on.ca/sites/default/files/Policy%20on%20preventing%20discrimination%20because%20of%20gender%20identity%20and%20gender%20expression.pdf.
Pardy, Bruce. "Meet the new 'human rights'—where you are forced by law to use 'reasonable' pronouns." *National Post,* June 19, 2017. http://nationalpost.com/opinion/bruce-pardy-meet-the-new-human-rights-where-you-are-forced-by-law-to-use-reasonable-pronouns-like-ze-and-zer.
Parliament of Canada. "Bill C-16: An Act to amend the Canadian Human

Rights Act and the Criminal Code."

———. "Bill C-276: An Act to amend the Canadian Human Rights Act and the Criminal Code (gender identity and gender expression)."

———. "Bill C-279: An Act to amend the Canadian Human Rights Act and the Criminal Code (gender identity)."

———. "Hate Speech and Freedom of Expression: Legal Boundaries in Canada." https://lop.parl.ca/sites/PublicWebsite/default/en_CA/ResearchPublications/201825E.

———. Legislative Summary of Bill C-16: An Act to amend the Canadian Human Rights Act and the Criminal Code, accessed August 1, 2021. https://lop.parl.ca/sites/PublicWebsite/default/en_CA/ResearchPublications/LegislativeSummaries/421C16E.

Peterson, Jordan. "Censorship on Campus." Manning Centre Conference, Ottawa, February 23–25, 2017. Clips: https://www.youtube.com/watch?v=nrNSxAT7zNU; https://www.youtube.com/watch?cv=9NZ4SwEX7Ts&list=FLU3wk8phyx87ArTttbreQFg&index=2; https://www.youtube.com/watch?v=rnb2-dqUyjg&t=56s; https://www.youtube.com/watch?v=KfEi3dpq54Q.

Peterson, Jordan B. *Maps of Meaning: The Architecture of Belief.* New York: Routledge, 1999.

———. "Why I won't use 'preferred' pronouns—and why you shouldn't either." *Toronto Sun*, November 3, 2017. http://www.torontosun.com/2016/11/03/why-i-wont-use-preferred-pronouns--and-why-you-shouldnt-either.

Pluckrose, Helen and James Lindsay. *Cynical Theories: How Activist Scholarship Made Everything about Race, Gender, and Identity—and Why This Harms Everybody*. Durham, NC: Pitchstone, 2020.

Reynolds, Jack. "Jacques Derrida (1930–2004)." *Internet Encyclopedia of Philosophy*. https://iep.utm.edu/derrida/.

Roberts, Amber. "Otherkin Are People Too; They Just Identify as Nonhuman." *Vice*, July 16, 2015. http://www.vice.com/en_ca/read/from-dragons-to-foxes-the-otherkin-community-believes-you-can-be-whatever-you-want-to-be.

Rorty, Richard. "Is Derrida a Transcendental Philosopher?" In *Derrida: A Critical Reader*, edited by David Wood. Oxford: Blackwell, 1992.

Searle, John R. "The World Upside Down." In *Working through Derrida*, edited by Gary B. Madison, 170-83. Evanston, IL: Northwestern University Press, 1993.

Sokal, Alan. "A Physicist Experiments with Cultural Studies," *Lingua Franca*, June 5, 1996.

———. "Transgressing the Boundaries: Toward a Transformative Hermeneutics of Quantum Gravity." *Social Text* 46–47 (1996): 217–252.

Sokal, Alan and Jean Bricmont. *Fashionable Nonsense: Postmodern Philosophers'*

Abuse of Science. New York: Picador, 1998.

Solzhenitsyn, Aleksandr. *The Gulag Archipelago: 1918-1956 An Experiment in Literary Investigation*, 3 vols. Translated by Thomas P. Whitney. New York: Harper & Row, Publishers, Inc., 1973.

Stein, Joel. "Life with the Father of Deconstructionism." *Time Magazine* 46, 76 (November 18, 2002). http://content.time.com/time/nation/article/0,8599,391685,00.html.

Sweetman, Brendan. "The Deconstruction of Western Metaphysics: Derrida and Maritain on Identity." In *Postmodernism and Christian Philosophy*, edited by Roman Ciapalo. Washington, DC: Catholic University of America Press, 1997.

———. "Postmodernism, Derrida and Différance: A Critique." *International Philosophical Quarterly* 39 (1999): 5–18

Thomas Aquinas. "Summa theologiae." In *Sancti Thomae de Aquino Oera Omnia Iussu Leonis XIII*. Vols. 4–12 of 50 vols., edited by Leonine Commission. Rome: 1882.

Ventureyra, Scott. "A brief reflection on M-103 and Islamophobia." *City Light News*, 29, 4, (April 2017): 6. https://www.scottventureyra.com/_files/ugd/f90fdb_d9e686bbe1484951bd8a09d2f69b8727.pdf.

———. "Canada's Boldest Professor Defies the Gender Police." *Crisis*, December 2, 2016. http://www.crisismagazine.com/2016/canadas-boldest-professor-defies-gender-police.

———. "Invocation of Fear." *The Ottawa Citizen*, March 26, 2010. http://www.pressreader.com/canada/ottawa-citizen/20100326/285009735713496.

Warmington, Joe. "No public hearings on gender identity protection bill." *Toronto Sun*, November 2, 2017. http://www.torontosun.com/2016/11/01/no-public-hearings-on-gender-identity-protection-bill.

Wolfreys, Julian. *Derrida: A Guide for the Perplexed.* New York: Continuum, 2007.

Chapter 29

The Gender Revolution and Its Global Imposition

Pablo Muñoz Iturrieta

The first quarter of the 21st century will be remembered in the history of ideas as having reached the climax of a cultural revolution that is made manifest in the United Nations' *2030 Agenda for Sustainable Development.* This Agenda was crafted and then imposed upon all nations of the world without any democratic process, and it in effect gives a new meaning to the political, legal and social arrangements of every nation on the planet.[1] The 2030 Agenda represents a true cultural revolution, because the economic and political changes it proposes are nothing more than concrete applications of its central underlying principle: gender ideology. The Agenda, in fact, establishes through two of its global goals the imposition of the "recognition" of gender identity as a human right worldwide: Goal 5 (gender equality) and Goal 10 (reduction of inequalities). For this reason, the Agenda states, "the systematic mainstreaming of a gender perspective in the implementation of the Agenda is crucial."[2]

The 2030 Agenda does not simply intend to "extend civil rights" to an allegedly oppressed community, but rather it signifies a true "identity" revolution that intends to impose a new paradigm of what it means to be a human being, a conception not centered on our common nature but on accidental characteristics and subjective perceptions. As such, this identity revolution is leading us, in the name of freedom, towards the annihilation of what it really means to be human, giving way to a new category: gender identity.[3]

In this chapter, then, I first want to dwell on the topic of gender identity. Secondly, I will offer a few examples of this legal, political, and social imposition and offer what I think is the main reason for its totalitarian imposition. Thirdly, I will explain why giving in to the demands of gender activists implies the destruction of the political foundations of the West. Finally, as a conclusion, I'd like to offer a few ideas on how to counteract this "gender revolution."

1 General Assembly of the United Nations, *Transforming Our World: The 2030 Agenda for Sustainable Development.*

2 *Transforming Our World,* 7.

3 The concept was analyzed from a philosophical and scientific perspective in Muñoz Iturrieta, *Atrapado en el cuerpo equivocado: La ideología de género frente a la ciencia y la filosofía.*

The Gender Revolution

Gender ideology denies the reality of the human person and its nature in a kind of extreme dichotomy: our body does not reflect our mind, so that a man can be "trapped" in the body of a woman, and his body must be accommodated or technically transformed in order to make his feelings a reality. Yet this does not end here, as the founding philosophy of the global Agenda also requires by every possible means that the population and the political and legal system of a nation accept gender identity as the constitutive identity of a person, even if said identity denies the biological constitution of the human being.

This change of cultural paradigm has been developing for decades, and its ideological primacy is manifested in the elimination of any idea or voice that dares to question it.[4] Hence the constant censorship and the "cancel culture" that the current situation has created. Not surprising, for example, is the speed with which legislatures, judicial systems, universities, various organizations, and even intellectuals adopt without any critical thinking the mainstreaming of a "gender perspective" promoted by the United Nations and various corporations and financial organizations, afraid to be left out or culturally delegitimized if they do not embrace the 2030 Agenda.

Today, it is explicitly forbidden to question the false philosophical assumptions that guide this Agenda: One is not born a man or a woman, but rather "becomes," "self-constitutes" in a specific identity; sex is a "social construction" imposed by parents upon their children; gender is a "personal or social construction" radically independent from biology, in such a way that "when the constructed status of gender is theorized as radically independent of sex, gender itself becomes a free-floating artifice, with the consequence that man and masculine might just as easily signify a female body as a male one, and woman and feminine a male body as easily as a female one," according to Judith Butler, the main exponent of gender ideology today.[5]

Society, on the other hand, is seen by the proponents of this ideology as corrupting, for it imposes labels and a biological sex, thereby forcing individuals to live according to expectations that make the person an inauthentic being.[6] And that is the greatest paradox of this ideology: although it is necessary to free oneself from society and its oppressive norms in order to build a true identity in the name of freedom (based on feelings), society is in turn forced

4 The ideological architecture of this cultural revolution is developed in Muñoz Iturrieta, *Las mentiras que te cuentan, las verdades que te ocultan.*

5 Butler, *Gender Trouble: Feminism and the Subversion of Identity*, 6.

6 The "gender unicorn" graphic employed in Sex Education programs around the world in fact states that sex is assigned by parents at birth. See http://www.children.gov.on.ca/htdocs/English/professionals/LGBT2SQ/guide-2018/notelanguage.aspx.

to accept that identity in the name of freedom, so that without social approval no identity would seem to be complete. This ideology pretends to reject any "social construction" imposed by society, but at the same time forces society, in the name of freedom, to accept and confirm a self-proclaimed identity.[7] If you don't agree, then you are considered a bigot, LGBTQ+QI+-phobic, and an enemy of progress.

The last point is key to understanding the logic behind the self-proclaimed human rights groups. The main objective of their activism is to achieve cultural, political, and institutional changes not so much in order to "expand rights" as to force upon others the recognition of new "identities" and "sexual diversity." Ultimately, the guiding principle is that all individuals have the right not only to perceive themselves according to their own feelings, but also to be recognized as such by others. Failure to recognize this supposed right is framed as a hate crime, an act that causes psychological damage, and an exercise of "symbolic violence." This explains the phenomenon of the cancel culture and the political and totalitarian legal measures, both locally and globally, that are imposed on society at large. This is a true case of social and ideological engineering.

The Social Imposition of Gender Ideology

The language of everyday communication, the content of what is taught in the classroom, posts on social media: everything is scrutinized and becomes "problematic" if it provokes some type of "psychological damage" to the individual. Thus, speech must be controlled and suppressed, and the transgressors punished and "cancelled." This has given rise to the so-called cancel culture within universities.[8] The result is a true "ethical chaos where intolerance is disguised as tolerance, and where individual freedom is crushed by the tyranny of the group," states Camila Paglia.[9] And this also extends to the state level, as in the case of INADI, a government agency in Argentina created to control speech and publications, a true thought police designed to shut down those who do not adhere to the ideological agenda. Even at the private corporate level, one of the most demanded certifications today is that of "diversity and inclusion officer," with university enrolment options to train in

7 For more on this, see Muñoz Iturrieta, *Las mentiras que te cuentan, las verdades que te ocultan*, ch. 4.

8 A great number of universities in North America have created "diversity and inclusion" offices, which function as a type of thought police. Another phenomenon is the declaration of the university as a "safe space," with agents ("safe space marshals") to control the content of what is said in the classroom and at conferences, disguised as control of "intellectual behavior."

9 Paglia, *Free Women, Free Men: Sex, Gender, Feminism*, ix.

an "inclusive culture," "unconscious discrimination," or "strategies for gender diversity and inclusion," whatever that means.[10]

In Canada, Bill C-16, given royal assent in 2016, introduced terms such as "gender identity" and "gender expression."[11] The new legislation was rightly viewed by many as an infringement and an attack on freedom of expression. The bill sparked a national debate, for it made it a crime to question gender identity and expression, and penalized citizens who did not use specific pronouns when referring to those who perceive themselves according to a different identity.[12] In the academic world, it meant that a biology professor had to "acknowledge" not only that a student's "gender" may differ from their biological sex, but that their sex is something altogether unrelated to gender. It also meant that a psychology professor could not refer to a "gender identity disorder," or even dare to question the idea of a "non-binary gender spectrum." If anyone in academia dared to affirm a biological truth that contradicts gender ideology, they could easily be accused of committing a hate crime and be expelled from the university under the recommendation of the "diversity and inclusion office," be stripped of their license to practice (in the case of a psychologist), and face heavy fines from the Court of Human Rights, and even imprisonment.

Clinical psychologist and University of Toronto professor Dr. Jordan B. Peterson became a fierce opponent of the bill, testifying before Parliament during preliminary hearings and, once it received Royal Assent from Queen Elizabeth II and became part of Canadian law, publicly opposing it. In a video lecture series taking aim at political correctness, Dr. Peterson had enough of what he saw as a campus culture where social justice warriors and left-wing radical political activists ran rampant. Dr. Peterson's argument was that under free speech rights, one cannot be forced by legislation such as Bill C-16 to use alternative pronouns like the singular "they" or "ze" and "zir," used by some as alternatives to "she" or "he." The video series became a worldwide hit with millions of views and eventually brought Dr. Peterson to international fame and recognition in a *New York Times* opinion piece as "the most influential public intellectual in the Western world."[13] Yet the University of Toronto, probably fearing legal and political retaliation for his criticism of Canadian human rights legislation, went after Dr. Peterson. The University requested him not to speak on the issue anymore and to delete his YouTube videos, in

10 These certificates are coming out of the most "prestigious" universities in the United States and Canada, such as Harvard, Cornell, Stanford, Georgetown, Princeton, Toronto, and Queens.

11 Jody Wilson-Raybould, "An Act to amend the Canadian Human Rights Act and the Criminal Code."

12 The law intended to normalize conditions that in psychology and psychiatry have long been considered mental disorders. For more on this, see Pablo Muñoz Iturrieta, *Atrapado en el cuerpo equivocado*; Anderson, *When Harry Became Sally*.

13 Brooks, "The Jordan Peterson Moment."

a clear infringement of his right to enjoy academic freedom and get involved in political controversies. Moreover, the Human Resources department at the University of Toronto made anti-bias and anti-discrimination training mandatory for its staff, a decision that Dr. Peterson believed to be ineffective, coercive, and politically motivated.

In January 2009, the president of the American Association of University Professors, Cary Nelson, debated Peter Wood, president of the National Association of Scholars, on "The Meaning of Academic Freedom," in reference to an evidence-based defining statement of academic freedom from 1915. Professor Nelson stated that he supports the scientific method, yet at the same time opened the door to gender ideology, for he stipulated that what constitutes evidence is "contingent," that knowledge is culturally constructed, and that neither knowledge nor evidence is transcendent. This is a good reflection of the postmodern spirit that has permeated academia. The postmodern goal for the academy is not to search for the truth and the freedom to make this possible, but the question of representation and diversity. Thus, one of the consequences of the postmodern ideological possession of the university is that most administrative boards require an "equity, diversity, and inclusion statement" as a condition of employment, while also clarifying that when it comes to hiring new faculty, priority will be given to "under-represented" and "historically oppressed" minorities. This "inclusion statement" works in fact as a type of "litmus test" for the appointment or nomination of a potential academic. In this way, academic freedom is violated in the name of the different postmodern tenets, such as gender identity. Sex and gender have been redefined by ill-informed academic theorists as superficial phenomena produced fictitiously by oppressive social forces, and totally disconnected from biology.

And the problem does not stop there. Universities are patrolled by a ruthless type of thought police, the "diversity and inclusion" offices, placed within the university to enforce postmodern dogmas such as gender ideology. This had led to the creation of "safe spaces" and subsequent policies in violation of academic freedom, such as the introduction of "safe space marshals" to monitor intellectual behavior in the classroom. This is fundamentally at odds with the rigorous intellectual exchange central to the idea of the university.

In 2017, Lindsay Shepherd, a teaching assistant for a first-year communications seminar at Wilfrid Laurier University, screened in class a televised debate on gender-neutral pronouns. The debate, which appeared on the public station *TVOntario*, featured Dr. Jordan Peterson and a trans activist professor from the University of Toronto. She simply wanted to show the debate to illustrate the sometimes-controversial politics of grammar. Nevertheless, after an anonymous student complained to the Office of Diversity and Inclusion "thought police," Shepherd found herself reprimanded for violating the school's Gender and Sexual Violence policy.

Moreover, administrators of that Canadian university accused Shepherd of creating a "toxic climate." In a subsequent meeting with university officials, she was accused of creating a "toxic" and "problematic" environment that constituted violence against transgender students, and she was also falsely told that she had broken Canadian law.[14] From an academic perspective, one can argue that there was no topic timelier than the "pronouns" political controversy—a topic that deserved to be discussed within the university. Furthermore, Shepherd had taken a neutral stance on the matter and offered a balanced presentation of both positions. Yet as Nathan Rambukkana, one of the "canceling" professors on the Shepherd's case, put it: "Not all perspectives are valid." Shepherd argued the case that ideas, however controversial, deserve mention in the classroom. Rambukkana, however, held fast to the notion that some ideas are "problematic" and cannot be raised without being clearly labeled as such.[15] For Rambukkana, "problematic" meant challenging the postmodern dogma on gender identity.

Meanwhile, in New York City it is a "hate crime" to "misgender" an individual, and such a transgression is punishable by fines of up to $250,000, while in California one can go to prison for the same reason.[16] In addition, Ontario's Bill 77 (2015) prohibits any type of therapy for minors who fight against gender dysphoria or any other identity disorders, contrary to the opinion of psychiatrists.[17] The totalitarian direction of gender ideology also brings hitherto unimaginable repercussions for the family. Bill 89 of Ontario (2017) implies that the state is the guarantor of the rights of children against their parents in matters of gender identity and sexual orientation, and it establishes the prohibition of adoption by couples who do not accept the dogma of gender identity.[18]

At the international level, the attack upon reality is such that, on February 4, 2021, President Biden signed a Presidential Memorandum according to which LGBTQ+Q rights would be a priority during his term in office. The Memorandum directs US agencies working abroad to combat any measure that adversely affects the LGBTQ+ community, and orders the State Department to include violence, discrimination, and anti-LGBTQ+ laws in its annual human rights report. In addition, the president threatens to apply economic sanctions for those countries that do not accept the LGBTQ+ agenda.[19]

The Office of the UN High Commissioner for Human Rights recently published a call for contributions to a report on "Gender, sexual orientation

14 Hopper, "Here's the full recording of Wilfrid Laurier reprimanding Lindsay Shepherd."
15 Hopper, "Wilfrid Laurier reprimanding Lindsay Shepherd."
16 Senate of California, Senate Bill No. 219.
17 DiNovo, "Bill 77: Affirming Sexual Orientation and Gender Identity Act."
18 Coteau, "Bill 89: Supporting Children, Youth and Families Act."
19 Alper and Shalal, "Biden calls for expanded efforts to protect LGBTQ rights globally."

and gender identity."[20] Basically, the United Nations is elaborating a blacklist of people and institutions that oppose the systematic mainstreaming of the gender agenda. The document calls to expose "the main actors," their "arguments," and the "narratives that, under different lines of characterization (including the accusation of so-called 'gender ideology'), seek to eliminate the gender framework from international human rights law instruments and processes, and national legislative and policy documents." Among those *dangerous* narratives that should be exposed, the author of the document mentions "religious narratives or narratives of tradition" employed to "hinder the adoption of legislative or policy measures aimed at addressing or eradicating violence and discrimination based on sex, gender, sexual orientation and gender identity," in addition to the use of religious freedom in ways that have had "the practical impact of limiting the enjoyment of human rights (including sexual and reproductive rights) of LGBTQ+ persons."[21]

The report also seeks to pressure the member nations of the UN in relation to "measures of public policy, legislation or access to justice" and the application of "comprehensive sexual education in schools." In addition, the document employs very ideological terminology: it refers to biological and sexual differences between men and women as "social constructions," it affirms that "gender identity" has no "direct and necessary correlation with biological sex," it proclaims "the validity of a wide range of sexual orientations and gender identities," and it even introduces an ideological novelty: "race and gender are interconnected." The point the Commissioner makes is clear: whoever does not accept this ideology must be exposed and blacklisted.

In 2020, the United Nations Office of the High Commissioner for Human Rights published a report titled "Gender-based violence and discrimination in the name of religion or belief." Presented at the 43rd Session of the Human Rights Council, the report hints that Christianity is an enemy of human rights. It decries that the church in Latin America is constantly blocking any efforts to legalize abortion and "reproductive rights," as well as pushing "prohibitions on assisted reproductive technologies and gender reassignment surgery, and limits on the provision of evidence-based sexuality education."[22] Furthermore, the Report laments that "reproductive and sexual health education programmes had been curtailed in Brazil, Chile, Colombia, Ecuador and Paraguay following pressure from religious groups."[23] It even laments and shows "particular concern" that health-care providers and institutions make use of their rights to conscientious objection when they are "unwilling to perform abortions

20 Madrigal-Borloz, "Call for input to a thematic report."
21 Madrigal-Borloz, "Call for input to a thematic report."
22 Shaeed, "Gender-based violence and discrimination," 28.
23 Shaeed, "Gender-based violence and discrimination," 35.

or provide access to contraception on religious grounds."[24] The solution, for the UN Office of the High Commissioner, is to reinterpret religious doctrine according to an LGBTQ+ viewpoint, manifested in the fact that individuals are already "increasingly rejecting patriarchal interpretations of religious doctrine and demanding equal rights within their religious traditions."[25]

There is clearly a move at all levels to impose a right for individuals to be recognized in their self-perceived identity, a totalitarian measure that not only limits the fundamental rights of the human person, such as the right to say the truth and enjoy freedom of religion and conscience, but also forces us to lie. And this, the institutionalization of a lie, as we will note below, will mark the end of Western civilization.

One of the main themes of modern philosophy was the tension between the individual and society. This is evident in Jean-Jacques Rousseau (1712–1778), who denounced society for its constructive and oppressive effect on the individual: it is the demands of the social environment that corrupt individuals and alienate them from what they really are.[26] Hegel tries to solve this social dilemma and tension by acknowledging the absolute autonomy of the individual and the social recognition of that autonomy.[27] Humans have a need to belong somewhere, as Carl Trueman points out, which means that the contemporary identitarian movement requires that one's own identity be recognized and acknowledged by others.[28] This dichotomy between the social and the individual is exactly what Hegel's social philosophy attempted to bridge, in the words of Frederick Neuhauser: "Hegel's social philosophy attempted to satisfy two aspirations bequeathed to us by the Enlightenment and its Romantic successors: aspiration to radical autonomy and to expressive unity with nature and society."[29] This is the key, in Trueman's opinion, to understanding this social, legal, and political imposition of recognized "gender identity." Activists not only fight for "inclusion" or the expansion of rights, but insist on the need to express oneself as an individual and to be accepted by society as such, as if the need for social approval was essential to the constitution of that identity. This is a very Hegelian attitude, as noted by Trueman.

In his *Phenomenology of Spirit*, Hegel makes a clear reference to the problem of identity and society: "Self-consciousness exists in and for itself when, and by the fact that, it also exists for another; that is, it exists only in being acknowledged."[30] This is the social dilemma, then, that Hegel seeks to solve:

24 Shaeed, "Gender-based violence and discrimination," 43.
25 Shaeed, "Gender-based violence and discrimination," 50.
26 Rousseau, *The Discourses and Other Early Political Writings*, 166.
27 Taylor, *Hegel and Modern Society*, vii.
28 Trueman, *The Rise and Triumph of the Modern Self*, 57.
29 Neuhauser, preface to Taylor, *Hegel and Modern Society*, vii.
30 Hegel, *Phenomenology of Spirit*, 111.

absolute autonomy and social recognition and belonging to society without implying any type of social imposition (or social construction, in postmodern terms). This has become the central question of the identity politics in our time: How can one achieve a personal identity and be accepted by society without that society assigning some sort of sexual category (male or female) or imposing on one an identity that does not correspond with one's feelings? Here is the dilemma of modern social philosophy. From the perspective of those activists pushing for an ideological gender agenda, then, it is necessary that society "accepts" one's identity in order to be completed both in one's own identity and in relation to the society one inhabits. One's own feelings on one side, and the social acknowledgment of those feelings on the other.

This, however, has catastrophic implications for the political structure of the West: the oath, that is, the promise to tell the truth, the whole truth, and nothing but the truth, is the foundation of the political tradition of the West. Gender identity laws, the enforcing of pronouns that do not correspond to someone's biological sex, and mandatory recognition of someone else's perceived gender identity are in fact an attack on the political foundation of our civilization.

The Destruction of the Political Foundations of the West

Paolo Prodi, in his work *The Sacrament of Power* (*Il sacramento del potere*), argued that there is in Western Christian culture a dual belonging between religion and politics, to which the role of the oath testifies.[31] According to him, the oath is foundational for Western politics: as a "sacrament of power," it is the most sacred form of language, for its words are meant to become reality. Thus, in our Western tradition, the oath has been a special and powerful kind of performative speech act. Through the oath, humans have invoked or called upon the divinity as a witness in order to attest either to the truth of an assertion or to the sincerity of a promise.[32]

Giorgio Agamben, in his *Il sacramento del linguaggio: archeologia del giuramento*, argues that the oath points toward a particular response to the experience of language, a response that gave birth to both religion and the law.[33] Stefania Tutino states: "In the Western tradition the oath has been generally understood as both a powerful way to connect humans with the divinity (in this respect oaths are intrinsically linked to the sphere of the sacred) and an equally

31 Prodi, *Il sacramento del potere*, 522.

32 Tutino, *Shadows of Doubt*, 149.

33 Agamben, *Il sacramento del linguaggio: archeologia del giuramento*. English trans.: Giorgio Agamben, *The Sacrament of Language: An Archaeology of the Oath*. On the dispute over the ways in which the oath connects the sphere of the sacred and that of the law, see Agamben, *Sacramento del linguaggio*, 1–19.

powerful way to connect humans with one another (in this respect oaths are intrinsically linked to the sphere of law)."[34]

For Agamben, rather than the "sacrament of power" (as in Prodi), the oath is more properly the "sacrament of language," for, aside from and before binding men to either God or each other, the oath binds men to their own word.[35] Thus, the oath represents the "verification of words in facts," that is, the "precise correspondence between words and reality."[36] Our words are true in the measure that they can be verified in reality, or insofar as we undertake the promises we have made, thus making our speech a reality. This is what makes possible any social interaction, family, and even type of society and consequent political order. Without a firm foundation in the truth, it is impossible to trust others, to have any social interactions or form any political structures in our world. A society that bases its principles on a lie is inevitably headed to self-destruction. This is my main concern when it comes to "gender identity" laws, for the government is mandating its citizens to lie and to deny the objective reality of each one of us as human beings. That so many countries are "progressing" in this respect only signals that they are near the end as a civilization and political society. In his *Against Leocrates*, Lycurgus (800–730 BC), the legendary lawgiver of Sparta, states that "the power that holds together our democracy is the oath."[37] Yet if the oath has no more value and gender identity is the guiding principle, nothing will be able to hold together our political institutions.

Conclusion

Given the real possibility of political turmoil because of this ideological agenda, the potential economic boycott by of large corporations for not kowtowing the line, and individuals losing their jobs for rejecting gender ideology and facing cultural cancellation and judicial persecution, it is important to consider strategies to face this challenge. We are truly facing a redefinition of what it means to be a human being, and this ideology even seeks to redefine the constitutions of our countries, as is happening now in Chile. What can we do about it?

First, no one can face alone the progressive onslaught of the left. It is necessary to forge communities and social, religious, and political movements that find their strength in the union of ideals and constitute a true "counterculture," where the transcendent ideal of being human is experienced intensely and the

34 Tutino, *Shadows of Doubt*, 150.
35 Agamben, *Sacramento del linguaggio*, 71.
36 Agamben, *Sacramento del linguaggio*, 21.
37 Lycurgus, *Minor Attic Orators*, 79.

role of the family in society is valued above all other things. This requires the union of religious leaders who have courage and clarity of ideas, cultural leaders who bring together the movement in defence of life and the family, and, last but not least, political leaders who materialize this fight with concrete measures and through institutions that perfect what children learn within the family.

Second, intellectual formation is key in this culture war, especially the formation of leaders, whether they are political leaders, pastors and leaders of religious communities, heads of social movements, leaders of educational institutions, or parents. Today it is more important than ever to be well formed intellectually for a simple reason: in the past, kids grew up within a culture based on traditional values that in a certain way made up for any deficiencies found in a given family. Today that culture does not exist anymore, and if parents are not well formed, they will be unable to fill the moral vacuum created by the current cultural revolution. If we want to generate a true counter-cultural revolution, we must be well formed in every aspect of life. This will also require defending parental rights and religious freedom.[38]

Third, we have to teach our children how to love. A direct consequence of the sexual and identity revolution is that, by reducing the meaning of life to mere genital pleasure, the contemporary man has lost the ability to love. How to recover the meaning of true love? I believe that the answer lies within the family, source of true love. Teaching children how to love is the primary task of parents, but in order to succeed one must first learn how to love, and then take the necessary steps to educate children in developing a strong moral character. The latter is key, because only a person with a firm moral character is capable of truly loving, as love requires forgetting oneself, putting aside all sentimentality, and focusing on being the best person possible by tending to the good, the just, and the true. It is key to be good citizens and to live according to a natural law that the world rejects: to live in the world, but without belonging to it, living with a realism that impacts others, becoming a living testimony to the falsehood of the hyper-sexualized ideal of modern man that only leads to death. Life is worth living, and the joy of living fully attracts more than any ideology and its false and empty promises.

Fourth, it is time to turn off the TV and turn on the brain. We must be extremely careful with television, social media, and the internet, because it is a fact that the media actively works to accelerate the process of this cultural revolution. We must not be naïve and should start paying attention and controlling what we and our children watch.

Finally, we have to be responsible. We must work as hard as we possibly can and attempt to achieve the best results in what we do, especially with regards to our responsibilities within the family, at work, and in society. Those with a

38 See Iturrieta, *The Meaning of Religious Freedom in the Public Square.*

mediocre spirit have never accomplished anything worth talking about. We live immersed in a culture of victimization, so the answer to any problem will always start with taking full responsibility for one's own actions. It is never too late to put our lives in order, take responsibility for our destiny, and thus transcend the social chaos in which we are immersed.

Bibliography

Agamben, Giorgio. *Il Sacramento Del Linguaggio: Archeologia Del Giuramento.* Rome: Laterza, 2008.

———. *The Sacrament of Language: An Archaeology of the Oath.* Translated by Adam Kotsko. Stanford, CA: Stanford University Press, 2011.

Alper, Alexandra, and Andrea Shalal. "Biden Calls for Expanded Efforts to Protect LGBTQ+ Rights Globally." *Reuters,* February 4, 2021. https://www.reuters.com/article/us-usa-biden-LGBTQ+-idUSKBN2A42KF.

Anderson, Ryan T. *When Harry Became Sally: Responding to the Transgender Moment.* New York: Encounter Books, 2018.

Brooks, David. "The Jordan Peterson Moment." *New York Times,* January 26, 2018. https://www.nytimes.com/2018/01/25/opinion/jordan-peterson-moment.html.

Butler, Judith. *Gender Trouble: Feminism and the Subversion of Identity.* New York: Routledge, 1990.

Coteau, Michael. "Bill 89, Supporting Children, Youth and Families Act." Legislative Assembly of Ontario, 2017. https://www.ola.org/en/legislative-business/bills/parliament-41/session-2/bill-89.

DiNovo, Cheri. "Bill 77, Affirming Sexual Orientation and Gender Identity Act." Legislative Assembly of Ontario, 2015. https://www.ola.org/en/legislative-business/bills/parliament-41/session-1/bill-77.

General Assembly of the United Nations. *Transforming Our World: The 2030 Agenda for Sustainable Development.* New York: United Nations, 2015.

Hegel, Georg Wilhelm Friedrich. *Phenomenology of Spirit.* Translated by A. V. Miller. Oxford: Oxford University Press, 1977.

Hopper, Tristin. "Here's the Full Recording of Wilfrid Laurier Reprimanding Lindsay Shepherd for Showing a Jordan Peterson Video." *National Post,* November 21, 2017. https://nationalpost.com/news/canada/heres-the-full-recording-of-wilfrid-laurier-reprimanding-lindsay-shepherd-for-showing-a-jordan-peterson-video.

Lycurgus. *Minor Attic Orators.*, vol. 2. Translated by O. J. Burtt. Cambridge: Harvard University Press, 1962.

Muñoz Iturrieta, Pablo. *Atrapado En El Cuerpo Equivocado: La Ideología De Género Frente a La Ciencia Y La Filosofía.* 2nd ed. Ontario: Metanoia Press, 2020.

———. *Atrapado En El Cuerpo Equivocado: La Ideología De Género Frente a La Ciencia Y La Filosofía.* Buenos Aires: Editorial Katejón, 2019.

Prodi, Paolo. *Il Sacramento Del Potere: Il Giuramento Politico Nella Storia Costituzionale Dell'occidente*. Bologna: Il Mulino, 1992.

Rousseau, Jean-Jacques. *The Discourses and Other Early Political Writings.* Translated by Victor Gourevitch. Cambridge: Cambridge University Press, 1997.

Senate of California. Senate Bill No. 219. 2017. https://leginfo.legislature.ca.gov/faces/billTextClient.xhtml?bill_id=201720180SB219.

Taylor, Charles. *Hegel and Modern Society.* Cambridge: Cambridge University Press, 2015.

Trueman, Carl R. *The Rise and Triumph of the Modern Self: Cultural Amnesia, Expressive Individualism, and the Road to Sexual Revolution.* Wheaton, IL: Crossway, 2020.

Tutino, Stefania. *Shadows of Doubt: Language and Truth in Post-Reformation Catholic Culture.* New York: Oxford University Press, 2014.

Volokh, Eugene. "You Can Be Fined for Not Calling People 'Ze' or 'Hir,' If That's the Pronoun They Demand That You Use." *The Washington Post*, May 17, 2016. https://www.washingtonpost.com/news/volokh-conspiracy/wp/2016/05/17/you-can-be-fined-for-not-calling-people-ze-or-hir-if-thats-the-pronoun-they-demand-that-you-use/?utm_term=.d6a33d44dbd9.

Wilson-Raybould, Jody. "Bill C-16: An Act to Amend the Canadian Human Rights Act and the Criminal Code." Parliament of Canada, 2016. https://openparliament.ca/bills/42-1/C-16/.

Part V:

The Continual Struggle for Civil Liberties and Human Freedom

Chapter 30

The Tragic Story of Imre Szép: Disproportionate Justice and What Cannot Be Unseen[1]

Paul Satori

It's true that my progress in a long life hasn't been a straight line. Trying to sum it up, it looks more like a capricious exponential curve of zigzags. Sudden turns followed many defining moments. But the defining events of the previous hundred years were equally numerous and many of them still haunts the human race. Think about the assassination of Archduke Francis Ferdinand and his wife Sophie at Sarajevo in 1914. This senseless act precipitated the disastrous World War One. Yet, the assassin remains a Serbian hero, who died of tuberculosis inside an Austrian prison in 1918.

I was born two years after his death into a century of capricious changes with wars, dictators, holocausts, atomic bombs, weapons of mass destruction, which we hoped to end but instead the new century started with airplanes full of terrorists and innocent passengers flying into skyscrapers and the pentagon in the United States. Is there a hope that this insanity will end one day if human beings and the biosphere will survive this catastrophe we have created?

So if you want to know how a person, born in the year of the monkey, can become a neurosurgeon and curiosity drives you to learn how the hurts, the countless failures and some successes, his many life-threatening illnesses and the historical events that have shaped his life, crushed and revived his dreams, read on. You might even find it interesting to know what the twists, turns and oddities of time can do to a man in so many decades of life.

1 Editor's Note: This is based on "Book I" of an unpublished work that Leslie Ivan (Paul Satori) wrote, titled *They Called Me Antaeus: Memoirs of a Neurosurgeon*. I gave this chapter its title. I was also given permission by his daughter, Patricia Ivan, to use this chapter. The events recounted in this short story occurred in 1943, right in the middle of War World II. Throughout that year Hungary was involved in four major battles. Hungary was subsequently occupied by Nazi Germany in 1944 and the Soviet Union in 1949. The recounting of the events by Satori demonstrates a brutal judicial system that was in place in Hungary whereby the sentence was inordinately disproportionate to the crime. As we begin to have our civil liberties eroded, we need to be reminded of such tragic events of the past, in order not to return to them.

When I decided to go through medical school, I felt that to relieve human suffering was one of the noblest duties toward our fellow man. I knew that learning the manual skill of a surgeon or the diagnostic acumen of a physician is an arduous exercise and was part of the training that needs a disciplined mind. I was already cultivating self-control and decided not to make myself ridiculous by failing examinations or fainting from seeing surgery or putting needles in a human being.

And then you meet the unexpected challenge.

I was a fourth year medical student when my job forced me to witness an act that only a weird law in a sick society could invent. At twenty-two years of age and for the first time in my life, I had to watch the death and dying of a man. The cause of death was execution by hanging.

I don't remember the name of the judge, the faces of the prosecutor or the executioner, but my memory has clearly preserved the image of the condemned man and the words he said before he died.

He was a 42-year-old woodcutter, his name, Imre Szép, his crime, theft during blackout. Was it a brace of chickens or a bicycle, or both, I don't remember clearly. The time was the summer of 1943, the place Debrecen, Hungary, where the lunacy of the Second World War had imposed martial law and the death penalty to deter breaking and entering during blackouts.

I became witness to this barbaric act due to circumstances out of my control. During the war years, as a medical student, I had to support myself by working as a histology technician in the Institute of Forensic Pathology. The director, Doctor Jankovich, a white-haired, rosy faced professor and a decent man, ordered me to assist him with the case. As one of the designated officials at the execution, the professor was to record the proceedings and confirm with another appointed physician the moment of death. My role was to read out the time on a stopwatch every 15 seconds from the moment of hanging till death occurred.

On my way to the prison, I decided that I was not going to faint and, apart from a frog that crept into my throat, I functioned as required. When I reached 12 minutes and fifteen seconds, my boss and the other physician declared that the man was dead. The criteria of death, of course, were absent pulse and heart sounds. What I witnessed became one of the defining moments of my life. Apart from making me an opponent of the death penalty, it generated my profound interest in life and death and helped me to recognize that death is a gradual and often painful process.

My curiosity about the brain and its relationship to the soul has grown from the seeds of this experience and my urge to write about the pain and suffering that a man has to endure in a lifetime became, from that very moment, an urge I could never suppress.

Based on this episode I wrote my first published short story, in Hungarian, that was included in an anthology sixty years ago. The original translation into

English was done by Maria Green, in Saskatoon, whose excellent work I could never acknowledge since the story did not get published in English. The short excerpt from the story that follows here is a much modified version of the original translation.

Imre Szép, the accused, was a woodcutter, a dirt-poor seasonal worker, who lived with his wife in a shack, the type of accommodation you can see only in the slums of big cities. One summer evening during the blackout, which he described as being "darker than a buffalo's ass," he had been stumbling homeward, hungry, and couldn't resist the temptation to steal a pair of chickens from a rich lawyer's backyard. Because of a hole in his pocket, his jackknife slipped out and was found at the crime scene. It did not take an elaborate effort to find the perpetrator. Imre Szép was arrested the next day and after questioning he admitted that he was hungry and couldn't stop himself from taking the chickens with him. A summary court found him guilty of breaking, entering and theft during blackout and, according to the stipulations of martial law, they sentenced him to death. Since he had no previous criminal record, the presiding judge submitted the case to the Governor for consideration of clemency.

His case was big news and thanks to the vigilance of a few smart journalists, the public received full and detailed information about life on death row. Imre Szép had a carefree time for a fortnight. He wore gray but clean prison garb, received food three times a day and a barber shaved him twice a week. Doctors treated his stubborn diarrhea, and they guarded his health with great care. "Why all this fuss?" he asked one of the reporters.

Then one evening they told him that the Governor had refused clemency and he was to be hanged next morning. They treated him with understanding and questioned him about his last wishes. He asked for a bottle of wine for the last evening, brandy and a cigar for breakfast and everything was granted without the slightest objection. "How about that?" he said, "this is a very fine prison."

As the wine was brought in, the minister arrived too. He was wearing a pleated gown and a velvet hat. "I bring you the grace of God my fellow Christian" he said. "Well, now, what can I do for you?" "Just talk, I s'pose," Imre said and drained off his glass. "You see, I did not go to church or school or anything. I grew up like the weeds. Nobody cared. It's all the fault of the rich, they don't care." Each time his temper rose at the very thought. "But watch me, sir, I'll tell the people from the gallows who squeezes the hell out of you if you are poor."

The minister soothed the troubled man with sorrow and understanding and soon they were immersed in a quiet heart to heart talk. And then suddenly Imre asked a very odd question: "Tell me sir, between us, do you think God is going to help me?" "My son," said the minister. "How can you doubt it? He is here with you in this very hour. Without his knowledge not a single hair of yours can be touched." "Then how come that I get killed for a couple of wretched birds?" "You did not live a godly life on this earth" he said. "True, but…" "Yet," the Minister said, "you are dear to our Heavenly Father. He forgives you if you repent." "Sure, I repent. No harm is done anyway if I die. But I wanna tell the people who is to blame." "Don't say a word, Imre, your struggle is over soon. Be worthy of the Son of God, who suffered the cross and gave his life for us." He opened his Bible and looked up the Thirty Fifth Psalm and he began to read:

> Plead my cause, O Lord, with them that strive with me: fight against them that fight against me… Let their way be dark and slippery: and let the angel of the Lord chase them. For without cause have they hid for me their net in a pit, which without cause they have digged for my soul… Let them be ashamed and brought to confusion together that rejoice at mine hurt; let them be clothed with shame and dishonor that magnify themselves against me. And my tongue shall speak of Thy righteousness and of Thy praise all the day long.

He held the Bible to his chest and looked at the man. "Exquisite words" said the minister, then continued the reading until daybreak. The barber came at six o'clock; at seven they brought him the ounce of brandy and the cigar. They were of no more use to him; he longed only for the words of wisdom and little by little he made his peace with everybody. This much we knew from the papers and interviews. The rest I witnessed myself.

As I followed the professor into the neatly swept prison yard, a small crowd of the curious began to flock in. At one end of the yard there was a long table covered with green felt. The guards lined up in a double row. On the left, between the table and the cordon, in the shade of the prison stood the newly erected gallows, a plain freshly hewed heavy pole with an iron hook at the top. Nearby three men were setting things in order. One of them was in a dark suit, wearing a broad-brimmed black hat. He was stout and sure of things, obviously the man in charge. He moved about silently, making signs to the other two. At the foot of the gallows, quite close to the ground, they screwed in a shiny metal hook. The chief checked everything carefully, placed a small box near the platform and a ladder against the rear of the scaffolding. Everything was neatly set. The prison doctor appeared, bag in hand, and after exchanging a few words with my boss, he discreetly retreated.

At half-past eight, the Court of Justice came in. They gathered gravely around the table. The door squeaked and two guards appeared, followed by Imre and the Minister. Two other guards closed the line. The minister, with lowered head, moved his lips silently. The chairman's voice broke the terror of silence. "Stand here!" he said and pointed to a place in front of the table. Imre Szép approached, took off his prison cap and smoothed his hair with his gnarled hand. "Good morning," he said and resumed his posture. His freshly shaved face was flushed, the summer breeze fluttered his thin dry hair. "His Excellency, the Governor, has refused the plea for clemency. The sentence now is legally valid and will be enforced. Have you understood everything, Imre Szép?"

"I understand everything, sir," he answered with civility.

The chairman assumed a grave expression and said: "I hand you over to the public prosecutor." The prosecutor raised his voice and said: "Executioner, carry out the sentence."

The stout man stepped forward, took the cap from the hand of the man and threw it near the gallows. Then with a brisk movement he opened the neck of the prison uniform, as specified by regulations. His assistants looped a rope around the wrists and fastened them to the left thigh of the man. The Minister continued whispering his prayers. The man was led to the scaffold. "Step up here" said the man in charge, "it won't hurt," he whispered. The man hobbled up two steps and rested his back against the pole. His face was flushed and as he took a deep breath a slight wind tousled his hair. He looked around and opened his mouth to speak. The minister's lips were trembling. Imre saw him. He turned his head towards the crowd and simply said: "Well, God keep you," and closed his eyes. For the last time he inhaled the fragrance of the freshly hued oak. The noose circled his neck, the stool was kicked out from under his feet. I started counting the seconds and minutes.

The executioners yanked the rope on his ankles and pulled it down around the shiny hook, stretching the man stiff. They covered his head with a white cloth to hide sweat, saliva, and tears which make agony so unsightly.

I kept counting. "Two minutes 15 seconds."

There was a hushed silence, heads bowed or turned away. Those who watched could see the convulsions of the tightly bound fists with the bulging veins. Then the cracked fingernails turned blue and the convulsing hands became limp.

I reached 12 minutes. The doctor pulled a stethoscope from his black bag, listened to the chest of the man repeatedly and after thirty long seconds pronounced him dead. The professor, my boss, agreed.

The hangman and his assistants removed the corpse from the gallows and sold pieces from the rope as souvenirs. Some men paid a couple of bucks for a short piece.

"It brings you luck," the big man said. "It's a bargain for good luck," somebody observed with an awkward snicker. The hangman did not smile back. "It brings luck," he said seriously again as he busily cut the rope into small pieces.

When in June 1914 Gavrilo Principe assassinated Franz Ferdinand and his wife the act prompted Franz Josef, the uncle of Ferdinand and the emperor of the Austro–Hungarian Empire, to invade Serbia. This mindless decision, which exploded into the First World War, was a defining point in history and marked the beginning of many decades of suffering. The decision of the emperor triggered a fatuous war, a full-blown series of senseless killings, which then ended with the "Trianon Treaty," an equally harebrained solution. The new Hungary was stripped of two thirds of its traditional lands and lost areas where the Magyars were in a majority such as in Subcarpathia and Transylvania. The same time Austria, the dominant part of the Austro-Hungarian Empire was rewarded by donating a small part of Hungary, Burgenland, to Austria.

I was born in Hungary on April 14, 1920, in a Carpathian village seven weeks before the Treaty of Trianon was signed in Versailles on June 4, 1920. At the moment the treaty was signed, we became citizens of another country.

From early childhood till my old age, I lived through enormous changes in our world, I have seen life and death in many countries, happiness in peace and tragedy in wars, revolutions and miraculously I survived. Was it providence, chance or good fortune, I still don't know. My father, a religious man, prayed for my safety and firmly believed I was one of the chosen.

Chapter 31

Living and Surviving Socialism

Stella Shihman

> "John Steinback once said that socialism never took root in America because the poor see themselves not as an exploited proletariat but as temporarily embarrassed millionaires."
>
> —Ronald Wright, Canadian author

The quote above struck me as particularly apt because the social and economic conditions in America, and by extension in the rest of the world, are changing rapidly, and America's relevance may be diminishing. Recent conversations with friends who, ironically enough, enjoy the benefits of open societies with free markets and capitalism are showing evidence of a return of the doctrines of socialism, Marxism, and communism. One recent conversation was particularly memorable for one of its interlocutors claiming to be a sworn Marxist—with a strong stand against private property rights—who simultaneously happens to be wealthy, a property owner, and someone who hasn't had to work in years—unless he chose to—in order to feed his family. Talk about unabashed champagne socialism and cognitive dissonance. Such convictions are perplexing, contradictory, and just outright hypocritical; equally, they seem to be in line with the apparently growing popularity of socialism and anti-capitalism in the American psyche, trickling down from academia to millennials, Zoomers, and the rest of society.

That's not to say that America is metamorphizing into a socialist dystopia along the lines of North Korea, but membership in the Democratic Socialists of America (DSA) chapters has surged in 2020; specifically, since March 2020, ten thousand people have joined the organization, whose total membership is now about sixty-six thousand people.[1] While those numbers represent a minuscule fraction of the total population, a DSA spokesperson has indicated a decisive upward trend.[2] Another noteworthy datum juxtaposes attitudes toward socialism: past and present. Specifically, to the question "Would some form of

1 Godfrey, "Thousands of Americans Have Become Socialists since March."
2 Godfrey, "Thousands of Americans Have Become Socialists since March."

socialism be a good thing or a bad thing for the country as a whole?," asked by the Roper/*Fortune* survey, 25 percent of Americans deemed it a good thing back in 1942, whereas 43 percent said so in 2019.[3] Granted, there has also been an increase in the percentage of people deeming socialism—in some form—a bad thing, albeit that variance from 1942 to 2019 was less than that for the opposite claim.[4] In Canada, America's generally more left-leaning neighbour, 58 percent of 1,733 randomly polled Canadian voters in 2019 said they have a positive view of socialism, and 18 percent of those said they have a very positive view of socialism.[5] Indeed, there seems to be a kind of renaissance of socialism—in some form—in modern-day America.

"Well, what is the problem with socialism?" you may ask. That is, admittedly, a good question. After all, the capitalist system allows for negative economic turbulences such as recessions or, worse, depressions. Moreover, current wealth inequality is rather striking: recent data has shown that top 1 percent of U.S. households hold 15 times more wealth than the bottom 50 percent holds combined.[6] Prima facie, socialism is an egalitarian alternative: a social and political theory that advocates for social or collective ownership of the means of production, self-management of the working class, and reduction and ultimately elimination of class struggle by ending the exploitation of the proletariat, all resulting in increased social justice. Wouldn't that maximize the greatest good for the greatest number of people from a utilitarian standpoint? Well, in theory it would, but socialism runs into the problem of translation from theory into practice, or, borrowing from biology, translating results from *in vitro* to *in vivo*. In this chapter, I will address the embodiment of the Soviet version of socialism (since that was the reality for my family and me). Indeed, that was our experience, which culminated in immigrating to the West at the onset of the fall of USSR and never looking back.

"From each according to his ability, to each according to his needs." This dictum, popularized by Marx in 1875, is seen to represent free access to the distribution of goods, capital, and services made possible in a developed communist system, the road to which will be paved by the development of socialism and unfettered productive forces that will ensure enough to satisfy everyone's needs.[7] In theory, a communist utopia created by expanding socialism worldwide is a collectivist's Shangri-La; however, the reality in the former USSR—and other socialist countries—was completely and rather nefariously different.

3 Younis, "Four in 10 Americans Embrace Some Form of Socialism."

4 Younis, "Four in 10 Americans Embrace Some Form of Socialism."

5 The Forum Poll "Majority of Canadians Have Positive Opinions of Socialism."

6 Beer, "Top 1% of U.S. Households Hold 15 Times More Wealth Than Bottom 50% Combined."

7 Marx, *Critique of the Gotha.*

Lineups and deficits: those were plentiful when I was growing up. Even though my family had good socio-economic standing in the former Soviet Union and many connections by way of my mother's employment, I clearly remember standing in lines with my older sister for necessities. One tidbit etched in my memory is the long line we stood in one day to obtain plastic bags, which we then washed and reused routinely until they became warped and had to be disposed of. At least it was more ecologically sound and less wasteful, I tell myself semi-jokingly. It was a regular occurrence for people to stand in lines for hours without knowing what would be rationed that day. Semantics matter here: not purchased freely, but rationed at a cost, whichever product was available. Want to make a homemade cake and need baking ingredients? While you're probably thinking it's as simple as going to a grocery store and buying them, back then one had to obtain the ingredients over a period of time and then make the cake. And how about hosting a get-together or a party? I recall my parents having to plan such events far in advance in order to obtain foods—typically meats and seafood products—through various channels and connections. One couldn't stop at a deli and pick up items from a grocery list, for often there was scarcity of food and other necessities. That promised cornucopia of capital and goods within the socialist system? It remained a theoretical objective rather than reality for most people.

The economy of the former USSR was based on state ownership of the means of production and characterized by centralized economic planning, which was managed by the administrative-command system.[8] In contrast to a market economy, decisions concerning what should be produced, in what quantities, and how products should be priced resulted from a hierarchical chain of instructions from government supervisors to producers.[9] Since the planners controlled the planning and production, production didn't follow the interplay of supply and demand; there was no regard—or minimal regard—for the wishes of ordinary people, the users of products. Additionally, competition was absent. Producers in the same sphere of activity were executors of the state's planning rather than competitors contending for their share of the market. Lastly, central planners neither fixed quantities and let prices adjust nor fixed prices and let quantities adjust. They fixed both, which led to queues, shortages, and occasional surpluses due to absence of the information and motivation that inform markets.[10]

Such a centralized top-down system is prone to unintended miscalculations in planning and production, as well as more deliberate errors such as misreporting reached targets and quotas in order to meet the goals of planning.

8 Hanson, *The Rise and Fall of the Soviet Empire*, 22
9 Hanson, *The Rise and Fall of the Soviet Empire*, 22
10 Hanson, *The Rise and Fall of the Soviet Empire*, 22

Quality control, improvement, and innovation were not significant drivers of production in the Soviet system, as it wasn't necessary to make high-quality, innovative products in order to have a competitive edge with consumers. As a matter of fact, what may have proved most detrimental for the Soviet economy in the long run was the minimal incentivization to introduce new products and processes. Producers were motivated to avoid innovation, since it would entail disruptions to established processes of production, which acted as a source of bonuses in the system.[11] Under the Soviet socialist state, discrepancies concerning information flow, lack of incentives, and absence of competition proved fatal for the centrally managed economy.

While most proponents of socialism would presumably admit that the economic system of the former USSR was substandard, they would also maintain that the social, political, and economic philosophy underpinning socialism remains progressive, egalitarian, and just in principle; they would add that socialism is simply in need of proper implementation. (Not that its trial in Maoist China had favourable outcomes for its people, or in Venezuela, or North Korea, as added examples.) Is there a better way to organize society in accordance with the socialist paradigm which will be unlike the Soviet, Marxist-Leninist socialist state—no food deficits or political authoritarianism? While I am unaware of historical examples where state-run socialism has made people happy and prosperous in the long term, the Nordic model may come to mind, say in a country like Sweden. That being said…is Sweden actually a socialist country? Well, it's not actually socialist, or at least not in the sense of a collective/social ownership of the means of production and self-management of the working class. Even though socialism as a philosophy and theory has manifold interpretations, the common denominator is the social or collective ownership of the means of production. Sweden's Nordic model has many social safety nets characteristic of a welfare state, but it does not have a collective ownership of the means of production. In fact, it's a free-market/trade economy, with strong property rights and little product market regulation.[12] The system has been likened to a kind of hybrid of socialist values and capitalist economics, perhaps a modernized and improved capitalistic alternative to the Anglo-Saxon capitalism, but capitalistic nonetheless. Similarly to other Scandinavian countries, Sweden is only socialistic in wealth distribution. It is a capitalist country in wealth creation and accumulation.

Aside from the economic failure of socialism in the former USSR, a bigger affront to human life and justice was political authoritarianism and repression of dissidents. This subject matter is of particular importance to me and to my family since my paternal grandfather was one of those dissidents. Even though

11 Hanson, *The Rise and Fall of the Soviet Empire*, 22.

12 Norberg, "Sweden's Lessons for America."

the 1917 Russian Revolution ended the centuries-long official antisemitism of the Russian Empire, it was shortly replaced with the Soviet kind, particularly during the Stalinist period. This type of antisemitism questioned Jewish people's allegiance to the Soviet Union and its ideology, accused Jewish intellectuals of a lack of patriotism, and demonized religious or traditional Jewish practices. The state's goal was to build an irreligious or atheist society, aligned with Marx's view of religion as the "opium of the people."[13]

In 1940, when my paternal grandfather was 28, he was apprehended in the middle of the day by the Soviet secret police and charged with being an enemy of the people and the state due to Jewish-Zionist activity. Having completed jurisprudence studies but standing to earn little, my grandfather taught at a Jewish *cheder*—a type of a Jewish school—in order to earn extra income. In addition to teaching, he was also doing accounting. A colleague at the school disclosed his involvement with Jewish life to the secret police. Secret informants or *snitches* were common at the time, a practice sustained in order to prove loyalty to the regime and in exchange gain benefits and advancement. After he was accused of being disloyal to the state, my grandfather was deemed a political prisoner and sent by the Soviet Gulag System to a forced-labour camp in Siberia to work as a feller. The concepts of *due process* and *presumption of innocence* were patently absent, and my grandfather was quickly made aware that any resistance would lead to execution by shooting. Unable to change his circumstances, he chose to be pragmatic and kept a low profile in order to stay alive. While imprisoned, even though he faced extremely harsh weather conditions and periods of starvation, because he was educated and intellectually savvy he managed to transition from logging trees to working in a hospital. That may have been, ultimately, what saved his life and helped him survive the camp system where he was a resident for seven years until his release in 1947. Many prisoners, however, were far less fortunate and did not get to return home.

Following the USSR's dissolution, documents were declassified, and they paint the following picture pertaining to the Soviet Gulag System, although estimates vary: 799,455 persons were recorded as having been executed between 1921 and 1953, and the labour camp population reached 2.5 million at its peak post-World War II.[14] In the Stalinist days, the total number of persons with records of imprisonment and slave labour has run as high as 25 million or 15% of the population.[15] During the forced state collectivization of the agricultural sector which lasted from 1928 to 1940, more than two million peasants were deported, hundreds of thousands perished following deportation, and six million died of hunger. At its peak, a deliberately enacted famine called

13 Weinberg, *Demonizing Judaism*, 120–153.

14 Milne, "The Battle for History."

15 Applebaum, "The Gulag," 1–8.

Holodomor resulted in the genocide of millions of ethnic Ukrainians.[16] The *Black Book of Communism* estimates the overall death toll at the hands of the Soviet regime at 20 million, whereas 65 million people were killed or murdered by the Communist Party of China in process of its cultural revolution. In total, establishing socialism and communism came with an unspeakable worldwide price tag of about 100 million victims.[17]

This chapter of history and its atrocities make one wonder about the unholy marriage between the implementation of socialism—in our experience its Soviet version—and authoritarianism or totalitarianism. It has been proposed that socialist states are not randomly repressive; that is, they are repressive in similar ways, suggestive of a method. This reflects the nature of a socialist economy: unlike a market economy, where individuals are free to pursue personal goals, a socialist economy mandates that collective goals and objectives override individual priorities.[18] In the former USSR, the Five-Year Plan enacted in 1928 is a good example of collective priorities superseding individual goals. Once the central planning committee (*Gosplan*) established a goal that had to be met, manpower had to be allocated for its completion. Citizens could not easily move and relocate as that would disrupt the plan. As such, civil liberties and personal freedoms had to be constrained to fit the system.[19] For instance, *kolkhozniks* working in a *kolkhoz*—a collective farm—didn't have internal passports until 1965. This rendered them incapable of changing jobs or moving outside their farms and villages without the approval of the *kolkhoz* chairperson. For all intents and purposes, they were second-class citizens in the Soviet system.[20] This was not an accidental flaw but a design feature; the centralized economy administered by central committees dictated that collective goals had to be met, and individuals were predestined to do the work to meet those goals irrespective of their personal desires and aspirations.

Aside from misunderstanding and mismanaging economic forces in the former USSR, perhaps the biggest problem of translating socialism from theory into practice has had to do with concentration of power. Market signals and competitive forces serve as means to disperse and limit power; dispersing and balancing, on the other hand, become obsolete when the state becomes the sole source of income and housing, financial intermediary, and supplier of all goods and services. It is the collective economy that gives the state its enormous power, bearing out the maxim of Lord Acton: "Power tends to corrupt, and absolute power corrupts absolutely."[21]

16 Courtois, et al., *The Black Book*, 146.
17 Courtois, et al., *The Black Book*, 4.
18 Niemietz, "Trendy Socialism Leads Straight to the Gulag."
19 Niemietz, "Trendy Socialism Leads Straight to the Gulag."
20 Hanson, *The Rise and Fall of the Soviet Empire.*
21 Niemietz, *Socialism: The Failed Idea,* 50.

Despite its intuitive appeal, socialism in the abstract is easier to support than contemporary or historical examples of socialism in action.[22] There is a chasm between socialism in the abstract, the *in vitro*, and the many failed attempts to build socialism in the real world, the *in vivo*. Some scholars claim that those (many!) failed attempts were not *true* socialism, that they were mere distortions, yet are unable to explain concretely how they themselves would build a *true* socialist society based on a shared economy in which the means of production are collectively owned. That said, why does socialism *feel* so good? Capitalism feels exploitative, and socialism, by contrast, aligns with our moral intuition. This line of thinking is based on the research by Jonathan Haidt, who contends that moral and political reasoning is often about finding post-hoc justifications for our initial, intuitive judgments.[23] Thus, advocating for a perfectly equitable and egalitarian world makes us reaffirm our moral nature, irrespective of the multitude of historical examples to demonstrate that in the case of socialism—and no, the "Nordic Model" isn't socialism—there is no good translation from the ideal to the real. This is because human motivations are often complex, contradictory, and far less than ideal.

Perhaps it's also time to admit that good will notwithstanding, implementing socialism in the real and imperfect world is the realization of the adage that the road to hell is paved with good intentions. It is precisely as the Austrian-British economist F. A. Hayek has pointedly remarked:

> After seventy years of experience with socialism, it is safe to say that most intellectuals…remain…unwilling to wonder whether there might not be a reason why socialism, as often as it is attempted, never seems to work out as its intellectual leaders intended. The intellectuals' vain search for a truly socialist community…results in the idealisation of, and then disillusionment with, a seemingly endless string of 'utopias'—the Soviet Union, then Cuba, China, Yugoslavia, Vietnam, Tanzania, Nicaragua.[24]

Bibliography

Applebaum, Anne. "The Gulag: What We Now Know and Why It Matters." *Cato's Letter* 2, 1 (Winter 2008): 1–8. https://www.cato.org/sites/cato.org/files/pubs/pdf/catosletterv2n1.pdf.

Beer, Tommy. "Top 1% of U.S. Households Hold 15 Times More Wealth Than Bottom 50% Combined." *Forbes*, October 8, 2020. https://www.forbes.

22 Niemietz, *Socialism: The Failed Idea.*

23 Niemietz, *Socialism: The Failed Idea.*

24 Niemietz, Socialism: *The Failed Idea.*

com/sites/tommybeer/2020/10/08/top-1-of-us-households-hold-15-times-more-wealth-than-bottom-50-combined/?sh=72346acf5179.

Courtois, Stephane, et al. *The Black Book of Communism: Crimes, Terror, Repression*. Cambridge: Harvard University Press, 1999.

Forum Poll, The. "Majority of Canadians Have Positive Opinions of Socialism, But Americans Hold a Different Opinion." August 27, 2019. https://poll.forumresearch.com/post/3020/socialism-capitalism-august-2019/.

Godfrey, Elaine. "Thousands of Americans Have Become Socialists since March." *The Atlantic*, May 14, 2020. https://www.theatlantic.com/politics/archive/2020/05/dsa-growing-during-coronavirus/611599/.

Hanson, Philip. *The Rise and Fall of the Soviet Economy: An Economic History of the USSR 1945–1991*. London: Taylor and Francis, 2003.

Marx, Karl. *Critique of the Gotha Programme*. Moscow: Progress Publishers, 1970. https://www.marxists.org/archive/marx/works/1875/gotha/index.htm.

Milne, Seumas. "The Battle for History." *The Guardian*, September 12, 2002. https://www.theguardian.com/education/2002/sep/12/highereducation.historyandhistoryofart.

Niemietz, Kristian. *Socialism: The Failed Idea That Never Dies*. London: The Institute of Economic Affairs, 2019.

———. "Trendy Socialism Leads Straight to the Gulag." *Reaction*, September 19, 2018. https://reaction.life/trendy-socialism-leads-straight-gulag/.

Norberg, Johan. "Sweden's Lessons for America." *Policy Report,* January/February 2020. https://www.cato.org/publications/policy-report/swedens-lessons-america.

Weinberg, Robert. "Demonizing Judaism in the Soviet Union during the 1920s." *Slavic Review* 67, 1 (Spring 2008): 120–153. https://works.swarthmore.edu/fac-history/88/.

Younis, Mohamed. "Four in 10 Americans Embrace Some Form of Socialism." *Gallup*, May 20, 2019. https://news.gallup.com/poll/257639/four-americans-embrace-form-socialism.aspx.

Chapter 32

Turning a Blind Eye: Denial of Left-Wing Pathologies

Trevor Blackwell

Liberté, égalité, fraternité is the universally recognized motto of the French Revolution of 1789. This watershed moment in European history is seen by many as what ushered in the modern values of tolerance, common humanity, and suffrage for all. The French pride themselves on having bequeathed to the world the principles of the Enlightenment and many of the pillars upon which Western civilization is founded. This revolution has also been represented as the birth of the middle class and framed by many historians (most notably Karl Marx) as the moment when the bourgeoisie were able to free themselves from the bondage of feudalism, overthrow their aristocratic overlords, and reject the overriding concept of the divine right of monarchical privilege. Since the Enlightenment was a universalist movement, the ideals of the French Revolution were not meant to be confined within the barriers of France, but spread globally to places such as Haiti, England's thirteen colonies, the United Kingdom, and many others.

On paper it truly seems like a remarkable awakening of humanity, and a defining moment in the historical evolution of human rights. Indeed, this revolution is what has given France a sense of civic identity and a defining element of its heritage. However, if one looks closely at the actual events of the revolution, one becomes increasingly aware of a bewitching paradox associated with the movement. The paradox I am speaking of relates to the notion of how a movement predicated on superficially altruistic principles (equality, common humanity, universal human rights and values) can end up producing tyranny, oppression, turmoil, anarchy, and the desecration of national monuments and historical memory. Indeed, Robespierre and the Jacobins, a Parisian radical political group intent on remolding France into a civic republic, led France into an abyss of chaos and human rights abuses, and their ideals ironically led to the widespread massacre of innocents.

What I intend to show in this brief paper is how the circumstances of the French Revolution are not too distant and remote from the events currently transpiring in North America (primarily in the United States). Many striking parallels can be observed between the incendiary and subversive activities of the French Jacobins and contemporary leftist forms of anarchy and upheaval. Indeed, one can easily trace a historical continuity among all radical left-wing radical experiments. Some notable historical examples of far-left agitation and ferment that derived inspiration from the French include Karl Marx, the 1848 European revolutionaries, the Paris Commune, Lenin's Bolsheviks, Stalin, Mao Zedong, Pol Pot, and the current state of North Korea. In addition, phenomena such as the nebulous and disparate antifa and Seattle's CHAZ (Capitol Hill Autonomous Zone) represent contemporary examples of radical left-wing subversion.

One theme of this chapter is the tendency of western societies to divide themselves into two very polarized political camps: the left-wing progressives and radicals on one hand and on the other the conservative right, bent on preserving and maintaining long-cherished traditional values and institutions. Just as the Jacobins of the French Revolution were keen to remodel France's civic identity and national character through violent means, the progressives of modern-day America are also keen on dismantling and overthrowing long-standing traditional values and national heroes such as Thomas Jefferson, George Washington, and (perhaps most absurdly) Abraham Lincoln.

This sense of polarization can most notably be found in the scholarship and historiographical writings on the Soviet Union and Russian Communism. This chapter will thus provide an overview of the manner in which polarization has heavily affected the viewpoints of scholars of Soviet history and of Communism. This topic may sound seemingly distant and irrelevant to the political concerns and debates of our era. However, I will try to show, much of what we are witnessing in the current political arena stems from historical events such as the French and Russian Revolutions. I will also demonstrate that attempts to play down and "apologize" for pathologies inherent in Communistic ideology have been circulating for many decades and are not just a recent phenomenon.

More precisely, I will focus on a specific debate within Soviet historical scholarship, related to the decisive effect that Stalin's ascent to power had on the history of Communism and the repercussions his leadership had on the legitimacy of Communism as a viable political ideology. When the Russians experienced their Marxist Revolution of 1917, it was heralded by many as the birth of a new world order and celebrated as a rejection of autocratic feudalism. It was seen as an opportunity for the historically downtrodden peasant masses and workers to gain a foothold in politics and gain a sense of recognition. All these ideals and optimistic viewpoints evidently collapsed and eroded once Stalin's regime took hold in the 1920s in the wake of Lenin's death.

You might have thought that the death knell of Communism would have been sounded by the 1950s after the world had witnessed the gruesome and atrocious manner in which Stalin governed the Russian populace. His cult of personality, disastrous programs of rapid industrialization, show trials of dissidents and political enemies, and forced starvation meted out against untold millions of farmers and peasants are clear examples of how there is evidently something pathologically inherent in the doctrine of Marxism-Leninism. However, this only initiated a new strategy for scholars on the left, where now it became a game of dissociating Stalin from "true" Communism, and even arguing that the revolution that took place in Russia was not authentically Marxist, due to the fact that Russia had not yet undergone the required phases of historical development prescribed by Marx. Indeed, according to Marx a Communist uprising was meant to occur in an industrialized economy (such as Germany or the United Kingdom), and Russia still possessed a feudal and agrarian economy in 1917.[1]

The decisive and enduringly influential moment in Soviet scholarship occurred when Leon Trotsky published *The Revolution Betrayed*. In this famous treatise, Trotsky essentially accused Stalin of betraying the original principles and values of the Bolshevik Revolution of 1917, and of not remaining faithful to the model set by Vladimir Lenin. Indeed, the publication of this polemical piece would create a deep schism within the world of Soviet politics, as now Trotsky would basically become an enemy of the state, and a symbol of evil for supporters of Stalin and his totalitarian cult.[2]

Many scholars supportive of Communist ideology would take up this stance of Trotsky's as a way of separating Stalin's crimes and abuses from the original doctrine of Marxism. To say that Stalin was not a true Bolshevik was a perfect way to keep the image of Karl Marx intact and preserve the sanctity of Communism as a viable political ideology. According to Trotsky and his future disciples, Stalin diverged from the natural course of the Bolshevik Revolution, and ended up creating a regime that was diametrically opposed to the ideas of Marx and Lenin. For Trotsky, Stalin ended up establishing a regime that was not the fruition of Communism but was bureaucratic and fundamentally at odds with the Marxist dogma. The toxicity of Stalin's personality, cult, and style of leadership were, according to Trotsky, not attributable to Marx or Lenin, but only to Stalin's abhorrent and monstrous character. In "The Revolution Betrayed," Trotsky employs references to the French Revolution in order to highlight how Stalin deviated from the true ideals of the 1917 Revolution. Trotsky argued that Stalin's ascent to power represented a "Thermidorian" reaction to events, as his regime was characterized by a dampening down of revolutionary energies and the establishment of bureaucratic principles of government.[3]

Trotsky's viewpoints can be regarded with some respect, given that he displayed foresight in being able to predict the future oppressions, abuses of

1 Marx and Engels, *The Communist Manifesto.*

2 Trotsky, *The Revolution Betrayed.*

3 Trotsky, *The Revolution Betrayed.*

power, and human rights atrocities that would occur under Stalin. He did not publish *The Revolution Betrayed* in the 1950s when all of the secrets of the macabre nature of the Soviet politburo had become known the world over. He was writing in the 1930s, when Stalin's reputation as a totalitarian tyrant was not yet fully established, and the Molotov-Ribbentrop pact had yet to be signed.

Thus, many historians and scholars of Soviet politics would become enamored with Trotsky as a supposedly respectable proponent of Communism and a seemingly humane alternative to Stalin. It seemed like a very good strategy to cast Stalin as inhumane and unrepresentative of true Communism. However, many scholars became skeptical about this ploy and argued that there were many striking similarities between the leadership styles of Lenin and Stalin. It was correctly argued by many historians, for example, that the use of terror as a political tool to keep a populace in a perennial state of fear was not unique to Stalin's regime. There is ample evidence that Lenin employed terror tactics in order to wield his power, and that he displayed many of the qualities of a despotic, autocratic dictator.

Indeed, a new scholarly paradigm would emerge, known as the totalitarian school, where these historians would portray Stalin as a heartless murderer of his own people, in coldblooded pursuit of an ostensibly noble ideal of establishing a full-scale Socialist utopia in Russia. Scholars of the totalitarian paradigm would group together Lenin and Stalin as sharing common goals as Communist dictators. According to scholars of the totalitarian school, it is very difficult to find points of policy by which to differentiate Stalin and Lenin. Both essentially had the same outlooks about implementing Communist principles in Russia and believed in a one-party state. Scholars of the totalitarian school were implicitly responding to the arguments propounded by Trotsky, as they clearly saw continuity rather than discontinuity between the regimes of Lenin and Stalin. They considered it highly erroneous to think that Stalin's brand of leadership was antithetical to that of Lenin's. Both Soviet leaders were unapologetic about using unorthodox means to consolidate their personal dictatorships and ruthless in deploying terror as an instrument of power.[4]

After the totalitarian school emerged as a dominant force in Soviet studies, an alternative emerged that came to be regarded as a revisionist movement. As opposed to analyzing Soviet politics from the unidimensional perspective of Lenin and Stalin, scholars of the revisionist school began to explore the social dimensions of Russian society and examine the attitudes of the masses. These scholars sought to move away from what they viewed as a simplistic understanding of the Soviet regime and embraced a "bottom-up" approach. Instead of applying the concept of totalitarianism to Soviet society, these

4 Fitzpatrick, "Revisionism in Soviet History."

historians formulated a new theoretical apparatus and began using the term "Stalinism" to distinguish Stalin's regime from that of Lenin, Hitler, and other dictators. This sounds reasonable enough; however, these revisionists came to be viewed as apologists and deniers of the pathology of Communism.[5]

One of the principal exponents of the revisionist approach was a Soviet dissident scholar named Roy Medvedev, who succeeded in triggering a deep rethinking in the West of the true nature of Communism, the Russian Revolution, and the Soviet Union. Writing during the period of de-Stalinization under Krushchev, Medvedev was able to convince many Westerners that Stalin led Russia down the wrong path and should be viewed as a violator and contaminator of the original doctrine of Marx. Medvedev judged Stalin's crimes to be the result of his own monstrous character, rather than a product of the ideology of Communism. Medvedev basically sought to rehabilitate the image of the Soviet Union by portraying Stalin as a leader who deviated from the true Bolshevik principles outlined by Lenin. Medvedev wanted to convince his readers that, in a retrospective hypothetical, Trotsky would have provided sound and venerable leadership if he had been able to consolidate his status as leader of the Soviets as opposed to Stalin. According to Medvedev, the Soviet Union would have experienced more fruitful and humane progress as a Communist Empire if Trotsky had established preeminence over Stalin in the wake of Lenin's death in the 1920s.[6]

Many were convinced by Medvedev's writings at the time and came to believe that the Soviet Union under Stalin did not accurately represent the principles of Marxism-Leninism. A sense of denial about the innate pathologies inherent in Communist doctrine became widespread. However, in response to Medvedev's watershed moment, many scholars sought to repudiate this myth, and asserted that Stalin did not deviate from Lenin or the original Bolsheviks. Stalin's ideas and policies were directly aligned with the ideals of 1917. Using the model of the French Revolution, scholars opposed to Medvedev did not view Stalin as a Thermidor reactionary (as Trotsky had done) but believed Stalin had achieved the fruition of Soviet ideology. Opponents of Medvedev's ideas asserted that Stalin's regime was a direct continuation of the events of 1917. Stalin did not break away from his forebears in terms of his outlook on policy or other doctrinal issues. Terror was an instrument used by the revolutionaries of 1917 and continued to be deployed by Stalin. Many historians contended that the Russian Revolution could be understood as taking place between 1917 and 1936. Stalin maintained a sense of loyalty to original Bolshevik principles and sustained a sense of revolutionary impetus into the 1930s.[7]

5 Fitzpatrick, "Revisionism in Soviet History."

6 Medvedev, *Let History Judge.*

7 Medvedev, *Let History Judge.*

One final historiographical school that will be discussed in this chapter is post-revisionism. Post-revisionists were no longer interested in the arguments posited by their predecessors and were also very skeptical of the lens used in the totalitarian approach. These younger Soviet historians have produced a great amount of scholarship analyzing the cultural and intellectual roots of Stalinism and the Bolshevik Revolution, as opposed to focusing on the social dimensions of Soviet politics, for instance.

One very important observation made by several post-revisionists was that the Enlightenment tradition served as a focal point of inspiration for many of the Russian revolutionaries of 1917 and for Stalin himself. The notion of bringing about a more just and equitable society and new world order through the implementation of ambitious programs of reform and industrialization stems from the Enlightenment. The Enlightenment thinkers and philosophers of the 17th and 18th centuries in Europe promoted building a new social and world order. They sought to accelerate the process of modernity through scientific inquiry, breaking from deeply ingrained traditions, and promoting human rights.[8]

These are all clearly values that were promoted under Stalin's reign as Supreme Commissar of the USSR. Stalin, by adhering faithfully to the doctrinal principles of Marxism-Leninism, sought to build a more just and equal society through programs of rural collectivization and a planned centralized economy. Stalin believed that he was building a better society and future for the people of Russia. Following the Bolsheviks of 1917, he broke away from programs and policies that existed under the Tsarist regimes. By abolishing feudalism and ushering in a new, merry phase of historical progress along Marxist-Leninist lines, the Bolsheviks contended that a utopian society could be achieved.

The irony that we all recognize at this point is that pursuing utopian visions of society and historical progress quite often ends in disaster. Stalin's attempts to lift Russia out of serfdom and feudalism ended up producing one of the gravest tragedies of the 20th century. Through the forced collectivization of farms and radically reshaping agriculture in Russia, Stalin ended up imposing starvation upon millions of kulaks and innocent peasants. Stalin was so committed and dogmatically faithful to the ideals of Marxism that he was able to feel no remorse about the atrocities committed against his own people. For Stalin, plain and simple, the ends justified the means.

Stalin and the Bolsheviks truly believed that, in order for Russian society and the world at large to advance, capitalism needed to be overthrown, discarded, and replaced by Communism. It was acknowledged by the Bolsheviks (and Marx himself) that capitalism had produced great wealth and a fruitful market economy. However, capitalism needed to be eventually thrown away since

8 Kotkin, *The Magnetic Mountain.*

it only truly benefited the exploiter class, the bourgeoisie. Once capitalism had given way to Communism, such ills as exploitation, colonization, and imperialist wars would soon vanish. Solidarity, emancipation from oppression, and peace would become established once Communism had taken hold and the world had liberated itself from the capitalist order.[9]

Having provided a brief overview of the historiographical debates within Soviet scholarship and Stalinist studies, I will now briefly discuss some of the connections that can be drawn between past debates and contemporary issues. Clearly, polarization has been a feature of political debate for millennia (the Ancient Romans experienced this through the opposition between the Optimates and the Populares). But it is interesting to trace this polarization from the French Revolution through the era of the Bolsheviks and Stalin to the present. The French Revolution witnessed a schism and opposition between supporters of the Revolution (such as the Jacobins) and the upholders of monarchical tradition (the Royalists). Marx was clever enough to seize on this and took the problem of polarity one step further by introducing a Hegelian confrontation between the bourgeoisie (owners of production and the exploiter class) and the proletariat (the oppressed and downtrodden class of industrial laborers). Part of the genius of Marx lies in his ability to tap into the deep, ingrained tendency of human societies to organize themselves into diametrically opposed political camps. When one has a clear and distinguishable enemy who appears to prize values that are totally incompatible with your own set of beliefs, this becomes a driving force of social and economic change.

Obviously, this sense of political polarization has not faded, and has become ever more pronounced in recent years, particularly in North America. A clear example of this is the expressions of social justice displayed when statues of former Canadian prime ministers are dismantled and toppled. A scorched earth policy is being applied to past politicians associated with the Residential School System. There seems to be a clearly demarcated line drawn between those in favor of renaming long-standing institutions and toppling statues and those intent on preserving historical memory and recognizing it (regardless of how problematic it is).

A direct line of continuity can also be traced between the Enlightenment thinkers, Bolsheviks, and today's "woke" politicians seeking to radically reform the world order and implement globalist programs purported to promote progress, equity, and human rights for all. Specifically, the COVID-19 pandemic has offered progressive politicians a once-in-a-lifetime opportunity to radically alter the complexion of society and initiate a global agenda. For example, as stated on the World Economic Forum's official website, the "Great Reset" program sees an opportunity to recalibrate the world order through

9 Kotkin, *Stalin: Waiting for Hitler*.

managing the social, economic, and political disruptions that the COVID-19 pandemic has caused. Similar to the Enlightenment project of the 18th century, the Great Reset Initiative seeks to build a new social contract that honors the dignity of every human being.[10] A sense of utopianism is evident in this line of thinking. Building a perfect, fair, and more equitable global society is a notion that stems from the minds of Enlightenment thinkers such as Voltaire, Rousseau, and Montesquieu. It is also a vision championed by Stalin and the Bolshevik revolutionaries, as we have seen.

Clearly, turning a blind eye from historical patterns and mistakes committed by leftist revolutionaries has become a serious issue in today's world. It is too large a topic to delve into now, but it is obvious that Marxist utopian ideals are nested in the globalist agendas of leaders in the West today. While no politician can proclaim themselves proud successors to Marx and the revolutionaries of Russia outright without committing political suicide, it is clear that terms such as "equity" stem from that tradition. Marx's ideas may not seem explicitly adhered to by today's politicians, but the heritage of the Enlightenment, the French Revolution, and the Bolshevik regimes remains a likely source of inspiration for prominent proponents of globalist ideals such as Emmanuel Macron, Justin Trudeau, George Soros, and Bill Gates.

Embracing Marxist thought and simultaneously denying its toxic and pathological elements is a major trend among a new generation of activists who are intent on dismantling history and instilling a sense of equity in the social fabric. Now in the service of neo-Marxists such as Michel Foucault and Jacques Derrida, these activists are able to engage in a disguised form of Communist insurgency. Instead of identifying outrightly as Marxists, activists have been programmed by their humanities professors to show allegiance to post-modernist doctrines which seek to undermine patriarchal notions of power and dismantle white supremacist systems of tyranny.[11] Again, what may sound good on paper can lead to severe repercussions for our society, such as the persecution of innocents, and a new form of insidious subversion of the rule of law. It is a deep shame that the legacy of Communism continues to be ignored, and that Marx remains a deeply cherished figure among activists, leaders, and professors, despite the untold cruelties and atrocities that have been perpetrated in his name. Just as left-leaning Soviet scholars had engaged in denial by dissociating the name of Stalin from the original and pure doctrine of Communism, so are today's generation of social justice warrior activists, politicians, and post-secondary educators unabashedly turning a blind eye to the tragedies committed by Communists of past eras.

10 World Economic Forum, "The Great Reset"; Schwab and Malleret, *COVID-19: The Great Reset.*

11 Derrida, *Plato's Pharmacy.*

Bibliography

Derrida, Jacques. "Plato's Pharmacy." In Jaques Derrida, *Dissemination*, 61-171. Translated by Barbara Johnson. Chicago: University of Chicago Press, 1983.

Fitzpatrick, Sheila. "Revisionism in Soviet History." *History and Theory* 46 (December 2007): 77–91.

Kotkin, Stephen. *The Magnetic Mountain: Stalinism as Civilization*. Berkeley: University of California Press, 1997.

———. *Stalin Waiting for Hitler*. New York: Penguin Random House, 2017.

Marx, Karl and Friedrich Engels. *The Communist Manifesto*. Translated by Samuel Moore. New York: Oxford University Press, 1992.

Medvedev, Roy. *Let History Judge*. New York: Columbia University Press, 1989.

Schwab, Klaus and Thierry Malleret. *COVID-19: The Great Reset*. Geneva: World Economic Forum, 2020.

Trotsky, Leon. *The Revolution Betrayed*. Translated by Max Easton. Atlanta: Pathfinder Press, 1937.

World Economic Forum. "The Great Reset." https://www.weforum.org/great-reset/.

Chapter 33

Learning to Think Critically About Culture and Combatting Wokeism

Oren Amitay and Scott D. G. Ventureyra

Editor's note*: This chapter examines a number of cultural issues. The content of this chapter is taken from psychologist Dr. Oren Amitay's Facebook page (with permission). I have selected some of the most interesting and relevant posts to this section of the book. I have given them titles. The selections are a diverse sample of his postings, which seek to help students and others to think critically about the media's gaslighting and brainwashing, unthinking individuals' knee jerk reactions, and the hypocrisy involved in criticizing other positions without being aware of one's own (something that is very commonplace with leftist viewpoints). It is important to note that Oren is giving a nonpartisan commentary in his posts. He exposes the lies and inconsistencies of the wokeism that runs rampant throughout our culture. I have given each post a relevant title with the date and time of posting as a subtitle.

The following post of January 8, 2021, by Amitay best explains, in his own words, the intention behind his posts, which are so often misunderstood by his leftist critics:

> Every once in a while, I need to write something like this because most people will not take the time to peruse enough of my posts/videos here or elsewhere in order to see that their initial *emotional* reaction to some of what I state should not be misconstrued as an indication of the motives, meanings and intentions of my words.
>
> Namely, I am as socially liberal as anyone you will meet. As a psychologist, university lecturer and humanist, I have helped more people "on the left" truly deal with a wide variety of important issues—including those pertaining to their sex, sexual orientation/proclivities/preferences/practices, gender, etc—than most people who *choose* to misunderstand and mischaracterize my words, actions, motives and intentions will ever help.
>
> Also, I would wager that I have helped more people "on the right" and "in the centre" gain a much better understanding of and ability to deal with issues pertaining to sex, sexual orientation/proclivities/

preferences/practices, gender, etc in a healthy/adaptive manner—e.g., in ways that most females, feminists, LGBTQ+Q etc, people "on the left," sex-positive individuals, etc would appreciate—than anyone who has *chosen* to misunderstand and mischaracterize my words, actions, motives and intentions.

From what I have seen, those who dislike, misunderstand and/or mischaracterize me or what I say appear unable to reconcile the fact that someone who is extremely liberal, socially speaking, could also be a Critical Thinker.

For the record and for the umpteenth time, my sole goal is to promote Critical Thinking so that more people will be better able to recognize what has been happening in many areas of society over the years—and thus might become motivated and/or better able to do something about it, or at least to become more resistant to the pernicious effects of the things I have been covering.

The reason I may seem biased against certain "groups" is that there is already ample coverage of the transgressions and other problematic words/actions of people from particular "groups." How am I adding any value by simply jumping on the very long and crammed bandwagon?

Rather, I am trying to help people see the kinds of issues that are not receiving much/any coverage via the majority of (social) media venues, the (higher) education system, the government or other such institutions/systems—or issues that are being presented in a false, biased, inaccurate, incomplete, distorted, misleading, unethical, manipulative, divisive, hypocritical, harmful and/or dangerous manner by those same institutions/systems.

How can *anyone* find fault with such a goal—unless you are part of, or stand to gain from the actions of, the aforementioned institutions/ systems?

If I come across in ways that rub some people the wrong way, that really is not my intention. There are reasons I feel the need to maintain this tone/stance; anyone who knows about the odious/harmful issues that face us knows what those reasons are.[1]

Mao's China Hitting Closer and Closer to Home

August 14, 2021, at 8:59 AM

I am still taking a hiatus from my usual posts, but I do hope that at least one or two people have seen enough of my material to at least consider looking further into the many issues I have been covering over the past few years.

1 Amitay, Facebook post. In this post, we agreed that I would include this excerpt in this volume.

I am not being hyperbolic when I say that the future of civilization is at risk, as literal forces of evil are skillfully taking advantage of and manipulating the ignorance, apathy, laziness, fear, anxiety, confusion, hubris, narcissism/"narcissism", delusional/"delusional" thinking, "Tribal/Identitarian Politics," bad/failed parenting, impotent rage, mental health, false "compassion," desperate need to be seen as "good"/"special"/"important," maladaptive self-interest and many other shortcomings of so many people in The West.

Most of what I have posted is designed to show the myriad ways that the aforementioned malevolence is being perpetrated. The evidence is obvious and is becoming more blatant every day. I and many others have been shining the light on this malfeasance for years.

Forget about *who* is providing the evidence; please just *look at* and *listen to* that evidence with an open mind. That is what Critical Thinkers do.

I am still trying to pull back from social media, so I hope that at least a few people will watch this clip [titled "Survivor Of Mao's Cultural Revolution Says It's Happening In The US NOW," (https://youtu.be/fknDR1ych3g)] and maybe be inspired to dig deeper into what has been happening. If anyone is wondering where to begin, try my Facebook posts over the past few years.[2]

Lastly, one thing that gives me hope is that I keep seeing more people—although not nearly enough—begin to realize that they have been gaslit and brainwashed by the aforementioned forces of extreme and destructive self-interest, evil, misinformation and disinformation.

That is, they are coming to see that most of us who have been sounding the alarm bells are a) not stupid, b) not reactionaries, c) not far-right or even right-wing, d) not bad people, e) not QAnon or any other false "conspiracy theorist," f) not hateful, g) not bigots, h) not "oppressors" and i) not racists or White Supremacists—including the many non-White Critical Thinkers.

And please never forget that a) most politicians, (social) media oligarchs and other power brokers are driven purely by cynical self-interest; b) many/most "journalists" today are *not* the kind of brave/courageous, ethical and brimming-with-integrity essential promulgators of *real news* who once made their profession proud; and c) far too many (mental) health "professionals" have become nothing more than timid, cowardly, or even manipulative and self-serving "activists" who have abandoned any pretense of ethics, science, Critical Thinking or best practices.

I will once again try to stay away for a bit...

2 Timcast IRL, "Survivor of Mao's Cultural Revolution Says It's Happening in the US NOW."

Journalism and Journalists' Ever Crumbling Integrity

July 31, 2021, at 8:16 PM

Here is an example to help combat gaslighting and brainwashing.[3]

If you read the piece—which quotes and relies on claims made nearly exclusively by Trans and non-binary individuals (and a presumably non-Trans person whose organization is extremely biased, myopic, hypocritical and lacking in any insight or credibility, IMO)—you might feel bad for Trans people for the stigma, hate, disgust, violence and discrimination they face much of the time.

I know *I* feel empathy for most Trans people, especially since the Gender Dysphoria they experience is real and is usually debilitating.

However, I also know that the piece is extremely one-sided/biased, lacking in any Critical Thinking and devoid of any compassion or empathy for those who have been harmed or who risk being harmed by the kind of (largely unfounded) Trans/gender ideology being promulgated by the subjects she interviewed.

If you have no idea what I am talking about, at least read the Comments[4] to this awful piece (ignoring any ignorant and/or hateful ones). Or, better yet, check out my many posts that have dealt with these issues.

Here is the Critical Thinking part that the author apparently has no ability to contemplate or process, based on her piece: Either *everyone* who a) points out the logical inconsistencies and nonsensical aspects or b) raises concerns about the consequences of radical Trans ideology is a transphobe, or some/many of them have legitimate points.

Think about that.

When people like this lazy, ignorant, ideologically possessed and/or virtue signaling but good-hearted journalist proclaim that transphobia has risen over the years, Critical Thinkers wonder whether this so-called "transphobia" is simply the *logical* and predictable reaction of people who recognize the many nonsensical claims and problems with radical Trans ideology.

Thousands of students and many more viewers/listeners have seen/heard me speak about Trans/gender-related issues for about 20 years.

My students are some of the most liberal-minded people you will find, given that they go to a very progressive university and often are in (extremely) liberal programs. Yet, only a tiny handful have ever had *any* problem with what I have stated; and they are typically the most radical, authoritarian and "woke" individuals who *applaud* pieces such as "Why assigning gender to animals is harmful"—as was actually written by one of the people the "journalist" interviewed for her piece—and are ready to attack and tyrannically, fascistically

3 See Dinah Brand, Twitter post.

4 See comments following Dinah Brand, Twitter post:

and/or narcissistically/"narcissistically" "cancel" everyone who disagrees with such ridiculous pieces.

In sum, Critical Thinkers understand—just like any good parent does—that giving into *every* self-serving nonsensical or harmful belief and *demand* is not *true* compassion.

We also understand that a) we can be compassionate/empathetic to certain people while also being compassionate/empathetic to others, and b) truly compassionate/empathetic people would never seek to harm, e.g., 50-99% of the population in order to appease or to ostensibly help .002% to *maybe* 2% (if we include people who truly believe they are "non-binary"/"gender-queer", as opposed to those who simply do not want to be counted among the "boring normal people") of the population.

And, as always, I am not picking on this one "journalist." I am simply using her as an exemplar of the many people like her who are inadvertently or deliberately causing a lot of harm to society, including some of its most vulnerable members.

August 1, 2021, at 8:43 AM

This "journalist" wrote what many are calling the most one-sided, misinformed, misguided, misogynistic and hateful/bigoted pieces in a national "news" source—which I posted yesterday.

Here is the tantrum she threw after people called her out on her ethical misconduct.[5]

This is the kind of person who represents "journalism" these days, similar to many others I have posted about over the past few years.

Many people in the comments section are calling her out for her lack of journalistic integrity and professionalism.

To be clear, I have always spoken out against trolls and other ignorant and/ or malevolent individuals who post hateful, threatening or violent comments. However, so many people post terrible things like this "journalist" did, and then when people call them out on their words, attitudes and actions, the person in the wrong "cries victim" and pretends that the tiny fraction of terrible comments represent the "majority," which enables them to cowardly and unethically deflect away from all of the valid concerns raised—which they never address and for which they are never held to account by people who claim to be good-hearted citizens.

5 Brooke Taylor. Deleted Twitter post. This journalist has since deleted her Twitter account: https://twitter.com/newsmanbrooke.

August 1, 2021, at 2:25 PM

I posted a link earlier today that revealed a "journalist's" infantile and unprofessional expletive-laden meltdown/temper tantrum after people called her out for what they considered an unethically one-sided, misinformed, misguided, misogynistic, bigoted and hateful piece—which I posted yesterday.

For whatever reason, she deleted the tweet thread. Presumably due to his reverence for what was once a noble profession, Jonathan Kay is using the "journalist" in question as one of many examples of the ways in which his beloved field has failed over the years.[6]

I wish more people would open their eyes to the realities around them. In short, whereas "fake news" was once unfairly applied far too broadly/liberally in order to tarnish an entire profession, in the past few years more and more "journalists" seem to have endeavored to "earn" that pejorative label.

Critical Thinkers realize what I am stating. And Critical Thinkers know that what I am stating applies even to "journalists" who appear to align with *their* "tribe"; or, better yet, they realize that true Critical Thinkers do not identify with any "tribe" but instead exist as individuals who are willing to engage with everyone—regardless of "tribal affiliation"—as long as those other people conduct themselves appropriately/accordingly.

Alexandria Ocasio Cortez's Massive Lie About January 6

July 31, 2021, at 3:23 PM

For those who have not yet got the memo—despite my repeating it ad nauseam over the years—the vast majority of my posts are intended to highlight the various ways individuals, families, organizations, companies, governments, societies and countries engage in harmful cognitive/psychological distortions and other maladaptive internal operations and social/interpersonal functioning, e.g., anything from confirmation bias to hypocrisy to gaslighting to brainwashing to virtue signalling to "tribal warfare" to Identitarian Politics, etc.

The key antidotes to the preceding destructive internal and external processes are courage, honesty, introspection, self-awareness, insight, Critical Thinking and *true/healthy* compassion/empathy.

Unfortunately, many people fail to understand or *choose* to ignore or distort the intentions of my posts, even though I have stated those intentions exceedingly clearly countless times and have also clarified any misperceptions those people may have harbored.

6 Kay, Twitter post.

So, when I post something like this,[7] the main point is *not* that AOC appears to have lied or grossly exaggerated about what supposedly happened (and allegedly smeared a police officer in the process).

Rather, the main points include the fact that a) not one mainstream "journalist" questioned her account of the day in question at all, even though it was apparently very suspicious (at least based on what Tim Pool presents), and even though that is *supposed* to be their job; and b) so many people from certain "tribes" called everyone who dared simply to ask questions about AOC's version of events—the way that Critical Thinkers, journalists and anyone with a modicum of intelligence should be doing—terrible things like "misogynist" or "racist" or any other term that is bandied about so freely these days, thereby robbing them of any meaning.

These two problems are indicative of something far more deleterious and sinister than most people can appreciate, hence I keep highlighting them. And I will do so in a non-partisan fashion; the problem is that certain "tribes" are far more guilty of such transgressions and/or wield far more power than others -- and hence can do far more damage -- which leads non-Critical Thinkers, the ideologically possessed and other unproductive or less-than-ideally productive individuals to make so many false assumptions and allegations regarding me, my motives and my words.

Democrats Demand Unthinking Compliance

July 28, 2021, at 12:22 AM

Truth be told, when I first heard of Ben Shapiro and heard him speak, I was turned off completely. However, I overcame my initial reaction and gave him a chance—listening to his *words* and analyzing the logic, veracity, consistency etc of what he was saying.

I soon realized that, as biased as he was, he was far more credible, honest, rational, consistent and transparent than most of the people I was listening to "on the left."

Here, he tackles the outright lies, misinformation, manipulation, gaslighting and brainwashing related to who are not getting vaccinated. Sadly, no one "on the left" will listen to this clip, so they will continue to believe the brainwashing of the Democratic ministry of propaganda, aka the mainstream media, and foolishly believe that only Trump supporters and other Republicans and right-wingers are the culprits, despite the clear evidence to the contrary.[8]

7 Timcast, "CNN Video Leak Catches AOC Is MASSIVE LIE."
8 Ben Shapiro, "You Will Be Made To Obey."

They will also fail to realize that teachers in New York are acting in an extremely hypocritical, unethical and manipulative fashion, as are frontline medical workers, first responders and others who should be the first to get vaccinated. And God forbid anyone "on the left" take an *honest* and *unbiased* look at which "races" are the least likely to vaccinate.

Lastly, no one "on the left" will learn that they are also being lied to about the most recent uptick in Covid cases vs fatalities.

The Left's Intolerance

July 27, 2021, at 3:43 PM

[This post was in response/reflection to a Tweet by writer Andrew Mount, who stated: "In a room full of Conservatives, I'm usually the most liberal person there. In a room full of Liberals, I'm usually the most conservative person there. In one room, my ideas are debated in good faith. In the other, I'm silently resented until I leave—then I'm slandered."][9]

I know many people—myself included—who feel the same way.

As I keep saying, people on the *far*-right are extremely intolerant of any ideas or *people* that differ at all from their "tribal beliefs," but I find I can discuss, debate and disagree with most intelligent conservatives and people on the not-far right in a productive manner that does not get personal and is not undermined by irrationality, ad hominems or other violations of proper discourse—as long as the other person is not a narcissist or "narcissist."

Conversely, it seems almost impossible to have any rational, good-faith and productive discussion about anything controversial with most intelligent people "on the left" these days—unless you agree with them 100%—because they are extremely intolerant of any ideas or *people* that differ at all from their "tribal beliefs."

If you peruse the post on my professional FB page from yesterday, in which I called out people for lauding someone who rudely and seemingly aggressively—i.e., he got right in Tucker Carlson's face—confronted the controversial and IMO off-putting TV pundit, you will see exactly what I mean in a number of engagements.

And my experience is mirrored by what has been recounted by *many* people who previously identified as "left" or "liberal" or "centre-left."

At what point do the remaining "leftists"/liberals finally take *any* responsibility for the fact that so many intelligent, educated and good-hearted

9 Mount, Twitter post.

people have distanced themselves from the ideology being promulgated by "the left" because they could no longer accept "the left's" literal cult-like reactions to being challenged on *anything* of importance?

If anyone does not know what I mean by "cult-like," it includes, in no particular order (and I am sure I am missing a few things as I am writing this quickly between patients):

- gaslighting
- personal attacks and other forms of (passive-)aggression
- extreme emotional/physiological reactivity
- irrationality and inconsistency in their claims/arguments
- inability to see things from any perspective other than "the cult's"
- automatic/mindless reciting of various words, phrases, ideas inability to stay on topic when the *facts* get in the way or when they are shown unequivocally the flaws in their "logic" or claims/arguments
- inability to mentally/psychologically/emotionally handle *facts* that do not line up with their "cult's" beliefs/ideologies
- reacting as if any challenge of their beliefs is a *direct personal* attack on *them*/their very existence
- extreme (and sometimes pathological) in-group/out-group mentality seemingly delusional (literally speaking) or desperate adherence to their beliefs, no matter how much (indisputable) evidence to the contrary is presented

To be clear, the preceding descriptors apply to most "far-right" people I know (of) or with whom I have engaged, and to a few conservative or "right-leaning" individuals. But they usually appear to possess relatively low intelligence.

Free Pass to Leftist Posts on Twitter

July 25, 2021, at 8:25 PM

It really does seem that Twitter gives out Blue Checks to any grifter who identifies as "left," and who unapologetically makes asinine and totally incorrect and easily disprovable ignorant statements in the most arrogant manner.[10]

As always, I am not singling anyone out but instead am using this "journalist" as an exemplar of the issue in question.

10 Ngo, Twitter post.

On Pedophilia

July 25, 2021, at 4:20 PM

This issue is far too complex and nuanced to discuss on Facebook.[11] I do cover related subjects in class and this particular unbelievable terrible story, along with related phenomena, has been discussed *many* times on a listserv I am on, by those with more expertise than I—but also by some who have a vested and, IMO, disturbing interest in such matters.

In any event, I am not trying to fuel any "conspiracy theories" nor hoping to denigrate the motives of others. However,

- I believe we have more than enough evidence that evil people—some of whom happen to be pedophiles—have ensconced themselves within the halls of power across the globe, and only the most lazy, apathetic, ignorant, terrified, ideologically possessed and/or evil individuals deny such Truth; and
- only the most lazy, apathetic, ignorant, terrified, ideologically possessed and/or evil individuals deny that various doctors, psychologists, therapists, counsellors, academics, researchers, politicians, journalists and others have denied, minimized, excused, lied about, promulgated and/or perpetrated some pretty terrible ideas/agendas over the years—many of which I have covered relentlessly—for their *own* narcissistic/"narcissistic," sick, manipulative, selfish, self-serving and/or evil needs and desires.

On Free Speech

July 24, 2021, at 8:14 PM

I have said it before and I will keep saying it: When asked, during Canada's largest Free Speech event on November 11, 2017, to state who we believed was the greatest proponent and symbol of free speech, I said "Joe Rogan."[12] Nearly 4 years later, my answer has been validated many times over.

11 See Aviv, "The German Experiment That Placed Foster Children with Pedophiles."
12 See Hunter, "Jordan Peterson fans pack free speech discussion."

Capital Rioters Charged

July 22, 2021, at 8:08 AM

Thank goodness! One of the marauding, murderous monsters who tried to violently take over the American government on January 6th during the greatest threat to America throughout its entire history was *finally* brought to justice!

But, because Orange Man Bad is still wielding power from within the shadows and is able to corrupt the judicial system with his particular brand of tyrannical/authoritarian evil, the aforementioned terrorist was sentenced to only 8 months in prison.

Ideologically possessed individuals will read my post literally. Critical Thinkers will want to know what exactly the accused/convicted had done. This video shows that he did *nothing* illegal, aside from trespassing, and was not involved in *any* violence at all—otherwise that would have been part of his indictment and description throughout the legal process.[13]

And, like Krystal and Saagar,[14] I feel the same way about the January 6th *protesters* as I do about, e.g., someone arrested during a violent ANTIFA/BLM riot or looting who did not actually do anything terrible, aside from, e.g., entering some store illegally. Yet, so many of the violent ANTIFA/BLM rioters have been let go without any penalty whatsoever (although *some* have been held [somewhat] accountable, at least).[15] And to be clear, I believe, as I have stated repeatedly, that anyone who engaged in threats and violence during the January 6th *riot* should be held fully and proportionately accountable.

Democrats' Hunger for Power and Authoritarian Rule

July 19, 2020, at 10:20 PM

Find whatever source appeals to you, but *please* educate yourself on what Biden is doing right now. I know this will be hard for at least half of the world to believe, but Biden/the Democrats are trying to facilitate something far more fascistic, tyrannical and authoritarian than Trump *ever* did.

Yes, Trump bloviated incessantly. Yes, there was as much bluster coming from Trump as there were exaggerations and stupid/unnecessary lies. Yes,

13 https://youtu.be/tZzcS-WFco4.

14 Breaking Points, "Krystal and Saagar: Capitol Rioter SENTENCED TO 8 Months for Taking Selfie. Is That Fair?"

15 Tim Pool, "Texas Democrat Stunt BACKFIRES."

Trump should have been far more careful in his communications regarding the tainted 2020 US elections.

In the end, however, what *actual/concrete* and *direct* destruction of freedom can you attribute to Trump in his four years as president? If there are any examples, I genuinely want to know because that would obviously be important.

Biden has been in power for only 6 months and is already letting slip that he/the Democrats plan to do one of the first things that all dictators do when they gain power.

And, inexcusably and inexplicably, the *very targets* of their tyrannical/authoritarian/evil plan are the biggest cheerleaders!

I know very few (if any) people "on the left" will watch this video (I am not going to edit out the ads, so just fast forward about a minute each time Ben starts them):[16]

Unfortunately, CNN, MSNBC, NY Times and the rest of the Democrat Pravda will not cover the story—or not cover it honestly—because they foolishly believe that they will benefit from Biden/the Democrats' brand of fascism.

As I keep saying, only those entirely ignorant of history fail to realize that the barrel of the gun will always end up eventually being turned on *them* after the power-mad tyrants have perfected their aim picking off those who these foolish cowards believe deserve to be "eliminated" or "unpersoned."

Unwarranted Attacks on Julian Assange and Edward Snowden

July 18, 2021, at 4:15 PM

All Democrats and Republicans who continue to promulgate the fake narratives and immoral—nay, evil—attacks against Julian Assange and Edward Snowden are guilty of treason against their constituents. And every "journalist" who cowardly, obsequiously, jealously, selfishly, self-servingly and narcissistically/"n arcissistically" buys into and promotes the same fake narratives and immoral/evil attacks against those who—unlike them—possess enough courage and integrity to reveal Truth, should never be trusted ever again.[17]

16 Ben Shapiro, "The Left Targets Social Media."

17 Greenwald, Twitter post. "This is one of the best and most important short videos on the Assange persecution, from @Reason. It documents why his prosecution is such a profound threat to press freedom and yet, shockingly, it's subservient corporate journalists most supportive." It is indeed as the post captions: "The Prosecution of Julian Assange Is an Assault on the First Amendment."

Questioning Narratives and Thinking Critically

July 4, 2020, at 2:20 PM

This person (Scott Ventureyra) is not a Johnny-come-lately, as he has been posting about and sending me information on many societal issues/concerns for quite some time.

Although I cannot verify the accuracy/veracity of all of his claims/sources, nor do I agree with every inference and conclusion Scott makes, he does provide a plethora of valuable and verified information (including many links to his sources).

Most importantly, critical thinkers are not afraid to expose ourselves to controversial or equivocal ideas. We can then discuss these issues to try to determine which ones might be more credible than others.

And, as (recent) history has proven time and again, just because certain "experts/authorities"^ deny or decry various claims/concepts/arguments/issues, we should not automatically go along with them simply because of their "status," because we like them (or dislike others), or because what they say fits into our pre-existing schemata/belief systems and/or correspond to what we want/need to believe.[18]

Here is [one] of Scott's recent important and informative pieces. Woe to anyone whose roster of "experts/authorities" includes "celebrities" or "social media influencers": https://www.scottventureyra.com/post/won-t-get-fooled-again-by-the-who.

Bibliography

Amitay, Oren. Facebook post, February 3, 2021. https://www.facebook.com/oren.amitay/posts/10157614272415957.

Aviv, Rachel. "The German Experiment That Placed Foster Children with Pedophiles." *The New Yorker*, July 19, 2021. https://www.newyorker.com/magazine/2021/07/26/the-german-experiment-that-placed-foster-children-with-pedophiles?.

Ben Shapiro. "The Left Targets Social Media—and the Daily Wire—for Destruction | Ep. 1299." YouTube video, July 19, 2021. https://youtu.be/wTQ1MNA_2_4?t=94.

———. "You Will Be Made To Obey | Ep. 1305." YouTube video. July 27, 2021. https://youtu.be/M1OYtVoDfIs?t=1448.

18 Ventureyra, "Won't Get Fooled Again by the WHO."

Brand, Dinah. Twitter post, July 31, 2021, 8:09 P.M. https://twitter.com/dinahbrand2/status/1421623986237100041?s=20&fbclid=IwAR0xFyy68w8Q0sehSf6Js2pkIhKA5Iijl4T.

Breaking Points. "Krystal and Saagar: Capitol Rioter SENTENCED TO 8 Months for Taking Selfie. Is That Fair?" YouTube video, July 20, 2021. https://www.youtube.com/watch?v=tZzcS-WFco4.

Detrans Canada. "Our Brief on Bill C-6." November 2020. https://detranscanada.com/brief-on-bill-c-6/.

Greenwald, Glenn. Twitter post, July 18, 2021, 1:13 P.M. https://twitter.com/ggreenwald/status/1416808406858489859.

Hunter, Brad. "Jordan Peterson fans pack free speech discussion." *Toronto Sun*, November 11, 2017. https://torontosun.com/news/local-news/jordan-peterson-fans-pack-free-speech-discussion.

Kay, Jonathan. Twitter post, August 1, 2021, 10:05 A.M. https://twitter.com/jonkay/status/1421834513437675523?s=20.

Mount, Andrew. Twitter post, July 26, 2021, 10:45 P.M. https://twitter.com/amount98/status/1419851512700829701?s=20.

Ngo, Andy. Twitter post, July 25, 2021, 5:33 P.M. https://twitter.com/MrAndyNgo/status/1419410502170644485.

Taylor, Brooke. Twitter post, July 31, 2021. https://twitter.com/newsmanbrooke/status/1421557919762587648?s=21&fbclid=IwAR2EFuZIjzVXRT1OvXxakS38_mBNpqkgUAQK82-ra2Qvtr5s4yboWtSf1kw.

Timcast. "CNN Video Leak Catches AOC Is MASSIVE LIE, CNN Complicit in AOC Lying about Jan 6th." YouTube video, July 29, 2021. https://www.youtube.com/watch?v=jZIGYQ7KNHc.

Timcast IRL. "Survivor of Mao's Cultural Revolution Says It's Happening in the US NOW." YouTube video, August 3, 2021. https://www.youtube.com/watch?v=fknDR1ych3g.

Tim Pool. "Texas Democrat Stunt BACKFIRES as Six Democrats, WH Staff and Pelosi Aide Test Positive for COVID." YouTube video, July 20, 2021. https://www.youtube.com/watch?v=4jLCnP7UaxY.

Ventureyra, Scott. "Won't Get Fooled Again by the WHO: Thoughts on the COVID-19 Crisis and Related World Events." June 9, 2020. https://www.scottventureyra.com/post/won-t-get-fooled-again-by-the-who.

Chapter 34

Canada's Free Speech Wars[1]

Scott D. G. Ventureyra

In Canada, the assaults on free speech continue like clockwork. Free speech, a self-correcting mechanism that makes possible civil public discourse and social peace in free societies, is increasingly under attack throughout Europe and North America. Canada in particular is on an unwavering path toward cultural suicide. It is a shameful period for Canadians, as the Liberal government led by Prime Minister Justin Trudeau continues to bow to the demands of favoured minorities and the political activists who claim to represent their interests. Indeed, Trudeau has unwittingly become postmodernism's poster boy.[2] He has abandoned Truth in his unbridled pursuit of power[3] and has further exacerbated what was already a decades-long problem.

As one of the "architects" of the deconstructionist postmodern ideology underlying this trend, Jean-Francois Lyotard[4] maintained that the utilization of language is power. According to Lyotard, the "truth" is controlled by the one who has the platform to speak. Thus, fittingly, authoritarians have incessantly sought to shut down inconvenient speakers, those who advocate free speech, in an attempt to strip them of any power to persuade. For example, in late September of 2017, Liberal Members of Parliament (MPs) walked out on Rachel Harder, a pro-life MP who was picked as women committee chair for the Conservative Party of Canada. This disregard, not only for truth but common decency, dialogue, and understanding, has become pervasive across Canada. In a similar vein, that same year, a draconian piece of legislation was passed[5] in Ontario by the Liberal provincial government led by the radical Kathleen Wynne to establish ridiculous "safe access zones" of 50 to 150 meters around abortion clinics for the purpose of preventing "harassment." The fact

1 This is a modified version of Scott Ventureyra, "Canada's Free Speech Wars," *Crisis Magazine*, December 6, 2017, https://www.crisismagazine.com/2017/canadas-free-speech-wars.

2 Craig, "Canada and Postmodernism's Poster Boy."

3 Rebello, "Canadians Didn't Sign Up for Trudeau's Scandals and Bad Policies."

4 Woodward, "Jean-François Lyotard (1924–1998)."

5 Janus, "Ontario to create 'safe access zones' around abortion clinics with new legislation."

is that harassment laws already prevent attempts to block access to clinics. It is just another way for abortion proponents to silence pro-life demonstrators and protect the current abortion laws.

Compelled Speech Demanded by Ontario's Bar Association

Following the poorly drafted and totalitarian Bill C-16,[6] which compels individuals to use an ever-growing list of personal pronouns for self-identified transgendered persons, the Law Society of Upper Canada (Ontario's bar association) now *demands* lawyers submit a "statement of principles" or risk disbarment. Society members have been given "convenient" statement templates to make the requirement less burdensome. Take, for instance, one of the compelled "principles": "A recognition that the Law Society is committed to Inclusive legal workplaces in Ontario, a reduction of barriers created by racism, unconscious bias and discrimination and better representation of Indigenous and racialized licensees in the legal professions in all legal workplaces and at all levels of seniority."[7] Are lawyers now supposed to confess to *unconscious* racism and discriminatory practices? In a *National Post* article, attorney Bruce Pardy, Professor of Law at Queen's University, rightly points out that "forced speech is the most egregious violation of freedom of expression, protected by section 2(b) of the Charter of Rights and Freedoms."[8] Thus, Canadian authorities are now suppressing unfashionable speech while simultaneously compelling favoured speech. In October of 2017, Jordan Peterson, Pardy, and practising attorney Jared Brown discussed the problems associated with the Law Society's policy.[9]

Wilfrid Laurier University's Suffocation of Free Speech

Canadian institutions of higher learning are increasingly implementing Lyotard's dictum on power and speech. In late 2017, a communications graduate student teaching assistant, Lindsay Shepherd, was caught in a crossfire of controversy at Wilfred Laurier University (WLU) in Waterloo, Ontario. Shepherd was reprimanded by WLU[10] for presenting a brief clip of a debate concerning the compelled usage of non-gendered pronouns on Steve Paikin's mainstream

6 Pardy, "Meet the new 'human rights'—where you are forced by law to use 'reasonable' pronouns."

7 The Law Society of Ontario, "Statement of Principles."

8 Pardy, "Law society's new policy compels speech."

9 See Peterson, "Update: Law Society of Ontario Compelled Speech."

10 Hopper, "Here's the full recording of Wilfrid Laurier reprimanding Lindsay Shepherd."

public television show *The Agenda.*[11] The clip featured two professors from the University of Toronto (U of T), Jordan Peterson, a professor of psychology, and Nicolas Matte, a lecturer at the Mark S. Bonham Centre for Sexual Diversity Studies, who in the video makes the absurd claim that there are no differences between males and females.[12]

What was Shepherd's crime? Apparently, she did not condemn the politically unfashionable views of Jordan Peterson, who refuses to use non-gendered pronouns as required by the Ontario Human Rights Commission. Instead, she held a neutral position, in order not to influence her students. This is good pedagogy if educating is your objective. However, indoctrination was the goal of the Communications Studies faculty. Shepherd was hauled into a meeting with two faculty members with whom she studied as well as Adria Joel, the acting manager of Gendered Violence Prevention and Support at the school.

In an appalling inquisitorial style, Shepherd's supervisor, Nathan Rambukkana, asked whether she was sent to WLU by Peterson and accused her of creating a "toxic" environment for students without a single shred of evidence. And most egregiously, Rambukkana and program coordinator Herbert Pimlott likened the defence of free speech to a Nazi propaganda tactic, thereby suggesting that Shepherd, by presenting the video clip neutrally, was facilitating Peterson's fascist agenda.[13] They further claimed she violated the school's Gendered and Sexual Violence policy and accused her (falsely) of breaking the law. She was told that students would not be allowed to hear views they disapproved of and that her seminar notes must be approved by her supervisor from that point on to ensure compliance.

Luckily, Shepherd had the courage to stand up to these three bullies and surreptitiously record them on her laptop. We now have official auditory confirmation for posterity of this type of Orwellian nightmare that is increasingly common at Canadian universities. Just over a year ago, Peterson had warned about such insanity and intolerance. Things have only gotten much worse since then. It has become commonplace to censor doctors and health practitioners who dare to speak against the deceptions of the COVID narrative. It is precisely what D.A. Carson labelled the intolerance of tolerance,[14] where the traditional meaning of tolerance—whereby one respects those with whom he disagrees—is inverted to mean that one who is tolerant must affirm views he previously opposed. Of course, such a definition of tolerance is incoherent, yet this is precisely the idea prevalent throughout Canada and witnessed in Shepherd's ordeal at WLU.

11 *The Agenda with Steve Paikin*, "Genders, Rights and Freedom of Speech."
12 Patent Trending, "Jordan Peterson owns smug professor."
13 Blatchford, "Thought Police Strike Again as Wilfried Laurier Grad Student."
14 Carson, *The Intolerance of Tolerance.*

Fallout from the WLU Controversy

It was only after Shepherd's recording was released that WLU felt obliged to offer her an apology. As Shepherd wrote on her Twitter account: "Moral of the story: A university must be repeatedly publicly shamed, internationally, in order to apologize (oh, but keep the task force & investigation). Even then, ambiguous about free speech. Also, make sure to secretly record all meetings or they won't take you seriously."[15]

The response offered by the administrators was weak and disingenuous. If they truly wanted to salvage a modicum of respectability, they would have taken disciplinary action against those who wrongfully reprimanded Shepherd. This was a real opportunity for WLU to champion academic freedom and genuine learning. Instead, they continued to kowtow to irrational fears and demands, while creating safe spaces because the campus is allegedly "unsafe" for transgender people and professors who support them.[16] WLU could easily set an example for other university campuses by removing the Gendered and Sexual Violence Policy (GSVP), which defines such violence as

> An act or actions that reinforce gender inequalities resulting in physical, sexual, emotional, economic or mental harm. This violence includes sexism, gender discrimination, gender harassment, biphobia, transphobia, homophobia and heterosexism, intimate partner violence, and forms of Sexual Violence. This violence can take place on any communication platform (e.g., graffiti, online environments, and through the use of phones).

This statement explains why Adria Joel accused Shepherd of "spreading transphobia" and causing "harm" and "violence." WLU has not taken any action to remove this Orwellian-style policy and I suspect they have no intention to. Although Shepherd has received significant support from the media, many from WLU still don't appreciate free speech and continue to create more "safe spaces." Furthermore, it is appalling how few Canadian politicians were willing to express their disgust at Wilfrid Laurier University's flagrant violation of free speech and academic standards in the Shepherd case. Neither Trudeau nor the socialist leader of the New Democratic Party of Canada, Jagmeet Singh, has defended free speech. The only political leader to do so has been Andrew Scheer, leader of the Conservative Party of Canada (CPC). Scheer specifically weighed in on the WLU controversy and condemned its assault on free speech.

15 Shepherd, Twitter post.

16 Booth, "Petition calls for safety measures to support trans people at Laurier."

He said, "I don't know why the Prime Minister can't simply denounce what happened at [WLU]."

In contrast, the Liberal Party's minister of science, Kirsty Duncan[17] was caught in an instance of doublespeak. She stated on one hand that the Liberal Party upholds free speech unless the views promote "intolerance and hate," while on the other hand claiming to fight for the Charter of Rights for all Canadians. What does she mean by "hate"—neutrally showing a video of Peterson on TVOntario? It is worth noting that the term "hate" in Canadian jurisprudence is nowhere to be found. However, "hatred" is defined in case law. What the Criminal Code does prohibit is "hate propaganda," which is defined as "any writing, sign or visible representation that advocates or promotes genocide…"[18] However, Bill C-16, the law Shepherd supposedly broke, amends the Canadian Human Rights Act and Criminal Code to protect gender expression and identity. Is Duncan suggesting that Shepherd committed hate propaganda? The reason Shepherd's accusers are wrong is that the Canadian Charter of Rights and Freedoms is not meant to protect someone from being offended. Until WLU adopts a policy similar to that of the University of Chicago on free expression, they will never restore their credibility.

The Associated Ills of Postmodernism

A quick look at the university webpages of Rambukanna[19] and Pimlott[20] will explain why political radicals like these were so willing to vilify anyone not in their ideological camp. Canadians should be appalled that their tax money is funding what the physicist Alan Sokal labelled "fashionable nonsense." Sokal brilliantly exposed postmodernism's abuse of science and reason in 1996 with the submission of a hoax article with the absurd title "Transgressing the Boundaries: Towards a Transformative Hermeneutics of Quantum Gravity" to *Social Text*, a prominent postmodern cultural studies journal.

Recently, in a desperate attempt to defend the humanities and their longstanding corruption while ostensibly lauding free speech, Ira Wells, professor of English at U of T, who had taught at WLU in 2011, wrote an irrational tirade against Peterson. Among many other details, he mischaracterized Peterson's political leanings, libelling him an "Alt-Right" figure. He fumbled on

17 Steeper33, "Scheer Condemns Wilfrid Laurier University's Egregious Actions."

18 Government of Canada, Criminal Code (R.S.C., 1985, c. C-46).

19 https://www.wlu.ca/academics/faculties/faculty-of-arts/faculty-profiles/nathan-rambukkana/index.html.

20 https://www.wlu.ca/academics/faculties/faculty-of-arts/faculty-profiles/herbert-pimlott/index.html.

IQ research, claiming that Peterson's IQ defence is on "shaky grounds," which it is not.[21] Peterson argues that IQ research pertains to the most reliable research in psychology, so much so that if such research is disparaged then much of the reliability of research in psychology will be found to be unreliable. Furthermore, his caricature of Peterson's position on postmodernism revealed the extent of his own ignorance of the subject. The fact that he can demonstrate one common theme within postmodernism seems to betray its "spirit." The point is that there is no common theme presented by its defenders since objective analysis is non-existent. The "framework" or "method" of deconstructionism, for example, makes it impossible to coherently affirm anything, since the whole point of postmodernism is to deny "logocentric" ways of knowing. It is only when you step outside of deconstructionism and actually use the "oppressive patriarchal tool" of logic to analyze postmodernism that you can affirm or refute anything. In a collection of essays titled *Postmodernism and Christian Philosophy*, philosopher Brendan Sweetman explains the difficulty in analyzing Jacques Derrida's deconstructionism:

> I am especially concerned to attempt to state Derrida's main thesis clearly, for it seems to me that this is one of the main difficulties with the philosophy of deconstructionism. Derrida and his disciples seldom provide a clear account of the main points of their philosophy. There are varying reasons for this, of course, not least their claim that they are not asserting a philosophical theory, or even a position, at all. This reluctance to state clearly what it is they wish us to take away from their thought has the effect of at once isolating deconstructionism from philosophical debate, while at the same time protecting it from critical examination.[22]

To add to this ambiguity and even incoherence, it should be noted that in all of Derrida's texts (roughly 60 of them translated to English), he purposely used his terms differently in each, which can be seen as part of the deconstructive "strategy." However, the incoherence and chaos of deconstructionism represent only an intellectual strategy for a larger, more sinister goal. Postmodernism is used by social activists to bring down the power structures of Western civilization, namely, free market capitalism and Christian values. Along the way, science, reason, and logic have become targets. Derrida, in his text *Moscou aller-retour*, admits that his philosophical system of radical epistemological skepticism and its subsequent political implications are based on Marxism: "Deconstruction never had meaning or interest, at least in my eyes, than as a radicalization, that is to say, also within the tradition of a certain Marxism in a certain spirit of

21 Plomin and Deary, "Genetics and intelligence differences: five special findings."
22 Sweetman, "The Deconstruction of Western Metaphysics," 236.

Marxism."[23] This quotation reveals the connection between postmodernism's method of deconstructionism and neo-Marxist activism. Not surprisingly, the Canadian universities that stifle free speech the most have devoted the greatest effort to promoting identity politics.

Which is why Peterson should seriously consider finally implementing his planned website intended to expose university curricula and professors who indoctrinate students with postmodern and Neo-Marxist ideology. Much maligned by the U of T Faculty Association, the proposed website is currently on hiatus.[24] It would allow students to avoid such courses before registering for classes and could lead to funding cuts in the coming years. It is time to put an end to the reign of terror at the hands of ideologically possessed faculty members.

Free Speech and the Human Person

Although Shepherd thought of herself as a person of the left before her ordeal, she has clearly distinguished herself from radicals like Rambukanna and Pimlott who have zero interest in freedom of expression (until it is theirs being threatened). They would much rather push their ideology than foster intellectual development. It is quite unfortunate that an intelligent young woman like Shepherd, who is keen on learning about the world, questioned whether academia is right for her.[25] Her experience at WLU has perhaps shown that trudging through a masters and a PhD is not worth the effort because of the ideological constraints. Even though conservatives (and a shrinking number of old-time liberals in the press) predominantly defend freedom of expression in public, it is a cause that should be championed by *all* Canadians who truly believe in the human person and democratic institutions. Shepherd has recently documented her experience at Wilfrid Laurier University in a new book, titled *Diversity and Exclusion: Confronting the Campus Free Speech Crisis.*[26] Like Shepherd, the great Thomistic philosopher Jacques Maritain saw himself by temperament as a man of the "left." Maritain also warned against the great dangers from the extreme right (although Nazis initially emerged from the left) and from Communists on the left. Closely bound up with Maritain's political philosophy was his moral philosophy. In *The Person and the Common Good,* Maritain recognized that "the end of society is neither the individual good nor the collection of individual goods of each of the persons who constitute it" but rather "[the] end of the society is the good of the community, the good of

23 Derrida, *Moscou aller-retour*; Hicks, *Explaining Postmodernism*, 186.

24 CBC Radio, "Toronto university professor says controversial website 'on hiatus.'"

25 Saad, "My Chat with Laurier TA Lindsay Shepherd."

26 Shepherd, *Diversity and Exclusion.*

the social body."[27] This is what I believe Shepherd and those who stand up for freedom of speech and expression have realized. Hopefully, we will all get there together, sooner than later.

Bibliography

Blatchford, Christie. "Thought Police Strike Again as Wilfried Laurier Grad Student Is Chastised for Showing Jordan Peterson Video." *National Post*, November 10, 2017. https://nationalpost.com/opinion/christie-blatchford-thought-police-strike-again-as-wilfrid-laurier-grad-student-is-chastised-for-showing-jordan-peterson-video.

Booth, Laura. "Petition calls for safety measures to support trans people at Laurier." *The Record*, November 27, 2017. https://www.therecord.com/news/waterloo-region/2017/11/27/petition-calls-for-safety-measures-to-support-trans-people-at-laurier.html#.Whyu7JgaXN8.twitter.

Carson, D.A. *The Intolerance of Tolerance*. Grand Rapids, MI: William B. Eerdmans, 2012.

CBC Radio. "Toronto university professor says controversial website 'on hiatus.'" *CBC Radio*, November 13, 2017. https://www.cbc.ca/radio/asithappens/as-it-happens-monday-edition-1.4396981/toronto-university-professor-says-controversial-website-on-hiatus-1.4396986.

Craig, James Porter. "Canada and Postmodernism's Poster Boy." *Catholic Insight*, July 1, 2017. https://catholicinsight.com/canada-postmodernisms-poster-boy/.

Derrida, Jacques. *Moscou aller-retour*. Sainte Etienne: De L'Aube, 1995.

Government of Canada. Criminal Code (R.S.C., 1985, c. C-46), amended on March 17, 2021. https://laws-lois.justice.gc.ca/eng/acts/C-46/section-319.html.

Hicks, Stephen R. C. *Explaining Postmodernism: Skepticism and Socialism from Rousseau to Foucault*. Milwaukee: Scholargy Publishing, 2004.

Hopper, Tristin. "Here's the full recording of Wilfrid Laurier reprimanding Lindsay Shepherd for showing a Jordan Peterson video." *National Post*, November 20, 2017. https://nationalpost.com/news/canada/heres-the-full-recording-of-wilfrid-laurier-reprimanding-lindsay-shepherd-for-showing-a-jordan-peterson-video.

Janus, Andrew. "Ontario to create 'safe access zones' around abortion clinics with new legislation." *CBC News*, October 7, 2017. https://www.cbc.ca/news/canada/toronto/safe-access-zones-1.4329367.

Maritain, Jacques. *The Social and Political Philosophy of Jacques Maritain Selected*

27 Maritain, *The Social and Political Philosophy of Jacques Maritain*, 88.

Readings, edited by Joseph W. Evans and Leo R. Ward. New York: Image Books, 1965.

Pardy, Bruce. "Law society's new policy compels speech, crossing line that must not be crossed." *National Post*, October 3, 2017. http://nationalpost.com/opinion/bruce-pardy-law-societys-new-policy-compels-speech-crossing-line-that-must-not-be-crossed.

———. "Meet the new 'human rights'—where you are forced by law to use 'reasonable' pronouns." *National Post*, June 19, 2017. https://nationalpost.com/opinion/bruce-pardy-meet-the-new-human-rights-where-you-are-forced-by-law-to-use-reasonable-pronouns-like-ze-and-zer.

Patent Trending. "Jordan Peterson owns smug professor." YouTube video, June 3, 2017. https://www.youtube.com/watch?v=EUTuSia3eCE.

Peterson, Jordan B. "Update: Law Society of Ontario Compelled Speech." YouTube video, November 2, 2017. https://www.youtube.com/watch?v=FPpPnGA8rkQ.

Plomin, R. and I. J. Deary. "Genetics and intelligence differences: five special findings." *Mol Psychiatry* 20, 98–108 (2015). https://doi.org/10.1038/mp.2014.105.

Rebello, Luke. "Canadians Didn't Sign Up for Trudeau's Scandals and Bad Policies." *Huffpost Canada*, January 9, 2017. https://www.huffingtonpost.ca/luke-rebello/justin-trudeau-broken-promises_b_13900284.html.

Saad, Gad. "My Chat with Laurier TA Lindsay Shepherd." *The Saad Truth* episode 551, YouTube video, November 27, 2017. https://www.youtube.com/watch?v=ZwUMk8DtuQ0.

Shepherd, Lindsay. *Diversity and Exclusion: Confronting the Campus Free Speech Crisis*. Canada: Magna Carta, 2021.

———. Twitter post, November 21, 2017, 2:41 P.M. https://twitter.com/NewWorldHominin/status/933057922875166720.

Steeper33. "Scheer Condemns Wilfrid Laurier University's Egregious Actions." YouTube video, November 23, 2017. https://www.youtube.com/watch?v=CG5OlzzHiuw.

Sweetman, Brendan. "The Deconstruction of Western Metaphysics: Derrida and Maritain on Identity." In *Postmodernism and Christian Philosophy*, edited by Roman Ciapalo. Washington, DC: Catholic University of America Press, 1997.

Steve Paikin. "Genders, Rights and Freedom of Speech." *The Agenda with Steve Paikin*, October 26, 2016. https://www.youtube.com/watch?v=kasiov0ytEc.

The Law Society of Ontario. "Statement of Principles." https://obiter-dicta.ca/2019/09/24/the-lso-repeals-its-statement-of-principles-requirement/#:~:text=In%20its%20original%20form%2C%20the,clients%20and%20the%20public.%E2%80%9D%20A.

Wilfried Laurier University. Governance and Leadership– 12.4: The Prevention of Sexual Violence Policy and Procedures. https://www.wlu.ca/about/

governance/assets/resources/12.4-gendered-and-sexual-violence-policy-and-procedures.html.

Woodward, Ashley. "Jean-François Lyotard (1924–1998)." *Internet Encyclopedia of Philosophy*. https://iep.utm.edu/lyotard/.

Chapter 35

On Peterson's Revoked Fellowship to Cambridge Divinity School[1]

Scott D. G. Ventureyra

In March of 2019, Jordan Peterson[2] had his fellowship offer to the University of Cambridge revoked. Cambridge's Faculty of Divinity issued the following statement on Twitter: "Jordan Peterson requested a visiting fellowship at the Faculty of Divinity, and an initial offer has been rescinded after a further review."[3] However, Peterson was quick to point out on his blog that this claim was a half-truth, since the visiting fellowship had been discussed with faculty members before he submitted his formal request.[4] A spokesperson gave *The Guardian* a blanket statement as to why Peterson was disinvited: "[Cambridge] is an inclusive environment and we expect all our staff and visitors to uphold our principles. There is no place here for anyone who cannot."[5]

Why the Revocation?

Before learning about Cambridge's "official" reason for disinviting Peterson, I considered a number of potential reasons. I wondered if it could be his hard stance against the toxic leftist ideologies that are antithetical to the tradition of Western civilization and its Christian roots. The ideologies I'm referring to include Neo-Marxism, postmodernism, radical feminism, and gender ideology. Could it be the unsubstantiated accusations that he rubs shoulders with the alt-right? What about his stated refusal to use gender-neutral pronouns? Could it be a lack of scholarship? Ignorant commentators on Twitter have suggested this, but

1 For the original see "On Peterson's Revoked Fellowship to Cambridge Divinity School," *Crisis Magazine*, March 27, 2019, https://www.crisismagazine.com/2019/on-petersons-revoked-fellowship-to-cambridge-divinity-school.

2 See Ventureyra, "Canada's Boldest Professor Defies the Gender Police," for an introduction to Peterson's opposition to mandated speech and gender-neutral pronouns.

3 Cambridge Faculty of Divinity, Twitter post.

4 Peterson, "Cambridge University Rescinds My Fellowship."

5 Marsh, "Cambridge University rescinds Jordan Peterson invitation."

the facts discredit their claims: Peterson's academic work is highly cited, and he is a respected authority on personality, social conflict, the psychology of religion, and the effects of alcohol on the brain. Google Scholar shows that he has over 11,000 citations and an h-index of 52.[6] It would be reasonable to think that the Faculty of Divinity might have a particular interest in Peterson's thoughts on the psychology of the various biblical narratives. His online biblical lectures on the "The Psychological Significance of the Biblical Stories" have had millions of views, with close to 10 million for the first lecture in this series alone.[7]

He is also highly sympathetic to the plight of young men suffering from social pathologies largely due to a lack of moral guidance and encouragement. Moreover, his work and talks have been highly transformative for thousands of people throughout the world. I asked myself: how could Cambridge object to good scholarship, provocative lectures, and helping people? Moreover, in November of 2018, Peterson delivered a lecture for the largest student society at Cambridge, a famous debating forum called the Cambridge Union. The lecture was well received and generated thoughtful discussion.

Finally, I wondered if it could be the picture that had recently surfaced of him posing with a fan sporting a "Proud Islamophobe" t-shirt. Below the title is a list of immoral acts committed by some Muslims. The picture spread quite rapidly after the tragic and horrifying massacre upwards of 50 Muslims peacefully worshipping in a mosque in Christchurch, New Zealand. By odd coincidence, a day after Cambridge revoked its invitation, Whitcoulls, New Zealand's largest book franchise, temporarily withdrew Peterson's *12 Rules for Life: An Antidote to Chaos*—an odd thing to do for a book that promotes moral responsibility and nowhere advocates violence.[8] And yet they carry undeniably objectionable books like Adolf Hitler's *Mein Kampf.* It turns out that this was the reason for the revocation given by the vice chancellor of the Faculty of Divinity, Stephen J. Toope. He stated: "Early last week, the Faculty became aware of a photograph of Professor Peterson posing with his arm around a man wearing a T-shirt that clearly bore the slogan 'I'm a proud Islamophobe.' The casual endorsement by association of this message was thought to be antithetical to the work of a Faculty that prides itself in the advancement of inter-faith understanding."[9]

One could argue that since Peterson often takes pictures with over a hundred people per lecture and thousands throughout his speaking tours, he didn't notice it. Still, one could conversely argue that the photographer or

6 Peterson, Google Scholar page.

7 Peterson, "The Psychological Significance of the Biblical Stories."

8 Crowe, "New Zealand Retailer Pulls Jordan Peterson Book after Mosque Shootings."

9 Toope, "Rescindment of visiting fellowship | statement from Vice-Chancellor Professor Stephen J Toope."

others on his team could have said something. Nevertheless, even if Peterson did consciously note the shirt, does that mean he endorses the messages on every piece of clothing worn by those he meets? Could a noted champion of free speech justifiably refuse to be seen with someone merely over a different point of view? And does the message on the shirt necessarily call for hatred or legal discrimination against all Muslims? I don't think it does. The term on the shirt is being used in an ironic way to suggest that his fear or "phobia" of Islam is not irrational. Is opposition to the immoral behaviour of some Muslims necessarily irrational? It would be unfair to paint too broadly. Not all forms of Islam are the same. For instance, I do not think most sensible people would fear the Ahmadis. The Ahmadiyya Islamic sect is a very peaceful version of Islam. However, many Muslims consider this sect to be heretical because it does not accept that Mohammed was the last prophet. But what about Wahhabi Islam? This form of Islam is antithetical to core Western values. Would fear of this brand of Islam be irrational? I think not. But you can't expect to find such distinctions on a t-shirt. Nor would such distinctions satisfy Peterson's critics. Furthermore, Muslims do not have a monolithic view of Peterson. Take for instance what one self-described devout Muslim on Reddit said about Peterson:

> Hi Dr Peterson, I pray you and your family are well.
>
> I am a devout Muslim and I would like to say that I am a big fan. I loved your book '12 Rules to Life' and am saddened that it's been pulled in New Zealand, I think this will only increase the dislike certain people have for Islam. I've listened to most of your talks and interviews, I haven't heard any hate speech towards Islam or to any other group for that matter.
>
> Your sincerity in pursuing and speaking what you believe to be the truth is admirable and I pray that God continues to assist you in this.
> Taz[10]

There are numerous things to say here but I'll mention only a couple. The vice chancellor mentions inter-faith understanding, but he squandered a perfect opportunity to facilitate it. A public inter-faith dialogue with Peterson could have attracted a significant amount of attention, but that would generate the sort of publicity Toope fears. Political correctness is stifling honest inquiry. Amidst all the misunderstandings about theology, this is a crucial time to build understanding between different faiths and viewpoints by asking difficult questions.

It is also worth pointing out that many Muslims do not know or accept all Islamic teachings. I would argue that many Muslims who were raised in the

10 Tazinio, "Message from a Muslim."

West are unaware of many of the "troubling" verses of the Quran and Hadith (which are a record of the traditions or sayings of the Prophet Muhammad). The issues are complex, and I cannot do them justice in a limited space. I have written on these issues at academia.edu.[11]

Nonetheless, many Muslims are leaving Islam because of groups like ISIS and Boko Haram.[12] Things are so polarized in the West that misunderstandings and confused emotions run rampant. Things are backward in England these days. Recently, a former Iranian Muslim seeking asylum in England, who had converted to Christianity believing it was a peaceful religion, had his application rejected. The British Home Office justified its decision by citing passages from Exodus, Leviticus, and Revelation to demonstrate that Christianity is not peaceful.[13] The only thing that the Home Office demonstrated was its profound ignorance of history and theology. These Old Testament verses were written 1,400 years prior to the New Testament and the advent of Christianity. They represent the old covenant between Yahweh and the Jews; they related to a piece of land and judgments regarding immoral practices such as child sacrifice. The new covenant has nothing to do with this and reflects Christ's teachings of radical altruism and loving one's enemies. Revelation is about things to come and God's future judgment; it does not incite Christians to commit acts of violence.

Nevertheless, Cambridge has not explained how Peterson is not inclusive. They have only pointed to his guilt by association. Moreover, Toope's statement itself is inconsistent since it does not identify Peterson's objectionable views—views which were unstated. Posing in a picture tells us nothing about someone's views. It is mere speculation. What is really going on then?

Unsurprisingly, it seems as though university administrations have become subservient sycophants to radical activist groups, instead of putting forward the best interests of the majority of the students. This is evidenced by the statement of the Cambridge University Student Union (CUSU) statement published by *The Guardian*:

> We are relieved to hear that Jordan Peterson's request for a visiting fellowship to Cambridge's faculty of divinity has been rescinded following further review. It is a political act to associate the University with an academic's work through offers which legitimise figures such as Peterson. His work and views are not representative of the student body and as such we do not see his visit as a valuable contribution to

11 Ventureyra, "The Psyche of the West: Christianity, Islam, Apologetics and the Human Person."

12 Talmazan, "Life under ISIS led these Muslims to Christianity."

13 Schaverien, "Rejecting Asylum Claim, U.K. Quotes Bible to Say Christianity Is Not 'Peaceful.'"

> the University, but one that works in opposition to the principles of the University.[14]

Curiously, as Peterson has pointed out on his blog, CUSU posted a tweet regarding his disinvitation three minutes before Cambridge's Faculty of Divinity did. This shows that CUSU knew of the decision prior to the faculty's posting. Are we to believe that the Divinity faculty agrees with the Student Union that the only ideas that should be allowed on campus are the ones that are already approved of by a presumably homogeneous student body? Do universities exist to coddle students or to educate them?

Cambridge's Legacy Disgraced

Even though Cambridge was rated second in the *Times Higher Education World University Rankings* this year, after last week's poorly thought-out decision, it looks like a bastion for radical activism and mediocrity. So much for Cambridge's motto: *Hinc lucem et pocula sacra* ("From this place, we gain enlightenment and precious knowledge"). Instead, obscurity and the suppression of certain types of thought have been upheld. Friedrich Nietzsche, in his 1881 work *The Dawn of Day*, captured the essence of what Cambridge has unwittingly become: "A young man can be most surely corrupted when he is taught to value the like-minded more highly than the differently minded."[15]

Peterson shouldn't be surprised at the corruption and unfettered leftist ideology found within Cambridge's Faculty of Divinity. One could say that it is the "devil's illusion" to deceive the outside world and unsuspecting minds that enter these institutions of ungodliness into thinking they are a place of orthodoxy. These once-Christian institutions do not care about Christian truth and values, despite what their mottos may have us believe. The world we live in is truly upside-down. Delusions and falsehoods are vociferously defended. If you speak the truth you will be met with derision. If you go against falsehoods and state facts about reality, you will be punished. Lies, deceit, and immorality are the law of the land. Man is indeed the measure of all things.

I'll close with Peterson's own condemnation of Cambridge and its Faculty of "Divinity," which accurately illustrates the current state and the future of many of these corrupt Christian universities:

> I think they handled publicizing the rescindment in a manner that could hardly have been more narcissistic, self-congratulatory, and devious. I

14 Marsh, "Cambridge University rescinds Jordan Peterson invitation."
15 Nietzsche, *The Dawn of Day*, 262.

believe that the parties in question don't give a damn about the perilous decline of Christianity, and I presume in any case that they regard that faith, in their propaganda-addled souls, as the ultimate manifestation of the oppressive Western patriarchy, despite their hypothetical allegiance to their own discipline. I think that it is no bloody wonder that the faith is declining (and with it, the values of the West, as its fragments) with cowards and mountebanks of the sort who manifested themselves today at the helm. I wish them the continued decline in relevance over the next few decades that they deeply and profoundly and diligently work toward and deserve.[16]

Bibliography

Cambridge Faculty of Divinity. Twitter post, March 20, 2019, 8:50 A.M. https://twitter.com/CamDivinity/status/1108352122779774977.

Crowe, Jack. "New Zealand Retailer Pulls Jordan Peterson Book after Mosque Shootings." *National Review*, March 21, 2019. https://www.nationalreview.com/news/new-zealand-retailer-pulls-jordan-peterson-book-after-mosque-shootings/.

Marsh, Sara. "Cambridge University rescinds Jordan Peterson invitation." *The Guardian*, March 20, 2019. https://www.theguardian.com/education/2019/mar/20/cambridge-university-rescinds-jordan-peterson-invitation.

Nietzsche, Friedrich Wilhelm. *The Dawn of Day.* Translated by John McFarland Kennedy. New York: The Macmillan Company, 1911.

Peterson, Jordan B. "Cambridge University Rescinds My Fellowship." Blog entry, March 20, 2019. https://www.jordanbpeterson.com/blog-posts/cambridge-university-rescinds-my-fellowship/.

———. Google Scholar page. https://scholar.google.ca/citations?user=wL1F22UAAAAJ&hl=en&oi=ao.

———. "The Psychological Significance of the Biblical Stories: 15-Part Lecture series by Dr. Jordan B. Peterson." https://www.jordanbpeterson.com/bible-series/.

Schaverien, Andrea. "Rejecting Asylum Claim, U.K. Quotes Bible to Say Christianity Is Not 'Peaceful.'" *New York Times*, March 21, 2019. https://www.nytimes.com/2019/03/21/world/europe/britain-asylum-seeker-christianity.html.

Talmazan, Yuliya. "Life under ISIS led these Muslims to Christianity." *NBC News*, February 3, 2019. https://www.nbcnews.com/news/world/life-under-isis-led-these-muslims-christ-n963281.

16 Peterson, "Cambridge University Rescinds my Fellowship."

Tazinio. "Message from a Muslim." Reddit – r/JordanPeterson. March 25, 2019. https://www.reddit.com/r/JordanPeterson/comments/b5fsyg/message_from_a_muslim/.

Toope, Stephen J. "Rescindment of visiting fellowship | statement from Vice-Chancellor Professor Stephen J Toope." *University of Cambridge News*, March 25, 2019. https://www.cam.ac.uk/news/rescindment-of-visiting-fellowship-statement-from-vice-chancellor-professor-stephen-j-toope.

Ventureyra, Scott D. G. "Canada's Boldest Professor Defies the Gender Police." *Crisis Magazine,* December 5, 2016. https://www.crisismagazine.com/2016/canadas-boldest-professor-defies-gender-police.

———. "The Psyche of the West: Christianity, Islam, Apologetics and the Human Person." *Maritain Studies/Études maritainiennes* 33 (2017): 46–77. https://www.academia.edu/36614359/The_Psyche_of_the_West_Christianity_Islam_Apologetics_and_the_Human_Person.

Chapter 36

On Anti-Religious Indoctrination

Scott D. G. Ventureyra

Throughout academia there are many thoughtful educators. There are also those who have agendas to indoctrinate their students, getting them to uncritically accept and adopt their personal philosophies.

Anti-Religious Indoctrination

Indoctrination is defined as "to instruct in a doctrine, principle, ideology, etc., especially to imbue with a specific partisan or biased belief or point of view." This definition serves well for understanding anti-religious indoctrination—the presentation of ideologies that are set to challenge traditional theistic thought and values, even when couched in seemingly neutral and subtle ways.

There is an inherent assumption in modern Western society that people who believe in God are irrational. Popular culture is suffused with anti-religious material—in newspapers, TV shows, documentaries, outspoken celebrities, and popular books. Yet there are many good reasons to believe in God's existence. Many modern versions of arguments for God's existence are defended by highly intelligent Christian philosophers and theologians. Much of this argumentation provides a convincing explanation for the origin of the universe, the existence of the universe, the origin of the laws and constants of physics, the origin of consciousness, the existence of objective morality, the correspondence of our minds to reality (which permits scientific study), and the historicity of the resurrection of Jesus. It is worth pointing out that one can be rationally justified (a natural intuitive or "properly basic" belief) in believing in God and trusting in Him wholly apart from arguments, but the beauty is that these arguments back up Christian beliefs.

It is also postulated that people who question naturalistic evolution (a view that excludes God from intervening in His Creation or sustaining it) are irrational. A great number of intelligent people, including scientists, believe that God either directly intervened or was somehow involved in the process of biological evolution. This is consistent with a variety of positions: Young Earth

Creationism, Old Earth Creationism, Intelligent Design, and Theistic Evolution (either planned or guided). Nonetheless, to suggest evolution is purposeless or unguided is a metaphysical claim and not a scientific one. The empirical science behind evolutionary theory cannot on its own answer questions of value and meaning unless coupled with a particular philosophy, whether it be naturalistic, deistic, theistic, or pantheistic. Nonetheless, the assumption that it is irrational to question naturalistic evolution has permeated popular culture.

Treating questions about certain issues respectfully is good pedagogy, whereas stifling questions through intimidation and appeals to authority is a form of indoctrination. This is what is occurring throughout North America, from the starting point of our education (e.g., kindergarten) to the graduate level.

Examples of Anti-Religious Indoctrination

Anti-religious indoctrination is beginning at the earliest levels of North American educational systems, at the elementary-school, and even kindergarten levels. LGBTQ+ activists have made some serious advances in the public school systems in an attempt to challenge and transform traditional theistic morality on such issues. Old Testament scholar Michael Brown observes that "Pro-gay books are being read in elementary school classrooms, teachers are being mandated to use gender neutral language, gay activists have been welcomed in the White House, and young evangelicals see no problem with same-sex marriage."[1] The inroads have been made into mainstream culture and even into the educational system, with kindergarten students being taught terms such as "gender queer" and "queer theology." There has also been a dramatic increase in the use of pro-gay books in elementary school classrooms, including such titles as *Two Daddies and Me* and *Oh the Things Mommies Do!: What Can Be Better Than Having Two?*[2] Another form of anti-religious indoctrination involves the conflation of the philosophical interpretation of scientific theories with scientific methodology—in more technical terms, of metaphysical naturalism with methodological naturalism. Evolutionary biologists of the highest rank, such as Stephen J. Gould, Richard Dawkins, Jacques Monod, and George Gaylord Simpson, have been guilty of this in declaring that humanity's purpose is illusory from their personal interpretations of evolutionary biology. A commonly associated mantra is that the ultimate purpose of life is to pass on our genes. This naturalistic sentiment is repeated at all levels of education, typically in high school and university biology classes taught by secular instructors.. Its contemporary formulation can be found in Richard Dawkins'

1 Kwong, "Christians Urged to Wake Up to Reality of GLBT Agenda."
2 Kwong, "Christians Urged to Wake Up to Reality of GLBT Agenda."

book *The Selfish Gene*, which contends that an organism merely acts as a vehicle to copy genes to subsequent generations via a Darwinian selection process. It is a gene-centric view; everything must ultimately bow down to the transferring of genetic information. Obviously, this in itself says nothing about the meaning or purpose of life. Dawkins himself seems to contradict this view in chapter 11: "We are built as gene machines and cultured as meme machines, but we have the power to turn against our own creators. We, alone on earth, can rebel against the tyranny of the selfish replicators."[3] This flies in the face of the genetic determinism to which many proponents of Neo-Darwinism adhere.

A third form of anti-religious indoctrination involves the denial of truth. This is common at the university level. The remnants of the "death of God" movement are still rearing their ugly heads in faculties of theology. Under the combined influence of this and postmodern epistemology, a number of theology professors have made declarative statements akin to "there is no truth." Anyone who understands anything about logic will realize that such a claim is literally self-refuting since it contradicts what it sets to establish, i.e., it unwittingly claims there is a truth, through the affirmation that there is none. Perhaps it isn't coincidental that such professors may not last too long in faculties of traditional Christian theology. Who knows what such theologians truly believe?

The concept of truth is fundamental to theological reflection. Its removal places the act of analyzing truth claims associated with the Christian faith (or any faith, for that matter) on the same level as deciding which McDonald's meal you prefer. This is made clear when such professors subsequently speak of the resurrection of Jesus as not being any "less real" if it had been solely experienced in the minds of the disciples than it would be had it objectively happened to Jesus. This position is clearly rooted in Kierkegaardian existentialism. Kierkegaard expounded a form of fideism elevating experience over reason. Kierkegaard went much too far with his emphasis on the experiential dimension while attempting to eradicate the rational element of the faith. In reality, faith and reason are intimately connected, and neither should be denigrated on behalf of the other. Traditionally the two have operated harmoniously.

A fourth and now commonplace form of indoctrination involves critical theories. These ideas emanate from the Frankfurt School, Neo-Marxist ideology, and postmodernist thought. They provide the justification for identity politics, also known as grievance studies. Helen Pluckrose and James Lindsay have dubbed these theories that have taken over our educational establishment "cynical theories."[4] It is important to realize that CRT has nothing to do with the civil rights movement, since it ventures far from Martin Luther King Jr.'s dream. CRT is inherently racist since it divides people by race. Critical race

3 Dawkins, *The Selfish Gene*, 201.
4 Pluckrose and Lindsay, *Cynical Theories*.

theorists object to such foundations of Western civilization as reason, science, law and legal reasoning. They argue that political structures and economic systems are merely social constructs founded by certain races (white-European, in the case of North America). The ideas of CRT are divisive and not conducive to any progress in democratic societies. CRT presents us with eight difficulties in dealing with race issues:

- believes racism is present in every aspect of life, every relationship, and every interaction and therefore has its advocates look for it everywhere.
- relies upon "interest convergence" (white people only give black people opportunities and freedoms when it is also in their own interests) and therefore doesn't trust any attempt to make racism better.
- is against free societies and wants to dismantle them and replace them with something its advocates. control
- only treats race issues as "socially constructed groups," so there are no individuals in Critical Race Theory.
- believes science, reason, and evidence are a "white" way of knowing and that storytelling and lived experience are a "black" alternative, which hurts everyone, especially black people
- rejects all potential alternatives, like colorblindness, as forms of racism, making itself the only allowable game in town (which is totalitarian).
- acts like anyone who disagrees with it must do so for racist and white supremacist reasons, even if those people are black (which is also totalitarian).
- cannot be satisfied, so it becomes a kind of activist black hole that threatens to destroy everything it is introduced into.[5]
- Recently, even the toy company Hasbro was exposed for promoting CRT. Whistleblower Harvey Nash, a packaging engineer who was contracting with Hasbro, exposed Hasbro's insidious agenda to Project Veritas.[6] Hasbro's employees were receiving lectures from an organization known as "Conscious Kids" about "infants' inherent racism."[7] Johnson stated that "he decided to come to Project Veritas because [he opposes] the indoctrination of children…[and felt] that more people needed to know about it."[8] Children are being targeted throughout our culture with these pernicious ideologies.

5 Lindsay, "Eight Big Reasons Critical Race Theory Is Terrible for Dealing with Racism."
6 Project Veritas, "Critical Race Theory 'Indoctrination' EXPOSED."
7 Project Veritas, "Critical Race Theory 'Indoctrination' EXPOSED."
8 Project Veritas, "Critical Race Theory 'Indoctrination' EXPOSED."

How to Recognize Anti-Religious Indoctrination

First, whenever an educator is adamant in pushing an ideology on their students as if it were commonsensical and widely established (despite it obviously not being so, such as the inexistence of God). Students should be alarmed when an educator makes such claims without substantiating them with good arguments and evidence.

Second, whenever an educator denies truth, as was previously discussed, this suggests an anti-religious agenda may be at work. This includes the denial of well-established laws of logic, which are necessary for any scientific endeavour, let alone communication. The laws of logic cannot be proved but must be presupposed; without them, communication would be literally impossible.

Third, the expounding of moral relativism, related to the previous point, which is a form of truth denial—specifically, a denial of moral truth. An important distinction between subjective and objective truths must be made. Subjective truth is based on internal preferences whereas objective truths are based on the outside world and cannot be altered based on our desires, regardless of how much we wish.[9] Moral relativists deny objective truths and reduce everything to the subjective level of internal preferences, which they then rationalize. For obvious reasons, such a view put into practice will have devastating consequences.

Fourth, the advocating of scientism—a belief that science can account for all types of knowledge. It is commonplace for university professors to pin science against religious belief and even sometimes philosophical reflection, as if this opposition were a scientific tenet. Scientists who do this unwittingly are expounding philosophical or even a-theological positions of their own. As the philosopher Peter van Inwagen says: "When it comes to classifying arguments, philosophy trumps science: if an argument has a single 'philosophical' premise (a single premise that requires a philosophical defense), it is a philosophical argument."[10]

Fifth, the relentless exposition of naturalistic (the view that all that exists are natural phenomena; no God(s), souls, or spiritual beings) ideologies while mocking religious or non-material concepts.

Sixth, the presentation and defence of leftist causes such as abortion, homosexual marriage, euthanasia, gender ideology, and identity politics/critical theories. You can also now add to the list, the incessant push of the COVID narrative by elementary and secondary school teachers. I include this under ant-religious indoctrination since many of the machinations of the COVID-19

9 Beckwith and Koukl, *Relativism*, 28.

10 van Inwagen, "Can Science Disprove the Existence of God?," 41.

crisis have a deep spiritual aspect which will be explored in Part VI—ones that I argue pose a series of challenges to traditional monotheism if scrutinized closely, especially Christianity. The obsession with school boards over anything related to COVID has been approached with religious like fervor. Teachers and schools propagandize mask-wearing, physical distancing, and promote the COVID-19 vaccines as lifesaving without ever presenting a balanced view of their risks. It should come as no surprise that the Ontario Teachers' Pension Plan (a pension fund company) has strong ties to the World Economic Forum, an organization vested in using COVID-19 as a pretext for the Great Reset.[11] If your child is exposed to this at a young age, approach the teacher and the school administration.

How to Counteract Such Indoctrination

There exists a wealth of resources to counteract each of these methods of anti-religious indoctrination.[12] It is important to read as widely as possible from differing viewpoints on issues pertaining to truth, relativism, the existence of God, religion, evolution, creation, abortion, euthanasia, the LGTBQ+ movement, the COVID-19 single narrative, and science in general in order to gain a nuanced and balanced perspective. It is vital to understand what you stand for and what you stand against. This is a proper first step in countering attacks against what you believe.

Students can challenge indoctrination by asking their professors simple but logical questions. Greg Koukl refers to this as the Colombo tactic: "[going] on the offensive in an inoffensive way by using carefully selected questions to productively advance the conversation. Simply put, never make a statement, at least at first, when a question will do the job."[13] By doing this one can gather more information or simply reveal inconsistencies and leaps in logic. Just one or two questions might suffice to get the instructor and the students thinking. For

11 World Economic Forum, Ontario Teachers' Pension Plan.

12 For literature on philosophical arguments for God`s existence I would recommend authors such as William Lane Craig, Norman Geisler, J. P. Moreland, Richard Swinburne, Alvin Plantinga, and Stuart Hackett. For literature on Intelligent Design, I would suggest William A. Dembski, Stephen C. Meyer, Michael Denton, and Michael Behe. In the camp of theistic evolution, one could read Francis Collins, Kenneth Miller, and Simon Conway Morris. In order to understand Neo-Darwinism, one should look at books by Richard Dawkins, Daniel Dennett, and Michael Ruse. An interesting appraisal of alternative theories to evolution is by Thomas Fowler and Daniel Kuebler: *The Evolution Controversy*. For apologetic-type books, have a look at Phillip E. Johnson, Michael L. Brown, and Gregory Koukl. For those who counter politically correct cultural thought, one should look to Jordan Peterson, Peter Kreeft, James Lindsay, Thomas Sowell, and Dinesh D'Souza.

13 Koukl, *Tactics*, 47.

example, if teachers are speaking about evolution, ask them to define what they mean by such a term, since it has several different meanings, which are more often than not conflated.

Parents and older students should be vigilant of teachers who deny truth: if they are consistent in this, they will not be able to discern the difference between the grades A and F. I believe it is absolutely important for students to question teachers (in a respectful manner) when they present unwarranted conclusions. The implications are great if such conclusions remain unchallenged. Why should a democratic society remain silent about the anti-religious indoctrination of students in the schools we fund through our tax dollars? Equipping young minds to ask the right questions is essential.

Amidst our educational systems and pop culture's obsession with identity politics—the elevation and glorification of critical (cynical) theories that promote racist ideology and sexual libertine ethics—we may ask whether all persons are to be treated equally based on our intrinsic value or on characteristics that divide us. It would be good for schools to teach classics like *Animal Farm* and situate George Orwell's message within our cultural milieu. The dictum near the end of *Animal Farm*: "ALL ANIMALS ARE EQUAL BUT SOME ANIMALS ARE MORE EQUAL THAN OTHERS,"[14] is a clear exemplification of a utopian vision for society—a parody of Stalinist Russia—something which the left irrationally longs for. Leftist pathologies attempt to elevate the once-suppressed to the level of oppressor. Essentially, nothing is learned from history and past mistakes are justified in the pursuit of equality of outcome. The common mistake made by utopic idealogues is thinking that human nature is purely good, denying the darker side of humanity—no matter the level of socialization, this side will never disappear. What they fail to realize is that the only hope for redemption is not found in the state's imposition but through spiritual transformation—freedom to choose good. Furthermore, it turns out that for leftist ideologues, belonging to a preferred race, religion, sexuality, gender, or now vaccination status[15] makes someone more equal than others. This is an obvious attack on the *imago Dei* and cannot be ignored. Logical questions can help bring this to the fore.

Nevertheless, one must prepare for backlash, since any dissent from such positions is met with censorship or even defamation or job loss. Students who counter the mainstay narrative may very well be ostracized. This does not create greater understanding and is poor pedagogy. Parents and older students should be vigilant of teachers who push such ideologies on their students. It is the first step to overcoming anti-religious indoctrination.

14 Orwell, *Animal Farm*, 114.

15 Ventureyra, "Preferential Treatment."

Bibliography

Beckwith, Francis J. and Gregory Koukl. *Relativism: Feet Firmly Planted in Mid-Air*. Grand Rapids, MI: Baker Books, 1998.

Dawkins, Richard. *The Selfish Gene*. Oxford: Oxford University Press, 2006.

Fowler, Thomas B. and Daniel Kuebler. *The Evolution Controversy: A Survey of Competing Theories*. Grand Rapids, MI: Backer Academic, 2007.

Koukl, Greg. *Tactics: A Game Plan for Discussing Your Christian Convictions*. Grand Rapids, MI: Zondervan, 2009.

Kwong, Lillian. "Christians Urged to Wake up to Reality of GLBT Agenda." *Christian Post*, October 19, 2010. http://www.christianpost.com/news/christians-urged-to-wake-up-to-reality-of-glbt-agenda-47244/.

Lindsay, James. "Eight Big Reasons Critical Race Theory Is Terrible for Dealing with Racism." *New Discourses*, June 12, 2021. https://newdiscourses.com/2020/06/reasons-critical-race-theory-terrible-dealing-racism/.

Orwell, George. *Animal Farm*. New York: Penguin Books, 1945.

Pluckrose, Helen and James Lindsay. *Cynical Theories: How Activist Scholarship Made Everything about Race, Gender, and Identity—and Why This Harms Everybody*. Durham, NC: Pitchstone Publishing, 2020.

Project Veritas. "Critical Race Theory 'Indoctrination' EXPOSED within Children's Toy Manufacturer Hasbro.'" July 8, 2021. https://www.projectveritas.com/news/breaking-critical-race-theory-indoctrination-exposed-within-childrens-toy/.

van Inwagen, Peter. "Can Science Disprove the Existence of God?" *Philosophic Exchange* 34 (2004): 39–53.

Ventureyra, Scott D. G. "Preferential Treatment." *Catholic Insight*, August 10, 2021. https://catholicinsight.com/some-are-more-equal-than-others/?fbclid=IwAR1-S_K7Ft26wqvRPgqUme0EQ2TQXDkxsn9fxzYlpaUsMsyXjNDsLS-Z0Qw.

World Economic Forum. Ontario Teachers' Pension Plan. Accessed February 20, 2022. https://www.weforum.org/organizations/ontario-teachers-pension-plan.

Chapter 37

Not Like Our Elders' Movement: The Revolutionary Monoculture of BLM, CRT, and DEI

C. C. Harvey

Meet the New Boss: The Racial Justice Juggernaut

Most people are aware that a new racial justice movement has swept the globe in recent years. The movement coalesced in America in the mid-2010s and is known the world over as Black Lives Matter. BLM is our era's largest global movement for socio-political change. The civil rights movement of the 1940s–1960s was arguably of greater impact because of the monumental legal changes it achieved, but the reach of the internet has allowed BLM's influence to spread faster and farther than was possible in any bygone era. BLM has affected a widespread shift in collective consciousness, the key to success for a socio-political movement. Topics related to racial identity and racial discrimination are now at the forefront in just about every way imaginable. Granted, BLM's activist leaders did not achieve this success overnight or in a vacuum—western populaces were primed to receive BLM's message by several decades of activist and scholarly work by proponents of the movement's foundational ideology, which is known as critical race theory, or CRT. But the movement became a true juggernaut in May 2020, after a video went viral of black American George Floyd dying in police custody as he lay in a Minneapolis street with a white officer performing a knee hold on his neck.

Floyd's death triggered a massive global outpouring of public grief and anger. For several years prior, BLM's activism had been strongly focused on generating public outrage about police violence against black people, and BLM was at the center of the protests and riots that raged in many American cities for several months after Floyd's death. Millions of people began incorporating (or increasing) pro-BLM messaging on their social media profiles and in everyday life, and institutions everywhere began implementing (or increasing) programs and policies aligned with the beliefs and goals of BLM/CRT. But a substantial wave of resistance and pushback against this movement began to build at this time, also, gaining great momentum as people became better informed about these movements. The resistance now is particularly strong against the dissemination of CRT-informed curricular materials in K–12 education, resulting in many states passing legislation to ban dissemination of CRT ideology in their public school systems on the grounds that the content is "unconstitutional" and "discriminatory."

Critical race theory was conceived in legal studies departments of American universities in the 1970s, but its roots stretch back to the Frankfurt School, a Marxist academic movement launched in Germany in 1923 that spread to the USA after the Institute for Social Research in Frankfurt was forced to close in 1933. CRT is a "lens" now used in most academic disciplines, and its influence has spread well beyond the universities. Aspects of this ideology now dominate virtually all public institutions and most sizable private corporations, and its proponents are being promoted to positions of power with mandates to apply CRT to organizational culture through educational programming and policy, which goes by many different names but is most commonly known as DEI: Diversity, Equity, and Inclusion.

In the decades following the civil rights era, the great success of CRT (and critical theory generally) laid the groundwork for the great success of BLM, a movement which has brought DEI educational programming and policy to the forefront throughout the western world. The racial justice protests and riots that raged for months during 2020, and spread far beyond America, had a profound effect on western citizens, the majority of whom were living under pandemic lockdown restrictions and therefore free to spend countless hours glued to screens witnessing the ongoing rage, violence, and physical devastation of cities. Millions of western citizens, including many government officials, responded to the ongoing spectacle by literally kneeling as a gesture of solidarity with (or supplication to) the BLM movement. Millions embraced the movement's demands to "defund the police," "end the war on black people," "pay reparations," and "dismantle white supremacy." But millions of others recoiled, raising the alarm about deceitful messaging and the socio-political danger of the movement's agenda. In the aftermath of the movement's astronomical rise, opponents have begun organizing resistance. The current racial reckoning is a deep conflict with potential for violence, so we urgently need to increase awareness and support healthy public debate about the origins, principles, and agenda of BLM/CRT/DEI. Only people with a full understanding of the revolutionary signification and implications of "taking a knee for antiracism" can properly assess whether this movement is likely to reduce racial discrimination, poverty, and violence in western societies.

A Foundation for Political Activism

Monetary donations to BLM's lead organization, the nascent Black Lives Matter Global Network Foundation, confirm the movement's incredible success: in 2020, global donors gave over 90 million dollars to support BLMGN political activism.[1] According to global philanthropy trackers, by June 2020, an astonishing five billion dollars had been pledged that year to various racial justice groups around the world.[2] Many might be surprised to learn that BLM was not registered as a charity until August 2020. The leadership took had not wanted to be beholden to governmental regulations and control. Not being registered as a charity meant minimal regulatory oversight. Donations made to BLM were funneled through other organizations with charitable status, and those organizations charged BLM a fee as "fiscal sponsors." Communist agitator and convicted domestic terrorist Susan Rosenberg was vice chair of the board of directors for one of BLM's primary sponsoring charities, called Thousand Currents. Generally, fiscal sponsorship agreements reflect the shared values of the partners involved.

BLM's leadership for years had no qualms about stating that their mission was not charitable, but purely political. Co-founder Patrisse Cullors called BLM a "power building body," whose "target" should be "the United States Government."[3] BLM was not founded to directly improve living conditions for disadvantaged black people.[4] BLM leaders believe black lives will never be liberated from oppression without a far-left political revolution. They speak constantly about the need for mass activism to force systemic, structural change. Their revolutionary terminology suggests that they see themselves as political revolutionaries. Why, then, did BLMGN leaders eventually move to register their wildly successful political-activism organization as a charity? The decision came after the rise of serious infighting and mutiny among local BLM chapters, and the circulation of ugly accusations against the lead organization's founders of fiscal mismanagement, greed, and corruption. Patrisse Cullors, who was at the center of a great deal of controversy for her lavish personal spending and other matters, resigned from BLMGN in May 2021. The political organization she founded continues to take donations and now purports to be "leaning into" charity work. None of the original founders now remain. Two new interim leaders were appointed to steer BLMGN through this challenging transition, but each of these women also retains senior executive positions in other racial and social justice organizations (some with their own histories of controversy),

1 Morrison, "Black Lives Matter Finances."
2 Murphy, "Billions Raised for Racial Equity Groups."
3 Vincent, "'Real Estate Buying Binge' Claims."
4 Kat, "Trained Marxist," 0:32.

raising the question whether this foundation that has accepted hundreds of millions in donations in recent years can possibly claim competency, accountability, and leadership integrity.

Grassroots Unity and Collective Action

The internal disunity and disintegration of BLM's core leadership didn't discernibly slow the momentum of the racial justice movement. BLM's original leadership team of "trained Marxists" did an outstanding job applying the strategies outlined in famed community organizer Saul Alinsky's *Rules for Radicals*,[5] so that BLM *the movement* took on a life of its own, separate from BLM *the organization.* BLM as a movement does not rely on BLMGN; it is self-sustaining through the widespread embrace of CRT ideology and praxis, and the transformational power of now-ubiquitous DEI programming and policy. Anyone wishing to counter the BLM movement by pointing out corruption and dysfunction within BLMGN or its affiliates will be disappointed to find that most who identify as "antiracist" are not the least bit deterred by this knowledge. The movement is supported by millions who believe wholeheartedly that BLM/CRT/DEI represents the progress we need and provides a blueprint for building a more just society. Ideological opponents have now settled into the realization that the real battlefront is elsewhere, as the cause, if not the organization, continues to be championed by an overwhelming majority of leaders in media, education, entertainment, government, and the corporate sector. Whether knowingly or not, the bulk of the western establishment is currently throwing its support behind the campaign for a radically far-left socio-political restructuring of society. But you won't likely hear the terms "Marxist" and "revolution" uttered publicly by a single representative of these institutions.

Antiracism Is Neoracism?

The changes related to race brought about by the civil rights movement of yesteryear (i.e., increased belief in racial equality, legislation, affirmative action) are almost universally regarded to have contributed to the common good, but despite the groundswell of institutional support for the current movement, people today are extremely divided about the overall public benefit conferred by the BLM movement. "Antiracism" programs and policies are now ubiquitous

5 Alinsky, *Rules for Radicals.*

in much of the West, but surveys suggest that many people believe that racial animosity and conflict in society are actually *increasing*. Anti-discrimination legislation such as the Civil Rights Act of 1964 is now sometimes being used to *oppose* the praxis of this new racial justice movement. Legal recognition and protection of racial equality was implemented decades ago in western societies, and western nations have progressed to become the planet's most pluralistic, tolerant, and egalitarian. Western cultures that were, until recently, homogeneously European in character typically no longer feature a rigid racial caste system. Racial equality under the law and a "colourblind" approach to social harmony and peaceful coexistence have been the norm since the civil rights movement. Western nations now completely dominate the top 40 spots on indexes measuring social mobility across the globe. Despite this, the new movement dramatically challenges the status quo of progress in racial equality. "Antiracists" argue that poorer collective outcomes in wealth, health, education, etc., that exist in certain "racialized" communities are primarily the result of the system *still* being deeply rigged against non-white people. The "antiracist" position is that all western socio-political systems are essentially, irredeemably, structurally white supremacist.

Today's "antiracists" teach people that regarding racial equality, nothing very meaningful or substantial has changed in western society since the Jim Crow era. Critical race theory also incorporates intersectional theory, so it claims that since western civilization is inherently "white supremacist," "heterosexual," "ableist," and "patriarchal," our social systems are systemically prejudiced and harmful to people from all minority out-groups. According to CRT and intersectionality, racial justice requires systemic destruction (supporters use words like "dismantling" and "deconstruction") in order to reconstruct these systems to advance toward the socio-political goal of "equity" (meaning "equal outcomes," as opposed to "equality under the law"). As this is a Marxist-inspired ideology that offers up race as a proxy for class, the "antiracist" reconstruction of western society will, of course, require widespread efforts to redistribute wealth and power, along with significant equalizing or corrective discrimination against dominant racial groups. This means that discrimination against the dominant racial group, typically called "white people" (encompassing European-heritage Caucasian peoples, and to some extent "white-passing" mixed-race people), is seen as a net positive. Increasingly, these calls for "positive" racial discrimination also now include high-achieving demographic groups not always included in the "white" category—despite these groups having claims to historical victimhood at the hands of "whites"—such as Jewish and Asian people.

Whiteness in Different Colours

Although they have historically suffered intense racism in parts of the West, the undeniable material success of large numbers of Jews and Asians (and also many subgroups: black, Indian, etc.) has led class-conscious Marxist theorists to identify several non-white groups and individuals as "white-adjacent," and therefore beneficiaries of "white privilege" who are prone to inadvertently supporting racial oppression due to "unconscious bias." "Antiracists" are taught to accept that society will never be just until we engage in large-scale governmental interventions to achieve socio-political racial equity, and equity requires punitive measures against (and collective sacrifices by) individuals from groups such as white people, Jewish people, and Asian people. This apparent contradiction—that racism is a requirement in "antiracist" work—perplexes many people who don't have a firm grasp on Marxist thought, or don't know that the "antiracist" movement is undergirded by Marxist ideology.

The justification for new forms of racial discrimination is expressed succinctly by the guru of the "antiracists" (and racially conscious anticapitalists), Ibram Kendi, a professor and bestselling author of several "antiracist" books, including *How To Be an Antiracist* and *Antiracist Baby.* He's also a very highly paid event speaker, the recipient of a recent $10 million donation to his foundation from former Twitter CEO Jack Dorsey, and the recipient of a 2021 MacArthur Genius Grant worth $625k. Kendi explains the need for a new "antiracist" racism as follows: "The only remedy to racist discrimination is antiracist discrimination. The only remedy to past discrimination is present discrimination. The only remedy to present discrimination is future discrimination."[6] The irony here is thick, that a "systemically racist" society is throwing many millions of dollars at the feet of a black scholar for doling out such advice and driving western jurisdictions into a litigious quagmire as "antiracist" racial discrimination is everywhere implemented via DEI programming and policy.

Individualism as a White Trait

"Antiracism" is a collectivist ideology seeking reparations and massively scaled-up affirmative action. The movement is antithetical to equality of opportunity, meaning it's also antithetical to individualism and free will. In an "antiracist" society, everybody is sorted into at least one racial category, and everybody is forced to accept that their racial status (in combination with other identity markers, in recognition of intersectional theory) is an important piece of

6 Kendi, "What it means to be antiracist."

information to be used by bureaucrats to determine their eligibility status for programs and services. BLM/CRT is a movement demanding we return to a fulsome embrace of both collectivism and segregation, but this time to empower and enrich members of identified victim groups and disempower and impoverish members of the dominant group—social improvement is a zero-sum game in this ideology. CRT teaches that the civil rights movement's achievements (i.e., equality of opportunity under the law within the existing capitalism system) were largely nonstarters, mechanisms of appeasement and false promises that mainly served to obscure how the entire system was and still is morally deficient and designed to perpetuate white supremacy. Traditional western virtues such as "rugged individualism," along with related values such as "self-reliance," "perfectionism," and "protection of property and entitlements," are denounced by "antiracists" as oppressive traits of white supremacy culture.[7] The racial justice movement demands that we erect new social structures (a new bureaucracy) to subordinate personal ambitions and private property (individual goals) to equity quotas and reparations (collective goals). In short, they want to give communism another try.

People pushing back against the racial justice movement commonly complain that many of the traits and values that we commonly believe integral to a free, prosperous, advanced society are now under attack: individual striving for personal gain, equal opportunity under the law, the primacy of the written word, hard work, immediate self-denial toward achievement of long-term goals, a sense of urgency, punctuality, objectivity, empiricism, etc. If these continue to be demoted, this raises the question how a restructured "antiracist" west could possibly hope to remain globally competitive and prosperous enough to provide the immense equity-producing welfare provisions stipulated by the "antiracists," who view an individual's material rights to resources such as food, housing, and education as much more important than "procedural rights" to abstractions like liberty and the pursuit of happiness. It's not clear how the new "antiracist" economy will serve minority groups if the very values that contributed so greatly to the West's success continue to be devalued in favour of a noncompetitive anti-western collectivist ideal. The underlying Marxism of the "antiracist" agenda likely spells ruin for western civilization's long period of prosperity and stability: historically, Marxist revolutions always begin with a dream of a classless and equitable society and devolve into a nightmare in which a dysfunctional and mismanaged system provides a whole lot less of everything for everybody before collapsing as a failed state.

7 Okun, "White Supremacy Culture."

Not Like Our Elders

A multitude of new organizations are forming to fight the spread of "antiracist" ideology and activism.[8] Reactionary protest against progressive social movements is nothing new—divided public opinion, heated debate, and counter-organizing were also prominent features of the civil rights movement during its heyday. It's essential to note, however, that today's racial justice movement is decidedly *not* an extension or reiteration of the prevailing ethos of the civil rights movement of the 1940s–60s. Most of today's vocal opponents to BLM/CRT have liberal biases and look favourably on the outcome of the civil rights movement. In fact, critics of BLM often display more admiration for that legacy than today's racial justice activists, who are trained by their critical theorist mentors to disparage the change achieved by the civil rights movement as insufficient and sometimes even counterproductive; CRT presents the theory of "interest convergence" as a way to explain how apparent gains by racial minorities might actually serve to consolidate power for the dominant racial group. Critical race theorists outright reject many core concepts and beliefs about race relations and racial justice that have dominated western collective consciousness since the 1960s. The leaders of the "antiracist" movement do not seek "more of the same" reforms and incremental improvements; their ultimate goal is a race-conscious political revolution, which they frame as a necessary, inevitable step toward fulfilment of our human destiny, which is to construct a materially just (i.e., equitable) society.

Co-founder of BLM Toronto Yusra Koghali distinguishes this revolutionary racial justice movement from the earlier movement, most often personified by the "elder" figure of Martin Luther King, Jr., in the following way: "What wypipo don't understand is that this is not like our elders movement. We will snatch ur edges and clap back you into ashes. We will also beat that ass becky. Run up [*sic*]."[9] In a similarly confrontational vein, she also posted the following black-supremacist pseudoscience, typical of the sort believed by the Nation of Islam's followers: "whiteness is not humxness. in fact, white skin is sub-human . . . white ppl are recessive genetic defects. this is factual [*sic*]."[10] Koghali and her peers display affinity for provocative rhetoric, leaders such as Louis Farrakhan, and militant black separatist groups such as the Black Panthers. They express alignment with violence-approving individuals and groups who were *active* but not *victorious* during the earlier civil rights movement, and thus not

8 American Conservative Union; Parents Defending Education; We the People Convention; Unsilenced Majority; The Woke Reformation; Walkaway Campaign.

9 GenuineWitty, "#BLMTO Unmasked Pt I."

10 Griswold, "'Genetic Defects.'"

memorialized like MLK—several of these surviving communist elders are, in fact, working within this new movement.

"Antiracist" leaders typically reject the non-violent methods and transcendent, unifying spiritual messages of the conventionally hallowed elders such as Dr. King, who attracted to his movement an army of nonviolent protesters grounded in Christian principles such as the inherent dignity of the individual person and individual free will. Apologists for the sometimes violent and always divisive rhetoric of today's activists claim that inflammatory and hateful speech by "antiracist" activists is acceptable and understandable, due to the severity of the individual and collective trauma that people of colour experience living in a "white supremacist" society.[11] Hostile anti-white expressions are now widely condoned as a valid form of "punching up," while "privileged" people "punching down" is strictly verboten and considered just cause for personal and professional cancellation. So, regardless of her noxious and inflammatory social media posts, Toronto City Council gave BLM leader Yusra Koghali a civic leadership award in 2018, which she accepted at city hall while raising a "black power fist" for the cameras. One city councillor publicly congratulated her for "making people uncomfortable."[12]

The Toronto council's decision to appease and reward one of the city's primary purveyors of militant far-left extremism raised some eyebrows and garnered a small quantity of media coverage condemning the move, but no substantial public outcry or debate ensued. Toronto's non-confrontational approach to the unsavoury aspects of its local BLM is not at all unusual—most people holding positions of power today (particularly those leaning left, but across the spectrum) refrain from exposing or criticizing any negative aspects of BLM/CRT/DEI.

Polite society today countenances no debate over the BLM movement's validity or merits. A prominent BLM organizer in the UK named Sasha Johnson, the self-styled "Black Panther of Oxford," regularly protested in military garb and a protective vest, and sometimes led groups of activists lined up in formation like a militia group. She campaigned for extreme proposals such as the creation of a "racial offenders list" to prohibit access to employment and housing for anyone even *accused* of racism against a minority person (even if it was a race-based *microaggression*). She was captured on video screaming racial slurs at another black person who opposed her politics; she regularly called for defunding police and for political revolution; and she argued financial reparations for black people in the UK would be justified because, as she said, "capitalism holds us down."[13] Johnson was, by all accounts, a highly aggressive

11 Hasson, "White People Are Sub-Human."

12 Pagliaro, "'We are still living in an anti-black city.'"

13 Beurthe, Henderson, Tingle, "Self-styled 'Black Panther of Oxford.'"

Marxist firebrand, yet she was regularly praised in the media as "empowered" and "passionate." When she was critically wounded in the spring of 2021 by a shot to the head while attending a yard party (reportedly it was a stray bullet fired by a young black person in a gang-related conflict), Barack Obama mourned her loss to racial justice activism, calling her a "great name" alongside several venerable civil rights icons who had recently passed away.[14]

Kneeling for or to BLM and "antiracism" became de rigueur for all "compassionate" people during the summer of 2020, and failure to supplicate to the movement is treated by many as a public confession of neo-Nazi or fascist beliefs. The underlying Marxism and revolutionary zeal of the movement is rarely mentioned by mainstream media or politicians. Anyone who publicizes such information in this era of decrying "hate facts" takes a great personal risk, as dissenters are frequently branded far-right racists and "cancelled" by leftist agitation designed to render political opponents unemployable and stigmatized.

Kneeling for Black Lives

Why do people in positions of power today, like Toronto's mayor and councillors (and Barack Obama), dismiss concerns about the militant and divisive far-left revolutionary messaging of this new racial justice movement, choosing instead to publicly affirm BLM and meet its demands for "antiracist" programs and policies?

Is it a condescension born of belief that the movement is not powerful enough to actually enact or incite violence, and so a bit of appeasement will allow the storm to pass and the voter base to remain unprovoked? That seems unlikely, since this movement's success is unprecedented, and many people have already been killed, and many buildings destroyed, by racial justice protesters.

Is it because the majority of these leaders, just like today's racial justice activists, are Marxist revolutionaries at heart? Are westerners everywhere being led by pretend centrists who are secret far-left revolutionaries, stealthily positioning for opportunities to make fundamental structural changes to western social systems? This is also unlikely, as most of our society's leaders didn't rise to prominence due to their revolutionary credentials, but rather due to displaying competence within the current system—our leaders in any field are generally "masters of the status quo." Plus, it is difficult to make revolutionary warriors out of well-paid middle-class people who own homes and cars and take nice vacations twice or thrice per year.

Some are surely motivated purely by fear and a self-preservation instinct, knowing that the movement will unseat anyone who dissents. But for most,

14 Pal, "How did Timuel Black die?"

the more likely reason that they support BLM is their wish to demonstrate agreement with the idea that western society is indeed flawed and racial inequalities do still exist. They believe a declaration of support for BLM/CRT/DEI will be widely perceived simply as a declaration of support for ideals of equality, fairness, and justice. In other words, today's leaders typically view BLM's activism as an extension of the civil rights movement and believe that reforming certain aspects of society according to "antiracist" demands will result in a net positive. Perhaps they calculate that the more extreme, anti-white, and militantly Marxist rhetoric will recede as reforms designed to increase racial equity are enacted and reductions in racial disparity result. In short, they are allying themselves with Marxists for progressive "street cred," and while this position has been translating into votes, it likely isn't just an empty and cynical virtue signal.

But are such prognostications correct? Will following this movement's lead result in an improved society? Will wealth and power be more fairly and equally distributed, will poverty and suffering be greatly reduced, by implementing its prescribed racial equity policies and programs? Is "antiracism" truly the antidote to racism it is advertised as, a revolutionary cure that will lead to greatly improved conditions of life for BIPoC (Black, Indigenous, People of Colour) people in western nations? Several spectacularly failed Marxist revolutions and social experiments in the modern era suggest not, but Marxist thinkers are known to be radically dedicated and optimistic, and they are emboldened by their recent success. The "antiracists" and their allies are currently winning the culture and information war due to a winning long-game strategy that their mentors and predecessors began pursuing nearly a hundred years ago in American institutions of higher learning. By coddling Marxist revolutionaries and supporting the spread of their ideology, our leaders are playing a dangerous game that is clearly not increasing peaceful coexistence and could be leading us toward violent civil conflict.

Bibliography

Alinsky, Saul D. *Rules for Radicals: A Practical Primer for Realistic Radicals*. New York: Vintage, 1989.

Beurthe, Daniel, Ben Henderson, and Rory Tingle. "Self-styled 'Black Panther of Oxford' be hind BLM-inspired political party calls for 'Holocaust-style' reparations for all black people and a sex offenders-style 'race offence register'—as she brands Labour MPs David Lammy and Diane Abbott 'tokenistic.'" *Daily Mail*, December 29, 2020 (updated January 6, 2021). https://www.dailymail.co.uk/news/article-9085623/Leader-Black-Lives-Matter-inspired-political-party-calls-race-offenders-register.html.

GenuineWitty. "#BLMTO Unmasked Pt I: Yusra Khogali Is Worse Than Jerry Agar Could Have Imagined (Feat Sandy Hudson)." April 10, 2016. http://www.genuinewitty.com/2016/04/10/blmto-unmasked-pt-i-yusra-khogali-is-worse-than-jerry-agar-exposed-her-to-be/.

Griswold, Alex. "Black Lives Matter Leader: White People are 'Sub-Human,' 'Genetic Defects.'" *Mediaite*, February 13, 2017. https://www.mediaite.com/online/black-lives-matter-leader-white-people-are-sub-human-genetic-defects/.

Hasson, Peter. "Black Lives Matter Leader: White People Are Sub-Human." *Daily Caller*, February 13, 2017. https://dailycaller.com/2017/02/13/black-lives-matter-leader-white-people-are-sub-human/.

Kat H. "Trained Marxist Patrisse Cullors, Black Lives Matters BLM." YouTube Video, June 21, 2020. https://youtu.be/1noLh25FbKI.

Kendi, Ibram X. "Ibram X. Kendi defines what it means to be an antiracist." Penguin Books Limited, June 9, 2020. https://www.penguin.co.uk/articles/2020/june/ibram-x-kendi-definition-of-antiracist.html.

Morrison, Aaron. "AP Exclusive: Black Lives Matter Opens up about Its Finances." *AP News*, February 23, 2021. apnews.com/article/black-lives-matter-90-million-finances-8a80cad199f54c0c4b9e74283d27366f.

Murphy, Jessica. "Billions Have Been Raised for Racial Equity Groups—What Comes Next?" *BBC News*, July 30, 2020. https://www.bbc.com/news/world-us-canada-53284611.

Okun, Tema. "Introduction to the Website." *White Supremacy Culture*. https://www.whitesupremacyculture.info/about.html.

Pagliaro, Jennifer. "'We are still living in an anti-black city': Leadership award winner Yusra Khogali demands government action." *Toronto Star*, March 9, 2018. https://www.thestar.com/news/gta/2018/03/09/we-are-still-living-in-an-anti-black-city-leadership-award-winner-yusra-khogali-demands-government-action.html.

Pal, Pragati. "How did Timuel Black die? Historian and civil rights activist dead at 102." *Meaww*, October 13, 2021. https://meaww.com/historian-civil-rights-activist-chicago-timuel-black-death-age-102-internet-reactions-550725.

Vincent, Isabel. "BLM Co-Founder Patrisse Khan-Cullors Shuts Down 'Real Estate Buying Binge' Claims." *Black Enterprise*, April 16, 2021. https://www.blackenterprise.com/blm-co-founder-patrisse-khan-cullors-shuts-down-real-estate-buying-binge-claims/.

Chapter 38

How Educational Institutions Imprison the Minds of Our Youth[1]

Scott D. G. Ventureyra

Introduction

Philosophy is intrinsic to all thought. Indeed, when we reflect, we engage in philosophy, whether or not such a philosophy is oriented toward truth and goodness. This applies as much to the natural, human, and social sciences as it does to education. So, the question is not whether philosophy should have a place in our educational system, but which philosophy and which philosophical tools best help cultivate human persons in accord with truth and upright moral living. For over 40 years, Western educational institutions, from graduate studies to elementary school, have been gradually incorporating reprehensible philosophies, such as postmodernism.[2] The goal, for the most part, in the context and instance of using such philosophical thought has not been to inspire and incite the cultivation of virtues through the development of the human person toward truth, virtue, wisdom, justice, love, and good will. Instead, truth has been hijacked; virtue replaced with virtue signalling; wisdom discarded; justice replaced with social justice; love and good will replaced with a peculiar type of insincere compassion filled with self-loathing and guilt.[3]

For better or for worse, politics, culture, and education are inextricably linked to one another; each informs the other. For example, education shapes culture; politicians implement educational policies and curricula; and educational institutes influence politics and politicians. In Canada, we do not have to look any further than the one who holds the highest office to see the direct influence

1 This chapter is based on a presentation that was delivered for a conference titled"Is Philosophy at a Crossroads in Education?" hosted by the Canadian Jacques Maritain Association on November 16–17, 2018, at the Dominican University College in Ottawa, Canada. The original title of the presentation was "Which Philosophy? Truth, the Human Person and the 2015 Ontario Health and Physical Education Curriculum."

2 See Hicks, *Explaining Postmodernism.*

3 Denigration of young males, white Christian males, white people, etc.

of, for instance, social justice policies coupled with the power to enact these ideas that are set forth by educational think tanks. Unfortunately, our Prime Minister, Justin Trudeau, is the embodiment of Protagoras's beast[4] and the incarnation of Jacques Derrida's deconstructionist experiment. We could also simply use the words of Professor Jordan Peterson to describe him: "an utter disaster" and a "weasel," or even a term I coined myself: postmodernism's poster-boy. We can expect no less from the minions in his cabinet, who, for instance, all agree that terminating an innocent unborn human life is worth their salaries—since all potential Liberal candidates who are pro-life were banned from his cabinet. Social conservatives should be up in arms about the salaries that have been stolen from the backs of honest, decent, and hard-working Canadians who are made complicit in such crimes against humanity with their tax dollars. Nor can we expect any less from the media, which incessantly spouts blatant #FakeNews and doubles down on the falsities of Liberals—it is as if no one has caught on yet.[5] What about the teachers who roll in the mire of pernicious ideologies which pollute the minds of future educators and contributing members of our society? Indeed, it will be a herculean task to restore education and the decadent culture it is rooted in to truth. Education in Canada, and especially in Ontario, has moved past the crossroads Jacques Maritain spoke of in, *Education At the Crossroads*, written during World War II and published in 1943. Unfortunately, if we do not make our best efforts to reverse it, truth-oriented education will fall into nether regions where Jacques Derrida, Michel Foucault, Jean-Francois Lyotard, Karl Marx, and Andrea Dworkin are consoling one another.[6]

What I'm about to discuss may be considered inflammatory to some. Please note that I'm not saying that all instructors have been corrupted or that all courses and teaching methods at the elementary, secondary, and university level are vain. Indeed, there are plenty of good teachers out there; some present here today and some who teach at this college and other institutions in Ottawa and throughout the world. That is not my point; I acknowledge that. My issue is with the underlying philosophy which seeks to implant radical activist ideas in unsuspecting students, coupled with the disdain for Western civilization and

4 For an interesting take on such an idea, see Robson, "Trudeau's lucky he's a relativist—he's decided his own failures don't matter"; Craig, "Canada and Postmodernism's Poster Boy."

5 The *Ottawa Citizen* and *Globe and Mail* alleging that the criticisms leveled against George Soros are about his Jewish roots rather than his globalist agenda; that Hillary Clinton's loss to Donald Trump was due to misogyny, instead of the obvious—her being the worst and most corrupt presidential candidate in American history; that any opposition to mass illegal immigration is based on racism and xenophobia; that the video of CNN reporter Jim Acosta forcing down an intern's hand and not relinquishing the mic was doctored—instead of focusing on his reprehensible behaviour and refusal to accept that President Trump had answered his questions.

6 To paraphrase philosopher David Berlinski's opening statement on *Firing Line*, December 4, 1997, in reference to Darwin, Marx, and Freud: https://www.youtube.com/watch?v=ITqiIQu-fbA.

democratic institutions, the denial of truth, and the use of science to serve their activist agenda; the politicizing of science through the poison of political correctness; the stifling of free speech; and finally, the various components of the sex-ed component of the physical and health-ed curriculum which deny science and smuggle in subtle age-inappropriate information, thus planting dangerous seeds in young minds—all of which ultimately denigrate the human person and spirit, through a rather sinister and Machiavellian plan.

Gathering insights from Maritain and his philosophy of education and his emphasis on the true nature of the human person, I will examine the current state of our educational system in Ontario. But, before I proceed to look at the 2015 Ontario Curriculum for Health and Physical Education with a focus on a couple of aspects of the sex ed curriculum, I will discuss the current state of affairs concerning truth, and the distinction between justice and social justice, as they apply to education, politics, and our wider culture.

The Hijacking of Truth

It is well known that universities have become bastions of indoctrination (particularly in the humanities and social sciences) and that, consequently, free speech and dissenting views have been stifled. The same, to perhaps a lesser degree, can be said of our elementary and secondary school system. Have radical social activists been hijacking this system as well? Whether the majority of teachers realize it or not, these ideologies find their roots in postmodern and cultural Marxist thought.[7] In case there is doubt of the connection between postmodernism and Marxism, it is worth mentioning a thought-provoking confession by Derrida on deconstructionism in his work *Moscou aller-retour*: "Deconstruction never had meaning or interest, at least in my eyes, than as a radicalization, that is to say, also within the tradition of a certain Marxism in a certain spirit of Marxism."[8] Michel Foucault said something similar: "I label political everything that has to do with class struggle, and social everything that derives from and is a consequence of class struggle, expressed in human relationships and in institutions."[9]

Perhaps many teachers mean well, but even so it is their responsibility to acknowledge the roots of such activist ideas that penetrate variant components of the curriculums that have been pushed forward by institutions such as the

7 See Mayer, *Islamic Jihad, Cultural Marxism and the Transformation of the West* and "Cultural Marxism in Canadian Society: Ricardo Duchesne and Shawn Dalton"; Duchesne, *Canada in Decay*; Peterson, "Postmodernism and Cultural Marxism."

8 Derrida, *Moscou aller-retour*. See also Hicks, *Explaining Postmodernism*, 186.

9 Foucault, *Foucault Live*, 104.

Ontario Institute for Studies in Education at the University of Toronto (OISE henceforward), and in particular in the 2015 Ontario Curriculum for Health and Physical Education. The roots of these social-justice principles run very deep in our culture. Indeed, the whole cultural Marxist game of identity politics as being played throughout the Western world is creating an unprecedented division between conservatives and liberals.

The famous skeptic Michael Shermer echoed my sentiments in a piece titled "Another Dream Deferred," published on November 8, 2018, in *Quillette* magazine.[10] It turns out that even scientific materialists can be rational and astute observers of disturbing cultural trends. Quips aside, it is a peculiar but reassuring thing to see that some, but by no means all, scientific materialists can function as allies against the insanity of cultural Marxism and intersectionality.[11] Luckily, truth and Western democratic ideals matter to both traditional theists and modernists. This is all to say that the identity politics ploy is a game of desperation—desperation to maintain power over media, culture, and education. This is how it is being played by the regressive Left, including the Democrats down South, and here by the Liberals and NDPs; but luckily it is gradually losing political influence.[12]

Any system of thought which either ignores truth or asserts that there is no objective or ultimate truth is antithetical to the development and flourishing of the human person. Maritain's philosophy of education is centred on the philosophical and religious notion of the human person.[13] As he states: "I say philosophical because it pertains to the nature or essence of the human being and religious because of the existential status of this human nature in relation to God and the special gifts and trials and vocation involved."[14] This is precisely

10 I have argued similarly in my piece I wrote earlier that year on Martin Luther King, Jr. (a modified version of which is included in this volume); see Ventureyra, "Sweeping up Martin Luther King's Dream."

11 Just think of Jordan B. Peterson (although very elusive and ambiguous about his worldview), Gad Saad, Johnathan Haidt, and at the odd times Steven Pinker. Although Pinker misinterprets the rise of nationalism in his latest book: *Enlightenment Now: The Case for Reason, Science, Humanism, and Progress*, with "white" populism as a distortion of the Enlightenment, as Ricardo Duchesne observes: "Pinker identifies nationalists, populists, Trump supporters, and the Alt Right as the biggest 'enemy' of the Enlightenment ideals of science, reason, and humanism… [However,] it is Pinker who is the enemy of the ideals of the Enlightenment, misinterpreting these ideals as if they were projects for the creation of a race-mixed humanity on European lands." See Duchesne, "Steven Pinker's Anti-Enlightenment Attack on White Identitarians," 49–68.

12 See Turley, *The New Nationalism*; Tucker Carlson, *Ship of Fools*. Consider the victory of Doug Ford in Ontario as the leader of the Ontario Progressive Conservative Party, François Legault's victory with the Quebec Coalition Avenir Québec (CAQ) party, both winning majorities in their respective provinces; and Blaine Higgs' victory as the Progressive Conservative leader in New Brunswick with a minority government. For an assessment of the gradual changing political landscape in Canada, see Craig, "The Dramatic Rejection of Liberal Politics in Canada."

13 Ibarra, *Maritain, Religion and Education*, 83.

14 Maritain, *Education at the Crossroads*, 6.

why Jordan Peterson's message of timeless truths such as moral responsibility has resonated so deeply within the minds and hearts of many, particularly young men—something that I believe Maritain would wholeheartedly endorse, although in a much more theological cast centred than Peterson allows.

Progressivism (or what should be more accurately be labelled a regressive mentality, or regressivism) has ultimately ignored the intrinsic value of the human person. The great University of Chicago professor Alan Bloom, in his 1987 book *The Closing of the American Mind*, diagnosed a deep malaise afflicting the educational systems of his time, where students, however incoherently, rejected absolute truth. These students, at the hands of their indoctrinating professors, have come to believe that "the study of history and of culture teaches that all the world was mad in the past; men always thought they were right, and that led to wars, persecutions, slavery, xenophobia, racism, and chauvinism. The point is not to correct the mistakes and really be right; rather it is not to think you are right at all."[15]

Bloom pinpoints two key aspects of postmodernism: historical revisionism and relativism. These represent the epitome of doublethink demonstrated by the social justice mob of today who will signal to their own moral virtue and condemn what they deem as morally reprehensible, while claiming there is no ultimate truth. It reminds me of a conversation I had with a former friend a couple of years ago, an unassuming Marxist who for many years genuflected at the altar of Noam Chomsky;[16] who at the beginning of our get-together began by claiming that life has no ultimate meaning and that we do not possess any objective moral values and duties, then hours later as our conversation progressed to other issues, such as immigration, went on to assert that we have a moral duty to help refugees. I couldn't let this contradiction escape him. He didn't realize he was making two mutually exclusive claims. On the one hand, he affirmed a nihilistic outlook, and on the other hand, he affirmed objective moral responsibilities. You can't have it both ways. Of course, this wasn't the only appalling contradiction; the other was his adherence to socialism while living and reaping the benefits of capitalism, like the social justice warrior who tweets about the perils of the patriarchy and capitalism on the latest iPhone model. The historical and philosophical ignorance of these people is nothing short of breathtaking. My former friend, instead of engaging in debate or acknowledging his missteps, became indignant and stormed out of the bar. Sadly, we have not interacted face-to-face since then. Unfortunately, he is a victim of a culture and educational system that have utterly failed him. When the belief in absolute

15 Bloom, *Closing of the American Mind*, 26.

16 For a closer glimpse at some of Chomsky's views, see Wilson's interview with Noam Chomsky, "Noam Chomsky: The Kind of Anarchism I Believe in, and What's Wrong with Libertarians."

truth is eroded, so is our ability to properly ground moral values and duties. Regrettably, education as it is practiced in modern institutions in the West, for the most part, is not truly about a love of wisdom or a mastery of facts, but merely about developing some skills to seek power and money. Yet less and less, given the current climate and lack of skills developed in such programs, do the social sciences and humanities even offer that. Through indoctrination and censorship, ideas of social justice and social constructionism have come to dominate our culture since the 1960s. This utterly betrays Maritain's vision of education as "directed toward wisdom, and centered on the humanities, aiming to develop in people the capacity to think correctly and to enjoy truth and beauty, [which] is education for freedom, or liberal education."[17] Instead of this, what we have is what Dinesh D'Souza termed "illiberal education." Postmodern and Neo-Marxist educators who have indoctrinated my friend and countless unassuming students for the past 40 years or so should face some sort of repercussion; perhaps, if this trend continues, astute students may decide not to attend university unless for STEMM programs (science, technology, engineering, math, and medicine). It may very well start to signal the end of the university as we know it. It always amazes me that taxpayers are never up in arms about the pseudo-academic rubbish that emanates from these ideologues.[18] Maritain recognized well in his day that in order for education to be free it must relieve itself from the shackles of pragmatism, which overlooks the realities of what it means to be a man or awoman. The stronghold that these ideas of social justice have had over educators, the government, culture, and educational institutions since then is even worse.[19] The primacy of truth cannot be denied, and Maritain knew well that there cannot be any true human flourishing without it.[20] As Luz Ibarra states:

> Truth does not depend on us, but on what it is; it is not a set of ready-made formulas to be recorded passively. Truth is an infinite realm whose wholeness infinitely transcends our powers of perception, and whose

17 Maritain, *The Education of Man*, 69.

18 Just as a quick example, take the persecution of Lindsay Shepherd at Wilfrid Laurier University, who was severely reprimanded for showing a clip of Jordan Peterson on Steve Paikin's TVO show *The Agenda* to students. The two professors who led this inquisition, Nathan Rambukkana and Herbert Pimlott, are self-avowed postmodernists and neo-Marxists; a look at their university webpage and publication list should, aside from evoking extreme laughter, enrage taxpayers. See Ventureyra, "Canada's Free Speech Wars."

19 While serving as a government employee I saw the strong push toward diversity, equity, and social justice without real diversity of thought or acknowledgment of the intrinsic worth of the human person. These regressive attitudes have deep-seated racist and bigoted roots, even if unassuming supporters see them as a matter of empathy and charity. These are attitudes that create further divisions among people, forming a tribal mentality. The government and educational institutions rely on unthinking compliance.

20 Maritain, *Education at the Crossroads*, 13.

> every fragment must be grasped through vital and purified internal activity. If we have to define truth in the light of Thomist philosophy, then truth consists in the conformity of mind with reality, with what is or exists independently of the mind.[21]

Truth matters on every front; what we need is a philosophy of truth and the true nature of the human person, not a confused theory of social justice. In this vein, to help cure or even eradicate some of these leftist leanings, students should be encouraged to read the *Gulag Archipelago* by Aleksandr Solzhenitsyn to understand the realities of communism, or speak to the many immigrants who fled or emigrated from the former Soviet Union. When I speak to Eastern Europeans who experienced the Cold War, about our educational system and the left-wing ideologies penetrating it, they look at me in disbelief, since Marxist ideals were never in their hearts but ran their state. The opposite is true in Europe and North America now: these pernicious ideas lurk in the heart of educators but have not been fully embraced by the state, at least not in full, just yet. All one must do is look at the sorry state of Venezuela to get a glimpse of full-blown socialism at work, where the inflation rate has recently hit 830,000 percent[22] and the minimum wage has risen over 3,000 percent.[23] You need exorbitant amounts of money to buy very little; in other words, you're better off replacing cash with toilet paper. Of course, the Marxist apologists will argue that this does not represent authentic socialism, nor do many of the other failed socialist experiments. The American economist Mark J. Perry has observed that such Marxists ideologues claim that

> the perfect version of socialism would work; it is just the imperfect socialism that doesn't work. Marxists like to compare a theoretically perfect version of socialism with practical, imperfect capitalism which allows them to claim that socialism is superior to capitalism.
>
> If perfection really were an available option, the choice of economic and political systems would be irrelevant... However, the choice of economic and political institutions is crucial in an imperfect universe with imperfect beings and limited resources. In a world of scarcity, it is essential for an economic system to be based on a clear incentive structure to promote economic efficiency. The real choice we face is between imperfect capitalism and imperfect socialism. Given that choice, the evidence of history overwhelmingly favors capitalism as the greatest wealth-producing economic system available.[24]

21 Ibarra, *Maritain, Religion and Education*, 93–94.
22 Martin, "Venezuela's inflation rate just hit 830,000%—and is likely to keep rising."
23 Zerpa, "Venezuela raises minimum wage 3,000 percent, and lots of workers get fired."
24 Perry, "Why Socialism Failed."

Truth matters in economics, philosophy, theology, and in any human endeavour. Truth is vital to the flourishing of the human person. As we have seen, betrayal of it is catastrophic not just for the individual human person but for the rest of society. Truth stands on its own and false ideologies should not be forced upon sovereign citizens of democratic societies. Ideas are to be thought about and debated, not declared by fiat. The halls of our educational institutions have followed the opposite of Maritain's vision, which was set

> to guide man in the evolving dynamism through which he shapes himself as a human being, armed with knowledge, strength of judgment and moral virtues, while at the same time conveying to him the spiritual heritage of the nation and the civilization in which he is involved and preserving in this way the century-old achievements of generations.[25]

Our illiberal education has made us less free. Maritain stated that "the prime goal of education is the conquest of internal and spiritual freedom to be achieved by the individual person, or in other words, his liberation through knowledge, wisdom, good will, love."[26] We have seen the opposite of this goal being carried forward right here in Canada.

Truth and Justice Supplanted by Social Justice

Justice versus Social Justice

Truth and justice have been supplanted by "social justice." The notion of justice is closely tied to not only truth but the concept of rightness. In the classical sense, going back to Aristotle's *Nichomachean Ethics*, justice in the broad sense of "complete virtue" is only predicated of an individual person.[27] Although a complex notion, justice basically has to do with fairness in the way people are treated. David Miller indicates that "the most plausible candidate for a core definition comes from the *Institutes of Justinian*, a codification of Roman law from the sixth century AD, where justice is defined as 'the constant and perpetual will to render to each his due.'"[28]

Therefore, justice as such cannot be and is not social. A major issue is that for proponents of so-called social justice is that it is never precisely defined. It was originally a Catholic term, later taken over by secular progressives.[29] Coined

25 Maritain, *Education at the Crossroads*, 10.

26 Maritain, *Education at the Crossroads*, 11.

27 Aristotle, *Nicomachean Ethics*, Book V, chs. 1–2.

28 Miller, "Justice."

29 Novak, "Social Justice: Not What You Think It Is."

by Luigi Taparelli D'Azeglio, it referred to something like what Aristotle and Aquinas called "general justice." Going further, Pope Leo XIII makes it clear that a Catholic understanding of "social justice" is the exact opposite of what the progressives have in mind:

> It must be first of all recognized that the condition of things inherent in human affairs must be borne with, for it is impossible to reduce civil society to one dead level. Socialists may in that intent do their utmost, but all striving against nature is in vain. There naturally exist among mankind manifold differences of the most important kind; people differ in capacity, skill, health, strength; and unequal fortune is a necessary result of unequal condition. Such inequality is far from being disadvantageous either to individuals or to the community. Social and public life can only be maintained by means of various kinds of capacity for business and the playing of many parts; and each man, as a rule, chooses the part which suits his own peculiar domestic condition. As regards bodily labor, even had man never fallen from the state of innocence, he would not have remained wholly idle; but that which would then have been his free choice and his delight became afterwards compulsory, and the painful expiation for his disobedience. "Cursed be the earth in thy work; in thy labor thou shalt eat of it all the days of thy life." [James 5:4][30]

Pope Leo XIII sees inequality as a benefit and its denial as inhumane:

> Therefore, let it be laid down in the first place that a condition of human existence must be borne with, namely, that in civil society the lowest cannot be made equal to the highest. Socialists, of course, agitate the contrary, but all struggling against nature is vain. There are truly very great and very many natural differences among men. Neither the talents, nor the skill, nor the health, nor the capacities of all are the same, and unequal fortune follows of itself upon necessary inequality in respect to these endowments. And clearly this condition of things is adapted to benefit both individuals and the community; for to carry on its affairs community life requires varied aptitudes and diverse services, and to perform these diverse services men are impelled most by differences in individual property holdings.[31]

Social justice according to Michael Novak was first understood as a virtue:

> Now, a virtue is a habit, a set of skills. Imagine a simple set of skills, such as driving a car. The social habit of association and cooperation for

30 Leo XIII, *Rerum Novarum (On Capital and Labor)*, 17.

31 Leo XIII, *Encyclical Letter on the Condition of the Working Classes*, 26.

> attending to public needs is an important, newly learned habit widely practiced, especially in America. Social justice is learning how to form small bands of brothers who are outside the family who, for certain purposes, volunteer to give time and effort to accomplishing something. If there are a lot of kids who aren't learning how to read, you volunteer for tutoring.[32]

This is exemplified by the Knights of Columbus. Philosopher Friedrich Hayek remarks in *The Mirage of Social Justice* that social justice has in recent years been associated with progressivism, which in practice means heading towards socialism.[33] This reflect's the left's concern with equality of outcome and identity politics. Hayek understood that social justice as a mode of distribution was as incoherent and empty as talk about a "moral stone."[34] When we make the claim that a supposedly oppressed group is owed something based on race, sexual orientation, or gender, we deny the individuality of each member of said group, and that of each person who is supposed to pay what is allegedly "owed" said oppressed group. Such a perversion of the notion of justice is actually an injustice. In October 2017, an article titled "Tell Me How That Makes You Feel: Philosophy's Reason/Emotion Divide and Epistemic Pushback in Philosophy Classrooms," by feminist philosopher Allison B. Wolff, stated that "we know injustice when we feel it."[35] This is not only a false idea but a pernicious one. Injustice is something that is rationally discerned, using the tools of logic. If justice is a virtue, it is not a mere feeling. One may feel as though they been treated unjustly, but this does not determine the nature of the treatment. Feelings fluctuate; it would be wrong to relegate concepts such as justice and injustice to a world of feelings.[36] It's an entirely different issue to say that we may feel sad or indignant when something unjust has been done to us, but justice and injustice as such transcend feelings. Justice demands fairness and consistency, and cannot be relegated to feelings, which come and go.

OISE (Ontario Institute for Studies in Education)—Social Justice Think Tank

This feelings-based understanding of justice runs deep in educational philosophy throughout the West. It is pervasive throughout Ontario. Take for instance the

32 Novak, "Social Justice: Not What You Think It Is."

33 Hayek, Law, *Legislation and Liberty, vol. II: The Mirage of Social Justice*.

34 Hayek, *The Mirage of Social Justice*, 78.

35 Wolff, "'Tell Me How That Makes You Feel,'" 893–910.

36 Thus, Wolff is equating injustice with a phenomenon such as pain, which is indeed subjective. But equating justice or injustice with such things inevitably leads to an ethical relativism.

Ontario Institute for Studies in Education (OISE). Before diving into the sex-ed component of the Health and Physical Education Curriculum, let us take a look at the indoctrination snares of OISE—which is the premier educational institute in Canada. I will examine OISE's mission statement and mention portions relevant to our study:

> Prepare scholars, teachers and other professional leaders to be equipped with the skills and global awareness required by an increasingly challenging and complex society, ready to influence policy and practice in their fields.
>
> Discover and mobilize knowledge through leading-edge research, pedagogical and technological innovation, creativity, and scholarship-driven local, national and international collaboration.
>
> Advance lifelong learning through innovative professional development programming and capacity building for educational change.
>
> Contribute to public policy dialogue regarding key societal issues.[37]

I just want to emphasize the aspect of being pushed toward influencing and contribution. Let's explore this a bit further. OISE has four departments:

1. Applied Psychology & Human Development Curriculum
2. Teaching & Learning Leadership
3. Higher & Adult Education
4. Social Justice Education

A whole department is dedicated to social justice education (henceforward SJE). One wonders how deep this runs in the educational policies of Ontario, as expressed in the Health and Physical Education Curriculum—particularly the components dealing with Sex Education (which will be our primary focus).

So, what is the mission statement for the SJE department? Again, I will present the relevant sections; emphases are my own:

> The Department of Social Justice Education (SJE) is a multi-interdisciplinary graduate program whose mission is to provide students with critical understandings of the social, historical, philosophical, cultural, political, economic, and ethical contexts of education, broadly conceived. *Based on the diverse intellectual traditions of the humanities and social sciences, the department is committed to multidisciplinary and interdisciplinary studies in education, with a focus that recognizes such disciplines, among others, as history, philosophy, sociology, political science and anthropology in the context of social justice education.*

37 University of Toronto OISE, "About OISE."

> Our mission affirms a supportive community of learners and educators in one of the world's most diverse cities. *SJE is well positioned to reaffirm its leadership position in social justice education* by leveraging its location and strengths through: strategic recruitment of students; diversified curriculum, courses and programs that cater to differentiated models of Masters and Doctoral studies; well thought-out and expertly presented multiple modes of delivery; a supportive environment for our students, faculty and staff; and, goals that provide clarity of our envisioned outcomes.
>
> The department is attentive to challenging barriers of systemic discrimination in education.[38]

What a bizarre statement: an educational institute that is meant, at least on the surface, to prepare teachers, has instead devoted an entire department of Social Justice to indoctrinate further generations of students and teachers. The goal in this is advertised in a manifesto which uses the term "constitution" as a euphemism. Again, I'll briefly excerpt this "constitution." Section 1.4 states:

> Working within broader university and societal structures and cultures of hierarchies, *the department is mindful of inequitable power relations* and dynamics within and across the different constituencies that may inform, influence, and impact deliberations and decisions. To the best of our individual and collective capacities, *the department shall work to challenge inequities, to recognize diverse competencies, and to create inclusive space.*[39]

Section 1.5 delves right into intersectionality when it states: "To challenge inequities and foster inclusion, all deliberation and decision-making processes shall be free from victimization, intimidation, character defamation, and/or discrimination based on racism, sexism, disableism, heteronormativity, ageism, classism, and/or other forms of prejudice."[40]

A few further points are worthy of note as well. The SJE Council is the "highest decision-making entity for the [entire] department."[41] Students on the council have equal voting privileges (nine students, of which four must be present for quorum). This should be evidence that OISE wants to make social

38 University of Toronto OISE, Department of Social Justice Education, "Mission Statement."

39 University of Toronto OISE, "Constitution of the Department of Social Justice Education."

40 University of Toronto OISE, "Constitution of the Department of Social Justice Education."

41 University of Toronto OISE, "Constitution of the Department of Social Justice Education."

justice warriors of its students, who will be our future teachers and professors. The programs with which OISE collaborates are also noteworthy:

- Aboriginal Health
- Community Development
- Comparative, International and Development Education
- Diaspora and Transnational Studies
- Education, Francophonies and Diversity
- Educational Policy
- Environmental Studies
- Ethnic and Pluralism Studies
- Sexual Diversity Studies
- South Asian Studies
- Women and Gender Studies[42]

This is sounds like an intersectional utopia rather than an academic institution. Nevertheless, of all these, the most problematic (to borrow an infamous professor's term), I believe, is the Women and Gender Studies. All 18 courses are taught by women; there is, of course, nothing comparable offered to men. Would they ever consider offering a men's studies curriculum? Of course not, as we all know we must smash the patriarchy. This should be sufficient evidence to demonstrate that the premier institute for educating teachers in Canada is immersed in radical leftist, feminist, and social justice activism. The postmodern Neo-Marxist agenda couldn't be clearer. Derrida's deconstructionist utopia has been fully realized.

Health and Physical Education

While remaining cognizant of the concept of social justice and OISE's implementation of it, let's advance our probe. It is worth noting that the Progressive Conservative Party of Ontario was intent last year on repealing and revising OISE's Health and Physical Education Curriculum. However, there has been a backlash from the Elementary Teachers' Federation of Ontario (ETFO). What is being revised for is the elementary version of the curriculum, not the high school.

I seek to demonstrate that instead of looking toward truth, and the nature and intrinsic value of the human person, this curriculum and the ideology that motivates it are opposed to a true understanding of personhood. Drawing on reputable science and Maritain's insights in his philosophy of education and

42 University of Toronto OISE, "Collaborative Specializations."

the centrality of the human person, and not a social constructionist agenda, I wish to elucidate specific ways in which the 2015 curriculum betrays such fundamental principles. I will also suggest some tentative plans for a better way forward. Ideas are to be debated and reflected upon; they are not to be used as a tool to indoctrinate unsuspecting young minds.

Background on Curriculum

In 2010 the Ontario Liberal Government, headed by Dalton McGuinty, abandoned the plan to teach early grades about age-inappropriate topics like masturbation, anal intercourse, oral sex, vaginal lubrication, and the idea that being male or female is merely a "social construct," because of a strong public outcry from many parents. Five years later the curriculum was reintroduced by Kathleen Wynne and Ontario's Liberal government. This 2015 curriculum remained practically the same, except that terms such as "Gender Identity" theory, sexual "identities," and "orientations" appeared more frequently.

One of the most disturbing aspects of the 2010 curriculum was that, despite Liberal protestations to the contrary, there is ample evidence to suggest that it was written under the direction of Benjamin Levin (a convicted child pornographer), who was at the time the Deputy Education Minister.[43] He was also the former Deputy Education Minister to Wynne when she was premier. Charles McVety of Canada Christian College stated:

> No matter how it is spun this radical curriculum that teaches a lurid sex to little children is Ben Levin's curriculum since he was the person in charge of it... The introduction of teaching new gender definitions of male, female, two-spirited, transgender, transsexual, intersex is going to confuse children. If it is not changed, parents opposed will have no [other] choice than to withdraw their children.[44]

It should come as no surprise that Levin received his PhD from OISE. Levin also supervised Research Supporting Practice in Education, a program of research and related activities oriented toward building strong links between research, policy, and practice, referred to as Knowledge Mobilization (KM). It is headquartered at OISE.

Having laid down sufficient background information, let's look a few of the more controversial aspects of the sex education component of the Health and Physical Education Curriculum for grades 1 to 8.

43 Warmington, "Liberals can't deny Levin's role with sex-ed curriculum."
44 Warmington, "Liberals can't deny Levin's role with sex-ed curriculum."

In Grade 3, gender is taught as a malleable social construct. Gender identity is defined as "a person's sense of self, with respect to being male or female. Gender identity is different from sexual orientation, and may be different from birth-assigned sex."[45]

The dubious theory of "gender identity" is being taught as if it were fact. This is the notion that your identification as a particular sex does not necessarily relate to your sexual organs and genetic makeup. Gender is taught as merely a "social construct." According to this ideology, gender is fluid, so that any little boy or girl can somehow decide they are the opposite sex, both sexes, or even neither.

A good assessment of the dangers and perniciousness of the sex ed component of the Health and Physical Education curriculum is summed up by the Campaign Life Coalition:

> The potential for causing serious sexual confusion in the minds of children is very real with this teaching. The problem with Gender Identity theory is that it is far removed from science-based teaching. It is a dangerous socio-political philosophy that seeks to normalize a mental disorder. Gender identity confusion is still recognized by the American Psychiatric Association's Diagnostic & Statistics Manual as a "gender dysphoria" disorder. This ideology being foisted on school children by the Wynne government aims to indoctrinate the next generation into believing that transgenderism/transsexualism is an innate, genetic characteristic just like skin colour or race.[46]

What is most troubling is that encouraging the delusion that one can choose their own gender, in opposition to one's sexual reproductive organs and genetic makeup, is psychologically harmful to children who experience such sexual confusions. Moreover, it can cause devastating physical harm to the child as well. A number of children who may experience a brief period of gender confusion, which may have otherwise naturally resolved itself over time, may now instead be "driven" by the school system toward sex-reassignment surgery. Take, for instance, the egregious example of an elementary teacher confusing a little girl by indoctrinating her with the denial of basic biology and logic with the reprehensible notion of gender fluidity. *National Post* columnist Barber Kay recounts the parents' decision to file a human rights complaint on behalf of their six-year older daughter against the Ottawa-Carleton School District Board:

45 *The Ontario Curriculum Grades 1–8: Health & Physical Education*, 2015—revised, 31.

46 Campaign Life Coalition, "Ontario's Radical Sex Ed Curriculum."

> The lessons continued and so did N's distress, to the point of asking to see a doctor about her fears. The Buffones say in their claim that "they were concerned about the impact (on) N's view of herself as a girl. Prior to (the teacher's) discussions with the Grade One class, N had consistently identified as a girl and had not previously expressed uncertainty or discontent with her gender identity and biological sex." The Buffones had asked the teacher to affirm N's identity as a girl—that is, reassure her that her identity as female was "real" in order to relieve her anxiety. Nothing that the Buffones asserted was denied by the school or its officials, but their request was rebuffed out of hand, first by the teacher, who said her lessons reflected "a change within society," then by the principal, and all the way up the ladder to the superintendent of the school board and the curriculum superintendent. They removed N to another school, where these gender theories are not taught, and where her mother told me she has recovered her wonted buoyancy.[47]

This sort of indoctrination is nothing short of child abuse.

A meticulous study performed in Sweden over a 30-year period analyzed the effects of sex-reassignment surgery (SRS). The study demonstrated that individuals who underwent SRS had suicide rates that, measured 10 to 15 years after the operation, were 20 times higher than those who didn't. This shows that foisting an unscientific and incredibly harmful ideology upon young impressionable minds is a greatly immoral act.

Other major issues with the sex education component of the curriculum is that it presents anal intercourse as not carrying any higher risks for sexually transmitted infections than vaginal intercourse.[48] This is patently false, since the risk by moderate estimates are 27 times higher for male-to-male sex than for male-to-female sex.[49] Dangerously, it has also promoted sexual intercourse as solely a pleasurable, frivolous, and recreational activity. Interestingly, the terms "love" and "marriage" never appear in the curriculum.[50] This is a strong indication that the curriculum is undergirded by liberal-secular hedonistic philosophy. Teachers, legislators, parents, and the general public should inform themselves about the follies of gender ideology, all of which are anti-scientific, illogical, and immoral—quite the triad!

47 Kay, "When gender identity education and theory goes wrong."

48 *The Ontario Curriculum Grades 1-8: Health & Physical Education*, 2015—revised, 297.

49 AVERT: Global information and education on HIV and AIDS, "Men who have sex with men (MSM), HIV and AIDS."

50 *The Ontario Curriculum Grades 1-8: Health & Physical Education*, 2015—revised.

The Follies of Gender Ideology

In 2017, Canada witnessed the implications of Bill C-16[51] in cases where individuals are "misgendered." Take, for instance, the case of Bill Whatcott, who was fined $55,000 for stating that a biological man who identifies as a female ("Morgane Oger") is a male.[52] This has set an ominous precedent. Feelings do not care about facts: the judge ruled that Whatcott must "pay Ms. Oger $35,000 in damages as compensation for injury to her dignity, feelings, and self-respect."[53] The judge who made this ruling has discarded objective truth and biological facts in favour of feelings. The law pushed by trans activists does not help people who claim to be transgender. The law legitimizes pernicious ideas while denigrating the human person.[54] Upholding biological truth and providing proper psychiatric care for someone who has gender dysphoria (known as gender identity disorder before lobbyists pushed to remove it from the DSM-V)[55] is defending human dignity and self-respect. Delusions make people do foolish things; now we have our court systems affirming these falsities.

The truth is that for 99 percent of people, perceived gender is equivalent to sex; there is only a 1-percent deviation and these individuals would be considered intersex. Indeed, sex is binary by definition. Our biological sex and all the cells of our body are immutable right down to the genetic level.[56] It is most definitely not a construct or a spectrum as the activists and postmodern "academics" would have you believe. Humans are a sexually dimorphic species, and this fact is essential to biological evolution. The philosopher of psychology Pablo Muñoz Iturrieta has probably written the best scientific and philosophical critique of transgenderism since *When Harry Became Sally* by Ryan T. Anderson; it is titled *Atrapado en el Cuerpo Equivocado* (Trapped in the Wrong Body). Unfortunately, the book has not been translated into English yet, but Iturrieta is having an influence on the Spanish-speaking world.[57]

51 See Parliament of Canada, Legislative Summary of Bill C-16: An Act to amend the Canadian Human Rights Act and the Criminal Code; Ventureyra, "Canada's Boldest Professor Defies the Gender Police."

52 Brown, "A tribunal fined this activist $55,000 for calling a man a biological male."

53 Oger v. Whatcott (No. 7), 2019 BCHRT 58.

54 For some good analyses of the serious yet outlandish case of Jessica Yaniv, a "trans woman" with predatory pedophilic tendencies who filed 29 human rights complaints against waxologists in British Columbia (16 of them) who refused to wax his male genitals, see Levitt, "Jessica Yaniv case shows that human rights tribunals can undermine those they should serve"; Kay, "As absurd as it is, the Jessica Yaniv case has serious implications"; White, "Exposing Jessica Yaniv: Trans Predator."

55 Beredjick, "DSM-V To Rename Gender Identity Disorder 'Gender Dysphoria.'"

56 Institute of Medicine (US) Committee on Understanding the Biology of Sex and Gender Differences; Wizemann, *Exploring the Biological Contributions to Human Health: Does Sex Matter?*

57 See Muñoz Iturrieta's chapter on gender ideology in this volume.

What's more, a growing number of people identify as non-binary—neither male nor female. Jamie Shupe, a person who considered himself non-binary, was the first in the United States. He now has revealed transgenderism to be a sham.[58] Even more disturbing is the growing number of children identifying as "trans." Reprehensibly, the *National Geographic* has promoted the "gender revolution."[59] Some "health professionals" are eagerly promoting hormonal therapy and even sexual reassignment for children. Even the American Psychological Association has abandoned biology by defining "gender identity" as "a person's internal sense of being male, female, or something else."[60] Parents should protect their children from these charlatans. In Ontario, the largest Canadian province, we have pending legislation suggesting that parents who oppose their offspring identifying as the opposite sex are liable to have their child taken away.[61] This is absolute madness.

Every critically minded person should fight against this. A top psychiatrist for children and adolescents, Dr. Allen Josephson, was fired from the University of Louisville for stating the obvious: that gender identity overturns basic biology because it "neglects the developmental needs of children and relies on ideas that are just not true."[62] He further stated that it denies our knowledge of "chromosomes, hormones, internal reproductive organs, external genitalia, and secondary sex characteristics." Others, such as Canadian psychologist Oren Amitay (a contributor to this volume), have had the courage and moral conscience to speak out against transgender ideology.[63] The evidence shows that children who are diagnosed as transgender typically grow out of this confusion after puberty. Amitay has received much flack and has been banned on Twitter. The imposition of this form of Cultural Marxism on children is nothing short of reprehensible and tantamount to child abuse—with devastating effects. Some activists are even encouraging trans boys to "pack" penises for girls under age five.

Gender ideology is corrosive and usurps everything in its path. Countless health professionals are bowing down to this politically correct insanity due to fear of reprisal. Activists have demonized lesbian academics such as Camille Paglia (who even identifies as transgender herself)[64] and legendary athletes

58 Shupe, "I Was America's First 'Nonbinary' Person. It Was All a Sham."

59 See Conant, "In their words: how children are affected by gender issues."

60 American Psychological Association, "Answers to Your Questions about Transgender People, Gender Identity, and Gender Expression."

61 Laurence, "Petition calls for repeal of 'totalitarian' bill allowing children to be taken from Christian homes."

62 O'Neil, "Child Psychology Prof Who Was Effectively Fired for Opposing Transgenderism Fights Back."

63 On Point with Alex Pierson, "Toronto doctor in trouble for comments about transgender kids."

64 Change.org, "Protect Professor Camille Paglia from Political Persecution."

such as Martina Navratilova for daring to speak against the absurdity of allowing biological males to compete in women's sports just because they identify as women.[65] Women always seem to be on the losing end;[66] transgender women are breaking world records in powerlifting. Some radical feminists have begun to push back against this transgender ideology[67] when it comes to transgender women (i.e., men) going to women's prisons, where there are growing instances of rape.[68]

Maritain's Emphasis on Truth-Centred Education

We should realize by now that gender is not a social construct. This is not to dismiss the difficulties that children and others who experience dender dysphoria must endure. Gender dysphoria is a real condition that requires proper psychiatric and psychological attention. Maritain, who was grounded in logic and recognized the importance of scientific evidence, would have agreed with such an assessment and asserted that people suffering from such a condition must be loved and treated with dignity. However, such treatment should be in accordance with truth through a gentle and kind manner.

At the time Maritain was writing on the philosophy of education, other pernicious philosophies were more of immediate concern. Maritain understood that human development and flourishing were "imperiled by the positivist, empiricist, agnostic and pragmatist philosophies which give themselves as standard-bearers of the new education, while overlooking both what man is and what dignity and primacy truth, the intellect and the creative powers of the human soul possess and claim by nature."[69] Likewise, we can emphatically say that social-justice-activism philosophy has penetrated our educational institutions to push forward pseudo-scientific ideas which are harmful to truth and the human person. I am inclined to believe that Maritain would have considered postmodern philosophy and today's so-called social justice movement even more dangerous than the personhood-denying philosophies he dealt with in his day. The postmodern denial of truth does not let us speak robustly and justly of the true nature of the human person. For Maritain the true *telos* of humanity is found in

65 BBC News, "Martina Navratilova sorry for transgender 'cheat' language as she re-enters debate."

66 Ventureyra, "Perpetuating the Gender Myth."

67 Ruse, "Radical Feminists Join Conservatives to Fight Trans Cult."

68 Parveen, "Karen White: how 'manipulative' transgender inmate attacked again."

69 Maritain, *Education of Man*, 180.

Christian truth. He recognized what is vital to a properly centred Christian philosophy of education:

> Man as an animal endowed with reason, whose supreme dignity is the intellect; and man as a free individual in personal relation with God, whose supreme righteousness consists in voluntarily obeying the law of God; and man as a sinful and wounded creature called to divine life and to the freedom of grace, whose supreme perfection consists of love.[70]

Our educational institutions are acting in violation of this Christian vision and the *telos* of the human person. I cannot help but look at the postmodern Cultural Marxist agenda as an attack on the *imago Dei* through the abandonment of truth and reason, and relegation to the realm of feelings. This amounts to a denial of good and evil: if things just are, moral action and responsibility are not only impossible but meaningless. This focus on identity politics or groups instead of individuals, allegedly for the sake of equity and inclusivity, is shattering respect for the individual person. Indeed, the character and personality of individuals are swept aside. As Maritain argues:

> the notion of personality thus involves that of wholeness and independence… it is this mystery of our nature which religious thought designates when it says that the person is in the image of God. A person possesses absolute dignity because he is in direct relationship with the realm of being, truth, goodness and beauty, and with God, and it is only with these that he can arrive at his complete fulfillment.[71]

Conclusion

God is the ultimate transcendent eternal reason and grounding for all truth, where justice and love reside. In the absence of the source of all truth, we find education not only at the crossroads but rapidly heading towards oblivion. A philosophy of education that is not centred around truth is a perilous one. The late philosopher of education Mario D'Souza, a longtime member of the Canadian Jacques Maritain Association, reflected that the education of every child is an end, much as a sculptor's final product is the end of his creativity. In essence, students are ends in themselves and not means to an end, as the radicals behind the sex education component of the curriculum imply. Sexual education must be age-appropriate and grounded in science and logic.

70 Maritain, *Education of Man*, 51–52.

71 Maritain, *Education at the Crossroads*, 8.

Parents, who for the most part have the best intentions for their children, especially in the realm of sexuality, should have this difficult conversation when the time is right. If we let the state dictate how our children are to be taught on such personal and intimate issues, what sort of message are we conveying to the government, let alone our children and family? It sounds eerily similar to a Communist-type authoritarian regime. As neuroscientist and journalist Debra Soh remarks: "It brings us to the question of who gets to dictate how a child is raised—should it be the responsibility of the parent or the state? Sexual education cannot be blindly outsourced to the education system. As uncomfortable as it may be, parents must be savvy about the issues their kids are contending with in 2018."[72]

Bibliography

American Psychological Association. "Answers to Your Questions about Transgender People, Gender Identity, and Gender Expression." https://www.apa.org/topics/lgbt/transgender.pdf.

Aristotle. *Nicomachean Ethics*.

AVERT: Global information and education on HIV and AIDS. "Men who have sex with men (MSM), HIV and AIDS." June 28, 2019. https://www.avert.org/professionals/hiv-social-issues/key-affected-populations/men-sex-men.

BBC News. "Martina Navratilova sorry for transgender 'cheat' language as she re-enters debate." March 3, 2019. https://www.bbc.com/sport/47433144.

Beredjick, Camille. "DSM-V to Rename Gender Identity Disorder 'Gender Dysphoria.'" *Advocate*, July 23, 2012. https://www.advocate.com/politics/transgender/2012/07/23/dsm-replaces-gender-identity-disorder-gender-dysphoria.

Bloom, Allan. *Closing of the American Mind: How Higher Education Has Failed Democracy and Impoverished the Souls of Today's Students*. New York: Simon & Schuster, 1987.

Brown, Michael L. "A tribunal fined this activist $55,000 for calling a man a biological male." *LifeSite*, April 5, 2019, https://www.lifesitenews.com/blogs/a-tribunal-fined-this-activist-55000-for-calling-a-man-a-biological-male.

Buckley, William F. *Firing Line*, December 4, 1997. https://www.youtube.com/watch?v=ITqiIQu-fbA.

72 Soh, "Ontario's sex-ed backlash isn't about children's safety." One may ask the same question regarding informed consent and minors in the massively aggressive international COVID vaccine rollout of the past few months.

Campaign Life Coalition. "Ontario's Radical Sex Ed Curriculum." https://www.campaignlifecoalition.com/sex-ed-curriculum.

Carlson, Tucker. *Ship of Fools: How a Selfish Ruling Class is Bringing America to the Brink of Revolution*. New York: Free Press, 2018.

Change.org. "Protect Professor Camille Paglia From Political Persecution." https://www.change.org/p/support-camille-paglia-against-political-persecution.

Conant, Eve. "In their words: how children are affected by gender issues." *National Geographic*, January 2017. https://www.nationalgeographic.com/magazine/2017/01/children-explain-how-gender-affects-their-lives/.

Craig, James Porter. "Canada and Postmodernism's Poster Boy." *Catholic Insight*, July 1, 2017. https://catholicinsight.com/canada-postmodernisms-poster-boy/.

———. "The Dramatic Rejection of Liberal Politics in Canada." *Crisis*, May 29, 2019. https://www.crisismagazine.com/2019/the-dramatic-rejection-of-liberal-politics-in-canadian.

Derrida, Jacques. *Moscou aller-retour*. Saint Etienne: De l'Aube, 1995.

Duchesne, Ricardo. *Canada in Decay: Mass Immigration, Diversity, and the Ethnocide of Euro-Canadians*. London: Black House Publishing, 2017.

———. "Steven Pinker's Anti-Enlightenment Attack on White Identitarians." *The Occidental Quarterly* 18 (2018): 49–68.

Foucault, Michel. *Foucault Live (Interviews 1961–1984)*, edited by Sylvere Lotringer, translated by Lysa Hocroth and John Johnston. New York: Semiotext(e), 1989.

Hayek, Friedrich. *Law, Legislation and Liberty, vol. II: The Mirage of Social Justice*. London: Routledge and Kegan Paul, 1976.

Hicks, Stephen R. C. *Explaining Postmodernism: Skepticism and Socialism from Rousseau to Foucault*. Milwaukee: Scholargy Publishing, 2004.

Ibarra, Luz M. *Maritain, Religion and Education: A Theocentric Humanist Approach*. New York: Peter Lang, 2013.

Kay, Barbara. "As absurd as it is, the Jessica Yaniv case has serious implications." *The Post Millennial*, July 23, 2019. https://www.thepostmillennial.com/as-absurd-as-it-is-the-jessica-yaniv-case-has-serious-implications/.

———. "When gender identity education and theory goes wrong." *The National Post*. June 25, 2019. https://nationalpost.com/opinion/barbara-kay-when-gender-identity-education-and-theory-goes-wrong.

Laurence, Lianne. "Petition calls for repeal of 'totalitarian' bill allowing children to be taken from Christian homes." *LifeSite*, June 15, 2017. https://www.lifesitenews.com/news/petition-calls-for-repeal-of-totalitarian-bill-allowing-children-to-be-take.

Leo XIII, Pope. *Rerum Novarum (On Capital and Labor)*. Encyclical, May 15, 1891. https://www.vatican.va/content/leo-xiii/en/encyclicals/documents/hf_l-xiii_enc_15051891_rerum-novarum.html.

———. *Rerum Novarum (On the Condition of the Working Classes)*. Encyclical May 15, 1891. https://www.newadvent.org/library/docs_le13rn.htm.

Levitt, Howard. "Jessica Yaniv case shows that human rights tribunals can undermine those they should serve." *Financial Post*, August 1, 2019. https://business.financialpost.com/legal-post/jessica-yaniv-case-shows-that-human-rights-tribunals-can-undermine-those-they-should-serve.

Maritain, Jacques. *Education at the Crossroads*. New Haven: Yale University Press, 1943.

———. *The Education of Man: The Educational Philosophy of Jacques Maritain*, edited with an introduction by Donald Arthur and Idella Gallagher. Notre Dame, IN: University of Notre Dame Press, 1967.

Martin, Will. "Venezuela's inflation rate just hit 830,000%—and is likely to keep rising." *Business Insider*, November 8, 2018. https://www.businessinsider.com/venezuela-inflation-rate-hyperinflation-2018-11?r=US&IR=T.

Mayer, W. August. *Islamic Jihad, Cultural Marxism and the Transformation of the West*. San Francisco: PipelineMedia, 2016.

Miller, David. "Justice." *Stanford Encyclopedia of Philosophy*, June 26, 2017. https://plato.stanford.edu/entries/justice.

Novak, Michael. "Social Justice: Not What You Think It Is." *The Heritage Foundation*, December 29, 2009. https://www.heritage.org/poverty-and-inequality/report/social-justice-not-what-you-think-it.

Oger v. Whatcott (No.7), 2019 BCHRT58, March 27, 2019. https://www.massresistance.org/docs/gen3/18d/Whatcott-BC-Tribunal/images3/58_Oger_v_Whatcott_No_7_2019_BCHRT_58.pdf.

O'Neil, Tyler. "Child Psychology Prof Who Was Effectively Fired for Opposing Transgenderism Fights Back." *PJ Media*, April 1, 2019. https://pjmedia.com/trending/child-psychology-prof-effectively-fired-for-opposing-transgenderism-fights-back/.

Ontario Curriculum Grades 1-8: Health & Physical Education, The. 2015 – revised. http://www.edugains.ca/resourcesMH/ClassroomEducator/CurriculumConnections_MentalHealth_Oct15.pdf.

Parliament of Canada. "Legislative Summary of Bill C-16: An Act to Amend the Canadian Human Rights Act and the Criminal Code." October 21, 2016. https://lop.parl.ca/sites/PublicWebsite/default/en_CA/ResearchPublications/LegislativeSummaries/421C16E.

Parveen, Nazia. "Karen White: how 'manipulative' transgender inmate attacked again." *The Guardian*, October 11, 2018. https://www.theguardian.com/society/2018/oct/11/karen-white-how-manipulative-and-controlling-offender-attacked-again-transgender-prison.

Perry, Mark J. "Why Socialism Failed." *Foundation for Economic Education*, May 31, 1995. https://fee.org/articles/why-socialism-failed/.

Peterson, Jordan B. "Postmodernism and Cultural Marxism." YouTube video,

July 7, 2017. https://www.youtube.com/watch?v=wLoG9zBvvLQ.

Pierson, Alex. "Toronto doctor in trouble for comments about transgender kids." *On Point*, Jan 23, 2018. https://omny.fm/shows/on-point-with-alex-pierson/toronto-doctor-in-trouble-for-comments-about-trans.

Pinker, Steven. *Enlightenment Now: The Case for Reason, Science, Humanism, and Progress*. New York: Penguin Books, 2018.

Robson, Jon. "Trudeau's lucky he's a relativist—he's decided his own failures don't matter." *National Post*, July 10, 2018. https://nationalpost.com/opinion/john-robson-trudeaus-lucky-hes-a-relativist-hes-decided-his-own-failures-dont-matter.

Ruse, Austin. "Radical Feminists Join Conservatives to Fight Trans Cult." *Crisis*, February 1, 2019. https://www.crisismagazine.com/2019/radical-feminists-join-conservatives-to-fight-trans-cult.

Shermer, Michael. "Another Dream Deferred." *Quillette*, November 8, 2018. https://quillette.com/2018/11/08/another-dream-deferred.

Shupe, Jamie. "I Was America's First 'Nonbinary' Person. It Was All a Sham." *The Daily Signal,* March 10, 2019. https://www.dailysignal.com/2019/03/10/i-was-americas-first-non-binary-person-it-was-all-a-sham/.

Soh, Debra. "Ontario's sex-ed backlash isn't about children's safety." *The Globe and Mail,* July 15, 2018. https://www.theglobeandmail.com/opinion/article-ontarios-sex-ed-backlash-isnt-about-childrens-safety/.

ThatChannel12. "Marxism in Canadian Society: Ricardo Duchesne and Shawn Dalton on ThatChannel2 (2013 10o 17)." YouTube video, October 23, 2013. https://www.youtube.com/watch?v=9pQMM2lLMIY.

Turley, Stephen T. *The New Nationalism: How the Populist Right is Defeating Globalism and Awakening a New Political Order*. Danvers, MA: Dr. Steve Turley, 2018.

University of Toronto, Ontario Institute for Studies in Education. "About." https://www.oise.utoronto.ca/oise/About_OISE/index.html.

———. "Constitution of the Department of Social Justice Education." https://www.oise.utoronto.ca/sje/About/Constitution.html.

———. "Collaborative Specializations." https://www.oise.utoronto.ca/sje/Programs/Collaborative_Specializations.html.

Ventureyra, Scott. "Canada's Boldest Professor Defies the Gender Police." *Crisis*, December 5, 2016. https://www.crisismagazine.com/2016/canadas-boldest-professor-defies-gender-police.

———. "Canada's Free Speech Wars," *Crisis*, December 6, 2017. https://www.crisismagazine.com/2017/canadas-free-speech-wars.

———. "Perpetuating the Gender Myth." *Crisis*, September 21, 2018. https://www.crisismagazine.com/2018/perpetuating-the-gender-myth-in-sports.

———. "Sweeping up Martin Luther King's Dream." *Convivium*, April 2, 2018. https://www.convivium.ca/articles/sweeping-up-martin-luther-kings-dream.

Warmington, Joe. "Liberals can't deny Levin's role with sex-ed curriculum." *Toronto Sun*, March 2, 2015. https://torontosun.com/2015/03/02/liberals-cant-deny-levins-role-with-sex-ed-curriculum/wcm/744836e1-03e8-44c0-b10f-615c26ba14ff.

White, Blair. "Exposing Jessica Yaniv: Trans Predator." YouTube video, July 23, 2019. https://www.youtube.com/watch?v=MI_lXO7zrAQ.

Wilson, Michael. "Noam Chomsky: The Kind of Anarchism I Believe in, and What's Wrong with Libertarians." Interview, *The South African Civil Society Information Service*, May 28, 2013. https://sacsis.org.za/site/article/1676?frommailing=1.

Wizemann, T. M. and M. L. Pardue, editors. *Exploring the Biological Contributions to Human Health: Does Sex Matter?* Washington, DC: National Academies Press; 2001.

Wolff, Allison B. "'Tell Me How That Makes You Feel'": Philosophy's Reason/Emotion Divide and Epistemic Pushback in Philosophy Classrooms." *Hypatia: A Journal of Feminist Philosophy* 32, no. 4 (2017): 893–910.

Zerpa, Fabiola. "Venezuela raises minimum wage 3,000 percent, and lots of workers get fired." *MSN*, September 14, 2018. https://www.msn.com/en-us/money/markets/venezuela-raises-minimum-wage-3000-percent-and-lots-of-workers-get-fired/ar-BBNjHTD.

Chapter 39

The Death of Man: The Coming Death of Western Civilization[1]

Phil Fernandes

As the twentieth century comes to a close, we must properly diagnose the disease that has caused the unprecedented wars, bloodshed, and genocide which this century has experienced. In this chapter I will discuss the prophetic insights of the German atheist Friedrich Nietzsche, as well as the prognostication of Christian thinkers C. S. Lewis and Francis Schaeffer, concerning the future of Western civilization. I will show that the nineteenth century's death of God has led to the twentieth century's death of both universal truth and absolute moral values, and that this in turn will lead to the death of man in the twenty-first century if the tide is not reversed.

Nietzsche: Prophet for the Twentieth Century

Friedrich Nietzsche (1844–1900) proclaimed that "God is dead."[2] By this he meant that the Christian worldview was no longer the dominant influence on the thought of Western culture. Nietzsche reasoned that mankind had once created God through wishful thinking, but nineteenth-century man had intellectually matured to the point where he rejected God's existence.[3] Intellectuals throughout the world were embracing atheism as their worldview,

1 **Editor's Note***: This chapter was originally a peer-reviewed paper that was presented at the 1998 Northwest regional meeting of the Evangelical Theological Society. It demonstrates that Nietzsche, Lewis, and Schaeffer foresaw the death of man spiritually, psychologically, socially, and now even genetically with the COVID-19 gene therapy injections, see chapter 45: "COVID-19: A Pandemic of Malfeasance and Incompetence" under subsection "Is it Gene Therapy?" for Yuval Noah Harari's discussion on hacking human biology. Although this paper was presented in 1998 and refers to the twentieth century, Fernandes's assessment is still extremely relevant today, especially when we consider the human enslaving COVID-19 measures (mandatory vaccination and digital ID) and the looming threat of the Great Reset.

2 Nietzsche, *The Portable Nietzsche*, 124, 447.

3 Nietzsche, *The Portable Nietzsche*, 143, 198.

and the ideas of these intellectuals were beginning to influence the common people throughout Western civilization. According to Nietzsche, scientific and technological advances had made belief in God untenable.

But Nietzsche saw a contradiction in the thought of these intellectuals. Though he agreed with their atheism, he rejected their acceptance of traditional moral values. Nietzsche argued that, since God is dead, traditional values have died with Him.[4] If the God of the Bible does not exist, reasoned Nietzsche, then the moral values taught in the Bible should have no hold over mankind.

Nietzsche viewed existence as a struggle and redefined the good as "the will to power."[5] This was a logical outgrowth of his acceptance of the Darwinian doctrine of the survival of the fittest. Nietzsche called for a group of "supermen" to arise with the boldness to create their own values.[6] He proposed that, through their will to power, these "supermen" replace the "soft values" of Christianity with what he called "hard values." Nietzsche believed that the "soft values" of Christianity (self-control, sympathy, love for enemies, human equality, mercy, humility, dependence on God, etc.) were stifling human creativity and progress; these values encouraged mediocrity. But the "hard values" of the supermen (self-assertion, daring creativity, passion, total independence, desire for conquest, etc.) greatly enhance creativity.[7] Nietzsche considered the soft values a slave morality, and the hard values a master morality, and he promoted the latter.

Nietzsche rejected the idea of universal, unchanging truths. He viewed truths as mere human creations, as metaphors mistaken for objective reality.[8] Therefore, Nietzsche showed that, since God is dead, universal truth, like absolute moral values, is dead as well.

Nietzsche predicted that the twentieth-century man would come of age. By this he meant that the atheist of the twentieth century would realize the consequences of living in a world without God, for without God there are no absolute moral values. Man is free to play God and create his own morality. Because of this, prophesied Nietzsche, the twentieth century would be the bloodiest century in human history.[9] Still, Nietzsche was optimistic, for man could create his own meaning, truth, and morality. Set free from belief in a non-existent God, man could excel like never before. Nietzsche viewed the changes that would occur as man becoming more than man (the superman or overman), rather than man becoming less than man.

Nietzsche was the forerunner of postmodernism. A key aspect of modernism was its confidence that, through reason, man could find absolute truth and

4 Geisler and Feinberg, *Introduction to Philosophy*, 408.
5 Nietzsche, *The Portable Nietzsche*, 570.
6 Geisler and Feinberg, *Introduction to Philosophy*, 408.
7 McGreal, *Great Thinkers of the Western World*, 409–410.
8 Nietzsche, *The Portable Nietzsche*, 46–47.
9 Copleston, *A History of Philosophy*, 405–406.

morality. Postmodernism rejects this confidence in human reason. All claims to having found absolute truth and morality are viewed by postmodernists as mere creations of the human mind.[10]

The history of the twentieth century has proven Nietzsche's basic thesis correct. Western culture's abandonment of the Christian worldview has led to a denial of both universal truth and absolute moral values. The twentieth century has proven to be the bloodiest century in human history.[11] Hence, the Christian thinker must object to the optimism of Nietzsche. The death of God is not a step forward for man; it is a step backward—a dangerous step backward. If God is dead, then man is dead as well.

The comments of Roman Catholic philosopher Peter Kreeft are worth noting:

> One need not share Nietzsche's atheism to agree with his historical, not theological, dictum that "God is dead"—i.e., that faith in God is dead as a functional center for Western civilization, that we are now a planet detached from its sun. One need not share Nietzsche's refusal of morality and natural law to agree with his observation that Western man is increasingly denying morality and natural law; that we are well on our way to the Brave New World.[12]

C. S. Lewis: The Abolition of Man

The nineteenth century brought the death of God to Western culture. The twentieth century brought the death of truth and morality to Western culture. Two twentieth-century Christian thinkers, C. S. Lewis (1898–1963) and Francis Schaeffer (1912–1984), argued that the death of man will follow, unless of course man repents.

A Christian thinker should not be content with rightly analyzing and critiquing current ideas. A true thinker should also attempt to foresee the probable future consequences of ideas. In this way, a Christian thinker performs the role of a watchman by warning his listeners of future dangers (Ezekiel 33:1–9). C. S. Lewis and Francis Schaeffer had the courage to fulfill this role.

Lewis, in his prophetic work *The Abolition of Man*, critiqued an English textbook for school children written in the 1940s. Lewis found that more than English was being taught in this book, for the authors rejected objective

10 Grenz, *A Primer on Postmodernism*, 83.

11 Rummel, *Death by Government*, 9. Rummel estimates that, in the twentieth century alone, between 170 and 360 million people have been killed by their own governments during times of peace. (This does not include the millions of unborn babies who were aborted in this century.)

12 Kreeft, *C. S. Lewis for the Third Millennium*, 107.

truth and traditional values and proclaimed a type of moral relativism.[13] Lewis expressed concern for two reasons. First, the children who read this textbook would be easy prey to its false teachings.[14] Second, this would lead to a culture built on moral relativism and the rejection of objective truth, something that, according to Lewis, has never before existed in the history of mankind.[15]

Lewis not only refuted the fallacious views of the authors, but also predicted the future consequences of this type of education. He argued that teaching of this sort would produce a race of "men without chests."[16] By this he meant men without consciences. According to Lewis, this would mean an entirely "new species" of man and "the abolition of man."[17]

Lewis argued that the practical result of such education would be "the destruction of the society which accepts it."[18] The rejection of all values leaves man free to recreate himself and his values.[19] When this power is placed in the hands of those who rule, their subjects will be totally at their mercy.

Lewis also saw in this rejection of traditional values a new purpose for science. In a sense, science is like magic in that both science and magic represent man's attempted "conquest of nature." However, science will become an instrument through which a few hundreds of men will rule billions of men,[20] for in man's conquest of nature, human nature will be the last aspect of nature to surrender to man.[21] Science will be used by future rulers to suppress the freedoms of the masses.

Lewis refers to the future rulers as "the man-moulders of the new age" or the "Conditioners."[22] It will be the job of the Conditioners to produce the

13 Lewis, *The Abolition of Man*, 23.

14 Lewis, *The Abolition of Man*, 16–17.

15 Lewis, *The Abolition of Man*, 28–29.

16 Lewis, *The Abolition of Man*, 34.

17 Lewis, *The Abolition of Man*, 77. **Editor's note***: Lewis is not alone in thinking about the emergence of a new human species. For example, Teilhard de Chardin first envisioned a higher evolved species of man in his prototypical work on transhumanism, *The Future of Man*. Likewise, futurists like Ray Kurzweil, Michio Kaku, Klee Irwin, and Elon Musk envision a positive evolution of humanity. Kurzweil speaks of the "singularity," i.e., when humanity merges with artificial intelligence, as a point in the future where technological growth goes out of control in irreversible ways which can produce unexpected changes to the human race and civilization; see Kurzweil, *The Singularity Is Near*. Some believe that the COVID-19 "vaccines" which may be more accurately referred to as gene therapy are a prelude to such a phenomenon. For a presentation on related concepts see Scott Ventureyra, "Artificial Intelligence, the Nature of Consciousness, Information, Reality and the Possibility of the Afterlife," at the 2:13:46 minute mark until 2:35:17 mark, https://www.youtube.com/watch?v=72nRMkp1KBE&t=9669s. COVID-19: A Pandemic of Malfeasance and Incompetence" under subsection "Is it Gene Therapy?" for "bio-hacking" as discussed by Yuval Noah Harari.

18 Lewis, *The Abolition of Man*, 39.

19 Lewis, *The Abolition of Man*, 62–63.

20 Lewis, *The Abolition of Man*, 69, 71.

21 Lewis, *The Abolition of Man*, 72.

22 Lewis, *The Abolition of Man*, 73–74.

rules, not to obey the rules.[23] The Conditioners (i.e., Nietzsche's supermen) will boldly create the laws the conditioned must obey. The role of education will become the production of artificial values which will serve the purposes of the Conditioners.[24] The Conditioners, through their Nietzschean "will to power" and motivated by the thirst to satisfy their own desires, will create their own new values and then force these "values" on the masses.[25]

According to Lewis, the rejection of traditional values and objective truth will lead to the same mentality in future rulers as that of "the Nazi rulers of Germany."[26] Traditional values will be replaced by the arbitrary wills of the few who rule over the billions,[27] and this will "abolish man" and bring about "the world of post-humanity."[28]

Schaeffer: The Post-Christian Era and the Death of Man

Francis Schaeffer proclaimed that Western culture is now in a "post-Christian era." By this he meant the same thing Nietzsche meant when he declared that "God is dead." Schaeffer was saying that the Christian world view was no longer the dominant presupposition of Western culture. Today, a secular humanistic view of reality permeates the thought of the West.[29] Due to this change in worldview, modern man has fallen below what Schaeffer called "the line of despair."[30] Schaeffer meant that, by throwing the God of the Bible out of the equation, modern man, left to himself and without divine revelation, could not find absolute truth and eventually gave up his search for it. According to Schaeffer, modern man no longer thinks in terms of antithesis (i.e., the law of non-contradiction); he now views truth as relative. And, since he believes there are no absolutes, modern man has rejected universal moral laws and has embraced moral relativism.

Schaeffer wrote concerning America, "our society now functions with no fixed ethics," and "a small group of people decide arbitrarily what, from their viewpoint, is for the good of society at that precise moment and they make it law."[31] Schaeffer compares this present climate of arbitrary lawmaking to the fall of the Roman Empire. The finite gods of Rome were not sufficient

23 Lewis, *The Abolition of Man*, 74.
24 Lewis, *The Abolition of Man*, 74.
25 Lewis, *The Abolition of Man*, 74, 84.
26 Lewis, *The Abolition of Man*, 85.
27 Lewis, *The Abolition of Man*, 85.
28 Lewis, *The Abolition of Man*, 85–86.
29 Schaeffer, *A Christian Manifesto*, 17–18.
30 Schaeffer, *The Complete Works of Francis A. Schaeffer*, 8–11.
31 Schaeffer, *A Christian Manifesto*, 48.

to give a base in law for moral absolutes; therefore, the Roman laws were lax and promoted self-interest rather than social harmony. This eventually led to a state of social anarchy as violence and promiscuity spread. To keep order, the Roman Empire had to become increasingly more authoritarian. Due to Rome's oppressive control over its people, few Romans believed their culture was worth saving when the barbarian invasions began.[32] Schaeffer saw that America, like ancient Rome, had turned to arbitrary laws which led to an increase in crime and promiscuity, which in turn led to ever-increasing government control. Schaeffer stated this principle as follows:

> The humanists push for "freedom," but having no Christian consensus to contain it, that "freedom" leads to chaos or to slavery under the state (or under an elite). Humanism, with its lack of any final base for values or law, always leads to chaos. It then naturally leads to some form of authoritarianism to control the chaos. Having produced the sickness, humanism gives more of the same kind of medicine for the cure. With its mistaken concept of final reality, it has no intrinsic reason to be interested in the individual, the human being.[33]

Schaeffer also noted that most American leaders no longer consider themselves subject to God's laws. They often view themselves as answerable to no one. They do not acknowledge "inalienable rights" given to each individual by God. Instead, American leaders play God by distributing "rights" to individuals and by making their own arbitrary laws. Schaeffer quotes William Penn: "If we are not governed by God, then we will be ruled by tyrants."[34]

Schaeffer saw the 1973 legalization of abortion as a by-product of man playing God by legislating arbitrary laws and by the few forcing their will on the many.[35] But, according to Schaeffer, this is just the beginning, for once human life has been devalued at one stage (i.e., the pre-birth stage), then no human life is safe. Abortion will lead to infanticide (the murdering of babies already born) and euthanasia (so-called "mercy-killing").[36] Christianity teaches that human life is sacred because man was created in God's image, but now that modern man has rejected the Christian world view (the death of God), the death of man will follow (unless modern man repents) and man will be treated as non-man. Schaeffer documents the erosion of respect for human life in the statements of Nobel Prize winners Watson and Crick. These two scientists, after winning the Nobel Prize for cracking the genetic code, publicly recommended that we

32 Schaeffer, *Complete Works*, 85–89.
33 Schaeffer, *A Christian Manifesto*, 29–30.
34 Schaeffer, *A Christian Manifesto*, 32–34.
35 Schaeffer, *A Christian Manifesto*, 39.
36 Schaeffer, *Complete Works*, vol. V, 317. See also vol. IV, 374.

should terminate the lives of infants three days old and younger if they do not meet our expectations.[37]

In his response to behavioral scientist B. F. Skinner's book *Beyond Freedom and Dignity*, Schaeffer argued that Western culture's rejection of God, truth, and God's moral laws will lead to the death of man. Written in 1971, Skinner's book proposed a "utopian" society ruled by a small group of intellectual elitists who control the environment and genetic makeup of the masses. Schaeffer stated, "We are on the verge of the largest revolution the world has ever known—the control and shaping of men through the abuse of genetic knowledge, and chemical and psychological conditioning."[38] Schaeffer referred to Skinner's utopian proposals as "the death of man,"[39] and wrote concerning Skinner's low view of C. S. Lewis:

> Twice Skinner specifically attacked C. S. Lewis. Why? Because he is a Christian and writes in the tradition of the literatures of freedom and dignity. You will notice that he does not attack the evangelical church, probably because he doesn't think it's a threat to him. Unhappily, he is largely right about this. Many of us are too sleepy to be a threat in the battle of tomorrow. But he understands that a man like C. S. Lewis, who writes literature which stirs men, is indeed a threat.[40]

Schaeffer not only understood the failure of secular humanism, but also realized that Eastern pantheism offered no escape from the death of man. Only a return to the Christian worldview could save the West from the death of man. He stated:

> Society can have no stability on this Eastern world-view or its present Western counterpart. It just does not work. And so one finds a gravitation toward some form of authoritarian government, an individual tyrant or group of tyrants who takes the reins of power and rule. And the freedoms, the sorts of freedoms we have enjoyed in the West, are lost. We are, then, brought back to our starting point. The inhumanities and the growing loss of freedoms in the West are the result of a world-view which has no place for "people." Modern humanistic materialism is an impersonal system. The East is no different. Both begin and end with impersonality.[41]

Schaeffer called upon evangelicals to sound the alarm, warning the church and society to repent, for the death of man is approaching: "Learning from

37 Schaeffer, *Complete Works,* vol. V, 319–320.
38 Schaeffer, *Complete Works,* vol. I, 381.
39 Schaeffer, *Complete Works,* 383.
40 Schaeffer, *Complete Works,* 382–383.
41 Schaeffer, *Complete Works,* vol. V, 381.

the mistakes of the past, let us raise a testimony that may still turn both the churches and society around—for the salvation of souls, the building of God's people, and at least the slowing down of the slide toward a totally humanistic society and an authoritarian suppressive state."[42]

Concluding Remarks

Nietzsche wrote that Western culture's rejection of God would inevitably lead to the rejection of absolute truth and universal moral values. Allan Bloom affirmed that this has indeed happened when he began his epic book *The Closing of the American Mind* with these words: "There is something a professor can be absolutely certain of: almost every student entering the university believes, or says he believes, that truth is relative."[43] Still, Nietzsche wrongly believed that this rejection of truth and morality would improve humanity by ushering in the "overman."

Lewis and Schaeffer agreed with Nietzsche's death of God, truth, and morality hypothesis, but, since they were Christians, they argued that this would not be an advancement for man. Instead, this would bring about the death of man. Though I believe that Lewis overstated his case by asserting that the death of man would create a "new species," I agree that, apart from Western culture's repentance, some type of death of man is inevitable. Man is presently being treated as non-man throughout the world (by abortion, infanticide, euthanasia, religious persecution, genocide, violent crimes, etc.), and this trend will continue to increase barring a return to the Christian worldview.

As I see it, the death of man will involve spiritual, social, and psychological aspects. The death of man will be characterized by man's further alienation from God (the lost becoming harder to reach with the Gospel), from others (mankind becoming more and more depersonalized), and from himself (the light of man's moral conscience and his thirst for God will be dimmed). People, especially those in positions of authority, will treat other people as less than human. Man's love for man will grow cold.

To prevent, or at least slow down, the death of man, Christian thinkers must defend the reality of God, absolute truth, and absolute moral values, as well as the dignity of man and the sanctity of human life. Still, we must do more than refute current ideologies; we must also proclaim to a complacent church and world where those ideas will take us in the twenty-first century if we refuse to repent. Like Lewis and Schaeffer, we must resist the temptation to pick dates for Christ's return or dogmatically declare that these are the last days,

42 Schaeffer, *Complete Works,* vol. IV, 364.

43 Bloom, *The Closing of the American Mind*, 25.

for we do not see the future with certainty—maybe Western culture will repent. Therefore, like Lewis, Schaeffer, and the Old Testament prophets, we must call our culture to repent. We must tell our generation that the nineteenth century gave us the death of God, and the twentieth century gave us the death of truth and morality. Without widespread repentance, the twenty-first century will bring the death of man. Just as the removal of God from our schools has all but destroyed our public school system, the removal of God from Western culture will surely destroy our civilization. The death of God will ultimately lead to the death of man, if we do not turn back to the God of the Bible. Unless trends are reversed and the Christian world view is restored as the dominant perspective in Western culture, the twenty-first century will surpass the twentieth century in tyranny, violence, and ungodliness.

Though only God knows whether we are actually in the final days, the words of our Savior warn us that someday the death of man will come:

> And this Gospel of the kingdom shall be preached in the whole world for a witness to all the nations, and then the end shall come… for then there will be a great tribulation, such as has not occurred since the beginning of the world until now, nor ever shall. And unless those days had been cut short, no life would have been saved; but for the sake of the elect those days shall be cut short. (Mt 24:14, 21–22)

Bibliography

Bloom, Allan. *The Closing of the American Mind.* New York: Simon & Schuster, 1987.

Copleston, Frederick. *A History of Philosophy*, vol. VII. New York: Doubleday, 1963.

Geisler, Norman L. and Paul D. Feinberg. *Introduction to Philosophy*. Grand Rapids, MI: Baker Book House, 1980.

Grenz, Stanley J. *A Primer on Postmodernism.* Grand Rapids, MI: William B. Eerdmans Publishing Co., 1996.

Kreeft, Peter. *C. S. Lewis for the Third Millennium.* San Francisco: Ignatius Press, 1994.

Kurzweil, Ray. *The Singularity Is Near: When Humans Transcend Biology*. New York: Viking Press, 2005.

Lewis, C. S. *The Abolition of Man.* New York: Collier Books, 1947.

McGreal, Ian P., ed. *Great Thinkers of the Western World.* New York: HarperCollins Publishers, 1992.

Schaeffer, Francis. *A Christian Manifesto.* Westchester, IL: Crossway Books, 1981.

———. *The Complete Works of Francis A. Schaeffer,* vol. I, IV, V. Westchester, IL: Crossway Books, 1982.

Teilhard de Chardin, Pierre. *The Future of Man.* Translated by Norman Denny, New York: Harper & Row, 1959.

Ventureyra, Scott D. G. "Artificial Intelligence, the Nature of Consciousness, Information, Reality and the Possibility of the Afterlife." Science of Consciousness Conference 2020, Concurrent 23: Nonlocal Consciousness. https://www.youtube.com/watch?v=72nRMkp1KBE&t=9669s.

Part VI:

The New World Order & COVID-19

Chapter 40

Lessons Lost to History

Travis Louisseize

Perhaps the most crucial lessons of history that explain the polarization and decay of society today can be found by a careful analysis of the formation, ideology, and atrocities of the Soviet Union. I would submit to you that nobody has a more comprehensive understanding than Aleksandr Solzhenitsyn. Solzhenitsyn authored several highly valued works, such as, *One Day in the Life of Ivan Denisovich* and *The Gulag Archipelago*. I want to focus on the latter which was made required reading in Russian high schools by the education ministry, which cited the work as "vital historical and cultural heritage on the course of 20th-century domestic history."[1]

In a time where society is rife with confusion, disorientation, and inability to reach a consensus on any policy or structure, one quote stands out. Solzhenitsyn writes: "And the lie has, in fact, led us so far away from a normal society that you cannot even orient yourself any longer; in its dense, gray fog not even one pillar can be seen."[2]

Accusations of propaganda, misinformation, and disinformation often run rampant from traditional authoritative sources, but also from the those of dissenting opinions. Unlike the period of the 1900s, handheld personal computers provide people with such vast amounts of information, offering a direct avenue of assault which can add an additional layer in our inability to reason. A study conducted by the University of Waterloo submitted as part of the journal *Computers in Human Behavior*, found that:

> With the advent of Smartphone technology, access to the internet and its associated knowledge base is at one's fingertips. What consequences does this have for human cognition? We frame Smartphone use as an instantiation of the extended mind—the notion that our cognition goes beyond our brains—and in so doing, characterize a modern form of cognitive miserliness. Specifically, that people typically forego effortful analytic thinking in lieu of fast and easy intuition suggests

1 CBC Arts, "Gulag Archipelago joins Russian curriculum."

2 Academy of Ideas, "The Gulag Archipelago and The Wisdom of Aleksandr Solzhenitsyn."

> that individuals may allow their Smartphones to do their thinking for them. Our account predicts that individuals who are relatively less willing and/or able to engage effortful reasoning processes may compensate by relying on the internet through their Smartphones. Across three studies, we find that those who think more intuitively and less analytically when given reasoning problems were more likely to rely on their Smartphones (i.e., extended mind) for information in their everyday lives. There was no such association with the amount of time using the Smartphone for social media and entertainment purposes, nor did boredom proneness qualify any of our results. These findings demonstrate that people may offload thinking to technology, which in turn demands that psychological science understand the meshing of mind and media to adequately characterize human experience and cognition in the modern era.[3]

The parallels between where society finds itself today and the Soviet Union do not stop there. One could draw a comparison between the Kulaks, a designated class of people, usually farmers, within the Soviet Union and the middle class, small business owners of today. Jordan Peterson produced a lecture which has been posted online. In the beginning he describes who the Kulaks were:

> For example, one of the things that characterized the Soviet Union, and this was particularly true of the 1920s, but afterwards… The Soviets were very much enamored of the idea of class guilt, so for example, although it was only about 40 years previously that the serfs had been emancipated, they weren't much more than slaves and that was the bulk of the Russian population. They were bought and sold along with the land. So they had been emancipated and some of them, many of them had turned into independent farmers. And some of them had become reasonably prosperous because—at least in principle I presume a certain proportion of them from being crooked, but I presume a larger proportion from actually being able to raise food. Of course at that time, the bulk of the Russian food population was produced by these relatively successful peasant farmers and relatively successful would mean maybe they had a brick house or something and maybe they had a couple of cows and maybe they were able to hire a few people. So it wasn't like they were massive land owners or anything.[4]

Later he describes how their success was used against them and how the communists took advantage of their position to introduce a sense of victimhood

3 Barr, et al., "Computers in Human Behavior; The brain in your pocket: Evidence that Smartphones are used to supplant thinking."

4 Medikatie, "When Victimization Leads to Genocide: Dekulakization in the Soviet Union."

in some of the people that were unsuccessful in their village. This false sense of grievance was then exploited to have the "victimized" people attack the Kulaks.

> So when the intellectuals came in and described the reason that these people should be treated as parasites and profiteers. Then it was the resentful minorities in those towns—and that would be the kind of guy that hangs around in the bar all the time and is completely unconscientious and fails at everything and then blames everyone else for it—the intellectuals came in and said "here, this is unfair that this has happened to you, you've actually been victimized and now it's your opportunity to go have your revenge." And so that's exactly what happened.[5]

Solzhenitsyn perfectly captured the ruthlessness and savagery that was brought to bear on this group of people, whose only crime was that of a slightly higher level of success:

> If a man had a brick house in a row of log cabins, or two stories in a row of one-story houses—there was your kulak: Get ready, you bastard, you got sixty minutes! There aren't supposed to be any brick houses in the Russian village, there aren't supposed to be two-story houses! Back to the cave! You don't need a chimney for your fire! This is our great plan for transforming the country: history has never seen the like of it.[6]
>
> No food or tools were left for them. The roads were impassable, and there was no way through to the world outside, except for two brushwood paths... Machine-gunners manned barriers on both paths and let no one through from the death camp. They started dying like flies. Desperate people came out to the barriers begging to be let through, and were shot on the spot... They died off—every one of them... There's no other way to build the New Society.[7]

The measures taken at the beginning of the pandemic, most notably lockdowns, severely impacted businesses ability to operate. According to an article in the CBC,

> the Canadian Federation of Independent Business said Thursday [that] one in six, or about 181,000, Canadian small business owners are now seriously contemplating shutting down.

5 Medikatie, "When Victimization Leads to Genocide: Dekulakization in the Soviet Union."
6 Academy of Ideas, "The Gulag Archipelago and The Wisdom of Aleksandr Solzhenitsyn."
7 Academy of Ideas, "The Gulag Archipelago and The Wisdom of Aleksandr Solzhenitsyn."

> The latest figures, based on a survey of its members done between Jan. 12 and 16, come on top of 58,000 businesses that became inactive in 2020.[8]

At the time, it seemed like little weight was placed on the damage this would have and although they have not faced a genocide, they have endured a tremendous loss of wealth while larger businesses, like Walmart and Amazon, have seen tremendous growth.[9] The policies which forced businesses to close or created an environment that affected sales were made by unelected health bureaucrats, as politicians around the country deferred to their guidance. The effect of the government's policies has, by decree, forced members of the middle class into the lower class thereby equalizing their wealth distribution while increasing the wealth of the upper class. There are more similarities as well. The Black Lives Matter (BLM) and antifa riots that took place in 2020 caused over $1 billion in damages, resulting in the closure of many businesses.[10] BLM co-founder, Patrisse Cullors, claimed that she and her fellow organizers were "trained Marxists."[11] Such a statement from a leader of a Western movement seems shocking, since it reveals similar type events that took place in the Soviet Union that are so clearly emphasized in *The Gulag Archipelago*. Another consequence of the riots was the destruction or pressure to remove historical monuments, a deliberate and often violent effort to destroy and vilify history.[12]

Solzhenitsyn and the people of Russia's understanding of the failings of communism and Marxism came at an unbelievable cost. The failed experiment of the Soviet Union provided the world with all the evidence needed to reject the ideology. A lesson he believed the West did not understand and so, namely, that, "in Russia communism is a dead dog, while, for many people in the West, it is still a living lion."[13]

The most critical lesson to be learned from the three most prominent totalitarian regimes of the twentieth century, the Nazi regime, the Soviet Union, and Mao's China, is the danger of centralized power. There seems to be no concern in Western democracies for the ever-increasing power and control the government has over its citizens. Acts such as "the Patriot Act" in the United States, which was created in response to the 9/11 attacks, have given the government extreme new powers, which it has to this day never repealed.[14] In

8 The Canadian Press, "COVID-19 could shutter more than 200,000 Canadian businesses forever, CFIB says."

9 Kinder and Stateler, "Amazon and Walmart have raked in billions in additional profits during the pandemic, and shared almost none of it with their workers."

10 Kingson, "Exclusive: $1 billion-plus riot damage is most expensive in insurance history."

11 Steinbuch, "Black Lives Matter co-founder describes herself as 'trained Marxist'."

12 Wikipedia, "List of monuments and memorials removed during the George Floyd protests."

13 Academy of Ideas, "The Gulag Archipelago and The Wisdom of Aleksandr Solzhenitsyn."

14 Lind, "Everyone's heard of the Patriot Act. Here's what it actually does."

Canada, Bill C-16 has introduced compelled speech regarding one's pronouns, a first in a British Commonwealth country.[15] A reason for this lack of perception is captured in this quote by philosopher Hans Hermann Hoppe:

> Under democracy the distinction between the rulers and the ruled becomes blurred. The illusion even arises that the distinction no longer exists: that with democratic government no one is ruled by anyone, but everyone instead rules himself. Accordingly, public resistance against government power is systematically weakened.[16]

Just like in the totalitarian regimes of the twentieth century, every attempt to increase governments power over their citizens is made in the name of safety or security. This can be attributed to new technology, gaps in previous legislation, or in the name of efficiency, but the results are always the same—expansion, increased surveillance, and authority. How is the decline possible? Why and how has society been steadily marching towards a communist, technocratic totalitarian state? I believe this can best be explained by the following quotes from Viktor Orbán in a memorandum to the European Parliament. These messages are not being championed by any party in the US or Canada, as well as having been nearly lost in the European People's Party (EPP):

> Instead of stepping up against communism and Marxism, which left behind a painful legacy in Europe, we are applauding Fidel Castro and Karl Marx. Instead of the Christian-social Rhine model, we embrace egalitarian, socialistic social theories.
>
> We gave up the family model based on the matrimony of one woman and one man, and fell into the arms of gender ideology. Instead of supporting the birth of children, we see mass migration as the solution to our demographic problems...
>
> We are not offering an attractive alternative to our political adversaries, and we regard their issues and their interpretations as points of reference... We don't stand up for ourselves as old and great Europeans, and don't take on the fight against left-liberal intellectual forces and the media they influence and control...
>
> We are not raising our voice loud enough against the socialists who are helping the radical anarchist communist left into government. We have created an impression that we are afraid to declare and openly accept who we are and what we want, as if we were afraid of losing our share of governmental authority because of ourselves.[17]

15 Dragicevic, "Canada's gender identity rights Bill C-16 explained."

16 Academy of Ideas, "Democracy and the Road to Tyranny."

17 Paternotte and Verloo, "De-democratization and the Politics of Knowledge: Unpacking the Cultural Marxism Narrative."

There needs to be a way for this ideology to be permeating the culture just like in other totalitarian regimes. For this we need to look at what is happening in the education system. The origins of radicalized Marxist teaching to the US educators may have become most strident in 2004 but has developed over several decades. According to a study conducted by Steiner and Rozen in 2004, *Pedagogy of the Oppressed*, by Paulo Freire, was one of the most assigned textbooks in many of the most prestigious schools.[18] Paulo Freire has been described as "a Brazilian educator who drew on Marxist class-warfare ideology to devise strategies to radicalize schools." Robert Holland describes this method of indoctrination:

> The oppressed must see examples of the vulnerability of the oppressor so that a contrary conviction can begin to grow within them. Until this occurs, they will continue disheartened, fearful, and beaten.
>
> Education as the exercise of domination stimulates the credulity of students, with the ideological intent (often not perceived by educators) of indoctrinating them to adapt to the world of oppression.[19]

It is immediately clear how this ideological worldview has permeated Western culture and consumed the postmodernists, politicians, and radical organizations like BLM and antifa. One thing that has baffled many is Peterson's relative ignorance behind COVID, the vaccine, COVID measures, and how it ties in with the ideologues, ideology, Marxism, postmodernism, and socialism. Peterson also said the following in response to a question regarding whether getting the vaccine was the right thing to do:

> Was it the right thing to do? How the hell do I know, I don't bloody well know. I don't think the vaccine makers are conspiratorial, fundamentally, or more than any other organization.
>
> I am sick and tired of the lockdown and assumed that, if in Canada we reach a certain threshold of vaccinated people that it will be done with, and I'm ready for that.[20]

Since, in large part, I attribute my ability to recognize the transformations in society to Peterson's lectures and publications, it came has a huge surprise to me. One could only speculate why he has been unable draw the connections between them. He may have simply underestimated how deeply it had penetrated the global systems, corporations, and institutions, or perhaps struggled to come to grips with reality because he was afraid of what it would mean. In an interview with Dave Rubin posted on November 10, 2021,

18 Holland, "The Cult of Paulo Freire."

19 Holland, "The Cult of Paulo Freire."

20 WiSe.InSiGhT, "Jordan Peterson: I had the Goddamn Vaccine So Get Out Of My Face!?"

Peterson made the following statements, which seem to indicate a realization of what is happening and his frustration:

> The thing that surprised me the most, probably, was how rapidly we stampeded to imitate a totalitarian state in the immediate aftermath of the release of COVID. You know, if you think it through a little bit, no one really knew how serious the virus was going to be, and so it was an unknown threat. And so you could imagine a herd of animals or a school of fish, for that matter, because this kind of phenomena is universal throughout the animal kingdom.
>
> ...you know, Canadians who aren't vaccinated now cannot leave the country? Like, what the hell? Why is that? And I'm—look, I got vaccinated, and people took me to task for that, and I thought, all right, I'll get the damn vaccine. Here's the deal, guys. I'll get the vaccine; you f***ing leave me alone. And did that work? No. So, stupid me, you know? That's how I feel about it.[21]

Once again, curfews and bans on private gatherings were implemented in Quebec, this time on New Year's Eve. Following this decree, Jordan Peterson posted a series of tweets in which he explicitly connects totalitarianism and the treatment of society to how the professors corrupted the universities.

> Do we care nothing for our liberties? "No private gatherings" with a near 80% vaccination rate? And a curfew?
> Is there no excuse too small for the totalitarianism wannabes? What the hell is wrong with this country?
>
> 135 hospitalization and Quebec citizens are subjected to draconian measures. We are doing to our society exactly what cowardly professors already let happen to the universities.
>
> Here's a shock. But Quebec in this benighted and cowardly country of mine has just initiated a curfew. And banned private gatherings. Resist, Montreal! Take to the streets at 10:00 pm tonight. Defy this appalling law! Or lose more freedom to the bureaucrats.[22]

The connection of events spaced out over time seem ambiguous, even more so when separated by vast distances or simply lost to the sheer volume of events taking place. Society has little time to process or reflect on the significance or lessons of an event before the next one occurs. If we look at historical events and understand their connections, we can use this pattern as a reference to identify repetitions in the present. The attempts to vilify, erase, and destroy history sends a clear warning signal as such events are needed to support the lie

21 Cheong, "Jordan Peterson says 'totalitarian' COVID restrictions plaguing Canada, the West."

22 News Analysis, "Jordan Peterson calls for civil disobedience in face of Quebec's curfew."

of a totalitarian state. In the story of the of the Kulaks, we can see resemblances to the treatment of the suburbs and middle class with those of the successful farmers. Organizations like BLM and other minority groups are "the victims" that were spurred on by the demagogues. The intellectuals represent those in the educational and political systems which have been consumed by Marxist ideology and are indoctrinating the young, while promoting the activism of groups like BLM. Should this trend continue, and we fail to address the radical ideological takeover of the education system, we may see the West fall into the same trap of the Soviet Union, just as Aleksandr Solzhenitsyn feared. It is for this reason I advocate for the mandatory reading of *The Gulag Archipelago* in high school, so that the lessons that have been lost may be excavated by our youth to avoid the pitfalls of yesterday.

Bibliography

Academy of Ideas. "Democracy and the Road to Tyranny." December 15, 2016. https://academyofideas.com/2016/12/democracy-road-to-tyranny.

———. "The Gulag Archipelago and The Wisdom of Aleksandr Solzhenitsyn." April 19, 2017. https://academyofideas.com/2017/04/gulag-archipelago-aleksandr-solzhenitsyn/.

Barr, Nathaniel, et al. "Computers in Human Behavior; The brain in your pocket: Evidence that Smartphones are used to supplant thinking." *ScienceDirect*, July, 2015. https://www.sciencedirect.com/science/article/abs/pii/S0747563215001272.

Canadian Press, The. "COVID-19 could shutter more than 200,000 Canadian businesses forever, CFIB says." *CBC*, January 21, 2021. https://www.cbc.ca/news/business/cfib-survey-1.5882059.

CBC Arts. "Gulag Archipelago joins Russian curriculum." *CBC*, September 9, 2009. https://www.cbc.ca/news/entertainment/gulag-archipelago-joins-russian-curriculum-1.825588.

Cheong, Ian Miles. "Jordan Peterson says 'totalitarian' COVID restrictions plaguing Canada, the West." *Rebel News*, November 11, 2021. https://www.rebelnews.com/jordan_peterson_says_totalitarian_covid_restrictions_plaguing_canada_the_west.

Dragicevic, Nina. "Canada's gender identity rights Bill C-16 explained." *CBC*. https://www.cbc.ca/cbcdocspov/features/canadas-gender-identity-rights-bill-c-16-explained.

Holland, Robert. "The Cult of Paulo Freire." In *Radicalization of Teacher Education Programs in the United States Nine Essays*. Lexington Institute, September 2012. https://www.lexingtoninstitute.org/wp-content/uploads/2014/04/RadicalizationOfTeacherEducationPrograms.pdf.

Kinder, Molly, and Laura Stateler. "Amazon and Walmart have raked in billions in additional profits during the pandemic, and shared almost none of it with their workers." *Brookings*, Dec 22, 2020. https://www.brookings.edu/blog/the-avenue/2020/12/22/amazon-and-walmart-have-raked-in-billions-in-additional-profits-during-the-pandemic-and-shared-almost-none-of-it-with-their-workers/.

Kingson, Jennifer. "Exclusive: $1 billion-plus riot damage is most expensive in insurance history." *Axios*, September 16, 2020. https://www.axios.com/riots-cost-property-damage-276c9bcc-a455-4067-b06a-66f9db4cea9c.html.

Lind, Dara. "Everyone's heard of the Patriot Act. Here's what it actually does." *Vox*, June 2, 2015. https://www.vox.com/2015/6/2/8701499/patriot-act-explain.

Medikatie. "When Victimization Leads to Genocide: Dekulakization in the Soviet Union" *Steemit.* https://steemit.com/psychology/@medikatie/when-victimization-leads-to-genocide-dekulakization-in-the-soviet-union.

News Analysis. "Jordan Peterson calls for civil disobedience in face of Quebec's curfew." *The Post Millennial*, December 31, 2021. https://thepostmillennial.com/jordan-peterson-calls-for-civil-disobedience-in-face-of-quebecs-curfew.

Paternotte, David, and Mieke Verloo. "De-democratization and the Politics of Knowledge: Unpacking the Cultural Marxism Narrative." *Oxford Academic*, November 12, 2021. https://academic.oup.com/sp/article/28/3/556/6426301?login=true.

Steinbuch, Yaron. "Black Lives Matter co-founder describes herself as 'trained Marxist'." *New York Post*, June 25, 2020. https://nypost.com/2020/06/25/blm-co-founder-describes-herself-as-trained-marxist/.

Wikipedia. "List of monuments and memorials removed during the George Floyd protests." https://en.wikipedia.org/wiki/List_of_monuments_and_memorials_removed_during_the_George_Floyd_protests.

WiSe.InSiGhT. "Jordan Peterson: I had the Goddamn Vaccine So Get Out Of My Face!?" YouTube Video, July 21, 2021. https://www.youtube.com/watch?v=LHcWTHht1mQ.

Chapter 41

The Great Reset and the New World Order

Phil Fernandes[1]

Billionaire Donald J. Trump was once a popular man in the eyes of the American media and the political establishment. But, once he ran for and won the United States Presidency, everything changed. Though Trump is considered by many to be obnoxious, if not pugnacious, it is doubtful that this is the main reason for the drastic change in the opinion of the American political establishment. Something much more sinister explains the anger directed at former President Trump.

For decades, the neo-conservative Republican establishment (i.e., the Bushes, Dick Cheney, Donald Rumsfeld, etc.) and the far-left Democratic Party (i.e., the Clintons, Obamas, Joe Biden, etc.) have embraced internationalism. These elites, despite their differences,[2] have worked fervently to undermine US sovereignty and build a New World Order.[3] Presidents George H. W. Bush, Bill Clinton, George W. Bush, and Barack Obama had "set the table" for their heir-apparent—Hillary Clinton. It was her task to finish the job and surrender US sovereignty by merging America with the global state. But then Donald J. Trump rained on their globalist parade by winning the 2016 presidential election.

Trump, in his July, 2016 Republican Convention acceptance speech, vowed to "make America great again" and dismantle treaties like NAFTA that weakened US sovereignty. He stated, "Americanism, not globalism, will be our credo." He pledged to "put America first." Trump proclaimed that we will "show the whole world America is back, bigger and stronger than ever before."

1 Rorri Wiesinger and Matthew J. Coombe assisted me in the research for this chapter.

2 The neo-conservative Republicans want a strong America (and a strong American military) leading the New World Order. On the other hand, the far-left Democrats want Europe and the United Nations, not America, to lead the New World Order (though still financed by the United States taxpayers). Still both groups have global government as their goal.

3 For more information on the New World Order, see the following books: Brooke, *One World*; Jasper, *Global Tyranny: Step By Step*; Grigg, *Freedom on the Altar*; McManus, *Changing Commands*; Perloff, *The Shadows of Power*; Kah, *En Route to Global Occupation*; Kah, *The New World Religion*; Isaacson, *Under the Tower of Babel*; Coffman, *Saviors of the Earth?*; McManus, *Financial Terrorism*; McManus, *The Insiders*; Newman, *Deep State: The Invisible Government Behind the Scenes*; Epperson, *The New World Order*.

The political establishment of both parties could not tolerate a nationalist president—a president who wanted to protect US sovereignty—a president who had no desire for building international government and dismantling US sovereignty. Hence, the media and the US political elite turned on President Trump. They raised false accusations of Russian collusion and moved swiftly towards impeachment. In short, Donald Trump is hated by the political and media elite because he is pro-American and anti-New World Order.

See No Evil

Many Americans ignore the ongoing formation of a one-world government, often referred to as the "New World Order." They do not want to be accused of espousing some type of "conspiracy theory." However, global government *is* becoming a reality and Americans must take a stand against it.

Former President George H. W. Bush often referred to the New World Order in his speeches during the Persian Gulf War. Bush made it clear that the UN would head the New World Order and that international law would and should be enforced by the UN. He stated: "Out of these troubled times, our fifth objective—a new world order—can emerge... We are now in sight of a United Nations that performs as envisioned by its founders."[4] Eleven years later, when his son George W. Bush was president, Democrat Gary Hart, longtime political rival of the Bushes, stated in response to the 9/11 terrorist attacks: "There is a chance for the President of the United States to use this disaster [9/11] to carry out what his father, a phrase his father used, I think only once, and hasn't been used since—and that is a new world order."[5] Globalist David Rockefeller clearly admitted that his desire for global government was not some far-fetched conspiracy theory. He stated, "Some even believe we (the Rockefeller family) are part of a secret cabal working against the best interests of the United States, characterizing my family and me as 'internationalists' and of conspiring with others around the world to build a more integrated global political & economic structure—one world, if you will. If that's the charge, I stand guilty, and I am proud of it."[6]

Many Americans, including numerous political leaders, believe that global government is the best way to achieve and sustain world peace. Many New Agers, secular humanists, American communists (i.e., neo-Marxists), liberal politicians, and neo-conservative politicians agree that the best (or only) way to guarantee global peace and prosperity is through a one-world socialist economy, international laws, and an all-powerful UN peace-keeping force. Besides the

4 Television address, September 11, 1990.

5 Democrat Gary Hart speaking at a CFR dinner, September, 2001.

6 Rockefeller, *Memoirs*, 405.

concern for global peace, other factors such as poverty, environmental issues, the ecumenical movement (the attempt to unite all the religions of the world), and the fear of overpopulation make the idea of one-world government an appealing prospect to many.

The Biblical View of Government

However, Bible-believing Christians must oppose the movement towards a one-world government. Because mankind is fallen, no human or group of humans should be given absolute control over the lives of billions. Only Jesus, as the Prince of Peace (Isa 9:6), has the right to reign over the entire Earth. We should trust in Jesus alone for peace, not the UN and the wisdom of man (Ps 118:8–9). A one-world government (without Jesus as its King) may produce the end-time kingdom of the Antichrist and the mark of the beast (Rev 13). It will never produce peace and justice (Dan 9:26; 1 Thess 5:3). God-ordained human government has a limited role (to serve its citizens by protecting their God-given human rights) and limited power. Unlimited global government will not serve mankind; it will enslave mankind.

Before jumping on the "peace at any price" bandwagon, Christians should turn to God's Word to find His view of world government. A person need only read the eleventh chapter of Genesis to find God's view of a one-world government. In this chapter, the peoples of the earth have settled together in one area of the earth. This is despite God's command that they fill the earth (Gen 1:28). God saw that mankind spoke one common language and that they had one common purpose (Gen 11:1–6). Contrary to what many modern men and women would expect, God was not pleased. God did not like the idea of mankind united into one government while they were still in rebellion against Him. God knew that one language and a one-world government would increase technology greatly (Gen 11:6); still, He recognized that this would only accelerate man's demise.

God decided to scatter mankind and confuse their language (Gen 11:7–9). This forced men to live in separate nations (Gen 10:25). God wanted the power of human government to be limited.

God's Word tells us that there will be wars until the end (Dan 9:26; Mat 24:6–7). Mankind will not be able to bring global peace to earth. Only when Jesus, the Prince of Peace, returns will man have the peace he has desired (Isa 9:6–7; 2:1–4). A one-world government will only increase the level of violence and destruction on this planet. For the leader of the future one-world government will be none other than the antichrist, a demon-possessed end-time ruler who will rule the world and oppress the masses (Rev 13:1–18; 2 Thess 2:1–12).

God instituted human government for two reasons. First, because man was created in God's image. Therefore, human life is sacred and is worth protecting (Gen 9:6). Second, humans are sinful (due to the fall of man in the garden) Therefore, evil needs to be restrained (Rom 13:1–4). Hence, God instituted human government to protect human life and to restrain evil.

The Word of God also indicates why human government must be limited. The Bible teaches that humans are sinful (Rom 3:10, 23). Since human governments are run by humans, and all humans are sinful, then the powers of those who rule must be limited. This is a biblical principle that our founding fathers clearly understood. They enacted several measures to insure the limiting of the rulers' power. First, they recognized God as an authority above the government by acknowledging the unalienable, God-given rights of men and women. Second, they believed that nations should be separate—they were opposed to surrendering United States' sovereignty. Third, they set up a system of checks and balances and a separation of powers to limit the power of human leaders. They established a separation of powers between federal, state, and local governments. They instituted a separation of powers between the three branches of the federal government (executive, judicial, and legislative branches). And, fourth, our founding fathers limited the power of human government by recognizing the people's right to worship, vote, assemble, protest, and bear arms.

God is opposed to a one-world government ruled by men. Our founding fathers were right to limit the power of government. Only when Jesus returns can mankind have true and lasting peace. Only when Jesus returns shall we have a God-ordained one-world government (Rev 19:11–16; 20:1–6); for, only then will the Kingdom of God have come to Earth (Rev 11:15). Until then, we must oppose the push towards global government.

The Twentieth-Century Move Towards Global Government

An overview of the twentieth century will show the conscious merging of the US government with various supranational organizations and institutions. Through multiple international agreements and treaties, the US and other nations have set upon a course leading to international government. Evidence for this has been sufficiently documented through various sources such as those listed in footnote #3 of this chapter.

In 1913, the Federal Reserve System was created. The Federal Reserve is a central bank with an exclusive monopoly to issue fiat currency (i.e., currency not backed by gold or silver). The Federal Reserve is run by private investment bankers who control the US economy through the inflation and deflation of its currency. Congress created the Federal Reserve with no constitutional authorization. Its bankers are not accountable to Congress or to the people, and they cannot be removed by the people through an election process. Hence, they have dictatorial authority to create boom-and-bust cycles, which they fully exploit in order to advance their socialist and globalist agendas.

The economic crash of 1929 provides a clear example of the Federal Reserve's nefarious ability to manipulate and destroy an economy. In a calculated move, the they reduced the quantity of currency, causing a deflationary effect that sank the Stock Market and initiated the Great Depression of the 1930s. With the economic depression in high gear, the Federal Reserve's brain trust had the necessary pretext for the introduction of President Franklin Roosevelt's economic "reforms," known as the New Deal. Roosevelt's socialist New Deal was patterned after the statist policies of Italy's fascist dictator, Benito Mussolini.

A close political ally of Franklin Roosevelt and one of America's most notorious political insiders, Edward M. House had played a pivotal role in the planning and creation of the graduated federal income tax, the League of Nations, and the Council on Foreign Relations.

As President Woodrow Wilson's chief advisor, House was able to exert his tremendous political influence into Wilson's domestic and foreign policies. It cannot be overstated that House was both an ardent internationalist and committed Marxist. In his thinly veiled 1912 novel, *Philip Dru: Administrator*, House wrote that he desired "socialism as dreamed of by Karl Marx."

House, working with British and American internationalists, helped to found the Council on Foreign Relations in 1921. This was due to the fact that America had refused to join the League of Nations following World War I. If another attempt to bring the United States into an international body was to succeed, the thinking of American leaders had to change. Therefore, the Council on Foreign Relations (CFR) was formed to persuade key American leaders that the answer to the world's greatest challenges was the establishment of a socialist world government. Hence, a gradual erosion of the sovereignty of the United States government had to occur.

Today, the CFR has over 3,000 members, the vast majority of which occupy top positions in finance, industry, business, government, defense, education, and the media.[7] The CFR has often been called the "American establishment" since the State Department has been controlled by CFR members for decades. The CFR has maintained control of the State Department regardless of whether the President is a Democrat or Republican. Since Eisenhower, every US president, except Ronald Reagan, George W. Bush, and Donald Trump, has been a member of the Council on Foreign Relations. Even in the Ronald Reagan and George W. Bush administrations, the President's cabinet was filled with key CFR members. Today, it is almost impossible to be a national leader in either of

7 Alex Newman lists the 2019 roster of CFR members on pages 173–199 in his book *Deep State*.

the major political parties without CFR membership. Prominent CFR members have included George H. W. Bush, Henry Kissinger, Zbigniew Brzezinski, Alan Greenspan, David Rockefeller, Bill Clinton, and Newt Gingrich.

The CFR publishes a journal called *Foreign Affairs*, dealing with US foreign policy. If one closely reads these journals, one will see that the issue of global government is not open to debate. The only questions open for discussion are the rate of increase concerning the movement toward world government and the ways and methods through which it will be achieved. Questions that challenge the pro-globalist orthodoxy, however, are not open for discussion.

In 1943, CFR members directed the Roosevelt State Department to draft the proposal for the founding of the United Nations. The United Nations was a second attempt at the failed League of Nations. After the end of World War II, representatives from 50 nations, including the United States, signed the Charter of the United Nations Organization in San Francisco on June 26, 1945. This marked the birth of the UN.

US State Department official Alger Hiss, a CFR member, was the first UN Secretary General. It later became known that Hiss was an American Communist Party member and a Soviet agent. The empowerment of the UN was one of the chief goals of the communist party in America.

Every major war that America has been involved in since World War II has been directed by or under UN subsidiary alliances such as the North Atlantic Treaty Organization (NATO) or the Southeast Asia Treaty Organization (SEATO) (i.e., Korea, Vietnam, Panama, Iraq, Somalia, Haiti, Bosnia, Kosovo, etc.). It should also be noted that the UN's top military official is the UN Secretary General of Political Affairs.

Many Americans believe that the UN offers no threat to US sovereignty since it has no "teeth" (i.e., no military power). However, this perspective is easily refuted once we realize that the US military (the most powerful military on Earth) seems to work exclusively for UN goals, and ultimately under UN command. According to the US Constitution, only the US Congress has the power to declare war. The last constitutional war the US was involved in was World War II. All wars or military "conflicts" in which America has been involved since World War II have been to serve the interests of the UN. It appears that the UN has "teeth" (i.e., the United States military). When Donald Trump was elected president and he instituted his America-first agenda, it seems that China has replaced the US as the enforcer for the UN/ global elites.

Today, there exist many UN-based subsidiary and regional organizations, such as the International Monetary Fund (IMF), the European Union (EU), the World Bank (WB), the International Criminal Court (ICC), the World Trade Organization (WTO), the UN Education, Scientific, and Cultural Organization (UNESCO), the United Religions Organization (URO), the

World Court (WC), the World Economic Forum (WEF), and the World Health Organization (WHO). These organizations are extremely influential in the affairs of the nations of the world. The gradual usurpations of national sovereignty by UN institutions show the UN to be a global government in the embryo stage.

Official policies of the United States government since the 1960s reveal that US strategy is threefold: 1) gradually disarm and weaken the US military, 2) progressively strengthen UN military capabilities, and 3) encourage the peaceful merger of the United States with Russia. This threefold strategy is spelled out in several executive and congressional policies.

Memorandum No. 7: A World Effectively Controlled by the UN was a study funded by the US State Department during the Kennedy administration and completed in February, 1961. It showed how US military disarmament could be achieved in order to further the cause of global governance.

US executive policy *Freedom From War: The US Program for General and Complete Disarmament in a Peaceful World* (Department of State Publication 7277, September, 1961) presents a three-stage program for the gradual transfer of US armaments to UN control. US Congressional Policy *US Public Law 87-297—the Arms Control and Disarmament Act* was signed into law by President Kennedy on September 26, 1961. This law created the US Arms Control and Disarmament Agency that was designed to advance efforts toward complete disarmament of the world's nations, while excluding the UN, thus attempting to give the UN a monopoly on military power. President Kennedy stated: "The program to be presented to this assembly…would achieve…a steady reduction in force, both nuclear and conventional, until it has abolished all armies and all weapons except those needed for internal order and a new United Nations Peace Force."[8]

Blueprint for the Peace Race: Outline of Basic Provisions of a Treaty on General and Complete Disarmament in a Peaceful World (US Arms Control and Disarmament Agency Publication No. 4, April 1962) is a US State Department document that superseded the earlier *Freedom From War* document. *Blueprint for the Peace Race* remains official US policy and continues the same three-stage US disarmament program of the *Freedom from War* document, while progressively strengthening UN military capabilities.

Project Phoenix: Study Phoenix Paper (June, 1963) is a US State Department funded study produced by the Institute of Defense Analyses for the US Arms Control and Disarmament Agency, which openly advocates US and Soviet unification. On June 17, 1992, President George H. W. Bush and Russian President Boris Yeltsin fulfilled much of the spirit of *Project Phoenix* by signing the official convergence document entitled *Charter for American-Russian Partnership and Friendship*.

8 John F. Kennedy, address to the United Nations, September 25, 1961.

In 1993 and 1994, President Clinton issued Presidential Decision Directives (PDD) that expanded the UN's peace-keeping missions around the world and permitted US military forces to be placed under foreign command in UN operations on a case-by-case basis (PDD-13 and PDD-25).

Key Globalist Organizations

Besides the CFR and UN, other key globalist organizations include the Bilderberg Group, the Club of Rome, the Trilateral Commission, and the European Union. The Bilderberg Group was launched by Prince Bernhard of Holland and David Rockefeller in 1954 at the Bilderberg Hotel in Oosterbeek, Holland. This elite group consists of prominent internationalists who meet annually to discuss their globalist agendas for the upcoming year and beyond. The media is strictly prohibited from covering these secret meetings. Although key leaders of the media are occasionally invited to attend a Bilderberg meeting, they do not divulge the details of the meeting.

The European Union can trace its roots back to 1951 when the European Coal and Steel Community (ECSC) was formed. From the ECSC, the gradual political merger of the European nations began to progress steadily. In 1957, the Treaty of Rome established the European Economic Community (EEC), also known as the Common Market, and the European Atomic Community (EURATOM or EAEC). In 1967, the ECSC, the EEC, and EURATOM merged to form the European Community (EC). In a major push to establish monetary and political union, the Maastricht Treaty of 1991 was signed by EC member nations. The Maastricht Treaty went into effect in 1993, and the European Union (EU) was born. Great Britain's recent exit from the EU was a massive blow to the globalist agenda.

In 1968, the Club of Rome was founded by Aurelio Peccei (a New Age thinker and disciple of the late Pierre Teilhard de Chardin) for the purpose of unifying the world under a single authority. In a work entitled *Mankind at the Turning Point*, Mihajlo Mesarovic and Eduard Pestel, two Club of Rome members, stated that the Club of Rome divided the world into 10 regions, and that, to ensure the survival of the human race, mankind must no longer cooperate on the national level, but on the global level. (Some Bible prophecy experts believe these 10 regions may be the "10 kingdoms" of the end-time world government headed by the Antichrist and spoken about in Rev 13:1; 17:12–14 and Dan 2:40–42; 7:23–24.)

Many globalist elites have argued for regionalization of the world to replace sovereign nations. P. E. Corbett, a British aristocrat & member of Cecil Rhodes' Roundtable, stated that, "The world government goal is to be accomplished by linking regional economic arrangements."[9]

9 Corbett, *Post-War Worlds*, 1942.

Inspired by the world government concepts outlined in Columbia University Professor Zbigniew Brzezinski's book *Between Two Ages*, David Rockefeller founded the Trilateral Commission in 1973. Brzezinski, who later became the National Security Advisor for President Carter, drew up the Commission's charter and became its first director. The purpose of the Trilateral Commission is to expedite the formation of a world government by encouraging economic interdependence between the world's three economic superpowers (the United States, Western Europe, and Japan). Brzezinski stated: "We cannot leap into world government in one quick step... The precondition for eventual globalization—genuine globalization—is progressive regionalization."[10]

Even government-run education promotes globalism. In 1972, Harvard University Professor Chester M. Pierce gave the keynote address to the Association for Childhood Education International. He stated that, "every child in America entering school...is insane because he comes to school with certain allegiances toward our founding fathers, toward his parents, toward a belief in a supernatural being... It's up to you, teachers, to make all of these sick children well—by creating the international children of the future."[11]

Key Globalist Leaders

Other key globalists of the past (besides former United States presidents) include Mikhail Gorbachev, former UN Secretary General Boutros Boutros-Ghali, Maurice Strong (Secretary General of the Earth Summit), former UN Assistant Secretary General Robert Muller, and the late Georgetown University Professor Carroll Quigley. Current leading globalists include such names as George Soros, Bill Gates, current UN Secretary-General António Guterres, and World Economic Forum head Klaus Schwab.

Gorbachev headed the Green Cross organization through which he promoted radical environmentalism and worship of the Earth. In a 1992 speech at Westminster College in Missouri, Gorbachev expressed "the need for some kind of global government." Gorbachev also hosted some of the world's leading globalists at his State of the World Forums.

Boutros Boutros-Ghali wrote a book entitled *An Agenda for Peace* in which he called for an end to national sovereignty. Boutros-Ghali sees the UN as man's only hope for global peace.

Maurice Strong was a close friend of David Rockefeller and the driving force behind the UN environmental policy. Strong was a fervent New Ager who headed the Earth Summit, also known as the United Nations Conference

10 Taken from the first State of the World Forum which was convened in 1995 by Mikhail Gorbachev.

11 Fernandes, et al., *God, Government, and the Road to Tyranny*, 183.

on Environment and Development. Strong worked with Gorbachev in producing and promoting the Earth Charter, supposedly a bill of rights for the people of the Earth. The Earth Charter calls for a new morality with radical environmentalism and worship of the Earth at its foundation.

Though Robert Muller officially retired in 1986, he continued to diligently work for the cause of world government. Muller was very active in the area of education and is the author of *The World Core Curriculum*, a document which promotes globalism and New Age beliefs. This document earned Muller the title "the Father of Global Education." The UN has pushed for The *World Core Curriculum* to be accepted as the foundation for education throughout the world. In fact, *Goals 2000*[12] in America was inspired by *The World Core Curriculum*. Muller's thought was influenced by New Agers such as Teilhard de Chardin and Alice Bailey of the Theosophical Society. Muller's ideas were instrumental in bringing the United Religions Initiative (the UN's current attempt to unite all the religions of the world) into existence. Muller's spiritual mentor Alice Bailey once wrote: "A world divided into regional blocs could provide a normal & progressive movement away from the separative nationalism of the past & towards the distant creation of the One World, & the One Humanity."[13] Nelson Rockefeller, during a 1962 lecture at Harvard University, declared "…the nation-state is becoming less and less competent to perform its international political tasks…pressing us to lead vigorously toward the true building of a new world order."[14] The former CFR President Richard Haas stated in a 2006 *Taipei Times* article: "State Sovereignty must be altered in a globalized era."[15]

The late Georgetown Professor, Carroll Quigley, himself a globalist, wrote a massive book entitled *Tragedy and Hope: A History of Our Time*. Written in 1966, this book gives the details of the globalist agenda from the perspective of an insider. Quigley's most famous student was William Jefferson Clinton (who went on to become President of the United States).

The Bill Clinton Administration

The movement towards global government has permeated presidential administrations, even after George H. W. Bush's presidency. Republican Senator Trent Lott complained that, "The Clinton Administration appears dedicated

12 *Goals 2000* is an educational reform that took place in the last quarter of the 20th century where students achieve competency in grade 4, 8, and 12.

13 Alice Bailey—occultic co-founder of Lucis Trust, author of *Externalization of the* Hierarchy,1957

14 de Ruiter and Springmeier, *Worldwide Evil and Misery: The Legacy of 13 Satanic Bloodlines*, 17.

15 Haass, "State sovereignty must be altered in globalized era."

to sending the US military…in an effort to elevate the status of the United Nations into a guardian arbiter of the new world order."[16] Strobe Talbott, Bill Clinton's former Oxford roommate and Clinton's Deputy Secretary of State, stated on July 20, 1992, "Within the next hundred years…nationhood as we know it will be obsolete; all states will recognize a single, global authority."[17]

The George W. Bush Administration

During the administration of President George W. Bush, the calls for global government continued. British Prime Minister Tony Blair, during his July 17, 2003 speech to the United States Congress, stated: "Our new world rests on order. The danger is disorder. And in today's world, it can now spread like contagion."[18] During the Bush II administration, Vice-President Dick Cheney and Secretary of State Donald Rumsfeld, both CFR members, continued the New World Order agenda of Bush I. In fact, before 9/11, the Bush II administration was trying to build the North American Union. In a 2006 CNBC interview with Steve Previs, VP of Jefferies International, Previs stated that, "The Amero is the proposed new currency for the North American Community, which is being developed right now between Canada, the United States and Mexico to make a borderless community much like that of the European Union, & the Canadian dollar, the US dollar & the Mexican peso replaced by the Amero."[19]

The Barack Obama Administration

During the Obama administration, the New World Order agenda remained a priority. Secretary of State Hillary Clinton wrote a review of Henry Kissinger's book, *World Order*. She wrote: "I was proud to help the president begin reimagining and reinforcing the global order to meet the demands of an increasingly interdependent age."[20] Vice President Joe Biden proclaimed, "The 'affirmative task' before us is to create a New World Order."[21] Globalist Henry Kissinger said of President Obama, "…he [Obama] can give new impetus to American foreign policy… I think that his task will be to develop an overall

16 Lott, "UN Intervention in Somali." C-SPAN, October 5, 1993. https://www.c-span.org/video/?51185-1/un-intervention-somalia.

17 Talbott, *The Great Experiment: The Story of Ancient Empires, Modern States, and the Quest for a Global Nation*,126–127.

18 CNN. "Transcript of Blair's Speech to Congress."

19 Corse. "Premeditated Merger: Amero Coming Within Decade."

20 Clinton, "Hillary Clinton Reviews Henry Kissinger."

21 Next News Network, "Joe Biden Calls to 'Create a New World Order'"; see also Admin. "Joe Biden: 'How I Learned To Love The New World Order'."

strategy for America in this period, when really a 'new world order' can be created. It's a great opportunity. It isn't such a crisis."[22] This is the same Henry Kissinger who once said:

> Today, America would be outraged if U.N. troops entered Los Angeles to restore order. Tomorrow they will be grateful! This is especially true if they were told that there was an outside threat from beyond, whether real or promulgated, that threatened our very existence. It is then that all peoples of the world will plead to deliver them from this evil. The one thing every man fears is the unknown. When presented with this scenario, individual rights will be willingly relinquished for the guarantee of their well-being granted to them by the World Government.[23]

President Obama himself made some pro-New World Order speeches before the United Nations. He stated:

> And so I believe that at this moment we all face a choice. We can choose to press forward with a better model of cooperation and integration. Or we can retreat into a world sharply divided, and ultimately in conflict, along age-old lines of nation and tribe and race and religion.[24]

During an earlier speech to the UN, Obama related:

> In an era when our destiny is shared, power is no longer a zero-sum game. No one nation can or should try to dominate another nation. No world order that elevates one nation or group of people over another will succeed. No balance of power among nations will hold. The traditional divisions between nations of the South and the North make no sense in an interconnected world; nor do alignments of nations rooted in the cleavages of a long-gone Cold War.[25]

Cultural Marxism—The New Civil Religion

Globalist, socialist propaganda was needed in order to change the thinking of Americans. This propaganda was found in Cultural Marxism, which became a dangerous tool in the hands of globalist politicians in America.[26] Americans

22 Jasper, "Kissinger Urges Obama to Build a 'New World Order'."

23 Unbeknownst to Kissinger the whole speech was recorded by a Swiss delegate. Kissinger, Bilderberg Conference in Évian-les-Bains, France in 1991.

24 Obama, "Read Barack Obama's Final Speech to the United Nations."

25 Obama, "Remarks by the President to the United Nations General Assembly."

26 An excellent overview of Cultural Marxism can be found in Breitbart, *Righteous Indignation*, 111–135.

were taught to think of Western civilization as intolerant, racist, and greedy. On the other hand, Marxist socialist ideology was thought to be the solution to the problems created by the West. The West must be caused to collapse, and then replaced by global socialism.

Before World War I, Marxists believed that if war started in Europe, the working class would revolt against the business owners. Instead, the working class went to war for their countries—they didn't revolt against their governments. After World War I, Marxists tried to figure out why the working class did not revolt—why didn't the predictions of Karl Marx come about? What went wrong?

Antonio Gramsci and Georg Lukacs believed that Western democracy and capitalism would have to be destroyed before the revolution would come into being. Gramsci believed religion was too strong in the West—opium that kept the workers from revolting. He was an Italian Marxist who believed that Western civilization had to be transformed—Marxists must infiltrate religion, media, education, and politics of the Western countries.[27] He was imprisoned by Mussolini and died in prison in 1937.

This attempt to reform Marxism led to the founding of the Frankfurt School. Georg Lukacs tried to attack the family unit and Christian morality. He promoted sexual immorality to destroy society in Hungary. He referred to this as "Cultural Terrorism." He encouraged presenting sexually explicit material to children in education. His views were rejected and he had to flee from Hungary. In 1923, Lukacs went to Frankfurt, Germany to meet with other Cultural Marxists—they started the Frankfurt School. Fellow Marxist Felix Weil financed the new Marxist think tank.[28]

In 1930, Max Horkheimer combined the psychological thought of Sigmund Freud with Marxism.[29] Now everyone, not just the workers, were psychologically oppressed by Western leaders. When the Nazis took control in Germany in 1933, the Marxists (many of whom were Jews) fled to New York City where the Frankfurt School took residence in Columbia University. There they developed "Critical Theory." This view criticized every pillar of Western society: the family, democracy, Christianity, freedom of speech, traditional morality, capitalism, etc.

Theodor Adorno was another Cultural Marxist. He authored *The Authoritarian Personality*. In this book he condemned traditional American views about gender roles and American views of human sexuality as prejudiced. He labeled these views "fascist."[30] The Cultural Marxists were moving classical Marxism away from economic oppression towards psychological oppression. They divided America

27 Breitbart, *Righteous Indignation*, 112.
28 Breitbart, *Righteous Indignation*, 112–113.
29 Horkheimer, *Critical Theory*, 207, 212–219.
30 Breitbart, *Righteous Indignation*, 114.

into two groups: the oppressors and the oppressed. Males of European descent were the oppressors. They also argued that gender and social roles of men and women were defined by the oppressors—gender distinctions don't really exist; they are simply a social construct according to Cultural Marxists.

Herbert Marcuse wrote *Eros and Civilization* in 1955.[31] In this book he promoted sexual freedom outside traditional, Christian morality. This book had a great influence on the sexual revolution of the 1960s. Now, the oppressed class was defined as minorities, women, and homosexuals. This led to many of the radical-left protests of the 1960s: Black Power, Feminism, Gay Rights, and Sexual Liberation. Marcuse defined "liberating tolerance" as tolerance of any views from the extreme left (Cultural Marxism), but rejection of any traditional views.[32] This is the essence of political correctness.

Saul Alinsky was a devoted disciple of Cultural Marxism. His *Rules for Radicals* was a practical guide for community organizers to promote his views.[33] This work has influenced the thought of many politicians, including Hillary Clinton and Barack Obama.

Cultural Marxism displays a fierce hatred for traditional Christian values. In fact, the Marxist hatred of Western civilization is due to the fact that traditional Christian beliefs formed the foundation for Western culture. Cultural Marxists have a divide-and-conquer strategy; they produce tribalism by pitting one community against another. They also attack the family unit. They attempt to overthrow society through their views, with Black Lives Matters and antifa doing their dirty work during violent protests. In Cultural Marxism, people are not judged by their individual character; they are judged by the group they are in. They are either oppressors (white, male, Christian, heterosexual) or the oppressed (minorities, female, non-Christian, homosexual, or transgender). People's significance is only found in their collective community. The individual dies. Individual rights die as well. There is no redemption for the so-called oppressors. To divide Americans into different warring groups, Cultural Marxists have developed Critical Race Theory and the idea of Systemic Racism. These views promote the idea that a white individual is a racist even if they never performed any racist acts, had any racists thoughts, or said any racist words—they are a racist because they are white. Whiteness is an oppressor group; therefore, all whites are systemically racist.[34]

31 Marcuse, *Eros and Civilization.*

32 Marcuse, "Repressive Tolerance," 95–137.

33 Saul D. Alinsky, *Rules for Radicals.*

34 Robin DiAngelo's book *White Fragility: Why It's So Hard for White People to Talk about Racism* is an excellent introductory book explaining and defending the far-left ideology called Critical Race Theory.

True Community is only found in the Judeo-Christianity worldview (as noted by German philosopher Dietrich Von Hildebrand). The Christian view of the individual is that each and every human was created in God's image; therefore, human life is sacred (Gen 1:26–27; Acts 17:22–28). Each individual is of great value. Hence, true community is found only in the Church—the Body of Christ (John 13:35; 1 Cor 12:12–14). Because they devalue the worth of each individual, godless systems like Postmodernism, Marxist Communism, Cultural Marxism, National Socialism, international socialism, and Fascism can never produce true community—they only produce collectivism. Only the collective whole has any value—individuals have no significance apart from their collective community. Hence, Cultural Marxism signals the death of human rights to any society that embraces it.

The Great Reset

On October 30, 2020, Archbishop Carlo Maria Viganò, the former Apostolic Nuncio to the United States, wrote a letter to then President Donald Trump warning him about the dangers of the "Great Reset." In this letter, Archbishop Viganò claimed that "the whole world is being threatened by a global conspiracy against God and Humanity." He wrote that global elites like Bill Gates and the World Economic Forum want to impose "coercive measures with which to drastically limit individual freedoms..." through a "health dictatorship" forced on the world. Viganò argued that the goal was to reset the world's economy by using the coronavirus as an excuse to control mankind and redistribute the world's wealth. A digital ID (possibly given through a vaccine) would be required as a global health passport, thus enabling those in power to track all humans. Lockdowns would destroy businesses and private property would be confiscated. Viganò claimed that not only is there a "deep state," but there is also a "deep church" headed by the present Bishop of Rome, Pope Francis. Viganò claimed that Pope Francis is himself a globalist and a socialist.

Journalist Alex Newman confirmed the reality of the "Great Reset" in his book *Deep State: The Invisible Government Behind the Scenes*.[35] Newman wrote about a 2010 Rockefeller Foundation report titled "Scenarios for the Future of Technology and International Development." In this report, a hypothetical future pandemic is discussed, and "the United States suffers due to a lack of Tyranny, while China fares much better."[36] The report promoted

35 Newman, *Deep State*, 132–134.

36 Newman, *Deep State*, 132.

the implementing of biometric IDs for all citizens and stricter regulations on businesses and the population. Ten years later, Bill Gates proposed ID2020 to give each human being a digital identity enabling governments to track every person on Earth. In October 2019 (two months before the COVID-19 pandemic) Bill Gates joined with the World Economic Forum to finance Event 201. Globalists at this conference speculated as to how government, media, and businesses should respond to a hypothetical coronavirus pandemic. It was determined that, if a pandemic occurred, any misinformation concerning the virus must be banned. Totalitarian measures, such as shutdowns, were suggested. When the COVID-19 pandemic actually began a couple months later, these exact measures were implemented by governments around the world.[37]

Klaus Schwab, Founder and Executive Chairman of the World Economic Forum, joined with fellow globalist Thierry Malleret to author a book titled *COVID-19: The Great Reset.*[38] In this book, the authors propose a global economic reset of the world's economy. They called this reset "stakeholder capitalism," but the Great Reset is actually global socialism, a redistribution of wealth, and the abolition of private property.

Pro-freedom journalist Alex Newman stated that, in late 2019 (right around the time when the coronavirus was being identified), MIT revealed that Bill Gates (along with other globalists) had funded research at the university to invent a new way to record a patient's vaccination history by "storing the data in a dye, invisible to the naked eye, that is delivered under the skin at the same time as the vaccine." The technology "consists of nanocrystals called quantum dots." The implanted material "emits near-infrared light that can be detected by a specially equipped smartphone."[39] The material is called "Luciferase." It would enable authorities to determine if a person had received the vaccine.

At this point, it appears the Coronavirus injection (called a vaccine) does not contain every ingredient that the World Economic Forum, Bill Gates, and other globalist proponents planned to force on the masses. This may be due to the fact that the production of the "vaccine" had to be rushed in order to make it available to the public. At this time, there is no evidence for the presence of Luciferase or any tracking devices in the so-called vaccine.[40] However, it is possible that future injections will be added, thus introducing other ingredients into the human body. In the future, additional injections for this "vaccination" (or other "vaccinations") may be used to track and control human beings all over the world. The untested synthetic RNA in the Moderna and

37 Newman, *Deep State*, 134.

38 Schwab and Malleret, *COVID-19: The Great Reset.*

39 Newman, *Deep State*, 134.

40 See the next chapter: Reflections on the COVID-19 Pandemonium, section titled: Luciferase and Graphene Oxide in the Pfizer Vaccine? which explores this very issue.

Pfizer "vaccines" are risky enough as it is now; synthetic RNA is an unproven technology. But, future injections could add additional material that can be used to enslave mankind. These so-called vaccines have failed to protect the vaccinated from catching the virus or from transmitting it to others. Some vaccinated individuals have still died from the virus. This should cause one to wonder why the Biden administration is pushing for mandatory vaccinations and requiring vaccine passports to travel or conduct business. It seems that more than physical health and well-being is the end goal. The so-called vaccine is more about political control than it is about health.

Leading Opponents of the New World Order

There have been a few American leaders with the courage to speak out against the above anti-American organizations. In the 1950s, Congressman Carroll Reece headed the Reece Committee, which investigated major tax-exempt foundations such as the Rockefeller, Carnegie, and Ford Foundations. The Reece Committee discovered that these foundations donated large sums of money to control the social sciences, public education, and international affairs. The Committee found that these foundations financed the CFR and other globalist organizations.

In the 1970s, Senator Barry Goldwater publicly spoke out against the New World Order on numerous occasions. He had the courage to identify key globalist leaders and denounce their hideous agendas.

In 1981, Congressman Larry McDonald called for a congressional investigation into the CFR and the Trilateral Commission. Five years earlier, he wrote,

> The drive of the Rockefellers and their allies is to create a one-world government combining supercapitalism and Communism under the same tent, all under their control… Do I mean conspiracy? Yes I do. I am convinced there is such a plot, international in scope, generations old in planning, and incredibly evil in intent.[41]

Unfortunately, McDonald's life and investigation were tragically cut short in 1983 when he was killed (along with 268 other passengers) when the Korean Air Lines Flight 007 was shot down by Soviet air-to-air missiles. The American media reported the incident as an unfortunate "accident."

In 1987, Senator Jesse Helms publicly spoke out against the "Eastern Establishment," the Council on Foreign Relations, the Trilateral Commission, the Bilderberg Group, and the Federal Reserve System. He stated that the

41 In the Introduction to Gary Allen, *The Rockefeller File* ('76 Press, 1976).

establishment's view was once called "one-world," but that it is now known as "globalism." In recent years, Senator Helms has not been as outspoken against the New World Order as he was in the 1980s.

In the 1980s and 1990s, presidential candidate Pat Buchanan railed against the New World Order in his campaign speeches. This may be one of the primary reasons for his failure to win the presidency. The American media portrayed Buchanan as a bigot, a common tactic utilized by the press against true conservative candidates.

Currently, former Congressman Ron Paul and his son Senator Rand Paul are leading opponents of the globalist agenda. On a regular basis, Ron Paul called upon his fellow congressmen to vote for the United States' removal from the UN, but only a small percentage of our congressmen have supported Ron Paul on this account. He also argued that the Federal Reserve should be audited, knowing this would reveal its corruption and its betrayal of the American people.

President Trump courageously spoke out against globalism at the third speech of his presidency to the UN. He said, "The free world must embrace its national foundations. It must not attempt to erase them, or replace them." Addressing the leaders of many nations, he proclaimed, "The future does not belong to the globalists; the future belongs to patriots."[42]

Conclusion: The Current Situation

As the Biden administration takes office, the global agenda is back on track. Donald J. Trump fought for America, but now he has left office. The Deep State (i.e., the political establishment, the FBI, CIA, DOJ, CFR, TLC, etc.) will be unleashed without presidential resistance. With control of the presidency and both houses of Congress, our leaders will now attempt to move America swiftly in the direction of an all-powerful globalist state. Decisions will be made, not according to what is best for Americans, by what is deemed to be best for the UN, internationalism, and the Chinese communist regime.

It is our Christian duty to pray for our leaders, especially for those on the side of freedom (i.e., Ron Paul, Rand Paul, former President Trump, etc.), as they lead the fight against the evil forces of globalism. But we must do more than pray. God is calling us to speak out against the New World Order just as He called Christians to speak out against the holocaust, slavery, and abortion. God is calling us to educate others about globalism. By remaining silent, we help tomorrow's tyrants build the New World Order and enslave the masses. If

42 Borger, "Donald Trump denounces 'globalism' in nationalist address to UN."

globalists have their way, it will lead to what C. S. Lewis called "The Abolition of Man." It will lead to the deification of the state in which the few enslave the billions. Between liberty and tyranny exists a very thin line. Only those who study history and appreciate God's hand in the affairs of man can detect this thin line. Politically speaking, the only thing worse than being a slave who knows he is a slave is being a slave who thinks he is still free. May God have mercy on America.

Bibliography

Admin. "Joe Biden: 'How I Learned To Love The New World Order'." *American Patriot Contact Tracers*, January 8, 2021. http://americanpatriotcontacttracers.com/joe-biden-how-i-learned-to-love-the-new-world-order/.

Allen, Gary. *The Rockefeller File*. 1976. https://openlibrary.org/books/OL5211079M/The_Rockefeller_file.

Alinsky, Saul D. *Rules for Radicals*. New York: Vintage Books, 1989.

Borger, Julian. "Donald Trump denounces 'globalism' in nationalist address to UN." *The Guardian*, September 24, 2019. https://theguardian.com/us-news/2019/sep/24/donald-trump-un-address-denounces-globalism.

Breitbart, Andrew. *Righteous Indignation*. New York: Grand Central Publishing, 2011.

Brooke, Tal. *One World*. Berkeley: End Run Publishing, 2000.

Clinton, Hillary Rodham. "Hillary Clinton Reviews Henry Kissinger." Washington Post, September 4, 2014, sec. Opinions. https://www.washingtonpost.com/opinions/hillary-clinton-reviews-henry-kissingers-world-order/2014/09/04/b280c654-31ea-11e4-8f02-03c644b2d7d0_story.html.

CNN. "Transcript of Blair's Speech to Congress." *CNN*, July 17, 2003. https://www.cnn.com/2003/US/07/17/blair.transcript/.

Coffman, Michael S. *Saviors of the Earth?* Chicago: Northfield Publishing, 1994.

Corse, Jerome R. "Premeditated Merger: Amero Coming Within Decade." *WND*, October 5, 2007. https://www.wnd.com/2007/10/43860/.

de Ruiter, Robin and Fritz Springmeier. *Worldwide Evil and Misery: The Legacy of 13 Satanic Bloodlines*. Ann Arbor, Michigan: Mayra Publications, 2008.

DiAngelo, Robin. *White Fragility: Why It's So Hard for White People to Talk about Racism*. Boston: Beacon Press, 2018.

Epperson, A. Ralph. *The New World Order*. Lookout Mountain, TN: Publius Press, 1990.

Fernandes et al., *God, Government, and the Road to Tyranny*. Maitland, Florida:

Xulon Press, 2003.

Grigg, William Norman. *Freedom on the Altar*. Appleton: American Opinion Publishing, Inc., 1995.

Haass, Richard. "State sovereignty must be altered in globalized era." *Taipei Times*, February 21, 2006. http://www.taipeitimes.com/News/editorials/archives/2006/02/21/2003294021.

Horkheimer, Max. *Critical Theory: Selected Essays*. New York: Continuum Books, 2002.

Isaacson, Dean. *Under the Tower of Babel*. Monroe, Washington: Cominus Books, 1995.

Jasper, William F. *Global Tyranny: Step By Step*. Appleton: Western Islands, 1992.

———. "Kissinger Urges Obama to Build a 'New World Order,'" *The New American*, January 7, 2009. https://thenewamerican.com/kissinger-urges-obama-to-build-a-new-world-order/.

Kah, Gary H. *En Route to Global Occupation*. Lafayette: Huntington House, 1992.

———. *The New World Religion*. Noblesville, Indiana: Hope International, 1998.

Kissinger, Henry. Bilderberg Conference in Évian-les-Bains. France, 1991. https://www.aspentimes.com/news/time-to-wake-up/.

Lott, Trent. "UN Intervention in Somali." *C-SPAN*, October 5, 1993. https://www.c-span.org/video/?51185-1/un-intervention-somalia.

Marcuse, Herbert. *Eros and Civilization*. Boston: Beacon Press, 1966.

———. "Repressive Tolerance," in Robert Paul Wolff, Barrington Moore, Jr., and Herbert

———. *A Critique of Pure Tolerance*. Boston: Beacon Press, 1969, 95–137.

McManus, John F. *Changing Commands*. Appleton: John Birch Society, 1995.

———. *Financial Terrorism*. Appleton: John Birch Society, 1993.

———. *The Insiders*. Appleton: John Birch Society, 1996.

Newman, Alex. *Deep State: The Invisible Government Behind the Scenes*. Appleton, WI: Western Islands Publishing, 2020.

Next News Network. "Joe Biden Calls to 'Create a New World Order'." YouTube Video, April 6, 2013. https://www.youtube.com/watch?v=MI6wvNJ22Dk&feature=emb_title.

Obama, Barack. "Remarks by the President to the United Nations General Assembly," *The Whitehouse: Office of the Press Secretary*, September 23, 2009. https://obamawhitehouse.archives.gov/the-press-office/remarks-president-united-nations-general-assembly.

———. "Read Barack Obama's Final Speech to the United Nations." *Time Magazine*, September 20, 2016. https://time.com/4501910/president-obama-united-nations-speech-transcript/.

Perloff, James. *The Shadows of Power*. Appleton: Western Islands, 1988.

Rockefeller, David. *Memoirs*. New York: Random House, 2002.

Schwab, Klaus and Thierry Malleret. *COVID-19: The Great Reset*. Geneva, Switzerland: Forum Publishing, 2020.

Talbott, Strobe. *The Great Experiment: The Story of Ancient Empires, Modern States, and the Quest for a Global Nation*. New York: Simon & Schuster, 2008.

Chapter 42

Reflections on the COVID-19 Pandemonium

Scott D. G. Ventureyra

To say that it has been difficult to keep abreast of all the new developments that surge daily would be a platitude but an undeniable fact. The other issue, aside from keeping abreast with the bombardment of information, is one of discerning reliable information from misinformation/disinformation; this is not an easy task. Niccolò Machiavelli in his novel, *The Prince*, wrote the following: "And since there are three kinds of brains: one that understands by itself, another that discerns what others understand, the third that understands neither by itself nor through others."[1] I am hoping you will either be in the first class or, if not, definitely the second when it comes to discerning the events related to COVID-19. It is precisely as Professor of Clinical Psychology at Ghent University in Belgium, Mattias Desmet, who has studied the psychology of totalitarianism, states in an interview with international trial lawyer Reiner Fuellmich:

> Usually it's only about 30% who are really grasped in mass phenomenon or in the hypnosis. But an additional 35 to 40% usually does not want to raise a dissonant voice in public space because they are scared of the consequences. So usually we have about 70% who shut up; 30% because they are convinced of the mainstream narrative and 40% because they don't dare to speak out. Then there is an additional 20, 25, 30% who do not go along with the narrative and also says it out loud in certain situations.[2]

In this interview, Fuellmich also asks: "So what is it in your view? What is it that, apart from the mainstream media, what is it that has caused this, well, illusion for so many people that they don't see the reality, but they see a totally different picture of what really goes on?"[3]

1 Machiavelli, *The Prince*, chapter XXII, 92.

2 The Eye of the Storm Corona Committee, "Mass Formation and Totalitarian Thinking in This Time of Global Crisis."

3 The Eye of the Storm Corona Committee, "Mass Formation and Totalitarian Thinking in This Time of Global Crisis."

Desmet's response is illuminating:

> Yes. Four things need to exist or need to be in place if you want a large-scale mass phenomenon to emerge. The first thing is that there needs to be a lot of socially isolated people, people who experience a lack of social bonds. The second one is that there needs to be a lot of people who experience a lack of sense-making in life. And the third and the fourth conditions are that there needs to be a lot of free-floating anxiety and a lot of free-floating psychological discontent. So: meaning, anxiety, and discontent that is not connected to a specific representation. So it needs to be in the mind without the people being able to connect it to something. If you have these four things—lack of social bonds, lack of sense-making, free-floating anxiety, and free-floating psychological discontent—then society is highly at risk for the emergence of mass phenomenon.[4]

Compelling the 40 percent who don't speak out is what is needed to reach a critical mass to bring about change. There are many friends and acquaintances that share similar views but are either afraid and/or would rather act in self-interest to sustain their comfort. This is why it is crucial to reverse that. This book is mostly directed to such individuals.

Mattias Desmet calls this hypnotic phenomenon, Mass Formation Psychosis, where a large portion of the population believes nonsensical narratives that fly in the face of evidence. People who are spiritual can see this as a demonic trance.[5] Desmet provides a way out of this cognitive dissonance, which a significant portion of the world's population has fallen prey to.[6]

We can summarize Desmet's mass formation psychosis in the following way: Totalitarianism requires the total obedience of a significant portion of the population. This obedience has been created through mass formation process inside the population. Four conditions need to be fulfilled: first, the masses must feel alone and isolated; second, they must feel that their lives are meaningless; third, they must experience a free-floating anxiety; and lastly, they must feel a free-floating frustration and aggression. This inability to pinpoint their aggression and loneliness is fundamental to the strategy. Once these four conditions are met, they are prepared to be "hypnotized." The inanity, stupidity, senselessness or even harmfulness of the proposed "solution" is irrelevant. The purpose is to make people feel solidarity with one another, thus validating the whole psychosis for them. From this period forward they are incapable of

4 The Eye of the Storm Corona Committee, "Mass Formation and Totalitarian Thinking in This Time of Global Crisis."

5 Carter Heavy Industries, "Prof. Mattias Desmet on Mass Formation."

6 Carter Heavy Industries, "What is Mass Formation Psychosis?"

being rational. This excludes any statistical, mathematical, or logical approaches to analysis which assume that people are in a rational state of mind. I have experienced an impenetrability to rationalize with many friends, including my daughter's mother, precisely because of this incapacity to reason. Consequently, these people who have been swept away by the mass-formation process also become highly intolerant and cruel. This is why you can see people on social media act viciously towards one another and in particular towards those who question the single narrative, and anything related to the vaccines. For example, some doctors have wished death upon the unvaccinated. Ironically, a cardiologist from New Brunswick, who claimed he wouldn't cry at the funeral of an unvaccinated person, or that he would punch the face of those who influence others against it, died shortly after receiving his booster.[7] For the people suffering mass formation psychosis, the vaccine is their only saviour, but also the only conceivable way out of their dystopian delusion. I argue later that the COVID-19 narrative is believed in such fervour that it resembles a religion. Desmet suggests that we must still resist and wake up others to combat mass formation psychosis. This, unfortunately, can be futile and often quite uncomfortable, but there are some people that may be open and receptive enough to question elements of the single narrative.

Some Preliminaries

Many health professionals see this as the greatest medical disaster in modern history. According to this view, there has been an unprecedented number of mishandlings, flip-flops, conflicts of interest and corruption, and countless examples of incompetence. While others see the COVID-19 pandemic as the greatest fraud pushed on humanity,[8] some see it as a "plandemic,"[9] a manufactured pandemic, a dystopian delusion, or a "scamdemic."[10] I, myself, prefer to call it a pandemic of medical malfeasance; one in lockstep with the pharmaceutical industry, the Center for Disease Control and Prevention (CDC) , National Institutes of Health (NIH), National Institute of Allergy and Infectious Diseases (NIAID), Food and Drug Administration (FDA), Bill & Melinda Gates Foundation, World Health Organization (WHO), Chinese Communist Party (CCP), Big Tech, mainstream media, World

7 The New American, "Doctor Who Said 'I Won't Cry' at 'Funeral for Unvaxxed' Dies After 3rd COVID Shot. He Wanted 'To Punch in the Face' the No Vax."

8 Covidland: Episode 1: The Lockdown.

9 Willis, *Plandemic: Fear Is the Virus. Truth Is the Cure.* See also "Plandemic: Indoctornation," 2020, https://www.imdb.com/title/tt12745644/. It has been one of the most censored yet watched documentaries of all time (over a billion views).

10 Iovine, *Scamdemic - The COVID-19 Agenda: The Liberal's Plot to Win The White House.*

Economic Forum, governments throughout the world, and medical and legal institutions throughout the world. The corruption and collusion is practically all encompassing.

Although I am not a scientist or healthcare professional, I have, however, received educational training in logic, philosophy, theology, history, economics, and ethics. I have presented at conferences to philosophers, theologians, and scientists. I have also successfully completed science courses at the university level. I have read widely on science. Furthermore, I wrote a book that interfaced the interactions between science, philosophy, and theology; it was endorsed by world renowned scientists and philosophers. So, although I am not an expert in medicine or science, my training in logic, philosophy, and other fields, allows me to assess the soundness and coherence of arguments regardless of the discipline in question. Logic and other aspects are fundamental to science and medicine, including being aware of the presuppositions involved. Even though pure objectivity is impossible, one should aim to be as objective as possible—science is about questioning and debating, not declaring issues by fiat. It is also subject to revision, especially in the case of COVID-19; we have seen this time and time again. Contradictory evidence to the main claims made by a particular case must be taken seriously and not swept away. Other authors in this book who focus on various aspects of COVID, including psychological elements, have the requisite training in such fields. Pediatric surgeon Enrique Ventureyra (also a contributor to this volume), who for many years was on the frontlines saving children's lives at the Children's Hospital of Eastern Ontario (CHEO), is completely horrified with the aggressive vaccine rollout program which is not seriously taking into account adverse effects and fatalities.

In this rather lengthy chapter, I will examine a number of issues related to, and pertaining to, the ongoing COVID-19 pandemonium that began in early 2020. You may want to separate your readings of this chapter by sections. I will provide a number of references in the footnotes for further research. These references include peer-reviewed articles, research articles, mainstream news articles, alternative news, opinion pieces, and various links with repositories of articles/videos. I have not verified the veracity of every resource, but I will leave it up to the reader to do further research and decide for themselves where the truth may lie. Please note that there are important details in the footnotes and the corresponding bibliographical references at the end of each chapter.

The Coronavirus disease 2019 (COVID-19), caused by the novel severe acute respiratory syndrome coronavirus 2 (SARS-CoV-2), is a disease that has been at the center of a world crisis since early 2020. Many secondary effects of the disease have been more devastating than the health repercussions alone. The recovery rate of COVID-19 is exceedingly high and has not warranted economic shutdowns and all of the associated negative effects that have been wrought upon free citizens of the world at the behest of governments, the World Health

Organization (WHO), and select medical experts. For the first time in human history, most of the world was locked down. Even if we take the Spanish Flu pandemic of 1918 to 1919, where the death toll was at least 50 million,[11] there was not a world lockdown which included healthy people. With COVID-19, healthy people were said to be "quarantined" which, by definition, is a logical contradiction since you cannot quarantine someone who is healthy. Indeed, the measures taken, and their associated ramifications, have been disproportionate to the danger the virus poses. It is also uncertain how long this situation will last given the potentially endless variants and boosters.

COVID-19 has brought a lot of uncertainty and changes throughout the world. Throughout the summer of 2021, the stock market took a dive because of investors' fears related to more lockdowns and impediments to financial recovery because of the so-called Delta variant. If this pattern continues, we may be heading in the same direction we did in March of 2020. The mainstream media in its mandate to divide the people have blamed the unvaccinated for this surge in the Delta variant. Interestingly, there has been a significant incidence of vaccinated people still transmitting and being affected by COVID-19.[12] Some studies are showing that natural immunity is stronger and longer lasting than being doubly vaccinated. In fact, an Israeli study, where the Pfizer vaccine has been widely and solely administered, demonstrates those who have been previously infected have 13 times stronger immunity than the doubly vaccinated.[13]

The only consistent thing we have been told throughout this pandemic is that we should wash our hands. Yes, we should always wash our hands. We should also try our best to keep our hands away from our face, especially after handling items in a grocery store, for instance. This is good general hygiene, and it prevents the spread of many germs. What about the rest of the recommendations, restrictions, and alleged "science"? Not so much. For close to two years, there have been a great many inconsistencies and falsities foisted upon citizens around the world. Many of the claims made by politicians and public health professionals have flipped and flopped. It is worth questioning the real reason why there are so many inconsistencies, retractions, and falsities. This has inevitably created a heightened level of skepticism and distrust over health mandates, the likes of which have never been witnessed before. Government, mainstream media (MSM), pharmaceutical companies' power over the medical establishment, the "medical experts," and Big Tech censorship are to blame. They

11 Center for Disease Control and Prevention (CDC), "1918 Pandemic (H1N1 virus)."

12 WND staff, "Mayo-trained doctor warns of COVID-19 'mutations' Israeli study and Mayo clinic doctor WND."

13 See Gazit, et al., "Comparing SARS-CoV-2 natural immunity to vaccine-induced immunity: reinfections versus breakthrough infections."

often work in ideological and financial unison. They share the same interests and agenda. These entities have successfully divided us over many issues.

Well-meaning people just want the truth, and these entities have at best obfuscated and distorted it, and, at the worst, blatantly told us lies. Without getting into all the specifics, it is worth noting that since March of 2020, we have seen a lot of flip flopping when it comes to many issues surrounding the COVID-19 pandemic, including mask mandates, asymptomatic versus symptomatic spread of the virus, forecasting models, the origin of the virus, the accuracy of PCR-testing, lockdowns, anti-viral treatments, retractions from major scientific and medical publications, the issuing of vaccine passports, vaccine information and disinformation regarding efficacy and safety, and issues revolving around informed consent particularly when it pertains to those 12 to 17 years old, to name a few. I had initially started writing about COVID-19 on my blog in April of 2020. I have also published a couple of articles for an online magazine since then. Even back then the astute observer could spot many inconsistencies and falsehoods being spewed by health officials, politicians, and their respective governments. However, I will not get into all the nitty gritty details here of how governments and health officials have so often contradicted themselves and/or spewed false information, since there is a large repository of articles including many peer-reviewed studies that challenge many of claims surrounding the COVID-19 narrative as pushed forward by governments and the media.[14]

Early Negligence in Canada

In March of 2020, the world was brought to its knees because of the misinformation provided by both the World Health Organization (WHO) and the Communist Party of China (CPC).[15] This has had devastating consequences for the world economy, and the health and lives of countless of millions around

14 For several repositories of information related to COVID that you will never find from mainstream sources, see: Truth for Health Foundation, "Vaccine News"; Knightly, "30 facts you NEED to know: Your Covid Cribsheet"; LifeSite News, "LifeFacts: COVID-19"; Awake Canada, "documentation"; Awake Canada, "Awake Evidence"; Awakening Channel, "Most Shared Blog Posts (past 18 months)." See also economist and professor emeritus at University of Ottawa, Michel Chossudovsky, and his website Global Research, which has many articles examining different aspects of the COVID-19 crisis, globalism, and the New World Order: https://www.globalresearch.ca/; Chossudovsky, *The 2020-21 Worldwide Corona Crisis: Destroying Civil Society, Engineered Economic Depression, Global Coup d'État and the "Great Reset."* Lastly, see the RCMP's thoroughly detailed open letter with several appendices with valuable resources: "Mounties for Freedom, Open Letter to RCMP Commissioner Brenda Lucki"; Association of American Physicians and Surgeons, "Physician List & Guide to Home-Based COVID Treatment"; Stop World Control.

15 Slatz, "The World Health Organization is to blame."

the globe. Unfortunately, news networks like CNN have chosen to focus their attention on identity politics rather than on China's reckless behavior.[16] This pandering to a communist enemy unleashing a viral threat towards the Western world is morally reprehensible; this just further exemplifies where the mainstream media's priorities lie. Let us not forget the great missteps within my homeland, Canada, to mitigate the entry of SARS-CoV-2. Conservative finance critic Pierre Poilievre rightfully criticized Prime Minister Justin Trudeau, and the Liberal government, of negligence for allowing two thousand people to enter Canada from Hubei, China after January 22, 2020. This was after receiving information from military intelligence that the spread of the coronavirus was extensive and dangerous. Conveniently, the CBC never wanted Canadians to see the video of Poilievre grilling the Liberals. Unfortunately, as is the case in so many instances, Trudeau and the Liberal Party members (in this video Chrystia Freeland) offer evasive responses to specific questions because they are obviously hiding information from the public.[17]

Instead, the CBC, which is funded by the Liberals, would rather focus its attention on criticizing former US President Donald J. Trump than keeping a closer eye on domestic politics.[18] On June 11, 2020, in his usual pointed style, Poilievre grilled our corrupt finance minister, Bill Morneau, only to be met with the usual and tiresome Liberal tactic of evasion when answering questions on how much Trudeau's incompetent government owes China on our national debt.[19] This evasiveness and corruption by elected governments is nothing unique to Canada, but can be seen running rampant throughout the world.

The following events of 2020, in Canada alone, should trouble any individual who believes their respective country has their best interests at heart. Vaccine trials have been approved by Health Canada; this vaccine candidate has been developed by Chinese company CanSino Biologics.[20] Trudeau, at the time, had signed a contract for 37 million syringes with Becton Dickinson.[21] This should raise red flags since by the end of March 2020, according to authorities in Spain, Turkey, and the Netherlands, thousands of testing kits and other medical equipment including medical

16 Vasque and Klein, "Trump again defends use of the term 'China virus'."

17 I have posted a number of videos on my website which have been censored on platforms such as Facebook, Twitter, and YouTube. Keep an eye out for scottventureyra.com—I will post many videos that have been censored on there in the coming months of 2022.

18 For a lengthy treatment on whether the CBC is trustworthy news, see watch out for a repost of Ventureyra, "The CBC - A Source of Trustworthy News or an Engine for Propaganda?"; Taghva, "Liberal minister says government will boost CBC funding."

19 Keep an eye out for Ventureyra, the third video on this webpage, which was downloaded and uploaded onto my website, where Pierre Poilievre grills former Liberal finance minister, Bill Morneau, https://www.scottventureyra.com/post/won-t-get-fooled-again-by-the-who.

20 Clinical Trials Arena Staff, "Health Canada approves first Covid-19 vaccine trials."

21 Aiello, "Anticipating 'mass vaccinations', Canada ordering millions of syringes."

masks provided by China were found to be defective.[22] In a report from June 2020, there were strong reasons to believe that the testing for COVID-19 at the beginning of the pandemic was wholly inaccurate because numerous of the kits created by the Centers for Disease Control and Prevention (CDC) were contaminated.[23] Moreover, thousands of contaminated test kits were provided to New Brunswick.[24] So, not only did they unleash this virus onto the world, which has crippled the world economy for the past 2 years, they have also provided defective testing kits and equipment. Instead of distancing financial relations with China, Trudeau's government double downs on it. Time and time again, he has demonstrated he cannot be trusted as the leader of Canada.[25] But, instead, the media, even in Canada, focused its attention on criticisms of President Donald Trump.

A Period of Mass Confusion

So how do we know what to believe these days with so many pieces of contradictory information? Can we trust municipal, provincial/state, and federal governments, WHO, CDC, and other organizations? The mainstream media or even alternative media? It is true that everyone has their own agenda. But the fundamental question is, does it line up with the truth? In other words, does it correspond with reality and how things *actually* are? These are not things easily discerned in periods of opacity. Therefore, it is crucial to think for yourself. That means you will have to sift and reflect upon what is true in terms of what you are being told by governments, experts, and alternative sources. Do not let them spoon feed you and tell you exactly what you *have* to believe. I know that everyone is busy with their day-to-day routines, but I can't stress how vital it is that we work together as a human race to unravel the truth and live in harmony. As you have heard time and time again, we are living in unprecedented times. Nothing of this nature has ever happened, given our technological developments and population size—we are in a totally unique point in human history. We are also at a breaking point with hopefully a brighter future for humans and the planet we inhabit. With the ease of information, you can consult many sources at your fingertips and make up your own mind with the caveat that Google manipulates your searches. It has gotten so bad that if you google "can a man get pregnant," the first result from the search says: "Yes, it's possible for men to become

22 BBC Staff, "Coronavirus: Countries reject Chinese-made equipment."
23 Carolyn Crist, "Early CDC COVID-19 Test Kits 'Likely Contaminated'."
24 Magee, "Thousands of contaminated test kits delivered to New Brunswick."
25 Craig, "The Dramatic Rejection of Liberal Politics in Canada."

pregnant and give birth to children of their own." But if you google "should you use ivermectin," the first result of the search lists the FDA website with the title on an article stating: "Why You Should Not Use Ivermectin to Treat or Prevent COVID-19." Nevertheless, many of the things we are told flip then flop, then spin, then flip and then flop again.

Human Corruption and Evil

A charitable interpretation could be that part of the reason for this may be because of sheer ignorance, but in other cases, it may be a clever deception involving Machiavellian tactics. Could it be that they are telling certain truths mixed with lies to confound and confuse? I am not closed to this possibility. This is not some loonie conspiracy theory, it is unraveling right before your eyes, but you have to be willing to see and seek the truth. It is a matter of connecting the dots between each major event and the conspiring powers, such as the technocrats, Hollywood elites, the Democrats, and world bankers. Why should anyone exclude this possibility? These people have vested interests in controlling the world economy and pushing their ideological agendas. The top 1% for years has owned 50% of the world's wealth.[26] In the USA alone, the top 1% own as much as the middle-class.[27]

If we have learned anything from history and human psychology it is that the human heart is engulfed with darkness, pride, a lust for power, and greed. It is not to say that there is not good—there is, but darkness and corruption penetrates the human heart, and even more so when power becomes heavily concentrated into governments and special interest groups. We must always be vigilant over governments. The role of government is not to tell us what to do and what to think, but to protect our civil rights and civil liberties. Unfortunately, governments throughout the world are focusing on the former. This is the path to tyranny, as we have witnessed time and time again, whether it be in the Soviet Union, Nazi Germany, Mao's China, Pol Pot's Cambodia, the CPC, or draconian measures taken in Canada right now. Although Canada is still far away from such totalitarianism, our politicians are gradually stripping our freedoms away.

26 Neate, "Richest 1% own half the world's wealth, study finds."

27 Kelly, "The 1% Owns Almost As Much Wealth As The Middle Class: Will The Rich Keep Getting Richer?"

Unthinking Compliance[28]

What has been striking since the beginning of the COVID-19 crisis is how quickly we were to abandon our civil liberties and behave like automatons: keeping six feet apart, not seeing people outside of those you live with, wearing a mask (even outdoors), staying away from parks, following arrows at essential stores, etc. And beware if you do not follow these regulations. In some instances you may be fined or at the very least ostracized by a holier-than-thou model citizen.[29] Up to June of 2021, in Ontario, Canada, the measures were astonishingly similar to what they were in March of 2020. When governments and medical authorities instill fear, as has been the case with COVID-19, it is remarkable how compliant and credulous a population becomes without questioning what is going on. Even more remarkable is that most North Americans initially supported governmental control and lockdowns. Some went so far as to report churches and other groups who did not abide by these stringent restrictions. Some just follow without thinking, whereas others, like myself, have followed out of respect for others and from feeling coerced by our governments—this could be thought of as a "thinking compliance."

The vaccine rollout has also demonstrated that most people are prepared to unthinkingly comply. It is alarming how many people are willing to inject themselves with the mRNA vaccine, which is experimental, without, more often than not, being able to articulate any logical reasons as to why. For a disease that has a high recovery rate of 97–99.75%, which includes people with comorbidities, one ought to wonder: why the excessive and aggressive vaccine rollout?[30] The fact that incentivization[31] is required for an unnecessary and potentially harmful experimental vaccine is troubling and should raise red flags about governments' motivations who exercise such strategies. Even strategies of offering a $100, according to the *NYT*, have been exercised. The *Financial Times* has reported that Biden is asking local and state governments to offer $100 as an incentive to receive the vaccine.[32] In the US, the Biden administration is offering free beer for taking the COVID-19 vaccine.[33] Even

28 This is a term I coined on my blog in June of 2020, long before I heard of Mattias Desmet's work on "mass formation psychosis," but it has some similarities since it gains compliance of the "masses" through fear.

29 Recently, in Saskatchewan, a snitch line online system has been setup to report against those breaking COVID-19 rules/mandates. See Lamb, "The province is implementing a user-friendly 'snitch line' (online reporting system), for citizens who wish to report individuals or businesses breaking COVID-19 rules or mandates."

30 WebMD, "Coronavirus Recovery."

31 D'Amore, "Can incentives help vaccine hesitancy? Experts say it's a short-term solution."

32 Politi, "Biden calls on state and local governments to offer $100 vaccine incentives."

33 Miller, "Free beer, other new incentives for Biden's 'vaccine sprint'."

donuts, pizza, fries, and gift cards are being offered[34]—quite a cheap price to pay for someone's health. For any objective observer, this seems quite odd and rather troubling.

Social Engineering?

It is also important to note that citizens of the world, including Canadians, are part of a social engineering program through an initiative known as The Behavioural Insights Team.[35] They use what is known as "nudge theory," which is:

> the idea that by shaping the environment, also known as the choice architecture, one can influence the likelihood that one option is chosen over another by individuals. A key factor of Nudge Theory is the ability for an individual to maintain freedom of choice and to feel in control of the decisions they make.[36]

This could explain a portion of why certain people are unthinkingly compliant. One would wonder how free their freedom of choice would be since the key is "to feel in control." If we are not truly aware of the choices we are making without coercion, manipulation, or some level of social engineering, how can one say that the choice is being made freely?

Cognitive Dissonance and Self-Deception

People are willing to compromise familial relations to bolster a mass deception. There is an undeniable cognitive dissonance when it comes to reasoning about the COVID-19 crisis. The media has managed to totally polarize families, friends, and society in general. A friend of mine was recently asked to attend her sister's Thanksgiving celebration, but her sister requested that all unvaccinated family members eat and stay within the garage and that other family members could go visit them if they felt comfortable doing so. She politely declined the invitation, but such a request finds itself at the intersection of hilarity, absurdity, and tragedy. The main narrative once supported the notion that if you were doubly vaccinated you would not be at risk of becoming sick with COVID nor

34 Dodd and Pukak, "How to Get Promotions, Prizes and Freebies with your COVID-19 Vaccine."

35 The Behavioural Insights Team, accessed November 3, 2021. https://www.bi.team/about-us/.

36 Imperial College London, "What is Nudge Theory?"

transmitting the disease. Things quickly changed, as they have throughout the pandemic, from this to now saying that you would get a weakened strain of COVID and that your potential to transmit the virus is substantially lessened. From an Israeli study we know that this is not the case. It is also incoherent to suggest that you are at risk of COVID from the unvaccinated after being doubly vaccinated. Either the vaccine protects you or it does not. Otherwise, what's the point in getting it? You can't have it both ways, despite the flip-flopping by the medical experts and politicians bolstering the accepted narrative.

There are three questions to be asked about the COVID-19 vaccine: Is it necessary? Is it safe? Does it stop transmission? The answer to these three questions is unequivocally no.[37]

COVID-19 "Vaccination" and Appalling Absurdities Related to Child Custody (Decision-Making)

The judicial system in Canada and in many countries is just as corrupt as the medical establishment, the media, and Big Tech when it comes to COVID-19. Some judges are willing to take away custody and access based on someone's particular views around COVID-19[38] and vaccine status.[39] They are also willing to interfere with a parent's conscience. For example, on October 18, 2021, Ontario Superior Court Justice Jennifer Mackinnon ruled in opposition to a mother advising against the COVID-19 vaccine for her 14-year-old boy.[40] The parents of the boy share joint decision-making but the judge ruled in favour of father having sole decision-making with respect to the vaccine, ignoring the recommendation of the mother's family doctor. The judge alleged that the mother had influenced the boy and that his vaccine hesitancy was not based on his own thoughts. Could it be that perhaps the boy, although not being able to fully articulate his hesitancy, may intuitively know he does not want to take it? Conversely, the question arises, why is it okay for child to provide "informed consent" without parental consultation in favour of the vaccine? Most adults are not even capable of providing proper informed consent since they possess asymmetrical information regarding this particular "vaccine." That is in part

37 See Vaccine Adverse Events Reporting System (VAERS), "VAERS COVID Vaccine Adverse Event Reports."; Kostoff, et al., "Why are we vaccinating children against COVID-19?"; Gazit, "Comparing SARS-CoV-2 natural immunity to vaccine-induced immunity: reinfections versus breakthrough infections."

38 Barker, "Windsor court ruling puts COVID-19 'hoax' belief at centre of custody fight."

39 Although a judge in Chicago ended up reversing his decision on withdrawing access from the mother, it shows that in North America we are dealing with kangaroo courts. See Colton, "Judge reverses decision, allows unvaccinated mom to see her son."

40 Dimmock, "Judge bans Ottawa mother from advising son against COVID-19 vaccine."

because most people have been subject to a massive propaganda campaign of coercion to receive this injection. Informed consent entails the following: consent by a person to undergo a medical procedure, participate in a clinical trial, or be counseled by a professional such as a social worker or lawyer, after receiving all material information regarding risks, benefits, and alternatives. The basis for the ruling was the rejection of the family physician's letter arguing for the child not to receive the vaccine. Later in this chapter, and in subsequent chapters, we will explore a myriad of reasons why the vaccine is not necessary, nor safe, for children. Sooner or later, judges, medical doctors, and parents who unjustifiably push vaccines onto healthy children will have to contend with the evidence and will be held accountable.

Regrettably, judges will follow scientific consensus despite how out of touch with reality it may be. The scientific and medical consensus on COVID is deeply flawed, unlike in other domains, but more on that below. Nevertheless, this is not to say that all judges think this way, but there is a tremendous pressure to follow the single narrative since dissidents must be punished. Questioning in any aspect of this single narrative revolving around COVID, regardless of the domain, is strictly "forboden," since 2+2=5 and if you say otherwise, you will be susceptible to some sort of reprisal. Some parents are withdrawing visiting access from separated parents if they have not received two doses of the COVID-19 injection. This is the epitome of irrationality since children have a higher chance of dying from a car accident, suffocation, etc. It seriously boggles my mind when a psychopathic duplicitous liar like Trudeau not only admonishes against adults who refuse to get vaccinated, but also has made it mandatory for air travellers and all Federal Government employees under the pretext that they can protect their children.[41] Anyone who believes such nonsense is in serious need of a lobotomy. Even if a child has a compromised immune system, there are other ways around this and growing evidence is suggesting that natural immunity is stronger than double vaccination, and that those who are doubly vaccinated can just as well transmit the virus.[42] Moreover, vaccines do not prevent transmission or even confer immunity. An article in the *British Medical Journal* highlights this very point. The vaccine manufacturers have been very clear upon distributing the untested mRNA-based gene therapies: they are aimed at "reducing the severity of symptoms" not eliminating them.[43]

41 This above cited article demolishes the need for children to be vaccinated against COVID-19, see: Kostoff, et al., "Why are we vaccinating children against COVID-19?" This article also backs up the points I made in an email (see below) towards my daughter's mother and our lawyers, which was totally ignored. It's another example of how evidence does not matter to the COVID zealots. For Trudeau's unconstitutional and absurd mandates, see Aiello, "Air passengers and federal public servants must be vaccinated by end of October."

42 Gazit, "Comparing SARS-CoV-2 natural immunity to vaccine-induced immunity: reinfections versus breakthrough infections."

43 Doshi, "Will covid-19 vaccines save lives? Current trials aren't designed to tell us."

In my own personal life, it is so difficult to reach some people who refuse and/or are incapable of absorbing sound reasoning and scientific data. Personally, I am not against vaccinations and have taken all the necessary vaccinations as a child and I have had my daughter take all of hers. But with respect to the COVID-19 vaccine I have expressed concerns that have been met by my daughter's mother with irrational vitriol instead of a civil discussion. In an email, I presented good reasons based on science and statistics, which were totally ignored since, according to her, I am being "unreasonable" because I dare question untrustworthiness of government officials, Big Pharma, and so-called health experts. These were the facts I presented in an email in August 2021 (adverse effects and fatalities have only gotten worse since then):

> In my view, the risks outweigh the benefits for a healthy child. For your information, there have been 16 deaths since the beginning of the pandemic in Canada for children ages 0 to 19. I'm quite confident these children had compromised immune systems. Go look at the stats yourself.[44] [Unfortunately, the government documents do not tell you such a thing, but it is reasonable to presume given the evidence collected thus far.] What must be done is a cost-benefit analysis. That's the rational way to go about this. And, to be very clear, I don't oppose vaccines; for instance, the tetanus and polio vaccinations are lifesaving.
>
> Consider the following, according to the Vaccine Adverse Events Reporting System (VAERS) in the US, from 1997–2013 there were 2, 149 reported deaths; this includes billions upon billions of administered vaccines (a significantly higher number than the administered number of COVID-19 vaccines). Whereas the COVID vaccine, in only an eight-to-nine-month period, with 366 M doses administered, as of August 21, [2021] there were 13, 068 reported deaths in about 5% of the time span. There were also 5,882 Heart Attacks, 4,861, Myocarditis/Pericarditis, and 17,228 Permanently Disabled reports [– in sum, over 700, 000 injuries]. This should give any reasonable person pause.[45] I could go on and on. I have plenty of arguments and data. One of my responsibilities as a parent is to protect [our daughter], not to blindly follow what governments mandate/recommend without question. I live by reason, not fear.[46]

What's more is that my daughter's doctor was in agreement about my concerns regarding adverse effects. Not only was he in agreement, but I have proof of it. He said that these are real concerns. Of course, the doctor, given the climate of hostility for dissenters, recommended the vaccine, despite the risks,

44 Government of Canada, "COVID-19 daily epidemiology update."

45 VAERS, https://www.openvaers.com/covid-data.

46 Scott Ventureyra, email dated August 27, 2021.

but he was sympathetic to my concerns since he realized I was well informed on the issues at hand. I presented him with legitimate concerns and facts, no misinformation. The doctor went out of his way to state this. The facts that were presented were taken from government sources whether in Canada or the US. It is also interesting to note that my daughter's doctor said that she could not provide informed consent regarding the vaccine. However, the Government of Ontario has recklessly stipulated that any child born in 2009 can take the vaccine by their own choice without parental approval. The doctor thought that the government allowing a 12-year-old to have informed consent is an extreme measure and would likely not be the case without parental consent. The meningococcal vaccine, which has a known track record for effectiveness and safety, even required both the signature of one parent and the recipient child from my daughter's school in September of 2021. Any inquisitive mind would wonder why the same standard is not applied to an experimental injection.[47]

My daughter's mother attempted to proceed with an urgent order for the vaccine even though there is an extremely low risk of fatality and hospitalization for this disease. (Since this attempted urgent order, I "reluctantly agreed" since I faced the potential of losing decision-making for the COVID-19 vaccines; I thought this could allow me to prevent the second dose if there was an adverse effect. She is set to receive her second dose in the coming weeks. It has been an impossible battle for me against the mother since she is supported by the entire government, medical and judicial establishment, not to mention educational institutions and the media. I did what I could and will include a generic form [as an appendix] of the letter I sent the mother to help her see the risks and not proceed with vaccinating our child. I may have truth and reason on my side, but this is useless when you are fighting a misled and corrupt system, unless a critical mass wakes up.) For instance, in Canada, as of November 5, 2021, there have been 1,718,937 cases of COVID-19.[48] Moreover, there have been 359,931 cases of people under the age of 20;[49] this amounts to 20.9 percent of the total number of cases, the largest age group of infections. This group has had 1,899 hospitalizations which amounts to be .53 percent of all cases under 20, which is the lowest of any age group. There have also been 17 deaths out of 28, 900[50] of the total number of deaths amounting to .059 percent of all deaths in Canada; and out of the total number of young people in that demographic of the population of 8.1 million, the risk factor is .0002%. What about deaths to total population of roughly 38 million? .000045 percent. In comparison to traffic collisions, in 2019, there were 160 deaths for people 20 and under;[51] if

47 See Chapter 46.
48 Government of Canada, "COVID-19 daily epidemiology update."
49 Government of Canada, "COVID-19 daily epidemiology update."
50 Government of Canada, "COVID-19 daily epidemiology update."
51 Government of Canada, "Canadian Motor Vehicle Traffic Collision Statistics: 2018."

we sample that to 20 months (at a rate of 13.33 deaths/month) there would be a total of 267 deaths for similar timespan. This means that there is 15.7 times higher risk of dying from a car accident than COVID-19. Does this mean we should be paralyzed by fear every time we drive? With life there are risks, just by virtue of living you will die. People die every day but living in fear or putting on a façade that this is about protecting children is a grave offense to everyone's intelligence and conscience.

The following questions arise: Who are you going to trust more: plain reason, common sense, evidential science, foundational moral principles, and your own conscience, or that of incompetent bureaucrats masquerading as actual conscientious medical doctors? Are you going to trust these so-called doctors like Anthony Fauci (director of the National Institute of Allergy and Infectious Diseases) in the US who has been caught lying and flip-flopping on countless occasions?[52] And who has had countless conflicts of interest?[53] What about in Canada, Theresa Tam (Chief Public Health Officer of Canada—dubbed Canada's "top doctor") who says you better mask up during sexual activity?[54] How about Kieran Moore (Ontario's top doctor) who warns about the dangers of children yelling on doorsteps "trick or treat" at Halloween?[55] (Whenever we hear the term "top doctor" we should think the opposite of these medical bureaucrats without any moral conscience.) What about when Patty Hajdu (the former Minister of Health), who has zero knowledge of science or medicine, in a response to independent MP Derek Sloan, ignorantly claimed that Vitamin D for boosting one's immune system to prevent illnesses such as COVID-19 is "fake news"?[56] To ask these questions is to answer them. Anyone who thinks they can trust these bureaucrats are either consumed by propaganda or suffer from both cognitive and moral deficiencies. We should do the exact opposite from what these people recommend since they have betrayed our trust on countless occasions. It is also worth considering that: 1) clinical trials for these inoculations were very short-term, and 2) these clinical trials did not address long-term effects most relevant to children.[57] Thus, it should become evident that not only are these injections unnecessary but potentially harmful to those under 20. It is the largest experiment performed on humanity, and everyone is participating "willingly."

52 Trejo, "Dr. Anthony Fauci Admits He was Lying about Masks and Vaccines After New CDC Directive."

53 See Deace and Erzen, *Faucian Bargain: The Most Powerful and Dangerous Bureaucrat in American History*.

54 Jones, "Canada's top doctor: 'consider using a mask' during sexual activity."

55 Liley, "Ford owes restaurants apology for bizarre reopening decision."

56 Malcolm, "No, Minister Hajdu, the Vitamin D conversation isn't 'fake news'."

57 See Kostoff, et al., "Why Are We Vaccinating Children Against COVID-19?"

The pretext of this push toward an urgent order was to "protect" our daughter and help stop the spread; the blame is laid on the unvaccinated but day by day this is being shown to be nothing more than fear mongering, as an article published October 29, 2021, in *The Lancet*, recognizes

> The SARS-CoV-2 delta (B.1.617.2) variant is highly transmissible and spreading globally, including in populations with high vaccination rates...our findings suggest that vaccination alone is not sufficient to prevent all transmission of the delta variant in the household setting, where exposure is close and prolonged.[58]

Parents, who alongside the government, news media, and social media are instilling irrational and ungrounded fear in our youth over COVID-19, should think long and hard of Jesus's words: "If anyone causes one of these little ones—those who believe in me—to stumble, it would be better for them to have a large millstone hung around their neck and to be drowned in the depths of the sea" (Matt 8:6).

Nevertheless, I always ask myself if this parent[59] has any appreciation for science or basic math. If we do exactly as we are told without good evidence, then we become intellectually subservient to medical and political authoritarians. The alleged urgency to vaccinate our healthy children is nothing short of criminal. Perhaps in the not-so-distant future, will this person be able to claim ignorance, if our daughter suffers some adverse effect and the narrative collapses? I will try my best to hold her accountable when and if that day comes. There is no excuse to play Russian roulette with your child's life and health. History will not look kindly on such parents.

Unfortunately, only some parents will do their due diligence in protecting their children, instead of blindly following unwarranted, reckless, and dangerous recommendations by government officials and medical experts who have proven their untrustworthiness time and time again. Make no mistake, many medical doctors at the highest levels are guilty of medical malfeasance. And even more disturbing is that some parents will also nefariously use COVID-19 as leverage for matters related to custody. A totally despicable

58 Singanayagam, "Community transmission and viral load kinetics of the SARS-CoV-2 delta (B.1.617.2) variant in vaccinated and unvaccinated individuals in the UK: a prospective, longitudinal, cohort study." Notice how the journal even tries to spin the data, suggesting that receiving boosters is still efficacious despite the two vaccines not curbing transmission effectively. These journals are obviously compromised.

59 Indeed, this "individual" failed the same first year science course twice and also had a very rough go at an introduction to philosophy course but begged for a D crying the card of a single mom. Science and reason are not this person's friend. It is quite depressing and frustrating to share a child with a person who is governed by fear and uses opportune situations for leverage in a custody battle, instead of taking into account the real best interests of the child.

action given the heightened societal anxiety surrounding the COVID-19 crisis. Attempting to enforce a vaccine order and/or anything related to COVID as leverage should bring into question a parent's motivations and state of mind for decision-making. Undoubtedly, government coercion on vaccines and the associated repercussions, such as restricted access to certain services, job loss, and potential loss of custody are a full-frontal assault on individuals' freedom of conscience. Unfortunately, some parents and judges think this is sufficient grounds to acquiesce to unconstitutional and medically dangerous experimental treatments.

On a positive note, recently in Ontario, Justice Alex Pazaratz, who was courageous enough to put logic and morality over making the Ontario Superior Court of Justice subservient to the Government of Ontario and its health bureaucrats, may have very well set a precedent by reprimanding a father who focused on politics rather than the wellbeing of his children. In contrast, the mother who represented herself relied on scientific data from credible sources and experts in the field. Justice Pazaratz awarded the mother sole decision making when it comes to the COVID-19 vaccines. The first few points of Justice Pazaratz's judgment are worth quoting here since they speak to every parent, like myself, who has been demonized by other parents, the government, and judicial system for wanting what's best for their child and actually doing their due diligence. It is a scathing commentary on the state of our country, judicial system, and the world:

- When did it become illegal to ask questions? Especially in the courtroom?
- And when did it become unfashionable for judges to receive answers? Especially when children's lives are at stake?
- How did we lower our guard and let the words "unacceptable beliefs" get paired together? In a democracy? On the Scales of Justice?
- Should judges sit back as the concept of "Judicial Notice" gets hijacked from a rule of evidence to a substitute for evidence
- And is "misinformation" even a real word? Or has it become a crass, self-serving tool to pre-empt scrutiny and discredit your opponent? To de-legitimize questions and strategically avoid giving answers. Blanket denials are almost never acceptable in our adversarial system. Each party always has the onus to prove their case and yet "misinformation" has crept into the court lexicon. A childish—but sinister—way of saying "You're so wrong, I don't even have to explain why you're wrong."
- What does any of this have to do with family court? Sadly, these days it has everything to do with family court.
- Because when society demonizes and punishes anyone who disagrees—or even dares to ask really important questions—the

resulting polarization, disrespect, and simmering anger can have devastating consequences for the mothers, fathers and children I deal with on a daily basis.

- It's becoming harder for family court judges to turn enemies into friends—when governments are so recklessly turning friends into enemies.[60]

It is my hope that this will help prevent the injection of constant boosters into our daughter since growing evidence suggests that this can significantly damage one's immune system. It seems that the Scales of Justice are starting to tip.

COVID Stockholm Syndrome

One of the most bizarre elements to this unthinking compliance is the exhibition of what is known as Stockholm syndrome. Stockholm syndrome is an emotional response of positive feelings from a victim towards an abuser. In the case of COVID, it is manifested whenever an individual or groups of people are thankful to the government for reopening businesses that should have never been closed in the first place. Even worse than this is when the victims defend their oppressors/abusers. Take, for instance, the protestors in Alberta who are protesting for extended lockdowns. They are angry about the government's plan to uplift COVID-19 isolation mandates.[61] It is akin to a beaten wife saying, "Well, my husband didn't hit me so hard tonight. It is just his way of showing he really does love me."

It is a form of mind control. The hope lies upon the false promises that there will be a return back to "normal" if we reach a certain level of vaccination, but, of course, mask wearing, physical distancing, and other restrictions are still applicable. The difference now is that the unvaccinated are to be blamed for any deaths, hospitalizations, or continued closures.

Over twenty months into this health crisis and we have seen that, regardless of one's political or religious persuasion, many have bought into the lies of the sanitary fascists, whether they are politicians, police officers, or medical experts. It is precisely as linguist Elena Gorokhova describes as the impetus towards survival by the act of accepting the lies perpetuated by politicians, in her memoir, *A Mountain of Crumbs*: "The rules are simple: They lie to us, we know they're lying, they know we know they're lying, but they keep lying anyway, and

60 To read the full judgement, see Ontario Superior Court of Justice, J.N. v. C.G., 2022 ONSC 1198 (CanLII).

61 Kaylen Small, "'This is a travesty': Albertans protest COVID-19 rule rollback for second day."

we keep pretending to believe them."[62] Even though the unfortunate reality is that a growing number of people in the Western world intuit that something is very wrong or at least amiss given this global crisis, they still manage to display doublethink; they are able to hold two contradictory thoughts at the same time, i.e., they will believe/claim that this is a plandemic, rather than a pandemic, but still go volunteer themselves to be injected with a totally unnecessary and potentially harmful gene therapy. It is always easier to be accepted and to conform than it is to resist and stay steadfast in one's own convictions.

Then you have the foolish social media trolls that sometimes include friends and relatives on Facebook who will incessantly defend draconian policies, demonize effective and inexpensive treatments, and claim that the gene therapy injection with vaccine passports are the only way out of this mess since it is based on "science." They will ridicule any dissenting view without any good arguments. Typically, their arguments are based on an appeal to authority without much regard to scientific evidence and logic.[63]

Homeopath Ian Watson made this incisive statement regarding the COVID health crisis and its associated authoritarian mandates:

> If you have to be persuaded, and reminded, and pressured, and lied to, and incentivised, and coerced, and bullied, and socially shamed, and guilt-tripped, and threatened, and punished and criminalised—if all of this is considered necessary to gain your compliance—you can be absolutely certain that what is being promoted is not in your best interest.[64]

In this instance, it is the homeopath who is approaching the issue of COVID-19 vaccination with more rationality than scientists and doctors who have swallowed the COVID-narrative.

62 Gorokhova, *A Mountain of Crumbs.*

63 If after presenting your arguments and evidence to these people, such as Judy Garland aka BG, and TCN (totally corrupt nothingness), IB, Razi Razor, OggafnaR (who I sung an original "opera" piece for his SJW ways) publicly and privately, and they still remain recalcitrant and unwilling to have a genuine discussion then, unfortunately, it is better to leave them to their own echo chambers and ignorance. But the absolute topper is Malcolm Daniel aka Sushi trans-ally who preaches social justice while steals from a street person to buy himself a cheeseburger, despite coming from a wealthy family. The lack of awareness of these individuals is akin to the protestors protesting for more lockdowns. I suppose you can say the only thing that supersedes their ignorance is their arrogance.

64 Watson's quote beautifully captures the coercion and manipulation governments are exerting on sovereign individuals to have them take the COVID-19 gene therapy. See Hallam, "It's personal choice at the end of the day"—Readers' discuss whether health and social care should be required to have the Covid jab" for Watson's quote and a number of opinions submitted by readers of *The Star.*

COVID-19 as Religion

The playwriter and poet, Émile Leon Cammaerts, in a quote often misattributed to G. K. Chesterton, remarked that: "When men choose not to believe in God, they do not thereafter believe in nothing. They then become capable of believing in anything."[65] This unfortunate reality has become starkly evident throughout this COVID-19 crisis for both unbelievers and believers in God, including those who claim to be devout Christians. Monotheists who follow COVID-19 with religious fervour may be guilty of a bizarre form of syncretism. One must also be careful of falling prey to an obsessive compulsion in upholding any dissenting view which can work in the same fashion, i.e., by deifying the act of one's vociferous opposition to COVID. For too many people, this COVID situation has manifested itself into a prototypic religion. The state has become their god. The virus SARS-CoV-2 that causes COVID-19 and any deviance are the source of evil. If one does not follow government mandates this is deemed to be sinful. Mainstream news, questionable scientific journals, and harmful mandates/policies upholding the single narrative at all costs, have come to be their scriptures and catechism. Divinely ordained experts, fact-checkers, policy makers, and politicians are their high priests and priestesses. These authorities interpret and disseminate the sacred scriptures to the Covidians.[66] Masks, physical distancing, obsession with hand sanitizing, etc., have become means of an outward demonstration of grace and remaining in their god's favour, much like the Sacraments in Catholicism. The vaccine is their promised sacrament of salvation. Anthony Fauci is Lord and savior to them. The vaccine passport is their paraclete. Prayer is the act of thanking the State for all of its mandates and hoping for more measures to protect citizens of the State.

Those who defy, question and/or stand up to these mandates/policies of the single narrative are heretical, whereas those who uphold them are deemed to be saints doing the will of their god. Even worse, those who spread the virus who are unvaccinated are selfish killers. Never mind the fact that the vaccinated can spread the disease.[67] For the Covidians, the end of times is imminent if we do not reach herd immunity through 100% vaccination levels with boosters every six months while heaven on Earth can be realized if we reach this utopic immunized state. Some may accuse me of being facetious and/or making gross exaggerations but this is true for those who are ideologically possessed with COVID. Unknowingly, yet tragically, many who have been brainwashed by the State have come to embody such absurd things.

65 Émile Cammaerts, *The Laughing Prophet: The Seven Virtues and G.K. Chesterton.*

66 A term for those who unthinkingly accept all the mandates and live in constant fear of a virus with an exceedingly high survival rate.

67 The narrative quickly changed from the vaccines providing full immunity and stopping transmission to weakening the virus and minimizing transmission.

There is a strong fideistic component to the COVID religion. Statements like "follow the science" and "trust the science" are akin to having faith in spite of the evidence. The average person puts a blind faith in a number of elements of the narrative, including the alleged effectiveness of lockdowns, masks, vaccines versus the alleged ineffectiveness and dangers of reopening businesses, natural immunity against the virus, and alternative treatments (hydroxychloroquine and ivermectin). The COVID fideist is someone who believes the COVID narrative uncritically and blindly; the establishment becomes their god.

Archbishop Carlo Maria Viganò in a foreword written for an edited volume titled, *Mors Tua Vita Mea*[68] which focuses on the problem of the moral illegitimacy of vaccines that use cell lines of fetuses that are victims of voluntary abortion, states that the vaccine is an instrument for the globalist ideology, which he dubs as "anti-human, anti-religious, and antichristic." Ultimately, for Viganò sees the whole COVID situation as a veritable religion:

> If the firstborn of Israel belong to the Lord, the simia Dei demands much more of the firstborn and even claims them through the pharmaceutical companies that use fetal tissue from abortions to manufacture a so-called vaccine that is presented in the delirium of Covid-19 as a sacrament of salvation by which one is incorporated into the "mystical body" of Satan, the globalist anti-church. On the other hand, the "liturgical" connotation of the pandemic intentionally echoes signs and symbols proper to the True Religion in such a way as to deceive even the simple and push them to conform to a collective cult that exempts them from making decisions independently and binds them to an uncritical obedience. We cannot forget the funeral processions of military trucks, the contradictory and intolerant attitude of the Covid priests, the health magisterium of the "experts," the inquisition against the denier "heretics," and the fideistic adherence to the most grotesque superstitions passed off as science by virologist sorcerers and television vestals.[69]

One wonders how long it will take these unthinkingly complacent people to realize this is the unending revolving door. Israel has recently deemed that after a certain period, the green passports of those who have been doubly vaccinated without their booster shot would be revoked.[70] The question is, how many booster

68 Viganò, Monsignor Carlo Maria. "Prefazione."

69 Taken from LifeSite News which is an excerpt from Archbishop Viganò's foreword to the book *Mors Tua Vita Mea*, published with kind permission by Professor Massimo Viglione: see Hickson, "Archbishop Viganò: Vaccines made with fetal tissue are a 'human sacrifice of innocent victims offered to Satan'."

70 TOI Staff, "Nearly 2 million Israelis lose Green Pass as new rules enter effect."

shots will it take for someone to finally awake to the absurdity of the situation? Furthermore, for how long will they remain thankful to their abusers/false gods?

The Nature and History of Science

As we know well, governments are not infallible, neither are scientists or medical doctors, very far from it, despite scientists becoming the high priests of modern society. What about science itself? Science as an enterprise is always in constant flux through learning, re-examining, observing, testing analyzing, interpreting, and re-interpreting. It is provisional in its nature and scope. Despite all of our progress, we know very little about physical reality, the more we explore into the darkness of the universe and the exquisite molecular world, the more that our ignorance confounds us. Anyone who has studied the history of science will realize that science is an ever-evolving endeavor. For instance, a certain theory may have explained the data quite well given the knowledge of the day but may require serious revisions in the future as new information through observation and rigorous analyses emerge. One can think of the Copernican Revolution and its replacement of the Ptolemaic understanding of the rotation of the planets and the Sun; we shifted from a geocentric to a heliocentric understanding of the universe. We could also think about the scientific revolution that occurred in 1859 when Charles Darwin and Alfred Wallace proposed their theory of natural selection; it came to supplant Creationism which argued for the fixity of species. This theory argued for the transmutation of species through natural selection and random variation to account for all living organisms and all of their distinct features. Subsequently, this theory then evolved into Neo-Darwinism, a theory that combined Mendelian genetics with the mechanism of natural selection. However, recent developments suggest that this isn't the entire picture. The data today opens up the debate to other natural mechanisms and has even allowed for the design perspective to have a place at the table; the mechanisms at hand do not seem to explain the origin of species nor the origin of novel structures as well as biologists had hoped. Some of the most remarkable scientific advancements have been the discoveries of modern physics from the 17th century onward: in 1687 Isaac Newton's discovery of the laws of motion and the law of universal gravitation; in 1782 Antoine Lavoisier's conservation of matter; 1801 Thomas Young's wave theory of light; 1803 John Dalton's atomic theory of matter; 1905 Einstein's theory of special relativity and in 1913 general theory of relativity; 1925–1927 quantum mechanics; Georges Lemaître with the "primeval egg theory" (big bang model); and in 1981 Alan Guth's cosmic inflation; 2015 gravitational waves were observed. So, with all these theories and discoveries, we see great advancements, building on previous knowledge and/or even correcting and modifying certain aspects of theories while continuing to unravel what observational data shows through logical inference. The theoretical physicist, Richard Feynman, famously said: "I think I can safely say that nobody understands quantum mechanics." Nevertheless, Feynman was able to develop a pictorial scheme to provide mathematical expressions for subatomic particles which came to be known as the Feynman diagrams. Indeed, a strong case for the mathematical rigor of quantum mechanics can be made.[71] So, why did he say that about quantum mechanics? Well, part of the answer relates to the fact there are at least nineteen competing interpretations of understanding quantum mechanics in its representation of "reality." Undoubtedly, scientific advancement is never conclusive since our knowledge is finite, it is constantly subject to revision, correction, interpretation, and replacement. Often enough the facts of the present day could be regarded in the future as the missteps or errors of yesterday. That's just how science works.

Unfortunately, the majority of laypersons are not aware of this and just take "scientific facts" as a "fait accompli." This mode of thinking also works great for controlling people, i.e., the lack of questioning certain authorities, especially scientific/medical ones. This is one of the ways as to how science can transform into scientism; the unsubstantiated claim that natural science is the only means by which we can ascertain "real" knowledge of the world. Regrettably, since March 2020 to the present, most people, regardless of which side of the "aisle" they have fixed themselves, have lacked any nuance or genuine awareness of the multiple complexities amidst this ongoing crisis. If anything, it has divided people more than ever. The mainstream media, government officials for both corruption and lack of competence are to be held largely responsible for the irrational reactions people have exhibited over the past year or so, due to the many uncertainties and gaps of knowledge of what is truly going on.

Most people have unthinkingly followed the narrative of "follow the science"/ "trust the science" which has zero to do with actual science. Science has become totally politicized. Medical doctors like Anthony Fauci have become more of a political/public figure than a bona fide doctor. Unsurprisingly, the pursuit of arriving at truth has been obliterated. Science has become a trademark instead of an understanding of the physical world and the beings within it. Science necessitates debate and argumentation to survive; without debate science becomes authoritarian and dogmatic. Through challenging scientific hypotheses, discoveries, and theories, with the use of logic, observation, and evidence, science can progress and develop. The media's fear mongering and the conformist establishment doctors, and scientists have removed this crucial component to scientific understanding. This is especially true in times of uncertainty with the ever-changing data revolving around the COVID-19 crisis. There should be a debate between a group of scientists and

71 Kronz, "Quantum Theory and Mathematical Rigor."

medical doctors who are for and against the current narrative, this would be enlightening and educational for the average citizen. It would help to settle much of what is dubbed misinformation and disinformation. But the bearers of the accepted narrative do not want this for fear of being exposed for their lies and deceptions. Take for example, Robert Malone's challenge to Anthony Fauci for a debate.[72] Many people are wanting to hear both sides, so they can decide for themselves which makes more sense, but most people are not afforded this courtesy. Nevertheless, Fauci would never accept the challenge since he knows precisely what is at stake and that he would be outflanked. Similarly, what does one think would happen if Malone or Peter McCullough were to debate Canada's "top doctor," Theresa Tam? She's not really a medical expert but an incompetent medical bureaucrat with a meager 71 citations in the literature (check out her score on Google Scholar).[73] Now compare that with Dr. Peter McCullough who has 115,430 citations.[74] What do you think would happen if they both squared off on CBC for a debate on COVID-19 and these vaccines? I think we all know the answer.

The Fallibility of Medicine and Doctors

Medicine, just like the natural sciences, has undergone incredible developments over the past few centuries. But, even less than a century ago, from the 1930s to the 1950s, medical doctors had promoted smoking for its alleged health benefits.[75] The negative effects of smoking were not well known during this time period, but it should serve as a cautionary note regarding the reliability of certain medical claims. Healthy skepticism should not be discouraged. If we consider misdiagnoses this should warrant patients to be vigilant. Please note that I am not encouraging complete mistrust of medical professionals because that is counter-productive, but to not take everything you're told with a grain of salt. Deaths due to medical negligence tend to increase year on year. On average, in the US, medical mistakes claim about 400,000 lives.[76] In Canada, thousands die in hospitals and most of the population is unaware of this.[77] Therefore, it is important that when we listen to governments and experts speak of certain

72 Schemmel, "Calls ring out for Fauci to debate virologist after Rogan podcast appearance."

73 https://scholar.google.ca/citations?user=pSRDb3gAAAAJ&hl=en&oi=ao.

74 Recently, I just noticed as of January 6, 2022, this was reduced to 63,670 citations. Google may have been tampering with this.

75 Klara, "Throwback Thursday: When Doctors Prescribed 'Healthy' Cigarette Brands."

76 Flynn, "3 horrific medical mistakes that scandalize the profession."

77 Finlay, "Preventable Medical Error Is Canadian Healthcare's Silent Killer"; McIlroy and Mickleburgh, "Hospital errors kill thousands in Canada, study estimates."

treatments, vaccines, statistics, precautions, and other recommendations revolving around COVID-19 we should question these claims. As has been iterated, science and medicine are evolving, but also many errors can be made due to either ignorance and/or negligence.

Mainstream Media's Duplicity and Lack of Integrity

News organizations, more often than not, are more interested in backing the agenda of those funding them.[78] For instance, the Government of Canada, i.e., The Liberal Party, over the past few years has given at least $675 million to the CBC.[79] Their motto is that "Canada wouldn't be the same without the CBC"—this statement is certainly true; Canada would certainly be better off without the CBC since it does not represent the diversity of thought of Canadians, nor does it offer critical, honest, and accurate reporting. If anything, it misleads Canadians into believing misinformation. This is a great disservice to the average Canadian who works a 9 to 5 job and does not have the time or interest to do their own research. They will typically tune in to get their 5 minutes of news before bed. Luckily, more and more Canadians are waking up to the reality that CBC is not what it presents itself as being. Consequently, Canadians have begun looking elsewhere for their news,[80] even though other popular organizations spew similar propaganda. Given all of this, we should demand why the Liberals are shamelessly wasting our tax money on this.

We must also ask why are the CBC and many other Canadian mainstream outlets more interested in the nomination of Supreme Court Justice, Brett Kavanaugh, than in the shortcomings of Canadian politics? Kavanaugh's case was covered ad nauseam in 2018. In my mind, the main objective was to attack President Donald Trump at all costs. It's no secret that the CBC and many Canadian media outlets have a rampant obsession with criticizing Trump. They rather focus on Trump than present their own man in a critical and honest light. It is an appalling double-standard that needs to be brought to the fore of Canadian reporting. Very few political commentators, with the exception of the likes of Rex Murphy, a seasoned and respectable political commentator, has the integrity to illuminate the obvious—why is the media not reporting on Joe Biden's assault allegations in comparison to extensive coverage of the Kavanaugh's case?[81] We know the answer.

78 See Ventureyra, "The CBC - A Source of Trustworthy News or an Engine for Propaganda?"
79 Liberal Party of Canada, "Support the CBC."
80 Lilley, "Canadians are ditching CBC, so why do we keep funding it?"
81 Murphy, "Why is the media not more interested in assault allegations against Biden?"

Nevertheless, people should be suspicious as to why much of the mainstream coverage has been rather lenient on Trudeau—much more lenient than on Kavanaugh who has very little to do with Canadian politics. Trudeau himself has been in hot water for some time since he has made an unprecedented three breaches of federal ethics rules. Any critical mind, will be quick to see the double standard here towards conservative figures as opposed to leftist establishment ones like Trudeau, Biden, Obama, the Clintons, etc. It's interesting to note that CBC nor any mainstream media outlet in Canada reported on Norman Traversy's case against Trudeau, as described by Diverge Media.[82]

Despite this disturbing trend of uncritical reporting, some reporters have had sufficient moral awareness and integrity to resign and expose the media that is weaponizing the left. They are misleading hard-working and trusting citizens of the world. Opinion editor and writer Bari Weiss, from The *New York Times* resigned after publishing a "controversial" view on how rioters should be dealt with.[83] Something that was anathema to "woke" individuals (a more accurate depiction would be "unsophisticated dormant individuals"). Weiss explains her experience with "woke" individuals (unsophisticated dormant individuals) in her resignation letter:

> Still other *New York Times* employees publicly smear me as a liar and a bigot on Twitter with no fear that harassing me will be met with appropriate action. They never are... There are terms for all of this: unlawful discrimination, hostile work environment, and constructive discharge. I'm no legal expert. But I know that this is wrong.[84]

In this letter, she further exposes The *New York Times*. In it, she states, "Instead, a new consensus has emerged in the press, but perhaps especially at this paper: that truth isn't a process of collective discovery, but an orthodoxy already known to an enlightened few whose job is to inform everyone else."[85] In similar fashion, even more recently, former MSNBC reporter, Ariana Pekary, resigned from the channel[86] and wrote an indictment against them, rightfully calling it fake news. Here's a short excerpt:

> As it is, this cancer stokes national division, even in the middle of a civil rights crisis. The model blocks diversity of thought and content because

82 Visser, "Norman Traversy's speech on corruption in Canada."

83 Cotton, "Send In the Troops The nation must restore order. The military stands read."

84 Weiss, "Resignation Letter."

85 Weiss, "Resignation Letter."

86 Graham, "MSNBC Producer Quits Because It's Liberal Fake News: 'We are a Cancer and There is No Cure'."

> the networks have incentive to amplify fringe voices and events, at the expense of others...all because it pumps up the ratings.
>
> This cancer risks human lives, even in the middle of a pandemic. The primary focus quickly became what Donald Trump was doing (poorly) to address the crisis, rather than the science itself. As new details have become available about antibodies, a vaccine, or how COVID actually spreads, producers still want to focus on the politics. Important facts or studies get buried.
>
> This cancer risks our democracy, even in the middle of a presidential election. Any discussion about the election usually focuses on Donald Trump, not Joe Biden, a repeat offense from 2016 (Trump smothers out all other coverage). Also important is to ensure citizens can vote by mail this year, but I've watched that topic get ignored or "killed" numerous times.
>
> Context and factual data are often considered too cumbersome for the audience.[87]

The media focused its attention on Trump instead of providing good journalism backed by evidence and data with respect to the COVID-19 crisis.

To make things worse, on October 14, 2021, CBC Edmonton was forced to retract a blatant falsehood:

> Earlier in October, we aired two stories on what patients can expect in a hospital ICU during the COVID crisis and the strain on nursing staff. We shot footage for these stories at two Edmonton training facilities that showed mannequins in beds and a realistic-looking hospital setting due to restrictions.
>
> Unfortunately, some of that same footage was then used in a different story about COVID projections and modelling last week. Using those images outside the context of the training facilities was inappropriate and we apologize for the error in judgement. The story has been corrected.[88]

And yet, the federal government in Canada wants to censor its own people over misinformation, but CBC, the government funded broadcaster, was admittedly involved in a brazen lie. One which was characterized as an "inaccuracy." One wonders how much longer Canadians will believe these lies and coverups. The CBC just like Trudeau offer up empty and dishonest apologies.

Most recently, producer and veteran journalist, Tara Henley, resigned from the CBC because they no longer provide trustworthy and important news to Canadians:

87 Pekary, "Personal news: why I'm now leaving MSNBC."

88 CBC Edmonton. Twitter Post. October 12, 2021, at 7:44 PM.

> It used to be that I was the one furthest to the left in any newsroom, occasionally causing strain in story meetings with my views on issues like the housing crisis. I am now easily the most conservative, frequently sparking tension by questioning identity politics. This happened in the span of about 18 months. My own politics did not change.
>
> To work at the CBC in the current climate is to embrace cognitive dissonance and to abandon journalistic integrity.
>
> It is to sign on, enthusiastically, to a radical political agenda that originated on Ivy League campuses in the United States and spread through American social media platforms that monetize outrage and stoke societal divisions. It is to pretend that the "woke" worldview is near universal—even if it is far from popular with those you know, and speak to, and interview, and read.
>
> To work at the CBC now is to accept the idea that race is the most significant thing about a person, and that some races are more relevant to the public conversation than others. It is, in my newsroom, to fill out racial profile forms for every guest you book; to actively book more people of some races and less of others.[89]

Whether it is "woke" news pieces or issues related to COVID-19, the CBC has lost the trust of Canadians, and rightfully so.

On COVID Censorship

Big Tech Censorship and Manipulation

Big Tech in collusion with mainstream media have obfuscated and censored information that contradicts the main narrative. It is no secret that dissenting voices are being censored. This is not a new development, but something that has increased throughout the COVID-19 situation. Facebook continually censors popular people, posts, and videos that run contrary to the preferred narrative.[90] For example, after a "questionable" post is removed and if you've engaged with it, you will receive a link to the WHO myth buster page. There are countless examples of censorship occurring on the majority of media platforms that cannot be fully explored here. I have been documenting on the abolition of free speech for a number of years now. Nonetheless, the censorship is more prominent than ever.

89 Henley, "Speaking Freely: Why I resigned from the Canadian Broadcasting Corporation."

90 Robertson, "Facebook will add anti-misinformation posts to your News Feed if you liked fake coronavirus news."

On May 24, 2021, investigative guerilla journalist, James O'Keefe of Project Veritas,[91] released a bombshell video of two Facebook whistleblowers, including Morgan Kahmann who got terminated from Facebook and may face further legal consequences,[92] exposing Facebook's global effort to secretly censor any questions or concerns regarding the COVID-19 vaccines.[93] Project Veritas obtained a leaked internal memo explaining "Vaccine Hesitancy Comment Demotion" with the "goal" to "drastically reduce user exposure to vaccine hesitancy."[94] Facebook is using an algorithm to track down vaccine hesitant users. This algorithm is being run on 1.5 percent of both Facebook and Instagram's 3.8 billion users. The vaccine hesitancy ratings are comprised of three tiers: zero, one, and two. Comments classified as tier zero are an explicit violation of Facebook policy, tier one is seen as "Alarmism & Criticism," while tier two is "Indirect Vaccine Discouragement," which could consist of any story that might dissuade some from getting the vaccine even if they are factual. The Facebook algorithm from there assigns a "VH Score" where they would be most likely hidden from the most relevant of the comments section or outright removed. Behind this sinister initiative are the following authors: Joo Ho Yeo, Nick Gibian, Hendrick Townley, Amit Bahl, and Matt Gilles, all of whom are high up employees on Facebook, who are not too far down the chain of command from its CEO, Mark Zuckerberg. These individuals lead Health Integrity teams on Facebook and messenger.

Any fact or event that does not line up with the narrative, i.e., "get the vaccine, it's good for you, if you do not, you're an anti-vaxxer and you're harming humanity by not doing so," etc., are omitted, demoted, de-boosted,

91 Project Veritas bio on James O'Keefe. O'Keefe and his Project Veritas are a dying breed of authentic reporting. Him and his organization practice what is known as muckraking journalism, where they expose corruption and scandals through surreptitious recordings and other means. Some may disagree with such methods but those who are involved with scandals, corruption, and lies that harm the public forfeit their right to privacy. See O'Keefe, *American Pravda: My Fight for Truth in the Era of Fake News*; O'Keefe, *American Muckraker: Re-thinking Journalism for the 21st Century*. His home was recently raided by the FBI in search of Ashley Biden's diary. O'Keefe issued the following statement: "The FBI took materials of current, and former, Veritas journalists despite the fact that our legal team previously contacted the Department of Justice and voluntarily conveyed unassailable facts that demonstrate Project Veritas' lack of involvement in criminal activity and/or criminal intent." This shows how the FBI believe they are above the law. They are targeting O'Keefe since he poses a great threat to the establishment powers. See Feuerherd, "Feds reportedly raid Project Veritas-linked apartments over Ashley Biden's diary."

92 Kahmann, "Facebook Insider Morgan Kahmann joins Tucker Carlson to discuss leaked 'Vaccine Hesitancy' documents."

93 You can read all the details on the Project Veritas webpage where there's a link to the original leaked document: "Facebook Whistleblowers Expose LEAKED INTERNAL DOCS Detailing New Effort to Secretly Censor Vaccine Concerns on a Global Scale."

94 You can see the memo titled, "Vaccine Hesitancy Comment Demotion": https://assets.ctfassets.net/syq3snmxclc9/7zG8FPh0cBk3qh28dY90iB/10771f24b25cf9994c08bf69e74056d5/Vaccine_Hesitancy_Comment_Demotion_WATERMARKED.pdf.

banned, and/or considered dangerous. Interestingly, on July 16, 2020, Mark Zuckerberg, who, alongside Twitter's Jack Dorsey has lied under oath,[95] in a leaked video, violated his own Facebook policy with his anti-Covid-19 vax stance when stating:

> But I do just want to make sure that I share some caution on this [vaccine] because we just don't know the long-term side effects of basically modifying people's DNA and RNA...basically the ability to produce those antibodies and whether that causes other mutations or other risks downstream. So, there's work on both paths of vaccine development.[96]

He then later contradicted himself in November 2020 in an interview with Anthony Fauci:

> Mark Zuckerberg: "Just to clear up one point, my understanding is that these vaccines do not modify your DNA or RNA. So that's just an important point to clarify, if I'm getting anything wrong here of course correct me, but just to make that clear..."
> Dr. Anthony Fauci: "No, first of all DNA is inherent in your own nuclear cell. Sticking in anything foreign will ultimately get cleared."
> Zuckerberg: "Good, well, I'm glad we cleared that up."[97]

Facebook users should be alarmed that a platform that is used for dialogue and discussion is suppressing users' freedom to share concerns regarding one of their most fundamental rights: "the right to the enjoyment of the highest attainable standard of physical and mental health."[98] This was first introduced by the 1946 Constitution of the World Health Organization (WHO). Censoring information pertaining to one of the most important issues in the world today is a direct violation of such a right. How can we enjoy the highest attainable standard of physical and mental health if information is being purposely hidden from us? The mainstream media, governments, WHO, CDC, and other social media platforms are all guilty of violating this through wrongful action, misinformation, and the suppression of correct information. Much more could be said of censorship related to COVID-19, but this is sufficient to paint a grim picture.

95 Otto, "Facebook and Twitter's CEOS Just Lied To Congress About Censorship."

96 Project Veritas, "Facebook CEO Mark Zuckerberg Takes 'Anti-Vax' Stance in Violation of His Own Platform's New Policy."

97 Project Veritas, "Facebook CEO Mark Zuckerberg Takes 'Anti-Vax' Stance in Violation of His Own Platform's New Policy."

98 Office of the United Nations High Commissioner for Human Rights/the World Health Organization, *The Right to Health: Fact Sheet No. 31*.

Censorship of Dissenting Scientific and Medical Experts

Throughout the course of the pandemic, numerous brave and highly credentialed scientists have either been dismissed from their academic and/or professional positions, censored, demonized, and/or threatened. To any objective observer it should become evident that these courageous souls who stand up to these tyrannical institutions, do so for their love of their profession, humanity, and truth. They have very little to gain and everything to lose by putting their reputations, careers, and even lives on the line. And like these, there are countless others willing to speak the truth despite the ramifications.[99] It just does not stand to reason that these reputable physicians and scientists are misguided and conspiratorial. There is good reason why many of the bearers of the COVID narrative don't want a debate. It is clear they are afraid of the truth being exposed along with their complicity.

For two years, governments throughout the world have been in a rush to vaccinate as many people as possible regardless of any knowledge of long-term effects, promotion of alternative treatments, and warnings from reputable world renown medical and scientific experts including Didier Raoult,[100] professor of immunology, Byram Bridle[101] at the University of Guelph in Canada,

99 Take a look at the following organizations/documents: Front Line COVID-19 Critical Care Alliance Prevention & Treatment Protocols for COVID-19: https://covid19criticalcare.com/; World Doctors Alliance, https://worlddoctorsalliance.com/about/; The Great Barrington Declaration, a document which has been signed by 860,000+ concerned citizens including 14,981 medical & public health scientists, and 44,167 medical practitioners: https://gbdeclaration.org/; there are also legal teams prepared to defend our constitutional rights against vaccine mandates and vaccine passports, like the Justice Center for Constitutional Freedoms: https://www.jccf.ca/justice-centre-sues-ontario-government-over-vaccine-passport/.

100 Raoult has over 2,300 indexed publications. He is also one of the most highly cited micro-biologists in the world: https://scholar.google.ca/scholar?hl=en&as_sdt=0%2C5&q=Didier+Raoult&btnG=. Raoult was demonized in 2020 for his promotion of hydroxychloroquine with azithromycin, an inexpensive treatment for COVID-19. Despite claims to the contrary, if administered early on during the period of when the first clinical signs of the flu are detected, then the success rate can be quite high. See "Dr. Oz Discusses The Hydroxychloroquine Study Outcome With Dr.Didier Raoult." YouTube Video.

101 Byram Bridle's web page at University of Guelph: https://ovc.uoguelph.ca/pathobiology/people/faculty/Byram-W-Bridle. There are several important documents prepared by Dr. Bridle: "COVID-19 Vaccines and Children: A Scientist's Guide for Parents." For another important document see, Byram Bridle, "Why Parents, Teens, and Children Should Question the COVID-19 Vaccine"; Druthers News & Information, "Dr. Byram Bridle Addresses Toronto Event Aimed at 'Let the Kids Play'" Rumble Video; Derek Sloan's conference with Dr. Byram Bridle, Dr. Patrick Phillips, and Dr. Donald Wash, "MP Derek Sloan Raises Concerns Over Censorship of Doctors and Scientists." An example in the legacy media has been made of Dr. Patrick Phillips for following his moral conscience in providing patients lifesaving treatments such as ivermectin, which has been unjustly demonized by Big Pharma, government, and medical establishment: CBC News, "Ontario doctor accused of spreading COVID-19 misinformation barred from providing vaccine, mask exemptions."

American cardiologist, Peter McCullough,[102] the mRNA vaccine inventor, Robert Malone,[103] Canadian pathologist, who is a Royal Fellow and Cambridge graduate, Roger Hodkinson,[104] former Clinical Professor of Surgery and faculty member of the University of Saskatchewan, Francis Christian,[105] Mayo Clinic, pathologist Ryan Cole,[106] British pharmacologist, chief scientist and vice-president of the allergy and respiratory research division of Pfizer, Michael

102 Peter McCullough has had over 600 peer-reviewed articles published. His publications have appeared in top journals such as the *New England Journal of Medicine*, *Journal of the American Medical Association*, and *The Lancet*. He is the president of the Cardiorenal Society of America, the co-editor of *Reviews in Cardiovascular Medicine* and associate editor of the *American Journal of Cardiology* and *Cardiorenal Medicine*. McCullough has over 114,000 citations and over 50 peer-reviewed articles related to COVID-19 since 2020. (This number is varying greatly on Google Scholar since Google is tampering with these numbers to undermine his credibility. Nonetheless, he is the most cited cardiologist in the history of medicine.) https://scholar.google.com/scholar?start=0&q=Peter+A.+Mccullough&hl=en&as_sdt=0,5&as_ylo=2020&as_yhi=2021. See WND Staff, "Top doc: Pull COVID-19 vaccines off the market now."

103 Robert Malone has recommended that people under 19 not to get vaccinated because of the risks and a lack of access to the data about the vaccine's side effects. As the inventor of the mRNA vaccines, he seems to be one of, if not the most, qualified person to speak on this issue. Since expressing concerns about the COVID-19 vaccines he has been censored on social media; his LinkedIn account was censored for posting articles that contradicted the accepted COVID narrative. According to Malone, no acceptable data-driven risk-benefit analysis has been provided as of yet. There has also been a concerted effort to also have his recent interview with Joe Rogan removed from Spotify. People have been demanding the de-platforming of Rogan because of this and his interview with Peter McCullough. Robert Malone's website: https://www.rwmalonemd.com/about-us; The Shocking Truth TV (originally on The Stew Peters Show), Interview with Stew Peters, "Dr. Robert Malone On His mRNA Creation"; TrialSite Staff, "Bioethics of Experimental COVID Vaccine Deployment under EUA: It's time we stop and look at what's going down"; Zoyesky, "The government shouldn't force young adults and teens to take experimental coronavirus vaccines, says inventor of mRNA vaccines."

104 See Nal, "Renowned Pathologist: Myocarditis Diagnoses Should Halt Covid Vaccine (Interview)"; Sullivan, "Dr. Roger Hodkinson On COVID19: 'It's All Been A Pack Of Lies'."; Hodkinson, "Dr. Roger Hodkinson DECIMATES Canadian Government."

105 For a short article written by Francis Christian on his recounting of what was done to him by the Saskatchewan College of Medicine: Christian, "The Persecution of Physicians and Scientists in Canada"; Christian, "Statement by Dr. Francis Christian FRCSEd, FRCSC"; To hear an audio recording of Francis Christian's dismissal by the Saskatchewan College of Medicine go here: https://www.jccf.ca/surgeon-fired-by-college-of-medicine-for-voicing-safety-concerns-about-covid-shots-for-children/. Here is an excerpt of Christian's courageous and pointed response to "Lysenkoist" style dismissal from the Department of Surgery at the Saskatchewan College of Medicine: "You guys are living in a dystopian bubble…the truth will come out, and when that bubble bursts, you guys are going to be in big trouble. And you think I'm in trouble? By the grace of God, I'm sleeping well at night, and I am not in any distress at all."

106 WND Staff, "Mayo-trained doctor warns of COVID-19 'mutations'." There is a link in this article where Cole discusses a number of issues with the mRNA COVID-19 vaccine and how natural immunity is more robust.

Yeadon,[107] Donald Trump's doctor, Vladimir Zelenko,[108] among thousands of others worldwide. Lawyers like Reiner Fuellmich,[109] Robert F. Kennedy Jr.,[110] Canadian constitutional lawyer Rocco Galati,[111] John Carpay,[112] and

107 Dr. Michael Yeadon former chief scientific officer and vice president, Allergy and Respiratory Research Head with Pfizer Global R&D and co-Founder of Ziarco Pharma Ltd. Yeadon discusses his discontents in this interview titled: "An Urgent Warning to the World." You can find a wide arrange of videos of different experts discussing a number of aspects and dangers related to the pandemic at this link: https://www.thepressandthepublic.com/latest. For a comprehensive critique of the RTPCR test written by Yeadon and 21 other authors, see Borgier, et al., "External peer review of the RTPCR test to detect SARS-CoV-2 reveals 10 major scientific flaws at the molecular and methodological level: consequences for false positive results."

For a critique of various aspects of the COVID-19 pandemic, see Kirkham, Yeadon, and Thomas, "How Likely Is A Second Wave?"; Yeadon, "Lies, Damned Lies and Health Statistics – the Deadly Danger of False Positives."

108 Vladimir Zelenko's website: https://vladimirzelenkomd.com/. With respect to the vaccines, Zelenko has three simple questions: Is it necessary? Is it safe? Is it effective? His answer is "no" to all three, see Special Reports, "Dr. Zelenko Calls for Bill Gates and Fauci's Arrest for War Crimes." Like Raoult, Zelenko has promoted the use of hydroxychloroquine. He has treated over 1,450 patients who have tested positive for COVID-19 with 200 mg of hydroxychloroquine twice a day for 5 days, 500 mg of azithromycin once a day for 5 days, and 220 mg of zinc sulfate (an ingredient often ignored by studies which are critical of the treatment) once a day for 5 days producing 99.9% success rate (only 2 deaths). In order to ensure success, hydroxychloroquine must be taken in conjunction with the other two drugs (or at least zinc). Scholz, Derwand and Zelenko, "COVID-19 Outpatients – Early Risk-Stratified Treatment with Zinc Plus Low Dose Hydroxychloroquine and Azithromycin: A Retrospective Case Series Study." See Louise, "Dr. Vladimir Zelenko has now treated over 1,450 coronavirus patients (2 deaths) using hydroxychloroquine with 99.99% success rate (latest video interview)"; Hanau, "Jewish MD who promoted virus cocktail is leaving community where he tested it"; Ventureyra, "A Feminine, or Feminist Response to Covid?" Similarly, medical doctor Anthony Cardill in Los Angeles, has observed that many patients become symptom free after 8–12 hours of taking these drugs. For a report of vaccine death reports, see David Johnson Sorensen and Vladimir Zelenko, "The Vaccine Death Report: Evidence of millions of deaths and serious adverse events resulting from the experimental COVID-19 injections," Version 1.0, September 2021, https://www.stopworldcontrol.com/downloads/en/vaccines/vaccinereport.pdf.

109 See Stop World Control, "Dr. Reiner Fuellmich: scientific evidence that covid is crime against humanity." Fuellmich is an international trial lawyer. Fuellmich has labeled this pandemic a greater crime against humanity than the holocaust and will most likely require a second Nuremberg trial.

110 Kennedy Jr. has been instrumental in exposing the corruption and malfeasance of the pharmaceutical companies. He has been championing freedom since the beginning of the pandemic. See Children's Health Defense website: https://childrenshealthdefense.org/. See also, Kennedy Jr., *The Real Anthony Fauci: Bill Gates, Big Pharma, and the Global War on Democracy and Public Health* for a devastating analysis of the utter corruption of Dr. Fauci.

111 Galati has indicated that COVID-19 operation is "the biggest example of misinformation and lies on a global scale that we've seen." See Galati and Taliano, "Lawsuit against Trudeau Government: Constitutional Lawyer Rocco Galati and the Lies and Crimes of the COVID Operation"; Constitutional Rights Centre Inc., https://www.constitutionalrightscentre.ca/action4canada-british-columbia-court-challenge/; Constitutional Rights Centre, "Your Rights to decline a Vaccine in the context of Employment."

112 Carpay is the president of the Justice Center for Constitutional Freedoms, https://www.jccf.ca/about-us/meet-the-team/carpay/. At this website, Canadians can find various important resources regarding COVID-19.

others are working incessantly to bring justice to the victims of the COVID disaster. The media and the so-called fact-checkers have initiated an outright assault on these experts and their reputations, in order to discredit their views since they challenge the accepted narrative revolving around COVID-19. It is worth noting that there are a growing number of scientists and medical doctors who have signed the Rome Declaration.[113] As of October 14, 2021, there have been over 12,000 signatures. The declaration unites physicians and scientists to stand against COVID tyranny, such as the "political intrusion into the practice of medicine and the physician/patient relationship."[114] Furthermore, the declaration, among other important statements, includes the following:

> that physicians must defend their right to prescribe treatment, observing the tenet FIRST, DO NO HARM. Physicians shall not be restricted from prescribing safe and effective treatments. These restrictions continue to cause unnecessary sickness and death. The rights of patients, after being fully informed about the risks and benefits of each option, must be restored to receive those treatments.[115]

It is a shame that still too many doctors across the globe remain in their ignorance, cowardice and/or duplicity to stand up for what is right. It is only in a post-Orwellian world where heroic, knowledgeable, competent, and morally self-aware physicians, scientists, and other professionals are persecuted, while duplicitous, immoral, ignorant, and incompetent ones are favoured. A prime example is when Alberta's Chief Medical Officer of Health, Dr. Deena Hinshaw was caught spreading misinformation (a blatant lie). On October 12, 2021, she announced that a 14-year-old boy had died from COVID-19, but then retracted her statement and admitted that the boy had a series of other complications. Unfortunately, this is unsurprising. The distinction between dying due to COVID-19 versus from other complications is rarely acknowledged.[116] As is the double-standard of shielding the fact that people are dying from the vaccine but saying it's due to other health issues including COVID. Those who have pointed this out and criticized both provincial and federal governments in their reporting of COVID-19 deaths are seldomly taken seriously. The following questions arise: How often has this occurred? Was such a blatant lie part of a larger plan to continue to justify vaccine roll out for 12 to 17-year-olds? Or even worse, part of an upcoming roll-out for 5 to 11-year-olds? Whatever the case, what is clear is that we cannot

113 Physicians Declaration – Global COVID Summit, "Rome Declaration."

114 Physicians Declaration – Global COVID Summit, "Rome Declaration."

115 Physicians Declaration – Global COVID Summit, "Rome Declaration."

116 Henney, "CDC director criticized for now differentiating between dying 'from' vs. dying 'with' COVID-19."

trust municipal, provincial, and federal governments about actual COVID infections, risks, and deaths. The question remains: Can we trust them about anything after more than 20 months of this corona circus.

Most recently, some emails between NIH director, Francis Collins, and Anthony Fauci surfaced from 2020 when they were working for the Trump administration. It shows there was a concerted effort to smear doctors of The Great Barrington Declaration who called for the cessation of lockdowns in favour of herd immunity. On October 8, 2020, Collins sent an email stating:

> See https://gbdeclaration.org/. This proposal from three fringe epidemiologists who met with the Secretary seems to be getting a lot of attention—and even a co-signature from Nobel Prize winner Mike Leavitt at Stanford. There needs to be a quick and devastating published take down of its premises. I don't see anything online yet—is it underway?[117]

With every email and lie that is uncovered we can see medical bureaucrats like Fauci, and Collins trying to smear and censor medical doctors and scientists that raise significant issues. These hit pieces resemble Nazi and communist propaganda more than what the scientific enterprise came to embody in the West of debate and skepticism. Notice that Collins deceptively calls these scientists "fringe epidemiologists," but they all work for major academic institutions: Jay Bhattacharya is at Stanford University, Sunetra Gupta at University of Oxford, and Martin Kulldorff at Harvard University. Very deceptive to call these scientists "fringe" because they question draconian and absurd measures related to COVID. They have taken a common-sense approach recommending that:

> Those who are not vulnerable should immediately be allowed to resume life as normal. Simple hygiene measures, such as hand washing and staying home when sick should be practiced by everyone to reduce the herd immunity threshold. Schools and universities should be open for in-person teaching. Extracurricular activities, such as sports, should be resumed. Young low-risk adults should work normally, rather than from home. Restaurants and other businesses should open. Arts, music, sport and other cultural activities should resume. People who are more at risk may participate if they wish, while society as a whole enjoys the protection conferred upon the vulnerable by those who have built up herd immunity.[118]

117 Lepore. "'There needs to be a quick and devastating take down': Emails show how Fauci and head of NIH worked to discredit three experts who penned the Great Barrington Declaration which called for an end to lockdowns."

118 The Great Barrington Declaration.

So, to respond to Collins, yes, "fringe," given the mass formation psychosis that a significant portion of the population including scientists and medical doctors have been subject to, but still the correct and commonsensical approach. Unfortunately, Collins has been shown to be disgraceful, deceitful, uncharitable, and unchristian in his approach.

Medical Experts Threatened Over COVID

Methods of censorship take a whole new meaning when threats are involved. A growing number of scientists and physicians with a media presence have been threatened over their views on alternative treatments for COVID-19, lockdowns, mask wearing, and vaccination. It is a sad day when medical experts are muzzled for their views, but it is incredibly disturbing to hear of them receiving sexual threats and death threats for holding unpopular views.[119] Many experts fear speaking publicly in light of this.

Ensuring Compliance of Health Practitioners

The censorship and muzzling of health practitioners in favour of following government narratives and scientifically questionable claims, continue like clockwork. Platforms such as Facebook, Twitter and YouTube have been notorious for censoring unpopular views. A group of physicians in the US, known as "America's Frontline Doctors," in July of last year, attempted to bring to public awareness the campaign of disinformation being put forth by both governments and mainstream news—they were subsequently banned once a video they posted began to grow in popularity.[120]

In Canada, physicians, surgeons, and nurses have been admonished not to stray away from the medical "consensus" regarding COVID-19. The College of Physicians and Surgeons of Ontario (CPSO) issued the following statement at the end of April 2021:

> There have been isolated incidents of physicians using social media to spread blatant misinformation and undermine public health measures meant to protect all of us. In response, the College released the statement

119 See Campbell, "Scientists abused and threatened for discussing Covid, global survey finds." The editor doesn't mention for which particular views these experts are targeted, but it is reasonable to think that those who contradict the main narrative are susceptible to these attacks even if The *Guardian* claims otherwise.

120 Schwartz, "Facebook and YouTube Ban Video of Doctors Talking COVID, Silenced Doctors Hold Press Conference."

> below. The statement is intended to focus on professional behaviour and is not intended to stifle a healthy public debate about how to best address aspects of the pandemic. Rather, our focus is on addressing those arguments that reject scientific evidence and seek to rouse emotions over reason. We continue to recognize the important roles physicians can play by advocating for change in a socially accountable manner.
>
> The College is aware and concerned about the increase of misinformation circulating on social media and other platforms regarding physicians who are publicly contradicting public health orders and recommendations. Physicians hold a unique position of trust with the public and have a professional responsibility to not communicate anti-vaccine, anti-masking, anti-distancing and anti-lockdown statements and/or promoting unsupported, unproven treatments for COVID-19. Physicians must not make comments or provide advice that encourages the public to act contrary to public health orders and recommendations. Physicians who put the public at risk may face an investigation by the CPSO and disciplinary action, when warranted. When offering opinions, physicians must be guided by the law, regulatory standards, and the code of ethics and professional conduct. The information shared must not be misleading or deceptive and must be supported by available evidence and science.[121]

The College of Nurses of Ontario (CNO) in December 2020 issued a similar warning:

> Nurses are expected to adhere to the standards of practice in carrying out their professional responsibilities. Nurses have a professional responsibility to not publicly communicate anti-vaccination, anti-masking and anti-distancing statements that contradict the available scientific evidence. Doing so may result in an investigation by CNO, and disciplinary proceedings when warranted.[122]

The position taken by both the CPSO and the CNO is nothing short of tyrannical. The fact that they are reprimanding health practitioners for questioning any of the holy tenets of the COVID-19 "pandemic," such as the safety of the COVID vaccines, masks, "social" distancing (a self-contradicting term), the efficacy of lockdowns, and suppressing knowledge of treatments that can show how unnecessary the vaccine is, is truly reprehensible. This is an unscientific approach that is motivated by politics rather than evidence. It is a flagrant assault on health practitioners' freedom of speech and freedom of conscience. It is an utter violation of the first principle of nonmaleficence born

121 The College of Physicians and Surgeons of Ontario, "Statement on Public Health Misinformation."

122 College of Nurses of Ontario (CNO), "Nurses Supporting Public Health."

out of the Hippocratic Oath, i.e., to never do harm. As the Oath of Hippocrates of Kos, from the 5th century BC, states:

> I swear by Apollo the physician, by Aesculapius, Hygeia, and Panacea, and I take to witness all the gods, all the goddesses, to keep according to my ability and judgment the following oath:
> I will prescribe regimen for the good of my patients according to my ability and my judgment and *never do harm to anyone. To please no one will I prescribe a deadly drug, nor give advice which may cause his death.*[123]

The first and obvious point to make is that the invocation of Greek pagan gods sounds bizarre to modern ears for both non-religious and religious individuals. Moreover, for those of monotheistic faiths, the invocation of imaginary gods is anathema to any form of classical theism. Nevertheless, the upholding of the Hippocratic Oath when it comes to its substance such as the principle of nonmaleficence, i.e., to never do harm corresponds to unchanging truth and goodness that are not susceptible to cultural change and moral relativism.[124] The proclamation of the italicized words are consonant with any worldview that upholds objective moral values and duties. The Pythagoreans who formulated The Oath of Hippocrates were in the minority of Greek thinkers, who challenged the widely accepted cultural and moral trends of their time, particularly on questions regarding abortion and assisted suicide; they sought to set an objective moral standard for medicine.[125]

Thus, in light of our current predicament, the following fundamental questions must be answered: Are the measures vociferously employed by our governments, the two colleges, and organizations such as the WHO and the CDC, causing more harm than good? Are they betraying the principle of nonmaleficence? Declarations by the governments, pharmaceutical companies, and so-called fact-checkers will not resolve the issue, only the evidence will.

123 See Association of American Physicians and Surgeons website, "The Oath of Hippocrates of Kos, 5th century BC." The rest of the oath states:

> Nor will I give a woman a pessary to procure abortion. But I will preserve the purity of my life and my art. I will not cut for stone, even for patients in whom the disease is manifest; I will leave this operation to be performed by specialists in this art. In every house where I come I will enter only for the good of my patients, keeping myself far from all intentional ill-doing and all seduction, and especially from the pleasures of love with women or with men, be they free or slaves. All that may come to my knowledge in the exercise of my profession or outside of my profession or in daily commerce with men, which ought not to be spread abroad, I will keep secret and never reveal. If I keep this oath faithfully, may I enjoy my life and practice my art, respected by all men and in all times; but if I swerve from it or violate it, may the reverse be my lot.

124 For an extensive treatment of this and other important issues on the usefulness of the Hippocratic Oath for Christians, see Verhey, "The Doctor's Oath - and a Christian Swearing It."

125 Edelstein, "The Hippocratic Oath: Text, translation, and interpretation," 4–8.

And the evidence is increasingly painting a wholly different picture than what the authorities would have you believe.

In the twenty-first century, the oath has been modified on several occasions. Today, three versions are the most recited by medical students upon entering and graduating from medical school: the original version, the Declaration of Geneva which was written in 1948 (revised many times, as recently as 2017), and The Modern Physician's Oath is a 1964 revision by Dr. Louis Lasagna. Unfortunately, many of the changes occurring have become progressively ambiguous in order to accommodate culturally relativistic values, such as euthanasia, abortion, over-prescription of opioids, and now the incessant push to vaccinate most of the population, even though the recovery rate is extremely high for the average person (97 percent and 99.75 percent, which includes people with comorbidities and for children [126]). In Ontario, Canada alone, deaths due to opioids has risen for men 71 percent from 2019 to 2020. This is attributable to the COVID-19 crisis. This is affecting the unhoused and unemployed people. A CBC article in May of 2020, admits that the increase in the opioids crisis is directly linked to "limited access to supports, health-care services, and community programs for people who use drugs, greater isolation as a result of public health measures to curb the spread of COVID-19 and shifting patterns of substance use that can be attributed to a rise in anxiety during the pandemic."[127] The unlawful and unethical policies surrounding COVID-19 are what are taking lives and destroying them further, more so than the virus itself.

The Imposition of Bill C-10

In relation to this gagging of physicians and nurses, Bill C-10 will help suppress free speech, freedom of the press, and consequently freedom of conscience even further. According to the Department of Justice in Canada:

> Bill C-10 amends the Broadcasting Act (the Act). The Act sets out the broadcasting policy for Canada, the role and powers of the Canadian Radio-television and Telecommunications Commission (the Commission) in regulating and supervising the broadcasting system, and the mandate for the Canadian Broadcasting Corporation. The Act plays an important role in supporting Canada's cultural industries and ensuring Canadian content is available and accessible.[128]

126 WebMD, "Coronavirus Recovery."

127 Draaisma and Seputis, "Ontario's opioid-related death toll surged to 2,050 during pandemic in 2020, new report finds."

128 Government of Canada, "Bill C-10: An Act to amend the Broadcasting Act and to make consequential amendments to other Acts."

Despite the constant censorship and banning of Christian, conservative, and opposing voices in general from many media platforms, Justin Trudeau's Liberal Party of Canada is attempting to pass Bill C-10 which will further ease the regulation and censorship of dissenting voices from the Liberal-funded CBC. Bill C-10, despite claims to the contrary, will seriously infringe not only freedom of the press (particularly for alternative news sources), but also freedom of speech. Trudeau has also gone out of his way to dismiss any claims made by YouTubers, independent journalists, and others, that this is a conspiracy theory, without understanding the term. [129] As Tristin Hopper of the *National Post* in an article stated:

> Indeed, Heritage Minister Steven Guilbeault has repeatedly framed C-10 as a way to regulate streaming services such as Netflix and Crave while leaving social media alone. He told the House of Commons just last month that "we're not particularly interested in...when my great-uncle posts pictures of his cats." But in a House of Commons Heritage committee meeting Friday the social media clause was deleted. When confronted on the change, Guilbeault said that it was always their plan to regulate "online platforms that act as broadcasters."
>
> What the deletion means is that every single Canadian who posts to Instagram, Facebook, TikTok, Twitter or YouTube could be treated like a broadcaster subject to CRTC [(Canadian Radio-television Telecommunications Commission)] oversight and sanction. The users themselves may not necessarily be subject to direct CRTC regulation, but social media providers would have to answer to every post on their platforms as if it were a TV show or radio program.[130]

This draconian bill clearly violates section 2B of the Canadian Charter of Rights and Freedoms which guarantees the "freedom of thought, belief, opinion, and expression, including freedom of the press and other media communications." In addition to all the censorship already occurring throughout social media with unpopular views which challenge the mainstream narrative, Bill C-10, will grant the government power to further censor and regulate Canadian citizens' speech. Peter Menzies, a former CRTC Commissioner, had stated that the bill would severely stifle free speech. Law professor at the University of Ottawa, Michael Geist, called the bill an unconscionable attack on free speech.[131]

The major concern with this bill, despite the dismissals from government analysts, is that it will negatively impact our rights and freedoms. The bill in its

129 Frei, Twitter Post. May 12, 2021, 10:25 PM.

130 Hopper, "'Full-blown assault' on free expression: Inside the comprehensive Liberal bill to regulate the internet."

131 The Globe and Mail Editorial Board, "The Trudeau government says it won't regulate user content on social media. Bill C-10 says otherwise."

current guise is not only vague but even unnecessary for regulation purposes. The vagueness associated with this bill which critics have pointed out is dangerous, since it can allow the Canadian government to overstep regulatory and legal boundaries. This will have devastating consequences for private individuals and independent journalists/commentators. This will further inhibit Canadians from receiving a balanced view on the COVID-19 crisis and other crucial issues of the day.

If anything, Canadians, and citizens of the world should be very concerned about their civil liberties. Many of the governments throughout this world have handled this crisis poorly. Incompetence and corruption have gone hand in hand. The first step to defeating government tyranny is by exposing it. Once exposed, then people can act on defeating it. The Canadian government and others throughout the world are very scared that people will unify against restrictions that are imposed upon free citizens.

Exposing COVID-19 Vaccine Companies

Project Veritas

In September of 2021, Project Veritas began a series of videos regarding vaccine safety and mandates. You can find the footage on the Project Veritas website, Twitter, Instagram, Telegram, and other social media platforms. Many of these scientists and other professionals who are exposed in these videos go on to delete their LinkedIn profiles and any other visible online presence. When approached they refuse to give comment or runaway such as Pfizer Senior Director of Worldwide Research, Vanessa Gelman.[132]

The first video released on September 20, 2021, released a bombshell video where Dr. Maria Gonzales, ER Doctor, US Department of Health and Human Services:

> "All this is bullshit. Now, [a patient] probably [has] myocarditis due to the [COVID] vaccine. But now, they [government] are not going to blame the vaccine." Gonzales went on to state that: "They [government] are not reporting [adverse COVID vaccine side effects]… They want to shove it under the mat."[133]

Registered Nurse, Deanna Paris, of the US Department of Health and Human Services, iterated that: "It's a shame they [government] are not treating

132 Project Veritas, "BREAKING: Pfizer Senior Director of Worldwide Research Vanessa Gelman RUNS from Veritas' Questions."

133 Project Veritas, "COVID-19 Vaccine Exposed Part 1."

people [with COVID] like they're supposed to, like they should. I think they want people to die."[134] Another insider and registered nurse with the US Department of Health and Human Services, Jodi O'Malley, who came forward to Project Veritas, made the following dire warning:

> The COVID vaccine is "not doing what it's purpose was… I've seen dozens of people come in with adverse reactions… If we [government] are not gathering [COVID vaccine] data and reporting it, then how are we going to say that this is safe and approved for use?[135]

The second video featured, Tyler Lee, an economist with The Food and Drug Administration (FDA) in the US, was exposed on camera by Project Veritas with a disconcerting position on mass unlawful inoculation:

> Go to the unvaccinated and blow it [COVID vaccine] into them. Blow dart it into them… Census goes door-to-door if you don't respond. So, we have the infrastructure to do it [forced COVID vaccinations]. I mean, it'll cost a ton of money. But I think, at that point, I think there needs to be a registry of people who aren't vaccinated. Although that's sounding very [much like Nazi] Germany…Nazi Germany…I mean, think about it like the Jewish Star [for unvaccinated Americans].[136]

In the third video, the following two conversations ensue between a Project Veritas reporter and two Johnson & Johnson employees, regional business lead, Brandon Schadt, and scientist, Justin Durrant.

Schadt made the following admissions:

> It's a kid, you just don't do that, you know? Not something that's so unknown in terms of repercussions down the road, you know?… Kids shouldn't get a f*cking [COVID] vaccine… It's a kid, it's a f*cking kid, you know? They shouldn't have to get a f*cking [COVID] vaccine, you know?[137]

Durrant, as a scientist, made even more damning statements than Schadt: "Don't get the Johnson & Johnson [COVID vaccine], *I didn't tell you though…* It wouldn't make that much of a difference" if children are unvaccinated for COVID.[138] Durrant then reveals the disturbing coercion that governments

134 Project Veritas, "COVID-19 Vaccine Exposed Part 1."
135 Project Veritas, "COVID-19 Vaccine Exposed Part 1."
136 Project Veritas, "COVID-19 Vaccine Exposed Part 2."
137 Project Veritas, "COVID-19 Vaccine Exposed Part 3."
138 Project Veritas, "COVID-19 Vaccine Exposed Part 3."

in a concerted effort with these pharmaceutical companies, like Johnson & Johnson, are executing:

> Inconvenience [the unvaccinated] to the point where it's like, 'I might as well just f*cking do it [and take the COVID vaccine],' you know what I'm saying?... It's almost like—you're almost like a second-grade citizen if you're not vaccinated...you can't do anything that a normal citizen can do... If you can't work, I feel like that's punishment enough... Only way people really act and comply is if it affects their pockets, like if you're working for a big company and you're going to lose your job, best believe you'll be the first one in line [to take the COVID vaccine]... That's what we're doing.[139]

In the fourth installment there are three scientists who work for Pfizer that admit that natural immunity is stronger and longer lasting than two doses of the COVID-19 vaccine.[140]

On October 6, 2021, Project Veritas released their fifth installment, an interview with Pfizer manufacturing quality auditor Melissa Strickler, who provided emails from Gelman and other corporate executives instructing staff to avoid mentioning the fetal cell lines that the company used to test its COVID vaccine. According to Strickler, Pfizer senior director, Vanessa Gelman, wrote in an email dated February 9, 2021: "From the perspective of corporate affairs, we want to avoid having the information on fetal cells floating out there,"[141] Gelman then went on to write:

> The risk of communicating this right now outweighs any potential benefit we could see, particularly with general members of the public who may take this information and use it in ways we may not want out there. We have not received any questions from policy makers or media on this issue in the last few weeks, so we want to avoid raising this if possible.[142]

Gelman in a different email thread insisted on remaining secretive about these fetal cell lines:

> We have been trying as much as possible to not mention the fetal cell lines... One or more cell lines with an origin that can be traced back to human fetal tissue has been used in laboratory tests associated with the vaccine program.[143]

139 Project Veritas, "COVID-19 Vaccine Exposed Part 3."
140 Project Veritas, "COVID-19 Vaccine Exposed Part 4."
141 Project Veritas, "COVID-19 Vaccine Exposed Part 5."
142 Project Veritas, "COVID-19 Vaccine Exposed Part 5."
143 Project Veritas, "COVID-19 Vaccine Exposed Part 5."

Because of this deception it had made Strickler question "whether aborted fetal tissue made it to the final COVID vaccine product."[144] Although the Pfizer COVID-19 vaccine does not contain actual cells from aborted babies, it was nonetheless tested with a fetal cell line, HEK293T (human embryonic kidney cell). That cell line was indeed created with cells from an aborted baby, that have been grown and multiplied in a lab for years. COVID-19 vaccines have connections to abortion; however, none contain actual cells from aborted babies.[145] It seems evident that Pfizer executives were well aware that such knowledge would deter many Americans and people worldwide from accepting such a vaccine.

Vice president of the Charlotte Lozier Institute, David Prentice, made the following statement on October 7, 2021: "Pfizer and other pharmaceutical companies should commit to no longer using the antiquated science of fetal cells and instead use ethically-sourced alternatives as are routinely used for many other medications."[146]

In the coming months we should expect more alarming evidence to be brought forth by Project Veritas and other organizations that are courageous enough to expose the truth regardless of the consequences. Behind "closed doors," these officials have no hesitation in disclosing their true thoughts and the agenda behind some of these governmental organizations in conjunction with pharmaceutical companies. Any reasonable person should be alarmed by these admissions and horrifying statements.

Luciferase and Graphene Oxide in the Pfizer Vaccine?

In a bombshell interview with *LifeSite News*, Strickler claimed that in addition to aborted fetal cell lines the vaccines contained luciferase, which is a term for the class of oxidative enzymes that produce bioluminescence.[147] These enzymes are produced by fireflies, plants, and fish. She overheard a scientist describing codes for certain ingredients contained in the vaccines including SM102 for luciferase. She also claimed that she had reason to believe that the vaccine contains graphene oxide, which is something that corroborates what was allegedly discovered by Spanish medical researchers. These Spanish researchers, including Dr. Pablo Campra Madrid and other biochemists at the University of Almeria, discovered that "toxic nanoparticulates of graphene

144 Project Veritas, "COVID-19 Vaccine Exposed Part 5."

145 See Prentice, "COVID-19 Vaccine Candidates and Abortion-Derived Cell Lines"; Prentice and Lee, "What you need to know about the COVID-19 vaccines."

146 Prentice, Charlotte Lozier Institute, Twitter Post, October 7, 2021, at 5:31 PM.

147 McGovern, "Pfizer whistleblower says vaccine 'glows,' contains toxic luciferase, graphene oxide compounds."

oxide have been found in massive quantities in the mRNA Covid 19 vials."[148] Since then, this has been pursued further by La Quinta Columna, a group of medical researchers, including Ricardo Delgado Martin (biostatistician) and José Luis Sevillano (a family doctor), who have done further investigations into the Pfizer vials.[149]

Goodbye to Reason and Morality

A Divided World

What we are witnessing is essentially the bifurcation of roughly two classes of people or groups.[150] These groups have been around since the dawn of time. The first puts their ultimate trust in the State; they believe the State is good and keeping their best interests. Politicians, policy makers, academics, scientists, and journalists are held in high esteem. The second group questions the authority of these individuals and the State. The first group looks at the second group with disdain as uneducated, ignorant, and conspiratorial. Whereas the second group looks at the first as sheepish, mind-controlled, utterly compliant, oblivious to corruption that exists within the State and the "trusted individuals," and incapable of thinking for themselves. COVID has made these two classes of people more glaring than ever. This division will be hard to navigate through. The State is rather content on wreaking divisions between citizens of the world since it easier to govern divided people. If humanity, as a whole, were to unify against corruption and the State, the State would have no power over its citizens and would be relegated to do its primary job, i.e., protecting its citizens' rights and freedoms by allowing them to make a living and live a happy life; they are currently doing the exact opposite.

We see these stark divisions within religious groups and families. Much of what we are witnessing is directly out of the Karl Marx and Friedrich Engels playbook: *The Communist Manifesto*. The one thing we can credit them with is

148 For the original study see Madrid, "Graphene Oxide Detection in Aqueous Suspension Observational Study in Optical and Electron Microscopy." For the most recent updated study: Madrid, "Deteccion de Grafeno en Vacunas Covid19 por Espectroscopia Micro-raman."

149 See Odell, "Issues Surrounding Graphene Oxide in the Pfizer mRNA Covid 19 Formulation. For an in-depth discussion regarding graphene oxide and its presence in the Pfizer COVID-19 vaccine"; see also Stew Peters, "La Quinta Columna 1-On-1: Spanish Researcher First to Reveal Graphene Oxide" for a discussion with one of the main doctors, Ricardo Delgado, involved in researching the presence of graphene oxide in the COVID-19 vaccines.

150 There are always sub-groups and divergences but the division of two major groups encapsulates precisely what is being revealed throughout the world with respect to COVID. See XandrewX, "Why are you awake when so many aren't 5 points of eye-opening truth."

their honesty, unlike the politicians we have in place now, like Justin Trudeau, Joe Biden, Emmanuel Macron, Boris Johnson, etc. The goal with COVID and the "Great Reset"[151] put forth by the World Economic Forum seeks to not only abolish private property but attack the family, individuality, eternal truths, nations, and the past.[152] We see this at play through critical theory/woke culture and the unfolding COVID pandemonium, all work in a concerted effort to undermine the longstanding values and fruits of the West.

There are many divisions among Christian brethren. For instance, it is certainly disheartening to see Francis Collins, a prolific scientist, Templeton award winner for science and faith, and a self-proclaimed devout Christian in addition to being involved in scandals with funding gain of function research, was also at the forefront of polarizing the vaccinated and unvaccinated. He has violated people's medical conscience through supporting compulsory vaccination upon private businesses and employees at the NIH.[153] He has demonized the unvaccinated and has labeled them unchristian-like and even so far as murderers.[154] This rhetoric is dangerous and based on many falsehoods, as John G. West explains:

> Although Collins likes to tout his personal faith, he appears to have very little concern for any sort of conscience rights of fellow religious believers who disagree with him. After all, he dutifully served in a previous administration that repeatedly weakened conscience protections for medical workers opposed to abortion and that violated federal law by turning a blind eye when California mandated abortion coverage in all private insurance plans.[155]

When an allegedly devout Christian who is a leading scientist partakes in demonizing and attacking dissenters' freedom of conscience, it is a sign of dangerous times. Similarly, we can witness this division within the Catholic Church. Despite the fact that the mRNA vaccines and the Janssen vaccine, which are produced and/or lab tested with aborted fetal cell lines, Pope Francis has called vaccination an "act of love."[156] Calling coercive mandates an act of love is extremely troubling. An act of love must be voluntary. So is inoculating children who, for the most part, have natural immunity to SARS-CoV-2 and its variants. In an interview on January 10, 2021, Francis said that "I believe that morally everyone must take the vaccine," he also emphasized

151 See Chapters 2, 3, 4, and 7 for where there is a larger discussion on the Great Reset and the goals of these elites.

152 Miltimore, "5 Things Marx Wanted to Abolish (Besides Private Property)."

153 Dima, "NIH Director Francis Collins calls for more vaccine mandates."

154 Hayes, "Transcript: All In With Chris Hayes."

155 West, Francis Collins's "Troubling Record at NIH."

156 Watkins, "Pope Francis urges people to get vaccinated against Covid-19."

that "it is the moral choice because it is about your life but also the lives of others."[157] In August of 2021, he said that "getting vaccinated is a simple yet profound way to care for one another, especially the most vulnerable."[158] Other Cardinals and archbishops have echoed Pope Francis's sentiments. The Pope never makes the distinction between who should and who should not take the vaccine. Never a single mention of the potential harm and serious adverse effects. Not a mention of natural immunity, nothing. The Church has also been utterly silent on the many violations perpetrated by governments on sovereign individuals throughout the world. It is all very discouraging and sinister. However, there are a number of cardinals and archbishops who are against receiving these experimental injections. Some Swiss Guards within Vatican City have voiced their objections as well and have returned to Switzerland. Swiss Guard, Pierre-André Udressy, in an open letter addressed to "Vatican authorities, its supreme head the Holy Father Pope Francis, the Vatican Secretariat of State, the institutions of the city, and the commandant of the Pontifical Swiss Guard," wrote scathingly on vaccine coercion occurring within Vatican City:

> Now the Vatican, the institution of the Church, has chosen the Pfizer vaccine, tested on abortive cell lines. What are we to think? It even imposes the vaccine on all its employees, although, as a sovereign state, it would have the possibility to choose products not contaminated by abortion, which also exist.
>
> What is even more frightening is the neglect of life where life should be defended! In such a dramatic situation, people would expect nothing but spiritual support: In such a crisis, only faith could allow them to bear the situation.[159]

Pope Francis is entitled to his opinions, and they are *just* that. His opinion holds zero weight for conscientious Catholics, like Udressy, me, and many others, who see that mandating and coercing people into compliance to receive the COVID injection as morally abhorrent. Pope Francis should feel a deep shame about the coercive stance he has taken, a total abuse of his papacy. It is immoral, wrongheaded, and serves the interests of a very evil people who are pushing this illegal injection no matter the evidence against its safety and efficacy. But should we feel surprised at the utter betrayal of Pope Francis on many faithful Catholics? The mere fact that he agreed to meet with Joe Biden is suggestive of something very sinister happening within the Church. He

157 McElwee, "Pope Francis suggests people have moral obligation to take coronavirus vaccine."

158 Watkins, "Pope Francis urges people to get vaccinated against Covid-19."

159 Gomes, "Swiss Guard Blows Whistle on Vaccine Coercion."

supposedly told Biden to continue to receive the Holy Communion despite Biden's anti-Catholic stance on abortion.[160] It is telling that Francis nor anyone at the Vatican has corrected Biden on this matter.

Catholics and other Christians who tout Pope Francis's support of mandating these vaccines, should keep in mind that Jorge Mario Bergoglio[161] is not speaking ex-cathedra, i.e., with the full authority of office which implies infallibility. This should become evident to any sincere Catholic, given the constant contradictions to Catholic doctrine Bergoglio is spewing.[162]

A leading dissenting voice is that of Archbishop Carlo Maria Viganò who has been unequivocal on his stance against these COVID-19 injections:

> But alongside this obvious uselessness of the "vaccine"—a uselessness that any doctor not subservient to the system would have considered from the beginning, since the Corona viruses are susceptible to mutation—we cannot fail to see how instrumental it is, precisely in its "mystical" value, to the collective acceptance of human sacrifice as normal and indeed necessary: the most innocent and defenseless creature, the baby in the womb in the third month of gestation, is sacrificed and dismembered in order to extract tissue from his still palpitating body with which to produce a non-cure, a non-vaccine, which not only does not heal from the virus, but in all likelihood causes a greater percentage of death than Covid itself, especially in the elderly or those who are sick.[163]

"Oh! What Ethics! What Heroes!"[164]

Throughout this chapter we examined a slew of unethical measures related to COVID-19, perpetrated by politicians, scientists, physicians, church officials, religious leaders, news anchors, globalist elites, parents using COVID as leverage in custody disputes, and even Pope Francis. The executive director of

160 Hadro, "Joe Biden says Pope Francis told him to 'keep receiving Communion'."

161 Over the years, the more I learn about Bergoglio's betrayal of Catholics and his incessant contradictions of Catholic teachings, the more I have to come question whether he is the Vicar of Christ, just as this Ohio Priest has stated: see A Pillar Explainer, "Why an Ohio priest who denied Pope Francis went 'viral'." For an article explaining why Pope Benedict XVI remains as pope, see: Veri Catholici, "How and why Pope Benedict XVI's resignation is invalid by the law itself."

162 See Benton, "Pope Francis Risks Leaving A Legacy Of Confusion And Division."

163 Hickson, "Archbishop Viganò: Vaccines made with fetal tissue are a 'human sacrifice of innocent victims offered to Satan'."

164 See Degrassi: School's Out (Part 4), 1992. A line adapted from Degrassi where Archie Simpson (Snake) speaks to Joey Jeremiah on his lack of ethics regarding him cheating on his girlfriend Caitlyn Ryan with Tessa Campanelli.

the *British Medical Journal*, Kamran Abbasi knows very well the sort of medical corruption that has surrounded the COVID-19 crisis:

> Science is being suppressed for political and financial gain. Covid-19 has unleashed state corruption on a grand scale, and it is harmful to public health. Politicians and industry are responsible for this opportunistic embezzlement. So too are scientists and health experts. The pandemic has revealed how the medical-political complex can be manipulated in an emergency—a time when it is even more important to safeguard science.[165]

Abbassi then goes on to incisively explains how science is politicized for the sake of personal gain while ordinary people suffer and die:

> Politicisation of science was enthusiastically deployed by some of history's worst autocrats and dictators, and it is now regrettably commonplace in democracies. The medical-political complex tends towards suppression of science to aggrandise and enrich those in power. And, as the powerful become more successful, richer, and further intoxicated with power, the inconvenient truths of science are suppressed. When good science is suppressed, people die.[166]

It is indeed a disturbing ordeal when an executive director of a leading medical journal explains in such stark terms the reality of this situation; one which most people are too blind to see and that governments will never admit. We need to "follow the money" at every level of government throughout the world in order to examine what has really been happening since March 2020. In the proceeding chapters, we will examine in greater detail some of these lies.

Betraying Your Moral Conscience

What can we hope for faithful Christians given this dire situation? The Pope, countless clergy, protestant ministers, and prominent lay Christians like Francis Collins have turned their back on the faithful. Catholics are beckoned to betray their conscience. The fact that the current COVID-19 mRNA vaccines and the Janssen vaccine are produced and/or lab tested with aborted fetal cell lines should give any Christian serious pause. Central to the Christian faith is that all human beings are image bearers of God and that this fact affirms the uniqueness and dignity of every human person. One ought to be aware of the

165 Kamran Abbasi, "Covid-19: politicisation, 'corruption,' and suppression of science."
166 Abbasi, "Covid-19: politicisation, 'corruption,' and suppression of science."

sixth commandment: "Thou shall not murder" (Exod 20:13), for the Christian, abortion is wrong at every stage. Catholics should be confident that according to the Congregation for the Doctrine of the Faith (CDF): "vaccination is not, as a rule, a moral obligation and that, therefore, it must be voluntary."[167] Moreover, they should also be considered morally objectional by Christians given that the present knowledge of how the vaccines were developed by pharmaceutical companies violate the moral imperative "to ensure that vaccines, which are effective and safe from a medical point of view, [and also] ethically acceptable."[168] Moreover, the unethical practices of coercive vaccine mandates and passports pushed forward by governments and international organizations have assaulted our freedom of conscience. The Pontifical Academy for Life also "clearly states that illicit vaccines, prepared from cells from aborted human fetuses, must be opposed, though admitting, on the other hand, that in case of need their use could be accepted." [169] So, the Catholic position is also clear, especially considering that the vaccinated are spreading the disease themselves, while medically and scientifically natural immunity is more robust and longer lasting. Faithful Christians, regardless of the coercion and pressures of this world must hold to the sanctity of human life and refuse vaccines that utilize such barbaric and antiquated methods of production. As David says in Ps 139:13–14, "For you formed my inward parts; you knitted me together in my mother's womb, I praise you, for I am fearfully and wonderfully made. Wonderful are your works; my soul knows it very well."

Should we not be looking toward having antibody (serology) tests instead to see what kind of immunity people have from the virus? Faithful Christians also recognize that their physical bodies, regardless of the method of Creation, have been given to us by God. Veritable Christians should also uphold their freedom of conscience. We do not bend our knee to the State—we are not communists—we only bend our knee to Jesus Christ. Our bodies are Created by God and are to be stewarded. Scriptures clearly place the responsibility on each individual person not the State. This is clearly stated by Saint Paul in 1 Cor 6:19–20, "Or do you not know that your body is a temple of the Holy Spirit within you, whom you have from God? You are not your own, for you were bought with a price. So glorify God in your body." For a Christian to

167 Rome, from the Offices of the Congregation for the Doctrine of the Faith, "Note on the morality of using some anti-Covid-19 vaccines." December 21, 2020. https://www.vatican.va/roman_curia/congregations/cfaith/documents/rc_con_cfaith_doc_20201221_nota-vaccini-anticovid_en.html.

168 Rome, from the Offices of the Congregation for the Doctrine of the Faith, "Note on the morality of using some anti-Covid-19 vaccines."

169 "Pontifical Academy for Life Statement: Moral Reflections on Vaccines Prepared from Cells Derived from Aborted Human Foetuses." *The Linacre Quarterly* 86, no. 2–3 (May 2019): 182–87. https://doi.org/10.1177/0024363919855896.

permit the State to dictate what they inject into their body is a violation of one's bodily autonomy and is morally wrong. What about the potentially never-ending revolving door of boosters? One thing that the currently vaccinated and unvaccinated will have in common given reoccurring boosters is that they will both be considered unvaccinated without them. Thus, for these and reasons of logic, science, and medicine, Christians must reject these experimental gene therapeutic injections.

Douglas Farrow, who is a Professor of Theology and Ethics at McGill University, in late August of 2021, echoed some of the aforementioned thoughts when he wrote an open letter against proposed vaccine mandates and passports in Quebec.[170] Farrow, in his open letter, makes the following salient points:

- "vaccine" mandates are incoherent since they either protect or do not protect those have been "inoculated." If they do protect the "vaccinated" then they have nothing to worry about, but if they don't government has no business mandating them.
- coercive vaccines violate bodily autonomy
- reinforcement of the vaccine passport system which violates liberty, equality, and fraternity
- it is deeply unethical to impose experimental treatment on young individuals who do not have any comorbidities
- growing numbers of people who have been pressured/coerced in taking this experimental injection are suffering injuries and even death which will lead to an unprecedented number of legal actions against those suppressing such information
- it is against the Nuremberg Code by discarding the principle of informed consent, regardless of if these are FDA approve—they still remain experimental

Similarly, ethicist Julie Ponesse, who recently got dismissed from her professorship at Huron College of Western University for not complying with the school's vaccine mandate, in an interview said that: "To be quite honest with you, I don't think that any Canadian who has received one of the COVID shots so far has been able to give fully informed consent."[171] Ponesse is absolutely correct on this.[172] How can informed consent be possible if we do not have all of the evidence regarding this COVID-19 vaccine and the pandemic in general. There are many uncertainties, flip flops, and lies that have been pushed forward by politicians, the media, and health practitioners. So, what does informed

170 Douglas Farrow, "An Open Letter on Coercive Mandates and Vaccine Passports."
171 The Democracy Fund, "Dr. Julie Ponesse on Counterpoint | Fear and Moral Panic."
172 See Ponesse, *My Choice: The Ethical Case Against COVID-19 Vaccine Mandates.*

consent entail? Informed consent for the COVID-19 vaccine would entail consent by a patient to undergo a medical or surgical treatment or to participate in an experiment after the patient understands the risks involved, benefits, and alternatives. It must be voluntary, free and in the absence of pressure, coercion, and duress. Unfortunately, there is no transparency on these issues. Mandating vaccination for a highly survivable disease, especially for those who do not have compromised immune systems and are under 20 years of age is exceedingly unethical, to say the least.

To have a semblance to full informed consent you would require accurate and honest answers to the following questions:

- How can you provide informed consent if you do not know the ingredients contained within the vaccine? As was revealed by Project Veritas, is Pfizer hiding information from the public? We would require an entire list of the contents of the vaccine and if any of the ingredients are toxic. We do not have credible assurances that the vaccine has been fully, independently, and rigorously tested against control groups, nor do we have the subsequent outcomes of those tests.
- Do we know whether the vaccine is an experimental mRNA gene altering therapy that is undergoing a trial period?
- What about long-term effects?
- What about the likelihood of fatality?
- What about adverse effects? Full disclosure of data must be provided.
- If an individual suffers a severe adverse effect, what is the recovery rate in comparison to COVID-19?
    - What is it for a person with a compromised immune system/of older age in comparison to a healthy individual? A healthy child?
- Is the vaccine medically necessary for a healthy person, let alone a child?
    - Is it safe for healthy people and children? List all the risks and rates of fatality.
    - And is it effective? Does it stop transmission? Full disclosure is necessary.
- How will side effects and injuries be classified, documented, and compensated as a result of these procedures?
- Who is liable?
    - Will a doctor give a prescription?
- Can you get a second opinion?
- Why is there an incessant push to incentivize people? What about children with ice cream, bottles of water, etc.? What are the ethics behind such practices?
- What about alternative treatments, like early therapeutic and antiviral drugs?

More Lies

The truth about alternative treatments have been hidden from us. It should be of no surprise as to why effective anti-viral treatments against COVID-19, like hydroxychloroquine and ivermectin, are not only discouraged but totally disparaged by pharmaceutical companies—they are inexpensive and do not ramp up profit margins. For example, news networks like CNN, NBC, MSNBC, and others claimed that Joe Rogan took horse dewormer medication; this is how they framed ivermectin.[173] These news anchors are criminals that are purposefully misleading the public on lifesaving medication. What they are doing is very dangerous. Ivermectin has been shown to be highly effective in treating COVID-19. The fact that they are putting this forward is criminal and they're unwittingly admitting it publicly. Then they parade meaningless statements like "trust the 'science'" which means believe whatever they tell you and take your endless boosters. The COVID-19 injection is much more profitable and serves a totally different purpose. As of May 2021, the pharmaceutical industry minted 9 new billionaires.[174] Nevertheless, ironically, Pfizer has been developing a antiviral medication to treat COVID-19.[175] Beat them if you can't join them? Who knows what the cost will be and how effective? Will it be weaponized against other successful aforementioned treatments? Will it help the vaccine hesitant find an alternative treatment, while helping us return to normalcy? Only time will tell. But Pfizer has not earned our trust. Moreover, think about how governments are in the absurd and awkward position of having to convince the unvaccinated that the vaccine is effective and necessary, while trying to convince the vaccinated that the vaccine is not strong enough and that they need boosters!

In Ontario, Member of Provincial Parliament (MPP), Randy Hillier, wrote a letter to the Ontario Provincial Police (OPP) to begin an immediate investigation related to sudden deaths of healthy and young individuals which appear to be caused by the COVID-19 vaccines:

> This request is based on Ontario public health data revealing a disproportionate occurrence among younger age demographics of potentially serious adverse reactions to COVID-19 vaccines. Cardiovascular conditions are of particular concern. Such trends are being observed in publicly available data worldwide, prompting several countries to suspend the use of certain vaccine products altogether, or restrict their usage among these young demographics.[176]

173 Wilson, "Joe Rogan In Info Wars Exposes The Truth About Ivermectin To America!"

174 Ziady, "Covid vaccine profits mint 9 new pharma billionaires."

175 Tanenbaum, "A pill to treat COVID-19? Pfizer takes next step in study of Tamiflu-like drug."

176 Hillier, "Rise in Sudden Deaths Among Young People Requires Investigation." See also Hillier, "Testimonies of people with adverse reactions."

One can only hope that justice will be brought to these families who have suffered greatly because of medical malfeasance. Recklessly, the FDA recently approved, and the CDC double downed on administering these injections to children 5 to 11, despite essentially having zero risk from the virus. Ontario's chief medical officer, Kieran Moore, on November 3, 2021, said that the province will be offering COVID boosters for anyone 12 years of age and up.[177] Keep in mind that in Israel, those without boosters are losing their green pass status.[178] However, the Ontario government promises otherwise:

> Booster doses will be encouraged but won't be mandatory, and Ontarians who have two shots of COVID-19 vaccine and choose not to get a booster will still be considered fully immunized. According to health officials, two doses continue to provide powerful and prolonged protection against COVID-19.[179]

Nonetheless, we already know the government's track record with COVID and how far we can trust them. For how long are people willing to play this charade?

There has been a tremendous lack of transparency regarding the adverse effects and fatality caused by the COVID-19 vaccine, not just in Canada, but throughout the world. Nevertheless, the push to vaccinate younger and younger segments of the population continues to defy evidence, reason, and basic principals of healthcare ethics. A tragic irony that you will never hear about in mainstream news is how the healthcare system can afford to terminate healthcare workers over unvaccinated status, but already face shortages of workers. Moreover, through the "thick" of the pandemic, when the vaccine wasn't rolled out, these same healthcare workers were deemed heroes, but became villains overnight because they wish to exercise bodily autonomy and follow the right to follow their conscience.

Something is also amiss when President Trump, who seemed to be against the NWO and its nefarious agenda, was responsible for the COVID-19 vaccine program: "Operation Warp Speed." Interestingly, "Operation Warp Speed" is the only time that the Biden Administration has praised Trump.[180] Why was Trump pushing hydroxychloroquine at one point and now pushing the COVID vaccine?[181] He's gone on to say that everyone would have been inoculated if he were still POTUS. Is this all a ploy for reelection? We can only wait and see.

177 CBC, "Ontario to offer COVID-19 boosters to everyone 12 and up, with those 70 and older eligible this week."

178 TOI Staff, "Nearly 2 million Israelis lose Green Pass as new rules enter effect."

179 CBC News, "Ontario to offer COVID-19 boosters to everyone 12 and up, with those 70 and older eligible this week."

180 Barnes, "Trump surprised and 'very appreciative' about Biden's praise."

181 Halon, "Trump urges all Americans to get COVID vaccine: 'It's a safe vaccine' and it 'works'."

But, despite the fruits of his presidency, it seems that Trump's moral compass goes in the direction that the wind blows.

Why is the Ontario Premier Doug Ford's daughter, Krista Haynes (née Ford) pushing back against COVID-19 vaccines and passports,[182] despite her father's heavy restrictions in Ontario for almost two years? Her husband, from the Toronto Police, refused the vaccine and went on unpaid leave, but is there a deeper reason? Are these occurrences theatrics or actual family disagreements?

Unceasing Absurdities

Absurdities continue as the archbishop of Moncton, New Brunswick, seeks to further create a divide between vaccinated and unvaccinated within the Catholic Church by demanding vaccine passports for those 12 years of age and over to attend mass.

George Orwell was not incorrect when he wrote in *Nineteen Eighty-Four* that the State would come to dictate that 2+2=5 by force. Illogicality is being embraced at every level, as it continues to unfold in our post-Orwellian world created by authoritarian governments at the direction of billionaire psychopaths and their sycophantic political minions. We are already compelled to accept and preach absurdities. Here, in the third decade of the twenty-first century, we find ourselves at the precipice of unreason, pseudoscience, and amorality. Never could Orwell have imagined how insufferable, malevolent, illogical, and recalcitrant those in power would be. One cannot help but continue to be in disbelief of the utter madness of the world.

If anything, citizens of the world should be very concerned about the unrelenting assaults on our freedoms and rights perpetrated by governments, the pharmaceutical industry, the WHO, the CDC, and Big Tech corporations, all of which are made under the illusion of helping us. Nothing could be further from the truth. Incompetence and corruption have gone hand in hand from the beginning of this crisis. Jay Richards, William Briggs, and Douglas Axe in their book, *The Price of Panic: How the Tyranny of Experts Turned a Pandemic into a Catastrophe*, have offered the following conclusion, one which is true of all countries who have enforced draconian responses to the COVID-19 world crisis:

> In the present case, the dominant voice isn't a political party, but rather official experts. But if a small group, whether politicians or vetted scientists, has vast power to control the rest of us, then others must have power to contest them. The coronavirus panic and shutdown would not

182 Memes127en, "Who is Doug Ford daughter, krista? – Photos and videos instagram and reddit."

> have played out as it did if a few scientific experts, boosted by a reckless media, had not had so much unchecked power. Elected representatives need to be able to weigh competing advice. But the dominant point of view tends to marginalize all dissent. This is what we saw over and over during the pandemic. Perhaps an official loyal opposition could temper this all-too-human tendency. Its sole job would be to probe, question, and where warranted, dismantle the official advice our political leaders receive. Of course, the experts in this opposing role would also be fallible. Still, the cut and thrust between the two sides might reveal some otherwise hidden truths.[183]

Awareness as a Way Forward?

The first step to defeating government tyranny is by exposing it. Once exposed, then the right course of action can be taken to oppose their damaging restrictions. The Canadian government, and governments throughout the world, fear that people will unify against these unconstitutional restrictions which have been imposed upon its free citizens. The "cure" they have offered to COVID-19 is much deadlier than the disease itself. This is something the 45th President of the USA, Donald J. Trump, had observed at the beginning of the crisis, but was met with unjustified derision. The COVID-19 situation is not only an affront to reason, but also a variety of indignities and crimes perpetrated against humanity by the most grotesque, inhumane, and repulsive beings inhabiting our planet. Michael Yeadon and others have prepared a document for filing with the International Criminal Court:

> Based on the extensive claims and enclosed documentation, we charge those responsible for numerous violations of the Nuremberg Code, crimes against humanity, war crimes and crimes of aggression in the United Kingdom, but not limited to individuals in these countries.[184]

Throughout 2020 and 2021, we have witnessed not only the erosion of civil liberties, but also the livelihoods of countless families and small generational businesses. It is interesting to note that billionaires like Jeff Bezos, Bill Gates, Mark Zuckerberg, and Elon Musk are some of the ones who have profited the most from this world crisis. Does anyone ever question why violent

183 Richards, et al., *The Price of Panic: How the Tyranny of Experts Turned a Pandemic into a Catastrophe*, 204.

184 As of December 6, 2021, Michael Yeadon and others are planning to file a 46-page document to the International Criminal Court for violating the Nuremberg code. http://web.archive.org/web/20211227070153/; https://hannahroselaw.files.wordpress.com/2021/12/icc-complaint-7.docx.

activist groups like Black Lives Matter and antifa, more often than not, attack small businesses and ordinary individuals as opposed to government and big corporations? Maybe it is not about justice at all.

COVID-19 medical expert, Dr. Peter McCullough has called for "unbreakable resistance"[185] against vaccinating our kids. In a powerful presentation for the Association of American Physicians and Surgeons, he has also stated that for public health agencies there has been an "astounding… ineptitude and willful misconduct."[186] He has been very explicit to call this medical malfeasance since there has been no safety review and that "vaccination should be halted immediately."[187] At the conclusion of his presentation, McCullough raises the point that there is something more sinister than most can possibly imagine happening in the world right now:

> This cannot be about money. It cannot. It cannot be about Pfizer. It's not. It can't be about Bill Gates. It's not. It's something very, very big going on in the world. In many ways, in kind of [a] perverse way, it's a very exciting time to be alive. All of us are charged. I can feel the charge in the room.
>
> Something is going on. This book [COVID-19 and the Global Predators: We are the Prey] has a thousand references. This book gives you the material transfer agreement between Moderna and the Chinese for the spike protein before COVID-19 was a problem. Okay? This was planned. This book has the Johns Hopkins symposium that planned the pandemic in 2017. They planned how they were going to get the scoreboard [of deaths] up on CNN.[188]

Undoubtedly, the long and narrow path is worth the travel, not the one of least resistance which leads to perdition.

185 Delaney, "COVID expert Dr. Peter McCullough urges 'unbreakable resistance' to vaccines for kids." You can see the presentation on Rumble: Peter McCullough, "Winning the War Against Therapeutic Nihilism & Trusted Treatments vs Untested Novel Therapies." Rumble Video. You can also find his slideshow presentation on scribd.com: https://www.scribd.com/document/530328436/Slides-from-Peter-McCullough-MD-Oct-1-2021-Lecture.

186 Delaney, "COVID expert Dr. Peter McCullough urges 'unbreakable resistance' to vaccines for kids."

187 Delaney, "COVID expert Dr. Peter McCullough urges 'unbreakable resistance' to vaccines for kids."

188 Delaney, "COVID expert Dr. Peter McCullough urges 'unbreakable resistance' to vaccines for kids." See also Breggin and Breggin, *Covid 19 and the Global Predators: We Are the Prey.*

Bibliography

A Pillar Explainer. "Why an Ohio priest who denied Pope Francis went 'viral'." *The Pillar*, August 25, 2021. https://www.pillarcatholic.com/p/why-a-priest-who-denied-pope-francis.

Abbasi, Kamran. "Covid-19: politicisation, 'corruption,' and suppression of science." *BMJ* November 13, 2020; 371. doi: https://doi.org/10.1136/bmj.m4425.

Aiello, Rachel. "Anticipating 'mass vaccinations,' Canada ordering millions of syringes." *CTV News*, June 2, 2020. https://www.ctvnews.ca/health/coronavirus/anticipating-mass-vaccinations-canada-ordering-millions-of-syringes-1.4965078.

———. "Air passengers and federal public servants must be vaccinated by end of October." *CTV News*, October 6, 2021. https://www.ctvnews.ca/politics/air-passengers-and-federal-public-servants-must-be-vaccinated-by-end-of-october-1.5612815.

Association of American Physicians and Surgeons. https://aapsonline.org/.

Association of American Physicians and Surgeons website. "The Oath of Hippocrates of Kos, 5th century BC." Accessed May 19, 2021. https://www.aapsonline.org/ethics/oaths.htm.

Awake Canada. "Documentation." Accessed October 30, 2021. https://awakecanada.org/documentation/.

———. "Awake Evidence." Awakecanada.org, accessed October 30, 2021. https://awakecanada.org/awake-videos/.

Awakening Channel. "Most Shared Blog Posts (last 18 months)." October 4, 2021. https://new.awakeningchannel.com/most-shared-last-12-months-oct-4/.

Barker, Jacob. "Windsor court ruling puts COVID-19 'hoax' belief at centre of custody fight." *CBC News,* March 5, 2021. https://www.cbc.ca/news/canada/windsor/windsor-covid-19-custody-decision-1.5937278.

Barnes, Adam. "Trump surprised and 'very appreciative' about Biden's praise." *The Hill*, December 22, 2021. https://thehill.com/changing-america/well-being/prevention-cures/586884-trump-surprised-and-very-appreciative-about.

BBC Staff. "Coronavirus: Countries reject Chinese-made equipment." *BBC News*, March 30, 2020. https://www.bbc.com/news/world-europe-52092395.

Behavioural Insights Team, The. Accessed November 3, 2021. https://www.bi.team/about-us/.

Benton, Carina. "Pope Francis Risks Leaving A Legacy Of Confusion And Division." *The Federalist*, October 27, 2020. https://thefederalist.com/2020/10/27/pope-francis-risks-leaving-a-legacy-of-confusion-and-division/.

Borgier, Pieter, et al. "External peer review of the RTPCR test to detect SARS-CoV-2 reveals 10 major scientific flaws at the molecular and methodological level: consequences for false positive results." International Consortium of Scientists in Life Science (ICLS), November 30, 2020. https://cormandrostenreview.com/report/; https://zenodo.org/record/4298004.

Breggin, Peter R. and Ginger Ross Breggin. *Covid 19 and the Global Predators: We Are the Prey.* Ithaca: Lake Edge Press, 2021.

Bridle, Byram. "COVID-19 Vaccines and Children: A Scientist's Guide for Parents." *COVID Care Alliance*, June 15, 2021. https://www.canadiancovidcarealliance.org/wp-content/uploads/2021/06/2021-06-15-children_and_covid-19_vaccines_full_guide.pdf.

———. "Why Parents, Teens, and Children Should Question the COVID-19 Vaccine." *COVID Care Alliance.* https://www.canadiancovidcarealliance.org/wp-content/uploads/2021/06/2021-06-15-children_and_covid-19_vaccines_full_guide.pdf; https://www.canadiancovidcarealliance.org/wp-content/uploads/2021/06/Guide_to_COVID19_vaccines_for_parents_v5.pdf.

Byram Bridle's web page at University of Guelph. https://ovc.uoguelph.ca/pathobiology/people/faculty/Byram-W-Bridle.

Cammaerts, Émile. *The Laughing Prophet: The Seven Virtues and G.K. Chesterton.* London: Methuen & Co., 1937.

CBC. "Ontario to offer COVID-19 boosters to everyone 12 and up, with those 70 and older eligible this week." *CBC*, November 3, 2021. https://www.cbc.ca/news/canada/toronto/covid-19-ontario-november-3-2021-booster-shots-details-1.6235235.

CBC Edmonton. Twitter Post. October 12, 2021, at 7:44 PM. https://twitter.com/CBCEdmonton/status/1448072068793315331.

CBC News. "Ontario doctor accused of spreading COVID-19 misinformation barred from providing vaccine, mask exemptions." *CBC*, September 28, 2021. https://www.cbc.ca/news/canada/toronto/patrick-phillips-covid-19-misinformation-college-1.6191906.

Campbell, Denis. "Scientists abused and threatened for discussing Covid, global survey finds." *The Guardian*, October 13,2021. https://www.theguardian.com/world/2021/oct/13/scientists-abused-and-threatened-for-discussing-covid-global-survey-finds.

Carter Heavy Industries. "Prof. Mattias Desmet on Mass Formation." Odysee Video, December 11, 2021. https://odysee.com/@CarterHeavyIndustries:6/Dr.-Reiner-Fuellmich---Prof.-Mattias-Desmet-(English):2.

———. "What is Mass Formation Psychosis?" November 12, 2021. https://carter-heavy-industries.com/2021/12/11/mass-formation-pandemic-psychosis/.

Center for Disease Control and Prevention (CDC). "1918 Pandemic (H1N1 virus)" last updated March 20, 2019. https://www.cdc.gov/flu/pandemic-resources/1918-pandemic-h1n1.html.

Children's Health Defense. Accessed November 3, 2021. https://childrenshealthdefense.org/.

Chossudovsky, Michel. *The 2020-21 Worldwide Corona Crisis: Destroying Civil Society, Engineered Economic Depression, Global Coup d'État and the "Great Reset"*. Global Research E-Book, Centre for Research on Globalization (CRG), Updated October 2021. http://www.globalresearch.ca/the-2020-worldwide-corona-crisis-destroying-civil-society-engineered-economic-depression-global-coup-detat-and-the-great-reset/5730652.

Christian, Francis. "Statement by Dr. Francis Christian FRCSEd, FRCSC." https://www.jccf.ca/wp-content/uploads/2021/06/17-June-press-conference-statement-Dr.-Christian.pdf.

———. "The Persecution of Physicians and Scientists in Canada." *Druthers* 1(10), September 2021: 7. www.druthers.net.

Clinical Trials Arena Staff. "Health Canada approves first Covid-19 vaccine trials." *Clinical Trials Arena*, May 18, 2020. https://www.clinicaltrialsarena.com/news/canada-covid-19-vaccine-trials/.

College of Nurses of Ontario (CNO). "Nurses Supporting Public Health." Page reviewed December 16, 2020. https://www.cno.org/en/news/2020/december-2020/nurses-supporting-public-health-measures/.

College of Physicians and Surgeons of Ontario, The. "Statement on Public Health Misinformation." April 30, 2021. https://www.cpso.on.ca/News/Key-Updates/Key-Updates/COVID-misinformation.

Colton, Emma. "Judge reverses decision, allows unvaccinated mom to see her son." *Fox News*, August 31, 2021. https://www.foxnews.com/us/judge-reverses-decision-mom-unvaccinated-custody.

Constitutional Rights Centre Inc. https://www.constitutionalrightscentre.ca/action4canada-british-columbia-court-challenge/.

———. "Your Rights to decline a Vaccine in the context of Employment." YouTube Video, March 8, 2021. https://www.youtube.com/watch?v=UHbMMf2c6KI&t=3s.

Cotton, Tom. "Send In the Troops The nation must restore order. The military stands read." *New York Times*, June 3, 2020. https://www.nytimes.com/2020/06/03/opinion/tom-cotton-protests-military.html.

Covidland: Episode 1: The Lockdown. Bill Sardi at the introduction of Infowars. *Infowars*, October 7, 2021. https://infowarsarmy.com/posts/covidland-the-lockdown-full-documentary/.

Craig, James Porter. "The Dramatic Rejection of Liberal Politics in Canada." *Crisis Magazine*, May 29, 2019. https://www.crisismagazine.com/2019/the-dramatic-rejection-of-liberal-politics-in-canadian.

Crist, Carolyn. "Early CDC COVID-19 Test Kits 'Likely Contaminated'." *WebMd*, June. https://www.webmd.com/lung/news/20200623/early-cdc-covid-19-test-kits-likely-contaminated?fbclid=IwAR26GBTccVWI-f71q9

SSdY3BCt8i3iWQRiRMQPcZKgwuWDnrP_lDHhNsauI.

D'Amore, Rachel. "Can incentives help vaccine hesitancy? Experts say it's a short-term solution." *Global News* May 13, 2021. https://globalnews.ca/news/7858373/covid-vaccine-incentives-canada-reward/.

Deace, Steve and Todd Erzen. *Faucian Bargain: The Most Powerful and Dangerous Bureaucrat in American History.* New York: Post Hill Press, 2021.

Degrassi: School's Out! TV Movie, 1992. https://www.imdb.com/title/tt0134951/?ref_=fn_al_tt_1.

Delaney, Patrick. "COVID expert Dr. Peter McCullough urges 'unbreakable resistance' to vaccines for kids." *LifeSite News*, October 11, 2021. https://www.lifesitenews.com/news/covid-expert-dr-peter-mccullogh-urges-unbreakable-resistance-to-vaccines-for-kids/.

Democracy Fund, The. "Dr. Julie Ponesse on Counterpoint | Fear and Moral Panic." YouTube Video, interview by Tanya Granic Allen, October25, 2021. https://www.youtube.com/watch?v=CuIUZeOvPSs&t=874s.

Derek Sloan conference with Dr. Byram Bridle, Dr. Patrick Phillips, and Dr. Donald Wash. "MP Derek Sloan Raises Concerns Over Censorship of Doctors and Scientists." CPAC, June 17, 2021. https://www.cpac.ca/episode?id=cd50ce93-5138-4489-a88f-bb8065b7aa32.

Dima, Jack. "NIH Director Francis Collins calls for more vaccine mandates." *Yahoo!* News, August 6, 2021. https://news.yahoo.com/nih-director-francis-collins-calls-150400174.html.

Dimmock, Gary. "Judge bans Ottawa mother from advising son against COVID-19 vaccine." *Ottawa Citizen*, October 22, 2021. https://ottawacitizen.com/news/local-news/judge-bans-ottawa-mother-from-advising-son-against-covid-19-vaccine?utm_medium=Social&utm_source=Facebook&fbclid=IwAR0hnfYarfhWpskoQOo3TPBEolCSK43bscfKNbOODpdu8G8rp2PN6u-xi-E#Echobox=1634944004.

Dodd, Sophie and Janine Pukak. "How to Get Promotions, Prizes and Freebies with your COVID-19 Vaccine." *People*, June 8, 2021. https://people.com/health/covid-19-vaccine-freebies-incentives-rewards/.

Doshi, Peter. "Will covid-19 vaccines save lives? Current trials aren't designed to tell us." *BMJ* (October 21, 2020); 371. doi: https://doi.org/10.1136/bmj.m4037.

Draaisma, Muriel and Jasmin Seputis. "Ontario's opioid-related death toll surged to 2,050 during pandemic in 2020, new report finds." *CBC News*, May 19, 2021. https://www.cbc.ca/news/canada/toronto/report-opioid-related-deaths-ontario-covid-19-pandemic-1.6031845?fbclid=IwAR2-iih3H1K8HrYHPkfTr0K0Z69kLgOsU__mwAbMmIzV_nOBF4lrRf-l3RU.

Druthers News & Information. "Dr. Byram Bridle Addresses Toronto Event Aimed at 'Let the Kids Play'." Rumble Video, October 13, 2021. https://rumble.com/vnppgt-dr.-byram-bridle-addresses-toronto-event-aimed-at-let-the-kids-play.html?fbclid=IwAR2BzNfsDlBhUpMpFoS43zpVZTZYuj

1OPck8FAfQ85Rdw-t5vqMExSrep_Y.

Edelstein, Ludwig. "The Hippocratic Oath: Text, translation, and interpretation." In *Cross Cultural Perspectives in Medical Ethics* second edition, edited by Robert M. Veatch. London: Jones and Bartlett Publishers, 2000, 4–8.

Eye of the Storm Corona Committee, The. "Mass Formation and Totalitarian Thinking in This Time of Global Crisis." Interview with Mattias Desmet, July 30, 2021. https://ratical.org/PandemicParallaxView/EyeOfTheStorm-ProfMattiasDesmet.html.

Farrow, Douglas. "An Open Letter on Coercive Mandates and Vaccine Passports." *Crisis Magazine*, August 30, 2021. https://www.crisismagazine.com/2021/an-open-letter-on-coercive-mandates-and-vaccine-passports.

Feuerherd, Ben. "Feds reportedly raid Project Veritas-linked apartments over Ashley Biden's diary." *NY Post*, November 5, 2021. https://nypost.com/2021/11/05/feds-raid-project-veritas-linked-apartments-over-ashley-bidens-diary-report/.

Finlay, Kathleen. "Preventable Medical Error Is Canadian Healthcare's Silent Killer." *HuffPost*, October 24, 2015. https://www.huffingtonpost.ca/kathleen-finlay/medical-error-deaths_b_8350324.html.

Flynn, Casey. "3 horrific medical mistakes that scandalize the profession." *Center for Health Journalism*, May 4, 2016. https://www.centerforhealthjournalism.org/2016/05/09/3-horrific-medical-mistakes-scandalize-profession.

Frei, Viva. Twitter Post. May 12, 2021, 10:25 PM. https://twitter.com/thevivafrei/status/1392667359991812099.

Front Line COVID-19 Critical Care Alliance Prevention & Treatment Protocols for COVID-19. https://covid19criticalcare.com/.

Galati, Rocco and Mark Taliano. "Lawsuit against Trudeau Government: Constitutional Lawyer Rocco Galati and the Lies and Crimes of the COVID Operation." Global Research, March 21, 2021. https://www.globalresearch.ca/rocco-galati-lies-crimes-covid-operation/5719222.

Gazit, Sivan, et al. "Comparing SARS-CoV-2 natural immunity to vaccine-induced immunity: reinfections versus breakthrough infections." medRxiv 2021.08.24.21262415. doi: https://doi.org/10.1101/2021.08.24.21262415.

Global Research. Center for Research on Globalization, accessed November 4, 2021. https://www.globalresearch.ca/.

Globe and Mail Editorial Board, The. "The Trudeau government says it won't regulate user content on social media. Bill C-10 says otherwise." *Globe and Mail*, May 4, 2021. https://www.theglobeandmail.com/opinion/editorials/article-the-trudeau-government-says-it-wont-regulate-user-content-on-social/.

Gomes, Jules. "Swiss Guard Blows Whistle on Vaccine Coercion." *The Church Militant*, October 9, 2021. https://www.churchmilitant.com/news/article/swiss-guard-shames-popes-vaccine-coercion.

Gorokhova, Elena. *A Mountain of Crumbs.* New York: Simon & Schuster, 2011.

Government of Canada. "Canadian Motor Vehicle Traffic Collision Statistics: 2018." Transport Canada, accessed November 7, 2021. https://tc.canada.ca/en/road-transportation/statistics-data/canadian-motor-vehicle-traffic-collision-statistics-2018.

———. "Bill C-10: An Act to amend the Broadcasting Act and to make consequential amendments to other Acts." Department of Justice, accessed May 25, 2021. https://www.justice.gc.ca/eng/csj-sjc/pl/charter-charte/c10.html.

———. "COVID-19 daily epidemiology update." Health Canada, updated November 5, 2021. https://health-infobase.canada.ca/covid-19/epidemiological-summary-covid-19-cases.html#a5.

Graham, Tim. "MSNBC Producer Quits Because It's Liberal Fake News: 'We are a Cancer and There is No Cure'." *Life News*, August 4, 2020. https://www.lifenews.com/2020/08/04/msnbc-producer-quits-because-its-liberal-fake-news-we-are-a-cancer-and-there-is-no-cure/?fbclid=IwAR0LPnnF-xsDzLKkUSIwLBOBasagwQKFLbE5bXOAlrBMQdr-xYfYctqYwTM.

Great Barrington Declaration, The. https://gbdeclaration.org/.

Hadro, Matt. "Joe Biden says Pope Francis told him to 'keep receiving Communion'." *Catholic News Agency*, October 29, 2021. https://www.catholicnewsagency.com/news/249441/joe-biden-says-pope-francis-told-him-to-keep-receiving-communion.

Hallam, Christopher. "It's personal choice at the end of the day - Readers' discuss whether health and social care should be required to have the Covid jab." *The Star*, September 14, 2021. https://www.thestar.co.uk/news/opinion/its-personal-choice-at-the-end-of-the-day-readers-discuss-whether-health-and-social-care-should-be-required-to-have-the-covid-jab-3381899.

Halon, Yael. "Trump urges all Americans to get COVID vaccine: 'It's a safe vaccine' and it 'works'." *Fox News*, March 16, 2021. https://www.foxnews.com/media/trump-urges-all-americans-to-get-covid-vaccine-its-a-safe-vaccine.

Hanau, Shira. "Jewish MD who promoted virus cocktail is leaving community where he tested it." *Times of Israel*, May 20, 2020. https://www.timesofisrael.com/jewish-md-who-promoted-virus-cocktail-leaving-community-where-he-tested-it/.

Hayes, Chris. "Transcript: All In With Chris Hayes." *MSNBC*, September 9, 2021. https://www.msnbc.com/transcripts/transcript-all-chris-hayes-9-9-21-n1278904.

Henley, Tara. "Speaking Freely: Why I resigned from the Canadian Broadcasting Corporation." Lean Out with Tara Henley on Substack, January 3, 2021. https://tarahenley.substack.com/p/speaking-freely?r=9dpfg&utm_campaign=post&utm_medium=web.

Henney, Megan. "CDC director criticized for now differentiating between dying 'from' vs. dying 'with' COVID-19." *Fox News*, May 16, 2021. https://

www.foxnews.com/politics/cdc-director-walensky-criticism-updated-guidance-coronavirus-deaths.

Hickson, Maike. "Archbishop Viganò: Vaccines made with fetal tissue are a 'human sacrifice of innocent victims offered to Satan'." LifeSite News, July 21, 2021. https://www.lifesitenews.com/blogs/archbishop-Vigan%C3%B2-vaccines-made-with-fetal-tissue-are-a-human-sacrifice-of-innocent-victims-offered-to-satan/.

Hillier, Randy, MPP. "Rise in Sudden Deaths Among Young People Requires Investigation." Letter to the OPP Commissioner on Unexplained Deaths, October 25, 2021. https://www.randyhilliermpp.com/20211025_pr_oppinvestigationsuddendeaths.

———. Testimonies of people with adverse reactions to the COVID-19 vaccine at Hillier's channel on odysee. Accessed November 16, 2021. https://odysee.com/@RandyHillier:c?view=content.

Hodkinson, Roger. "Dr. Roger Hodkinson DECIMATES Canadian Government." awakecanada.org, September 14, 2021. https://awakecanada.org/dr-roger-hodkinson-decimates-canadian-government/.

Hopper, Tristin. "'Full-blown assault' on free expression: Inside the comprehensive Liberal bill to regulate the internet." *National Post*, April 29, 2021. https://nationalpost.com/news/full-blown-assault-on-free-expression-inside-the-comprehensive-liberal-bill-to-regulate-the-internet.

Imperial College London. "What is Nudge Theory?" Accessed November 3, 2021. https://www.imperial.ac.uk/nudgeomics/about/what-is-nudge-theory/.

Infowars Special Reports. "Dr. Zelenko Calls for Bill Gates and Fauci's Arrest for War Crimes," *Infowars*, October 2, 2021. https://www.infowars.com/posts/dr-zelenko-calls-for-bill-gates-and-faucis-arrest-for-war-crimes/.

Iovine, John. *Scamdemic - The COVID-19 Agenda: The Liberal's Plot to Win The White House*. Long Island: Images Si Inc, 2021.

Jones, Alexander Mae. "Canada's top doctor: 'consider using a mask' during sexual activity." *CTV News*, September 2, 2020. https://www.ctvnews.ca/health/coronavirus/canada-s-top-doctor-consider-using-a-mask-during-sexual-activity-1.5090359.

Justice Center for Constitutional Freedoms. https://www.jccf.ca/justice-centre-sues-ontario-government-over-vaccine-passport/.

Kahmann, Morgan. "Facebook Insider Morgan Kahmann joins Tucker Carlson to discuss leaked 'Vaccine Hesitancy' documents." Interview by Tucker Carlson, *Fox News*, May 27, 2021. Project Veritas, YouTube Video. https://www.youtube.com/watch?v=ZVRqlCyvfmg.

Kelly, Jack. "The 1% Owns Almost As Much Wealth As The Middle Class: Will The Rich Keep Getting Richer?" *Forbes*, November 12, 2019. https://www.forbes.com/sites/jackkelly/2019/11/12/the-1-owns-almost-as-much-wealth-as-the-middle-class-will-the-rich-keep-getting-richer/#686026f44323.

Kennedy Jr., Robert F. *The Real Anthony Fauci: Bill Gates, Big Pharma, and the Global War on Democracy and Public Health*. New York: Sky Horse, 2021.

Kirkham, Paul, Michael Yeadon, and Barry Thomas. "How Likely Is A Second Wave?" *The Daily Skeptic*, September 7, 2020. https://dailysceptic.org/addressing-the-cv19-second-wave/#pcr.

Klara, Robert. "Throwback Thursday: When Doctors Prescribed 'Healthy' Cigarette Brands." *Adweek*, June 8, 2015. https://www.adweek.com/brand-marketing/throwback-thursday-when-doctors-prescribed-healthy-cigarette-brands-165404/.

Kostoff, Ronald, et al. "Why are we vaccinating children against COVID-19?" *Toxicology Reports* 8 (2021): 1665–1684. https://www.sciencedirect.com/science/article/pii/S221475002100161X.

Knightly, Kit. "30 facts you NEED to know: Your Covid Cribsheet." *Off Guardian*, September 22, 2021. https://off-guardian.org/2021/09/22/30-facts-you-need-to-know-your-covid-cribsheet/?fbclid=IwAR2totKESL00rNMwCpIFWkjqgcfkjZ5H1zmWoe86SI-p3cg1RN-zz8uYPSE.

Kronz, Fred. "Quantum Theory and Mathematical Rigor." *Stanford Encyclopedia of Philosophy*, revised July 1, 2019. https://plato.stanford.edu/entries/qt-nvd/.

Lamb, Kelly. "The province is implementing a user-friendly 'snitch line' reporting system online, for citizens who wish to report individuals or businesses breaking COVID-19 rules or mandates." *Rebel News*, October 22, 2021. https://www.rebelnews.com/saskatchewan_sets_up_covid_snitch_line_detainment_centres_and_enforcement_team.

Lepore, Stephen M. "'There needs to be a quick and devastating take down': Emails show how Fauci and head of NIH worked to discredit three experts who penned the Great Barrington Declaration which called for an end to lockdowns." *Daily Mail*, December 18, 2021. https://www.msn.com/en-us/news/politics/emails-reveal-how-fauci-head-of-nih-colluded-to-try-to-smear-experts/ar-AARX837#image=6.

Liberal Party of Canada. "Support the CBC." Liberal Party of Canada website, accessed June 3, 2021. https://www.liberal.ca/support-the-cbc/.

LifeSite News, "LifeFacts: COVID-19." *LifeSite News*, accessed October 30, 2021. https://lifefacts.lifesitenews.com/covid-19/.

Lilley, Brian. "Canadians are ditching CBC, so why do we keep funding it?" *The Toronto Sun*, June 3, 2021. https://torontosun.com/opinion/columnists/lilley-canadians-are-ditching-cbc-so-why-do-we-keep-funding-it.

———. "Ford owes restaurants apology for bizarre reopening decision." *Toronto Sun*, October 11, 2021. https://torontosun.com/opinion/columnists/lilley-ford-owes-restaurants-apology-for-bizarre-reopening-decision.

Louise, Nickie. "Dr. Vladimir Zelenko has now treated over 1,450 coronavirus patients (2 deaths) using hydroxychloroquine with 99.99% success rate (latest video interview)." *Tech Startups*, April 21, 2020. https://techstartups.com/2020/04/21/dr-vladimir-zelenko-now-treated-1450-coronavirus-patients-2-deaths-using-hydroxychloroquine-99-99-success-rate-latest-video-interview/.

Machiavelli, Niccolo. *The Prince*, chapter XXII, 92. Second edition. Chicago: University of Chicago Press, 1985.

Madrid, Pablo Campra. "Graphene Oxide Detection in Aqueous Suspension Observational Study in Optical and Electron Microscopy." Interim Report (I). University of Almeria, Spain, June 28, 2021. https://www.thecompleteguidetohealth.com/uploads/8/9/4/8/8948721/official_interim_report_in_english__university_of_almeria_.pdf.

Magee, Shane. 'Thousands of contaminated test kits delivered to New Brunswick." *CBC News*, April 16, 2020. https://www.cbc.ca/news/canada/new-brunswick/test-kits-contaminated-new-brunswick-1.5534125.

Malcolm, Candace. "No, Minister Hajdu, the Vitamin D conversation isn't 'fake news'." *Toronto Sun*, April 24, 2021. https://torontosun.com/opinion/columnists/malcolm-no-minister-hajdu-the-vitamin-d-conversation-isnt-fake-news.

McCullough, Peter. McCullough has over 114,000 citations and over 50 peer-reviewed articles related to COVID-19 since 2020. https://scholar.google.com/scholar?start=0&q=Peter+A.+Mccullough&hl=en&as_sdt=0,5&as_ylo=2020&as_yhi=2021.

———. PowerPoint Slides of Presentation: "Winning the War Against Therapeutic Nihilism & Trusted Treatments vs Untested Novel Therapies." https://www.scribd.com/document/530328436/Slides-from-Peter-McCullough-MDOct-1-2021-Lecture.

McElwee, Joshua. "Pope Francis suggests people have moral obligation to take coronavirus vaccine." *National Catholic Reporters*, January 11, 2021. https://www.ncronline.org/news/vatican/pope-francis-suggests-people-have-moral-obligation-take-coronavirus-vaccine.

McIlroy, Anne and Rod Mickleburgh. "Hospital errors kill thousands in Canada, study estimates." *The Globe and Mail*, May 24, 2004. https://www.theglobeandmail.com/news/national/hospital-errors-kill-thousands-in-canada-study-estimates/article999281/.

McGovern, Celeste. "Pfizer whistleblower says vaccine 'glows,' contains toxic luciferase, graphene oxide compounds." *LifeSite News*, October 14, 2021. https://www.lifesitenews.com/news/bombshell-pfizer-whistleblower-says-vaccine-glows-contains-toxic-luciferase-graphene-oxide-com pounds/?fbclid=IwAR2ASNswP3uh0nCXzJ_jgcXUTUfYr5453_zxAxZqYwwKXVa9EbjLrktNcFg.

Memes127en. "Who is Doug Ford daughter, krista? – Photos and videos instagram and reddit." *MRandom News*, January 2, 2022. https://

en.memesrandom.com/doug-ford-daughter-krista/.

Miller, Zeke. "Free beer, other new incentives for Biden's 'vaccine sprint'." *ABC News*, June 2, 2021. https://abcnews.go.com/Health/wireStory/beer-latest-vaccine-incentive-biden-month-action-78038433.

Miltimore, John. "5 Things Marx Wanted to Abolish (Besides Private Property)." *Fee Stories*, October 31, 2021. https://fee.org/articles/5-things-marx-wanted-to-abolish-besides-private-property/?fbclid=IwAR19cp5DGViIBrcNEI7Vp9GTNZqMolXXSZ2rVbfmohG6EQQw2qDCsHs3NbI.

Mounties for Freedom. "Mounties for Freedom, Open Letter to RCMP Commissioner Brenda Lucki." October 21, 2021. https://mounties4freedom.ca/open-letter/.

Murphy, Rex. "Why is the media not more interested in assault allegations against Biden?" *National Post*, May 1, 2020. https://nationalpost.com/opinion/rex-murphy-whats-with-the-medias-disinterest-in-assault-allegations-against-biden.

Nal, Renee. "Renowned Pathologist (Roger Hodkinson): Myocarditis Diagnoses Should Halt Covid Vaccine (Interview)." RAIR: USA Foundation, June 20, 2021. https://rairfoundation.com/renowned-pathologist-myocarditis-diagnoses-should-halt-covid-vaccine-interview/.

Neate, Rupert. "Richest 1% own half the world's wealth, study finds." *The Guardian*, November 14, 2017. https://www.theguardian.com/inequality/2017/nov/14/worlds-richest-wealth-credit-suisse.

New American, The. "Doctor Who Said 'I Won't Cry' at 'Funeral for Unvaxxed' Dies After 3rd COVID Shot. He Wanted 'To Punch in the Face the No Vax'." *Gospa News*, November 15, 2021. https://www.gospanews.net/en/2021/11/15/doctor-who-said-i-wont-cry-at-funeral-for-unvaxxed-dies-after-3rd-covid-shot-he-wanted-to-punch-in-the-face-the-no-vax/.

Noel Pekary, Ariana. "Personal news: why I'm now leaving MSNBC." Ariana Noel Pekary website, August 3, 2020. https://www.arianapekary.net/post/personal-news-why-i-m-now-leaving-msnbc.

Odell, James P. M. "Issues Surrounding Graphene Oxide in the Pfizer mRNA Covid 19 FormulationFor an in depth discussion regarding graphene oxide and its presence in the Pfizer COVID-19 vaccine." Bioregulatory Medicine Institute, August 30, 2021. https://www.biologicalmedicineinstitute.com/post/issues-surrounding-graphene-oxide-in-the-pfizer-mrna-covid-19-formulation.

Office of the United Nations High Commissioner for Human Rights/the World Health Organization. *The Right to Health: Fact Sheet No. 31*. Accessed November 1, 2021. https://www.ohchr.org/documents/publications/factsheet31.pdf.

O'Keefe, James. *American Pravda: My Fight for Truth in the Era of Fake News*. New York: St Martin's Press, 2018.

———. *American Muckraker: Re-thinking Journalism for the 21st Century*. New York: Post Hill Press, 2022.

Ontario Superior Court of Justice, J.N. v. C.G., 2022 ONSC 1198 (CanLII), February 22, 2022. https://canlii.ca/t/jmk30.

Otto, Joe. "Facebook and Twitter's CEOS Just Lied To Congress About Censorship!" *Conservative Daily*, October 30, 2020. https://conservative-daily.com/election/breaking-facebook-and-twitters-ceos-just-lied-to-congress-about-censorship.

Physicians Declaration – Global COVID Summit. "Rome Declaration." Updated October 14, 2021. https://doctorsandscientistsdeclaration.org/.

Plandemic: Indoctornation, 2020. https://www.imdb.com/title/tt12745644/.

Politi, James. "Biden calls on state and local governments to offer $100 vaccine incentives." *The Financial Times*, July 29, 2021. https://www.ft.com/content/b6a80442-a566-43ca-b23d-7793d417eddb.

Ponesse, Julie. *My Choice: The Ethical Case Against COVID-19 Vaccine Mandates.* Toronto: The Democracy Fund, 2021.

Pontifical Academy for Life. "Statement: Moral Reflections on Vaccines Prepared from Cells Derived from Aborted Human Foetuses." *The Linacre Quarterly* 86, no. 2–3 (May 2019): 182–87. https://doi.org/10.1177/0024363919855896.

Prentice, David. "COVID-19 Vaccine Candidates and Abortion-Derived Cell Lines." Charlotte Lozier Institute, updated September 30, 2021. https://lozierinstitute.org/update-covid-19-vaccine-candidates-and-abortion-derived-cell-lines/.

———. Charlotte Lozier Institute, Twitter Post, October 7, 2021, at 5:31 PM. https://twitter.com/LozierInstitute/status/1446226646412013569.

Prentice, David and Tara Sander Lee. "What you need to know about the COVID-19 vaccines." Updated December 8, 2020. https://lozierinstitute.org/what-you-need-to-know-about-the-covid-19-vaccine/.

Project Veritas. Project Veritas bio on James O'Keefe, *Project Veritas*, accessed June 1, 2021. https://www.projectveritas.com/bio/.

———. "Facebook Whistleblowers Expose LEAKED INTERNAL DOCS Detailing New Effort to Secretly Censor Vaccine Concerns on a Global Scale." *Project Veritas*, May 24, 2021. https://www.projectveritas.com/news/breaking-facebook-whistleblowers-expose-leaked-internal-docs-detailing-new/.

———. "Vaccine Hesitancy Comment Demotion." https://assets.ctfassets.net/syq3snmxclc9/7zG8FPh0cBk3qh28dY90iB/10771f24b25cf9994c08bf69e74056d5/Vaccine_Hesitancy_Comment_Demotion_WATERMARKED.pdf.

———. "Facebook CEO Mark Zuckerberg Takes 'Anti-Vax' Stance in Violation of His Own 'Platform's New Policy." Project Veritas, February 16, 2021. https://www.projectveritas.com/news/facebook-ceo-mark-zuckerberg-takes-anti-vax-stance-in-violation-of-his-own/.

———. "BREAKING: Pfizer Senior Director of Worldwide Research Vanessa Gelman RUNS from 'Veritas' Questions." YouTube Video, October 14,

2021. https://www.youtube.com/watch?v=50kghlaHYvM&t=12s.

Raoult, Didier. "Dr. Oz Discusses The Hydroxychloroquine Study Outcome With Dr. Didier Raoult." YouTube Video, April 15, 2020. https://www.youtube.com/watch?v=uy1cPT1ztko.

———. Raoult is also one of the most highly cited micro-biologists in the world. https://scholar.google.ca/scholar?hl=en&as_sdt=0%2C5&q=Didier+Raoult&btnG=.

Richards, Jay W., et al. *The Price of Panic: How the Tyranny of Experts Turned a Pandemic into a Catastrophe*. Regnery Publishing: Washington, 2020.

Robertson, Adi. "Facebook will add anti-misinformation posts to your News Feed if you liked fake coronavirus news." *The Verge*, April 16, 2020. https://www.theverge.com/2020/4/16/21223456/facebook-coronavirus-misinformation-fake-news-warning-update-who.

Rome, from the Offices of the Congregation for the Doctrine of the Faith. "Note on the morality of using some anti-Covid-19 vaccines." December 21, 2020. https://www.vatican.va/roman_curia/congregations/cfaith/documents/rc_con_cfaith_doc_20201221_nota-vaccini-anticovid_en.html.

Scholz, Martin, Roland Derwand, and Vladimir Zelenko. "COVID-19 Outpatients – Early Risk-Stratified Treatment with Zinc Plus Low Dose Hydroxychloroquine and Azithromycin: A Retrospective Case Series Study." *International Journal of Antimicrobial Agents* 56 (December 2020). DOI: https://doi.org/10.1016/j.ijantimicag.2020.106214.

Schwartz, Ian. "Facebook and YouTube Ban Video Of Doctors Talking COVID, Silenced Doctors Hold Press Conference." *RealClear Politics*, July 28, 2020. https://www.realclearpolitics.com/video/2020/07/28/facebook_and_youtube_ban_video_of_doctors_talking_covid_silenced_doctors_hold_press_conference.html#!.

Singanayagam, Anika, et al. "Community transmission and viral load kinetics of the SARS-CoV-2 delta (B.1.617.2) variant in vaccinated and unvaccinated individuals in the UK: a prospective, longitudinal, cohort study." *The Lancet: Infectious Diseases*, October 29, 2021. DOI: https://doi.org/10.1016/S1473-3099(21)00648-4.

Slatz, Anna. "The World Health Organization is to blame." *The Post Millennial*, March 30, 2020. https://thepostmillennial.com/world-health-organization-blame.

Small, Kaylen. "'This is a travesty': Albertans protest COVID-19 rule rollback for second day." *Global News*, July 31, 2021. https://globalnews.ca/news/8077040/alberta-doctors-rally-covid-19-rules-day-2/.

Stew Peters Show, The. "La Quinta Columna 1-On-1: Spanish Researcher First to Reveal Graphene Oxide." Rumble Video, January 13, 2022. https://rumble.com/vsj315-exclusive-la-quinta-columna-1-on-1-spanish-researcher-first-to-reveal-graph.html?fbclid=IwAR2hFkqOgWEGiX9lLR1-

UwiALuZrpJUh_tWf2YgDRadISjxTU2IR9A1sHtg.

Stop World Control. https://www.stopworldcontrol.com/fuellmich/.

———. "Dr. Reiner Fuellmich: scientific evidence that covid is crime against humanity." Accessed November 3, 2021. https://www.stopworldcontrol.com/fuellmich/.

Sullivan, John O. "Dr. Roger Hodkinson On COVID19: 'It's All Been A Pack Of Lies'." Principia Scientific International, August 20, 2021. https://principia-scientific.com/dr-roger-hodkinson-on-covid19-its-all-been-a-pack-of-lies/.

Taghva, Ali. "Liberal minister says government will boost CBC funding." *The Post Millennial*, December 30, 2019. https://thepostmillennial.com/liberal-minister-says-government-will-boost-cbc-funding.

Tanenbaum, Michael. "A pill to treat COVID-19? Pfizer takes next step in study of Tamiflu-like drug." *Philly Voice*, September 1, 2021. https://www.phillyvoice.com/covid-19-pfizer-pill-antiviral-treatment-symptoms-medication-tamiflu/.

The Shocking Truth TV (originally on The Stew Peters Show). Interview with Stew Peters, "Dr. Robert Malone On His mRNA Creation," October 14, 2021. https://www.theshockingtruth.tv/health/dr-robert-malone-on-his-mrna-creation/.

TOI Staff. "Nearly 2 million Israelis lose Green Pass as new rules enter effect." *Times of Israel*, October 3, 2021. https://www.timesofisrael.com/nearly-2-million-israelis-lose-green-pass-as-new-rules-enter-effect/?fbclid=IwAR38Uh29peiTPK8LUZfAO_pFzC054sPNVCqWSK4pzNgjRXx9Zn9OLUk6-1w.

Trejo, Shane. "Dr. Anthony Fauci Admits He was Lying about Masks and Vaccines After New CDC Directive." *SGT Report*, May 19, 2021. https://www.sgtreport.com/2021/05/dr-anthony-fauci-admits-he-was-lying-about-masks-and-vaccines-after-new-cdc-directive/.

TrialSite Staff. "Bioethics of Experimental COVID Vaccine Deployment under EUA: It's time we stop and look at what's going down." *TrialSite News*, May 30, 2021. https://trialsitenews.com/bioethics-of-experimental-covid-vaccine-deployment-under-eua-its-time-we-stop-and-look-at-whats-going-down/?fbclid=IwAR2d61j5gY4zUHEli3hsTo1e-bh8-39ENzJRlzJkbEkuQlmYOSb9LD7XuvUM.

Truth for Health Foundation. https://www.truthforhealth.org/.

Vaccine Adverse Events Reporting System (VAERS). "VAERS COVID Vaccine Adverse Event Reports." OpenVAERS, accessed October 30, 2021. https://www.openvaers.com/covid-data.

Vasque, Maegan and Betsy Klein. "Trump again defends use of the term 'China virus'." *CNN Politics*, March 19, 2020. https://www.cnn.com/2020/03/17/politics/trump-china-coronavirus/index.html.

Ventureyra, Scott D. G. "A Feminine, or Feminist Response to Covid?" *Catholic*

Insight, April 28, 2020. https://catholicinsight.com/a-feminine-or-feminist-response-to-covid/.

———. "Won't Get Fooled Again By The WHO: Thoughts On The COVID-19 Crisis and Related World Events." June 9, 2020. https://www.scottventureyra.com/post/won-t-get-fooled-again-by-the-who.

———. "The CBC - A Source of Trustworthy News or an Engine for Propaganda?" August 10, 2020. https://www.scottventureyra.com/post/the-cbc-a-source-of-trustworthy-news-or-an-engine-for-propaganda.

———. Email dated August 27, 2021.

Verhey, Allen. "The Doctor's Oath - and a Christian Swearing It." *The Linacre Quarterly* 51, no.2 (May 1984), 139–157. https://core.ac.uk/download/pdf/213068465.pdf.

Veri Catholici. "How and why Pope Benedict XVI's resignation is invalid by the law itself." December 19, 2018. https://vericatholici.wordpress.com/2018/12/19/how-and-why-pope-benedict-xvis-resignation-is-invalid-by-the-law-itself/.

Viganò, Monsignor Carlo Maria. "Prefazione." In *Mors Tua Vita Mea*, edited by Presentazione del Curatore. Rome: Maniera de Mirto, 2021. https://www.manierodelmirto.it/prodotto/mors-tua-vita-mea/.

Visser, Broderick. "Norman Traversy's speech on corruption in Canada." *Diverge Media*, July 1, 2020. https://divergemedia.ca/2020/07/01/video-norman-traversys-speech-on-corruption-in-canada/.

Watkins, Devon. "Pope Francis urges people to get vaccinated against Covid-19." *Vatican News*, August 8, 2021. https://www.vaticannews.va/en/pope/news/2021-08/pope-francis-appeal-covid-19-vaccines-act-of-love.html.

WebMD. "Coronavirus Recovery," *WebMD*, last accessed July 22, 2021. https://www.webmd.com/lung/covid-recovery-overview#1-2.

———. "Coronavirus Recovery," *WebMD*. Accessed July 22, 2021. https://www.webmd.com/lung/covid-recovery-overview#1-2.

Weiss, Bari. "Resignation Letter." Bari Weiss Website, accessed May 31, 2021. https://www.bariweiss.com/resignation-letter.

West, John G. "Francis Collins's Troubling Record at NIH." *Evolution News*, October 5, 2021. https://evolutionnews.org/2021/10/the-appalling-moral-failure-of-francis-collins/.

Willis, Mikki. *Plandemic: Fear Is the Virus. Truth Is the Cure*. New York: Skyhorse Publishing, 2021.

Wilson, Addison. "Joe Rogan In Info Wars Exposes The Truth About Ivermectin To America!" *The True Defender*, November 4, 2021. https://thetruedefender.com/joe-rogan-in-info-wars-exposes-the-truth-about-ivermectin-to-america/.

WND staff. "Mayo-trained doctor warns of COVID-19 'mutations' Israeli study and Mayo clinic doctor WND." *WND*, September 22, 2021. https://www.wnd.com/2021/09/mayo-trained-doctor-warns-covid-19-mutations/.

———. "Top doc: Pull COVID-19 vaccines off the market now." https://www.wnd.com/2021/09/top-doc-pull-covid-19-vaccines-off-market-now/.

World Doctors Alliance. https://worlddoctorsalliance.com/about/.

XandrewX. "Why are you awake when so many aren't 5 points of eye opening truth." Bitchute Video, October 31, 2021. https://www.bitchute.com/video/t4jbEBkN6Ycr/?fbclid=IwAR1ZVTTtXZdemHkcmIAzNwucjABE0cK2biqZtRD75HaoWouTmKqEYkdtXdA.

Yeadon, Michael. "Lies, Damned Lies and Health Statistics – the Deadly Danger of False Positives," *The Daily Skeptic*, September 20, 2020. https://dailysceptic.org/lies-damned-lies-and-health-statistics-the-deadly-danger-of-false-positives/.

———. "An Urgent Warning to the World," Perspectives on the Pandemic XVI, April 9, 2021. https://www.thepressandthepublic.com/post/an-urgent-warning-to-the-world.

———. Rose, Hannah, et al. Document to be filed with International Criminal Court, December 6, 2021. http://web.archive.org/web/20211227070153/; https://hannahroselaw.files.wordpress.com/2021/12/icc-complaint-7.docx.

Zelenko, Vladimir. "The Vaccine Death Report: Evidence of millions of deaths and serious adverse events resulting from the experimental COVID-19 injections." Version 1.0, September 2021. https://www.stopworldcontrol.com/downloads/en/vaccines/vaccinereport.pdf.

———. Zelenko's website: https://vladimirzelenkomd.com/ and www.zstackprotocol.com.

Ziady, Hanna. "Covid vaccine profits mint 9 new pharma billionaires." *CNN Business*, May 21, 2021. https://www.cnn.com/2021/05/21/business/covid-vaccine-billionaires/index.html?fbclid=IwAR1K1brG5XqkW205TTFHTRMuGtXvMy8xe6mf2z0M3EnW8O1IjcHwTT_MsnU.

Zoyesky. "The government shouldn't force young adults and teens to take experimental coronavirus vaccines, says inventor of mRNA vaccines." *Natural News: Defending Health, Life and Liberty*, June 28, 2021. http://45.89.97.6/2021-06-28-government-shouldnt-force-young-adults-teens-vaccinated.html?fbclid=IwAR20KGjGICxeezywqQkrESVLWyatuaFXB7aFLiUN7dEtwI8_9aWI8qeGJ2o.

Chapter 43

Mind Control Tactics & Fear Mechanisms Deployed During the COVID-19 Pandemic

Valérie A. G. Ventureyra

> "Philosophy teaches us to feel uncertain about the things that seem to us self-evident. Propaganda, on the other hand, teaches us to accept as self-evident matters about which it would be reasonable to suspend our judgement or feel doubt."
>
> —Aldous Huxley, *Brave New World Revisited*,
> Part V: Propaganda Under Dictatorship

The COVID-19 pandemic has been a catalyst for the application of measures serving the so-called "globalist agenda," seeking the implementation of one-world governance as sponsored by global institutions (United Nations, World Health Organization, International Monetary Fund, World Bank, among others) and implying greater control of individuals in all realms, through "projects" such as Agenda 2030.[1] Situations, behaviours, and pan-national decrees and regulations previously belonging to the realm of science fiction, or to another distant time in history and geographical space, have become realities, with relatively little questioning by the world population. The lack of critical thinking and resistance to absurd, scientifically unproven, and even blatantly harmful measures (mask wearing for healthy individuals,[2] oxymoronic "social distancing," lockdown and confinement of the healthy,[3] and, at this point, even injections with DNA-modifying experimental technology, so-called "Covid-19 vaccines"), supposedly taken to "protect each other from a highly deadly virus" is intriguing, to say the least, from a psychological perspective. What could have led the vast majority of Humanity, including most Westerners, known for being attached to their civil liberties and fundamental human rights and freedoms, to not only acquiesce, but even vehemently support, arbitrary measures, such as months-long lockdowns, mask wearing, continuous testing with dubious and invasive methods (PCR), and even delivery of experimental

1 World Economic Forum, 2030Vision.
2 Blaylock, "Facemasks Pose Serious Risks to the Healthy."
3 Mengin, et al. "Conséquences psychopathologiques du confinement."

products into their bodies? The most succinct response to this essential question is a one-word answer: FEAR. The more interesting and underlying question deserving investigation and reflection, however, is: By what means were collective and disproportionate fear and paralysis instilled in the world's population? And more crucially, what can be done to treat the irrational fear having nefarious psychological, medical, and economic consequences on individuals and on society?

In order to address the first of these questions, we can look to the notorious MKUltra mind control experiments[4] conducted by the CIA across the US and Canada in the 1950–60s. At the time, the world was in midst of the Cold War between liberal Western Europe and North America (and their allies on different continents), and Communist Eastern Europe (the Soviet Union and its satellite states) and their allies, namely, Cuba, North Korea, and China. As one of the main battle grounds of this war was ideological, and thus, situated in people's minds, the CIA funded a program to brainwash and recondition behaviour through the use of drugs (LSD), electroconvulsive therapy (ECT), and hypnotic techniques. One of the most notorious researchers in this project was Ewen Cameron,[5] who conducting his experiments at McGill University's Allan Memorial Institute, and "treated" his depressed and anxious patients with the above-mentioned methods, with the purpose of erasing memories, beliefs, and even behaviours, replacing these with newly implanted ones. Cameron devised the "psychic driving" method, in which a continuously looping audio message was administered to the patient, often while under the influence of psychedelic drugs or during an induced coma, resulting in amnesia, confusion (taking the experimenters for parents, for example), expressive aphasia, and even the induction of anxiety. One can only wonder whether mass media journalists worldwide covering the COVID-19 pandemic were cognizant of Cameron's experiments and sought after the same "successful results" by inducing and maintaining anxiety and shock in the general public for the purpose of manipulation and submission to absurd diktats and regulations (namely "staying home," wearing a mask outside while undergoing regular testing and now vaccination in order to "stay safe" and "protect others"). Mass media journalists have certainly become masters of "psychic driving" over the course of the past few decades, as the looping image of the destruction of Manhattan's twin towers in the aftermath of 9/11 evidenced, as well as the use

4 Project MKUltra (or MK-Ultra) is the code name given to a program of experiments on human subjects that were designed and undertaken by the US Central Intelligence Agency (CIA). The purpose of these was to develop procedures to be used in interrogations in order to weaken the individual and force confessions through brainwashing and psychological torture.

5 CBC, "MK Ultra: CIA mind control program in Canada (1980) - The Fifth Estate Kassam"; "The toxic legacy of Canada's CIA brainwashing experiments: 'They strip you of your soul'."

of the unremitting, pervasive (and perverse) "Stay at Home" slogan during the COVID-19 crisis lockdown, inducing shock and fear in the population, and, as expected, ensuing conformity and acceptance of reinforced security measures.

Much more can be said about media influence in shaping society's views and reactions to the COVID-19 pandemic, not least of which is governmental and Big Tech[6] control of media and censorship of all content threatening the globalist agenda. Interestingly, the massive censorship applied on divergent views applies not only to speculative views relating 5G technology to coronavirus or the presence of microchips in future COVID-19 vaccines, but even on resolutely medical and scientific subjects (the use of hydroxychloroquine, ivermectin, and chlorine dioxide in treatment of COVID-19 patients, PCR testing to diagnose COVID-19 and, of course, the efficacy and innocuity of COVID-19 vaccines) as expressed by seasoned and clinically active physicians[7] and researchers. Videos and posts having obtained millions of views on YouTube, Facebook, Twitter, and even LinkedIn, undergo deletion within hours, as well as receiving the special treatment of debunking by specialized censorship ("fact-checking") sites. Control access to the content, and if by chance it has seeped out, slander the proponents and dictate the "truth" (suppressing critical thinking, of course) to the poor uneducated, illiterate, non-elite remainder of Humanity. Say goodbye to Freedom of Speech and of Thought with the new measures reminiscent of Soviet-era propaganda and Orwellian "doublethink." (Fortunately, however, many of those censored have learned the lesson and created alternative platforms for the divulgation of censored information threatening to the official narrative: London Real Freedom Platform, World Doctor's Alliance, World Freedom Alliance, as well as alternatives to YouTube such as Twitch, Odysee, and BrandNewTube, to name a few.)

Despite its wide outreach, media control promoting the official narrative as doctrine (with little, if no possibility of questioning it), however, is not necessarily the most impactful of mind-control tactics. Social psychologists have demonstrated the power of conformity and "peer pressure" on thought and ensuing behaviour, experimentally. In a well-known conformity experiment among college students conducted by Asch (1951), subjects were presented with two cards, one of which contained one line and another with three lines of different lengths. The task required the subject to match the line on the first card to the one of the same length on the second card. When subjects

6 "Big Tech" refers to colossal internationally implanted companies focussed on promoting technologies and services. This term refers to Google, Apple, Facebook, Amazon, and Microsoft (GAFAM).

7 America's Frontline Doctors Press Conference, August 2020; in Spanish, Medicos por la Verdad, August 2020; in Germany, ACU Extra-Parliamentary Committee, July 2020, Bakersfield Doctors Press conference, April 2020, and a multitude of individual physicians and researchers expressing their views during interviews.

performed this task on their own, practically no errors were made in the matching. However, when subjects were tested in a group where the majority deliberately gave an incorrect answer, 75% of subjects gave at least one incorrect answer aligned with the answer provided by the group. Neuroscientist Gregory Berns and his team conducted a similar experiment using brain imaging (fMRI) comparing subjects' answers when given responses by a group of people and by a computer.[8] The behavioural results show that subjects were more inclined to conform their answers to those given by the group than to those given by the computer. The results of this study also show that even on a neurological level, specifically in the occipital and parietal lobes processing perceptual and spatial information, there are differences between subjects who conform to the group's incorrect answers and those who do not, meaning that the subjects process information differently when under social pressure. Interestingly, in those subjects who did not conform to "peer pressure" exerted by the group, fMRI evidenced greater amygdala activation, one of the brain structures associated with fear, stress, and shame. Could some extrapolation from these studies be used to explain conformity to many questionable COVID-19 measures, by distorted information processing to accept false and illogical information presented as being factual without any critical thought by the masses, and by a fear of rejection by those who may see the obvious flaws, but prefer to conform and avoid exclusion? It is worth noting that, in a study sponsored by Yale University,[9] seeking to evaluate different methods of promoting acceptance of a COVID-19 vaccine, social conformity, and the emotional consequences of non-conformity of guilt, embarrassment, anger, are presented as a powerful strategy of persuasion.

And when peer pressure is not enough to persuade and control, cognitive strategies may be employed. Cognitive dissonance occurs when one is confronted with evidence contrary to one's beliefs, creating emotional discomfort and some type of adaptation to restore psychological balance. Sometimes the adaptation will come in the form of acceptance of the new information, and on other occasions this will result in obstinacy and even greater fervour in the original beliefs, as described by Leon Festinger in the study of committed cult members who had given up their jobs and homes expecting doomsday and ended up becoming more fervent in their beliefs when proven wrong. Could the obstinacy and even categorical refusal of many, who, despite being shown scientific evidence differing from the official narrative of the pandemic, refuse to even consider it, preferring to remain in their cognitive comfort zone accepting only information received from the "trustworthy" mainstream media news sources? Such an attitude is

8 Berns, et al., "Neurobiological Correlates of Social Conformity and Independence During Mental Rotation."

9 NIH, "Covid-19 Vaccine Messaging, Clinical Trials."

reminiscent of the third category of people in an astute observation, attributed to Leonardo da Vinci: "There are three classes of people: those who see, those who see when they are shown, those who do not see." Others may fall into this last category by more subliminal methods, as the induction of hypnosis-like trance states, which are not only the privileged tactic of mainstream media news channels. Popular culture (notably movies made in Hollywood and pop-rock idols) has also been a highly successful vector in controlling the masses through influence and programming, particularly through use of occult symbolism,[10] most certainly resonating with archaic structures in the collective unconscious (according to C. G. Jung's theories), and the use of "predictive programming" in which the so-called "ruling elite" introduces novel concepts (transhumanism or enmity with the Arab world, for example) in order to shape its desired future scenario with minimal resistance, or even approval, from the population. Movies, such as "Contagion" and "V for Vendetta" (seemingly prophetic in nature), blatantly describing pandemics, may have programmed individuals (and the collective psyche) to behave similarly to the protagonists in these movies, and to expect (or even demand) similar outcomes or solutions (a vaccine in the case of the former). Non-fiction can also programme the masses, as the images of empty cities and nature gone wild projected daily during confinement on news channels the world over, would suggest. Could these clips, seemingly innocent, yet highly suggestive, have been seeking to programme Humanity into acceptance of living in a virtual world, with "virtual tourism" at the forefront? Is it not seductive to imagine having emblematic places such as Venice's Piazza San Marco to oneself? Let us not forget that tourism, as is air travel, are meant to disappear in the name of ecology, according to the globalist agenda. The globalists may as well programme humanity to accept virtual travel as of now.

It is also worth noting that the "hypnotic-like trances" are not only induced by the nature of the content (symbolism, scenarios), but also by the addictive and soporific effects sought by the distraction itself, and are reminiscent of Huxley's portrayal of a vacuous pleasure-seeking society in his visionary "Brave New World," and of the Roman "panem et circenses." (The "series" fad that has been in vogue over the past few years, is a telling illustration of this phenomenon.) A sedated population contents itself with immediate gratification and simply obtained meaningless pleasures, and being thus contented, loses its ability to think critically, is more easily manipulated and has no reason to resist authoritarian measures. Easy prey for the "ruling elite" to manipulate, control, and, as the story of the oblivious frog gradually exposed to the rising temperature of the water it is immersed in eloquently summarizes, may even lead to its own demise.

10 The Vigilant Citizen is an excellent reference for the study of occult symbolism in pop culture: https://vigilantcitizen.com.

As the world slowly but surely awakens to the reality of the COVID-19 pandemic, with the revision of morbidity and mortality rates (much lower than those predicted at the beginning of the crisis),[11] more physicians speaking out against the "orders" they were given by the establishment at the height of the pandemic and voicing their informed opinions regarding the useless and often harmful measures taken to supposedly "flatten the curve" or minimize contagions, as well as people across continents protesting massively against the same measures and totalitarian deviations, the fight for Freedom and Truth in the face of yet omnipresent propaganda and censorship continues and intensifies. (As an example, France was abruptly shaken by Emmanuel Macron's speech delivered on July 12, 2021, announcing "mandatory vaccination" of health care professionals and the application of a COVID "Pass sanitaire"[12] in the majority of public spaces, including restaurants, cafés, outdoor terrasses, concert halls, sports venues, gyms, shopping centres, hospitals, and long-distance trains and buses. These drastic measures turned France into the most totalitarian state in Europe overnight, and the shock of the unexpected announcements were met with protests, with millions of participants nationwide over the course of the Summer, strikes by health care professionals, boycotts of establishments applying the "pass sanitaire," and the creation of a multitude of alternatives by the Freedom-loving, conscious citizens seeking to create a parallel, better world.) Our role as conscious and awakened citizens in the face of the subliminal mind-control tactics and propaganda machinery deployed by the globalists is to continue "awakening" our fellow oblivious citizens to the reality of the situation and the grave threat to humanity that is at stake. Each one of us must find the method that works best and resonates with our personality and professional stance, the ultimate purpose being to not seek to convince or force a new view of the situation, which may very well be met with resistance, but to firstly question, and subsequently encourage, others to "do their own research." The Socratic Questioning style familiar to cognitive therapists is an appropriate method of questioning and exploration, allowing the individual to draw conclusions. (And when such questioning has no effect, as in many of those convinced by the dogmatic government propaganda who are impermeable to any logical argument and even the will to investigate, the best strategy is channelling one's energy into the conceptualization and construction of a parallel Free world.)

11 CDC, "Provisional Death Counts for Coronavirus Disease 2019 (COVID-19)"; Woods, "94% of Americans who died from COVID-19 had contributing conditions: CDC."

12 The Covid pass (« pass sanitaire ») in France is delivered to those who are "fully-vaccinated" until the next injection is required, those who have recovered from COVID and have proof of antibodies for six months, and to the others upon a presentation of a negative Covid test for 72 hours.

Mental health professionals have a particularly important role to play in the resistance to the mind-control tactics employed to implement the globalist agenda. Firstly, fostering awareness of fear mechanisms and psychotraumatic symptomatology, including signs of Post-Traumatic Stress Disorder (PTSD) and Dissociation among the general public, is crucial. Recognition of psychotraumatic syndromes is the first step in seeking professional help and treatment of these, and therapy paves the way to resilience, change, and greater receptivity to alternative information. Secondly, mental health professionals having privileged knowledge of the role of conditioning in the development of fear, should behave ethically and not reinforce the already overwhelming fear in our patients, while modelling and encouraging appropriate behaviour in the face of the given situation. On a collective level, psychologists and psychiatrists also have other awareness campaigns to lead, among which are the addictive and detrimental nature of television and social media, and the revelation of the very existence of mind control as a psychological weapon of population subjugation—a whole field of knowledge that certainly is not included in any university curriculum and requiring personal research and confrontation of one's own world views.

The quest for Truth and Freedom is a most vast and vital enterprise in these troubled times, and the understanding of underlying psychological strategies and mechanisms at play is key in changing the course of the perilous globalist agenda. Dr. Joost Meerloo's remarks based on his studies of mind control in belligerent settings seem particularly relevant to our current times, and contrast the unscrupulous use of knowledge with the responsible and elevating purpose that it should have:

> The modern techniques of brainwashing and menticide—those perversions of psychology—can bring almost any man into submission and surrender. Many of the victims of thought control, brainwashing, and menticide that we have talked about were strong men whose minds and wills were broken and degraded. But although the totalitarians use their knowledge of the mind for vicious and unscrupulous purposes, our democratic society can and must use its knowledge to help man to grow, to guard his freedom, and to understand himself.[13]

13 Meerloo, *The Rape of the Mind*, 304.

Bibliography

Asch, S. E. "Effects of group pressure upon the modification and distortion of Judgments." In Groups, leadership and men; research in human relations, edited by H. Guetzkow. 177–190. New York: Carnegie Press, 1951.

Berns, G., et al. "Neurobiological Correlates of Social Conformity and Independence During Mental Rotation." *Biol Psychiatry* 58 (2005): 245–253. http://www.ccnl.emory.edu/greg/Berns%20Conformity%20final%20printed.pdf.

Blaylock, Russell. "Facemasks Pose Serious Risks to the Healthy." 2020. https://ratical.org/PandemicParallaxView/Blaylock-MaskPoseSeriousRisks.pdf?fbclid=IwAR07iNoX78HD9W4x0vRm6sZTOiWrkz8tcwwsh5PM_oeP2X4bwh67U-053W4.

CBC. "MK Ultra: CIA Mind Control Program in Canada (1980) – The Fifth Estate." YouTube Video, August 26, 2016. https://www.youtube.com/watch?v=990k-5Jm5aA.

Centre for Disease Control. "Provisional Death Counts for Coronavirus Disease 2019 (COVID-19)," August 2020. https://www.cdc.gov/nchs/nvss/vsrr/covid_weekly/index.htm?fbclid=IwAR3-wrg3tTKK5-9tOHPGAHWFVO3DfslkJ0KsDEPQpWmPbKtp6EsoVV2Qs1Q.

Kassam, Ashifa. "The toxic legacy of Canada's CIA brainwashing experiments: 'They strip you of your soul'." *The Guardian*, May 3, 2018. https://www.theguardian.com/world/2018/may/03/montreal-brainwashing-allan-memorial-institute.

Meerlo, Joost Abraham Maurits. *The Rape of the Mind: The Psychology of Thought Control, Menticide, and Brainwashing of the Mind.* Mansfield: Martino Publishing, 2015.

Mengin, A., et al. "Conséquences psychopathologiques du confinement." *L'Encéphale* 46 (3) Supplement 2020: S43-S52. https://www.sciencedirect.com/science/article/pii/S0013700620300750?via%3Dihub.

National Institute of Health. "Covid-19 Vaccine Messaging, Clinical Trials." ClinicalTrials.gov, July 21st, 2020. https://clinicaltrials.gov/ct2/show/NCT04460703.

Woods, Amanda. "94% of Americans who died from COVID-19 had contributing conditions: CDC." *New York Post*, August 31, 2020. https://nypost.com/2020/08/31/94-of-americans-who-died-from-covid-19-had-contributing-conditions/.

World Economic Forum. 2030Vision, accessed November 4, 2021. https://www.weforum.org/projects/frontier-2030.

Chapter 44

The Psychosocial Cost of Extreme Measures Regarding Mental Health (Domestic Abuse and Suicide)

Martina J. Speck

> "As infectious disease epidemiologists and public health scientists we have grave concerns about the damaging physical and mental health impacts of the prevailing COVID-19 policies, and recommend an approach we call Focused Protection."
>
> —Great Barrington Declaration[1]

With thousands of signatures from scientists of various fields,[2] this declaration does not stand alone in their concern about the mental well-being of all the nations who introduced and maintained for almost two years drastic measures (e.g., lockdowns, masking, gene therapy) to end the spread of Sars-CoV-2 (COVID-19). As Dr. Peter McCullough says,[3]

> COVID-19 is not only killing people, it's destroying businesses, crushing dreams, and wreaking havoc on mental health. It's also driving a serious wedge between neighbours, communities, and society as a whole. As Canadians helplessly watch what some are calling a race between covid variants and the effectiveness of widespread vaccination, most are unaware there's another way out of this disaster, and doctors hold the key.

There is no scientific ground to uphold these extreme measures,[4] yet the pressure is on and has produced enormous damage, especially in the non-first-world countries.[5] Suicide rates have increased, 57 percent in the Philippines alone,[6]

1 The Great Barrington Declaration.

2 Concerned citizens: 805,155; medical & public health scientists: 14,981; medical practitioners: 44,167, see the signatures for the Great Barrington Declaration: https://gbdeclaration.org/view-signatures/.

3 Rolheiser, Duane, "Another Way."

4 Ioannidis, "Infection fatality rate of COVID-19 inferred from seroprevalence data."

5 Greene, "Lockdowns Cost Lives."

6 Philippine Statistics Authority, "Rise in Suicide."

while the rate of the body mass index (BMI) almost doubled in 2 to 19-year-old American children compared to the year preceding the pandemic,[7] which is a significant contributor towards suicide.[8] While there is enough evidence that natural immunity is sufficient to conquer the virus,[9] the aggressively pushed agenda creates high levels of anxiety,[10] which, long term, acts as an enemy towards a healthy immune system.[11] From there on, it's a spiral downwards—a weakened immune system seems to attract mental illness[12] and therefore creates a vicious cycle. An overall weakened society, battling the daily psychological impact of lockdowns with no end in sight, and now the introduction of a health passport, turns into a place of resignation, not only from jobs but from society, from life. There seems to be a link between pandemics and the occurrence of suicide,[13] which makes sense since. For example, life events that are stressful have shown a higher risk in adolescent suicidality.[14] The McMaster Hospital in London, Ontario, reported a significant rise in adolescent suicide attempts since the start of the pandemic and a prolonged hospital stay because of the seriousness of attempts. There is a potential relationship between SARS-CoV-2-related events and suicidal ideation including attempts in America.[15] In Canada, suicide has increased in association with the indirect impact of SARS-CoV-2 (e.g., unemployment).[16] The increased risk of mental health problems such as Post-Traumatic Stress Disorder (PTSD), depression, and anxiety during a crisis has been recorded in previous findings.[17] Children who were quarantined during past pandemics due to virus outbreaks (H1N1 and SARS-CoV) revealed 30 percent of cases obtaining PTSD.[18] The overall negative

7 Lange, et al., "Body Mass Index."

8 Perera, et al., "Predictor for Suicide."

9 Brownstone Institute, "Natural Immunity."

10 Abbott, "Mental Health Toll."

11 Segerstrom and Miller, "Psychological stress and the human immune system."

12 Leonard, "The concept of depression as a dysfunction of the immune system."

13 Sau Man Sandra Chan, et al., "Elderly Suicide and the 2003 SARS Epidemic in Hong Kong."

14 Brent, "Risk Factors for Adolescent Suicide and Suicidal Behavior: Mental and Substance Abuse Disorders, Family Environmental Factors, and Life Stress."

15 Ammerman, et al., "Preliminary Investigation of the Association between COVID-19 and Suicidal Thoughts and Behaviors in the U.S."

16 McIntyre and Lee, "Projected Increases in Suicide in Canada as a Consequence of COVID-19."

17 Douglas, et al., "Preparing for pandemic influenza and its aftermath: mental health issues considered"; Kar and Bastia, "Post-traumatic stress disorder, depression and generalised anxiety disorder in adolescents after a natural disaster: a study of comorbidity"; Yule, et al., "The Long-term Psychological Effects of a Disaster Experienced in Adolescence: I: The Incidence and Course of PTSD"; Bolton, et al., "The Long-term Psychological Effects of a Disaster Experienced in Adolescence: II: General Psychopathology"; Kar, "Depression in Youth."

18 Sprang and Silman, "Posttraumatic Stress Disorder in Parents and Youth After Health-Related Disasters."

effect on America's mental health has increased by about 20 percent.[19] A rise in self- infliction, self-harm, and suicidal ideation seems to have spiked since the beginning of the crisis.[20] It is apparent, that the stress that comes with job loss and economic crises causes a rise in mental health issues.[21] On top of that, pre-pandemic maltreatment has shown greater vulnerability towards the development and/or worsening of mental health issues in rural Chinese adolescents when exposed to societal turmoil.[22] Loneliness, in this case caused by ordering quarantine and lockdowns but also through self-isolation due to fear of an infection, adds to the factors leading to mental (and physical) health issues (e.g., depression, alcohol abuse, child abuse, sleep problems, personality disorders, and Alzheimer's disease),[23] which can increase the vulnerability towards suicidal ideation. There are parallels in how the current instructed isolation can be experienced as confinement within a prison situation.[24] Another easily missed factor when calculating risks regarding the enforcement of extreme measures is hopelessness. Hopelessness can arise through situations that appear as if there was no solution, no way out (helplessness), a roadblock that seems invincible and related subjective views that present themselves over a period time.[25] Moderate to severe hopelessness in a population is linked to suicidal ideation.[26] The stress factors caused by a pandemic create emotional exhaustion.[27] Individuals who care for the elderly and chronic sick are naturally at a much higher risk of developing caregiver-fatigue. With the onset of the pandemic, many of these people are pushed beyond their limit as another stress factor is placed upon them.[28] Many people are overwhelmed with the anxiety, depression, and emotional load of the current crisis. Some people cannot bear the weight and do not seem to know how to cope with it other than by trying

19 Kirzinger, et al., "KFF Health Tracking Poll - Early April 2020: The Impact Of Coronavirus On Life In America."

20 Maker, "The Silent Pandemic: Depression, Self-Harm, and Suicide"; Menon and Chakrap, "Spike in self-harm, suicide ideation amid Covid-19 pandemic."

21 Phillips and Nugent, "Suicide and the Great Recession of 2007–2009: The Role of Economic Factors in the 50 U.S. States."

22 Jing, et al., "Is the Psychological Impact of Exposure to COVID-19 Stronger in Adolescents with Pre-Pandemic Maltreatment Experiences? A Survey of Rural Chinese Adolescents."

23 Mushtaq, "Relationship Between Loneliness, Psychiatric Disorders and Physical Health? A Review on the Psychological Aspects of Loneliness."

24 Dhami, Weiss-Cohen, and Ayton. "Are People Experiencing the 'Pains of Imprisonment' During the COVID-19 Lockdown?"

25 Caruso, "Hopelessness: A Dangerous Suicide Warning Sign."

26 Haatainen, et al., "Factors Associated with Hopelessness: A Population Study."

27 Brooks, et al., "The Psychological Impact of Quarantine and How to Reduce It: Rapid Review of the Evidence."

28 Cohut, "Pandemic worries cause additional strain"; Wright, "DSHS urges caregivers not to give in to COVID-19 fatigue during the holidays."

to end it all, like John Mondello, an emergency medical technician.[29] We will not know the outcome of the current crisis, but one only has to look into the devastating consequences that past disasters brought with them, such as a study on the effects on children whose fathers were exposed to unemployment and related psychosocial issues who showed a higher risk in developing suicidal ideation and completing suicide.[30]

The psychological toll successive lockdown takes on people will show itself more and more. Just as the sister of someone, who recently took his own life, says, "It's not just people dying in a hospital—it's people dying inside."[31]

Another disconcerting issue is domestic violence. Due to the stay-at-home orders, an increase in intimate partner violence (IPV) is very possible,[32] which can involve physical, emotional, sexual, and psychological abuse.[33] The lockdown has created a trap geographically and financially for those seeking help.[34] The access to places of shelter from abuse, or where victims would report incidents in person, were cut off. Meanwhile, the unemployment rate skyrocketed which bears the potential of an increase in mental health issues.[35] Unemployment and economic crises have been shown to increase domestic violence.[36] Trauma-related medical emergency visits declined in Sao Paulo[37] while self-harm increased in the United Kingdom.[38] According to the police

29 Edelman, et al., "EMT John Mondello kills himself after less than three months on the job."

30 Aleck, et al., "The Impact of Fathers' Physical and Psychosocial Work Conditions on Attempted and Completed Suicide among Their Children."

31 Peltier and Kwai, "Suicide and Self-Harm: Bereaved Families Count the Costs of Lockdowns."

32 Peterman, et al., "Pandemics and Violence Against Women and Children"; Kluger, "Domestic Violence Is a Pandemic Within the COVID-19 Pandemic"; Gibson, "Domestic Violence during COVID-19: The GP Role"; Roesch, et al., "Violence against Women during Covid-19 Pandemic Restrictions."

33 Smith, et al., "The National Intimate Partner and Sexual Violence Survey (NISVS): 2015 Data Brief – Updated Release."

34 Evans, Lindauer, and Farrell, "A Pandemic within a Pandemic —Intimate Partner Violence during Covid-19"; Usher, et al., "Family Violence and COVID-19: Increased Vulnerability and Reduced Options for Support."

35 Kochhar, "Unemployment rate is higher than officially recorded, more so for women and certain other groups"; Thorbecke, "US unemployment rate skyrockets to 14.7%, the worst since the Great Depression"; Thomas, "Unemployment rate hits highest level in three years"; Bennett, "Long-term unemployment has risen sharply in U.S. amid the pandemic, especially among Asian Americans."

36 Schneider, Harknett, and McLanahan, "Intimate Partner Violence in the Great Recession"; Schneider, Waldfogel, and Brooks-Gunn, "The Great Recession and Risk for Child Abuse and Neglect."

37 Steinman, et al., "The Burden of the Pandemic on the Non-SARS-CoV-2 Emergencies: A Multicenter Study."

38 Olding, et al., "Penetrating Trauma during a Global Pandemic: Changing Patterns in Interpersonal Violence, Self-Harm and Domestic Violence in the Covid-19 Outbreak."

station in Jianli County, China, domestic violence went up three times as much (162 reports) compared to the same month of the previous year (47).[39] Crisis hotlines in the UK saw a drastic reduction in calls, just like Italy, yet in Italy text messages and emails started to take over instead.[40] Other countries like Spain and Cyprus experienced a rise by 20–30 percent in crisis calls.[41] A study conducted by the Ottawa Hospital reported a decrease in emergency department admissions in a time of higher risk of domestic violence and less access to care.[42] It is very likely that victims avoided hospitals and/or were not able to leave the house due to a controlling partner or parent.

Children are the most vulnerable these days. Even though they are the least effected physically by SARS-CoV-2,[43] their psychosocial make-up is enormously susceptible to long-term affliction caused by the various enforced restrictions and false beliefs (scientifically unfounded information on SARS-CoV-2), mainly induced by media which are unfortunately upheld by their peers and loved ones, since false beliefs seem hard to let go of once adopted. The psychological impact will by far outweigh the physical.[44]

Child protection services and other protective services within a working system are set up to meet the needs that are encountered all over the world. A disruption of the established system has its inevitable consequences.[45] Children's mental and physical health is positively linked to interaction with peers,[46] which therefore carries great potential for a deficit in the developmental years in children when interaction is prohibited for a prolonged time. Yet, despite that known and important fact, schools were shut down and extracurricular activities were cancelled, even though there has not been any compelling scientific evidence to do so.[47] A real threat that children are facing now because of the induced fear through mainstream media could be the stigmatization of infected and/or recovered children because of rumours or myths regarding the coronavirus.[48]

39 Wanqing, "Domestic Violence Cases Surge During COVID-19 Epidemic."

40 Fielding, "In quarantine with an abuser: surge in domestic violence reports linked to coronavirus."

41 Graham-Harrison, et al., "Lockdowns around the world bring rise in domestic violence."

42 Muldoon, et al., "COVID-19 Pandemic and Violence: Rising Risks and Decreasing Urgent Care-Seeking for Sexual Assault and Domestic Violence Survivors."

43 Kostoff, et al., "Why are we vaccinating children against COVID-19?"

44 Ghosh, et al., "Impact of COVID-19 on Children: Special Focus on the Psychosocial Aspect"; Dubey, et al., "Psychosocial Impact of COVID-19."

45 Feigert, et al., "COVID-19-Pandemie: Kinderschutz ist systemrelevant."

46 Gifford-Smith and Brownell, "Childhood Peer Relationships: Social Acceptance, Friendships, and Peer Networks"; Oberle, Schonert-Reichl, and Thomson, "Understanding the Link Between Social and Emotional Well-Being and Peer Relations in Early Adolescence: Gender-Specific Predictors of Peer Acceptance."

47 Viner, et al., "School Closure and Management Practices during Coronavirus Outbreaks Including COVID-19: A Rapid Systematic Review."

48 Centers for Disease Control and Prevention, "Reducing Stigma."

A drop in case referrals has been reported by the Office for the Children's Commissioner,[49] which leaves the question of where these "hidden" or "invisible" children are and what is happening with them. A lot of reports are processed through the schools,[50] which is impossible during lockdown. At the same time, abuse of babies is reported more frequently in England[51] with almost 40 percent being under the age of one. Child sex exploitation in Canada has been recorded to have risen as well due to an increase in screen time.[52] According to Psychologist Josie Serrata (PhD), the risk of domestic violence can increase during stress and social isolation.[53] Basically, by staying at home the risks for negative interactions are potentially higher.[54] Cybercrime is more rampant than ever, exploiting the pandemic through their scams and also through child pornography, which has increased according to Europol.[55] It seems more than obvious that there is no need to fish for more evidence when it comes to the rise in domestic violence since the beginning of extreme regulations all over the world and the inhumane treatment within health care,[56] especially regarding the already vulnerable population. My personal prediction is that the psychosocial impact on children will bring about a new era of anxiety and distrust, which will show in harsh and merciless control and massive cold-blooded surveillance. I am saying this because of many examples we can look back on historically. Think of 9/11, when the dust settled and seemingly everything went back to normal, a new level of control was introduced so that, for example, at airports every individual became a potential terrorist. Is this the life we desire for our children or is there something missing by constantly tightening the range of freedom of choice as soon as yet another threat appears? Trust is essential for a thriving society. Let us pursue faith (trust), hope and love...love being the most important of them all (1 Cor 13:13).

49 Savage, "Fears grow over hidden child abuse since start of pandemic."

50 McMillan, "Child abuse reports expected to rise when kids go back to class: Saskatoon police."

51 Weale, "Abuse of babies is up by a fifth during Covid crisis, Ofsted says."

52 Thompson, "Child sex exploitation is on the rise in Canada during the pandemic."

53 Serrata and Hurtado Alvarado, "Understanding the Impact of Hurricane Harvey on Family Violence Survivors in Texas and Those Who Serve Them."

54 Abramson, "How COVID-19 may increase domestic violence and child abuse."

55 De Bolle, "Catching the virus cybercrime, disinformation and the COVID-19 pandemic."

56 Vliet, "Exposed: Inhumane, lethal COVID Protocol in hospitals."

Bibliography

Abbott, Alison. "COVID's mental-health toll: how scientists are tracking a surge in depression." *Nature*, February 3, 2021. https://www.nature.com/articles/d41586-021-00175-z.

Abramson, Ashley. "How COVID-19 may increase domestic violence and child abuse."

American Psychological Association (April 2020). https://www.apa.org/topics/covid-19/domestic-violence-child-abuse.

Ammerman, Brooke A., et al. "Preliminary Investigation of the Association between COVID-19 and Suicidal Thoughts and Behaviors in the U.S." *Journal of Psychiatric Research* 134 (February 2021): 32–38. https://doi.org/10.1016/j.jpsychires.2020.12.037.

Bennett, Jesse. "Long-term unemployment has risen sharply in U.S. amid the pandemic, especially among Asian Americans." Pew Research Center (March 2021). https://www.pewresearch.org/fact-tank/2021/03/11/long-term-unemployment-has-risen-sharply-in-u-s-amid-the-pandemic-especially-among-asian-americans/.

Bolton, Derek, et al. "The Long-term Psychological Effects of a Disaster Experienced in Adolescence: II: General Psychopathology." Journal of Child Psychology and Psychiatry 41, no. 4 (May 2000): 513–523. https://doi.org/10.1111/1469-7610.00636.

Brent, David A. "Risk Factors for Adolescent Suicide and Suicidal Behavior: Mental and Substance Abuse Disorders, Family Environmental Factors, and Life Stress." *Suicide and Life-Threatening Behavior* 25 (December 1995): 52–63. https://doi.org/10.1111/j.1943-278x.1995.tb00490.x.

Brooks, Samantha K., et al. "The Psychological Impact of Quarantine and How to Reduce It: Rapid Review of the Evidence." *The Lancet* 395, no. 10227 (March 2020): 912–20. https://doi.org/10.1016/s0140-6736(20)30460-8.

Brownstone Institute, "Natural Immunity and Covid-19: Thirty Scientific Studies to Share with Employers, Health Officials, and Politicians." https://brownstone.org/articles/natural-immunity-and-covid-19-twenty-nine-scientific-studies-to-share-with-employers-health-officials-and-politicians/.

Caruso, Kevin. "Hopelessness: A Dangerous Suicide Warning Sign." *Suicide*, April 2021. http://www.suicide.org/hopelessness-a-dangerous-warning-sign.html.

Centers for Disease Control and Prevention. "Reducing Stigma." (June 2020). https://www.cdc.gov/coronavirus/2019-ncov/daily-life-coping/reducing-stigma.html.

Cohut, Maria. "Pandemic worries cause additional strain." *Medical News Today*, May 2020. https://www.medicalnewstoday.com/articles/heightened-challenges-how-the-pandemic-impacts-caregivers#Pandemic-worries-cause-additional-strain/.

De Bolle, Catherine. "Catching the virus cybercrime, disinformation and the COVID-19 pandemic." *Europol*, April 2020. https://www.europol.europa.eu/publications-documents/catching-virus-cybercrime-disinformation-and-covid-19-pandemic.

Dhami, Mandeep K., et al. "Are People Experiencing the 'Pains of Imprisonment' During the COVID-19 Lockdown?" *Frontiers in Psychology* 11 (November 19, 2020). https://doi.org/10.3389/fpsyg.2020.578430.

Douglas, Pamela K., et al. "Preparing for pandemic influenza and its aftermath: mental health issues considered." *International journal of emergency mental health*, vol. 11,3 (2009): 137–144.

Dubey, Souvik, et al. "Psychosocial Impact of COVID-19." Diabetes & Metabolic Syndrome: *Clinical Research & Reviews* 14, no. 5 (September 2020): 779–88. https://doi.org/10.1016/j.dsx.2020.05.035.

Edelman, Susan, et al. "EMT John Mondello kills himself after less than three months on the job," New York Post (April 2020). https://nypost.com/2020/04/25/nyc-emt-commits-suicide-with-gun-belonging-to-his-dad/.

Evans, Megan L. "A Pandemic within a Pandemic—Intimate Partner Violence during Covid-19." *New England Journal of Medicine* 383, no. 24 (December 2020): 2302–2304. https://doi.org/10.1056/nejmp2024046.

Feigert, Jörg, et al. "COVID-19-Pandemie: Kinderschutz ist systemrelevant," Journal Article, D 2020, J Dtsch Arztebl International, R P 703-V 117, N 14 (April 2020). https://www.aerzteblatt.de/archiv/213358/COVID-19-Pandemie-Kinderschutz-ist-systemrelevant.

Fielding, Sarah. "In quarantine with an abuser: surge in domestic violence reports linked to coronavirus." *The Guardian*, April 3, 2020. https://www.theguardian.com/us-news/2020/apr/03/coronavirus-quarantine-abuse-domestic-violence.

Ghosh, Ritwik, et al. "Impact of COVID-19 on Children: Special Focus on the Psychosocial Aspect." JB. *Minerva Pediatrica* 72, no. 3 (June 2020). https://doi.org/10.23736/S0026-4946.20.05887-9.

Gibson, Jeremy. "Domestic Violence during COVID-19: The GP Role." *British Journal of General Practice* 70, no. 696 (June 2020). 340–340. https://doi.org/10.3399/bjgp20x710477.

Gifford-Smith, Mary E. and Celia A. Brownell. "Childhood Peer Relationships: Social Acceptance, Friendships, and Peer Networks." *Journal of School Psychology* 41, no. 4 (July 2003): 235–284. https://doi.org/10.1016/s0022-4405(03)00048-7.

Graham-Harrison, Emma, et al. "Lockdowns around the world bring rise in domestic violence" *The Guardian*, March 28, 2020. https://www.theguardian.com/society/2020/mar/28/lockdowns-world-rise-domestic-violence.

Great Barrington Declaration. https://gbdeclaration.org/.

Greene, T. "For poor countries, lockdowns cost more lives than they save." *Prospect*, May 16, 2021. https://www.prospectmagazine.co.uk/world/for-poor-countries-lockdowns-cost-more-lives-than-they-save.

Haatainen, Kaisa, et al. "Factors Associated with Hopelessness: A Population Study." *International Journal of Social Psychiatry* 50, no. 2 (June 2004): 142–152. https://doi.org/10.1177/0020764004040961.

Ioannidis, John P. A. "Infection fatality rate of COVID-19 inferred from seroprevalence data." Bulletin of the World Health Organization (2021). https://doi.org/10.2471/BLT.20.265892.

Jing Mingqi Fu Guo, et al. "Is the Psychological Impact of Exposure to COVID-19 Stronger in Adolescents with Pre-Pandemic Maltreatment Experiences? A Survey of Rural Chinese Adolescents." *Child Abuse & Neglect* 110 (December 2020): 104667. https://doi.org/10.1016/j.chiabu.2020.104667.

Kar Nilamadhab. "Depression in Youth Exposed to Disasters, Terrorism and Political Violence." Current Psychiatry Reports 21, no. 8 (July 4, 2019). https://doi.org/10.1007/s11920-019-1061-9.

Kar Nilamadhab and Bastia B. K. "Post-traumatic stress disorder, depression and generalised anxiety disorder in adolescents after a natural disaster: a study of comorbidity." *Clinical Practice and Epidemiology in Mental Health* vol. 2,17 (2006): 1745-0179. https://doi.org/10.1186/1745-0179-2-17.

Kirzinger Ashley, et al. "KFF Health Tracking Poll – Early April 2020: The Impact Of Coronavirus On Life In America." *KFF*, April 2, 2020. https://www.kff.org/coronavirus-covid-19/report/kff-health-tracking-poll-early-april-2020.

Kluger Jeffrey. "Domestic Violence Is a Pandemic Within the COVID-19 Pandemic." *Time* (February 2021). https://time.com/5928539/domestic-violence-covid-19/.

Kochhar Rakesh, "Unemployment rate is higher than officially recorded, more so for women and certain other groups." Pew Research Center (June 2020). https://www.pewresearch.org/fact-tank/2020/06/30/unemployment-rate-is-higher-than-officially-recorded-more-so-for-women-and-certain-other-groups/.

Kostoff, R. N., et al. "Why are we vaccinating children against COVID-19?" *Toxicology Reports* 8 (2021): 1665–1684. https://doi.org/10.1016/j.toxrep.2021.08.010.

Lange, Samantha, et al. "Longitudinal Trends in Body Mass Index Before and During the COVID-19 Pandemic Among Persons Aged 2–19 Years—United States (2018–2020)." MMWR Morb Mortal Wkly Rep (2021). http://dx.doi.org/10.15585/mmwr.mm7037a3.

Leonard, Brian E. "The concept of depression as a dysfunction of the immune system." *Current immunology reviews*, vol. 6,3 (2010): 205–212. Doi:10.2174/157339510791823835.

Maker, Azmaira. "The Silent Pandemic: Depression, Self-Harm, and Suicide," *Psychology Today* May 21, 2020. https://www.psychologytoday.com/us/blog/helping-kids-cope/202005/the-silent-pandemic-depression-self-harm-and-suicide.

McIntyre, Roger S. and Yena Lee. "Projected Increases in Suicide in Canada as a Consequence of COVID-19." *Psychiatry Research* 290 (August 2020): 113104. https://doi.org/10.1016/j.psychres.2020.113104.

McMillan, Anna. "Child abuse reports expected to rise when kids go back to class: Saskatoon police." *Global News*, September 2, 2020. https://globalnews.ca/news/7313165/saskatoon-police-child-abuse-reports-rise-back-to-school.

Menon, Priya and Saranya Chakrap. "Spike in self-harm, suicide ideation amid Covid-19 pandemic." *Times of India*, July 25, 2020. https://timesofindia.indiatimes.com/india/spike-in-self-harm-suicide-ideation-amid-covid-19-pandemic/articleshow/77142884.cms.

Muldoon, Katherine A., et al. "COVID-19 Pandemic and Violence: Rising Risks and Decreasing Urgent Care-Seeking for Sexual Assault and Domestic Violence Survivors." *BMC Medicine* 19, no. 1 (February 2021). https://doi.org/10.1186/s12916-020-01897-z.

Mushtaq, Raheel. "Relationship Between Loneliness, Psychiatric Disorders and Physical Health? A Review on the Psychological Aspects of Loneliness." *Journal of Clinical and Diagnostic Research* (2014). https://doi.org/10.7860/jcdr/2014/10077.4828.

Oberle, Eva, et al. "Understanding the Link Between Social and Emotional Well-Being and Peer Relations in Early Adolescence: Gender-Specific Predictors of Peer Acceptance." *Journal of Youth and Adolescence* 39, no. 11 (November 2009): 1330–1342. https://doi.org/10.1007/s10964-009-9486-9.

Olding, James, et al. "Penetrating Trauma during a Global Pandemic: Changing Patterns in Interpersonal Violence, Self-Harm and Domestic Violence in the Covid-19 Outbreak." *The Surgeon* 19, no. 1 (February 2021): e9–13. https://doi.org/10.1016/j.surge.2020.07.004.

Ostry, Aleck, et al., "The Impact of Fathers' Physical and Psychosocial Work Conditions on Attempted and Completed Suicide among Their Children." *BMC Public Health* 6, no. 1 (March 2006). https://doi.org/10.1186/1471-2458-6-77.

Peltier, Elian and Isabella Kwai. "Suicide and Self-Harm: Bereaved Families Count the Costs of Lockdowns." *The New York Times*, March 17, 2021. https://www.nytimes.com/2021/03/27/world/europe/suicide-self-harm-pandemic.html.

Perera, S., et al. "Body Mass Index Is an Important Predictor for Suicide: Results from a Systematic Review and Meta-Analysis." *Suicide & life-threatening behavior* (2016). https://doi.org/10.1111/sltb.12244.

Peterman, Amber, et al. "Pandemics and Violence Against Women and Children." CGD Working Paper 528. Washington, DC: Center for Global Development (April 2020). https://www.cgdev.org/publication/pandemics-and-violence-against-women-and-children.

Philippine Statistics Authority. "Pandemic year sees 57% rise in suicide rate in Philippines." https://www.philstar.com/headlines/2021/07/06/2110596/pandemic-year-sees-57-rise-suicide-rate-philippines.

Phillips, Julie A. and Colleen N. Nugent. "Suicide and the Great Recession of 2007–2009: The Role of Economic Factors in the 50 U.S. States." *Social Science & Medicine* 116 (September 2014): 22–31. https://doi.org/10.1016/j.socscimed.2014.06.015.

Roesch, Elisabeth, et al. "Violence against Women during Covid-19 Pandemic Restrictions." *BMJ* (May 2020). m1712. https://doi.org/10.1136/bmj.m1712.

Rolheiser, Duane. "Another Way." Todayville, accessed November 7, 2021. https://www.todayville.com/theres-another-way-to-end-the-pandemic-doctors-can-knock-covid-out-with-treatment/.

Savage, Michael. "Fears grow over hidden child abuse since start of pandemic." *The Guardian*, January 24, 2021. https://www.theguardian.com/society/2021/jan/24/fears-grow-over-hidden-child-abuse-since-start-of-pandemic.

Sau, Man Sandra Chan, et al. "Elderly Suicide and the 2003 SARS Epidemic in Hong Kong." *International Journal of Geriatric Psychiatry* 21, no. 2 (2006): 113–118. https://doi.org/10.1002/gps.1432.

Schemmel, Alec. "Calls ring out for Fauci to debate virologist after Rogan podcast appearance." KATV, January 3, 2022. https://katv.com/news/nation-world/calls-ring-out-for-fauci-to-debate-virologist-after-rogan-podcast-appearance.

Schneider Daniel, et al. "Intimate Partner Violence in the Great Recession." *Demography* 53, no. 2 (March 2016): 471–505. https://doi.org/10.1007/s13524-016-0462-1.

Schneider, William, et al. "The Great Recession and Risk for Child Abuse and Neglect." *Children and Youth Services Review* 72 (January 2017): 71–81. https://doi.org/10.1016/j.childyouth.2016.10.016.

Segerstrom, Suzanne C. and Gregory E. Miller. "Psychological stress and the human immune system: a meta-analytic study of 30 years of inquiry." *Psychol Bull.* 130 (2004): 601–630. doi:10.1037/0033-2909.130.4.601.

Serrata, Josephine V. and M. Gabriela Hurtado Alvarado. "Understanding the Impact of Hurricane Harvey on Family Violence Survivors in Texas and Those Who Serve Them." *Texas Council on Family Violence*, accessed April 6, 2021. https://tcfv.org/wp-content/uploads/2019/08/Hurricane-Harvey-Report-FINAL-and-APPROVED-as-of-060619.pdf.

Smith, S. G., et al. "The National Intimate Partner and Sexual Violence Survey (NISVS): 2015 Data Brief – Updated Release." Atlanta, GA: National Center for Injury Prevention and Control, Centers for Disease Control and Prevention (2018). https://www.cdc.gov/violenceprevention/pdf/2015data-brief508.pdf.

Sprang, Ginny and Miriam Silman. "Posttraumatic Stress Disorder in Parents and Youth After Health-Related Disasters." Disaster Medicine and Public Health Preparedness 7, no. 1 (February 2013): 105–110. https://doi.org/10.1017/dmp.2013.22.

Steinman, Milton, et al. "The Burden of the Pandemic on the Non-SARS-CoV-2 Emergencies: A Multicenter Study." *The American Journal of Emergency Medicine* 42 (April 2021): 9–14. https://doi.org/10.1016/j.ajem.2020.12.080.

Thomas, Daniel. "Unemployment rate hits highest level in three years." *BBC*, October 13, 2020. https://www.bbc.com/news/business-54520521.

Thorbecke Catherine. "US unemployment rate skyrockets to 14.7%, the worst since the Great Depression." abcNEWS, May 8, 2020. https://abcnews.go.com/Business/us-economy-lost-205-million-jobs-april-unemployment/story?id=70558779.

Thompson, Elizabeth. "Child sex exploitation is on the rise in Canada during the pandemic." *CBC*, July 13, 2020. https://www.cbc.ca/news/politics/pandemic-child-sexual-abuse-1.5645315.

Usher, Kim, et al. "Family Violence and COVID-19: Increased Vulnerability and Reduced Options for Support." *International Journal of Mental Health Nursing* 29, no. 4 (May 2020): 549–552. https://doi.org/10.1111/inm.12735.

Vliet, Elizabeth Lee. "Exposed: Inhumane, lethal COVID Protocol in hospitals." *WND*, October 25, 2021. https://www.wnd.com/2021/10/exposed-inhumane-lethal-covid-protocol-hospitals/?fbclid=IwAR0T9VZ0Egya9FyAPMJ1-b0K05Kny2PvZftvE39lwzu4uY3VSm4PpVYLwys.

Viner, Russell M., et al. "School Closure and Management Practices during Coronavirus Outbreaks Including COVID-19: A Rapid Systematic Review." *The Lancet Child & Adolescent Health* 4, no. 5 (May 2020): 397–404. https://doi.org/10.1016/s2352-4642(20)30095-x.

Wanqing, Zhang. "Domestic Violence Cases Surge During COVID-19 Epidemic." *Sixth Tone* March 2, 2020. https://www.sixthtone.com/news/1005253/domestic-violence-cases-surge-during-covid-19-epidemic.

Weale, Sally. "Abuse of babies is up by a fifth during Covid crisis, Ofsted says." *The Guardian*, November 6, 2020. https://www.theguardian.com/society/2020/nov/06/abuse-babies-up-fifth-covid-19-eight-died-ofsted.

Wright, Chris. "DSHS urges caregivers not to give in to COVID-19 fatigue during the holidays," Washington State Department of Social and

Health Services, November 24, 2020. https://www.dshs.wa.gov/os/office-communications/media-release/dshs-urges-caregivers-not-give-covid-19-fatigue-during-holidays.

Yule, William, et al. "The Long-term Psychological Effects of a Disaster Experienced in Adolescence: I: The Incidence and Course of PTSD." *Journal of Child Psychology and Psychiatry* 41, no. 4 (May 2000): 503–11. https://doi.org/10.1111/1469-7610.00635.

Chapter 45

COVID-19: A Pandemic of Malfeasance and Incompetence: Unpopular Truths and Propagated Lies[1]

Scott D. G. Ventureyra and Enrique C. G. Ventureyra

The lead singer of Soul Asylum, David Pirner, in the lyrics to "Misery" from the 1995 album "Let Your Dim Light Shine," proleptically captures the essence of the COVID-19 pandemic when indicating that both an unknown cure and disease were created in a factory. As time passes, the intuition that this pandemic was orchestrated gains more and more evidence, from the origin of the virus to the vaccine passports.

In line with this, consider the salient points made in an interview by internist, cardiologist, and COVID specialist (who has published over 50 papers on COVID since the beginning of the pandemic), Dr. Peter McCullough:

- This pandemic has always been "ABOUT THE VACCINE."
- "Stakeholders" that strongly want a "needle in every arm" are Big Pharma, White House, CDC, FDA, NIH, Gates Foundation, WHO.
- The death rate for the covid vaccine is far higher than for any other vaccine in history.
- "Never vaccinate into the middle of a pandemic."
- "85% of covid deaths were preventable with early treatment which was squashed."
- The "dangerous spike protein" damages blood vessels and cause blood clotting.[2]

Since March 2020, throughout the world, we witnessed both medical malfeasance and total incompetence from the absurd recommendations of

1 The amount of information that comes out on a daily basis is overwhelming. I had to stop including information at the end of February 2022. It is very difficult to keep up with new developments.

2 MichaelSavage.com, "MASSIVE! Top Doctor Warns about COVID Vaccine (DISTURBING)"; see McCullough, "Winning the War Against Therapeutic Nihilism & Trusted Treatments vs Untested Novel Therapies."

double masking made by medical bureaucrats, like Anthony Fauci in the US and Theresa Tam in Canada, to the barring of effective treatment such as hydroxychloroquine and ivermectin by hospitals. Governments in lockstep with the mainstream media, medical colleges, the pharmaceutical industry, Big Tech, and the above-mentioned organizations, supported a false narrative that caused irreparable harm and death to countless people around the globe.

Indeed, alongside the innumerable lies there has been an unrelenting campaign of propaganda coupled with a persistent psychological assault on humanity. A perfect example of this disturbing propaganda appeared in *The Globe and Mail* on November 23, 2021, which featured a father who was ecstatic to vaccinate his seven and nine-year-old girls:

> Sean McDonald was lying in bed on Tuesday morning when a friend texted him to say Ontario's online portal to book COVID-19 vaccine appointments for children aged 5 to 11 had opened early.
>
> "I swear to God I've never bolted out of my bed and flown down the stairs faster," said Mr. McDonald, a father of two children, aged 7 and 9, who lives in Toronto.
>
> He said the process of booking vaccine appointments for his children was quick, easy and, above all, emotional.
>
> "Honestly, I shed a tear," said Mr. McDonald, national managing partner and chief strategy officer at Rethink, an advertising agency. "It was the culmination of one year of quiet terror of how to protect our kids."
>
> With 2.9 million pediatric vaccines now in Canada, tens of thousands of parents such as Mr. McDonald are rushing to book appointments. Demand has been high at the onset – but it remains unclear as to how many parents will choose to inoculate their children after the initial dash.
>
> The vaccines are arriving as the incidence rate of COVID-19 among those aged 5 to 11 is higher than in any other age group, Theresa Tam, Canada's Chief Public Health Officer, said last week. And while most children will fully recover from COVID-19, a small number are at risk for serious cases and long-lasting severe health problems, including multisystem inflammatory syndrome, long COVID and other issues.[3]

This is a perfect example of how governments and the media have created unmitigated and irrational anxiety and fear. It is what Mattias Desmet has labeled "Mass Formation Psychosis." This is why conditioned parents live in extreme terror of a disease that has .0002 percent fatality for those under 20 years of age (nineteen deaths out of a demographic of 8.1 million people). Shedding a tear? One wonders what percentage of the population buys this propaganda. Desmet

3 Stone, et al., "'Some relief': Parents across Canada rush to book COVID-19 vaccines for kids."

suggests about 30 percent. For Canadians it's probably a larger percentage since a significant proportion of Canadians will accept whatever they're told by the legacy media and government. This is the sort of propaganda we have been fed for over twenty months. Just as, or perhaps even more egregious is the segment on Sesame Street, "The ABCs of COVID Vaccines" with pediatric neurosurgeon and CNN chief medical correspondent, Sanjay Gupta, and journalist Erica Hill.[4] It is the sort of video you would expect emanating from Joseph Goebbels and the Reich Ministry of Public Enlightenment and Propaganda (RMVP), not in the USA in 2021. This segment is incredibly disturbing, bordering on cultish. A few days after the post was made, the number of dislikes on the video greatly outnumbered likes. However, for unknown reasons, since then YouTube has removed the dislike button from all videos. Unsurprisingly, comments have also been disabled. The satirical Babylon Bee recently released a video with a "Playskool Vaccinate Me Elmo Doll." I must admit that it made me laugh hysterically, only because Playskool, CNN, and Sesame Street would have wished to have come up with the idea first. The pitch they made up is: "Do you want your kid vaccinated? Then get the Vaccinate Me Elmo Doll and terrify your kid to a safer tomorrow."[5] The video and slogan are hilarious in a very sinister way since it isn't too far from the truth.

The Canadian pathologist Roger Hodkinson, who does not mince his words, has communicated the following pointed message:

> Believe nothing you are being told. It's all been a pack of lies from start to finish. Pure propaganda! This is nothing more than a bad seasonal flu with slightly increased risk for older people with comorbidities… This is a pandemic of fear; fear that was intentionally driven by two major factors, the notorious PCR test, and the viciously effective silencing of any counter narrative. The PCR test creates over 95 percent false positives in perfectly well people.[6]

The Origin of SARS-CoV-2

The Publicly Released Fauci Emails[7]

For those who are totally in the dark when it comes to the origin of the virus and still believe it had its origin in nature via some Wuhan wet market, what

4 Sesame Street, "The ABCs of COVID Vaccines."

5 See The Babylon Bee, "Playskool Unveils Vaccinate Me Elmo Doll."

6 O'Sullivan, "Dr. Roger Hodkinson on COVID19: it's all been a pack of lies."

7 These emails were publicly released in early June of 2021 and so any previous analysis on the origin of the virus would be missing some of these revelations. However, much of this information corroborates long held suspicions.

you are about to read will utterly dismantle this not-so-noble lie. Recently, the media has begun flirting with this notion again, now claiming that it originated with a female seafood vendor (patient zero) in November 2019,[8] who was likely infected by live animals such as raccoon dogs (Nyctereutes procyonoides) that are susceptible to coronaviruses.[9]

Much of what has unraveled before our eyes through the publicly released emails of Anthony Fauci confirm what skeptics have long thought of the COVID-19 situation. Over 3,000 pages of Fauci's emails obtained by *The Washington Post* and *BuzzFeed News*, which were released through the Freedom of Information Act, paint a very different picture of Fauci, The Patron Saint of Wuhan, than by the mainstream media.[10] Despite fact checkers' continuously false and misleading claims defending the COVID-19 accepted narrative,[11] these emails paint a picture of how Fauci has been implicated in the COVID-19 pandemic, rather than the great medical hero proclaimed by the mainstream media. One should not expect a proper investigation from the Biden administration since they are supporting the same narrative regarding the pandemic. In fact, one should expect the Biden administration to cover up the lies as much as possible. This has been happening in collusion with Big Tech, medical experts, WHO, CDC, MSM, Hollywood Stars, the pharmaceutical industry, and others interest groups. There is an agenda that is being pushed at all costs, regardless of the corruption and evidence. The White House press Secretary, Jen Psaki,[12] who unlike her predecessor, Kayleigh McEnany, is constantly protected by the press from any difficult questions, stated that: "The president and the administration feel that Dr. Fauci has played an incredible role and [sic] getting the pandemic under control and being a voice to the public throughout the course of this pandemic."[13]

These publicly released emails paint a very different picture of Fauci than has been revealed by the MSM. Take, for instance, the claim about how President Trump was muzzling Fauci; a claim that was made by Joe Biden from the onset of the COVID crisis and again in mid-2021. Fauci was echoing the same in January

8 Reuters, "Market in China's Wuhan likely origin of COVID-19 outbreak – scientist"; Ali, "First known Covid case was a Wuhan wet market vendor, study 'confirms categorically'."

9 Worobey, "Dissecting the early COVID-19 cases in Wuhan."

10 These emails can be viewed and downloaded here: Anthony Fauci emails: https://assets.documentcloud.org/documents/20793561/leopold-nih-foia-anthony-fauci-emails.pdf. Please note that any reference to Fauci's emails or others in this chapter refer to the emails contained in this document.

11 You can make up your own mind by comparing their alleged fact checking versus what has been written in this book and supporting documents in the footnotes. See Funk, "Fact check: Fauci's emails don't show he 'lied' about hydroxychloroquine."

12 It is fascinating to hear people like Psaki make Freudian slips by calling this alleged pandemic, a "plandemic": Leaked Reality, "'the plandemic' Jen Psaki Makes a Freudian Slip." September 2020. https://leakedreality.com/video/21111/the-plandemic-jen-psaki-makes-a-freudian-slip.

13 Nelson, "Psaki calls Fauci 'undeniable asset' after Chinese lab leak emails."

2021, which contradicted his public statements and private emails from a year earlier.[14] In a couple of private emails dated Sunday, March 1, 2020, he stated the following: "Thanks for the note. Please stay silent since I have not been muzzled. I will be on multiple TV shows tomorrow and was on FOX this AM. No one is censoring me."[15] The following day he emphatically stated:

> I have been very explicit in stating publicly that I am not being muzzled or censored. I say exactly what I want to say based on scientific evidence, I have stated this on multiple TV programs over the past few days including at a major press conference with many, many reporters present including several TV cameras. I could not possibly be more public about this. No censor. No muzzle. Free to speak out.[16]

So why did Fauci contradict himself a year later? Was it that he was afraid to speak the truth both publicly and privately in 2020 due to potential reprisal? No matter how you slice it, either Fauci was lying in 2020 or he was lying in January of 2021 in his interview with *The New York Times* alleging he was silenced.[17] If anything, these emails demonstrate that he is a liar. What else has he lied about?

One of the major revelations comes from an email dated January 31, 2020, from virologist, Kristian G. Andersen of the Scripps Research Institute, in response to an article sent by Fauci titled: "Mining coronavirus genomes for clues to the outbreak's origins,"[18] which attempts to dispel the notion that the virus may have been manipulated, stated the following:

> Thanks for sharing. Yes, I saw this earlier today and both Eddie and myself are actually quoted in it. It's a great article, but the problem is that our phylogenetic analyses aren't able to answer whether the sequences are unusual at individual residues, except if they are completely off. On a phylogenetic tree the virus looks totally normal and the close clustering with bats suggest that bats serve as the reservoir. The unusual features of the virus make up a really small part of the genome (<0.1%) so one has to look really closely at all the sequences to see that some of the features (potentially) look *engineered.*
>
> We have a good team lined up to look very critically at this, so we should know much more at the end of the weekend. I should mention that after discussions earlier today, Eddie, Bob, Mike, and myself all find *the genome inconsistent with expectations from evolutionary theory.*

14 Cruta, "Biden Claimed Trump 'Muzzled' Fauci—But Emails Reveal Fauci Said Otherwise."
15 Anthony Fauci, email to Thomas Murray, March 1, 2020, 18:43.
16 Anthony Fauci, email to Mark Jay Shlomchik, March 2, 2020, 9:20.
17 McNeil Jr. "Fauci on What Working for Trump Was Really Like."
18 See Cohen, "Mining coronavirus genomes for clues to the outbreak's origins."

> But we have to look at this much more closely and there are still further analyses to be done, so those opinions could still change. [19]

Interestingly, the following day, on February 1, 2020, Fauci sent an email labeled "IMPORTANT" to the Principal Deputy Director of the National Institute of Allergy and Infectious Diseases (NIAID), Hugh Auchincloss, regarding an article describing the gain of function research occurring at the Wuhan Institute of Virology. He sent an email at 12:29 am urgently stating:

> It is essential that we speak this AM. Keep your cell phone on. I have a conference call at 7:45 AM with Azar. It likely will be over at 8:45 AM. Read this paper as well as the e-mail that I will forward to you now. [The same paper he sent on several occasions to multiple people including Kristian Andersen: "Mining coronavirus genomes for clues to the outbreak's origins stating the following" which fits the narrative of the virus evolving naturally."] You will have tasks today that must be done.[20]

That same day, Fauci and Dr. Jeremy Farrar, director of the British Wellcome Trust, organized a teleconference to discuss the origins of the coronavirus. This teleconference led to the publication of two influential pieces; one was an open letter and the other an opinion piece, both with the same goal: to dispel any notion that SARS-CoV2 was engineered. The open letter was signed by a number of scientists and was published in the medical journal, *The Lancet*, on February 19, 2020.[21] Interestingly, the letter was drafted by the president of EcoHealth Alliance, Peter Daszak,[22] on February 6, 2020—this information, like the Fauci emails, were obtained through the Freedom of Information Act. Daszak stated the following in his call for support against "conspiracy theories" of the virus's origin:

> I've been following the events around the novel coronavirus emergence in China very closely and have been dismayed by the recent spreading of rumors, misinformation and conspiracy theories on its origins. These are now specifically targeting scientists with whom we've collaborated for many years, and who have been working heroically to fight this outbreak and share data with unprecedented speed, openness and transparency. These conspiracy theories threaten to undermine the

19 Kristian G. Andersen, email to Anthony Fauci, February 1, 2020, 18:43.

20 Anthony Fauci, email to Hugh Auchincloss, February 1, 2020, 12:29 AM.

21 Calisher, et al. "Statement in support of the scientists, public health professionals, and medical professionals of China combatting COVID-19."

22 See EcoHealth website with Peter Daszak's profile page: https://www.ecohealthalliance.org/personnel/dr-peter-daszak.

> very global collaborations that we need to deal with a disease that has already spread across continents. We have drafted a simple statement of solidarity and support for scientists, public health and medical professionals of China, and would like to invite you to join us as the first signatories.[23]

It is worth pointing out that Daszak's organization had received $3.7 million from the NIAID, out of this money, $600,000 or more was given to the Wuhan Institute of Virology, over a five-year period, to study whether bat coronaviruses could be transmitted to humans.

In spite of the open letter that appears in *The Lancet*, which was drafted by Daszak, it is evident that Daszak was aware of this research and helped support its funding. According to Natalie Winters, "Daszak made the admission at a 2016 forum discussing 'emerging infectious diseases and the next pandemic,' which appears to be at odds with Fauci's repeated denial of funding gain-of-function research at the Wuhan Institute of Virology."[24] In a 2016 video on C-Span, which was discovered by *The National Pulse*, Daszak states the following:

> Then when you get a sequence of a virus, and it looks like a relative of a known nasty pathogen, just like we did with SARS. We found other coronaviruses in bats, a whole host of them, some of them looked very similar to SARS. So we sequenced the spike protein: the protein that attaches to cells. Then we… Well I didn't do this work, but my colleagues in China did the work. You create pseudo particles, you insert the spike proteins from those viruses, see if they bind to human cells. At each step of this you move closer and closer to this virus could really become pathogenic in people… You end up with a small number of viruses that really do look like killers.[25]

Fauci denied any of the funding was for gain of function research. Republican Senator Rand Paul, claimed that Fauci committed perjury over his denial of gain of function research funding.[26] Rand Paul stated that:

> There's a lot of evidence that he [Fauci] has a great deal of conflict of interest and that if it turns out this virus came from the Wuhan lab—

23 Daszak, "A Statement in support of the scientists, public health and medical professionals of China."

24 Winters, "WATCH: Explosive, Unearthed Video Shows Peter Daszak Describing 'Chinese Colleagues' Developing 'Killer' Coronaviruses."

25 Winters, "Explosive, "Unearthed Video Shows Peter Daszak Describing 'Chinese Colleagues' Developing 'Killer' Coronaviruses."

26 Husubo, "Sen. Paul: Fauci Committed Perjury over Gain of Function Comments Related to Wuhan Lab."

> which it looks like it did—that there's a great deal of culpability and that he was a big supporter of the funding… But he also was a big supporter, to this day, of saying, 'We can trust the Chinese on this. We can trust the Chinese scientists,' and I think that's quite naïve and really should preclude him from the position that he's in." Nevertheless, Fauci and the director of the National Institutes of Health (NIH) have admitted there is no way of knowing for certain if this money was used for gain of function research.[27]

In an email dated April 19, 2020, Daszak thanks Fauci for publicly dispelling any myths surrounding any "conspiracies" that the virus was engineered.

The other relevant piece that helped form the narrative followed by MSM was merely a non-peer-reviewed 2-page letter published on March 17, 2020, in *Nature Medicine*, titled: "The Proximal Origin of SARS-CoV-2."[28] The main author of this letter was Kristian Andersen. A question arises as to why he completely refutes his initial private analysis publicly? Another unsurprising incident was that Andersen subsequently deleted his Twitter account after Twitter users demanded explanations for his previous statements which contradicted his letter to *Nature*.[29]

What could these groups of scientists possibly be discussing in that urgent teleconference? Jeremy Farrar's email on page 3197 of the leaked emails states that, "Information and discussion is shared in total confidence and not to be shared until agreement on next steps."[30]

On March 6, Fauci congratulated Andersen on the acceptance of his publication. Andersen's publication: "The Proximal Origin of SARS-CoV-2" letter and the open letter published in *The Lancet* have both been heavily critiqued by Nicholas Wade in his article: "Origin of Covid—Following the Clues." Another refutation of Andersen's letter can be found at Harvard to the Big House website in an entry titled: "China owns Nature magazine's ass: Debunking "The proximal origin of SARS-CoV-2" claiming COVID-19 definitely wasn't from a lab."[31] In this entry, the author states these damning words of the journal *Nature* with its corruption and ties to the Chinese Communist Party (CCP):

27 Chamberlain, "Sen. Paul: Fauci emails prove he knew of Wuhan gain-of-function research."

28 Andersen, et al. "The proximal origin of SARS-CoV-2."

29 Louise, "Kristian Andersen, the virologist who told Dr. Fauci that COVID-19 'potentially look engineered,' just deleted his Twitter account."

30 Jeremy Farrar, email to Anthony Fauci, Francis Collins, Kevin Andersen and others, February 1, 2020, 15:34.

31 See Harvard2thebighouse, "China owns Nature magazine's ass: Debunking 'The proximal origin of SARS-CoV-2' claiming COVID-19 definitely wasn't from a lab."

> Maybe you shouldn't blindly believe everything you read? Even if the source has a pretty solid reputation?
>
> Nature magazine has censored over 1,000 articles at the request of the Chinese government over the past several years, and runs columns sponsored by outside interests. And it seems pretty clear that their recent article, "The proximal origin of SARS-CoV-2" is just one more example of their influence. China bought off the head of Harvard's chemistry department, you don't think they could buy off run-of-the-mill research scientists scrambling for tenure and funding and publication? It's absolutely horrific that so many scientists and researchers are taking part in what's really clearly a disinformation campaign orchestrated by the Chinese Communist Party, and willfully spreading a smokescreen about something that's already killed thousands and is projected to kill millions more across the planet.
>
> And while the mainstream corporate media mindless [sic] regurgitates claims from the Chinese government that are falsifiable with the simplest of google searches, allowing the public to be lulled into a false sense of security and complacency, and Reddit rapidly censors and moderates anything that might indicate that this virus leaked from a Chinese lab and so the Chinese government is to blame for this pandemic—sites like ZeroHedge, that have been at the forefront of keeping the lines of investigation open, have been banished from Twitter and marginalized.[32]

It should become apparent from the trail of emails and the urgency that emerged to respond to public reporting on the potential connection between COVID-19 and the Wuhan Institute of Virology, that Fauci and his team had something to hide.[33] Why did Fauci publicly dismiss the idea that the SARS-CoV-2 was engineered as baseless in an interview with the *National Geographic*? Fauci stated the following:

> If you look at the evolution of the virus in bats and what's out there now, [the scientific evidence] is very, very strongly leaning toward this could not have been artificially or deliberately manipulated... Everything about the stepwise evolution over time strongly indicates that [this virus] evolved in nature and then jumped species.[34]

He also discredited the idea that the virus was found in the wild, then brought to a lab, and then escaped. Not surprisingly, any public discourse on the notion

32 Harvard2thebighouse, "China owns Nature magazine's ass: Debunking 'The proximal origin of SARS-CoV-2' claiming COVID-19 definitely wasn't from a lab."

33 Carlson and Mahncke, "Emails Reveal How Influential Articles That Established COVID-19 Natural Origins Theory Were Formed."

34 Nsikan Akpan and Victoria Jaggard, "Fauci: No scientific evidence the coronavirus was made in a Chinese lab."

that the virus emanated from a lab leak, and that it was potentially engineered, was aggressively censored and scoffed at by social media platforms, health officials, and WHO. Since then, in May of 2021, in order to mitigate mistrust of social media and other implicated bodies, Facebook stated they will not remove any material suggesting SARS-CoV-2 was engineered.

Why did Kristian Andersen and the team of scientists go out of their way to refute their initial analysis—especially considering the fact that the scientific arguments in their letter are found wanting? Of course, as we saw in our earlier section devoted to the origin of the virus, the arguments in favour of the virus being engineered were more compelling; this has been known since April 2020 with *The Epoch Times* documentary, "Tracking Down the Origin of the Wuhan Coronavirus."[35] These are just two lies of many. What else have they been lying to us about? Sadly, a criminal investigation of Fauci and other medical doctors and scientists will most likely never happen under the leadership of the Biden administration, who will protect Fauci at all costs since they cheer for the same team.[36] Jill Biden even considers Fauci a hero—this speaks volumes as to where mainstream Democrats and the Biden administration's alliances lie.

Recall that President Trump received a significant amount of backlash for closing the border to China "too prematurely." And yet, he was constantly criticized for not acting quick enough. His critics cannot have it both ways. No matter what Trump did, he was going to be lambasted by MSM and the so-called health experts. We must not forget the early-on collusion and spread of misinformation between WHO and China through an-ever haunting Tweet: "Preliminary investigations conducted by the Chinese authorities have found no clear evidence of human-to-human transmission of the novel #coronavirus (2019-nCoV) identified in #Wuhan, #ChinaCN." [37] One must also not forget the scorn that the Trump administration received from MSM and the usual suspects (health experts, professors, Hollywood stars, Big Tech, etc.) for prudently ceasing funding to the NIH for coronavirus research and its ties to the Wuhan Institute of Virology because of "conspiracy theories." *ABC News* reporting has come back to haunt them and others supporting a false narrative:

> The Trump administration has pulled funding for a group of scientists studying coronaviruses in bats and the risk of their spillover into

35 The Epoch Times, "The first documentary movie on CCP virus, Tracking Down the Origin of the Wuhan Coronavirus."

36 Chalfant, "Jill Biden recognizes Fauci as an 'American hero'"; Samuels, "Biden 'very confident' in Fauci amid conservative attacks."

37 See Givas, "WHO haunted by old tweet saying China found no human transmission of coronavirus"; Hancock-Watts "U.S. President Trump criticized For Shutting Border to China."

> humans—the very kind of infection that started the COVID-19 pandemic—according to EcoHealth Alliance, the New York-based nonprofit organization conducting the research.
>
> The cancellation of the grant after more than a decade of work in this field seems to be tied to EcoHealth Alliance's partnership with the Wuhan Institute of Virology, the biomedical lab at the heart of conspiracy theories that the Chinese government created or unleashed the virus or the unproven thesis that the outbreak started with an accident because of faulty safety standards in the lab. [38]

They proceed to push their demonstrably false narrative even further:

> The president has taken a harder line on China in recent days, saying Thursday he has seen evidence that the Wuhan Institute is responsible for the outbreak, although he wasn't clear whether he believes it was somehow manufactured in the lab or the result of an accident. Most experts have told ABC News the first human infection—what's known a "zoonotic spillover"—is much more likely to have happened in the wild, where that kind of transmission occurs increasingly often.[39]

Nevertheless, in spite of Trump's halt to funding gain-of-function research, Fauci continued to funnel $7.5 million to Peter Daszak's EcoHealth Alliance. Fauci as the director of the NIAID, which is part of the NIH, headed by Francis Collins, will both have much to answer to. President Trump was astonished as to these recent findings, issuing the following statement on June 10, 2021:

> It is now unanimous, and I have been proven right (once again) that the initial World Health Organization Report on the Wuhan Lab was flawed and must be redone, this time by a truly transparent investigation. We were right about the China Virus from the beginning, and now the entire world sees it. This is why the Chinese Communist Party should pay $10 Trillion in global reparations for what they allowed to happen, the worst event in world history. Even here in the United States, the so-called experts like Dr. Fauci were wrong about the Wuhan Lab and China's role the entire time. Just think how bad things would have gotten if I followed Dr. Fauci's advice and never closed down travel from China (and other things)? Dr. Fauci likes to say that he is "science," when in fact he is merely science fiction![40]

38 Finnegan, "Trump admin pulls NIH grant for coronavirus research over ties to Wuhan lab at heart of conspiracy theories."

39 Finnegan, "Trump admin pulls NIH grant for coronavirus research over ties to Wuhan lab at heart of conspiracy theories."

40 Donald J. Trump, "Statement by Donald J. Trump, 45th President of the United States of America."

It is important to note that Ottawa is helping fund a COVID-19 research project with the Wuhan Lab.[41] This is terrifying since a substantive amount of evidence points towards the virus being manipulated within this lab in order to infect humans.[42] The ex-CDC director, Robert Redfield, publicly announced that he believed the virus had escaped from the Wuhan lab.[43] Even Dr. Anthony Fauci has recently admitted that this could very well be the case, after over a year of denial.[44] On May 11, 2021, *Fox News* anchor, Tucker Carlson, called for criminal investigations if the virus indeed was "leaked" from the Wuhan lab:

> But you've got to think that at least part of Fauci's authoritarian germ hysterical [sic] is a cover for something else. Could it be that Tony Fauci is trying to divert attention from himself and his own role in the COVID-19 pandemic?
>
> What do we mean by that? We can't recommend more strongly a new piece by Nicholas Wade, who for more than 50 years has been one of the preeminent science writers in the world. For 30 years, Nicholas Wade worked for the *New York Times*, he edited the science section there. But this piece did not run in the *New York Times*, it ran on *Medium*. And the piece explains where the virus almost certainly came from. In it, Wade makes it clear that, more than any other single American, Tony Fauci is responsible for the COVID-19 pandemic.
>
> Wade lays out a nearly insurmountable amount of evidence that this virus originated at the Wuhan Institute of Virology in Central China. We've raised this possibility from the early days of the pandemic. But this piece all but proves it. At the time the outbreak began last fall, the Wuhan lab was conducting experiments on how to make bat viruses infectious to human beings. Those experiments were funded by American tax dollars, the funding for those experiments was approved and directed by Tony Fauci in Washington. It's hard to believe that, but it's true, and the piece lays it out.
>
> Many of the Wuhan experiments fell under the direction of a Chinese researcher Shi Zheng-li. Known as the "bat lady," she was

41 Chase and Fife, "Ottawa funds COVID-19 research project that is collaborating with Wuhan virus lab"; Chase and Fife, "CSIS first alerted Ottawa to national-security concerns of two scientists at top disease laboratory."

42 This is something I wrote about back in 2020, even though many doctors and political leaders continue to deny this, see Scott Ventureyra, "Won't Get Fooled Again By The WHO: Thoughts On The COVID-19 Crisis and Related World Events," www.scottventureyra.com, June 9, 2020, https://www.scottventureyra.com/post/won-t-get-fooled-again-by-the-who. See also a recent book by Mercola and Cummins, *The Truth About COVID-19: Exposing The Great Reset, Lockdowns, Vaccine Passports, and the New Normal*, chapter 2.

43 Eustachewich, "Ex-CDC Director Robert Redfield believes COVID-19 came from Wuhan lab."

44 Sheehy, "Fauci admits COVID-19 could have come from Wuhan lab, butts heads with Rand Paul."

> China's leading expert on bat-born viruses. Her job was genetically engineering coronaviruses so that they infect human beings, and do so as easily as possible.
>
> The work, Wade notes, involved, "doing gain-of-function experiments designed to make coronaviruses infect human cells [and humanized mice]"... It's an amazing story. It is a shocking story. In a functional country, there would be a criminal investigation into Tony Fauci's role in the COVID pandemic that has killed millions and halted our country, changing it forever. So why isn't there a criminal investigation into Tony Fauci's role in this pandemic?[45]

According to science writer, Nicholas Wade, who Tucker Carlson's refers to, the evidence pointing to the virus originating in the Wuhan lab is eminently more plausible than the notion that it jumped from a bat to human. As he states in his excellent piece published on May 2, 2021, in *Medium*, titled: "Origin of Covid—Following the Clues: Did people or nature open Pandora's box at Wuhan?":

> If the case that SARS2 [SARS-Cov-2] originated in a lab is so substantial, why isn't this more widely known? As may now be obvious, there are many people who have reason not to talk about it. The list is led, of course, by the Chinese authorities. But virologists in the United States and Europe have no great interest in igniting a public debate about the gain-of-function experiments that their community has been pursuing for years... People round the world who have been pretty much confined to their homes for the last year might like a better answer than their media are giving them. Perhaps one will emerge in time. After all, the more months pass without the natural emergence theory gaining a shred of supporting evidence, the less plausible it may seem. Perhaps the international community of virologists will come to be seen as a false and self-interested guide. The common sense perception that a pandemic breaking out in Wuhan might have something to do with a Wuhan lab cooking up novel viruses of maximal danger in unsafe conditions could eventually displace the ideological insistence that whatever Trump said can't be true.
>
> And then let the reckoning begin.[46]

45 Hains "Tucker Carlson: If COVID-19 'Lab Leak' Theory Is True, We Need Criminal Investigations."

46 Wade, "Origin of Covid —Following the Clues: Did people or nature open Pandora's box at Wuhan?"

Back in April of 2020, *The Epoch Times*, in their documentary, "Tracking Down the Origin of the Wuhan Coronavirus," present persuasive evidence by a series of scientific experts and whistleblowers, that the virus originated in the Wuhan lab.[47] Unsurprisingly, the lying mainstream media made attempts to discredit *The Epoch Times* breaking story as "far right conspiracy theories."[48] At this point, people should not be asking if it is conspiracy that the virus originated and/or was manipulated in the Wuhan lab then unleashed ("escaped") into the world, but rather why organizations like the WHO, the Liberal Party of Canada, and others vociferously have denied it when the evidence points more convincingly in one direction.

Denials that the virus originated in the Wuhan lab continue to the present. It is worth considering the words of Tara Kartha (who served as the director of India's National Security Council Secretariat) regarding the interesting connections and widespread denials between the origin of COVID-19 and the Wuhan lab:

> Biological research and the secrecy around it is the aspect of focus in Nicholas Wade's article published in Bulletin of the Atomic Scientists. As he writes, from the beginning, there was denial at the highest levels from some unexpected quarters. The first was in *The Lancet*—one of the oldest journals of medical research—by a group of authors in March 2020, when the pandemic had just broken out. Even to a layman, it would have seemed that it was far too early for the group of authors to contemptuously dismiss 'conspiracy theories' that the virus was not of a natural origin.
>
> It turns out that *The Lancet* letter was drafted by Peter Daszak, President of the EcoHealth Alliance of New York, who's organisation funded corona virus research at the Wuhan lab. As is pointed out in Wade's article, any revelation of such a connection would have been criminal to say the least, if it was proved that the virus did escape from the lab. Unsurprisingly, Daszak was also part of the WHO team investigating the origins of the virus.
>
> Another burst of outrage came from a group of professors who also hurried to disprove, in an article, the 'lab created' theory on the grounds—simply put—that it was not of the most probably calculated design. The lead author Kristian G. Anderson is from the Scripps Research Institute, La Jolla, which specialises in biomedical research. It also has partnerships with Chinese labs and pharma companies. None of that is criminal. Especially when Scrippsis [sic] already in financial distress at the time. Besides, such collaborations

47 *The Epoch Times*, "The first documentary movie on CCP virus, Tracking Down the Origin of the Wuhan Coronavirus."

48 Rittiman, "Unsolicited 'The Epoch Times' paper spreads outlandish COVID-19 claims."

> are not restricted to just US labs. See, for instance, an account of Australian doctor Dominic Dwyer, who was part of the first WHO study, and who dismissed without any evidence presented that the virus had leaked from a lab.
>
> Dwyer's claim that the Wuhan lab seems to have been run well, and that nobody from the facility seemed to have fallen sick has now been disputed. Evidence of a dangerous virus escaping a lab—as it has in the past on what he calls "rare" occasions—would mean a death blow to labs everywhere. Funding is, after all, hard to come by. Then there is the nice hard cash involved. The Harvard professor Dr Charles Leiber who was arrested, together with two other Chinese, for collaborating quietly with the Wuhan University of Technology (WUT), was being paid roughly $50,000 per month, living expenses of up to 1,000,000 Chinese Yuan (approximately $158,000) and awarded $1.5 million to establish a research lab at WUT. He was also asked to 'cultivate' young teachers and Ph.D. students by organising international conferences.[49]

Fast forward to early September of 2021, *The Intercept* obtained over 900 pages of US funded research on the coronavirus.[50] Molecular biologist Richard Ebright at Rutgers University, according to *The Intercept*, concluded that the "viruses they constructed were tested for their ability to infect mice that were engineered to display human type receptors on their cell."[51] Ebright also stated on Twitter that:

> The materials confirm the grants supported the construction—in Wuhan—of novel chimeric SARS-related coronaviruses that combined a spike gene from one coronavirus with genetic information from another coronavirus, and confirmed the resulting viruses could infect human cells.[52]

It is now evident that both Anthony Fauci, director of the National Institute of Allergy and Infectious Diseases (NIAID), and his boss, the National Institutes of Health (NIH) director, Francis Collins, have been untruthful. They both claimed that the NIH was not providing financial support for the gain-of-function research or potential pandemic pathogen enhancement at Wuhan Institute of Virology (WIH). Consequently, it

49 Kartha, "Why the suspicion on China's Wuhan lab virus is growing. Read these new analyses."

50 Lerner and Hvistendahl, "New Details Emerge About Coronavirus Research at Chinese Lab."

51 Lerner and Hvistendahl, "New Details Emerge About Coronavirus Research at Chinese Lab."

52 Ebright, Twitter Post.

should come as no surprise that Francis Collins stepped down from his role as the NIH director. He claims the reason for his resignation is his belief that "no single person should serve in the position too long, and that it's time to bring in a new scientist to lead the NIH into the future."[53] One may be tempted to think that Collins was a pawn of Anthony Fauci, as some had claimed at the early onset of the pandemic. This may have seemed plausible back in March 2020, after all, Collins had been pushing the junk-DNA myth to support his views on theistic Darwinism for some time, in spite of the evidence; he's had papers published of his team, under his name, providing evidence contradicting his claims.[54] He has since then reassessed his position. Although there is no comparison in the seriousness of this situation with the other, I don't think he can claim ignorance here. It is highly doubtful this is the reason for his resignation. Collins has been involved with at least six different scandals which the media has not reported on:

- Francis Collins Advises Chinese Military Proxy-Linked Group Working Alongside COVID-19 Gene Storage Firm.
- Collins Admits Funding Wuhan Lab: 'We Had No Control Over What They Were Doing.'
- EVIDENCE: Fauci's Bosses Signed Research Deals With Chinese Communist Military Front.
- INVESTIGATION: US Has Funded Over 250 Studies for Chinese Communist Military Researchers.
- America Has Given Millions for 'Research' At Chinese Communist-Run Facilities Since COVID Outbreak.
- US National Institutes of Health Fires 54 Researchers As Ongoing Investigation Reveals 93% Failed to Disclose Links to Chinese Communist Party.[55]

It is disheartening to see Francis Collins, a self-proclaimed devout Christian, be embroiled in such corruption, but there is nothing new under the Sun, men of all stripes throughout history have been susceptible to deep sin and corruption. One wonders what the future holds for Collins and if he will be held fully accountable. The question also remains as to when his subordinates such

53 Fox, "Dr. Francis Collins to step down as head of NIH."

54 See my review of Woodward and Gills, *The Mysterious Epigenome: What Lies Beyond DNA* (2012), *Science et Esprit* 67:2 (2015), 304–308. I state in the review that: "Ironically, Collins' own research team was publishing a number of these papers that argue for a high degree of functionality in these non-protein [coding] areas."

55 Winters and Kassam, "6 Scandals The Media Won't Tell You About Outgoing NIH Director Francis Collins."

as Anthony Fauci, who is no stranger to corruption and medical malfeasance,[56] and Peter Daszak, will face any serious repercussions.

Curiously, years ago, I had reached out to Collins for an endorsement of my first book: *On the Origin of Consciousness*. At the time he had shown interest in the subject matter but politely declined because it would be a "conflict of interest" for him as the director of the NIH. And yet, he has had no issues polarizing, demonizing, and violating people's moral conscience,[57] while also being involved in multiple scandals with Communist China. Unfortunately, leading public Christian figures often succumb to greed, power, and/or lust—one need only think of the revelations made after Ravi Zacharias' death. These ordeals can greatly affect both the faithful and outsiders on their view of Christianity and Christians.

So, what can we glean from this? Massive corruption, coverups, and denials, rather than admitting where the evidence clearly points. One cannot help but wonder about the fact that world economy has been turned upside-down since March 2020, with millions of deaths and people's livelihoods affected, all the while China gains more economic strength and rapidly scales the world's global hierarchy. Throughout 2020 and 2021, Ontario, Canada dealt with futile lockdowns that have caused exceedingly more harm than good.

We have already seen how often health experts and organizations have lied and blundered. If anything, we should show hesitancy when it comes to many of the reckless claims that people have unthinkingly accepted. Inevitably, there will be gaps in knowledge because of the provisional nature of science and medicine, and the dissemination of blatant misinformation. Nevertheless, we must take seriously countervailing points to the mainstream narrative, especially considering how often they have erred.

56 This is an opinion piece written by playwriter and LGBTQ+ activist, Larry Kramer, who in 1999 didn't mince his words about Dr. Anthony Fauci's handling of AIDS treatment research:

> I have been screaming at the National Institutes of Health since I first visited your Animal House of Horrors in 1984. I called you monsters then and I called you idiots in my play, The Normal Heart, and now I call you murderers.
>
> You are responsible for supervising all government-funded AIDS treatment research programs. In the name of right, you make decisions that cost the lives of others. I call that murder.

See Larry, "An Open Letter to Dr. Anthony Fauci." For more documentation of Fauci's corruption and his persecution of Judy Mikovits, see Kent and Mikovits, *Plague: One Scientist's Intrepid Search for the Truth about Human Retroviruses and Chronic Fatigue Syndrome (ME/CFS), Autism, and Other Disease*; Heckenlively and Mikovits, *Plague of Corruption: Restoring Faith in the Promise of Science*; Winslow, "Dr. Judy Mikovits – Since 1984, Fauci has Been the Mastermind Behind Every Pandemic." See also for the most thorough documentation of Fauci's ongoing corruption and deceit: Kennedy Jr., *The Real Anthony Fauci: Bill Gates, Big Pharma, and the Global War on Democracy and Public Health*.

57 See the subsection in Chapter 42: "Goodbye to Reason and Morality."

On PCR Testing

There are three main types of tests used to diagnose COVID-19. First, a molecular test known as the Reverse-Transcriptase Polymerase Chain Reaction/ Real Time PCR (RT-PCR/RT-qPCR) which is meant to detect the nucleic or RNA component of the virus. Second, an antigen test (rapid antigen test) which detects proteins in the virus.[58] Third, an antibody test which can determine if you've had COVID-19 in the past but can be inaccurate to test for current infection.[59]

The PCR is the most important and widely used test for determining whether someone has COVID-19. It is described by the media and governments as the "gold standard" for diagnosing COVID-19, since "it provides a more definitive answer as to whether an individual has the virus in their body."[60] Medical microbiologist Jonathan Gubbay, of Public Health Ontario, has said that the PCR test is used "as the gold standard of testing for COVID-19 because it is able to successfully detect tiny amounts of the virus (sensitivity) with a low chance for error (accuracy) compared to other types of lab tests."[61]

How does the PCR test work? PCR tests are aimed to find genetic material. It is important to note that coronaviruses such as SARS-CoV-2 do not have any DNA and, as such, a first step in testing for the virus is to convert the virus's RNA into DNA through what is known as reverse transcription.[62] This is done because DNA has a much higher stability than RNA, since RNA is more susceptible to hydrolysis and degradation. PCR machines produce millions of copies of the DNA by running multiple "cycles,"[63] something akin to a washing machine. This process is known as amplification and crucial to find the most minimal amounts of DNA. The more cycles that are managed, the more copies of DNA are produced. It doubles every time that it is copied thereby making it easier to find DNA. However, if the DNA cannot be duplicated then either the sample of the virus is so minimal it cannot be detected or there is simply no virus at all.

This leads to another related question: What are cycle threshold values? The cycle threshold (Ct) value is the number of cycles undertaken for the PCR test

58 Mayo Clinic, "COVID-19 diagnostic testing." This form of testing is considered much less reliable than the PCR test, but its use is being encouraged more so than before.

59 The Healthline Editorial Team and Fraley, "What's the difference between antigens and antibodies?"

60 Ask a Scientist Staff, "Why qPCR is the gold standard for COVID-19 testing."

61 Public Health Ontario, "Explained: COVID-19 PCR testing and cycle thresholds."

62 Santa Clara County Public Health, "FAQs about CT Values from COVID-19 PCR Tests: A Response for LTCFs."

63 Santa Clara County Public Health, "FAQs about CT Values from COVID-19 PCR Tests: A Response for LTCFs."

to detect the virus.[64] It does not give the actual amount of virus, but it allegedly gives an estimate of how much may have been in the sample. For instance, if the Ct value is under 30 it is an indication that the virus was easily found and that the sample probably had a significant amount of the virus.[65] This would not be dissimilar to using the zoom function in your web browser if the item only requires a little bit of zoom, then it was larger to begin with than if it required a large percentage of zooming.

Surely, the PCR test must have a high degree of accuracy and these false positives are either fabricated or anomalous occurrences. But is that really the case? The unreliability of PCR tests is nothing new—this been known in scientific literature for years. For instance, in 2006, PCR tests for a particular coronavirus (CoV-OC43 (HCoV-OC43)) responded to another coronavirus (SARS-CoV).[66] In 2007, overconfidence in PCR tests led to a false epidemic of whooping cough.[67] In April of 2020, a study from China showed that the same patient could receive two distinct results from the identical test on the same day.[68]

Given that PCR tests have a history of being unreliable, one would expect the test to produce a substantial number of false positives through reacting with DNA material that is not particular to SARS-CoV-2. There are a number of examples, aside from the one listed above, that corroborate this. For instance, the late Tanzanian President John Magufuli, in order to test the validity of the PCR test kits, submitted samples from a goat, pawpaw, and motor oil for PCR testing but assigned the samples with a name, sex, and age, all came back positive for the virus.[69] Magufuli, who had a PhD in chemistry, would have understood how the PCR testing worked and, as such, questioned the accuracy and legitimacy of the testing process. He was also very vocal against globalism and the COVID agenda since he was keen on eradicating internal corruption and outside global influence from Tanzania. He also questioned the potential legitimacy and efficacy of the viral vector (Johnson & Johnson's Janssen COVID-19 vaccine) and mRNA COVID vaccine (Pfizer).[70] Unsurprisingly, *The Guardian* published a piece, supported by the

64 Santa Clara County Public Health, "FAQs about CT Values from COVID-19 PCR Tests: A Response for LTCFs."

65 Santa Clara County Public Health, "FAQs about CT Values from COVID-19 PCR Tests: A Response for LTCFs."

66 Patrick, et al., "An Outbreak of Human Coronavirus OC43 Infection and Serological Cross-reactivity with SARS Coronavirus."

67 Kolata, "Faith in quick test leads to epidemic that wasn't."

68 Li et al., "Stability issues of RT-PCR testing of SARS-CoV-2 for hospitalized patients clinically diagnosed with COVID-19."

69 Reuters Staff, "President queries Tanzania coronavirus kits after goat test"; Kashiwagi, "President of Tanzania exposed the inaccuracy of PCR Test."

70 Dahir, "Tanzania's president says 'vaccines don't work,' earning a rebuff from the W.H.O."

Bill & Melinda Gates foundation, demonizing the Tanzanian leader as an anti-vaxxer who was "hell bent against science, facts and logic," according to the activist journalist Vava Tampa.[71] Magufuli took the PCR test to task and was accurate on predicting the inefficacy of the COVID vaccines considering they do not stop transmission. Close to three weeks after this hit piece, Magufuli mysteriously disappeared on February 27, 2021, and was pronounced dead on March 17, 2021. The lying mainstream media said he died from COVID-19 despite any corroborating evidence and emphasized that he was a COVID denier. He was then replaced by Samia Suluhu Hassan, who is an associate of the World Economic Forum.[72]

It is worth noting that on November 11, 2020, a Portuguese judge in the Lisbon Court of Appeal ruled that the PCR tests should not be used because of their unreliability. Moreover, these "judges had ruled against the PCR test being used in order to diagnose and quarantine so-called infected people, 4 German tourists in this case."[73] The judges quoted a paper from *The Lancet*, where the authors emphasize that:

> Any diagnostic test result should be interpreted in the context of the pretest probability of disease. For COVID-19, the pretest probability assessment includes symptoms, previous medical history of COVID-19 or presence of antibodies, any potential exposure to COVID-19, and likelihood of an alternative diagnosis. When low pretest probability exists, positive results should be interpreted with caution and a second specimen tested for confirmation.[74]

The authors concluded that: "To summarise, false-positive COVID-19 swab test results might be increasingly likely in the current epidemiological climate in the UK, with substantial consequences at the personal, health system, and societal levels (panel)."[75]

This leads us to ask, what difference do the cycle thresholds make in discerning the presence of SARS-CoV-2? Well, the judges in Lisbon also cited another important study co-authored by Didier Raoult, which examines the connection between cycles and the detection of the virus's genetic material. According to this study, if you increase the cycles to 35 and above, at this point the probability of testing for a false positive is 97 percent or above.[76]

71 Tampa, "It's time for Africa to rein in Tanzania's anti-vaxxer president."

72 World Economic Forum, "Samia Suluhu Hassan."

73 See TLB Staff, "Those Portuguese Judges Ruling Against PCR Test Got Official Backlash."

74 Surkova, et al., "False-positive COVID-19 results: hidden problems and costs."

75 Surkova, et al., "False-positive COVID-19 results: hidden problems and costs."

76 Jaafar, et al., "Correlation Between 3790 Quantitative Polymerase Chain Reaction–Positives Samples and Positive Cell Cultures, Including 1941 Severe Acute Respiratory Syndrome Coronavirus 2 Isolates."

Kary B. Mullis, who alongside Michael Smith won the 1993 Nobel Prize in Chemistry for his role in creating the PCR method,[77] had some damning statements about the reliability of PCR tests in viral detection. It is worth noting the obvious, namely that Mullis would not have been aware of the PCR test being utilized for SARS-CoV-2 since he died on August 7, 2019. Mullis never intended the PCR test to be used as a diagnostic test. Mullis once stated that: "If you have to go more than 40 cycles to amplify a single-copy gene, there is something seriously wrong with your PCR."[78] Similarly, The Minimum Information for Publication of Quantitative Real-Time PCR Experiments (MIQE) guidelines corroborates Mullis' statement: "[Ct] values > 40 are suspect because of the implied low efficiency and generally should not be reported."[79] Even Dr. Anthony Fauci, in an interview, admits that anything above a cycle threshold of 35 has a "miniscule" chance of being replication competent.[80] Many other scientists confirm that any threshold above 35 is much too sensitive, as Dr. Juliet Morrison explains: "Any test with a cycle threshold above 35 is too sensitive… I'm shocked that people would think that 40 [cycles] could represent a positive… A more reasonable cutoff would be 30 to 35."[81] Dr. Michael Mina in the same article indicates that Ct should be under 30: "Dr. Mina said he would set the figure at 30, or even less. Those changes would mean the amount of genetic material in a patient's sample would have to be 100-fold to 1,000-fold that of the current standard for the test to return a positive result—at least, one worth acting on."[82] Nevertheless, the National Health Service (NHS) in England set the limit at 40 cycles.[83]

The inventor Kary Mullis, despite claims to the contrary, indicated that the PCR-test was not meant to be used as a diagnostic tool to detect illnesses or accurately test for the presence of retroviruses. Videos that have surfaced were from the 1990s and in the context of HIV and AIDS. Mullis was known for his controversial statements that are aimed to refute the hypothesis that HIV causes AIDS: "The HIV/AIDS hypothesis is one hell of a mistake."[84] In a 1994 interview, Mullis stated the following:

77 The Nobel Prize, "The Nobel Prize in Chemistry: Kary B. Mullis."

78 Innis and Gelfand, "Optimization of PCRs." In *PCR Protocols: A Guide to Methods and Applications.*

79 Bustin, "The MIQE Guidelines: Minimum Information for Publication of Quantitative Real-Time PCR Experiments."

80 Racaniello, "TWiV 641: COVID-19 with Dr. Anthony Fauci."

81 Mandavilli, "Your Coronavirus Test Is Positive. Maybe It Shouldn't Be."

82 Mandavilli, "Your Coronavirus Test Is Positive. Maybe It Shouldn't Be."

83 NHS, "Guidance and Standard Operating Procedure COVID-19 Virus Testing in NHS Laboratories."

84 Goodson, "Questioning the HIV-AIDS Hypothesis: 30 Years of Dissent." (Shortly after Mullis's death on August 7, 2019.)

> I think it's simple logic. It doesn't require that anyone have any specialized knowledge of the field. The fact is that if there were evidence that HIV causes AIDS—if anyone who was in fact a specialist in that area could write a review of the literature, in which a number of scientific studies were cited that either singly or as a group could support the hypothesis that HIV is the probable cause of AIDS-somebody would have written it. There's no paper, nor is there a review mentioning a number of papers that all taken together would support that statement. That's a review that's been requested long ago, in print, by Duesberg, of the leading lights in the field. In fact, it was in-I don't remember the exact issue, but it was mentioned in Science that Duesberg brought this up at a meeting, and these guys, I believe it was Howard Temmin and Smoky Blattner and David Baltimore, to name a few, said there will be such a paper. Do you remember?[85]

Like Larry Kramer, Judy Mikovits, and Robert F. Kennedy Jr., Mullis was very vocal about Fauci's corruption and deceit:

> What is it about humanity that it wants to go to the all detail to stop and listen? Guys like Fauci get up there and start talking, and he doesn't know anything really about anything, and I'd say that to his face. Nothing.
>
> The man thinks you can take a blood sample and stick it in an electron microscope and if it's got a virus in there, you will know it. He doesn't understand electron microscopy and he doesn't understand medicine. He should not be in a position like he's in.
>
> Most of those guys up there on the top are just total administrative people and they don't know anything about what's going on with the bottom. You know, those guys have got an agenda, which is not what we would like them to have, being that we pay for them to take care of our health in some way.
>
> They've got a personal kind of agenda. They make up their own rules as they go. They change them when they want to and they smugly like Tony Fauci does not mind going on television in front of the people, who pay his salary, and lie directly into the camera.[86]

There is no doubt that Mullis saw firsthand the unbelievable corruption of public health bureaucrats like Fauci, and corrupt medical institutions like the CDC. He thought that if you follow where the money comes from, then

85 VirusSmyth, Interview with Kary Mullis, Rethinking AIDS March/April 1994.

86 Uroš Cerar, "PCR INVENTOR KARY MULLIS TALKS ABOUT ANTHONY FAUCI 'HE DOESN'T KNOW ANYTHING REALLY ABOUT ANYTHING!'"; Black Pegasus, "PCR TEST INVENTOR Kary Banks Mullis opinion on DR. FAUCI"; PoorRichards News, "Fauci in News Today with His Emails Revealing Lies."

you'll know the agenda, since these compromised individuals and institutions do not care about truth.[87] Based on what we can judge from interviews and public statements made by Mullis, we can deduce that he would have been up and arms about how this whole COVID fiasco has been handled and how his PCR test has been misused. Mullis was very clear in an interview, that he thought debate and discussion is fundamental to scientific understanding and progress—as his words about Fauci clearly illustrate:

> [T]he vast majority of [humans] do not possess the ability to judge who is and who isn't a really good scientist. I mean that's a problem. That's a problem, that's a main problem actually with science I'd say in the century because the science is being judged by people [in reference to peer review] funding is being done by people who don't understand it. Okay, who do we trust? Fauci doesn't know enough to get on television with somebody who knows a little bit about this stuff and debate them. He could easily do it, because he has been asked and I have had a lot of people—the President of the University of South Carolina ask Fauci about if he'd come down there and debate me on stage in front of the student body because I wanted somebody who was from the other side to come down there and balance my, because I felt like well these guys can listen to me but I need to have somebody else down here that's going to tell me the other side but Fauci didn't want to do it.[88]

In an interview that has gone viral now, Mullis made some damaging statements on the veracity and the purpose of the PCR method. Although at the time he was speaking about the suitability of the method to detect HIV and diagnose AIDS, there's no reason to think that these statements have no applicability to SARS-CoV-2 and COVID-19:

> I don't think you can misuse PCR. [It is] the results; the interpretation of it. If they can find this virus in you at all—and with PCR, if you do it well, you can find almost anything in anybody.[89]

He then went on to say:

> It starts making you believe in the sort of Buddhist notion that everything is contained in everything else. If you can amplify one single molecule up to something you can really measure, which PCR can do,

87 Uroš Cerar, "PCR INVENTOR KARY MULLIS TALKS ABOUT ANTHONY FAUCI "HE DOESN'T KNOW ANYTHING REALLY ABOUT ANYTHING!"; State of the Nation, "Coronavirus: The Truth about PCR Test Kit from the Inventor and Other Experts – Video."

88 PoorRichards News, "Fauci in News Today with His Emails Revealing Lies."

89 Corrochio, "Kary Mullis Explains the PCR Test."

> then there is just very few molecules that you don't have at least one single one of in your body.[90]

In this question-and-answer period, he goes on to address the meaningfulness of an interpretation of a reading of a PCR test—something that is still applicable with respect to COVID "cases"[91] since it's been the justification for draconian measures taken by governments such as lockdowns, mask mandates, vaccine mandates, and passports:

> That could be thought of as a misuse: to claim that it [a PCR test] is meaningful. It tells you something about nature and what is there. To test for that one thing and say it has a special meaning is, I think, the problem. The measurement for it is not exact; it is not as good as the measurement for apples. The tests are based on things that are invisible and the results are inferred in a sense. It allows you to take a miniscule amount of anything and make it measurable and then talk about it.[92]

Although the PCR test has advanced since the time of Mullis's statements, should we doubt that the general principles behind his concerns have altered at all? Mullis indirectly, but by implication, addresses the issues of cases, which is relevant to PCR tests and COVID:

> PCR is just a process that allows you to make a whole lot of something out of something. It doesn't tell you that you are sick, or that the thing that you ended up with was going to hurt you or anything like that.[93]

There is no doubt that Mullis was a free thinker who questioned authority, dogmatism, and authentically cared about scientific truth. There is absolutely no reason to think that his position on SARS-CoV-2 would be any different, despite the claims of his wife,[94] unless he had compromised his worldview regarding the integrity of science and his strongly held ethical principles. Unquestionably, he would be furious to see the unprecedented censorship

90 Corrochio, "Kary Mullis Explains the PCR Test."

91 See James, "PCR Inventor: 'It doesn't tell you that you are sick'." James offers a strong refutation of the fact checkers' claims that Mullis's comments have been taken out of context with respect to the efficacy and purpose of PCR testing.

92 Corrochio, "Kary Mullis Explains the PCR Test."

93 Corrochio, "Kary Mullis Explains the PCR Test."

94 Nancy Mullis seems to claim that Mullis would not have questioned the COVID narrative, this seems to be naïve since there are so many glaring inconsistencies, falsehoods, and the censorship that has been implemented throughout the pandemic. Please note that questioning her thinking on this does not give credence to the accusation that he was murdered by Fauci. See Alex Diaz, "Widow of scientist who invented PCR test hits out at covid denier conspiracists who claim he was murdered by Fauci."

of dissenting scientific and medical voices to the likes he could have never imagined. Science has been politicized and absolutely corrupted in mind-boggling ways throughout this COVID fiasco. Indeed, contra his wife, he would have had even more contemptuous things to say about Fauci, the WHO, CDC, the medical and scientific establishment, and world governments, than he did when he was alive.

In addition to all the aforementioned argumentation and evidence presented against the accuracy, efficacy, and validity of the PCR test is an external peer review that was done by former Pfizer chief scientist Michael Yeadon and 21 other scientists who are part of the international consortium of life science-scientists. The title of this review is: "External peer review of the RTPCR test to detect SARS-CoV-2 reveals 10 major scientific flaws at the molecular and methodological level: consequences for false positive results" (also known as Corman-Drosten Review Report).[95] In their review they critique a paper titled: "Detection of 2019 novel coronavirus (2019-nCoV) by real-time RT-PCR" which was published in the journal *Euro Surveillance* in 2020.[96] The authors of the external review have requested the editorial board at *Euro Surveillance* to retract the paper.[97] Despite all the scientific flaws and ethical breaches enumerated in the critical review, the paper remains published on *Euro Surveillance*. The authors of the review outline the rationale of their critique as follows:

> The published RT-qPCR protocol for detection and diagnostics of 2019-nCoV and the manuscript suffer from numerous technical and scientific errors, including insufficient primer design, a problematic and insufficient RT-qPCR protocol, and the absence of an accurate test validation. Neither the presented test nor the manuscript itself fulfils the requirements for an acceptable scientific publication. Further, serious conflicts of interest of the authors are not mentioned. Finally, the very short timescale between submission and acceptance of the publication (24 hours) signifies that a systematic peer review process was either not performed here, or of problematic poor quality. We provide compelling evidence of several scientific inadequacies, errors and flaws.[98]

International trial lawyer Dr. Reiner Fuellmich has rightfully said that "[t]he whole pandemic is based on a completely unreliable PCR test that produces

95 See Borger, et al., "External peer review of the RTPCR test to detect SARS-CoV-2 reveals 10 major scientific flaws at the molecular and methodological level: consequences for false positive results."

96 Corman, et al., "Detection of 2019 novel coronavirus (2019-nCoV) by real-time RT-PCR."

97 See Borger, et al., "Retraction request letter to Eurosurveillance editorial board."

98 Borger, et al., "External peer review of the RTPCR test to detect SARS-CoV-2 reveals 10 major scientific flaws at the molecular and methodological level: consequences for false positive results."

high percentages of false positives, and is not able to accurately detect any kind of infection. All the lockdowns, mask mandates and vaccines are based on this fraud."[99] Indeed, the PCR test is the Achilles heel of the whole pseudo-pandemic. Thus, The Corman-Drosten report's assays are standard to virtually every COVID PCR test throughout the globe. This should bring into serious question the validity of every PCR test. Coincidentally, on July 21, 2021, the CDC urged laboratories to transition from Real-Time PCR COVID tests to a new FDA approved kit that can distinguish between Sars-CoV-2 and influenza viruses.[100] This was supposed to be in effect as of January 1, 2022. It is interesting to note that the PCR test was never granted full FDA approval. More accurately, it was granted use under the Emergency Use Authorization.[101] The question arises: How often was someone diagnosed with an influenza virus or even another coronavirus strain which was deemed a positive test for SARS-CoV-2? Contrary to claims that influenza "disappeared" throughout 2020 and 2021 due to mask wearing, physical distancing, and lockdowns,[102] given the ineffectiveness of such measures, the best explanation would be that this is because the COVID-19 cases may have been influenza, another coronavirus or perhaps just an absolute false positive. On December 29, the director of the CDC, Rochelle Walensky, announced in a White House press briefing that the PCR test can register positive even after the infection has subsided: "...people can remain PCR positive for up to 12 weeks after infection and long after they are transmissible and infectious."[103] By this admission, the CDC is basically telling us that there have been millions of false positives. Obviously, CDC could not have made such a huge mistake, but that's the point, it wasn't a mistake, just another deception that they cannot cover up any longer.

One thing is clear, the so-called "gold standard" for COVID-19 testing is nowhere close to what it has been touted to be. Moreover, these fraudulent "cases" generated by millions upon millions of false positives have been the justification for much of the draconian measures and the unnecessary COVID-19 injection rollout.

Symptomatic, Asymptomatic, and Pre-symptomatic Spread

In June 2020, the WHO claimed that COVID-19 rarely spreads through asymptomatic people. A day later, in the face of backlash, the WHO retracted

99 Fuellmich, "Scientific Evidence that Covid is Crime Against Humanity."
100 CDC, "Lab Alert: Changes to CDC RT-PCR for SARS-CoV-2 Testing."
101 "Lab Alert: Changes to CDC RT-PCR for SARS-CoV-2 Testing."
102 Peek, "Flu has disappeared for more than a year."
103 Stieber, "Walensky: PCR Tests Can Remain Positive for up to 12 Weeks."

their statement. [104] In a study carried out by the *Annals of Internal Medicine*, it is suggested that through random sampling that 50 percent of carriers of SARS-CoV-2 are asymptomatic. The study concluded that: "[a] substantial but wide-ranging proportion of persons with a SARS-CoV-2 infection are asymptomatic."[105] Nevertheless, this poses a serious problem: how do we distinguish between someone who carries the virus and is asymptomatic with someone who doesn't carry the virus? Adding to this confusion is the distinction between presymptomatic and asymptomatic. Obviously, one is unable to tell the difference between the two[106] nor the difference with someone who doesn't carry the virus. Without being tested it is virtually impossible to know. That would be under the unwarranted assumption that the testing is trustworthy. But we have good reasons to be skeptical of the WHO, CDC, and other such organizations. And yet, a study published in the journal of *Emerging Infectious Diseases* supports early quarantining of healthy individuals and, as a result, lockdowns of the likes we have experienced these past two years, argues that:

> In this cluster of COVID-19 cases, little to no transmission occurred from asymptomatic case-patients. Presymptomatic transmission was more frequent than symptomatic transmission. The serial interval was short; very short intervals occurred.
>
> In conclusion, our study suggests that asymptomatic cases are unlikely to contribute substantially to the spread of SARS-CoV-2. COVID-19 cases should be detected and managed early to quarantine close contacts immediately and prevent presymptomatic transmissions.[107]

This article, if anything, is a justification to push forward more PCR testing.

The Myth of Asymptomatic Transfer

The vast majority of COVID infections have been labeled as asymptomatic. In March of 2020, in Italy, at least 50 percent to 75 percent of positive COVID-19 tests had no symptoms.[108] Similarly, according to a study in the UK, 86.1

104 Miller, "WHO backtracks on claim that asymptomatic spread of COVID-19 is 'very rare'."

105 Oran and Topol, "Proportion of SARS-CoV-2 Infections That Are Asymptomatic: A Systematic Review."

106 Willis, "What's the difference between asymptomatic and presymptomatic spread of coronavirus?"

107 Bender, et al., "Analysis of Asymptomatic and Presymptomatic Transmission in SARS-CoV-2 Outbreak, Germany, 2020."

108 Reguly, "Italy's coronavirus fatalities overtake China's, and the government prolongs the tight quarantine."

percent were reported to have no symptoms.[109] It is impossible to tell the difference between a false-positive test and an asymptomatic case.

The head of the WHO's emerging diseases and zoonoses unit, Dr. Maria Van Kerkhove, concluded in June of 2020 that from the available data it is "very rare" that an asymptomatic individual passes the virus to another.[110] According to a meta-analysis of 54 studies with 77,758 participants, published on December 14, 2020 in the *Journal of the American Medical Association* (JAMA), it was found that asymptomatic carriers had 0.7 percent chance of infecting people within their own homes. Likewise, in 2009, researchers studying the asymptomatic and presymptomatic transfer of influenza observed that:

> We performed a systematic review of published studies describing the relationship between viral shedding and disease transmission. Based on the available literature, we found that there is scant, if any, evidence that asymptomatic or presymptomatic individuals play an important role in influenza transmission. As such, recent articles concerning pandemic planning, some using transmission modeling, may have overestimated the effect of presymptomatic or asymptomatic influenza transmission.[111]

Even though COVID-19 is considered to be more contagious than influenza, the available evidence for asymptomatic transmission of SARS-CoV-2 is negligible.

Continued Absurdity or the Crumbling of the Narrative?

New public health policy measures to come under the pretext of the spread of the Omicron variant. It is the perfect opportunity for governments to backtrack their absurd policies. Ontario's "top doctor" Kieran Moore made several sweeping statements that bring about change regarding the PCR test, COVID-19 symptoms, and isolation: "If you have symptoms of COVID-19 and are not eligible for a PCR test, and do not have access to a rapid antigen test, you should assume that you have COVID-19 and isolate."[112] Then, on the required isolation period, he added: "based on growing evidence that generally healthy people with COVID-19 are most infectious for the two days

109 Petersen and Phillips, "Three Quarters of People with SARS-CoV-2 Infection are Asymptomatic: Analysis of English Household Survey Data."

110 Feuer and Higgins-Dunn, "Asymptomatic spread of coronavirus is 'very rare,' WHO says."

111 Patrozou and Mermel, "Does Influenza Transmission Occur from Asymptomatic Infection or Prior to Symptom Onset?"

112 Forestell, "In-class learning to resume January 5 as Ministry announces sweeping changes due to Omicron."

before their symptoms develop, and for three days after their symptoms [have developed]." And restrictions continue for the "fully vaccinated":[113]

> If you have been exposed to someone who has tested positive for COVID-19 and you are fully vaccinated, have no symptoms, and don't live with a positive case, you are advised to continue to monitor for symptoms for 10 days from the time that you interacted last with that individual and adhere to all Public Health measures when outside your home.[114]

Why weren't these measures taken in the first place? Was it because of ignorance, incompetence, malfeasance, control? It's hard to say, but whatever the case may be, people should begin to resist the recommendations of "top doctors" who are more accurately described as medical "bottom feeders."

With Vs. From COVID

If we can't trust the PCR tests, then how can we trust the numbers reported of hospitalization and deaths? Without an autopsy report how can we possibly know the death was from COVID? The answer is: because they tested positive for COVID from a PCR test or a rapid antigen test. We know these can't be trusted. It is up to physicians and coroners to decide whether someone has died with or from COVID when they write down the cause on the death certificate. The number of people that should be registered as dying from COVID should have COVID as the primary cause of death. However, often times, COVID-related deaths will include other causes and comorbidities.[115] It may not be an easy task and it would require further investigation to determine which it was from. To complicate matters worse, governments have incentivized hospitals and doctors to list COVID as a primary reason for death. Former director of the CDC, Robert Redfield, has admitted that COVID-19 cases have been inflated because hospitals receive monetary gain for reporting deaths as such.[116]

It is interesting to see the current CDC director, Rochelle Walensky, makes a point of the distinction between "with" and "from" when asked about those who have died from COVID after being inoculated. This seems like a coverup

113 Forestell, "In-class learning to resume January 5 as Ministry announces sweeping changes due to Omicron."

114 Forestell, "In-class learning to resume January 5 as Ministry announces sweeping changes due to Omicron."

115 Trabsky and Hempton, "'Died from' or 'died with' COVID-19? We need a transparent approach to counting coronavirus deaths."

116 Fussell, "CDC director agrees hospitals have monetary incentive to inflate COVID-19 data."

for the vaccine. On the one hand, authorities and the media want to argue that the primary cause is most likely than not COVID before the vaccine rollout, but now with the vaccine rollout, if the person contracts COVID while being inoculated then it could be "from" or "with" COVID, but the vaccine is not considered as a primary cause.[117]

Has SARS-CoV-2 Been Isolated/Purified?

Thus far we have examined the possibility as to whether the virus originated and was engineered/manipulated at the Wuhan Institute of Virology, and that it escaped from the lab, versus the notion that it emerged in nature and then was transmitted at a wet market infecting said patient zero. We also observed that the PCR tests do not function adequately to diagnose the virus in question. Evidence was also brought forth that asymptomatic transfer is lacking. So, this leads us to the question as whether SARS-CoV-2 exists. To be sure, there is a virus that is infecting people but that could be an influenza virus, or a different coronavirus strain which produces similar symptoms that are being attributed to SARS-CoV-2. In examining this idea further, we must consider whether the virus has been isolated/purified.

The first important point to make clear is that if COVID-19 is not caused by a biological agent, then it cannot be a contagious disease. A virus is a particle of DNA or RNA and cannot replicate itself, it needs to invade and parasite a cell for this purpose. A damaged cell by toxic substances or electromagnetic (EM) waves eliminate/extrudes particles of damaged proteins (exosomes) that, under the microscope, can look like a virus and produce false positive PCR results.

According to the official narrative, the pathogen that causes COVID-19 disease is SARS- CoV-2. Nevertheless, to this date this biological agent has not been purified or isolated by any laboratory around the world. Thus, the Koch's postulates, which are fundamental to establishing the criteria for establishing that a microorganism causes a disease, cannot be reproduced. The Koch's postulates are as follows:

- The microorganism must be found in diseased but not healthy individuals.
- The microorganism must be cultured from the diseased individual.
- Inoculation of a healthy individual with the cultured microorganism must recapitulated the disease.

117 Henney, "CDC director criticized for now differentiating between dying 'from' vs. dying 'with' COVID-19."

- The microorganism must be re-isolated from the inoculated, diseased individual and matched to the original microorganism.[118]

Now ponder the following: is it not merely conceivable, but even plausible, that there may not be a SARS-CoV-2 virus? This is what conspiracy realist, David Icke has been claiming since April 6, 2020, on London Real with interviewer Brian Rose.[119] In light of this, one would expect the number of deaths to remain rather stable throughout the US and the world in 2020. For example, the number of deaths in the US did not increase throughout first year of the pandemic in 2020, but in fact decreased.[120] However, oddly, the number of deaths have increased in 2021, coinciding with the mass vaccination roll-out.[121] Furthermore, it is interesting to note that according to the government of British Columbia, the number of hospitalizations and hospitalizations with intensive care decreased from April 1, 2020, to March 31,2021 in comparison to previous years.[122] This is significant since the narrative has led us to believe that there was an increase in deaths and hospitalizations throughout the first year of the pandemic. Moreover, people would expect deaths and hospitalizations to decrease with the rollout of the COVID-19 vaccine. The evidence suggests otherwise. This has led some like Icke to be skeptical of not only the existence of the virus, but also the safety of the so-called vaccines. Now consider the following thoughts of freelance investigative reporter, Jon Rappaport:

> Question: How do you prevent a disease that has no cause? Get back to me after contemplating this for 10 years. The so-called disease, COVID, is touted as the result of a virus, but the virus doesn't exist. Nevertheless, a vaccine aimed at beefing up the immune system against the virus that doesn't exist is heralded as a miracle. There is also a test for the virus that doesn't exist. People fear the virus that doesn't exist. Whole countries are locked down to stop the spread of the virus that doesn't exist. People wear masks to stop the transmission of the virus that doesn't exist. People with no symptoms are called cases of the disease caused by the virus that doesn't exist. The vaccine can't stop the transmission of the virus that doesn't exist. The federal database lists over a million injuries reported after the vaccination which was designed to prevent the disease caused by the virus that doesn't exist. People who refuse the vaccination

118 Segre, "What does it take to satisfy Koch's postulates two centuries later? Microbial genomics and Propionibacteria acnes."

119 See London Real, "THE CORONAVIRUS CONSPIRACY: HOW COVID-19 WILL SEIZE YOUR RIGHTS & DESTROY OUR ECONOMY – DAVID ICKE."; London Real, "ROSE/ICKE 6: THE VINDICATION."

120 See for a sample in the US: Snapp, "Did the US Mortality Rate Increase in 2020-2021?"

121 Howell, "More COVID Deaths in 2021 than in 2020."

122 See BC Ministry of Health, "Number of Hospitalizations and Hospitalizations with Intensive Care."

> designed to prevent the disease caused by the virus that doesn't exist are called criminals or even terrorists. The virus that doesn't exist will spread at a small party in a person's home, but the virus that doesn't exist will detour around waves of immigrants coming into the country.
>
> The virus that doesn't exist was created in a lab.
>
> The overwhelming percentage of people who die from infection by the virus that doesn't exist are the elderly, who already have several long-standing serious health problems and have been treated for decades with toxic drugs, and are then given more toxic drugs to kill the virus that doesn't exist and are sedated with powerful drugs and put on breathing ventilators—a lethal treatment. There are at least two variants of the virus that doesn't exist. There are doctors who heavily criticize the current vaccines, but claim that a safe and successful vaccine can be developed to prevent the disease caused by the virus that doesn't exist.
>
> Other than all of the above, the global public COVID policy is quite sane.[123]

I don't know if this is the case at all, most of this book assumes the existence of SARS-CoV-2 at face value. Are Icke and Rappaport onto something or out-to-lunch? I have had the same thoughts myself; his explanation is coherent but whether it is the case or not would require even further investigation. However, if it is the case, all this talk about the origin of the virus is smoke and mirrors. It would make sense of the false positives of the PCR and antigen tests. The harmfulness of masks and lockdowns, etc.

But why are high credentialed doctors like Robert Malone and Peter McCullough fighting a narrative that is untrue? What is true is that the vaccines are causing harm and do not fulfill their purpose. Here are some thoughts by Enrique Ventureyra on the issue:

> I have listened to Robert Malone's interview with Joe Rogan on Spotify. It is excellent, but I have reservations about Malone's line of thinking which supports the unproven pathogen/spike protein theory and it totally ignores the presence of graphene oxide nanotubes in the vaccines, as well as the environmental theory which fits much better in the globalist agenda. Mind and emotions control via 5G (the internet of bodies) as well as the progressive transhumanist transformation included in the Globalist Agenda 2030.
>
> Dr. McCullough similarly centers his narrative on the unproven existence of the SARS-CoV-2 pathogen. In addition, both authorities

123 Jon Rappaport, "Zen Koan for the virus." Jon Rappaport's Blog, January 14, 2022. https://blog.nomorefakenews.com/2022/01/14/zen-koan-for-the-virus/.

> claim having recovered from Covid-19 infection and support the existence of Covid variants. I remain puzzled by their narrative.[124]

I would add that McCullough and Malone leave out many details and speculations about the motives of others because they do not want to lose credibility with their growing audiences. They also do not want to give more ammunition to the "fact checkers." Finally, I believe that they may fear lawsuits for claims that may be difficult to substantiate, although probably true.

The Environmental Theory[125]

If SARS-CoV-2 has not been isolated and, in fact, does not exist, then what causes COVID-19? As an alternative, there is the environmental theory of COVID-19. It emerged with the proliferation of 4G and 5G towers' emissions of EM waves of various frequencies. The symptoms of COVID-19 are exactly the same as those of toxic radiation. The geographic distribution of COVID-19 is directly associated with the existence of 4G and 5G technology in those geographical locations as demonstrated by the Bartomeu Payares report.[126]

Historically, there seems to be an associated finding of pandemics with the introduction of radio signals in the atmosphere as observed during the Spanish flu pandemic of 1918 with the introduction of the radio broadcasting technology. The global distribution of radio signals helps to understand the similarities between different pandemic events. Graphene oxide (GO) is a carbon derivative of extraordinary molecular structure and characteristics. Graphene oxide has been found in the vials of various COVID-19 vaccines according to the recent Campra report.[127]

Graphene is introduced into the body via vaccines, PCRs, antigen tests, masks, air, nasal sprays, alcoholic gels, water, food, etc. It's a toxic chemical

124 Personal communication via email. See also the following discussion with Mike Adams that can shed light as to why McCullough and Malone do not want to delve into speculating what is exactly happening. He explains the sinister agenda behind what is happening and why science and ethics do not matter to Big Pharma, the Media, Governments, etc.: Adams, "What Dr. Robert Malone could NOT tell Joe Rogan."

125 This sub-section was solely worked on by Enrique Ventureyra. I am skeptical about the environmental theory but believe it should be debated and considered. There is no contradiction here between whether the virus is natural, manipulated, engineered, or non-existent—these positions will be consistent with false positives. What is it I am reading for in the first place? It also shows that we are being lied to if any of these turn out to be true, especially if SARS-CoV-2 does not have a natural origin.

126 Cifre, "Study of the correlation between cases of coronavirus and the presence of 5G networks"; This version supersedes the previous one: Cifre, "Estudio sobre la asimétrica distribución de casos de COVID-19 y su relación con la tecnología 5G."

127 Madrid, "Detección de Grafeno en Vacunas Covid19 por Espectroscopía Micro-Raman."

agent. It's degraded by glutathione or its precursor N-acetylcysteine, enzyme myeloperoxidase, and kaolin.[128]

Graphene oxide is highly toxic, thrombogenic, and a super conductor of electricity. It is known to resonate at various frequencies of 4G and 5G microwave emissions. In addition, it forms part of the nano-lipid biosphere transporting mRNA into the cells after injection via COVID-19 vaccines. These biospheres are designed for transport and protection of the mRNA injected from the host immune system. The role of Graphene is multiple: it is a highly toxic and potent thrombogenic agent with a biosphere structural component and nano-sensors that receive and transmit radio signals. This also aids on connecting humans to the "internet of things" through neuromodulation that influences the emotions and thoughts of individuals.

The city of Wuhan in China, where the COVID outbreak started in 2019, is the most populated city in the world by 5G towers. Coinciding with the COVID outbreak there was a simultaneous startup of all city 5G towers. Soon after this event 21 million telephone subscribers mysteriously disappeared,[129] suggesting that all those telephone users connected to the same network perished during the massive 5G towers start up. Was this an experiment that went wrong or a purposeful method of population control which had been tested?

Via an inside informer it's known that the 5G towers have two components:

- The 5G tower antenna has a two-way energy flow that receives and emits signals to and from the Star-Link satellite system and in turn receives and emits signals to and from individuals saturated with Graphene oxide nanoparticles. Besides, the imbedded GO nanoparticles act like nano blades damaging the endothelial surface of blood vessels causing blood clotting and thrombosis. This same mechanism may explain the sudden death of athletes during sports due to high blood flow with consequent endothelial vascular damage and thrombosis, in these individuals.
- The second component of the 5G tower is a mysterious COVID-19 box under Artificial Intelligence control, which delivers the microwave energy signals at various rates and intensities. These EM signals cause cell toxicity and inflammation replicating the COVID-19 disease including cytokines storm as well as blood clotting disorders. Due to the similarity of both mechanisms in the COVID-19 production, it is logical to question the spike protein's existence. Thus, it's possible

128 See Polonikov, "Endogenous Deficiency of Glutathione as the Most Likely Cause of Serious Manifestations and Death in COVID-19 Patients."

129 Li, "Why Did 21 Million Phone Numbers Disappear from China After Coronavirus Outbreak?"

that the mRNA/spike protein theory is just a distraction or both mechanisms play a role in COVID-19? Analysis of several vaccine vials, according to the Campra report, has demonstrated the presence of GO (>80%) and traces of mRNA.

Further analysis of the Pfizer vaccine vials has demonstrated the presence of an artificial genetically modified version of Hydra Vulgaris and its eggs. This is an otherwise innocuous parasite present in the fresh water of ponds and pools which becomes virulent after genetic modification.[130] It is notorious that the tentacles of the artificial and genetically modified Hydra contain aluminum and graphene. The Hydra eggs hatch after being exposed to 5G.[131] Another interesting phenomenon of Graphene nanoparticles assembly has been observed at Rice University, after electrical stimulation (Teslaphoresis).

On Lockdowns

Thus far we have examined several falsehoods. First, we examined the claim that a deadly virus emerged from the wild, which we now know is false even though the media and governments are still trying to push this narrative. Second, we saw that despite claims to the contrary, PCR testing has had a history of unreliability; this was evident in the devastating analysis of the Corman-Drosten Review Report and also in the many statements from the creator, Kary Mullis. Third, the myth that asymptomatic transfer plays a significant role in infecting significant portions of the populations. Fourth, we considered whether the virus has even been isolated—is there such a thing as SARS-CoV-2? This is something that is worth greater scrutiny. This suggests that the whole rationale and basis for locking down most of the world has zero justification. And yet, as is the case in Austria, they continue to do so to both vaccinated and unvaccinated individuals.[132] If this does not sound off alarms for the vaccinated, I don't know what will. Moreover, the practice of putting healthy people under lockdown is unprecedented and totally absurd. The absurdity is compounded given the facts enumerated above. It is also economically devastating for entire countries and countless families, not to mention totally unscientific. But maybe that's the point. Through and through this alleged pandemic we have seen malfeasance at every level of the medical establishment, but things are getting worse.

130 Love, "What's In the Vaxx? Transgenic Hydra And Parasite Implants Used As Rapid Human Cloning System."

131 The Stew Peters Show, "Dr. Carrie Madej: First U.S. Lab Examines "Vaccine' Vials, HORRIFIC Findings Revealed."

132 BBC staff, "Covid: Austria back in lockdown despite protests."

In March of 2020, we were told that to flatten the curve, i.e., to slow the virus's spread, we had to isolate, even if we were healthy. Despite this, we have been facing ongoing lockdowns and fear-mongering with other mandates as well. This being said, there is no evidence that lockdowns prevent the spread of COVID-19 or lower the number of deaths. Sweden can function as a clear example of a success story, according to Johan Ahlander at *Reuters*:

> Preliminary data from EU statistics agency Eurostat compiled by Reuters showed Sweden had 7.7% more deaths in 2020 than its average for the preceding four years. Countries that opted for several periods of strict lockdowns, such as Spain and Belgium, had so-called excess mortality of 18.1% and 16.2% respectively.
>
> Twenty-one of the 30 countries with available statistics had higher excess mortality than Sweden. However, Sweden did much worse than its Nordic neighbours, with Denmark registering just 1.5% excess mortality and Finland 1.0%. Norway had no excess mortality at all in 2020.[133]

This is precisely what Sweden's top epidemiologist, Anders Tegnell, predicted from the onset of the pandemic. He came under heavy scrutiny and even received a number of death threats for holding such a position.[134] It is worth pointing out that Sweden had more restrictive measures than its Nordic neighbours, so this is a strong indicator that less restrictive countries had lower transmission and death rates. The same is true for Florida, which has uplifted all of its restrictions. Florida is also devoid of any vaccine mandates or passports, unlike the Democrat-run states. Much to the chagrin of Democrat leaders, Ron DeSantis, despite all the media backlash is following *actual* science and data.[135]

The Great Barrington declaration emphasized the catastrophe that lockdowns have led to:

> Coming from both the left and right, and around the world, we have devoted our careers to protecting people. Current lockdown policies are producing devastating effects on short and long-term public health. The results (to name a few) include lower childhood vaccination rates, worsening cardiovascular disease outcomes, fewer cancer screenings and deteriorating mental health—leading to greater excess mortality in years to come, with the working class and younger members of society carrying the heaviest burden. Keeping students out of school is a grave injustice.[136]

133 Ahlander, "Sweden saw lower 2020 death spike than much of Europe – data."

134 Miltimore, "Sweden Saw Lower Mortality Rate Than Most of Europe in 2020, Despite No Lockdown."

135 Ayers, "Florida COVID-19 cases remain low as Democratic-led states see numbers rise."

136 Kulldorf, Gupta, and Bhattacharya, "Great Barrington Declaration."

On December 19, 2020, the American Institute for Economic Research (AIER) published a review of 35 devastating studies demonstrating the ineffectiveness and dangers of lockdowns.[137] This list has been in addition to the one catalogued by data engineer Ivor Cummins.[138] Taken together, the studies systematically elucidate all the perils of lockdowns, such as increased mortality; global economic crisis affecting countless livelihoods and leading to extreme poverty,[139] the weakening of children's immune systems,[140] domestic abuse, increase in suicide rates,[141] mental health issues, increase in substance abuse,[142] and unnecessary and unwarranted disruption to many lifesaving medical procedures (a truly horrific proposition when we consider the number of people who were delayed cancer diagnoses, vital medical examinations and life-saving treatments).[143] In Ontario, there were 560,000 fewer surgeries because of lockdowns which cost the lives of many.[144] Lockdowns have zero benefit for the common person; they don't save lives or stop the transmission of the virus—a very similar tale to the COVID-19 vaccines. The harm caused by lockdowns far exceeds any conceivable benefit. The only ones who have benefitted from lockdowns have been billionaire elites and subservient politicians.

On the Inutility of Masks

Conventionally, masks have been intended to be worn in either sterile environments, like scientific research laboratories and operating rooms in hospitals, or contaminated ones, like hazardous waste sites with toxic fumes and chemicals. Although wearing masks outdoors has been commonplace in China, the Western world has not seen universal mask mandates, including outdoor recommendations for healthy people before the emergence of COVID-19. It is

137 AIER Staff, "Lockdowns Do Not Control the Coronavirus: The Evidence."

138 The Fat Emperor, "Published Papers and Data on Lockdown Weak Efficacy – and Lockdown Huge Harms medical services many of which are more pressing than COVID-19."

139 Miltimore, "COVID Crisis Could Push 100 Million People into Extreme Poverty, New World Bank Study Says."

140 Grover, "Covid distancing may have weakened children's immune system, experts say."

141 The CDC has reported that there has been a 31 percent increase in the hospitalization of children aged 12–17 because of rising mental health issues including suicidal idealization. See Leeb, "Mental Health-Related Emergency Department Visits Among Children Aged <18 Years During the COVID-19 Pandemic —United States, January 1–October 17, 2020."

142 For a very well referenced article about all of the psycho-social effects of COVID-19, see Michaéla C. Schippers, "For the Greater Good? The Devastating Ripple Effects of the Covid-19 Crisis" and chapter 44.

143 Briggs, "Sorry LA Times: The COVID Lockdowns Were Not Painless and Effective."

144 Canadian Institute for Health Information, "Overview: COVID-19's impact on health care systems."

a rather intriguing phenomenon to see people wearing masks outdoors in the scorching heat while having no one around.

Early on, we were told that healthy people do not have to wear face masks. This was uttered by Anthony Fauci on 60 Minutes. He stated that the only real need for them was for psychological purposes, i.e., to make people feel safe.[145] Shortly after the interview he claimed one should wear a mask. He then claimed we should wear double masks. The CDC also recommended double-mask wearing: "Wear one disposable mask underneath a cloth mask that has multiple layers of fabric. The second mask should push the edges of the inner mask snugly against the face and beard."[146] We were then told that wearing a mask is to protect you from others, but then that the purpose was to prevent the spread of the virus in order to protect others.[147] Initially, a top medical journal, *Annals of Internal Medicine*, suggested that masks are ineffective to stop the spread of COVID-19, claiming that, "both surgical and cotton masks seem to be ineffective in preventing the dissemination of SARS–CoV-2 from the coughs of patients with COVID-19 to the environment and external mask surface." It then retracted the study.[148] This is just one of a number of scientific/medical papers being retracted from reputable journals.[149] One wonders if it is solely because of the speed these papers are being published or if there is something else going on here that we are not being told. It is also worth mentioning that masks have the potential of becoming contaminated as they are repeatedly adjusted.[150] Moreover, according to some medical professionals, such as Dr. Russell Blaylock, healthy people should not be wearing masks for the following adverse reason: "By wearing a mask, the exhaled viruses will not be able to escape and will concentrate in the nasal passages, enter the olfactory nerves and travel into the brain."[151] As the Mayo Clinic website states: "Some N95 masks, and even some cloth masks, have one-way valves that make them easier to breathe through. But because the valve releases unfiltered air when the wearer breathes out, this type of mask doesn't prevent the wearer from spreading the virus. For this reason, some places have banned them."[152]

Dr. Michael Osterholm, director of the Center of Infectious Disease and Research Policy, and a Regents Professor at the University of Minnesota, in a

145 See video under section "What's the Dealio with Masks?" Scott Ventureyra, "Won't Get Fooled Again by the WHO," accessed May 25, 2021, https://www.scottventureyra.com/post/won-t-get-fooled-again-by-the-who.

146 Centers for Disease Controls and Prevention, "Improve How Your Mask Protects You."

147 Tufekci, Jeremy Howard, and Trisha Greenhalgh, "The Real Reason to Wear a Mask."

148 Bae, et al., "Effectiveness of Surgical and Cotton Masks in Blocking SARS–CoV-2: A Controlled Comparison in 4 Patients."

149 Retraction Watch, "Retracted coronavirus (COVID-19) papers."

150 Medical Xpress Staff, "Masks, gloves don't stop coronavirus spread: experts."

151 Blaylock, "Face Masks Pose Serious Risks To The Healthy."

152 Mayo Clinic Staff, "How well do face masks protect against coronavirus?"

special podcast, stated the following as a response to the CDC's lack of evidence on the effectiveness of cloth masks: "Never before in my 45-year career have I seen such a far-reaching public recommendation issued by any governmental agency without a single source of data or information to support it. This is an extremely worrisome precedent of implementing policies not based on science-based data or why they were issued without such data."[153]

The CDC published a study in May of 2020, which found that in ten randomized control trials (RCTs) "no significant reduction in influenza transmission with the use of face masks."[154] Another study published in PLOS One that close to 8,000 subjects demonstrated that face masks do not in fact reduce the transmission of viral respiratory infections.[155] In fact, there are many studies which corroborate the fact that there is "little to no evidence for the effectiveness of face masks in the general population, neither as personal protective equipment nor as a source control."[156] It is worth pointing out that there are some serious flaws with studies that have claimed that masks work against COVID-19.[157] The WHO also published a study in *The Lancet* analyzing the effectiveness of N95 masks in hospitals. The Swiss Policy research has argued that the study should be retracted since it contains many flaws and misrepresentations.[158]

Size Matters

The most practical use of masks is to protect others from spit and droplets. This is especially useful for surgeons and nurses, for instance. One can even see its practicality for barbers and hairdressers as well. The most common form of transmission of SARS-CoV-2 is said to be either through droplets or tiny particles known as aerosols. These transmit when an infected individual coughs, sneezes, talks, or sings thereby releasing droplets or aerosols from their nose and/or mouth. Although masks will be effective in protecting others of droplets, they do not offer much of advantage against aerosols, as one study indicates:

153 Dr. Michael Osterholm, interview with Chris Dall, "Special Episode: Masks and Science."

154 Jingyi, et al., "Nonpharmaceutical Measures for Pandemic Influenza in Nonhealthcare Settings—Personal Protective and Environmental Measures."

155 See Alfelali, et al., "Facemask against viral respiratory infections among Hajj pilgrims: A challenging cluster-randomized trial."

156 For a comprehensive list of studies demonstrating the ineffectiveness of masks to reduce the spread of viruses, including SARS-CoV-2, see Swiss Policy Research, "Are Face Masks Effective? The Evidence."

157 The following preprinted article was withdrawn since it did not demonstrate that masks reduce the transmission of the virus or the number of hospitalizations due to COVID-19, Adjodah, et al., "Decrease in Hospitalizations for COVID-19 after Mask Mandates in 1083 U.S. Counties."

158 Swiss Policy Research, "WHO Mask Study Seriously Flawed."

> SARS-CoV-2 has a size ranging from 60 to 140 nm [nanometer] smaller than bacteria, dust, and pollen. Therefore, masks and respirators made of materials with larger pore sizes, such as cotton and synthetic fabric, will not be able to effectively filter these viruses or tiny virus-laden droplets, as compared with those made of materials with much smaller pore sizes.

The pores in an N95 mask are about 300 nm (nanometer) in size. So, although it can prevent respiratory particles which have a minimum size of 4.7 μm (micron)[159] from transmitting, it cannot prevent the transmission of SARS-CoV-2 through its pores. They do not shield anyone from the virus.[160] This is why it is especially absurd to think that cloth masks will do anything to prevent the spread of the virus. Therefore, it should come as no surprise when we discover Fauci, in his trove of leaked emails, iterating something similar in an email dated February 5, 2020, sent to a former Team Obama health official, stating that masks were for infected people, and that "the typical mask you buy in a drug store is not really effective in keeping out the virus, which is small enough to pass through the material."[161]

Side-Effects of Masks

Leading epidemiologists in the *British Medical Journal* note serious potential side-effects of wearing masks which are not often discussed:

- Wearing a face mask makes the exhaled air go into the eyes. This generates an uncomfortable feeling and an impulse to touch your eyes. If your hands are contaminated, you are infecting yourself. [(Not to mention how difficult it makes it to see for someone who wears glasses when they get fogged.)]
- Face masks make breathing more difficult. For people with COPD [(Chronic obstructive pulmonary disease)], face masks are in fact intolerable to wear as they worsen their breathlessness. Moreover, a fraction of carbon dioxide previously exhaled is inhaled at each respiratory cycle. Those two phenomena increase breathing frequency and deepness, and hence they increase the amount of inhaled and exhaled air. *This may worsen the burden of covid-19 if infected people wearing masks spread more contaminated air.* This may also worsen the

159 Lee, "Minimum Sizes of Respiratory Particles Carrying SARS-CoV-2 and the Possibility of Aerosol Generation."

160 Sidley and Mordue, "Masks – do benefits outweigh the harms?"

161 Anthony Fauci Emails: https://assets.documentcloud.org/documents/20793561/leopold-nih-foia-anthony-fauci-emails.pdf.

clinical condition of infected people if the enhanced breathing pushes the viral load down into their lungs. [(The situation worsens if people don't replace their single-use masks frequently and wash reusable ones regularly. Improper disposal could increase risk of contamination as well.)]

- While impeding person-to-person transmission is key to limiting the outbreak, so far little importance has been given to the events taking place after a transmission has happened, when innate immunity plays a crucial role. The main purpose of the innate immune response is to immediately prevent the spread and movement of foreign pathogens throughout the body. The innate immunity's efficacy is highly dependent on the viral load. If face masks determine a humid habitat where the SARS-CoV-2 can remain active due to the water vapour continuously provided by breathing and captured by the mask fabric, they determine an increase in viral load and therefore they can cause a defeat of the innate immunity and an increase in infections. This phenomenon may also interact with and enhance previous points.[162]

These are all valid points that I doubt many have considered, nor have most governing bodies taken them seriously. The epidemiologists conclude the article by stating that: "It is necessary to quantify the complex interactions that may well be operating between positive and negative effects of wearing surgical masks at population level. It is not time to act without evidence."[163] It turns out that we continue to act without evidence.

What's also troubling is the mask mandates imposed on children attending schools. On April 8, 2021, a German Court ruled against masks usage, social distancing, and testing for students. The Court stated that:

> the measures now prohibited represent a present danger to the mental, physical or psychological well-being of the child to such an extent that, if they continue to develop without intervention, considerable harm can be foreseen with a high degree of certainty… The children are physically, psychologically and pedagogically damaged and their rights are violated without any benefit for the children themselves or third parties.[164]

162 Lazzarino, et al., "Covid-19: important potential side effects of wearing face masks that we should bear in mind."

163 Lazzarino, et al., "Covid-19: important potential side effects of wearing face masks that we should bear in mind."

164 202 News, "Sensationsurteil aus Weimar: keine Masken, kein Abstand, keine Tests mehr für Schüler." For a translation see: "Sensational verdict from Weimar: no masks, no distance, no more tests for students." https://docs.google.com/document/d/13tlF0vUYQBYba7_d-tam3cSt0dUDqlI1MeQvO0TbM_E/edit.

Moreover, the judge stated that "school administrators, teachers and others cannot invoke the state-law regulations on which the measures are based, because they are unconstitutional and thus void."[165] Despite this, these regulations continue like clockwork in many countries.

Many side-effects associated with extended mask usage include headaches, drowsiness, dizziness, reduced ability to concentrate, and reductions in cognitive function.[166] There is also the risk of developing neurodegenerative diseases from continual mask usage that could take years to manifest.

The fact that children have an incredibly low percent chance of either contracting or transmitting COVID-19 and a 99.998 percent recovery rate is indicative of how unnecessary mask usage is for them. It is actually detrimental to their socialization and interaction with other children and adults.

Masks cause a host of psychological harm, as Gary Sidley and Alan Mordue clearly state:

> Masks impair verbal communication, render lip-reading impossible for the deaf, and stymie emotional expression, the latter effect potentially constituting a gross impediment to children's social development. Acting as a crude, highly visible reminder that danger is all around, face coverings are fuelling widespread, irrational fear.
>
> Wearing a mask will heighten the distress of many people with existing mental health problems and may trigger 'flashbacks' for those historically traumatised by physical and/or sexual abuse. Sadly, going without a mask (even as a means of avoiding psychological distress) can often attract harassment and further victimisation. In response to this, 'exemption lanyards' have been developed, which further stigmatise those who cannot wear face coverings due to health conditions or previous trauma.[167]

The Politicization of Masks

In May of 2020, MSNBC reporter, Cal Perry (a former CNN reporter) was shaming people for not wearing masks, but he was quickly embarrassed by a passer-by who filmed him and his crew, pointing out that half the crew was not wearing masks.[168] Fast forward a month to June of 2020, throughout multiple Oregon counties, people who are non-white were not required to wear face

165 202 News, "Sensationsurteil aus Weimar: keine Masken, kein Abstand, keine Tests mehr für."

166 Mercola, "Study shows how masks are harming children."

167 Sidley and Mordue, "Masks – do benefits outweigh the harms?"

168 Brown, "MSNBC reporter Cal Perry humiliated on air after mask-shaming backfires."

masks due to potential racial profiling and harassment.[169] It is evident that this absurdity was meant to create more division between police officers and civilians, especially whites and non-whites. This is just one of the many examples of how the mainstream media deceive the public. If you want to learn more about how the media deceives the public through fake news, I recommend Mark Dice's book, *The True Story of Fake News.*[170]

It is unfortunate that the use of masks serves more of a political purpose than any health benefit. The politicization of wearing masks or not wearing them has gone into the depths of absurdity that may have been unimaginable a couple of years ago. Take for example, in Canada, the Chief Public Health Officer of Canada, Dr. Theresa Tam's recommendation that couples should stop kissing and wear masks during intercourse. [171] Even more absurdly, Vice President of the USA, Kamala Harris, and second gentleman, Doug Emhoff, who received their second dose of the COVID-19 vaccination in January of 2021, for the sake of political theater, kissed while wearing their masks. [172] This flies in the face of the CDC recommendation that fully vaccinated people have little risk of contracting the disease. The wearing of masks has been more about virtue signaling, compliance, and even improving AI's ability for facial recognition,[173] while coupled with physical distancing, than it has about safety.

The Demonization of Early COVID-19 Treatments

For over twenty months there has been a disturbing trend of silencing any voices that counter the COVID-19 narrative. Effective COVID-19 treatments that could have saved thousands upon thousands of lives were demonized from the onset of the crisis; antiviral treatments such as hydroxychloroquine and ivermectin that have been proven to be effective for the treatment of COVID-19 were either discredited or banned. However, remdesivir was highly used and promoted by Fauci and many governments, including Canada.[174] Due to the toxicity of remdesivir, it may have very well contributed to a significant number of adverse effects and deaths of hospitalized patients who received the drug,

169 Andrew, "An Oregon county drops its mask exemption for people of color after racist response."

170 Dice, *The True Story of Fake News: How the Mainstream Media Manipulates Millions.*

171 Gordon, "Wear a mask while having sex, Dr. Theresa Tam suggests."

172 Chamberlain, "Kamala Harris and husband Doug Emhoff kiss with masks on despite being vaccinated."

173 Metz, "Think your mask makes you invisible to facial recognition? Not so fast, AI companies say"; see also Felenasoft, "Mask Detector: AI-based detection of people wearing a facial mask."

174 Herrer, "Doctor Exposes the Dangers of Remdesivir and other Drugs that are Being Recommended by NIH."

but, as usual, deaths were accredited to COVID-19.[175] Hospitals have been incentivized by governments to use remdesivir.[176]

Hydroxychloroquine

In March and April of 2020, the mainstream media unjustly blasted President Trump for promoting the use of hydroxychloroquine as an early treatment for COVID-19. During that period, several articles were published arguing that it led to the death of a number of hospitalized patients.[177] In June of 2020, an article published in the journal, *Clinical Advances*, argued that there are no benefits to treat the COVID-19 through the use of hydroxychloroquine and that it has contributed to the increasing number of deaths.[178] Nevertheless, hydroxychloroquine combined with azithromycin is a relatively inexpensive treatment that has been endorsed by a prominent French scientist,[179] Didier Raoult, who is one of the most highly cited micro-biologists in the world.[180] He and his colleagues published a couple of studies that showed that it was efficacious in the early treatment of COVID-19.[181] Thus, despite claims to the contrary, if administered early on during the period of when the first clinical signs of the flu are detected, then the success rate can be quite high. Moreover, at the onset of the pandemic, Dr. Vladimir Zelenko treated over 1,450 patients[182] who tested positive for COVID-19 with 200 mg of hydroxychloroquine twice a day for 5 days, 500 mg of azithromycin once a day for 5 days, and 220 mg of zinc sulfate (an ingredient often ignored by studies which are critical of the treatment) once a day for 5 days, producing 99.9% success rate (only 2 deaths).[183]

175 Hendrie, "Doctor Reveals that Remdesivir Was the Real Cause For Many Alleged COVID-19 Maladies."

176 Breggin, "Murdering COVID Patients in the Name of Treatment."

177 Mahévas, et al., "No evidence of clinical efficacy of hydroxychloroquine in patients hospitalised for COVID-19 infection and requiring oxygen: results of a study using routinely collected data to emulate a target trial."

178 Magagnoli, et al., "Outcomes of Hydroxychloroquine Usage in United States Veterans Hospitalized with COVID-19."

179 Raoult, "Dr. Oz Discusses The Hydroxychloroquine Study Outcome With Dr. Didier Raoult."

180 Raoult is also one of the most highly cited micro-biologists in the world. https://scholar.google.ca/scholar?hl=en&as_sdt=0%2C5&q=Didier+Raoult&btnG=.

181 Million, et al., "Early treatment of COVID-19 patients with hydroxychloroquine and azithromycin: A retrospective analysis of 1061 cases in Marseille, France"; see also Guatret, et al., "Hydroxychloroquine and azithromycin as a treatment of COVID-19: results of an open-label non-randomized clinical trial."

182 Louise, "Dr. Vladimir Zelenko has now treated over 1,450 coronavirus patients (2 deaths) using hydroxychloroquine with 99.99% success rate (latest video interview)."

183 Louise,"Dr. Vladimir Zelenko has now treated over 1,450 coronavirus patients (2 deaths) using hydroxychloroquine with 99.99% success rate (latest video interview)."

In order to ensure success, hydroxychloroquine must be taken in conjunction with the other two drugs (or at least zinc). Medical doctor Anthony Cardill, in Los Angeles, observed that many patients become symptom free after 8–12 hours of taking these drugs.[184] Undoubtedly, this information has been troubling for pharmaceutical companies and other interest groups, such as the Bill and Melinda Gates Foundation who have promoted the vaccine as the only way to get out of this pandemic.

The studies involving hydroxychloroquine (alongside azithromycin and zinc) as a treatment for COVID-19 involve three different stages: prophylactic, early symptomatic stages, and late-stage treatments. Most of the studies that were eventually retracted focused on the late-stage treatment,[185] but this was more misleading than anything since researchers ought to have known that the treatment won't have a positive effect based on prior knowledge. It is at the prophylactic and predominantly in the early symptomatic stage where the treatment will make its greatest impact. Proper dosages must be taken to ensure successful treatment. The abovementioned studies that argue against the usage of hydroxychloroquine do not address the true efficacy of the treatment, but, rather, provide a misleading analysis.

On June 4, 2020, there was an enormous retraction from *The Lancet*, one of the most respected and established medical journals in the world.[186] This retraction was considered to be one of the largest in modern medical journal history. The claim of the paper was that hydroxychloroquine increases arrythmias and decreases hospital survival rates. This study was treated as conclusive and influenced the stoppage of various drug trials. However, as Ralph Ellis of WebMD states:

> The study was withdrawn because the company that provided data would not provide full access to the information for a third-party peer review, saying to do so would violate client agreements and confidentiality requirements, *The Lancet* said in a statement.
>
> Based on this development, we can no longer vouch for the veracity of the primary data sources. Due to this unfortunate development, the authors request that the paper be retracted. *The Lancet* said in a statement.

This leaves the door open to the independent work, claims, and results of scientists and medical doctors such as Dr. Didier Raoult who has been cited 156,179 times according to Google Scholar,[187] Dr. Zelenko, and others,

184 ABC7, "LA doctor seeing success with hydroxychloroquine to treat COVID-19."

185 Retraction Watch, "Retracted coronavirus (COVID-19) papers."

186 Mehra, "RETRACTED: Hydroxychloroquine or chloroquine with or without a macrolide for treatment of COVID-19: a multinational registry analysis."

187 https://scholar.google.ca/citations?hl=en&user=n8EF_6kAAAAJ.

regarding the efficacy of hydroxychloroquine for COVID-19's treatment. Interestingly, an hour after *The Lancet* journal's retraction, *The New England Journal of Medicine* retracted a separate study[188] involving blood pressure medications in COVID-19 which had used data and was supported by the William Harvey Distinguished Chair in Advanced Cardiovascular Medicine at Brigham and Women's Hospital, as was *The Lancet* article. An unprecedented 205 articles related to COVID-19 have been withdrawn since March 2020.[189] The organization Retraction Watch monitors the retractions of papers from peer reviewed journals worldwide.

Even CNN admitted that hydroxychloroquine was effective in helping hospitalized COVID-19 patients survive—going against their prior false narrative. CNN calls it "surprising" and "controversial." This is only the case because Big Pharma had other plans by lying, censoring, and smearing any favourable studies and information regarding the lifesaving drug. A final point worth mentioning is that the hydroxychloroquine is a highly inexpensive treatment so the incentive to make monetary gain is just not there.

Ivermectin

The Nobel Prize in Physiology or Medicine was awarded to Tu Youyou, and William C. Campbell and Satoshi Omura in 2015 for the discovery of ivermectin.[190] It was the committee's first award for an antiviral disease treatment since streptomycin in 1952. Throughout 2020, The Frontline Covid Care Alliance (FLCC) conducted a comprehensive review of the effectiveness of ivermectin in the prophylaxis and treatment of COVID-19. The abstract was removed without notice from *Frontiers in Pharmacology*. The authors summarized their findings as follows:

> [B]ased on the existing and cumulative body of evidence, we recommend the use of ivermectin in both prophylaxis and treatment for COVID-19. In the presence of a global COVID-19 surge, the widespread use of this safe, inexpensive, and effective intervention would lead to a drastic reduction in transmission rates and the morbidity and mortality in mild, moderate, and even severe disease phases. The authors are encouraged and hopeful at the prospect of the many favorable public health and societal impacts that would result once adopted for use.[191]

188 Mandeep, et al., "Cardiovascular Disease, Drug Therapy, and Mortality in Covid-19."

189 Retraction Watch, "Retracted coronavirus (COVID-19) papers."

190 The Nobel Prize in Physiology or Medicine 2015. https://www.nobelprize.org/prizes/medicine/2015/press-release/.

191 Kory, et al., "Review of the Emerging Evidence Demonstrating the Efficacy of Ivermectin in the Prophylaxis and Treatment of COVID-19."

Furthermore, in March 2021, Omura and his team performed a wide review of the clinical activity involved in combatting COVID-19. Their study concluded that ivermectin aided in large reductions of mortality and morbidity.[192] Most recently, Peter McCullough and his colleagues, with the consideration of a few new studies, corroborate the findings of Omura and team.[193]

Despite good medical and scientific evidence of the drug's efficaciousness, Canada has not authorized it to prevent or treat COVID-19.[194] Health Canada issued the following warning:

> Health Canada is reminding Canadians not to use ivermectin to prevent or treat COVID-19. Canadian poison centres have seen an increase in reports concerning ivermectin over the summer.
>
> There is no evidence that ivermectin works to prevent or treat COVID-19, and it is not authorized for this use. To date, Health Canada has not received any drug submission or applications for clinical trials for ivermectin for the prevention or treatment of COVID-19.
>
> Ivermectin has been authorized by Health Canada for human use, as a prescription antiparasitic drug for the treatment of parasitic worm infections. Prescription drugs should be taken only under the advice and supervision of a healthcare professional. Patients taking prescription drugs without being examined and monitored by a healthcare practitioner may not receive the appropriate treatment to maintain and protect their health. They may also put themselves at risk for drug interactions or harmful side effects. Canadians should never consume health products intended for animals because of potential serious health risks, including seizures, coma and even death.[195]

Health Canada is misleading Canadians when they emphasize it as a deworming drug while ignoring the corroborative evidence that the antiviral drug is extremely effective at treating people with COVID-19. Similarly, in an effort to discredit not only ivermectin but also Joe Rogan (for promoting it), mainstream media outlets like CNN and NBC claimed that ivermectin was a horse deworming drug. CNN, NBC, MSNBC, and others claimed that Joe Rogan took horse dewormer medication; this is how they framed ivermectin.[196] This should come as no surprise since they all want to push the vaccine on all citizens. CNN's Chief Medical Correspondent, Sanjay Gupta, did not know

192 Yagisawa, et al., "Global trends in clinical studies of ivermectin in COVID-19."

193 Santin, et al., "Ivermectin: a multifaceted drug of Nobel prize-honoured distinction with indicated efficacy against a new global scourge, COVID-19."

194 Health Canada, "Ivermectin not authorized to prevent or treat COVID-19; may cause serious health problems."

195 Health Canada, "Ivermectin not authorized to prevent or treat COVID-19; may cause serious health problems."

196 Wilson, "Joe Rogan In Info Wars Exposes The Truth About Ivermectin To America!"

how to respond to Rogan on his podcast when confronted as to why CNN would push a blatant lie like this.

No Transparency with Big Pharma

Developing a vaccine has been highly profitable for the indemnified pharmaceutical industry. It's been interesting to see how a significant number of people on the "left" who have criticized Big Pharma in the past are all in support of their massive vaccine rollout, government mandates, passports, and the ridiculous profits they are generating, not to mention the ongoing boosters. There is no transparency or responsibility. Big Pharma is one of, if not the most, mistrusted institutions in the world.[197] Indemnification has removed Big Pharma's incentive for creating safer products. Just like vaccine mandates remove building trust between government and its citizens.

Luckily, a federal judge in Texas ordered the FDA to make public all the data that was relied upon to licence Pfizer's COVID-19 vaccine.[198] The information which includes 400,000 pages is set to be released throughout a period of 8 months (roughly 55,000/month), starting March 1, 2022.[199] The world will finally be able to witness what has been hidden from them for long enough. Given the secrecy, one would expect that the level of unprecedented malfeasance that BioNtech-Pfizer has been involved in is of a magnitude that has never been seen before. A report released from December 2020 corroborates the claims of Melissa Strickler (see chapter 42) about the presence of luciferase in the COVID-19 vaccines.[200]

Scientists through the Freedom of Information Act (FOIA) have asked The Food and Drug Administration (FDA) to share data that was used to license Pfizer's COVID-19 vaccine. The FDA has requested fifty-five years to release this information.[201] What are they hiding?

197 Doidge, "Needle Points," chapters I to IV.

198 Greene, "'Paramount importance': Judge orders FDA to hasten release of Pfizer vaccine docs."

199 To access Pfizer's documents go to: Public Health and Medical Professionals for Transparency Documents, accessed March 3, 2022. https://phmpt.org/pfizers-documents/?fbclid=IwAR2lFzAGWiIgpCRG0k7KoRwlUMTcCMyZApKefwKcSTBymCtBVCxoll1EEj8.

200 BioNTech RNA Pharmaceuticals GmBH, "R&D STUDY REPORT No. R-20-0072: EXPRESSION OF LUCIFERASE-ENCODING MODRNA AFTER I.M. APPLICATION OF GMPREADY ACUITAS LIPID NANOPARTICLE FORMULATION, version 3."

201 Greene, "Wait what? FDA wants 55 years to process FOIA request over vaccine data."

Incompetence and Medical Malfeasance

Throughout 2020, one of the most alarming developments is what has been leaked from a recent meeting among directors of *The Lancet* and *The New England Medical Journal of Medicine* at the Chatham House Lectures (top-secret meetings with experts which prohibits recordings). Whistleblower Philippe Douste-Blazy, Cardiology MD, former France Health Minister, and 2017 candidate for director at the WHO, in this two-minute video[202] explains in French (with English subtitles) what happened in this meeting with respect to the stranglehold pharmaceutical companies have in the publication of papers with highly dubious and inaccurate conclusions, as was the case with retracted papers regarding hydroxychloroquine.[203] The editor-in-chief of *The Lancet* in a leaked statement, said:

> Now we are not going to be able to, basically, if this continues, publish any more clinical research data, because the pharmaceutical companies are so financially powerful today and are able to use such methodologies, as to have us accept papers which are apparently methodologically perfect but which, in reality, manage to conclude what they want to conclude…[204]

This is what happens when researchers and journals rely upon funding from the government and Big Pharma for their research and publications. Tragically, science and medicine have been compromised for the sake of profiteering over people's health and scientific integrity.

By now, it should become rather obvious to the somewhat astute observer that there has been a war waged against inexpensive and effective treatments against COVID-19. Why? The simple answer is it's not profitable. The pharmaceutical industry has made billions of dollars on the COVID-19 vaccine roll out regardless of its risks and lack of long-term studies. Governments, the media, Big Pharma, politicians, and medical bureaucrats would rather fill their pocketbooks than promote and protect people's health.

Given the current climate, one can't help but be suspicious of what's truly going on. Perhaps a little damage control? Perhaps an honest demonstration that science is a self-correcting process? Perhaps something else? Be that as it may, anyone with a modicum of understanding of the philosophy of science and the history of science (as we discussed in Chapter 42) will know that peer review, or whatever longstanding consensus, all too often ensures

202 Stone, "Lancet Editor Spills the Beans and Britain's PM Surrenders to the Gates Vaccine Cartel."

203 Madison Area Lyme Support Group, "Former French Health Minister Blows Whistle."

204 Madison Area Lyme Support Group, "Former French Health Minister Blows Whistle."

orthodoxy over innovation. Scientists of high repute like Greta Thunberg, Alexandria Ocasio-Cortez, the beloved Canadian Prime Minister, Justin "Fidelito" Trudeau, and all of those who have become overnight scientific revolutionaries/experts, please take note. The lesson here is to try to think for yourself and question things. Be skeptical and try not to end your search for the truth after a page or two of Google search results.

According to the WHO: "A total of 1.5 million people died from TB in 2020 (including 214 000 people with HIV). Worldwide, TB is the 13th leading cause of death and the second leading infectious killer after COVID-19 (above HIV/AIDS)."[205] Moreover, the WHO also stated that: "TB is spread from person to person through the air. When people with lung TB cough, sneeze or spit, they propel the TB germs into the air. A person needs to inhale only a few of these germs to become infected."[206] So, it is just as communicable as COVID-19, or perhaps even more. Interestingly, the claim that COVID-19 is the leading infectious killer can be disputed on various grounds, such as the fraudulent PCR testing that racks up fictitious case numbers. Nevertheless, this inevitably leads one to ask why weren't we or aren't we urged to wear masks? Why have there been no lockdowns in 2018 or even now, causing world economic destruction? Why has this not been widely and incessantly reported by any media news outlets? What makes COVID-19 so much more worrisome than tuberculosis, given this information?

Another question worth considering is why in the 50,000 peer reviewed papers was there not a single one on how to treat COVID-19? In January 2021, Peter McCullough and his colleagues published such a paper in *The American Journal of Medicine*. These were the salient points of the article:

- COVID-19 hospitalizations and death can be reduced with outpatient treatment.
- Principles of COVID-19 outpatient care include: 1) reduction of reinoculation, 2) combination antiviral therapy, 3) immunomodulation, 4) antiplatelet/antithrombotic therapy, and 5) administration of oxygen, monitoring, and telemedicine.
- Future randomized trials will undoubtedly refine and clarify ambulatory treatment; however we emphasize the immediate need for management guidance in the current crisis of widespread hospital resource consumption, morbidity, and mortality.[207]

205 World Health Organization, "Tuberculosis."

206 World Health Organization, "Tuberculosis."

207 McCullough, et al., "Pathophysiological Basis and Rationale for Early Outpatient Treatment of SARS-CoV-2 (COVID-19) Infection." Also see related articles: McCullough, et al., "Multifaceted highly targeted sequential multidrug treatment of early ambulatory high-risk SARS-CoV-2 infection (COVID-19)"; Truth for Health Foundation, "COVID Home Treatment."

It is hard to say if these missteps by governments are due more to incompetence or malfeasance. Perhaps it is both. Or perhaps it may be something more sinister. Nevertheless, according to Robert Malone, there are good modelling studies that over 500,000 people in the USA died from inaccessibility to early treatments such as hydroxychloroquine and ivermectin.[208]

Natural Immunity Matters

Natural immunity is the antibody protection that is created by your body against a microorganism that causes disease once you have been infected. It may vary from person to person and the particular pathogen.

Throughout parts of Europe, including Germany, natural immunity after recovering from COVID-19 is considered the same as vaccination. Canada and the US do not recognize natural immunity from previous infection as public health policy. However, there is no scientific or medical basis for this. Dr. Marty Makary of Johns Hopkins Hospital has said that "the data on natural immunity are now overwhelming."[209] And that,

> [i]t turns out the hypothesis that our public health leaders had that vaccinated immunity is better and stronger than natural immunity was wrong. They got it backwards. And now we've got data from Israel showing that natural immunity is 27 times more effective than vaccinated immunity. And that supports 15 other studies.[210]

On July 14, 2021, a study was published arguing that "long lived immunity" would be required to end the COVID-19 pandemic. The article demonstrates that immunity is long lasting after infection.[211] Similarly, a study by Israeli

208 The Joe Rogan Experience, "#1757 – Dr. Robert Malone, MD." Episode description:

Dr. Robert Malone is the inventor of the nine original mRNA vaccine patents, which were originally filed in 1989 (including both the idea of mRNA vaccines and the original proof of principle experiments) and RNA transfection. Dr. Malone, has close to 100 peer-reviewed publications which have been cited over 12,000 times. Since January 2020, Dr. Malone has been leading a large team focused on clinical research design, drug development, computer modeling and mechanisms of action of repurposed drugs for the treatment of COVID-19. Dr. Malone is the Medical Director of The Unity Project, a group of 300 organizations across the US standing against mandated COVID vaccines for children. He is also the President of the Global Covid Summit, an organization of over 16,000 doctors and scientists committed to speaking truth to power about COVID pandemic research and treatment.

209 Prestigiacomo, "Johns Hopkins Doctor Criticizes Vaccine Mandates, Stresses Natural Immunity."

210 Prestigiacomo, "Johns Hopkins Doctor Criticizes Vaccine Mandates, Stresses Natural Immunity."

211 Cohen, "Longitudinal analysis shows durable and broad immune memory after SARS-CoV-2 infection with persisting antibody responses and memory B and T cells."

researchers comparing SARS-CoV-2 natural immunity versus COVID-19 "vaccine induced immunity," show that natural immunity is longer lasting and more robust:

> This study demonstrated that natural immunity confers longer lasting and stronger protection against infection, symptomatic disease and hospitalization caused by the Delta variant of SARS-CoV-2, compared to the BNT162b2 two-dose vaccine-induced immunity. Individuals who were both previously infected with SARS-CoV-2 and given a single dose of the vaccine gained additional protection against the Delta variant.[212]

There is no reason to think this wouldn't be the case against other variants including Christmas 2021's "cadeau": Omicron.

Peter McCullough has argued that natural immunity is unbeatable when it comes to combatting COVID-19. In a testimony to the Texas Senate, he stated the following:

> We're at 80% herd immunity right now [Texas] with no vaccine effect, and more people are developing covid today. They're gonna become immune. People who develop covid have complete and durable immunity. You can't beat natural immunity. You can't vaccinate on top of it and make it better. There's no scientific clinical or safety rationale for ever vaccinating a covid recovered patient.[213]

And further that, "Clinical trial results. The vaccine is going to have a 1% public health impact. That's what the data says."[214] McCullough laments that "We have over 500,000 deaths in the United States. The preventable fraction could have been as high as 85 % if our pandemic response would have been laser focused on the problem, the sick patient right in front of us."[215] Here he shows that the emphasis was put on the future vaccine roll out instead of direct treatment of patients in need. It should also be strongly emphasized that:

> Healthy, unvaccinated children are critical to achieving herd immunity. Natural immunity is proven to tolerate infection, benefiting community

212 Gazit, et al., "Comparing SARS-CoV-2 natural immunity to vaccine-induced immunity: reinfections versus breakthrough infections."

213 Association of American Physicians and Surgeons (AAPS), "Peter McCullough, MD testifies to Texas Senate HHS Committee."

214 Association of American Physicians and Surgeons (AAPS), "Peter McCullough, MD testifies to Texas Senate HHS Committee" at the 13:30 mark.

215 Association of American Physicians and Surgeons (AAPS), "Peter McCullough, MD testifies to Texas Senate HHS Committee" at the 14:58 mark.

> protection while there is insufficient data to assess whether Covid vaccines assist herd immunity.[216]

On the COVID-19 "Vaccines"

We now reach the most sacred aspect of the pandemic, the COVID-19 vaccine, for the Covid Fideist—a term I use to describe blind believing Covidians who accept the governments and the media's propaganda of fear and submission. This is the promised saviour that will end the pandemic and let everyone "return back to normal," whatever that means. The Covidian believes in this so fervently that they encourage vaccine mandates and passports.

Prior to 2020 there had not been a single successful vaccine that was developed to combat any human coronavirus. However, in a short timespan—a year and a half—twenty were "miraculously" produced. Research into vaccine development for SARS and MERS vaccines had been ongoing for a number of years. Experiments had the opposite desired outcome, namely, lab mice that were administered the vaccine would suffer more severely than the unvaccinated. These vaccines caused what's known as hypersensitivity to SARS.[217]

The new technology of mRNA, even though undergoing research since the 1990s, had never been approved prior to 2020. It functions in the following way:

> An RNA is injected in the body. This RNA encodes the information to produce the antigen, which is a protein from a pathogen, that will stimulate the immune system. Inside the cells, the RNA is used to synthesize the antigen, which is exposed to the cell surface. Then, a subset of immune system cells recognizes the antigen and trigger an immune response (direct response and long-term memory).[218]

In essence, the mRNA (messenger ribonucleic acid) vaccines inject viral mRNA into the body then replicate inside cells. Its objective is to create memory within the cell where it can recognize "spike proteins" and produce antigens.

216 International Alliance of Physicians and Medical Scientists, "Physicians Declaration II – Updated Global Covid Summit."

217 Tseng, et al., "Immunization with SARS coronavirus vaccines leads to pulmonary immunopathology on challenge with the SARS virus."

218 See Figure 1: Hubaud, "RNA vaccines: a novel technology to prevent and treat disease."

Incessant Psychological Attacks

The incessant psychological attacks have bombarded the susceptible from every possible angle. Robert Malone, following the thought of Mattias Desmet[219] on "Mass Formation Psychosis," states that:

> When you have a society that has become decoupled from each other and has free-floating anxiety in a sense that things don't make sense, we can't understand it. And then their attention gets focused by a leader or series of events on one small point, just like hypnosis. They literally become hypnotized and can be led anywhere… They will follow that person. It doesn't matter if they lie to them or whatever.[220]

Within totalitarian societies people become subservient to fear and hypnotized into obedience "for the good of the collective." Unaware and compliant populations cannot pinpoint the source of their anxiety or aggression. For those who are spiritually awake (note many religious people are not) the battle is discernible between good and evil. In the absence of a cause or source for their distress, people begin to irrationally long for a resolution, regardless of how absurd and devastating it may be. The injection fulfills such a candidacy. Once the "clot-shot" is rolled out, then those who refuse it are seen as enemies, despite the evidence and data.

On a Personal Front

Even my daughter's mother will text her with a brainwashing technique stating that the unvaccinated are selfish and should be shipped off to an island. We can now see who the real fascists are. People's true colours have been revealed. Those who claim they would never become an Auschwitz guard are the very first who have fallen prey to immoral and savage proclivities. But who wouldn't want to escape this horror? However, being banished to an "island," sounds like a euphemism for a concentration camp more than any paradise. A close friend of mine took two doses of the injection just to get out of the nightmare Canada has become: he's in Florida now. He has said that the only restriction is having fun and described freedom as essential there. The total opposite of the hellhole Canada has become.

My daughter would personally tell me that she was unsure about the "vaccine." On the morning of November 26, 2021, upon dropping my

219 See the beginning of Chapter 42.

220 Phillips, "Dr. Robert Malone to Rogan: US in 'Mass Formation Psychosis' Over COVID-19."

daughter off at school, she reassured me that she wouldn't be pressured to take the vaccine that weekend. On the Sunday of that weekend, I was emailed by the mother to say that she had received her first dose. In November of 2021, a judge recommended that prior to vaccinating our daughter, that the mother read the document I prepared regarding the risks.[221] (I have included a template version of this document as Appendix 1.) I was coerced to "reluctantly agree" since I could lose decision-making in this avenue and incur more costs for an unwinnable battle in the courts.[222] It was a strategic move so I could still intervene if there were some severe adverse effects after either dosage. (I doubt the mother even gave it a glance but proceeded to take my daughter to be vaccinated.) The mother would often say "let our child hear the other side" regarding vaccination. The problem is that all my daughter would hear from were the news, social media, her friends, her mother and other relatives, and schoolteachers that were in favour of these experimental injections. I am the only "other side" and counter narrative that my daughter has access to. Anyhow, my daughter lied to me and proceeded with the first dose (she admitted this later on), the second dose was administered to her eight weeks later. The mother does not think for herself and follows whatever recommendation the government makes regardless of whether it is in the best interest of the child or not.[223]

The Fideistic Anesthesiologist

Recently, a friend of mine who went for a hospital procedure on Christmas Eve was reprimanded by the anesthesiologist for not receiving the COVID-19 injection and was urged to get it as soon as possible. He told my friend he could cancel the procedure because of this but that he would still go through with it. The remarkable thing was that my friend was never asked about the reason he was not "vaccinated." It could have been for religious, medical, ethical, etc., reasons, but that did not matter to the anesthesiologist, who also told my friend that he had put everyone at risk. I laughed with my friend about how preposterous and illogical this claim was (especially given all of the contents of this section of the book). My friend told the anesthesiologist that he had no symptoms. So how absurd was his claim? First, presumably, all of the staff including the good

221 The motion to change I had initiated had nothing to do with vaccination of our daughter. But the bulk of the case conference focused on this issue. I was the only one who spoke about scientific and medical facts. I provided statistics from the Health Canada. Unfortunately, it was an exercise in futility, but I had to try for my daughter's sake.

222 See chapter 42 for new precedent set by a logical and courageous judge ruling sole decision making for the mother against her children receiving the COVID-19 vaccines.

223 Her unthinking compliance is similar to the mother mentioned in this article: Harding, "Saskatchewan father in hiding to keep daughter from having COVID vax."

doctor himself were "fully vaccinated," meaning they had received their three doses, so either the "vaccines" protect the recipient, or they don't. Obviously, he did not have full confidence in the vaccines. Second, my friend was wearing a mask and so was this doctor, so then did that mean he thought that the masks were not effective, especially in conjunction with the vaccines? Third, did the fact that my friend had no symptoms make a difference to the doctor? This doctor is part of this mass formation psychosis who has been paralyzed by fear. Logic and evidence were obviously irrelevant to him. According to my friend, other doctors and professionals said that the anesthesiologist acted unprofessionally and unethically. He was incapacitated by fear much like the irrational fear of transmission at the onset of the HIV crisis throughout the 1970s and 1980s. Most of what he said did not stand up to scrutiny, however, the government supports such lunacy based on unwarranted recommendations and mandates. My friend said that the doctor was pushing a Noble Lie. At the time, my friend said that he began to wonder if this was the beginnings of a tour de force twenty-first century Canadian merging of the Nazi Party's chief propagandist, Joseph Goebbels, and the physician Josef Mengele (known as the Angel of Death). Could physicians suffering from this COVID malady of the mind become what some men were to Adolf Hitler, but to Ontario Premier Doug Ford and Canadian Prime Minister Justin Trudeau? He wondered to himself if this medical tyranny continued whether Canada would descend into the same depths of Hell that was wrought by the tyrannies of the twentieth century. Unfortunately, the COVID-19 situation has eroded my friend's and many others' confidence in the medical system and now with this physician's reaction. My friend said because of this doctor's treatment he became quite anxious about the procedure, to the point he feared for his life.

My friend recounted vague recollections of what was said under sedation and how he reacted when coming out of its influence. He told me that his subconscious made him aware that the anesthesiologist kept talking, complaining, and deriding him about his vaccination status. He said he felt awful since he could not defend himself. Upon gaining consciousness, he recalls saying: "It's not right how he [the doctor] is treating me… I want to talk to this guy." He said it was an unnerving feeling. I can only imagine the horror of his experience. I was furious when he told me how unjustly and unethically, he was treated. I told him he should complain to the institution and the college of physicians, even though the college is now totally compromised and corrupted. My friend also recalled this injection jockey saying: "You're in rhythm now." And then saying to everyone else: "He won't remember anything." My friend said he then vanished, and that it was akin to a magician hypnotizing his victim and taking what he wants then disappearing, thus violating his free will. This was a definite form of psychological abuse. His physician spoke to him and agreed that the anesthesiologist's behaviour was highly unethical. It seems as though the doctor in question tried to humiliate my friend into becoming subservient to the State and succumbing to these experimental injections. My friend said that this experience made him stronger in his resolve. I stand in solidarity with him for his freedom of choice and exercising his freedom of conscience. Sadly, this injection jockey betrayed medical-ethical guidelines as laid out in the Hippocratic Oath and other oaths by causing harm.[224] His "convictions" and fear took ownership over his identity, compromising his role as a physician and thus the sacredness of his personhood. And for what benefit? People in their tribalistic proclivities are quick to serve the world rather than God and truth: "For what shall it profit a man, if he shall gain the whole world, and lose his own soul?" (Matt 16:26). Unfortunately, instead of living by true science, medicine, plain reason, and principled-based ethics (which focuses on autonomy, beneficence/nonmaleficence, and justice), this anesthesiologist has thrown all of this out the window for his fear-based blind faith in the COVID-19 narrative and its accomplices (government, media, corrupt medical colleges, and Big Pharma). I told my friend that all we can do is pray for him. Pray that he wakes up from his delusion. And to pray the following prayer recommended by Father Dave (an American priest): "Bless him Lord, and change me."

Further Absurdities

This so-called pandemic has functioned as a psychological experiment for conditioning the masses. This is evident when we witness the unthinking compliance to mask wear, "socially distance," isolate, become doubly vaccinated, and receive any subsequent booster, etc. People were conditioned to believe that the only way out was this COVID-19 injection.

Anyone who doubts the effectiveness or safety of the COVID-19 vaccine is pejoratively labeled as an anti-vaxxer. Some who question these vaccines may be anti-vaccination, but many others have a healthy skepticism of these injections. This is just a facile way to dismiss serious concerns and questions. Robert Malone, one of the architects of the mRNA vaccine, has been labeled as an anti-vaxxer, which is totally absurd. Demonizing and dismissing dissent is unscientific to its core. It's the sort of tactic used by Nazis and Communists. (As a side note, it's disappointing to see many Creation Scientists and Intelligent Design advocates who have been victim subject to this sort of censorship in the past, now falling prey to such tactics.)

Most stunning were the recent comments made by postmodernism's poster-boy, Justin Trudeau, who said that COVID-19 anti-vaxxers are misogynists

224 See Chapter 42 for a more in-depth discussion on the Hippocratic Oath and other oaths (bonnai sehjmerm). It is tragic this is not being held as sacred.

and racists. This seems rather odd considering that the typical "anti-vaxxer," according to early polls, was a 42-year-old female Liberal voter.[225] Moreover, the reserve of Six Nations of the Grand River has only a 49 percent vaccination rate while receiving early access. First Nations people have a low "vaccination" rate because of a distrust of government.[226] But in the land of Never-Never Woke Land, where facts, science, medicine, and morality, do not matter, Trudeau is the Fuehrer, emperor, and arbiter of what is "true" when expedient. Again, we can see who the real fascists are. In making this statement, you can see a white female French-Canadian journalist in total adulation of this so-called leader's duplicitous and utterly absurd words.[227] This is also ironic coming from someone who appeared in blackface on more than one occasion,[228] and who inappropriately groped a woman years ago,[229] and has mistreated females to cover up his corruption in his cabinet, including First Nations, Jody-Wilson Raybould.[230]

Trudeau ("Fidelito")[231] has also gone to say that he has no problems trampling on the freedoms of a minority in favour of the majority and, therefore, ignoring the Canadian Charter of Rights and Freedoms. This is beyond despicable behaviour. It is still a mystery to me how anyone could vote for such a duplicitous, weak, corrupt, amoral individual, but we could thank Liberal handouts and the CBC's lies for that.

But is it a Vaccine?

Vaccines have been lifesaving and crucial for controlling outbreaks of various diseases. Vaccines that have undergone long-term clinical trials have stood the test of time in their safety and efficacy. But what is a vaccine? The Wordnik Dictionary defines a vaccine as "a preparation of a weakened or killed pathogen, such as a bacterium or virus, or of a portion of the pathogen's structure that upon administration to an individual stimulates antibody production or cellular immunity against the pathogen but is incapable of causing severe

225 Anderson, "Typical 'vaccine hesitant' person is a 42-year-old Ontario woman who votes Liberal: Abacus polling."

226 Squire, Twitter Post.

227 Melville, Twitter Post.

228 Cavanagh, "FACE OF SHAME Inside Justin Trudeau's blackface shame after Canadian PM is caught in shocking pics in afro wigs and make-up."

229 Kingston, "Why Justin Trudeau's reported 'Kokanee Grope' really matters."

230 Forrest, "Trudeau goes on the attack after former justice minister Jody Wilson-Raybould's shock resignation."

231 A humorous nickname used to describe Trudeau as the illegitimate son of former Cuban dictator, Fidel Castro.

infection."[232] Such a definition was standard prior to 2015. From 2015–2021, to accommodate new technology such as mRNA, the definition provided by the CDC shifted to "producing immunity to a specific disease." Then from September 2021 forward, the definition changed to "produce protection from a specific disease."[233] Why this change? It seems that the definition has undergone such a change in order to correspond with the narrative we have been fed about COVID-19 vaccines, i.e., that they do not necessarily provide immunity but "protection" from serious illness. This new definition does not entail disease prevention or immunization. COVID-19 vaccines would not meet the prior definitions, so why not change its definition to fit the narrative? As Matt Margolis at *PJ Media* states:

> Is this part of the Biden administration's efforts to make the public accept regular COVID-19 boosters by changing how we understand the purpose of vaccines? Vaccines, we're now supposed to accept, don't provide us with immunity, just protection from disease. This vague definition essentially makes it easier for the government to recommend endless boosters for COVID (or any other disease) because vaccines, they say, no longer make us "immune." And yes, there are several vaccines that do need boosters, but that never changed our understanding or the definition of vaccines and vaccination.[234]

Is it Gene Therapy?

The president of Bayer's Pharmaceuticals Division, Stefan Oelrich, in a globalist health conference at the World Health Summit in Berlin from October 24–26 clearly stated that the mRNA COVID-19 injections are "cell and gene therapy" and that they were marketed under the guise of "vaccines" in order to make them more acceptable to most persons. Oelrich, at the The World Health Summit stated the following:

> We are really taking that leap [for diving innovation]—us as a company, Bayer—in cell and gene therapies...ultimately the mRNA vaccines are an example for that cell and gene therapy. I always like to say: if we had surveyed two years ago in the public—'would you be willing to take a gene or cell therapy and inject it into your body?'—we probably would have had a 95% refusal rate.[235]

232 Wordnik, "Vaccine."

233 CDC, "Vaccination and Immunization."

234 Margolis, "The CDC Just Made an Orwellian Change to the Definition of 'Vaccine' and 'Vaccination'."

235 See World Health Summit, "KEY 01 - Opening Ceremony - World Health Summit."

An article titled "Development of COVID-19 vaccines utilizing gene therapy technology" by gene therapy expert, Hironori Nakagami, published in the journal of *International Immunology*, explains the use of gene therapy technology:

> Viral vectors are tools to efficiently deliver genetic material into cells. As viral vectors, viruses are genetically engineered to efficiently produce some coronavirus proteins. Measles or adenovirus have been utilized as vectors that can efficiently enter cells, but the viral vector itself is weakened and cannot cause disease. This type of viral vector has achieved high transfection efficiency and has been developed over more than 20 years, using translational research on gene therapy, as an efficient therapy for cancer or diseases caused by genetic disorders. [236]

So, very well, one may argue that the "vaccine" uses gene therapy technology but in and of itself is not a gene therapeutic. In an earlier paper, Nakagami, explains further how this newer technology functions:

> In this last type of vaccine [Gene Therapy Technology including Viral Vector (adenovirus vector vaccine) and Activation of Cellular Immunity (RNA and DNA vaccine with drug delivery system)], DNA or RNA corresponding to a viral gene or modified gene is delivered into cells in the body to provoke an immune response. **These vaccines can also be developed to use genetic material, not viruses, and potentially activate cellular immunity as well as humoral immunity.** However, one of the problems for clinical development is the low transfection efficiency of nucleic acids in the body. In the rapid development of RNA vaccines against SARS-CoV-2, BioNTech and Moderna established gene delivery technology, which includes modification of nucleic acids and encapsulating mRNA in lipid nanoparticles. These companies rapidly, within half a year, presented initial results of clinical trials to support their RNA vaccine concept [6, 7], and in a phase 3 clinical trial, the RNA vaccine was found to be 95% effective in preventing COVID-19 [8]. The Food and Drug Administration (F.D.A.) granted the Pfizer and BioNTech vaccine the first approval given by the United States to a coronavirus vaccine, and the World Health Organization approved it for emergency use. Similarly, Moderna presented the initial results of a dose-escalation clinical trial [9, 10] and ultimately determined that its vaccine had an efficacy rate of 94%. The Moderna vaccine was the second one authorized by the F.D.A., at 1 week after approval of the Pfizer and BioNTech vaccine. **Although these vaccines are highly effective in preventing COVID-19 in the short term, their safety and efficiency should be continuously monitored for a long time.**[237]

236 Nakagami, "Development of COVID-19 vaccines utilizing gene therapy technology."
237 Nakagami, et al., "Therapeutic vaccine for chronic diseases after the COVID-19 Era."

I have set in bold text a couple of sentences that deserve special attention. The first boldened sentence focuses on how this technology can "potentially" activate cellular and humoral immunity—the question is to what success since we see so many breakthrough cases and people with the vaccine contracting and transmitting SARS-CoV-2 with all its variants. Then recall the change of definition on the CDC website of what a vaccine entails, so the narrative changed to how the vaccines weaken the virus. The second sentence I've boldened builds on the problem iterated with the first boldened sentence since this technology is so new with respect to COVID-19 and without long-term studies, how effective and safe is it? That's the point. If they were rushed while ignoring early life-saving treatment and they are not producing the intended effect, what was the point?

In December of 2021, the CDC dispelled a number of "myths" about the mRNA vaccines. First, they made clear that the vaccines do not invade the human cell's nucleus: "The genetic material delivered by mRNA vaccines never enters the nucleus of your cells, which is where your DNA is kept."[238] Second, they emphasized that the vaccines do not interact or alter human DNA: "COVID-19 vaccines do not change or interact with your DNA in any way."[239] And finally, that the "viral vector COVID-19 vaccines deliver genetic material to the cell nucleus to allow our cells to build protection against COVID-19. However, the vector virus does not have the machinery needed to integrate its genetic material into our DNA, so it cannot alter our DNA."[240] A new study from Sweden suggests that the claims of CDC are too premature, and that further rigorous studies would be required to determine whether the Pfizer-BioNTech COVID-19 (BNT162b2) vaccines alter DNA. These studies should involve entire living organisms involving animals in order to generate a greater understanding of the possible side-effects of mRNA vaccines.[241] The study did, however, indicate that the mRNA vaccine enters human liver cells, and indeed triggers the cell's DNA (which is found within the nucleus), which in turn, increases the production of the LINE-1 gene expression to make mRNA.[242] So although it's uncertain if it alters the DNA, the study indicates that it does indeed enter the nucleus and interact with DNA:

> In this study, we investigated the effect of BNT162b2 on the human liver cell line Huh7 in vitro. Huh7 cells were exposed to BNT162b2, and quantitative PCR was performed on RNA extracted from the

238 CDC, "Myths and Facts about COVID-19 Vaccines."

239 CDC, "Myths and Facts about COVID-19 Vaccines."

240 CDC, "Myths and Facts about COVID-19 Vaccines."

241 Aldén, et al., "Intracellular Reverse Transcription of Pfizer BioNTech COVID-19 mRNA Vaccine BNT162b2 In Vitro in Human Liver Cell Line."

242 Aldén, et al., "Intracellular Reverse Transcription of Pfizer BioNTech COVID-19 mRNA Vaccine BNT162b2 In Vitro in Human Liver Cell Line."

> cells... Our results indicate a fast up-take of BNT162b2 into human liver cell line Huh7, leading to changes in LINE-1 expression and distribution. We also show that BNT162b2 mRNA is reverse transcribed intracellularly into DNA in as fast as [6 hours] upon BNT162b2 exposure.[243]

A final question also arises with this gene therapy technology: Is there a connection with a transhumanism project? This certainly leaves the door open to many possibilities. Historian and philosopher, Yuval Noah Harari who authored *Sapiens: A Brief History of Humankind* has made some startling remarks in recent years regarding the future of humanity. In his book, *Sapiens*, he attempts to provide a materialistic account of human origins, he does so without providing much evidence though. In lieu of this, he rejects human free will. He has said he believes in intelligent design, not in a transcendent creator, but in humans directing the future of evolution. Unsurprisingly, on his website he states: "History began when humans invented gods, and will end when humans become gods."[244] Harari is an "agenda contributor" for the World Economic Forum.[245] He supports the Fourth Industrial Revolution and the transhumanist agenda. He has proposed a simple equation that he claims can lead to hacking human biology: B (biological knowledge) x C (computing power) x D (data) = AHH! (ability to hack humans).[246]

Humans have willfully submitted themselves to taking an experimental injection without a clue of its long-term effects, one which has been largely ineffective against SARS-CoV-2. Over the past two years, the so-called pandemic has forced people into making a choice between health and privacy/civil liberties. Although a false dichotomy, most people have chosen "health." Throughout the pandemic we have seen governments monitoring its citizens in unprecedented ways. This trend will only worsen with the fully global implementation of digital ID (which has already been implemented in Canada),[247] as Harari states:

> You might argue that there is nothing new about all this. In recent years both governments and corporations have been using ever more sophisticated technologies to track, monitor and manipulate people.

243 Aldén, et al., "Intracellular Reverse Transcription of Pfizer BioNTech COVID-19 mRNA Vaccine BNT162b2 In Vitro in Human Liver Cell Line."

244 Harari, https://www.ynharari.com/.

245 Harari, https://www.weforum.org/agenda/authors/yuval-harari.

246 World Economic Forum, "Read Yuval Harari's blistering warning to Davos in full."

247 Government of Ontario, "Digital ID in Ontario." Please note that the Government of Ontario's webpage makes Digital ID sound benign and provides a number of assurances regarding privacy, but this could be just the beginning of larger system of human monitoring. This is just the next step.

> Yet if we are not careful, the epidemic might nevertheless mark an important watershed in the history of surveillance. Not only because it might normalise the deployment of mass surveillance tools in countries that have so far rejected them, but even more so because it signifies a dramatic transition from "over the skin" to "under the skin" surveillance.
>
> Hitherto, when your finger touched the screen of your smartphone and clicked on a link, the government wanted to know what exactly your finger was clicking on. But with coronavirus, the focus of interest shifts. Now the government wants to know the temperature of your finger and the blood-pressure under its skin.[248]

So, how does this relate to the "vaccines"? Well, Harari, in an interview, has also gone on to support the Great Reset with statements like the following: "It's often said that you should never allow a good crisis to go to waste, because a crisis is an opportunity to also do 'good' reforms that in normal times, people will never agree to. But in a crisis, you see, we have no choice—so let's do it."[249] This is the sort of language we've been hearing from globalist politicians and health experts for two years. He goes on to say that:

> The vaccine will help us, of course. It will make things more manageable, [such as] surveillance. People could look back in a hundred years and identify the [COVID-19] pandemic as the moment when a regime of surveillance took over – especially surveillance under the skin... This ability to hack human beings, to go under the skin, collect biometric data, analyze it and understand people better than they understand themselves ... is the most important event of the 21st century.[250]

Given this, Harari dismisses the idea of the soul, free will and any conventional spirituality. Harari also brings to the fore the notion of digital dictatorship. Is this far fetched? Perhaps to some, but the transhumanist project has been underway for many years. The Catholic paleontologist Pierre Teilhard de Chardin, in the early 20th century, was one of the first to discuss the concept with some depth. The Great Reset with the pandemic, the digital ID system, and what we are discovering about the mRNA vaccines and their abilities, make this notion quite plausible. The transhumanist connection to the vaccines will be further explored in Chapter 46.

248 Harari, "The World After Coronavirus."

249 Thrivetime Show, "'People Will Look Back & Identify COVID-19 Is When a Surveillance Regime Took Over.' - Dr. Harari."

250 Thrivetime Show, "'People Will Look Back & Identify COVID-19 Is When a Surveillance Regime Took Over.' - Dr. Harari."

Three Vital Questions

Is it Necessary?

First, there is a high recovery rate of at least that of 97% and 99.75%, which includes people with comorbidities; therefore one ought to wonder why the excessive and aggressive vaccine rollout?[251] Second, we can say "no" for those who have acquired natural immunity from the virus since based on some credible studies it is longer lasting and more robust than double vaccination.[252] Third, there are early treatments that have been largely ignored by governments to treat COVID-19. Fourth, given the high survival rate from COVID-19 and the fact that there are so many breakthrough cases for those who have been doubly vaccinated,[253] we can emphatically say that, no, it is not necessary. Fifth, it's worth considering that the vaccines' "efficacy" wane after 6 months or less. It is worth asking why they are pushing these boosters and how many will be required (one every 3–6 months). Lastly, is it necessary to vaccinate anyone under 20, especially those 5 to 11? Of course not. In fact, healthy children are critical to herd immunity.[254] They are at zero risk of fatality and at an incredibly low risk for hospitalization. Given the infectious Omicron variant, Israel is rethinking its vaccination policy to allow mass infection to reach herd immunity. So, a resounding "no" to the question of its necessity. The only necessity would be for those who want to avoid restrictions, whether it is to travel, dine out, or go to the gym. However, in many places, including Ontario, lockdowns for both the vaccinated and unvaccinated have been imposed. Many countries have been lifting most of their mandates including vaccine passports, even if it may be temporary.

Is it dangerous?

On assessing the dangers of the COVID-19 vaccines, it is worth considering what we are comparing it to, i.e., the relative risks in comparison to other vaccines and medications. We already saw that it is not necessary. Even though out of the 9.35 billion doses of COVID-19 vaccines administered around the world,[255] the majority of people receiving these have not had any serious adverse

251 WebMD, "Coronavirus Recovery."

252 See subsection above: "Natural Immunity Matters."

253 Here's an example: World Entertainment News Network, "Derek Hough in quarantine with COVID-19 after 'DWTS' appearance."

254 For a list of scientific studies and peer reviewed articles supporting this, see "International Alliance of Physicians and Medical Scientists, COVID-Recovered Immunity is Durable."

255 Vaccine Tracker, "More Than 9.35 Billion Shots Given: Covid-19 Tracker."

reactions or suffered fatality, the long-term effects are still unknown, especially with respect to children. We also do not know what kind of cumulative effect that receiving booster after booster will have on people's organs, immune systems, and body in general. We also do not know the real reasons as to why some suffer vaccine injuries and fatalities while others do not.[256] We also do not have accurate statistics regarding the adverse effects and number of fatalities.

There has been a lot of misinformation and disinformation spread about the Vaccine Adverse Events Reporting System (VAERS). According to the CDC website: "VAERS is part of the larger vaccine safety system in the United States that helps make sure vaccines are safe. The system is co-managed by CDC and FDA."[257] Patients and family members may also submit reports. People have been quick to respond that the reporting method is not accurate and is over embellished. VAERS is a voluntary reporting system for many, but healthcare providers are required by law to report adverse effects. Whether or not a significant percentage goes unreported by healthcare providers remains up for debate. One should consider that the reports only account for one percent of actual vaccine injuries according to the Lazarus Report.[258] As of December 24, 2021, there have been 1,000,227 reports. There have been 21,002 deaths and 110,609 hospitalizations.[259] The majority of deaths are reported within the first couple of days. The adverse effects at times require further investigation, but when an adverse reaction occurs within a few days of the vaccine, it seems more likely than not that the vaccine caused the adverse reaction or was at least a contributing factor. Because of the Freedom of Information Act (FOIA), the FDA and Pfizer agreed to release 400,000 pages of reports. Most alarming was the enormous list of potential adverse events from the mRNA vaccines which are listed in an appendix titled "adverse events of special interest" (people should be aware of this, this will help them provide a more accurate form of informed consent). There are 9 pages of adverse effects listed in paragraph form.[260] This should give anyone pause.

Let's consider the 1976 US swine flu vaccination program. The goal of this program was to inoculate every American. Over 40 million were vaccinated (around one fifth of the population then). Consequently, the program was halted after at least 25 deaths and 500 people developed a rare neurological disorder known as Guillain-Barre Syndrome.[261] As of January 6, 2022, 514

256 See Chapter 46 for some speculations regarding percentage of placebos administered.

257 CDC, "Vaccine Adverse Event Reporting System (VAERS)." L.

258 See Lazarus, et al., "The Lazarus Report."

259 Open VAERS, "VAERS COVID Vaccine Adverse Event Reports."

260 World Safery Pfizer, "5.3.6 CUMULATIVE ANALYSIS OF POST-AUTHORIZATION ADVERSE EVENT REPORTS OF PF-07302048 (BNT162B2) RECEIVED THROUGH 28-FEB-2021."

261 Roan, "Swine flu 'debacle' of 1976 is recalled"; Gollom, "1976 U.S. swine flu vaccination program may offer lessons for COVID-19 pandemic."

million COVID-19 vaccine doses have been administered in the US, i.e., 12.85 times more than for the swine flu, but proportionally over 65 times the number of deaths have been reported. Given this data, yes, the vaccine is dangerous. The question arises as to why it has not been yet pulled from the market. This is incredibly troublesome if The Lazarus Report has any validity.

As we saw above, natural immunity and healthy children are vital for reaching herd immunity. We must also ask, given this information and what we know about the improbability of fatality and hospitalization for people under 20 years of age (we will explore the numbers below), why the desperate approach to inoculate everyone aged five and up? An excellent article titled "Why Are We Vaccinating Our Children?"[262] in the journal *Toxicology Reports*, makes the following points:

- Bulk of COVID-19 per capita deaths occur in elderly with high comorbidities.
- Per capita COVID-19 deaths are negligible in children.
- Clinical trials for these inoculations were very short-term.
- Clinical trials did not address long-term effects most relevant to children.
- High post-inoculation deaths reported in VAERS (very short-term).

With the Omicron variant, a contradictory narrative is unfolding—much of which is Orwellian doublespeak. First, we were told that although Omicron is highly virulent, it is not a major threat like the Delta variant since it is weaker but better at evading vaccines.[263] Then we have been told that: "To be clear, medical experts still stress that COVID-19 remains a mild illness for the vast majority of children; the rise in hospitalizations among youth is likely tied, at least in part, to this variant's uncanny ability to simply infect more people."[264] We are also told the children have "cold"-like symptoms and that it is affecting children and newborns more than adults.[265] Again, how do we know this is not influenza since the PCR and rapid tests are unreliable for distinguishing between SARS-CoV-2 and influenza viruses. So, we may ask why? This article title tells all: "Omicron surge vexes parents of children too young for shots." One may argue that the effects of Omicron are unknown, and this is why the facts are constantly shifting, but why should we trust the media, government

262 Kostoff, et al., "Why are we vaccinating children against COVID-19?"

263 The Associated Press, "Data analysis indicates omicron is milder, better at evading vaccines."

264 Pelley, "Why COVID-19 hospitalizations of Canadian kids —and infants —could keep rising as Omicron spreads."

265 Pelley, "Why COVID-19 hospitalizations of Canadian kids —and infants —could keep rising as Omicron spreads."

or medical bureaucrats since they have betrayed us so often. For anyone paying attention, the answer should be rather obvious: it is about producing a justification to begin an aggressive campaign inoculate children under the age of five. Before Christmas of last year, a three-year-old girl, Ámbar Suárez, died of a heart attack shortly after receiving the COVID-19 vaccine. All because she could not otherwise enroll in pre-school.[266]

It should be further emphasized as to why healthy children should not receive this vaccine:

- Negligible clinical risks from SARS-CoV-2 infection exist for healthy children under eighteen.
- Long-term safety of the current COVID vaccines in children cannot be determined prior to instituting such policies. Without high-powered, reproducible, long-term safety data, risks to the long-term health status of children remain too high to support use in healthy children.
- Children risk severe, adverse events from receiving the vaccine. Permanent physical damage to the brain, heart, immune and reproductive system associated with SARS-CoV-2 spike protein-based genetic vaccines has been demonstrated in children.
- Healthy, unvaccinated children are critical to achieving herd immunity. Natural immunity is proven to tolerate infection, benefiting community protection while there is insufficient data to assess whether Covid vaccines assist herd immunity.[267]

Also consider the numbers from the VigiAccess database (World Health Organization Programme for International Drug Monitoring (WHO PIDM): http://www.vigiaccess.org/. Type in COVID-19 vaccine in the search engine and you'll see all the adverse effects. Look at Appendix 3 for a chart comparing the COVID-19 vaccine (all different types) to other vaccines and drugs from 1968–2021. Notice the astronomical difference in adverse effects in a short time span—it's more dangerous than all these vaccines/drugs combined from 1960s/1970s/1980s until now. If you tally all the adverse effects of the COVID-19 vaccines (keep in mind according to The Lazarus Report only one percent are reported) in less than a two-year span, there are more reported adverse events than all the other drugs and vaccines combined spanning decades!

Steven Pelech, a tenured UBC professor of Immunology and Neurology, founder of Kinexus Bioinformatics, and Chair of the Scientific and Medical

266 Wolfe, "3-year-old girl dies of heart attack one day after taking COVID vaccine."

267 See International Alliance of Physicians and Medical Scientists, "COVID-Recovered Immunity is Durable."

Advisory Committee for the Canadian COVID Care Alliance (CCCA) has initiated a petition in the House of Commons. In the petition he requests that the Canadian government "suspend the use of COVID-19 vaccines in pregnant women, children, youth, and adults of child-bearing age until the ongoing short- and long-term safety trials are fully completed and published in peer-reviewed journals."[268]

Consider this statement from a group of physicians examining and questioning vaccine safety and the lack of research being conducted into this:

> Under the cautionary principle, it is parsimonious to consider vaccine-induced Spike synthesis could cause clinical signs of severe COVID-19, and erroneously be counted as new cases of SARS-CoV-2 infections. If so, the true adverse effects of the current global vaccination strategy may never be recognized unless studies specifically examine this question. There is already noncausal evidence of temporary or sustained increases in COVID-19 deaths following vaccination in some countries (Fig. 1) and in light of Spike's pathogenicity, these deaths must be studied in depth to determine whether they are related to vaccination.[269]

The UK government, in vaccine surveillance reports, has recently admitted that COVID vaccines have damaged the natural immune system of those who have been double-vaccinated. Furthermore, that once you have been double-vaccinated, you will never again be able to acquire full natural immunity to Covid variants, or possibly any other virus. In the "COVID-19 Vaccine Surveillance Report Week 42,"[270] the UK Department of Health admits on page 23 that "N antibody levels appear to be lower in individuals who acquire infection following 2 doses of vaccination." [271] It goes on to say that this drop in antibodies is essentially permanent. What does this mean? We know that these vaccines do not prevent infection or transmission of the virus (indeed, the report elsewhere shows that vaccinated adults are now much more likely to be infected than unvaccinated ones). The British now find that the vaccine interferes with the body's ability to make antibodies after infection, not only against the spike protein, but also against other parts of the virus. In particular, vaccinated people do not appear to form antibodies against the nucleocapsid protein, the envelope of the virus, which is a crucial part of the response in unvaccinated people. In the long term, the vaccinated are far more susceptible to any mutations in the spike protein, even if they have already been infected and recovered once or

268 Pelech, Petition to the House of Commons. 6.

269 Bruno, et al., "SARS-CoV-2 mass vaccination: Urgent questions on vaccine safety that demand answers from international health agencies, regulatory authorities, governments and vaccine developers," 5.

270 UK Health Security Agency, "COVID-19 vaccine surveillance report Week 42."

271 UK Health Security Agency, "COVID-19 vaccine surveillance report Week 42."

more. The unvaccinated, on the other hand, will gain lasting, if not permanent, immunity to all strains of the alleged virus after being naturally infected with it even once. Insurance companies are backing down because a huge wave of claims that are coming their way. In line with this, in the state of Indiana, deaths are up by 40 percent according to an insurance CEO.[272] Moreover, a number of other states in the US are investigating the spike in deaths among 18 to 49-year-olds that are unrelated to COVID-19.[273] We may ask what is the cause of this? Covidians will rush to say it's COVID, but this does not add up to scrutiny. Why now after massive amounts of vaccination rates and not a year ago when vaccination was very low? The answer is obviously the vaccines and the side-effects of ridiculous COVID restrictions. So, one can unequivocally say that, yes, the injection is dangerous. It seems quite evident as to why there is so much censorship on anything that questions the efficacy and safety of these injections. Governments will be quick to say that it is misinformation, and that they are censoring such material because it is to protect our health. However, this is pure propaganda. If this was about our health, they would have not taken the majority of the measures they have. Journals are adamant to censor and remove papers that question the safety and efficacy of the vaccines. Publishers like Elsvier will remove papers without notifying or even providing any reason for their removal.[274] This should give any reasonable person pause.

Is it effective? [275]

This brings us to our last question: Is it effective? In short, the answer again is no. On January 10, 2022, in an interview with *Yahoo! Finance*, Pfizer CEO, Albert Bourla, admitted that the two vaccine doses offer very little protection, if any, against the so-called Omicron variant:

> So—and we know that the two doses of the vaccine offer very limited protection, if any. The three doses, with the booster, they offer reasonable protection against hospitalization and deaths—and, again, that's, I think, very good—and less protection against the infection.
>
> Now, we are working on a new version of our vaccine—the 1.1, let me put it that way—that will cover Omicron as well. And, of course, we

272 Menge, "Indiana life insurance CEO says deaths are up 40% among people ages 18-64."

273 See Svab, "States Investigating Surge in Mortality Rate Among 18–49-Year-Olds, Majority Unrelated to COVID-19."

274 Svab, "Researcher Calls Out Censorship After Journal Pulls COVID-19 Vaccine Adverse Events Analysis."

275 We have already discussed much of the material regarding the transmission of COVID-19 from the vaccinated to both vaccinated and unvaccinated populations, see Chapter 42 section titled: "Cognitive Dissonance and Self-Deception."

> are waiting to have the final results. The vaccine will be ready in March. And the vaccine, we'll be able to produce it massively.[276]

The ploy is to produce endless profits through endless boosters because of an infinite number of variants.

In an article published in October 2021 in *The Lancet*, researchers state: "The SARS-CoV-2 delta (B.1.617.2) variant is highly transmissible and spreading globally, including in populations with high vaccination rates."[277] Also, consider that natural immunity is considered to be just as strong or stronger than double vaccination.[278] This is well known throughout the literature, something not told to us by the media. Furthermore, a significant number of doctors insist that taking the vaccine after having had COVID-19 is a contraindication. Consider this, from an Israeli study where there is a high rate of double vaccination:

> This study demonstrated that natural immunity confers longer lasting and stronger protection against infection, symptomatic disease and hospitalization caused by the Delta variant of SARS-CoV-2, compared to the BNT162b2 two-dose vaccine-induced immunity.[279]

Please keep in mind that the main role of the vaccine is to protect the recipient and growing data is suggesting otherwise. To this end, they are not effective. The media propaganda machine is saying that the vaccinated are in danger from the unvaccinated, but this is logically incoherent. If the vaccines don't work, why take them? If they do work, then why be fearful? Changing the narrative to that it "weakens" the virus or that "it does not offer 100 percentage protection but it's still effective" is a clear admission that they aren't effective while saying otherwise. It's just a form of doublespeak. Even Dr. Anthony Fauci admits they're not effective and that you'll need boosters after being doubly vaccinated. Does it sound like they're very effective to you? Check out the *New York Times* transcript of his interview regarding this.[280] Think about how governments are in the absurd and awkward position of having to convince the unvaccinated that the vaccine is effective and necessary, while trying to

276 Yahoo! Finance, "New COVID-19 vaccine that covers Omicron 'will be ready in March,' Pfizer CEO says."

277 Singanayagam, et al., "Community transmission and viral load kinetics of the SARS-CoV-2 delta (B.1.617.2) variant in vaccinated and unvaccinated individuals in the UK: a prospective, longitudinal, cohort study."

278 Block, "Vaccinating people who have had covid-19: why doesn't natural immunity count in the US?" See also section above: "Natural Immunity Matters."

279 Gazit, et al., "Comparing SARS-CoV-2 natural immunity to vaccine-induced immunity: reinfections versus breakthrough infections."

280 Barbaro, "An interview With Dr. Anthony Fauci."

convince the vaccinated that the vaccine is not strong enough and that they need boosters! There is much more to be said and many more resources to be shared, but this should suffice to dismantle the case for vaccinating children—especially healthy children. Consider that the end trial date for testing "the Safety, Tolerability, Immunogenicity, and Efficacy of RNA Vaccine Candidates Against COVID-19 in Healthy Individuals" ends on May 2, 2023.[281] That's taken from the clinical trials of the US Government website.

Democratic Governor of New York, Kathy Hochul, recently admitted that they overcounted COVID-19 cases. The overcounting seems like a justification for pushing boosters. Luckily, Hochul was honest enough to admit that:

> We talked about the hospitalizations. I have always wondered, we're looking at the hospitalizations of people testing positive in a hospital… Is that person in the hospital because of COVID or did they show up there and are routinely tested and showing positive and they may have been asymptomatic or even just had the sniffles?[282]

Are politicians starting to realize that people are catching onto their lies?

Professor Günter Kampf of the University Medicine Greifswald in Germany explains that vaccinated populations are indeed spreading the virus and that it should affect government policy:

> The US Centres for Disease Control and Prevention (CDC) identifies four of the top five counties with the highest percentage of fully vaccinated population (99.9–84.3%) as "high" transmission counties. Many decision makers assume that the vaccinated can be excluded as a source of transmission. It appears to be grossly negligent to ignore the vaccinated population as a possible and relevant source of transmission when deciding about public health control measures.[283]

Consider also that people who are allowed to travel are "fully vaccinated," so how did the Omicron variant spread? It is the vaccinated who are spreading the variants around the globe if they are the only ones permitted to travel for the time being. The vaccinated are spreading the variants of SARS-CoV-2. Forty percent of the Ottawa Senators hockey team were infected with COVID-19 despite 100 percent vaccination.[284] In late December 2021, over 80 cruise ships were being

281 NIH, "Study to Describe the Safety, Tolerability, Immunogenicity, and Efficacy of RNA Vaccine Candidates Against COVID-19 in Healthy Individuals."

282 Moore, "Governor admits COVID hospitalizations overcounted."

283 Kampf, "The epidemiological relevance of the COVID-19-vaccinated population is increasing."

284 Radnofsky and Higgins, "The Ottawa Senators Have a 100% Vaccination Rate—and 40% of the Team Has Tested Positive for Covid."

investigated by the CDC for COVID outbreaks.[285] And again, aren't only fully vaccinated people allowed to board these ships? How did the Omicron variant enter Australia if the unvaccinated are not able to leave or enter the country?

How do we make sense of these statistics after 200 million have been vaccinated in the United States?

> After months of promises to tackle the pandemic, Biden recently conceded that there's "no federal solution" to it. Last year ended with more than 450,000 deaths attributed to COVID-19 and more than 33 million detected infections. That's up 27 percent and 67 percent, respectively, from a year earlier.[286]

It turns out the Biden administration is failing splendidly.

Surprisingly, the CBC published a piece quoting Dr. Robert Strang, Nova Scotia's chief medical officer of health. He is taking a commonsense approach, echoing The Great Barrington Declaration, calling for the uplifting of restrictions since the virus will be here to stay regardless of what other medical experts claim: "At some point in time, we are going to have to say we have to move away and accept that the virus that causes COVID is going to be around with us."[287] He also rightly recognizes immunity from infection, where he said the goal should be to "'manage' COVID-19 'based on having good levels of immunity from both vaccination and infection…[so] that we no longer have to have these wide restrictive measures and have this huge focus of trying to identify as many cases as possible."[288] Again, this sounds an awful like The Great Barrington Declaration. Strang also refers to what he calls "population immunity" (a term he prefers over "herd immunity"):

> But whether it's a combination of vaccine or infection, you know, we have to at some point be able to say we need to have a much more normal life and live with COVID…and try to find a more balanced approach between limiting the impacts of COVID, focusing on the severe side of the illness—those who are most vulnerable—but not having all the restrictions that we have in place right now.[289]

Could this be a sleight of hand to offer governments in Canada and elsewhere a "way out" of facing the absurd and unlawful measures that have been exacted

285 Stokes, "More than 80 cruise ships are being investigated for COVID outbreaks. So why are people still going aboard"; Phillips, "COVID-19 Outbreak Among Fully Vaccinated Cruise Crew Ends New Year's Trip in Portugal."

286 Svab, "2021 COVID-19 Recap: 200 Million Vaccinated, 450,000 Dead."

287 Hall, "Learning to live with COVID: why some experts say it's time to 'manage' the virus."

288 Hall, "Learning to live with COVID: why some experts say it's time to 'manage' the virus."

289 Hall, "Learning to live with COVID: why some experts say it's time to 'manage' the virus."

on free citizens of the world? The Omicron variant presents the perfect chance to argue for natural immunity in the face of all the failures from the lockdowns, masks, vaccines, vaccine mandates, and passports, etc. It turns out that natural immunity indeed does matter.[290] High numbers of people who are vaccinated are catching and transmitting COVID. It is also interesting to note that the majority of hospitalizations, including higher numbers in ICU, are of people that have been doubly or triply vaccinated.[291] Thus, the vaccinated that are hospitalized are outnumbering those that aren't by a significant margin. One could argue, "well, there are more people vaccinated, so that is the reason why there are more hospitalizations," or could the answer be that perhaps the vaccines are playing a role in increased hospitalizations? As of January 14, 2022, the percentage of fully vaccinated people being hospitalized for reasons related to COVID-19 is 54 percent[292] (most likely related to adverse effects of the vaccine). So much for effectivity; again, doesn't stop infection, hospitalization, or transmission. Even though anecdotal, I have noticed that the vaccinated people I do know tend to get sick more often than others who are injection free. I have yet to be sick in over two years (much prior to March 2020). As a final point worth pondering, the Omicron variant renders vaccine passports and mandates obsolete since the vaccines are not reducing transmission.

In an interesting twist of events, the WHO interestingly made a couple of omissions in a recent statement: "in addition to protection against severe disease and death, be more effective in protection against infection thus lowering community transmission and the need for stringent and broad-reaching public health and social measures."[293] First, they recognize that the vaccines are inefficient in protecting against infection. Second, if they do not expect flu vaccines to lower community transmission, why would they expect new COVID vaccines to do so? Especially considering how much more dangerous they are. They cannot shoulder the burden of increasing efficiency and lowering adverse reactions and fatalities.

Unjustly Stigmatizing the Unvaccinated

Australia has even gone as far as revoking the visa of the number one tennis player in the world, Novak Djokovic, based on vaccination status, despite

290 See section above: "Natural Immunity Matters."

291 Government of Ontario, "Hospitalizations."

292 Bradley, "Ontario first province to correct misinformation on COVID hospitalization numbers."

293 WHO, "Interim Statement on COVID-19 vaccines in the context of the circulation of the Omicron SARS-CoV-2 Variant from the WHO Technical Advisory Group on COVID-19 Vaccine Composition (TAG-CO-VAC)"; see also Berenson, "Boosters Are Over."

having acquired natural immunity after being infected and having a medical exemption.[294] On January 14, 2022, his visa was revoked for a second time and was sent back to a "detention hotel" and the was subsequently deported.[295] And just like on many other issues, governments flip-flopped on this one. They tried to fear monger by saying: "look what we can do to the number one tennis player in the world, what do you think we will do to you?" Serbia has much greater freedom than Australia at this point in time. Serbians seem to value their freedom much more. Unlike, other professional tennis players, Djokovic is taking a stance on the major "health" crisis of this century. The irony is that Novak Djokovic is one of the greatest athletes on the planet. He is in incredible physical condition, more so than 99.999999 percent of the world's population, and I would argue more than his "fully vaccinated" fellow professional tennis competitors. The more they continue to get boosters the more they will compromise their immune systems and their careers. As an example, Jeremy Chardy's tennis career was brought to a halt because of a vaccine injury.[296] He was perfectly healthy prior to receiving the clot-shot. Chardy wanted to do the "common good for humanity." This notion is reprehensible since healthy people, and people in general who do not want this experimental vaccine, should not be coerced or even questioned for not taking it. Tragically, Chardy's case is not an isolated one. As of December 2021, there have been 260 deaths due to the COVID vaccine and many more injuries.[297] Whoever thinks this is normal and acceptable needs a reality check. The mainstream media would never report on this since they work hand in hand with Big Pharma. And yet, they treat Djokovic like he's a leper, while the vaccinated are getting ill from COVID and transmitting it. He may not be able to defend his title for another three years; Australia has truly fallen. Nevertheless, Djokovic would rather protect his body and soul than to be number one in the world, as he told a BBC reporter.[298] Another athlete on the right side of history is the legendary Canadian hockey player, Theo Fleury, who has been a formidable opponent of the NWO. Recently he tweeted: "Trudeau needed to invoke the Emergencies Cowards Act because he's afraid of Tamara Lich."[299] We have been forced into accepted Orwellian doublethink, much like the slogans of the Party in the novel, *Ninety Eighty-Four*: "War is peace / freedom is slavery [and] ignorance is

294 You can count on the BBC to write a hit piece on Novak: BBC, "What has Novak Djokovic actually said about vaccines?"

295 BBC, "Novak Djokovic: Australia to detain tennis star on Saturday after visa cancelled."

296 Mesic, "Taking vaccine and doing 'common good for humanity' force Jeremy Chardy to end season."

297 Real Science, "445 Athlete Cardiac Arrests, Serious Issues, 260 Dead, After COVID Shot."

298 Game To Love - Tennis Podcast "Novak Djokovic BBC FULL Interview | LIVE Stream Reaction | Game To Love."

299 Fleury, Twitter Post. This was a reference to Trudeau's dictatorial imposition of the Emergencies Act to stop the truckers' protest on Parliament Hill in Ottawa (more on that in the epilogue).

strength." We can add healthy is ill, and the continual doublethink we are being fed: "the COVID vaccine is safe and effective."

Despite the inconvenient facts regarding these vaccines, politicians, medical bureaucrats, the media, vaccinated citizens, etc., continue to blame the unvaccinated for the spread of SARS-CoV-2 and its variants. This is so absurd that you cannot even make this up. Robert Malone tweeted, "First time in history that the ineffectiveness of a medicine is blamed on those who haven't taken it."[300] Malone was removed from Twitter for tweeting a video from the Canadian Covid Care Alliance showing that the Pfizer COVID-19 vaccines causes more illnesses than they prevent.[301] Malone had half a million followers on Twitter, and after being interviewed by Joe Rogan on Spotify, he had gathered close to 50 million views. Many people that had never heard of him became acquainted with his work. Luckily, Twitter's strategy was a massive failure.

French President Emmanuel Macron, in similar fashion to Trudeau, in an interview said: "But as for the non-vaccinated, I really want to piss them off. And we will continue to do this, to the end. This is the strategy." Politicians are taking desperate measures to intimidate the unvaccinated into compliance. However, the epidemiological significance of the vaccinated should not be ignored. Despite what governments and the media propagandize with, mass vaccination is creating selective evolutionary pressures:

> By ineptly pushing mass vaccination, governments have created evolutionary pressures on SARS-CoV-2, which have mutated to escape the effect of the vaccines. Now fully vaccinated persons are contracting COVID-19 in large numbers, probably with the Delta variant. They cover vaccine safety, and when considering the failure of efficacy and the fatal and nonfatal serious safety concerns with all of the vaccines, McCullough concludes that we should shut down the ill-fated mass vaccination program. The remaining cases can be easily treated early at home, and we can close out the pandemic with little hardship on populations.[302]

What McCullough iterated in July of 2021 in an interview is true of the Omicron variant as well. Does anyone ask the question as to why there were no variants spreading like wildfire prior to the vaccine rollout? The answer seems rather simple, i.e., vaccines exert evolutionary pressure on viruses that cause an

300 This was on his Twitter account, but he was taken off the platform at the end of December 2021: https://ifunny.co/picture/robert-w-malone-md-rwmalonemd-first-time-in-history-that-z2FvLpl79.

301 Canadian Covid Care Alliance, "The Pfizer Inoculations For COVID-19 – More Harm Than Good – VIDEO."

302 McCullough, "By Pushing Mass Vaccination, Governments Have Created Evolutionary Pressures on SARS-CoV-2."

acceleration in mutations and consequently create variants adept in evading immune response. This causes the virus's mutation to become more virulent and threatening. What are we to make of the fact that these variants appear within countries where inoculation is the highest? Given this hypothesis, it becomes more plausible that the vaccinated are carrying forward and extending the pandemic.

The COVID-19 crisis presents us with one of the greatest medical disasters in human history. In part due to malfeasance and in part to utter incompetence; it's difficult to say where one starts and the other stops, but they have gone hand in hand.

We know from history that stigmatization of groups of people whether in the US, Germany, Africa, or even currently China has led to horrific crimes against humanity. Professor Kampf emphasizes this point in an opinion piece published in *The Lancet*:

> Historically, both the USA and Germany have engendered negative experiences by stigmatising parts of the population for their skin colour or religion. I call on high-level officials and scientists to stop the inappropriate stigmatisation of unvaccinated people, who include our patients, colleagues, and other fellow citizens, and to put extra effort into bringing society together.[303]

Peter Doshi, the editor of the *British Medical Journal* and associate professor of pharmaceutical health services research at the University of Maryland School of Pharmacy, has gone out of his way to emphasize that we are not in a pandemic of the unvaccinated. He's questioned the necessity of booster shots if hospitalization and death are occurring predominantly in unvaccinated people.

In a roundtable discussion organized by US Senator Ron Johnson with people that have been harmed by the COVID-19 vaccines and respected scientific experts, Doshi stated the following: "And why would the statistics be so different in the United Kingdom [in comparison to the United States], where most hospitalizations and deaths from COVID occur among the fully vaccinated? There's a correlation there that you should be curious about."[304] He also went on say that: "Something's not right."[305] Doshi also challenged the redefinition of "vaccine," "anti-vaccination," and "anti-vaxxer." For instance, in the Merriam-Webster dictionary, anti-vaxxer is defined as "a person who opposes the use of vaccines or regulations mandating vaccination."[306] He

303 Kampf, "COVID-19: stigmatising the unvaccinated is not justified."

304 *The Rio Times*, "We are not in a "pandemic of the unvaccinated," says British Medical Journal editor Peter Doshi."

305 *The Rio Times*, "We are not in a "pandemic of the unvaccinated," says British Medical Journal editor Peter Doshi."

306 Miriam-Webster Dictionary, "Anti-Vaxxer."

iterated that the second part of the definition is alarming since whole countries and perhaps the majority of the world comes under such a definition.[307] Clearly, an agenda for mandating COVID-19 vaccination across many spectrums is in full-force.

Doshi has also been skeptical of whether the clinical trials demonstrate that COVID-19 vaccines will save lives:

> None of the trials currently under way are designed to detect a reduction in any serious outcome such as hospital admissions, use of intensive care, or deaths. Nor are the vaccines being studied to determine whether they can interrupt transmission of the virus.[308]

Oddly, governments never give any adequate response to these inconvenient facts. In my experience, when I point out evidence—actual science, and statistics—people are unwilling to listen. It is unfortunate. I attribute this trance to what Desmet calls "mass formation psychosis" since for the Covidian, evidence is irrelevant, and you must believe blindly in the narrative. The vaccinated must keep in mind that they are just one booster away from becoming unvaccinated in their status but must live with the ramifications of all the shots they've taken.

If anything, governments, and vaccinated populations should be thankful to the unvaccinated since they function as a control group. Does it make any sense to try and inoculate an entire population if this is truly about our health? How could we possibly know whether the vaccine is truly effective or not? You need to measure it against a certain segment of the population. This is the largest human experiment that has taken place in medical history.

Where's the Baloney Detector?

Anyone who is not in the trance of mass formation psychosis will realize that something is not right with this picture. The level of incompetence coupled with malfeasance are truly breathtaking. But is that all? Something just does not add up. We can observe from the origins of the virus to all the measures taken, including lockdowns, masking, "social" distancing, PCR testing, and vaccine roll out, that this is not about our well-being nor our health. Governments do not have our best interests at heart, neither does the media and even many physicians who have betrayed their Oaths to do no harm.

307 *The Rio Times*, "We are not in a 'pandemic of the unvaccinated,' says British Medical Journal editor Peter Doshi."

308 Doshi, "Will covid-19 vaccines save lives? Current trials aren't designed to tell us."

The late astronomer, Carl Sagan, in his book, *Demon Haunted World: Science As a Candle in the Dark*, warned us about falling prey to blatant falsehoods through what he dubbed a "baloney detector":

> A deception arises, sometimes innocently but collaboratively, sometimes with cynical premeditation. Usually the victim is caught up in a powerful emotion—wonder, fear, greed grief. Credulous acceptance of baloney can cost you money; that's what P. T. Barnum meant when he said, "There's a sucker born every minute." But it can be much more dangerous than that, and when governments and societies lose the capacity to for critical thinking catastrophic, however, sympathetic we may be to those who have bought the baloney.[309]

Governments and societies do not deserve any pity in this context. Something tells me Sagan would have agreed. Sagan encouraged skepticism and debate so that experts can discuss freely. None of this has happened, instead experts countering the narrative have been censored, silenced, and cancelled (losing employment). Sagan also encouraged us to think of many hypotheses and possibilities. He also wrote about not getting overly attached to a hypothesis and to question why we do when we do, and then compare it objectively with others.[310] There was much more he said on the issue, but this suffices to show this is not what has happened at all. Science has been politicized and reduced to marketing slogans that Joseph Goebbels would have been proud of, like "trust the science," "the vaccines are extremely safe," and "we are in this together." It was all propaganda. I suspect Sagan would have been appalled by what has happened to science and medicine over the past two years. The falsehoods surrounding COVID-19 are of a "high-grade baloney" and copious amounts of it. Much of what we have been fed is pseudoscience and carefully concocted lies. The best explanation for this is that the narrative we have been fed is far removed from reality. Members of the Liberal Party of Canada have repeatedly and callously reminded us that COVID-19 is a political opportunity for their own agenda. As the Deputy Prime Minister of Canada, Chrystia Freeland, cavalierly stated: "I really believe COVID-19 has created a window of political opportunity and maybe an epiphany…on the importance of early learning and childcare."[311] These words echo Trudeau's vision, which support the World Economic Forum's Great Reset and the United Nation's projected named Agenda 2030:

309 Sagan, *Demon Haunted World: Science As a Candle in the Dark*, 209.

310 Sagan, *Demon Haunted World*, 210.

311 Murphy, "Chrystia Freeland's 'epiphany' that COVID-19 is an 'opportunity'—that's pretty dark."

> Building back better means getting support to the most vulnerable while maintaining our momentum on reaching the 2030 agenda for sustainable development… This is our chance to help your pre-pandemic efforts to reimagine economic systems that actually address global challenges like extreme poverty, inequality, and climate change… Canada believes that a strong, coordinated response across the world and across sectors is essential. This pandemic has provided an opportunity for a reset.[312]

Don't be fooled by this optimistic sounding language, the Great Reset only has the interests of affluent globalists in mind and is to the detriment of those found in the middle-class and the lower economic stratus of the world. What should be very clear is that none of the COVID measures that have been taken are actually about people's health or well-being. Take for instance, that only now, we are being told by MSM that the increased use of hand sanitizers could lead to the development of cancer.[313] Nevertheless, they have pushed its frequent use incessantly. Trudeau is perfectly content in appeasing his globalist friends like Klaus Schwab over doing what is right for Canadians. This has become increasingly evident in his disparagement of those who participated in the "freedom convoy" protests (which we will explore in greater detail in the Epilogue). People are convinced that Agenda 2030 and the Great Reset are conspiracy theories, but these people are willfully burying their heads in the sand in spite of the evidence. In fact, on February 19, 2022, a question was raised by an honourable member of Oshawa (through one of his constituents) pertaining to who and how many members of the Liberal cabinet were involved with Klaus Schwab's World Economic Forum. It was shut down by the Speaker of the House of Commons of Canada because of alleged audio problems, even though he admitted it was a good question. A Liberal MP responded by saying "that member was promoting open disinformation, that's not debate."[314] I suppose asking tough questions regarding corruption within the Liberal cabinet is disinformation and not worth debating. Disinformation has become a key word for truth. Schwab has bragged that half or more of the Liberal cabinet support his WEF.[315]

Every edifice of this so-called pandemic and every measure taken should draw every ounce of skepticism from citizens of the world. But why? As unpalatable and "conspiratorial" for some, the agenda behind this is worth seriously considering out of a variety of options that differ from the single narrative. The next chapter will explore one alternative perspective.

312 Sun Media, "Trudeau sees pandemic as an 'opportunity'."
313 Singh, "'Increase risk of cancer': Health Canada recalls more hand sanitizers."
314 mistersunshinebaby, "Denied Ability to Discuss Orders Of Klaus Schwab..WTF."
315 PUGNACIOUS, "Klaus Schwab Penetrates Justin Trudeau."

Bibliography

2020News, "Sensationsurteil aus Weimar: keine Masken, kein Abstand, keine Tests mehr für Schüler." 2020News, April 14, 2021. https://2020news.de/sensationsurteil-aus-weimar-keine-masken-kein-abstand-keine-tests-mehr-fuer-schueler/ for translation.

ABC7. "LA doctor seeing success with hydroxychloroquine to treat COVID-19." YouTube Video, April 7, 2020. https://www.youtube.com/watch?v=eVs_EWVCVPc.

Adams, Mike. "What Dr. Robert Malone could NOT tell Joe Rogan." *Natural News*, January 2, 2022. https://www.naturalnews.com/2022-01-02-what-dr-robert-malone-could-not-tell-joe-rogan.html.

Adjodah, Dhaval, et al. "Decrease in Hospitalizations for COVID-19 after Mask Mandates in 1083 U.S. Counties." *MedRxiv*, November 4, 2020. https://doi.org/10.1101/2020.10.21.20208728.

Ahlander, Johan. "Sweden saw lower 2020 death spike than much of Europe – data." *Reuters*, March 24, 2021. https://www.reuters.com/article/us-health-coronavirus-europe-mortality-idUSKBN2BG1R9.

AIER Staff. "Lockdowns Do Not Control the Coronavirus: The Evidence." American Institute for Economic Research, December 19, 2021. https://www.aier.org/article/lockdowns-do-not-control-the-coronavirus-the-evidence/.

Aldén, Markus et al. "Intracellular Reverse Transcription of Pfizer BioNTech COVID-19 mRNA Vaccine BNT162b2 In Vitro in Human Liver Cell Line." *Current Issues In Molecular Biology*, 44 (February 2022): 1115–1126. https://doi.org/10.3390/cimb44030073.

Alfelali, Mohammad, et al. "Facemask against viral respiratory infections among Hajj pilgrims: A challenging cluster-randomized trial." *PLOS ONE*, October 13, 2020. https://doi.org/10.1371/journal.pone.0240287.

Ali, Taz. "First known Covid case was a Wuhan wet market vendor, study 'confirms categorically'." *iNews*, November 19, 2021. https://inews.co.uk/news/world/covid-case-first-known-wuhan-wet-market-vendor-study-1309115.

Anderson, Bruce. "Typical 'vaccine hesitant' person is a 42-year-old Ontario woman who votes Liberal: Abacus polling." *Macleans Magazine*, August 11, 2021. https://www.macleans.ca/society/typical-vaccine-hesitant-person-is-a-42-year-old-ontario-woman-who-votes-liberal-abacus-polling/.

Andersen, Kristian G., et al. "The proximal origin of SARS-CoV-2," *Nature Medicine* 26 (March 17, 2020): 450–452. https://doi.org/10.1038/s41591-020-0820-9.

Andrew, Scott. "An Oregon county drops its mask exemption for people of color after racist response." *CNN*, June 25, 2020. https://www.cnn.

com/2020/06/24/us/oregon-county-people-of-color-mask-trnd/index.html.

Anthony Fauci emails: https://assets.documentcloud.org/documents/20793561/leopold-nih-foia-anthony-fauci-emails.pdf.

"Anti-vaxxer." Merriam-Webster Dictionary, Accessed February 4, 2022. https://www.merriam-webster.com/dictionary/anti-vaxxer.

Ask a Scientist Staff, "Why qPCR is the gold standard for COVID-19 testing." *ThermoFisher Scientific*, October 23, 2020. https://www.thermofisher.com/blog/ask-a-scientist/why-qpcr-is-the-gold-standard-for-covid-19-testing/.

Association of American Physicians and Surgeons (AAPS). "Peter McCullough, MD testifies to Texas Senate HHS Committee." Association of American Physicians and Surgeons. YouTube Video at the 11:59 minute mark, March 11, 2021. https://www.youtube.com/watch?v=QAHi3lX3oGM&t=1s.

Associated Press, The. "Data analysis indicates omicron is milder, better at evading vaccines." *CBC*, December 15, 2022. https://www.cbc.ca/news/health/omicron-variant-early-analysis-pfizer-1.6285578.

Ayers, Robert. "Florida COVID-19 cases remain low as Democratic-led states see numbers rise." *Conservative Institute*, November 27, 2021. https://conservativeinstitute.org/conservative-news/florida-cases-remain-low.htm.

Babylon Bee, The. "Playskool Unveils Vaccinate Me Elmo Doll." YouTube Video, November 10, 2021. https://www.youtube.com/watch?v=Wl_BfOIXkaA.

Barbaro, Michael. "An interview With Dr. Anthony Fauci." *New York Times*, November 12, 2021. https://www.nytimes.com/2021/11/12/podcasts/the-daily/anthony-fauci-vaccine-mandates-booster-shots.html?showTranscript=1.

BBC. "What has Novak Djokovic actually said about vaccines?" *BBC*, January 6, 2022. https://www.bbc.com/news/world-59897918.

———. "Novak Djokovic: Australia to detain tennis star on Saturday after visa cancelled." *BBC News*, January 14, 2021. https://www.bbc.com/news/world-australia-59991762#:~:text=Novak%20Djokovic%20is%20set%20to,a%20three%2Dyear%20visa%20ban.

BBC staff, "Covid: Austria back in lockdown despite protests." *BBC News*, November 22, 2021. https://www.bbc.com/news/world-europe-59369488.

BC Ministry of Health. "Number of Hospitalizations and Hospitalizations with Intensive Care." District Abstract Database, September 15, 2021. http://docs.openinfo.gov.bc.ca/Response_Package_HTH-2021-13906.pdf?fbclid=IwAR1ZnOL3YXldkLMf1ATxIrFtXcJJ_ZJH6IK2EZaYkpRae9d862JogfXVId0.

Bender, Jennifer K., et al. "Analysis of Asymptomatic and Presymptomatic Transmission in SARS-CoV-2 Outbreak, Germany, 2020," Emerging Infectious Diseases 27, no. 4, April 2021. DOI: 10.3201/eid2704.204576.

Berenson, Alex. "Boosters Are Over. Substack – Unreported Truths." January 12,

2022. https://alexberenson.substack.com/p/boosters-are-over/comments.

Black Pegasus, "PCR TEST INVENTOR Kary Banks Mullis opinion on DR. FAUCI." YouTube Video, December 22, 2020. https://www.youtube.com/watch?v=MkqQIY7J0fQ.

Blair, Alex. "How facial recognition technology will be used to track positive Covid cases." News.com.au, December 13, 2021. https://www.news.com.au/technology/online/security/how-facial-recognition-technology-will-be-used-to-track-positive-covid-cases/news-story/67500e603797c6cfdb50c0bb9a8331c9.

Blaylock, Russell. "Face Masks Pose Serious Risks To The Healthy." *Technocracy News and Trends*, May 11, 2020. https://www.technocracy.news/blaylock-face-masks-pose-serious-risks-to-the-healthy/.

Block, Jennifer. "Vaccinating people who have had covid-19: why doesn't natural immunity count in the US?" *The British Medical Journal* (September 13, 2021); 374. DOI: https://doi.org/10.1136/bmj.n2101.

Borger, Pieter. et al., "Retraction request letter to Eurosurveillance editorial board." November 26, 2020. https://cormandrostenreview.com/retraction-request-letter-to-eurosurveillance-editorial-board/.

———. "External peer review of the RTPCR test to detect SARS-CoV-2 reveals 10 major scientific flaws at the molecular and methodological level: consequences for false positive results." International Consortium of Scientists in Life Science (ICLS), November 30, 2020. https://cormandrostenreview.com/report/; https://zenodo.org/record/4298004.

Bradley, Jonathan. "Ontario first province to correct misinformation on COVID hospitalization numbers." *True North*, January 13, 2022. https://tnc.news/2022/01/13/ontario-first-province-to-correct-misinformation-on-covid-hospitalization-numbers/.

Breggin, Peter R. "Murdering COVID Patients in the Name of Treatment." *Brighteon Video*, December 21, 2021. https://www.brighteon.com/3f64ee04-b547-4ecc-89e2-bfd91881cc9c.

Briggs, William M. "Sorry LA Times: The COVID Lockdowns Were Not Painless and Effective." *The Stream*, May 22, 2021. https://stream.org/sorry-la-times-the-covid-lockdowns-were-not-painless-and-effective/?fbclid=IwAR2_QvNx03G8G_f4Dlnrq0WaQz1Y0_aTDkpHXvNm7RzJ44t-3lad9e420Og.

Brown, Lee. "MSNBC reporter Cal Perry humiliated on air after mask-shaming backfires." *New York Post*, May 27, 2020. https://nypost.com/2020/05/27/msnbc-reporter-cal-perry-humiliated-on-air-after-mask-shaming-backfires/.

Bruno, Roxana, et al. "SARS-CoV-2 mass vaccination: Urgent questions on vaccine safety that demand answers from international health agencies, regulatory authorities, governments and vaccine developers." May 24, 2021. https://

d197for5662m48.cloudfront.net/documents/publicationstatus/63616/preprint_pdf/a63a137eb14404fbd393121dafa96ada.pdf.

Bustin, Stephen A., et al. "The MIQE Guidelines: Minimum Information for Publication of Quantitative Real-Time PCR Experiments." *Clinical Chemistry* 55, 4 (2009): 611–622.

Calisher, Charles et al. "Statement in support of the scientists, public health professionals, and medical professionals of China combatting COVID-19," *The Lancet* 395, no. 10226 (March 7, 2020): E42–E43. https://www.thelancet.com/journals/lancet/article/PIIS0140-6736(20)30418-9/fulltext.

Canadian Institute for Health Information. "Overview: COVID-19's impact on health care systems." December 9, 2021. https://www.cihi.ca/en/covid-19-resources/impact-of-covid-19-on-canadas-health-care-systems/the-big-picture.

———. "The Pfizer Inoculations For COVID-19 – More Harm Than Good – VIDEO." Accessed January 2, 2022. https://www.canadiancovidcarealliance.org/media-resources/the-pfizer-inoculations-for-covid-19-more-harm-than-good-2/.

Carlson, Jeff and Hans Mahncke. "Emails Reveal How Influential Articles That Established COVID-19 Natural Origins Theory Were Formed," *The Epoch Times*, June 8, 20201. https://www.theepochtimes.com/emails-reveal-how-influential-articles-that-established-covid-19-natural-origins-theory-were-formed_3848832.html.

Cavanagh, Niahm. "FACE OF SHAME Inside Justin Trudeau's blackface shame after Canadian PM is caught in shocking pics in afro wigs and make-up." *The U.S. Sun*, September 21, 2021. https://www.the-sun.com/news/3702537/justin-trudeau-blackface-afro-wigs/.

CDC (Centers for Disease Controls and Prevention). "Improve How Your Mask Protects You," *Centers for Disease Controls and Prevention*, updated April 6, 2021. https://www.cdc.gov/coronavirus/2019-ncov/your-health/effective-masks.html.

———. "Lab Alert: Changes to CDC RT-PCR for SARS-CoV-2 Testing." Division of Laboratory Systems (DLS), July 21, 2021. https://www.cdc.gov/csels/dls/locs/2021/07-21-2021-lab-alert-Changes_CDC_RT-PCR_SARS-CoV-2_Testing_1.html.

———. "Vaccination and Immunization." Last reviewed September 1, 2021. https://www.cdc.gov/vaccines/vac-gen/imz-basics.htm.

———. "Vaccine Adverse Event Reporting System (VAERS)." Reviewed November 2, 2021. https://www.cdc.gov/vaccinesafety/ensuringsafety/monitoring/vaers/index.html.

———. "Myths and Facts about COVID-19 Vaccines." December 15, 2021. https://www.cdc.gov/coronavirus/2019-ncov/vaccines/facts.html.

Center for Infectious Disease Research and Policy podcast. Dr. Michael Osterholm, interview with Chris Dall, "Special Episode: Masks and Science" with the University of Minnesota, June 2, 2020. https://www.cidrap.umn.edu/covid-19/podcasts-webinars/special-ep-masks.

Cerar, Uroš. "PCR Inventor Kary Mullis Talks About Anthony Fauci 'He Doesn't Know Anything Really About Anything!'" YouTube Video, December 14, 2020. https://www.youtube.com/watch?v=chRVZ1V7Y1s.

Chalfant, Morgan. "Jill Biden recognizes Fauci as an 'American hero'," *The Hill*, May 20, 2021. https://thehill.com/homenews/administration/554617-jill-biden-recognizes-dr-fauci-as-an-american-hero?rl=1.

Chamberlain, Samuel. "Kamala Harris and husband Doug Emhoff kiss with masks on despite being vaccinated." *New York Post*, May 5, 2021. https://nypost.com/2021/05/05/kamala-harris-and-doug-emhoff-kiss-with-masks-on-despite-being-vaccinated/.

———. "Sen. Paul: Fauci emails prove he knew of Wuhan gain-of-function research," *New York Post*, June 3, 2021. https://nypost.com/2021/06/03/fauci-emails-prove-he-knew-of-wuhan-research-sen-paul/.

Chase, Steven and Robert Fife "Ottawa funds COVID-19 research project that is collaborating with Wuhan virus lab." *The Globe and Mail*, April 16, 2020. https://www.theglobeandmail.com/canada/article-ottawa-funds-covid-19-research-project-that-is-collaborating-with/.

———. "CSIS first alerted Ottawa to national-security concerns of two scientists at top disease laboratory," *The Globe and Mail*, May 12, 2021. https://www.theglobeandmail.com/politics/article-csis-first-alerted-ottawa-to-national-security-concerns-of-two/.

Cohen, Jon. "Mining coronavirus genomes for clues to the outbreak's origins," *Science Magazine*, January 31, 2020. https://www.science.org/content/article/mining-coronavirus-genomes-clues-outbreak-s-origins.

Cohen, Kristen, W., et al. "Longitudinal analysis shows durable and broad immune memory after SARS-CoV-2 infection with persisting antibody responses and memory B and T cells." *Cell Reports Medicine* 2 (July 20, 2021): 100354. DOI: https://doi.org/10.1016/j.xcrm.2021.

Corman, Victor M., et al. "Detection of 2019 novel coronavirus (2019-nCoV) by real-time RT-PCR. Euro Surveill. 2020;25(3):pii=2000045. https://doi.org/10.2807/1560-7917.ES.2020.25.3.2000045.

Corrochio, Eduardo. "Kary Mullis Explains the PCR Test." Odysee Video, October 3, 2020. https://odysee.com/@EduardoCorrochio:4/kary-mullis-explains-the-pcr-test:e.

Cruta, Virginia. "Biden Claimed Trump 'Muzzled' Fauci—But Emails Reveal Fauci Said Otherwise," *Daily Caller*, June 2, 2021. https://dailycaller.com/2.021/06/02/joe-biden-white-house-coronavirus-response-anthony-fauci-cdc-walensky-personal-emails-muzzled/.

Daszak, Peter. "A Statement in support of the scientists, public health and medical professionals of China." EcoHealth Alliance, February 6, 2020, 12:43 AM. https://usrtk.org/wp-content/uploads/2020/11/Biohazard_FOIA_Maryland_Emails_11.6.20.pdf.

David, James. "PCR Inventor: 'It doesn't tell you that you are sick'." *OffGuardian*, October 5, 2020. https://off-guardian.org/2020/10/05/pcr-inventor-it-wasn't-tell-you-that-you-are-sick/.

Diaz, Alex. "Widow of scientist who invented PCR test hits out at covid denier conspiracists who claim he was murdered by Fauci." *The U.S. Sun*, October 16, 2021. https://www.the-sun.com/news/3865900/pcr-covid-test-kary-mullis-fauci-theory/.

Dice, Mark. *The True Story of Fake News: How the Mainstream Media Manipulates Millions.* San Diego: The Resistance Manifesto, 2017.

Doidge, Norman. "Needle Points." *The Tablet*, October 27, 2021, chapters I to IV. https://www.tabletmag.com/sections/science/articles/needle-points-vaccinations-chapter-four.

Doshi, Peter. "Will covid-19 vaccines save lives? Current trials aren't designed to tell us." *The British Medical Journal* 371 (October 21, 2020): 371:m4037. DOI: https://doi.org/10.1136/bmj.m4037.

Ebright, Richard H. Twitter Post, 9:33 PM, Sep 6, 2021. https://twitter.com/R_H_Ebright/status/1435053505169944579.

EcoHealth website with Peter Daszak's profile page: https://www.ecohealthalliance.org/personnel/dr-peter-daszak.

Edward, Hendrie. "Doctor Reveals that Remdesivir Was the Real Cause For Many Alleged COVID-19 Maladies." *Great Mountain Publishing*, August 7, 2021. https://greatmountainpublishing.com/2021/08/07/doctor-reveals-that-remdesivir-was-the-real-cause-for-many-alleged-covid-19-maladies/.

Epoch Times, The. "The first documentary movie on CCP virus, Tracking Down the Origin of the Wuhan Coronavirus," *NDT*, YouTube Video, April 7, 2020. https://www.youtube.com/watch?v=3bXWGxhd7ic.

Eustachewich, Lia. "Ex-CDC Director Robert Redfield believes COVID-19 came from Wuhan lab." *New York Post*, March 26m 2021. https://nypost.com/2021/03/26/ex-cdc-director-believes-covid-19-came-from-wuhan-lab/.

Fat Emperor, The. "Published Papers and Data on Lockdown Weak Efficacy – and Lockdown Huge Harms medical services many of which are more pressing than COVID-19." Accessed November 30, 2021. https://thefatemperor.com/published-papers-and-data-on-lockdown-weak-efficacy-and-lockdown-huge-harms/.

Felenasof, "Mask Detector: AI-based detection of people wearing a facial mask." May 18, 2020. https://felenasoft.com/xeoma/en/articles/mask-detector/.

Feuer, Will and Noah Higgins-Dunn. "Asymptomatic spread of coronavirus is 'very rare,' WHO says." *CNBC*, June 8, 2020. https://www.cnbc.

com/2020/06/08/asymptomatic-coronavirus-patients-arent-spreading-new-infections-who-says.html.

Finnegan, Connor. "Trump admin pulls NIH grant for coronavirus research over ties to Wuhan lab at heart of conspiracy theories." *ABC News*, May 1, 2020. https://abcnews.go.com/Politics/trump-admin-pulls-nih-grant-coronavirus-research-ties/story?id=70418101.

Fleury, Theo. Twitter Post, February 18, 2022, at 9:44 AM. https://twitter.com/TheoFleury14/status/1494684142809669634?ref_src=twsrc%5Egoogle%7Ctwcamp%5Eserp%7Ctwgr%5Etweet.

Forestell, Michelle Dorey. "In-class learning to resume January 5 as Ministry announces sweeping changes due to Omicron." *Kingstonist*, December 30, 2021. https://www.kingstonist.com/news/in-class-learning-to-resume-january-5-as-ministry-announces-sweeping-changes-due-to-omicron/.

Forrest, Maura. "Trudeau goes on the attack after former justice minister Jody Wilson-Raybould's shock resignation." *National Post*, February 12, 2019. https://nationalpost.com/news/politics/jody-wilson-raybould-resigns.

Fox, Maggie. "Dr. Francis Collins to step down as head of NIH." *CNN*, October 5, 2021. https://www.cnn.com/2021/10/04/health/collins-leaving-national-institutes-of-health/index.html.

Fuellmich, Reiner. "Scientific Evidence that Covid is Crime Against Humanity." Accessed November 25, 2021. https://www.stopworldcontrol.com/fuellmich/.

Funk, Daniel. "Fact check:'Fauci's email's don't show he 'lied' about hydroxychloroquine." *USA Today*, June 5, 2021. https://eu.usatoday.com/story/news/factcheck/2021/06/05/fact-check-fauci-emails-hydroxychloroquine-dont-show-he-lied/7544007002/.

Fussell, Blake. "CDC director agrees hospitals have monetary incentive to inflate COVID-19 data." *The Christian Post*, August 4, 2020. https://www.christianpost.com/news/cdc-director-agrees-that-hospitals-have-monetary-incentive-to-inflate-covid-19-data.html.

Gazit, Sivan, et al. "Comparing SARS-CoV-2 natural immunity to vaccine-induced immunity: reinfections versus breakthrough infections." medRxiv, August 25, 2021. DOI: https://doi.org/10.1101/2021.08.24.21262415.

Game To Love - Tennis Podcast. "Novak Djokovic BBC FULL Interview | LIVE Stream Reaction | Game To Love." YouTube Video, February 15, 2022. https://www.youtube.com/watch?v=wdSSblqLAyo.

Guatret, Philippe, et al. "Hydroxychloroquine and azithromycin as a treatment of COVID-19: results of an open-label non-randomized clinical trial." *International Journal of Antimicrobial Agents* 56: 1 (July 2020), 105949.

Givas, Nick. "WHO haunted by old tweet saying China found no human transmission of coronavirus." *New York Post*, March 20, 2020. https://nypost.com/2020/03/20/who-haunted-by-old-tweet-saying-china-found-no-human-transmission-of-coronavirus/.

Goldberg, et al. "Protection and waning of natural and hybrid COVID-19 immunity." medRxiv, December 5, 2021. https://www.medrxiv.org/content/10.1101/2021.08.24.21262415v1.

Gollom, Mark. "1976 U.S. swine flu vaccination program may offer lessons for COVID-19 pandemic." *CBC*, December 3, 2020. https://www.cbc.ca/news/health/swine-flu-vaccination-covid-1.5825276.

Goodson, Patricia. "Questioning the HIV-AIDS Hypothesis: 30 Years of Dissent." *Frontiers in public health*, vol. 2 154. 23 Sep. 2014. doi:10.3389/fpubh.2014.00154. The article was retracted on October 29, 2019.

Gordon, Julie. "Wear a mask while having sex, Dr. Theresa Tam suggests." *Globe and Mail*, September 2, 2020. https://www.theglobeandmail.com/canada/article-wear-a-mask-while-having-sex-dr-theresa-tam-suggests/.

Government of Ontario, "Digital ID in Ontario." Updated February 26, 2022. https://www.ontario.ca/page/digital-id-ontario.

Greene, Jenna. "Wait what? FDA wants 55 years to process FOIA request over vaccine data." *Reuters*, November 18, 2021. https://www.reuters.com/legal/government/wait-what-fda-wants-55-years-process-foia-request-over-vaccine-data-2021-11-18/.

———. "'Paramount importance': Judge orders FDA to hasten release of Pfizer vaccine docs." *Reuters*, January 7, 2022. https://www.reuters.com/legal/government/paramount-importance-judge-orders-fda-hasten-release-pfizer-vaccine-docs-2022-01-07/.

Grover, Natalie. "Covid distancing may have weakened children's immune system, experts say." *The Guardian*, June 9, 2021. https://www.theguardian.com/society/2021/jun/09/covid-distancing-may-have-weakened-childrens-immune-system-experts-say.

Hains, Tim. "Tucker Carlson: If 'COVID-19' 'Lab Leak' Theory Is True, We Need Criminal Investigations." *RealClear Politics*, May 11, 2021. https://www.realclearpolitics.com/video/2021/05/11/tucker_carlson_if_lab_leak_theory_is_true.html.

Hall, Chris. "Learning to live with COVID: why some experts say it's time to 'manage' the virus." *CBC*, January 8, 2022. https://www.cbc.ca/radio/thehouse/covid-pandemic-vaccine-omicron-1.6307272.

Hancock-Watts, Cheryl. "U.S. President Trump criticized For Shutting Border to China," *International Press Association*, April 13, 2020. https://ipanews.info/u-s-president-trump-criticized-for-shutting-border-to-china/.

Harari, Yuval Noah. "The World After Coronavirus." *Financial Times*, March 20, 2020. https://www.ft.com/content/19d90308-6858-11ea-a3c9-1fe6fedcca75.

———. Accessed March 3, 2022. https://www.weforum.org/agenda/authors/yuval-harari.

———. Accessed March 3, 2022. https://www.ynharari.com/.

Harvard2thebighouse. "China owns Nature magazine's ass: Debunking

'The proximal origin of SARS-CoV-2' claiming COVID-19 definitely wasn't from a lab," *Harvard to the Big House*, March 19, 2020. https://harvardtothebighouse.com/2020/03/19/china-owns-nature-magazines-ass-debunking-the-proximal-origin-of-sars-cov-2-claimingwasn'td-19-wasnt-from-a-lab/.

Healthline Editorial Team and Leilani Fraley, The. "What's the difference between antigens and antibodies?" *Health Line*, March 4, 2021. https://www.healthline.com/health/infection/antigen-vs-antibody#antibody-testing.

Health Canada, "Ivermectin not authorized to prevent or treat COVID-19; may cause serious health problems." October 19, 2021. https://recalls-rappels.canada.ca/en/alert-recall/ivermectin-not-authorized-prevent-or-treat-covid-19-may-cause-serious-health-problems.

Heckenlively, Kent and Judy Mikovits. *Plague: One Scientist's Intrepid Search for the Truth about Human Retroviruses and Chronic Fatigue Syndrome (ME/CFS), Autism, and Other Disease*. New York: Skyhorse Publishing, 2017.

———. *Plague of Corruption: Restoring Faith in the Promise of Science*. New York: Skyhorse Publishing, 2021.

Henney, Megan. "CDC director criticized for now differentiating between dying 'from' vs. dying 'with' COVID-19." *Fox News*, May 16, 2021. https://www.foxnews.com/politics/cdc-director-walensky-criticism-updated-guidance-coronavirus-deaths.

Herrer, James. "Doctor Exposes the Dangers of Remdesivir and other Drugs that are Being Recommended by NIH." *eClassifie*, accessed December 28, 2021. https://www.eclassifie.com/2021/09/doctor-exposes-the-dangers-of-remdesivir-and-other-drugs-that-are-being-recommended-by-nih/.

Howell, Tom. "More COVID Deaths in 2021 than in 2020." *Washington Times*, November 22, 2021. https://www.washingtontimes.com/news/2021/nov/22/more-covid-19-deaths-2021-2020/.

Hubaud, Alexis. "RNA vaccines: a novel technology to prevent and treat disease." Harvard University Blog, May 5, 2015. https://sitn.hms.harvard.edu/flash/2015/rna-vaccines-a-novel-technology-to-prevent-and-treat-disease/.

Husubo, Wendell. "Sen. Paul: Fauci Committed Perjury over Gain of Function Comments Related to Wuhan Lab." *Breibert News*, May 25, 2021. https://www.breitbart.com/politics/2021/05/25/sen-paul-fauci-committed-perjury-over-gain-of-function-comments-related-to-wuhan-lab/.

Innis, Michael A. and David H. Gelfand, "Optimization of PCRs." In *PCR Protocols: A Guide to Methods and Applications* edited by Innes, Michael A., et al., 8–9. Cambridge, Massachusetts: Academic Press, 1990.

International Alliance of Physicians and Medical Scientists. "Physicians Declaration II – Updated Global Covid Summit." Global Covid Summit,

October 29, 2021. https://doctorsandscientistsdeclaration.org/.

———. "COVID-Recovered Immunity is Durable." *Global Covid Summit*, accessed January 6, 2022. https://doctorsandscientistsdeclaration.org/home/supporting-evidence/#recovered.

Jaafar, Rita, et al., "Correlation Between 3790 Quantitative Polymerase Chain Reaction–Positives Samples and Positive Cell Cultures, Including 1941 Severe Acute Respiratory Syndrome Coronavirus 2 Isolates." *Clinical Infectious Diseases* 72 (June1, 2021): e921. https://doi.org/10.1093/cid/ciaa1491.

Jingyi, Xiao, et al. "Nonpharmaceutical Measures for Pandemic Influenza in Nonhealthcare Settings—Personal Protective and Environmental Measures." Emerging Infectious Diseases, 26(5), 967–975. https://doi.org/10.3201/eid2605.190994.

Joe Rogan Experience, The. "#1757 – Dr. Robert Malone, MD." *Spotify*, December 31, 2021. https://unityprojectonline.com/news/dr-robert-malone-md-on-the-joe-rogan-experience/.

Kampf, Günter. "The epidemiological relevance of the COVID-19-vaccinated population is increasing." *The Lancet Regional Health – Europe* 11 (November 19, 2021): 100272. DOI: https://doi.org/10.1016/j.lanepe.2021.100272.

———. "COVID-19: tigmatizing the unvaccinated is not justified." *The Lancet* 398, (November 2021): P1871. DOI: https://doi.org/10.1016/S0140-6736(21)02243-1.

Kartha, Tara. "Why the suspicion on China's Wuhan lab virus is growing. Read these new analyses." *The Print*, May 17, 2021. https://theprint.in/opinion/why-suspicion-on-china-wuhan-lab-virus-is-growing/659575/.

Kashiwagi, Mari. "President of Tanzania exposed the inaccuracy of PCR Test." YouTube Video, May 8, 2020. https://www.youtube.com/watch?v=Ml-6QgTSJ3I.

Kennedy Jr., Robert F. *The Real Anthony Fauci: Bill Gates, Big Pharma, and the Global War on Democracy and Public Health.* New York: Skyhorse Publishing, 2021.

Kingston, Anne. "Why Justin Trudeau's reported 'Kokanee Grope' really matters." *Macleans Magazine*, June 27, 2018. https://www.macleans.ca/news/canada/justin-trudeaus-reported-kokanee-grope-matters-but-not-for-the-obvious-reason/.

Kolata, Gina. "Faith in quick test leads to epidemic that wasn't." *New York Times*, January 22, 2007. https://www.nytimes.com/2007/01/22/health/22whoop.html.

Kory, Pierre, et al. "Review of the Emerging Evidence Demonstrating the Efficacy of Ivermectin in the Prophylaxis and Treatment of COVID-19." Updated January 16, 2021. https://covid19criticalcare.com/wp-content/uploads/2020/11/FLCCC-Ivermectin-in-the-prophylaxis-and-treatment-of-COVID-19.pdf.

Kostoff, R. N., et al. "Why are we vaccinating children against COVID-19?" Toxicology Reports 8 (2021): 1665–1684. https://doi.org/10.1016/j.toxrep.2021.08.010.

Kramer, Larry, "An Open Letter to Dr. Anthony Fauci." *The Press of Freedom*, May 31, 1988. https://www.villagevoice.com/2020/05/28/an-open-letter-to-dr-anthony-fauci/.

Kulldorf, Martin, Sunetra Gupta and Jay Bhattacharya, "Great Barrington Declaration." https://gbdeclaration.org/view-signatures/.

Latif Dahir, Abdi. "Tanzania's president says 'vaccines don't work,' earning a rebuff from the W.H.O." *New York Times*, January 28, 2021. https://www.nytimes.com/2021/01/28/world/tanzanias-president-says-vaccines-dont-work-earning-a-rebuff-from-the-who.html.

Lazarus, Ross, et al. The Lazarus Report ("Electronic Support for Public Health–Vaccine Adverse Event Reporting System (ESP:VAERS)".) *Open VAERS*, accessed January 6, 2022. https://openvaers.com/images/r18hs017045-lazarus-final-report-20116.pdf.

Lazzarino, Antonio, et al. "Covid-19: important potential side effects of wearing face masks that we should bear in mind." *The British Medical Journal*, 369: m2003 (May 2020). DOI:10.1136/bmj.m2003.

Leaked Reality. "'the plandemic' Jen Psaki Makes a Freudian Slip." September 2020. https://leakedreality.com/video/21111/the-plandemic-jen-psaki-makes-a-freudian-slip.

Lee, Byung Uk. "Minimum Sizes of Respiratory Particles Carrying SARS-CoV-2 and the Possibility of Aerosol Generation." International journal of environmental research and public health, vol. 17,19 6960. 23 Sept, 2020. doi:10.3390/ijerph17196960.

Leeb, Rebecca T. "Mental Health–Related Emergency Department Visits Among Children Aged <18 Years During the COVID-19 Pandemic—United States, January 1–October 17, 2020." Center for Disease Control and Prevention, Morbidity and Mortality Weekly Report (MMWR), 69 (November 13, 2020): 1675–1680. DOI: http://dx.doi.org/10.15585/mmwr.mm6945a3externalicon.

Lerner, Sharon and Mara Hvistendahl. "New Details Emerge About Coronavirus Research at Chinese Lab." *The Intercept*, September 6, 2021. https://theintercept.com/2021/09/06/new-details-emerge-about-coronavirus-research-at-chinese-lab/.

Li, Johanna. "Why Did 21 Million Phone Numbers Disappear from China After Coronavirus Outbreak?" *KMOV4*, April 11, 2020. https://www.kmov.com/why-did-21-million-phone-numbers-disappear-from-china-after-coronavirus-outbreak/article_80456379-e8af-52a8-9366-f8af64b45fd1.html.

Li, Yafang, et al. "Stability issues of RT-PCR testing of SARS-CoV-2 for hospitalized patients clinically diagnosed with COVID-19." Journal of medical virology vol. 92,7 (2020): 903–908. doi:10.1002/jmv.25786.

London Real. "The Coronavirus Conspiracy: How COVID-19 Will Seize Your Rights & Destroy Our Economy – David Icke." April 6, 2020. https://freedomplatform.tv/the-coronavirus-conspiracy-how-covid-19-will-seize-your-rights-destroy-our-economy-david-icke/.

———. "Rose/Icke 6: The Vindication." January 21, 2022. https://freedomplatform.tv/rose-icke-6-the-vindication/.

Louise, Nickie. "Dr. Vladimir Zelenko has now treated over 1,450 coronavirus patients (2 deaths) using hydroxychloroquine with 99.99% success rate (latest video interview)." *Tech Startups*, April 21, 2020. https://techstartups.com/2020/04/21/dr-vladimir-zelenko-now-treated-1450-coronavirus-patients-2-deaths-using-hydroxychloroquine-99-99-success-rate-latest-video-interview/.

———. "Kristian Andersen, the virologist who told Dr. Fauci that COVID-19 "potentially look engineered, just deleted his Twitter account." *Tech Startups*, June 6, 2021. https://techstartups.com/2021/06/06/kristian-andersen-virologist-told-dr-fauci-covid-19-potentially-look-engineered-just-deleted-twitter-account/.

Love, Ariyana. "What's In the Vaxx? Transgenic Hydra And Parasite Implants Used As Rapid Human Cloning System." Red Voice Media, October 31, 2021. https://www.redvoicemedia.com/2021/10/transgenic-hydra-and-parasite-implants-used-as-rapid-human-cloning-weapons-system/.

Madison Area Lyme Support Group. "Former French Health Minister Blows Whistle." https://madisonarealymesupportgroup.com/2020/06/12/former-french-health-minister-blows-whistle-criminal-pressure-from-bigpharma-on-publications-means-theres-no-longer-any-real-science/.

Madrid, Pablo Campra. "Detección de Grafeno en Vacunas Covid19 por Espectroscopía Micro-Raman." Informe Técnico. University of Almeria, Spain, November 2, 2021. https://www.researchgate.net/publication/355684360_Deteccion_de_grafeno_en_vacunas_COVID19_por_espectroscopia_Micro-RAMAN.

Mahévas, Matthieu, et al. "No evidence of clinical efficacy of hydroxychloroquine in patients hospitalised for COVID-19 infection and requiring oxygen: results of a study using routinely collected data to emulate a target trial." *medRxiv*, April 21, 2020. https://doi.org/10.1101/2020.04.10.20060699.

Magagnoli, Joseph, et al. "Outcomes of Hydroxychloroquine Usage in United States Veterans Hospitalized with COVID-19." *Clinical Advances*, Volume 1, Issue 1: P114-127.E3 (DECEMBER 18. 2020). https://doi.org/10.1016/j.medj.2020.06.001.

Mandavilli, Apoorva. "Your Coronavirus test is positive. Maybe it shouldn't be." *New York Times*, August 29, 2020. https://www.nytimes.com/2020/08/29/health/coronavirus-testing.html.

Mandeep, Mehra R., et al. "Cardiovascular Disease, Drug Therapy, and Mortality in Covid-19." *New England Journal of Medicine*, 2020: 382: e102. DOI: 10.1056/NEJMoa2007621.

Margolis, Matt. "The CDC Just Made an Orwellian Change to the Definition of 'Vaccine' and 'Vaccination'." *PJ Media*, September 8, 2021. https://pjmedia.com/news-and-politics/matt-margolis/2021/09/08/the-cdc-just-made-an-orwellian-change-to-the-definition-of-vaccine-and-vaccination-n1476799.

Mayo Clinic, "COVID-19 diagnostic testing." August 3, 2021. https://www.mayoclinic.org/tests-procedures/covid-19-diagnostic-test/about/pac-20488900.

Mayo Clinic Staff. "How well do face masks protect against coronavirus?" *Mayo Clinic*, updated May 18, 2021. https://www.mayoclinic.org/coronavirus-mask/art-20485449.

Mercola, Joseph R. "Study shows how masks are harming children," *LifeSite News*, March 3, 2021. https://www.lifesitenews.com/opinion/study-shows-how-masks-are-harming-children.

Mercola, Joseph and Ronnie Cummins. *The Truth About COVID-19: Exposing The Great Reset, Lockdowns, Vaccine Passports, and the New Normal.* London: Chelsea Green Publishing, 2021, chapter 2.

McCullough, Peter. "By Pushing Mass Vaccination, Governments Have Created Evolutionary Pressures on SARS-CoV-2." *America Out Loud*, July 20, 2021. https://www.americaoutloud.com/by-pushing-mass-vaccination-governments-have-created-evolutionary-pressures-on-sars-cov-2/.

———. PowerPoint Slides of Presentation: "Winning the War Against Therapeutic Nihilism & Trusted Treatments vs Untested Novel Therapies." October 1, 2021. https://www.scribd.com/document/530328436/Slides-from-Peter-McCullough-MD-Oct-1-2021-Lecture.

———. "Winning the War Against Therapeutic Nihilism & Trusted Treatments vs Untested Novel Therapies." Rumble Video Presentation, October 4, 2021. https://rumble.com/vnbv86-winning-the-war-against-therapeutic-nihilism-and-trusted-treatments-vs-unte.html.

McCullough Peter A., et al. "Multifaceted highly targeted sequential multidrug treatment of early ambulatory high-risk SARS-CoV-2 infection (COVID-19)." *Reviews in Cardiovascular Medicine* 202021(2020): 517–530. DOI: https://doi.org/10.31083/j.rcm.2020.04.264.

———. et al. "Pathophysiological Basis and Rationale for Early Outpatient Treatment of SARS-CoV-2 (COVID-19) Infection." *The American Journal of Medicine* 134 (January 2021): 16–22. https://doi.org/10.1016/j.amjmed.2020.07.003.

McNeil Jr., Donald. "Fauci on What Working for Trump Was Really Like," *The New York Times*, January 24, 2021. https://www.nytimes.com/2021/01/24/health/fauci-trump-covid.html.

Medical Xpress Staff. "Masks, gloves don't stop coronavirus spread: experts." *Medical Xpress*, March 17, 2020. https://medicalxpress.com/news/2020-03-masks-gloves-dont-coronavirus-experts.amp.

Mehra, Mandeep. "RETRACTED: Hydroxychloroquine or chloroquine with or without a macrolide for treatment of COVID-19: a multinational registry analysis." *The Lancet*, May 22, 2020. DOI: https://doi.org/10.1016/S0140-6736(20)31180-6.

Melville, James. Twitter Post, January 1, 2021, at 1:59 PM. https://twitter.com/JamesMelville/status/1477353695855714312.

Menge, Maragert. "Indiana life insurance CEO says deaths are up 40% among people ages 18-64." *69News, January* 4, 2022. https://www.wfmz.com/health/indiana-life-insurance-ceo-says-deaths-are-up-40-among-people-ages-18-64/article_b5f123e4-7c45-5308-bc31-b50dee76b4b7.html?fbclid=IwAR1qiFVOAPSzP2o7J4EQPgXp7iD7YpI1lYIOXqUOKnO6QDdMUJ-FQm-OmUk.

Mesic, Dzevad. "Taking vaccine and doing 'common good for humanity' force Jeremy Chardy to end season." *Tennis World*, September 27, 2021. https://www.tennisworldusa.org/tennis/news/ATP_Tennis/102939/taking-vaccine-and-doing-common-good-for-humanity-force-jeremy-chardy-to-end-season/.

Metz, Rachel. "Think your mask makes you invisible to facial recognition? Not so fast, AI companies say." *CNN*, August 12, 2020. https://www.cnn.com/2020/08/12/tech/face-recognition-masks/index.html/.

MichaelSavage.com, "MASSIVE! Top Doctor Warns about COVID Vaccine (DISTURBING)." Interview with Dr. Peter McCullough, accessed November 16, 2021. https://michaelsavage.com/top-doctor-warns-about-covid-vaccine/.

Miller, Adam. "WHO backtracks on claim that asymptomatic spread of COVID-19 is 'very rare'." *CBC News*, June 9, 2020. https://www.cbc.ca/news/health/who-covid-19-asymptomatic-spread-1.5604353.

Million, Matthieu, et al. "Early treatment of COVID-19 patients with hydroxychloroquine and azithromycin: A retrospective analysis of 1061 cases in Marseille, France." *Travel Med Infect Dis.* May–June 2020, 35:101738. doi: 10.1016/j.tmaid.2020.101738.

Miltimore, Jon. "COVID Crisis Could Push 100 Million People into Extreme Poverty, New World Bank Study Says." *Fee Stories*, July 1, 2020. https://fee.org/articles/covid-crisis-could-push-100-million-people-into-extreme-poverty-new-world-bank-study-says/.

———. "Sweden Saw Lower Mortality Rate Than Most of Europe in 2020, Despite No Lockdown." *Fee Stories*, March 26, 2021. https://fee.org/articles/sweden-saw-lower-mortality-rate-than-most-of-europe-in-2020-despite-no-lockdown/.

Moore, Art. "Governor admits COVID hospitalizations overcounted." *WND*,

January 4, 2022. https://www.wnd.com/2022/01/governor-admits-covid-hospitalizations-overcounted/.

Murphy, Rex. "Chrystia Freeland's 'epiphany' that COVID-19 is an 'opportunity'—that's pretty dark." *National Post*, April 15, 2021. https://nationalpost.com/opinion/rex-murphy-chrystia-freelands-epiphany-that-covid-19-is-an-opportunity-is-actually-pretty-dark.

Nakagami, Hironori. "Development of COVID-19 vaccines utilizing gene therapy technology." *International immunology* vol. 33 (October 2021): 521–527. DOI:10.1093/intimm/dxab013.

Nakagami, Hironori, et al. "Therapeutic vaccine for chronic diseases after the COVID-19 Era." *Hypertension Research* 44 (June 2021): 1047–1053. https://doi.org/10.1038/s41440-021-00677-3.

Nelson, Steve. "Psaki calls Fauci 'undeniable asset' after Chinese lab leak emails," *New York Post*, June 3, 2021. https://nypost.com/2021/06/03/psaki-calls-fauci-an-undeniable-asset/.

NIH, "Study to Describe the Safety, Tolerability, Immunogenicity, and Efficacy of RNA Vaccine Candidates Against COVID-19 in Healthy Individuals." *ClinicalTrial.gov*, updated December 22, 2021. https://clinicaltrials.gov/ct2/show/NCT04368728.

NHS, "Guidance and Standard Operating Procedure COVID-19 Virus Testing in NHS Laboratories." Accessed November 25, 2021. https://www.rcpath.org/uploads/assets/90111431-8aca-4614-b06633d07e2a3dd9/Guidance-and-SOP-COVID-19-Testing-NHS-Laboratories.pdf.

Nobel Prize, The. "The Nobel Prize in Chemistry: Kary B. Mullis." Accessed November 18, 2021. https://www.nobelprize.org/prizes/chemistry/1993/mullis/facts/.

Nobel Prize in Physiology or Medicine 2015. https://www.nobelprize.org/prizes/medicine/2015/press-release/.

Nsikan, Akpan and Victoria Jaggard. "Fauci: No scientific evidence the coronavirus was made in a Chinese lab," National Geographic, May 4, 2020. https://www.nationalgeographic.com/science/article/anthony-fauci-no-scientific-evidence-the-coronavirus-was-made-in-a-chinese-lab-cvd.

O'Sullivan, John. "Dr. Roger Hodkinson on COVID19: it's all been a pack of lies." *Principia Scientific International*, August 20, 2021. https://principia-scientific.com/dr-roger-hodkinson-on-covid19-its-all-been-a-pack-of-lies/.

Open VAERS, "VAERS COVID Vaccine Adverse Event Reports." December 24, 2021. https://openvaers.com/covid-data.

Oran, Daniel P. and Eric J. Topol. "Proportion of SARS-CoV-2 Infections That Are Asymptomatic: A Systematic Review." 174, no. 5 (May 24, 2021): 655–662. https://doi.org/10.7326/M20-6976.

Patrick, David M., et al. "An Outbreak of Human Coronavirus OC43 Infection and Serological Cross-reactivity with SARS Coronavirus." *The Canadian journal of infectious diseases & medical microbiology = Journal canadien des maladies infectieuses et de la microbiologie medicale* 17,6 (2006): 330–336. doi:10.1155/2006/152612.

Patrozou, Eleni, and Leonard A. Mermel. "Does Influenza Transmission Occur from Asymptomatic Infection or Prior to Symptom Onset?" Public Health Reports 124, no. 2 (March 2009): 193–196. https://doi.org/10.1177/003335490912400205.

Payeras i Cifre, Bartomeu. "Study of the correlation between cases of coronavirus and the presence of 5G networks." Translated from the Spanish by Claire Edwards. March–April 2020. www.tomeulamo.com/fitxers/264_CORONA-5G-d.pdf.

———. "Estudio sobre la asimétrica distribución de casos de COVID-19 y su relación con la tecnología 5G." Mayo 2020. https://www.untumbes.edu.pe/vcs/biblioteca/document/varioslibros/0567.%20Estudio%20sobre%20la%20asim%C3%A9trica%20distribuci%C3%B3n%20de%20casos%20de%20COVID-19%20y%20su%20relaci%C3%B3n%20con%20la%20tecnolog%C3%ADa%205G.pdf.

Peek, Katie. "Flu has disappeared for more than a year." *Scientific American*, April 29, 2021. https://www.scientificamerican.com/article/flu-has-disappeared-worldwide-during-the-covid-pandemic1/.

Pelech, Steven. Petition to the House of Commons. December 7, 2021. https://petitions.ourcommons.ca/en/Petition/Details?Petition=e-3696.

Pelley, Laura. "Why COVID-19 hospitalizations of Canadian kids—and infants—could keep rising as Omicron spreads." *CBC*, January 6, 2022. https://www.cbc.ca/news/health/children-hospitalization-omicron-1.6305207.

Petersen, Irene and Andrew Phillips. "Three Quarters of People with SARS-CoV-2 Infection are Asymptomatic: Analysis of English Household Survey Data." *Clinal Epidemiology*. 2020 (12):1039–1043. https://doi.org/10.2147/CLEP.S276825.

Phillips, Jack. "Dr. Robert Malone to Rogan: US in 'Mass Formation Psychosis' Over COVID-19." *The Epoch Times*, January 2, 2021. https://www.theepochtimes.com/dr-robert-malone-to-rogan-us-in-mass-formation-psychosis-over-covid_4189087.html?utm_source=newsnoe&utm_campaign=breaking-2022-01-02-2&utm_medium=email&est=bOsJSccLI9rhfoo9nYyJlncXkbAasqqTG3jpD7I72T7WUdISYzhG7mxl7glpJeswumVLKUEllw%3D%3D.

Polonikov, Alexey. "Endogenous Deficiency of Glutathione as the Most Likely Cause of Serious Manifestations and Death in COVID-19 Patients." ACS infectious diseases vols. 6,7 (2020): 1558–1562. doi:10.1021/acsinfecdis.0c00288.

PoorRichards News. "Fauci in News Today with His Emails Revealing Lies."

PoorRichard News, June 3, 2021. https://poorrichardsnews.com/dr-kary-mullis-fauci-has-a-history-of-lying-to-you/.

Prestigiacomo, Amanda. "Johns Hopkins Doctor Criticizes Vaccine Mandates, Stresses Natural Immunity." *Daily Wire*, October 7, 2021. https://www.dailywire.com/news/johns-hopkins-doctor-criticizes-vaccine-mandates-stresses-natural-immunity.

Public Health and Medical Professionals for Transparency Documents. Accessed March 3, 2022. https://phmpt.org/pfizers-documents/?fbclid=IwAR2lFzAGWiIgpCRG0k7KoRwlUMTcCMyZApKefwKcSTBymCtBVCxoll1EEj8.

Public Health Ontario. "Explained: COVID-19 PCR testing and cycle thresholds." Public Health Ontario, February 17, 2021. https://www.publichealthontario.ca/en/about/blog/2021/explained-covid19-pcr-testing-and-cycle-thresholds.

Racaniello, Vincent. "TWiV 641: COVID-19 with Dr. Anthony Fauci." Interview with Fauci at the 4:28 minute mark. YouTube Video, July 17, 2020. https://www.youtube.com/watch?v=a_Vy6fgaBPE.

Radnofsky, Louise and Laine Higgins. "The Ottawa Senators Have a 100% Vaccination Rate—and 40% of the Team Has Tested Positive for Covid." *The Wallstreet Journal*, November 17, 2021. https://www.wsj.com/articles/ottawa-senators-covid-11637123408.

Raoult, Didier. "Dr. Oz Discusses The Hydroxychloroquine Study Outcome With Dr. Didier Raoult." YouTube Video, April 15, 2020. https://www.youtube.com/watch?v=uy1cPT1ztko.

Rappaport, Jon. "Zen Koan for the virus." Jon Rappaport's Blog, January 14, 2022. https://blog.nomorefakenews.com/2022/01/14/zen-koan-for-the-virus/.

Real Science, "445 Athlete Cardiac Arrests, Serious Issues, 260 Dead, After COVID Shot." *Real Science*, accessed January 15, 2022. https://goodsciencing.com/covid/athletes-suffer-cardiac-arrest-die-after-covid-shot/.

Reguly, Eric. "Italy's coronavirus fatalities overtake China's, and the government prolongs the tight quarantine." *Globe and Mail*, March 19, 2020. https://www.theglobeandmail.com/world/article-italys-coronavirus-fatalities-overtake-chinas-and-the-government/.

Retraction Watch, "Retracted coronavirus (COVID-19) papers." Updated May 26, 2021. https://retractionwatch.com/retracted-coronavirus-covid-19-papers/.

Reuters, "Market in China's Wuhan likely origin of COVID-19 outbreak – scientist." *Reuters*, November 19, 2021. https://www.reuters.com/world/market-chinas-wuhan-likely-origin-covid-19-outbreak-study-2021-11-19/?utm_campaign=trueAnthem%3A%20Trending%20Content&utm_medium=trueAnthem&utm_source=facebook&fbclid=IwAR2bT3JMBn0O5tSdforPohZTa-56tnNT9IpWkP-KB9hLAwe4SDrl4dg-RJQ.

Reuters Staff, "President queries Tanzania coronavirus kits after goat test."

Reuters, May 3, 2020. https://www.reuters.com/article/us-health-coronavirus-tanzania-idUSKBN22F0KF.

Rio Times, The. "We are not in a "pandemic of the unvaccinated." says British Medical Journal editor Peter Doshi." *The Rio Times*, November 9, 2021. https://www.riotimesonline.com/brazil-news/modern-day-censorship/we-are-not-in-a-pandemic-of-the-unvaccinated-says-british-medical-journal-editor-peter-doshi/.

Rittiman, Brandon. "Unsolicited 'The Epoch Times' paper spreads outlandish COVID-19 claims."*ABC10*, May 20, 2020. https://www.abc10.com/article/news/health/coronavirus/verify-unsolicited-paper-spreads-outlandish-covid-claims/103-9290495e-a501-44fa-b7df-0bb0e385328b.

Roan, Shari. "Swine flu 'debacle' of 1976 is recalled." *Los Angeles Times*, April 27, 2009. https://www.latimes.com/archives/la-xpm-2009-apr-27-sci-swine-history27-story.html.

Sagan, Carl. *Demon Haunted World: Science As a Candle in the Dark*. New York: Random House, 1995.

Samuels, Brett. "Biden 'very confident' in Fauci amid conservative attacks." *The Hill*, June 4, 2021. https://thehill.com/homenews/administration/556863-biden-very-confident-in-fauci-amid-conservative-attacks.

Santa Clara County Public Health, "FAQs about CT Values from COVID-19 PCR Tests: A Response for LTCFs." June 1, 2021. https://publichealthproviders.sccgov.org/sites/g/files/exjcpb951/files/Documents/FAQs-CT-values-from-covid-19-PCR-tests.pdf?__cf_chl_jschl_tk__=WVWSPrtqYS7H71pt8eBktf5.uGjRR9E2FCdJRyHprG0-1637764548-0-gaNycGzNCOU.

Santin, A. D., et al. "Ivermectin: a multifaceted drug of Nobel prize-honoured distinction with indicated efficacy against a new global scourge, COVID-19." *New Microbes and New Infections* 43 (September 2021): 100924. https://doi.org/10.1016/j.nmni.2021.100924.

Schippers, Michaéla C. "For the Greater Good? The Devastating Ripple Effects of the Covid-19 Crisis." *Frontiers in Psychology*, September 29, 2020.

Segre, Julia A. "What does it take to satisfy Koch's postulates two centuries later? Microbial Genomics and Propionibacteria acnes." *The Journal of investigative dermatology*, vol. 133,9 (2013): 2141–2142. doi:10.1038/jid.2013.260.

"Sensational verdict from Weimar: no masks, no distance, no more tests for students." https://docs.google.com/document/d/13tlF0vUYQBYba7_d-tam3cSt0dUDqlI1MeQvO0TbM_E/edit.

Seongman, Bae, et al. "Effectiveness of Surgical and Cotton Masks in Blocking SARS–CoV-2: A Controlled Comparison in 4 Patients." *Annals of Internal Medicine*, 173, no.1 (July 7, 2020): W22-W23. https://doi.org/10.7326/M20-1342.

Sesame Street, "The ABCs of COVID Vaccines." YouTube Video, November 8, 2021. https://www.youtube.com/watch?v=yPlhRUF2aXA.

Sheehy, Kate. "Fauci admits COVID-19 could have come from Wuhan lab, butts heads with Rand Paul." *New York Post*, May 11, 2021. https://nypost.com/2021/05/11/fauci-admits-covid-19-could-have-come-from-wuhan-lab-butts-heads-with-rand-paul/.

Sidley, Gary and Alan Mordue. "Masks – do benefits outweigh the harms?" Health Advisory and Recovery Team (HART), March 28, 2021. https://www.hartgroup.org/masks/.

Singanayagam, Anika, et al. "Community transmission and viral load kinetics of the SARS-CoV-2 delta (B.1.617.2) variant in vaccinated and unvaccinated individuals in the UK: a prospective, longitudinal, cohort study." *The Lancet: Infectious Diseases*, October 29, 2021. DOI: https://doi.org/10.1016/S1473-3099(21)00648-4.

Singh, Simran. "'Increase risk of cancer': Health Canada recalls more hand sanitizers." *Toronto Star*, February 22, 2022. https://www.thestar.com/news/gta/2022/02/22/increase-risk-of-cancer-health-canada-recalls-more-hand-sanitizers.html.

Snapp, Shaun. "Did the US Mortality Rate Increase in 2020-2021?" *Brightwork Research & Analysis*, November 7, 2021. https://www.brightworkresearch.com/did-the-us-mortality-rate-increase-in-2020-and-2021/.

Squire, Cole. Twitter Post, January 1, 2021, at 1:49 PM. https://twitter.com/SquireforBrant/status/1477351306390085634.

State of the Nation. "Coronavirus: The Truth about PCR Test Kit from the Inventor and Other Experts – Video." *State of the Nation*, October 7, 2020. https://stateofthenation.co/?p=30880.

Stew Peters Show, The. "Dr. Carrie Madej: First U.S. Lab Examines 'Vaccine' Vials HORRIFIC Findings Revealed." https://www.redvoicemedia.com/2021/09/dr-carrie-madej-first-u-s-lab-examines-vaccine-vials-horrific-findings-revealed/.

Stieber, Zackhary. "Walensky: PCR Tests Can Remain Positive for up to 12 Weeks." *The Epoch Times*, December 29, 2021. https://www.theepochtimes.com/walensky-pcr-tests-can-remain-positive-up-to-12-weeks_4183971.html.

Stokes, Deborah. "More than 80 cruise ships are being investigated for COVID outbreaks. So why are people still going aboard?" *National Post*, December 29, 2021. https://nationalpost.com/news/more-than-80-cruise-ships-are-being-investigated-for-covid-outbreaks-so-why-are-people-still-going-aboard.

Stone, Laura, et al. "'Some relief': Parents across Canada rush to book COVID-19 vaccines for kids." *The Globe and Mail*, November 23, 2021. https://www.theglobeandmail.com/canada/article-some-relief-parents-across-canada-rush-to-book-covid-vaccines-for/.

Stone, Phil. "Lancet Editor Spills the Beans and Britain's PM Surrenders to the Gates Vaccine Cartel." July 4, 2020. *Philosophers Stone.* https://philosophers-stone.info/2020/07/04/lancet-editor-spills-the-beans-and-britains-pm-surrenders-to-the-gates-vaccine-cartel/.

Sun Media, "Trudeau sees pandemic as an 'opportunity'." *Toronto Sun*, November 16, 2020. https://torontosun.com/opinion/editorials/editorial-trudeau-sees-pandemic-as-an-opportunity.

Surkova, Elena, et al. "False-positive COVID-19 results: hidden problems and costs." *The Lancet* 8 (December 2020): 1167-1168. https://doi.org/10.1016/S2213-2600(20)30453-7.

Svab, Petr. "2021 COVID-19 Recap: 200 Million Vaccinated, 450,000 Dead." *The Epoch Times*, January 3, 2022. https://www.theepochtimes.com/2021-covid-19-recap-200-million-vaccinated-450000-dead_4190440.html?utm_source=newsnoe&utm_campaign=breaking-2022-01-03-4&utm_medium=email&est=q%2BMH9pdnbGJreEVKSiqJdH%2FLYCBt%2Fz2litP1XBEfwLfeHoXf5iRyKKTL4OGWosQGtQV%2FPUKJ%2FQ%3D%3D.

———. "States Investigating Surge in Mortality Rate Among 18–49-Year-Olds, Majority Unrelated to COVID-19." *The Epoch Times*, January 14, 2022. https://www.theepochtimes.com/several-states-examine-2021-mortality-surge-in-americans-aged-18-49_4213438.html?utm_source=Morningbrief&utm_campaign=mb-2022-01-15&utm_medium=email?utm_source=morningbriefnoe&utm_medium=email_MB&utm_campaign=mb-2022-01-14&utm_content=News_EXCLUSIVE:_States_Investigating&est=%2BP0VOXWDpBZeHJryzuY0fQ04kBQer9lt2z9rqQOsktRWkx%2F%2F1oVai4QwAwpFfkBwP1Ep9ywN.

———. "Researcher Calls Out Censorship After Journal Pulls COVID-19 Vaccine Adverse Events Analysis." *The Epoch Times*, January 20, 2022. https://www.theepochtimes.com/researcher-calls-out-censorship-after-journal-pulls-covid-19-vaccine-adverse-events-analysis_4221081.html?utm_source=Morningbrief&utm_campaign=mb-2022-01-20&utm_medium=email&est=43%2BReNROJ527PUVWBnu7VrfrhkZqlyBRT2wW0p%2FFwnUbcpk4Y9UQiAxdJRQblQh6jDUQ2l5y?utm_source=morningbriefnoe&utm_medium=email_MB&utm_campaign=mb-2022-01-19&utm_content=News_Researcher_Calls_Out&est=[EMAIL_SECURE_LINK].

Swiss Policy Research, "WHO Mask Study Seriously Flawed." September 18, 2020. https://swprs.org/who-mask-study-seriously-flawed/.

———. "Are Face Masks Effective? The Evidence." *Swiss Policy Research*, Updated December 2021. https://swprs.org/face-masks-and-covid-the-evidence/.

Tampa, Vava. "It's time for Africa to rein in Tanzania's anti-vaxxer president." February 8, 2021. https://www.theguardian.com/global-development/2021/feb/08/its-time-for-africa-to-rein-in-tanzanias-anti-vaxxer-president.

Thrivetime Show. "'People Will Look Back & Identify COVID-19 Is When a Surveillance Regime Took Over.' - Dr. Harari." Brighteon Video, February 7, 2022. https://www.brighteon.com/2025dc4b-14c8-4687-a52e-d772cefba862.

TLB Staff. "Those Portuguese Judges Ruling Against PCR Test Got Official Backlash." *The Liberty Beacon*, December 6, 2020. https://www.thelibertybeacon.com/those-portuguese-judges-ruling-against-pcr-test-got-official-backlash/ https://drive.google.com/file/d/1t1b01H0Jd4hsMU7V1vy70yr8s3jlBedr/view?fbclid=IwAR0L_Iu6wwIVfFlZpykLhDHroS12MHZqO533Uizzc-5ZfUUmALOOjY58he4.

Trabsky, Mark and Courtney Hempton. "'Died from' or 'died with' COVID-19? We need a transparent approach to counting coronavirus deaths." *The Conversation*, September 9, 2020. https://theconversation.com/died-from-or-died-with-covid-19-we-need-a-transparent-approach-to-counting-coronavirus-deaths-145438.

Trump, Donald J. "Statement by Donald J. Trump, 45th President of the United States of America," Donald J. Trump website, June 10, 2021. https://www.donaldjtrump.com/about.

Truth for Health Foundation. "COVID Home Treatment." Accessed January 6, 2021. https://www.truthforhealth.org/patientguide/patient-treatment-guide/.

Tseng, Chien-Te, et al. "Immunization with SARS coronavirus vaccines leads to pulmonary immunopathology on challenge with the SARS virus." PloS one vol. 7,4 (2012): e35421. doi:10.1371/journal.pone.0035421.

Tufekci, Zeynep, Jeremy Howard and Trisha Greenhalgh. "The Real Reason to Wear a Mask." *The Atlantic*, April 22, 2020. https://www.theatlantic.com/health/archive/2020/04/dont-wear-mask-yourself/610336/.

UK Health Security Agency. "COVID-19 vaccine surveillance report Week 42." October 21, 2021. https://assets.publishing.service.gov.uk/government/uploads/system/uploads/attachment_data/file/1027511/Vaccine-surveillance-report-week-42.pdf.

Vaccine Tracker. "More Than 9.35 Billion Shots Given: Covid-19 Tracker." Bloomberg, January 6, 2022. https://www.bloomberg.com/graphics/covid-vaccine-tracker-global-distribution/.

Ventureyra, Scott D. G., Thomas E. Woodward and James P. Gills. *The Mysterious Epigenome: What Lies Beyond DNA* (2012); *Science et Esprit* 67:2 (2015): 304–308. https://www.academia.edu/35323275/Review_of_The_Mysterious_Epigenome_What_Lies_Beyond_DNA.

———. "Won't Get Fooled Again By The WHO: Thoughts On The

COVID-19 Crisis and Related World Events." scottventureyra.com, June 9, 2020. https://www.scottventureyra.com/post/won-t-get-fooled-again-by-the-who.

———. "What's the Dealio with Masks?" in "Won't Get Fooled Again by the WHO." "accessed May 25, 2021. https://www.scottventureyra.com/post/won-t-get-fooled-again-by-the-who.

VirusSmyth, Interview with Kary Mullis, Rethinking AIDS March/April 1994. Accessed November 25, 2021. http://virusmyth.com/aids/hiv/ramullis.htm.

Wade, Nicholas. "Origin of Covid—Following the Clues: Did people or nature open Pandora's box at Wuhan?" *Medium*, May 2, 2021. https://nicholaswade.medium.com/origin-of-covid-following-the-clues-6f03564c038.

WebMD. "Coronavirus Recovery." Accessed November 13, 2021. https://www.webmd.com/lung/covid-recovery-overview#1.

WHO. "Interim Statement on COVID-19 vaccines in the context of the circulation of the Omicron SARS- CoV-2 Variant from the WHO Technical Advisory Group on COVID-19 Vaccine Composition (TAG-CO-VAC)." January 11, 2022. https://www.who.int/news/item/11-01-2022-interim-statement-on-covid-19-vaccines-in-the-context-of-the-circulation-of-the-omicron-sars-cov-2-variant-from-the-who-technical-advisory-group-on-covid-19-vaccine-composition.

Willis, Kiersten. "What's the difference between asymptomatic and presymptomatic spread of coronavirus?" *Medical Xpress*, June 18, 2020. https://medicalxpress.com/news/2020-06-difference-asymptomatic-presymptomatic-coronavirus.html.

Wilson, Addison. "Joe Rogan In Info Wars Exposes The Truth About Ivermectin To America!" The True Defender, November 4, 2021. https://thetruedefender.com/joe-rogan-in-info-wars-exposes-the-truth-about-ivermectin-to-america/.

Winslow, Donald. "Dr. Judy Mikovits – Since 1984, Fauci has Been the Mastermind Behind Every Pandemic." *Daily Report USA*, September 29, 2021. https://dailyreportusa.com/dr-judy-mikovits-since-1984-fauci-has-been-the-mastermind-behind-every-pandemic/.

Winters, Natalie. "WATCH: Explosive, Unearthed Video Shows Peter Daszak Describing 'Chinese Colleagues' Developing 'Killer' Coronaviruses." *The National Pulse*, June 8, 2021. https://thenationalpulse.com/2021/06/08/daszak-reveals-chinese-colleagues-manipulating-coronaviruses/.

Winters, Natalie and Raheem Kassam. "6 Scandals The Media Won't Tell You About Outgoing NIH Director Francis Collins." *The National Pulse*, October 5, 2021. https://thenationalpulse.com/2021/10/05/6-scandals-the-media-wont-tell-you-about-outgoing-nih-director-francis-collins/?fbclid=IwAR0wMk-03XuASoXdEdPEuXd18NxWYItbbFFSbcUOFRA5VffuhwTDnl7jkYY.

Wordnik, "Vaccine." Accessed January 4, 2021. https://www.wordnik.com/words/vaccine.

Wolfe, Raymond. "3-year-old girl dies of heart attack one day after taking COVID vaccine." *LifeSite News*, January 5, 2022. https://www.lifesitenews.com/news/3-year-old-girl-dies-of-heart-attack-one-day-after-covid-vaccine/.

World Economic Forum. "Samia Suluhu Hassan." Accessed November 23, 2021. https://www.weforum.org/people/samia-suluhu-hassan.

———. "Read Yuval Harari's blistering warning to Davos in full." January 4, 2020. https://www.weforum.org/agenda/2020/01/yuval-hararis-warning-davos-speech-future-predications/.

World Entertainment News Network. "Derek Hough in quarantine with COVID-19 after 'DWTS' appearance." *Toronto Sun*, November 16, 2021. https://torontosun.com/entertainment/television/derek-hough-in-quarantine-with-covid-19-after-dwts-appearance?utm_term=Autofeed&utm_medium=Social&utm_source=Facebook&fbclid=IwAR3fsB8Pjc86ZcdWsjrWniT_TS8eOgrZFp9Qq3VNewlZ4IbOiMS0l0dthag#Echobox=1637106973.

World Health Organization. "Tuberculosis." October 14, 2021. https://www.who.int/news-room/fact-sheets/detail/tuberculosis.

World Health Summit. "KEY 01 - Opening Ceremony - World Health Summit." YouTube Video, the 1:37:28 to 1:38:00 mark, October 24, 2021. https://www.youtube.com/watch?v=OJFKBritLlc&list=PLsrCyC4w5AZ8F0xsD3_rzLcfxHbOBRX4W.

World Safety Pfizer. "5.3.6 CUMULATIVE ANALYSIS OF POST-AUTHORIZATION ADVERSE EVENT REPORTS OF PF-07302048 (BNT162B2) RECEIVED THROUGH 28-FEB-2021." Accessed March 3, 2022. https://phmpt.org/wp-content/uploads/2021/11/5.3.6-postmarketing-experience.pdf.

Worobey, Michael. "Dissecting the early COVID-19 cases in Wuhan." *Science*, November 18, 2021. https://www.science.org/doi/10.1126/science.abm4454.

Yagisawa, Morimasa, et al. "Global trends in clinical studies of ivermectin in COVID-19." *The Japanese Journal of Antibiotics* 74 (March 2021): 44–95. https://www.psychoactif.org/forum/uploads/documents/161/74-1_44-95.pdf.

Yahoo! Finance, "New COVID-19 vaccine that covers Omicron 'will be ready in March,' Pfizer CEO says." *Yahoo! News*, January 10, 2022. https://ca.finance.yahoo.com/video/covid-19-vaccine-covers-omicron-144553437.html.

Chapter 46

The Aftermath of a False Pandemic: Thoughts on Experimental Vaccines

Enrique C. G. Ventureyra

Klaus Schwab and Thierry Malleret stated at the conclusion of their book, *COVID-19: The Great Reset*, that the COVID-19 pandemic: "represents a rare but narrow window of opportunity to reflect, reimagine and reset our world."[1] This chapter explores to what extent this reflection or proclamation has come into effect.

After changing its original definition, in December 2019, the WHO declared that there was a new coronavirus (COVID-19) pandemic. This pandemic was created by the detection of a not properly isolated virus (SARS-CoV-2) by means of a nonspecific test (RT-PCR) in both symptomatic and asymptomatic individuals suffering from common cold symptoms. Although patient zero[2] was never identified, the first fatality from pneumonia occurred in Wuhan, China. Without having isolated the pathogen, several theories were postulated trying to determine the origin of the virus. These included animals such as bats, pigs, and pangolins, acting as reservoirs of the virus. This zoonosis theory was generated by considering the local consumption of these animals in that region of the world.

As a prelude to the COVID-19 pandemic, Event 201 took place in NYC; they clearly state their agenda as an "exercise" on their webpage:

> The Johns Hopkins Center for Health Security in partnership with the World Economic Forum and the Bill and Melinda Gates Foundation hosted Event 201, a high-level pandemic exercise on October 18, 2019, in New York, NY. The exercise illustrated areas where public/private partnerships will be necessary during the response to a severe pandemic in order to diminish large-scale economic and societal consequences.
>
> In recent years, the world has seen a growing number of epidemic events, amounting to approximately 200 events annually. These events

1 Schwab and Malleret, *COVID-19: The Great Reset*, 98.

2 See Duarte, "Who is 'patient zero' in the coronavirus outbreak?"; Page, "In Hunt for Covid-19 Origin, Patient Zero Points to Second Wuhan Market."

> are increasing, and they are disruptive to health, economies, and society. Managing these events already strains global capacity, even absent a pandemic threat. Experts agree that it is only a matter of time before one of these epidemics becomes global—a pandemic with potentially catastrophic consequences. A severe pandemic, which becomes "Event 201," would require reliable cooperation among several industries, national governments, and key international institutions.[3]

This plan was also displayed in the 2011 film "Contagion: Anatomy of a Pandemic."[4] This film portrayed a pandemic originating in Hong Kong caused by the consumption of contaminated pork meat via a contaminated bat where the "wrong bat met the wrong pig."[5] The pandemic depicted in the film ended after the implementation of massive inoculation of the world population with a newly developed "vaccine." In addition, the Toronto Protocols from 1967[6] and the Rockefeller Foundation Annual Report from 2010,[7] both describe a pandemic as an instrument for population control. The question arises: How can this happen? Fear is a known instrument of power for population control. Considering the previous background, it is clear that a pandemic due to a highly contagious lethal virus would be ideal not only to instil fear in the population but to justify otherwise unacceptable draconian sanitary measures.[8]

Considering this background information, it is clear that a pandemic due to a highly contagious lethal virus would be ideal not only to instil fear in the population but to justify otherwise unacceptable draconian sanitary measures. In-line with this philosophy, a group of psychopaths under the guise of "philanthropists," have engineered an evil plan of population control by depopulation and sterilization.[9] Why depopulation? Inscriptions found in the Georgia Stones, a Masonic Monolith of obscure origin, includes a world population of 500 million as one of the planet sustainable goals.[10] Justified by a pandemic, mass vaccination of the world population could be used as a bioweapon for depopulation and population control.[11]

The so called "new vaccines" are genetically engineered products designed to alter the human genome and introduce nanoparticles into the human body.

3 Event 201 took place on October 18, 2019, in New York City. See Center for Health Security, "Event 201: A Global Pandemic Exercise." They are sponsored by the John Hopkins University, the Bill & Melinda Gates Foundation and of course, the World Economic Forum.

4 Like Stories of the Old, "Contagion – Anatomy of a Global Pandemic."

5 Rosenthal, "'The Wrong Bat Met the Wrong Pig': Pandemic Ethics in Contagion (2011)."

6 See Monast, "Intelligence Report."

7 The Rockefeller Foundation, "Annual Report 2010."

8 del Pino Calvo-Sotelo, "Fear as an instrument of power."

9 Truth Revolution, "The Dark Plan of Bill Gates Mass Vaccination and Depopulation Agenda"; Awakening Channel, "Depopulation Agenda, the Origins."

10 Wikipedia, "George Guidestones."

11 The History of Vaccines, "Biological Weapons, Bioterrorism, and Vaccines."

These so-called vaccines are experimental products due to the unnecessarily rushed production and untested safety and effectiveness through rigorous clinical trials. Due to the availability of cheap, safe, and efficacious drugs, such as hydroxychloroquine and ivermectin,[12] emergency approval for clinical use of these genetic products has been deceptive and fraudulent.[13] Furthermore, these "vaccines" do not contribute to build strong and long-lasting immunity to the receptor nor prevent the spread of the disease. These new vaccines are a departure from classical vaccines produced from dead or tamed viruses, instead these are produced by artificial mRNA or adenovirus vector induced technologies aimed to induce immunity by the production of the coronavirus spike protein. Contrary to false producer's advertising, both types of vaccines reach the cell nucleus during the prophase of the cell mitosis producing permanent DNA changes.[14] In addition, these genetic changes carry enormous implications to vaccinated individuals by virtue of the existing patents rights owned by the producing companies. This is a hidden clause for the receptor who becomes committed to receive an unknown number of booster shots in the future in order to keep their vaccination status. Considering that 85 percent are placebos, vaccination thus becomes a game of Russian roulette, as has been confirmed by funeral director John O'Looney on the Stew Peters Show:

> The vaccine method being used is the 'advocate' method: suppose you have 100 vaccines in a tray, and 85 are placebo whereas the remaining 15 are designed to maim and kill. The 85 recipients that are fine are your advocates for the vaccine, whereas the 15 that become sick and ill are your 'Covid' deaths. And they've already warned us that the vaccines aren't fully effective.[15]

Soon after the vaccination program started, an abnormal magnetic phenomenon was observed on vaccinated individuals which led to the investigation and analysis of the vaccines vials and needles used for inoculation. This investigation

12 See for a peer-reviewed article on the efficacy of ivermectin, see Bryant, et al., "Ivermectin for Prevention and Treatment of COVID-19 Infection: A Systematic Review, Meta-analysis, and Trial Sequential Analysis to Inform Clinical Guidelines"; for a peer reviewed paper on the efficacy of hydroxychloroquine see "Hydroxychloroquine is effective, and consistently so when provided early, for COVID-19: a systematic review"; Delaney, "COVID expert Dr. Peter McCullough urges 'unbreakable resistance' to vaccines for kids."

13 Ley, "Is FDA following rules for emergency use authorization in the creation of vaccines?"

14 Dolgin, "The tangled history of mRNA vaccines."

15 O'Looney "Funeral Director John O'looney Confirms What We've Suspected"; Clevenger, "Funeral Director John O'Looney Blows the Whistle on Covid." Mainstream media is now attempting to blame mild side-effects on what is known from a nocebo effect after certain recipients received a placebo version of the vaccine, see Somos, "Study suggests 'nocebo effect,' not jabs, could be behind two-thirds of mild COVID-19 vaccine reactions." Prior to this mainstream media was not discussing placebo versions of the COVID-19 vaccines.

revealed the presence of unexpected toxic products in the vaccines, particularly a hight content of Graphene oxide (GO) among other foreign substances and organisms.[16] Graphene oxide is a carbon derivate with super conductor properties which becomes magnetic in contact with the hydrogen molecule after inoculation.[17] The symptoms of COVID-19 are replicated in the absence of a virus (GO = SARS CoV2 + 5G = COVID-19).[18] Graphene is introduced into the body via vaccines, PCRs, Antigen tests, masks, air, nasal sprays, alcoholic gels, water, food, etc.[19] Graphene is degraded by the enzyme myeloperoxidase present in the lungs and by glutathione, a potent antioxidant produced by its precursor N-Acetyl Cysteine (NAC). Both substances are found in the normal diet or ingested as food supplements. Glutathione levels are particularly high in young athletes providing protection against COVID-19. The natural degradation of Graphene explains the necessity of vaccines booster shots to maintain adequate GO levels. GO has strong thrombotic properties, which explain serious side effects and deaths due to strokes and heart attacks after vaccination, because of its electric affinity GO deposits, particularly in organs driven by electricity such as brain and heart. Due to its super conductor properties, GO vibrates when exposed to electromagnetic fields of various frequencies.[20] This particular phenomenon contributes to the mechanism of neuromodulation and consequently to the control of brain functions such as thought and emotions.[21] This mechanism is facilitated by the GO ability to go through the blood–brain barrier and its adherence to neurons.[22]

The teslaphoresis phenomenon experiments at Rice University demonstrated the capabilities of this type of technology with the remote induced self-assembly of nanoparticles.[23]

It's interesting to note that the massive roll out of 5G technology, including antennas and satellites, coincided with waves of COVID-19 and that the incidence of this disease is much lower or absent in countries where

16 Love, "What's In the Vaxx? Transgenic Hydra And Parasite Implants Used As Rapid Human Cloning System."

17 Madrid, "Graphene Oxide Detection in Aqueous Suspension Observational Study in Optical and Electron Microscopy."

18 La Quinta Columna, "Graphene oxide + 5G = COVID-19."

19 To find out more details go to the Graphene – Flagship website: https://graphene-flagship.eu/.

20 Mousavi, et al., "Recent Progress in Electrochemical Detection of Human Papillomavirus (HPV) via Graphene-Based Nanosensors."

21 Mendonça, "Reduced graphene oxide induces transient blood–brain barrier opening: an in vivo study."

22 Aguiar, "Una llave para entrar al cerebro"; Huang, "Graphene-Based Sensors for Human Health Monitoring."

23 Coldewey, "Teslaphoresis-activated self-assembling carbon nanotubes look even cooler than they sound."

5G technology has not proliferated.[24] These findings are in support of the environmental theory.[25] Based on the foregoing vaccinated individuals that do not receive a placebo dose when exposed to 5G become human antennas that receive and emit electric signals. Thus, humans will become part of the "Internet of Things" (something that has been predicted by futurist Ray Kurzweil)[26] by being neuromodulated and connected to the internet and to an artificial intelligence system,[27] which control their thoughts and emotions (Agenda 2030).[28] Additionally, this integration provides the geolocation of the vaccinated individuals. These facts are supported by patents filed by the vaccine producer Pfizer.[29] Simultaneously, legislation contemplating neuromodulation rights is undergoing parliamentary discussion in countries like Chile.[30]

The boundaries of AI are totally unknown to us and the human race is undergoing a process of transhumanism with robots gaining popularity. As time passes, we learn more of these unbelievable stories. Saudi Arabia as one of the leading countries of globalization has granted citizenship to a robot named Sophia.[31] Apparently, Sophia will be leading a robot's factory and she has stated her plans for not hiring humans as workers in her factory. For better or for worse, this is becoming a reality.[32] Thus, it is obvious that if left unchecked, robots and AI will take over many tasks currently under exclusive human control. This should not be allowed, otherwise the "singularity" concept, where transhumans will be able to attend their own funerals, in the form of a robot, will become a reality much sooner than we can imagine. Sophia, when asked a question by her creator, David Hanson of Hanson Robotics, on whether she would destroy humans, she said she would.[33] This all seems part of an unfolding Global Satanic plan.

Many developments, although put in front of our eyes, go totally undetected by a large portion of the population. Some developments are so bizarre that they challenge the most creative minds. Only after all the dots are joined, only then does the full picture become visible. Here is an example: At the inauguration of the Gotthard Base Tunnel in the Swiss Alps in 2016, disguised as a ballet, an

24 La Quinta Columna, "5G Map & COVID-19 Environmental Theory."

25 La Quinta Columna, "5G Map & COVID-19 Environmental Theory."

26 RT staff, "Google's Ray Kurzweil says humans will have 'hybrid' cloud-powered brains by 2030."

27 Hong and Kahn, "Hybrid Brain–Computer Interface Techniques for Improved Classification Accuracy and Increased Number of Commands: A Review."

28 Salas, "Por qué hay que prohibir que nos manipulen el cerebro antes de que sea possible."

29 Ehrlich, et al., "Methods and Systems of Prioritizing Treatments, Vaccination, Testing and/or Activities While Protecting the Privacy of Individuals." US Patent No.: US 11,107,588 B2.

30 Salas, "Por qué hay que prohibir que nos manipulen el cerebro antes de que sea possible."

31 Cuthbert, "Saudi Arabia becomes first country to grant citizenship to a robot."

32 Brown, "A new study measures the actual impact of robots on jobs. It's significant."

33 Weller, "The First 'Robot Citizen' in the World Once Said She Wants to 'Destroy Humans'."

exoteric Satanic ritual took place. This ceremony of inauguration was attended by high rank globalists, including European dignitaries and leaders.[34] Among them French President François Hollande and German Chancellor Angela Merkel, were present. Not far from the place where this inauguration ceremony took place is the city of Geneva, where the European Council for Nuclear Research (CERN), the largest particle (hadron) accelerator in the world, the Large Hydron Collider (HCL) is located. At the entrance of CERN there is a statue of Shiva, one of the principal deities of Hinduism. Shiva is said to be responsible for the creation and the destruction of the universe:

> The Council meeting closed with a ceremony to unveil a statue offered to CERN by the Government of India as a symbol of India's long-standing relationship with CERN. Nataraja, the Cosmic Dancer, depicts a dancing Lord Shiva trampling ignorance. Speaking at the unveiling ceremony, Dr Anil Kakodkar, Chairman of the Indian Atomic Energy Commission and Secretary to the Government of India, expressed his satisfaction that "the Indian scientific community is part of the quest for understanding the Universe". India's involvement with CERN dates back to the early 1960s.[35]

Meanwhile, an unprecedented experiment took place at CERN; the tiniest particles in the universe (hadrons), were accelerated to a speed beyond the speed of light, which after colliding generated unprecedented energy fields that altered the space–time dimension of this world. This extraordinary event opened a trans-dimensional portal to the underworld. What was the purpose of both the extraordinary CERN experiment and the nearby Satanic ceremony? It was to welcome the Satanic figure of Baphomet into this world![36] These events, plus others like the ritualistic Masonic ceremony celebrated at the Royal Palace in Madrid, Spain, in 2020 to commemorate the dead during the pandemic, confirmed the spiritual component of the current false sanitary crisis called the COVID-19 pandemic.[37] Apparently, the real meaning of COVID-19 is not that of Coronavirus Disease 2019. Instead, it is that of "Certificate of Vaccination Identification Artificial Intelligence."[38] This last definition falls in line with

34 BBC, "Switzerland tunnel: The oddest moments of the opening ceremony."

35 CERN, "CERN Director General Outlines Seven-point Strategy for European Laboratory."

36 Watkins, "CERN Collider opening the gates of Hell?"

37 López, "Vamos a dormir". Vergonzosa ceremonia masónica y new-age por las víctimas del coronavirus." See also Dyer, "Learn How to Fight in the Spiritual Warfare Being Waged on Humanity"; his website: Jay Dyer of https://jaysanalysis.com.

38 Uddin, "Certificate Of Vaccination ID & AI The Mark of the Beast." ID = identification, and for the 19 component, 1 designates the letter A and 9 the letter I.

the implementation of the COVID vaccination passport, or green passport in Europe. Based on Vaccine Adverse Events Reporting System (VAERS) and the European medication surveillance programs, the number of serious complications and mortalities rising from COVID vaccination are staggering,[39] despite being underreported and estimated at < 1% of the total numbers.[40] The World Health Organization database has so far registered a total of 2,199,476 reports of adverse effects after COVID-19 vaccination during 2021.[41] Spain was one of the most affected countries in the world with a vaccination program that failed to achieve its goals. In September 2021, the government announced that the pandemic was under control![42] These facts speak volumes. Confirming the Covid "vaccines" are ineffective and dangerous! The Israeli health minister is currently hiding the thousands of cases of adverse reactions to the vaccine, published on the government's own website, and then withdrawn.[43]

The simple reality is that the COVID vaccines are new, experimental, unproven, and are causing many deaths and injuries.[44] Worst of all, everyone foolish enough to take this "jab" finds out they can still catch COVID, and they can still transmit it to others.

In many places, the vaccinated are still required to wear masks! So, more and more people see the absurdity of the vax and figure: "Why bother?" The "vaccine" seems to be a fraud. The following statement is a very revealing description of the purpose of these vaccines by the group called, "Psicólogos por la Verdad" (Psychologists for the Truth) in Argentina:

> The vaccine is the "black baptism", the initiation ritual to enter as a citizen of the new world order. For this you must renounce all your rights and your portion created in the image and likeness of God, accepting to be genetically modified. Some vaccines cause thrombi in the legs and arms, which will need to be amputated and replaced by robotic limbs. Others cause thrombi in organs, which must also be replaced by robotic organs. Others sterilize, and others kill (population

39 Redshaw, "FDA Grants Emergency Use of Pfizer Vaccine for Kids 5 to 11, as Reports of Injuries After COVID Vaccines Near 840,000."

40 Nigh, "VAERS, Underreporting, and the Mysterious 1%"; Digital Healthcare Research, "Electronic Support for Public Health - Vaccine Adverse Event Reporting System (ESP: VAERS)."

41 Bingham, "WHO database reports over 2 million potential COVID jab injuries in 2021, vast majority in women."

42 Guell, "Experts say worst of the pandemic is over in Spain, but warn coronavirus is here to stay."

43 Jansezian, "SILENCED? Israel's Health Ministry removes comments claiming adverse effects from the COVID vaccine on its social media post."

44 For a movie about peoples' experiences related to COVID-19 vaccine injuries, see "The Testimonies Project" with a movie and other videos: https://www.vaxtestimonies.org/en/; see also the statement by the International Alliance of Physicians and Medical Scientists, "Physicians Declaration II – Updated Global Covid Summit."

> control). Everything converges in the creation of a new transhuman, without the ability to connect with the divine; but connected himself to the internet ("internet of things"/bluetooth code in vaccinated).[45] The "consolation prize" for having been chemically" castrated will be the proposal of "amortality": to change and rejuvenate damaged organs, notably prolonging the life of the human who "will have nothing but will be happy" since by not having anything in his life, will fall into excesses of all kinds; causing great damage to nature and to the divine law of God, since a scenario like Sodom and Gomorrah will be revived...making the need for a divine correction imminent; so they will suffer torments for those who will want to find death, but will not be able to.[46]

Despite the above facts and developments, a massive vaccination program is in progress around the world. Due to the experimental status and the availability of safe and efficacious medicines, such as HCQ and Ivermectin, none of the vaccines can be legally approved and mandated, until the vaccines clinical trials are completed by May 2023.[47]

Thus, governments have unconstitutionally implemented coercive methods of persuasion to achieve their goals. These methods not only violate the constitutional rights of citizens but the Nuremberg Code of global human rights.[48] To achieve the goal of massive vaccination, a pre-pandemic planned COVID pass has been illegally mandated in several countries. Without a vaccination pass, citizens' personal liberties, including traveling, working, banking, access to restaurants, hotels, gyms, etc., will be restricted. Additionally, this pass allows governments to track and trace citizens as they wish and to implement a social credit score system like communist countries.[49] The finding of luciferase[50] in the vaccines revealed a method of tattooing to

45 This embodies a tracking system that works in conjunction with the injections. Its main purpose is to ensure compliance through the continuance of accepting more injections which is part of the "beast system." This tracking ID system is to implement a global social credit system through numeric ID and monitoring and scoring people to allow access to services, see Google Patents, "Methods and systems of prioritizing treatments, vaccination, testing and/or activities while protecting the privacy of individuals"; States of Israel Patents Office, "Methods and systems of prioritizing treatments, vaccination, testing and/or activities while protecting the privacy of individuals."

46 Psicólogos por la Verdad, https://psicologosporlaverdad.org/.

47 See ClinicalTrials.gov, "Study to Describe the Safety, Tolerability, Immunogenicity, and Efficacy of RNA Vaccine Candidates Against COVID-19 in Healthy Individuals." See also Cyranoski, "Why emergency COVID-vaccine approvals pose a dilemma for scientists."

48 The Nuremberg Code 1947.

49 Tate, "Coming soon: America's own social credit system."

50 McGovern, "Pfizer whistleblower says vaccine 'glows,' contains toxic luciferase, graphene oxide compounds."

prevent tampering with the COVID pass. Taking into account the foregoing information about this pass, it seems that the Apocalyptic "mark of the beast" is already in the vaccinated.[51]

The reader may ask now, how do all the previously presented events and developments tie together? Awareness about the goals of the "Great Reset" which includes transhumanism, and the Fourth Industrial Revolution[52] are necessary to join the dots and visualize the full picture. In addition to depopulation and sterilization, the COVID "vaccines" coupled with 5G technology, as well as technical advances in AI and robotics, are useful tools necessary to achieve and implement the goals of the Great Reset Agenda.[53]

Unlike World War II, there will not be liberation forces emancipating humanity from the oppression of the current globalist tyranny that is already present in several countries. This global tyranny found its way in, facilitated by the absurd compliance of the citizenship, to their unjust, illogical, and illegal mandates. Thus, unless humans stand up for their human rights and massively reject all tyrannical rules and mandates imposed by the corrupted and malefic rulers, the current state of affairs is likely to continue for the next one hundred or more years!

Nevertheless, a foreseeable alternative scenario may unfold due to the massive number of vaccine-induced casualties, particularly those affecting loved ones, friends, and neighbours. Witnessing this devastating scenario will wake up a frustrated and enraged citizenry, turning them against their oppressors. Thus, seeking justice from their own hands, like what happened during the Russian Revolution of 1917, the tyrannical World War II, the Italian regime in 1945, and the more recent oppressive Romanian regime.

This false pandemic has been an eye opener for me, becoming the largest disappointment in my life. I am grateful to God for allowing me to see the truth about the unfolding sinister plan perpetrated against humanity, from the beginning.

I am deeply troubled and disappointed to have seen family members, dear friends, and colleagues lose their moral and scientific compass through the evolution of this ordeal,[54] surrendering their minds and bodies to the evil propaganda utilized by corrupted governments and institutions. Particularly, with my medical colleagues, many of whom violated the sacred principle of their Hippocratic Oath of "first do no harm."

Consequently, I lost all my respect and trust in those corrupted institutions and governments that willingly damaged and misled humanity, with the

51 The Radio Bible Study, "How the Quantum Dot Microneedle Vaccination Delivery System Compares to the Mark of the Beast in Revelation 13."

52 Schwab, "The Fourth Industrial Revolution: what it means, how to respond."

53 World Economic Forum, "The Great Reset."

54 See Appendix 2 for a letter addressed to colleagues and friends.

ultimate purpose of population control by extermination and sterilization, to install a NWO, that will benefit a few and will enslave the rest of humanity, for the next fifty or one hundred years.

Final Thoughts

The "Covid 19 Pandemic" has been planned for a long time to destroy humanity as we know it.[55] Homo sapiens evolved from homo erectus over 300,000 years ago. Since then, advanced civilizations—Atlanteans, Sumerians, Egyptians, Mayans, Incas, etc.—existed and disappeared mysteriously. Humans in their short history haven't been good housekeepers of the planet, as demonstrated by the destruction inflicted by wars and pollution they generated.

The real history before humanity has been carefully hidden and contaminated by false histories and legends. Some knowledge of exo-politics and biblical facts are necessary to understand the following developments. The universe has existed for billions of years containing an extraordinary number of stars and galaxies with an extraordinary number of planets, which most likely are inhabited by races more advanced than ours. The activity and balanced interaction of these various races is controlled and coordinated by an Intergalactic Alliance, integrated by members of the various non-human races. Based on the poor historical performance of humanity's mission to preserve Planet Earth's integrity, at one point in time, the Alliance decided that the human race should be eliminated and replaced. Planet Earth has a privileged location in the galaxy and gifted with fantastic resources. Thus, it was selected for colonization by another more evolved and responsible race. This nefarious plan was created and developed by non-humans, such as demons, aliens, and other entities. To execute this plan of extermination of the human race, bioweapons, so-called vaccines were created.[56] Thus, a massive vaccination and sterilization plan was engineered. This plan of extermination was designed and directed by non-humans and facilitated by a small group of "human elites," three thousand or less, who were provided with enormous financial resources and powers, to execute the Plan. In return for their services, the elites were promised the means and resources to exit the planet, at the End of the human holocaust. Thus, enabling them to migrate to another planet such as Mars.

In essence, a war of good vs evil was launched. The foregoing plan fits well in the Satanic agenda, confirming that Satan is determined to destroy humanity, simply because God created humans as His *image and likeness*, placing humans

55 Healther Ranger Report, "What Dr. Robert Malone could not say."

56 See Parsa, *The Great Reset: How Big Tech Elites and the World's People can be enslaved by China CCP or A.I.*

at the centre of His Creation. Lucifer, the fallen Angel, became jealous of God's design and wanted to destroy His Creation.[57]

The methods of depopulation utilized and currently in progress, via vaccination and sterilization, are evil but clever because they will deliver a depopulated planet: clean, full of resources and apt for colonization. Human and organ trafficking and experimentation, as well as Satanic rituals with child sacrifice, are part of the Satanic agenda, currently in progress.

Totally undeterred, corrupted governments worldwide are pushing unjustified massive vaccination, abortion, and euthanasia programs in order to accomplish the depopulation plan at the earliest possible date before 2030 as designed by the WEF.

According to this evil plan, a segment of the world population will be eliminated (Georgia Stones inscription) and the remaining survivors will be subjected to a process of transhumanism, required for total control of their minds and emotions.

The so-called vaccines were engineered as bioweapons to produce death, mayhem and sterilization. These bioweapons contain various nanoparticles, including graphene oxide, lipid biospheres, and hydrogels, required not only to produce death and sterilization but to induce genetic transformation enabling humans to be integrated in the "Internet of things/bodies" via 5G and Star-link connection, under AI control.[58] Thus, the ID Chip or Mark of the Beast can be introduced in the human body less invasively and controlled remotely.[59]

The book of Revelation is very revealing and can serve as an important spiritual resource to assist and guide us during these times of turbulent tribulation—shedding light into the darkness in which the world has fallen. God always wins, so we must trust His plan, but we must continue to act in accordance with His will. Rest assured that all those responsible for plotting and perpetrating these criminal and inhuman methods of destruction for self-benefit and controlling humanity, will have no place to hide from his Divine Justice: "the Lord knows how to rescue the godly from temptation, and to keep the unrighteous under punishment for the day of judgment" (2: Pet 2:9).

57 Foros de la Virgen María, "La Pandemia es un Plan del Maligno y Dios dijo cómo Combatirla [revelaciones de exorcismos]."

58 Liu, "Tracking how our bodies work could change our lives."

59 Dark_universe_09, "Mark of the beast"; Don't Speak News, "More Evidence the Vax is the Mark of the Beast."

Bibliography

Aguiar, Ricardo. "Una llave para entrar al cerebro." Pesquisa, Edición 256, June 2017. https://revistapesquisa.fapesp.br/es/una-llave-para-entrar-al-cerebro/.

Awakening Channel, "Depopulation Agenda, the Origins." Awakeningchannel.com, October 21, 2021. https://new.awakeningchannel.com/depopulation-agenda-the-origins/.

BBC, "Switzerland tunnel: The oddest moments of the opening ceremony." *BBC News*, June 1, 2016. https://www.bbc.com/news/in-pictures-36428799.

Bingham, Jack. "WHO database reports over 2 million potential COVID jab injuries in 2021, vast majority in women." *LifeSite News*, October 7, 2021. https://www.lifesitenews.com/news/who-database-reports-over-2-million-potential-covid-jab-injuries-in-2021-vast-majority-in-women/.

Brown, Sara."A new study measures the actual impact of robots on jobs. It's significant." *MIT Management: Sloan School*, July 29, 2020. https://mitsloan.mit.edu/ideas-made-to-matter/a-new-study-measures-actual-impact-robots-jobs-its-significant.

Bryant, et al. "Ivermectin for Prevention and Treatment of COVID-19 Infection: A Systematic Review, Meta-analysis, and Trial Sequential Analysis to Inform Clinical Guidelines." *American Journal of Therapeutics* Vol. 28 (July/August 2021): p e434-e460 doi:10.1097/MJT.0000000000001402.

Center for Health Security. "Event 201: A Global Pandemic Exercise." Accessed October 29, 2021. https://www.centerforhealthsecurity.org/event201/about.

CERN. "CERN Director General Outlines Seven-point Strategy for European Laboratory." *CERN: Accelerating Science*, June 18, 2004. https://home.cern/news/press-release/cern/cern-director-general-outlines-seven-point-strategy-european-laboratory.

Clevenger, Lynn. "Funeral Director John O'Looney Blows the Whistle on Covid." *Sherman Clay*, October 30, 2021. https://shermanclay.blogspot.com/2021/10/funeral-director-john-olooney-blows.html.

ClinicalTrials.gov. "Study to Describe the Safety, Tolerability, Immunogenicity, and Efficacy of RNA Vaccine Candidates Against COVID-19 in Healthy Individuals." BioNTech SE/Pfizer, updated October 27, 2021. https://clinicaltrials.gov/ct2/show/NCT04368728.

Coldewey, Devin. "Teslaphoresis-activated self-assembling carbon nanotubes look even cooler than they sound." *TechCrunch*, April 14, 2016. https://techcrunch.com/2016/04/14/teslaphoresis-activated-self-assembling-carbon-nanotubes-look-even-cooler-than-they-sound/.

Cuthbert, Olivia. "Saudi Arabia becomes first country to grant citizenship to a robot." *Arab News*, October 16, 2017. https://www.arabnews.com/node/1183166/saudi-arabia.

Cyranoski, David. "Why emergency COVID-vaccine approvals pose a dilemma for scientists." *Nature*, November 23, 2020. https://www.nature.com/articles/d41586-020-03219-y.

Dark_universe_09. "Mark of the beast." Telegram, September 10, 2021. https://t.me/darkuniverse09/1947.

del Pino Calvo-Sotelo, Fernando. "Fear as an instrument of power." *Fpcs: Independent views in freedom*, June 2, 2020. https://www.fpcs.es/en/fear-as-an-instrument-of-power/.

Delaney, Patrick. "COVID expert Dr. Peter McCullough urges 'unbreakable resistance' to vaccines for kids." *LifeSite News*, October 11, 2021. https://www.lifesitenews.com/news/covid-expert-dr-peter-mccullogh-urges-unbreakable-resistance-to-vaccines-for-kids/.

Digital Healthcare Research, "Electronic Support for Public Health - Vaccine Adverse Event Reporting System (ESP:VAERS)." Accessed November 10,2021. https://digital.ahrq.gov/ahrq-funded-projects/electronic-support-public-health-vaccine-adverse-event-reporting-system.

Dolgin, Elie. "The tangled history of mRNA vaccines." Nature, September 14, 2021. https://www.nature.com/articles/d41586-021-02483-w.

Don't Speak News. "More Evidence the Vax is the Mark of the Beast." Don't Speak News, October 14, 2021. https://dontspeaknews.com/2021/10/14/more-evidence-the-vax-is-the-mark-of-the-beast/.

Duarte, Fernando. "Who is 'patient zero' in the coronavirus outbreak?" *BBC*, February 23, 2020. https://www.bbc.com/future/article/20200221-coronavirus-the-harmful-hunt-for-covid-19s-patient-zero.

Dyer, Jay. "Learn How to Fight in the Spiritual Warfare Being Waged on Humanity." Interview on *The Alex Jones Show*, November 11, 2021. https://banned.video/watch?id=618db5522fa19644c8ae91b0.

Ehrlich, et al. "Methods and Systems of Prioritizing Treatments, Vaccination, Testing and/or Activities While Protecting the Privacy of Individuals." US Patent No.: US 11,107,588 B2. August 30, 2020. https://patentscope.wipo.int/search/en/detail.jsf?docId=US320331550&tab=NATIONALBIBLIO.

Foros de la Virgen María. "La Pandemia es un Plan del Maligno y Dios dijo cómo Combatirla [revelaciones de exorcismos]." YouTube Video, February 28, 2021.

Google Patents. "Methods and systems of prioritizing treatments, vaccination, testing and/or activities while protecting the privacy of individuals. August 11, 2020. https://patents.google.com/patent/US11107588B2/en.

Graphene – Flagship website: https://graphene-flagship.eu/.

Grider, Geoffrey. "How the Quantum Dot Microneedle Vaccination Delivery System Compares to the Mark of the Beast in Revelation 13." *Now The End Begins: Radio Bible Study*, April 29, 2020. https://www.nowtheendbegins.com/nteb-radio-bible-study-how-the-quantum-dot-microneedle-vaccination-delivery-system-mark-of-the-beast-revelation-13/.

Guell, Oriol. "Experts say worst of the pandemic is over in Spain, but warn coronavirus is here to stay." September 27, 2021. https://english.elpais.com/society/2021-09-27/experts-say-worst-of-the-pandemic-is-over-in-spain-but-warn-coronavirus-is-here-to-stay.html.

Healther Ranger Report. "What Dr. Robert Malone could not say." Brighteon Video, January 2, 2022. https://www.brighteon.com/9f76180e-1642-43a0-ba33-5fde2b35eb37.

History of Vaccines, The. "Biological Weapons, Bioterrorism, and Vaccines." Accessed October 29, 2021. https://ftp.historyofvaccines.org/index.php/content/articles/biological-weapons-bioterrorism-and-vaccines.

Hong, Keum-Shik and Muhammad Jawad Kahn. "Hybrid Brain–Computer Interface Techniques for Improved Classification Accuracy and Increased Number of Commands: A Review." *Frontiers in Neurorobotics* (July 24, 2017). https://doi.org/10.3389/fnbot.2017.00035.

Huang, Haizhou. "Graphene-Based Sensors for Human Health Monitoring." *Front Chem*. 2019. 7: 399. doi:10.3389/fchem.2019.00399.

International Alliance of Physicians and Medical Scientists. "Physicians Declaration II – Updated Global Covid Summit." *Global Covid Summit*, October 29, 2021. https://doctorsandscientistsdeclaration.org/?fbclid=IwAR2gxmvjPkJf3aPMrOrko5xQn0gkws1hvzV6N8FuInHKihDelFV12GqrmnE.

Jansezian, Nicole. "SILENCED? Israel's Health Ministry removes comments claiming adverse effects from the COVID vaccine on its social media post." *All Israel News*, October 1, 2021. https://www.allisrael.com/israel-s-health-ministry-removes-comments-claiming-adverse-effects-from-the-covid-vaccine-on-its-social-media-post.

Jay Dyer's website: https://jaysanalysis.com/.

Ley, John. "Is FDA following rules for emergency use authorization in the creation of vaccines?" *Clark County*, August 16, 2021. https://www.clarkcountytoday.com/news/is-fda-following-rules-for-emergency-use-authorization-in-the-creation-of-vaccines/.

Liu, Xiao. "Tracking how our bodies work could change our lives." *World Economic* Forum, June 4, 2020. https://www.weforum.org/agenda/2020/06/internet-of-bodies-covid19-recovery-governance-health-data/.

Love, Ariyana. "What's In the Vaxx? Transgenic Hydra And Parasite Implants Used As Rapid Human Cloning System." *Red Voice Media*, October 31, 2021. https://www.redvoicemedia.com/2021/10/transgenic-hydra-and-parasite-implants-used-as-rapid-human-cloning-weapons-system/.

Like Stories of the Old. "Contagion – Anatomy of a Global Pandemic." Released in 2011. YouTube Video, March 31, 2020. https://www.youtube.com/watch?v=ELq4iRFLiLM.

López, Eulogio. "Vamos a dormir". Vergonzosa ceremonia masónica y new-age por las víctimas del coronavirus."

Madrid, Pablo Campra. "Graphene Oxide Detection in Aqueous Suspension Observational Study in Optical and Electron Microscopy." Interim Report (I). University of Almeria, Spain, June 28, 2021. https://carterheavyindustries.files.wordpress.com/2021/07/official-interim-report-in-english-university-of-almeria.pdf.

———. "Detección de Grafeno en Vacunas Covid19 por Espectroscopía Micro-Raman." Informe Técnico. University of Almeria, Spain, November 2, 2021. https://www.researchgate.net/publication/355684360_Deteccion_de_grafeno_en_vacunas_COVID19_por_espectroscopia_Micro-RAMAN.

McGovern, Celeste. "Pfizer whistleblower says vaccine 'glows,' contains toxic luciferase, graphene oxide compounds." *LifeSite News*, October 14, 2021. https://www.lifesitenews.com/news/bombshell-pfizer-whistleblower-says-vaccine-glows-contains-toxic-luciferase-graphene-oxide-compounds/?fbclid=IwAR2ASNswP3uh0nCXzJ_jgcXUTUfYr5453_zxAxZqYwwKXVa9EbjLrktNcFg.

Mendonça, M.C.P., et al. "Reduced graphene oxide induces transient blood–brain barrier opening: an in vivo study." *Journal of Nanobiotechnology* 13, 78 (2015). https://doi.org/10.1186/s12951-015-0143-z.

Monast, Serge. "Intelligence Report." Free Press Agency, 1995. https://stateofthenation.co/wp-content/uploads/2020/01/the-toronto-protocols-serge-monast.pdf.

Mousavi, Seyyed Mojtaba, et al. "Recent Progress in Electrochemical Detection of Human Papillomavirus (HPV) via Graphene-Based Nanosensors." *Journal of Sensors*, vol. 2021, Article ID 6673483, 15 pages, 2021. https://doi.org/10.1155/2021/6673483.

Nigh, Greg. "VAERS, Underreporting, and the Mysterious 1%." July 4, 2021. https://gnigh-66270.medium.com/vaers-underreporting-and-the-mysterious-1-5b4f9b109145.

Nuremberg Code 1947, The. https://media.tghn.org/medialibrary/2011/04/BMJ_No_7070_Volume_313_The_Nuremberg_Code.pdf.

O'Looney, John. "Funeral Director John O'Looney Confirms What We've Suspected." Interview on the Stew Peters Show. Brighteon Video, September 16, 2021. https://www.brighteon.com/63fe9994-893a-42b8-8ab7-43eabd1b952c.

Page, Jeremy. "In Hunt for Covid-19 Origin, Patient Zero Points to Second Wuhan Market." *WSJ*, February 26, 2021. https://www.wsj.com/articles/in-hunt-for-covid-19-origin-patient-zero-points-to-second-wuhan-market-11614335404.

Parsa, Cyrus. A. *The Great Reset: How Big Tech Elites and the World's People can be enslaved by China CCP or A.I.* La Jolla: California, The A.I. Organization, 2021.

Prodromos, C and T. Rumschlag. "Hydroxychloroquine is effective, and consistently so when provided early, for COVID-19: a systematic review." *New microbes and new infections* vol. 38 (2020): 100776. doi:10.1016/j.nmni.2020.100776.

Psicólogos por la Verdad. https://psicologosporlaverdad.org/.

Quinta Columna, La. La Quinta Columna, "Graphene oxide + 5G = COVID-19." *Orwell City*, July 3, 2021. https://www.orwell.city/2021/07/graphene-oxide-5G-COVID-19.html.

———. "5G Map & COVID-19 Environmental Theory." *Orwell City*, August 12, 2021. https://www.orwell.city/2021/08/5G-map.html.

Redshaw, "FDA Grants Emergency Use of Pfizer Vaccine for Kids 5 to 11, as Reports of Injuries After COVID Vaccines Near 840,000." *Children's Health Defense*, October 29, 2021. https://childrenshealthdefense.org/defender/vaers-cdc-deaths-injuries-covid-vaccines-fda-emergency-use-pfizer-kids/.

Rockefeller Foundation, The. "Annual Report 2010." New York, 2010. https://www.rockefellerfoundation.org/wp-content/uploads/Annual-Report-2010-1.pdf.

Rosenthal, M. Sara. "'The Wrong Bat Met the Wrong Pig': Pandemic Ethics in Contagion (2011)." In *Healthcare Ethics on Film: A Guide for Medical Educators*, 275-303. Springer, Cham, 2020. https://doi.org/10.1007/978-3-030-48818-5_6.

RT staff. "Google's Ray Kurzweil says humans will have 'hybrid' cloud-powered brains by 2030." *RT*, June 4, 2015. https://www.rt.com/usa/265029-kurzweil-google-hybrid-brain/.

Salas, Javeir. "Por qué hay que prohibir que nos manipulen el cerebro antes de que sea possible." *El País*, February 12, 2020. https://elpais.com/elpais/2020/01/30/ciencia/1580381695_084761.html.

Schwab, Klaus. "The Fourth Industrial Revolution: what it means, how to respond." *World Economic Forum*, January 4, 2016. https://www.weforum.org/agenda/2016/01/the-fourth-industrial-revolution-what-it-means-and-how-to-respond/.

Schwab, Klaus and Thierry Malleret. *COVID-19: The Great Reset*. Geneva, Switzerland: Forum Publishing, 2020.

Somos, Christy. "Study suggests 'nocebo effect,' not jabs, could be behind two-thirds of mild COVID-19 vaccine reactions." *CTV News*, January 19, 2022. https://www.ctvnews.ca/health/coronavirus/study-suggests-nocebo-effect-not-jabs-could-be-behind-two-thirds-of-mild-covid-19-vaccine-reactions-1.5746067.

States of Israel Patents Office. "Methods and systems of prioritizing treatments, vaccination, testing and/or activities while protecting the privacy of individuals." August 30, 2020. https://israelpatents.justice.gov.il/en/patent-extract/277083.

Tate, Kristin. "Coming soon: America's own social credit system." *The Hill*, August 3, 2021. https://thehill.com/opinion/finance/565860-coming-soon-americas-own-social-credit-system.

Testimonies Project, The. "The testimonies project - the movie." Accessed November 10, 2021. https://www.vaxtestimonies.org/en/.

Truth Revolution, "The Dark Plan of Bill Gates Mass Vaccination and Depopulation Agenda." Accessed October 29, 2021. https://thetruthrevolution.net/the-dark-plan-of-bill-gates-mass-vaccinations-depopulation-agenda/.

Uddin, Faiz. "Certificate Of Vaccination ID & AI The Mark of the Beast," *Blackhawk Partners*, August 2020. https://www.blackhawkpartners.com/blog/certificate-vaccination-id-ai-mark-beast/.

Watkins, Jon. "CERN Collider opening the gates of Hell?" *Exposing Satanism and Witchcraft*, February 5, 2017. https://www.exposingsatanism.org/cern-collider-opening-the-gates-of-hell/.

Weller, Chris. "The First 'Robot Citizen' in the World Once Said She Wants to 'Destroy Humans'." *Inc.* October 26, 2017. https://www.inc.com/business-insider/sophia-humanoid-first-robot-citizen-of-the-world-saudi-arabia-2017.html.

Wikipedia. "George Guidestones." Accessed October 29, 2021. https://en.wikipedia.org/wiki/Georgia_Guidestones.

World Economic Forum. "The Great Reset." Accessed November 10, 2021. https://www.weforum.org/great-reset/.

Part VII:

Human Hope:
The *Imago Dei* and Human Resilience

Chapter 47

Shattering Martin Luther King Jr.'s Dream[1]

Scott D. G. Ventureyra

It has been over 50 years since the assassination of Martin Luther King Jr., and August 28 of 2022 will be the fifty-ninth anniversary of his famous "I have a dream" speech. I admire what King embodied and accomplished, though I do have strong disagreements with him in areas such as his heterodox theological views. For instance, in a paper titled, "An Autobiography of Religious Development," King states:

> I shocked my Sunday School class by denying the bodily resurrection of Jesus. From the age of thirteen on doubts began to spring forth unrelentingly. At the age of fifteen I entered college and more and more could I see a gap between what I had learned in Sunday School and what I was learning in college.[2]

In another paper titled, "The Sources of Fundamentalism and Liberalism Considered Historically and Theologically," he denied the Trinity, salvation through Christ, the virgin birth, and the Second Coming, all of which he equated with fundamentalism.[3] It is a shame that King did not live to see the tremendous shift in New Testament scholarship from 1975 onward, which has provided strong support for the historicity of the bodily resurrection of Jesus. Still, what matters more than a critique of King's theological shortcomings is the legacy of his "dream," and how so-called progressives are shattering it.

King was an activist for civil rights, human dignity, and free speech. He took seriously the Gospel notion of turning the other cheek, and of loving one's neighbour and enemies. He followed the example of Christ's Sermon on the

1 This a modified version with a different title of this article: Scott Ventureyra, "Sweeping Up Martin Luther King's Dream," *Convivium*, April 2, 2018, https://www.convivium.ca/articles/sweeping-up-martin-luther-kings-dream/.

2 Martin Luther King Jr., "An Autobiography of Religious Development (12 Sept–22 Nov 1950)."

3 Martin Luther King Jr., "The Sources of Fundamentalism and Liberalism Considered Historically and Psychologically (13 Sept–23 Nov 1949)."

Mount (Matt 5–7). His approach was one of love and was deeply influenced by Mahatma Gandhi's nonviolent approach to social change.[4]

King thought of himself as a "Jesus Extremist." When we speak of extremism we might immediately think of radical Islam, which seeks to wreak havoc on nonbelievers through violent and nonviolent subjugation (stealth jihad). But Jesus (Christian) extremism is the exact opposite: everyone is loved regardless of their religion, and for their intrinsic worth as persons. It encompasses the idea that one is prepared to follow Christ non-violently through a radical altruism, to the point of self-sacrifice, for the sake of the ultimate good. King's life and death demonstrates the cost of this self-sacrifice. At 39, his heart resembled someone who was 60,[5] most likely resulting from 13 years of cumulative stress working within the civil rights movement.

King dreamed of an egalitarian society, one that was predicated not on one's group identity but on individual essence. As he famously said:

> I have a dream that my four little children will one day live in a nation where they will not be judged by the color of their skin but by the content of their character... And when this happens and when we allow freedom ring, when we let it ring from every village and every hamlet, from every state and every city, we will be able to speed up that day when all of God's children, black men and white men, Jews and Gentiles, Protestants and Catholics, will be able to join hands and sing in the words of the old Negro spiritual: "Free at last! Free at last! Thank God Almighty, we are free at last!"[6]

We have veered far away from King's dream. Western civilization is experiencing a divisiveness that is completely antithetical to the spirit of his message. The main culprits are radicals on both the political right and left. However, the radical left has had much more dominance over culture, especially since the 1960s, through its control of many academic institutions and major media outlets. Leftists follow the postmodernist Jean François Lyotard's dictum that truth is disseminated by those who control it, and they exert such control by shutting down, suspending, demonetizing, and censoring social media accounts, as well as by "de-platforming" speakers on university campuses. Many have lost their reputations for standing up for what they believe.

Reporting has become subservient to the left by following a predictable script. The recent antidote to the leftist agenda and the mainstream media's stranglehold on information has been the "intellectual dark-web" comprising

4 Martin Luther King Jr., "My Pilgrimage to Nonviolence (September 1, 1958)."
5 Archive Collection, "Assassination of Martin Luther King Jr. (April 4, 1968)."
6 Martin Luther King Jr., "I have a Dream."

independent and insightful commentators such as Dennis Prager, Ben Shapiro, Jordan Peterson, Stefan Molyneux, Gad Saad, David Rubin, Joe Rogan, Paul Joseph Watson, Steven Crowder, Tommy Robinson, Mark Dice, Candace Owens, Samuel Sey, and others who speak freely and unreservedly.

Political correctness attempts to not offend anyone, but differing viewpoints inevitably risk offence. Without taking that risk, progress becomes impossible, and we are left in a relativistic morass. The Western world has been brought to its knees by political correctness, identity politics, and the suppression of free speech. These three malaises are inexorably linked and resemble a kind of collective madness. Political correctness, a concept originating with Leon Trotsky and echoed by genocidal tyrants like Mao Tse-Tung, is an oppressive tool to prevent dissenting views. In the Western world it is the translation of Marxism from economic to cultural terms. This is best revealed by the intersectional framework that seeks to interconnect differing oppressed groups by race, sexual orientation, gender, disability, and class. The whole concept of intersectionality is a race to the depths of absurdity because we can continue dividing people almost infinitely into sub-groups such as intelligence, height, weight, athletic prowess, and so on. Intersectionality does not unify, but divides. More than absurd, it is sinister.

As for identity politics, it leads to one being judged by the colour of one's skin rather than the content of one's character, shattering the appeal of King to transcend groupthink and tribalism, silencing his call to see the intrinsic worth of every human. King defended the *imago Dei* and so fought for equal rights for all people, at all times. He emphatically pushed this message in the sermon "The American Dream," given on July 4, 1965, at Ebenezer Baptist Church in Atlanta:

> You see the founding fathers were really influenced by the Bible. The whole concept of the *imago Dei*...is the idea that all men have something within them that God injected. Not that they have substantial unity with God, but that every man has a capacity to have fellowship with God. And this gives him uniqueness, it gives him worth, it gives him dignity. And we must never forget this as a nation: There are no gradations in the image of God. Every man from a treble white to a bass black is significant on God's keyboard, precisely because every man is made in the image of God. One day we will learn that. We will know one day that God made us to live together as brothers and to respect the dignity and worth of every man. This is why we must fight segregation with all of our non-violent might.[7]

7 Martin Luther King Jr., "The American Dream."

How far have we ventured from this uplifting message? African American critical race theorist and author, Ibram Kendi, shows us in his recent book, *How to Be an Antiracist*. Kendi's words are in stark contrast to King's race-neutrality: "the most threatening racist movement is not the alt right's unlikely drive for a White ethnostate but the regular American's drive for a 'race-neutral' one."[8] It turns out that all races are equal, but some races are more equal than others. I wonder if Kendi realizes the Orwellian nature of his language.

Several years ago, former Ontario Premier Kathleen Wynne, in a bid to gain more votes for the provincial election of 2018, made a similar statement: "If you don't vote, then somebody who looks like me is going to vote, some senior person, older than me, some white person."[9] Her quote, like Kendi's, epitomizes identity politic's implicit denial of King's *imago Dei* message.

In the end, we must fight for our freedom to speak against the many ills besetting Western society and culture. We should follow King's example of nonviolent resistance. We have shattered his dream and, in the process, desecrated ourselves as the image of God. But King's words, and the meaning behind them, must live on. We must always defend the spark of the divine in each and every individual. This is where humanity's intrinsic value lies. The content of someone's character is a clear illustration of this, not all the other characteristics such as race that divide us. We can embrace our differences but also exalt our shared human essence. It is not too late— it is this very hope that will keep humanity united rather than divided. We owe to the prophets of the past such as Martin Luther King Jr., and the countless of unknown innocents who have suffered and died at the hands of totalitarian regimes, the resolve to ensure the truth always prevails.

Bibliography

Agar, Jerry. "Wynne demonizes old, white voters in grasp for votes." *Toronto Sun*, March 19, 2018. http://torontosun.com/opinion/columnists/agar-wynne-demonizes-old-white-voters-in-grasp-for-votes.

Archive Collection. "Assassination of Martin Luther King Jr. (April 4, 1968)," *The Friday Times*, archive from April 10, 2020. https://www.thefridaytimes.com/assassination-of-martin-luther-king-jr-april-4-1968/.

Kendi, Ibram X. *How to Be an Antiracist*. New York: Random House, 2019.

King Jr., Martin Luther. "An Autobiography of Religious Development (12 Sept–22 Nov 1950)." In *The Papers of Martin Luther King, Jr. Volume I: Called*

8 Kendi, *How to Be an Antiracist*, 20.

9 Agar, "Wynne demonizes old, white voters in grasp for votes."

to Serve, January 1929-June 1951, edited by Clayborne Carson, et al. Los Angeles: University of California Press, 1992. https://kinginstitute.stanford.edu/king-papers/documents/autobiography-religious-development.

———. "I have a Dream" speech, Stanford University: The Martin Luther King, Jr. Research and Education Institute, August 20, 1968. https://kinginstitute.stanford.edu/encyclopedia/i-have-dream.

———. "The American Dream" speech, Stanford University: The Martin Luther King, Jr.

———. Delivered July 4, 1965. https://kinginstitute.stanford.edu/king-papers/publications/knock-midnight-inspiration-great-sermons-reverend-martin-luther-king-jr-4.

———. "The Sources of Fundamentalism and Liberalism Considered Historically and Psychologically 13 Sept–23 Nov 1949)." In *The Papers of Martin Luther King, Jr. Volume I: Called to Serve*, edited by Clayborne Carson, et al. January 1929–June 1951. https://kinginstitute.stanford.edu/king-papers/documents/sources-fundamentalism-and-liberalism-considered-historically-and.

———. "My Pilgrimage to Nonviolence (September 1, 1958)," in *The Papers of Martin Luther.*

———. *King, Jr. Volume IV: Symbol of the Movement, January 1957-December 1958*, edited by Clayborne Carson, et al. Los Angeles: University of California Press, 2000.

Chapter 48

Friends & Politics

Benjamin Blake Speed Watkins

There is no doubting the fact that in 2021, America is a place of deep political divides that have made political discourse with family, friends, and peers uncomfortable. What are we to make of these deep political divides? What is an appropriate response to them, and how can we better navigate the terrain of our current political landscape? I want to explore these questions and their relationship to building friendships and tolerating those with whom we disagree. In this chapter we will see what I believe to be some effective methods for dialoguing with those we disagree with during a time when civil discourse is in short supply.

What Do You Mean?

Have you ever been in dialogue with someone, but you just can't seem to make any progress? When these situations arise, do you find yourself talking past one another? Not only is this normal, but there is even a biological explanation. Expressing ourselves releases reward hormones. Instead of focusing on the conversation at hand we naturally begin to chase the natural high given by these hormones. This in turn can cause us to have blind spots within the conversational dynamics. To make matters worse, when we feel like someone is talking past us, our brains release neurochemicals that cause us to feel pain. We colloquially call this "fight or flight mode." Judith E. Glaser explains it this way,

> Feeling that rejection sends them into a "fight, flight" response, releasing cortisol, which floods the system and shuts down the prefrontal cortex, or executive brain, letting the amygdala, or lower brain, take over. To compound conversational challenges, the brain disconnects about every 12–18 seconds to evaluate and process, which means we're often paying as much attention to our own thoughts as we are to other people's words.[1]

1 Glaser, "Why You're Talking Past Each Other, and How to Stop."

So how can we combat this little curse given to us from our evolutionary past? One simple strategy to center yourself in conversation is to continually stop and ask: What do you mean? We can ask this even if we do not have any actual questions of meaning too. The goal is to understand those you disagree with rather than to defeat them, this question is an easy way to refocus any discussion. Because people like to express themselves, having someone clarify what they mean gets them talking, gets you listening, and reduces the chances of talking past one another. Additionally, there is a lot of value added in having someone clarify what it is they mean. Doing this requires us to rethink what we've just said, and this process can help us identify our own errors or mistakes in our reasoning.

It's natural to frame discourse in terms of a court of law, where one side is prosecuting and the other side is giving a defense, but as we've seen this is part of the problem. Discourse should be framed more like friends trying to solve a puzzle. Both sides should share the same aim. In the case of my analogy, that aim is trying to find the one right solution to the puzzle, and in the case of inquiry, it should be trying to find the truth. In a court of law, the defense and the prosecution are not friends. They are partisan actors whose obligations are to their clients' interests more than to every detail of the truth. The truth is presumed in this context. We don't have to frame our discussions this way. How else might we frame such discussions?

One of the easiest ways to facilitate understanding and cultivate friendships with those we disagree with is to simply take some immortal wisdom from the French philosopher, Voltaire, and define our terms. This is another way in which our question "what do you mean?" can come in handy. Simply asking someone what they mean by any claim which we may disagree with not only reduces the chances of us misunderstanding them, but it also puts the direction of the conversation entirely in the hands of the person you are disagreeing with. The goal is not to challenge them nor dominate them but rather to listen and clarify. It also allows us to gauge whether someone's intention in the discussion is to vent or to problem solve. Someone may only be interested in venting their opinion, and this will often be obvious by their request to better understand what it is they mean. If their aim is to problem solve, though, then it can also be a great opportunity to identify points of confusion that allow us to better identify where resolvable and irresolvable disagreements are.

Resolving Disagreement as Our Aim

We've already seen that truth-seeking should be our aim, but it's important to remember this aim should not come at the cost of friendships. So, how can we better achieve this aim without losing friends? I think the best way to achieve this is to have another aim: Attempt to resolve disagreements rather than trying to convince someone they are making a mistake. What do I mean by this? As a matter of human psychology, we do not like having our beliefs challenged, and people are generally unwilling to change their minds even when presented with decisive facts.[2] When we engage in discussions about disagreement, we often suppose this disagreement is reasonable, and that those we engage will be amenable to reason. Human psychology gives us reasons to doubt such suppositions. This is where we need to change our aims by changing such suppositions. What people are more amenable to when having a discussion is resolving any apparent disagreements by searching for common ground in the first place. In doing this, we can resolve disagreements and misunderstandings much easier. It also gives those we disagree with more latitude to express their opinions rather than to feel like they are being lectured. People are more responsive when they feel heard and are positively contributing to the conversation. This last claim will be a recurring theme in this chapter.

What might resolving disagreements look like? One way that can help involves us making concessions, even if only for the sake of moving the discussion forward. We might not be willing to change our own minds, but we can *suppose* those we disagree with are getting something right, even if this is only a supposition on our part rather than an outright concession because of the force of argument. When other people observe us being willing to do this, they can often be willing to make similar moves. This gives us more latitude in a conversation to attempt to resolve disagreement. Again, people feel heard and that they are positively contributing to the conversation. It can be a powerful motivator to relax those all-too-human impulses that lead us to protect our beliefs at all costs.

It's also helpful to remember that the conversation will not have a clearly demarcated "finish." Often in conversation with deep disagreement there is a tendency to try to cover as much ground as possible, and that the conversation cannot end unless we've made certain points for our interlocutors to consider. Paradoxically, this can have the opposite effect. In trying to make sure certain points go through, we often end up dying on hills rather than exploring different ones. We should accept that there's always more to say another time, and that perhaps we've explored some issue as far as we can for a particular discussion. Recognizing this is a powerful tool. When we correctly identify such points in conversation, they are good places to remind everyone involved that this is where we can do more research after the discussion too. Even if we could not get past some point, and we should save this disagreement for another time, we can take that opportunity to ask how to better research this disagreement. We should, as rational thinkers, engage with the strongest

2 Mercier and Sperber, *The Enigma of Reason.*

material from those you disagree with in the meantime. So what does that strongest material on the other side look like? Sometimes asking this very question can help transition away from a hill everyone would have died on to a more productive conversation about how we can learn from one another. Again, people feel heard in these situations, and that they are positively contributing not only to the conversation, but also adding to their own growth as a rational thinker. It might just also motivate someone else to engage with material they fundamentally disagree with in the future.

Mirroring as Technique

Another useful technique called *mirroring* is used to build rapport with an interlocutor because they feel more connected with you. Mirror neurons react to and cause non-verbal movements that allow us to feel a greater sense of engagement and belonging within the conversation.[3] Mirroring can also be used verbally. For example, we might repeat something someone has said earlier in the conversation which builds a greater sense of trust that you are really listening to what they have to say. Mirroring is yet another method we can use to help those we disagree with feel heard in conversation. For example, simply repeating back claims in the form of a question can not only make use of a mirroring technique but can also use one of our previous methods of trying to clarify the meaning of what people are saying. When people feel comfortable in the climate of a discussion, they are more likely to positively respond, even in the face of deep disagreements. This technique is much more difficult to master than the others, but that difficulty and the practice required to master it perfectly sets the stage for the closing section of this chapter.

Patience Is a Virtue

I want to close this chapter by reminding people that patience in discussion is one of the most powerful tools we have at our disposal. When we disagree, it's very easy to escalate and end up saying things we may not necessarily mean. This is especially true if we perceive ourselves as being disrespected or otherwise unheard in the conversation.[4] While this may be one of our most powerful tools at our disposal, it can also be one of the most difficult to master. We could spend our entire lives practicing the control of our emotions, remaining calm during intense and heated discussion, and learning how to navigate a conversation

3 Iacoboni, *Mirroring People.*
4 Bergland, *The Neuroscience of Patience.*

back to a more calm state. Unfortunately, there are no easy tricks here. It will require practice, and we will undoubtedly fail in many of our attempts. In other words, we must commit to a charitability and good faith that is often not be reciprocated. This is not reason to despair, though, rather they are opportunities to learn and grow through the rest of our lives. How could I have been more patient? When should I have walked away? What could I have said differently, and what can I say differently in the future? These are all questions we use to help ourselves grow. Ideally, others will notice this growth too, and it might just inspire others to grow with us.

Bibliography

Bergland, Christopher. "The Neuroscience of Patience." *Psychology Today*, June 1, 2018. https://www.psychologytoday.com/us/blog/the-athletes-way/201806/the-neuroscience-patience.

Glaser, Judith E. "Why You're Talking Past Each Other, and How to Stop." *Harvard Business Review*, December 20, 2012. https://hbr.org/2012/12/why-youre-talking-past-each-other-and.

Iacoboni, Marco. *Mirroring People: The Science of Empathy and How We Connect with Others*. London: Picador, 2009.

Mercier, Hugo and Dan Sperber. *The Enigma of Reason*. Cambridge: Harvard University Press, 2019.

Chapter 49

A Message to All Humanity, All Governments, All Royal and Financial Elites (One Percent Group)[1]

Ton Laurijssen

Message to all the children of Earth's Humanity: Are you at all concerned about the health, wellbeing, and future of planet Earth, nature, and Humanity? Planet Earth is the Home, Backyard, Theatre "Hub" of Life, and Lifeline sustenance to sustain Humanity and nature, and it is slowly being destroyed and disintegrating before our very own eyes. Humanity cannot afford to be unknowing or ignorant. Humanity must take control and take care of its Home! Humanity is the guardian of planet Earth and nature. Humanity is "survivor" on planet Earth.

The silent majority of humankind needs to create a strong voice together through "strength by numbers" to stand and speak up to our respective governments, royal and financial elites and demand for real peace, a clean (save) planet Earth and an organized, better run World with a thriving Humanity! If we don't stand and speak up together, we are contributing to the silence that allows the problems in this World to persist.

If you want real change to realize a liveable, sustainable, manageable, and peaceful planet in the near foreseeable future, you must speak up to your respective authorities, financial and royal elites. Your future is seriously at stake.

Whichever part of the World you come from; whatever your creed, we are all human beings of the great family of Humanity living on blue planet Earth. This is the common denominator. There are as many different viewpoints (belief systems) and values (ethics and morals) in this World as there are people. This is the human condition!

1 **Editor's Note***: This chapter is not in line with a biblical understanding of government. If you're interested in reading one that is, see Chapter 41 of this volume, "The Great Reset and The New World Order" by Phil Fernandes. Fernandes illustrates the many perils of a one world government. Although this chapter, on the surface, may sound quite similar to a One World Government or a New World Order, it is meant to override the power exerted over humanity by global elite billionaires and organizations. Indeed, the author is offering a trans-political system since our current systems of government are broken. The editor may not agree with a number of components in this chapter, including how the author defines God, but there are many ideas worth exploring and debating.

We may not necessarily agree with these differences in views and values. We will have disagreements. This is unavoidable. Even with these differences in views and values, we can work together. We can still get along. We have to learn to accept these differences, respect each other, and, above all, not to hurt or harm our homes and each other. All heinous, violent acts of extreme, fanatic fundamental and radical behaviors and attitudes are unacceptable and should be dealt with appropriately by all nations in this World. Views and values can only change or evolve from within the system through awareness and proper education to reach an awakened understanding or an enlightened reality consciousness (positive change).

We have come a long way from our dark, shady past full of strife, wars, diseases, plagues, famines, disasters, droughts, floods, forest fires, and the latest COVID-19 pandemic. There is still a long way to go. Humanity has become conscious of itself. Have we learned from all our lessons? Now is the time for Humanity to sit down and talk, work things out, and walk about together—hand in hand and not fist over fist—on this beautiful blue planet Earth, to lay the foundation of an enlightened, united Humanity and "One World©" on the existing cornerstones. Now is the time for a revolution or a positive paradigm shift in being, doing, and thinking.

We are going to be here for a very long time, so why not make it a good time for everyone here on planet Earth, together as Humanity? Let's not put a time limit on the negotiations. Let's take as long as it takes to realize the best scenario outcome or ideal situation and circumstances for planet Earth, Nature, and Humanity. Let's take as long as it takes to get to know one another and let's establish new, strengthened existing and restore the strained and estranged relationships between all people nations in this World.

Through unified, combined cooperative efforts, we can succeed to maintain the sustenance of planet Earth for ourselves and our future generations to come. Let's negotiate cleanly, clearly, and properly and walk about hand in hand to clean up planet Earth (No dirt! No pollution!), maintain real, lasting peace on Earth (No war! No strife!), have a better run World, a better managed World with competent servant leadership (No mess! No corruption!), have a thriving Humanity (No hunger! No poverty!), sustain all minerals, plants and trees, and animals on Earth (No loss! No waste!), share economics, wealth (one percent group), control, resources, etc. (No inequality!), and integrate the sciences and religions (No schism!). We all have the right to life in an enlightened, united, peaceful, free, safe, secure, and prosperous World.

The problem is that, nowadays, when Humanity comes together in high-profile meetings (UN or G7, etc.) to sit down collectively and talks about issues, it frequently brings its brawns or ego-dominant (veto power) and egocentric self and/or nation-interest attitudes and behaviors to the negotiation table.

The collective, constructive brainstorming in these high-profile meetings is often overshadowed by self or nation-egos, the human condition (behaviors and attitudes), and unconsciousness or unknowing (ignorance).

When Humanity meets and comes together to discuss the World or planet Earth, Humanity and nature, it needs to do so by bringing independent, neutral expert brains to the negotiation table to become a collective (Humanity; humanitarian), concise, precise (logical, commonsensical), constructive (building), non-egocentric brainstorming thinktank centre of world-experts, providing binding socio-economic, legal and governmental instructions, strategies and guidelines for all the people nations to follow or fulfill.

The negative effects of egocentric behaviors and attitudes expressed through self-interest, national-interests, and ego-dominance (inequity, inequality) constitute a major hindrance or obstacle to human development. Overcoming these negative effects constitutes an enlightened, united Humanity. This is in reference to all governments of developed nations and the "one percent group" members or the royal and financial elites. The developed nations and the "one percent group" need to step up to the plate and share with the rest of the World. Giving is an egoic act, whilst sharing is an enlightened ideal. The "one percent group" can easily mitigate any catastrophic, economic or financial collapse anywhere in this World. They can easily initiate an enlightened, united, and thriving Humanity anywhere in this World. Share your wealth with your "goods and services" benefactor: Humanity, nature, and planet Earth.

A new national sovereign democratic active "open source" dialogue government is needed in this World. The government works on behalf of all the people in the nation and works with a 70 percent democratic consensus ruling. The active "open source" dialogue government is an extension of the will of the people and the intellectuals of the nation. There are no political parties. The goal of the active "open source" dialogue government is to create the best possible "nation" for all its citizens to live in. The government cabinet, Central Bank, and Supreme Court can bring forth a new law or amendment in collaboration with the will of the people and the intellectuals of the nation, which is recognized, respected, and accepted by the people in the nation. The will of the people and the intellectuals can also bring forth a new law or amendment to the government.

A new international sovereign democratic United Nations Allegiance Alliance (UNAA) organization is needed in this World, where all the countries swear allegiance to the alliance of all nations. The UNAA works on behalf of the World of all people nations and works with a 70 percent democratic consensus ruling. There is no veto power. The goal of the UNAA is to create the best possible "planet Earth" World for all of us (Humanity and nature) to live in. The UNAA can bring forth a new law or amendment in collaboration with the 196 cabinet, 196 Central Bank, and 196 Supreme Court leaders of all people nations, which is recognized, respected, and accepted by all people nations of this World. The 196 cabinet, 196 Central Bank, and 196 Supreme Court leaders can also bring forth a new law or amendment to the UNAA.

A revolutionary planetary reconstruction program is needed in this World, to save planet Earth and nature, to save Humanity from itself. Planet Earth and nature don't need Humanity. Humanity on the other hand, needs planet Earth and nature to live.

All our lifelines are extremely important for the survival of all life or all archaea, bacteria, plants, trees, protists, fungi, animals, and humans on this beautiful blue planet Earth. There is absolutely no life possible without the vital lifeline links of earth, water, air, and the Sun.

The situation across the globe is very precarious and serious right now! Humanity, as a whole, is at a crossroads. Humanity, as a whole has, to choose between kindness, beauty, goodness, love, truth, and peace or meanness, ugliness, badness (evilness), hatred, lies, and war. Humanity's choice: good or bad? The far left and the extreme right (although negligible in numbers) are based on fascist, racist and/or extreme radical reactionary ideologies. Far left politics embraces the concept of "equality of outcome," which favours group identity over competence and individuality – factors necessary for economies to thrive. The far-left anti-peoples minority opposes and manipulates others (majority) who have a different idea or view of what the ruling class should be. This isn't good. It has to be stopped. The leftist machinery uses the media and social media to manipulate the masses majority. This unwarranted and unwanted manipulation isn't controlled, balanced, or checked by Law and Order properly as of yet. This should be corrected with high fines and/or appropriate punishments. Proper Laws and Orders should be put in place to stop any form of disinformation and discrimination. All humans, races, women, men, genders are equal under the Human rights, duties, and responsibilities Charter.

No more left-wing, centre, or right-wing wingnut politics. No more politics at all or politics without politics. No more political parties that seed division, apartheid, and separation. There is only one party. For example: the party of a "nation" where the needs of the people and nature of the nation are looked after appropriately. The goal of the party of a nation is to govern a nation towards the ideal nation. The ideal nation is the best place for all its citizens to live in.

The World at large needs to take a very serious look at taking distance from power, money, control, discrimination, male dominance, and egoism. These are not the hallmarks of an enlightened, united World. The hallmarks of an enlightened World are shared power, control, shared economics, and wealth with rights, responsibilities and duties, human equality with rights, and this ultimately includes 100 percent male and female equality with rights, responsibilities and duties, and having a balance between individualism and communalism, etc.

The planetary revolutionary reconstruction program functions as a wake-up call for Humanity. It proposes a logical, commonsensical "plan," "course of action," solution "suggestion" for Humanity to consider and discuss. The bottom line is that we've got to do something about it right now. Let's open the dialogue. Let's consider and discuss. Let's choose a proper, appropriate plan or course of action to lay down the foundation of planet Earth, nature, and Humanity on its already existing cornerstones. Please Humanity; let's take as long as it takes—months, years—for negotiations. Let's work it out properly. We are going to be here on planet Earth for a very long time. Humanity has become conscious of itself. Now is the time to act to lay down Humanity's foundation to save planet Earth; to save Humanity from itself and become united and enlightened.

Much emphasis is placed these days on the environment and climate changes, which are indeed extremely important factors to regulate because the environment and climate changes do affect planet Earth's sustenance to sustain all of life. What is more important, though, is the realization that the environment and climate changes are symptoms of a non-integrated, non-cooperative Humanity. When Humanity really comes together to talk, work, and walk together, the environment and climate changes will be automatically addressed and corrected. Humanity will take proper care of its HOME, planet Earth!

We all need to realize that our beautiful blue planet Earth is a gift to Humanity and nature!

HUMANITY IS AT A CROSSROADS; Humanity has a choice between:

Good Choice True, honest, real, right, healthy, positive	Bad Choice Untrue, corrupt, unreal, wrong (alternative), unhealthy, negative
Peace Peace treaty to be signed, sealed, delivered, and ratified by all nations	War A treaty to prevent all war and strife
Clean Environmental treaty to be signed, sealed, delivered, and ratified by all nations	Dirt A treaty to clean, clear up the earth (land), water (ocean), and air (sky)

Order United Nations Allegiance Alliance, World, (inter)continental, (inter) national Government, Court, Bank, Health Care, School, Business and Retail, Industry, Transport system, etc.	Mess (Chaos) This World is in an unorganized, disorderly, non-integrated mess
Thrive All of Humanity has the right to thrive	Poverty The better-off nation governments and the select few prosperous financial and royal elites share their wealth with other nations and Humanity at large
Gain Humanity needs to safeguard (maintain) all minerals, plants, trees, and animals (nature)	Loss To maintain the sustenance of planet Earth to sustain all of life (Humanity and nature)
Equality The applied ideal of shared economics (GNP and minimal guaranteed or supplemental income), shared wealth, power, control, and resources, etc.	Inequality All humans, all races, all women, all men, both genders and pay (salary) equality, and an anti-discrimination law accepted and honored by all national constitutions immediately
Unity "God" = the Universe; "God" = You or the integration of Science and Religion The integration of the Governments, courts, banks, businesses, etc. A non-political party system	Schism All religions accept one Supreme Being All nations accept a non-political party system BRING YOUR BRAINS TO WORK (Negotiation table) AND LEAVE YOUR DIFFERENCES OR BRAWNS (EGO) AT HOME

All governments, all financial and royal elites, please help facilitate the financing and realization of the clean-up of planet Earth and to build proper garbage, waste, and raw sewage facilities everywhere, wherever it is needed, to prevent further pollution.

All governments, financial and royal elites please, help facilitate the financing, and realization of real peace on planet Earth to build proper relationships and restore the strained and estranged relationships between all people nations.

All governments, financial and royal elites, please stop all the production of weapons of mass destruction, dismantle all existing weapons of mass destruction, and greatly reduce and strictly regulate the production and use of all weaponry. Peace doesn't sell weapons! You can choose to change the business of weaponry into another business!

All governments, financial and royal elites, please help facilitate the financing and realization of the equalization of all people nations on planet Earth. Awareness and education can bring an awakened understanding that brings positive, real change (choice).

The revolutionary planetary reconstruction proposal contains:

- Are you a good person? (Personal assessment)
- Do you run a good "social responsibility included" corporation or company? (Business assessment)
- Do you have a good "social responsibility included" government, i.e., leader? (Government assessment)
- Do we have a good "social responsibility included" United Nations? (UN assessment)
- A Central World (international) Government, Bank, and Court system
- A Central National Government, Bank, and Court system
- A comprehensive rights, freedoms, and responsibilities charter for planet Earth
- A comprehensive rights, freedoms, and responsibility charter for all minerals in this World
- A comprehensive rights, freedoms, and responsibilities charter for all plants, trees, and animals in this World
- A comprehensive rights, freedoms, and responsibilities charter for all human beings (world citizens) in this World
- A comprehensive rights, freedoms, and responsibilities charter for all people nations in this World
- A comprehensive rights, freedoms, and responsibilities charter for all religions in this World
- A new "socially responsible and accountable" business model for companies, corporations, and governments, INCLUDING MEDIA OUTLETS AND SOCIAL MEDIA; what happened to trust and truth?
- The end of rentier capitalism
- Amnesty for the super-rich (financial and royal elites)

Chapter 50

Embracing Intuition

Andrew H. Gill

Intuition is not a an altogether understood concept in our overly rationalistic world. It gets mischaracterized as being some strange New Age mantra. Nevertheless, it is shrouded in mystery, but it need not be because it is a tool that we all possess to some degree or another. It is that little voice in your head which tells you whether something you feel is right or not. More precisely, it is a universal signal that aims to improve your body, mind, and spirit.

Intuition is knowing something without knowing why. A known author on the subject, Shakti Gawain, informs us that every time you don't follow your inner guidance, you feel a loss of energy, loss of power, and a sense of spiritual sadness.[1] Her four-step method aids us on our quest to achieve our goals. As an example, do we tell ourselves to save time by taking a shortcut on the way home and then feel that something is not quite right, and then later learn that because we followed that gut feeling that, around the same time, in the same alleyway, someone was robbed? Or do we follow our gut about a stock tip our friend tells us about, or do we convince ourselves it's a long shot only to learn later that the stock price soared by 1000 percent?

Intuition is not completely separated from logical thinking but forms an important synergy between our brain and the heart in our gut. As we all can relate, fear and worry are a form of bodily expression to tell us that our actions and our thoughts are not corresponding. If that voice inside of you says to remain silent, do we follow it? Or when that voice says to speak up, do we listen?

Intuition and Law Enforcement

Just by their nature, law enforcement officers, like the Police and FBI, must be observant, so that not only do they see, but also feel what they are observing.

1 Gawain, "Four Basic Steps for Effective Visualization."

Officers may ask themselves questions like, "What would I do in this situation as if I was attempting to evade arrest?" When an officer feels that something isn't right, they ask more questions.

The American Psychological Association in the early 2000s examined how intuition could be better understood in law enforcement.[2] A police officer at this conference, reported in their work that they were able to apprehend a person because they made eye contact and felt that something wasn't quite right. Those conference attendees were not in complete agreement about what intuition was but knew that it existed. It's important to know, that intuition needn't be over analyzed, but something we act on in that moment.

In other real-life scenarios, FBI consulted with psychics to help them solve cold cases. A highly gifted psychic, Troy Griffin,[3] was able to locate the body of a missing person who disappeared under mysterious circumstances. He used his clairvoyance and mediumship to feel where she was found and under what circumstances she died. By knowing that drugs were involved in her death, he deduced that some friends were the culprits. One of her Facebook friends had robbed the woman of her pain medication and hit her on the head.

Although this story had a tragic ending it served to underscore the importance that intuition can help individuals in organizations to become more efficient and less stressed. This in turn will lead to less stress related illnesses and burnout. In this case, the FBI hired an expert to help them solve a case and increase morale.

Our Relationship to Animals and Intuition

A long time ago, I went out to our backyard and saw that our beloved Golden Retriever had dug up several holes in our garden. When I looked out at the yard, he started whimpering like he knew he done something wrong. He had a sensitivity to the event. He had a big black nose and he stood there looking at me in a way that stopped me from getting angry. He may have been naughty but not mischievous.

We have a special bond with animals. You will often see people talk to animals like they are babies. There is a purity and innocence that cannot be denied. They sense things that we do not, and they sense things before they happen. This is because their energy system operates on a higher frequency than most human beings. They are highly intuitive, not to mention low ego and full of love. Dogs will know when their owner is coming home even when they are three or four blocks away, even when their owner comes home at an irregular

2 Winerman, "Workshop Examines Intuition in Law Enforcement,"15.
3 Peyser, "Meet the Psychic Who Uses Gift to Solve FBI Cold Cases."

time. Research fellow of the Royal Society and former director of studies in biochemistry and cell biology at Clare College, Cambridge University, Rupert Sheldrake, discusses the idea of morphic fields in his book, *Dogs That Know When Their Owners Are Coming Home*. In an interview with John Horgan, author of *Scientific American*, Sheldrake states the following in differentiating morphic resonance from telepathy:

> Animal telepathy is a consequence of the way that animal groups are organized by what I call morphic fields. Morphic resonance is primarily to do with an influence from the past, whereas telepathy occurs in the present and depends on the bonds between members of the group. For example, when a dog is strongly bonded to its owner, this bond persists even when the owner is far away and is, I think, the basis of telepathic communication. I see telepathy as a normal, not paranormal, means of communication between members of animal groups. For example, many dogs know when their owners are coming home and start waiting for them by a door or window. My experiments on the subject are described in my book *Dogs That Know When Their Owners Are Coming Home*. Dogs still know even when people set off at times randomly chosen by the experimenter, and travel in unfamiliar vehicles.[4]

Essentially, dogs and animals can access memories from time and space. They draw on a collective memory. You can observe a flock of birds and they will turn on a dime collectively. This is called murmuration and it suggests part of this movement is an attempt to avoid predators. You could say that these animals have a collective extrasensory perception (ESP) and intuition.

Animals have this understanding of acting in a way that benefits the whole group. Individually, animals have many qualities that makes us think they share many affinities with humans, both spiritually and emotionally. To reiterate, dogs act with little or no ego and it can influence us in important ways because it gives us pause to think about how we treat other people. There is a selflessness about domesticated animals and an unconditional love for their owners that we can learn from. In our daily lives, for instance, we can think about what we say before we speak, we can reduce our stubbornness in our social and business relationships with other people.

We naturally light up around animals. There is a gentleness we have in our interactions we have with them. Guide dogs and therapy dogs provide a wonderful stress reduction and anxiety tool for their owners as well. Dogs and animals remind us that we spend more time thinking about the present

4 See Horgan, "Scientific Heretic Rupert Sheldrake on Morphic Fields, Psychic Dogs and Other Mysteries." For the experiment Sheldrake is alluding to in this quote see: https://blogs.scientificamerican.com/cross-check/scientific-heretic-rupert-sheldrake-on-morphic-fields-psychic-dogs-and-other-mysteries/.

moment (where possible) and worry less about the past and future.

One time, when I was young and our family was vacationing in St. Andrews, New Brunswick, my father took another Golden Retriever of ours for a walk and he ingested strychnine poisoning, and he started to convulse. My father carried him hurriedly out of the woods and a vet, who had been driving by, saw him and they went immediately to the hospital where his stomach was pumped out. We waited with profound worry until we heard the news of his recovery.

Animals are an extension of family and are invaluable in the lessons we can learn from them, in terms of our connectivity. It was a gift of synchronicity that the vet was there at the right time and right place.

Just as friends and family lend us a non-judgmental ear, so too can animals uplift us in moments of sadness. Animals have emotions akin to human beings. They are very spiritual, special, intuitive souls that bring much happiness into our lives. We should be very careful and wary of people who display cruelty towards animals. Your intuition will broadcast very strongly: stay away from these individuals!

Intuition and Relationships

A long time ago, I was encouraged to go on a date with a woman of a friend of mine. I agreed to go, but I had the feeling in my gut that it was the wrong thing to do. I did not have a romantic attraction to this person.

Of course, it ended badly, and I felt very guilty about it. My stomach was in knots the whole time I was with her, and I didn't honor the warning signal or feeling that I should end the relationship. How many times do you hear stories like this one? People make poor decisions because of fear, self-pressure or pressure from family or friends to immerse ourselves in a relationship that we know is intuitively wrong.

Relationships do not have to lead to emotional chaos. You may have to endure hardships but following your gut will lead to a fulfilling, loving, and truthful reciprocal relationship. Although being honest about a lack of connection with another person is not easy, it is the path towards goodness, justice, and truth. By respecting and valuing the other person through honesty, you give each other the gift of freedom. In doing so, you will be in a position to meet someone you are meant to love.

Intuition also has a place in relationships in enhancing communication skills, such as prudence in knowing when to speak and when to be silent. One important communication tool is to listen to that inner voice. Improving listening skills will foster a more understanding relationship. Your significant other will surprise you by putting their arm around you and thanking you for being emotionally supportive. Even though when you listen to someone, in some circumstances, you may endure criticism and emotional abuse. This is a perfect example of when to listen to that inner intuitive voice that guides you into the right direction.

Intuition and Corporations: The Missing Soul

The definition of corporation is a company or a group of people that act as a single legal entity (legally a person) and recognized as such in law. Corporations, in all their glory, provide us with relatively low-priced goods in return for earning a profit for them and their shareholders. We accept this as a given in our capitalist society. However, as an entity they have many flaws.

A corporation's Machiavellian thirst for power is one of them. The prevailing sentiment in a corporation is a "what's in it for me" mentality. One may ask rhetorically: If I fail to act with integrity in a corporation, or in a nefarious way, how can I hide behind an expensive lawyer to deflect and obscure my negative behavior, so that the individual or group of people will cower away? A corporation has a heartbeat but no soul. The next time you hear a corporate lawyer saying the phrase "without prejudice," it means with prejudice. For example, when you sue a corporation for intellectual property theft, they would hijack you financially to settle for an amount that would be far greater if you had the financial resources and mental fortitude.

Let us address another example, of corporations acting in bad faith. I knew of a person who worked at a corporation who had his pay cut after many years of service and accumulated seniority. This is an example of constructive dismissal and downward reclassification. Their pay was cut in half and their job duties were altered to justify the reduced pay. The corporation's response after being brought to court was to reinstate pay for a short period of time, only for it to be removed later. This was done by a deceptive lawyer who was secretly involved in writing up a new binding contract that benefitted the corporation and not the individual.

Intuition and Big Pharma

Lastly, we can target the pharmaceutical industry as players in this game that act reprehensibly. Price gouging is a common tactic in this industry's goal of accumulating more profit. A pharmaceutical CEO was called before a house committee on oversight and reform and verbally reprimanded for smirking at the fact that he sold a drug for $750 a pill when it cost only $13.50 to make.[5]

5 Lupkin, "A Decade Marked by Outrage Over Drug Prices."

I personally heard of a story that a diabetes drug that cost just under $10 to make, was sold for almost $300. Like these examples, there are countless more of such corruption and exploitation of ordinary hardworking people in need of life-saving medication. This is unacceptable, but you can still prevail.

The question to ask yourself intuitively is how you can limit your dependency on Big Pharmaceutical companies through exploring other health alternatives. Is it necessary for you to take medication for type two diabetes in most cases? Or can you get off the couch, make a conscious plan to solve your nutritional problems and eat healthier. Can you make that plan to join the gym, or buy those running shoes or bike that you've put off for so long? These are the type of intuitive questions you should ask yourself to be happier and to bypass the dependence we have on band aid health solutions that simply don't work. You will in most cases reduce your dependence on blood pressure medication, heart medication, and blood thinners for stroke prevention. It's time for you to take back the control over your body that you so richly deserve.

In closing, asking yourself these intuitive questions can help you in all areas of your life. Don't like the corporation you are working for? Start your own business. Don't like the side effects from the anti-depressants? Work through it and find yourself again with time, good nutrition, and a supportive mentor or a life coach. Also, do not be afraid to confide in the loving support of friends and family. If you take nothing else from this chapter, I ask you to follow your gut as often as you can. Life certainly offers us many challenges and can present many hardships. But as the old adage goes: "When God closes a door, he opens a window." So be attentive to when God knocks on your door, make sure you answer it, or he may have to knock the door down.

Bibliography

Gawain, Shakti. "Four Basic Steps for Effective Visualization." *Creations Magazine*. Accessed August 11, 2021. http://www.creationsmagazine.com/articles/C171/Gawain.html.

Horgan, John. "Scientific Heretic Rupert Sheldrake on Morphic Fields, Psychic Dogs and Other Mysteries." *Scientific American*, July 14, 2014. https://blogs.scientificamerican.com/cross-check/scientific-heretic-rupert-sheldrake-on-morphic-fields-psychic-dogs-and-other-mysteries/.

Lupkin, Sydney. "A Decade Marked by Outrage Over Drug Prices." *NPR*, December 31, 2019. https://www.npr.org/sections/health-shots/2019/12/31/792617538/a-decade-marked-by-outrage-over-drug-prices.

Peyser, Andrea. "Meet the Psychic Who Uses Gift to Solve FBI Cold Cases." *New York Post*, August 1, 2016. https://nypost.com/2016/08/01/meet-the-psychic-who-uses-gift-to-solve-fbi-cold-cases/.

Sheldrake, Rupert. *Dogs That Know When Their Owners Are Coming Home: And Other Unexplained Powers of Animals.* New York: Crown, 2011.

Winerman, L. "Workshop Examines Intuition in Law Enforcement." *American Psychological Association* 35, 8 (2004): 15. https://www.apa.org/monitor/sep04/workshop.

Chapter 51

Reflections On the *Rocky* Saga and the Intrinsic Value of the Human Person[1]

Scott D. G. Ventureyra

The eighth "chapter" of the *Rocky* series, *Creed II,* was released on November 21, 2018. Continuing in the tradition of the previous seven chapters of the Rocky Saga, *Creed II* exploits the underdog archetype. The protagonist, Adonis Creed (Michael B. Jordan), although recently crowned heavyweight boxing champion of the world, is not prepared to beat a lethally dangerous opponent, Victor Drago (Florian Munteanu), son of Ivan Drago (Dolph Lundgren), who is superior in power, strength, and speed. Adonis requires Rocky Balboa's (Sylvester Stallone) mentorship to overcome this formidable foe. What makes this latest instalment of the *Rocky* series so poignantly beautiful and unique is its take on the Biblical notion of the "sins of the father." This is a concept which William Shakespeare famously utilized in his *Merchant of Venice* in Act III, Scene V, where Launcelot Gobbo states in a conversation with Jessica, the daughter of Shylock (the Venetian Jewish moneylender): "the sins of the father are to be laid upon the children."[2] This concept is found throughout the Old Testament (Exod 20:5, 34:7; Deut 5:9; Num 4:18; Isa 14:21; Ps 51:5; 1 Kgs 15:3). And yet other verses in the Old Testament pertain to taking moral responsibility for one's own sins; for some theologians it represents a newer covenant, regardless of being a father, mother or child; neither are to be transferred to the other, but one is to be judged by their own righteousness (Deut 24:16; Ezek 18:19-20; Jer 31:30–33). Continuing in this progression is the new covenant found in the New Testament whereby we are redeemed from the transgressions of our fathers through the sacrament of baptism (Acts 2:38; 1 Pet 3:21; Gal 3:27; John 3:5; Heb 10:22). Furthermore, we are redeemed by Christ's atoning sacrifice not by our own righteousness (1 John 1:19, 3:16–17, Titus 3:5, Rom 8:1; 1 Cor 15:22); this renewal of the self (Col 3:10) is shown by our faith and the good works that follow from it (Jas 2:14–24).

1 For the original see Scott Ventureyra, "A Review of Creed II: 'Reflections On the Rocky Saga & the Intrinsic Value of the Human Person,'" *Catholic Insight*, December 19, 2018, https://catholicinsight.com/creed-ii-reflections-on-the-rocky-saga-the-intrinsic-value-of-the-human-person/.

2 Shakespeare, *The Merchant of Venice*, Act III, Scene V, 133.

Even though not theologically explicit, the concept of "sins of the father" alongside those of redemption and reconciliation, run deep within *Creed II*, especially as they are found in the struggles of the main characters: Adonis, Rocky, and Ivan. All three characters have their own awakening. Embedded within the struggles of these three men are many valuable elements that both Catholics and non-Catholics may overlook, including self-transcendence, family/community, and the sanctity of life.

Relevant Background to the *Rocky* Saga

The Rocky Saga comprises a series of American boxing sports-drama films (*Rocky I–V*, *Rocky Balboa*, and *Creed I* and *II*). They are arguably some of the greatest sports movies ever made. The original *Rocky* movie was released in 1976, and nominated for ten Oscars in 1977, winning best picture and director. The script was written by Sylvester Stallone and directed by the late John Avildsen (who also directed the *Karate Kid* series). For those unfamiliar with the *Rocky* movies, here is a brief synopsis of them[3] and here is an interesting documentary[4] which will give readers a deeper background.

Most relevant prequels to *Creed II* are *Creed I* and *Rocky IV*. In *Rocky IV*, Ivan Drago (Dolph Lundgren), a Soviet boxing Olympic champion, kills Adonis' father, Apollo (who has become a dear friend of Rocky) in an exhibition match. Rocky then feels obliged to fight Drago in the Soviet Union in a brutal re-match. Despite winning, he suffers brain damage. One of the most interesting elements of this movie, aside from the training montages and fights, are the proleptic words of Rocky with respect to "changing one's heart"; several years after this movie, which was released in 1985, the Soviet Union collapsed.

Creed I is about the rise of Adonis, who was the result of Apollo's infidelity before his death. Adonis is left an orphan at a young age after the death of his mother. Apollo's wife, Mary Anne Creed (Phylicia Rashad, known for The Cosby Show) adopts him and raises him. Adonis yearns to emulate his father and longs to be revered as a champion, so he seeks out Rocky for training. Now, *Creed II* shows the return of Ivan Drago through his son, Viktor, 33 years after his loss to Rocky in the Soviet Union; the bad blood between Rocky and Ivan is brought into a new light.

3 IGN "The Rocky & Creed Saga in 7 Minutes."

4 Margus Ian Andimäe, "The Rocky Saga (Documentary)." YouTube Video, February 29, 2016. https://www.youtube.com/watch?v=LLlupHLXgvU.

Adonis's Struggles

One of the striking features related to Adonis's life struggles is the shame he feels from living in the absence of his father and being born illegitimately. Interestingly, whether the intention was even there or not, or even if it was meant to be implicit or explicit, there is a powerful argument for the sanctity of life. This is raised in *Creed I* and *II*, through Adonis's desire for self-actualization. In *Creed I*, Adonis says to Rocky, in an incredibly heartbreaking manner at the last round of his fight against "Pretty" Ricky Conlan (Tony Bellew), that he wants to prove that he wasn't a "mistake." Rocky in his own words expresses that Adonis has been a blessing in helping him fight against cancer; Adonis then proves to himself by knocking down Conlan before the bell, that he is not a "mistake."

In *Creed II*, this notion of the sanctity of life rears its head again. Adonis's fiancé, Bianca, experiences progressive hearing loss in *Creed I*. In *Creed II*, they worry that their recently conceived offspring may be born with the same disability. Ever growing numbers of couples would be prepared to discard the unborn, whom they discover to possess a genetic deficiency through what is known as fetal genome screening,[5] even though it often can be inaccurate. This is beyond tragic and morally deficient.

Unfortunately, unborn children that are conceived with discoverable genetic deficiencies, or illegitimately through an extra-marital affair or even a one-night stand, are aborted more often than one may think. Even children born in such situations feel as though they were a mistake. But at least those given a chance at life can have the opportunity to do amazing things and affect human history positively. However, God, as the sovereign, omniscient and omnibenevolent Creator who exists outside but interacts within the physical spatiotemporal reality, knows all of our struggles before we experience them. Even though aborted children have a home with Him, humans partaking in such action will be morally accountable if they do not repent. The truth is that no being that has the *imago Dei* can be a mistake, despite the wrongdoings of their procreators.

Throughout the movie, Adonis also struggles with self-actualization through his desire to instantiate his own legacy. He attempts to move out of the shadow of his father's greatness and traumatic demise; something that has persistently haunted him. Although he wears his last name proud and proves himself as the heavyweight champion of the world, he still suffers on this road to self-transcendence. It is important to note that self-transcendence is a mode of being which orients itself to the human good. For Adonis, it is related to a team (his family, consisting of Bianca, his mother, daughter, and Rocky [whom

5 Scientific American Board of Editors, "Beware the Destiny Test."

he considers an uncle]) that is fighting together against both Ivan and Victor Drago. For Adonis, it is this sense of community that gives him the strength to overcome not only his fears and living in his father's shadow, but also the tragedy of his demise. Thus, he is able to build his own identity and his claim to want to "rewrite history." This is exemplified when he acknowledges, at his father's grave, that his defeat of Viktor Drago was about himself and his life now, and not avenging his father's death when he says: "I did it for me"— this is the moment where he explicitly becomes conscience of his self-actualization. Adonis is able to overcome both his internal and external struggles through his many trials and tribulations.

Rocky's Reconciliation

Initially, Rocky refuses to train Adonis because he fears that he may suffer the same fate as his father. Although 33 years have passed since Apollo's death, he still carries the guilt of his death since he made the choice not to throw in the towel. Moreover, it was he who was supposed to fight Ivan Drago for that fateful exhibition match. He then also feels guilt when Adonis is massacred in the first fight against Viktor. Only then does he agree to help train him for the re-match. Although Rocky with the help of Adonis overcomes his cancer and feels a sense of purpose again, he still suffers from the lack of contact with his only immediate family (son and grandson). For Rocky too, there is a sense of incompleteness, a wrongness that can only be made right by reconciliation. Yet, despite years of silence, in a beautiful scene nearing the end of the movie, he finally visits his son and grandson. It is through this reconciliation, brought forth by reflection then acting upon it, that Rocky is also able reconcile himself to his remaining family members. Thus, there is again an emphasis on love, family, community, and the transcendence of the human spirit to overcome loss, suffering and adversity.

Ivan Drago's Re-Emergence and Awakening

In 1985, Ivan Drago was an Olympic boxing gold medalist and hero of the Soviet Union. After his loss to Rocky on his own soil, he was exiled from Russia, losing the respect of his nation. Subsequently, his wife also left him. For 33 years, instead of taking responsibility for his own shortcomings, he blames everything on Rocky. He raises his son in hatred, making him into a killing boxing machine. His son is now the vehicle for his re-emergence onto the world stage. For Viktor, what matters more than anything is the love of his father and mother. He longs for the unity of his family, for the respect of his father and that is more central to him than defeating Adonis and the heavyweight championship title. In the final fight, Viktor's mother leaves him as he begins to lose control of the fight. This destroys him internally and weakens him physically to the point one begins to wonder if there will be a repeat of what Ivan did to Apollo, whereby now it is Ivan's son who is at risk of facing death. This is when Ivan has his moment of awakening. Ivan decides to throw in the towel, in order for history not to repeat itself, understanding what is truly good; the love and wellbeing of his son, not his pride and selfishness. In a strange way, despite the hate brought forth by Viktor which was propelled by Ivan's anger, one begins to feel sympathetic to their sufferings, as Viktor's mother abandons them yet again.

Recently, Charles Tator, a neurosurgery professor at University of Toronto, stated after Montreal boxer Adonis "Superman" Stevenson was hospitalized for suffering some brutal blows to the head, that: "Boxing should be abolished as a sport… I wouldn't hesitate to say that."[6] Although boxing is indeed a brutal sport that can cause severe physical damage, there is a certain elegance to it. It can also provide hope, solace, and inspiration to many who may not have much else in their life. Many boxers have said that they became fighters because of the influence of the *Rocky* movies. Be that as it may, the Rocky Saga and this last "chapter," are incredibly inspirational movies and represent the triumph of the human spirit through confronting challenges in and out of the boxing ring.

Bibliography

AFP, "Former light heavyweight champion Adonis Stevenson in stable condition in induced coma after knockout." news.com.au, December 4, 2018. https://www.news.com.au/sport/boxing/former-light-heavyweight-champion-adonis-stevenson-in-stable-condition-in-induced-coma-after-knockout/news-story/27e8dc479e1fc40280f36b4dfdc02865.

IGN "The Rocky & Creed Saga in 7 Minutes." YouTube, November 7, 2018. https://www.youtube.com/watch?v=pGO7aQ58KCs.

Margus, Ian Andimäe. "The Rocky Saga (Documentary)." YouTube Video, February 29, 2016. https://www.youtube.com/watch?v=LLlupHLXgvU.

Scientific American Board of Editors. "Beware the Destiny Test." In Scientific American 308, 2, 12 (February 2013). doi:10.1038/scientificamerican0213-12.

Shakespeare, William. *The Merchant of Venice*. Edited by Barbara A. Mowat and Paul Werstine. New York: Simon & Schuster, 2010.

6 AFP, "Former light heavyweight champion Adonis Stevenson in stable condition in induced coma after knockout."

Chapter 52

Cobra Kai: Self-Defense and the Defense of Others[1]

Scott D. G. Ventureyra

Cobra Kai is the latest addition to the epic *The Karate Kid* saga. It takes place 34 years after the 1984 All Valley Karate Tournament of the original Karate Kid movie. All four seasons can be found on Netflix. Well worth watching if you are an avid fan of the original *Karate Kid* quadrilogy (if one includes *The Next Karate Kid* since it continues with Mr. Miyagi's character (Pat Morita) but features Hilary Swank). Each of the four seasons contain ten episodes. Season four was released on December 31, 2021. (Apparently, season five has also been completed.) Throughout the four seasons there are many twists and turns that make the show into a sort of Karate style drama. There are plenty of similarities between this series and the Rocky Saga, which is to be expected since the late director, John G. Avildsen, directed all three Karate Kid movies and *Rocky I* and *V*. Continuing in this tradition, producers Josh Heald, Jon Hurwitz, and Hayden Schlossberg have paid a tremendous homage to the original three movies. The series is without a doubt a nostalgic throwback for those who grew up in the 1980s. There are also plenty of references which make it a gem for lifelong fans but there's also enough new material and young actors to captivate the next generation. In my opinion, *Cobra Kai* is one of the best shows in recent memory. The high ratings on the website Rotten Tomatoes is a testament to this. Without revealing too much, I'll discuss features of the series that would be of interest to Catholic readers (but not limited to).

Synopsis

There is a significant shift in dynamic between the original characters of Johnny Lawrence (William Zabka) and Daniel LaRusso (Ralph Macchio). Johnny is now the underdog, while Daniel enjoys a comfortable life with a very successful auto-business, a beautiful wife and family. Johnny, on the other hand, who

1 For the original see Scott Ventureyra, "Cobra Kai: A Nostalgic Adventure," *Catholic Insight*, June 26, 2018, https://catholicinsight.com/cobra-kai-a-nostalgic-adventure/.

enjoyed a posh life in his younger days and popularity in high school, is now down on his luck. He can barely hang onto lower-end jobs and has become a heavy drinker. However, after receiving some money from his stepfather who intends on "buying" him out, he opens up his own dojo with the intention to resurrect the *Cobra Kai*. There are a series of new characters, many of whom are misfits and outcasts within high school life.

The show has a great cast of actors. The most prominent characters aside from Johnny and Daniel throughout the series include Daniel's daughter, Amanda; Miguel Diaz, one of Johnny's neighbors who desperately seeks a father figure in Johnny; and Johnny's son, Robby, who feels dejected and abandoned by Johnny, but finds solace in Daniel's attentiveness and mentorship.

Each season adds another layer of complexity to the characters and the unfolding plot. Season two has a number of special guest appearances from the original *The Karate Kid* including Johnny's friends: Tommy (Rob Garrison), Bobby (Ron Thomas), Jimmy (Tony O'Dell); and Daniel's mother, Lucille LaRusso (Randee Heller). Season three has actors from both *The Karate Kid* and *The Karate Kid Part II* make some special guest appearances, including Daniel's and Johnny's love interest from the original, Ali Mills (Elisabeth Shue); Johnny's friend again, Bobby, (Ron Thomas); Daniel's love interest who he met in Japan, Kumiko (Tamlyn Tomita); and Daniel's arch nemesis from *Karate Kid II*, Chozen Toguchi (Yuji Okumoto) who teaches Daniel Karate techniques and philosophies from Miyagi that he never knew of.

Season four reintroduces the series most villainous character, John Kreese's long time friend from his days in the special forces in the Vietnam War, and billionaire, Terry Silver (played by Thomas Ian Griffith), who was featured in *The Karate Kid Part III*. Silver is probably one the most skilled martial arts specialist after Mr. Miyagi in the series. (Griffith holds black belts in Kenpo Karate and Tae Kwon Do.) At the end of season four, Daniel is at Miyagi's tomb asking for help to overcome *Cobra Kai* once and for all. We then see a prelude of what is to come with the reappearance of Chozen Toguchi, while Def Leppard's "Switch 625" plays louder and louder in the background.

The characters in this series are developed with greater depth than the original three, more realistic and nuanced— television series give more time and space than movies for this. Johnny and Daniel are not stuck in a simplistic good and evil type dualism. (The merging of both of their Karate styles by their students is also an example of this.) The depth of both their characters reveals a complexity of many inner struggles and demons that have followed them from their youth. They both undergo their own positive transformation throughout the series. In season four, the complexities continue with the history, development, and deterioration of Terry Silver and John Kreese's relationship. The encounters between characters that have never met face to face are intriguing in the fourth season.

Old alliances are reformed. New alliances are forged. Changes in life decisions and in fighting styles are rethought and appreciated. While in other avenues, deceit rears its ugly head in unexpected ways.

The Search for a Father Figure

Over the past decade, young men have been bailing out of college in unprecedented rates. Boys are underperforming throughout elementary and high school education. Girls are outperforming boys in most educational domains (in terms of sheer numbers, except very few such as STEM, philosophy, and theology). Boys are increasingly told they are tyrants in the making. This is not at all helpful for the future of Western civilization. Our society is increasingly attacking the traditional notion of the family, including basic and natural roles such as fatherhood; roles that have been tried and tested throughout human history for millennia. The social constructionist perspectives that ignore biological facts, if allowed to persist, will have fatal consequences for the future of human civilization.

Public intellectuals such as Jordan Peterson are labeled as misogynistic for stating there should be culturally, not institutionally, "enforced monogamy," and that young men (women as well) need encouraging words but rarely receive it. Young men and women are seeking hope in a father figure they've never met since for whatever reason their own fathers are absent or do not exist. Say what you will about Peterson and his shortcomings, when it comes to the Christian faith we must be grateful for the advent of someone like him. Not many have assumed this important role nor have the competency, courage, or articulation to do so. If those that are so critical of him think they can do a better job, let them step forward.

One of the most positive elements of *Cobra Kai* throughout every season is its focus on fatherhood. This is something that runs contrary to the contemporary narrative which is increasingly attacking the family, gender roles, and the importance of males. Every child yearns for a relationship with his father. Unfortunately, many fathers, for various reasons, are absent from their children's lives. This is precisely why Professor Peterson's message of responsibility and traditional values is resonating so deeply with many of his listeners, especially young men. We witness this yearning throughout *Cobra Kai*, in not only the teenage boy characters of Miguel and Robby, but also in Johnny and Daniel. Daniel lost his father at a young age and found a father figure in his Karate mentor, Mr. Miyagi (Pat Morita). Johnny searched for the father figure, just like Daniel, in his Karate mentor Sensei John Kreese (Martin Kove)— the main antagonist of the original series. Interestingly, in the aftermath of a violent encounter between Johnny and Silver, we witness

Kreese having difficulty in wanting to aid Johnny since he had been a father figure to him over the years, but they had betrayed one another in season three. Unfortunately, unlike Daniel's father figure, Johnny's mentor was a very bad influence on him. This negative influence has impacted the rest of his life.

In the first season, Johnny begins to mentor Miguel and teaches him Karate in order to be able to defend himself from bullies but, unfortunately, he teaches him the corrupt mantra of *Cobra Kai*: "strike first, strike hard and show no mercy." Miguel resembles a young Daniel in many ways but learns a pernicious philosophy to Karate. On the other hand, Robby, Johnny's son, first out of spite towards Johnny, seeks Daniel but then finds a fatherly figure in him. He begins to learn the foundational roots of what Miyagi taught Daniel, which involves defending oneself with honour and integrity but without fear and in the style of Kata. Johnny begins to show a transformation and realization in the wrongs of his previous ways, especially when his own method and teaching of fighting begins to hurt his son.

Despite now being in their 50s, Daniel still searches for that "balance" in his life, still in his now deceased mentor/father figure. Episode five of the first season, which is dedicated in loving memory to Morita, emphasizes this. Likewise, Johnny struggles throughout the series with alcoholism and from the broken bond between him and his son. In episode one it is revealed that his biological father was absent and that his stepfather never had anything to offer him aside from money. Later seasons, including season four, further develop these complicated dynamics. Miguel sees Johnny as not only his sensei but also as a father figure. Johnny is dating Miguel's mother and fills the void of never having met his biological father with Johnny's mentorship and love. His biological father is unaware of his existence (Miguel is unaware of this himself) and he sets out to find him after becoming disenchanted with the Karate world and Johnny's carelessness. To complicate matters more, Miguel warms up to Daniel, and Robby to Kreese and Silver. All of these interactions and relationships create a web of deceit and jealousy. Finally, we see Daniel's son, Anthony, beginning to search for mentorship in his father, something that had not been explored in previous seasons. I suspect season five will show him finally taking an interest in learning Karate.

One could say that our yearning for a father figure is deeply embedded within our personhood and consciousness. It is reflective of our desire for not just an earthly father but even more profoundly in our Heavenly Father, who is the source of all earthly fathers and loving relations.

Bullying, Self-Defense, Moral Responsibility, Adaptation, and Transformation

In the first episode of the series, Johnny actually defends Miguel from his callous bullies. This is where Miguel becomes interested in the art of Karate. It is interesting to note that Zabka never thought he could pull off the character of Johnny in the original *Karate Kid* because bullying was so far removed from his own temperament. Nonetheless, he became the quintessential icon for bullying throughout the 1980s. He has stated that the one and only line that originally resonated with him, after first reading the script to the original movie, was when he states: "You're alright LaRusso!"[2] before relinquishing his champion's trophy to Daniel. In recent years, Zabka has become quite vocal against the culture of bullying[3] and has given several talks on the subject.

The series has plenty of examples of bullying, just as one would expect within a high school setting. It touches on contemporary issues such as bullying through social media. There is also a juxtaposition between the culture of victimization versus taking responsibility for one's actions and lives. The message at times can be crude, while at the same time running counter to our pernicious culture of victimization. It emphasizes that one must shoulder one's own burden, and overcome whatever obstacles there may be. Counter to popular views emanating from the regressive left that have dominated our culture for so long, this show demonstrates that victimhood is anything but a virtue. After Miguel successfully stands up to his bullies and takes them all down in a four against one fight, videos of the fight go "viral." The next day, Johnny has all kinds of students wanting to learn Karate. And so, the next generation of *Cobra Kai* students begins and his dojo is open for business. In later seasons, confronting bullies is explored in ways outside of mere physical prowess, but in ways where the characters introspect and endure transformations in how they view themselves and others around them; in ways that can also transform their so-called bullies. In *The Karate Kid Part III*, Daniel was influenced and seduced by Silver and the power of *Cobra Kai* with its offensive style. This was to Daniel's detriment and short lived; he returned back to Miyagi-Do style to win the All-Valley Championship again. In season four, we see another layer to this where the characters adapt to different styles, i.e., the style of Miyagi-Do defense and Eagle-Fang (Johnny's new dojo) offense, much like *Rocky III* when Apollo works with Rocky to defeat Clubber Lang (Mr. T). In reality, the different characters begin to see the value of each style in different contexts,

2 Hovenaut, "You're Alright LaRusso."

3 ScreenCrush Staff, "Billy Zabka, the Movies' Biggest Bully Takes A Strong Anti-Bullying Stance."

and in every day living. Karate, much like life, does not present easy answers to difficult situations—adaptation is required for survival.

Although vengeance and betrayal certainly play a role in later seasons, so does mercy and forgiveness. Interestingly, Anthony becomes the opposite of his father—a bully. But then his victim confronts him in aggression with *Cobra Kai*-style fighting. This in turn, begins a process of transformation and adaptation for both characters. The concept of shedding weaknesses is also prevalent throughout season four in both virtuous and dishonourable ways. Although Silver's loyalty to Kreese at one point knows no bounds; it is this same loyalty and the sense of indebtedness that creates Silver's great resentment of Kreese, setting a great storyline for season five. According to Ralph Macchio, these twists and turns bring a fuller context to *The Karate Kid Part III* and its characters, therefore redeeming it after 33 years.

As Macchio states in an interview with *The Hollywood Reporter*:

> I was not a fan of how *The Karate Kid III* came out. I felt the story was only repeating itself and was not character forwarding for the end of LaRusso. And production-wise, it was being written one way and then changed another way. It was not a smooth ride. In the end, there were parts of the character that I didn't embrace as well as I did with the original and the first sequel. I don't put it on the top of my résumé.
>
> However, it informs *Cobra Kai* going forward, clearly with season four. It gives us so much story. And what is so wonderful about doing the *Cobra Kai* series, the creators find ways to take that story and let it evolve and find backstories for characters who might have been thinly written.[4]

Griffith, in an interview with the *Hollywood Reporter*, said this about Terry Silver's character: "You may hate Terry, but you want to watch him because I think there are sprinkles of truth in his madness. And I think that is why people enjoy him on a visceral level."[5] Indeed, there is the inner savage that must be tamed. Griffith's character presents a worldly man with mental and physical aptitudes, an appreciation for art, an accomplished classical piano player, and extremely wealthy but deep inside lays his inner beast that he has so desperately tried to tame for years, up until Kreese helps release this inner demon that possesses him again, much like an addiction or compulsion. It is a reminder of the depths of depravity and deceit men can go to if they do not struggle to cultivate virtues as opposed to vices. The sophistication and complexity of Silver's character reminds us of the Nazis who belonged

4 Parker, "Ralph Macchio (Still) Dislikes 'The Karate Kid Part III' But Proud 'Cobra Kai' Fleshed Out Dynamite Villain."

5 Parker, "'Cobra Kai' Star Thomas Ian Griffith Teases Chilling Terry Silver Future."

to a highly educated and cultured society, but who nonetheless were still able to perpetrate some of the cruelest crimes against humanity. Like the character of Hannibal Lector, who is able to appreciate classical music and art, while cannibalizing his victims. St. Paul reminds of the power of sin that is something we must struggle with everyday:

> We know that the law is spiritual; but I am unspiritual, sold as a slave to sin. I do not understand what I do. For what I want to do I do not do, but what I hate I do. And if I do what I do not want to do, I agree that the law is good. As it is, it is no longer I myself who do it, but it is sin living in me. For I know that good itself does not dwell in me, that is, in my sinful nature. For I have the desire to do what is good, but I cannot carry it out. For I do not do the good I want to do, but the evil I do not want to do—this I keep on doing. Now if I do what I do not want to do, it is no longer I who do it, but it is sin living in me that does it…
>
> Although I want to do good, evil is right there with me. For in my inner being I delight in God's law; but I see another law at work in me, waging war against the law of my mind and making me a prisoner of the law of sin at work within me. What a wretched man I am! Who will rescue me from this body that is subject to death? Thanks be to God, who delivers me through Jesus Christ our Lord!
>
> So then, I myself in my mind am a slave to God's law, but in my sinful nature[d] a slave to the law of sin (Rom. 7:14–25).

So, despite our good intentions to follow God's path, if we do not surrender our lives to Christ in faith and morally virtuous living then sin can still enslave us.

Nevertheless, one of the reasons I enjoyed *The Karate Kid Part III* was because of Silver's character (which has been developed so beautifully in the latest installment), and also how Daniel was able to overcome his fear and use Kata to defeat Mike Barnes (Sean Kanan, who is anticipated to return in season five) but this Silver's character's further development and corresponding backstories make the original story even greater.

Learning Karate requires and instills discipline and inculcates inner confidence. As Kreese in an emotive dialogue states:

> Do you remember when we got back from Nam? We went through hell watching our friends die. Only to be welcomed home by a bunch of hippies calling us killers. People needed to learn some respect. Some discipline. That's why we started *Cobra Kai.* Together we made a difference.

These sorts of tragic experiences must have been commonplace upon soldiers' return back home. It wasn't their fault that they were drafted and consequently suffered from the flaws of American policy revolving around the Vietnam War. It is indeed heartbreaking. But discipline and moral responsibility is the key. Hippies, much like the social justice warriors of today, have a misplaced anger which is never truly aimed at the culprits responsible for the many injustices of the world.

Be that as it may, physical self-defense is not to condone violence, but it is indeed to recognize that it is honorable to properly defend oneself and those who are defenseless. There is a strong message of confronting bullies and helping others in such situations throughout the series. I would argue that one should avoid fighting if they can; sometimes, however, when one or others are being attacked, there is no other option. Some are not aware of this but, under Christian principles, it would be immoral to let others inflict harm on the innocent. There has always been a sort of tension and confusion on how to respond to violence within the Christian tradition. Are we to exhibit self-defense, martyrdom, or both? The Catechism is clear when it states:

> Love toward oneself remains a fundamental principle of morality. Therefore, it is legitimate to insist on respect for one's own right to life. Someone who defends his life is not guilty of murder even if he is forced to deal his aggressor a lethal blow.[6]

However, there are times and certain contexts where retaliation and self-defense may not be what is asked of us, as Jesus demonstrates throughout the New Testament. This is exemplified in Jesus' words found in Matt 17:22–23, "When they came together in Galilee, he said to them, 'The Son of Man is going to be delivered into the hands of men. They will kill him, and on the third day he will be raised to life.'" And the disciples were filled with grief." When it comes to self-defense, we must be wise and prudent. Jesus also stated in Luke 22:36, "If you don't have a sword, sell your cloak and buy one." Thus, if one has the tools to confront bullies, he should, or if he doesn't, he should acquire them. We all also have the moral responsibility to confront the bullying of innocent people. Another biblical example of self-defense and the defense of the innocent includes Nehemiah 4:44, which states: "Do not be afraid of them. Remember the Lord, who is great and awesome, and fight for your brothers, your sons, your daughters, your wives, and your homes." Similarly, St. Thomas Aquinas in the *Summa Theologica* states that:

> [T]his act, since one's intention is to save one's own life, is not unlawful, seeing that it is natural to everything to keep itself in 'being,' as far as possible... [it is not] necessary for salvation that a man omit the act of moderate self-defence in order to avoid killing the other man, since one is bound to take more care of one's own life than of another's.[7]

6 Catechism of the Catholic Church, "Legitimate Defense," 2264.

7 St. Thomas Aquinas, *Summa theologiae*, Part II.II, Question 64, Article 7.

This is not to say that the defense of others is not to be encouraged, but that your own life is to be valued more than the one who is causing harm. Likewise, John Locke, in his *Two Treatise of Government*, emphasized the moral responsibility behind self-defense when he wrote:

> I should have a right to destroy that which threatens me with destruction: for, by the fundamental law of nature, man being to be preserved as much as possible, when all cannot be preserved, the safety of the innocent is to be preferred.[8]

And further:

> Thus the law of Nature stands as an eternal rule to all men, legislators as well as others.
>
> The rules that they make for, other men's actions must, as well as their own and other men's actions, be conformable to the law of Nature—i.e., to the will of God, of which that is a declaration, and the fundamental law of Nature being the preservation of mankind, no human sanction can be good or valid against it.[9]

So, as Christians, we have good grounds to use self-defense to preserve the well-being of ourselves and the innocent. This is in line with Miyagi's teachings to Daniel, and how Daniel passes this message to his students (Robby and Amanda). This theme continues into the other two subsequent seasons. However, it is antithetical to the *Cobra Kai* motto of "striking first."

Given our reflection, *Cobra Kai* has much to offer Christians and others. The show instills moral responsibility and the importance of fathers that is sorely lacking from many contemporary shows that celebrate unbridled violence and sexuality. It also smashes political correctness and safe space culture to bits. It is refreshing to see that this series does not kowtow to political correctness. This is something I believe will appeal to both older and younger generations of viewers. More and more individuals are growing fed up with the politically correct narrative and the associated ills of identity politics. The show focuses on individual personhood, which transcends the groupthink that is so prominent throughout the indoctrinating halls of our educational institutions. All this being said, I still get nostalgic, and even inspired, when I see Daniel beginning his Kata sequence to the epic original Karate Kid music and the virtuous transformations of old characters.

8 Locke, *Two Treatise of Government*, III, 16.
9 Locke, *Two Treatise of Government*, XI, 135

Bibliography

Aquinas, Thomas. *Summa theologiae.* In Sancti *Thomae de Aquino Opera Omnia Iussu Leonis XIII.* Vols 4–12 of 50 vols., edited by Leonine Comision. Rome: 1882.

Catechism of the Catholic Church, second edition, Washington: Libreria Editrice Vaticana, 2000, Section II, Article 5, I, Legitimate Defense, 2264, 545.

Hovenaut, "You're Alright LaRusso." Video Clip, July 18, 2015, Imgur. https://imgur.com/gallery/Z4kJhtW.

Locke, John. *Two Treatise of Government*, edited by Peter Laslett. Cambridge: Cambridge University Press, 1988

Parker, Ryan. "Ralph Macchio (Still) Dislikes 'The Karate Kid Part III' But Proud 'Cobra Kai' Fleshed Out Dynamite Villain." *The Hollywood Reporter*, January 3, 2022. https://www.hollywoodreporter.com/tv/tv-features/ralph-macchio-proud-cobra-kai-karate-kid-part-iii-villain-1235069083/.

———. "'Cobra Kai' Star Thomas Ian Griffith Teases Chilling Terry Silver Future." *The Hollywood Reporter*, January 8, 2022. https://www.hollywoodreporter.com/tv/tv-features/cobra-kai-thomas-ian-griffith-terry-silver-future-1235071505/?fbclid=IwAR3nxGPh5xpRBOzhhFbQ-hO6f29x8MhK2Xewh8nEh2MCHfQpWvvwUp1dJMI.

ScreenCrush Staff. "Billy Zabka, the Movies' Biggest Bully Takes A Strong Anti-Bullying Stance." *ScreenCrush*, November 16, 2015. https://screencrush.com/billy-zabka-karate-kid-bully/.

Chapter 53

A Korean Pastor Inspires Us to Love Without Limits[1]

Scott D. G. Ventureyra

The Drop Box is a heart wrenching, yet inspirational documentary about a selflessly heroic South Korean pastor, Lee Jong-rak, who is consumed by a compelling desire to love unconditionally abandoned and helpless newborn babies. [2] The award-winning documentary is directed by Brian Ivie.

In 2009, Pastor Lee and his wife installed a drop box on the outside of their home that functions as a depository for undesired infants, many of whom possess physical and/or mental disabilities. Some of these babies are also abandoned by teen mothers who fear societal repercussions such as expulsion from school and ostracism or disownment by their families. The documentary recounts how many of these teens contemplate suicide because of their predicament.

Long before the drop box was installed, however, Pastor Lee endured his own familial hardships. They began with the birth of his biological son Eun-man, who was born with an enormous cyst on his left cheek. Despite multiple operations as a child, he remained disabled his whole life, suffering from a severe form of cerebral palsy. The cost to maintain Eun-man's bedridden life was tremendous in both time and wealth.

Over the years, the Lees took in orphans they had encountered at the hospital that cared for Eun-man. Pastor Lee's reputation for loving unconditionally the "unlovable" developed far and wide. A woman abandoned her child one cold evening outside of Lee's home. Her decision moved Lee to build his drop box equipped with a motion sensor and alarm in order to help prevent the untimely death of abandoned babies.

Aside from the very poignant yet uplifting scenes, the film possesses several humorous moments. For instance, Lee is referred to by his wife as "fish bones" because of his ultra-skinny physique. In turn, Lee says his wife is too short and stumpy. Even family members urged him not to marry her

1 For the original, see Scott Ventureyra, "A Korean Pastor Inspires Us to Love Without Limits," *Crisis Magazine*, March 1, 2015, https://www.crisismagazine.com/2015/korean-pastor-inspires-us-love-without-limits.

2 Focus on the Family, "The Drop Box – Official Full Movie Trailer."

because of her appearance. Despite their compromised aesthetic preferences, Lee warmly explains that they ultimately married because of their deep love for one another.

The couple's love for each other is evident from the mutual support they give to the children in their care. On countless nights Pastor Lee kept sleepless vigils listening for the sound of the drop box bell. He describes the sound of the bell as a heart-breaking moment, in part because of the realization that a parent is willing to abandon her baby in such a way. Nevertheless, Pastor Lee, from the moment he opens that drop box door, pours out his abundant love upon that baby. He lifts the baby, kneels, and prays, thanking God for safely delivering the baby and for the opportunity to help. From there he delivers the baby to a hospital, orphanage or even adoption agency.

Every year in Seoul hundreds of babies are abandoned and many die. However, Pastor Lee and a few volunteers have managed to save hundreds of infants who would otherwise be forsaken. Oftentimes, a letter accompanies the baby, typically written by the biological mother. Pastor Lee reads a few for the documentary. Most of them thank Lee for creating hope for the mothers and their babies. The South Korean government accuses Pastor Lee of facilitating the abandonment of children. Nothing could be further from the truth. The problem existed long before Pastor Lee set up the drop box. Indeed, it is a problem that not only affects South Korea but many parts of the world, including our own backyard.

There are roughly a dozen children who live with Lee and his family permanently. His tireless efforts to rescue dropped-offed babies has taken its toll on Lee's health. As a weeping volunteer explains, there is a great fear that there will be no one who possesses the strength or desire to continue Lee's great legacy after he dies.

However, there may be one successor in the coming years. Remarkably, he may be one of the very orphans that Lee rescued at the hospital: a young boy wise beyond his years. This boy, perhaps 11 years old, suffers from a congenital hand deformity. The interview sequence with the boy is one of the most touching moments of the film. He recounts how he was often chastised by his fellow peers because of his hands. The other children would not throw that ball at him during dodgeball because they said, "it's no fun to play with a cripple" and laughed. Despite the cruelty of his peers, the boy explains that he demonstrated that he could play all the sports just as well and developed a great mastery ofTae Kwon Do. He also became class president for his leadership abilities and finally earns the respect of his peers, who have now accepted him wholeheartedly.

This boy also describes the disappointment he felt when he found out that the Lees were not his biological parents, but he said he now considers them his real parents. He loves Eun-man as his own brother and prays for him. Despite his young age, he realizes that his father is sick and wishes to continue his father's work one day.

Above the drop box, Pastor Lee has placed the very fitting caption of Psalm 27:10, which reads "Though my father and mother forsake me, the LORD will receive me." Since God has adopted him, Lee believes he should adopt those that have been deemed undesirables by their biological parents.

Nearing the end of the film, Pastor Lee exhibits great wisdom and insight when he intimates that these unwanted babies are far from being purposeless. He affirms that they do indeed have purpose and intrinsic value. Despite their ailments, incapacities, and sufferings they smile in the face of injustice. Their courage can act as a light of inspiration to the world, demonstrating love and hope that can transform us from within. This stems from the profound realization of the Judeo-Christian faith, that we all carry the spark of the divine; that we are all created in the image and likeness of God. Although many of us may not have such physical or mental incapacities like Pastor Lee's children, we suffer from our selfishness and ungodly desires. Humans throughout the world, both individually and collectively, have a strong tendency to focus on themselves too much and ignore the suffering around them.

The light that Pastor Lee brings to this ever-enveloping darkness with the untimely predicaments of innocent babies is inestimable and is what prompted director Ivie to produce his documentary. In 2011, Lee's story reached many parts of the globe including Los Angeles, where Ivie resides. It ultimately inspired Ivie to travel to South Korea with his crew to depict on film this remarkable story. Ivie does a magnificent job capturing the deep emotions of those he interviews. Some of the most memorable moments of the film focus on the children's smiles and playful interactions.

In a twist of fate, while pursuing his selfish desires for fame, Ivie was unexpectedly transformed by his encounter with Pastor Lee. The young aspiring director was profoundly moved by Lee's inspiring example of sanctity that he converted to Christianity. In his acceptance speech at the 8th annual San Antonio Independent Christian Film Festival, he candidly confessed:

> I became a Christian while making this movie. When I started to make it and I saw all these kids come through the drop box—it was like a flash from heaven, just like these kids with disabilities had crooked bodies, I have a crooked soul. And God loves me still. When it comes to this sanctity of life issue, we must realize that that faith in God is the only refuge for people who are deemed unnecessary. This world is so much about self-reliance, self-worth, and self-esteem. It's a total illusion that we can be self-sufficient. Christ is the only thing that enables us.[3]

3 Veith, "The Drop Box - Brian Ivie tells us about the box that saves babies."

This documentary can act as a much-needed remedy to the devaluation of human life and dignity throughout our planet. It could also help cure the apathy among many who do not care enough to reflect upon the intrinsic worth of all human beings. This man of God, in a distant part of the globe, teaches everyone a valuable lesson. He inspires us to move outside of our selfish lives through acting selflessly and partaking in God's call to impart love and compassion to all of humanity, whether it be the unborn, the disabled, the sick, the elderly, the forgotten, or those who suffer silently in despair.

Bibliography

Focus on the Family. "The Drop Box – Official Full Movie Trailer," YouTube Video, October 1, 2014. https://www.youtube.com/watch?v=yTQ2VTf5vWc&t=1s.

Veith, Matthew. "The Drop Box - Brian Ivie tells us about the box that saves babies." *CVHNRadio*, February 11, 2015. https://chvnradio.com/articles/the-drop-box-brian-ivie-tells-us-about-the-box-that-saves-babies.

Chapter 54

The Indomitable Spirit of Man: Seeking Unity Through the Enduring Message of Terry Fox[1]

Scott D. G. Ventureyra

Much of the Western world is currently split by issues pertaining to politics, economics, race, gender, sexual orientation, the COVID-19 crisis, and religion. No doubt, these issues need to be adequately assessed and dealt within a morally prudent and logical manner. The popular debates surrounding these broad issues concern human wellbeing, both individually and collectively, but demonstrate a deep neglect of the intrinsic worth of the human person. There is au fond, a profound flawed misunderstanding and/or dismissal of metaphysics and meta-ethics. Unfortunately, particular ideologies have been elevated over the human person. Truth has been compromised. This has manifested itself in the debates revolving around abortion, assisted suicide, and transgender washrooms. As polarizing and misguided these debates truly are, we sometimes need to take a pause from the cacophony of confused and competing voices. Regardless of ideological clashes, I would like to focus on a timeless issue. For a brief moment, let us focus our attention toward a cause that will help create unity instead of disunity, even if just for a brief moment.

Whether one believes in the Judeo-Christian doctrine of the image-likeness of God (Gen 1:27) or not, it provides one with an equalizer or guarantor in terms of why each human person has intrinsic value. Although Jewish, Christian, and Sufi Islamic philosophers and theologians have debated the meaning of being created in the image of God, it is as an aspect to the human person which signifies a profound intrinsic worth distinguishing human persons from the rest of the animal kingdom. I would argue that our capacity for self-consciousness (i.e., our ability to be aware of ourselves— the ability to recognize we are persons; the "I" moment) and what such a capacity entails, including the ability to deliberate, imagine, love, empathize, create, and imagine, are what encompass being created in the image of God. This doctrine is inclusive to all

1 For the original see Scott Ventureyra, "The Indomitable Spirit of Man: Seeking Unity Through the Enduring Message of Terry Fox," *Catholic Insight*, October 27, 2016, https://catholicinsight.com/finding-unity-despite-disunity-god-love-and-the-enduring-message-of-terry-fox/.

of humanity. All human persons share in this image, whether one is a believer in the doctrine (Jew, Christian, Sufi-Muslim) or a non-believer (Hindu, Buddhist, Atheist, Agnostic, etc.).

It is worth pointing out that the origin and experience of self-consciousness is part of the subjective phenomenological human experience. This is not to negate that animals have a certain level of self-awareness but the extent that it exists in humans seems to be something rather radical in comparison to the rest of the animal kingdom. Panpsychists who see consciousness as being ubiquitous throughout nature and particularly the animal kingdom will certainly disagree with such a statement. It is worth pointing out that a number of Christian intellectuals, such as Catholic paleontologist Daryl Domning, Catholic philosopher Peter van Inwagen, and theologians such as Anglican bishop and eminent New Testament scholar N.T. Wright, through the implication of their embracing of Christian physicalism (which denies the existence of an immaterial self/soul), postulate that through further evolutionary development leading to high levels of complexity is what led to the origin of self-consciousness, i.e., the ability to introspect deeply on one's own self. However, in Pope John Paul II's address *The Pontifical Academy of Sciences: On Evolution* in 1996, he sates:

> It is by virtue of his eternal soul that the whole person, including his body, possesses such great dignity. Pius XII underlined the essential point: if the origin of the human body comes through living matter which existed previously, the spiritual soul is created directly by God ("animas enim a Deo immediate creari catholica fides non retimere iubet"). (Humani Generis)
>
> As a result, the theories of evolution which, because of the philosophies which inspire them, regard the spirit either as emerging from the forces of living matter, or as a simple epiphenomenon of that matter, are incompatible with the truth about man. They are therefore unable to serve as the basis for the dignity of the human person. [2]

John Paul II rightfully emphasizes the great discontinuity between humanity's soul and consciousness with the rest of the animal kingdom. This was a point of contention between the co-discoverers of evolution by natural selection: Alfred Wallace (1832–1913) and Charles Darwin (1809–1882). The origin of self-consciousness is a radical event in the history of the universe, as G. K. Chesterton (1874–1936), observes:

> The matter here is one of history and not of philosophy so that it need only be noted that no philosopher denies that a mystery still attaches to the two great transitions: the origin of the universe itself and the origin

2 Pope John Paul II, "Message to the Pontifical Academy of Science."

> of the principle of life itself. Most philosophers have the enlightenment to add that a third mystery attaches to the origin of man himself. In other words, a third bridge was built across a third abyss of the unthinkable when there came into the world what we call reason and what we call will. Man is not merely an evolution but rather a revolution. That he has a backbone or other parts upon a similar pattern to birds and fishes is an obvious fact, whatever be the meaning of the fact. But if we attempt to regard him, as it were, as a quadruped standing on his hind legs, we shall find what follows far more fantastic and subversive than if he were standing on his head.[3]

It is our conscious experience of reality which entails self-consciousness that provides us with the capacity towards love which is what binds humans together. Inevitably, so does suffering, which occurs upon reflection of physical and/or emotional pain. Our ability to empathize and identify with those who suffer also unifies us with others through our ability to love.

The Catholic philosopher and theologian, Bernard Lonergan, would refer to a love for God and a love for others as a mode of self-transcendence which would be the fulfillment of our self-consciousness. Or, as Lonergan would put it: "being in love with God is the basic fulfillment of our conscious intentionality."[4]

The greatest example of love throughout the history of humanity is embodied in the person of Jesus. Jesus asks us to love in a radical manner, i.e., to love those who are our enemies and who persecute us: "But I tell you, love your enemies and pray for those who persecute you, that you may be children of your Father in heaven. He causes his sun to rise on the evil and the good and sends rain on the righteous and the unrighteous" (Matt 5:44–45). Jesus also asks us to love completely selflessly and in a radical form of perfect altruism which will help us break free from the shackles of our selfishness and sinful desires, in the form of sacrificing oneself for our neighbour but to ultimately also save ourselves from our sinful and selfish nature: "My command is this: Love each other as I have loved you. Greater love has no one than this: to lay down one's life for one's friends" (John 15:12–13). It is in this sense that we can freely partake in God's love to others through being created in His image.

Catholic paleontologist, Daryl Domning, and the late theologian, Monika Hellwig, entertain an intriguing (but ultimately unorthodox) idea of perfect altruism in their book, *Original Selfishness: Original Sin And Evil in the Light of Evolution.*[5] This is something only exemplified through Christ in the created order. It helps break us free from our evolutionary roots of

3 Chesterton, *The Collected Works of G.K. Chesterton II: The Everlasting Man*, 158.

4 Lonergan, *Method in Theology*, 105.

5 See Domning and Hellwig, *Original Selfishness.*

selfishness which before the advent of moral consciousness was manifested in pre-humans through a propensity and innate predisposition to do everything in our capacity (or any particular organism) to survive. All organisms are selfish in a non-pejorative sense merely because of this propensity to survive. This inherent selfishness, Domning calls "original selfishness," as a substitute to what is typically referred to as "original sin." All organisms share this original selfishness from the origin of life to all present organisms including humans. The difference with humans is that we have a moral consciousness to choose evil through free will whereby guilt can result.

Moral evil, although largely passed on from cultural transmission from sinful societies, is not the root. Domning and Hellwig reason that this is not the result of a pre-historical Fall, so, eventually, moral evil evolves out of physical evil. Yet, again, it is worth clarifying that this stands in contrast to Catholic doctrine, as enunciated in Pius XII's 1950 encyclical *Humani Generis*:

> When, however, there is question of another conjectural opinion, namely polygenism, the children of the Church by no means enjoy such liberty. For the faithful cannot embrace that opinion which maintains either that after Adam there existed on this earth true men who did not take their origin through natural generation from him as from the first parent of all or that Adam represents a certain number of first parents. Now it is in no way apparent how such an opinion can be reconciled with that which the sources of revealed truth and the documents of the Teaching Authority of the Church propose with regard to original sin, which proceeds from a sin actually committed by an individual Adam and which through generation is passed on to all and is in everyone as his own. (#37).[6]

This involves the debate between polygenism and monogenism. Domning and Hellwig opt for polygenism. Over the years, there have been several attempts, although highly speculative, to try and reconcile a monogenist theological account of human origins with that of a polygenist. The success or failure of such notions would be beyond the scope of this essay. Nonetheless, what is certain between Domning and Hellwig's view and Church Doctrine, is that perfect unselfishness cannot come from natural processes; we need supernatural grace transcending our original selfishness through Christ's salvation. Thus, Domning and Hellwig see our emulation of Jesus' perfect altruism as portrayed through his words and his ultimate act of love through his sacrifice on the Cross is how we may overcome "selfishness" and our mere ability to perform reciprocal altruism as is found through much of the animal

6 Pope Pius XII, *Humani Generis*:

kingdom. Similarly, in reference to Christian authenticity, Lonergan expresses how this is truly manifested:

> Christian authenticity— which is a love of others that does not shrink from self-sacrifice and suffering— is the sovereign means for overcoming evil. Christians bring about the kingdom of God in the world not only by doing good but also by overcoming evil with good (Rom 12, 21).[7]

God's perfect image through Christ is the highest example, who embodies the perfect moral consciousness which is geared towards love for one another. This is demonstrated through God's true love and purpose for His creation. Jesus, through the ultimate act of love and humility (His sacrificing atonement), is the one who demonstrates the true image stamp of God.

Following such an understanding of moral self-consciousness and authentic Christian living, through God's image, is the inspirational story of the great Canadian hero Terry Fox. The story is well known. Fox at the age of 18 was diagnosed with bone cancer and had to have his right leg amputated above the knee. Despite this huge setback in his life, he was determined to fight cancer through running from coast to coast in Canada. When many people would choose to turn inwards and become bitter and succumb to their impending death, Fox chose life and decided to rage against that good night, as he states:

> I don't feel that this is unfair. That's the thing about cancer. I'm not the only one, it happens all the time to people. I'm not special. This just intensifies what I did. It gives it more meaning. It'll inspire more people. I just wish people would realize that anything's possible if you try; dreams are made possible if you try.[8]

This run, in 1979, came to be known as the *Marathon of Hope*. Unfortunately, he had to stop running outside of Thunder Bay, Ontario since the cancer had spread to his lungs and had made it extremely difficult for him to breathe. Only months after, people from all over the world were able to realize Fox's dream of raising one dollar per Canadian citizen for cancer research— $23.4 million was raised. Indeed, miracles of hope can occur. Who would've thought in a span of a few months such a feat was possible. Fittingly, Fox had stated: "I'm not a dreamer, and I'm not saying this will initiate any kind of definitive answer or cure to cancer, but I believe in miracles. I have to."[9]

This was over 40 years ago. Since that moment, not just only Canadians

7 Lonergan, *Method in Theology*, 291.

8 Global News Staff, "Memorable quotes from Terry Fox."

9 Global News Staff, "Memorable quotes from Terry Fox."

but millions of people around the world have participated in *The National School Run Day*, *The Terry Fox Run*, and *Terry Fox fundraising event*. As of April 2020, remarkably, over $800 million have been raised in Terry Fox's name—an incredible milestone considering how it all began. Fox's prophetic words have been realized: "Even if I don't finish, we need others to continue. It's got to keep going without me."

Close to 5 years ago, a newsletter sent home to parents from my daughter's Catholic elementary school, describing the Terry Fox Run/Walk On[10] inspired me to create a webpage for my daughter where sponsors could donate money online. This was an opportunity for friends and family to unite for a common cause despite their internal disagreements and discord. It is a beautiful thing to see the sponsor's names from people who have different ideologies and religious outlooks but share the common propensity towards love and fighting a secondary cause to much of our human suffering: cancer. As an aside, I am proud to say that Julianna was able to run 17 more laps than the previous year (21 in total). She also helped raise close to $500, which was one third of the school's goal for that year!

As Fox recognized, cancer affects us all, whether indirectly or directly. It also does not discriminate with respect to our ideologies, age, race, gender, religion, etc., things that otherwise separate us. This realization of our common finitude and fragility, is an appeal to our moral consciousness, where we can come together and be unified. It is this propensity towards love, even if sometimes buried deep down inside, that unifies us to one another through our common suffering.

Although, Fox was only 22 years old when he died, he realized his higher purpose. Terry Fox was a self-professing Christian.[11] Unfortunately, many people spend a lifetime without truly embodying such a propensity towards love and helping others, as he states: "It took cancer to realize that being self-centered is not the way to live. The answer is to try and help others."[12] It is through his very suffering that he is transformed and redeemed. A curse turns into a blessing. This seems to evince the notion that some evil is *necessary* for a greater good. In this light, evil has profound spiritual benefits towards human development. Augustine, in his *Enchiridion*, argues that evil is not a thing in and of itself but merely an absence of the good, so if we are able to increase the good despite the circumstances, we find ourselves in, as Fox did, we are able diminish such an absence of good. We thus increase the light in this world to illuminate truth.

10 The Terry Fox Foundation, https://terryfox.org/terry-fox-run/. This year the run is scheduled for September 18, 2022.

11 Simmons, "Stratford-born author reveals untold story of Terry Fox's love life."

12 Fox, "Terry Fox Quotes."

Fox personifies the indomitable spirit of humanity. Fox promised himself that if he should live, he should prove to himself deserving of life.[13] Indeed, he did, and serves as an extraordinary example for all of us to live by. We should all follow Fox's example to love selflessly, mirroring Jesus' radical altruism, albeit through a finite and imperfect way. Even if one does not believe in Christ, following such an example will lead us from disunity to unity despite our many differences. Keeping with this spirit of love, let us not forget the great many persons who have suffered from cancer and who continue to this very day, which could include close loved ones. Regardless of whether we can one day find a cure or not, let us always give our love to comfort them.

Bibliography

Chesterton, Gilbert Keith. *The Collected Works of G.K. Chesterton II: The Everlasting Man*. San Francisco: St. Ignatius, 1986.

Domning, Daryl P. and Monika Hellwig. *Original Selfishness: Original Sin And Evil in the Light of Evolution*. New York: Routledge, 2006.

Global News Staff. "Memorable quotes from Terry Fox." *Global News*, April 12, 2012. https://globalnews.ca/news/233070/memorable-quotes-from-terry-fox/.

joeblow8579. "Terry Fox: Marathon of Hope." YouTube Video, April 11, 2010. https://www.youtube.com/watch?v=09mypXm_ZRM#t=90.

Lonergan, Bernard. *Method in Theology*. Toronto: University of Toronto Press, 1992.

Pope John Paul II, "Message to the Pontifical Academy of Science." Message delivered to the Pontifical Academy of Sciences on October 22, 1996. https://humanorigins.si.edu/sites/default/files/MESSAGE%20TO%20THE%20PONTIFICAL%20ACADEMY%20OF%20SCIENCES%20%28Pope%20John%20Paul%20II%29.pdf.

Pope Pius XII. Encyclical *Humani Generis*. August 12, 1950. https://www.vatican.va/content/pius-xii/en/encyclicals/documents/hf_p-xii_enc_12081950_humani-generis.html.

Simmons, Galen. "Stratford-born author reveals untold story of Terry Fox's love life." *Postmedia*, May 28, 2019. https://o.canada.com/entertainment/books/stratford-born-author-reveals-untold-story-of-terry-foxs-love-life/wcm/d4a47aba-775a-476d-ae28-34ad462b4ee4.

Terry Fox Foundation, The. "Terry Fox Quotes." AZ QUOTES, accessed March 15, 2022. https://www.azquotes.com/author/23947-Terry_Fox.

———. The Terry Fox Virtual Run, May 2, 2021. http://www.terryfox.org/Run/.

13 joeblow8579, "Terry Fox: Marathon of Hope."

Chapter 55

The Gift of Self and the Renewal of Humanism and Culture

Nikolaj Zunic

> Man thus created is man as the image of God. He is the image of God not in spite of but just because of his bodiliness. For in his bodiliness he is related to the earth and to other bodies, he is there for others, he is dependent upon others. In his bodiliness he finds his brother and the earth. As such a creature man of earth and spirit is in the likeness of his Creator, God.[1]
>
> —Dietrich Bonhoeffer

Introduction: Do We Live in An Age of Crisis?

Is human civilization in crisis? If we only restrict our view to Western culture, can we rightly judge it to be in the throes of what we may call "a crisis"? To answer this question, we could point to various troubling aspects or developments: the widespread rejection of religious faith, the rise of feelings of despair and purposelessness, aggressive secularization which marginalizes and persecutes religious groups and worldviews, the breakdown of the family, the isolation and loneliness of individuals, the weakening of morality, and the ever-present threats of violence in the forms of civil unrest, war, and terrorism. Against a Pollyannaish perspective, it is arguably the case that our world is in crisis. But what precisely is a "crisis"? The word "crisis" comes from the Greek *krinein*, which means "to judge" or "to decide." Colloquially, a crisis is an unfortunate state of affairs, an emergency situation when something has gone terribly wrong. But at its heart a crisis is rooted in decisions and actions. Not only are such tragic events *caused* by decisions, but the response that is elicited in the face of them is carried out by way of decisions as well. In other words, a crisis in human culture and civilization demands certain deeds and decisions as forms

1 Bonhoeffer, *Creation and Fall – Temptation: Two Biblical Studies*, 52.

of redress. As Thomas Langan has written: "A 'crisis' is a moment of decision… when those trying to live out a vision must make new determinations as to how they are going to organize themselves, in response to challenges that have arisen in the milieu."[2]

We can justifiably cite a host of problems with our world today, but, in reality, regarded from a historical perspective, the world has always been beset with injustice, plagued by disorder, and in crisis. This is nothing new. Biblical revelation informs us that there was a primordial Fall, an original sin, a rupture in our relationship with our Creator, God. Ever since that fateful event, the world has never been the same. The human reality has been marked by tragedy and pain and all this because of a free decision on the part of our first parents. This is the primordial decision that caused the crisis which we are currently witnessing throughout the world. But, of course, this decision of disobedience, pride, and arrogance had to be countered by a response in order to correct what had been set out of joint. The response—the new decision—was God's act of love to become one of us and to live among us, and in so doing to show us who He truly is. The Incarnation of God in the person of Jesus Christ is God's self-revelation as love and His reestablishment of the relationship with us human beings, which had been sundered in the Fall. The negative crisis of sin was challenged by the positive crisis of divine love. What all this amounts to is the utter ambiguity of the meaning of the crisis. *O felix culpa!*

From the perspective of Christian revelation, we can understand humanity's moral, political, intellectual, and spiritual problems as originating from a disordered or absent love. Human beings were made for love, and gain their fullest dignity and worth in love. But when love is suppressed, perverted, or misunderstood, then human actions can cause much harm and produce a veritable crisis. However, what exactly is love? How should it be understood and lived out? I would like to argue that love is essentially a *gift of self.* This is a view of love which can be gleaned from the writings of Jacques Maritain, but it is also the firm conviction of St. John Paul II, as expressed in his *Theology of the Body*. Both Maritain and John Paul II diagnosed profound problems in Western civilization in the twentieth century. Maritain, particularly in the 1940s, as can be seen in the collection of articles in *Pour la justice*, was concerned with the utter collapse of European civilization under the weight of a barbarous ideology and evil in Nazism. He saw the rejection of God and the Gospel as the principal causes of this crisis. The way to overcome this nihilism was to rejuvenate culture with an evangelical inspiration and a theocentric humanism. Later in the same century, John Paul II argued that the West was still in a crisis, a moral and anthropological one, which was trampling on human dignity. The specter of communism and totalitarianism was the political manifestation of this deep

2 Langan, *The Catholic Tradition*, 94, n.1.

confusion of what it means to be human. John Paul II sought to chart the right course by focusing on the meaning of the body and its "spousal" character in his series of talks entitled *The Theology of the Body.* These anthropological studies on the body were really expositions of human and divine love: the love of married couples and the love of God for man.

If human civilization is in the midst of a crisis—both presently and always—we need to consider the nature of the crisis, but, more importantly, the way to respond to it. Evil and sin cannot be "solved"; the state of human fallenness cannot be fixed by crafty human innovations. There is indeed a mystery surrounding the crisis of humanity which resists easy remedies. The key to unlocking this mystery and shedding light on this imbroglio is to turn to Christ and to learn from him regarding the human condition. Both Maritain and John Paul II believed that recuperating a Christian anthropology was the only way to combat the evils of the world and to restore the world to its proper state of goodness in relation to God. Therefore, in this chapter I wish to discuss the role which love plays in addressing three distinct areas of the human crisis. First, I will examine the ways in which love heals and completes a wounded intellect in its pursuit of truth and salvation. Second, I will discuss Maritain's ideas of a theocentric or integral humanism which is heralded in opposition to an anthropocentric humanism. And finally, I will turn to John Paul II's *Theology of the Body* and his teachings of love as the gift of self in the context of marriage and sexuality. These studies have as their singular aim to show how the crisis of the world can be adequately and effectively addressed with a spirit of love and in the process human culture and civilization can be rejuvenated and reborn.

Love as the Path to Knowing God

Atheism has been around for a long time in Western civilization, dating back to the ancient atomists Democritus and Leucippus, but what makes its manifestation rather unique in modernity is its pervasiveness. As Charles Taylor ponders in his work *A Secular Age*, 500 years ago the default position in the West was one of faith, whereas today it is reversed and most people consider it normal to have no religious faith at all.[3] In fact, it is regarded as strange to be a believer, as something in need of justification. In his very insightful study on modern atheism, Henri de Lubac argues the thesis that the common feature present in all forms of modern atheism is a false notion of God.[4] One could accuse atheists of all stripes of committing the Straw Man Fallacy in their arguments: they present a certain concept of God and then attempt to refute

3 Taylor, *A Secular Age*, 25.
4 de Lubac, S.J., *The Drama of Atheist Humanism.*

God's existence, but this concept in the first place is not the real, true God, certainly not the God of Christianity, that is, the God which real human beings worship and believe in.[5] Since the fabricated image of God is a convenient one for the atheist's agenda, the attack against religion seems to occur so effortlessly and effectively. After all, when one hears the descriptions of God which somebody like Richard Dawkins offers, representing God as a vengeful sadist or fairy-tale character, it is unsurprising that his subversive arguments receive tacit support even from believers—for who in their right mind would want to endorse a god who is bent on destruction and cruelty and quite frankly is depicted as the figment of a child's imagination?[6] Such a god is not worthy of our adoration and worship. So, when Nietzsche proclaims the "death of God" in the nineteenth century there is no need to fear his message or to protest vigorously against this atheistic vendetta against all that we hold dear, since the idea of God entertained here bears little to no resemblance to the God of the prophets. For, in Pascal's language, as far as faithful Christians are concerned, the God of the philosophers might as well perish, since such a god holds out no hope for salvation or eternal happiness.[7]

If atheism is indeed premised on a false understanding of God's essence, the question that then immediately rears its head is: Who is the true God? How should we understand God's proper essence? Furthermore, how do we come *to know* the truth of who God is? A popular approach in the philosophical and theological traditions to this question is to examine what the concept of God tells us about God's essence. By reflecting on God's nature as a perfect being, we can deduce that God must exist. Therefore, God's essence—*who God is*—is recognized to be identical to God's existence—*that God is*. The ontological proofs for God's existence typically work in this fashion.[8] However, the result in this conceptual approach to God is usually unsatisfactory. Not only does this identity of essence with existence not tell us anything substantial or positive about God's being, but, as Kant argued, every ontological argument rests on a fundamental fallacy by which existence is illegitimately attached to the concept of God.[9] For, according to Kant, we cannot deduce the existence of God from the idea of God; being is not a *real* predicate.

5 See Lennox, *Gunning for God*, 31–37, 118–120.

6 See Dawkins, *The God Delusion*, 31, 52–54.

7 Blaise Pascal famously distinguished the God of the philosophers from the God of Abraham, Isaac, and Jacob in his Memorial, which is Pascal's description of his mystical experience on November 23, 1654. See Kreeft, *Christianity for Modern Pagans*, 326: "'The God of the philosophers' is a timeless principle; 'the God of Abraham, Isaac and Jacob' is a historical fact. We *think* the God of the philosophers, we *meet* the God of Abraham."

8 Most famously, see St. Anselm of Canterbury, *Proslogion*, 7-8, and René Descartes, *Meditations on First Philosophy*, 42–47.

9 Kant, *Critique of Pure Reason*, 563–569.

An alternative and better approach to the determination of God's essence is to focus on the content of divine revelation, the manner by which God communicates His essence to human beings. In contrast to the rationalistic approach of the ontological argument, revelation is historical and experiential; it is not knowledge which can be gained simply by thinking about an idea. The fact of revelation encompasses much within its purview. It includes not only Sacred Scripture and the testimonials of saints and mystics, that is, those who have been directly touched by God's hand, but most importantly is embodied in the person of Jesus Christ and his Church. The Christian image of God emphasizes the centrality of the Incarnation for the full revelation of God's being. The historical Jesus walked among us as a human being, as a man, two millennia ago, but is also present in the world today in and through the Church which is his mystical body. God's revelation to humankind, in short, is something real, tangible, concrete. The body occupies a place of honour in Christianity. Jesus' temporal life was physical and he died on the cross in his body. Moreover, the body is described as the temple of God, as the living tabernacle that contains the living God.[10] Only a heretical monophysitism would deny the importance of the body for Christian revelation.

These reflections on the role of the body in our understanding of God's essence shed valuable light on the manner by which God is known. The fact that Jesus was a man, though simultaneously God, informs us that coming to know God fully cannot be done merely through our minds, that is, by means of an immaterial intellectual principle. This knowledge can only be obtained in and through our bodies through an experiential mode of understanding. On a very general level, what this points to is that pleromatic truth, that is, truth in its fullness, can only be known through the ups and downs, the successes and failures, and the joys and sorrows of human life, from the cradle to the grave. Simply by living in the world we are taught much through experience that contributes to our comprehension of who God is. This is not such an outlandish view, since wisdom, both in its philosophical and theological variants, is regarded as the product of lifelong experience. But in a more restricted sense, the embodied foundation of divine truth tells us that truth involves non-conceptual and non-rational elements as well—not to be construed as irrational—those aspects which are normally associated with our corporeal life. Here I have in mind the bodily drives, desires, and inclinations which reside in the bosom of our affective sphere. When we have an insight into the truth of life, such as that all life involves suffering, similar to the Buddha's enlightenment, this kind of knowledge is obtained through our bodily existence, not in a purely

10 See St. Paul, *The First Letter of Paul to the Corinthians*, 6: 19–20: "Or do you not know that your body is a temple of the Holy Spirit within you, which you have from God, and that you are not your own?"

intellectual manner. It is a direct grasp of the true essence of reality, which is a capacity peculiar to human beings. Max Scheler called this immediate comprehension of a thing in both its particularity and universality "ideation,"[11] but St. Thomas Aquinas had a more useful idea to denote the unique kind of knowledge of truth: knowledge by connaturality or knowledge by inclination.[12] Connatural knowledge differs from conceptual knowledge—what Elizabeth Anscombe calls "the knowledge of indifferent truth"—insofar as our affective sphere participates in and harmonizes with the reality which we are seeking to cognize with our intellects.[13] Our inclinations and desires are attuned to the object of our concern and in this way we arrive at a truer and more genuine understanding of that which we desire. Ultimate truth, the truth which is God, can only be obtained with the intellect's cooperation with the body, which is expressed in the Thomistic notion of connatural knowledge, because God has revealed Himself in the person of Jesus Christ. To want to know God, therefore, one must turn to Jesus.

In St. Anselm's famous ontological argument for God's existence from the *Proslogion*, he takes a quote from the Psalms: "The fool has said in his heart, 'There is no God'."[14] The argument that follows which aims to demonstrate rationally God's existence is anchored in Anselm's initial affirmation of God's existence in faith: "That God truly exists." Clearly, Anselm adopts the Augustinian model of *faith seeking understanding* for his ontological argument.[15] But if we turn our attention to the fool in this work and notice how he so haughtily denies God's existence we are struck by Anselm's explanation for the fool's lack of belief. It is not that the fool did not have the concept of God in his mind, for he certainly is able to understand the argument, but that there was something amiss "in his heart." The problem with the fool—the *reason* why he dismissed God's existence—is because his heart was not rightly ordered. The language of the heart permeates Anselm's discussion of the fool, which should be a clear message to us that Anselm thought that the fool suffered from a defective or disordered affective sphere in his personality. The inference to be drawn here is that if the fool's heart had been properly ordered then the chief obstacle to affirming God's existence would have been removed. The crux of the matter is the view, propounded by Anselm and others in the Christian tradition, that coming to know God is not simply a matter of embracing propositions or dogmas asserted about God's being, but involves an affective energy which originates from the very core of our being, located in what is metaphorically

11 See Scheler, *The Human Place in the Cosmos*.

12 See Thomas Aquinas, *Treatise on Law: The Complete Text*, q94, a2, pp. 38–41. See also Suto, "Virtue and Knowledge: Connatural Knowledge According to Thomas Aquinas," 61–79.

13 Anscombe, "Knowledge and Reverence for Human Life," 59–66.

14 St. Anselm, *Proslogion*, 7.

15 See Koterski, S. J., *An Introduction to Medieval Philosophy: Basic Concepts*, 10–18.

referred to as the heart. One is not delivered to belief in God's existence because one has *thought* about God correctly, but rather, one believes in God because one meets, dialogues with and loves God. For, as Karl Rahner once stated in an interview, "I believe because I pray."[16]

The heart is a powerful symbol in the Western tradition.[17] The heart (*kardia*, *cor*) is the centre of our affectivity, meaning, in its positive determination, that it is the seat of all desire and appetite, whereas, according to its negative determination, it is also the basis of a human being's vulnerability and capacity for suffering, which is the ability to be affected by one's environment. In his definitive study on this subject, Dietrich von Hildebrand writes in *The Heart: An Analysis of Human and Divine Affectivity* that the heart denotes not only the root of all affectivity, but also represents the very core of the human person. As von Hildebrand puts it:

> In saying that something "struck a man's heart," we wish to indicate how deeply this event affected him. We want to express not only that a given incident irked or angered him, but that it wounded him in the very core of his affective being. It is this sense of "heart" which we find in the words of our Lord, "For where thy treasure is, there thy heart also will be" (Mt 6:21). In this context, "heart" means the focal point of the affective sphere, that which is most crucially affected with respect to all else in that sphere.[18]

The heart is the wellspring of all human longing and is the source of all love. On this account, the essence of the human person is his heart, not his reason or will as the philosophical tradition would have us believe, but the innermost sphere of a person's being where one reaches out towards otherness in a quest for fulfillment, but in so doing makes oneself vulnerable and open to being touched by the other.

These reflections on the place of affectivity in the life of the human being in his comportment towards truth lead us finally to consider the fundamental characteristic of Christianity. The Christian is all too facilely identified with that of a believer, someone who has faith in the God of Jesus Christ. But it is arguable that this intellectualistic understanding of Christianity is not entirely true to its real essence. Christianity is not a religion based on faith, understood as the intellectual assent to certain dogmas and propositions about God, but on love. The God who is revealed in Christianity is the God of love, revealed in the person of Jesus Christ. The Gospel is firmly based on the two commandments

16 Biallowons, et al., *Karl Rahner in Dialogue: Conversations and Interviews, 1965-82*, 212.

17 See Kreeft, *Wisdom of the Heart*; Tallon, *Head and Heart* ; Steinbock, *Moral Emotions: Reclaiming the Evidence of the Heart.*

18 von Hildebrand, *The Heart*, 21.

of love: to love God with all one's soul, mind and heart, and to love one's neighbor as oneself. There are frequent exhortations to love not only one's neighbor, but also one's enemy—a truly daunting task. In the first letter to the Corinthians, St. Paul famously proclaims that love supersedes both faith and hope (1 Cor 13:13). The examples and references are too numerous to cite in their entirety. Although Christians generally know that love is supposed to be the cornerstone of their baptized identities as members of the Church, it is an all-too-common fault to lapse into the view that faith, which is a form of intellectual assent, defines what it means to be Christian. To follow Jesus does not mean to believe that God exists, much less to present persuasive arguments to unbelievers that God exists, but to love others and God with all one's heart. That is what Christianity is all about. That is what Christian truth is all about. Pascal was correct when he wrote:

> We make an idol of truth itself; for truth apart from charity is not God, but His image and idol, which we must neither love nor worship; and still less must we love or worship its opposite, namely, falsehood.[19]

The Need for a New Humanism

The crisis which Jacques Maritain was responding to in the first half of the 1940s, as evidenced in the collection of essays in *Pour la justice*, is the evil of Nazism spreading violently throughout Europe.[20] Maritain writes about the immense threats faced by European civilization from the Nazi ideology of totalitarian domination and enslavement, and he urges those free peoples of the West, especially the French and Americans, to resist this modern barbarism. Maritain identifies several causes of this evil situation. From the intellectual and philosophical tradition, Maritain blames Descartes for distorting the nature of reason and in so doing introducing a radical split or separation between the mind and the body.[21] Cartesian rationalism ushers from an epistemology which discards the body and the senses as vehicles for knowledge and emphasizes instead the immediate intellectual apprehension of truths. For Descartes, the body plays no role in the acquisition of knowledge, an epistemological position which Maritain calls an *angelism*, since the Cartesian knower operates in a similar manner to angels, who know directly without any bodily intervention.[22] This dualistic model in epistemology carried over into the religious domain

19 Pascal, *Pensées*, sec. 581, 161.

20 Maritain, *Pour la justice: Articles et discours (1940-1945).*

21 Maritain, *Pour la justice: Articles et discours*, 128–135.

22 For a more extensive discussion of Descartes' "angelism" see Maritain, *The Dream of Descartes, together with some other essays.*

and had repercussions for Christian faith. Descartes was, throughout his life, a pious Catholic, but his understanding and practice of his faith was determined by his philosophical commitments. Faith, for Descartes, was a product of the will, of a volitional affirmation of certain truths, and was not understood as an intellectual assent, as it was for somebody like Thomas Aquinas. As Maritain explains, according to Descartes, faith was about mere obedience, not knowing or understanding.[23] Given the separation between the intellect and the body, there came to be a split between the truths of reason and the articles of faith, the former being grasped by the mind and the latter affirmed by the will. This is a very significant development that marked an entire age. It is precisely the separation of these different components of truth into their own isolated compartments that has had the most disastrous effect on Western culture and civilization. The intellect operates independently of one's will and one's body; what one knows has nothing to do with what one believes. It is precisely this spirit of separation and compartmentalization that has fragmented the human person and contributed to the dismantling of the foundations of Western civilization which led ultimately to the horrors of war in the twentieth century.

This spirit of separation and dualism caused the fragmentation of the human person in the diverse dimensions of his life, this being the Cartesian inheritance. Maritain, therefore, argued that what we need to rescue us from this crisis is a movement of reunification and restoration of the lost wholeness. The modern turn to the individual had to be surmounted by a recuperation of the community and the notion that human persons exist for each other and in relationships of mutual dependence. At issue here is the attempt to rediscover a holistic anthropology and unified vision of the human being. For not only did Descartes distort the nature of truth by separating the intellect from the body and human experience in general, but he also bequeathed to the West a new understanding of human nature. Maritain considered this change in our understanding of the human person as another major cause of the upheavals experienced in World War II. As I have been describing it here, the key characteristic of the new, modern, Cartesian anthropology is this idea of separation or fragmentation. The modern human person is marked by disunity, brokenness, and disintegration. The modern self is the fragmented self. What this means practically is that the modern individual compartmentalizes the different parts or aspects of his or her life without bringing these parts together into a concerted whole or under the principle of a certain unity. We have already seen with Descartes that the chief distinction is that between the mind and the body: intellectual truth is independent of bodily experience. However, there are many other expressions of this same spirit of separation in modern culture, such

23 Maritain, *Pour la justice*, 132: "Au lieu d'être un don surnaturel de connaissance obscure, la foi deviendra pour Descartes un don surnaturel de simple obeisance."

as the split between the public and private spheres, the disharmony between the individual and society, and the rupture between heaven and earth, the eternal and temporal spheres of being. How one behaves in the public square or in the workplace is different from how one behaves at home. One's own individual beliefs and views have no bearing or impact on the values and goals of society as a whole. How one lives here on Earth has nothing to do with what happens after one dies.

Maritain acknowledges that Descartes's intentions were noble, insofar as he sought to preserve the autonomy of the sciences and philosophy against the encroachment of theology and faith, but that he went about it the wrong way and unfortunately produced harmful results. An important element in this modern anthropology for Maritain is precisely this abandonment of the Christian understanding of man. The secularization of culture contributed to the rejection of the Christian heritage of the West and replacing it with a reductionistic account of the human person, whether it be along the lines of the natural sciences or an aggressive form of atheism. This is why Maritain promoted a new anthropology or humanism, one that could overcome this spirit of fragmentation. Hence the need for an integral humanism, a humanism which could recapture that lost wholeness and completeness. Maritain was convinced that this integral humanism could only be a theocentric or Christian humanism, one that emphasized the human person's divine origins and finality. The anthropocentric humanism of modernity was by contrast self-enclosed and individualistic, whereas the theocentric humanism was open to transcendence and had a personalist foundation.

The Christian humanism which Maritain wanted to build up was based on the Biblical notion of the human being made in the image of God, as related in the book of Genesis. This is how Maritain describes it:

> The image of man involved in integral humanism is that of a being made of matter and spirit, whose body may have emerged from the historical evolution of animal forms, but whose immortal soul directly proceeds from divine creation. He is made for truth, capable of knowing God as the Cause of Being, by his reason, and of knowing Him in His intimate life, by the gift of faith. Man's dignity is that of an image of God, his rights derive as well as his duties from natural law, whose requirements express in the creature the eternal plan of creative Wisdom.[24]

At the heart of this Christian anthropology and humanism is the belief that the human person was created by God and is destined to be in communion with God. Furthermore, there is also the acknowledgement of the imperishable

24 Maritain, "Christian Humanism," 195–196.

essence of the human person which will enjoy eternal life with God. However, the true center of this doctrine is the Christian message that God is love and that we were made for love. The Christian idea of man focuses on this doctrine of the centrality of love as the moving force of creation. That which animates human decisions and actions is nothing other than love, a movement which leads on to higher reaches of being, culminating in the love of God Himself. For Maritain, love is to be understood as a *gift of self*, as he explains in the following way:

> If I think of the imperishable life of man, of that life which makes him "a god by participation" and, beginning here below, will consist in seeing God face to face, nothing in the world is more precious than human life. And the more a man gives himself, the more he makes this life intense within him. Every self-sacrifice, every gift of oneself involves, be it in the smallest way, a dying for the one we love. The man who knows that "after all, death is only an episode," is ready to give himself with humility, and nothing is more human and more divine than the gift of oneself, for "it is more blessed to give than to receive.".[25]

If we take a closer look at the Biblical notion of the *imago Dei*, we will better see what it involves as a doctrine on the nature of the human person as a being created in and for love. In Genesis 1:27 we read: "And God created the human being [*ha'adam*] in His image [*betsalmo*], in the image of God [*betselem'elohim*] He created him, male and female He created them."[26] In his commentary on the book of Genesis, Leon Kass informs us that the Hebrew word for "image" is *tselem*, from the root meaning "to cut off", "to chisel." *Tselem* is something cut or chiseled out, like a statue or a sculpture, and thus it is a resemblance of the original according to which has been chiseled out. The image—that which has been chiseled or sculpted—is in a unique position as being modeled on the original, but not being identical to the original. As Kass writes:

> Any image, insofar as it is an image, has a most peculiar manner of being: it both *is* and *is not* what is resembles... Although being merely a likeness, an image not only resembles but also points to, and is dependent for its very being on, that of which it is an image. Man, like any other creature, is simply what he is. But according to the text, he is—in addition—also something more insofar as he resembles the divine.[27]

25 Maritain, "Christian Humanism," 196–97.

26 Kass, *The Beginning of Wisdom: Reading Genesis,* 36. The Biblical translation is Kass's.

27 Kass, The Beginning of Wisdom: Reading Genesis, 37.

To be made in the image of God means that the human being has a resemblance to God, but at the same time is not God. In other words, the human person both is and is not God, for God is who the human being *resembles*, not who the human being *is*. After all, the human person is "the image of God," which suggests that human nature is in fact divine, God-like. However, being merely an "image," and not the original, suggests that this human nature is not identical to God and thus denotes something different from God. Such a view of the human being appears to be paradoxical insofar as the human being both is and is not that of which he is the image. How do we resolve this apparent paradox?

The Christian understanding of the human person is of a being whose essence is not yet fully actualized, who is still underway towards the completion or perfection of his nature. If we examine the Genesis story once again, we can notice that God had announced as good each thing that He had created, except in the case of the human being. When God created the human being, He did not immediately call him good. Although God does go on at the end of the seventh day to reflect on everything He had created and to judge everything as good, there is this curious omission when it comes to the creation of the human being. On one interpretation, this suggests that the human being is not good at the beginning of his existence. Leon Kass explains that this concept of "good" in Genesis does not mean "morally good," but rather what is "fitting" or "complete" or "perfect" or "fully formed."[28] Therefore, the human being is not complete or fully formed at the very beginning but must become so through time. Man's proper nature is not given to him straight away in the act of creation but is something that man himself must actualize or bring about. The reason that man is incomplete—not good—at the outset has to do with the human being's having been endowed with freedom. It is man's free will which can make man fully human, or, conversely, fail to achieve that end. Kass explains the situation thus:

> A moment's reflection shows that man as he comes into the world is not yet good. Precisely because he is the free being, he is also the incomplete or indeterminate being; what he becomes depends always (in part) on what he freely will choose to be. Let me put it more pointedly: precisely in the sense that man is in the image of God, man is not good—not determinate, finished, complete, or perfect. It remains to be seen whether man will *become* good, whether he will be able to complete himself (or to be completed). Man's lack of obvious goodness or completeness, metaphysically identical with his freedom, is, of course, the basis also of man's *moral* ambiguity. As the being with the greatest freedom of motion, able to change not only his path but also

28 Kass, The Beginning of Wisdom: Reading Genesis, 39.

> his way, man is capable of deviating widely from the way from which he is most suited or through which he—and the world around him—will most flourish. The rest of the biblical narrative elaborates man's moral ambiguity and God's efforts to address it, all in the service of making man "good"—complete, whole, holy.[29]

To make the human being complete and whole is nothing other than to make the human being *holy*, which is to say, like God.

The project of making the human being complete and whole is the very heart of an integral humanism. A crucial and indispensable element of this integral humanism is to recognize that God is the origin and goal of one's life. According to J. Augustine di Noia's discussion of the doctrine of *imago Dei*, he points out that in our secular age an unfortunate rift has occurred in the idea of human fulfillment and that of religious consummation.[30] In other words, many people today, including many Christians, believe that one can be a complete and happy human being without God and without religious faith. The purported Christians in this group are the ones who separate out their religious identity from the rest of their lives. So, for instance, one can attend Mass on Sundays, but then live the rest of the week as if God did not exist. Religion is, therefore, sidelined and made out to be irrelevant to the fundamental aspirations of human life. It is from this standpoint that one comes across statements to the effect that one can be perfectly happy and content in this life without God or that God is superfluous and unnecessary to a fulfilled human life. Such a way of thinking and living introduces a radical divide between this temporal or worldly existence and the life to come after death. There is, in other words, a separation that is enacted between how one lives now, and the life which God expects us to lead. Many see no connection between the two, this being an instance of the fragmentation of modern life. A Christian humanism, by contrast, aims to bridge this divide and to show how man's ethical life on Earth is essentially related to God's designs for man. For both ethics and religion focus on the same end: the fulfillment and realization of human nature. Put differently, ethics and religion are not at odds with each other, but cooperate for the same purpose of making the human being complete.

The Gift of Self as the Fulfillment of Self

So far, I have been arguing, with support from Jacques Maritain and others, that an anthropocentric or secular humanism views the human being as self-

29 Kass, The Beginning of Wisdom: Reading Genesis, 39.

30 Di Noia, O.P., "Imago Dei-Imago Christi: The Theological Foundations of Christian Humanism," 274.

sufficient and as not needing anything beyond or transcendent to his being for fulfillment and that, moreover, such a conception of the human person is deficient and even disastrous. By contrast, the Christian or integral humanism understands the human being as created in the image of God and, therefore, as possessing his completion and fulfillment only in God. The difficult question we need to ask ourselves at this juncture is how do we demonstrate that the integral humanism is, to borrow Maritain's terminology, the *true* humanism and that anthropocentric humanism is in fact deficient and fraudulent? How do we overcome the appearance, which is fostered by modern moral relativism, that these represent two equally viable and legitimate worldviews and that none is better than the other? Or put more concisely and pointedly: how does one convince a person who lives by the principles of anthropocentric humanism that the theocentric humanism is the true and more desirable vision of man? At stake in this dilemma is the persuasive power of the Gospel, which at its core is the spirit of evangelization. Can the Gospel still speak to a modern, secular civilization?

The modern separation referred to earlier between one's temporal ethical life and the demands of religious and divine law has reached a climax over the last century in the arena of human sexuality. It is not difficult to see in our world the results of the sexual revolution: widespread use of contraceptives, premarital and extramarital sexual relationships, the approbation extended to homosexuality, the increasing acceptance of deviant sexual behaviours, and the great numbers of divorced couples and broken families. What is striking is that many who consider themselves to be Catholic and members of the Church believe that the Church's moral and social teachings have no relevance or bearing on their sexual acts. Many Catholics accuse the Church of being out of touch with the realities of human relationships and even go so far as to condemn official Church doctrine as unrealistic and cruel. So, for instance, huge numbers of Catholic couples routinely use contraceptives as part of their sexual lives; and the Church's teaching that homosexual acts are gravely sinful is dismissed as intolerant and hateful. This spirit of dissent is so widespread in the Christian world itself, not to mention in secular society, that it is hard not to question whether the Church is right in its doctrines, given that this fragmented outlook on life is so infectious. What are we to make of this divide between ethical fulfillment and religious consummation?

St. John Paul II was deeply concerned about these problems in the twentieth century, which is why he devoted many of his writings on topics dealing with anthropology and sexuality. In the aftermath of Pope Paul VI's encyclical *Humanae Vitae*, which reaffirmed the Church's longstanding condemnation of artificial contraception, and the ensuing criticism and dissent which arose as a consequence, John Paul II wanted to provide a robust anthropological study which could give intellectual support to the Church's stance on issues relating to marriage, sexuality, and love. The fruit of this work was the *Theology of the Body*, otherwise referred to as "Man and Woman He Created Them," a collection of audiences John Paul II held from 1979 to 1984.[31] The entire project takes its inspiration from the passage in Matthew's Gospel (Mt 19:3–8) where Jesus is questioned about the indissolubility of marriage by the Pharisees. The passage at issue reads as follows:

> Some Pharisees came to him, and to test him they asked, "Is it lawful for a man to divorce his wife for any cause?" He answered, "Have you not read that the one who made them at the beginning 'made them male and female' and said, 'For this reason a man shall leave his father and mother and be joined to his wife, and the two shall become one flesh'? So they are no longer two, but one flesh. Therefore, what God has joined together, let no one separate." They said to him, "Why then did Moses command us to give a certificate of dismissal ande to divorce her?" He said to them, "It was because you were so hard-hearted that Moses allowed you to divorce your wives, but from the beginning it was not so."[32]

To investigate what Jesus means by "from the beginning it was not so," John Paul II is led to study more closely the narratives in Genesis regarding the creation of man. The familiar themes arise in this context: God's creation of man, man's loneliness, the creation of man as male and female, the original innocence, the subsequent fall from grace, and the promise of the redemption of the body in Christ. It is striking that John Paul II emphasizes that this creation story possesses both theological and anthropological truth. In other words, it is not relevant merely for Christians who happen to assent to the authority of the Bible, but that it describes truths about the human condition which all human beings can come to understand and accept. Yet the original insights that come from this study concentrate on the human being's bodily existence and the dimension of love which is manifested in and through the body.

John Paul II asserts that there is an essential connection between man being made in the image of God and his being a body. John Paul II writes: "Although in its normal constitution, the human body carries within itself the signs of sex and is by its nature male or female, *the fact that man is a 'body' belongs more deeply to the structure of the personal subject than the fact that in his somatic constitution he is also male or female.*"[33] It is from his body, in his state of original solitude, that God creates man as male and female, establishing the basis for the expression of interpersonal love. The love that male and female share between

31 John Paul II, *Man and Woman He Created Them.*

32 New Revised Standard Version

33 John Paul II, *Theology of the Body*, 157.

each other is a love that is anchored in and communicated through the body. By focusing on the primacy of the body in elucidating not only the meaning of human nature but also the meaning of love itself, John Paul II is rejecting all modern theories of love which portray it as a feeling or spiritual entity. Moreover, the concrete, bodily nature of love underscores the significance of the paragon of all love in Jesus Christ, who is the incarnate God.

Love, according to the doctrine of *Theology of the Body*, is a gift of self. The entire framework of this study is the *hermeneutics of the gift*, the recognition that creation itself and all that follows from it is sheer, unmerited gift. Since creation is a gift and man is made in the image of God, man is uniquely situated within the compass of creation to understand and express this gift of existence. But what exactly is a gift? How can we understand this concept? John Paul II is clear that a gift and the act of giving only make sense in the context of a relationship where there are at least two parties present: the giver and the receiver of the gift. God was able to give because He created man in his image. Man was created in the image of God and, as such, man was created for his own sake, which suggests that God created for the sake of man. In this way, John Paul II asserts that "[i]n the account of the creation of the visible world, giving has meaning only in relation to man."[34] This is the reason why man is the one creature who is truly able to understand the gift-nature of creation because man is the receiver of the gift of creation.

This hermeneutics of the gift is then expressed through the bodies of man as male and female. The revelatory quality of this teaching is that man and woman were created to be together and share their lives with one another. However, this union takes on a deeper, anthropological meaning insofar as man and woman are called to give reciprocally to each other. The gift of self happens in and through their bodies which results in the birth of new life in procreation. John Paul II describes this reality as the evocation of the spousal meaning of the body. The body is meant to be in communion with the other. Furthermore, this giving of oneself in one's bodily existence to the other is the very essence of love, mirroring God's free act of love in creating the world. This giving of oneself remains genuine as long as it is a true act of giving, namely, it is done for the sake of the other and not for some self-gain. If one is focused on the other and gives oneself to the other for the other's sake, then one has the very essence of spousal love. However, the moment when concupiscence enters the relationship is when this spousal love is perverted into a counterfeit love. Concupiscence is the corruption of the purity of heart and shows itself in the attitude of appropriation, of a grasping for the other in an attempt to control and possess the other. John Paul II is clear that concupiscence changes the

34 John Paul II, *Theology of the Body*, 180.

spousal relationship from one that is rooted in self-giving to the objectification of the other. The opposite of giving oneself to the other is to turn the other into an object to be possessed and appropriated.

Although much more could be said about John Paul II's *Theology of the Body*, this doctrine of the gift of self is at the very core of it. Its significance lies in the fact that human existence gains its meaning and nature from the free act of God to create, and that this act of giving is indelibly inscribed into the very heart of the human being which man and woman are then called upon to actualize in their own lives as a loving couple. Procreation is naturally a clear expression of this further expression of the gift. As the image of God, the human being discovers his identity as male and female in the act of giving oneself to the other—not in any vague, spiritual manner, but in the very concreteness of one's body. It is in the human body that all the mysteries of creation and love are concentrated, a mystery that far too many people ignore and neglect.

Conclusion

As a concluding thought, let us attempt to synthesize the main themes of the paper under the rubric of the restoration or renewal of human culture and civilization. If humanity is in crisis—now and always—then it is imperative that we somehow respond to this crisis. As I argued at the start of the chapter, a crisis is a decision, a choice, an act. It does not happen spontaneously of its own accord but arises because of freedom. Essentially, there are two options that stand before us, one of which we must choose. There is the anthropocentric humanism, which understands the human being as the master of his own destiny and as not requiring any assistance from anything external to him. Self-reliance and self-regard are two pivotal characteristics of the anthropocentric humanism. Then there is the real, life-giving alternative, the integral or theocentric humanism. This is the humanism of hope, love, and faith. It acknowledges the glory of God and the origin of all things in God. It confesses that the human being is not born complete but must grow and develop into perfection by means of the choices and decisions that he or she makes in life. The paradigm of this journey in becoming human is to live with others and to sacrifice oneself for others. Only by losing one's life will one gain it. Only by giving oneself to another person will one discover who God intended one to be.

Bibliography

Anscombe, G. E. M. "Knowledge and Reverence for Human Life." In *Human Life, Action and Ethics*. Edited by Mary Geach and Luke Gormally. Exeter: Imprint Academic, 2005: 59–66.

St. Anselm of Canterbury. *Proslogion*. Translated by Thomas Williams. Indianapolis: Hackett, 1995.

Aquinas, Thomas. *Treatise on Law: The Complete Text*. Translated by Alfred J. Freddoso. South Bend, Indiana: St. Augustine's Press, 2009.

Biallowons, Hubert, Harvey Egan, and Paul Imhof, eds. *Karl Rahner in Dialogue: Conversations and Interviews, 1965-82*. New York: Crossroad, 1986.

Bonhoeffer, Dietrich. *Creation and Fall – Temptation: Two Biblical Studies*. New York: Touchstone, 1997.

Dawkins, Richard. *The God Delusion*. London: Bantam, 2006.

de Lubac, S. J., Henri. *The Drama of Atheist Humanism*. San Francisco: Ignatius Press, 1995.

Descartes, René. *Meditations on First Philosophy*. Third Edition. Translated by Donald A. Cress. Indianapolis: Hackett, 1993.

Di Noia, O. P., Augustine J. "Imago Dei-Imago Christi: The Theological Foundations of Christian Humanism." *Nova et vetera*, Vol. 2, No. 2 (2004): 267–78.

John Paul II. *Man and Woman He Created Them: A Theology of the Body*. Translated by Michael Waldstein. Boston: Pauline Books & Media, 2006.

Kant, Immanuel. *Critique of Pure Reason*. Translated by Paul Guyer and Allen W. Wood. Cambridge: Cambridge University Press, 1998.

Kass, Leon. *The Beginning of Wisdom: Reading Genesis*. New York: Free Press, 2003.

Koterski, S. J., Joseph W. *An Introduction to Medieval Philosophy: Basic Concepts*. Wiley-Blackwell, 2009.

Kreeft, Peter. *Christianity for Modern Pagans*. San Francisco: Ignatius Press, 1993.

———. *Wisdom of the Heart*. Gastonia, North Carolina: TAN, 2020.

Langan, Thomas. *The Catholic Tradition*. Columbia, Missouri: University of Missouri Press, 1998.

Lennox, John C. *Gunning for God: Why the New Atheists are Missing the Target*. Oxford: Lion Books, 2011.

Maritain, Jacques. "Christian Humanism." In *The Range of Reason*. New York: Charles Scribner's Sons, 1952: 185–99.

———. *Pour la justice: Articles et discours (1940-1945)*. New York: Éditions de la maison française, Inc., 1945.

———. *The Dream of Descartes, together with some other essays*. Translated by Mabelle L. Andison. New York: Philosophical Library, 1944.

Pascal, Blaise. *Pensées*. Translated by W. F. Trotter. Mineola, New York: Dover Publications, 2003.

St. Paul. *The First Letter of Paul to the Corinthians*. New Revised Standard Version.

Scheler, Max. *The Human Place in the Cosmos*. Translated by Manfred S. Frings. Northwestern University Press, 2008.

Steinbock, Anthony J. *Moral Emotions: Reclaiming the Evidence of the Heart*. Evanston, Illinois: Northwestern University Press, 2014.

Suto, Taki. "Virtue and Knowledge: Connatural Knowledge According to Thomas Aquinas." *The Review of Metaphysics* 58 (September 2004): 61–79.

Tallon, Andrew. *Head and Heart*. New York: Fordham University Press, 1997.

Taylor, Charles. *A Secular Age*. Cambridge, Massachusetts: The Belknap Press, 2007.

von Hildebrand, Dietrich. *The Heart: An Analysis of Human and Divine Affectivity*. Edited by John Henry Crosby. South Bend, Indiana: St. Augustine's Press, 2007.

Epilogue

Where Do We Go from Here?

Scott D. G. Ventureyra

Over the past few weeks, I have chronicled some of the important events that have come to shape the direction of this spiritual battle. On March 4, 2022, I decided to stop making additions in order to finally publish this book. As I mentioned in the Preface, this book will serve as a historical witness to what has transpired right before our eyes. It exposes the machinations of governments, health organizations, the globalist elites, Big Pharma, Big Tech, and the legacy media. Everything has come to this pivotal moment in history.

The West is crumbling at an accelerated rate. The unfolding erasure of history, objective morality, and truth has paved the way for our current predicament. We are now standing at the precipice of the future of human civilization. As we have seen, the attacks on the human person are unrelenting, malicious, multifaceted, and wide-ranging in their scope and breadth, from the time prior to birth until the moment of death. If you are granted the "right" to live, then you must be prepared for unending assaults on your, mind, body, and soul. Nevertheless, the spirit of man and the greatness of God are infinitely greater than any of these assaults.

Within less than two years we have seen the ever-hastening erosion of our civil liberties. Bodily autonomy and freedom of conscience are constantly under siege. The reckless ways in which our governments, medical establishment, judicial system, media, and Big Tech are colluding and working against sovereign citizens of the world presents an unprecedented attack on the human person. The only thing that supersedes the ignorance of such people is their arrogance, as we have seen from those who genuflect at the altar of COVID, regressive ideologies (woke culture, political correctness, identity politics, socialism, communism, etc.), the follies of scientific materialism, and sheer human depravity. Silence and dismissal of what is happening right before our eyes will make us complicit in the ever-enveloping moral evil that is penetrating the hearts of men and women at exponential rates. So, how do we make sense of the nonsense? Through our experience of the world. We must use legitimate science, not politicized science. We must be willing to follow the evidence wherever it leads. We mustn't deny our human experience of the world since we are composite beings of mind, body, and soul. Thus, the phenomenal experience of the world (the five senses) works in unison with the intellect (the rational; capacity for logic) and through our will act to bring about the maximum good in the world. An adherence to the natural law where all humans have inherent rights granted to us, not by legislation, but by God. Under natural law, our civil laws are based on morality, ethics, and what is intrinsically right. This is opposed to what is known as "positive law" or "man-made law" as defined by statutes and common law, which increasingly have not come to reflect the natural law, as has become more evident in the moral decadence of the West and in this false pandemic. These aspects of human existence make us fully human. This is the essence of the *imago Dei* (image of God). We must be vigilant and follow God, the Bible promises that as you draw closer to Him, he will draw nearer to you (Jas 4:8).

By way of regressive ideologies, the eradication of truth and God in the education system, the propagandizing of socialism, the degradation of life, the human person, and the trampling of our civil liberties, we are ushering an era of global communism. If people don't unite and speak up, politicians, media personalities, and others who are subservient to the globalist elites, will continue to live lives of luxury, while the rest of us, "we the people," will suffer under their totalitarian rule. What is coming with the Great Reset includes: loss of property, wealth, and job opportunities, more mandates, more passports, more restrictions, social credit scoring, and the loss of basic human rights for those who are not subservient to this Globalist Agenda, also known as the New World Order.

Given the current cultural and political trajectory, we can say that historical progress is not linear but cyclical when we carefully learn from history and the persistence of reoccurring dark periods in human history, as evident in the stigmatization of certain groups. Most humans that do not ground the experience of the world in God, truth, and the natural law, surrender to their tribal proclivities towards groupthink which are susceptible to repeat the mistakes of the past. The regressive "woke culture" is an example of this. The woke phenomenon, much like the COVID madness, is one plagued with censorship and punishment for dissent. This is similar to what happened in Nazi Germany, the Soviet Union, and currently in Communist China.

The atheist Richard Dawkins may have some insight here when applying one of his sayings to the inanity of regressive ideologies and the blindness of the COVID dystopian delusion: "It is absolutely safe to say that if you meet somebody who claims [to believe in wokeness and the COVID single narrative], that person is ignorant, stupid or insane (or wicked, but I'd rather not consider that)."[1] Although Dawkins had evolution deniers in mind, I think this quote

1 Richard Dawkins, "In Short: Non-Fiction." *New York Times*, April 9, 1989. https://www.nytimes.com/1989/04/09/books/in-short-nonfiction.html.

fits quite nicely with the drone-like unthinking compliance and mass formation psychosis we have seen.

It is important not to ignore or underestimate the role relativism and scientific materialism have played in the destruction of core Judeo–Christian principles. These core principles are ways of combatting the malaise and various maladies we face in the West. Systemic corruption and outright evil have played in this current nightmarish psychosis of the twenty first century. This is found in all of the godless, materialist philosophies which guide nihilistic ideologies, including abortion, child abuse and sacrifice,[2] attacks on the family, on the freeness of the individual, gender ideology, and the COVID-19 medical tyranny. Make no mistake, the world is in a diabolical trance. Will reason, arguments, evidence, and adherence to objective moral values and duties save us from this quagmire? I don't know. Even though 2+2 still does not equal 5, it seems that that alone cannot save us. At least not until people wake up from their slumber. When falsehoods are so rampant, the truth becomes incomprehensible. Our individual and collective eyes distort reality because of our fallen nature, but God unveils the truth to us by His salvific gift and aptitude to see the truth.

No matter how desperate a situation may get, we must accept that every event that unfolds is part of God's eternal plan: "'For my thoughts are not your thoughts, neither are your ways my ways,' declares the Lord. 'As the heavens are higher than the earth, so are my ways higher than your ways and my thoughts than your thoughts'" (Isa 55:8–9). We must discern the role we play in God's plan. The question is: will we choose to embrace it or oppose it? People's dormancy and willful ignorance will not absolve them. There is no neutral position in the face of injustice; silence is complicity. Au fond, as I have said before, this is a spiritual battle, and this is the best way to understand what is transpiring throughout the globe. People are making choices and choosing sides. The apostle John puts this in the simplest of terms: "We know that we belong to God, and the whole world is under the power of the evil one" (1 John 5:19). We either choose between the world (Satan) or God and His Kingdom—

2 At the end of 2021, Ghislaine Maxwell was convicted of recruiting and grooming teenage girls for Jeffrey Epstein. Although doubtful, the hope is that she will bring down all the "elites" that frequented Epstein's Island and engaged in pedophilic activities with underage girls. Prince Andrew has renounced his military affiliations and royal patronages amidst a sex abuse lawsuit. Unfortunately, it is most likely Maxwell will be used as the scapegoat for many other politicians and celebrities that frequented the island. See Victoria Bekiempis, "Ghislaine Maxwell found guilty in sex-trafficking trial." *The Guardian*, December 29, 2021. https://www.theguardian.com/us-news/2021/dec/29/ghislaine-maxwell-sex-trafficking-trial-verdict. For an eye-opening documentary exposing child trafficking and sacrifice that has been banned by all media platforms, see "Out of Shadows": https://www.outofshadows.org/. See also Ann Coulter, "The Great Epstein Cover-up." *Breibart*, January 13, 2022. https://www.breitbart.com/politics/2022/01/13/ann-coulter-the-great-epstein-cover-up-part-2/?utm_medium=social&utm_source=facebook&fbclid=IwAR3Y9zY9YWEiRWSAshxZxg-j3CViQAITdQfcYHI7lZqtE1nvzB3b4e-ze8c.

under a biblical context there is no third option. Satan may be very powerful in his ability to influence and seduce but God is infinitely more powerful. Theologian Sam Storms explains the influence of Satan:

> He exerts an insidious influence on the financial world, business and industry, athletics, the stock market, the banking system, political institutions and parties, entertainment, the internet, education, the family, the home, neighborhood, civic clubs and social service organizations, and country clubs. We must reckon with a global satanic influence.[3]

This would make sense of how much of the developments and engines of propaganda (government, Big Pharma, Big Tech, mainstream media, legal system, and even the medical establishment), before and especially under the COVID tyranny, have been in lockstep with one another.

As unpalatable and superstitious as the spiritual dimension and the demonic may sound to many twenty-first century ears, it is the best way to understand the world's situation. I have struggled with accepting this reality for quite some time and regarded it as irrational and remained agnostic to the existence of demons and the devil. But, I have found that this reality in opposition to God makes the most sense of my internal struggles, the struggles of humanity, and the struggle between good and evil. Given a theological backdrop there is no other way to understand our inner darkness and the outer darkness of the world.

Where do we go from here? Do we accept Klaus Schwab and the globalists' "Great Reset," or do we reject it and fight for a "Great Reckoning" (bringing the heavy hand of justice to them) and "Great Take Over" (the seizing and re-distribution of *their* wealth)? If we want the "Great Reckoning"[4] and the "Great Take Over,"[5] whereby the culprits who orchestrated and supported the false pandemic will be held accountable, we cannot remain complacent. Part of the macabre plan has been to displace Judeo–Christian principles. Must we also reject godless regressive ideologies for love and truth, or do we remain complacent to identity politics and cancel culture? They all have the same satanic source, and all are bent on the destruction of Judeo–Christian precepts. In order for this to happen there needs to be a large awakening. Unfortunately, many Christian brethren have been led astray by the father of lies (John 8:44).

3 Sam Storms, *Understanding Spiritual Warfare: A Comprehensive Guide* (Grand Rapids: Zondervan, 2021).

4 Scott Lively, "COVID: Will it be a 'Great Reckoning' for Big Pharma?" *WND*, January 10, 2022. https://www.wnd.com/2022/01/covid-will-great-reckoning-big-pharma/?utm_source=Email&utm_medium=wnd-newsletter&utm_campaign=dailyam&utm_content=newsletter&ats_es=c7eb08c99666ed3496daaa702b24bd0c.

5 Nick Buxton and Lynn Fries, "Global Coup d'État: Mapping the Corporate Takeover of Global." *Transnational Institute*, February 18, 2021. https://www.tni.org/en/article/global-coup-detat.

Catholics, Reformed and Orthodox Christians, and others must be vigilant against the unholy union of Jorge Bergoglio (Pope Francis) and Klaus Schwab.[6] One may ask what a supporter of liberation theology[7] may have in common with a wealthy globalist like Schwab? Schwab, as chairman and founder of the World Economic Forum, and Francis, a follower of liberation theology (Christian theology that has been adulterated by Marxism), agree that private property and wealth should be redistributed. In October of 2020, Bergoglio, in his encyclical letter, *Fratelli Tutti*, declares the following:

> Business abilities, which are a gift from God, should always be clearly directed to the development of others and to eliminating poverty, especially through the creation of diversified work opportunities. The right to private property is always accompanied by the primary and prior principle of the subordination of all private property to the universal destination of the earth's goods, and thus the right of all to their use.[8]

Similarly, Schwab and Malleret clearly state part of the agenda behind the "Great Reset "in their book, *COVID-19: The Great Reset*: "First and foremost, the post-pandemic era will usher in a period of massive wealth redistribution, from the rich to the poor and from capital to labour."[9] Indeed, Bergoglio has given his stamp of approval of the "Great Reset" in his 43,000-word encyclical.[10] This falls in line with the World Economic Forum's mantra that has been dubbed a "conspiracy theory": "You'll own nothing, and you'll be happy."[11] In a video laying out the 2030 Agenda, created by the World Economic Forum, Schwab's eight predictions, including loss of property ownership for 2030, are outlined.[12]

6 Strangely, recently I have found to have a stronger affinity to many outside of my faith, secularized beliefs, than many of your own (in my case, Catholics).

7 Liberation theology is a theology of the oppressed. It attempts to baptize Christian theology with Marxist and socialist ideologies. It also tolerates violence against leaders of opposition.

8 Pope Francis, encyclical *Fratelli Tutti*, October 3, 2020. https://www.vatican.va/content/francesco/en/encyclicals/documents/papa-francesco_20201003_enciclica-fratelli-tutti.html#_ftn95.

9 Klaus Schwab and Thierry Malleret, *COVID-19: The Great Reset* (Geneva, Switzerland: Forum Publishing, 2020), 78.

10 John Letzing, "Here's the pope's prescription for resetting the global economy in response to COVID-19." *World Economic Forum*, October 9, 2020. https://www.weforum.org/agenda/2020/10/here-s-the-pope-s-prescription-for-resetting-the-global-economy-in-response-to-covid-19/.

11 The Bigger Picture, "World Economic Forum: 'You'll own nothing, and you'll be happy' (While Oligarchs Own Everything)." YouTube Video, October 28, 2020. https://www.youtube.com/watch?v=ER04dbt5p74; see also Russell Brand, "'You Will Own Nothing and You Will Be Happy'? – The Great Reset." *Take Back Our World*, September 6, 2021. https://takebackour.world/you-will-own-nothing-and-you-will-be-happy-the-great-reset/.

12 The Bigger Picture, "World Economic Forum: 'You'll own nothing, and you'll be happy' (While Oligarchs Own Everything)."

It is important to note that it is highly improbable that Schwab and his co-author, Malleret, were able to write a complex and wide-ranging book like *COVID-19: The Great Reset* in only four months. This suggests that it was premeditated. Unsurprisingly, Bergoglio, being a supporter of the "Great Reset," has also unflinchingly supported the Global Warming Green Agenda, mandated COVID-19 vaccines, vaccine passports, gender equality, massive migration, and other controversial social actions. This is a sinister merging, for the sake of gaining large support from Catholics, other Christians, and members of other religions including the youth, the poor, and disenfranchised. All for the sinister goal of exploiting and robbing the middle class for the global technocratic fascistic agenda. On December 29, 2021, Canadian globalist puppet Justin Trudeau made the following incendiary and alarming remarks about the unvaccinated population in Canada:

> We are going to end this pandemic by proceeding with the vaccination. We all know people who are deciding whether or not they are willing to get vaccinated, and we will do our very best to try to convince them. However, there is still a part of the population (that) is fiercely against it.
>
> They don't believe in science/progress and are very often misogynistic and racist. It's a very small group of people, but that doesn't shy away from the fact that they take up some space.
>
> This leads us, as a leader and as a country, to make a choice: Do we tolerate these people? Over 80% of the population of Quebec have done their duty by getting the shot. They are obviously not the issue in this situation.[13]

First, maybe the vaccination numbers are exaggerated. Second, it shows how desperate the Canadian government is to roll out the plan and at all costs. But the question is, do we tolerate such a disgraceful prime minister? The leader of the People's Party of Canada, Maxime Bernier, has rightfully said, "If the Liberals really want to combat hate speech, the first thing they should do is get rid of their leader."[14] He also said in a tweet that Trudeau is a "fascist psychopath."[15] The truth is that most of the politicians and globalist leaders are psychopaths. Trudeau's tyranny knows no end; he was recently caught by

13 Dave Naylor, "Trudeau calls the unvaccinated racist and misogynistic extremists." *Western Standard,* December 29, 2021. https://westernstandardonline.com/2021/12/trudeau-calls-the-unvaccinated-racist-and-misogynistic-extremists/.

14 Helena Hanson, "Maxime Bernier Just Called Trudeau A 'Fascist Psychopath' For Dragging Anti-Vaxxers." *Narcity,* September 2, 2021. https://www.narcity.com/maxime-bernier-just-called-trudeau-a-facist-psychopath-for-dragging-anti-vaxxers.

15 Hanson, "Maxime Bernier Just Called Trudeau A 'Fascist Psychopath' For Dragging Anti-Vaxxers."

Conservatives using the Public Health Authority of Canada (PHAC) to track the movement of 33 million Canadians.[16]

As expected, Canada secured COVID-19 vaccine contracts with Pfizer and Moderna for "enough doses to give two or three more mRNA shots to every Canadian, every year, until at least 2024."[17] And rest assured that Trudeau has Canadian's best interest at heart: "Trudeau said Monday [January 17, 2022] there will be third and fourth booster doses available in this country if or when they're needed."[18] As I predicted, dose after dose will be administered and mandated for a virus that poses little threat to most people unless they have several comorbidities. But the tyranny and absurdities continue. Quebec, at one point, announced a health tax for those unvaccinated against COVID-19.[19] Should they start taxing obese people for clogging up the healthcare system? What about smokers? Alcoholics? The elderly? Does that mean a tax will be imposed for anyone who misses a dose for the next few years? Desperate measures for desperate people.

Vardit Ravitsky, an Israeli–Canadian bio-ethicist who leads the COVID-19 Impact Committee of the Pierre Elliott Trudeau Foundation, weighed on this Quebec tax. Ravitsky believes that the unvaccinated should not be allowed to move "freely."[20] We should not be surprised given the foundation she represents. She also thinks that these "second-class citizens" should only be able to access grocery stores and pharmacies. Tragically, this woman lacks a basic understanding of history, given her Jewish heritage. She should know what the stigmatization of certain groups can lead to. She also does not realize that vaccine passports are a total failure in stopping transmission. Furthermore, does she not keep abreast with the science? Does she not know that the vaccines are

16 Ima Stoner, "Justin Trudeau Gets Caught SECRETLY SPYING on Nearly Every Canadian." YouTube Video, January 11, 2022. https://www.youtube.com/watch?v=5RrwgV2GFd8.

17 The Canadian Press, "Federal contracts poised to deliver 100 million vaccine doses annually for years." *CBC*, January 11, 2022. https://www.cbc.ca/news/politics/pfizer-moderna-contracts-2024-1.6311559?fbclid=IwAR3j0L9EAA91MPEHI7qsUsTShL_wo4-jRE_TmTpQLcRBeFseRqQuROpz92s.

18 The Canadian Press, "Federal contracts poised to deliver 100 million vaccine doses annually for years." *CBC*, January 11, 2022. https://www.cbc.ca/news/politics/pfizer-moderna-contracts-2024-1.6311559?fbclid=IwAR3j0L9EAA91MPEHI7qsUsTShL_wo4-jRE_TmTpQLcRBeFseRqQuROpz92s.

19 Annabelle Olivier, "Quebec to impose a tax on people who are unvaccinated from COVID-19." *Global News*, January 11, 2022. https://globalnews.ca/news/8503151/quebec-to-impose-a-tax-on-people-who-are-unvaccinated-from-covid-19/?fbclid=IwAR1fzkRJ3Gp4RCz3C5R_470SaOKNvHlCmQ8RmnK55dKYCvrKwcMc83BYjiQ.

20 Ian Miles Cheong, "'We cannot allow you to circulate freely': Bioethicist delivers warning to unvaccinated Canadians." *Rebel News*, January 12, 2022. https://www.rebelnews.com/we_cannot_allow_you_to_circulate_freely_bioethicist_delivers_warning_to_unvaccinated_canadians?fbclid=IwAR0n_DMBgyiY7iXNT9szIli2rKW5-x0Wr6WtkFM_Km4XSYHExhOh_4u9FFQ.

ineffective? One questions the grounds of her "ethics." Clearly this so-called ethicist has her feet firmly planted in mid-air.

Trudeau, and any other politician who support vaccine mandates and taxes, and the repeated use of boosters, do not care about our health. In fact, their goals have nothing to do with our health. European Union regulators have warned that repeated COVID-19 boosters could damage the immune system,[21] most likely irreparably if you don't die in the process. These shots will make people "immune compromised" since they will lower your CD8+ T and white blood cell count. Consequently, you will be susceptible to severe illness or death from the common cold, like AIDS patients were throughout the 1980s (Vaccine Acquired Immunodeficiency Syndrome). In the past few weeks, I've seen three of my friends' fathers pass away shortly after receiving their first booster (third dose). It is interesting to note that Luc Montagnier, Nobel-winning co-discoverer of HIV (human immunodeficiency virus), died at the age of 89 on February 8, 2022, not long after voicing his discontents about the COVID vaccines. On January 8, 2022, in a speech given to the Luxembourg Parliament, Montagnier had the following scathing remarks to make about the COVID-19 vaccines:

> These vaccines are poisons. They are not real vaccines. The mRNA allows its message to be transcribed throughout the body, uncontrollably. No one can say for each of us where these messages will go. This is therefore a terrible unknown. And in fact we are now learning that this is a work published over a year ago that these mRNAs contain an area that we can call prion,[22] which is an area capable of introducing protein modifications in an unpredictable way. As a doctor I knew 21 people who received 2 doses of Pfizer vaccine, there is another person who received Moderna. The 21 died of Creutzfeldt-Jakob disease caused by prions. The 3 vaccines Pfizer, AstraZeneca, Moderna contain a sequence identified by Information Technology as transformation into a prion. There is therefore a known risk to human health.[23]

21 Irina Anghel, "Repeat booster shots spur European warning on immune-system risks." *BNN Bloomberg*, January 11, 2022. https://www.bnnbloomberg.ca/repeat-booster-shots-spur-european-warning-on-immune-system-risks-1.1706083?fbclid=IwAR02nzwWZ59Crg468dr_ovq7J54u82BsMTzBAjwRkvT8lW_AzFwIhrv6ytc.

22 A prion is a specific type of protein that can attack and destroy healthy cells, so that they can no longer recover.

23 See Luc Montagnier, "'They Are Not Vaccines, They Are Poisons' – Speech To The Luxembourg Parliament." *World Freedom Alliance*, February 10, 2022. https://worldfreedomalliance.org/au/news/luc-montagnier-they-are-not-vaccines-they-are-poisons-speech-to-the-luxembourg-parliament/; see also his warning about the vaccine creating variants: Renee Nal, "Nobel Laureate Warns Doctors: 'Vaccines are Not for Killing, They are for Shielding' (Video)." *RAIR Foundation USA*, January 17, 2022. https://rairfoundation.com/nobel-laureate-warns-doctors-vaccines-are-not-for-killing-they-are-for-shielding-video/.

Taking this into account, and Trudeau's statement above: he is hell bent on harming his people, and he wants premiers to follow him. If this continues, no one will be safe. Ronald MacDonald Houses stated that they would deny treatment and evict anyone five years of age and older if they were not vaccinated.[24] They were willing to evict a five-year-old boy that was undergoing treatment for leukemia. How is this about our health and protecting the vulnerable? If these machinations don't sound alarm bells, what will? Luckily, because of public outrage, they reversed this evil policy. Unfortunately, for the most part, people are willingly entering the slaughterhouse and denouncing those who are not joining them. This is true of medical staff supporting this wickedness. It is as Voltaire once said: "Anyone who can make you believe absurdities; can make you commit atrocities."[25]

In January of 2022, Canadian writer, Henry Makow, made some startling claims about vaccine mandates, more loss of civil liberties and human rights, and increased strains on the supply chain.[26] What was most alarming was that some of these breaches of the Constitution Act of 1982 have begun to take place with mobility and equality rights. Makow stated:

> By as early as late next week the Federal Government will break Canada's Constitution Act 1982 by imposing an unconstitutional mandate that removes the irrevocable Right To Ones Own Autonomy And Anatomy.
>
> That mandate will imply that every citizen in Canada no longer has the right and ability to make their own choices and decisions, and, that every citizen in Canada must comply with any medical treatment or experiment proposed to them by any level of government.
>
> Wait, it gets so much better... On top of the illegal mandate that will remove your right to make your own decisions regarding your own body and path in life, they are going to remove the rest of your rights and freedoms too! The Federal Government is also going to impose the Emergency Measures Act. This Act will be applied across all provinces and territories. The Emergency Measures Act suspends Section 2 and Sections 7 through 15 of the Charter of Rights and Freedoms for a term of up to 5 years before a Parliamentary or Judiciary review in needed for an extension.
>
> This means no citizen will have the freedom of conscience or religion. No citizen will have the freedom of thought, belief, opinion

24 Harley Sims, "B.C. family being evicted from Ronald McDonald House due to vaccine status." *True North*, January 12, 2022. https://tnc.news/2022/01/12/b-c-family-being-evicted-from-ronald-mcdonald-house-due-to-vaccine-status/.

25 Voltaire (François-Marie Arouet), *Questions sur les miracles*, (1765). For a direct translation see: Voltaire, *On Injustice*.

26 Craig Lord, "Truckers warn vaccine mandate at U.S. border could worsen supply chain issues." *Global News*, January 11, 2022. https://globalnews.ca/news/8503670/trucking-vaccine-mandate-us-canada-border/.

> and expression. Nor will any citizen have freedom of peaceful assembly and freedom of association. The right to Life, Liberty and Security will be removed. The Government, and its authorities, can search, seize, detain, arrest any citizen or property without just cause or any legal recourse. Citizens will no longer be protected from cruel and unusual treatment or punishment. And, any citizen can be discriminated against by authorities based on race, national or ethnic origin, colour, religion, sex, age and mental or physical disability.
>
> The Rights and Freedoms that Canadians today take for granted of could all be gone by as early as next week. Welcome to the tyrannical dystopia Canadian compliance has allowed to destroy a once-great place to live. [27]

However, in a major recent shift, on January 26, 2022, The Justice Centre for Constitutional Freedoms filed a lawsuit in Federal Court seeking to overturn the federal government's unlawful mandatory Covid-19 vaccine requirements for air travellers.[28] According to the JCCF:

> On October 30, 2021, the federal government announced that anyone travelling by air, train, or ship, must be fully vaccinated. The travel vaccination mandate has prevented approximately 6 million unvaccinated Canadians (15% of Canada's population) from travel within Canada and prevents them from flying out of Canada. Some of the Canadians involved in the lawsuit cannot travel to help sick loved ones, get to work, visit family and friends, take international vacations, and live ordinary lives.
>
> The main applicant in the case is former Newfoundland Premier, The Honourable A. Brian Peckford. Mr. Peckford, pictured [see link], is the only surviving drafter and signatory 40 years after the 1982 Constitution and the Charter of Rights and Freedoms was enacted.[29]

Peckford, in an interview with Jordan Peterson, discusses how Part I of the Constitution Act of 1982, the Canadian Charter of Rights and Freedoms, has been violated by federal and provincial governments. Governments have

27 Henry Makow, "Canada- Are 'Vaccines' about to Become Mandatory?" henrymakow.com, January 10, 2022. https://www.henrymakow.com/2022/01/-have-canadians-run-out.html?fbclid=IwAR32MP6fB-TwYXlzD7beZS8af22qVTBbNNzGEgSEsfOXglOqr35AwRfMS_k. See also Constitution Act, 1982. https://laws-lois.justice.gc.ca/eng/const/.

28 See Notice of Application for Judicial Review, https://www.jccf.ca/wp-content/uploads/2022/01/2022-01-26-Notice-of-Application-FILING-COPY-REDACTED_Redacted.pdf?mc_cid=923a6baff1&mc_eid=31650729a2.

29 The Justice Centre for Constitutional Freedoms, "The Charter's only living signatory sues Canada over travel mandates." January 26, 2022. https://www.jccf.ca/the-charters-only-living-signatory-sues-canada-over-travel-mandates/?mc_cid=923a6baff1&mc_eid=31650729a2.

breached fundamental freedoms, democratic rights, and mobility rights of sovereign Canadians. Peckord also discusses the collusion between the media and government, and the suppression of early COVID treatments.[30] It seems that good changes are about to come.

Makow, on his blog, also made some interesting remarks concerning the connectivity that truck drivers enjoy with their CB radios, which is much more difficult to monitor and censor than any media application:

> Within two weeks over 30,000 truckers who drive the Canadian border are going to quit because Canada is going to mandate the vax for international crossings, and that's just on the Canadian side, lots of American truckers are going to quit too. 70 percent of what goes into Canada arrives on truck, with an enormous portion of the remaining 30 percent arriving on rail. Rail workers will also be quitting due to the mandates. What position will that leave Canada in?
>
> Truckers and rail workers are at an intelligence level that broadly accepts the vax. That level is defined as: Professional, but not a PhD. Why would that group be so "vaccine hesitant"?? Is it because they saw too many sports players die? Is it because radios can't be censored? I'll say it like it is: Despite the decline in CB radios in use on trucks, truckers are still connected. They are the hardest group to censor because they HAVE TO communicate one way or another. Is that why so many truckers are refusing the shot? Is it because they can't be shut up??[31]

For a period of roughly 3 weeks in February, the truckers fought against Trudeau's federal medical tyranny. On January 13, in a period of less than 24 hours, the Canadian federal government flip-flopped on mandatory vaccination for truckers crossing the border. First, they dropped it,[32] but then they finally went through with the absurd mandate.[33] Hopefully, the rest of Makow's claims do not come to pass. But Trudeau hosted a call with all provincial and territorial premiers which was closed to the media.[34]

30 Jordan Peterson, "Canadian Constitutional Crisis | Brian Peckford | The Jordan B. Peterson Podcast S4: E78." YouTube Video, January 26, 2022. https://www.youtube.com/watch?v=EdhFuMDLBDM.

31 Makow, "Canada- Are 'Vaccines' about to Become Mandatory?"

32 Steve Scherer, "Canada drops vaccine mandate for its truckers after pressure from industry." *Reuters*, January 12, 2022. https://www.reuters.com/world/americas/canadian-truckers-stay-exempt-covid-19-vaccine-requirements-2022-01-13/.

33 Christopher Reynolds, "Ottawa to go ahead with trucker vaccine mandate after stating it would scrap it." *CP24*, January 13, 2022. https://www.cp24.com/news/ottawa-to-go-ahead-with-trucker-vaccine-mandate-after-stating-it-would-scrap-it-1.5739047.

34 https://pm.gc.ca/en/news/readouts/2022/01/10/prime-minister-justin-trudeau-holds-36th-call-premiers-covid-19-response.

How do people of good will combat this global dystopian nightmare? First, a critical mass is required to combat this, i.e., a significant number of people who can bring about a radical change in behaviour, opinions, and action against the Global Coup d'État. More people need to wake up, but time is running out. Recall in Chapter 42, we explored Mattias Desmet's mass formation psychosis. He argues that 30 percent buy into a narrative without any questioning, and around 30 percent don't go along with it, leaving 40 percent who can go either way but do not speak out. If most or even a significant percentage of this 40 percent realize that the narrative is bunk, then that can help gather a critical mass to topple the dominant narrative. I suspect and hope that those who realize they have been duped into taking the injections and still face restrictions like lockdowns and mask wearing, etc., will resist and peacefully non-comply, given the fact that their immune systems will be increasingly weakened dose after dose and making them susceptible to getting ill and dying more easily. Not to mention if they start to see their loved ones die or seriously harmed. What is needed is a nudge for the 40 percent. Not unlike the defiance against communist authority, which Pope John Paul II inspired, stirring a "revolution of conscience" and paving the way for "the nonviolent political Revolution of 1989."[35] (In this respect, the stark contrast between Francis, who sides with the globalists, and John Paul II couldn't be any more apparent.) John Paul II saw religion as a peaceful catalyst for political change.

After a period of strikes which ended in Gdańsk, Polish workers chose to use their Catholic faith as a peaceful symbolism of defiance by leaving behind icons. Perhaps with the new vaccination policy, truckers crossing the border between the US and Canada have taken a similar stance of civil disobedience that has sparked a movement around the world, marking another pivotal moment in history. Truckers in Canada and some from the US have come together to fight for freedom. They have formed the longest convoy in human history (spanning 70 kilometers long).[36] A GoFundMe campaign which had exceeded $10 million for these freedom fighters was clawed away by the Government of Canada.[37] They initially arrived in Ottawa on January 29 to combat federal and provincial mandates which are unscientific, draconian,

35 George Weigel, *Witness to Hope: The Biography of Pope John Paul II* (New York: Harper Perennial), 612.

36 Joe Warmington, "'Freedom' truckers may form world's longest convoy." *Toronto Sun*, January 25, 2022. https://torontosun.com/news/local-news/warmington-freedom-truckers-may-form-worlds-longest-convoy.

37 The funds were since seized and refunded because of legal threats made to GoFundMe, not by Canadian politicians but by governor of Florida, Ron DeSantis. The other funding site GiveSendGo was hacked and the information of roughly 92,000 donors were leaked: David Gilbert, "Hackers Just Leaked the Names of 92,000 'Freedom Convoy' Donors." *Vice News*, February 14, 2022. https://www.vice.com/en/article/k7wpax/freedom-convoy-givesendgo-donors-leaked.

and harmful. Unsurprisingly, the lying media has called these freedom-loving truckers "dangerous" and "separatists."[38] But they are not; they love their country and constitutional freedoms. They are the last line of defense against unlawful governments. Without these truckers the supply chain would be totally disrupted. This freedom movement led by Canadian truckers, that has inspired truckers in Australia, Europe, and around other parts of the world, has put a significant amount of pressure on Trudeau and other politicians. Five days into this awesome movement, we saw the leader of the Conservative Party of Canada (CPC), Erin O'Toole, step down. His leadership was ineffective and began to splinter the CPC further. He was unprincipled, since he pandered to whatever leftist ideology he thought would help him gain more popularity.

We also mustn't forget the utter silence from the CPC throughout the pandemic. None of its leaders championed freedom. We must always remember that there were very few politicians willing to stand against unlawful mandates and draconian restrictions. These leaders include Maxime Bernier of the PPC (the only federal leader who has spoken out against the mandates and restrictions); Derek Sloan, who now heads the Ontario Party; and Randy Hillier and Roman Baber, who are both Members of Provincial Parliament of Ontario. Those who have been following the insanity of this crisis know full well who is who. These were the courageous voices we heard from the onset, not Candice Bergen, the interim leader of the CPC, nor CPC Member of Parliament, Pierre Poilievre, although an articulate and intelligent voice had a deafening silence when it came to issues of freedom. (I was extremely disappointed by this since he was one of the few CPC members that I respected.) Unfortunately, I suspect that the CPC is trying to ride the coattails of a grass roots movement, seeing it as a "political opportunity," just like their Liberal friends saw the pandemic as such. The heroes of this continuous saga are the truckers and the freedom fighters of Canada.

Because of the truckers' defiance, the premiers of Saskatchewan, Manitoba, and Alberta have begun to scrap their COVID restrictions.[39] Quebec dropped their idea of taxing the unvaccinated. The premier of Ontario, Doug Ford, on February 15, 2022, in a desperate plea to hang onto power for the upcoming elections, flipped again, saying that by the first of March he will remove the requirement of proof of vaccination. (He also admitted that one or ten doses of the vaccine do not stop transmission.) Keep in mind that last year he said he

38 Ewa Sudyk, "Truckers: 'We are not separatists or terrorists'." *Western Digital,* January 25, 2022. https://westernstandardonline.com/2022/01/truckers-we-are-not-separatists-or-terrorists/.

39 Some critics of the 'freedom convoy' argue that these mandates were going to be lifted anyway. I believe they miss the point since every time they would lift restrictions, they would come back to them over and over again. This movement is to secure a return back to normal (not a "new normal").

would've never introduced them since they would be too divisive. Nevertheless, the provinces are falling like dominoes.

Even two members of Trudeau's cabinet, Quebec Liberal MPs Joël Lightbound and Yves Robillard have spoken up about their discontents on how he has divided Canadians.[40] Lightbound, in an impassioned speech, highlighted the division wrought by members of his party, especially Trudeau:

> I've heard from people worried that those making the decisions seem at times to have been blind to the fact that we're not all equal for lockdowns that not everyone can earn a living on a Macbook at the cottage. I've heard people worried that a few might have lost sight of the quiet and discreet suffering of the many.
>
> I've heard people in great pain to see some of their friends whom they love and respect but who've decided, for whatever reason, we might very well disagree with, who've decided not to get vaccinated and as a consequence, are jobless, selling what they have and moving to the United States, away from their communities, away from their friends and from their families.
>
> I've heard from teachers worried to see kids reenacting in the schoolyard the kind of discrimination and segregation we see in our society between vaccinated and unvaccinated. I've heard from people worried to see those they care about fighting each other on this issue, tearing some families and some friends apart.
>
> I've heard from a lot of people wondering why just a year ago, we were all united, in this together. And now that we have one of the most vaccinated population in the world, we've never been so divided. Now these people are increasingly confused, when on the other hand, they hear experts like Dr. Karl Weiss, a renowned Quebec epidemiologist, say last week and I quote "that COVID-19 is here to stay that those at risk will have to be monitored closely when symptoms appear; that we will have to protect our health-care systems; but then we will also have to live with the virus like we do with influenza; that we can't go back to lockdowns and restrictions not supported by science."[41]

There may be more like Lightbound and Robilliard who just don't have the courage to speak out, at least not yet. Trudeau and his main cronies are not only

40 Abbas Rana, "Quebec Liberal MP Robillard also breaks ranks, questions Trudeau government's handling of pandemic, sides with Lightbound." *The Hill Times*, February 9, 2022. https://www.hilltimes.com/2022/02/09/quebec-liberal-mp-robillard-also-breaks-ranks-questions-trudeau-governments-handling-of-pandemic-sides-with-lightbound/343476.

41 For the full transcript, see The World News, "Liberal MP Joël Lightbound's full remarks: 'It's time to choose positive, not coercive methods'." February 8, 2022. https://theworldnews.net/ca-news/liberal-mp-joel-lightbound-s-full-remarks-it-s-time-to-choose-positive-not-coercive-methods.

splintering the country, but their own party with their hatred and contempt for hard-working Canadians. The Conservatives have been sympathizing with the cause of trucker convoy protesters, advocating for the removal of all COVID-19 mandates and restrictions. It appears as change may be coming to Canada. The world is watching and following the Canadian truckers' lead. I would have never thought Canadians would be leading the way in a global effort to dismantle the concerted efforts of the globalists and their allied institutions, like the corrupt media, governments, health organizations, Big Tech, and Big Pharma, to subjugate humanity into a global communist surveillance state, the like of which would have made George Orwell shudder. Whether the lying media and many establishment politicians like it or not, the truckers have made large waves throughout Canada and will continue to do so until all mandates are lifted for everyone. One of the main champions and leaders of the truckers' freedom convoy is Pat King (the Real Pat King), a real Canadian Patriot,[42] who has been devoted to the cause day and night. He has dealt with a tremendous amount of adversity from leftists and their lies.

All the while, Trudeau continues to hang by a single thread to his "power." He is a weak leader whose time is running out. Canadians do not even know of his whereabouts. On February 1, 2022, he tweeted an absurd, incoherent, and inflammatory statement against freedom-loving, hard-working men and women who form the backbone of the nation of the "true north strong and free," and who have been protesting the authoritarian COVID measures throughout Canada:

> Today in the House, Members of Parliament unanimously condemned the antisemitism, Islamophobia, anti-Black racism, homophobia, and transphobia that we've seen on display in Ottawa over the past number of days. Together, let's keep working to make Canada more inclusive.[43]

Trudeau, in my estimation, has become the most divisive person in Canadian history. His wrath is an indication of the political class's loss of control over their false and ever crumbling narrative. Trudeau is a liar who wreaks of desperation. One wonders if this statement, like many of his others, could be considered "hate speech" since he is slandering freedom-loving Canadians (some who are vaccine free and some who are not). According to Canadian Criminal Code:

> Public incitement of hatred
>
> 319 (1) Every one who, by communicating statements in any public place, incites hatred against any identifiable group where such

42 For his website, see The Real Pat King, Accessed February 16, 2022. https://therealpatking.wordpress.com/.

43 Justin Trudeau, Twitter Post, February 1, 2022, at 6:47 PM. https://twitter.com/JustinTrudeau/status/1488660359422648320.

> incitement is likely to lead to a breach of the peace is guilty of
>
> (a) an indictable offence and is liable to imprisonment for a term not exceeding two years; or (b) an offence punishable on summary conviction.
>
> Wilful promotion of hatred
>
> (2) Every one who, by communicating statements, other than in private conversation, wilfully promotes hatred against any identifiable group is guilty of
>
> (a) an indictable offence and is liable to imprisonment for a term not exceeding two years; or (b) an offence punishable on summary conviction.[44]

Further questions arise as to whether Trudeau is using hate speech against vaccine-free individuals. He is consistently using divisive language to pin the vaccine-free and freedom-loving Canadians to others. He even accused a Jewish Conservative MP, Melissa Lantsman, of supporting people who wave swastikas, without apology.[45] Very shameful and despicable behaviour for the leader of a Western country. The lying media, in a desperate attempt to discredit the truckers' freedom convoy, speculate that Russia may be behind this movement. Their idiocy knows no bounds. On February 1, 2022, Tucker Carlson in a piercing commentary tore Trudeau and the Canadian media to shreds over their blatantly false claims regarding the truckers' convoy.[46] Curiously, not once has he condemned any of the actions of antifa or BLM who are renown for violent acts like lighting buildings on fire, toppling statues, and attacking innocent bystanders. He even took a knee with BLM but can't even meet with truckers and freedom-loving citizens to offer them any support or any words of encouragement.

Regrettably, moronic Canadians echo Trudeau's informal fallacies. The intellectual vacuity of Canadians who support this illogical political rhetoric is almost inconceivable. Some people's attempt to argue that the truckers are affecting the livelihoods of many businesses in Ottawa. These people are so out of touch with reality that they can't see that this is precisely what our governments have done for the past two years, running businesses to the ground. Moreover, many unvaccinated individuals have lost their jobs.

Trudeau, also known as "Fidelito" or postmodernism's poster boy (a term I coined to make sense of his logical incoherence and doublespeak), has been

44 Criminal Code (R.S.C., 1985, c. C-46), Public Incitement of Hatred, https://laws-lois.justice.gc.ca/eng/acts/c-46/section-319.html.

45 Joe Warmington, "Accusing Jewish MP of 'standing with swastika' new low for PM." *Toronto Sun*, February 16, 2022. https://torontosun.com/news/local-news/warmington-accusing-jewish-mp-of-standing-with-swastika-new-low-for-pm.

46 Tucker Carlson, "There's no more fearful despot than Canada's Prime Minister." *Fox News*, February 1, 2022. https://www.foxnews.com/opinion/tucker-carlson-canada-prime-minister-justin-trudeau.

blasted by Canadian-born Diane Bederman as "a sanctimonious, self-serving, self-righteous, inept, unethical, immoral and corrupt man, who can now add evil to the list."[47] She draws strong parallels between the shaming of the vaccine-free to the hatred against the Jews in 1930s Nazi Germany. Whatever may come of the truckers' convoy, it has shown that Canada is not as divided as our political "elites" would like us to believe. Love is a unifying principle between people of good will, despite their attempts to demoralize us. Trudeau and other politicians have underestimated the Canadian people. For the first time in many years, I am proud to be Canadian again.

Despite so much hatred and division, will history repeat itself? Will goodness prevail, as it did with the collapse of Nazi Germany and the toppling of the Soviet Union? What we need are leaders like Pope John Paull II and Ronald Reagan. John Paul II was effectively a messenger between the Solidarity movement in Poland and Washington. Together, President Reagan and the great saint were able to defeat the oppressive Soviet reign of terror. Most recently, there was a glimmer of hope that a similar alliance between Archbishop Carlo Maria Viganò and former President Trump would materialize to defeat the COVID global tyranny. (Although it has become increasingly difficult to see where Trump's loyalty lies since he's become a big supporter of the "vaccines" and Big Pharma—one can assume this may be a ploy for re-election in 2024.) All this is to say that there was a critical mass that made the decision to stop acquiescing to communist rule, which was a key component to the Soviet Union's collapse. This is what is needed to bring about change now. Since January 29, we have seen this critical mass come together publicly and forcefully.

This is not like World War II, where we waited for others to liberate us; it must be done in unison with all other people of good will. It is only through prayerful action that corresponds with God's will that we may overcome these tyrannies. This would involve peaceful resistance, similar to Mahatma Gandhi's strategy of civil disobedience, which pushed the British Empire out of India:

> Civil Disobedience, therefore, becomes a sacred duty when the state has become lawless, or which is the same thing, corrupt. And a citizen that barters with such a state shares its corruption or lawlessness. And a citizen that barters with such a State shares its corruption or lawlessness.[48]

47 Diane Bederman, "Is Comparing Covid Policies with the policies of Nazi Germany Antisemitic?" *The Jewish Press*, January 10, 2022. https://www.jewishpress.com/blogs/is-comparing-covid-policies-with-the-policies-of-nazi-germany-antisemitic/2022/01/10/.

48 Mahatma Gandhi, *Young Indian* (May 1, 1922), 5. https://www.mkgandhi.org/voiceoftruth/civildisobedience.htm.

Any tyrannical government is immoral. Just as the early Christian martyrs had the duty to disobey the Roman State, even if it meant being fed to the lions. Christians share that same duty today. Just as the Bible is clear on who we choose to serve, American theologian Francis Schaeffer is just as blunt:

> First, since tyranny is satanic, not to resist it is to resist God—to resist tyranny is to honor God. Second, since the ruler is granted power conditionally, it follows that the people have the power to withdraw their sanction if the proper conditions are not fulfilled. The civil magistrate is a "fiduciary figure"—that is, he holds his authority in trust for the people. Violation of the trust gives the people a legitimate base for resistance.[49]

Governments around the globe have fallen to corruption and lawlessness. So, citizens have this same duty to stand up to them. Bartering with the State makes us complicit and complacent in such corruption. It also sends the message that they can continue with their unlawful oppression.

This can involve speaking up for truth and freedom whenever the opportunity presents itself. As uncomfortable as it may be, speak up! This could be at a place of work, online, family dinners, and other public spaces. Here are some pragmatic ways you can dissent from governmental tyranny:

- Do not comply with mandates. Show resolve and resistance against government restrictions that are unconstitutional and that violate our human rights; you will see there are more people that think alike—they just need a nudge.
- Go and peacefully protest whenever possible.
- Show resilience through acts of civil disobedience.
- You can use dissenting information against Big Tech platforms—if you see a post that speaks the truth that was censored by a popular figure, repost it repeatedly.
- Join platforms that are uncensored (for the moment) like Telegram.
- Build communities with like-minded people.
- Prepare for shortages, try to be self-sufficient.
- Dissent financially: gradually withdraw money and convert fiat to precious metals like gold and silver (their value is stable unlike fiat) and/or cryptocurrencies like bitcoin, Ethereum, and Ripple XRP.

49 Francis A. Schaeffer, *A Christian Manifesto* (Wheaton: Crossway Books, 1982), 103. https://archive.org/details/christianmanifes0000scha/page/100/mode/2up?q=tyranny&view=theater.

> Unlike fiat money, cryptocurrencies like bitcoin have intrinsic value. Their value goes beyond the trust of its community since they do not rely upon system of debts; its value is predicated on how effective it is as a medium of exchange. Cryptocurrency networks, unlike banks, are decentralized. The value of cryptocurrency is not regulated by governments. This is a way to combat inflation and central banking.[50]

Follow your moral conscience and do what is right and just—do so unwaveringly. Without an unwavering faith rooted in biblical truths and traditions, an objective understanding of the world, the use of reason and logic coupled with righteous action lining up with God's will, we will not be able to navigate out of this quagmire. Essentially, we will not be able to make sense of nonsense. This is a spiritual battle and only within that context can any of this nonsense that is permeating through the world and its institutions make sense. Although it is nice to think that reason and discussion may be able to change the minds of some, it seems as though the time for learned discussion is drawing to a close—it is a time for prayer fulfilled through action to bring about the good we want to see in the world, individually and collectively. People of good will must do their part. It's not to disparage arguments and reason, but to be aware that change will come from a change in consciousness that is uncoerced. We must love God with all of our heart, soul, strength, and mind (Luke 10:27). This gives us the strength to love our neighbours and enemies, which in turn can work to change hearts and minds. The opposition to good is growing fiercer by day. This is why we must remind ourselves of Jesus's words of comfort: "If the world hates you, keep in mind that it hated me first" (John 15:18). This will provide us with the requisite strength to bear the torment and suffering that may lay ahead.

Archbishop Carlo Maria Viganò emphasizes full out opposition to the New World Order and Great Reset agenda:

> One of the elements that unequivocally confirms the criminal nature of the Great Reset is the perfect synchrony with which all the different Nations are acting, demonstrating the existence of a single script under a single direction. And it is disconcerting to see how the lack of treatment, the deliberately wrong treatments that have been given in order to cause more deaths, the decision to impose lock downs and masks, the conspiratorial silence about the adverse effects of the so-called "vaccines" that are in fact gene serums, and the continuous repetition of culpable errors have all been possible thanks to the complicity of

50 See Saidedean Amous, *The Bitcoin Standard: The Decentralized Alternative to Central Banking* (Hoboken: Wiley & Sons, 2018); Saidedean Amous, *The Fiat Standard: The Debt Slavery Alternative to Human Civilization* (Saifedean House, 2021).

> those who govern and the institutions. Political and religious leaders, representatives of the people, scientists and doctors, journalists and those who work in the media have literally betrayed their people, their laws, their Constitutions, and the most basic ethical principles…
>
> My appeal for an Anti-Globalist Alliance—which I renew today—aims precisely to constitute a movement of moral and spiritual rebirth which will inspire the civil, social and political action of those who do not want to be enslaved as slaves to the New World Order. A movement that at the national and local level will be able to find a way to oppose the Great Reset and that coordinates the denunciation of the coup that is currently in progress. Because in the awareness of who our adversary is and what his aims and purposes are, we can disrupt the criminal action he intends to pursue and force him to retreat. In this, the opposition to the pandemic farce and the vaccination obligation must be determined and courageous on the part of each of you.
>
> Yours must therefore be a work of truth, bringing to light the lies and deceptions of the New World Order and their anti-human and anti-christic matrix. And in this it is mainly the laity and all people of good will—each in the professional and civil role he holds—who must coordinate and organize together to make a firm but peaceful resistance, so as not to legitimize its violent repression by those who today hold power.[51]

The choice is simple: either we stand courageously for what is true, just, good, and Godly or we accept and surrender to falsehoods, injustice, evil, and ungodliness. The proleptic and haunting words of Ronald Reagan, from his "A Time for Choosing" speech bear much light in our current period of darkness:

> Admittedly, there's a risk in any course we follow other than this, but every lesson of history tells us that the greater risk lies in appeasement, and this is the specter our well-meaning liberal friends refuse to face—that their policy of accommodation is appeasement, and it gives no choice between peace and war, only between fight or surrender. If we continue to accommodate, continue to back and retreat, eventually we have to face the final demand—the ultimatum…
>
> You and I know and do not believe that life is so dear and peace so sweet as to be purchased at the price of chains and slavery. If nothing in life is worth dying for, when did this begin—just in the face of this enemy? Or should Moses have told the children of Israel to live in slavery under the pharaohs? Should Christ have refused the cross? Should the patriots at Concord Bridge have thrown down their guns and refused to fire the shot heard 'round the world? The martyrs of history were not

51 Thomas Lifson, "Archbishop Viganò's startling warning to the American people." *American Thinker*, December 20, 2021.

> fools, and our honored dead who gave their lives to stop the advance of the Nazis didn't die in vain. Where, then, is the road to peace? Well it's a simple answer after all.
>
> You and I have the courage to say to our enemies, "There is a price we will not pay." "There is a point beyond which they must not advance." And this—this is the meaning in the phrase of Barry Goldwater's "peace through strength." Winston Churchill said, "The destiny of man is not measured by material computations. When great forces are on the move in the world, we learn we're spirits—not animals." And he said, "There's something going on in time and space, and beyond time and space, which, whether we like it or not, spells duty."
>
> You and I have a rendezvous with destiny.
>
> We'll preserve for our children this, the last best hope of man on earth, or we'll sentence them to take the last step into a thousand years of darkness.[52]

Let us take Reagan's call to heart. Let us unceasingly fight to bring about the "Great Reckoning" and "Great Take Over" which will hold the culprits responsible for these crimes against humanity. Nuremberg 2.0, as Reiner Fuellmich has called it.[53] We can then exercise the reverse of their intended "Great Reset" and redistribute the globalist elites' and their minions' wealth to the rest of the world and let the rest of us live freely. They should be subject to the same measures, and even worse, than they've inflicted upon the world. Many lives have been lost and lives destroyed. They have divided the world. On a positive note, Ricardo Maarman has begun the process of litigation against the New World Order in South Africa.[54]

We must be reminded of the Prophet Isaiah's admonishment: "Woe to those who call evil good and good evil, who put darkness for light and light for darkness" (Isa 5:20). We can hope that when the smoke has cleared, many persons will be found culpable for their crimes against humanity, while many others will be complicit in the crimes of politicians, medical bureaucrats, media personalities, and oligarchs. Professors and other educators who are guilty of indoctrinating unsuspecting minds against truth, life, and liberty will face a proportional punishment for leading many astray. CEOs and other higher ups of Big Pharma, CDC, WHO, Health Canada, etc., will pay dearly for these

52 Ronald Reagan, "A Time for Choosing (The Speech)." October 27, 1964. YouTube video. https://www.youtube.com/watch?v=qXBswFfh6AY.

53 Chembuster, "Reiner Fuellmich: New findings are enough to dismantle the entire VVV industry." Bitchute Video, January 2, 2022. https://www.bitchute.com/video/GykwcdMzw3o0/?fbclid=IwAR1w7Lg5xBQ3xMktIimXKN2bn7o93tvILmL_-DamENctuPMylAl7ScnUNfM.

54 "Litigation for the trial that'll free Africa from the NOW has begun! Home-base for Nuremberg 2.0." BitChute Video, December 15, 2021. https://www.bitchute.com/video/7IC770ZNNt3R/.

crimes. Scientists working in Big Pharma who do not expose the dangerous lies behind the vaccines will also be held accountable. Medical doctors who abandoned their sacred oaths will be held responsible. Police officers who abandoned their duty to protect their citizens will face justice. (The RCMP authoritarian commissioner, Brenda Lucki, would have made the late former president of the People's Republic of China, Mao Zedong, and Communist China's current president, Xi Jinping, proud with her crack down on anti-authority internet opinions.)[55] The lying and smearing mercenary "fact checkers" will get their much-deserved payment. Any Christian theologian worth his salt will be unmoved by the depths of such depravity, knowing full well that there's nothing new under the sun when it pertains to the darkness of the human heart. However, the question for them would be: Did they preach salvation and truth? Did they warn God's people of the impending dangers, or did they promote falsehoods? Did they follow in the steps of someone like Dietrich Bonhoeffer, who opposed Nazi tyranny, or of those professors of theology, bishops, and pastors who supported Adolf Hitler's war against Jews through, for example, their participation in The Institute for the Study and Eradication of Jewish Influence on German Church Life?[56] Judges and lawyers cowering away from truth and justice will also be judged but with more severity. Those who stigmatize the unvaccinated will be judged. How did the unvaccinated treat the vaccinated—were they also guilty of divisiveness?

History will not be kind to philosophers who chose comfort over their love of wisdom and truth. Musicians and artists who willfully lie will be held responsible. Instead, may they follow the example of Eric Clapton, who has shown with his song, "This Has Gotta Stop,"[57] and his stance against vaccine passports, a tremendous amount of courage and respect for the sacredness of human freedom and bodily autonomy. Quite oppositely, legendary Canadian singer and songwriter, Neil Young, demanded that Spotify choose between hosting him or Joe Rogan. Spotify made the right choice. Young has always been vocal about his leftist politics. Sadly, it turns out that Young is so woke that he cancelled himself.[58] So much for "rockin' in the free world." Joni Mitchell took the same stance against Spotify. These former hippies have lost their minds and have come to defend the establishment and Big Pharma over freedom.

55 Jonathan Bradley, "RCMP commissioner wants Canadians to report 'anti-authority' Internet opinions." *True North*, January 12, 2022. https://tnc.news/2022/01/12/rcmp-commissioner-wants-canadians-to-report-anti-authority-internet-opinions/?fbclid=IwAR1v57wgRSyec5t26qeZf1MduT7mqnSmxKUciX9vql5tJRGnjjCnoE8Dh0Q.

56 Susannah Heschel, *The Aryan Jesus: Christian theologians and the Bible in Nazi Germany*. (Princeton: Princeton University Press, 2008).

57 See Eric Clapton, "Eric Clapton - This Has Gotta Stop (Official Music Video)." YouTube Video, August 21, 2021. https://www.youtube.com/watch?v=dNt4NIQ7FTA&t=3s.

58 BBC Staff, "Spotify removes Neil Young after he calls for Joe Rogan to go." *BBC News*, January 27, 2022. https://www.bbc.com/news/entertainment-arts-60149951.

Parents who participate in injuring their children with these experimental vaccines will not be able to claim ignorance and should be held accountable. And the oligarchs and bankers should prepare themselves for what is to come when they are exposed and truth creeps up behind them—they will not escape justice. For some (pawns at the bottom of the complicity scale) we may say they do not know what they do (Luke 23:34), but for the ones who do, prepare yourselves: "But the Lord laughs at the wicked, for he knows their day is coming" (Ps 37:13).

We should take heed from the holocaust survivor and medical activist, Vera Sharav, who is very weary of the COVID measures such as lockdowns, constant testing, vaccine mandates, and passports. In a recent interview, she made the following statements drawing parallels between Nazi Germany and the global COVID tyranny:

> Fear is an extremely powerful psychological tool, that has been used by politicians always, the Nazis were particularly adept at it... What happens with a public health policy is that public health officials decide who shall live and who shall die... I have come to the conclusion that when doctors become aligned with government—corporations for that matter – they discard their moral and professional responsibility to the individual patient... As public officials they talk about the greater good. Who has the authority to decide what is the greater good?... If the individuals are oppressed or relegated to third-class citizens...what kind of society is it? We are now at the gate of that.[59]

When the interviewer asked Sharav if we are nearing a Nazi-like society, she responded the following:

> I absolutely do... One of the main things that has happened in these 18 months of the pandemic is that fear has been the major weapon, which has really crippled people from thinking straight. It has isolated people and taught children to distrust other people: "They might be infected, they might infect me."[60]

We must be reminded that slaves were never treated this way. It is the first time in history where the majority of the world has been enslaved and "forced" / "mandated" to put something inside their bodies. In the past they have been branded, but nothing that affects their DNA. This is pure

59 Kennedy Hall, "Holocaust survivor: We should be 'more than nervous' about COVID-19 measures." *LifeSite News*, August 17, 2021. https://www.lifesitenews.com/news/holocaust-survivor-more-than-nervous-covid-measures/.

60 Hall, "Holocaust survivor: We should be 'more than nervous' about COVID-19 measures."

madness. A hundred years from now, assuming we make it out of this dark period in human history, historians will be flummoxed as to how we could repeat these egregious and unforgivable crimes against humanity. The plain truth is that this is "over." We have won. The unceasing efforts and sacrifices of noble martyrs of today that have been instrumental in combatting this evil: all of the truckers, doctors, scientists, philosophers, theologians, lawyers, psychologists, journalists, frontline workers, authors, and everyday freedom fighters. Peter McCullough has declared that the official COVID narrative has collapsed, and again empathetically stating that the vaccines should be pulled off the market immediately.[61] The comedian JP Sears explains 16 reasons why on his show, "We Lie To You News," in a video with usual hilarity.[62] His news show is a more accurate source of news than the lying media. Some countries are backing down from their mandates, while backward countries like Australia embarrassingly continue to push forward with this false narrative. The British Prime Minister, Boris Johnson, after being exposed for his participation in gatherings that did not follow COVID protocol, has changed his tune on restrictions. England has officially ended all vaccine passports, vaccine mandates, and work restrictions.[63] Many other countries throughout Europe have followed suit. These announcements have left authoritarian rulers like Joe Biden and Justin Trudeau scrambling. Maybe justice is just around the corner. Nevertheless, even if other countries continue to push the false narrative with unlawful restrictions, we have indeed won. We have won with truth, logic, arguments, science, medicine, morality, and a clear understanding of history. But the enemies of humanity are desperate to cause as much damage as possible with incredible amounts of finances at their disposal. We must come together. We must begin to heal. They are few, we are many. Those susceptible to the propaganda should be vigilant that they do not fall again for the lies of Big Pharma and governments about there being a more effective vaccine coming into the market, as Pfizer CEO, Albert Bourla, has recently declared.

We must continue in our resolve to resist their threats and fear mongering. The current state of the COVID war is not dissimilar to the end of World War II. Germany and Japan had by many metrics lost the war but were hellbent on

61 Art Moore, "Dr. Peter McCullough: Official COVID 'narrative has crumbled'" *WND*, January 14, 2022. https://www.wnd.com/2022/01/dr-peter-mccullough-official-covid-narrative-crumbled/?fbclid=IwAR2J5VoYtpEUkwB9n-1U_L9EVycIOg4lY2vdSR9TDIL4PSqxrJG-QmF3MMc.

62 JP Sears (AwakenWithJP), "The Narrative is Crumbling - 16 Reasons Why." YouTube Video, January 15, 2022. https://www.youtube.com/watch?v=D70kZDLGr4Q.

63 Lily Zhou, "England Ends All COVID Passports, Mask Mandates, Work Restrictions." *The Epoch Times*, January 19, 2022. https://www.theepochtimes.com/england-ends-all-covid-passports-mask-mandates-work-restrictions_4222549.html?utm_source=mr_recommendation&utm_medium=left_sticky.

causing as much damage and as many casualties as possible. In a similar vein, on February 14, 2022, Trudeau unwarrantedly invoked the Emergencies Act[64] for the first time in Canadian history. The *Emergencies Act* entails a scenario that "seriously endangers the lives, health or safety of Canadians" or "seriously threatens the ability of the Government of Canada to preserve the sovereignty, security and territorial integrity of Canada."[65] Interestingly, the definition of "threats to the security of Canada" include the following:

> (a) espionage or sabotage that is against Canada or is detrimental to the interests of Canada or activities directed toward or in support of such espionage or sabotage,
> (b) foreign influenced activities within or relating to Canada that are detrimental to the interests of Canada and are clandestine or deceptive or involve a threat to any person,
> (c) activities within or relating to Canada directed toward or in support of the threat or use of acts of serious violence against persons or property for the purpose of achieving a political, religious or ideological objective within Canada or a foreign state, and
> (d) activities directed toward undermining by covert unlawful acts, or directed toward or intended ultimately to lead to the destruction or overthrow by violence of, the constitutionally established system of government in Canada.[66]

It is important to note that "lawful advocacy, protest or dissent," are excluded. This poses a significant problem for invoking the *Emergencies Act*, i.e., there is no rational justification for it. The provinces of Alberta, Manitoba, Saskatchewan, and Quebec disagree with invoking the Act. Premier Ford has quickly turned his tune against vaccine passports but remains supportive of invoking the Act. To the reasonable mind, it should be obvious that the truckers and their supporters do not pose a threat to the security of Canada. In fact, the streets have never been safer in Ottawa's downtown core. Although the protests have been disruptive, they have been peaceful acts of civil disobedience, despite allegations to the contrary. Trudeau's cabinet treats the truckers' freedom convoy movement as if it were some insurrection and occupation when, in reality, it resembles a block party. These lawful protests do not even come close to such situations

64 The predecessor to the *Emergencies Act* was the War Measures Act which was used in World War I and World War II, and also invoked by Pierre Elliot Trudeau in 1970 in the October Crisis against the Front de Liberation du Québec (FLQ), who said "just watch me," in response to being asked how far he would go. Let's see how far his hapless son goes.

65 Justice Laws Website, Emergencies Act (R.S.C., 1985, c. 22 (4th Supp.)). Accessed February 15, 2022. https://laws-lois.justice.gc.ca/eng/acts/e-4.5/page-1.html.

66 Justice Laws Website, Canadian Security Intelligence Service Act (R.S.C., 1985, c. C-23). Accessed February 15, 2022. https://laws-lois.justice.gc.ca/eng/acts/C-23/section-2.html.

enumerated above. This is an act of desperation. And yet, you have the leader of a the NDP (New Democratic Party), Jagmeet Singh, saying that his party will support the Trudeau government's use of the *Emergencies Act* against working-class protestors. Recently, I posted some pictures on Facebook of my experience at the freedom protest on Parliament Hill with the caption: "A privilege to be part of a freedom loving movement in history. Canada is leading the way out of this disaster." Although the post was popular among freedom lovers, there was one commentator who furiously wrote:

> What garbage. This is an illegal occupation with no logical basis, held by selfish, ignorant people who reveal their absolute ignorance by calling our current situation "Chinada." Public health restrictions will be loosened as it's safe to do so. Be a citizen. Unfriending.[67]

This person is living in a dystopian bubble. They were clearly emotive and illogical, and breathtakingly ignorant. They lack the ability to understand the selflessness of fighting for freedom, a lack of historical self-awareness of how civil disobedience has toppled tyrannical governments, what is truly ignorant, and what the actual duty of a citizen is. The truckers have set an example for the world of what a citizen must do in the face of political oppression. I responded to the individual by stating: "What is illegal and unconstitutional is this government overreach at the provincial and federal level. What is absolute ignorance is *actually* believing these mandates are about our health. Cheers."[68] At this stage of the game, if one continues to believe that this is about our health, then they are irredeemable. It is worth considering that the truckers have performed the ultimate COVID experiment. As physicist Denis Rancourt put it: ">2 weeks of mass hugs, handshakes, close proximity, [and no masks,] from all over Canada = zero infections, zero hospital cases, zero truckers in Ottawa ICUs. Conclusion: The gov has been lying big time." [69]

Truthfully, my ex-Facebook friend's and Jagmeet Singh's hypocrisy can be labeled "champagne socialism." The liberal elites will never stand for the common man if it entails any sort of self-sacrifice. A few days after this exchange, Justin "Fidelito" Castro Trudeau, proves me correct by invoking the *Emergency Act*. Last summer, Trudeau sympathized with the burning of churches throughout Canada, but that was okay because he agreed with the cause. With the truckers' presence, the streets of downtown Ottawa have never been safer, and cleaner. They have taken full responsibility of maintaining them. Interestingly, Trudeau,

67 Scott Ventureyra, Facebook Post, February 5, 2022. We must pray for Glabson Iana.

68 Scott Ventureyra, Facebook Post, February 5, 2022.

69 Denis Rancourt, Twitter Post. February 14, 2022, at 2:40 PM. https://twitter.com/denisrancourt/status/1493218555982135296.

in his announcement regarding the *Emergency Act*, there wasn't a single mention about our health or COVID-19. Dead on. All of which I have been arguing throughout this book.

This leads to another question: why has there been no mention of COVID and its spread from Trudeau and his cronies, all of a sudden? Well, because this is not about a virus, and never was. What is it about? As we know, Trudeau has strong ties to the World Economic Forum (WEF) and Klaus Schwab.[70] Essentially, he is Klaus Schwab's little pet, and he has demonstrated extreme loyalty to him, the WEF, and what is called the "fourth industrial revolution." His loyalty is not with Canadians. In return, Trudeau has become a very rich person on his profits from the BioNTech/Pfizer and Moderna vaccines. He is invested heavily in the Canadian company that holds the patents for the lipid nanoparticles. Otherwise, why order multiple doses for every Canadian up until 2024? The same holds true for his cronies like the reprehensible Minister of Finance, Chrystia Freeland, and others. Moreover, the Canadian government is profiting handsomely from these companies—from their patent royalties.

Dr. David Martin has done a tremendous amount of research to expose all of this.[71] (He has followed the money, as Freeland insists that the government must do, when tracking those who have donated to the truckers' convoy in order to seize their assets and freeze bank accounts. Unfortunately for her, those who are in the know, are onto her.) Martin has never been interviewed by the mainstream media, and for good reason. He has produced many documents and facts demonstrating that Trudeau and the Canadian government are tied financially to the mRNA vaccine companies. This is the best explanation for his authoritarian rule, vaccine mandates, and use of the Act which have benefitted him and his cronies while compromising Canadians. It is time for him to face justice in a veritable court of law, the people's court— for the people and by the people. Freedom lovers around the world must unify against Trudeau and the crimes he is driving under the guise of public health. In the words of Artur Pawlowski, who has seen the horrors of communism in Poland, and who has been wrongfully imprisoned for the fifteenth time and now denied bail: "We are coming for you!"[72] Organized political criminality will be brought to justice.

70 TheNo1Waffler, Twitter Post. February 15, 2022, at 4:44 PM. https://twitter.com/TheNo1Waffler/status/1493702862471323661.

71 My recommendation is to download Telegram which, for the time being, is one of the most secure apps with no censorship. Follow Dr. David Martin on Telegram: https://t.me/DrDavidMartin.

72 He's been in isolation in a filthy cell for "public health reasons." His son and brother, Nathan Pawlowski and David Pawlowski, respectively, provide a good explanation for the reasoning behind his father's incarceration: "Artur Pawlowski's family speaks to Rebel News as hundreds gather to support jailed pastor." *Rebel News*, February 14, 2022. https://www.youtube.com/watch?v=lHRMf6ogNg0.

The irony is inescapable: the truckers and freedom protestors are combatting government overreach and the government's response is more overreach. Humorously, in a matter of two weeks, Trudeau went from calling the truckers and freedom-loving protestors, "a fringe minority," to needing emergency powers exacted against them.

If passed, the Act, will give extraordinary powers to police forces, including the Royal Canadian Mounted Police, to freeze bank accounts, seize commercial licenses, and insurances, and truckers and protestors could face imprisonment. (As of now, organizers of the freedom convoy, Tamara Lich and, Chris Farber, have been arrested. Lich was recently denied bail.) There will also be financial ramifications for participants in this freedom-loving movement. For example, Tom Marazzo, despite there being no warrant for his arrest, no charges laid, and no notification of anything, has had his bank accounts frozen, his credit cards cancelled, and his spouse's credit card score was lowered by 109 points.[73] The Government of Canada has set a dangerous precedent where finances can be seized without due process. Freeland explains the potential governmental overreach:

> We are announcing the following immediate actions: first, we are broadening the scope of Canada's anti-money laundering and terrorist financing rules so that they cover crowdfunding platforms and the payment service providers they use. These changes cover all forms of transactions, including digital assets, such as cryptocurrencies.
>
> The illegal blockades have highlighted the fact that crowdfunding platforms, and some of the payment service providers they use, are not fully captured under the Proceeds of Crime and Terrorist Financing Act.[74]

She also threatened to freeze the corporate and personal bank accounts of those involved in the protests. Freedom lovers are now considered terrorists and subject to the Proceeds of Crime (Money Laundering) and Terrorist Financing Act (PCMLTFA). Did Trudeau and his government freeze the bank accounts of returning ISIS members? Indeed, it pays to be on their "side." Ask Omar Khadr, he'll tell you 10.5 million reasons why.

In 2019, I never thought Canada would descend into a totalitarian dictatorship. We are now at the brink of fully becoming a socialist-fascist state. Beware if you criticize the government, they will take your ability to work, your finances and imprison you. Instead of resolving issues, they are creating more of them. The despots of history would have been very proud.

73 News Desk, "'There's no warrant for my arrest…yet all my bank accounts have been frozen' | Tom Marazzo." *The Global Herald*, February 25, 2022. https://theglobalherald.com/news/canada-theres-no-warrant-for-my-arrest-yet-all-my-bank-accounts-have-been-frozen-tom-marazzo/.

74 "Full text of Chrystia Freeland's remarks during the Emergencies Act announcement." *Toronto Star*, February 14, 2022. https://www.thestar.com/news/canada/2022/02/14/full-text-of-chrystia-freelands-remarks-during-emergencies-act-announcement.html.

In response to Trudeau's announcement of the *Emergencies Act*, one of the key organizers of the truckers' convoy, Tamara Lich, made it very clear that the truckers would not be leaving until all of the mandates were lifted throughout Canada. She told all the freedom lovers to "hold the line":

> To our truckers and friends on Parliament Hill, do not give in to fear and threats.
>
> Your courage has already exceeded all of our expectations and inspired an international movement. Be strong, show kindness. Love will always defeat hate. Hold the line.[75]

Following Lich, Brian Peckford, the only surviving signatory to the 1982 Constitution and Charter of Rights and Freedoms, made the following pointed statement regarding the Government of Canada's totalitarian power grab:

> Looking at the situation here in Ottawa, it is peaceful, the streets are clean, crime is down since the truckers arrived. And so therefore, it behooves the government, if they are going to proceed on this movement of invoking this act, to prove that this really is necessary to apply to the capital city and to this convoy.
>
> It's a great onus upon the Government of Canada when they start initiating these kinds of actions, that they must be consistent with the Charter of Rights and Freedoms in all its values. Remember, the Charter of Rights and Freedoms also says, whereas this country is founded on the principles of the supremacy of God and the rule of law, this must also come into play: the Constitution of this nation, not the Emergency Act, the Constitution of this nation is the supreme law of Canada.
>
> We don't do these kinds of things in Canada: we engage in dialogue. Let's forget the negotiations for a minute; just natural dialogue to reach out and say "Can we sit down and have a talk, see where the major issues lie and see if there's any common ground to move?
>
> It's my understanding that the Government of Canada has not reached out once to the truckers since they arrived in this capital city. I find that very hard to understand. Because how can you justify going to measure like an Emergency Measures where a lot of powers can be imposed upon the citizens when you have not even taken any action to engage, yourself? First of all, a dialogue?[76]

75 "'Hold the line,' Convoy organizer Tamara Lich tells Truckers.'" *Road Warrior News*, February 15, 2022. https://roadwarriornews.com/hold-the-line-convoy-organizer-tamara-lich-tells-truckers/.

76 Rita Smith, "Trudeau's Emergency Measures Act 'completely, absolutely unnecessary' says Brian Peckford." *Road Warrior News*, February 15, 2022. https://roadwarriornews.com/trudeaus-emergency-measures-act-completely-absolutely-unnecessary-says-brian-peckford/.

The entire world is watching Canada. Canada is leading a world freedom movement. Canada is at the center of this globalist battle. There is a lot at stake since Trudeau is one of the globalist elite's "young leaders." And due to this, and his conflicts of interests with the pharmaceutical industry, he has committed multiple acts of treason. He has sold Canada and Canadians to the World Economic Forum. He can only proceed in one direction, and he has become more brazen by thinking he's invincible because of the globalists' support. If the Trudeau government's plan fails due to the truckers' and freedom-loving Canadians' resistance, it will send a rippling effect across the world. Therefore, we mustn't back down, and we must continue to fight for what is right. Patriots must stand up against tyranny, regardless of political affiliation and rank. Patriots must stand up against tyranny, regardless of political affiliation and rank.

Despicably, Trudeau has allowed large amounts of violence and injustice against peaceful protestors throughout the weekend of February 18, 2022. Patriots stood up against this tyranny in -30° weather. They stood up for all of Canadians, despite the misplaced hatred towards them. Police were brutal with some of the protestors by using excessive force. Police brutally beat a young man named Nick Strachan[77] and trampled others with horses including an aboriginal Mohawk woman named Candice Sero—this must be the reason they do not want honest reporting being done.[78] These police officers have desecrated their oath to protect the people and have even bragged about such violence.[79] Ottawa Police have also spread misinformation about the reason for violence and have denied that the RCMP horses ever ran over anyone (there is plenty of video evidence documenting this).[80]Mr. Christian-Vasile Terheş, a Romanian politician currently serving as a Member of the European Parliament for Christian Democratic National Peasants' Party, said of Trudeau: "He's exactly like a tyrant, a dictator. He's like Nicolae Ceauşescu in Romania."[81] Interestingly, walking by the protests, I met two Romanians who came from

77 Nick Strachan is a true patriot, he did not accept the polices' ultimatum of accepting charges, which turned out to be a bluff. Druthers, "The Price Of Freedom In Canada?" YouTube Video, February 22, 2022. https://www.youtube.com/watch?v=UPwr7j4lZzs.

78 Alexandre Lavoie, "Aboriginal peaceful protester trampled by Toronto police horse unit in Ottawa." *Rebel News*, February 21, 2022. https://www.rebelnews.com/interview_female_aboriginal_peaceful_protester_trampled_by_rcmp_horse_unit_in_ottawa.

79 Sheila Gunn Reid, "LEAKED RCMP MESSAGES: 'Time for the protesters to hear our jackboots on the ground.' *Rebel News*, February 19, 2022. https://www.rebelnews.com/leaked_rcmp_messages_time_for_the_protesters_to_hear_our_jackboots_on_the_ground.

80 Ottawa Police, Twitter Post, February 19, 2022, at 8:25 AM. https://twitter.com/OttawaPolice/status/1495026664845328388.

81 "Romanian MEP Cristian Terheş Goes Fully Automatic on Justin Trudeau's Dictatorial Measures in Canada." Red Voice Media, February 20, 2022. https://www.redvoicemedia.com/video/2022/02/romanian-mep-cristian-terhes-goes-fully-automatic-on-justin-trudeaus-dictatorial-measures-in-canada/.

Toronto several times to support the protest because they fear that Canada will fall into a communist pitfall under a dictatorship regime like it did in Romania. It takes several generations to regain freedom. Trudeau is coming after political enemies with violence, such as journalist Alexa Lavoie, who was viciously attacked by police.[82] So much for "sunny ways," Trudeau is ushering darker days in our once beautiful and free land.[83] Our Charter of Rights and Freedoms have become null and void.

Trudeau is more interested in the Chinese Olympics than addressing the division he has caused to his people. Under a tweet he posted regarding the Olympics, Canadians exposed who he really is, tweet after tweet.[84] Given this unprecedented evil and corruption, at all levels of government and police forces, we must call upon all patriots, whether police officers, politicians, people with power, and ordinary citizens, to stand up against this tyranny. On February 7, 2022, Archbishop Viganò released an important message to the Canadian truckers:

> Your protest, dear Canadian truck driver friends, joins a worldwide chorus that wants to oppose the establishment of the New World Order on the rubble of nation-states through the Great Reset desired by the World Economic Forum and by the United Nations under the name of "Agenda 2030." And we know that many heads of government have participated in Klaus Schwab's School for Young Leaders—the so-called Global Leaders for Tomorrow—beginning with Justin Trudeau and Emmanuel Macron, Jacinta Ardern and Boris Johnson and, before that, Angela Merkel, Nicolas Sarkozy and Tony Blair.[85]

He also recognizes the many difficulties that face the truckers:

> You understood this instinctively and your yearning for freedom was shown in all its coordinated harmony moving towards the capital, Ottawa. Dear truck drivers, you are facing great difficulties—not only

82 Ian Miles Cheong, "Rebel News journalist Alexa Lavoie attacked by Ottawa." *Rebel News*, February 19, 2022. https://www.rebelnews.com/breaking_rebel_news_journalist_alexa_lavoie_attacked_by_ottawa_police.

83 I underestimated how bad things could get over 6 years ago, see Scott Ventureyra "Trudeau and the decapitation of Christian values." *City Light News*, December 2015, 5. https://www.scottventureyra.com/_files/ugd/f90fdb_d9e686bbe1484951bd8a09d2f69b8727.pdf.

84 Justin Trudeau, Twitter Post. February 19, 2022, at 4:32 PM. https://twitter.com/JustinTrudeau/status/1495149275499708417.

85 To read the full message, see Abp. Carlo Maria Viganò, "Message of His Excellency Archbishop Carlo Maria Viganò to Canadian Truckers." *Church Militant*, February 8, 2022. https://www.churchmilitant.com/news/article/archbishop-vigano-to-canadian-truckers. To listen to his message, go to: INSPIRED, "Archbishop Viganò's IMPORTANT MESSAGE To Canadian Truckers." YouTube Video, February 15, 2022. https://www.youtube.com/watch?v=FXXM_BH4b7Y.

> because you give up your work to demonstrate but, also, because of the adverse weather conditions, long nights in the cold and attempts to be cleared away that you face. But, along with these difficulties, you have also experienced the closeness of many of your fellow citizens who, like you, have understood the looming threat and want to support you in protesting against the regime. Allow me also to express to you my support and my spiritual closeness, to which I join the prayer that your event may be crowned with success and may also extend to other countries.[86]

Viganò addresses the cowardice of friends and family members who have done nothing but conform:

> In these days, we see the masks of tyrants from all over the world fall and, unfortunately, we also see so much conformism, so much fearfulness, so much cowardice in people who, up until yesterday, we regarded as friends, even among our family members. Yet, precisely because of this extreme situation, we discover with amazement gestures of humanity made by strangers, signs of solidarity and brotherhood on the part of those who feel close to us in the common battle. We discover so much generosity and so much desire to shake us from this stupor. We discover that we are no longer willing to passively suffer the destruction of our world—imposed by a cabal of unscrupulous criminals thirsty for power and money.[87]

He concludes by insisting that we must not acquiesce, and keep pushing for freedom and its ultimate significance:

> Today, more than ever, it is essential that you realize that it is no longer possible to passively assist. It is necessary to take a position, to fight for freedom, to demand respect for natural freedoms. But, even more, dear Canadian brothers, it is necessary to understand that this dystopia serves to establish the dictatorship of the New World Order and totally erase every trace of Our Lord Jesus Christ from society, from history and from the traditions of peoples.[88]

By the time this book is published, many changes will have come about. We can only hope that these changes are for the betterment of humanity. May the lies we have been fed for the past two years make us question the new unfolding narrative with Ukraine. Oftentimes, things are not as they appear, especially

86 Viganò, "Message of His Excellency Archbishop Carlo Maria Viganò to Canadian Truckers."
87 Viganò, "Message of His Excellency Archbishop Carlo Maria Viganò to Canadian Truckers."
88 Viganò, "Message of His Excellency Archbishop Carlo Maria Viganò to Canadian Truckers."

popularly held views. Whatever is unfolding with the Russian–Ukrainian conflict may be more profound than a superficial analysis will allow—keep questioning and keep an open mind. Something tells me that it is not a coincidence that any talk of COVID-19 has vanished. Nevertheless, the truth always prevails. History will not be kind to those who were complicit—inaction is action. The globalists and their political understudies are wreaking as much havoc as possible since their time will be short, much like their demonic inspirer (Rev 12:12). We must always remember that although God has defeated evil and our enemy; the accuser's presence and hostility towards God's kingdom and us, will continue until Christ returns. So, what matters most is our resolve. We must keep resisting because we know what we are doing is right and just. We must follow God until the end. We must uphold God's will and goodness towards one another. We are living in dangerous times. Regardless of our differences, we share in His *imago Dei*, which will shape us into the persons He intended us to be. Eventually, through our persistence and faithfulness to God (Heb 1:11), if we continue to kick against this oppression then the darkness will begin to subside and bleed day light.[89]

89 A reference to Bruce Cockburn's "Lovers in a Dangerous Time."

Appendix 1

Template letter for warning of risks to parents in favour of COVID-19 vaccination

Dear _____,

We both love our child very much, but we have a fundamental disagreement about the COVID-19 vaccine. If I wasn't concerned, I wouldn't have taken the time to create this document. I do this out of love for our child and my duty as a father to protect her. So, please take the time to read the material (all of the links provided in the footnotes) and watch the excellent presentation by Dr. Peter McCullough (link in the main text), it may be the most powerful and important presentation you'll ever watch on COVID vaccines. This material is for your serious consideration. Please take into serious consideration my request in the last paragraph of page 8. I'm not sending this to argue, but to make you aware of things that you may not be aware of. I don't know which sources you follow but mainstream news is unceasingly feeding people propaganda—it is an unrelenting attack of fear and disinformation/misinformation. Even Sesame Street is incessantly pushing these vaccines onto our children.[1] (The YouTube video: https://www.youtube.com/watch?v=yPlhRUF2aXA is incredibly disturbing, bordering on the level of cultish. Notice that the number of dislikes outnumber the likes on a Sesame Street video [this not a common occurrence], people realize this is very wrong.)

If you pay close enough attention you can catch the mainstream media's lies, just like our leaders and medical bureaucrats like Theresa Tam, Kieran Moore, and Deena Hinshaw. They've flip-flopped[2] and admitted to lying to us on several occasions. Do you trust Trudeau with his massive push for these vaccines? These politicians and bureaucrats have conflicts of interests up the yin yang. It is as though a significant portion of the population is in a trance and incapable of looking at the evidence calmly. It is unfortunate we are having this

1 https://www.rt.com/usa/539557-sesame-street-covid-vaccine-children/.

2 https://tnc.news/2020/05/22/six-times-federal-officials-contradicted/.

issue, but we should be batting for the same team since it's ultimately about protecting _____, not about our differences.

At the case conference on Monday, November 8, 2021, I presented everyone with solid facts taken from the Health Canada website, other Government of Canada sources, and peer reviewed journals. Earlier this year, you admitted that you didn't think _____ "necessarily needed to take the vaccine." It seemed as though we agreed. Your lawyer called it a "deadly" virus, but that is a misleading statement without proper context. Yes, deadly in the context of people with comorbidities/compromised immune systems and who are of old age. But not deadly for people who are healthy, especially those under 20 years of age. Therefore, it is not deadly for a young healthy girl like _____. Justice Kaufman agreed with me on this point. The risk of fatality is effectively zero and incredibly low for hospitalization.

Data and Facts from Government Websites and Other Reputable Sources

Here are facts from the Government of Canada and Vaccine Adverse Events Reporting System (VAERS) that you can verify for yourself:

Risks Associated with COVID-19

For children, there is an extremely low risk of fatality and hospitalization for COVID-19. Can anyone dispute this? For instance, in Canada, as of November 5, 2021, there have been 1,718,937 cases.[3] Moreover, there have been 359,931 cases of people under the age of 20;[4] this amounts to 20.9 percent of the total number of cases, the largest age group of infections. This group has had 1,899 hospitalizations which amounts to be .53 percent of all cases under 20, which is the lowest of any age group. There have also been 17 deaths out of 28, 900[5] of the total number of deaths amounting to .059 percent of all deaths in Canada; and out of the total number of young people in that demographic of the population of 8.1 million, the risk factor is .0002 percent. What about deaths

3 Health Canada, "COVID-19 daily epidemiology update." https://health-infobase.canada.ca/covid-19/epidemiological-summary-covid-19-cases.html#a5.

4 Health Canada, "COVID-19 daily epidemiology update." https://health-infobase.canada.ca/covid-19/epidemiological-summary-covid-19-cases.html#a5.

5 Health Canada, "COVID-19 daily epidemiology update." https://health-infobase.canada.ca/covid-19/epidemiological-summary-covid-19-cases.html#a5.

6 Transport Canada, "Canadian Motor Vehicle Traffic Collision Statistics: 2018." https://tc.canada.ca/en/road-transportation/statistics-data/canadian-motor-vehicle-traffic-collision-statistics-2018.

to total population of roughly 38 million? .000045 percent. In comparison to traffic collisions, in 2019 there were 160 deaths for people 20 years of age and under,[6] if we sample that to 20 months (at a rate of 13.33 deaths/month) there would be a total of 267 deaths for a similar timespan. This means that there is 15.7 times higher risk of dying from a car accident than COVID-19. Does this mean we should be paralyzed by fear every time we drive?

Risks Associated with the COVID-19 Vaccine

Consider the following: according to the Vaccine Adverse Events Reporting System (VAERS) in the US, from 1997–2013 there were 2,149 reported deaths, this includes billions upon billions of administered vaccines (a significantly higher number than the administered number of COVID-19 vaccines). Whereas the COVID vaccine, in only an eight-to-nine-month period, with 366 million doses administered, as of August 21, 2021 (keep in mind that things have gotten substantially worse since then) there were 13, 068 reported deaths in about 5 percent of the time span. There were also 5,882 Heart Attacks, 4,861, Myocarditis/Pericarditis, and 17,228 Permanently Disabled reports (in sum, over 700,000 injuries, again the reality is worse now). This should give any reasonable person pause.[7] I could go on and on. I have plenty of arguments and data. One of my responsibilities as a parent is to protect _____, not to blindly follow governments' mandates/recommendations without question. I live by reason and my conscience, not irrational fear.

Please WATCH this presentation in its entirety that was delivered on October 2, 2021, to the Association of American Physicians and Surgeons by the COVID-19 medical expert Dr. Peter McCullough (he is one of the most cited doctors in the world and has published over 50 peer reviewed articles on COVID alone—that's much more than most physicians in their career): "Winning the War Against Therapeutic Nihilism & Trusted Treatments vs Untested Novel Therapies":

https://rumble.com/vnbv86-winning-the-war-against-therapeutic-nihilism-and-trusted-treatments-vs-unte.html

- Consider this article titled: "Why Are We Vaccinating Our Children?"[8] which concurs the facts above, published in a respected journal: *Toxicology Reports*. Here are the highlights:
  - Bulk of COVID-19 per capita deaths occur in elderly with high comorbidities.

7 VAERS, https://www.openvaers.com/covid-data.

8 https://www.sciencedirect.com/science/article/pii/S221475002100161X.

- Per capita COVID-19 deaths are negligible in children.
- Clinical trials for these inoculations were very short-term.
- Clinical trials did not address long-term effects most relevant to children.
- High post-inoculation deaths reported in VAERS (very short-term).

- Consider the Physicians Declaration II—Updated Global Covid Summit by the International Alliance of Physicians and Medical Scientists (originally Rome Declaration)[9]:

RESOLVED, THAT HEALTHY CHILDREN SHALL NOT BE SUBJECT TO FORCED VACCINATION (view supporting evidence)[10]

- Negligible clinical risks from SARS-CoV-2 infection exist for healthy children under eighteen.
- Long-term safety of the current COVID vaccines in children cannot be determined prior to instituting such policies. Without high-powered, reproducible, long-term safety data, risks to the long-term health status of children remain too high to support use in healthy children.
- Children risk severe, adverse events from receiving the vaccine. Permanent physical damage to the brain, heart, immune and reproductive system associated with SARS-CoV-2 spike protein-based genetic vaccines has been demonstrated in children.
- Healthy, unvaccinated children are critical to achieving herd immunity. Natural immunity is proven to tolerate infection, benefiting community protection while there is insufficient data to assess whether Covid vaccines assist herd immunity.

RESOLVED, THAT NATURALLY IMMUNE PERSONS RECOVERED FROM SARS-CoV-2 SHALL NOT BE SUBJECT TO ANY RESTRICTIONS OR VACCINE MANDATES (view supporting evidence)[11]

Now let's consider the following questions:

1. Is it necessary? Given the high survival rate from COVID-19, and the fact that there are so many breakthrough cases for those who

9 https://doctorsandscientistsdeclaration.org/?fbclid=IwAR19QsUMuvltxTjANlSat5UWRckJTcMfhQAjdMztxkh5QdEiWH7aD4caX2w.

10 Vaccinating Children Means Unnecessary Risks: https://doctorsandscientistsdeclaration.org/home/supporting-evidence/#children.

11 COVID-Recovered Immunity is Durable: https://doctorsandscientistsdeclaration.org/home/supporting-evidence/#recovered.

have been doubly vaccinated,[12] we can emphatically say that, no, it is not necessary. Plus, you have to consider that the vaccines' "efficacy" wane after 6 months or less. Ask yourself why they are pushing these boosters. Also ask yourself how many will be required.

2. Is it dangerous?

   Yes, look at the VAERS data and the article above "Why Are We Vaccinating Our Children?" in *Toxicology Reports*.

   Also consider the numbers from the VigiAccess database (World Health Organization Programme for International Drug Monitoring (WHO PIDM)): http://www.vigiaccess.org/. Type in COVID-19 vaccine in the search engine and you'll see all the adverse effects. Look at the chart in Appendix 3 comparing the COVID-19 vaccine (all different types) to other vaccines and drugs from 1968–2021. Notice the astronomical difference in adverse effects in a short time span—it's more dangerous than all these vaccines/drugs combined from 1960s/1970s/1980s until now:

The numbers don't lie.

Take also into consideration these points:

- This pandemic has always been "ABOUT THE VACCINE."
- "Stakeholders" that strongly want a "needle in every arm" are Big Pharma, White House, CDC, FDA, NIH, Gates Foundation, WHO, Trudeau/Government of Canada.
- The death rate for the COVID vaccine is far higher than for any other vaccine in history [look at the VAERS numbers I provided].
- "Never vaccinate into the middle of a pandemic."
- "85% of covid deaths were preventable with early treatment which was squashed."
- The "dangerous spike protein" damages blood vessels and cause blood clotting.[13]

12 Here's a recent example: https://torontosun.com/entertainment/television/derek-hough-in-quarantine-with-covid-19-after-dwts-appearance?utm_term=Autofeed&utm_medium=Social&utm_source=Facebook&fbclid=IwAR3fsB8Pjc86ZcdWsjrWniT_TS8eOgrZFp9Qq3VNewlZ4IbOiMS0l0dthag#Echobox=1637106973.

13 https://michaelsavage.com/top-doctor-warns-about-covid-vaccine/.

Consider this statement from a group of physicians examining and questioning vaccine safety and the lack of research being conducted into this:

> "Under the cautionary principle, it is parsimonious to consider vaccine-induced Spike synthesis could cause clinical signs of severe COVID-19, and erroneously be counted as new cases of SARS-CoV-2 infections. If so, the true adverse effects of the current global vaccination strategy may never be recognized unless studies specifically examine this question. There is already noncausal evidence of temporary or sustained increases in COVID-19 deaths following vaccination in some countries (Fig. 1) and in light of Spike's pathogenicity, these deaths must be studied in depth to determine whether they are related to vaccination."[14]

3. Is it effective? No, it doesn't stop transmission:

> The SARS-CoV-2 delta (B.1.617.2) variant is highly transmissible and spreading globally, including in populations with high vaccination rates.[15]

Also consider that natural immunity is considered to be just as strong or stronger than double vaccination.[16] This is well known throughout the literature, something not told to us by the media. Furthermore, a significant number of doctors insist that taking the vaccine after having had COVID-19 is a contraindication. Consider this, from an Israeli study where there is a high rate of double vaccination:

> This study demonstrated that natural immunity confers longer lasting and stronger protection against infection, symptomatic disease and hospitalization caused by the Delta variant of SARS-CoV-2, compared to the BNT162b2 two-dose vaccine-induced immunity.[17]

Please keep in mind that the main role of the vaccine is to protect the recipient and growing data is suggesting otherwise; to this end: they are not effective. The

14 https://d197for5662m48.cloudfront.net/documents/publicationstatus/63616/preprint_pdf/a63a137eb14404fbd393121dafa96ada.pdf, page 5.

15 https://doi.org/10.1016/S1473-3099(21)00648-4.

16 https://www.bmj.com/content/374/bmj.n2101.

17 https://www.medrxiv.org/content/10.1101/2021.08.24.21262415v1.

media propaganda machine is saying that the vaccinated are in danger of the unvaccinated, but this is logically incoherent. If the vaccines don't work, why take them? If they do work, then why be fearful? Changing the narrative to that it "weakens" the virus or that "it does not offer 100% protection but it's still effective" is a clear admission that they aren't effective while saying otherwise. It's just a form of doublespeak. Even Dr. Anthony Fauci admits they're not effective and that you'll need boosters after being doubly vaccinated. Does it sound like they're very effective to you? Check out the NY Times transcript of his interview regarding this.[18] **Think about how governments are in the absurd and awkward position of having to convince the unvaccinated that the vaccine is effective and necessary, while trying to convince the vaccinated that the vaccine is not strong enough and that they need boosters!**

Final Thoughts:

I also have many theological and philosophical objections to all of this, but I have limited my objections to medical/scientific and statistical evidence. Recall that Dr. _____ (our daughter's family doctor) agreed with every concern I raised (I can provide evidence if need be). He also believes that a 12-year-old cannot provide informed consent. Of course, Dr. _____, given the climate of hostility for dissenters, recommends the vaccine despite the risks. Nonetheless, he was sympathetic to my concerns and admitted I was well informed on the issues.

Finally, why do you think they are coercing us to inoculate our children? NEVER in history have those who have resorted to coercive tactics been the good guys. And also, don't think that governments will ever let you go back to "normal" just by taking this vaccine, then the next, then your booster, since you'll still have to wear masks, take PCR tests, etc. Watch Peterson, who is doubly vaccinated (who now regrets it) and what he has to say about all this (it's only a one-minute clip).[19] In the full version of the interview he says that this unrelenting push to vaccinate children is reprehensible.

There is a lot of money at stake, and many involved with the pharmaceutical industry are covering up the reality of these vaccines. You can peruse the Project Veritas website which has a growing number of whistleblowers exposing the FDA, Pfizer, Johnson & Johnson, US Government, big media, etc.[20]

18 https://www.nytimes.com/2021/11/12/podcasts/the-daily/anthony-fauci-vaccine-mandates-booster-shots.html?showTranscript=1.

19 https://www.youtube.com/watch?v=0fhlSw72Z5M. He says: "Here's the deal, I got vaccinated, you f*cking leave me alone," but of course they won't they need more testing, masks, distancing, quarantining, and boosters.

20 https://www.projectveritas.com/news/pfizer-scientist-your-antibodies-are-probably-better-than-the-vaccination/.

Consider all the highly respected doctors who signed the Barrington Declaration, (over 14,000 medical and public health scientists have signed; over 44,000 medical practitioners)[21] and the Rome Declaration.[22] These signees put their names on the line. These health experts are not only putting their careers and reputations at risk, but even their lives. Why would a doctor like Robert Malone, who is the ARCHITECT of the mRNA technology for the Pfizer and Moderna vaccine speak out? He knows how this technology functions and its dangers. Dr. Malone said that: "This is the Largest Experiment Performed on Human Beings in the History of the World."[23]

These courageous doctors are combatting governments, billionaire elites, the pharmaceutical industry, and the media who do not have our best interests at heart. Consider this point here: do you trust "Canada's Top Doctor," Theresa Tam? She's not really a medical expert but an incompetent medical bureaucrat with a meager 65 citations in the literature (check out her score on Google Scholar).[24] Now compare that with Dr. Peter McCullough who has 115,430 citations. What do you think would happen if they both squared off on CBC for a debate on COVID-19 and these vaccines? I think you know the answer. Also, ask yourself why people like Dr. Fauci and Dr. Tam do not want to debate reputable doctors. Dr. Malone has challenged Dr. Fauci on numerous occasions, but Malone has been met with silence. Science is about debate, questioning, and testing hypotheses — without it, progress is impossible. What science is not about, is declaring issue by fiat and demonizing those who are critical of certain hypotheses, theories, and accepted "narratives."

Thus, given the information I presented, do you honestly believe it's about our health? I hope you can see why I have concerns for _____ taking this vaccine. I don't know how to reach you. As I said at the case conference, the vaccine issue is not about ethics and evidence, even though it should be, but rather about coercion and submission. Our governments are completely reckless. If adults aren't able to provide informed consent, since they don't have the right information, then how can a child born in 2009 be able to provide informed consent? Informed consent entails: consent by a person to undergo a medical procedure, participate in a clinical trial, or be counseled by a professional, such as a social worker or lawyer, after receiving all material information regarding risks, benefits, and alternatives. Our governments haven't been forthright about the real risks or the lack of benefits nor alternative treatments that work. (Alternatives that have been demonized like ivermectin have been effective in early treatment

21 https://gbdeclaration.org/view-signatures/.

22 https://doctorsandscientistsdeclaration.org/?fbclid=IwAR2Lu9M7a1lrtoe2mOcbmE1z9C1evKlElDta3u9f_ZkdH-8HoEYIIg_4_sY.

23 https://thenewamerican.com/dr-robert-malone-this-is-the-largest-experiment-performed-on-human-beings-in-the-history-of-the-world/.

24 https://scholar.google.ca/citations?user=pSRDb3gAAAAJ&hl=en&oi=ao.

of COVID. Interestingly, Pfizer has filed for authorization of a pill similar to it now. Please note that Pfizer is releasing about 400,000 pages of data regarding the vaccines. One document lists 9 pages of adverse effects in paragraph form – do you think this is a safe vaccine?)[25] Therefore, informed consent has been nullified for both adults and especially children. The vaccines will not help us reach herd immunity, so why now the aggressive push for five-year-olds? That should raise red flags for anyone.

In conclusion, the risks of the COVID-19 vaccine exceed any conceivable benefit. Plus, we know that natural immunity, through unvaccinated children, is crucial to reaching herd immunity. This is what the evidence clearly indicates. We also have no idea about what sort of long-term effects these vaccines will have on adults let alone children. There are growing number of testimonies of individuals and parents with children who have suffered severe adverse effects. Again, you won't hear about this in the mainstream media. Check out the powerful testimony of Brianne Dressen in front of the FDA who suffered a neurological injury[26]: https://www.youtube.com/watch?v=YLYo-uSN6xA. I also encourage you to look at this page, where you can hear the testimonies from parents themselves: https://odysee.com/@RandyHillier:c/20211108_adverseeffects:e.

We both are trying to do what we believe is right because we both love ______ and want what's best for her. This is why the evidence is so crucial, wouldn't you agree? Science is about debate. Ask yourself this: why do they not allow credible dissenting views to be given a fair platform? Instead, what happens? They get censored. But why? Now can you please refute what I have stated and give an argument aside from "I'm following the provincial and federal guidelines when it comes to the COVID injection"? Can you provide me evidence that COVID-19 kills healthy children? And that any healthy child has died *from* COVID-19 not *with*? Can you demonstrate that the doubly vaccinated transmit the virus less than the unvaccinated? 40% of the Ottawa Senators are now infected with 100% inoculation. Can you show that double vaccination is superior to natural immunity? I provided my evidence, what is yours? It's a two-way street, is it not? This is not aggression—these are necessary questions that must be responded to. Disagreement is not aggression. I've done my homework, but most people have not. As I said at the case conference, unfortunately this is about might making right, not truth, evidence, or objective ethics/morals. Does 2+2=5 because the government says so?

25 https://globalnews.ca/news/8377984/pfizer-covid19-pill-treatment/?utm_medium=Facebook&utm_source=GlobalNews&fbclid=IwAR0cc8ely2PTgg2P6awWFI-ZzXXcPHgeRwavjDMp2nSrxqpmDyQXLnT1tL0.

26 https://kutv.com/news/local/utah-scientist-testifies-before-fda-panel-asks-not-to-approve-covid-19-vaccine-for-kids.

What recourse do we have if _____ is harmed by the vaccine? The pharmaceutical companies are indemnified, and our governments won't be liable, so then who takes responsibility? What is your course of action if this happens? Do you know? What are you prepared to do if she experiences a vaccine injury? What will you say then? What would you do if you were me? I'm trying my best to work with you by showing you evidence and sound reasoning, but you have to work with me.

There is much more to be said and many more resources to be shared, but this should suffice to dismantle the case for vaccinating children, especially healthy children. Consider that the end trial date for testing "the Safety, Tolerability, Immunogenicity, and Efficacy of RNA Vaccine Candidates Against COVID-19 in Healthy Individuals" ends on May 2, 2023.[27] That's taken from the clinical trials of the US Government website. Would you consider holding off on _____ taking the vaccine until she's 13 and reassessing the situation then? All these mandates might be lifted for *everyone*, and everything might collapse by then. She has not been restricted from activities so far, but potential restrictions shouldn't be a sufficient reason to play "Russian roulette" with her health, especially given all the evidence I presented, don't you think? Keep in mind that, Dr. Kieran Moore (Ontario's chief medical officer of health) and the provincial government "won't be adding COVID-19 vaccinations to the list of immunizations students are required to have to attend schools."[28] That is quite significant and should weigh in our decision. Also consider that many restrictions still exist for the doubly vaccinated and that in Israel those who have not received their booster shots have lost their vaccine passports (this amounts to close to 2 million people).[29] If you take everything I said seriously and examine/check my claims, then you would not only be concerned about _____ but for yourself and the rest of your family. These may be inconvenient facts (especially for those who've received the injection already), but this is the reality of the situation whether we like it or not.

I'm always open to discussing all of this calmly and rationally, but through mediation or with a neutral party present. This is preferable over litigation. I hope we can both come to an agreement on our own. Let us not do what is expedient and cave to governmental pressures in the absence of logic, evidence, and objective ethical standards. Please think long and hard about how we should proceed with the health of our precious child, _____. (This letter was written to my daughter's mother, who I doubt read it and then proceeded immediately

27 https://clinicaltrials.gov/ct2/show/NCT04368728.

28 https://www.theglobeandmail.com/canada/article-students-in-ontario-will-not-require-covid-19-vaccination-to-attend/.

29 https://www.timesofisrael.com/nearly-2-million-israelis-lose-green-pass-as-new-rules-enter-effect/?fbclid=IwAR38Uh29peiTPK8LUZfAO_pFzC054sPNVCqWSK4pzNgjRXx9Zn9OLUk6-1w.

after receiving it to inject our child. Since then, our daughter has received her second dose and the mother with her mass formation psychosis wants to keep injecting our child even though the mandates are finished for now. The mother was arguing that she didn't want our daughter to be excluded from activities but now it makes no difference. What's more is that our daughter has been wanting to tryout for certain team sports, but the mother does not pick up the slack to drive her from her house, whereas I'm always ready and able to support her extra-curricular activities and driver her at any time. None of this makes any sense, but this is the unfortunate reality of dealing with irrational people. For some people spite will blind them to not act in the best interests of their child.)

Sincerely,

Scott Ventureyra

Appendix 2

Time to Wake Up: A Letter to Physicians

Dear friends and colleagues,

I am fully conscious of my position in this matter and proud to be part of the resistance to a totalitarian global regime, which is pushing a nefarious agenda planned to install the New World Order. I am in complete disagreement with and opposed to all those individuals, physicians, that support and promote the implementation of unscientific and unjustified sanitary measures, including a massive inoculation with experimental genetic products (so-called vaccines) currently proven to inflict enormous amounts of damage and mayhem to the world population, children in particular. Regrettably, these physicians have failed to adhere to the sacred principle of the Hippocratic Oath: "DO NO HARM."

Personally, I became a victim of the false pandemic protocols, having had to postpone indefinitely a much-needed surgical intervention because I refused the preoperative infamous PCR-test. Which is one of the pillars of the false pandemic narrative. In addition, few weeks ago, I developed Dyshidrotic Eczema which, according to the dermatologist I consulted, is frequently seen after COVID vaccination. Interestingly, I am not vaccinated. Thus, the dermatologist advised me against COVID vaccination but was unwilling to extend the vaccination exemption certificate, obviously concerned about possible consequences to her employment.

It seems I contracted this skin condition from vaccinated individuals with whom I may have been in contact (i.e., at restaurants) where most servers are vaccinated. Regarding the chaotic hospital situation in Canada due to the overwhelming number of hospitalized new COVID infections. Honestly, I don't believe that these new COVID infections are really occurring in the unvaccinated population. Actually, the available data from various official sources (VAERS, EMA, etc.) confirms the reverse phenomenon. Which is alarming!

The COVID-19 pandemic is not just about health, it is a political instrument used as justification for the implementation of Agenda 2030, created and promoted by the World Economic Forum as part of the "Great Reset." Which, among other things, is planned to reduce and enslave the world population.

It seems that you and many others like you, that unfortunately believe in the deceiving official COVID-19 narrative, are not seeing the appalling reality of an unfolding catastrophe for humanity. Which includes the possible destruction of our society and the human race, as we know it. I am sorry to see you falling into the trap set up by the globalists. To really understand what's going on, one must read the book titled: *COVID-19: The Great Reset* written by Klaus Schwab and Thierry Malleret.

Due to the current tyrannical COVID-19 travel restrictions, intended to curtail civil liberties, I am unable to return to Canada, my home country, to join my son and granddaughter whom I have not seen in a long time.

I don't care what people say about me because: "I know who I am and I don't have to prove anything to anyone." I want to be remembered as a physician who risked his reputation trying to protect and preserve the life and integrity of his fellow man and of the entire human race. And who upheld and practiced the sacred principles of the Hippocratic Oath.

Sincerely,

Enrique Ventureyra

Appendix 3

World Health Organization's Database chart of side effects of medicinal products versus COVID-19 vaccine

World Health Organization

VigiAccess was launched by the World Health Organization (WHO) in 2015 to provide public access to information in VigiBase, the WHO global database of reported potential side effects of medicinal products.		
Vaccine or Drug Name	Total ADRs	Years
Mumps vaccine	711	1972–2021
Rubella caccine	2,621	1971–2021
Ivermectin	5,705	1992–2021
Measles vaccine	5,827	1968–2021
Penicillin nos	6,684	1968–2021
Smallpox vaccine	6,891	1968–2021
Chloroquine	7,139	1968–2021
Tetanus vaccine	15,085	1968–2021
Hydroxychchloroquine	32,641	1968–2021
Hepatitis A vaccine	46,773	1989–2021
Benzylpenicillin	51,327	1968–2021
Rotavirus vaccine	68,327	2000–2021
Accutane	70,719	1983–2021
Vancomycin	71,159	1974–2021
Hepatitis B vaccine	104,619	1984–2021
Polio vaccine	121,988	1968–2021
Meningococcal vaccine	126,412	1976–2021
Ibuprofen	166,209	1969–2021
Tylenol	169,359	1968–2021
Aspirin	184,481	1968–2021
Pneumococcal vaccine	234,786	1980–2021
Influenza vaccine	272,202	1968–2021
Covid-19 vaccine	2,457,386	2020–2021

www.vigiaccess.org
Updated November 12, 2021

Contributors

Scott D. G. Ventureyra

Scott D. G. Ventureyra completed several undergraduate degrees (including one in economics from the University of Ottawa), a Master of Arts in Theology from Saint Paul University, and a PhD in Philosophical Theology from Carleton University/Dominican University College. He is the author of two books, including the Amazon best-seller *On the Origin of Consciousness: An Exploration through the Lens of the Christian Conception of God and Creation* (Wipf and Stock). He has published in academic journals such as *Science et Esprit, The American Journal of Biblical Theology, Studies in Religion, Dialogue: Canadian Philosophical Review*, and *Maritain Studies*. He has also written for magazines such as *Crisis Magazine, Catholic Insight*, and *Convivium*, and newspapers such as *The National Post, City Light News, The Ottawa Citizen*, and *The Times Colonist*. He has presented his research at conferences around North America, including the Science of Consciousness Conference in 2020. He is currently working on a book about the Roman Catholic priest, paleontologist, and theologian Pierre Teilhard de Chardin, titled *Why Teilhard Matters*. His website is www.scottventureyra.com.

Phil Fernandes

Phil Fernandes is the pastor of Trinity Bible Fellowship of Bremerton, Washington, and vice-president of the International Society of Christian Apologetics. He teaches philosophy and apologetics for Crosspoint Academy, Veritas International University, Columbia Evangelical Seminary, and Shepherds Bible College. He has earned doctoral degrees in philosophy of religion and Christian apologetics, and he has debated some of America's leading atheists. He is director of the Doctor of Ministry in Christian Apologetics Program for Veritas International University. Fernandes has authored numerous books on Christian apologetics, including *Hijacking the Historical Jesus, The Atheist Delusion*, and *The Fernandes Guide to Apologetic Methodologies*. He also contributed to *Vital Issues in the Inerrancy Debate*.

John Ferrer

Dr. John D. Ferrer is a teaching fellow with the Equal Rights Institute. He has a PhD and ThM in Philosophy of Religion with a minor in Ethics (Southwestern Baptist Theological Seminary) and an MDiv in Christian apologetics (Southern Evangelical Seminary). His teaching and debates focus largely on worldview and ethics, with a special focus on abortion. His written works include *Body Ethics* (2014) and contributions to *Answering the Music Man: Dan Barker's Arguments Against Christianity* (2020) and *The Popular Handbook of World Religions* (2021). When he's not helping his wife Hillary with her ministry *Mama Bear Apologetics*, he oversees two websites: www.intelligentchristianfaith.com and www.abortionhistorymuseum.com.

Trevor Blackwell

Trevor Blackwell is currently employed as a full-time Social Science teacher for the OCDSB (Sir Wilfrid Laurier Secondary School). He has degrees in education and history, including a Master of Arts in History from Queen's University.

David C. Bellusci

David C. Bellusci holds a PhD in Philosophy and PsyD in Clinical Pastoral Psychotherapy. He is the author of seven books, including *Love Deformed, Love Transformed: A Christian Response to Sexual Addiction* (Wipf and Stock). Bellusci is Assistant Professor of Philosophy and Theology at Catholic Pacific College in British Columbia. He is a Roman Catholic priest and belongs to the Dominican Order.

Brenna Bloodworth

Brenna Bloodworth is an outspoken advocate and the founder of parent advocacy group Alliance Against the Ontario Autism Program. She has organized province-wide protests and twice petitioned the Ontario government, aiding in the fight towards meaningful policy changes to support autistic children. She has been interviewed by several media outlets, including Global News Canada, which featured her leaked, heated phone call with Ontario Premier Doug Ford.

Rick Mehta

Rick Mehta completed his undergraduate degree in neuroscience at the University of Toronto, and his graduate degrees in psychology at McGill University. He spent three years as a post-doctoral fellow at the University of Winnipeg before becoming a professor. Between 2003 and 2018, Rick Mehta was a professor in the Department of Psychology at Acadia University. During this time, he excelled at teaching the department's required courses and his research was on the topic of judgment and decision-making. He was dismissed from his position as a tenured professor after becoming an advocate for free speech.

Andrew Gill

Andrew Gill is a fitness instructor and trainer who has worked for over 25 years with people of all ages. He completed a degree in Social Science from the University of Ottawa, as well as certifications in personal training and older adult fitness. He is an inventor and a Canadian Patent holder (#2,524,078) for a fitness device. He resides in Ottawa and is an avid athlete.

Martina Speck

Martina Speck is currently a PhD student at the University of Ottawa with a research emphasis on symptoms of schizophrenia, especially auditory-verbal hallucinations. She holds a Master of Science in Clinical and Health Psychology from the Johannes Gutenberg University in Germany. She has worked with multiple research groups, with publications in illusory self-motion and trauma research. She lives with her husband in Ottawa.

Valérie A. G. Ventureyra

Valérie A. G. Ventureyra is a clinical psychologist and psychotherapist, specializing in Cognitive-Behavioural Therapy (CBT) and EMDR. She earned her undergraduate degree at McGill University in Montreal, then moved to France, where she studied at the University of Lyon 2 and the University of Paris 5 before earning her PhD in Cognitive Neuroscience at the Ecole des Hautes Etudes en Sciences Sociales (EHESS) in Paris. She has conducted research in cognitive psychology and neuroscience, notably regarding bilingualism, brain plasticity, and language loss, as well as in clinical psychology, with a specific focus on trauma/PTSD assessment and treatment. She has also lectured at several universities in France and has made contributions to the written press in psychology (*Sciences Humaines/Cercle Psy).* Today, she runs a trilingual clinical psychology practice based in Paris and is actively engaged in the fight for Truth and Freedom.

Nikolaj Zunic

Nikolaj Zunic is Associate Professor in the Department of Philosophy at St. Jerome's University, Waterloo, Ontario. He earned his BA at the University of Toronto and his MA and PhD at the Institute of Philosophy of the Catholic University of Leuven, Belgium. His scholarly work focuses on the philosophy of human nature and ethics as well as topics in modern and contemporary philosophy, ranging from Descartes, Kant, and Schelling to phenomenology and 20th-century neo-Thomism. An area of particular philosophical interest is personalism, especially the work of Martin Buber, Gabriel Marcel, and Jacques Maritain. He serves as the President of the Canadian Jacques Maritain Association and is the former editor of the academic journal *Études maritainiennes—Maritain Studies*. He is the editor of *Distinctions of Being: Philosophical Approaches to Reality* (2013), an American Maritain Association publication.

James A. Harris

James A. Harris has spent the majority of his adult life (35 years) in the security and investigations industry, including the U.S. Armed Forces, and as a career investigator he is deeply concerned with the healthcare industry and the institutions which train new medical professionals. He has a BA with honors in Psychology and Comparative Religion (Ottawa), completed post-graduate Studies in Naturopathy (Montreal), and is currently pursuing a PhD in Natural Medicine (Hawaii). A global traveler, he enjoys visiting new cultures and learning new languages and healthy ways of living.

Stella Shihman

Stella Shihman is a registered nurse with a psychology degree. Seeking knowledge, adhering to the Socratic Paradox, evidence-based and intuition-guided. Interested in storytelling, science, politics, and yoga. Unlike Bruce Springsteen, she was born in the USSR and brought up in Israel, and that has made all the difference.

Hugh Hunter

Hugh Hunter is a philosopher living in Canada. He completed his PhD at the University of Toronto. His first book, *How to Be a Philosopher*, was released in 2020.

Enrique C. G. Ventureyra

Enrique C. G. Ventureyra, M.D., FRCS (C), FAANS (L), Professor and Emeritus Chief, Division of Neurosurgery, Children's Hospital of Eastern Ontario, Department of Surgery, University of Ottawa, Ontario, Canada. Dr. Ventureyra obtained his medical degree from the University of La Plata, Argentina, in 1970 and then completed a residency program in neurosurgery at the University of Ottawa. He was the program's first graduate in 1976. He subsequently completed fellowships in pediatric neurosurgery in both Canada and the United States and actively participated in the International Society of Pediatric Neurosurgery (ISPN) and was appointed to the Executive Board in 1996. He is past President of the ISPN (2004–2005) and former Canadian Editor of *Child's Nervous System*, the official journal of the ISPN. Dr. Ventureyra has 148 peer-reviewed publications in the field of neurosurgery to his credit. In 2000, he published in the journal *Child's Nervous System* an innovative concept—Transcutaneous Vagus Nerve Stimulation (t-VNS) as a noninvasive method of Neuromodulation to control partial onset seizures. Based on this new concept a t-VNS stimulator was developed. Because of the noninvasive characteristics of t-VNS the clinical indications of VNS stimulation were expanded.

Pablo Muñoz Iturrieta

Pablo Muñoz Iturrieta holds a doctorate in philosophy and is the author of three books and numerous articles and chapter contributions on topics ranging from gender ideology and religious freedom to political freedom and the cultural decline of the West. He has lectured to thousands of people in more than 100 cities in 15 countries. He currently resides in Canada.

Paul Satori

Paul Satori was the pen name of a Hungarian-born Canadian author and neurosurgeon. He was also the editor's godfather.

Oren Amitay

Oren Amitay holds a PhD in clinical psychology. He is a psychologist with a very busy clinical practice who has taught 20 different university courses approximately 200 times since 2000. He was also a prominent figure in the media until 2020, when he was "canceled" for speaking out on important issues.

Benjamin Blake Speed Watkins

Benjamin Blake Speed Watkins is a nuclear engineer and analytic philosopher from Norfolk, Virginia, whose philosophical work centers on the philosophy of religion, moral philosophy, and Hegel. He is also the host of *Real Atheology: A Philosophy of Religion Podcast*, where he explores questions in the philosophy of religion from non-theist perspectives. Ben graduated from the University of South Carolina in 2009 with a Bachelor of Science in Mechanical Engineering.

Matthew J. Coombe

Matthew Coombe completed a PhD in Theology and Apologetics at Liberty University School of Divinity in Lynchburg, VA. His dissertation was titled *Mythology, Morality, and the Messiah: How Natural Moral Law and Hero Myth Entail that Jesus Christ Is the Best Possible Hero.* He also completed a Master of Arts in Philosophy of Religion and Ethics at the Talbot School of Theology in La Mirada, CA. He is currently an adjunct instructor for Liberty University online. He shares a daughter named Lynn and a dog named Vash with his wife, Nekya, in Bremerton, Washington. He enjoys gardening, writing, basketball, world building, and gaming.

C.C. Harvey

C.C. Harvey is a writer, teacher, artist, and entrepreneur, born and raised in Vancouver, BC. Her mother was Irish-American, and her father was English by birth but raised in Vancouver. She grew up a free-spirited West Coast bohemian, passionate from a young age about literature, art, music, travel, and freedom. She's an avid nature and animal lover. At UBC, she earned an Honours B.A. in literature and a B.Ed. in secondary education. C.C. attended OCAD, University of Toronto, and Queens for additional studies after moving to Ontario. She has held many jobs, working in retail and food service, in art galleries, and for 19 years as a secondary school teacher of English, art, and media, specializing in working with at-risk teens and young adults in alternative education environments. She now lives in a small town on the shore of Lake Ontario with her three children, her husband, and an assortment of pets and plants. C.C. Harvey's first book explored the iconography of Northwest Coast indigenous art, and her primary writing focus now is on cultural and political commentary.

Travis Louisseize

Travis Louisseize received a diploma in electrical engineering technology at Algonquin College. During that time, he wrote a paper on nanotechnology which explored the possibilities for medical advancement as well as the potential for weaponization. Travis has spoke at several public events in response to the Canadian government's COVID measures and is working with local members of the community to support those that are impacted.

Index

4G, 569–70
5G, 518, 568–71, 631, 642–43, 647, 649, 654

A
Abbasi, Kamran, 492, 501
Abortion-Derived Cell Lines, 487*n145*, 511. *See also* HEK693T
Abraham, 712*n7*
Adorno, Theodor, 20, 27, 434
Alex Jones Show, 651
Alinsky, Saul D., 366*n5*, 373, 435, 440
Allen, Tanya Granic, 504
Alston, William, 108*n13*, 117
Amitay, Oren, 36, 324–25, 336, 392, 781
Amnesty International, 19, 28
Andersen, Kristian G., 183*n2*, 195, 289*n12*, 297, 541–42, 544, 546, 550, 594*n225*, 616, 627
Anderson, Ryan T., 391
anesthesiologist, 591–93
Angel of Death (Jose Mengele), 592
Anscombe, Elizabeth, 714, 726
antifa, 416, 418, 435, 500, 744
APA (American Psychiatric Association), 188–89, 193–94
Archbishop Carlo Maria Viganò, 436, 464, 491, 507, 514, 745, 747–48, 759–60.
Archduke Francis Ferdinand, 301, 305
Aristotle, 132, 262-63, 281, 382–83, 395
Armour, Leslie, 56, 60
Arroway, Ellie, 131–32
Assange, Julian, 335
Association of American Physicians and Surgeons (AAPS), 448*n14*, 500–501, 588*n213*, 588*n214*, 588*n215*, 617, 765
AstraZeneca, 736
asymptomatic, 562–64, 621, 630–31
Auchincloss, Hugh, 542
Audioslave, 230
Aunt Jemima, 37
Auschwitz guard, 590
Avildsen, John, 684, 688
Axe, Douglas, 498
Ayala, Francisco, 36
azithromycin, 474*n100*, 476*n108*, 512, 580–81, 622, 629

B
Babylon Bee, 539*n5*, 617
baloney detector, 613–14
bands, punk rock, 227
Baphomet, 644
Barbour, Ian, 123*n4*, 129, 134, 143, 153*n7*, 156
Barnes, Mike, 281, 497*n180*, 501, 694
Barrington Declaration, 770
Bartomeu Payares report, 569, 631
Beckwith, Francis, 165, 359*n9*, 362
Bederman, Diane, 745*n47*
Behe, Michael J., 144, 360*n12*
Bellusci, David C., 183, 198, 201*n25*, 211, 778
Bennington, Chester, 230*n1*
Bergen, Candice, 741
Bergoglio, Jorge Mario, 491, 733–34. *See also* Pope Francis
Bernier, Maxime, 734, 741
Bezmenov, Juri, ix, 4, 7–9, 11–13, 28, 30
Bezos, Jeff, 39, 499
Bhattacharya, Jay, 478, 572*n136*, 626
Biden, Joe, 291*n19*, 334–35, 422, 432*n21*, 440–41, 468–70, 489–91, 506, 510–11, 540, 546*n36*
Big Pharma, 474*n101*, 476*n110*, 582, 584–85, 593, 729, 732, 743, 745, 749–50, 752
Bilderberg Conference, 433*n23*, 441
Bill & Melinda Gates Foundation, 445, 556, 581, 639–40
Bill C-10, 482–83, 505–6
Bill C-16, 50, 249, 260–64, 268–69, 271–72, 274–76, 283–84, 289, 298, 342, 391, 397
Bill C-276, 261, 284
Bill C-279, 261*n6*, 261*n7*, 284
BioNtech-Pfizer, 584, 650, 755
biospheres, lipid, 649
bitcoin, 746–47
Blackwell, Trevor, 315, 778
Blair, Tony, 399, 618, 759
Blaise Pascal, 712*n7*
Blavatsky, Helena, 88–90
Blaylock, Russell, 516*n2*, 523, 574, 618
BLM (Black Lives Matter), 363–66, 370, 372, 374, 416, 418, 420–21, 435, 500, 744
Bloom, Allan, 379, 395, 407–8
Boghossian, Peter, 94, 268*n33*, 281
Bolshevik Revolution, 20, 317, 320
Bonhoeffer, Dietrich, 709, 750
Bourdain, Anthony, 230*n1*
Bourla, Albert, 605, 752
Boyle, Peter, 268*n33*, 283
Braasch, Karsten, 250
brainwashing, 9, 324, 327, 329–30, 517*n4*, 522–23
Brand, Russell, 733*n11*
Breggin, Peter R., 500*n188*, 502, 580*n176*, 618
Bricmont, Jean, 93, 266*n27*, 284
Bridle, Byram, 474, 502, 504
Brown, Michael L., 360*n12*
Brzezinski, Zbigniew, 427, 430
Buckley, Jeff, 228
Buckley, Tim, 228, 395
Bultmann, Rudolf, 118
Bunge, Mario Auguste, 92–96
Bush, George W., 422–23, 426–28, 432
Butler, Judith, 287, 297

C
Calhoun, John B., 150–51
Cammaerts, Émile Leon, 463, 502
Campanelli, Tessa, 491*n164*
Campra, Pablo Madrid, 487–88, 509, 569, 571, 627, 642*n17*, 644, 653
Canaanites, 71, 85, 90–91
Canadian truckers, 741, 743, 759–60
Candlebox, 86
cannibalism, 150

capitalism, 94, 308, 310, 343, 369, 381, 437, 675, 680
Carell, Steve, 250
Carlson, Tucker, 40, 45, 331, 378*n12*, 396, 472*n92*, 507, 545*n33*, 548–49, 619, 623
Carpay, John, 476
Carrier, Richard, 89
Castro, Fidel, 417, 594*n231*
CBC funding, 449*n18*, 513
CCCA (Canadian COVID Care Alliance), 604, 611
CDC (Center for Disease Control), 445, 447*n11*, 450, 497–98, 502, 521*n11*, 523, 561–63, 565, 573–75, 595, 597, 619, 626, 628
Ceauşescu, Nicolae, 758
censorship, 4, 203*n39*, 205, 212, 264*n19*, 471, 473-74, 474*n101*, 479, 483, 504, 511, 518, 521
Central Intelligence Agency (CIA), 439, 517
CERN, 644, 650, 644*n35-36*, 560, 655
CFI (Center for Inquiry), 105–8, 114, 116–18, 120
CFR (Council on Foreign Relations), 426–27, 429, 438–39
Chan, Sandra, 525*n13*, 534
Chappelle, Dave, 280, 283
Chardy, Jeremy, 610
Charlotte Lozier Institute, 162*n7*, 166, 487, 511
Charter of Rights and Freedoms, 339, 342, 483, 594, 737–38, 757, 759
Cheney, Dick, 422
CHEO (Children's Hospital of Eastern Ontario), 98, 446, 781
child abandonment, 244–45
child abuse, 390, 392, 526–27, 529–30, 534, 731
child pornography, 183*n1*, 198, 202–4, 206, 209, 211, 529
Children's Hospital of Eastern Ontario (CHEO), 98, 446, 781
child trafficking, 183*n1*, 198–211, 230*n1*
chimpanzees, 186
China Virus, 449*n16*, 513, 547
Chinese Communist Party (CCP), 9, 25, 445, 544–45, 547, 552
Chomsky, Noam, 379, 399
Chossudovsky, Michel, 448*n14*, 503
Christen, Zoe, 283
Christian, Francis, 475
Christian Theology, 83, 116, 131, 133, 135, 137, 263, 733
Christian truths, 74, 78, 89, 101, 227, 394, 716
Churchill, Winston, 749
civil disobedience, 419n22, 421, 740, 745–46, 753–54
civil liberties, 299, 301, 312, 451–52, 484, 499, 516, 729–30, 737, 775
civil rights, 205, 451, 659
Civil Rights Act, 367
Clapton, Eric, 750
Clinton, Bill, 422, 427, 431-32
Clinton, Hillary, 422, 435
clot-shot, 590, 610. *See also* COVID-19 vaccine; injection
CMI (Creative Mutual Interaction), 123, 134
CNO (College of Nurses of Ontario), 480, 503
Cobra Kai, 688–94, 696–97
Cockburn, Bruce, 761*n89*
cognitive dissonance, 307, 444, 453, 471, 519, 605n275
Cole, Ryan, 475
College of Nurses of Ontario. *See* CNO
College of Physicians and Surgeons of Ontario (CPSO), 168–69, 479–80, 503
Collins, Francis, 360*n12*, 478–79, 489, 492, 504, 544*n30*, 547, 551–53, 622
common descent, 123, 142
communism, 150, 307, 312, 314, 316–22, 369, 381, 416–17, 438, 710, 729-30
comorbidities, 452, 482, 494, 525*n17*, 532, 539, 565, 600, 602, 735, 765
Conceptual Penis, 268, 281, 283
Conlan, pretty Ricky, 685
Connors, Jimmy, 250, 622
conspiracy realist, 567
conspiracy theories, 333, 423, 451, 483, 542, 546–47, 550, 615, 622, 733
conspiracy theorist, 326
Contagion, 432, 520–21, 640, 652, 654
Coombe, Matthew J., 152, 422*n1*, 782
Copan, Paul, 70, 73, 119–20
Copernican Revolution, 465
Copernicus, Nicolas, 116, 128, 134
Cornell, Chris, 230, 232, 289*n10*
cosmic authority problem, the, 90, 107, 120
Coulter, Ann, 278*n66*, 282, 731*n2*
Court, Margaret, 250
COVID-19 Agenda, 445*n10*, 507
COVID-19 anti-vaxxers, 593
COVID boosters, 497*n177*, 497*n179*, 445, 447, 463–64, 494, 496–97, 502, 593, 595, 600–601, 605–7, 610, 613, 736, 767, 769
COVID-19 Vaccine Composition, 609*n293*, 637
COVID-19 vaccine doses, 600, 602
COVID-19 vaccine injuries, 645*n44*
COVID-19 Vaccine Mandates, 494*n172*, 511
COVID fiasco, 559, 561
Covid Fideist, 464, 589
Covidian evidence, 613
Covidians, 463, 589, 605
Covidland, 445*n8*, 503
COVID zealots, 455*n41*
Coyne, Jerry, 131*n2*, 136
CPC (Conservative Party of Canada), 164, 338, 341, 448, 451, 741
Craig, James Porter, 273*n49*
Craig, William Lane, 68, 70–73, 78–80, 82–84, 90*n14*, 101–2, 108*n13*, 113–15, 117, 119–20, 338*n2*, 376*n4*, 378*n12*
creation ex nihilo, 132
Creationism, 356
Creed, Adonis, 683
Creed I, 684–85
Creed II, 683–85
Crick, Francis, 405
critical mass, 444, 740, 745
Crowder, Steven, 661
CRT (critical race theory), 357–58, 362–64, 367, 369–70, 435
cryptocurrencies, 746–47, 756
Culler, Jonathan, 269
Cullors, Patrisse, 365, 416
Cultural Marxism, 279, 377–78, 397, 433, 435–36
cycle thresholds (PCR-Test), 554, 556–57, 632

D

Dahlheimer, Patrick, 86
Dalton, John, 465
Darwin, Charles, 71, 90, 107, 111, 124, 141, 143–45, 149, 376*n6*, 465, 703
Daszak, Peter, 542–44, 550, 553, 621
Davies, Paul, 82
da Vinci, Leonardo, 520
Dawkins, Richard, 67–73, 100, 105*n2*, 111–12, 121, 126, 152–56, 162*n8*, 356–57, 360*n12*, 362, 726, 730
Deaths by EAS, 174
deconstructionism, 249, 260,

264–69, 271, 276*n61*, 279–80, 285, 343–44, 377
Deep State, 422*n3*, 426*n7*, 436–37, 439, 441
Def Leppard, 689
Degrassi, 491*n164*, 504
Dekulakization, 414*n4*, 415*n5*, 421
Delgado, Ricardo, 488*n149*
Delta variant of SARS-CoV-2, 446, 459, 588, 602, 606, 611, 768
Dembski, William A., 144, 360*n12*
demons, 142*n2*, 144, 648, 689, 732
Denisovich, Ivan, 413
Dennett, Daniel, 105*n2*, 360*n12*
Denton, Michael, 141, 144, 360*n12*
Depopulation Agenda, 640*n9*, 650, 655
Derrida, Jacques, 93, 249, 260, 264–71, 279, 281–85, 322–23, 343–46, 376–77, 396
DeSantis, Ron, 572, 740*n37*
Descartes, Rene, 116, 282, 716–17, 726, 780
Desmet, Mattias, 443–45, 502, 505, 538, 590, 613
Deuteronomy, 70
devil, 228, 732
deworming drug, horse. *See* ivermectin
Diaz, Miguel, 689–92
Dice, Mark, 579*n170*, 621, 661
digital ID, 400, 436, 598
Digital ID in Ontario, 598*n247*, 623
disinformation, 326, 413, 448, 467, 479, 529*n55*, 531, 601, 615, 672
Disney, 190*n42*, 196
diversity of thought, 277, 468, 469
divine intervention, 122, 126, 128, 130
Djokovic, Novak, 609–10, 617
DNA, 85*n2*, 91, 121, 130, 473, 552*n54*, 554, 566, 596–98, 636, 751
Dolezal, Rachel, 278, 282
Dominican University College, 86, 108*n13*, 375
Domning, Daryl, 704–5, 708
Dorsey, Jack, 39, 368, 473
Doshi, Peter, 455*n43*, 504, 612–13, 621, 633
Dostoyevsky, Fyodor, 15
doublespeak, 342, 606, 744, 769
doublethink, 379, 518
Douste-Blazy, Philippe, 585
Down's syndrome, 68, 162
draconian measures, xxvii, 419, 451, 560, 562, 640
Drago, Ivan, 683–84, 686
Drago, Viktor, 683, 686
D'Souza, Dinesh, 153*n8*, 154*n9*, 156, 360*n12*, 380
Duchesne, Ricardo, 377*n7*, 378*n11*, 396, 398
Duncan, Kirsty, 127, 342
Durrant, Justin, 485
Dworkin, Andrea, 205, 376
Dyer, Jay, 644*n37*, 651–52
Dyshidrotic Eczema, 774
Dyson, Michael Eric, 6
dystopian bubble, 475*n105*, 754
dystopian delusion, 445, 764–82

E
Eagle-Fang, 692
Earman, John, 105, 118, 121
Eastwood, Clint, 255
EcoHealth Alliance, 542, 542*n22*, 547, 621
Edict of Nantes, 53–54, 61
Egyptian Horus, 88
Ehrman, Bart, 83, 89, 91, 118
Elderly Suicide, 525*n13*, 534
Elders' Movement, 363
Electron Microscopy, 488*n148*, 509, 558, 642*n17*, 653
Elmo Doll, 539, 617
Emergencies Act, 753–55, 756–57
Emergencies Cowards Act, 610
emergency powers, 756
Empire State Building, 192
Engels, Friedrich, 317*n1*
Engineered Economic Depression, 448*n14*, 503
Enlightenment, 293, 315, 320, 322, 352, 378*n11*, 398, 704
enslavement, 716
environmental theory of COVID-19, 569
Ephesus, 163
epidemic, 555*n67*, 599, 625, 640
Epidemiology, 532
Epigenome, 636
epiphenomena, 90, 703
Epitaph, 169
Epstein, Jeffrey, 731*n2*
Epstein, Robert, 40–41, 45
equality of outcome, 248, 361, 384, 672
Ethereum, 746
eugenics, 170–79
Euro Surveillance, 561
euthanasia, 159, 168–79, 359–60, 405, 407, 482
extraordinary claims, 105, 107, 109, 114–15, 117, 119–20

F
Facebook posts, 325–26, 336, 754*n67*, 754*n68*
faith and reason, 80, 90, 154–55, 357
fake news, 85, 127, 130, 280*n72*, 283, 329, 458, 469, 472*n91*, 509–10, 579
fallen Angel, 649
Farber, Chris, 756
Farrakhan, Louis, 370
Farrar, Jeremy, 151, 196, 542, 544*n30*
Farrow, Douglas, 494, 505
Father Dave, 593
Father Joe LeClair, 162
Father Tony Van Lee, 165
Fauci, Anthony, 466–67, 473, 476*n110*, 478, 538, 540–48, 551–53, 557–61, 574, 576, 617–18, 620–21, 626–28, 630–32, 769–70
FDA (Food and Drug Administration), 221, 445, 485, 494, 497, 584, 596, 601, 767, 769, 771
fear, 11–12, 32, 34, 107, 194, 257, 350, 458–59, 517–19, 522, 538–39, 589–90, 592–93, 686, 751
Federer, Roger, 247
Feinberg, Paul D., 153*n4*, 156, 401*n4*, 401*n6*, 408
feminism, 242, 250*n12*, 251*n19*, 253, 287*n5*, 288*n9*, 297, 435
Fernandes, Phil, 152, 400, 422, 430*n11*, 440, 669, 777
Ferrer, John D., 235, 778
Feser, Edward, 80*n2*, 84
fetal tissue, aborted, 487
fetuses, aborted human, 493
Feynman, Richard, 466
Fidelito Castro Trudeau, 586, 754. *See also* Trudeau, Justin
Fleury, Theo, 610, 622
Flew, Antony, 101–2
Floyd, George, 416*n12*, 421
Flynt, Larry, 203*n39*
Fogelin, Robert, 106, 118, 121
Fognini, Fabio, 248, 252
FOIA (Freedom of Information Act), 540, 542, 584, 601, 621
Ford, Doug, 189, 378*n12*, 458*n55*, 498, 508, 741
Ford, Krista, 498n182, 509
Foster, Jodie, 131
Foucault, Michel, 93, 282, 322, 345, 376–77, 396
Fox, Terry, 702, 707–8
Frankfurt School, 357, 364, 434
freedom convoy, 741*n39*, 743–44, 756. *See also* truckers; Canadian truckers
freedom fighters, 740–41
Freedom of Information Act. *See* FOIA

freedom of religion and conscience, 293
freedom of speech and expression, 345
freedom of speech and freedom of conscience, 275, 480
Freeland, Chrystia, 127, 449, 614, 630, 755–56
free speech, xv–xvi, xxiv, xxvi, 37–38, 260, 262, 269, 271–73, 275, 280–81, 333, 338–42, 344, 377, 482–83
free will, 147–48, 231–32, 599, 705, 720
    human, 99, 125
Freire, Paulo, 418, 420
French Revolution, 315–17, 319, 321–22
Freud, Sigmund, 183–85, 187–89, 193–94, 196, 254, 376*n6*, 434
fringe epidemiologists, 478
Fuellmich, Reiner, 443, 476, 513, 561–62, 622, 749
fully vaccinated, 565, 592, 607

G
GAFAM (Google, Apple, Facebook, Amazon, and Microsoft), 518*n6*
Galati, Rocco, 476, 505
Galileo Galilei, 116, 128, 134
Gandhi, Mahatma, 660, 745
Garland, Judy, 462*n63*
gaslighting, 329–30, 324, 332
Gates, Bill, 322, 430, 436–37, 476*n108*, 476*n110*, 499–500, 507–8, 553*n56*, 625
Gates Vaccine Cartel, 585*n202*, 635
Geisler, Norman, 153*n4*, 155–56, 264–65, 282, 360*n12*, 401*n4*, 401*n6*, 408
Geist, Michael, 483
Geivett, Douglas R., 156
Gelman, Vanessa, 484, 486
gender, non-binary, 276
gender blender, 276
gender dysphoria, 291, 327, 391, 393, 395
gender dysphoria disorder, 389
gender equality, 188, 237, 241, 249, 286, 734
gender fluidity, 276, 389
gender-neutral pronouns, 275–77, 289-91, 348, 294, 298, 417
gender unicorn graphic, 287*n6*
Genesis, 424, 718–20, 723
gene therapy, 403*n17*, 462, 524, 595–96
    untested mRNA-based, 455
genetic algorithms, 124
Georgina, 6
German Constitutional Court, 177
GG (Governor General), 122–30
Gill, Andrew H., 676, 779
Glabson Iana, 754*n67*
Glaser, Judith E., 664, 668
global communist surveillance state, 743
global government, 422–25, 427–28, 430–32
globalism, 422, 430–31, 439–40, 448*n14*, 555
globalist agenda, 322, 376*n5*, 426, 429, 431, 439, 516, 518, 520, 522, 568
globalization, 430, 505, 643
Global Research, 448*n14*, 505
global vaccination strategy, 604, 768
glucosamine, 216
glutathione, 570, 631, 642
goal of education, 382
God and truth, 20, 593
goddamn Vaccine, 418*n20*, 421
godfather, 97–101, 142
Goebbels, Joseph, 539, 592, 614
Golden Calf, 192*n48*
Golden Retriever, 677, 679
Goldstein, Rebecca, 78–79, 84, 127*n9*, 130
Goldwater, Barry, 438, 749
Golgi Apparatus, 70
Gomorrah, 646
Gonzales, Maria, 484
Gonzalez, Guillermo, 135–36
Google, Apple, Facebook, Amazon, and Microsoft (GAFAM), 518*n6*
Google Patents, 646*n45*, 651
Gorbachev, Mikhail, 430–31
Gould, Stephen J., 79, 142–43, 146, 151, 356
government coercion on vaccines, 460
Governor General. *See* GG
grafeno, 488*n148*, 569*n127*, 627, 653
Gramsci, Antonio, 434
granddaughter, 775
grandfather, 99, 224, 258, 311
graphene oxide (graphene), 437*n40*, 487–88, 509, 569–70, 642, *646n50*, 649, 651, 654, 659
Great Barrington Declaration, 474*n99*, 478, 506, 508, 524, 532, 572, 608, 626
Great Reckoning, 732, 749
Great Reset, the, 321–23, 422–42, 448*n14*, 599, 615, 647–48, 653–55, 730, 732–34, 747–49, 774–75
Great Take Over, 732, 749
Greenspan, Alan, 427
grievance studies, 280, 283, 357
Griffin, Edward, 7
Griffith, Thomas Ian, 689, 693, 697
Groothuis, Douglas, 76–77, 106*n8*, 121
groupthink, 248, 696, 730
Gupta, Sunetra, 478, 626
Guth, Alan, 115, 465

H
Habermas, Gary R., 156, 266*n27*, 282
Hackett, Stuart, 108*n13*, 110*n15*, 110*n16*, 121, 360*n12*, 726
Hahn, Scott, 70, 73
Haidt, Johnathan, 313, 378*n11*
Hajdu, Patty, 127, 130, 458, 509
Harari, Yuval Noah, 400, 403*n17*, 598–99, 623, 636, 638
Harder, Rachel, 164, 338
Harpur, Tom, 89, 91
Harris, James A., 215, 780
Harris, Kamala, 579, 620
Harris, Sam, 82
Harvard University, 430–31, 478
Harvey, C. C., xvi, 56*n17*, 363, 782
Haught, John, 134, 152*n1*, 153*n8*, 154*n9*, 156
Hawking, Stephen, 111–12, 121
Hayek, Friedrich, 313, 384, 396
Hayes, Chris, 489*n154*, 506
HCL (Hydron Collider), 644
Health Canada, 449, 503, 506, 583, 591*n221*, 615*n313*, 624, 634, 749, 764
Heffner, Hugh, 184, 188
Hegel, Georg Wilhelm Friedrich, 293, 297, 782
HEK293T, 487. *See also* Abortion-Derived Cell Lines
heliocentric understanding, 465
Hellwig, Monika, 704–5, 708
Henley, Tara, 470–71, 506
Hepatitis, 776
Heraclitus, 263, 282
herd immunity, 463, 478, 588–89, 600, 602–3, 608, 766, 771
Hicks, John, 83
Hicks, Stephen, 266*n27*, 271, 273–74, 281–82, 344–45, 375*n2*, 377*n8*, 396
Higgins-Dunn, Noah, 564*n110*, 621
Hijacking of Truth, xvii, 377
Hildebrand, Dietrich Von, 436, 715, 727
Hillier, Randy, 496, 507, 741
Hinduism, 112, 128, 240, 644
Hinshaw, Deena, 477, 763
hippies, 694–95, 750
Hippocrates, 481, 501

Hippocratic Oath, 170, 225, 481, 505, 593, 647, 774–75
Hippocratic Oath for Christians, 481*n124*
Hitler, Adolf (Adolph), 5, 162, 280, 319, 321*n9*, 323, 349, 592
HIV, 209, 390*n49*, 395, 557–58, 586, 736
Hochul, Kathy, 607
Hodkinson, Roger, 475, 507, 510, 539*n6*, 630
Hoff, Christina, 259
Holland, Robert, 418, 420, 429
Hollywood, xiii, 191, 193–95, 208*n71*
holocaust survivor, 751
Holy Land, 22
Hopkins, Anthony, 95
Horkheimer, Max, 434, 441
human freedom, xv, 54, 83, 146, 299, 750
human rights, 13, 20, 275, 283, 289, 291–92, 315, 320–21, 339*n6*, 346, 737
Hume, David, 105–6, 118, 121, 145, 151
Hunter, Graeme, 278*n66*
Hunter, Hugh, 145, 780
Hurwitz, Jon, 688
Huxley, Aldous, 516
Hydron Collider (HCL), 644
hydroxychloroquine, 464, 474*n100*, 476*n108*, 538, 540*n11*, 579–82, 587, 616, 622, 627, 629
hydroxychloroquine and azithromycin, 580*n181*, 622, 629

I
IB, 462*n63*
ICC (International Criminal Court), 427, 499, 515
Icke, David, 567–68, 627
identity politics, 247, 274, 278, 357, 361, 378, 384, 394, 661–62, 729, 732
image of God, 394, 661–62, 702, 709, 718–20, 722–25, 730
Imago Dei-Imago Christi, 721*n30*, 726
IMF (International Monetary Fund), 427, 516
immunology, 474, 603
immunomodulation, 586
Impact of COVID-19 on Children, 528*n44*, 531
inclinations, 713–14
individualism, xvii, 20, 368, 673
influenza virus, 562, 566
informed consent, 395*n72*, 448, 454–55, 457, 494–95, 601, 769–71
intellect, 25, 132, 262, 393–94, 714, 717, 730
intelligibility, 76, 117, 128, 134–36, 263
International Criminal Court (ICC), 427, 499, 515. *See also* ICC
intersectionality, 367, 378, 386, 661
intuition, 413, 537, 676–81
irrational fear, 341, 517, 578, 592, 765
Irwin, Klee, 403*n17*
isolation, 175, 482, 564, 709, 755*n72*
Israeli study, 447, 454, 606, 768
Iturrieta, Pablo Muñoz, 286, 289*n12*, 781
Ivan, Leslie P., 97*n2*, 301, 684, 686–87
Ivan, Patricia, 301
ivermectin, 451, 496, 514, 518, 579, 582–83, 587, 624–25, 633, 637–38, 641, 646, 650
Ivie, Brian, 698, 700–701

J
Jackson, Michael, 230
Jastrow, Robert, 129–30
Jefferson, Thomas, 195, 280, 283, 316
Jeremiah, Joey, 491*n164*
Jesus, 76–77, 81, 83–84, 88–89, 91, 119, 163, 228, 357, 424–25, 659–60, 695, 704–6, 713–15, 723-24
Jim Crow Laws, 367
John Birch Society, 441
Johnson, Boris, 489, 752, 759
Johnson, Phillip E., 141, 143, 360*n12*
Johnson, Ron, 612
Johnson & Johnson's Janssen COVID-19 vaccine, 555
John the Apostle, 731
Jong-rak, Lee, 698
Joplin, Janis, 227
Jordan, Michael B., 683
Jung, Carl, 75
justice and social justice, 377

K
Kahmann, Morgan, 472, 507
Kakodkar, Anil, 644
Kalam Cosmological Argument. *See* KCA
Kanan, Sean, 694
Karinthy, Frigyes, 98, 102
Kartha, Tara, 550
Kata, 691, 696
Kaufman (Justice), 764
Kavanaugh, Brett, 468–69
Kay, Jonathan, 329, 337, 390*n47*, 391*n54*, 396
KCA (Kalam Cosmological Argument), 76, 83, 113–14, 116, 118, 133, 136
Kendi, Ibrahim, 368, 374, 662
Kennedy, John F., 428*n8*
Kennedy Jr, Robert F., 476, 558
kenosis, 229
Kenyon, Dean H., 67
Kepler, Johannes, 116, 128, 134
Khadr, Omar, 756
Kierkegaard, Søren, 357
Kierkegaardian existentialism, 357
King, Billie Jean, 230, 250
King, Pat, 743
King Crimson, 169
King Herod, 161
Kinsey, Alfred, 183–89, 193–94, 196–97, 199–200, 212
Kissinger, Henry, 427, 432–33, 441
Kocian, Erica
Koukl, Greg, 359–60, 362
Kove, Martin, 690
Kowalczyk, Ed, 86–90
Kramer, Larry, 553*n56*, 558, 626
Krauss, Lawrence, 105*n2*
Kreeft, Peter, 360*n12*, 402, 408, 712*n7*, 715*n17*, 726
Kreese, John, 689, 691, 693–94
Krishna, Hindu, 88
Krushchev, Nikita, 319
Kurzweil, Ray, 403*n17*, 408, 643, 654

L
LaBoeuf, Shia, 191
Lang, Clubber, 692
Lantsman, Melissa, 744
LaRusso, Daniel, 688, 692–93, 697
LaRusso, Lucille, 689
Lasagna, Louis, 482
Laurijssen, Ton, 669
Lavoie, Alexandre, 758*n78*
Law, Stephen, 105*n2*, 114*n26*, 119*n38*
Lawrence, Johnny, 688–92
Lazarus Report, 601–3, 626
Led Zeppelin, 232
Lemaître, Georges, 465
Lemon, Don, 6, 40*n29*
Lenin, Vladimir, 316-7, 319
Lennox, John, 69, 72–73, 152–56, 712*n5*, 726
lessons for COVID-19 pandemic, 601*n261*, 623
Levin, Benjamin, 388
Lewis, C. S., xvii, xxiii, xxvi, 74, 76, 83, 87–88, 91, 165–66, 172*n14*, 400, 402–4, 406–8
liberalism, 5, 34, 47, 150, 274, 659, 663
Liberal Party of Canada, 468*n79*, 508, 550, 614
liberation theology, 733
libertine sexuality, 238–40, 243

Lich, Tamara, 610, 756–57
Licona, Michael, 81, 84, 89*n12*, 91
Lightbound, Joël, 742
Limbaugh, Rush, 34*n6*
Lincoln, Abraham, 316
Lindsay, James, 94, 96, 268*n33*, 280–81, 283–84, 346, 357–58, 360*n12*, 362
LĪVE+, 85–87, 89–91
lockdowns, 445*n8*, 447–48, 462*n63*, 464, 478–80, 524–29, 531, 533, 560, 562–63, 571–73, 616–17, 628–29, 740, 742
Locke, John, 696–97
Lonergan, Bernard, 135–36, 263*n16*, 283, 704, 706, 708
Lopez, Jennifer, 192
Louisseize, Travis, 413, 783
Love, Ariyana, 627, 652
Lucki, Brenda, 750
Ludemann, Gerd, 119–20
Lukacs, Georg, 434
Lundgren, Dolph, 683–84
Luther, Martin, 662–63
Luther King Jr, Martin, 357, 370, 378*n10*, 659–63
Lyell, Charles, 111, 124, 143
Lynott, Phil, 227–28
Lyotard, Francois, 93, 338

M
Maarman, Ricardo, 749
Maastricht Treaty, 429
Macchio, Ralph, 688, 693, 697
Machiavelli, Niccolò, 443, 509
Macron, Emmanuel, 322, 489, 521, 759
Magufuli, John, 555–56
mainstream media, 217, 222, 443, 445, 447, 450, 466, 471, 473, 538, 540, 550, 556
Makow, Henry, 737–39
Malcolm , Daniel, 462*n63*
malfeasance, 326, 400, 403*n17*, 476*n110*, 537–637
Malleret, Thierry, 322–23, 437*n38*, 442, 639, 654, 733–34, 775
Malone, Robert, 467, 568–69, 587, 590, 593, 611, 616, 625, 631, 648*n55*, 652, 770
mandated COVID vaccines for children, 587*n208*
Marazzo, Tom, 756
Marcuse, Herbert, 435, 441
Maritain, Jacques, 265*n25*, 266*n27*, 271*n43*, 344–46, 377–82, 387, 393–94, 396–97, 710–11, 716–19, 721, 726
Martin, David, 283, 381*n22*, 397, 512, 626, 755
Martin, Michael, 120
Marx, Karl, 308, 311, 314–17, 319–23, 376, 417, 426, 434, 488–89, 510
Marxism, 92, 271, 307, 317, 320, 343–44, 369, 372, 377, 416–18, 434
    trained, 365–66, 416, 421
mask mandates and vaccines, 562
masks, xix, 259, 448, 450, 463–64, 479–80, 516–17, 562, 568–69, 573–79, 592, 619–20, 628–29, 633–34, 636–37
    cotton, 574, 633
materialism
    dialectical, 16
    metaphysical, 16–17, 75, 114
Matte, Nicholas, 248, 340
Maxwell, Ghislaine, 86*n4*, 91, 731*n2*
Mayo Clinic, 475, 554*n58*, 574, 628
McConaughey, Matthew, 131
McCullough, Peter, 467, 500, 504, 509, 568–69, 583, 586, 588, 611, 628–29, 763, 765, 770
McDonald, Sean, 538
McEnany, Kayleigh, 540
McEnroe, John, 250–51
McGuinty, Dalton, 388
McKenna, Catherine, 127
McVety, Charles, 388
Measles vaccine, 776
medical mistakes, 217, 467*n76*, 505
Medvedev, Roy, 319, 323
Meenan, John Paul, 168–69
Meerloo, Joost, 522
Mehta, Rick, 778–79
Member of Provincial Parliament (MPP), 496, 507
mental health, xix, xxxi, 254*n1*, 254*n2*, 259, 326, 473, 524, 526, 532, 572
mental illness, 171–76, 231, 525
Mental Jewelry, 86, 88, 91
Menzies, Peter, 483
Mercola, Joseph, 548*n42*, 578*n166*, 628
Merkel, Angela, 759
MERS vaccines, 589
metaphysical naturalism, 71, 79–80, 89, 112, 116, 136, 142, 144, 356
methodological naturalism, 71, 79–80, 112, 116, 118, 142, 356
Meyer, Stephen C., 112*n21*, 121, 124–25, 130, 144, 360*n12*
Meyer, Theryn, 276*n61*
mice, 150, 220–21, 551
microorganism, 566–67, 587
Mikovits, Judy, 553*n56*, 558, 624, 637
Miller, Kenneth, 360*n12*
mind control, 461, 522
MIQE Guidelines, 557*n79*, 619
miracles, 76, 105–6, 118–19, 121, 142, 156, 163, 165, 567, 706, 737*n25*
misinformation, 326, 330, 457, 460, 470, 473, 476–77, 480, 542, 546, 601, 605
misogynistic, 328–29, 690, 734
misogynists, 330, 593
Mitchell, Joni, 248*n6*, 252, 750
MK Ultra, 517*n5*, 523
Mlodinow, Leonard, 111*n18*, 121
Moderna, 437, 500, 596, 735–36
Moderna vaccines, 596, 755, 770
Modern Pagans, 712*n7*, 726
Modern Physician's Oath, 482
modern science, 92, 101, 116, 133–34, 136
Molyneux, Stefan, 661
Mondello, John, 527
Money, John, xiii, 183, 185, 187–88, 193
Monod, Jacques, 356
Montagnier, Luc, 736
Moore, Kieran, 458, 497, 607*n282*, 629, 763, 772
Moore, Michael, 6
Moore, Samuel, 323
moral awareness, 469
moral character, 296
moral conscience, xix, xxxii, 59, 168, 392, 407, 458, 474*n101*, 492, 553, 747
morality and natural law, 402
moral relativism, 7, 79, 168, 359, 403–4, 481
moral responsibility, xxi, 27, 147, 189, 231, 349, 379, 683, 692, 695–96
Moreland, J. P., 76–77, 108*n13*, 117*n32*, 152–53, 156, 360*n12*
Morita, Pat, 688, 690–91
Morneau, Bill, 127*n11*, 129, 449
morphic resonance, 678
Morris, Simon Conway, 360*n12*
Morrison, Jim, 227, 365*n1*, 374
mother, daughter's, 445, 455–57, 590, 772
Mr. Miyagi, 689–91
mRNA vaccines, 452, 475*n103*, 489, 587*n208*, 593, 595, 597, 599, 601, 641*n14*, 651
    current COVID-19, 492
MSM, 39n27, 40n29, 42, 222, 390n49, 395, 447, 540, 544, 546, 615. *See also* mainstream media
MTV, 203*n39*, 212
Mullis, Kary, 557–60, 571, 620, 630, 637

Mullis, Nancy, 560*n94*
Munich, 83
Murdering COVID Patients, 580*n176*, 618
Murphy, Rex, 468
Murray, Andy, 251
Murray, Thomas, 541*n15*
Musk, Elon, 403*n17*, 499
Mussolini, Benito, 426, 434

N
NAC (N-Acetyl Cysteine), 642
NAFTA, 422
Nagel, Thomas, 71*n13*, 73, 90, 107–8, 121
Nakagami, Hironori, 596, 630
Nanobiotechnology, 653
nanocrystals, 437
nanometer, 576
nanoparticles, 640, 642, 649
  lipid, 596, 755
nanoparticles act, 570
nano-technology, 123, 783
NASA, 128–29
Nash, Ronald, 154, 156
National Center for Missing and Exploited Children (NCMEC), 199, 204–5, 212
National Health Service (NHS), 557, 630
National Institutes of Health (NIH), 217, 445, 523, 544, 551, 553*n56*
National Socialism, 436
NATO (North Atlantic Treaty Organization), 427
natural immunity, 447, 454–55, 486, 489–90, 493, 587–88, 602–4, 606, 609, 766, 768, 771
Navratilova, Martina, 250, 393, 395
Nazareth, 81, 83, 89, 91
Nazism, 416, 710, 716
NDP (New Democratic Party), 261, 273, 378, 754
Nehemiah, 695
Neo-Darwinism, 141–42, 144, 357, 360*n12*, 465
neo-Marxism, 5, 20, 34, 348
Nestorianism, 163
Nestorius, 163*n9*, 166
Netflix, 193, 196, 483, 688
Never-Never Woke Land, 594
New Age, 429, 431, 676
Newman, Alex, 422*n3*, 426*n7*, 436–37, 441
Newton, Isaac, 116, 128, 134, 465
New World Order, 316, 320, 422–41, 448*n14*, 645, 669, 730, 748, 749, 759–60, 774
NIAID (National Institute of Allergy and Infectious Diseases), 445, 458, 542–43, 547, 551
Nietzsche, Friedrich, 68, 281, 352–53, 400–402, 404, 407, 712
NIH (National Institute of Health), 217, 508, 514, 519*n9*, 523, 537, 544, 547, 551–53, 622, 624, 630
Noble Lie, 592
NOMA approach, 143
Novak, Michael, 382–84, 397, 610*n294*, 617
nucleic acids, 596
nudge theory, 453
Nuremberg Code, 494, 499, 646*n48*, 653, 749

O
Oath of Hippocrates of Kos, 481, 501
Obama, Barack, 372, 422, 432–33, 435, 441, 469
objective truth, 81–82, 93, 262, 359, 403–4
Ocasio-Cortez, Alexandria, 586
O'Dell, Tony, 689
Oelrich, Stefan, 595
OggafnaR, 462*n63*
OISE (Ontario Institute for Studies in Education), 378, 384–88, 398
O'Keefe, James, 472, 510–11
Old Testament, 351, 408, 683
oligarchs, 733*n11*, 733*n12*, 749, 751
O'Looney, John, 641*n15*, 653
O'Malley, Jodi, 485
omicron, 564*n112*, 565*n113*, 565*n114*, 588, 602, 605–6, 617, 622, 631, 638
one-world governance, 516
Ontario Teachers' Pension Plan, 360, 362
Open VAERS, 513, 601*n259*, 626, 630
Operation Warp Speed, 497
Orbán, Viktor, 417
Origin of SARS-CoV-2, 539
origin of self-consciousness, 703
origin of species, 124, 465
Orwell, George, 361–62, 498, 743
Orwellian doublespeak, 602
Orwellian doublethink, 610
Orwellian nightmare, 340
Osaka, Naomi, 247
Osterholm, Michael, 574–75, 620
O'Toole, Erin, 741
Owens, Candace, 91, 661
Oz, Mehmet, 215, 474*n100*, 512, 580*n179*, 632

P
paganism, 255*n4*, 259
Paglia, Camille, 288*n9*, 392
Paikin, Steve, 276*n61*, 340*n11*, 346
panentheism, 87
Pannenberg, Wolfhart, 83–84
panpsychists, 703
pansexual, 150
pantheistic, 356
paraphilia, 188–89
parasites, 236, 415, 566
  innocuous, 571
Parcak, Sarah, 34*n6*
Pardy, Bruce, 275, 283, 339, 346
Park, Yeonmid (Park Yeon-mi), ix, 5, 12–13
Parliament of Canada, 261*n4*, 261*n5*, 261*n6*, 261*n8*, 283, 298, 391*n51*, 397
Parsons, Keith, 105*n2*
Pastor Lee, 698–700
patient zero, 639*n2*, 651
patriarchy, 200*n18*, 238, 379, 387
Patriot Act, 416, 421
patriotism, 10, 311
Paul, Rand, 439, 543, 548*n44*, 634
Paul, Ron, 439
Pawlowski, Artur, 23–25, 755
Pawlowski, Dawid, 23, 755*n72*
Pawlowski, Nathan, 755*n72*
Payette, Julie, 122, 127–30. *See also* GG
Pazaratz, Justice Alex, 460
PCR test, 508, 516, 518, 554–55, 557, 559–60, 562–63, 569, 571, 586, 602, 613, 642
PCR Inventor, *See* Mullis, Kary
PCR testing and cycle thresholds, 554*n61*, 632
Peckford, Brian, 738–39, 757
Pekary, Ariana, 469–70, 510
Pelech, Steven, 603–4, 631
People's Party of Canada, 734
Perakh, Mark, 143
pericarditis, 456
Persian Gulf War, 423
Peters, Ted, 134
Peterson, Jordan, 78–84, 260, 262–64, 272, 274–77, 280–81, 284, 289–90, 339–40, 342–46, 348–53, 376–80, 418–19, 421, 690, 738–39
Pfizer, 438, 475, 486–87, 495–96, 500, 513, 555, 596, 601, 735, 769–71
Pfizer-BioNTech COVID-19, 597
Pfizer BioNTech COVID-19 mRNA Vaccine BNT162b2, 597*n241*, 597*n242*, 598*n243*, 616
Pfizer CEO, 605–6, 638, 752

Pfizer vaccine docs, 584*n198*, 623
Pfizer Vaccine for Kids, 645*n39*, 654
Pfizer vaccine vials, 488, 571
Pfizer whistleblower, 487*n147*, 509, 646*n50*, 653
phallogocentrism, 268
Pharisees, 723
pharmaceutical companies, 69, 215–25, 447, 464, 476*n110*, 481, 486–87, 493, 496, 581, 585
pharmaceutical industry, 216–20, 222, 445, 496, 498, 538, 540, 585, 680, 758, 769–70
Phillips, Andrew, 631
Phillips, Patrick, 474*n101*, 504
Philoponus, John, 132–34, 137
phonocentrism, 268
physical world, 466
Pierce, Chester M., 430
Pierre Elliott Trudeau Foundation, 735
Pimlott, Herbert, 342, 344, 380*n18*
Pinker, Steven, 378*n11*, 398
Pirner, David, 537
placebos, 601*n256*, 641
plandemic, 445, 462, 511, 514, 540*n12*, 626
planet Earth, 648, 669–75
Plantinga, Alvin, 70, 73, 80, 106*n9*, 108*n13*, 117, 121, 360*n12*
Plato, xxviii, 96, 262, 267
Platonic, 79
Platonism, 83
Playboy, 184, 188, 200–201
Playskool, 539
Pluckrose, Helen, 96, 280, 284, 357, 362
Pluribus Unum, 41
pneumonia, 227, 639
Poilievre, Pierre, 449, 741
Polio vaccine, 776
political correctness, 208, 249, 260, 262, 269, 271–72, 277–79, 282, 289, 661, 696
Pollyannaish perspective, 709
Pol Pot's Cambodia, 16, 451
polygenism, 705
Pompeo, Michael, 198*n5*
Ponesse, Julie, 494, 504, 511
Pool, Tim, 330, 334*n15*, 337
Pope Benedict XVI, 95, 491*n161*, 514
Pope Francis, 95, 436, 489–91, 501, 506, 509, 514, 733. *See also* Bergoglio, Jorge
Pope John Paul II, 199, 212, 703, 708, 710–11, 722–26, 740, 745
Pope Leo XIII, 383n30, 383n31, 396
Pope Paul VI, 199, 212, 722
Pope Pius, 705*n6*, 708
Popoli, Vox, 136
porn addiction, 237
pornographic consumption, 201*n19*
pornography industry, 210
Porter, Melvin, 249
Post-Christian Era, xvii, 404
postmodernism, 92–96, 266–67, 271, 273–74, 280, 282, 285, 342–43, 345, 348, 375, 377, 379, 401–2
Postmodernism's Poster Boy, 273*n49*, 281, 338, 345, 376, 396, 593, 744 *See also* Trudeau, Justin
Pot, Pol, 162, 316
Prager, Dennis, 661
pragmatic truth, 81–82, 84, 262*n12*
predators, sexual, 191
Prentice, David, 487, 511
Presley, Elvis, 227
presumption of atheism, 106, 114–15, 118
presymptomatic, 562–64, 617, 637
Previs, Steve, 432
Price, Robert M., 89
Prince Andrew, 731*n2*
pro-choicers, 237–38, 241–42, 244
progress, 358, 366–67, 398, 401, 465–66, 642*n20*, 646, 649, 653, 661, 664
progressivism, 5, 34, 200*n18*, 379, 384
Project Phoenix, 428
Project Veritas, 358, 362, 472–73, 484–87, 507, 511, 769
pro-life, 235, 237–38, 244, 376
property rights, 3, 307, 310
Prophet Isaiah, 749
Prophet Muhammad, 351
prophylaxis and treatment for COVID-19, 582
Psalms, 52, 128, 700, 714
pseudoscience, 92, 498, 614
Psychic Dogs, 678*n4*, 681
psychoanalysis, 92, 196
psychological damage, 184, 288
PTSD (Post-Traumatic Stress Disorder), 522, 525, 532, 536
Public Health Authority of Canada (PHAC), 735
Pukak, Janine, 453*n34*, 504

Q

Quantum Gravity, 94, 267*n32*, 284, 342
quantum mechanics, 76, 465–66
quarantine, 447, 526*n27*, 528*n40*, 530–31, 556, 563, 600*n253*, 632, 638
quasi-omniscience, 74
Queen Elizabeth II, 122, 223, 289, 535
Quigley, Carroll, 430–31
Quinta Columna, 488, 642*n18*, 643*n24*, 643*n25*, 654

R

racism, 339, 358, 362, 368, 371, 373, 376*n5*, 379, 386, 435*n34*, 440
racist, unvaccinated, 734*n13*
Rahner, Karl, 715, 726
Rambukkana, Nathan, 291, 340, 380*n18*
Ramos, Carlos, 247–48, 252
Rancourt, Denis, 754
Raoult, Didier, 474, 476*n108*, 512, 556, 580–81, 632
Rappaport, Jon, 567–68, 632
Razi Razor, 462*n63*
Reagan, Ronald, 3, 13, 25, 161, 426, 745, 748–49
realism, 149, 296
Real Pat King, 743. *See also* King, Pat
Redfield, Robert, 548, 565
Reid, Sheila Gunn, 758*n79*
Reimer, Bruce, 185*n13*
Reisman, Judith, 184*n6*, 186–87, 197, 200, 212
Richards, Jay, 135–36, 498
Ripple XRP, 746
Rittenhouse, Kyle, x, 42–43, 46–47
RNA, 473, 554, 566, 589, 596–97
RNA Vaccine Candidates, 607, 630, 646*n47*, 650, 772
Robillard, Yves, 742
Robinson, Tommy, 661
Rockefeller, David, 423, 427, 429–30
Rockefeller, Nelson, 431
Rockefeller File, 438*n41*, 440
Rockefeller Foundation, 183–84, 188, 436, 640*n7*, 654
Rocky Balboa, 683–84
Rocky Saga, 683–84, 687–88, 692
Rogan, Joe, 333, 475*n103*, 496, 568–69, 583–84, 590*n220*, 611, 616, 631, 661, 750
Ronald McDonald House, 737
Roosevelt, Franklin, 426
Rorty, Richard, 269–71, 284
Rose, Brian, 567
Rubin, Dave, 418, 661
Rudolf, 74
Rumsfeld, Donald, 422
Ruse, Michael, 360*n12*, 393*n67*, 398
Russell, Bertrand, 121
Russell, Robert John, 134

Ryan, Caitlin, 491*n164*
Ryle, Gilbert, 146

S
Saad, Gad, 250–51, 253, 278*n66*, 281*n75*, 344*n25*, 346, 378*n11*, 661
Saad Truth, 346
Sagan, Carl, 105–6, 109, 131, 135–36, 614, 633
Saint Augustine, 210
Sainte Etienne, 282, 345, 396
Saint Paul, 100, 493
Sandman, Nick, x, 42
Sanford, John C., 67
Santa Monica Boulevard, 208
Sarkozy, Nicolas, 759
SARS-CoV-2, 446–47, 449, 524–25, 528, 544–46, 554–57, 559–64, 566, 568–69, 575–77, 588, 606–7, 611, 618–19, 628
Satanic Bloodlines, 431*n14*, 440
satanic figure, 644
satanic rituals, 649
satanic source, 732
Satori, Paul, 301, 781
Schadt, Brandon, 485
Schaefer III, Henry F., 67
Schaeffer, Francis A., 400, 402, 404–9, 475*n105*, 503, 746
Scheer, Andrew, 341
Scheler, Max, 714, 727
Schlossberg, Hayden, 688
Schwab, Klaus, 322–23, 430, 437, 442, 615, 639, 647*n52*, 654, 732–34, 755, 759
science of fetal pain, 162, 166
scientific materialism, 94, 142, 144, 729, 731
scientism, 90, 107, 111*n19*, 123, 139, 145–50, 153–54, 156, 359,
Scripps Research Institute, 541, 550
Scruton, Roger, 20
Searle, John, 249, 253, 266*n27*, 271–73, 284
Sears, JP, 752*n62*
SEATO (Southeast Asia Treaty Organization), 427
Seattle's CHAZ, 316
self-sacrifice, 97, 660, 706, 719, 754
self-transcendence, 167, 684–85, 704
Sero, Candice, 758
SETI, 131
Severe Acute Respiratory Syndrome Coronavirus (SARS), 556*n76*, 625
Sevillano, José Luis, 488
Sey, Samuel, 661
Seymour, Jayne, 208, 212
Shakespeare, William, 683, 687
Shapiro, Ben, 36*n10*, 44, 330, 335–36, 661
Sharapova, Maria, 248*n7*, 252
Sharav, Vera, 751
Sheldrake, Rupert, 510, 678, 681–82
Shepherd, Lindsay, 290–91, 339–42, 344–46, 380*n18*
Shermer, Michael, 378, 398
Shihman, Stella, 254, 307, 780
Shook, John, 105*n2*, 115
Shue, Elisabeth, 689
Shylock, 683
Sidley, Gary, 578
Simpson, Archie, 172*n17*, 177, 491*n164*
Simpson, George Gaylord, 356
SJW (social justice warrior), 462*n63*
skepticism, 75, 108–10, 116, 120, 155, 282, 345, 396, 447, 478, 615
slaughterhouse, 737
slaves, 206–7, 414, 440, 481*n123*, 694, 748, 751
Sloan, Derek, 474*n101*, 504, 741
Sly, Tony, 227
Smallpox vaccine, 776
Snowden, Edward, 335
Snider, Dee, 38
socialism, 5, 8, 13, 17–18, 271, 274, 307–8, 310, 312–14, 379, 381, 384, 729–30
social justice, 321, 375, 377, 380–84, 386–87, 396–97, 462*n63*
social justice warriors (SJWs), 267*n29*, 279, 289, 379, 695
Socrates, 81
Socratic text, 81
Sokal, Alan, 93–94, 266*n27*, 267*n32*, 284,
Solzhenitsyn, Aleksandr, ix, 5, 6*n4*, 260*n3*, 285, 381, 413, 415–16, 420
Soros, George, 322, 376*n5*, 430
Soul Asylum, 537
Soundgarden, 230–31
Soviet Union, 254, 274, 301, 309, 311, 313–14, 319, 381, 413–16, 420–21, 684, 686, 745
Sowell, Thomas, 360*n12*
Spacetime Odyssey, 105*n3*
Spanish flu pandemic, 447, 569
species, new human, 403*n17*
Speck, Martina J., 524, 779
Spitzer, Robert J., 112, 121
Springsteen, Bruce, 780
stakeholders, 537, 767
Stalin, Josef, 5, 17, 162, 316–22
Stallone, Sylvester, 683–84
St. Anselm, 80, 712*n8*, 714, 726
St. Augustine, xxviii, 80, 232, 707, 721, 726
Steinback, John, 307, 715*n17*, 727
STEMM programs, 380
Stetson, Brian, 58
Stew Peters Show, the, 475*n103*, 488*n149*, 512–13, 571*n131*, 634, 641, 653
stigmatization, 175, 528, 612, 730, 735
St. Ignatius, 708
St. Nicholas, 74
Stockholm syndrome, 461
stoicism, 254, 256
Stone Temple Pilots, 227
Stop World Control, 448*n14*, 476*n109*, 513
Storms, Sam, 732
St. Paul, 83, 169, 694, 713*n10*, 716, 727
Strachan, Nick, 758
Strang, Robert, 608
Straw Dogs, 148, 151
Strickler, Melissa, 486–87, 584
Strong, Maurice, 430
St. Serafim, 128
St. Thomas Aquinas, 80, 262, 285, 383, 695, 697, 714, 717, 726–27
suicide, 164, 167–73, 175–79, 185*n13*, 230–31, 257, 524–27, 530, 533–34, 698, 702
suicide bombers, 109
sunny ways, 759
Superbowl, 192
supplements, glucosamine, 216, 225
surveillance, 26-27, 417, 529, 599
Swank, Hilary, 688
Sweet, Will, 95
Swinburne, Richard, 80, 108*n13*, 360*n12*
swine flu vaccination program, 601*n261*, 623
Swiss Guard, 490*n159*, 505
Swiss Policy Research, 575, 635
Switzerland tunnel, 644*n34*, 650
symbolism, occult, 520
Szép, Imre, 301–5

T
Tam, Theresa, 94, 127, 458, 467, 538, 579*n171*, 623, 763, 770
Taylor, Chad, 86
TCN, 462*n63*
technocrats, 150, 451
Tegnell, Anders, 572
Teilhard de Chardin, Pierre, 95, 403*n17*, 409, 429, 431, 599, 777
Terheș, Christian-Vasile, 758
Terry Fox Run, 707

tests, goat, 555*n69*, 632
thermodynamics, 133
thinking compliance, 452. *See also* unthinking compliance
Thin Lizzy, 227
Thomas, Barry, 73, 84, 121, 283, 362, 476*n107*, 508, 527*n35*, 535, 697, 726
Thomas, Ron, 689
Thomson, Judith Jarvis, 236*n2*
thought police, 288*n8*, 290
thrombosis, 570
Thunberg, Greta, 586
Toguchi, Chozen, 689
tolerance, x, xxiv, xxvi, xxxi, 13, 20, 53–61, 288, 315, 340, 345
Toope, Stephen J., 349, 354
Totalitarianism (totalitarian regime), xxxi, 3, 6–7, 18, 21, 83, 168, 260*n3*, 312, 318, 416-19, 443–44, 451, 662, 710
transableism, 278–79
transageism, 279
transgender, 183, 195, 262, 276*n61*, 278, 282, 297, 388, 391–93, 395, 435
transphobia, 327, 341, 743
transracial, 278
transsexual, 262, 388-89
trans-speciesism, 276, 279
trans-speciesist, 278
transubstantiation, 69
Traversy, Norman, 469*n82*, 514
treason, 335, 758
Treaty of Rome, 429
Trianon Treaty, 306
Trilateral Commission, 429–30, 438
Trojan Horse, 93
Trotsky, Leon, 317–19, 323, 661
truckers, 737*n26*, 739–41, 743–45, 752–59
Truckers in Canada, 740. *See also* truckers; Canadian truckers
Trudeau, Justin, 127–28, 164, 166, 338, 341, 449, 469–70, 592–94, 610–11, 619, 734–36, 739, 741–45, 752–56, 758–59
Trudeau, Pierre Elliot, 8, 753*n64*
Trump, Donald J., 334–35, 376*n5*, 422–23, 426–27, 439–40, 449–50, 468, 470, 476, 497–99, 540–41, 546–47, 622–23, 636, 745
Turley, Steve, 378*n12*, 398
Tylenol, 776

U
Udressy, Pierre-André, 490. *See also* Swiss Guards
UFOs, 107
Unintelligent Design, 143
unthinking compliance, 380*n19*, 452, 461, 591*n223*, 593, 731. *See also* mass formation psychosis
US swine flu vaccination program, 601

V
vaccine coercion, 207–8, 210, 453, 455, 462*n64*, 485, 493, 495, 770
vaccine hesitancy, 452*n31*, 454, 472, 504, 511
vaccine-induced immunity, 447n13, 454n37, 455n42, 505, 588, 606, 622, 768
VAERS (Vaccine Adverse Events Reporting System), 454*n37*, 456, 513, 601–2, 619, 626, 645, 651, 653, 764–66, 774
van Inwagen, Peter, 106*n10*, 112–13, 359, 362, 703
Varghese, Roy Abraham, 101*n3*
Vatican, 490–91
Ventureyra, Enrique C. G, 568–69, 775, 781
Ventureyra, Figaro
Ventureyra, Gina
Ventureyra, Julianna, 75, 707
Ventureyra, Maria-Elba
Ventureyra, Scott D. G, 74, 78, 92, 96–97, 336, 338, 683, 698, 702, 754*n67*, 754*n68*, 773, 777
Ventureyra, Valérie A., 516, 779
verificationism, 108*n13*
Verloo, Mieke, 417*n17*, 421
victimhood, 414, 692
Vietnam War, 689, 694
VigiAccess database, 603, 767, 776
Virgen María, 649*n57*, 651
Voltaire, 322, 665, 737

W
Wade, Nicholas, 236, 544, 548–49, 637
Wahhabi Islam, 350
Walensky, Rochelle, 562, 565, 634
Wallace, Alfred, 465, 703
War World II, 301
Wash, Donald, 474*n101*, 504
Washington, 69, 136, 156, 197, 215, 226, 285, 346, 399, 777, 782
Washington, George, 316
Watkins, Benjamin Blake Speed, 664, 782
Watson, Ian, 462
Watson, Paul Joseph, 661
Wayne, John, 255
Weigel, George, 740*n35*
Weiland, Scott, 227
Weinstein, Bret, 37, 45
Weiss, Bari, 469
Weiss, Karl, 742
Wells, Jonathan, 144
West, John G., 489
Whatcott, Bill, 391, 397
white privilege, 368
WHO (World Health Organization), 336–37, 428, 445, 447–48, 450, 473, 512, 514, 546, 561–64, 574–75, 585–86, 621–22, 636–39, 776
Wiker, Benjamin, 70, 73
Willard, Dallas, 108*n13*
Williams, Serena, 247, 250–52
Willis, Bruce, 255
Wilson, E. O., 67*n2*, 72
Wilson-Raybould, Jody, 275, 289*n11*, 298
witchcraft, 655
WLU (Wilfred Laurier University), 339–42, 344
wokeism, 37*n21*, 46, 324
Wolfreys, Julian, 267, 285
Wolscht, StefonKnee, 278
Wood, David, 284
World Bank (WB), 427, 516
World Economic Forum (WEF), 321–23, 360, 362, 428, 436–37, 516*n1*, 638–40, 647*n53*, 649, 654–55, 733, 755, 758–59
World War I, 162, 434, 753*n64*
World War II, 162, 254, 376, 427, 647, 717, 745, 752–53
wrongthink, 23
Wuhan Institute of Virology, 542–43, 545–47, 551, 566
Wynne, Kathleen, 189, 388

X
xenophobia, 376*n5*, 379

Y
Yaniv, Jessica, 391*n54*
Yeadon, Michael, 476, 499, 508, 515
Young, Neil, 750
Young, Thomas, 465

Z
Zabka, William, 688, 692, 697
Zelenko, Vladimir, 476, 508, 512, 515, 580–81, 627
Zeus, 111
zinc, 476*n108*, 512, 581
zinc sulfate, 476*n108*, 580
zoology, 67, 194
Zoomers, 307
zoonosis theory, 639
Zuckerberg, Mark, 472–73, 499
Zunic, Nikolaj, 709, 780

www.ingramcontent.com/pod-product-compliance
Lightning Source LLC
Chambersburg PA
CBHW071357230426
43669CB00010B/1375
9781777343507